Do More

McGraw-Hill Connect Student Quick Tips for Blackboard Users

Use this McGraw-Hill Connect Student Quick Tips for Blackboard Users guide for a quick and easy start with your assignments within McGraw-Hill Connect or ConnectPlus. You'll get valuable tips on doing assignments, accessing resources, and support.

"Register Now" or "Sign In"

TIP: To start using Connect assignments within Blackboard, you will be asked to "Register Now" or "Sign In" the first time you click on a Connect assignment. Consider these points as you make your selection:

- If this is your first experience with a McGraw-Hill Connect assignment in Blackboard, select "Register Now" and follow the prompts to establish an account

- If this is not your first experience with a McGraw-Hill Connect assignment, simply select "Sign In" and enter the email address and password that you used for previous McGraw-Hill Connect assignments

- Enter the Connect Access Code purchased with your new textbook or choose "Buy Online" to purchase access online.

TIP: If you are creating a new account with McGraw-Hill, please choose your Security Question and Answer carefully. We will ask you for this information if you forget your password.

TIP: If you do not have an access code, or have not yet secured your tuition funds, you can click "Free Trial" during registration. This trial will provide temporary Connect access (typically three weeks) and will remind you to purchase online access before the end of your trial.

Home (Assignments)

TIP: If you are unable to begin an assignment, verify the following:

- The assignment is available (check start dates and due dates)

- You have not exceeded the maximum number of attempts for the assignment

- You have not achieved a score of 100%

NOTE: If an assignment contains questions that require manual grading, you can attempt to complete the assignment again if your instructor has enabled multiple attempts; however, you won't receive credit for the manually graded questions until the instructor reviews and enters a grade.

Do More

TIP: If you are unable to complete your assignment in one sitting, utilize the "*Save & Exit*" button to save your work and complete it at a later time. Once you have completed your assignment, utilize the "*Submit*" button in order for your assignment to be graded.

TIP: There may be limitations on your assignment, based on your instructor's settings. You may encounter the following limitations when working on your assignment(s):

- Ability to "Print" an assignment
- Once you begin a timed assignment, the timer will not stop

Library

TIP: For shortcuts to various resources, go to the **My Connect Section** under the McGraw-Hill Higher Education link in the "Tools" area.

- If you purchased ConnectPlus, you will see an eBook link, which can also be accessed from the course section information widget of the "Home" tab

- Recorded lectures can be accessed if your instructor is using Tegrity Campus to capture lectures. You may also access recorded lectures when beginning an assignment by clicking on the projector icon in the navigation bar

- Many McGraw-Hill textbooks offer additional resources such as narrated slides and additional problem sets, which are accessible via the "Student Resources" link

Do More

Grades

TIP: Your grades and results are available in the **Grade Book** immediately.

NOTE: Your instructor has the ability to limit the amount of information (e.g. questions, answers, scores) you can view for each submitted assignment

Need More Help with Connect Assignments?

CONTACT US ONLINE:

Visit us at:

www.mcgrawhillconnect.com/support

Browse our support materials including tutorial videos and searchable knowledge base. If you cannot find an answer to your question, click on Contact Us to send us an email.

GIVE US A CALL

Call us at:

1-800-331-5094

Our live support is available:
Mon-Thurs:	8 am – 11 pm CT
Friday:	8 am – 6 pm CT
Sunday:	6 pm – 11 pm CT

THE SCIENCE OF

PSYCHOLOGY ³

AN APPRECIATIVE VIEW

LAURA A. KING

University of Missouri, Columbia

PSY2012
General Psychology
Valencia College

1 2 3 4 5 6 7 8 9 0 BRN BRN 17 16 15 14

ISBN-13: 978-1-259-34637-8
ISBN-10: 1-259-34637-4

Learning Solutions Consultant: Salim Bradley
Project Manager: Catherine Bethke
Cover Photo Credits: 101534012 © Kheng guan Toh

for *Sam*

LAURA KING

Laura King did her undergraduate work at Kenyon College, where, an English major, she declared a second major, in psychology, during the second semester of her junior year. She completed her AB in English with high honors and distinction and in psychology with distinction in 1986. Laura then did graduate work at Michigan State University and the University of California, Davis, receiving her PhD in personality psychology in 1991.

Laura began her career at Southern Methodist University in Dallas, moving to the University of Missouri in 2001, where she is now a Curators' Professor of Psychological Science. In addition to seminars in the development of character, social psychology, and personality psychology, she has taught undergraduate lecture courses in introductory psychology, introduction to personality psychology, and social psychology. At SMU, she received six different teaching awards, including the "M" award for "sustained excellence" in 1999. At the University of Missouri, she received the Chancellor's Award for Outstanding Research and Creative Activity in 2004.

Her research, which has been funded by the National Institute of Mental Health and the National Science Foundation, has focused on a variety of topics relevant to the question of what it is that makes for a good life. She has studied goals, life stories, happiness, well-being, and meaning in life. In general, her work reflects an enduring interest in studying what is good and healthy in people. In 2001, she earned recognition for her research accomplishments with a Templeton Prize in Positive Psychology. In 2011, she received the Ed and Carol Diener Award for Distinguished Contributions to Personality Psychology. Laura's research (often in collaboration with undergraduate and graduate students) has been published in *American Psychologist,* the *Journal of Personality and Social Psychology, Psychological Bulletin,* and *Psychological Science.*

Currently editor-in-chief of the Personality and Individual Differences section of the *Journal of Research in Personality and Social Psychology,* Laura has also served as editor-in-chief of the *Journal of Research in Personality* and associate editor for the *Journal of Personality and Social Psychology* and *Personality and Social Psychology Bulletin,* as well as on numerous grant panels. She has edited or coedited special sections of the *Journal of Personality* and *American Psychologist.*

In "real life," Laura is an accomplished cook and enjoys listening to music (mostly jazz vocalists and singer-songwriters), running with her faithful dog Bill, and swimming and roller-skating with her son Sam.

BRIEF CONTENTS

CONTENTS

3
Biological Foundations of Behavior 60

4
Sensation and Perception 102

5
States of Consciousness 142

Alternative Chapter: Thinking and Language

Alternative Chapter: Intelligence

9
Human Development 288

Alternative Chapter: Human Development (topical approach)

10
Motivation and Emotion 326

PREFACE

When Things Go Right for Students... Things Go Right for Instructors

Focusing on why things go right, *The Science of Psychology: An Appreciative View,* Third Edition, helps students understand and appreciate psychology as a science and as an integrated whole. Informed by student data, the third edition's program extends these themes and enhances their pedagogical value by guiding students toward topics they find the most challenging and then offering new learning resources to help students master them.

Appreciating Student Data

For this new edition, data were analyzed to identify the concepts students found to be the most difficult, allowing for expansion upon the discussion, practice and assessment of the challenging topics. The revision process for a new edition used to begin with gathering information from instructors about what they would change and what they would keep. Experts in the field were asked to provide comments that pointed out new material to add and dated material to remove. Using all these reviews, authors would revise the material. But now, a new tool has revolutionized that paradigm.

McGraw-Hill Education authors now have access to student performance data to analyze and to inform their revisions. This data is anonymously collected from the many students who use *LearnSmart,* the adaptive learning system that provides students with an individualized assessment of their own progress. Because virtually every text paragraph is tied to several questions that students answer while using LearnSmart, the specific concepts with which students are having the most difficulty are easily pinpointed through empirical data in the form of a "heat map" report.

> *" Because virtually every text paragraph is tied to several questions that students answer while using LearnSmart, the specific concepts with which students are having the most difficulty are easily pinpointed through empirical data in the form of a "heat map" report. "*

For example, based on thousands of student responses, LearnSmart's heat map report showed that only 38 percent of students successfully mastered the learning objective "Identify the differences between top-down and bottom-up processing" when first assessing their understanding through the adaptive learning system. In response, we

- Expanded the explanation of the concept in the chapter

- Added additional, assignable pre-test, reading, and post-test questions targeting this learning objective

- Developed multiple new digital Learning Resources for this learning objective

Appreciating Student Learning

Today's students are as different from the learners of the last generation as the discipline of psychology is now from the field 30 years ago. Students now learn in multiple modalities; rather than sitting down and reading traditional printed chapters from beginning to end, their work preferences tend to be more visual and interactive. They like to access information in multiple ways and expect their course material to be engaging and personalized. *The Science of Psychology: An Appreciative View,* Third Edition, supports learning by showing students what they know and do not know through LearnSmart Advantage, adaptive learning products, by providing assignable assessments through Connect Psychology, and by presenting key concepts in engaging ways.

Mc Graw Hill Education | LEARNSMART™
ADVANTAGE

LearnSmart Advantage is a new series of adaptive learning products fueled by LearnSmart—a widely used and adaptive learning resource that has been proven to strengthen memory recall, increase retention, and boost grades.

LEARNSMART

Millions of students have answered over a billion questions in LearnSmart since 2009. This most effective and successful study tool has been shown to keep students in class and to improve their grades. Students using LearnSmart are 13 percent more likely to pass their classes and 35 percent less likely to drop out.

By clearly distinguishing what the student knows from what the learner is less sure of or more likely to forget, LearnSmart continuously adapts to each student's needs by building an individualized learning path. This allows the student to study smarter and to retain more knowledge. Turnkey reports provide valuable insight to instructors so that precious class time can be spent on higher-level concepts and discussion.

LEARNSMART ACHIEVE

LearnSmart Achieve is a revolutionary new learning system that combines a continuously adaptive learning experience with necessary course resources to focus students on mastering concepts they do not already know. Developed with the aim of helping students retain more knowledge, stay in class, and earn better grades, "just-in-time" learning experiences from the program adjust to each student's needs. This model has been shown to accelerate learning and strengthen memory recall. A convenient time management feature and turnkey reports for instructors also ensure that the student stays on track.

SMARTBOOK

Fueled by LearnSmart, SmartBook is the first and currently the only adaptive reading experience available. By clearly distinguishing what a student knows from what he or she does not, and by focusing on concepts the student is most likely to forget, SmartBook personalizes the content for each student in a continuously adapting reading experience. Reading is no longer passive and linear, but is instead an engaging and dynamic experience. Students using SmartBook are more likely to master and retain important concepts and be better prepared for class. Instructors receive valuable reports giving them insight into how students are progressing through textbook content, allowing instructors to shape their in-class time and assessments. As a result of the adaptive reading experience found in SmartBook, students are more likely to retain knowledge, stay in class, and earn better grades.

Connect Psychology includes assignable and assessable videos, quizzes, exercises, and interactivities, all associated with learning objectives for *The Science of Psychology: An Appreciative View,* Third Edition. Videos, interactive assessments, and simulations invite engagement and add real-world perspective to the introductory psychology course. With Connect Psychology, students can study whenever and wherever they choose.

Student-Focused Content

The content of *The Science of Psychology: An Appreciative View,* Third Edition, was developed with effective student learning in mind. Chapters are built around learning objectives and scaffolding designed to guide students and help them confirm their understanding.

Concept Clips, designed to help students comprehend some of the most difficult concepts in introductory psychology, include colorful graphics and stimulating animations to break down core concepts in a step-by-step manner, engage students, and increase retention. Powered by Connect Psychology, Concept Clips can be used as both a lively presentation tool for the classroom or for student assessment purposes.

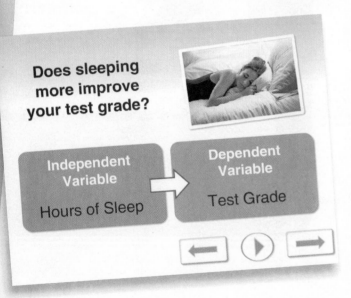

Appreciating Why Things Go Right

The third edition of *The Science of Psychology: An Appreciative View* continues to emphasize function before dysfunction. Rather than focusing on why things go wrong, the focus is first on *why things go right.*

One of the challenges instructors face as a result of this alternative focus is that it goes against human nature. Research in psychology itself tells us that the negative captures our attention more readily than the positive. There is no question that bad news makes headlines. A terrorist attack, the global recession, disturbing climate changes, political scandals, and the everyday demands of juggling work, family, and finances—these and other issues loom large for us all. We strive and struggle to find balance and to sculpt a happy life. The science of psychology has much to offer in terms of helping us understand the choices we make and the implications of these choices for ourselves and for others around the world.

The Science of Psychology: An Appreciative View, Third Edition, communicates the nature and breadth of psychology, and its value as a science, with an appreciative perspective. Its primary goal is to help students to think like psychological scientists.

Appreciating Psychology as an Integrated Whole

As with the previous editions, the continuing goal of *The Science of Psychology: An Appreciative View* is to present psychology as an integrated field in which the whole is greater than the sum of its parts, but the parts are essential to the whole. Accordingly, this third edition illuminates many areas where specialized subfields overlap and where research findings in one subfield support important studies and exciting discoveries in another. Students come to appreciate, for example, how neuroscientific findings inform social psychology and how discoveries in personality psychology relate to leadership in organizational settings. **Intersection** features showcase research at the crossroads of two areas and shed light on these intriguing connections.

The third edition includes many new Intersections showing the influence of work in one field of psychology on another. For example, the Intersection in the chapter on psychological disorders, Chapter 15, links work in clinical psychology with personality psychology to explore the topic "Are Aspects of Psychopathy Related to Leadership Success?"

Related NewsFlash exercises, powered by Connect, tie current news stories to key psychological principles and learning objectives. After interacting with a contemporary news story, students are assessed on their ability to make the connection between real life and research findings. Cases are revisited across chapters, encouraging students to consider multiple perspectives.

INTERSECTION

Clinical Psychology and Personality Psychology: Are Aspects of Psychopathy Related to Leadership Success?

Scott Lilienfeld and his colleagues (2012) gathered a host of information about each of the U.S. presidents up to and including George W. Bush. Historians who were experts on each president made ratings of his personality. Those ratings were used as measures of psychopathy, including antisocial/impulsiveness and fearless dominance. The researchers collected evidence about each man's presidency, such as the amount of legislation passed, foreign policy accomplishments, willingness to take risks, and ability to avoid crucial mistakes, as well as surveys among historians about presidential effectiveness.

Overall, being antisocial and impulsive was unrelated to presidential performance, but fearless dominance predicted many indicators of success. Presidents who scored higher on fearless dominance had higher overall performance ratings and were higher in public persuasiveness, crisis management, leadership, and agenda setting (Lilienfeld & others, 2012).

Which presidents were highest on fearless dominance? These are the rankings for the top five as well as all the living presidents:

4. Ronald Reagan
5. Rutherford B. Hayes
7. Bill Clinton
10. George W. Bush
18. Jimmy Carter
30. George H. W. Bush

Certainly, this work does *not* indicate that any U.S. presidents were psychopaths. Rather, it suggests that aspects of personality indicating boldness related to especially high levels of presidential success. Lilienfeld and his colleagues suggest that fearless dominance, although part of a very undesirable constellation of traits, may be important for individuals who are engaged in extremely high-stakes decision making in the uppermost positions

Can you recognize fearless dominance in the leaders in your life?

Appreciating Psychology as a Science

The Science of Psychology: An Appreciative View, Third Edition, communicates the nature and breadth of psychology and its value as a science from an appreciative perspective. Its primary goal is to help students think like psychological scientists, which includes asking them questions about their own life experiences. Throughout, students' curiosity is nurtured through timely, applied examples and a focus on what psychological science means for people going about daily life.

The third edition's attention to function before dysfunction, up-to-date coverage, and broad scope reflect the field of psychology *today.* These qualities underscore psychology's vital and ongoing role as a *science that ever advances knowledge* about ourselves and our interactions in the world. Psychology is a vigorous young science and one that changes quickly. The text narrative interweaves the most current research with classic findings to give students an appreciation of this vitality. In Chapter 13, for instance, the treatment of Milgram's classic study on obedience is complemented by an analysis of Burger's recent attempts to recreate the study.

The **Psychological Inquiry** feature stimulates students' analytical thinking about psychology's practical applications. The selections reinforce student understanding of central aspects of research design, such as the difference between correlational and experimental studies and the concepts of independent and dependent variables. The selections in each chapter guide students' analysis of a figure, graph, or other illustration and include a set of critical thinking questions. For example, one of the Psychological Inquiry features in Chapter 6 on learning prompts students to analyze graphical schedules of reinforcement and different patterns of responding to them.

In conjunction with creating current and contemporary course materials, *The Science of Psychology: An Appreciative View,* Third Edition, includes citations that bring the most important recent and ongoing research into the text. These updated references give students and instructors the very latest that psychology has to offer on each topic.

Appreciating science also means appreciating disagreements in the field. Each chapter contains a **Critical Controversy** feature highlighting current psychological debates and posing thought-provoking questions that encourage students to examine the evidence on both sides. For example, Chapter 6's Critical Controversy explores whether *learning styles* matter to learning and Chapter 11's Critical Controversy investigates whether autism represents the behavior of an "extreme male brain."

Two special features, **Touring the Brain and Nervous System** and **Touring the Senses,** offer detailed full-color overlays (transparencies in the print text; digital versions through Connect) of important figures. The overlays provide students hands-on practice in grasping key biological structures and processes that are essential to an appreciation of the role of science in psychology and success in the course.

Appreciating Psychology's Role in Health and Wellness

The Science of Psychology: An Appreciative View, Third Edition, continues to emphasize the relevance of psychology to the health and well-being of students and the people in their lives. As in prior editions, substantial discussion and examples focus on the scientific understanding of human strengths and capacities, health, and wellness in order to cultivate students' appreciation for how extensively psychology applies to their lives.

Appreciating Our Dynamic Field: Chapter-by-Chapter Changes

Key content changes, chapter by chapter, include but are not limited to the following:

CHAPTER 1: WHAT IS PSYCHOLOGY?

- New coverage of generational differences in teen narcissism.
- Expanded coverage of introspection; neuroscience; the sociocultural approach; the cognitive approach; and the influence of culture on psychological perception.
- Expanded research on the psychology of forgiveness and positive psychology.
- Updated Critical Controversy feature, "Are Young Americans in the Middle of a Narcissism Epidemic?"
- Updated Intersection selection, "Social Psychology and Cross-Cultural Psychology: How Does Culture Influence the Meaning of Success?"

CHAPTER 2: PSYCHOLOGY'S SCIENTIFIC METHOD

- Expanded intensive coverage of foundational concepts in research, including independent and dependent variables, operational definition, experimental and control groups, confederates, hypotheses, and predictions.
- New comparison of terms clarifying central tendency and measure of dispersion, as well as the difference between correlation and causation.
- New example of a meta-analysis.
- Expanded coverage of replication as part of the process of drawing conclusions; the application of meta-analysis; experimentation in a natural setting; case studies and generalizability; replication in practice; common uses of mode, median, and mean in data analysis; the application of inferential statistics; the use of deception in a research study; and the application of correlational research.
- New Intersection feature, "Personality and Social Psychology: Does Sociability Lead to Happiness or Is It the Other Way Around?"
- New Critical Controversy selection, "Is It Ethical to Use Deception in Research?"

CHAPTER 3: BIOLOGICAL FOUNDATIONS OF BEHAVIOR

- New coverage of a study of the impact of elevated levels of oxytocin in the brains of new lovers.
- New comparison between neurons and glial cells.
- Expanded coverage of the relationship between the brain and an individual's personality or behavior; the parasympathetic and sympathetic nervous systems; plasticity; the functions of specialized neurons; the structure and purpose of the myelin sheath; nerve impulse, and the way that it travels through an axon.
- Expanded coverage of unresolved questions regarding neurotransmitters in the brain; neurochemical responses to stress; the role of dopamine in personality trait expression; the use and function of EEGs in research; and the Human Genome Project's exploration of diseases with genetic links.
- Expanded comparison between afferent and efferent nerves, as well as between the functions of the Broca's and Wernicke's areas of the brain.
- New Critical Controversy selection, "Do Mirror Neurons Hold the Key to Social Understanding?"
- New Intersection box, "Neuroscience and Emotion: How Does the Brain Recognize What Is Funny?"

CHAPTER 4: SENSATION AND PERCEPTION

- New coverage of senses that can detect energies outside of the "normal" range.
- New example illustrating the process of determining differences between stimuli.
- New Figure 4.1, "Top-Down and Bottom-Up Processes in Perception."
- Expanded coverage of top-down and bottom-up processing; species' adaptations of sense organs for greater protection in natural environments; subtle differences in perception of stimuli (such as candlelight compared to a searchlight); threats to the hearing system; outcomes of research on mirror therapy; differences in timbre; information acquisition and criterion in signal detection theory; the visual system's response to stimuli; and perceiving "whole" stimuli.
- New Critical Controversy feature, "Can We Feel the Future?"
- New Intersection selection, "Emotion and Sensation: What Do Feelings Smell Like?"

CHAPTER 5: STATES OF CONSCIOUSNESS

- New coverage of the important topic of *executive function*.
- New coverage of daydreaming and the purpose served by this state of consciousness; a study indicating that students who "pulled all nighters" learned less new material and had more academic problems in the future; studies indicating the relationship between concentration abilities and duration of sleep.
- New research on the relationship between psychological disorders and sleep-related conditions; the impact of sleep apnea (such as the population most commonly affected and related negative outcomes); the impact of psychoactive drugs on human consciousness; and the legitimization of hypnosis in Western medicine.
- Expanded coverage of stream of consciousness, explored by psychology pioneer William James; the impact of stream of consciousness on perceptions; the parts of the brain responsible for consciousness, awareness, and arousal; theory of mind and developmental phases; automatic behaviors and associated indications; controlled and automatic processes; subconscious brain activity; and the phenomenon of incubation.
- Expanded coverage of the role of subconscious brain activity in the learning process; the relationship between sleep duration and stress levels; the five sleep stages; sleep throughout the life span, comparing average cycles in different age cohorts; problems associated with sleeping too much; and current psychological thinking about the nature of dreams, as well as the enigmatic nature of dreams in history and pop culture.
- Updated coverage of brain activity as understood through the lens of cognitive-behavior theory; different types of prescription medications commonly taken recreationally (such as prescription tranquilizers); the rate of tobacco and marijuana use in the United States; the incidence of alcoholism in the U.S. teen population; and potential negative outcomes related to substance use.
- Expanded coverage of the state of hypnosis and its use in psychotherapy, as well as positive outcomes of meditation practice.
- New Critical Controversy selection, "Does Conscious Reflection Matter to Matters of Conscience?"
- New Intersection box, "Consciousness and Neuroscience: Can We Tell What the Brain Is Dreaming About?"

CHAPTER 6: LEARNING

- New coverage of mechanisms of applied behavior analysis, as well as the contexts in which observational learning can occur.
- New comparisons of fixed-ratio schedules and fixed-interval schedules, with examples; in addition, new discussion of insight learning and how it differs from learning through trial and error.
- New examples of classical conditioning (E*TRADE commercials and embedded marketing) and variable-interval schedules (random drug testing).

- Expanded coverage of neutral stimulus; classical conditioning; taste aversion and links to classical conditioning; principles of reinforcement; positive reinforcement; secondary reinforcers; fixed-ratio schedules; the benefits of multicultural learning; and various learning styles.
- New Intersection box, "Learning and Clinical Psychology: Can Classical Conditioning Help Us Understand Drug Abuse?"
- New Critical Controversy selection, "Do Learning Styles Matter to Learning?"

CHAPTER 7: MEMORY

- New coverage of the impact of fMRIs on memory-related research; double-blind studies indicating ways of reducing faulty memory; and the social symbolism of memory (such as, the importance of remembering someone's name).
- Expanded coverage of the negative impact of divided attention; the benefits of elaborate processing; mental imagery as a memorization tool and its use in daily life; improving short-term memory through rehearsal; and the components of working memory.
- Updated discussion of the impact of the Internet on memory use; episodic memory; flashbulb memory; the impact of stress-related hormones on memory; the impact of trauma on memory; repression as a form of motivated forgetting and the controversy surrounding the concept of repression; and the faultiness of memory, with mistaken eyewitness testimony as an example.
- Expanded coverage of mnemonic devices; the impact of sleep on the quality of memory; the relationship between autobiographical memories and sense of identity, with an example involving Alcoholics Anonymous autobiographical memories; mental imagery as a memorization tool; and the differences between anterograde and retrograde amnesia.
- New Intersection feature, "Cognitive and Cultural Psychology: How Does Culture Influence Episodic Memory?"
- New Critical Controversy selection, "Can Adults Tell If Children's Memories Are Accurate?"

CHAPTER 8: THINKING, INTELLIGENCE, AND LANGUAGE

- Two-chapter treatment of the topics—Thinking and Language; and Intelligence—available through Create for those who want to dedicate more time to these topics.
- New coverage of ways to avoid cognitive biases; the relationship between creative genius and psychological disorders; multiple-intelligences evaluations; the neural correlates of cognitive ability; and the bias blind spot.
- Expanded coverage of the uses of AI systems; the structure and function of concepts; heuristics; the relationship between heuristics and biases; the availability heuristic; functional fixedness; and cognitive flexibility.
- Updated coverage of the process of reasoning; bottom-up processing; inductive reasoning; decision making and reasoning; intuitive judgment; confirmation bias; and hindsight bias.
- Expanded coverage of actively open-minded thinking and intelligence; criteria of good intelligence tests; mental age; the Stanford-Binet test for intelligence; the Weschler Scale; the impact of genetic and environmental influences on intelligence; heritability of intelligence; the controversy around heritability estimates; the Flynn effect; the role of language in cognitive activity; and the impact of cognitive appraisal on stress.

- New Intersection selection, "Cognitive Psychology and Personality: Do Sophisticated Thinkers Avoid the Bias Blind Spot?"
- New Critical Controversy box, "Is There a Link Between Creative Genius and Psychopathology?"

CHAPTER 9: HUMAN DEVELOPMENT

- Topical approach to human development available through Create for those who prefer that organization.
- New coverage of infant eye-tracking research.
- New coverage of information-processing approaches to cognitive development.
- Expanded coverage of research on infant perceptual and cognitive skills, including nativist and empiricist approaches; executive functioning in cognitive development; Bowlby's attachment theory and Erikson's developmental theory; the controversy around Kohlberg's developmental theory; parenting styles thought to result in well-developed children; and socioemotional development in adolescence.
- Updated coverage on the physical changes in older adults; the impact of meditation on telomerase activity; the role of free radicals in the body; the role of cognitive engagement in maintaining cognitive functioning in late adulthood; happiness reports from different age cohorts; and meaningful life themes, with examples of celebrities participating in humanitarian causes.
- New Intersection box, "Developmental and Social Psychology: Is Attachment an Enduring Aspect of Life?"
- New Psychological Inquiry feature, "Looking at Identity Exploration."
- New Critical Controversy selection, "Is Parenthood Associated with Happiness?"

CHAPTER 10: MOTIVATION AND EMOTION

- New coverage of psychological factors relating to overeating.
- New coverage of international rates of obesity; disordered eating patterns; and binge-eating disorder (causes and treatments).
- New coverage of the reliability of the polygraph exam and the two-factor theory of emotion.
- Expanded coverage of optimal arousal theory; the link between arousal and performance, with Reeshemah Taylor discussed as an example of being able to perform well in an emergency; the role of the hypothalamus in regulating hunger; eating disorders; and the potential links between social factors and eating disorders.
- Updated coverage of intrinsic and extrinsic motivations; the relationship between long-term goal setting and self-regulation; self-regulation mechanisms; the James-Lange theory; the relationship between dopamine and endorphins and emotional states; and the role of the limbic system in emotions.
- Updated coverage of the differences between the theories of Zajonc and Lazarus on the role of thinking in emotions; facial expressions and their relationship to emotions; the broaden-and-build model of positive emotion; and the pursuit of happiness.
- New Intersection selection, "Emotion and Health Psychology: Can a Smile Protect Against Stress?"

CHAPTER 11: GENDER, SEX, AND SEXUALITY

- Updated coverage of gender identities of individuals born with disorders of sexual development (DSD) or ambiguous genitalia; the debate over the sex assignment process for individuals with DSD; the change in terminology from *gender identity disorder* to *gender dysphoria,* and the controversy over whether affected individuals should be considered as having a disorder at all; and common treatments for transgender individuals seeking to change genders.

- New coverage of the importance of emotion, empathy, and helping and the intersections among the three; the gender similarities hypothesis; research indicating gender differences in pursuing casual sex; the rate of Americans who identify as straight, lesbian, gay, or bisexual; prenatal androgens and their impact on sexual orientation; 2D:4D ratio and sexual orientation; and the association between sexual orientation and brain differences.
- Updated coverage of the incidence of discrimination in the United States based on sexual orientation and the growing support for marriage equality of same-sex couples; the factors contributing to higher relationship satisfaction in LGBTQ communities; and the rights of same-sex relationships internationally.
- Expanded coverage of the similarities and differences between males and females in expression of emotions; theories of gender development; evolutionary psychology and gender differences; the development of children's concepts of gender; social role theory; research indicating differences between male and female infants in terms of eye-tracking abilities; and gender differences in sexual expression.
- Expanded coverage of research indicating bisexuality is a stable orientation; modeling or observational theory of LGBTQ development; the typical age at which Americans start having sex; comprehensive sex education; and the psychology of gender differences.
- New Critical Controversy box, "Does Autism Spectrum Disorder Represent an Extreme Male Brain?"
- New Intersection selection, "Gender and Neuroscience: Are There His and Hers Brains (and Should We Even Ask That Question)?"

CHAPTER 12: PERSONALITY

- Expanded and updated coverage of defense mechanisms; Maslow's approach; Rogerian theory; research on authenticity as related to self-esteem; Allport's personality theory; factor analysis; and the big five factors of personality.
- Updated coverage of the trait approach to personality development; the stability of personality traits over the life course; evaluation of the trait perspectives; Bandura's social cognitive theory; new research indicating stability of personality and behavior across interpersonal situations; Mischel's CAPS model; Gray's reinforcement sensitivity theory; and the heritability of personality traits.
- Expanded coverage of criticism of the validity and reliability of the Rorschach test; description of conscientiousness as a personality trait; the impact of optimism on lifestyles; and the Type D behavior pattern.
- New Critical Controversy feature, "Do Defense Mechanisms Underlie Homophobia?"
- New Intersection selection, "Personality and Health Psychology: Are Traits Linked to Obesity?"

CHAPTER 13: SOCIAL PSYCHOLOGY

- New coverage of research on the accuracy of first impressions; downward social comparisons; the link between behavior and attitudes; the impact of different mediums of communication; and biological and sociocultural factors in prosocial behavior.
- New coverage of the impact of socioeconomic status on prosocial behavior; the relationship between personality and displays of aggression; culture-bound differences in norms of acceptable social behavior and rules for interpreting that behavior; comparisons of collectivistic and individualistic cultures in terms of social norms; the Stanford prison experiment (studying obedience in humans); research on the ways that individuals exert personal control; and the role of intimate relationships in social life.

- Expanded coverage of research indicating that traits can be conveyed in face structure; research indicating how beauty is perceived; the fundamental attribution error; heuristics in social information processing; the false consensus effect (with examples); self-objectification; and the negative impact of social comparison.
- Updated coverage of cognitive dissonance; altruism; egoism; empathy; trait agreeableness; conformity; informational social influence; normative social influence; group influence; group polarization effect; groupthink; and open discourse.
- Expanded discussion of the role race plays in social interactions and racial biases; the impact of heuristics on cognitive processing; and the role of genes in social behavior.
- New Psychological Inquiry feature, "Improving Group Relations Through Cooperative Activities."
- New Intersection box, "Social Psychology and Cross-Cultural Psychology: Why Are Some Nations More Conforming Than Others?"
- New Critical Controversy feature, " Is Intelligence Related to Prejudice and Political Beliefs?"

CHAPTER 14: INDUSTRIAL AND ORGANIZATIONAL PSYCHOLOGY

- Expanded coverage of the role of I-O psychology in job analysis; I-O psychology as related to job interviews; interviewer-interviewee relationships; and research on how successful job applicants find those jobs.
- Updated coverage of the impact of personality on the quality of leadership; types of leaders and types of followers; I-O psychology research on the impact of downsizing; I-O psychology studies related to workplace violence; and the role of unemployment in health and wellness.
- New Critical Controversy selection, "Does Self-Efficacy Always Lead to Better Performance?"
- New Intersection box, "I-O Psychology and Personality Psychology: Are Transformational Leaders in the Eye of the Beholder?"

CHAPTER 15: PSYCHOLOGICAL DISORDERS

- Revisions based on *DSM-5.*
- New coverage of the biopsychosocial model; the vulnerability-stress hypothesis; the structure and critiques of *DSM-5;* biopsychosocial factors related to generalized anxiety disorder; symptoms of panic disorder; the underlying factors (biological, psychological, and social) of panic disorder, with examples of social anxiety disorder; and the symptoms of and underlying factors (biopsychosocial) of specific phobia.
- New coverage of disorders related to anxiety, including symptoms and underlying factors of obsessive-compulsive disorder (OCD); the symptoms and underlying factors (biopsychosocial) of OCD-related disorders (hoarding, excoriation, trichotillomania, and body dysmorphic disorder); and new coverage of post-traumatic stress disorder (PTSD), including its symptoms and underlying biopsychosocial factors.
- New coverage of disorders of emotion and mood; research on the biopsychosocial factors of depressive disorders; and *DSM-5's* diagnosis of disruptive mood dysregulation disorder in children.
- New coverage of the changes to the schizophrenia spectrum in *DSM-5;* early-intervention treatment plans for schizophrenia; research on the link between antisocial personality disorder (ASPD) and low activation in different parts of the brain; studies on the link between ASPD and childhood abuse; symptoms of

borderline personality disorder (BPD), symptom splitting, and research on treatments for BPD.

- Expanded coverage of the role of context in determining the appropriateness of a behavior; the role of culture in establishing deviance and context boundaries; the impact of social roles on mental health; research indicating prevalence of depression in the United States; prevalence of dissociative identity disorder in the United States and abroad; underlying factors (biopsychosocial) of schizophrenia spectrum disorders; and suicide.
- New Critical Controversy feature, "Does *Everyone* Have ADHD?"
- New Psychological Inquiry box, "Depression Among Women and Men Across Cultures."
- New Intersection selection, "Clinical Psychology and Personality Psychology: Are Aspects of Psychopathy Related to Leadership Success?"

CHAPTER 16: THERAPIES

- New opening section comparing psychological and biological approaches to treatment; and new description of the controversy over prescription privileges for clinical psychologists.
- New organizational structure, lending prominence to psychological approaches to treatment.
- New coverage of the impact of social media for alerting others of the need for treatment; new research on empirically supported treatments and the controversy of whether samples used in studies are representative of the individuals clinicians see in practice.
- New coverage of research on applied behavior analysis in treating individuals with autism; and research studying the success of early and intense behavioral treatment for autism spectrum disorders.
- New coverage of cross-cultural competence as a factor in therapy.
- Expanded coverage of the effectiveness of psychotherapy and the factors involved with successful treatment; systematic desensitization; distinctions between different therapies (insight versus immediate symptoms/skills and directive or nondirective); research on cognitive-behavior therapy in treating many disorders, including anxiety disorders, disorders of emotion and mood, schizophrenia (in combination with drug therapy), and personality disorders; and research on integrative therapy to adjust the treatment to the individual client.
- Updated listing of medications for treating anxiety, depression, bipolar disorder, and schizophrenia; new research on the side effects of antipsychotic medications.
- New Intersection feature, "Clinical and Cultural Psychology: How Does Culture Influence Responses to Treatment?"

CHAPTER 17: HEALTH PSYCHOLOGY

- New coverage of obstacles to engaging in physical activity.
- Expanded coverage of the theory of reasoned action and the theory of planned behavior; ways to mitigate the impact of stress; theoretical models of change; the impact of habitual and endurance exercise on health; and different types of health interventions.
- New Intersection feature, "Health Psychology and Cross-Cultural Psychology: How Does Culture Influence the Meaning of Social Support?"
- New Critical Controversy selection, "How Powerful Is the Power of Positive Thinking?"

Appreciating Course Materials and Instructor Support

With McGraw-Hill, you can development and tailor the course you want to teach.

Create Easily rearrange chapters, combine material from other content sources, and quickly upload content you have written, such as your course syllabus or teaching notes, using McGraw-Hill Create. Find the content you need by searching through thousands of leading McGraw-Hill textbooks. Arrange your book to fit your teaching style. Create even allows you to personalize your book's appearance by selecting the cover and adding your name, school, and course information. Order a Create book, and you will receive a complimentary print review copy in 3 to 5 business days or a complimentary electronic review copy via e-mail in about an hour. Experience how McGraw-Hill empowers you to teach *your* students *your* way. **www.mcgraw-hillcreate.com**

Three *Science of Psychology: An Appreciative View* chapters are available exclusively through Create. These include:

- **Development,** a topical organization based on the textbook's Chapter 9, "Human Development"
- **Thinking and Language,** an expanded treatment of the topics found in the text's Chapter 8, "Thinking, Intelligence, and Language"
- **Intelligence,** an expanded treatment of this topic based on the text's Chapter 8, "Thinking, Intelligence, and Language"

CourseSmart e-Textbook This text is also available as an e-book where through CourseSmart your students can take advantage of significant savings off the cost of a print textbook, reduce the impact on the environment, and gain access to powerful web tools for learning. CourseSmart e-textbooks can be viewed online or downloaded to a computer. The e-textbooks allow students to do full-text searches, add highlighting and notes, and share comments with classmates. Visit **www.coursesmart.com** to learn more and to try a sample chapter.

Tegrity Capture lessons and lectures in a searchable format for use in traditional, hybrid, "flipped classes," and online courses by using Tegrity. Its personalized learning features make study time efficient, and its ability to affordably scale brings this benefit to every student on campus. Patented search technology and real-time LMS integrations make Tegrity the market-leading solution and service.

Instructor's Manual by Lorelei A. Carvajal, Triton Community College The Instructor's Manual provides a wide variety of tools and resources for presenting the course, including learning objectives, ideas for lectures and discussions, and handouts. The Connections section lists instructional resources and Connect-assignable assets to support each chapter.

Test Bank By increasing the rigor of the test bank development process, McGraw-Hill has raised the bar for student assessment. A coordinated team of subject-matter experts prepared over 3,000 questions. The team methodically vetted each question and set of possible answers for accuracy, clarity, effectiveness, and accessibility, and each question is annotated for level of difficulty, Bloom's taxonomy, APA learning outcomes, and corresponding coverage in the text. Organized by chapter, the questions are designed to test factual, applied, and conceptual understanding.

PowerPoint Presentations by Victor Broderick, Lakeland Community College Two sets of PowerPoint Presentations are available. The first includes the key points of the chapter. The second includes the key points of the chapter and supporting visuals. All of the slides can be modified to meet individual needs.

Image Gallery The Image Gallery features the complete set of figures and tables from the text. These images are available for download and can be easily embedded into PowerPoint slides.

McGraw-Hill Campus McGraw-Hill Campus (www.mhcampus.com) provides faculty with true single sign-on access to all of McGraw-Hill's course content, digital tools and other high quality learning resources from any Learning Management System (LMS). This innovative offering allows for secure and deep integration enabling seamless access for faculty and students to any of McGraw-Hill's course solutions such as McGraw-Hill Connect® (all-digital teaching and learning platform), McGraw-Hill Create™ (state-of-the-art custom-publishing platform), McGraw-Hill LearnSmart™ (online adaptive study tool) or Tegrity® (a fully searchable lecture capture service).

McGraw-Hill Campus includes access to McGraw-Hill's entire content library, including eBooks, assessment tools, presentation slides and multimedia content, among other resources, providing faculty open, unlimited access to prepare for class, create tests/quizzes, develop lecture material, integrate interactive content, and more.

ACKNOWLEDGMENTS

APPRECIATING VALUABLE INSTRUCTOR AND STUDENT FEEDBACK

The quality of *The Science of Psychology: An Appreciative View*, Third Edition, is a testament to the skills and abilities of so many people, and I am tremendously grateful to the following individuals for their insightful contributions during the project's development and production.

Angela Adame-Smith, *Seminole State College of Florida*

Judi Addelston, *Valencia College–East*

Cheryl Anagnopoulos, *Black Hills State University*

Benjamin Anderson, *Bethel University*

Gene Ano, *Mt. San Antonio College*

Nicole Arduini-Van Hoose, *Hudson Valley Community College*

Jeffrey Armstrong, *Northampton Community College*

Sandra K. Arntz, *Carroll University*

Irwin Badin, *Montclair State University*

Steven H. Baron, *Montgomery County Community College*

Colleen Bartels, *Hudson Valley Community College*

Karen Bedell, *Baker College–Flint*

Daniel R. Bellack, *Trident Technical College*

Nora Benjamin, *College of Lake County*

William Bennett, *Bluefield State College*

Kate Bieda, *College of Lake County*

Christopher Michael Blake, *Baton Rouge Community College*

Emilia Boeschen, *Black Hills State University*

David Brackin, *Young Harris College*

Scott Brandhorst, *Southeast Missouri State University*

Kathy J. Brewster, *Cloud County Community College*

Tara Broccoli, *Mitchell College*

Kathy E. Brooks, *Community College of Philadelphia*

Brad Brubaker, *Indiana State University*

Amy Buckingham, *Red Rocks Community College*

Myra Beth Bundy, *Eastern Kentucky University*

Lucy Capuano-Brewer, *Ventura College*

David Carlston, *Midwestern State University*

Lorelei Carvajal, *Triton College*

Mark A. Casteel, *Pennsylvania State University–York*

Michelle L. Caya, *Trident Technical College*

Sharon E. Chacon, *Northeast Wisconsin Technical College*

Daniel P. Chadborn, *Southeastern Louisiana University*

Diana Ciesko, *Valencia College–East*

Jennifer Clark, *Butler Community College*

Sharon Clark, *College of Lake County*

Jamie Clopton, *Palomar College*

Abby Coats, *Westminster College*

Herbert Coleman, *Austin Community College*

Doreen Collins-McHugh, *Seminole State College of Florida*

Melanie Conti, *Kean University*

Seth Corley, *Austin Community College*

Alexander M. Czopp, *Western Washington University*

Thomas C. Davis, *Nichols College*

Dianne DeSousa, *Prairie State College*

Penny Devine, *Florida State College–Kent*

Mike Devoley, *Lone Star College*

George Diekhoff, *Midwestern State University*

John Dilworth, *Kellogg Community College*

Stephanie Ding, *Del Mar College*

Christopher Dyszelski, *Madison Area Technical College*

Kenneth C. Elliott, *University of Maine–Augusta*

Jim Ellison, *Triton College*

Mark Evans, *Tarrant County College*

Jeanne Face, *J. Sargeant Reynolds Community College*

Linda Fayard, *Mississippi Gulf Coast Community College–Jackson County*

Jamie Fearrington, *Appalachian State University*

Yuna Ferguson, *Pennsylvania State University–Shenango*

Linda Kay Fernandes, *Trident Technical College*

Roy Fish, *Zane State College*

Laura Flewelling, *Johnston Community College*

Kristin Flora, *Franklin College*

Lela M. Foxx, *University of Memphis*

Fatima Gibbs, *Great Lakes Institute of Technology*

Rachael Giovenco-Bicknell, *Triton College*

Paul R. Gladden, *Middle Georgia State College*

Ryan Godfrey, *East Los Angeles College*

William Goggin, *University of Southern Mississippi*

Jessica Goodwin, *Gloucester County College*

Cameron Gordon, *University of North Carolina–Wilmington*

Raymond M. Gordon, *Bristol Community College*

Gladys S. Green, *State College of Florida–Manatee-Sarasota*

Shelia P. Greenlee, *Christopher Newport University*

Gregory Harris, *Polk State College*

Julia Heberle, *Albright College*

Raquel Henry, *Lone Star College–Kingwood*

Linda E. Hoffman, *McKendree University*

Natalie Homa, *Webster University*

Becky Howell, *Forsyth Technical Community College*

David Hurley, *Stonehill College*

Darren Iwamoto, *Chaminade University of Honolulu*

Alisha Janowsky, *University of Central Florida*

Margaret Jenkins, *Seminole State College of Florida*

Joan Jensen, *Central Piedmont Community College–Cato*

Andrew Johnson, *Park University*

James J. Johnson, *Illinois State University*

Lance Jones, *University of Toledo*

Amy Kausler, *Jefferson College*

Scott Keiller, *Kent State University–Tuscarawas*

Yuthika Kim, *Oklahoma City Community College*

Rosalyn M. King, *Northern Virginia Community College–Loudoun*

Norman Kinney, *Southeast Missouri State University*

Cheri L. Kittrell, *State College of Florida–Manatee-Sarasota*

Kristina T. Klassen, *North Idaho College*

Kimberly Knesting-Lund, *University of Wisconsin–Whitewater*

Sandra J. Knode, *Anne Arundel Community College*

Donald Knox, *Wayland Baptist University*

Burton F. Krain, *College of Lake County*

Kelly Leonhard, *Valencia College–Orlando*

Deranda Lester, *University of Memphis*

Irv Lichtman, *Lone Star College*

Shayn Lloyd, *Tallahassee Community College*

Shane Long, *Southern Maine Community College*

Cynthia Lonsbary, *SUNY Jefferson Community College*

Randy Lowell, *University of South Carolina–Union*

Ayanna M. Lynch, *Bowie State University*

Lynda Mae, *Arizona State University–Tempe*

Jon Mandracchia, *University of Southern Mississippi*

Diane Martichuski, *University of Colorado–Boulder*

Beena Mathew, *Triton College*

Catherine Matson, *Moraine Valley Community College*

Douglas McHugh, *Quinnipiac University*

Michael R. Meager, *Georgia Regents University*

Yuvonie Mickel, *Coahoma Community College*

Will Miller, *Flagler College*

Peggy Motsch, *Siena Heights University*

Dan Muhwezi, *Butler Community College*

Taryn Myers, *Virginia Wesleyan College*

David P. Nalbone, *Purdue University*

Bryan Neighbors, *Southwestern University*

Ryan Newton, *Metropolitan Community College*

Fabian Novello, *Clark State Community College*

Alan Y. Oda, *Azusa Pacific University*

Eirini Papafratzeskakou, *Mercer County Community College*

Joseph Pelletier, *California Baptist University*

Dick Pelley, *Tennessee Wesleyan College*

James Previte, *Victor Valley College & Antelope Valley College*

Anna Pullara, *Triton College*

Linda Raasch, *Normandale Community College*

Jill Ramet, *Metropolitan Community College*

Belinda Ramos, *Chandler-Gilbert Community College*

Sadhana Ray, *Delgado Community College*

Gregory Reichhart, *SUNY Potsdam*

Hugh H. Riley, *Baylor University*

Kim Roberts, *California State University–Sacramento*

Rebecca Roberts, *Franklin College*

Darla Rocha, *San Jacinto College–North*

Christopher Roddenberry, *Wake Technical Community College*

William B. Sammons, *Des Moines Area Community College*

Karen Savarese, *Southern Connecticut State University*

Sharon Sawatzky, *Butler Community College*

Theresa Schrantz, *Tarrant County College*

John Schulte, *Cape Fear Community College*

Alan Searleman, *St. Lawrence University*

Sandra Sego, *American International College*

Keith Shafritz, *Hofstra University*

Shannon Shepard, *Lewis and Clark Community College*

Stuart Silverberg, *Westmoreland County Community College*

David Simpson, *Carroll University*

Debbie Skousen, *Treasure Valley Community College*

Cynthia M. Sodini, *Morton College*

Jason S. Spiegelman, *Community College of Baltimore County*

Emily Stark, *Minnesota State University–Mankato*

Stephen P. Stelzner, *College of Saint Benedict*

Betsy Stern, *Milwaukee Area Technical College*

Anne E. Stuart, *American International College*

Lauren Stutts, *Davidson College*

Julie Suek, *Lower Columbia College*

William Travis Suits, *Seminole State College of Florida*

Jennifer Sullivan, *Mitchell College*

Shawn D. Talbot, *Kellogg Community College*

Danielle Tallent, *Red Rocks Community College*

Marianna Tanguy, *Austin Community College*

Rachelle Tannenbaum, *Anne Arundel Community College*

Holly E. Tatum, *Randolph College*

Lara Tedrow, *Tidewater Community College*

Mark D. Thomas, *University of Wisconsin–Whitewater*

Albert K. Toh, *University of Arkansas–Pine Bluff*

Susan M. Troy, *Northeast Iowa Community College*

Margot Underwood, *Joliet Junior College*

JoAnne Uthe-Gibson, *Northeast Iowa Community College*

Michael A. Vandehey, *Midwestern State University*

Jonathan Waldron, *Virginia Tech*

Stacy A. Walker, *Lone Star College*

Janet Weigel, *Black Hawk College*

Susan Wells, *Iowa Central Community College*

Adam Wenzel, *Saint Anselm College*

Matthew Wiediger, *MacMurray College*

Roberta Wiediger, *Lincoln Land Community College*

Travis Wilkerson, *Ozarka College*

Glenda S. Williams, *Lone Star College, North Harris*

Khara Williams, *University of Southern Indiana*

James Woolcock, *Baker College–Flint*

Shelly Wooldridge, *University of Arkansas Community College–Batesville*

Jennifer R. Yates, *Ohio Wesleyan University*

Mona Yektaparast, *Central Piedmont Community College*

Since the publication of the first edition, I have met hundreds of faculty members across the country, and I continue to be awestruck by the hard work, dedication, and enthusiasm of introductory psychology instructors. So, I wanted to say thank you. You all continue to inspire me—to be a better teacher myself, to develop the best learning solutions for the introductory psychology course, and to make our field fun and relevant to today's students. I appreciate you!

Thanks as well to the manuscript reviewers whom I have not met in person. Your critical and thoughtful appraisals of the book will benefit students in innumerable ways. I thank you for sharing your expertise with me.

PERSONAL ACKNOWLEDGMENTS

I would like to extend my deepest appreciation to the many energetic and talented individuals at McGraw-Hill who have contributed so much to this work. Certainly, I owe a debt of gratitude to the amazing sales representatives whose hard work allowed the previous editions of *The Science of Psychology* to be such successes. In addition, I thank Nancy Welcher, Krista Bettino and Mike Ryan for their encouragement throughout the process of this third edition. Thanks also to Sheryl Adams, and Dawn Groundwater for wonderful ideas and contributions along the way, as well as to A. J. Laferrera and Ann Helgerson for finding ways to "let me be me" in the service of the book.

Readers of this third edition will benefit from the conscientious efforts of development editor Cara Labell, who added her personal energies and gifts to make the third edition a special and exciting new introduction to psychology. Cara was extraordinarily helpful in navigating the data from the LearnSmart heat maps, identifying places where the students needed more or different material. It allowed me to "hear" students' needs in a way that was truly invaluable. A very special thanks to copyeditor Jennifer Gordon for her indefatigable sensibility and attention to detail. Her thoughtfulness, her "ear" for the written word, and her willingness to take on responsibilities have been incredible. This third edition is better for her efforts. And I am grateful to Content Project Manager April Southwood for her deep well of professionalism and skill. Thanks also to Design Manager Michelle Whitaker, Designer Matt Backhaus, Content Licensing Specialist Carrie Burger, and Buyer Laura Fuller for their hard work on this project.

I also have to thank my students at the University of Missouri, Columbia, especially my introductory psychology students, who manage (even at 8 A.M.) to keep me on my toes and thinking. They have been a fabulous testing ground for ideas. Thanks as well to Samantha Heintzelman, Sarah Harrison, Jerry Mitchell, and Jason Trent, my graduate students, who have patiently managed to build scholarly careers while their advisor has juggled her writing and editing.

Finally, I thank my family for their love, support, patience, and encouragement. I would especially like to acknowledge my father, Robert C. King, who died while I was completing this third edition. He was an amazing father and an amazing person who always modeled a good life, in every sense, for me. One of my most cherished memories of my dad is seeing his smiling face in the back of a lecture hall when I was teaching at SMU. As someone who never went to college, my father might be excused for not quite "getting" what it means to be an academic. But he showed again and again that he did get it. I will be forever grateful for his support of my career and my life. When we were going through the many mementoes he'd collected over the years, I was gratified to find a copy of the second edition of the *Science of Psychology* on a shelf. I miss him and I wish he could add a copy of the third edition to that shelf. But I don't have to imagine what he'd say to me about it because he told me himself, so many times: "Honey, you work harder than anyone I know. I love you, and I am proud of you."

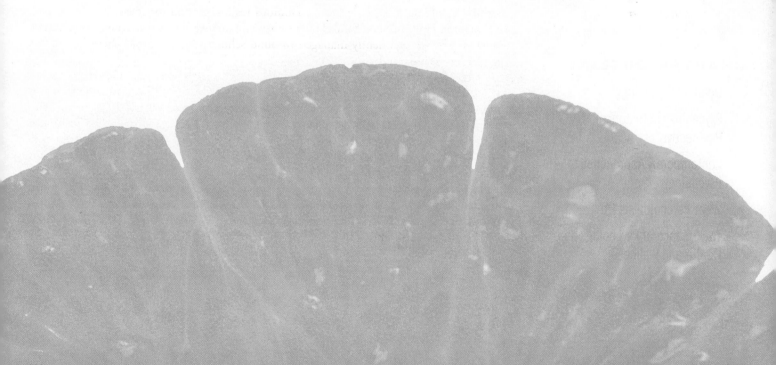

PSYCHOLOGY

THE SCIENCE OF

AN APPRECIATIVE VIEW

3

CHAPTER 1

What Is Psychology?

The Mystery That Is You

Do you have a hero? When you think of someone you truly admire, a celebrity or star athlete might come to mind. In a December 2012 Gallup poll, the most admired man in America was President Barack Obama. Nelson Mandela was second, followed by Mitt Romney (Newport, 2012). Hillary Rodham Clinton was the most admired woman followed by Oprah Winfrey and Michelle Obama. These are all famous people who have made significant contributions in public life.

At the right moment, though, an "ordinary" person can become a hero. In October 2012, Hurricane Sandy hit the northeastern United States, devastating areas of New York and New Jersey. Jesús Ayala, a public school custodian, responded to the emergency by turning his school into a makeshift shelter for displaced New Yorkers. The school became a haven for over 168 people, including families with children, the elderly, homeless people, and psychiatric patients from a local hospital. Night and day, Ayala and his team kept the peace and did all they could to provide comfort to these individuals rendered refugees by the storm. Once Sandy passed, Ayala and his crew transformed the school back to a place of learning, in a single weekend (Ruiz, 2012). Their dedication meant that children could get back to their regular lives. Everyday, ordinary people who work tirelessly at their jobs can sometimes be invisible heroes, noticed only when called upon to take action.

Even in less extraordinary circumstances, people make choices that we might call heroic. They are generous when they might be selfish. They forgive when they could hold a grudge, work hard when they could slack off. You might not think of psychology as focusing on admirable aspects of human behavior, but in fact the science of psychology is about *all* of human behavior.

Ordinary human behavior is extraordinary when viewed in the right light, with a close lens. Scientists, including psychologists, look at the world with just such a lens. Right now, dedicated scientists are studying things about you that you might have never considered, like how your eyes adjust to a sunny day. There is not a single thing about you that is not fascinating to some psychologist somewhere. Psychologists are passionate about what they study—and what they study is you. ●

PREVIEW

This introductory chapter begins by formally defining psychology and then gives context to that definition by reviewing the history and the intellectual underpinnings of the field. We next examine a number of contemporary approaches to the subject. We explore what psychologists do, including therapeutic practice and research, and consider the areas of specialization within psychology. Our introduction to this dynamic, practical field closes with a look at how understanding and applying psychological findings can positively influence human health and wellness.

1. DEFINING PSYCHOLOGY

● **psychology** The scientific study of behavior and mental processes.

● **science** The use of systematic methods to observe the natural world, including human behavior, and to draw conclusions.

When you think of the word *psychology,* what first comes to mind? Formally defined, **psychology** is the scientific study of behavior and mental processes. Let's consider the three key terms in this definition: *science, behavior,* and *mental processes.*

As a **science,** psychology uses systematic methods to observe human behavior and draw conclusions. The goals of psychological science are to describe, predict, and explain behavior. In addition, psychologists are often interested in controlling or changing behavior, and they use scientific methods to examine interventions that might help, for example, reduce violence or promote happiness.

Researchers might be interested in knowing whether individuals will help a stranger who has fallen down. The investigators could devise a study in which they observe people walking past a person who needs help. Through many observations, the researchers could come to *describe* helping behavior by counting how many times it occurs in particular circumstances. They may also try to *predict* who will help, and when, by examining characteristics of the individuals studied. Are happy people more likely to help? Are women or men more likely to help? After psychologists have analyzed their data, they also will want to *explain* why helping behavior occurred when it did. Finally, these investigators might be interested in changing helping behavior by devising strategies to increase helping.

● **behavior** Everything we do that can be directly observed.

● **mental processes** The thoughts, feelings, and motives that each of us experiences privately but that cannot be observed directly.

Behavior is everything we do that can be directly observed—two people kissing, a baby crying, a college student riding a motorcycle to campus. **Mental processes** are the thoughts, feelings, and motives that each of us experiences privately but that cannot be observed directly. Although we cannot see thoughts and feelings, they are nonetheless real. They include *thinking* about kissing someone, a baby's *feelings* when its mother leaves the room, and a student's *memory* of a motorcycle trip.

The Psychological Frame of Mind

What makes for a good job, a good marriage, or a good life? Although there are a variety of ways to answer the big questions of life, psychologists approach these questions as scientists. Psychology is a rigorous discipline that tests assumptions, bringing scientific data to bear on the questions of central interest to human beings (Gravetter & Forzano, 2012; Stanovich, 2013). Psychologists conduct research and rely on that research to provide evidence for their conclusions. They examine the available evidence about some aspect of mind and behavior, evaluate how strongly the data (information) support their hunches, analyze disconfirming evidence, and carefully consider whether they have explored all of the possible factors and explanations. At the core of this scientific approach are four attitudes: critical thinking, skepticism, objectivity, and curiosity.

Like all scientists, psychologists are critical thinkers. **Critical thinking** is the process of reflecting deeply and actively, asking questions, and evaluating the evidence (Bonney & Sternberg, 2011; Smith & Davis, 2013). Thinking critically means asking ourselves *how* we know something. Critical thinkers question and test what some people say are facts. They examine research to see if it soundly supports an idea (Rosnow & Rosenthal, 2013). Critical thinking reduces the likelihood that conclusions will be based on unreliable personal beliefs, opinions, and emotions. Thinking critically will be very important as you read *The Science of Psychology*. Some of the things you read will fit with your current beliefs, and some will challenge you to reconsider your assumptions. Actively engaging in critical thinking is vital to making the most of psychology. As you read, think about how what you are learning relates to your life experiences and to your assumptions about others.

In addition, scientists are characterized by *skepticism* (Stanovich, 2013). Skeptical people challenge whether a supposed fact is really true. Being skeptical can mean questioning what "everybody knows." There was a time when "everybody knew" that women were morally inferior to men, that race could influence a person's IQ, and that the earth was flat. Psychologists, like all scientists, look at such assumptions in new and questioning ways and with a skeptical eye. You might use scientific skepticism the next time you encounter an infomercial about the latest diet craze that promises to help you lose weight "without diet or exercise." A skeptic knows that if something sounds too good to be true, it probably is.

Psychology researchers often find the unexpected in human behavior. For example, it might seem obvious that couples who live together before marriage (cohabitation) have a better chance of making the marriage last. After all, practice makes perfect, right? Yet, in general, researchers have found a higher rate of marital success for couples who did *not* live together before marriage (Manning & Cohen, 2012; Rhoades, Stanley, & Markman, 2009).

Scientists are driven to pursue more precise information about particular issues or topics. In the case of cohabiting prior to marriage, researchers recently have found two conditions in which cohabiting does *not* lead to a decrease in marital satisfaction and an increase in divorce: (1) when cohabitation occurred only with the eventual marital partner (Jose, O'Leary, & Moyer, 2010); and (2) when the couple got engaged prior to cohabitation (Stanley & others, 2010). Research is an ongoing process for seeking knowledge, and future studies likely will require further modifications so that we can better understand whether cohabiting prior to marriage predicts negative marital outcomes.

Related to critical thinking and skepticism is the distinction between science and pseudoscience. *Pseudo* means "fake," and *pseudoscience* refers to information that is couched in scientific terminology but is not supported by sound scientific research. Astrology is an example of a pseudoscience. Although astrologers may present detailed information about an individual, supposedly based on when that person was born, no

A baby's interactions with its mother and the infant's crying are examples of behavior because they are observable. The feelings underlying the baby's crying are an example of a mental process that is unobservable.

● **critical thinking** The process of reflecting deeply and actively, asking questions, and evaluating the evidence.

"According to this rubbish I'm going on a long journey."

© Roy Nixon. www.CartoonStock.com.

● **empirical method** Gaining knowledge through the observation of events, the collection of data, and logical reasoning.

scientific evidence supports these assumptions and predictions. One way to tell that an explanation is pseudoscientific rather than scientific is to look at how readily proponents of the explanation will accept evidence to the contrary.

Being open to the evidence means thinking *objectively*. To achieve this goal, scientists apply the empirical method to learn about the world (Graziano & Raulin, 2013). Using the **empirical method** means gaining knowledge through the observation of events, the collection of data, and logical reasoning. Being objective involves seeing things as they really are, *not as we would like them to be.* Objectivity means waiting to see what the evidence tells us rather than going with our hunches. Does the latest herbal supplement truly help relieve depression? An objective thinker knows that we must have sound evidence before answering that question.

Last, scientists are *curious*. Scientists notice things in the world (a star in the sky, an insect, a happy person) and want to know what it is and why it is that way. Science involves asking questions, even very big questions, such as where did the earth come from, and how does love between two people endure for 50 years? Thinking like a psychologist means opening your mind and imagination to wondering why things are the way they are. Once you begin to think like a psychologist, you might notice that the world looks like a different place. Easy answers and simple assumptions will not do.

As you can probably imagine, psychologists have many different opinions about many different things, and psychology, like any science, is filled with debate and controversy. Throughout this book, we will survey areas of hot debate in psychology in a feature called Critical Controversy. As the first example, check out this chapter's Critical Controversy concerning whether the generation of Americans born since the 1980s is experiencing an epidemic of self-love.

Debate and controversy are a natural part of thinking like a psychologist. Psychology has advanced as a field *because* psychologists do not always agree with one another about why the mind and behavior work as they do. Psychologists have reached a more accurate understanding of human behavior *because* psychology fosters controversies and *because* psychologists think deeply and reflectively and examine the evidence on all sides. A good place to try out your critical thinking skills is by revisiting the definition of psychology.

Psychology as the Science of All Human Behavior

As you consider the definition of psychology as the science of human behavior, you might be thinking, okay, where's the couch? Where's the mental illness? Psychology certainly does include the study of therapy and psychological disorders. *Clinical psychologists* in particular specialize in studying and treating psychological disorders (Routh, 2013). By definition, though, psychology is a much more *general* science (Fuchs & Evans, 2013). Surely, psychological disorders are very interesting, and the media often portray psychologists as therapists. Yet the view of psychology as the science of what is wrong with people started long before television was invented. So how did we end up with the idea that psychology is only about mental illness?

When they think about psychology, many people think of Sigmund Freud (1856–1939). Freud believed that most of human behavior is caused by dark, unpleasant, unconscious impulses clamoring for expression. For Freud, even the average person on the street is a mysterious well of unconscious desires. Certainly, Freud has had a lasting impact on psychology and on society; as recently as March 2006, on the occasion of his 150th birthday, Freud was featured on the cover of *Newsweek*. Consider, though, that Freud based his ideas about human nature on the patients whom he saw in his clinical practice—individuals who were struggling with psychological problems. His experiences with these clients, as well as his analysis of himself, colored his outlook on all of humanity. Freud once wrote, "I have found little that is 'good' about human beings on the whole. In my experience most of them are trash" (Freud, [1918] 1996).

Freud's view of human nature has crept into general perceptions of what psychology is all about. Imagine, for example, that you are seated on a plane, having a pleasant conversation with the woman (a stranger) sitting next to you. At some point you ask your seatmate what she does for a living, and she informs you she is a psychologist.

CRITICAL CONTROVERSY

Are Young Americans in the Middle of a Narcissism Epidemic?

"Just had a delicious cappuccino!"

"Hate waiting in line. Grrrr."

Reading status updates posted to Facebook and Twitter, we can easily get the impression that many young adults think even the smallest details of their lives are fascinating. A lively controversy in psychology concerns whether young people in the United States today are more likely to think of themselves as special and extraordinary compared to their counterparts in previous generations. Jean Twenge and her colleagues (Twenge, 2006; Twenge & Campbell, 2009; Twenge, Campbell, & Freeman, 2012; Twenge & Foster, 2008) argue that Americans born since the 1980s are different in being unusually self-confident, self-assertive, and self-centered.

Examining evidence from nationally representative surveys of U.S. high school students over 30 years, Twenge and Keith Campbell (2008) found that students in 2006 rated themselves higher as compared to students in 1975 in terms of their positive expectations as spouses, parents, and workers. Indeed, students in 1975 on average rated themselves as likely to be "good" in these roles, whereas students in 2006 rated themselves as likely to be "very good" (Twenge & Campbell, 2008). Additional studies have shown that compared to baby boomers (born between 1946 and 1961) and Gen Xers (born from 1962 to 1981), Millennials (those born after 1982) tend to be less dedicated to community goals and to value money, image, and fame over goals such as helping others (Twenge, Campbell, & Freeman, 2012). Millennials were especially unlikely to embrace the importance of taking action to preserve the environment, compared to Gen Xers.

Imagine: An entire generation of self-focused, swollen heads. Twenge refers to these individuals as Generation Me and suggests that there is an epidemic of *narcissism* (a condition of intense, unhealthy self-love) in this age group (2006). The popular media—including CBS News, National Public Radio, and several major newspapers—have jumped on the bandwagon to cover this "epidemic" (Associated Press, 2007).

Other psychologists sharply disagree with these conclusions. They argue that the positivity of Americans' self-views has remained stable over time (Donnellan, Trzesniewski, & Robins, 2009; Trzesniewski, Donnellan, & Robins, 2008). For example, Kali Trzesniewski and Brent Donnellan (2009) looked at Twenge and Campbell's data and noted that small differences in the order of the questions could produce the differences in the ratings students made. In most of their analyses, Twenge and Campbell focused on 1975, but 1975 might not have been a representative year, Trzesniewski and Donnellan assert, because the order of the questions was changed after that year. These changes may have rendered 1975 an unusually modest year (Trzesniewski & Donnellan, 2009). Looking at the data for 1975, 1976, and 1977 and comparing these to 2006, Trzesniewski and Donnellan found no evidence that students had developed increasingly positive self-views over time (2009). Thus, Trzesniewski and Donnellan caution against assuming that the young adults of today are especially likely to think of themselves as special or extraordinary (Trzesniewski & Donnellan, 2009, 2010).

This debate illustrates a number of important aspects of the science of psychology. First, solid scientific evidence is a vital part of psychology, and claims must be supported by that evidence. Further, scientists can look at the same data and reach strikingly different conclusions. The lesson here is that no matter how popular a research conclusion might be, it must be evaluated critically and objectively. In their search for answers to fascinating questions, psychologists rely on the empirical method for solid evidence.

WHAT DO YOU THINK

- Where do you stand in this debate? What kind of research would be needed to change your mind about whether there is a narcissism epidemic among young Americans?
- What problems are inherent in drawing conclusions about the members of an entire generation?

© Kate Taylor. www.CartoonStock.com.

You might think to yourself, "Uh oh. What have I already told this person? What secrets does she know about me that I don't know about myself? Has she been analyzing me this whole time?" Would you be surprised to discover that this psychologist studies happiness? Or intelligence? Or the processes related to the experience of vision? The study of psychological disorders is a very important aspect of psychology, but it represents only one part of the science of psychology.

Psychology seeks to understand the truths of human life in *all* its dimensions, including people's best and worst experiences. Psychologists acknowledge that sometimes an individual's best moments emerge amid the most difficult circumstances. Research on the human capacity for forgiveness demonstrates this point (Bono, McCullough, &

The murder in 2006 of five Amish schoolgirls evoked feelings in the community not of hatred and revenge but of forgiveness.

● **positive psychology** A branch of psychology that emphasizes human strengths.

test yourself

1. What makes psychology a science? What are the goals of psychological scientists?
2. What four attitudes are at the core of the scientific approach?
3. Which particular Freudian views of human nature have influenced general perceptions of what psychology is all about?

Root, 2008; Flanagan & others, 2012). Forgiveness is the act of letting go of our anger and resentment toward someone who has harmed us. Through forgiveness we cease seeking revenge or avoiding the person who did us harm, and we might even wish that person well.

One such example is a tragic event from October 2006. Charles Carl Roberts held 10 young Amish girls hostage in a one-room schoolhouse in Pennsylvania, eventually murdering 5 of them and wounding 5 others before killing himself. The grief-stricken Amish community focused not on hatred and revenge but on forgiveness. In addition to raising money for the victims' families, the Amish insisted on establishing a fund for the murderer's family. As they prepared simple funerals for the dead girls, the community invited the killer's wife to attend. The science of psychology has much to offer to our understanding of not only the perpetrator's violence but also the victims' capacity for forgiveness.

The willingness of the Amish community to forgive this horrible crime is both remarkable and puzzling. Can we scientifically understand the human ability to forgive even what might seem to be unforgivable? A number of psychologists have taken up the topic of forgiveness in research and clinical practice (Balliet, Li, & Joireman, 2011; Burnette & others, 2012; McCullough, Kurzban, & Tabak, 2011; Peets, Hodges, & Salmivalli, 2013; Tabak & others, 2012). Michael McCullough and his colleagues (2010, 2012) have shown that the capacity to forgive is an unfolding process that often takes time. For the Amish, their deep religious faith led them to embrace forgiveness, where many people might have been motivated to seek revenge and retribution. Researchers also have explored the relationship between religious commitment and forgiveness (McCullough, Bono, & Root, 2007), the cognitive skills required for forgiveness (Pronk & others, 2010), and even the potential dark side of forgiveness, which might emerge, for example, when forgiveness leads an abusive spouse to feel free to continue a harmful behavior (McNulty, 2011).

Some argue that psychology has focused too much on the negative while neglecting qualities that reflect the best of humanity (Seligman & Csikszentmihalyi, 2000). From these criticisms positive psychology has emerged. **Positive psychology** is a branch of psychology that emphasizes human strengths. Research in positive psychology centers on topics such as hope, optimism, happiness, and gratitude (Diener, 2012b; Lopez, 2013). One goal of positive psychology is to bring a greater balance to the field by moving beyond focusing on how and why things go wrong in life to understanding how and why things go right (Lopez & Gallagher, 2012). Positive psychology is not without its own critics, though. Indeed, some psychologists insist that human weaknesses are the most important topics to study (Lazarus, 2003).

To be a truly general science of human behavior, psychology must address *all* sides of human experience. Surely, controversy—such as that concerning positive psychology—is a part of any science. The healthy debate that characterizes the field of psychology can give rise to new psychological perspectives, and this is a sign of a lively discipline.

2. PSYCHOLOGY IN HISTORICAL PERSPECTIVE

Psychology seeks to answer questions that people have been asking for thousands of years—for example:

■ How do we learn?

■ What is memory?

■ Why does one person grow and flourish while another struggles?

It is a relatively new idea that such questions might be answered through scientific inquiry. From the time human language included the word *why* and became rich enough to enable people to talk about the past, people have created folklore to explain why things are the way they are. Ancient myths attributed most important events to the pleasure or displeasure of the gods. When a volcano erupted, the gods were angry; if two people fell in love, Cupid's arrows had struck them. Gradually, myths gave way to *philosophy*—the rational investigation of the underlying principles of being and knowledge. People attempted to explain events in terms of natural rather than supernatural causes.

Western philosophy came of age in ancient Greece in the fourth and fifth centuries B.C.E. Socrates, Plato, Aristotle, and others debated the nature of thought and behavior, including the possible link between the mind and the body. Later philosophers, especially René Descartes, argued that the mind and body were completely separate, and they focused their attention on the mind. Psychology grew out of this tradition of thinking about the mind and body. The influence of philosophy on contemporary psychology persists today, as researchers who study emotion still talk about Descartes, and scientists who study happiness often refer to Aristotle (Biswas-Diener, Kashdan, & King, 2009).

In addition to philosophy, psychology also has roots in the natural sciences of biology and physiology (Jacobs, 2013; Clark & others, 2013). Read on to trace how the modern field of psychology developed.

William Wundt (1832–1920) Wundt founded the first psychology laboratory (with his coworkers) in 1879 at the University of Leipzig.

Wundt's Structuralism and James's Functionalism

Wilhelm Wundt (1832–1920), a German philosopher-physician, integrated pieces from philosophy and the natural sciences to create the academic discipline of psychology. Some historians say that modern psychology was born in December 1879 at the University of Leipzig, when Wundt and his students performed an experiment to measure the time lag between the instant a person heard a sound and the moment he or she pressed a telegraph key to signal having heard it. What was so special about this experiment? Wundt's study was about the workings of the brain: He was trying to measure the time it took the human brain and nervous system to translate information into action. At the heart of this experiment was the idea that mental processes could be measured. This notion ushered in the new science of psychology.

Wundt and his collaborators concentrated on discovering the basic elements, or "structures," of mental processes. Their approach was thus called **structuralism** because of its focus on identifying the structures of the human mind, and their method of study was *introspection*. Introspection means looking inside our own minds, by focusing on our own thoughts (literally, "looking inside"). For this type of research, a person in Wundt's lab would be asked to think (introspect) about what was going on mentally as various events took place. For example, the individual might be subjected to a sharp, repetitive clicking sound and then might have to report whatever conscious thoughts and feelings the clicking produced. Introspection relies entirely on the person's conscious reflection. What made this method scientific was the systematic, detailed self-report required of the person in the controlled laboratory setting.

Although Wundt is most often regarded as the founding father of modern psychology, it was psychologist and philosopher William James (1842–1910), perhaps more than anyone else, who gave the field an American stamp. From James's perspective, the key question for psychology is not so much what the mind *is* (that is, its structures) as what it *is for* (its purposes or functions). James's view was eventually named *functionalism*.

In contrast to structuralism, which emphasized the components of the mind, **functionalism** probed the functions and purposes of the mind and behavior in the individual's adaptation to the environment. Whereas structuralists were looking inside the mind and searching for its structures, functionalists focused on human interactions with the outside world and the purpose of thoughts. If structuralism is about the "what" of the mind, functionalism is about the "why." Unlike Wundt, James did not believe in the existence of rigid structures in the mind. Instead, James saw the mind as flexible and fluid, characterized by constant change in response to a continuous flow of information from the world. James called this natural flow of thought a "stream of consciousness."

● **structuralism** Wundt's approach to discovering the basic elements, or structures, of mental processes; so called because of its focus on identifying the structures of the human mind.

● **functionalism** James's approach to mental processes, emphasizing the functions and purposes of the mind and behavior in the individual's adaptation to the environment.

William James (1842–1910) James's approach became known as functionalism.

A core question in functionalism is, why is human thought *adaptive*—that is, why are people better off because they can think than they would be otherwise? When we talk about whether a characteristic is adaptive, we are focusing on how it makes an organism better able to survive. As we will see next, functionalism fit well with the theory of evolution through natural selection proposed by British naturalist Charles Darwin (1809–1882).

Darwin's Natural Selection

● **natural selection** Darwin's principle of an evolutionary process in which organisms that are best adapted to their environment will survive and produce offspring.

In 1859, Darwin published his ideas in *On the Origin of Species* (1979). A centerpiece of his theory was the principle of **natural selection,** an evolutionary process in which organisms that are best adapted to their environment will survive and, importantly, produce offspring.

Darwin noted that the members of any species are often locked in competition for scarce resources such as food and shelter. Natural selection is the process by which the environment determines who wins that competition. Darwin asserted that organisms with biological features that led to survival and reproduction would be better represented in subsequent generations. Over many generations, organisms with these characteristics would constitute a larger percentage of the population. Eventually, this process could change an entire species.

Importantly, a characteristic cannot be passed from one generation to the next unless it is recorded in the *genes,* those collections of molecules that are responsible for heredity. Genetic characteristics that are associated with survival and reproduction are passed down over generations. According to evolutionary theory, species change through

psychological *inquiry*

Explore Evolution from Giraffes to Human Beings

Evolution through natural selection and genetic mutation is a slow process that explains the various characteristics we see in creatures in the natural world. Darwin developed his theory of evolution through natural selection by observing phenomena in nature.

Let's take a look at a familiar creature of our natural world—the giraffe. Giraffes are the tallest mammals on earth, with some reaching a soaring height of 19 feet. Much of that height comes from the giraffe's very long neck. That neck poses a mystery that fascinates scientists: Why does the giraffe have such a long neck? Critically explore some possible reasons below, and answer the questions with each.

1. An evolutionary explanation for the giraffe's neck would begin by assuming that, ages ago, some giraffes were genetically predisposed to have longer necks, and others were genetically predisposed to have shorter necks. Take this evolutionary argument one step further: Why do we now see *only* giraffes with long necks?

2. You might reasonably guess that giraffes have long necks in order to reach leaves growing on tall trees—in other words, so that they can eat and survive. However, giraffes often prefer to eat from bushes and relatively low tree branches. Instead, male giraffes use their long necks in fights with other giraffes as they compete over mates. Those that win the fights are more likely to reproduce. Over time, were the winners those with the longer necks or the shorter necks? Explain.

3. The process of evolution sheds light on why members of a particular species share common characteristics. If you were to apply evolutionary theory to human beings, what kinds of characteristics would you focus on and why? Choose one human characteristic and apply the same kinds of questions you considered about the giraffe's long neck. Why are we humans the way we are?

random genetic mutation. That means that, essentially by accident, some members of a species are born with genetic characteristics that make them different from other members. If these changes are adaptive (if they help those members compete for food, survive, and reproduce), they become more common in the species. If environmental conditions were to change, however, other characteristics might become favored by natural selection, moving the process in a different direction.

Evolutionary theory implies that the way we are, at least in part, is the way that is best suited to survival in our environment (Buss, 2012; Durrant & Ellis, 2013). The Psychological Inquiry feature lets you critically apply the principles of Darwin's theory of evolution.

Darwin's theory continues to influence psychologists today because it is strongly supported by observation. We can make such observations every day. Right now, for example, in your kitchen sink, various bacteria are locked in competition for scarce resources in the form of those tempting food particles from your last meal. When you use an antibacterial cleaner, you are playing a role in natural selection, because you are effectively killing off the bacteria that cannot survive the cleaning agents. However, you are also letting the bacteria that are genetically adapted to survive that cleanser to take over the sink. The same principle applies to taking an antibiotic medication at the first sign of a sore throat or an earache. By killing off the bacteria that may be causing the illness, you are creating an environment in which their competitors (so-called antibiotic-resistant bacteria) may flourish. These observations powerfully demonstrate Darwinian selection in action.

If structuralism won the battle to be the birthplace of psychology, functionalism won the war. To this day, psychologists continue to talk about the adaptive nature of human characteristics, although they have branched out to study more aspects of human behavior than Wundt or James might ever have imagined. In a general way, since the days of those pioneers in the field, psychology has defined itself as the science of human behavior. The question of what exactly counts as human behavior, however, has fueled debate throughout the history of the field. For some psychologists, behavior has meant only observable actions; for others, it has included thoughts and feelings; for still others, unconscious processes have been the focal point. Traces of this debate can be seen today in the various contemporary approaches to the science of psychology that we will consider next.

3. CONTEMPORARY APPROACHES TO PSYCHOLOGY

In this section we survey seven different approaches that represent the intellectual backdrop of psychological science: biological, behavioral, psychodynamic, humanistic, cognitive, evolutionary, and sociocultural.

The Biological Approach

Some psychologists examine behavior and mental processes through the **biological approach,** which is a focus on the body, especially the brain and nervous system. For example, researchers might investigate the way your heart races when you are afraid or how your hands sweat when you tell a lie. Although a number of physiological systems may be involved in thoughts and feelings, the emergence of neuroscience has

test yourself

1. What is structuralism? How does functionalism contrast with structuralism?
2. What is meant when we say that a particular characteristic of an organism is adaptive?
3. In what ways is Darwin's work relevant to psychology?

● **biological approach** An approach to psychology focusing on the body, especially the brain and nervous system.

B. F. Skinner was a tinkerer who liked to make new gadgets. Deborah, the younger of his two daughters, was raised in Skinner's enclosed Air-Crib. Some critics accused Skinner of monstrous experimentation with his children; however, the early controlled environment has not had any noticeable harmful effects. Deborah, shown here as a child with her parents, is today a successful artist whose work strongly reflects her unique early childhood experience.

perhaps contributed the most to physiological psychology (Bavelier & others, 2012; Mercado & Henderson, 2013).

Neuroscience is the scientific study of the structure, function, development, genetics, and biochemistry of the nervous system. Neuroscience emphasizes that the brain and nervous system are central to understanding behavior, thought, and emotion. Neuroscientists believe that thoughts and emotions have a physical basis in the brain. Electrical impulses zoom throughout the brain's cells, releasing chemical substances that enable us to think, feel, and behave. Our remarkable human capabilities would not be possible without the brain and nervous system, which constitute the most complex, intricate, and elegant system imaginable.

Although neuroscience is perhaps most often linked with research on human thought, it has spread to many research areas. Today, psychologists from diverse perspectives study topics such as behavioral neuroscience, developmental neuroscience, social neuroscience, and so forth. Although biological approaches might sometimes seem to reduce complex human experience into simple physical structures, developments in neuroscience have allowed psychologists to understand the brain as an amazingly complex organ, perhaps just as complex as the psychological processes linked to its functioning.

The Behavioral Approach

The **behavioral approach** emphasizes the scientific study of observable behavioral responses and their environmental determinants. It focuses on an organism's visible interactions with the environment—that is, behaviors, not thoughts or feelings. The principles of the behavioral approach have been widely applied to help people change their behavior for the better (Craighead & others, 2013; Miltenberger, 2012). The psychologists who adopt this approach are called *behaviorists.* Under the intellectual leadership of John B. Watson (1878–1958) and B. F. Skinner (1904–1990), behaviorism dominated psychological research during the first half of the twentieth century.

Skinner (1938) emphasized that psychology should be about what people do—their actions and behaviors—and should not concern itself with things that cannot be seen, such as thoughts, feelings, and goals. He believed that rewards and punishments determine our behavior. For example, a child might behave in a well-mannered fashion because her parents have previously rewarded this behavior. We do the things we do, behaviorists say, because of the environmental conditions we have experienced and continue to experience.

Contemporary behaviorists still emphasize the importance of observing behavior to understand an individual, and they use rigorous methods advocated by Watson and Skinner (Miller & Grace, 2013; Rehfeldt, 2011). However, not every behaviorist today accepts the earlier behaviorists' rejection of thought processes, which are often called *cognition* (Bandura, 2011).

The Psychodynamic Approach

The **psychodynamic approach** emphasizes unconscious thought, the conflict between biological drives (such as the drive for sex) and society's demands, and early childhood family experiences (Josephs & Weinberger, 2013). Practitioners of this approach believe that sexual and aggressive impulses buried deep within the unconscious mind influence the way people think, feel, and behave.

Sigmund Freud, the founding father of the psychodynamic approach, theorized that early relationships with parents shape an individual's personality. Freud's (1917) theory was the basis for the therapeutic technique that he called *psychoanalysis,* which involves an analyst's unlocking a person's unconscious conflicts by talking with the individual about his or her childhood memories, as well as the individual's dreams, thoughts, and feelings. Certainly, Freud's views have been controversial, but they

● **neuroscience** The scientific study of the structure, function, development, genetics, and biochemistry of the nervous system, emphasizing that the brain and nervous system are central to understanding behavior, thought, and emotion.

● **behavioral approach** An approach to psychology emphasizing the scientific study of observable behavioral responses and their environmental determinants.

● **psychodynamic approach** An approach to psychology emphasizing unconscious thought, the conflict between biological drives (such as the drive for sex) and society's demands, and early childhood family experiences.

Sigmund Freud (1856–1939)
Freud was the founding father of the psychodynamic approach.

remain a part of contemporary psychology. Today's psychodynamic theories tend to place less emphasis on sexual drives and more on cultural and social experiences as determinants of behavior.

The Humanistic Approach

The **humanistic approach** emphasizes a person's positive qualities, the capacity for positive growth, and the freedom to choose one's destiny. Humanistic psychologists stress that people have the ability to control their lives and are not simply controlled by the environment (Maslow, 1971; Rogers, 1961). They theorize that rather than being driven by unconscious impulses (as the psychodynamic approach dictates) or by external rewards (as the behavioral approach emphasizes), people can choose to live by higher human values such as *altruism*—unselfish concern for other people's well-being—and free will. Many aspects of this optimistic approach appear in research on motivation, emotion, and personality psychology (Greenberg & others, 2013).

The Cognitive Approach

According to cognitive psychologists, the human brain houses a "mind" whose mental processes allow us to remember, make decisions, plan, set goals, and be creative (Diederich & Busemeyer, 2013; Leahey, 2013). The **cognitive approach,** then, emphasizes the mental processes involved in knowing: how we direct our attention, perceive, remember, think, and solve problems. Many scientists who adopt this approach focus on *information processing,* the ways that the human mind interprets incoming information, weighs it, stores it, and applies it to decision making. Cognitive psychologists seek answers to questions such as how we solve math problems, why we remember some things for only a short time but others for a lifetime, and how we use our imagination to plan for the future.

Cognitive psychologists view the mind as an active and aware problem-solving system (Leighton & Sternberg, 2013). This view contrasts with the behavioral view, which portrays behavior as governed by external environmental forces. In the cognitive view, an individual's mental processes are in control of behavior through memories, perceptions, images, and thinking.

The Evolutionary Approach

Although arguably all of psychology emerges out of evolutionary theory, some psychologists emphasize an **evolutionary approach** that uses evolutionary ideas such as adaptation, reproduction, and natural selection as the basis for explaining specific human behaviors. David Buss (2012) argues that just as evolution molds our physical features, such as body shape, it also influences our decision making, level of aggressiveness, fears, and mating patterns. Thus, evolutionary psychologists argue, the way we adapt is traceable to problems early humans faced in adapting to their environment (Durrant & Ellis, 2013).

Evolutionary psychologists believe their approach provides an umbrella that unifies the diverse fields of psychology (Bjorklund, 2012). Not all psychologists agree with this conclusion, however. For example, some critics stress that the evolutionary approach provides an inaccurate explanation of why men and women

● **humanistic approach** An approach to psychology emphasizing a person's positive qualities, the capacity for positive growth, and the freedom to choose any destiny.

● **cognitive approach** An approach to psychology emphasizing the mental processes involved in knowing: how we direct our attention, perceive, remember, think, and solve problems.

● **evolutionary approach** An approach to psychology centered on evolutionary ideas such as adaptation, reproduction, and natural selection as the basis for explaining specific human behaviors.

According to humanistic psychologists, warm, supportive behavior toward others helps us to realize our capacity for self-understanding.

have different social roles and does not adequately account for cultural diversity and experiences (Eagly, 2012; Matlin, 2012). Yet, even psychologists who disagree with applying the evolutionary approach to psychological characteristics still agree with the general principles of evolutionary theory.

The Sociocultural Approach

● **sociocultural approach** An approach to psychology that examines the ways in which social and cultural environments influence behavior.

The **sociocultural approach** examines the ways in which social and cultural environments influence behavior. Socioculturalists argue that understanding a person's behavior requires knowing about the cultural context in which the behavior occurs (Gauvain, 2013; Matsumoto & Juang, 2013). Researchers who focus on sociocultural influences might compare people from different cultures to see whether they are similar or different in important ways (Schwartz & others, 2012).

The sociocultural view focuses not only on comparisons of behavior across countries but also on the behavior of individuals from different ethnic and cultural groups within a country (Leong & others, 2013; Mistry, Contreras, & Dutta, 2013; Spring, 2013). Rising cultural diversity in the United States in recent years has prompted increasing interest in the behavior of ethnic minority groups, especially the factors that have restricted or enhanced their ability to adapt and cope with living in a predominantly non-Latino White society (Gollnick & Chinn, 2013). Further, as the nations of the world grow increasingly economically interdependent, it becomes especially important to understand cultural influences on human interaction. For example, psychologists are interested in studying how cultural differences may help or hinder business negotiations (Rosette & others, 2012).

Research on the influence of culture on behavior has led to important findings about psychological processes and especially about the role of culture in the psychological experience of our own sense of self (Wan & others, 2011), as we will see in the Intersection later in this chapter.

Summing Up the Seven Contemporary Approaches

These seven psychological approaches provide different views of the same behavior, and all of them may offer valuable insights that the other perspectives miss. Think about the simple experience of seeing a cute puppy. Looking at that puppy involves physical processes in the eyes, nervous system, and brain—the focus of the biological approach to psychology. The moment you spot that puppy, though, you might smile without thinking and reach down to pet the little guy. That reaction might be a response based on your past learning with your own dog (behavioral perspective), or on unconscious memories of a childhood dog (psychodynamic perspective), or on conscious memories that you especially like this dog breed (cognitive perspective), or even evolutionary processes that promoted cuteness to help offspring survive (evolutionary approach). You might find yourself striking up a conversation with the puppy's owner, based on your shared love of dogs (humanistic perspective). Further, sociocultural factors might play a role in your decision about whether to ask the owner if you could hold the puppy, whether you share those warm feelings about the puppy with others, and even whether (as in some cultures) you might view that puppy as food.

test yourself

1. What are two differences between the cognitive and psychodynamic approaches to psychology?
2. How are the biological and evolutionary perspectives on psychology similar and how are they different?
3. What specific ideas did B. F. Skinner's behaviorist approach emphasize?

4. WHAT PSYCHOLOGISTS DO

People who think of themselves as psychologists work in a wide range of settings and engage in many different activities. Figure 1.1 shows the various settings in which psychologists practice their profession. In this section we look at what psychologists do, and then we zoom in on the areas of specialization.

Careers in Psychology

Individuals with undergraduate training in psychology might use their expertise in occupations ranging from human resources and business consulting to doing casework for individuals struggling with psychological disorders. Those with graduate training in psychology might work as therapists and counselors, researchers and teachers in universities, or as business consultants or marketing researchers.

Individuals who are primarily engaged in helping others are often called *practitioners* of psychology. They spend most of their time in clinical practice, seeing clients and offering them guidance as they work through problems. However, even psychologists who are primarily concerned with clinical practice pay attention to scientific research. For these individuals, rigorous research guides their therapeutic practice and their efforts to make improvements in the lives of their patients. Increasingly, psychologists who primarily provide therapy engage in *evidence-based practice*—that is, they use therapeutic tools whose effectiveness is supported by empirical research (Barkham & others, 2012; Duncan & Reese, 2013).

An important distinction that is often not well understood is the difference between a clinical psychologist and a psychiatrist. A clinical psychologist typically has a doctoral degree in psychology, which requires approximately four to five years of graduate work and one year of internship in a mental health facility. In contrast, a psychiatrist is a physician with a medical degree who subsequently specializes in abnormal behavior and psychotherapy. Another difference between a psychiatrist and a clinical psychologist is that a psychiatrist can prescribe drugs, whereas a clinical psychologist generally cannot. Despite these differences, clinical psychologists and psychiatrists are alike in sharing an interest in improving the lives of people with mental health problems.

Many psychologists who are employed at universities divide their time between teaching and doing research. Research in psychology creates the knowledge that is presented in this book and that you will be learning about in your introductory psychology course.

Human behavior is a vast, complex topic. Most psychologists specialize in a particular area of study, as we consider next.

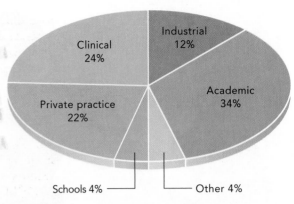

FIGURE 1.1   Settings in Which Psychologists Work More psychologists work in academic environments (34 percent), such as colleges and universities, than in any other setting. However, clinical (24 percent) and private practice (22 percent) settings—both of them contexts in which many psychologists in the mental health professions work—together make up almost half of the total settings.

Areas of Specialization

Psychology has many areas of specialization. Currently, there are 56 divisions in the American Psychological Association, each focusing on a specific subfield of psychology. Division 1, the Society of General Psychology, seeks to provide a coherent integration of the vast science of psychology. Division 2, the Society for the Teaching of Psychology, is dedicated to devising the best ways to help students learn about this fascinating science. The other main specializations in the field of psychology include the following:

Physiological Psychology and Behavioral Neuroscience

Researchers who study *physiological psychology* are interested in the physical processes that underlie mental operations such as vision and memory. Physiological psychologists may use animal models (that is, they may employ animals, such as rats, to study processes that are difficult or impossible to study in the same way in humans) to examine such topics as the development of the nervous system. The field of *behavioral neuroscience* also focuses on biological processes, especially the brain's role in behavior (Eichenbaum, 2013). In Chapter 3 we will examine the many ways that physiological processes relate to psychological experience.

Sensation and Perception   Researchers who study *sensation and perception* focus on the physical systems and psychological processes that allow us to experience the world—to listen to a favorite song (Yost, 2013) and to

Richard J. Davidson of the University of Wisconsin, Madison, shown with the Dalai Lama, is a leading researcher in behavioral neuroscience.

The research of Carol S. Dweck of Stanford University spans developmental and social psychology. Her influential work looks at how our ideas of self play a role in motivation, self-regulation, and achievement.

see the beauty of a sunset (Proffitt & Caudek, 2013). These complex processes are the subject of Chapter 4.

Learning *Learning* is the intricate process by which behavior changes in response to changing circumstances (Miller & Grace, 2013). Many researchers study the basic principles of learning using animals such as rats and pigeons (Capaldi & Martins, 2013). Learning has been addressed from the behavioral and cognitive perspectives (Craighead & others, 2013). This topic is covered in Chapter 6.

Cognitive Psychology *Cognitive psychology* (explored in Chapters 7 and 8) is the broad name given to the field of psychology that examines attention, consciousness, information processing, and memory. Cognitive psychologists are also interested in skills and abilities such as problem solving, decision making, expertise, and intelligence, topics covered in Chapter 8 (Siegler, 2013; Sternberg, 2013a, 2013b). Researchers in cognitive psychology and sensation perception are sometimes called *experimental psychologists*.

Developmental Psychology *Developmental psychology* is concerned with how people become who they are, from conception to death. In particular, developmental psychologists concentrate on the biological and environmental factors that contribute to human development (Kagan, 2013). Developmentalists study child development (Deater-Deckard, 2013) but also adult development and aging (Schaie, 2012). Their inquiries range across the biological, cognitive, and social domains of life (Dweck, 2013; Thompson, 2013). Chapter 9 reviews the key findings in this fascinating area.

Motivation and Emotion Researchers from a variety of specializations are interested in *motivation and emotion,* two important aspects of experience. Scientists who study motivation address research questions such as how individuals persist to attain a difficult goal and how rewards affect the experience of motivation (Anderman, Gray, & Chang, 2013). Emotion researchers delve into topics including the physiological and brain processes that underlie emotional experience, the role of emotional expression in health, and the possibility that emotions are universal (Christenfeld & Mandler, 2013; Lewis, 2013). These fascinating questions are examined in Chapter 10.

Psychology of Women and Gender Those researchers studying the *psychology of women* consider the psychological, social, and cultural influences on women's development and behavior. This field stresses the integration of information about women with current psychological knowledge and beliefs and applies that information to society and its institutions (Hyde & Else-Quest, 2013; Leaper, 2013). Psychologists are also interested in understanding the broad topic of *gender* and the ways in which our biological sex influence our ideas about ourselves as men and women. We consider these important topics in Chapter 11.

Personality Psychology *Personality psychology* considers personality, consisting of the relatively enduring characteristics of individuals. Personality psychologists study such topics as traits, goals, motives, genetics, personality development, and well-being (McCrae, Gaines, & Wellington, 2013). Researchers in personality psychology are interested in those aspects of your psychological makeup that make you uniquely you. The field of personality is explored fully in Chapter 12.

Social Psychology *Social psychology* deals with people's interactions with one another, relationships, social perceptions, social cognition, and attitudes (Bodenhausen & Morales, 2013). Social psychologists are interested in the influence of groups on individuals' thinking and behavior and in the ways that the groups to which we belong

Social psychologists explore the powerful influence of groups (such as, clockwise, Chinese Americans, members of motorcycle clubs, gay Americans, inner-city youths, and military families) on individuals' attitudes, thinking, and behavior.

influence our attitudes. The research questions that concern social psychologists include understanding and working to reduce racial prejudice, determining whether two heads really are better than one, and exploring how the presence of others influences performance. Social psychologists also study the important domain of close interpersonal relationships (Mikulincer & Shaver, 2013a, 2013b, 2013c). Chapter 13 reviews the major research findings of social psychology.

Industrial and Organizational Psychology

Industrial and organizational psychology (I-O psychology) centers on the workplace—both the workers and the organizations that employ them. I-O psychology is often divided into *industrial psychology* and *organizational psychology*. Among the main concerns of industrial psychology are personnel matters and human resource management (Sackett, Walmsley, & Laczo, 2013). Thus, industrial psychology is increasingly referred to as *personnel psychology*. *Organizational psychology* examines the social influences in organizations (Ostroff, Kinicki, & Muhammad, 2013), as well as organizational leadership (Avolio, Sosik, & Berson, 2013). Chapter 14 investigates the key concerns and findings of I-O psychology.

Clinical and Counseling Psychology

Clinical and counseling psychology is the most widely practiced specialization in psychology. Clinical and counseling psychologists diagnose and treat people with psychological problems (Hammen & Keenan-Miller, 2013). Counseling psychologists sometimes work with people to help solve practical problems in life (Baker & Joyce, 2013). For example, counseling psychologists may work with students, advising them about personal problems and career planning. Clinical psychologists are interested in **psychopathology**—the scientific study of psychological disorders

● **psychopathology** The scientific study of psychological disorders and the development of diagnostic categories and treatments for those disorders.

We've run out of lab rats, Henderson... Put this on and come with us.

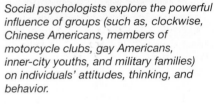

and the development of diagnostic categories and treatments for those disorders. Chapters 15 and 16 explore the intriguing world of psychological disorders and therapies.

Health Psychology *Health psychology* is a multidimensional approach to human health that emphasizes psychological factors, lifestyle, and the nature of the healthcare delivery system (Corsica & Perry, 2013). Many health psychologists study the roles of stress and coping in people's lives (Xanthopoulos & Daniel, 2013). Health psychologists may work in physical or mental health areas. Some are members of multidisciplinary teams that conduct research or provide clinical services. Health psychology is examined in Chapter 17.

This list of specialties cannot convey the extraordinarily rich knowledge you will be gaining as a student in introductory psychology. To whet your appetite for what is to come, check out the Psychological Inquiry feature on page 19 and try answering some of the questions that fascinate psychologists.

The specialties that we have discussed so far are the main areas of psychology that we cover in this book. However, they do not represent an exhaustive list of the interests of the field. Other specializations in psychology include the following.

Community Psychology *Community psychology* concentrates on improving the quality of relationships among individuals, their community, and society at large. Community psychologists are practitioner scientists who provide accessible care for people with psychological problems. Community-based mental health centers are one means of delivering services such as outreach programs to people in need, especially those who traditionally have been underserved by mental health professionals (Dalton & others, 2013).

Community psychologists strive to create communities that are more supportive of their residents by pinpointing needs, providing services, and teaching people how to access resources that are already available (Moritsugu, Wong, & Duffy, 2010). Community psychologists are also concerned with prevention. That is, they try to prevent mental health problems by identifying high-risk groups and then intervene with appropriate services and resources in the community.

School and Educational Psychology *School and educational psychology* centrally concerns children's learning and adjustment in school (Miller & Reynolds, 2013). School psychologists in elementary and secondary school systems test children, make recommendations about educational placement, and collaborate on educational planning teams (Fagan, 2013). Educational psychologists work at colleges and universities, teach classes, and do research on teaching and learning.

Environmental Psychology *Environmental psychology* is the study of the interactions between people and their physical environment. Environmental psychologists explore the effects of physical settings in most major areas of psychology, including perception, cognition, learning, development, abnormal behavior, and social relations (Hartmann & Apaolaza-Ibanez, 2010). Topics that an environmental psychologist might study range from how different building and room arrangements influence behavior to what strategies might be used to reduce human behavior that harms the environment.

Forensic Psychology *Forensic psychology* is the field of psychology that applies psychological concepts to the legal system (Grisso & Brigham, 2013). Social and cognitive psychologists increasingly conduct research on topics related to

Feeling lost, lonely, desperate?

When it seems like there's no hope, there is help.

If you feel trapped…If you feel you have no one to turn to…If you've been feeling down for a while and you're not exactly sure why…

It's important to talk to someone. You can talk to someone right now by calling the Lifeline. Help is available at any time of the day or night—and it's completely free and confidential. We're here to listen and to help you find your way back to a happier, healthier life.

If you or someone you know is thinking about suicide, call the National Suicide Prevention Lifeline:

1-800-273-TALK (8255)

With help comes hope.

NATIONAL SUICIDE PREVENTION LIFELINE
1-800-273-TALK
www.suicidepreventionlifeline.org

U.S. DEPARTMENT OF HEALTH AND HUMAN SERVICES
Substance Abuse and Mental Health Services Administration
www.samhsa.gov

Community psychologists provide accessible care to local populations, often through efforts such as the suicide-prevention program advertised in this poster.

psychological *inquiry*

Questions That Psychology Specialists Ask

This table identifies, by chapter, the topics we will investigate in this book (column 1). For each topic, a question is posed that the chapter will answer (column 2). What do you think the research will show about each of these questions? In the space provided in the note pad, jot down your guesses. Be bold—there are no right answers (yet)!

Chapter and Topic	Question
2 Psychology's Scientific Method	How is deception used in psychological research?
3 Biological Foundations of Behavior	How does behavior change the brain?
4 Sensation and Perception	Is there evidence for the existence of ESP?
5 States of Consciousness	What do dreams mean?
6 Learning	How do pop quizzes influence studying?
7 Memory	Are you likely to remember what you've learned in intro psychology this year 50 years from now?
8 Thinking, Intelligence, and Language	Is creativity related to psychological disorders?
9 Human Development	What kind of parenting is associated with children who are responsible and kind?
10 Motivation and Emotion	Does pursuing happiness make people happier?
11 Gender, Sex, and Sexuality	Where does sexual orientation come from?
12 Personality	Are personality characteristics genetically determined?
13 Social Psychology	How can we best combat racial prejudice?
14 Industrial and Organizational Psychology	What kind of leadership leads to success?
15 Psychological Disorders	What role do genes play in psychological disorders?
16 Therapies	Does psychotherapy work?
17 Health Psychology	What is the role of religion and spirituality in influencing healthy choices?

Your Hunch

2.
3.
4.
5.
6.
7.
8.
9.
10.
11.
12.
13.
14.
15.
16.
17.

Social Psychology and Cross-Cultural Psychology: How Does Culture Influence the Meaning of Success?

The influence of culture—the shared meanings that characterize a particular social group—on psychological experience has long fascinated psychologists. Researchers have distinguished between individualistic and collectivistic cultures (Matsumoto & Juang, 2013; Triandis, 2007). *Individualistic cultures* (such as those of the United States and western European nations) emphasize the uniqueness of each individual and his or her thoughts, feelings, and choices. In contrast, *collectivistic cultures* (such as those in East Asia) emphasize the social group and the roles the individual plays in that larger group. Cultural psychologists believe that these differences influence people's sense of self. Individualists experience the self as independent, separate from his or her social group. Collectivists experience the self as interdependent, embedded in a social context. These differences have been linked to different responses to the experience of success.

Imagine that you are in a psychological study in which you are asked to solve a number of puzzles. Some of the puzzles are easy, and you complete them with no problem. The other puzzles are difficult, and you cannot figure them out. Then, you are left alone with the puzzles, and the researchers inform you that if you would like, you can keep working the puzzles while they prepare the rest of the study materials. Which puzzles will you be more likely to choose?

If you are like most individualists, you will gravitate toward the easy puzzles, choosing to work on what you know you are already good at. However, if you are like most collectivists, you will pick up the difficult puzzles and keep working on those that you have not yet solved (Heine, 2005; Heine & Hamamura, 2007), a pattern that has been shown in Asian cultures (Falk & others, 2009; Heine & Hamamura, 2007), in Chile (Heine & Raineri, 2009), and among Mexican Americans (Tropp & Wright, 2003) and Native Americans (Fryberg & Markus, 2003). Psychologists have sought to identify the processes that led to these cultural differences.

> *How does your cultural experience influence your perceptions of success and failure?*

For example, Toshie Imada and Phoebe Ellsworth (2011) proposed that cultural differences in responses to success are due to the different ways that individualists and collectivists explain or *appraise* their successes. The researchers predicted that when appraising the reasons for their success, individualists would focus on their own personal qualities and abilities ("I did well because I am smart"), while collectivists would more likely point to situational factors—those that reflect a given situation ("I did well because the test was easy"). Moreover, they predicted that these cultural differences in appraisal would affect the emotion experienced after success, with individualists feeling pride and collectivists feeling lucky. They conducted a study comparing U.S. and Japanese students that supported these predictions: After a successful experience, the U.S. students felt proud, and the Japanese students felt lucky (Imada & Ellsworth, 2011). Such studies allow psychologists to shed light on the ways that cultural differences are reflected in our thoughts and feelings.

psychology and law. Forensic psychologists are hired by legal teams to provide input about many aspects of trials, such as jury selection. Those forensic psychologists with clinical training may also testify as experts in trials, such as when they are asked to evaluate whether a person is likely to be a danger to society.

Sport Psychology *Sport psychology* applies psychology's principles to improving sport performance and enjoying sport participation (Rotella, 2010). Sport psychology is a relatively new field, but it is rapidly gaining acceptance. It is now common to hear about elite athletes working with a sport psychologist to improve their game.

Cross-Cultural Psychology Cross-cultural psychology is the study of culture's role in understanding behavior, thought, and emotion (Bullock, 2013). Cross-cultural psychologists compare the nature of psychological processes in different cultures with a particular focus on whether psychological phenomena are universal or culture-specific.

Keep in mind that psychology is a collaborative science in which psychologists work together to examine a wide range of research questions. It is common for scholars from different specialties within psychology to join forces to study some aspect of human behavior. The Intersection feature reviews research that represents collaboration among scientists from different specialties to investigate the same question. See how looking at psychology through the lens of culture can influence our conclusions by checking out this chapter's Intersection.

test yourself

1. What are some career options for a person with an undergraduate degree in psychology? What careers might someone with a graduate degree in psychology pursue?
2. What important distinctions are there between a clinical psychologist and a psychiatrist?
3. Name five areas of specialization in psychology and describe the primary concerns of each.

5. THE SCIENCE OF PSYCHOLOGY AND HEALTH AND WELLNESS

We have reviewed a variety of ways that psychologists approach human behavior, and psychologists have learned much about behavior that is relevant to you and your life. By tying research in psychology to your physical health and psychological wellness, in *The Science of Psychology* we seek to answer the question, what does psychology have to say about *you?* At the close of each chapter, we will consider how the topics covered matter to your physical body and your mind. This link between the mind and the body has fascinated philosophers for centuries. Psychology occupies the very spot where the mind and body meet.

How the Mind Impacts the Body

When you think about psychology, your first thought might be about the mind and the complex feelings—love, gratitude, hate, anger, and others—that emanate from it. Psychologists have come to recognize more and more the degree to which that mind is intricately connected to the body. As you will see when we examine neuroscience in Chapter 3, observations of the brain at work reveal that when mental processes change, so do physical processes (Hagner, 2007).

Health psychologists talk about health behavior as just a subset of behaviors that are relevant to physical health. These behaviors might include eating well, exercising, not smoking, performing testicular and breast self-exams, brushing your teeth, and getting enough sleep. But think about it: Is there ever really a time when your behavior is *not* relevant to your body, and therefore to your health? Is there ever a time when you are doing something—thinking, feeling, walking, running, singing—when your physical body is not present? As long as your body is there—with your heart, lungs, blood, and brain activated—your health is affected. In short, *everything* we do, see, think, and feel is potentially important to our health and well-being.

It might be instructive to think concretely about the ways the mind and body relate to each other, even as they are united in the physical reality of a person. Let's say you see an infomercial on TV for a fitness program, like P90X. You decide to embark on a quest for ripped abs and toned buttocks. Commitment, goal setting, and self-discipline will be among the many mental processes necessary to resculpt your body. In this example, the mind works on the body by producing behaviors that change its shape and size.

How the Body Impacts the Mind

Similarly, the body can influence the mind in dramatic ways. Consider how fuzzy your thinking is after you stay out too late and how much easier it is to solve life's problems when you have had a good night's sleep. Also recall your outlook on the first day of true recovery from a nagging cold: Everything just seems better. Your mood and your work improve. Clearly, physical states such as illness and health influence the way we think.

The relationship between the body and mind is illustrated in a major question that psychologists regularly encounter: What is the impact of nature (genetic heritage) versus nurture (social experience) on a person's psychological characteristics? The influence of genetics on a variety of psychological characteristics, and the ways that genetic endowments can themselves be altered by social experience, will be addressed in many of the main topics in this book, from development (Chapter 9) to personality (Chapter 12) to psychological disorders (Chapter 15). You will see that your physical and mental selves are intertwined in ways you may have never considered (Diamond, Casey, & Munakata, 2011).

Throughout *The Science of Psychology*, we investigate the ways that all of the various approaches to psychology matter to your life. Psychology is crucially about you, essential to your understanding of your life, your goals, and the ways that you can use the insights of thousands of scientists to make your life healthier and happier. In taking introductory psychology, you have an amazing opportunity. You will learn a great deal about human beings, especially one particular human being: you. Whether the psychological research presented is about emotions and motivation or the structures of the nervous system, it is still essentially about the mystery that is you.

test yourself

1. What has psychology increasingly come to recognize about the relationship between the mind and the body?
2. What are some mental processes that might be involved in efforts to change your physical body, as through diet or exercise?
3. What is some real-life evidence of the body's impact on the mind? Give examples that are different from those in the text.

SUMMARY

1. DEFINING PSYCHOLOGY

Psychology is the scientific study of human behavior and mental processes. Psychologists approach human behavior as scientists who think critically and are curious, skeptical, and objective. Behavior includes everything organisms do that can be observed. Mental processes are thoughts, feelings, and motives.

As a truly general science, psychology addresses all sides of human experience—positive and negative, strengths and weaknesses. Psychology is characterized by controversy and debate, and new psychological perspectives sometimes arise when one scientist questions the views of another.

2. PSYCHOLOGY IN HISTORICAL PERSPECTIVE

Psychology emerged as a science from the fields of philosophy and physiology. Two founders of the science of psychology are Wilhelm Wundt and William James. Wundt's structuralism emphasized the conscious mind and its structures. James's functionalism focused on the functions of the mind in human adaptation to the environment. The functionalist emphasis on the mind's adaptive character fit well with the new understandings that came from Charles Darwin's theory of evolution.

3. CONTEMPORARY APPROACHES TO PSYCHOLOGY

Different approaches to psychology include biological, behavioral, psychodynamic, humanistic, cognitive, evolutionary, and sociocultural views. All of these consider important questions about human behavior from different but complementary perspectives.

The biological approach focuses on the body, especially the brain and nervous system. Technological advances in brain imaging have allowed researchers to examine the brain in all its complexity. The behavioral approach emphasizes the scientific study of observable behavioral responses and their environmental determinants. John B. Watson and B. F. Skinner were important early behaviorists. The psychodynamic approach emphasizes unconscious thought, the conflict between biological instincts and society's demands, and early family experiences. Sigmund Freud was the founding father of the psychodynamic approach. The humanistic approach emphasizes a person's capacity for positive growth, freedom to choose a destiny, and positive qualities. The cognitive approach emphasizes the mental processes involved in knowing. Cognitive psychologists study attention, thinking, problem solving, remembering, and learning. The evolutionary approach stresses the importance of adaptation, reproduction, and "survival of the fittest." The sociocultural approach focuses on the social and cultural determinants of behavior and encourages us to attend to the ways that our behavior and mental processes are embedded in a social context.

4. WHAT PSYCHOLOGISTS DO

Psychologists work in a wide range of settings and engage in many different activities. Individuals with undergraduate training in psychology hold occupations ranging from human resources and business consulting to doing casework for individuals struggling with psychological disorders. Those with graduate training in psychology might work as therapists and counselors, researchers and teachers in universities, or as business consultants or marketing researchers.

A clinical psychologist typically has a doctoral degree in psychology, whereas a psychiatrist is a medical doctor who specializes in treating people with abnormal behavior. A psychiatrist treats patients with psychotherapy and can prescribe drugs; a clinical psychologist generally cannot prescribe medication.

Main areas of specialization in psychology include physiological psychology and behavioral neuroscience, developmental psychology, sensation and perception, cognitive psychology, learning, motivation and emotion, personality psychology, social psychology, industrial and organizational psychology, clinical and counseling psychology, and health psychology. Other specialties include community psychology, school and educational psychology, environmental psychology, the psychology of women, forensic psychology, sport psychology, and cross-cultural psychology.

5. THE SCIENCE OF PSYCHOLOGY AND HEALTH AND WELLNESS

Psychologists recognize that the mind and the body are intricately related. The mind can influence the body. The way we think has implications for our nervous system and brain. Our motives and goals can influence our bodies as we strive to be physically fit and eat well. In turn, the body can have an impact on the mind. We think differently when our bodies are rested versus tired, healthy versus unhealthy.

Plan to make the most of your experience in taking introductory psychology by applying your learning to your life. Psychology is, after all, the scientific study of you—your behavior, thoughts, goals, and well-being.

key *terms*

psychology, p. 4
science, p. 4
behavior, p. 4
mental processes, p. 4
critical thinking, p. 5

empirical method, p. 6
positive psychology, p. 8
structuralism, p. 9
functionalism, p. 9
natural selection, p. 10

biological approach, p. 11
neuroscience, p. 12
behavioral approach, p. 12
psychodynamic approach, p. 12
humanistic approach, p. 13

cognitive approach, p. 13
evolutionary approach, p. 13
sociocultural approach, p. 14
psychopathology, p. 17

apply your *knowledge*

1. Ask 10 friends and family members to tell you the first thing that comes to mind when they think of psychology or a psychologist. After hearing their answers, share with them the broad definition of psychology given in this chapter. How do they react?

2. Visit the website of a major book retailer (such as Amazon) and enter "psychology" as a search term. Read the descriptions of five to seven of the most popular psychology books listed. How well do the themes covered represent your perceptions of what psychology is? How well do they represent the approaches to psychology discussed in the text? Are any perspectives over- or underrepresented? If so, why do you think that is?

3. In the directory for your school (or for another institution), look up the psychology faculty. Select several faculty members and see what the areas of specialization are for each person (be careful, they may not be the same as the classes they teach). How do you think their areas of academic training might affect the way they teach their classes?

4. Human beings evolved long ago in a very different environment than we occupy today. The survivors were those who were most able to endure extremely difficult circumstances, struggling to find food, avoid predators, and create social groups. What do you think were the most adaptive traits for these early humans? Are those traits still adaptive? To what specific environments are humans adapting today?

5. Adopt Wilhelm Wundt's approach to understanding the human mind and behavior. Invite three friends to listen to a piece of music, and then ask them to reflect on the experience. Examine what they each say about various aspects of the music. What does this exercise tell you about the subjectivity of introspection? In what ways do you think the method is worthwhile, and in what ways is it limited?

CHAPTER 2

Psychology's Scientific Method

The Psychology of the Jinx

On Sunday, August 12, 2012, the Los Angeles Dodgers were locked in battle against the Miami Marlins. Dodgers' pitcher Chris Capuano had pitched six innings without allowing a hit. Was he on his way to a no-hitter? The TV announcers did what everyone knows you should never do. They began to *openly* discuss the possibility. Instantaneously, Twitter lit up with fan outrage: How could these announcers jinx Capuano's chances? As if right on cue—indeed, as if by magic—in the seventh inning, Marlin Jose Reyes ended Capuano's quest with a single to centerfield. The announcers did not *cause* Reyes's hit, but, for fans, the conclusion was inescapable.

Baseball fans and players are famously superstitious, but magical thinking is common in everyday life. Who hasn't thought, "Of course, the professor who never calls on me will call on me the one day I haven't done the reading!"?

Psychologists Jane Risen and Tom Gilovich (2008) conducted a series of studies to explore the psychology of jinxes or tempting fate. They asked students to consider Jon, a college senior applying to graduate school. Knowing his first choice was Stanford, Jon's mom bought him a Stanford T-shirt. Half of the students read that Jon stuffed the shirt in his bottom drawer, while the other half read that Jon tempted fate: He wore the shirt. If Jon had worn the shirt, students thought he would be less likely to be accepted by Stanford, and once rejected, he would feel even worse than if he had simply tucked it away. Risen and Gilovich suggested that these strong negative feelings associated with negative events after tempting fate make those events vivid in our minds. When we or someone else tempts fate, the possibility of failure pops into mind, like magic.

This is an example of scientific inquiry: Psychologists can take an observation from everyday life, develop a theory that might explain that observation, and then test their ideas systematically using the scientific method. ●

PREVIEW

Being a psychologist means being a scientist who studies psychology. In this chapter, we review the scientific method. You will read about the ways that psychologists have applied this general method to a variety of important topics and about the steps that are involved in recognizing research questions, developing methods to test them, and using statistical techniques to understand the results. Later in the chapter we consider some of the ethical issues that are involved in scientific inquiry. Psychology shares a great deal with other sciences, but as you will see, topics that psychologists study sometimes require special methodological and ethical consideration. To close the chapter, we examine the role of psychological research in health and wellness.

Science is defined not by what it studies but by how it investigates. Photosynthesis, butterflies, and happiness all can be studied in a scientific manner.

● **variable** Anything that can change.

● **theory** A broad idea or set of closely related ideas that attempts to explain observations and to make predictions about future observations.

1. PSYCHOLOGY'S SCIENTIFIC METHOD

Science is defined not by *what* it investigates but by *how* it investigates. Whether you want to study photosynthesis, butterflies, Saturn's moons, or happiness, the *way* you study your question of interest determines whether your approach is scientific. The scientific method is how psychologists gain knowledge about mind and behavior.

It is the use of the scientific method that makes psychology a science (Fuchs & Evans, 2013; Rosnow & Rosenthal, 2013). Indeed, most of the studies published in psychological research journals follow the scientific method, which comprises these five steps (Figure 2.1):

1. Observing some phenomenon
2. Formulating hypotheses and predictions
3. Testing through empirical research
4. Drawing conclusions
5. Evaluating the theory

Step 1. Observing Some Phenomenon

The first step in conducting a scientific inquiry involves observing some phenomenon in the world. The curious, critically thinking psychologist—much like a detective—sees something in the world and wants to know why or how it is the way it is (Smith & Davis, 2013). As an example, recall the research on the psychology of the jinx from the opening of this chapter. Psychologists noticed that people seem to believe that positive things are less likely to happen if we jinx them by tempting fate, so the researchers then designed studies to investigate this belief.

The phenomena that scientists study are called *variables*, a word related to the verb *to vary*. A **variable** is anything that can change. In the studies of jinxing, the variables included whether or not students read that Jon wore that Stanford T-shirt, their estimates of his likelihood of admission to Stanford, and how they imagine Jon would feel if rejected. All the different things psychologists study are variables, including experiences like happiness, gratitude, aggression, belongingness, conformity, and so forth.

As scientists consider answers to such questions, they often develop theories. A **theory** is a broad idea or set of closely related ideas that attempts to explain observations. Theories tell us about the relations between variables on a conceptual level. They seek

1

Observing Some Phenomenon

We feel good when we give someone a gift. However, do we genuinely feel better giving something away than we might feel if we could keep it? Elizabeth Dunn, Lara Aknin, and Michael Norton (2008) decided to test this question.

2

Formulating Hypotheses and Predictions

These researchers hypothesized that spending money on other people would lead to greater happiness than spending money on oneself.

3

Testing Through Empirical Research

In an experiment designed to examine this prediction, the researchers randomly assigned undergraduate participants to receive money ($5 or $20) that the students had to spend on either themselves or someone else by 5 P.M. that day. Those who spent the money on *someone else* reported greater happiness that night.

4

Drawing Conclusions

The experiment supported the hypothesis that spending money on others can be a strong predictor of happiness. Money might not buy happiness, the researchers concluded, but spending money in a particular way, that is, on other people, may enhance happiness.

5

Evaluating the Theory

The experimental results were published in the prestigious journal *Science*. Now that the findings are public, other researchers might investigate related topics and questions inspired by this work, and their experiments might shed further light on the original conclusions.

FIGURE 2.1   Steps in the Scientific Method: Is It Better to Give Than to Receive? This figure shows how the steps in the scientific method were applied in a research experiment examining how spending money on ourselves or others can influence happiness (Dunn, Aknin, & Norton, 2008).

to explain why certain things have happened and can be used to make predictions about future observations. For instance, some psychologists theorize that the most important human need is the need to belong to a social group (Baumeister & Leary, 2000).

Step 2. Formulating Hypotheses and Predictions

The second step in the scientific method is stating a hypothesis. A **hypothesis** is an educated guess that derives logically from a theory. It is a prediction that can be tested. A theory can generate many hypotheses. If more and more hypotheses related to a theory turn out to be true, the theory gains in credibility. So, a researcher who believes that social belonging is the most important aspect of human functioning might predict that people who belong to social groups will be happier than those who do not. Another hypothesis from the theory that belongingness is important to human functioning might be that individuals who have been socially excluded should feel less happy than those who have been socially included.

● **hypothesis** An educated guess that derives logically from a theory; a prediction that can be tested.

Step 3. Testing Through Empirical Research

The next step in the scientific method is to test the hypothesis by conducting *empirical research,* that is, by collecting and analyzing data. At this point, it is time to design a study that will test predictions that are based on the theory. To do so, a researcher first needs a concrete way to measure the variables of interest.

An **operational definition** provides an objective description of how a variable is going to be measured and observed in a particular study. Operational definitions eliminate the fuzziness that might creep into thinking about a problem. Imagine, for instance,

● **operational definition** A definition that provides an objective description of how a variable is going to be measured and observed in a particular study.

Researchers have identified Duchenne smiling (notice the wrinkles) as a sign of genuine happiness.

that everyone in your psychology class is asked to observe a group of children and to keep track of kind behaviors. Do you think that all your classmates will define "kind behaviors" in the same way? Establishing an operational definition ensures that everyone agrees on what a variable means.

To measure personal happiness, for example, prominent psychologist Ed Diener and his students (1985) devised a self-report questionnaire that measures how satisfied a person is with his or her life, called the Satisfaction with Life Scale. (You will get a chance to complete the questionnaire later in this chapter.) Scores on this questionnaire are then used as measures of happiness. Research using this scale and others like it has shown that certain specific factors—marriage, religious faith, purpose in life, and good health—are strongly related to being happy (Diener, 1999, 2012b).

Importantly, there is not just one operational definition for any variable. Although Diener and his colleagues used a questionnaire, researchers have used diverse operational definitions for this variable. For instance, in a study of the relationship between happiness and important life outcomes, researchers used the facial expressions displayed by women in their college yearbook pictures as a measure of happiness. The women in the pictures had graduated 30 years prior. The researchers coded the photographs for the appearance of *Duchenne smiling* (Harker & Keltner, 2001). This type of smiling is genuine smiling—the kind that creates little wrinkles around the outer corner of the eyes—and it has been shown to be a sign of true happiness. (If you want to see whether someone in a photograph is smiling genuinely, cover the bottom of the person's face. Can you still tell that he or she is smiling? A genuine smile is evident in the eyes, not just the mouth.) In addition to coding those photos, the researchers followed up on the women's life experiences since graduating and found that happiness, as displayed in yearbook pictures, predicted positive life outcomes, such as successful marriages and satisfying lives, some 30 years later (Harker & Keltner, 2001).

So, in Diener's research, happiness was operationally defined as a score on a questionnaire; however, in this second study, happiness was operationally defined as Duchenne smiling. These definitions are just two among the many ways that psychologists have operationalized happiness. Another way to operationally define happiness is to *make* people happy, for example, by giving them an unexpected treat like candy or cookies or having them watch an amusing video-clip.

Devising effective operational definitions for the variables in a study is a crucial step in designing psychological research (Kirk, 2013). To study anything, we must have a way to see it or measure it. Clearly, to establish an operational definition for any variable, we first have to agree on what we are trying to measure. If we think of happiness as something that people know about themselves, then a questionnaire score might be a good operational definition of the variable. If we think that people might not be aware of how happy they are (or are not), then a facial expression might be a better operational definition. In other words, our definition of a variable must be set out clearly before we operationally define it. You might try your hand at operationally defining the following variables: generosity, love, maturity, exhaustion, and physical attractiveness. What are some things that *you* find interesting? How might you operationally define these variables?

Because operational definitions allow for the measurement of variables, researchers have a lot of numbers to deal with once they have conducted a study. A key aspect of the process of testing hypotheses is data analysis. *Data* are all the information (all those numbers) researchers collect in a study—say, the questionnaire scores or the behaviors observed. Data analysis means "crunching" those numbers mathematically to see if they support predictions. We will cover some of the basics of data analysis later in this chapter.

Let's consider an example that demonstrates the first three steps in the scientific method. One theory of well-being is *self-determination theory* (Deci & Ryan, 2000, 2012a; Ryan & Deci, 2009). According to this theory, people are likely to feel fulfilled when their lives meet three important needs: relatedness (warm relations with others), autonomy (independence), and competence (mastering new skills).

One hypothesis that follows logically from this theory is that people who value money, material possessions, prestige, and physical appearance (that is, *extrinsic rewards*) over the needs of relatedness, autonomy, and competence (which are *intrinsic rewards*) should be less fulfilled, less happy, and less well adjusted. In a series of studies entitled "The Dark Side of the American Dream," researchers Timothy Kasser and Richard Ryan asked participants to complete self-report measures of values and of psychological and physical functioning (Kasser & Ryan, 1993, 1996; Kasser & others, 2004). Thus, the operational definitions of values and psychological functioning were questionnaire scores. The researchers found that individuals who value material rewards over more intrinsic rewards do indeed tend to suffer as predicted.

Step 4. Drawing Conclusions

Based on the results of the data analyses, scientists then draw conclusions from their research. Do the data support the predictions or not? What do the findings tell us about the theory that guided the study? Psychologists write articles presenting those findings. The articles are submitted for publication in scientific journals. Once submitted, they undergo rigorous review by other scientists who evaluate the work for its scientific merit. If the paper and the research it reports are judged to be of sufficiently high quality, the paper is published for all to see and read.

Step 5. Evaluating the Theory

The final step in the scientific method is one that never really ends. Once a paper is published, the community of scientists continues to evaluate it in light of other research. When many studies have been conducted on the same topic, scholars go back and consider the theory that started it all. Do the studies really support the theory? It is important to keep in mind that usually a theory is revised only after a number of studies produce similar results.

A key step after a study has been published is *replication*. Replicating a study means repeating it and getting the same results. Scientific conclusions rely on showing that the results remain the same, regardless of the specific scientist who conducts the study or the specific group of people who were studied. *Direct replication* means doing the study precisely as it was conducted in its original form. *Conceptual replication* means doing the study with different methods or different types of samples. For instance, a researcher might want to know if a particular strategy to enhance social skills works not only for college students but for older adults or for individuals with autism. If a research finding is shown again and again—that is, if it is *replicated*—across different researchers and different specific methods, it is considered *reliable*. It is a result on which we can depend.

One special type of study involves a meta-analysis. **Meta-analysis** is a statistical procedure that summarizes a large body of evidence from the research literature on a particular topic. For a meta-analysis, a researcher tries to find all of the studies that have been done on a topic of interest. The researcher then compares all the studies and their findings. A meta-analysis allows researchers to conclude whether a result is consistent in the literature and to estimate the magnitude of the relationship between variables (Schmidt, 2013).

● **meta-analysis** A method that allows researchers to combine the results of several different studies on a similar topic in order to establish the strength of an effect.

Meta-analytic results are more powerful than the results of any single study because they combine many findings in the literature. For example, within I-O psychology (our focus in Chapter 14), a large number of studies have examined the question, is it better for employees to avoid making mistakes, preventing disaster, or to seek out opportunities for advancement, always looking for the next chance at success? Those who show the first orientation are said to be "prevention focused" whereas those showing the second are "promotion focused" (Higgins, 2005). A recent meta-analysis summarized the findings of 97 different articles, presenting data from 148 different samples (Lanaj,

● **descriptive research** Research that determines the basic dimensions of a phenomenon, defining what it is, how often it occurs, and so on.

Chang, & Johnson, 2012). The meta-analysis concluded that promotion focus, seeking out new opportunities, was associated with superior task performance, greater innovation at the workplace, and a tendency to engage in helpful activities at work even if they were not a job requirement. In contrast, prevention focus was related to counterproductive work behaviors such as leaving work early, gossiping, or undermining one's colleagues.

The research community maintains an active conversation about what scientists know, and this dialogue constantly questions conclusions (Stanovich, 2013). From published studies, a scholar may come up with a new idea that will eventually change the thinking on a particular topic. Steps 3, 4, and 5 in the scientific method are part of an ongoing process. That is, researchers go back and do more research, revise their theories, hone their methods, and draw and evaluate their new conclusions.

2. TYPES OF PSYCHOLOGICAL RESEARCH

Psychologists commonly use three types of research. *Descriptive research* involves finding out about the basic dimensions of some variable (for example, what the average level of happiness is for men in the United States). *Correlational research* is interested in discovering relationships between variables (for instance, whether being married predicts greater happiness for men). *Experimental research* concerns establishing causal relationships between variables (such as, whether women perceive men as more attractive if the men are smiling). In this section, we examine each of these types of research.

Descriptive Research

Just as its name suggests, **descriptive research** is about describing some phenomenon—determining its basic dimensions and defining what this thing is, how often it occurs, and so on. By itself, descriptive research cannot prove what causes some phenomenon, but it can reveal important information about people's behaviors and attitudes (Leedy & Ormrod, 2013). Descriptive research methods include observation, surveys and interviews, and case studies.

OBSERVATION

Imagine that you are going to conduct a study on how children who are playing together resolve conflicts that arise. The data that are of interest to you concern conflict resolution. As a first step, you might go to a playground and simply observe what the children do—how often you see conflict resolution occur and how it unfolds. You would likely keep careful notes of what you observe.

This type of scientific observation requires an important set of skills (Graziano & Raulin, 2013). Unless you are a trained observer and practice your skills regularly, you might not know what to look for, you might not remember what you saw, you might not realize that what you are looking for is changing from one moment to the next, and you might not document and communicate your observations effectively. Furthermore, you might not realize the value of having one or more others do the observations as well, so that you develop a sense of the accuracy of your observations. In short, for observations to be effective, they must be systematic. You must know whom you are observing, when and where you will observe, and how you will make the observations. Also, you need to know in advance in what form you will document them: in writing, by sound recording, or by video.

SURVEYS AND INTERVIEWS

Sometimes the best and quickest way to get information about people is to ask them for it. One technique is to interview people directly. A related method that is especially useful when information from many is needed is the *survey,* or questionnaire. A survey presents a standard set of questions, or *items,* to obtain people's self-reported attitudes or beliefs about a particular topic.

Although surveys can be a straightforward way to measure psychological variables, constructing them requires care (Leedy & Ormrod, 2013). For example, surveys can measure only what people think about themselves. Thus, if we are interested in studying a variable that we believe is unconscious, such as a psychodynamic drive, we cannot use a survey. Furthermore, people do not always know the truth about themselves. If you were answering a survey that asked, "Are you a generous person?" how might your answer compare to that of a friend who is asked to make that same rating about you? One particular problem with surveys and interviews is the tendency of participants to answer questions in a way that will make them look good rather than in a way that communicates what they truly think or feel (Reynolds & Suzuki, 2013).

Another challenge in survey construction is that when a questionnaire is used to define variables operationally, it is crucial that the items clearly measure the specific topic of interest and not some other characteristic. The language used in a survey therefore must be clear and understandable if the responses are to reflect the participants' actual feelings.

Surveys and interviews can examine a wide range of topics, from religious beliefs to sexual habits to attitudes about gun control (Rosnow & Rosenthal, 2013). Some survey and interview questions are unstructured and open-ended, such as "How fulfilling would you say your marriage is?" Such questions allow for unique responses from each person surveyed. Other survey and interview questions are more structured and ask about quite specific things. For example, a structured question might ask, "How many times have you talked with your partner about a personal problem in the past month: 0, 1–2, 3–5, 6–10, 11–30, every day?"

Questionnaires often use rating scales as a way for participants to indicate their agreement with a statement. Such scales, sometimes called *Likert scales* (after their inventor, Rensis Likert) usually involve the subject selecting a number that indicates the person's level of agreement with a statement. For example, in response to the item, "I am outgoing and sociable," the respondent might be asked to select a number from 1 (indicating not at all) to 7 (indicating very much). Later in this chapter, you will be completing a questionnaire that uses such a scale.

CASE STUDIES

A **case study,** or **case history,** is an in-depth look at a single individual. Case studies are performed mainly by clinical psychologists when, for either practical or ethical reasons, the unique aspects of an individual's life cannot be duplicated and tested in other individuals. A case study provides information about one person's goals, hopes, fantasies, fears, traumatic experiences, family relationships, health, and anything else that helps the psychologist understand the person's mind and behavior. Case studies can also involve in-depth explorations of particular families or social groups.

An example of a case study is the analysis of India's spiritual leader Mahatma Gandhi (1869–1948) by psychodynamic theorist Erik Erikson (1969). Erikson studied Gandhi's life in great depth to discover how his positive spiritual identity developed, especially during his youth. In piecing together Gandhi's identity development, Erikson described the contributions of culture, history, family, and various other factors that might affect the way people form an identity.

A case history provides a dramatic, detailed portrayal of a person's life, but we must be cautious about applying what we learn from one person's life to others. The subject of a case study is unique, with a genetic makeup and personal history that no one else shares. Case studies can be very valuable as the first step of the scientific method, in that they often provide vivid observations that can then be tested in a variety of ways through psychological research. However, and importantly, an in-depth study of a single case may not be generalizable to the general population. This means that a case study

● **case study** or **case history** An in-depth look at a single individual.

Mahatma Gandhi was India's spiritual leader in the mid-twentieth century. Erik Erikson conducted an extensive case study of Gandhi's life to determine what factors contributed to his identity development.

may tell us a great deal about the individual person being studied but not very much about people in general.

THE VALUE OF DESCRIPTIVE RESEARCH

Descriptive research allows researchers to get a sense of a subject of interest, but it cannot answer questions about how and why things are the way they are. Nevertheless, descriptive research does explore intriguing topics, such as the experience of happiness in different cultures. Before reading about and considering the value of that research, complete the measure below. Specifically, using the 7-point scale, indicate your agreement with each item that follows the scale.

1	2	3	4	5	6	7
Strongly Disagree	Disagree	Slightly Disagree	Neither Agree nor Disagree	Slightly Agree	Agree	Strongly Agree

1. In most ways my life is close to my ideal.

2. The conditions of my life are excellent.

3. I am satisfied with my life.

4. So far I have gotten the important things I want in life.

5. If I could live my life over, I would change almost nothing.

You have just completed the Satisfaction with Life Scale (or SWLS; Diener & others, 1985), one operational definition of happiness. To find out your score, add up your ratings and divide by 5. This average rating could be considered your level of general happiness. Many different kinds of studies from many different countries have used this scale and others like it to measure happiness levels. Based on such research, Ed and Carol Diener (1996) concluded that most people are pretty happy because they score above the midpoint, 4, on the scale you just completed. However, research on happiness in various cultures has generally centered on relatively developed countries. What about developing societies that are not as prosperous?

One study examined levels of happiness in groups of people who have not generally been included in psychological studies (Biswas-Diener, Vitterso, & Diener, 2005). The research assessed three groups: the Inughuits (Inuits) of Greenland, the Maasai of southern Kenya, and the American Old Order Amish. All three groups completed measures that were essentially the same as the one you just did.

The Inuit tribe studied (the Inughuits) live at 79 degrees latitude (very far north), in the harshest climate inhabited by a traditional human society. Rocks, glaciers, and the sea dominate the landscape. Farming is impossible. The Inughuits have some modern conveniences, but they generally adhere to a traditional hunting culture. It is not uncommon to find an Inughuit hunter carving a seal or caribou on the kitchen floor while children watch TV in the next room. Most of us might feel a little blue in the winter months when gloomy weather seems to stretch on, day after day. For the Inughuits, however, the sun never rises at all throughout the winter months, and in the summer, it never sets. How happy could an individual be in such a difficult setting? Pretty happy, it turns out, as the Inughuits averaged a 5.0 on the Satisfaction with Life Scale.

The Maasai are an indigenous (native) African nomadic group who live in villages of about 20 people, with little exposure to the West. Maasai are fierce warriors, and their culture has many traditional ceremonies built around a boy's passage from childhood to manhood. Boys are circumcised between the ages of 15 and 22, and they are forbidden from moving or making a sound during the procedure. Girls are also circumcised as they enter puberty, in a controversial ritual that involves the removal of the clitoris and that makes childbirth extremely difficult. The Maasai practice child marriage and polygamy. Maasai women have very little power and are generally expected to do most of the work. How happy could an individual be in this context? Maasai men and women who completed the measure orally in their native tongue, Maa, averaged a 5.4 on the Satisfaction with Life Scale (Biswas-Diener, Vitterso, & Diener, 2005).

Finally, the Old Order Amish of the midwestern and northeastern United States belong to a strict religious sect that explicitly rejects modern aspects of life. The Amish separate themselves from mainstream society and travel by horse and buggy. The women wear bonnets, and the men sport beards, dark clothes, and dark brimmed hats. The Amish farm without modern machinery and dedicate their lives to simplicity—without washing machines, cars, computers, TVs, DVDs, iPods, and smartphones. Still, the Amish are relatively happy, averaging 4.4 on the 7-point happiness scale (Biswas-Diener, Vitterso, & Diener, 2005).

Like a host of other studies in developed nations, these results indicate that most individuals are pretty happy. Such descriptive findings provide researchers of well-being a valuable foundation for further exploring the processes that lead to these feelings of happiness in different cultural settings. If researchers wanted to extend these findings to investigate predictors of happiness in different cultures, they would then turn to a correlational design.

Correlational Research

We have seen that descriptive research tells us about the basic dimensions of a variable. In contrast, **correlational research** tells us about the relation between two variables. The purpose of correlational research is to examine whether and how two variables *change together*. That is, correlational research looks at a *co*-relation. For instance, if one of the variables increases, what happens to the other one? When two variables change together, we can predict one from the other, and we say that the variables are correlated.

● **correlational research** Research that examines the relations between variables with the purpose of determining whether and how two variables change together.

Correlational research is so named because of the statistical technique *correlation* that is typically used to analyze these types of data. The key feature of a correlational study is that the factors of interest are measured or observed to see how they are related (Kiess & Green, 2010; Levin & Fox, 2011). If we want to know whether shy people are happy, we might give the same people two questionnaires—one that measures shyness and another that assesses happiness. For each person we would have two scores, and we would then see whether shyness and happiness relate to each other in a systematic way.

The degree of relation between two variables is expressed as a numerical value called a *correlational coefficient,* which is most commonly represented by the letter *r*. The correlation coefficient is a statistic that tells us two things about the relationship between two variables—its strength and its direction. The value of a correlation always falls between −1.00 and +1.00. The number or magnitude of the correlation tells us about the *strength* of the relationship. The closer the number is to ±1.00, the stronger the relationship. The sign (+ or −) tells us about the *direction* of the relation between the variables. A positive sign means that as one variable increases, the other also increases. A negative sign means that as one variable increases, the other decreases. A zero correlation means that there is no systematic relation between the variables.

Examples of scatter plots (a type of graph that plots scores on the two variables) showing positive and negative correlations appear in Figure 2.2. Note that every dot in this figure represents both scores for one person.

CORRELATION IS NOT CAUSATION

Look at the terms in bold type in the following newspaper headlines:

Researchers **Link** Coffee Consumption to Cancer of Pancreas

Brain Size Is **Associated** with Gender

Psychologists Discover **Relationship** Between Religious Faith and Good Health

Reading these headlines, one might conclude that coffee causes pancreatic cancer, gender causes differences in brain size, and religious faith causes good health. The boldface words are synonymous only with correlation, however, not with causality.

Correlation does not equal causation. Remember, correlation means only that two variables change together. Being able to predict one event based on the occurrence

FIGURE 2.2 Scatter Plots Showing Positive and Negative Correlations A positive correlation is a relationship in which two factors vary in the same direction, as shown in the two scatter plots on the left. A negative correlation is a relationship in which two factors vary in opposite directions, as shown in the two scatter plots on the right.

Positive Correlations

The longer the lecture, the more you yawn.

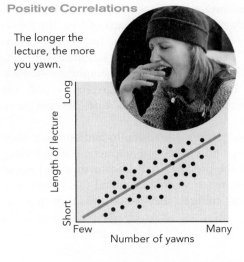

The more you study, the higher your test grade.

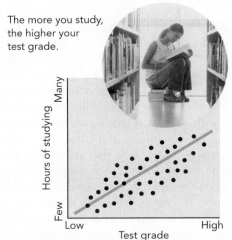

Negative Correlations

The longer the lecture, the lower your attentiveness.

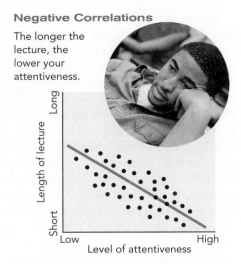

The more you party, the lower your test grade.

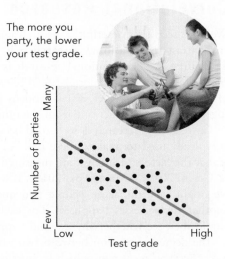

● **third variable problem** The circumstance where a variable that has not been measured accounts for the relationship between two other variables. Third variables are also known as confounds.

of another event does not necessarily tell us anything about the cause of either event (Rossi, 2013). At times some other variable that has not been measured accounts for the relationship between two others. Researchers refer to this circumstance as the **third variable problem.**

To understand the third variable problem, consider the following example. A researcher measures two variables: the number of ice cream cones sold in a town and the number of violent crimes that occur in that town throughout the year. The researcher finds that ice cream cone sales and violent crimes are positively correlated, to the magnitude of +.50. This high positive correlation would indicate that as ice cream sales increase, so does violent crime. Would it be reasonable for the local paper to run the headline "Ice Cream Consumption Leads to Violence"? Should concerned citizens gather outside the local Frosty Freeze to stop the madness? Probably not. Perhaps you have already thought of the third variable that might explain this correlation—heat. Indeed, when it is hot outside, people are more likely both to purchase ice cream and to act aggressively (Anderson & Bushman, 2002). Such a third variable is also called a *confound*.

Consider that interesting study on smiling in college yearbook pictures and happy marriages. What are some third variables that might explain that association? If we think about the reasons women might not be smiling in those yearbook pictures, we might come up with a few possibilities. Perhaps those women experienced parental divorce during their college years. Perhaps they experienced a recent romantic breakup. Perhaps they were having trouble with their coursework, leading them to less successful occupations. Even very compelling correlational studies might be open to alternative explanations.

Further, if a causal link did exist between two variables, a correlation between them cannot tell us about the *direction* of that link. A correlation cannot tell us which variable is the cause and which is the effect. Imagine a study that shows that happiness and physical health are positively correlated in a group of elderly people. We cannot tell, based on that positive correlation, if happiness leads to better health or if health leads to greater happiness.

This example also illustrates a specific type of correlational study known as a cross-sectional design. A **cross-sectional design** is a type of correlational study in which variables are measured at a single point in time. Observations from this single measurement are then compared.

● **cross-sectional design** A type of correlational study in which variables are measured at a single point in time.

THE VALUE OF CORRELATIONAL RESEARCH

Given the potential problems with third variables and the difficulty in drawing causal conclusions, why do researchers bother to conduct correlational studies? There are several very good reasons. Although correlational studies cannot show a causal connection between variables, they do allow us to use one variable to predict a person's score on another (Caldwell, 2013). This is the reasoning behind tests such as the SAT and ACT, which provide a measure of academic ability that predicts performance in college. In addition, some important questions can be investigated only through correlational studies. Such questions may involve variables that can only be measured or observed, such as biological sex, personality traits, genetic factors, and ethnic background.

Another reason why researchers conduct correlational studies is that sometimes the variables of interest are real-world events, such as hurricanes and earthquakes, that influence people's lives. Researchers might compare individuals who have been exposed to a natural disaster to a similar group not so exposed. Such studies are called *quasi-experimental* (see p. 40).

Correlational research is also valuable in cases where it would not be ethical to do the research in any other way. For example, it would be unethical for an experimenter to direct expectant mothers to smoke varying numbers of cigarettes in order to see how cigarette smoke affects birth weight or infant development.

Although we have focused mainly on relations between just two variables, researchers often measure many variables in their studies. In this way, they can assess whether a connection between two variables is explained by a third variable (or a fourth or fifth variable). An interesting question that researchers have examined in this fashion is, do happy people live longer? In one study, 2,000 Mexican Americans ages 65 and older were interviewed twice over the course of two years (Ostir & others, 2000). In the first assessment, participants completed measures of happiness but also reported about potential third variables such as diet, physical health, smoking, marital status, and distress. Two years later, the researchers contacted the participants again to see who was still alive. Even with these many potential third variables taken into account, happiness predicted who was still living two years later.

Correlational studies also are useful when researchers are interested in studying everyday experience. For example, correlational researchers often use daily reports that track experiences, known as the *experience sampling method (ESM),* to assess people in their natural settings. ESM studies involve having people report on their experiences in a diary a few times a day or to complete measures of their mood and behavior whenever they are beeped by an electronic organizer or by a smartphone (Ebner-Priemer &

Correlational research is useful for studying the impact on people's lives of events such as Hurricane Sandy in 2012.

psychological *inquiry*

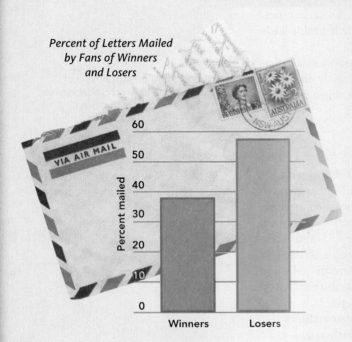

Percent of Letters Mailed by Fans of Winners and Losers

Miserable but Helpful?

Many studies have shown that happy individuals are more helpful than people in a negative mood. Social psychologist R. F. Soames Job (1987) was interested in examining how mood relates to helping. In a clever study, he used naturally occurring mood and an unusual measure of helpfulness.

The study took place outside a major rugby match pitting Canterbury-Bankstown against St. George, in Sydney, Australia. Rugby is enormously popular in Sydney, and more than 40,000 people attended the match.

While the game was going on, the researchers placed 100 stamped letters on the windshields of cars parked around the sporting grounds. The letters were addressed to the same person, and a handwritten note on each letter said, "Found near your car." The researchers identified which cars belonged to supporters of each team by the different colored streamers, team stickers, and posters. Fifty letters were placed on the cars of supporters of each team. The researchers then waited to see which type of fan was most likely to put the letter in the mailbox—a fan of the winning team or of the losing team.

The figure shows the results. Try your hand at the questions below.

1. What were the variables of interest in this study?

2. How did the study operationally define these variables?

3. Why is this a correlational study?

4. Job concluded that these data support the notion that negative mood relates to helping. Is this conclusion justified, in your opinion? Why or why not?

5. Identify at least one third variable that might explain the results of this study.

Trull, 2012). A similar method, *event-contingent responding,* asks participants to complete a report each time they engage in a particular behavior, such as drinking alcohol or having sex (Cooper, 2010). Such methods allow researchers to get close to real life as it happens.

Although the correlation coefficient is often used to express the relation between two variables, it is important to keep in mind that what makes a study correlational is not the statistic researchers use to analyze the data. Rather, a study is correlational when it relies on measuring variables to see how they are related. To get a sense of this distinction and learn about some clever ways in which psychologists have operationalized variables, check out the Psychological Inquiry above.

LONGITUDINAL DESIGNS

● **longitudinal design** A special kind of systematic observation, used by correlational researchers, that involves obtaining measures of the variables of interest in multiple waves over time.

One way that correlational researchers can deal with the issue of causation is to employ a special kind of systematic observation called a **longitudinal design.** Longitudinal research involves obtaining measures of the variables of interest in multiple waves over time (Windle, 2012). (Note that longitudinal designs differ from cross-sectional designs in that cross-sectional designs measure the variables only once.) Longitudinal research can suggest potential causal relationships because if one variable is thought to cause changes in another, it should at least come before that variable in time.

One intriguing longitudinal study is the Nun Study, conducted by David Snowdon and his colleagues (Grossi & others, 2007; Mortimer, Snowdon, & Markesbery, 2009; Snowdon, 2003). The study began in 1986 and has followed a sample of 678 School Sisters of Notre Dame (SSND) ever since. The nuns ranged in age from 75 to 103 when the study began. These women complete a variety of psychological and physical measures annually. This sample is unique in many respects. However, certain characteristics render the participants an excellent group for correlational research. For one thing, many potential extraneous third variables are relatively identical for all the women in the group. Specifically, their biological sex, living conditions, diet, activity levels, marital status, and religious participation are essentially held constant, so there is little chance that differences would arise in these variables that might explain the study's results.

Researchers assessed the link between happiness and longevity using this rich dataset. All of the nuns had been asked to write a spiritual autobiography when they entered the convent (for some, up to 80 years prior). In one study, these documents were used as indicators of happiness earlier in life by counting the number of positive emotions expressed in the autobiographies (note that here we have yet another operational definition of happiness) (Danner, Snowdon, & Friesen, 2001). Higher levels of positive emotion expressed in autobiographies written at an average age of 22 were associated with a 2.5-fold difference in risk of mortality when the nuns were in their 80s and 90s. That is, women who included positive emotion in their autobiographies when they were in their early 20s were 2.5 times more likely to survive some 60 years later.

Recently, researchers replicated this finding using autobiographies of 88 famous psychologists. They found that the more active positive emotion words (such as *lively* and *excited*) the psychologists used to describe their life, the longer they lived (Pressman & Cohen, 2012).

Longitudinal designs provide ways by which correlational researchers may attempt to demonstrate causal relations among variables (Gibbons, Hedeker, & DuToit, 2010). Still, it is important to be aware that even in longitudinal studies, causal relationships are not completely clear. Even an excellent longitudinal study cannot prove causation. For example, the nuns who wrote happier autobiographies may have had happier childhood experiences that might be influencing their longevity, or a particular genetic factor might explain both their happiness and their survival.

As you read about correlational research studies throughout this book, do so critically, and with a modicum of skepticism; consider that even the brightest scientist may not have thought of all of the potential third variables that could have explained the results. It is easy to assume causality when two events or characteristics are merely correlated. Remember those innocent ice cream cones, and critically evaluate conclusions that may be drawn from simple observation.

Experimental Research

To determine whether a causal relationship exists between variables, researchers must use experimental methods (Kirk, 2013). An **experiment** is a carefully regulated procedure in which the researcher manipulates one or more variables that are believed to influence some other variable. Researchers cannot demonstrate causation without experimental research. Imagine, for example, that a researcher notices that people who listen to classical music seem to be of above average intelligence. A correlational study on this question would not tell us if listening to classical music *causes* increases in intelligence. In order to demonstrate causation, the researcher would manipulate whether or not people listen to classical music. He or she might create two groups: one that listens to classical music and one that does not. To test for differences in intelligence, the researcher would then measure intelligence.

If that manipulation led to differences between the two groups on intelligence, we could say that the manipulated variable *caused* those differences: The experiment has demonstrated cause and effect. This notion that experiments can demonstrate causation

● **experiment** A carefully regulated procedure in which the researcher manipulates one or more variables that are believed to influence some other variable.

● **random assignment** Researchers' assignment of participants to groups by chance, to reduce the likelihood that an experiment's results will be due to preexisting differences between groups.

● **independent variable** A manipulated experimental factor; the variable that the experimenter changes to see what its effects are.

In laboratory experiments by King and her colleagues (Hicks & others, 2012; King & others, 2006), participants who listened to happy music rated their lives as more meaningful than those who listened to neutral music.

is based on the idea that if participants are *randomly assigned* to groups, the only systematic difference between them must be the manipulated variable. **Random assignment** means that researchers assign participants to groups *by chance*. Random assignment is an essential aspect of experimental research, and it is because psychologists use random assignment that they can assume that there are no preexisting differences between groups (Graziano & Raulin, 2013).

The logic of random assignment is this: If participants in an experiment are assigned to each group only by chance, the potential differences between the groups will cancel out over the long run. So, for instance, in the example of classical music and intelligence, we might wonder if it is possible that the groups differed on intelligence to begin with. Because participants were randomly assigned, we assume that intelligence is spread across the groups evenly.

Random assignment does not always work. One way to improve its effectiveness is to start with a relatively large pool of people. Let's say that you decided to do that study—examining whether listening to classical music (as compared to no music) prior to taking an intelligence test leads to higher scores on the test. Although you wisely use random assignment, you begin with just 10 people. Unbeknownst to you, there are two geniuses (people with extraordinarily high IQs) in that small pool of participants. Each person has a 50–50 chance of ending up in either group, so there is 25 percent chance that both geniuses will end up in the same group, meaning there is a 25 percent chance that your groups will differ systematically in intelligence before you even start the study.

In contrast, if your study had begun with, say, 100 people, intelligence scores would likely be more evenly distributed throughout the overall pool. When these individuals are randomly assigned to groups, differences in intelligence would be much more likely to cancel out across the two groups. That is why it is important that random assignment is allowed to work its magic on a larger pool of people.

To get a sense of what experimental studies, as compared to correlational studies, can reveal, consider the following example. Psychologists have long assumed that experiencing one's life as meaningful is an important aspect of psychological well-being (Frankl, [1946] 2006; Steger, 2012). Because surveys that measure meaning in life and well-being correlate positively (that is, the more meaningful your life, the happier you are), the assumption has been that experiencing meaning in life causes greater happiness. However, because the studies involved in exploring this relationship have been correlational, the cause is unclear. Meaning in life may lead people to be happier, but the reverse might also be true: Happiness might make people feel that their lives are more meaningful.

To address this issue, Laura King and her colleagues (Hicks & others, 2012; King & others, 2006) conducted a series of laboratory experiments. In one study, the researchers put some participants in a positive mood by having them listen to happy music. Other participants listened to neutral music. Participants who listened to happy music rated their lives as more meaningful than did individuals who listened to neutral music (King & others, 2006). Note that participants were randomly assigned to one of two conditions, happy music or neutral music, and then rated their meaning in life using a questionnaire. In this case happiness was operationally defined by the type of music participants heard, and meaning in life was operationally defined by ratings on a questionnaire. Because participants were randomly assigned to conditions, we can assume that the only systematic difference between the two groups was the type of music they heard. As a result, we can say that the happy music caused people to rate their lives as more meaningful.

INDEPENDENT AND DEPENDENT VARIABLES

Experiments have two types of variables: independent and dependent. An **independent variable** is a manipulated experimental factor. The independent variable is the variable that the experimenter changes to see what its effects are; it is a potential cause. In the example of listening to classical music and intelligence, the independent variable is whether or not participants listened to music. In the study of positive mood and meaning in life, the independent variable is mood (positive versus neutral), operationally defined by the type of music participants heard.

A **dependent variable** in an experiment is the variable that may change as a result of manipulations of the independent variable. It represents the outcome (effect) in an experiment. As researchers manipulate the independent variable, they measure the dependent variable to test for any effect of the manipulated variable. In the example of listening to classical music and intelligence, the dependent variable is intelligence. In the study by King and others of positive mood and meaning in life, meaning in life is the dependent variable.

Any experiment may include several independent variables, or factors that are manipulated, to determine their effect on the outcome. Similarly, many experiments include more than one dependent variable as well, to examine the effects of manipulations on a number of outcomes.

Independent and dependent variables are two of the most important concepts in psychological research. Despite their similar names, they are very different. Remember that the independent variable is the *cause,* and the dependent variable is the *effect.* The independent variable is the one that is manipulated, and the dependent variable is the outcome.

Independent and dependent variables can be operationalized in many ways. Sometimes the independent variable involves an individual's social context. Social psychologists often manipulate the social context with the help of a confederate. A **confederate** is a person who is given a role to play in a study so that the social context can be manipulated.

Let's consider one more example to review the process of experimental research step-by- step. Have you ever noticed how sometimes when a friend tells you about an upsetting event in his or her life that you start to feel the same emotions your friend is feeling, as if that event had happened to you? A team of social psychologists led by David Cwir was interested in studying this phenomenon (Cwir & others, 2011). They hypothesized that being socially connected to someone *causes* us to experience that person's experience as if it were our own. To test this hypothesis in an experiment, they needed to manipulate social connection and then measure how a person might be affected by someone else's experience.

Here's what they did. First, a few weeks before the experiment, all of the participants completed a survey gauging their favorite music, TV shows, movies, actors, books, and so forth. When participants came to the lab for the experiment, they were told that the study was about the effects of physical exercise on cardiovascular function, and their heart rate and blood pressure were measured. Next, participants were introduced to the confederate (who the participants thought was just another participant in the study). The experimenter told the participant and confederate to chat to get to know each other.

What the participants did not know is that the confederate had been given a script to follow during this chat. Participants were, in fact, randomly assigned to interact either with a confederate who mentioned interests very similar to their own, as noted on the earlier measure, or with a confederate who did not mention those interests.

Next, the participant and confederate completed different activities. The confederate was instructed to run in place, vigorously, for 3 minutes while the participant sat and watched. Finally, the researchers measured participants' heart rate and blood pressure (a second time). The results showed that the group that had interacted with a confederate to whom they felt connected had greater change in heart rate and blood pressure (from the initial measure) after watching that confederate run in place, compared to the group that watched a confederate to whom they did not have a sense of connection (Cwir & others, 2011).

Let's review the concepts covered so far in the context of this clever experiment. The researchers had hypothesized that being socially connected to someone would lead to greater responsiveness to that other person's experience. The independent variable (the

● **dependent variable** The outcome; the factor that can change in an experiment in response to changes in the independent variable.

● **confederate** A person who is given a role to play in a study so that the social context can be manipulated.

cause) in this study is social connection. The operational definition of that variable is interacting with someone who shared participants' interests (or not). The dependent variable (the effect) is the responsiveness of participants to the other person's experience. The operational definition of this variable is participants' heart rate and blood pressure. Participants were randomly assigned to groups, so that the researchers could be sure that the groups did not differ systematically from each other (in this case, on variables such as heart rate or blood pressure, or on psychological characteristics like empathy). The confederate is the individual who acted like just another participant but was actually part of the manipulation of the independent variable.

This study involved two groups: one that experienced social connection with the confederate and one that did not. Why did the researchers need *both* of these groups? They were only interested in how social connection influences shared feelings, so why did they have a group that did not feel a social connection? Notice that if they did not have that second group, they would have nothing with which to compare their results, no way to determine whether social connection mattered. This is the basic logic behind the concepts of experimental and control groups, our next topic.

EXPERIMENTAL AND CONTROL GROUPS

● **experimental group** The participants in an experiment who receive the drug or other treatment under study—that is, those who are exposed to the change that the independent variable represents.

● **control group** The participants in an experiment who are as much like the experimental group as possible and who are treated in every way like the experimental group except for a manipulated factor, the independent variable.

Experiments involve comparing different groups that have been exposed to differing versions of the independent variable. These groups have names. An **experimental group** consists of the participants in an experiment who are exposed to *the change* that the independent variable represents. A **control group** in an experiment is as much like the experimental group as possible and is treated in every way like the experimental group *except for that change*. The control group provides a comparison against which the researcher can test the effects of the independent variable.

We now have reviewed three examples of experimental and control groups:

- In our imaginary study of music and intelligence, the experimental group is the group that listened to classical music; the no-music group is the control group.
- In the study of happiness and meaning in life, participants who listened to happy music are the experimental group; those who heard neutral music are the control group.
- In the study of social connection and shared experiences, participants who interacted with a confederate who shared their interests are the experimental group; those who interacted with a confederate who did not share their interests are the control group.

Many research questions can be addressed both experimentally and correlationally. To see how experimental and correlational research can illuminate the relations between variables, check out the Intersection.

QUASI-EXPERIMENTAL DESIGNS

Another approach to experimental research is to use a *quasi-experimental design*. As the prefix *quasi-* ("as if") suggests, this type of design is similar to an experiment, but it is not quite the same thing. The key difference is that a quasi-experimental design does not randomly assign participants to conditions because such assignment is either impossible or unethical (Reichardt, 2009; Thyer, 2012).

Quasi-experimental designs might be used for studies that assess the differences between groups of people who have had different experiences—say, soldiers who have seen combat versus those who have not, children whose school was destroyed by a tornado versus those in a neighboring town where the school was not affected, or adults who are single, divorced, or remarried. In a quasi-experimental design, researchers examine participants in varying groups, but their group assignment is not determined randomly.

For example, researchers interested in the influence of using online learning tools on performance in introductory psychology classes might compare students from two

Personality and Social Psychology: Does Sociability Lead to Happiness or Is It the Other Way Around?

Psychologists who study happiness have found a very strong connection between social relationships and positive feelings (Diener & Seligman, 2002). Spending time in social situations is related to greater positive emotions than spending time alone (Fredrickson, 2013a, 2013b). Furthermore, people who describe themselves as being more sociable also describe themselves as happier (Diener & others, 1999; Smillie & others, 2012). Even individuals who are generally socially reserved report greater happiness when they are acting in an outgoing, social manner (Fleeson, Malanos, & Achille, 2002).

Are you more likely to seek out friends when you are happy or sad?

It seems that one key to happiness is being around others. But is it possible that the causal arrow goes in the other direction as well? Finding out that social activities lead to happiness does not rule out the possibility that being happy leads people to be more sociable. Does happiness also cause greater desire to be with others? To answer this question, we need an experiment that manipulates the independent variable, happiness, to examine its effects on the dependent variable, sociability.

Deanna Whelan and John Zelenski (2012) completed two such studies. In their experiments, they randomly assigned college student participants to one of three mood groups:

- In the *positive mood* groups, the students watched film clips that were selected to make them happy, including scenes from *E.T.: The Extra-Terrestrial* (the scenes where ET recovers from his injuries, and the kids are able to help him return to his spaceship so he can go home) and *Akeelah and the Bee* (the scenes of Akeelah winning the spelling bee).
- In the *neutral mood* groups, they watched either a documentary about an artist or a roundtable discussion of *Beowulf*.
- In the *negative mood* groups, they watched scenes from *My Girl* (in which the girl's friend dies from an allergic reaction to a bee sting) or from *Stepmom* (in which a

woman reveals that she is dying of cancer, celebrates her last Christmas, and says good-bye to her two young children).

Note that in this example, the positive and negative groups are the experimental groups, whereas the neutral group is the control, or comparison, group. Further, the independent variable, mood, is operationalized by the type of film students watched. Participants were randomly assigned to groups to ensure that the groups did not differ systematically on sociability prior to the experiment.

After watching the clips, all of the participants completed measures of the dependent variable, sociability. In this case, they rated how much they felt like being with other people and the desirability of being in social and nonsocial situations. Those in the positive mood groups reported feeling more social and had a stronger desire to be in social situations. In contrast, those in the negative mood groups reported lower levels of sociability and a greater desire to be in nonsocial situations. Those in the neutral mood groups placed in the middle between the two extremes.

This research illustrates that there can be complex links between variables. Sociability and happiness are positively correlated, but this correlation appears to reflect a two-way street: Although being with others can make us happy, being happy can also spur us to seek out social activities.

different sections of a class—one that uses online tools and one that does not. Because students typically choose which section of a course they take, the experimenter cannot randomly assign them to sections. Assessing differences between the groups might provide information about the merits of online learning tools. However, there might be confounding factors (whether students are morning people or not, for example) that could account for differences between the groups. Although quasi-experimental designs are common, it is important to keep in mind that they do not allow for the strong causal conclusions that can be drawn from true experiments that employ random assignment (Thyer, 2012).

SOME CAUTIONS ABOUT EXPERIMENTAL RESEARCH

Earlier we noted that psychologists are interested in drawing conclusions not just from a single study but from a whole body of research on a given topic. We discussed the idea that if a finding is replicated (that is, found again and again), it is considered *reliable,* a finding that we expect to stand the test of time. However, even a reliable finding may not be *valid.*

Validity refers to the soundness of the conclusions that a researcher draws from an experiment. In experimental designs, there are two broad types of validity that matter. The first is **external validity,** which refers to the degree to which an experimental design actually reflects the real-world issues it is supposed to address. Often, operationalizing variables in the lab involves creating analogues to real-world experiences. External validity is concerned with how well those analogues represent the real-world contexts they are meant to represent. In other words, the researcher assesses external validity to see whether the experimental methods and the results *generalize*—whether they apply—to the real world.

● **external validity** The degree to which an experimental design actually reflects the real-world issues it is supposed to address.

Imagine, for example, that a researcher is interested in the influence of stress (the independent variable) on creative problem solving (the dependent variable). The researcher randomly assigns individuals to be blasted with loud noises at random times during the session (the high-stress or experimental group) or to complete the task in relative quiet (the control group). As the task, the researcher gives all participants a chance to be creative by asking them to list every use they can think of for a cardboard box. Counting up the number of uses that people list, the researcher discovers that those in the high-stress group generated fewer uses of the box. This finding might seem to indicate that stress reduces creativity. In considering the external validity of this study, however, we might appropriately ask some questions: How similar are the blasts of loud, random noises to the stresses people experience every day? Is listing uses for a cardboard box really an indicator of creativity? Even if a large number of laboratory studies demonstrated this effect, we would still need to consider whether this result generalizes to the real world. We are asking, in other words, if these operational definitions do a good job of reflecting the real-world processes they are supposed to represent.

The second type of validity is **internal validity,** which refers to the degree to which changes in the dependent variable are genuinely due to the manipulation of the independent variable. In the case of internal validity, we want to know whether the experimental methods are free from biases and logical errors that may render the results suspect.

● **internal validity** The degree to which changes in the dependent variable are due to the manipulation of the independent variable.

Although experimental research is a powerful tool, it requires safeguards. Expectations and biases can, and sometimes do, tarnish results (Kirk, 2013), as we next consider.

Experimenter Bias Experimenters may subtly (and often unknowingly) influence their research participants. **Experimenter bias** occurs when the experimenter's expectations influence the outcome of the research. No one designs an experiment without wanting meaningful results. Consequently, experimenters can sometimes subtly communicate to participants what they want the participants to do. **Demand characteristics** are any aspects of a study that communicate to participants how the experimenter wants them to behave. The influence of experimenter expectations can be very difficult to avoid.

● **experimenter bias** The influence of the experimenter's expectations on the outcome of research.

● **demand characteristics** Any aspects of a study that communicate to the participants how the experimenter wants them to behave.

In a classic study, Robert Rosenthal (1966) turned college students into experimenters. He randomly assigned the participants rats from the same litter. Half of the students were told that their rats were "maze bright," whereas the other half were told that their rats were "maze dull." The students then conducted experiments to test their rats' ability to navigate mazes. The results were stunning. The so-called maze-bright rats were more successful than the maze-dull rats at running the mazes. The only explanation for the results is that the college students' expectations, conveyed in their behaviors, affected the rats' performance.

Often the participants in psychological studies are not rats but people. Imagine that you are an experimenter, and you know that a participant is going to be exposed to disgusting pictures in a study. Is it possible that you might treat the person differently than you would if you were about to show him photos of cute kittens? The reason experimenter bias is important is that it introduces systematic differences between the experimental group and the control groups; this means that we cannot know if those who looked at disgusting pictures were more, say, upset because of the pictures or because of different treatment by the experimenter.

Like third variables in correlational research, these systematic biases are called *confounds*. In experimental research, confounds are factors that "ride along" with the experimental manipulation, systematically and undesirably influencing the dependent variable. Experimenter bias, demand characteristics, and confounds may all lead to biased results.

Research Participant Bias and the Placebo Effect

Like experimenters, research participants may have expectations about what they are supposed to do and how they should behave, and these expectations may affect the results of experiments (Gravetter & Forzano, 2012). **Research participant bias** occurs when the behavior of research participants during the experiment is influenced by how they think they are supposed to behave or by their expectations about what is happening to them.

One example of the power of participant expectations is the placebo effect. The **placebo effect** occurs when participants' expectations, rather than the experimental treatment, produce a particular outcome. Participants in a drug study might be assigned to an experimental group that receives a pill containing an actual painkiller or to a control group that receives a placebo pill. A **placebo** is a harmless substance that has no physiological effect. This placebo is given to participants in a control group so that they are treated identically to the experimental group except for the active agent—in this case, the painkiller. Giving individuals in the control group a placebo pill allows researchers to determine whether changes in the experimental group are due to the active drug agent and not simply to participants' expectations.

Another way to ensure that neither the experimenter's nor the participants' expectations affect the outcome is to design a **double-blind experiment.** In this design, neither the experimenter administering the treatment nor the participants are aware of which participants are in the experimental group and which are in the control group until the results are calculated. This setup ensures that the experimenter cannot, for example, make subtle gestures signaling who is receiving a drug and who is not. A double-blind study allows researchers to distinguish the specific effects of the independent variable from the possible effects of the experimenter's and the participants' expectations about it.

"We close at six!"

© Mike Williams. www.CartoonStock.com.

● **research participant bias** In an experiment, the influence of participants' expectations, and of their thoughts on how they should behave, on their behavior.

● **placebo effect** A phenomenon in which the participants' expectations, rather than an actual treatment, produce an outcome.

● **placebo** In a drug study, a harmless substance that has no physiological effect, given to participants in a control group so that they are treated identically to the experimental group except for the active agent.

● **double-blind experiment** An experimental design in which neither the experimenter nor the participants are aware of which participants are in the experimental group and which are in the control group until the results are calculated.

Advertisements for prescription drugs usually describe not only the side effects on people taking the actual drug but also the effects experienced by individuals receiving a placebo.

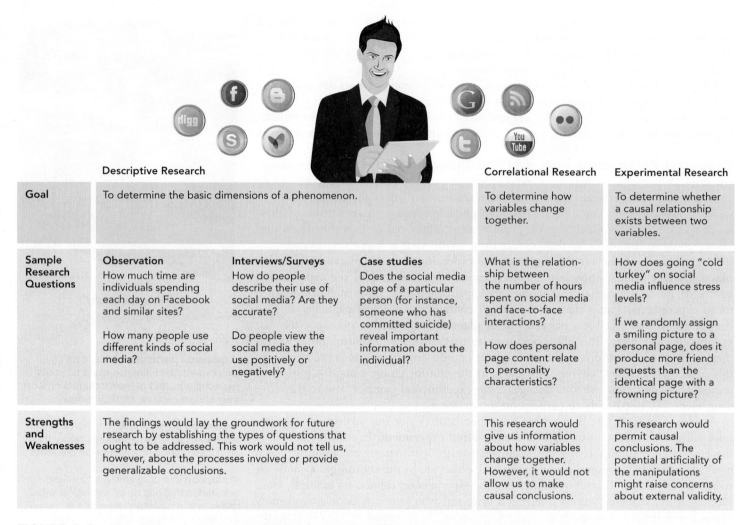

	Descriptive Research			Correlational Research	Experimental Research
Goal	To determine the basic dimensions of a phenomenon.			To determine how variables change together.	To determine whether a causal relationship exists between two variables.
Sample Research Questions	**Observation** How much time are individuals spending each day on Facebook and similar sites? How many people use different kinds of social media?	**Interviews/Surveys** How do people describe their use of social media? Are they accurate? Do people view the social media they use positively or negatively?	**Case studies** Does the social media page of a particular person (for instance, someone who has committed suicide) reveal important information about the individual?	What is the relationship between the number of hours spent on social media and face-to-face interactions? How does personal page content relate to personality characteristics?	How does going "cold turkey" on social media influence stress levels? If we randomly assign a smiling picture to a personal page, does it produce more friend requests than the identical page with a frowning picture?
Strengths and Weaknesses	The findings would lay the groundwork for future research by establishing the types of questions that ought to be addressed. This work would not tell us, however, about the processes involved or provide generalizable conclusions.			This research would give us information about how variables change together. However, it would not allow us to make causal conclusions.	This research would permit causal conclusions. The potential artificiality of the manipulations might raise concerns about external validity.

FIGURE 2.3 **Psychology's Research Methods Applied to Studying Social Media** Use Psychologists can apply different methods of study to the same phenomenon. The popularity of social media has opened up a host of new research questions for psychologists.

Applications of the Three Types of Research

All three types of research—descriptive, correlational, and experimental—can be used to address the same topic (Figure 2.3). For instance, various researchers have used different research methods to explore the role of intensely positive experiences in human functioning, as follows.

Abraham Maslow believed that people who were the healthiest and the happiest were capable of having intense moments of awe; he used the descriptive case study approach (1971) to examine the role of such "peak experiences" in the lives of such individuals, who seemed to enjoy the best of life. In contrast, Dan McAdams (2001) used correlational research to probe individuals' descriptions of their most powerful positive experiences. He found that individuals who were motivated toward warm interpersonal experiences tended to mention such experiences as the best memories of their lives. Finally, experimental researchers have also investigated this topic by randomly assigning individuals to write about their most intensely positive experiences for a few minutes each day for two or three days. Those who wrote about emotional and happy topics experienced enhanced positive mood as well as fewer physical illnesses two months later, as compared to individuals in control groups who wrote about topics that were not emotional (Burton & King, 2004, 2009). So, researchers coming from many different methodological perspectives can address the same topic, leading to different but valuable contributions to knowledge.

3. RESEARCH SAMPLES AND SETTINGS

Regardless of whether a study is correlational or experimental, among the important decisions to be made about collecting data is whom to choose as the participants and where to conduct the research. Will the participants be people or animals? Will they be children, adults, or both? Where will the research take place—in a lab or in a natural setting?

The Research Sample

When psychologists conduct a study, they usually want to be able to draw conclusions that will apply to a larger group of people than the participants they actually study. The entire group about which the investigator wants to draw conclusions is the **population.** The subset of the population chosen by the investigator for study is a **sample.** The researcher might be interested only in a particular group, such as all children who are gifted and talented, all young women who embark on science and math careers, or all gay men. The key is that the sample studied must be representative of the population to which the investigator wants to generalize his or her results. That is, the researcher might study only 100 gifted adolescents, but he or she wants to apply these results to all gifted and talented adolescents. A representative sample for the United States would reflect the U.S. population's age, socioeconomic status, ethnic origins, marital status, geographic location, religion, and so forth.

To mirror the population as closely as possible, the researcher uses a **random sample,** a sample that gives every member of the population an equal chance of being selected. Random sampling improves the chances that the sample is representative of the population. In actual practice, however, random sampling typically only *approximates* this ideal—for example, by randomly sampling people who have telephones or people who live in a particular town or state. Note that a random sample is *not* the same thing as random assignment. Random assignment is about making sure experimental and control groups are equivalent, and a random sample is about selecting participants from a population so that the sample is representative of that population.

In selecting a sample, researchers must strive to minimize bias, including gender bias (Hyde & Else-Quest, 2013). Because psychology is the scientific study of human behavior, it should pertain to *all* humans, and so the participants in psychological studies ought to be representative of humanity as a whole. Early research in the field often included just the male experience—not only because the researchers themselves were often male, but also because the participants too were typically male (Matlin, 2012). For a long time, the human experience studied by psychologists was primarily the male experience.

There is also a growing realization that psychological research needs to include more people from diverse ethnic groups (Leong & others, 2013). Because a great deal of

- **population** The entire group about which the investigator wants to draw conclusions.

- **sample** The subset of the population chosen by the investigator for study.

- **random sample** A sample that gives every member of the population an equal chance of being selected.

The research sample might include a particular group, such as all gay men or all women runners.

psychological research involves college student participants, individuals from groups that have not had as many educational opportunities have not been strongly represented in that research. Given the fact that individuals from diverse ethnic groups have been excluded from psychological research for so long, we might reasonably conclude that people's real lives are more varied than past research data have indicated.

These issues are important because scientists want to be able to predict human behavior broadly speaking, not just the behavior of non-Latino White, male college students. Imagine if policymakers planned their initiatives for a wide range of Americans based on research derived from only a small group of individuals from a particular background. What might the results be?

The Research Setting

All three types of research you studied in the preceding section can take place in different physical settings. The setting of the research does not determine the type of research it is. Common settings include the research laboratory and natural settings.

Because psychology researchers often want to control as many aspects of the situation as possible, they conduct much of their research in a laboratory—a controlled setting with many of the complex factors of the real world, including potential confounding factors, removed. Although laboratory research provides a great deal of control, doing research in the laboratory has drawbacks. First, it is almost impossible to conduct research in the lab without the participants knowing they are being studied. Second, the laboratory setting is not the real world and therefore can cause the participants to behave unnaturally. A third drawback of laboratory research is that individuals who are willing to go to a university laboratory may not be representative of groups from diverse cultural backgrounds. Those who are unfamiliar with university settings and with the idea of "helping science" may be intimidated by the setting. Fourth, some aspects of the mind and behavior are difficult if not impossible to examine in the laboratory.

● **naturalistic observation** The observation of behavior in a real-world setting.

Research can also take place in a natural setting. **Naturalistic observation** is viewing behavior in a real-world setting (Leedy & Ormrod, 2013). Psychologists conduct naturalistic observations at sporting events, child-care centers, work settings, shopping malls, and other places that people frequent. If you wanted to study the level of civility on your campus for a research project, most likely you would include naturalistic observation of how people treat one another in such gathering places as the cafeteria and the library reading room. In another example of a natural setting, researchers who use survey methods are increasingly relying on web-based assessments that allow participants to complete the measures using the Internet.

Natural settings and laboratories are common locales for psychological studies. (Left) Jane Goodall, who specializes in animal behavior, has carried out extensive research on chimpanzees in natural settings. Her work has contributed a great deal to our understanding of these intelligent primates. (Right) Barbara L. Fredrickson (on the right in the photo, pointing to the monitor) is a psychologist at the University of North Carolina, Chapel Hill, whose work investigates topics such as positive emotions and human flourishing. Here she conducts a laboratory study.

The type of research a psychologist conducts, the operational definitions of the variables of interest, and the choice of sample and setting are decisions that ideally are guided by the research question itself. However, sometimes these decisions represent a compromise between the psychologist's key objective (for example, to study a representative sample of Americans) and the available resources (for instance, a sample of 100 college students). For a closer look at the process of conducting an experiment in a real-world setting, check out the Psychological Inquiry on page 48.

4. ANALYZING AND INTERPRETING DATA

Once psychologists collect data, whether in a lab or a natural setting, it is time to analyze and interpret those data. For this task they use *statistics,* mathematical methods for reporting data (Rossi, 2013). There are two basic categories of statistics: descriptive statistics, which are used to describe and summarize data, and inferential statistics, which are used to draw conclusions about those data.

Psychology students are sometimes surprised to learn that a statistics course is often a requirement for the major. In this section, as we look at how psychologists analyze and interpret research data, you will get a flavor of the ways in which math plays an important role in the science of psychology.

Descriptive Statistics

Most psychological studies generate considerable numerical data. Simply listing all of the scores (or other measures) generated by a study—for each individual in the study—is not very meaningful. **Descriptive statistics** are the mathematical procedures researchers have developed to describe and summarize sets of data in a meaningful way. Descriptive statistics reveal the "big picture"—the overall characteristics of the data and the variation among them.

MEASURES OF CENTRAL TENDENCY

A *measure of central tendency* is a single number that indicates the overall characteristics of a set of data. The three measures of central tendency are the mean, the median, and the mode.

Most quantitative techniques in psychological science begin with the mean. The **mean** is what people often call the average. The mean is calculated by adding all the scores in a set of scores and then dividing by the number of scores. As a good indicator of the central tendency for a group of scores, the mean is the measure that is used most often. When your instructor provides students with their exam grades, he or she might mention the test mean, because this average gives the class a general idea of how the group performed.

The mean is not so helpful, however, when a group of scores contains a few extreme scores, especially if the number of cases in the group is small. Consider the annual earnings for the two groups of five people shown in the table below.

Group 1		Group 2	
	$19,000		$19,000
	19,000		19,000
	23,000		23,000
	24,000		24,000
	25,000		45,000,000
Mean	$22,000	Mean	$9,017,000
Median	$23,000	Median	$23,000
Mode	$19,000	Mode	$19,000

test yourself

1. What is a population in a research study? What is a sample?
2. What is the difference between a random sample and random assignment?
3. What are two common physical settings for research?

● **descriptive statistics** Mathematical procedures that are used to describe and summarize sets of data in a meaningful way.

● **mean** A measure of central tendency that is the average for a sample.

psychological *inquiry*

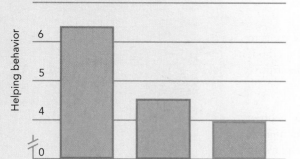

Target Employee Helping as a Function of Mood Condition

Adapted From Forgas, Dunn, & Granland, 2008.

Experimentation in a Natural Setting

A team of social psychologists was interested in studying how mood influences helping behavior in the real world (Forgas, Dunn, & Granland, 2008). They hypothesized that, especially among the less experienced members of a sales staff, mood would guide behavior, so that happy salespeople would be most helpful to customers and unhappy salespeople less so. The researchers conducted an experiment in a Target department store, as follows.

First, the experimenters trained two confederates. The first confederate was in charge of manipulating the employees' mood across three conditions:

- In the *positive mood condition,* the confederate said, "I just wanted to let someone know that I am so impressed with the service at this store! The store looks great, and the staff is so nice. I was able to get what I wanted and will be coming back to this store again."

- In the *negative mood condition,* the confederate said, "I just wanted to let someone know that I am so disappointed with the service at this store. The store looks terrible, and the staff is rude. I couldn't get anything I wanted and won't be coming back here again."

- In the *neutral mood condition,* the confederate simply observed, "Interesting, I have been coming here quite regularly, and this store seems always the same, nothing much changes."

Employees were chosen randomly by the confederate and were randomly assigned to the conditions.

Then, after the first confederate interacted with the employees, the second confederate, who was blind to the mood procedure (meaning unaware of the mood condition for each participant), approached the employees individually and asked, "Excuse me, could you tell me where I could find the book *The White Bear*?" This second confederate surreptitiously recorded (1) the number of helpful responses, (2) the number of actual attempts to help, and (3) the time spent helping. These three values were averaged to create an overall helpfulness score. (If the staff salesperson saw the confederate jotting things down, the confederate pretended to be checking a shopping list.) The researchers were also interested in how workers' experience level influenced the results.

The figure shows the results for the less experienced sales staff. As you can see, those in a positive mood were most helpful. The researchers concluded that mood caused these differences. Now, answer these questions to see how much you remember about experimental design.

1. Despite the natural setting, this was an experiment. Why?
2. What was the independent variable and what was its operational definition?
3. What was the dependent variable and what was its operational definition?
4. Why is it important that the second confederate was "blind" to the mood condition?
5. Why were the employees assigned to mood condition randomly?
6. The store management was aware of the study, but the employees were not. Do you think the experiment was ethical? Why or why not?

Group 1 lists the earnings of five ordinary people. Group 2 is composed of the earnings of four ordinary people plus the approximate earnings of movie director Steven Spielberg. Now look at the means that have been calculated for the two groups. The vast difference between them is due to the one extreme score. In such a situation, one of the other two measures of central tendency, the median or the mode, would give a more accurate picture of the data overall.

The **median** is the score that falls exactly in the middle of the distribution of scores after they have been arranged (or ranked) from highest to lowest. When you have an odd number of scores (say, five or seven), the median is the score with the same number of scores above it as below it. In the table above, each group has a median income of $23,000. Notice that, unlike the mean, the median is unaffected by extreme scores. The medians are the same for both groups ($23,000), but their means are extremely different ($22,000 versus $9,017,000). Of course, if there is an even number of scores, there is no "middle" score. This problem is dealt with by averaging the scores that share the middle location.

The **mode** is the score that occurs most often in a dataset. In our earnings example, the mode is $19,000, which occurs twice in each group. All of the other annual incomes occur only once. The mode is the least used measure of central tendency. Yet the mode can be particularly useful, for example, in cases in which information is desired about preference or popularity. Consider a teacher who wants to know the most popular or least popular child in her classroom. She might create a questionnaire and ask students which of their classmates they like the most or the least. The most frequently nominated child would be the mode in these instances.

Although the mode and the median of a dataset can provide useful information, the most commonly used measure of central tendency in psychological research is the mean. As you will see, the mean is also a key component of calculating other important descriptive statistics—measures of dispersion.

MEASURES OF DISPERSION

In addition to revealing the central characteristics of a sample, descriptive statistics can also give us *measures of dispersion,* which describe how much the scores in a sample differ from one another. That is, these measures give us a sense of the spread of scores, or how much variability exists in the data. Like measures of central tendency, measures of dispersion involve a single number that characterizes a dataset. But although measures of central tendency involve numbers that tell us about the scores in that dataset, measures of dispersion tells us about the differences among those scores. Let's look at some common ways that researchers measure dispersion.

To begin, suppose that four students rate their positive mood on a scale from 1 (not at all positive) to 7 (extremely positive), as follows:

Positive Mood

Sarah	7
Sun Mee	6
Josh	2
Rodney	5

(You might note that the mean for these data is 20/4, or 5.) One common measure of dispersion is the **range,** which is the distance between the highest and the lowest scores. In the example above, the range in positive mood is 5 (that is, the highest score, 7, minus the lowest score, 2). Generally speaking, the range is a rather simplistic estimate of the variability within a group of scores. Because the range takes into account only the lowest and highest scores, it can produce a misleading picture of how different from one another scores in the dataset actually are. Note that for positive mood, most people in the example have fairly similar scores, but using the range alone gives the impression that scores are widely dispersed.

A more informative measure of dispersion, and the one most commonly used in psychological research, is the standard deviation. The **standard deviation** measures how

- **median** A measure of central tendency that is the middle score in a sample.

- **mode** A measure of central tendency that is the most common score in a sample.

- **range** A measure of dispersion that is the difference between the highest and lowest scores.

- **standard deviation** A measure of dispersion that tells us how much scores in a sample differ from the mean of the sample.

much scores vary, on average, around the mean of the sample. There is a little hitch, however. One of the mathematical properties of the mean is that if you add up each person's difference from the mean, the sum will always be 0. So, we cannot calculate the average difference (or deviation) from the mean and get a meaningful answer.

To get around this problem, we take each person's difference from the mean and multiply it by itself (or square it). This removes the negative numbers, and the sum of these differences will no longer equal 0. We add these squared deviations together and then divide by the number of cases (minus 1). Finally, we take the square root of that number (to get rid of the squaring we did earlier). Essentially, then, the standard deviation is the square root of the average squared deviation from the mean. The smaller the standard deviation, the less variability in the dataset. A small standard deviation indicates that, on average, scores are close to the mean.

The following table presents the information needed to calculate the standard deviation for the positive mood ratings given above.

Participant	A Rating	B Difference from the mean (5)	C *Squared* difference from the mean (5)
Sarah	7	2	4
Sun Mee	6	1	1
Josh	2	−3	9
Rodney	5	0	0
MEAN $= \dfrac{(7 + 6 + 2 + 5)}{4} = 5.0$		Sum of this column = 0	Sum of these differences = 4 + 1 + 9 + 0 = 14

Column A presents the ratings by each participant. Column B shows the differences of these scores from the mean (5). Notice that if we add up Column B, the answer is 0. Column C shows the squared deviations from the mean for each participant. Adding up those squared differences, we get 14. Next, we divide 14 by the number of participants minus 1, in this case 14 divided by 3, which is 4.67, and then we take the square root of that number, which is 2.16. This is the standard deviation of our sample, which, compared to the range of 5, tells us that the group is actually fairly closely arranged around the mean.

The mean and standard deviation together yield a lot of information about a sample. Indeed, given the raw scores, the means, and the standard deviations of two variables, we can calculate the correlation coefficient in no time. The correlation coefficient is not a descriptive statistic but rather an inferential statistic, our next topic.

Inferential Statistics

Imagine that, inspired by the research of Lee Anne Harker and Dacher Keltner on college yearbooks (see p. 28), you conduct a study on the relationship between expressions of positive emotion and interpersonal success. In your project, you video-record job candidates being interviewed, code the videos for Duchenne smiling by the candidates, and document which of the job seekers were called back for a second interview. Let's say you calculate that the mean number of smiles for candidates who were not called back is 3.5, and the mean number of smiles for candidates who were called back is 6.5. So, those who were called back generated, on average, 3 more smiles than those who were not called back. Does that difference matter? It seems pretty big, but is it big enough? Could we have obtained the same difference simply by chance?

To draw conclusions about differences we observe in studies, we want to know that the difference is likely to be one that can be replicated or found consistently in a variety of studies. Inferential statistics are the tools that help us to state whether a difference is unlikely to be the result of chance. More specifically, **inferential statistics** are the mathematical methods used to indicate whether data sufficiently support a research

● **inferential statistics** Mathematical methods that are used to indicate whether results for a sample are likely to generalize to a population.

hypothesis (Rossi, 2013). A psychologist conducting a study would certainly calculate the means and standard deviations to describe the sample, but in order to *test predictions* about that sample, the researcher needs inferential statistics.

The logic behind inferential statistics is relatively simple. Inferential statistics yield a statement of probability about the differences observed between two or more groups; this probability statement gives the odds that the observed differences were due simply to chance. In psychological research the standard is that if the odds are 5 out of 100 (or .05) or less that the differences are due to chance, the results are considered *statistically significant*. In statistical language, this is referred to as the .05 level of statistical significance, or the .05 *confidence level*. Put another way, statistical significance means that the differences observed between two groups are large enough that it is highly unlikely that those differences are merely due to chance. The .05 level of statistical significance is considered the minimum level of probability that scientists will accept for concluding that the differences observed are real, thereby supporting a hypothesis.

Recall that although we study a sample, we typically wish to generalize our findings to a population. Inferential statistics are the bridge between a sample and a population, because they tell us the likelihood that the results we found with a sample reflect differences in the larger population. It makes sense that the larger our sample is, the more likely it is to represent that population. Thus, significance tests are based in part on the number of cases in a sample. The higher the number of cases, the easier it is to get statistical significance. As a result, with a very large sample, even very small differences may be significant.

However, statistical significance is not the same thing as real-world significance. Even if a difference is found to be statistically significant, its real-world value remains to be evaluated by critically thinking scientists.

5. CONDUCTING ETHICAL RESEARCH

Ethics is a crucial consideration for all science. This fact came to the fore in the aftermath of World War II, for example, when it became apparent that Nazi doctors had forced concentration camp prisoners to participate in experiments. These atrocities spurred scientists to develop a code of appropriate behavior—a set of principles about the treatment that participants in research have a right to expect. In general, ethical principles of research focus on balancing the rights of the participants with the rights of scientists to ask important research questions (Smith & Davis, 2013).

The issue of ethics in psychological research may affect you personally if at some point you participate in a study. In that event, you need to know your rights as a participant and the researchers' responsibilities in ensuring that these rights are safeguarded. Experiences in research can have unforeseen effects on people's lives.

One investigation of young dating couples asked them to complete a questionnaire that coincidentally stimulated some of the participants to think about potentially troublesome issues in the relationship (Rubin & Mitchell, 1976). One year later, when the researchers followed up with the original sample, 9 of 10 participants said they had discussed their answers with their dating partners. In most instances, the discussions helped to strengthen the relationships. In some cases, however, the participants used the questionnaire as a springboard to discuss problems or concerns previously hidden. One participant said, "The study definitely played a role in ending my relationship with Larry." In this case, the couple had different views about how long they expected to be together. She was thinking of a short-term dating relationship, whereas he was thinking in terms of a lifetime. Their answers to the questions brought the disparity in their views to the surface and led to the end of their relationship. Researchers have a responsibility to anticipate the personal problems their study might cause and, at least, to inform the participants of the possible fallout.

Ethics comes into play in every psychological study. Even smart, conscientious students sometimes think that members of

test yourself

1. What is meant by a measure of central tendency? Name three measures of central tendency.
2. What do measures of dispersion describe?
3. What does standard deviation measure?

Being part of a research study can potentially lead to unintended consequences for the participants. After taking part in a study of young dating couples (Rubin & Mitchell, 1976), some participants identified problems in their relationship and ended it.

their church, athletes in the Special Olympics, or residents of the local nursing home present great samples for psychological research. Without proper permission, though, the most well-meaning and considerate researchers still violate the rights of the participants.

Ethics Guidelines

A number of guidelines have been developed to ensure that research is conducted ethically. At the base of all of these guidelines is the notion that people participating in psychological research should be no worse off coming out of the study than they were on the way in.

Today colleges and universities have a review board that is typically called the *institutional review board (IRB)* that evaluates the ethical nature of research conducted at their institutions. Proposed research plans must pass the scrutiny of a research ethics committee before the study can be initiated. In addition, the American Psychological Association (APA) has developed ethics guidelines for its members. The code of ethics instructs psychologists to protect their participants from mental and physical harm. The participants' best interests need to be kept foremost in the researcher's mind (Graziano & Raulin, 2013). The APA's guidelines address four important issues:

- *Informed consent:* All participants must know what their participation will involve and what risks might develop. For example, participants in a study on dating should be told beforehand that a questionnaire might stimulate thoughts about issues in their relationships that they have not considered. Participants also should be informed that in some instances a discussion of the issues might improve their relationships but that in others it might worsen the relationships and even end them. Even after informed consent is given, participants must retain the right to withdraw from the study at any time and for any reason.

- *Confidentiality:* Researchers are responsible for keeping all of the data they gather on individuals completely confidential and, when possible, completely anonymous. Confidential data are not the same as anonymous. When data are confidential, it is possible to link a participant's identity to his or her data.

- *Debriefing:* After the study has been completed, the researchers should inform the participants of its purpose and the methods they used. In most cases, the experimenters also can inform participants in a general manner beforehand about the purpose of the research without leading the participants to behave in a way that they think that the experimenters are expecting. When preliminary information about the study is likely to affect the results, participants can at least be debriefed after the study's completion.

- *Deception:* This is an ethical issue that psychologists debate extensively. In some circumstances, telling the participants beforehand what the research study is about substantially alters the participants' behavior and invalidates the researcher's data. Recall the study of social connectedness and cardiovascular function described earlier. The participants were not told that the person they interacted with was a confederate following a script. Had the psychologist informed the participants beforehand that this was the case, the whole study would have been ruined. Thus, the researcher deceived participants about the purpose of the study (recall they were told it was about cardiovascular function and physical activity) as well as about the nature of their relationship with the interaction partner. In all cases of deception, the psychologist must ensure that the deception will not harm the participants and that the participants will be told the true nature of the study (will be debriefed) as soon as possible after the study is completed.

Note that when a study uses deception, the principle of informed consent is violated. This is why participants in studies involving deception should have the option of withdrawing consent after they find out what the study is actually about. To read more about the use of deception in psychological research, see the Critical Controversy.

CRITICAL CONTROVERSY

Is It Ethical to Use Deception in Research?

Imagine that you have signed up to participate in a study that the experimenter tells you concerns decision making and timing. Your task is to solve a list of word jumbles. For each jumble you solve correctly, you and a randomly selected participant from another study will each receive a dollar. The experimenter cautions that you must solve the jumbles *in the order presented*. If you fail to solve an early jumble, you will not receive payment for any subsequent jumbles on the list.

The experimenter then leaves you alone with a list of nine scrambled words to solve. A quick glance at the list reveals that the first two words are a cinch, but the third one is tricky: UNAAGT. The rest of the words look pretty easy too, except the last one: YOMSEELVD. When the experimenter returns, he gives you another copy of the list and asks you to check off the jumbles you got correct but *does not ask you for the actual answers*.

At the end of the study, the experimenter tells you that, actually, this study was not about decision making and timing at all. Instead, it was about *lying*. This experiment, which was, in fact, conducted by Scott Wiltermuth (2011), tested the prediction that people would be more likely to lie if doing so benefited not only themselves but another person (as in the condition described above). Wiltermuth found that participants were more likely to lie and say they solved the seemingly impossible jumbles (UNAAGT and YOMSEELVD) if doing so benefited not just themselves but another person as well. (By the way, those impossible jumbles do have solutions: The *taguan* is a large nocturnal flying squirrel, and *semovedly* is a little used synonym for *separately*.)

Certainly this interesting study has implications for understanding ethical behaviors. Many real-world situations involve unethical behaviors that benefit not only the person engaging in the behavior but others too. Think of athletes in team sports who take steroids to benefit their teammates as well as themselves, and accountants who cheat on their clients' taxes to benefit those clients. These are important human behaviors for scientists to investigate.

But, consider the irony for a moment: A study about *lying*, an unethical behavior, employed *deception*. A study on lying involved lying to participants. Is that really okay?

Deception in psychological research can range from what is called deception by omission to active deception. *Deception by omission* means simply not telling participants what a study is really about. *Active deception* means actually misleading participants about what is going on in a study, such as giving participants false feedback about their performance on a task or leading them to believe that a confederate is just another participant in a study.

The use of deception in research has been criticized on a variety of grounds (Hertwig & Ortmann, 2008; Kimmel, 2012). First, religions and cultures around the world regard lying as morally wrong. We do make exceptions, of course, in situations that call for "little white lies." Are psychological studies also an exception to this rule?

Second, using deception in psychological research is criticized because of its influence on availability of naïve participants. Once individuals have been deceived in a study, they may be less likely to believe researchers in later studies, even when no deception is involved, threatening the validity of future studies (Hertwig & Ortmann, 2008). Such a possibility has led to a general prohibition against deception in experiments in economics (Ariely & Norton, 2007).

Finally, deception in psychological research may erode public trust in the science of psychology itself (Kimmel, 2012). If everyone believes psychological researchers regularly engage in unethical behavior, why should they believe anything these scholars have to say?

As you continue your journey through introductory psychology, you will encounter many studies that use deception. That deception can be as great as leading people to believe they are administering harmful electrical shock to another person (in classic and controversial research by Stanley Milgram, which we will review in Chapter 13). Researchers who employ deception in their studies must be able to justify lying to participants, because doing so is vital to the scientific merit of their work (Benham, 2008).

Although it might seem like fun to fool people, psychological researchers take deception seriously and employ it only when no other options would allow them to ask the questions they seek to answer.

WHAT DO YOU THINK
- How do you feel about the use of deception in psychological research?
- If you participated in a study and later found out it involved deception, would that experience change your perspective in future studies? Why or why not?

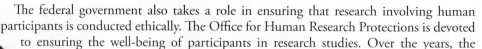

The federal government also takes a role in ensuring that research involving human participants is conducted ethically. The Office for Human Research Protections is devoted to ensuring the well-being of participants in research studies. Over the years, the office has dealt with many challenging and controversial issues—among them, informed consent rules for research on mental disorders, regulations governing research on pregnant women and fetuses, and ethical issues regarding AIDS vaccine research.

Ethical Treatment of Research Animals

For generations, psychologists have used animals in some research. Animal studies have provided a better understanding of and solutions for many human problems (Dewsbury, 2013). Neal Miller (1985), who has made important discoveries about the effects of biofeedback on health, listed the following areas in which animal research has benefited humans:

- Psychotherapy techniques and behavioral medicine for a variety of issues
- Rehabilitation for neuromuscular disorders
- Alleviation of the effects of stress and pain
- Drug treatments for anxiety and severe mental illness
- Methods for avoiding drug addiction and relapse
- Treatments for premature infants to help them gain weight
- Methods for alleviating memory deficits in elderly people

About 5 percent of APA members use nonhuman animals in their research. Rats and mice account for 90 percent of all psychological research with animals. It is true that researchers sometimes use procedures with animals that would be unethical with humans, but these scientists are guided by standards for housing, feeding, and maintaining the psychological and physical well-being of their animal subjects. Researchers are required to weigh potential benefits of the research against possible harm to the animal and to avoid inflicting unnecessary pain. In short, researchers must follow stringent ethical guidelines, whether animals or humans are the subjects in their studies.

test yourself

1. What two things do the ethical principles used in research seek to balance?
2. With respect to the participants in a study, what do the various ethical guidelines covering research all fundamentally seek to protect?
3. What four key issues do the APA's ethics guidelines address?

6. THINKING CRITICALLY ABOUT PSYCHOLOGICAL RESEARCH

Not all psychological information presented for public consumption comes from professionals with excellent credentials and reputations at colleges or universities or in applied mental health settings (Norcross & others, 2013; Stanovich, 2013). Because journalists, television reporters, online bloggers, and other media personnel are not usually trained in psychological research, they often have trouble sorting through the widely varying material they find and making sound decisions about the best information to present to the public. In addition, the media often focus on sensationalistic and dramatic psychological findings to capture public attention. Media reports may go beyond what actual research articles and clinical findings really say. For example, recall from Chapter 1 the research controversy over the alleged epidemic of narcissism in Millennials, those born in the early 1980s. The popular media and online sources latched on to this study, although subsequent research has called its conclusions into question.

Even when the media present the results of excellent research, they sometimes have trouble accurately informing people about the findings and their implications for people's lives. *The Science of Psychology* is dedicated to carefully introducing, defining, and elaborating on key concepts and issues, research, and clinical findings. The media, however, do not have the luxury of so much time and space to detail and specify the limitations and qualifications of research. In the end, *you* have to take responsibility for

Snapshots

"This just in from the AMA: New studies reveal that life is bad for you."

© Jason Love. www.CartoonStock.com.

evaluating media reports on psychological research. To put it another way, you have to consume psychological information critically and wisely. Five guidelines follow.

Avoid Overgeneralizing Based on Little Information

Media reports of psychological information often leave out details about the nature of the sample used in a given study. Without information about sample characteristics— such as the number of participants, their sex, or their ethnic representation—it is wise to take research results with a grain of salt. For example, research that demonstrated the classic "fight or flight" response to stress has had great impact on how we understand the body's response to threatening situations. Yet the original work on this topic included only male participants (Taylor, 2011a). The implications of the lack of women in these studies will be explored in Chapter 3.

Distinguish Between Group Results and Individual Needs

Just as we cannot generalize from a small group to all people, we also cannot apply conclusions from a group to an individual. When you learn about psychological research through the media, you might be disposed to apply the results to your life. It is important to keep in mind that statistics about a group do not necessarily represent each individual in the group equally well. Imagine, for example, taking a test in a class and being told that the class average was 75 percent, but you got 98 percent. It is unlikely that you would want the instructor to apply the group average to your score.

Sometimes consumers of psychological research can get the wrong idea about whether their own experience is "normal" if it does not match group statistics. New parents face this issue all the time. They read about developmental milestones that supposedly characterize an entire age group of children; one such milestone might be that most 2-year-olds are conversing with their parents. However, this group information does not necessarily characterize *all* children who are developing normally. Albert Einstein did not start talking until he was the ripe old age of 3.

Look for Answers Beyond a Single Study

The media might identify an interesting piece of research and claim that its conclusions are phenomenal and have far-reaching implications. Although such pivotal studies do occur, they are rare. It is safer to assume that no single study will provide conclusive answers to an important question, especially answers that apply to all people. In fact, in most psychological domains that prompt many investigations, conflicting results are common. Answers to questions in research usually emerge after many scientists have conducted similar investigations that yield similar conclusions. Remember that you should not take one research study as the absolute, final answer to a problem, no matter how compelling the findings.

Avoid Attributing Causes Where None Have Been Found

Drawing causal conclusions from correlational studies is one of the most common mistakes the media make. For example, the results of the Nun Study described earlier suggest that happy people live longer. However, we cannot state that happiness *caused* them to live longer. When a true experiment has not been conducted—that is, when participants have not been randomly assigned to treatments or experiences—two variables might have only a non-causal relation to each other. Remember from the discussion of correlation earlier in the chapter that causal interpretations cannot be made when two or more factors are simply correlated. We cannot say that one causes the other. When you hear about correlational studies, be skeptical of words indicating causation until you know more about the particular research.

Consider the Source of Psychological Information

Studies conducted by psychologists are not automatically accepted by the rest of the research community. The researchers usually must submit their findings to an academic journal for review by their colleagues, who make a decision about whether to publish the paper, depending on its scientific merit. Although the quality of research and findings is not uniform among all psychology journals, in most cases journals submit the findings to far greater scrutiny than do the popular media (Stanovich, 2013).

Within the media, though, you can usually draw a distinction. The reports of psychological research in respected newspapers such as the *New York Times* and the *Washington Post,* as well as in credible magazines such as *Time* and the *Atlantic Monthly,* are far more trustworthy than reports in tabloids such as the *National Enquirer* and *Star* or online bloggers without scientific credentials. Yet whatever the source—serious publication, tabloid, blog, or even academic journal—you are responsible for reading the details behind the reported findings and for analyzing the study's credibility.

test yourself

1. For what reasons are media reports on psychological studies often problematic?
2. Why is it wise to look beyond the conclusions of just one research study?
3. How does the submission of research findings to a respectable academic journal aid both researchers and the public?

7. THE SCIENTIFIC METHOD AND HEALTH AND WELLNESS

Throughout this book we examine a host of ways that psychological research has implications for health and wellness. In this chapter's concluding section, we focus on a research topic in which the scientific method has played a particularly important role in the conclusions drawn—the power of expressive writing to enhance health and wellness.

James Pennebaker has conducted a number of studies that converge on the same conclusion: that writing about one's deepest thoughts and feelings concerning one's most traumatic life event leads to a number of health and well-being benefits (Pennebaker & Chung, 2007). This research began with a correlational study comparing two groups of individuals—those who had lost a spouse to suicide and those who had lost a spouse to an accident (Pennebaker & O'Heeron, 1984). The results of the study showed that survivors of a suicide were more likely to have become sick in the months after the death, compared to accident survivors. Importantly, the difference was explained by the fact that individuals whose spouses had committed suicide were much less likely to talk about their loss, compared to the other participants.

These correlational findings led Pennebaker to wonder whether it might be possible to manipulate expressing one's thoughts and feelings about a traumatic event *experimentally* and thereby to receive the benefits of socially sharing the trauma. So, in subsequent studies, participants were randomly

The research of James Pennebaker of the University of Texas, Austin, explores the connections among traumatic life experience, expressive writing, physical and mental health, and work performance.

assigned to write about one of two topics—either the individual's most traumatic life event or a relatively uninteresting topic (for example, his or her plans for the day). Assignment of the specific topic was meant to control for the act of writing itself so that the control group was as much like the experimental group as possible (Baddeley & Pennebaker, 2009; Pennebaker & Graybeal, 2001).

The participants wrote about the same topic for three or four consecutive days for about 20 minutes each day. Weeks or months after writing, participants in the trauma writing group had better physical health than those in the control group. Since the first traumatic writing study, a host of researchers have replicated these effects, showing that writing about trauma is associated with superior immune function, better response to a vaccine, higher psychological well-being, better adjustment to coming to college, and more quickly finding employment after being laid off from work (Lepore & Smyth, 2002; Pennebaker, 1997a, 1997b, 2004). Thus, we might conclude that documenting one's deepest thoughts and feelings about traumatic life events is necessary to attain the health benefits of writing.

Note, however, that the participants in the trauma group were not just writing about a trauma. They were also documenting an important personal experience. Thinking about these results in terms of the internal validity of the conclusions, we might ask if focusing on a trauma is the key ingredient in producing health benefits. Might there be other, less negative aspects of life that are equally meaningful and that might promote good health when they are the subject of personal writing? Indeed, subsequent research has shown that health benefits can emerge from writing about a variety of topics, including how one has grown from a negative experience (King & Miner, 2000; Low, Stanton, & Danoff-Burg, 2006), one's life dreams (King, 2001), and one's most intensely positive experiences (Burton & King, 2004, 2009). In one study, participants who wrote about either a traumatic life event or an extremely positive event for just 2 minutes a day over 2 days reported fewer illnesses a month later (Burton & King, 2008).

The body of evidence for the effects of expressive writing on health is substantial and has been subjected to two meta-analyses, the procedure described earlier in this chapter. These meta-analyses indicate that individuals who write over days that are spaced apart tend to benefit most from writing, and that feeling distressed while writing is not necessary to enjoy these benefits (Frattaroli, 2006; Smyth, 1998).

If you would like to explore the benefits of writing in your own life, use the simple guidelines below:

- Find a quiet place to write.
- Pick just one topic to explore through writing.
- Dedicate yourself to a few minutes of writing each day, perhaps writing once a week for a few weeks.
- While writing, do not worry about punctuation, grammar, or spelling—just let yourself go and write about all of the thoughts, emotions, and feelings associated with the experience you are documenting.
- If you feel that writing about something negative is not for you, try writing about your most positive life experiences, the people you care about, or all the things for which you feel grateful.

The long and growing literature on the effects of expressive writing on health demonstrates how research methods influence the conclusions that scientists reach and how the process of scientific research builds from one study to the next. This literature also demonstrates how psychological research is relevant to the daily life of everyone with a story to write—and how an individual can benefit from writing that story.

test yourself

1. Briefly describe Pennebaker's initial correlational study comparing two groups of individuals who had lost a spouse.
2. What did Pennebaker's subsequent experimental research show?
3. What does the accumulated body of evidence indicate about the effects of expressive writing on health?

1. PSYCHOLOGY'S SCIENTIFIC METHOD

Psychologists use the scientific method to address research questions. This method involves starting with a theory and then making observations, formulating hypotheses, testing these through empirical research, drawing conclusions, and evaluating the theory. The science of psychology is an ongoing conversation among scholars.

2. TYPES OF PSYCHOLOGICAL RESEARCH

Three types of research commonly used in psychology are descriptive research (finding out about the basic dimensions of some variable), correlational research (finding out if and how two variables change together), and experimental research (determining the causal relationship between variables). Descriptive research includes observation, surveys, interviews, and case studies. Correlational research often includes surveys and interviews as well as observation. Experimental research often occurs in a lab but can also be done in a natural setting.

In an experiment, the independent variable is manipulated to see if it produces changes in the dependent variable. An experiment involves comparing two groups: the experimental group (the one that receives the treatment or manipulation of the independent variable) and the control group (the comparison group or baseline that is equal to the experimental group in every way except for the independent variable). Experimental research relies on random assignment to ensure that the groups are roughly equivalent before the manipulation of the independent variable. Quasi-experimental designs are similar to experiments, but they do not involve random assignment of participants to groups.

3. RESEARCH SAMPLES AND SETTINGS

Two important decisions that must be made for psychological research are whom to study and where to study them. A sample is the group that participates in a study; a population is the group to which the researcher wishes to generalize the results. A random sample is the best way of ensuring that the sample reflects the population.

Research settings include both the laboratory and real-world, naturalistic contexts. The laboratory allows a great deal of control, but naturalistic settings may give a truer sense of natural behavior.

4. ANALYZING AND INTERPRETING DATA

Descriptive statistics are used to describe and summarize samples of data in a meaningful way. Two types of descriptive statistics are measures of central tendency and measures of variability. Measures of central tendency are the mean (or the mathematical average), the median (the middle score), and the mode (the most common score). Measures of variability include the range (the difference between the highest and lowest scores) and the standard deviation (the square root of the average squared deviation from the mean).

Inferential statistics are used to draw conclusions about data. Inferential statistics aim to uncover statistical significance, which means that the differences observed between groups (or the correlation between variables) are unlikely to be the result of chance.

5. CONDUCTING ETHICAL RESEARCH

For all kinds of research, ethical treatment of participants is crucial. Participants should leave a psychological study no worse off than they were when they entered. Some guiding principles for ethical research in psychology include informed consent, confidentiality, debriefing (participants should be fully informed about the purpose of a study once it is over), and explaining the use of deception in a study. Researchers must follow stringent ethical guidelines, whether animals or humans are the subjects in their studies.

6. THINKING CRITICALLY ABOUT PSYCHOLOGICAL RESEARCH

In your everyday life and in introductory psychology, you will be exposed to psychological research findings. In approaching psychological research in the media, you should adopt the attitude of a scientist and critically evaluate the research presented. This means being careful to avoid overgeneralizing based on little information, realizing that group results may not apply to every individual, looking for answers beyond a single study, and avoiding attributing causation when none has been found. Finally, it is important to consider the source when you encounter research in the popular media.

7. THE SCIENTIFIC METHOD AND HEALTH AND WELLNESS

A great deal of psychological research has relevance to health and wellness. An example is research by James Pennebaker on the effects of expressive writing on health and well-being. This research has shown that individuals who are randomly assigned to write about a traumatic life event for a few minutes a day over three or four days show a host of health and well-being benefits compared to those in a control condition. Subsequent research has shown that these health benefits can be obtained by writing about very positive life experiences and even just writing for a couple of minutes.

This research demonstrates how a research question can begin as a correlational study and then move to the laboratory to demonstrate causation. When many studies have been done on a topic, a meta-analysis can provide a sense of the overall importance of the results. This example also shows how psychological research can have important implications for everyday life.

key *terms*

SUMMARY

experimenter bias, p. 42

demand characteristics, p. 42

research participant bias, p. 43

placebo effect, p. 43

placebo, p. 43

double-blind experiment, p. 43

population, p. 45

sample, p. 45

random sample, p. 45

naturalistic observation, p. 46

descriptive statistics, p. 47

mean, p. 47

median, p. 49

mode, p. 49

range, p. 49

standard deviation, p. 49

inferential statistics, p. 50

apply your *knowledge*

1. It's time to get out those old photos from the prom, wedding, or family reunion and see just how happy people were (or weren't). Look at some pictures from your own life and see who was genuinely smiling and who was faking it. Just cover the mouths with your finger—you can see who is happy from their eyes.

2. Is an old diary of yours hanging around somewhere? Pull it out and take a look at what you wrote. Count up your positive emotion words or negative emotion words. Are there themes in your diary from years ago that are still relevant to your life today? Does looking at your own diary change the way you might think about the results of the Nun Study? Explain.

3. What are some positive and negative correlations that you have observed in your own experience? What are some third variables that might explain these relationships? Do you think these relationships may be causal? How would you design an experiment to test that possibility?

4. In the next few days, look through several newspapers and magazines for reports about psychological research. Also notice what you find on the Internet and on television about psychology. Apply the guidelines for being a wise consumer of information about psychology to these media reports.

5. The opening of this chapter presented research on magical thinking in college students. Design a replication of this work using a different population of participants. How might you study this phenomenon among middle-aged adults, elderly individuals, or children?

6. Pick a topic of interest to you and define the variables. Then list as many ways to operationalize the variables as you can. Come up with at least one behavioral measure of the variable. Would your topic be best studied using a correlational or an experimental method? How would you conduct the study?

CHAPTER 3

Biological Foundations of Behavior

Changing the Brain, Changing the Person

Our brains are involved in every aspect of our lives. Every behavior, every thought is an event in the brain. When the brain is changed, it can change a person's very personality—in ways that can be tragic or redeeming. When people experience a brain injury, personality change can be so dramatic that a spouse may feel that he or she is married to a different person. In many cases, these individuals must face the challenge of forging a new relationship with someone they have known and loved for years (Wheaton, 2012).

Yet, such changes are not always negative.

Consider Jason Padgett, a futon store clerk in Tacoma, Washington. After a brutal mugging, Jason suffered what doctors thought was a concussion. But during the months of recovery, Jason noticed a dramatic change in himself. A college dropout who had never been particularly interested in math, he suddenly began seeing the world as made up of intricate mathematic patterns. And he discovered he had a special talent for creating artwork based on the arithmetic laws he saw everywhere in his world. During his recovery, Jason's brain seems to have unlocked capacities he had never known before (Karlinsky & Frost, 2012). With his new abilities, Jason plans on a career in teaching so that he can share the beauty that he now recognizes all around him.

These examples illuminate the brain's role in precious human experiences as well as its sometimes mysterious nature. Imagine: This intricate 3-pound structure that you are reading about is the engine that is doing the work of reading itself. The brain is also the structure responsible for the research presented here. The brain is at once the object of study and the reason we are able to study it. ●

PREVIEW

In this chapter, our focus is the the biological foundations of human behavior We review the essentials of what we know about the nervous system and its command center—the brain. We then look at how genetic processes influence who we are as individuals and how we behave. Finally, we explore the role of the brain and nervous system in the experience of stress and consider ways to unlock the brain's unique resources to better meet life's challenges and maintain health and well-being.

1· THE NERVOUS SYSTEM

● **nervous system** The body's electrochemical communication circuitry.

The **nervous system** is the body's electrochemical communication circuitry. The field that studies the nervous system is called *neuroscience,* and the people who study it are *neuroscientists.*

The human nervous system is made up of billions of communicating nerve cells, and it is likely the most intricately organized aggregate of matter on the planet. A single cubic centimeter (about the size of a snack cube of cheese) of the human brain consists of well over 50 million nerve cells, each of which communicates with many other nerve cells in information-processing networks that make the most elaborate computer seem primitive.

Characteristics of the Nervous System

The brain and nervous system guide our interactions with the world around us, move the body through the world, and direct our adaptation to the environment. Several extraordinary characteristics allow the nervous system to command our behavior: complexity, integration, adaptability, and electrochemical transmission.

COMPLEXITY

The human brain and nervous system are enormously complex. This complexity is demonstrated in the orchestration of the billions of nerve cells in the brain—to allow you to talk, write, sing, dance, and think. This capacity is simply awe-inspiring. As you read *The Science of Psychology,* your brain is carrying out a multitude of functions, including seeing, reading, learning, and (we hope) breathing. Extensive assemblies of nerve cells participate in each of these activities, all at once.

INTEGRATION

Neuroscientist Steven Hyman (2001) has called the brain the "great integrator," meaning that the brain does a wonderful job of pulling information together. Think of everything going on around you right now, as well as the multitude of processes happening in your body—like breathing, the digestion of your last meal, the healing of a cut. Somehow, you need to make sense of all of these various stimuli. Similarly, the shapes on this page are not simply splashes of ink but letters, and those letters compose words that make sense. It is your brain that draws your experiences together into a coherent whole. Sounds, sights, touches, tastes, and smells—the brain integrates all of these sensory inputs so that you can function in the world.

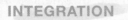

As we dance, write, play sports, talk, think, and connect with the world in countless other ways, the brain and the nervous system guide our every interaction, movement, and adaptation.

The nervous system has different levels and many different parts. Brain activity is integrated across these levels through countless interconnections of brain cells and extensive pathways that link different parts of the brain and body. Each nerve cell communicates, on average, with 10,000 others, making an astronomical number of connections (Bloom, Nelson, & Lazerson, 2001). The evidence for these connections is observable, for example, when a loved one takes your hand. How does your brain know, and tell you, what has happened? Bundles of interconnected nerve cells relay information about the sensation in your hand through the nervous system in a very orderly fashion, all the way to the areas of the brain involved in recognizing that someone you love is holding your hand. Then the brain might send a reply and prompt your hand to give your loved one a little squeeze.

ADAPTABILITY

The world around us is constantly changing. To survive, we must adapt to new conditions. The brain and nervous system together serve as our agent for adapting to the world. Although nerve cells reside in certain brain regions, they are not unchanging structures. They have a hereditary, a biological foundation, but they are constantly adapting to changes in the body and the environment (Mercado & Henderson, 2013).

The term **plasticity** refers to the brain's special physical capacity for change. Jason Padgett's recovery from his brain injury demonstrates the brain's plasticity. Less dramatic examples of plasticity occur in all of us. Because the brain has plasticity it can change in response to experience. For example, you might believe that thinking is a mental process, not a physical one. Yet thinking *is* a physical event, because every thought you have is reflected in physical activity in the brain.

● **plasticity** The brain's special capacity for change.

Moreover, the brain can be changed by experience. London cab drivers who have developed a familiarity with the city show increases in the size of the area of the brain thought to be responsible for reading maps (Maguire & others, 2000). Think about that: When you change the way you think, you are *literally* changing the brain's physical processes and even its shape. Our daily experiences contribute to the wiring or rewiring of the brain, just as the experiences of those London cab drivers did (Bavelier & others, 2012; Petrosini, Cutuli, De Bartolo, 2013).

ELECTROCHEMICAL TRANSMISSION

The brain and the nervous system function essentially as an information-processing system powered by electrical impulses and chemical messengers (Emes & Grant, 2012). When an impulse travels down a nerve cell, or *neuron,* it does so electrically. When that impulse gets to the end of the line, it communicates with the next neuron using chemicals, as we will consider in detail later in this chapter.

Pathways in the Nervous System

As we interact with and adapt to the world, the brain and the nervous system receive and transmit sensory input (like sounds, smells, and flavors), integrate the information taken in from the environment, and direct the body's motor activities. Information flows into the brain through input from our senses, and the brain makes sense of that information, pulling it together and giving it meaning. In turn, information moves out of the brain to the rest of the body, directing all of the physical things we do (Alstermark & Isa, 2012).

The nervous system has specialized pathways that are adapted for different functions. These pathways are made up of afferent nerves, efferent nerves, and neural

● **afferent nerves or sensory nerves**
Nerves that carry information about the external environment *to* the brain and spinal cord via sensory receptors.

● **efferent nerves or motor nerves** Nerves that carry information *out of* the brain and spinal cord to other areas of the body.

● **central nervous system (CNS)** The brain and spinal cord.

● **peripheral nervous system (PNS)** The network of nerves that connects the brain and spinal cord to other parts of the body.

● **somatic nervous system** The body system consisting of the sensory nerves, whose function is to convey information from the skin and muscles to the CNS about conditions such as pain and temperature, and the motor nerves, whose function is to tell muscles what to do.

● **autonomic nervous system** The body system that takes messages to and from the body's internal organs, monitoring such processes as breathing, heart rate, and digestion.

● **sympathetic nervous system** The part of the autonomic nervous system that arouses the body to mobilize it for action and thus is involved in the experience of stress.

● **parasympathetic nervous system** The part of the autonomic nervous system that calms the body.

test yourself

1. Name and explain four characteristics that allow the nervous system to direct human behavior.
2. What is the difference between afferent and efferent nerves?
3. What are the two main parts of the autonomic nervous system, and what is the function of each?

networks (discussed later in the chapter). **Afferent nerves,** or **sensory nerves,** carry information *to* the brain and spinal cord. These sensory pathways communicate information about the external environment (for example, the sight of a sunrise) and internal conditions (for example, fatigue or hunger) from sensory receptors to the brain and spinal cord. **Efferent nerves,** or **motor nerves,** carry information *out of* the brain and spinal cord—that is, they carry the nervous system's output. These motor pathways communicate information from the brain and spinal cord to other areas of the body, including muscles and glands, instructing them, in a sense, to get busy. Notice that the fact that we have separate afferent and efferent nerves tells us something interesting about neurons: Each neuron is a one-way street in the nervous system.

These terms can be complicated. Remember that sensory nerves are afferent nerves. They bring the brain and spinal cord information about the world. Motor nerves are efferent nerves that send information out from the brain and spinal cord. It might help to remember the functions of afferent and efferent nerves by noting that *a*fferent nerves *a*rrive at the brain and spinal cord, and *e*fferent nerves *e*xit these components of the nervous system.

Divisions of the Nervous System

This truly elegant system is highly ordered and organized for effective function. Figure 3.1 shows the two primary divisions of the human nervous system: the central nervous system and the peripheral nervous system.

The **central nervous system (CNS)** is made up of the brain and spinal cord. More than 99 percent of all nerve cells in our body are located in the CNS. The **peripheral nervous system (PNS)** is the network of nerves that connects the brain and spinal cord to other parts of the body. The functions of the peripheral nervous system are to bring information to and from the brain and spinal cord and to carry out the commands of the CNS to execute various muscular and glandular activities.

The peripheral nervous system has two major divisions: the somatic nervous system and the autonomic nervous system. The **somatic nervous system** consists of sensory nerves, whose function is to convey information from the skin and muscles to the CNS about conditions such as pain and temperature, and motor nerves, whose function is to tell the muscles what to do. The function of the **autonomic nervous system** is to take messages to and from the body's internal organs, monitoring such processes as breathing, heart rate, and digestion.

The autonomic nervous system also is divided into two parts. The first part, the **sympathetic nervous system,** arouses the body to mobilize it for action, while the second, the **parasympathetic nervous system,** calms the body. The sympathetic nervous system is involved in the "fight or flight" response, the body's reaction to a threat (an incident that you can either stay and fight or flee). When you feel your heart pounding and your hands sweating under stress, those experiences reveal the sympathetic nervous system in action. If you need to run away from a dangerous situation, the sympathetic nervous system sends blood out to your extremities to prepare you for taking off. The parasympathetic nervous system is responsible for the ways you calm down once you have escaped the danger. While the sympathetic nervous system is associated with "fight or flight," the parasympathetic nervous system might be thought of as the system that "rests and digests."

In an emergency, the sympathetic nervous system also triggers the body's release of powerful hormones (Maggio & Segal, 2009). These stress hormones allow you to focus attention on what needs to be done *now*. For example, in an emergency, people sometimes report feeling strangely calm and doing what has to be done, whether calling 911 or applying pressure to a serious wound. Such experiences reveal the benefits of stress hormones for humans in times of acute emergency (Dougall & others, 2013). We will revisit the relationship between the experience of stress and the nervous system at the close of this chapter.

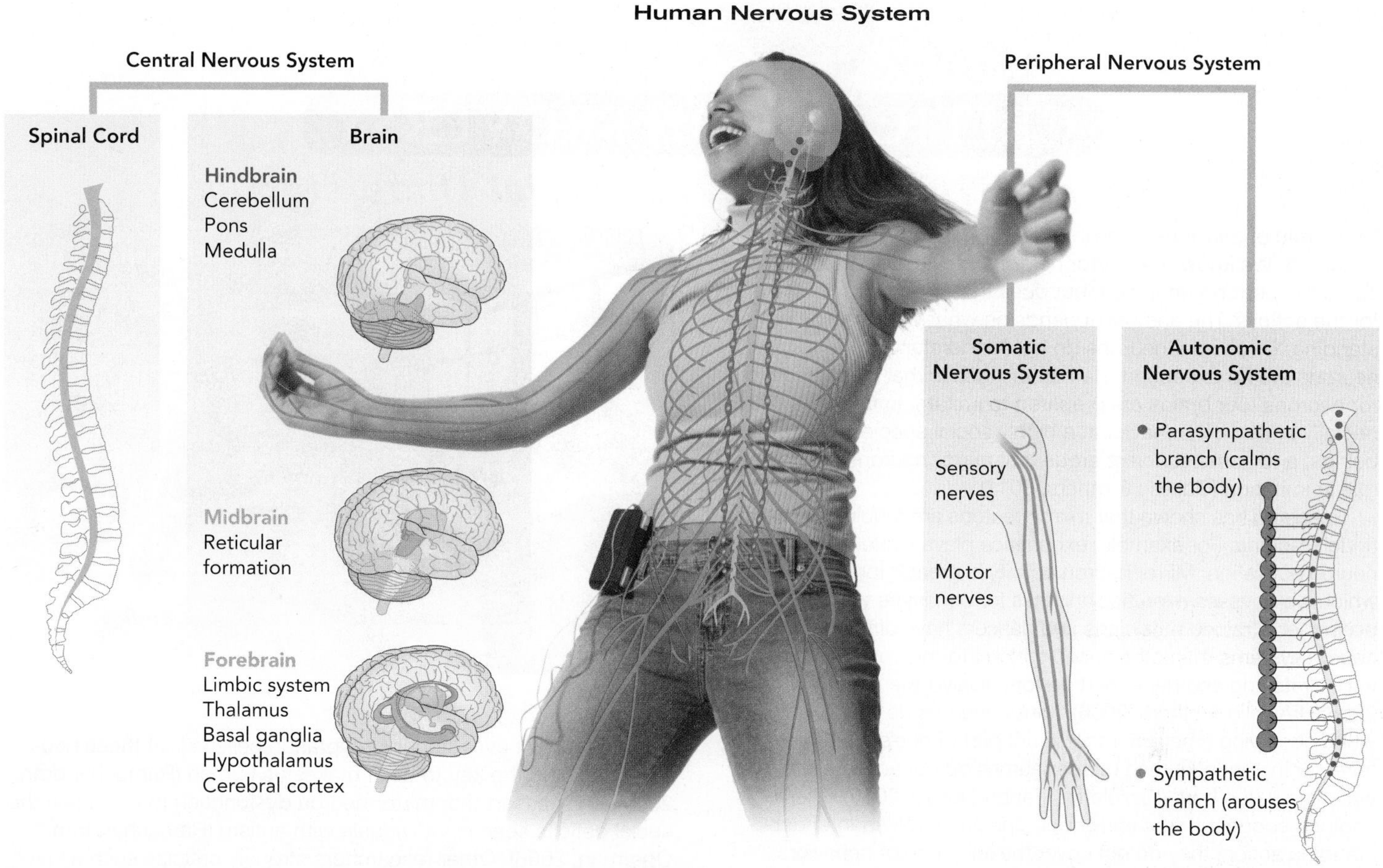

Human Nervous System

FIGURE 3.1 **Major Divisions of the Human Nervous System** The nervous system has two main divisions. One is the *central nervous system* (*left*), which comprises the brain and the spinal cord. The nervous system's other main division is the *peripheral nervous system* (*right*), which itself has two parts—the *somatic nervous system*, which controls sensory and motor neurons, and the *autonomic nervous system*, which monitors processes such as breathing, heart rate, and digestion. These complex systems work together to help us successfully navigate the world.

2· NEURONS

Within each division of the nervous system, much is happening at the cellular level. Nerve cells, chemicals, and electrical impulses work together to transmit information at speeds of up to 330 miles per hour. As a result, information can travel from your brain to your hands (or vice versa) in a matter of milliseconds (Rand & Shimansky, 2013). Just how fast is 330 miles per hour? Consider that the NASCAR speed record was set in 1987 by Bill Elliott, who completed a lap driving at 212.8 miles per hour.

There are two types of cells in the nervous system: neurons and glial cells. **Neurons** are the nerve cells that handle information processing; we will generally concentrate on neurons in this chapter. The human brain contains about 100 billion neurons. The average neuron is a complex structure with as many as 10,000 physical connections with other cells.

Recently, researchers have been particularly interested in a special type of neuron called a *mirror neuron.* Mirror neurons are activated (in human and nonhuman primates) both when we perform an action and when we watch someone else perform that same activity (Fontana & others, 2012; Hickok, 20090; Oztop, Kawato, & Arbib, 2013). You might be wondering why that is such a big deal. Remember, neurons are

● **neurons** One of two types of cells in the nervous system; neurons are the nerve cells that handle the information-processing function.

CRITICAL CONTROVERSY

Do Mirror Neurons Hold the Key to Social Understanding?

The role of mirror neurons in social understanding is hotly debated. We know that mirror neurons are active while observing someone perform an action, but does that indicate *understanding* for the action? The answer depends on what we mean by understanding. Of course, neurons do not "understand," and mirror neurons are no exception. Rather, the idea is that because of mirror neurons, our brains are prepared to imitate. Imitation is an especially important behavior in a highly social species like human beings, and some scholars argue that mirror neurons play a key role in imitation (Gallese & others, 2011).

Research has shown that mirror neurons are required for social understanding. For example, experience plays a role in mirror neuron activation. Mirror neuron activity is greater for behaviors for which we possess expertise and less for behaviors we have never performed. Trained musicians and dancers have different mirror neuron systems than others, and their mirror neurons fire differently while watching another expert perform (Calvo-Merino & others, 2006; D'Ausilio & others, 2006). Mirror neurons do not respond when observing a behavior that is not part of one's typical repertoire; for instance, human mirror neurons do not activate while watching a dog bark (Rizzolatti & Fabbri-Destro, 2010). These findings suggest that if mirror neurons are involved in understanding action, they do not cover the full range of behaviors we understand. If you watch someone play a violin, having never played one yourself, you still understand what the person is doing (Hickok, 2009; Hickok & Hauser, 2010). So, we can understand behavior even without the involvement of mirror neurons.

Although acknowledging that there are many ways to gain an understanding of another person's action, others argue that mirror neurons provide a unique route—from the inside out (Rizzolatti & Sinigaglia, 2010). Consider that mirror neurons suggest a kind of mental telepathy, a direct connection between an observer's brain and a person being observed (Heyes, 2010). If I see you performing an act, my mirror neurons put my brain in the very same state that you are in, without you ever speaking a word. Even if I am not intending to imitate your behavior, mirror neurons will fire. My brain, somehow, seems to "know" what you are doing and starts mentally doing it too.

The potential role of mirror neurons in autism is especially controversial (Glenberg, 2011). Those who champion mirror neurons

as an important evolutionary adaptation believe that these neurons may hold the key to what makes us human (Ramachandran, 2000). They assert that mirror neuron dysfunction may explain the social deficits seen in individuals with autism (Ramachandran & Oberman, 2006). Other researchers strongly criticize such a view, contending that we know far too little about mirror neurons to claim a central role for them in autism (Gallese & others, 2011; Pascolo & Cattarinussi, 2012). They point to mixed results in research linking mirror neuron function to autism and warn that such claims appear to label individuals with autism as somehow "less human" (Gallese & others, 2011).

Mirror neurons have powerfully captured neuroscientists' attention. This fascination perhaps reveals an important truth: The mystery of human social behavior is an immensely compelling area of scientific inquiry.

WHAT DO YOU THINK

- Why do you think the discovery of mirror neurons has led to such excitement and controversy among scientists?

- What do you think are the characteristics that make human beings different from other animals? How would you study those characteristics?

specialized: Motor neurons do not respond to sensory information, and sensory neurons do not respond to motor information. Yet, mirror neurons appear to respond to both kinds of information, doing and seeing (Gallese & others, 2011; Oztop, Kawato, & Arbib, 2013). This responsiveness to two different kinds of input is one characteristic that makes mirror neurons so fascinating.

The discovery of mirror neurons has led to provocative predictions about the function of these neurons in imitation, social cognition (that is, thinking about oneself and others),

Touring the Nervous System and the Brain

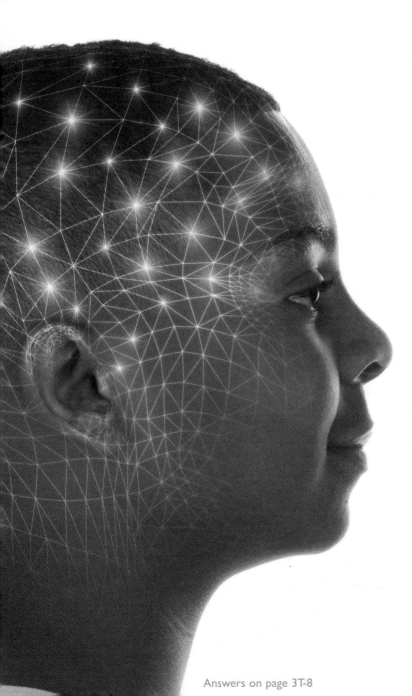

GOALS OF THE TOUR

1 **The Neuron and Synapse.** Identify parts of the neuron and synapse and describe how they communicate information.

2 **The Resting Potential and Action Potential.** Describe the ions used in maintaining the resting potential and in producing the action potential.

3 **Structures and Functions in the Human Brain.** Identify the brain's key structures and functions.

4 **Cerebral Cortex Lobes and Association Areas.** Identify the location and describe the function of the four cerebral lobes.

5 **Visual Information in the Split-Brain.** Describe hemispheric lateralization and communication in the brain.

6 **Central and Peripheral Nervous Systems.** Identify the parts of the central and peripheral nervous systems and describe the body functions they control.

Answers on page 3T-8

The Neuron and the Synapse

1 Identify parts of the neuron and synapse and describe how they communicate information.

Sending Neuron

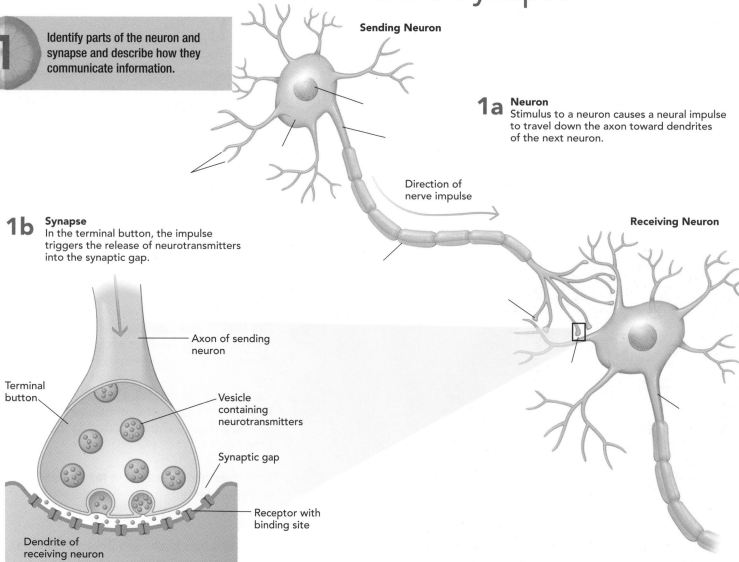

1a **Neuron**
Stimulus to a neuron causes a neural impulse to travel down the axon toward dendrites of the next neuron.

Direction of nerve impulse

Receiving Neuron

1b **Synapse**
In the terminal button, the impulse triggers the release of neurotransmitters into the synaptic gap.

Axon of sending neuron

Terminal button

Vesicle containing neurotransmitters

Synaptic gap

Receptor with binding site

Dendrite of receiving neuron

The Resting Potential and Action Potential

2a Resting Potential

The electrical potential across the membrane when the neuron is not stimulated. −70 mV inside relative to the outside of the membrane.

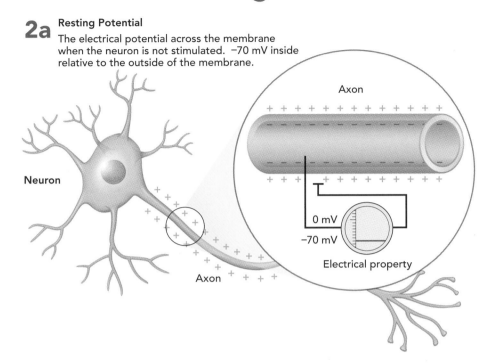

Axon

0 mV
−70 mV

Electrical property

Neuron

Axon

2b Action Potential

The action potential is generated by an impulse within a neuron that causes a brief wave of positive electrical charge to sweep down the axon.

Axon at time 1

Voltage

Time 2

Voltage

Time 3

Voltage

Positive charge within the axon

Negative charge

Direction of impulse

Structures and Functions of the Human Brain

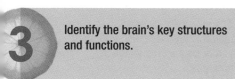

3 Identify the brain's key structures and functions.

3a Brain Stem Structures

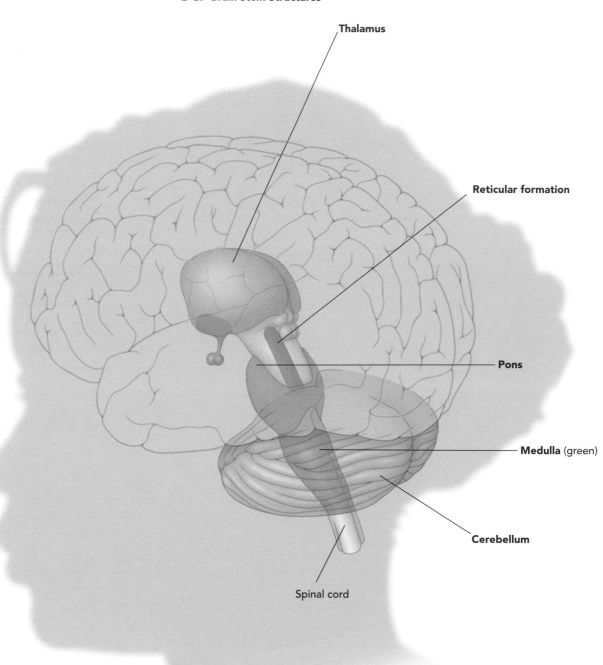

Thalamus

Reticular formation

Pons

Medulla (green)

Cerebellum

Spinal cord

Cerebral Cortex Lobes and Association Areas

Identify the location of the four cerebral cortex lobes and describe their primary functions.

4

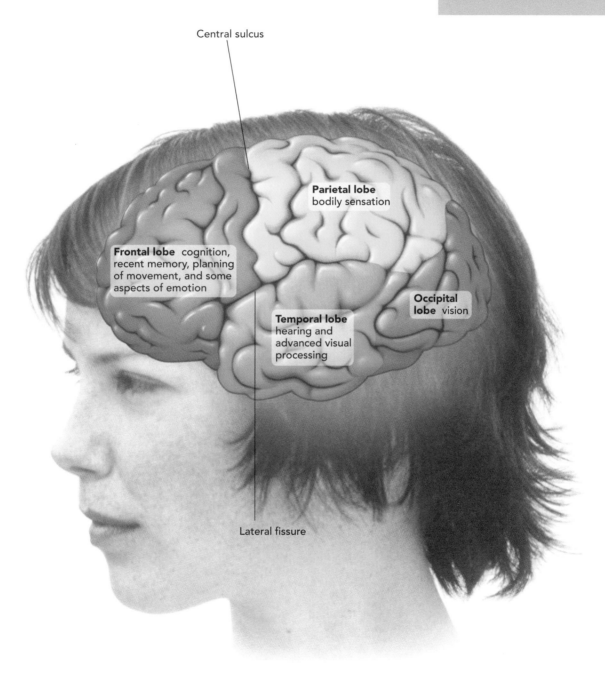

Central sulcus

Parietal lobe bodily sensation

Frontal lobe cognition, recent memory, planning of movement, and some aspects of emotion

Occipital lobe vision

Temporal lobe hearing and advanced visual processing

Lateral fissure

Visual Information in the Split-Brain

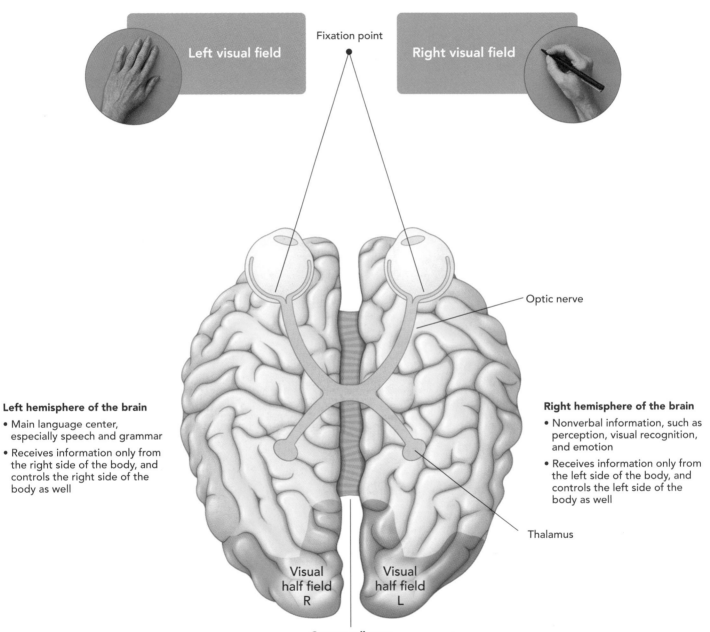

Fixation point

Left visual field

Right visual field

Optic nerve

Thalamus

Left hemisphere of the brain

- Main language center, especially speech and grammar
- Receives information only from the right side of the body, and controls the right side of the body as well

Right hemisphere of the brain

- Nonverbal information, such as perception, visual recognition, and emotion
- Receives information only from the left side of the body, and controls the left side of the body as well

Visual half field R

Visual half field L

Corpus callosum

A thick band of axons that connect brain cells in one hemisphere to the other. In healthy brains, the two sides engage in a continuous flow of information via this neural bridge and share information.

Central and Peripheral Nervous Systems

6a The Central Nervous System

Brain

Spinal cord

Identify the parts of the central and peripheral nervous systems and describe the bodily functions they control.

6

1. THE NEURON AND SYNAPSE

The *neuron* consists of a *cell body*, *dendrites*, and an *axon*. The cell body is the structure of the neuron that contains the nucleus, which consists of the genetic material including the chromosomes. The dendrites are branches of the neuron that receive information from other neurons. The axon sends information away from the cell body to other neurons or cells.

When a neuron fires, it sends an electrical impulse down the axon, known as the *action potential*. When the impulse arrives at the axon terminal buttons, it causes the release of *neurotransmitter* molecules into the *synapse*. The synapse is the gap junction between two neurons. Neurons communicate with one another by means of chemical signals provided by neurotransmitters that cross the synapse.

The neurotransmitter released by the sending neuron enters the synaptic gap and attaches to a *binding site* located on a *receptor* on the receiving neuron. The receptor contains a channel that is typically closed when the receiving neuron is in the resting state (*resting potential*). When the neurotransmitter binds to the receptor, it causes an opening of the receptor channel that then allows a particular *ion* to enter or leave the receiving neuron. If a neurotransmitter causes the opening of channels on the receiving neuron to a positively charged ion like sodium (Na^+), it will become less negative in charge. The entry of sodium will cause a change in the electrical charge (potential) of the receiving neuron that may make it more likely to generate its own action potential.

2. THE RESTING POTENTIAL AND ACTION POTENTIAL

The neuron maintains electrical properties called an *electrical gradient*, displaying a difference in the electrical charge inside and outside of the cell. The electrical gradient is created because the membrane of the neuron is *selectively permeable*. Some molecules can pass through it more freely than others. The membrane is not permeable to large negatively charged protein molecules that are trapped inside the neuron. Inside and outside of the neuron are various electrically charged particles called *ions* that vary in concentrations. The ions that play an important role in the function of the neuron are sodium (Na^+), potassium (K^+), and chloride (Cl^-). These ions enter or leave the neuron through special channels provided by protein molecules that line the neuron.

The *resting potential* is the electrical property of the neuron when it is not stimulated or not sending a nerve impulse. In a typical neuron this is seen as a -70 mV charge inside relative to the outside of the membrane. During the resting potential, the sodium channels are closed, leaving a higher concentration of sodium ions outside of the neuron membrane. The negative charge of a neuron during the resting state is largely maintained by the negatively charged protein molecules trapped inside the neuron and by the inability of positively charged sodium ions to cross the membrane into the neuron.

The *action potential* occurs when the neuron is stimulated to generate a nerve impulse down the axon. This is often referred to as the firing of the neuron. During the action potential, there is a rapid and slight reversal in the electrical charge from -70 mV to +40 mV. The action potential occurs as a brief wave of positive charge that sweeps down the axon.

3. STRUCTURES AND FUNCTIONS IN THE HUMAN BRAIN

The brain stem structures are embedded within the core of the brain and provide a number of vital functions for survival. These include the medulla, pons, cerebellum, reticular formation, and the thalamus.

The *medulla* is a brain structure just above the spinal cord. It controls a number of life-sustaining reflexes and functions including breathing, coughing, vomiting, and heart rate. The *pons* lies just above the medulla and is involved in functions including sleep and arousal. The *cerebellum* is a large structure at the base of the brain with many folds. It is traditionally known to be involved in motor coordination and balance but also plays a role in attention of visual and auditory stimuli and the timing of movements. The *reticular formation* is an elaborate diffuse network of neurons that runs through the core of the medulla and pons to the base of the thalamus. It plays a role in arousal, attention, sleep patterns, and stereotyped patterns such as posture and locomotion. The *thalamus* is a central structure in the brain that relays auditory, visual, and somatosensory (bodily senses) information to the cerebral cortex.

The limbic system comprises a number of brain structures involved in motivation, emotion, and memory. The *hypothalamus* is a small structure that is located just below the thalamus. It controls the autonomic nervous system as well as the release of hormones from the pituitary gland. It is involved in a number of functions including eating, drinking, and sexual behavior, and plays an important role in the expression of emotions and stress responses. The *hippocampus* is located in the temporal lobe and plays a role in learning and memory. Adjacent to the hippocampus is the amygdala, which is involved in fear and anxiety.

The *cerebral cortex* is the outer layer of the brain and is involved in higher-order functions such as thinking, learning, consciousness, and memory.

4. CEREBRAL CORTEX LOBES AND ASSOCIATION AREAS

The *cerebral cortex* is anatomically divided into four lobes: occipital lobe, parietal lobe, temporal lobe, and frontal lobe. The *occipital lobe* is located in the posterior end (back region) of the cortex and is involved in processing *visual information*. The *parietal lobe* lies between the occipital lobe and the *central sulcus*, which is one of the deepest grooves in the surface of the cortex. The parietal lobe is involved in *bodily senses*. The area just posterior to the central sulcus is called the primary somatosensory cortex because it is the primary target for the *touch senses* of the body and information for muscle-stretch receptors and joint receptors. The *temporal lobe* is the large portion of each hemisphere near the temples and lies behind the frontal lobe and below the *lateral fissure*. It is the primary region of the cortex that processes *auditory information*. The *frontal lobe* extends from the central sulcus to the anterior limit (forward region) of the brain. The region of the frontal lobe immediately adjacent to the central sulcus is called the *motor cortex* because it controls *fine movements*. The most anterior region is called the *prefrontal cortex;* it is involved in higher brain functions including *cognition* (thought processes), recent *memory*, the *planning of movement*, and some aspects of *emotion*.

Association areas are not primarily sensory or motor areas but, rather, associate sensory and motor inputs that give rise to higher mental functions such as perception, learning, remembering, thinking, and speaking.

5. VISUAL INFORMATION IN THE SPLIT-BRAIN

Lateralization refers to the division of labor between the two cerebral hemispheres of the brain. The *left hemisphere* receives sensory information from and controls the movements in the right side of the body. Likewise, images of objects in the right visual field are projected to the left half of the retina of each eye, which in turn sends the information to the visual cortex in the left hemisphere. The left hemisphere also contains the main language area involved in the comprehension and production of language.

The *right hemisphere* receives sensory information from and controls the movements in the left side of the body. Likewise, images of objects in the left visual field are projected to the right half of the retina of each eye, which in turn sends the information to the visual cortex in the right hemisphere. The right hemisphere processes nonverbal information, such as perception, visual recognition, and emotion.

In the healthy brain the two cerebral hemispheres share information with each other across the broad band of axons called the *corpus callosum*. In some instances the corpus callosum is surgically cut, a procedure called the *split-brain*. In the split-brain, information in one cerebral hemisphere is confined to that side of the brain.

6. CENTRAL AND PERIPHERAL NERVOUS SYSTEMS

The nervous system is made up of the *central nervous system* and the *peripheral nervous system*. The central nervous system is comprised of the brain and the spinal cord. The peripheral nervous system consists of all nerve fibers outside of the brain and spinal cord. The peripheral nervous system is made up of two major divisions: the *somatic division* and the *autonomic division*.

The *somatic division* consists of nerve fibers conveying information from the brain and spinal cord to skeletal muscles; this information controls movement and sends information back to the brain via the spinal cord from sensory receptors located in various parts of the body.

The *autonomic division* controls the glands and muscles of the internal organs such as the heart, digestive system, lungs, and salivary glands, and it consists of the sympathetic and the parasympathetic branches. The *sympathetic branch* arouses the body, mobilizes its energy during physical exercise and in stressful situations, and activates the adrenal gland to release epinephrine into the bloodstream. The *parasympathetic branch* calms the body and conserves and replenishes energy.

empathy, and understanding behavior (Vanderwert, Fox, & Ferrari, 2013). Some scientists have argued that "broken mirror neurons" play an important role in autism, a disorder of neural development characterized by impairment in communication and social interaction (Lauvin & others, 2012; Ramanchandran & Oberman, 2006). Indeed, some scholars hail mirror neurons as a promising new direction in understanding the origins of human sociability (Ramachandran, 2000). Others charge that such claims far overstep the evidence (Gernsbacher & Pripas-Kapit, 2012; Hickok, 2009). To read more about this controversy, see the Critical Controversy.

Glial cells or **glia** are the other type of cell that provides support, nutritional benefits, and other functions in the nervous system (Selvaraj & others, 2012). Glial cells keep neurons running smoothly. These cells are not specialized to process information in the way that neurons are, and there are many more of them in the nervous system than there are neurons. In fact, for every neuron there are about 10 glial cells. You might think of the glial cells as the pit crew in the raceway of the nervous system.

Neuroscientists know much less about the function of glial cells than neurons, but dramatic new discoveries have shed light on ways in which glial cells might be involved in behavior (Edgar & Sibille, 2013). Until recently, it was thought that glia do not have synapses or release neurotransmitters, both of which, as we will see, are crucial for neural transmission. However, research now suggests that some glial cells are not just passive bystanders to neural transmission but may detect neural impulses and send signals to other glial cells (Chakraborty & others, 2010). Glial cells may play a role in vision (Lin & others, 2013); memory (Hassanpoor, Fallah, & Raza, 2012); neurogenerative diseases such as Alzheimer disease (Melo & others, 2011); pain (Gao & Ji, 2010; Yamamoto & others, 2013); psychological disorders such as schizophrenia (Mitterauer, 2011) and mood disorders (Cobb & others, 2013; Edgar & Sibille, 2013); and the development of neural stem cells (Hattiangady & Shetty, 2012), which we will examine later in this chapter. Still, by far the majority of information processing in the brain is done by neurons, not glial cells.

● **glial cells or glia** The second of two types of cells in the nervous system; glial cells provide support, nutritional benefits, and other functions and keep neurons running smoothly.

Specialized Cell Structure

Not all neurons are alike, as they are specialized to handle different functions. However, all neurons do have some common characteristics. Most neurons are created very early in life, but their shape, size, and connections can change throughout the life span. The way neurons function reflects the major characteristic of the nervous system described at the beginning of the chapter: plasticity. That is, neurons can and do change.

Every neuron has a cell body, dendrites, and an axon (Figure 3.2). The **cell body** contains the *nucleus,* which directs the manufacture of substances that the neuron needs for growth and maintenance. **Dendrites,** treelike fibers projecting from a neuron, receive information and orient it toward the neuron's cell body. Most nerve cells have numerous dendrites, which increase their surface area, allowing each neuron to receive input from many other neurons. The **axon** is the part of the neuron that carries information away from the cell body toward other cells. (Remember that *axon* and *away* both start with the letter *a*). Although extremely thin (1/10,000th of an inch—a human hair by comparison is 1/1000th of an inch), axons can be very long, with many branches. In fact, some extend more than 3 feet—all the way from the top of the brain to the base of the spinal cord. Finally, covering all surfaces of the neurons, including the dendrites and axons, is a very thin cellular membrane that allows substances to move in and out of the cell. We will examine this membrane and its functions in more detail later.

A **myelin sheath,** a layer of cells containing fat, encases and insulates most axons. By insulating the axons, myelin sheaths speed up transmission of nerve impulses (de Boer, Peper, & Beek, 2012). The myelin sheath developed as the nervous system evolved.

● **cell body** The part of the neuron that contains the nucleus, which directs the manufacture of substances that the neuron needs for growth and maintenance.

● **dendrites** Treelike fibers projecting from a neuron, which receive information and orient it toward the neuron's cell body.

● **axon** The part of the neuron that carries information away from the cell body toward other cells.

● **myelin sheath** A layer of fat cells that encases and insulates most axons.

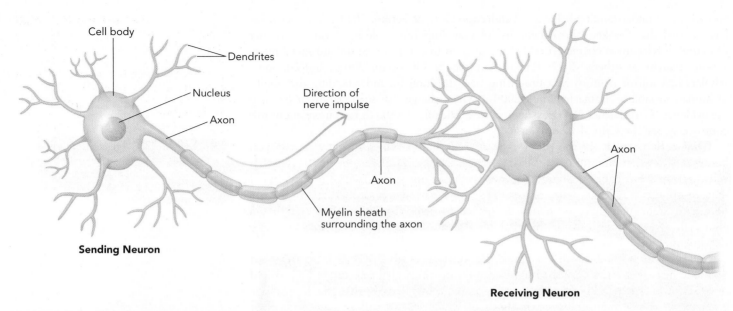

FIGURE 3.2 **The Neuron** The drawing shows the parts of a neuron and the connection between one neuron and another. Note the cell body, the branching of dendrites, and the axon with a myelin sheath.

Jack Osbourne, son of musician Ozzy Osbourne, announced he has multiple sclerosis (MS) in 2012.

As brain size increased, it became necessary for information to travel over longer distances in the nervous system. Axons without myelin sheaths are not very good conductors of electricity. However, with the insulation of myelin sheaths, axons transmit electrical impulses and convey information rapidly (D. J. Miller & others, 2012). We can compare the myelin sheath's development to the evolution of interstate highways as cities grew: Highways keep fast-moving, long-distance traffic from getting snarled by slow, local traffic.

Numerous disorders are associated with problems in either the creation or the maintenance of myelin. One of them is multiple sclerosis (MS), a degenerative disease of the nervous system in which myelin tissue hardens, disrupting neuronal communication. In MS, scar tissue replaces the myelin sheath. Symptoms of the disease include blurry and double vision, tingling sensations throughout the body, and general weakness.

The Neural Impulse

To transmit information to other neurons, a neuron sends brief electrical impulses (let's call them "blips") through its axon. As you reach to turn this page, hundreds of such impulses will stream down the axons in your arm to tell your muscles when to flex and how quickly. By changing the rate of the signals, or blips, the neuron can vary its message. Those impulses traveling down the axon are electrical. How does a neuron—a living cell—generate electricity? To answer this question, we need to take a moment to examine the axon and the cellular membrane that surrounds it.

The axon is a tube encased in a membrane. There are fluids both inside and outside the axon. Floating in those fluids are electrically charged particles called *ions*. Some of these ions, notably sodium and potassium, carry positive charges. Negatively charged ions of chlorine and other elements also are present. The membrane surrounding the axon prevents negative and positive ions from randomly flowing into or out of the cell. That membrane has thousands of tiny gates in it. These gates are generally closed, but they can open. We call the membrane *semipermeable* because fluids and ions can sometimes flow into and out of it. In fact, the neuron creates electrical signals by moving positive and negative ions back and forth through its outer membrane.

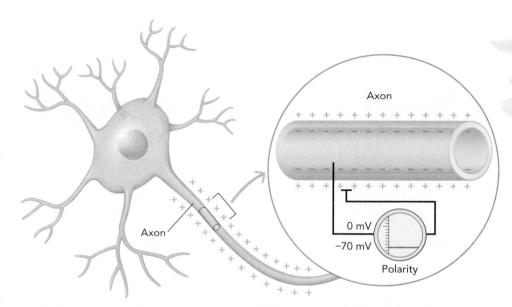

FIGURE 3.3   The Resting Potential
An oscilloscope measures the difference in electrical potential between two electrodes. When one electrode is placed inside an axon at rest and one is placed outside, the electrical potential inside the cell is −70 millivolts (mV) relative to the outside. This potential difference is due to the separation of positive (+) and negative (−) charges along the membrane.

Normally, when the neuron is resting—that is, not transmitting information—the tiny gates in the membrane, called *ion channels,* are closed, and a slight negative charge is present along the inside of the cell membrane. On the outside of the cell membrane, the charge is positive. Because of the difference in charge, the membrane of the resting neuron is said to be *polarized,* with most negatively charged ions on the inside of the cell and most positively charged ions on the outside. This polarization creates a voltage between the inside and outside of the axon wall (Figure 3.3). That voltage, called the neuron's **resting potential,** is between –60 and –75 millivolts. A millivolt (mV) is 1/1000th of a volt.

How does the movement of ions across the membrane occur? Those ion channels open and close to let the ions pass into and out of the cell. For ions, it is true that opposites attract. The negatively charged ions on the inside of the membrane and the positively charged ions on the outside of the membrane will rush to each other if given the chance. Impulses that travel down the neuron do so by opening and closing ion channels, allowing the ions to flow in and out.

A neuron becomes activated when an incoming impulse—a reaction to, say, a pinprick or the sight of someone's face—raises the neuron's voltage, and the sodium gates at the base of the axon open briefly. This action allows positively charged sodium ions to flow into the neuron, creating a more positively charged neuron and *depolarizing* the membrane by decreasing the charge difference between the fluids inside and outside of the neuron. Then potassium channels open, and positively charged potassium ions move out through the neuron's semipermeable membrane. This outflow returns the neuron to a negative charge. Then the same process occurs as the next group of channels flips open briefly.

So it goes all the way down the axon, like a long row of cabinet doors opening and closing in sequence. It is hard to imagine, but this system of opening and closing tiny doors is responsible for the beautiful fluid movements of a ballet dancer and the flying fingers of a pianist playing a concerto.

The term **action potential** describes the brief wave of positive electrical charge that sweeps down the axon (Figure 3.4). An action potential lasts only about 1/1000th of a second, because the sodium channels can stay open for only a very brief time. They quickly close again and become reset for the next action potential. When a neuron sends an action potential, it is commonly said to be "firing."

The action potential abides by the **all-or-nothing principle,** meaning that once the electrical impulse reaches a certain level of intensity, called its *threshold,* it fires and moves all the way down the axon without losing any of its intensity. The impulse traveling

resting potential The stable, negative charge of an inactive neuron.

action potential The brief wave of positive electrical charge that sweeps down the axon.

all-or-nothing principle The principle that once the electrical impulse reaches a certain level of intensity (its threshold), it fires and moves all the way down the axon without losing any intensity.

FIGURE 3.4 The Action Potential
An action potential is a brief wave of positive electrical charge that sweeps down the axon as the sodium channels in the axon membrane open and close. (a) The action potential causes a change in electrical potential as it moves along the axon. (b) The movements of sodium ions (Na$^+$) and potassium ions (K$^+$) into and out of the axon cause the electrical changes.

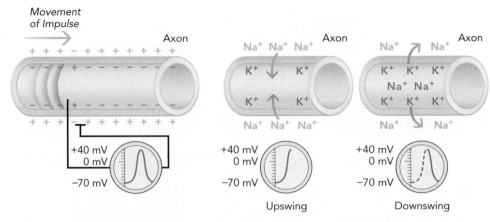

(a) Action potential generated by an impulse within a neuron

(b) Movement of sodium (Na$^+$) and potassium (K$^+$) ions responsible for the action potential

down an axon is comparable to the burning fuse of a firecracker. Whether you use a match or blowtorch to light the fuse, once the fuse has been lit, the spark travels quickly and with the same intensity down the fuse. So, the intensity of the impulse is communicated not by the size of the electrical charge but by the rate of the blips coming down the axon.

Synapses and Neurotransmitters

The movement of an impulse down an axon may be compared to a crowd's doing "the wave" in a stadium. With the wave, there is a problem, however—the aisles. How does the wave get across the aisle? A similar problem arises for neurons, because they do not touch one another directly, and electricity cannot cross the space between them. Yet somehow neurons manage to communicate.

Here is where the chemical part of electro*chemical* transmission comes in. Neurons communicate with one another through chemicals that carry messages across the space. This connection between one neuron and another is one of the most intriguing and highly researched areas of contemporary neuroscience (Emes & Grant, 2012). Figure 3.5 gives an overview of how this connection between neurons takes place.

SYNAPTIC TRANSMISSION

● **synapses** Tiny spaces between neurons; the gaps between neurons are referred to as synaptic gaps.

Synapses are tiny spaces (the aisle in our stadium analogy) between neurons, and the gap between neurons that the synapses create is referred to as the *synaptic gap*. Most synapses lie between the axon of one neuron and the dendrites or cell body of another neuron (Chapeton & others, 2013). Before an impulse can cross the synaptic gap, it must be converted into a chemical signal.

● **neurotransmitters** Chemical substances that are stored in very tiny sacs within the terminal buttons and involved in transmitting information across a synaptic gap to the next neuron.

Each axon branches out into numerous fibers that end in structures called *terminal buttons*. Stored in very tiny synaptic vesicles (*sacs*) within the terminal buttons are chemicals called **neurotransmitters.** As their name suggests, neurotransmitters transmit, or carry, information across the synaptic gap to the next neuron. When a nerve impulse reaches the terminal button, it triggers the release of neurotransmitter molecules from the synaptic vesicles (Parpura & others, 2013; Santos, Torcato, & Castanho, 2012). The neurotransmitter molecules flood the synaptic gap. Their movements are random, but some of them bump into receptor sites in the next neuron.

The neurotransmitters are like pieces of a puzzle, and the receptor sites on the next neuron are differently shaped spaces. If the shape of a receptor site corresponds to the shape of a neurotransmitter molecule, the neurotransmitter fits into the space opening the receptor site, so that the neuron receives the signals coming from the previous

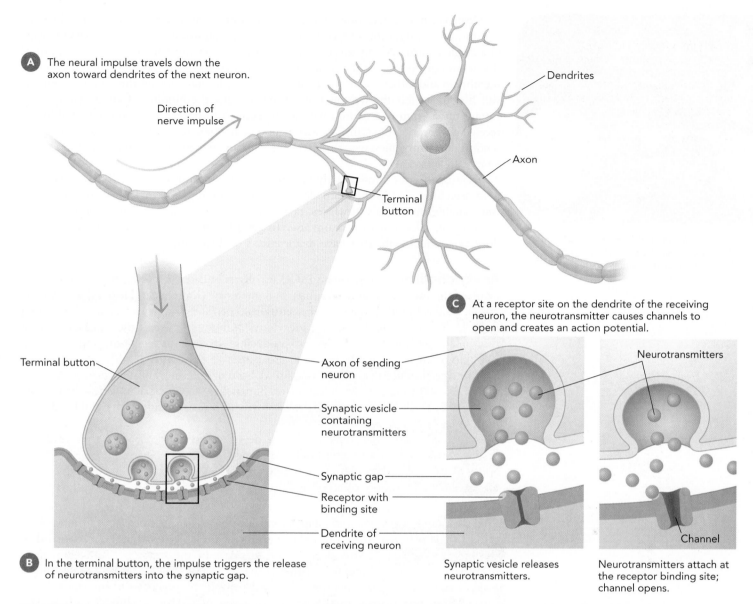

A The neural impulse travels down the axon toward dendrites of the next neuron.

Direction of nerve impulse

Dendrites

Axon

Terminal button

Terminal button

Axon of sending neuron

Synaptic vesicle containing neurotransmitters

Synaptic gap

Receptor with binding site

Dendrite of receiving neuron

C At a receptor site on the dendrite of the receiving neuron, the neurotransmitter causes channels to open and creates an action potential.

Neurotransmitters

Channel

Synaptic vesicle releases neurotransmitters.

Neurotransmitters attach at the receptor binding site; channel opens.

B In the terminal button, the impulse triggers the release of neurotransmitters into the synaptic gap.

FIGURE 3.5   How Synapses and Neurotransmitters Work (*A*) The axon of the presynaptic (sending) neuron meets dendrites of the postsynaptic (receiving) neuron. (*B*) This is an enlargement of one synapse, showing the synaptic gap between the two neurons, the terminal buttons, and the synaptic vesicles containing a neurotransmitter. (*C*) This is an enlargement of the receptor site. Note how the neurotransmitter opens the channel on the receptor site, triggering the neuron to fire.

neuron. You might think of the receptor site as a keyhole in a lock and the neurotransmitter as the key that fits that lock. After delivering its message, some of the neurotransmitter is used up in the production of energy, and some of it is reabsorbed by the axon that released it to await the next neural impulse. This reabsorption is called *reuptake*. Essentially, a message in the brain is delivered across the synapse by a neurotransmitter, which pours out of the terminal button just as the message approaches the synapse.

NEUROCHEMICAL MESSENGERS

There are many different neurotransmitters. Each plays a specific role and functions in a specific pathway. Whereas some neurotransmitters stimulate or excite neurons to fire, others can inhibit neurons from firing (Zorumski & others, 2013). Some neurotransmitters are both excitatory *and* inhibitory.

The neurotransmitter-like venom of the black widow spider does its harm by disturbing neurotransmission.

Most neurons secrete only one type of neurotransmitter, but often many different neurons are simultaneously secreting different neurotransmitters into the synaptic gaps of a single neuron. At any given time, a neuron is receiving a mixture of messages from the neurotransmitters. At the neuron's receptor sites, the chemical molecules bind to the membrane and either excite the neuron, bringing it closer to the threshold at which it will fire, or inhibit the neuron from firing. Usually the binding of an excitatory neurotransmitter from one neuron will not be enough to trigger an action potential in the receiving neuron. Triggering an action potential often requires a number of neurons sending excitatory messages simultaneously, or fewer neurons sending rapid-fire excitatory messages.

Scientists do not know exactly how many neurotransmitters exist. To date, over 100 have been identified in the brain alone, each with a unique chemical makeup. In organisms ranging from snails to whales, neuroscientists have found the same neurotransmitter molecules that our own brains use. To get a better sense of what neurotransmitters do, let's consider eight that have major effects on behavior.

Acetylcholine *Acetylcholine (ACh)* usually stimulates the firing of neurons and is involved in muscle action, learning, and memory (Kalmbach, Hedrick, & Waters, 2012). ACh is found throughout the central and peripheral nervous systems. The venom from the bite of the black widow spider causes ACh to gush out of the synapses between the spinal cord and skeletal muscles, producing violent muscle spasms and weakness. The role of ACh in muscle function also comes to light in the working of Botox, a brand-name product made from botulin. A bacterial poison, botulin destroys ACh, so that when someone gets an injection of Botox, his or her facial muscles—which are activated by ACh—are prevented from moving, with the result that wrinkles do not form (Akaike & others, 2013).

Individuals with Alzheimer disease, a degenerative brain disorder that gradually destroys memory, have an acetylcholine deficiency (Pepeu, Giovannini, & Bracco, 2013). Some of the drugs that alleviate Alzheimer symptoms do so by compensating for the loss of the brain's supply of acetylcholine.

GABA *GABA (gamma aminobutyric acid)* is found throughout the central nervous system. It is believed to be the neurotransmitter present in as many as one-third of the brain's synapses. GABA plays a key function in the brain by inhibiting many neurons from firing (Richter & others, 2012); indeed, GABA is the brain's brake pedal, helping to regulate neuron firing and control the precision of the signal being carried from one neuron to the next. Low levels of GABA are linked with anxiety (Koester & others, 2012). Valium and other antianxiety drugs increase the inhibiting effects of GABA.

Glutamate *Glutamate* has a key role in exciting many neurons to fire and is especially involved in learning and memory (Gao, van Beugen, & de Zeeuw, 2012). Too much glutamate can overstimulate the brain and trigger migraine headaches or even seizures. Researchers have recently proposed that glutamate also is a factor in anxiety, depression, schizophrenia, Alzheimer disease, and Parkinson disease (Serafini & others, 2013; Valenti & others, 2013). Because of the widespread expression of glutamate in the brain, glutamate receptors have increasingly become the targets of drug treatment for a number of neurological and psychological disorders (Kato & others, 2013).

Norepinephrine Stress stimulates the release of another of the body's neurotransmitters—*norepinephrine* (Martino & others, 2012). When we respond to stress, multiple things must happen at once, and so it is not surprising that norepinephrine (also called *noradrenaline*) has a number of effects on the body. If you think of all the things your body does when you are experiencing extreme fear, for instance, you might be able to guess some of the ways norepinephrine affects your body. It *inhibits* the firing of neurons in the central nervous system, but it simultaneously *excites* the heart muscle, intestines, and urogenital tract.

This neurotransmitter also helps to control alertness. Too much norepinephrine triggers agitation or jumpiness. For example, amphetamines and cocaine cause hyperactive, manic states of behavior by rapidly increasing brain levels of norepinephrine (Janak, Bowers, & Corbit, 2012). However, too little norepinephrine is associated with depression.

Recall from the beginning of the chapter that one of the most important characteristics of the brain and nervous system is integration. In the case of neurotransmitters, they may work in teams of two or more. For example, norepinephrine works with acetylcholine to regulate states of sleep and wakefulness.

Dopamine   *Dopamine* helps to control voluntary movement and affects sleep, mood, attention, learning, and the ability to recognize opportunities for rewarding experiences in the environment (Meyer, 2012). Stimulant drugs such as cocaine and amphetamines produce excitement, alertness, elevated mood, decreased fatigue, and sometimes increased motor activity mainly by activating dopamine receptors (Mariani & Levin, 2012). Dopamine is related to the personality trait of extraversion (being outgoing and gregarious), as we will see in Chapter 12.

Low levels of dopamine are associated with Parkinson disease, a degenerative neurological disorder in which a person develops jerky physical movements and a tremor and has difficulty with speech and walking (Berthet & others, 2012). This disease affects about a million people in the United States (D. H. Park & others, 2009); actor Michael J. Fox has been diagnosed with this disease. Parkinson impairs coordinated movement to the point that just walking across a room can be a major ordeal.

High levels of dopamine and elevated numbers of dopamine receptors are associated with schizophrenia (Brunelin, Fecteau, & Suad-Chagny, 2013). We examine this severe psychological disorder in Chapter 15.

Serotonin   *Serotonin* is involved in the regulation of sleep, mood, attention, and learning. In regulating states of sleep and wakefulness, it teams with acetylcholine and norepinephrine. Lowered levels of serotonin are associated with depression (Karg & Sen, 2012). The antidepressant drug Prozac works by slowing down the reuptake of serotonin into terminal buttons, thereby increasing brain levels of serotonin (Little, Zhang, & Cook, 2006). There are 15 known types of serotonin receptors in the brain (Hoyer, Hannon, & Martin, 2002), and each type of antidepressant drug has its effects on different receptors. Figure 3.6 shows the brain pathways for serotonin.

Endorphins   *Endorphins* are natural opiates—substances that depress nervous system activity and eliminate pain—that mainly stimulate the firing of neurons. As opiates, endorphins shield the body from pain and elevate feelings of pleasure. A long-distance runner, a woman giving birth, and a person in shock after a car wreck all have elevated levels of endorphins (Mahler & others, 2009).

As early as the fourth century B.C.E., the Greeks used wild poppies to induce euphoria. More than 2,000 years later, the magical formula behind opium's addictive action was finally discovered. In the early 1970s, scientists found that opium plugs into a sophisticated system of natural opiates that lie deep within the brain's pathways (Pert, 1999; Pert & Snyder, 1973). Morphine (the most important narcotic of opium) mimics the action of endorphins by stimulating receptors in the brain involved with pleasure and pain (Jiang & others, 2010).

Oxytocin   *Oxytocin* is a hormone and neurotransmitter that plays an important role in the experience of love and social bonding. A powerful surge of oxytocin is released in mothers who have just given birth, and oxytocin is related to the onset of lactation (milk production) and breastfeeding (Vrachnis & others, 2011). Oxytocin, however, is involved in more than a mother's ability to provide nourishment for her baby. It is also

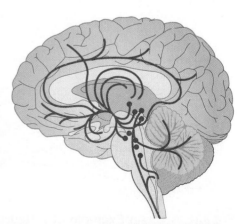

FIGURE 3.6   Serotonin Pathways
Each of the neurotransmitters in the brain has specific pathways in which it functions. Shown here are the pathways for serotonin.

a factor in the experience of parents who find themselves "in love at first sight" with their newborn (Young, 2009).

Oxytocin is released as part of sexual orgasm and is thought to play a role in the human tendency to feel pleasure during orgasm and to form emotional bonds with romantic partners (Magon & Kalra, 2011). A recent study found that a higher level of oxytocin was present in new lovers and persisted at a higher level 6 months later compared to non-attached single young adults (Schneiderman & others, 2012). In this study, higher oxytocin levels were associated with positive affect, affectionate touch, and preoccupation with one's partner and the relationship.

Provocative research also has linked oxytocin to the way that some individuals respond to stress (Neumann & Landgraf, 2012). According to Shelley Taylor (2011a, 2011b), women under stress do not experience the classic "fight or flight" response—rather, the influx of oxytocin they experience suggests that women may seek bonds with others when under stress. Taylor refers to this response as "tend and befriend" and believes that it more accurately represents the stress response of women.

DRUGS AND NEUROTRANSMITTERS

Recall that neurotransmitters fit into the receptor sites like keys in keyholes. Other substances, such as drugs, can sometimes fit into those receptor sites as well, producing a variety of effects. Many animal venoms, such as that of the black widow spider mentioned above, act by disturbing neurotransmission. Similarly, most drugs that influence behavior do so mainly by interfering with the work of neurotransmitters (Fields, 2013).

Drugs can mimic or increase the effects of a neurotransmitter, or they can block those effects. For example, the drug morphine mimics the actions of endorphins by stimulating receptors in the brain and spinal cord associated with pleasure and pain, producing feelings of pleasure. Other drugs can block a neurotransmitter's action by preventing it from getting into the receptor site. Drugs used to treat schizophrenia, for example, interfere with the activity of dopamine.

Neural Networks

So far, we have focused mainly on how a single neuron functions and on how a nerve impulse travels from one neuron to another (Lefaucheur, 2012; McCarrey & others, 2012). Now let's look at how large numbers of neurons work together to integrate incoming information and coordinate outgoing information.

● **neural networks** Networks of nerve cells that integrate sensory input and motor output.

Most information processing occurs when information moves through **neural networks**—interconnected pathways of nerve cells that integrate sensory input and motor output. For example, as you read your class notes, the input from your eyes is transmitted to your brain and then passed through many neural networks, which translate the characters on the page into neural codes for letters, words, associations, and meanings. Some of the information is stored in the neural networks, and, if you read aloud, some is passed on as messages to your lips and tongue.

Neural networks can take years to develop and make up most of the brain. Working in networks allows neurons to amplify the brain's computing power (Wolf, Grein, & Queisser, 2013). Figure 3.7 shows a simplified drawing of a neural network and gives you an idea of how the activity of one neuron is linked with that of many others.

Some neurons have short axons and communicate with other nearby neurons. Other neurons have long axons and communicate with circuits of neurons some distance away. These neural networks are not static. They can be altered through changes in the strength of synaptic connections.

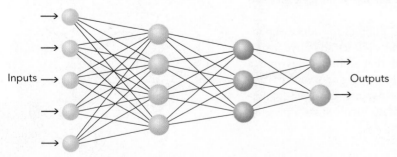

FIGURE 3.7   **An Example of a Neural Network** *Inputs* (information from the environment and from sensory receptors, such as the details of a person's face) become embedded in extensive connections between neurons in the brain. This embedding process leads to *outputs* such as remembering the person's face.

Any piece of information, such as a name, might be embedded in hundreds or even thousands of connections between neurons (Angel & others, 2013). In this way, human activities such as being attentive, memorizing, and thinking are distributed over a wide range of connected neurons. The strength of these connected neurons determines how well the information is remembered (Dinkelbach & others, 2012). Differences in these neural networks are responsible for the differences observed in those London cab drivers discussed earlier in this chapter.

3· STRUCTURES OF THE BRAIN AND THEIR FUNCTIONS

The extensive and intricate networks of neurons in the living brain are invisible to the naked eye. Fortunately, technology is available to help neuroscientists form pictures of the structure and organization of neurons and of the larger systems they make up without harming the organism being studied. This section explores the techniques that scientists use in brain research, and we consider what these tools reveal about the brain's structures and functions. We pay special attention to the cerebral cortex, the region of the brain that is most relevant to the topics in this book.

How Researchers Study the Brain and Nervous System

Early knowledge of the human brain came mostly from studies of individuals who had suffered brain damage from injury or disease or who had brain surgery to relieve another condition. Modern discoveries have relied largely on technology that enables researchers to "look inside" the brain while it is at work. Let's examine some of these innovative techniques.

BRAIN LESIONING

Brain lesioning is an abnormal disruption in the tissue of the brain resulting from injury or disease. In a lab setting, neuroscientists produce lesions in laboratory animals to determine the effects on the animal's behavior (Kirby & others, 2012; Lieu & Subramanian, 2012). They create the lesions by surgically removing brain tissue, destroying tissue with a laser, or eliminating tissue by injecting it with a drug. Examining the person or animal that has the lesion gives the researchers a sense of the function of the part of the brain that has been damaged.

Do you know anyone who has experienced a stroke or brain-damaging head injury? These experiences create lesioned areas in the brain.

ELECTRICAL RECORDING

An *electroencephalograph (EEG)* records the brain's electrical activity. Electrodes placed on the scalp detect brain-wave activity, which is recorded on a chart known as an *electroencephalogram* (Figure 3.8). This device can assess brain damage, epilepsy, and other problems (Cojan & others, 2013; Rosenthal, 2012).

EEGs have been used in research examining the brain and happiness. Paul Ekman, Richard Davidson, and Wallace Friesen (1990) measured EEG activity during emotional experiences provoked by watching film clips. Individuals in

test yourself

1. What are neurons, and what are their three parts?
2. What is meant by the neuron's action potential? How does the all-or-nothing principle apply to it?
3. What do neurotransmitters do? Name four specific neurotransmitters and describe the role each plays.

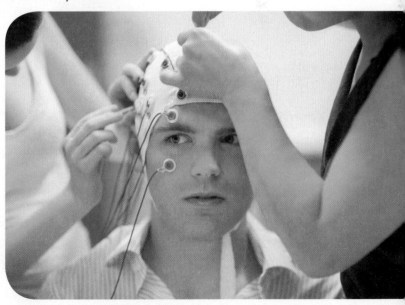

FIGURE 3.8 An EEG Recording The electroencephalograph (EEG) is widely used in sleep research. The device has led to some major breakthroughs in understanding sleep by showing how the brain's electrical activity changes during sleep.

this study watched amusing clips (such as a puppy playing with flowers and monkeys taking a bath) as well as clips likely to provoke fear or disgust (a leg amputation and a third-degree burn victim). How does the brain respond to such stimuli? The researchers found that while watching the amusing clips, people tended to exhibit more left than right prefrontal activity, as shown in EEGs. In contrast, when the participants viewed the fear-provoking films, the right prefrontal area was generally more active than the left.

Do these differences generalize to overall differences in feelings of happiness? They just might. Heather Urry and her colleagues (2004) found that individuals who have relatively more left than right prefrontal activity (what is called *prefrontal asymmetry*) tend to rate themselves higher on a number of measures of well-being, including self-acceptance, positive relations with others, purpose in life, and life satisfaction.

Not every recording of brain activity is made with surface electrodes that are attached to the scalp. In *single-unit recording*, which provides information about a single neuron's electrical activity, a thin probe is inserted in or near an individual neuron. The probe transmits the neuron's electrical activity to an amplifier so that researchers can "see" the activity (Warden & others, 2013).

BRAIN IMAGING

For years, medical practitioners have used X rays to reveal damage inside the body, both in the brain and in other locations. A single X ray of the brain is hard to interpret, however, because it shows a two-dimensional image of the three-dimensional interior of the brain. An improved imaging technique called *computerized axial tomography* (*CAT scan* or *CT scan*) produces a three-dimensional image obtained from X rays of the head that are assembled into a composite image by a computer. The CT scan provides valuable information about the location and extent of damage involving stroke, language disorder, or loss of memory (Knox & Kavanagh, 2012).

Another imaging method, *positron-emission tomography (PET scan),* is based on metabolic changes in the brain related to activity. PET measures the amount of glucose in various areas of the brain and sends this information to a computer for analysis. Neurons use glucose for energy, so glucose levels vary with the levels of activity throughout the brain. Tracing the amounts of glucose generates a picture of the brain's activity levels (Nozaki & others, 2013).

An interesting application of the PET technique is the work of Stephen Kosslyn and colleagues (1996) on mental imagery—the brain's ability to create perceptual states in the absence of external stimuli. For instance, if you were to think of your favorite song right now, you could "hear" it in your mind's ear; or if you reflected on your mother's face, you could probably "see" it in your mind's eye. Research using PET scans has shown that often the same area of the brain—a location called Area 17—is activated when we think of seeing something as when we are actually seeing it. However, Area 17 is not always activated for all of us when we imagine a visual image. Kosslyn and his colleagues asked their participants to visualize a letter in the alphabet and then directed those individuals to answer some yes or no questions about the letter. For instance, a person might be thinking of the letter *C* and have to answer the question "Does it have curvy lines?" The answer would be yes. If the person was thinking of *F,* the answer would be no. The fascinating result of this work is that individuals who showed brain activation on the PET scan in Area 17 while engaged in the visualization task answered the questions faster than those who were not using Area 17. Even though they were doing the same task, some people used Area 17 and others did not. Although all human brains are similar in some ways, in other ways each person's brain is unique.

Another technique, *magnetic resonance imaging (MRI)*, involves creating a magnetic field around a person's body and using radio waves to construct images of the person's tissues and biochemical activities. The magnetic field used to create an MRI image is over 50,000 times more powerful than the earth's magnetic field (Parry & Matthews, 2002). MRI takes advantage of the fact that the human brain contains a great deal of water (like the rest of the body, the brain is 70 percent water). Within each water molecule there are hydrogen atoms (remember, water is H_2O). These hydrogen atoms can be thought of as tiny magnets. When these magnetlike hydrogen atoms encounter a very strong magnetic field, they align themselves with it. Neurons have more water in them than do other brain tissues, and that contrast is what provides the nuanced brain images that MRI is able to produce (Parry & Matthews, 2002).

MRI generates very clear pictures of the brain's interior, does not require injecting the brain with a substance, and (unlike X rays) does not pose a problem of radiation overexposure (Nyberg, 2004). Getting an MRI scan involves lying still in a large metal tunnel, similar to a barrel. MRI scans provide an excellent picture of the architecture of the brain and allow researchers to see if and how experience affects brain structure.

In one MRI study, Katrin Amunts and colleagues (1997) documented a link between the number of years a person has practiced musical skills (playing the piano or violin, for example) and the size of the brain region that is responsible for controlling hand movements, demonstrating again that behavior can influence the very structure of the brain. Note that these brain changes reflect the development of neural networks.

Although MRI scans can reveal considerable information about brain *structure*, they cannot portray brain *function*. Other techniques, however, can serve as a window on the brain in action. One such method, *functional magnetic resonance imaging*, or *fMRI*, allows scientists literally to see what is happening in the brain while it is working (Figure 3.9). The use of fMRI in psychological studies has increased dramatically in the twenty-first century (Rugg & Vilberg, 2013). The field of *cognitive neuroscience*, which involves linking cognitive processes and their underlying neural bases, has especially benefited from progress in fMRI (Brent & others, 2013; Groenewold & others, 2013).

Like the PET scan, fMRI rests on the idea that mental activity is associated with changes in the brain. Although PET relies on the use of glucose as fuel for thinking, fMRI exploits changes in blood oxygen that occur in association with brain activity. When part of the brain is working, oxygenated blood rushes into the area. This oxygen, however, is more than is needed. In a sense, fMRI is based on the fact that thinking is like running sprints. When you run the 100-yard dash, blood rushes to the muscles in your legs, carrying oxygen. Right after you stop, you might feel a tightness in your legs, because the oxygen has not all been used. Similarly, if an area of the brain is hard at work—for example, solving a math problem—the increased activity leads to a surplus of oxygenated blood. This "extra" oxygen allows the brain activity to be imaged.

Getting an fMRI involves reclining in the same large metal barrel as does an MRI, but in the case of fMRI, the person is actively doing something during the procedure. The individual may be listening to audio signals sent by the researcher through headphones or watching visual images on a screen that is mounted overhead. During these procedures, pictures of the brain are taken, both while the brain is at rest and while it is engaging in an activity such as listening to music, looking at a picture, or making a decision. By comparing the at-rest picture to the activity picture, fMRI tells us what specific brain activity is associated with the mental experience being studied.

Note that saying that fMRI tells us about the brain activity *associated* with a mental experience is a *correlational* statement. As we saw in Chapter 2, correlations point to the association between variables, not to the potential causal link between them. For example, although identifying a picture as a cat may relate to activation in a particular brain area, we do not know if recognizing the cat *caused* the brain activity (Dien, 2009).

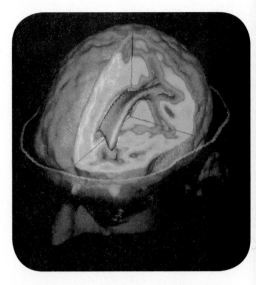

FIGURE 3.9 **Functional Magnetic Resonance Imaging (fMRI)** Through fMRI, scientists can literally see what areas of the brain are active during a task by monitoring oxygenated blood levels.

An additional method for studying brain functioning, and one that *does* allow for causal inferences, is *transcranial magnetic stimulation (TMS)* (Ma & others, 2013; Temel & others, 2012). First introduced in 1985 (Barker, Jalinous, & Freeston, 1985), TMS is often combined with brain-imaging techniques to establish causal links between brain activity and behavior, to examine neuronal functioning following brain-injuring events such as accidents and strokes, and even to treat some neurological and psychological disorders.

In the TMS procedure, magnetic coils are placed over the person's head and directed at a particular brain area. TMS uses a rapidly changing magnetic field to induce brief electrical current pulses in the brain, and these pulses trigger action potentials in neurons (Berlim, Van den Eynde, & Daskalakis, 2013; Tremblay & others, 2013). Immediately following this burst of action potentials, activity in the targeted brain area is inhibited, causing what is known as a *virtual lesion*. Completely painless, this technique, when used with brain imaging, allows scientists to examine the role of various brain regions. If a brain region is *associated* with a behavior, as demonstrated using fMRI or PET, then the temporary disruption of processing in that area should disrupt that behavior as well. So, for instance, if researchers were doing a study involving the cat recognition example described above, they might use TMS to disrupt the brain area that was associated with cat recognition and see whether the study's participants are temporarily unable to identify a picture of the feline.

How the Brain Is Organized

● **hindbrain** Located at the skull's rear, the lowest portion of the brain, consisting of the medulla, cerebellum, and pons.

● **brain stem** The stemlike brain area that includes much of the hindbrain (excluding the cerebellum) and the midbrain; it connects with the spinal cord at its lower end and then extends upward to encase the reticular formation in the midbrain.

As a human embryo develops inside its mother's womb, the nervous system begins forming as a long, hollow tube on the embryo's back. At 3 weeks or so after conception, cells making up the tube differentiate into a mass of neurons, most of which then develop into three major regions of the brain: the hindbrain, which is adjacent to the top part of the spinal cord; the midbrain, which rises above the hindbrain; and the forebrain, which is the uppermost region of the brain (Figure 3.10).

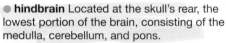
HINDBRAIN

The **hindbrain,** located at the skull's rear, is the lowest portion of the brain. The three main parts of the hindbrain are the medulla, cerebellum, and pons. Figure 3.11 locates these brain structures.

The *medulla* begins where the spinal cord enters the skull. The medulla controls many vital functions, such as breathing and heart rate. It also regulates our reflexes. The *pons* is a bridge in the hindbrain that connects the cerebellum and the brain stem. It contains several clusters of fibers involved in sleep and arousal (Thankachan, Kaur, & Shiromani, 2009).

Taken together, the medulla, pons, and much of the hindbrain (as well as the midbrain, discussed below) are called the **brain stem,** which gets its name because it looks like a stem. Embedded deep within the brain, the brain stem connects with the spinal cord at its lower end and then extends upward to encase the reticular formation in the midbrain. The most ancient part of the brain, the brain stem evolved more than 500 million years ago, when organisms needed to breathe out of water (Hagadorn & Seilacher, 2009). Clumps of cells in the brain stem determine alertness and regulate basic survival functions such as breathing, heartbeat, and blood pressure (R. E. Brown & others, 2012).

The *cerebellum* extends from the rear of the hindbrain. It consists of two rounded structures thought to play important roles in motor coordination (Hardwick & others, 2013). The cerebellum coordinates leg and arm movements; for example, when we walk, play golf, and practice the piano, the cerebellum is hard at work. If another portion of the brain

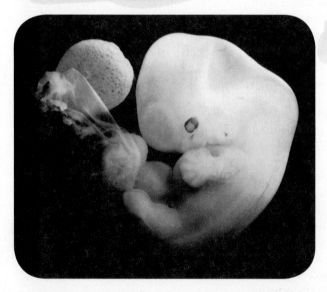

FIGURE 3.10 Embryological Development of the Nervous System The photograph shows the primitive tubular appearance of the nervous system at 6 weeks in the human embryo. The drawing shows the major brain regions and spinal cord as they appear early in the development of a human embryo.

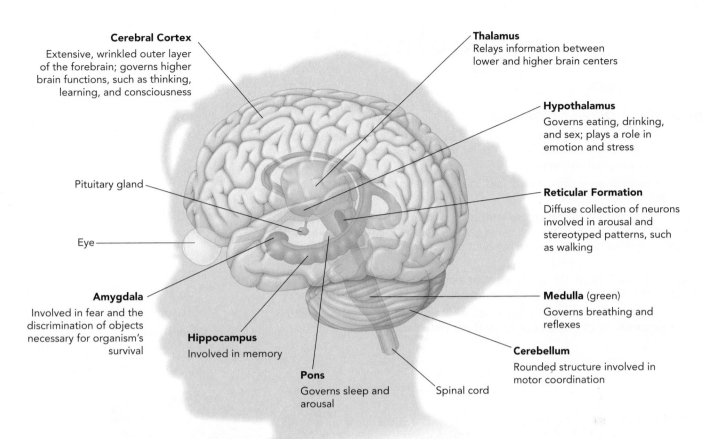

Cerebral Cortex
Extensive, wrinkled outer layer of the forebrain; governs higher brain functions, such as thinking, learning, and consciousness

Thalamus
Relays information between lower and higher brain centers

Hypothalamus
Governs eating, drinking, and sex; plays a role in emotion and stress

Pituitary gland

Reticular Formation
Diffuse collection of neurons involved in arousal and stereotyped patterns, such as walking

Eye

Amygdala
Involved in fear and the discrimination of objects necessary for organism's survival

Hippocampus
Involved in memory

Pons
Governs sleep and arousal

Spinal cord

Medulla (green)
Governs breathing and reflexes

Cerebellum
Rounded structure involved in motor coordination

FIGURE 3.11 **Structure and Regions in the Human Brain** To get a feel for where these structures are in your own brain, use the eye (pictured on the left of the figure) as a landmark. Note that structures such as the thalamus, hypothalamus, amygdala, pituitary gland, pons, and reticular formation reside deep within the brain.

commands us to send a quick text message to a friend, it is the cerebellum that integrates the muscular activities required to do so. Damage to the cerebellum impairs the performance of coordinated movements (Fouad & others, 2013). When this damage occurs, people's movements become awkward and jerky. Extensive damage to the cerebellum makes it impossible to stand up.

MIDBRAIN

The **midbrain,** located between the hindbrain and forebrain, is an area in which many nerve-fiber systems ascend and descend to connect the higher and lower portions of the brain (Watabe-Uchita & others, 2012). In particular, the midbrain relays information between the brain and the eyes and ears. The ability to attend to an object visually, for example, is linked to one bundle of neurons in the midbrain.

Parkinson disease damages a section near the bottom of the midbrain called the *substantia nigra* (Wright & Harding, 2013), causing deterioration in body movement, rigidity, and tremors. The substantia nigra contains a large number of dopamine-producing neurons. This part of the midbrain feeds dopamine into the *striatum,* the central input station for the basal ganglia, to which we will turn our attention in a moment.

Another important system in the midbrain is the reticular formation (see Figure 3.11). The **reticular formation** is a diffuse collection of neurons involved in stereotyped patterns of behavior such as walking, sleeping, and turning to attend to a sudden noise (Jones & Benca, 2013; Vanini, Lydic, & Baghdoyan, 2012).

● **midbrain** Located between the hindbrain and forebrain, an area in which many nerve-fiber systems ascend and descend to connect the higher and lower portions of the brain; in particular, the midbrain relays information between the brain and the eyes and ears.

● **reticular formation** A system in the midbrain comprising a diffuse collection of neurons involved in stereotyped patterns of behavior such as walking, sleeping, and turning to attend to a sudden noise.

psychological *inquiry*

The Brain in Different Species

The below illustration compares the brain of a rat, a cat, a chimpanzee, and a human. In examining the figure, keep in mind that each species is adapted to differing environmental challenges.

1. In what ways is each brain well suited to the challenges faced by its particular species?

2. What structures are similar across all the species? Why do you think certain brain structures are common for these various species? What challenges do all of these species face that would account for the common features of their brains?

3. Note how much larger the cerebral cortex becomes as we go from the brain of a rat to the brain of a human. Why don't rats have a large cerebral cortex?

4. We often think of the human brain as an amazing accomplishment of nature. How might life be different for a rat or a cat with a human brain?

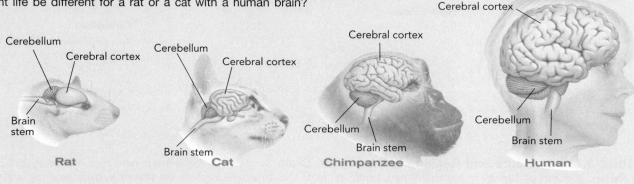

FOREBRAIN

You try to understand what all of these terms and parts of the brain mean. You talk with friends and plan a party for this weekend. You remember that it has been 6 months since you went to the dentist. You are confident you will do well on the next exam in this course. All of these experiences and millions more would not be possible without the **forebrain**—the brain's largest division and its most forward part.

Before we explore the structures and function of the forebrain, though, let's stop for a moment and examine how the brain evolved. The brains of the earliest vertebrates were smaller and simpler than those of later animals. Genetic changes during the evolutionary process were responsible for the development of more complex brains with additional parts and interconnections (Durrant & Ellis, 2013). The Psychological Inquiry above compares the brain of a rat, a cat, a chimpanzee, and a human. In both the chimpanzee's brain and (especially) the human's brain, the hindbrain and midbrain structures are covered by a forebrain structure called the *cerebral cortex.* The human hindbrain and midbrain are similar to those of other animals, so it is the relative size of the forebrain that mainly differentiates the human brain from the brain of animals such as rats, cats, and chimps. The human forebrain's most important structures are the limbic system, thalamus, basal ganglia, hypothalamus, and cerebral cortex.

● **forebrain** The brain's largest division and its most forward part.

● **limbic system** A loosely connected network of structures under the cerebral cortex, important in both memory and emotion. Its two principal structures are the amygdala and the hippocampus.

Limbic System The **limbic system,** a loosely connected network of structures under the cerebral cortex, is important in both memory and emotion. Its two principal structures are the amygdala and the hippocampus (see Figure 3.11).

The **amygdala** is an almond-shaped structure located inside the brain toward the base. In fact, there is an amygdala (the plural is *amygdalae*) on each side of the brain. The amygdala is involved in the discrimination of objects that are necessary for the organism's survival, such as appropriate food, mates, and social rivals. Neurons in the amygdala often fire selectively at the sight of such stimuli, and lesions in the amygdala can cause animals to engage in incorrect behavior such as attempting to eat, fight with, or even mate with an object like a chair.

In both humans and animals, the amygdala is active in response to unpredictable stimuli (Herry & others, 2007). In humans, damage to the amygdala can result in an inability to recognize facial expressions of distress (Adolphs, 2009). The amygdala also is involved in emotional awareness and expression through its many connections with a variety of brain areas (Whalen & others, 2013). Throughout this book you will encounter the amygdalae whenever we turn to discussions of intense emotions.

The **hippocampus** has a special role in memory (Wasserman & Castro, 2013). Individuals who suffer extensive hippocampal damage cannot retain any new conscious memories after the damage. It is fairly certain, though, that memories are not stored "in" the limbic system. Instead, the limbic system seems to determine what parts of the information passing through the cortex should be "printed" into durable, lasting neural traces in the cortex. The hippocampus seems to help us recall things by waking up the areas of the brain that were used when we originally encountered the information (Trinkler & others, 2009).

Thalamus   The **thalamus** is a forebrain structure that sits at the top of the brain stem in the central core of the brain (see Figure 3.11). It serves as a very important relay station, functioning much like a server in a computer network. That is, an important function of the thalamus is to sort information and send it to the appropriate places in the forebrain for further integration and interpretation (Bonath & others, 2013). For example, one area of the thalamus receives information from the cerebellum and projects it to the motor area of the cerebral cortex. Indeed, most neural input to the cerebral cortex goes through the thalamus. Whereas one area of the thalamus works to orient information from the sense receptors (hearing, seeing, and so on), another region seems to be involved in sleep and wakefulness, having ties with the reticular formation.

Basal Ganglia   Above the thalamus and under the cerebral cortex lie large clusters, or *ganglia,* of neurons called **basal ganglia.** The basal ganglia work with the cerebellum and the cerebral cortex to control and coordinate voluntary movements (Fouad & others, 2013). Basal ganglia enable people to engage in habitual activities such as riding a bicycle and vacuuming a carpet. Individuals with damage to basal ganglia suffer from either unwanted movement, such as constant writhing or jerking of limbs, or too little movement, as in the slow and deliberate movements of people with Parkinson disease (Lenglet & others, 2012; Starkstein, 2012).

Hypothalamus   The **hypothalamus,** a small forebrain structure just below the thalamus, monitors three rewarding activities—eating, drinking, and sex—as well as emotion, stress, and reward (see Figure 3.11 for the location of the hypothalamus). As we will see later, the hypothalamus also helps direct the endocrine system.

Perhaps the best way to describe the function of the hypothalamus is as a regulator of the body's internal state. It is sensitive to changes in the blood and neural input, and it responds by influencing the secretion of hormones and neural outputs. For example, if the temperature of circulating blood near the hypothalamus is increased by just one or two degrees, certain cells in the hypothalamus start increasing their rate of firing. As a result, a chain of events is set in motion. Increased circulation through the skin and sweat glands occurs immediately to release this heat from the body. The cooled blood circulating to the hypothalamus slows down the activity of some of the neurons there, stopping the process when the temperature is just right—37.1 degrees Celsius (98.6 degrees Fahrenheit). These temperature-sensitive neurons function like a finely tuned thermostat in maintaining the body in a balanced state.

● **amygdala** An almond-shaped structure within the base of the temporal lobe that is involved in the discrimination of objects that are necessary for the organism's survival, such as appropriate food, mates, and social rivals.

● **hippocampus** The structure in the limbic system that has a special role in the storage of memories.

● **thalamus** The forebrain structure that sits at the top of the brain stem in the brain's central core and serves as an important relay station.

● **basal ganglia** Large neuron clusters located above the thalamus and under the cerebral cortex that work with the cerebellum and the cerebral cortex to control and coordinate voluntary movements.

● **hypothalamus** A small forebrain structure, located just below the thalamus, that monitors three pleasurable activities—eating, drinking, and sex—as well as emotion, stress, and reward.

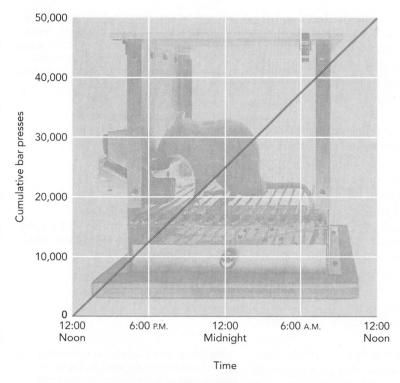

FIGURE 3.12 **Results of the Experiment on the Role of the Hypothalamus in Pleasure** The graphed results for one rat show that it pressed the bar more than 2,000 times an hour for a period of 24 hours to receive stimulation to its hypothalamus. One of the rats in Olds and Milner's (1954, 1958) experiments is shown pressing the bar.

● **cerebral cortex** Part of the forebrain, the outer layer of the brain, responsible for the most complex mental functions, such as thinking and planning.

● **neocortex** The outermost part of the cerebral cortex, making up 80 percent of the cortex in the human brain.

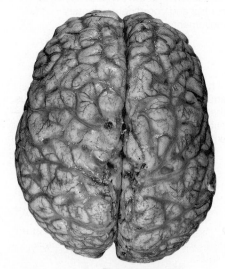

FIGURE 3.13 **The Human Brain's Hemispheres** The two halves (hemispheres) of the human brain can be seen clearly in this photograph.

The hypothalamus also is involved in emotional states and stress, playing an important role as an integrative location for handling stress. Much of this integration is accomplished through the hypothalamus's action on the pituitary gland, an important endocrine gland located just below it (Di Iorgi & others, 2012).

If certain areas of the hypothalamus are electrically stimulated, a feeling of pleasure results. In a classic experiment, James Olds and Peter Milner (1954) implanted an electrode in the hypothalamus of a rat's brain. When the rat ran to a corner of an enclosed area, a mild electric current was delivered to its hypothalamus. The researchers thought the electric current would cause the rat to avoid the corner. Much to their surprise, the rat kept returning to the corner. Olds and Milner believed they had discovered a pleasure center in the hypothalamus. Olds (1958) conducted further experiments and found that rats would press bars until they dropped over from exhaustion just to continue to receive a mild electric shock to their hypothalamus. One rat pressed a bar more than 2,000 times an hour for a period of 24 hours to receive the stimulation to its hypothalamus (Figure 3.12).

Today researchers agree that the hypothalamus is involved in pleasurable feelings, but they have found that other brain areas, such as the limbic system and two other structures—the nucleus accumbens and the ventral tegmental area, to be discussed in Chapter 5—are also important in the link between the brain and pleasure (Hernandez Lallement & others, 2013).

Certainly, the Olds studies have implications for drug addiction (Ludlow & others, 2009). We will explore the effects of drugs on the reward centers of the brain in Chapter 5. These reward centers have also been implicated in the experience of humor, as we explore in the Intersection.

The Cerebral Cortex

The **cerebral cortex** is part of the forebrain and is the most recently developed part of the brain in the evolutionary scheme. The word *cortex* means "bark" (as in tree bark) in Latin, and the cerebral cortex is in fact the outer layer of the brain. It is in the cerebral cortex that the most complex mental functions, such as thinking and planning, take place.

The **neocortex** (or "new bark") is the outermost part of the cerebral cortex. In humans, this area makes up 80 percent of the cortex (compared with just 30 to 40 percent in most other mammals). The size of the neocortex in mammals is strongly related to the size of the social group in which the organisms live. Some scientists theorize that this part of the human brain, which is responsible for high-level thinking, evolved so that human beings could make sense of one another (Adolphs, 2009).

The neural tissue that makes up the cerebral cortex covers the lower portions of the brain like a sheet that is laid over the brain's surface. In humans the cerebral cortex is greatly convoluted with a lot of grooves and bulges, and these considerably enlarge its surface area (compared with a brain with a smooth surface). The cerebral cortex is highly connected with other parts of the brain (Bueno-Junior & others, 2012). Millions of axons connect the neurons of the cerebral cortex with those located elsewhere in the brain.

LOBES

The wrinkled surface of the cerebral cortex is divided into two halves called *hemispheres* (Figure 3.13). Each hemisphere is subdivided into four regions, or *lobes*—occipital, temporal, frontal, and parietal (Figure 3.14).

Neuroscience and Emotion: How Does the Brain Recognize What Is Funny?

- "I'm good friends with 25 letters of the alphabet . . . I don't know why."
- "I was raised as an only child, which really annoyed my sister."

What do you think of these one-liners? Hilarious? Silly? Or just not amusing at all? These jokes, from comics Chris Turner and Will Marsh, placed in the top-10 one-liners at the Edinburgh Fringe Festival in 2012 (Handley, 2012).

When it comes to humor, we might say there is no accounting for taste. One person might find *The Hangover* movies sidesplitting and another not so much. Thinking that something is funny is, like other experiences, an event in the brain. Even if the specific stimuli that provoke a laugh vary from person to person, the experience of humor itself is rooted in systematic brain processes. What are the processes involved in making something funny?

Research with adults has shown that a network of brain regions called the *temporal-occipital-parietal junction (TOPJ)* is active while adults are viewing funny stimuli, ranging from cartoons to standup comics (Bartolo & others, 2006; Franklin & Adams, 2011; Mobbs & others, 2003). Interestingly, this region of the brain is involved in the ways we understand other people and pick up on their intentions (Saxe & Kanwisher, 2005). Such findings tell us that part of "getting" a joke is getting inside the head of the person telling it.

Further, humor often involves detecting and resolving conflict. Think about it: If you found one of those jokes above pretty funny, why was that? Theories of humor often focus on the ways that jokes set up an expectation and then violate

that expectation in a way that evokes humor (McGraw & others, 2012). In other words, finding something funny involves detecting an incongruity and then resolving it in a funny way. So, if a comedian mentions letters, we might be thinking of *Y*. In that context, the word *why* is funny. Sure enough, research has shown that brain regions involved in detecting and resolving conflict are active during exposure to amusing stimuli (in this case, sitcoms) (Moran & others, 2004).

How might the brain explain what different people find to be funny?

Of course, jokes are (supposed to be) pleasurable. So, we might expect brain regions such as the nucleus accumbens to be active when we encounter funny things. Although some research has shown activity in these brain areas in response to humorous stimuli (Franklin & Adams, 2011), other research with adults has not (Bartolo & others, 2006). A recent study by Michelle Neely and colleagues (2012) may help shed light on these mixed results. In that study, children ages 6 to 12 watched age-appropriate funny video clips and neutral clips during neuroimaging. The research showed that activity in the TOPJ was also present in children. Interestingly, the nucleus accumbens was especially active with the youngest kids in the study as they watched the humorous videos. It might be that the sheer reward of funny experiences is especially powerful for young children. Perhaps it takes a bit more for adults to feel the deep pleasure of laughter.

Studying how the brain recognizes and appreciates what is funny can help to illuminate the processes of humor itself. Through brain imaging, scientists can study the activity of the brain regions known to function in understanding the intentions of others, detecting incongruity, or experiencing pleasure—those areas that are active when we find something to be funny.

Clearly, the brain's funny bone is a complex interconnected system, combining social understanding, expectancy violation, and resolution. Maybe it also involves a strong reward in the experience of a good laugh.

The **occipital lobes,** located at the back of the head, respond to visual stimuli. Connections among various areas of the occipital lobes allow for the processing of information about aspects of visual stimuli such as their color, shape, and motion (C. I. Baker, 2013). A person can have perfectly functioning eyes, but the eyes only detect and transport information. That information must be interpreted in the occipital lobes in order for the viewer to "see it." A stroke or a wound in an occipital lobe can cause blindness or, at a minimum, can wipe out a portion of the person's visual field.

- **occipital lobes** Structures located at the back of the head that respond to visual stimuli.

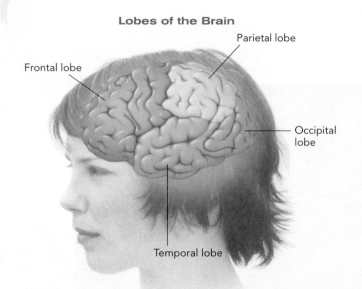

Lobes of the Brain

Frontal lobe
Parietal lobe
Occipital lobe
Temporal lobe

Functional Regions Within the Lobes

Motor cortex
Somatosensory cortex
Sensory association cortex
Motor association cortex
Prefrontal cortex
Auditory association cortex
Auditory cortex (mostly hidden from view)
Visual cortex
Visual association cortex

FIGURE 3.14 **The Cerebral Cortex's Lobes and Association Areas** The cerebral cortex (*left*) is roughly divided into four lobes: occipital, temporal, frontal, and parietal. The cerebral cortex (*right*) also consists of the motor cortex and somatosensory cortex. Further, the cerebral cortex includes association areas, such as the visual association cortex, auditory association cortex, and sensory association cortex.

● **temporal lobes** Structures in the cerebral cortex that are located just above the ears and are involved in hearing, language processing, and memory.

● **frontal lobes** The portion of the cerebral cortex behind the forehead, involved in personality, intelligence, and the control of voluntary muscles.

● **parietal lobes** Structures at the top and toward the rear of the head that are involved in registering spatial location, attention, and motor control.

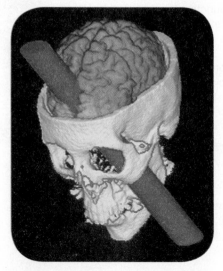

A computerized reconstruction of Phineas T. Gage's accident, based on measurements taken of his skull.

The **temporal lobes,** the part of the cerebral cortex just above the ears, are involved in hearing, language processing, and memory. The temporal lobes have a number of connections to the limbic system. For this reason, people with damage to the temporal lobes cannot file experiences into long-term memory (Narayanan & others, 2012).

The **frontal lobes,** the portion of the cerebral cortex behind the forehead, are involved in personality, intelligence, and the control of voluntary muscles. A fascinating case study illustrates how damage to the frontal lobes can significantly alter personality. Phineas T. Gage, a 25-year-old foreman who worked for the Rutland and Burlington Railroad, was the victim of a terrible accident in 1848. Phineas and several coworkers were using blasting powder to construct a roadbed. The crew drilled holes in the rock and gravel, poured in the blasting powder, and then tamped down the powder with an iron rod. While Phineas was still tamping it down, the powder exploded, driving the iron rod up through the left side of his face and out through the top of his head. Although the wound healed in a matter of weeks, like the individuals described in the opening of this chapter, Phineas had become a different person. Previously he had been mild-mannered, hardworking, and emotionally calm, well liked by all who knew him. Afterward, he was stubborn, hot-tempered, aggressive, and unreliable. Damage to the frontal lobe area of his brain had dramatically altered Phineas's personality.

The frontal lobes of humans are especially large when compared with those of other animals. For example, in rats the frontal cortex barely exists; in cats, it occupies just 3.5 percent of the cerebral cortex; in chimpanzees, 17 percent; and in humans, approximately 30 percent.

An important part of the frontal lobes is the *prefrontal cortex,* which is at the front of the motor cortex (see Figure 3.14). The prefrontal cortex is involved in higher cognitive functions such as planning, reasoning, and self-control (Teffer & Semendeferi, 2012; van Noordt & Segalowitz, 2013). Some neuroscientists refer to the prefrontal cortex as an executive control system because of its role in monitoring and organizing thinking (Zelazo, 2013).

The **parietal lobes,** located at the top and toward the rear of the head, are involved in registering spatial location, attention, and motor control (K. L. Roberts & others, 2013). Thus, the parietal lobes are at work when you are judging how far you have to throw a ball to get it to someone else, when you shift your attention from one activity to another (look away from the TV to a noise outside), and when you turn the pages of this book. The brilliant physicist Albert Einstein said that his reasoning often was best when he imagined objects in space. It turns out that his parietal lobes were 15 percent larger than average (Witelson, Kigar, & Harvey, 1999).

A word of caution is in order about going too far in localizing function within a particular lobe. Although this discussion has attributed specific functions to a particular lobe (such as vision in the occipital lobe), considerable integration and connection occur between any two or more lobes and between lobes and other parts of the brain.

SOMATOSENSORY CORTEX AND MOTOR CORTEX

Two other important regions of the cerebral cortex are the somatosensory cortex and the motor cortex (see Figure 3.14). The **somatosensory cortex** processes information about body sensations. It is located at the front of the parietal lobes. The **motor cortex,** at the rear of the frontal lobes, processes information about voluntary movement.

The map in Figure 3.15 shows which parts of the somatosensory and motor cortexes are associated with various parts of the body. It is based on research done by Wilder Penfield (1947), a neurosurgeon at the Montreal Neurological Institute. He worked with patients who had severe epilepsy, and he often performed surgery to remove portions of the epileptic patients' brains. However, he was concerned that removing a portion of the brain might impair some of the individuals' functions. Penfield's solution was to map the cortex during surgery by stimulating different cortical areas and observing the responses of the patients, who were given a local anesthetic so that they would remain awake during the operation. He found that when he stimulated certain somatosensory and motor areas of the brain, patients reported feeling different sensations, or different parts of a patient's body moved.

● **somatosensory cortex** A region in the cerebral cortex that processes information about body sensations, located at the front of the parietal lobes.

● **motor cortex** A region in the cerebral cortex that processes information about voluntary movement, located just behind the frontal lobes.

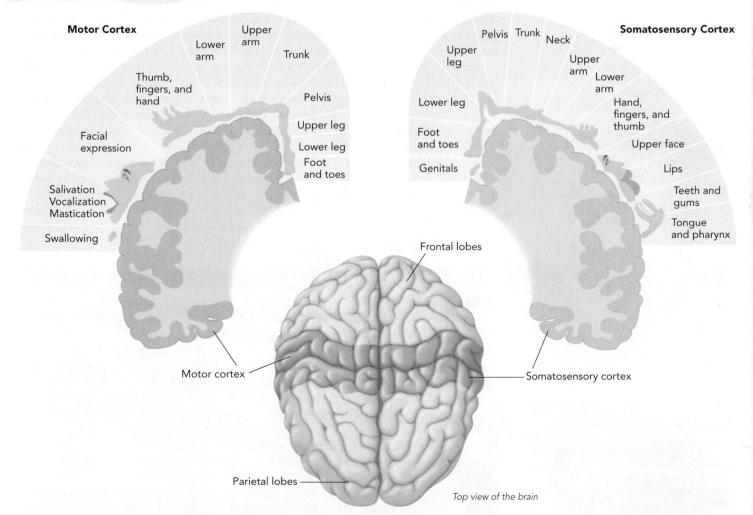

FIGURE 3.15   Disproportionate Representation of Body Parts in the Motor and Somatosensory Areas of the Cortex The amount of cortex allotted to a body part is not proportionate to the body part's size. Instead, the brain has more space for body parts that require precision and control. Thus, the thumb, fingers, and hand require more brain tissue than does the arm.

Penfield's approach is still used today when neurosurgeons perform certain procedures—for example, the removal of a brain tumor. Keeping the patient awake allows the neurosurgeon to ask questions about what the individual is seeing, hearing, and feeling and to be sure that the parts of the brain that are being affected are not essential for consciousness, speech, and other important functions. The extreme precision of brain surgery ensures that life-saving operations do as little harm as possible to the delicate human brain.

For both somatosensory and motor areas, there is a point-to-point relation between a part of the body and a location on the cerebral cortex. In Figure 3.15, the face and hands are given proportionately more space than other body parts because the face and hands are capable of finer perceptions and movements than are other body areas and therefore need more cerebral cortex representation.

The point-to-point mapping of somatosensory fields onto the cortex's surface is the basis of our orderly and accurate perception of the world (Hsiao & Gomez-Ramirez, 2013). When something touches your lip, for example, your brain knows what body part has been touched because the nerve pathways from your lip are the only pathways that project to the lip region of the somatosensory cortex.

ASSOCIATION CORTEX

● **association cortex or association area** The region of the cerebral cortex that is the site of the highest intellectual functions, such as thinking and problem solving.

Association cortex or **association area** refers to the regions of the cerebral cortex that integrate sensory and motor information. (The term *association cortex* applies to cortical material that is not somatosensory or motor cortex—but it is not filler space.) There are association areas throughout the brain, and each sensory system has its own association area in the cerebral cortex. Intellectual functions, such as thinking and problem solving, occur in the association cortex. Embedded in the brain's lobes, association cortex makes up 75 percent of the cerebral cortex (see Figure 3.14).

Interestingly, damage to a specific part of the association cortex often does not result in a specific loss of function. With the exception of language areas, which are localized, loss of function seems to depend more on the extent of damage to association cortex than on the specific site of the damage. By observing brain-damaged individuals and using a mapping technique, scientists have found that association cortex is involved in linguistic and perceptual functioning.

The largest portion of association cortex is located in the frontal lobes, directly behind the forehead. Damage to this area does not lead to somatosensory or motor loss but rather to problems in planning and problem solving, or what are called *executive functions* (Carlson, Zelazo, & Faja, 2013). Personality also may be linked to the frontal lobes. Recall the misfortune of Phineas Gage, whose personality radically changed after he experienced frontal lobe damage.

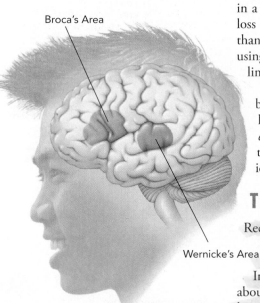

Broca's Area

Wernicke's Area

FIGURE 3.16 Broca's Area and Wernicke's Area Broca's area is located in the brain's left hemisphere and is involved in the control of speech. Individuals with damage to Broca's area have problems saying words correctly. Also shown is Wernicke's area, the portion of the left hemisphere that is involved in understanding language. Individuals with damage to this area cannot comprehend words; they hear the words but do not know what they mean.

The Cerebral Hemispheres and Split-Brain Research

Recall that the cerebral cortex is divided into two halves—left and right (see Figure 3.13). Do these hemispheres have different functions? A discovery by French surgeon Paul Broca provided early evidence that they do.

In 1861 Broca saw a patient who had received an injury to the left side of his brain about 30 years earlier. The patient became known as Tan because *tan* was the only word he could speak. Tan suffered from *expressive aphasia* (also called *Broca's aphasia*), a language disorder that involves the inability to produce language. Tan died several days after Broca evaluated him, and an autopsy revealed that the injury was to a precise area of the left hemisphere. Today we refer to this area of the brain as *Broca's area,* and we know that it plays an important role in the production of speech.

Another area of the brain's left hemisphere that has an important role in language is *Wernicke's area.* This area is named for Carl Wernicke, a German neurologist, who noticed in 1874 that individuals with injuries in the left hemisphere had difficulties in understanding language. Damage to this region causes problems in comprehending language; although an individual with an injury to Wernicke's area can produce words, he or she may not be able to understand what others are saying. Figure 3.16 shows the locations of Broca's area and Wernicke's area. It is easy to confuse Broca's area (associated with speech production) and Wernicke's area (associated with language comprehension). You might remember that Broca's famous patient was called Tan because that was the only word he could produce, so Broca's areas is about speech production.

Today there continues to be considerable interest in the degree to which the brain's left hemisphere or right hemisphere is involved in various aspects of thinking, feeling, and behavior (Meng & others, 2012). For many years, scientists speculated that the **corpus callosum,** the large bundle of axons that connects the brain's two hemispheres, has something to do with relaying information between the two sides (Figure 3.17).

Roger Sperry (1974) confirmed this in an experiment in which he cut the corpus callosum in cats. He also severed certain nerves leading from the eyes to the brain. After the operation, Sperry trained the cats to solve a series of visual problems with one eye blindfolded. After a cat learned the task—say, with only its left eye uncovered—its other eye was blindfolded, and the animal was tested again. The "split-brain" cat behaved as if it had never learned the task. In these cats, memory was stored only in the left hemisphere, which could no longer directly communicate with the right hemisphere.

Further evidence of the corpus callosum's function has come from studies of patients with severe, even life-threatening, forms of epilepsy. Epilepsy is caused by electrical "brainstorms" that can flash uncontrollably across the corpus callosum. In one famous case, neurosurgeons severed the corpus callosum of an epileptic patient now known as W. J. in a final attempt to reduce his unbearable seizures. Sperry (1968) examined W. J. and found that the corpus callosum functions the same in humans as in animals— cutting the corpus callosum seemed to leave the patient with "two separate minds" that learned and operated independently.

As it turns out, the right hemisphere receives information only from the left side of the body, and the left hemisphere receives information only from the right side of the body. When you hold an object in your left hand, for example, only the right hemisphere of your brain detects the object. When you hold an object in your right hand, only the left hemisphere of the brain detects it (Figure 3.18). In individuals with a normally functioning corpus callosum, both hemispheres receive this information eventually, as it travels between the hemispheres through the corpus callosum. In fact, although we might have two minds, we usually use them in tandem.

You can appreciate how well the corpus callosum rapidly integrates your experience by considering how hard it is to do two things at once (Stirling, 2002). Maybe as a child you tried to pat your head and rub your stomach at the same time. Even with two separate hands controlled by two separate hemispheres, such dual activity is hard.

In people with intact brains, hemispheric specialization of function occurs in some areas. Researchers have uncovered evidence for hemispheric differences in function by sending different information to each ear. Remember, the left hemisphere gets its information (first) from the right ear, and the right hemisphere hears what is going on (first) in the left ear. Such research has shown that the brain tends to divide its functioning into one hemisphere or the other, as we now consider.

LEFT HEMISPHERE FUNCTION

The most extensive research on the brain's two hemispheres has focused on language. Although it is a common misconception that *all* language processing occurs in the brain's left hemisphere, *much* language processing and production does come from this hemisphere (Ibrahim & Eviatar, 2012; Prat, 2013). For example, when we are reading, the left hemisphere recognizes words and numbers and comprehends syntax (rules for forming phrases and sentences) and grammar (Dien, 2009), but the right hemisphere does not. The left hemisphere is also keenly involved when we sing the words of a song. In addition, although not generally associated with spatial perception, the left hemisphere

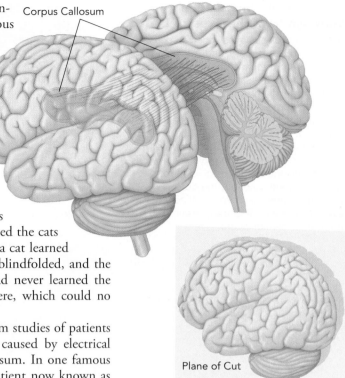

Corpus Callosum

Plane of Cut

FIGURE 3.17   The Corpus Callosum The corpus callosum is a thick bundle of fibers (essentially axons) that connects the brain cells in one hemisphere to those in the other. In healthy brains, the two sides engage in a continuous flow of information via this neural bridge.

● **corpus callosum** The large bundle of axons that connects the brain's two hemispheres, responsible for relaying information between the two sides.

FIGURE 3.18   Information Pathways from the Eyes to the Brain Each of our eyes receives sensory input from both our left and our right field of vision. Information from the left half of our visual field goes to the brain's right hemisphere (which is responsible for simple comprehension), and information from the right half of our visual field goes to the brain's left hemisphere (the brain's main language center, which controls speech and writing). The input received in either hemisphere passes quickly to the other hemisphere across the corpus callosum. When the corpus callosum is severed, however, this transmission of information cannot occur.

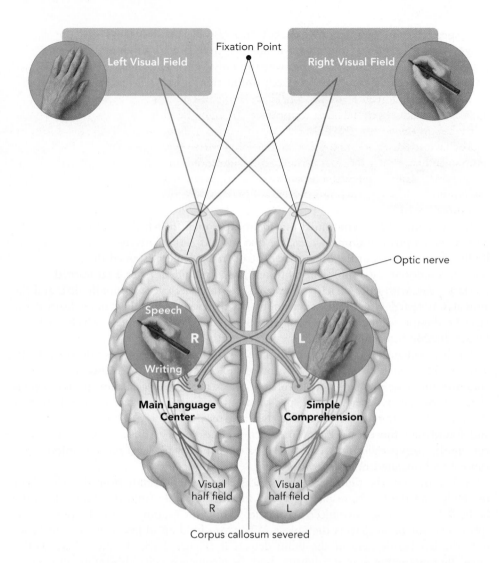

can direct us in solving some basic spatial puzzles, such as identifying whether an object is inside or outside a box.

RIGHT HEMISPHERE FUNCTION

The right hemisphere is not as verbally oriented as the left hemisphere, but it does play a role in word recognition, especially if the words are difficult to see (Dien, 2009). The reason we know that the right hemisphere is the source of some human verbal abilities is that people with split brains can draw (with their left hand) pictures of things that are communicated to them in words that are spoken to them (in their left ear). Also, researchers have found increasing evidence that following damage to the left hemisphere, especially early in development, the right hemisphere can take over some language functions (Staudt, 2010). Moreover, the right hemisphere is adept at picking up the meaning of stories and the intonations of voices, and it excels at catching on to song melodies. Furthermore, a recent study revealed that the right hemisphere is involved in conversation processing (Holtgraves, 2012).

The real strength of the right hemisphere, however, appears to lie in the processing of nonverbal information such as spatial perception, visual recognition, and emotion (Kensinger & Choi, 2009). With respect to interpreting spatial information, the right hemisphere is involved in our ability to tell if something is on top of something else, how far apart two objects are, and whether two objects moving in space might crash.

The right hemisphere is the one mainly at work when we process information about people's faces (Kanwisher, 2006). How do we know? One way we know is that researchers have asked people to watch images on a computer screen and to press a button with either their right or left hand if they recognize a face. Even right-handed people are faster to recognize faces with their left hand because the information goes directly from the part of the brain that recognizes faces (the right hemisphere) to the left hand (Gillihan & Farah, 2005).

Research by Nancy Kanwisher and her colleagues has provided evidence for the role of a specialized area in the brain for processing faces (Kanwisher & Yovel, 2010; McKone, Crookes, & Kanwisher, 2010; Pitcher & others, 2012). This area, located in the fusiform gyrus in the right temporal lobe, is called the *fusiform face area (FFA)*. The FFA is a dime-size spot just behind your right ear. Using fMRI, researchers have shown that the FFA is especially active when a person is viewing a face—a human face, a cat's face, or a cartoon face—but not cars, butterflies, or other objects (Tong & others, 2000).

The right hemisphere may be more involved than the left hemisphere, too, in processing information about emotions—both when we express emotions ourselves and when we interpret others' emotions (Carmona, Holland, & Harrison, 2009). People are more likely to remember emotion words if they hear them in the left ear. As well, much of our sense of humor resides in the right hemisphere (Bartolo & others, 2006; Coulson & Wu, 2005). If you want to be sure that someone laughs at your joke, tell it to the person's left ear!

Our emotions in turn can influence the hemisphere that is relied upon at any given moment. In one experiment (Papousek, Schulter, & Lang, 2009), participants were randomly assigned to experience a variety of different emotional states by watching videos of a woman expressing intense feelings, such as sadness, cheerfulness, and anger. Then the participants completed a set of verbal tasks (thought to be strengths of the left hemisphere) and a set of figural tasks (thought to be strengths of the right hemisphere). The results showed that when participants were in an intense mood state, they were better at completing figural tasks than the verbal exercises. Thus, the experience of intense emotion may shift processing over to the right hemisphere (Papousek, Schulter, & Lang, 2009). With respect to emotion, though, the dominance of the right hemisphere in processing emotions is still under debate (Beraha & others, 2012).

RIGHT-BRAINED VERSUS LEFT-BRAINED

Because differences in the functioning of the brain's two hemispheres are known to exist, people commonly use the terms *left-brained* (meaning logical and rational) and *right-brained* (meaning creative or artistic) as a way of categorizing themselves and others. Such generalizations have little scientific basis, however—and that is a good thing. We have both hemispheres for a reason: We use them both. In most complex activities in which people engage, interplay occurs between the brain's two hemispheres (Hinkley & others, 2012).

Integration of Function in the Brain

How do all of the regions of the brain cooperate to produce the wondrous complexity of thought and behavior that characterizes humans? Neuroscience still does not have answers to questions such as how the brain solves a murder mystery or composes an essay. Even so, we can get a sense of integrative brain function by using a real-world scenario, such as the act of escaping from a burning building.

Imagine that you are sitting at your computer, writing an e-mail, when a fire breaks out behind you. The sound of crackling flames is relayed from your ear through the thalamus, to the auditory cortex, and on to the auditory association cortex. At each stage, the stimulus is processed to extract information, and at some stage, probably at the association cortex level, the sounds are finally matched with something like a neural memory representing sounds of fires you have heard previously.

The association "fire" sets new machinery in motion. Your attention (guided in part by the reticular formation) shifts to the auditory signal being held in your association cortex and on to your auditory association cortex, and simultaneously (again guided by reticular systems) your head turns toward the noise.

● **endocrine system** The body system consisting of a set of glands that regulate the activities of certain organs by releasing their chemical products into the bloodstream.

● **glands** Organs or tissues in the body that create chemicals that control many of our bodily functions.

Now your visual association cortex reports in: "Objects matching flames are present." In other regions of the association cortex, the visual and auditory reports are synthesized ("We have things that look and sound like fire"), and neural associations representing potential actions ("flee") are activated. However, firing the neurons that code the plan to flee will not get you out of the chair. For that task, the basal ganglia must become engaged, and from there the commands will arise to set the brain stem, motor cortex, and cerebellum to the work of transporting you out of the room. All of this happens in mere seconds.

So, which part of your brain did you use to escape? Virtually all systems had a role. By the way, you would probably remember this event because your limbic circuitry would likely have started memory formation when the association "fire" was triggered. The next time the sounds of crackling flames reach your auditory association cortex, the associations triggered would include this most recent escape. In sum, considerable integration of function takes place in the brain (Rissman & Wagner, 2012). All of the parts of the nervous system work together as a team to keep you safe and sound.

4· THE ENDOCRINE SYSTEM

The nervous system works closely with another bodily system—the endocrine system. The **endocrine system** consists of a set of glands that regulate the activities of certain organs by releasing their chemical products into the bloodstream. **Glands** are organs or tissues in the body that produce chemicals that control many of our bodily functions. The endocrine glands consist of the pituitary gland, the thyroid and parathyroid glands, the adrenal glands, the pancreas, the ovaries in women, and the testes in men (Figure 3.19). The chemical messengers produced by these glands are called **hormones.** The bloodstream carries hormones to all parts of the body, and the membrane of every cell has receptors for one or more hormones. Let's take a closer look at the function of some of the main endocrine glands.

The **pituitary gland,** a pea-sized gland just beneath the hypothalamus, controls growth and regulates other glands (Figure 3.20). The anterior (front) part of the pituitary is known as the master gland, because almost all of its hormones direct the activity of target glands elsewhere in the body. In turn, the anterior pituitary gland is controlled by the hypothalamus.

The **adrenal glands,** located at the top of each kidney, regulate moods, energy level, and the ability to cope with stress. Each adrenal gland secretes epinephrine (also called *adrenaline*) and norepinephrine (also called *noradrenaline*). Unlike most hormones, epinephrine and norepinephrine act quickly. Epinephrine helps a person get ready for an emergency by acting on smooth muscles, the heart, stomach, intestines, and sweat glands. In addition, epinephrine stimulates the reticular formation, which in turn arouses the sympathetic nervous system, and this system subsequently excites the adrenal glands to produce more epinephrine.

Norepinephrine also alerts the individual to emergency situations by interacting with the pituitary and the liver. You may remember that norepinephrine functions as a neurotransmitter when it is released by neurons. In the adrenal glands, norepinephrine is released as a hormone. In both instances, norepinephrine conveys information—in the first case, to neurons; in the second case, to glands (Brooker & others, 2010). The activation of the

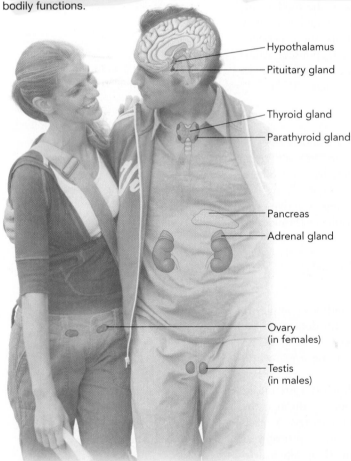

Hypothalamus
Pituitary gland
Thyroid gland
Parathyroid gland
Pancreas
Adrenal gland
Ovary (in females)
Testis (in males)

FIGURE 3.19 The Major Endocrine Glands The pituitary gland releases hormones that regulate the hormone secretions of the other glands. The pituitary gland is regulated by the hypothalamus.

adrenal glands has an important role to play in stress and physical health, as we will see at the end of this chapter (Dougall & others, 2013).

The **pancreas,** located under the stomach, is a dual-purpose gland that performs both digestive and endocrine functions. The part of the pancreas that serves endocrine functions produces a number of hormones, including insulin. This part of the pancreas, the *islets of Langerhans,* busily turns out hormones like a little factory. Insulin is an essential hormone that controls glucose (blood sugar) levels in the body and is related to metabolism, body weight, and obesity.

The **ovaries,** located in the pelvis on either sides of the uterus in women, and **testes,** located in the scrotum in men, are the sex-related endocrine glands that produce hormones involved in sexual development and reproduction. These glands and the hormones they produce play important roles in developing sexual characteristics, as we will discover in Chapter 11. They are also involved in other characteristics and behaviors, as we will see throughout this book.

Neuroscientists have discovered that the nervous system and endocrine system are intricately interconnected. They know that the brain's hypothalamus connects the nervous system and the endocrine system and that the two systems work together to control the body's activities (Boonen & others, 2010). Recall from earlier in the chapter that the autonomic nervous system regulates processes such as respiration, heart rate, and digestion. The autonomic nervous system acts on the endocrine glands to produce a number of important physiological reactions to strong emotions, such as rage and fear.

The endocrine system differs significantly from the nervous system in a variety of ways. For one thing, as you saw in Figure 3.19, the parts of the endocrine system are not all connected in the way that the parts of the nervous system are. For another, the endocrine system works more slowly than the nervous system, because hormones are transported in our blood through the circulatory system. Our hearts do a mind-boggling job of pumping blood throughout the body, but blood moves far more slowly than the neural impulses do in the nervous system's superhighway.

5· BRAIN DAMAGE, PLASTICITY, AND REPAIR

Recall from the discussion of the brain's important characteristics earlier in this chapter that plasticity is an example of the brain's remarkable adaptability. Neuroscientists have studied plasticity, especially following brain damage, and have charted the brain's ability to repair itself (Sozzi & others, 2012; Zelazo, 2013). Brain damage can produce horrific effects, including paralysis, sensory loss, memory loss, and personality deterioration. When such damage occurs, can the brain recover some or all of its functions? Recovery from brain damage varies considerably, depending on the age of the individual and the extent of the damage (Anderson & Arciniegas, 2010; Kolb & Teskey, 2012).

The Brain's Plasticity and Capacity for Repair

The human brain shows the most plasticity in young children, before the functions of the cortical regions become entirely fixed (Spencer-Smith & Anderson, 2011). For example, if the speech areas in an infant's left hemisphere are damaged, the right hemisphere assumes much of this language function. However, after age 5, damage to the left hemisphere can permanently disrupt language ability. We examine the brain's plasticity further in Chapter 4 on sensation and perception and Chapter 9 on human development.

A key factor in recovery is whether some or all of the neurons in an affected area are just damaged versus whether they are destroyed (Huang & Chang, 2009). If the

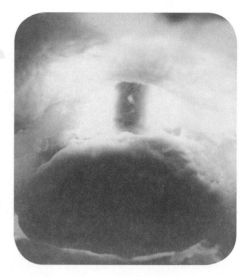

FIGURE 3.20 **The Pituitary Gland** The pituitary gland, which hangs by a short stalk from the hypothalamus, regulates the hormone production of many of the body's endocrine glands. Here it is enlarged 30 times.

test yourself

1. What is the endocrine system's function, and what role do hormones play in it?
2. What two adrenal gland secretions prepare the body to react quickly to emergencies, and what specifically do they do?
3. Through what brain structure are the nervous and the endocrine systems connected, and what do the two systems work together to control?

● **hormones** Chemical messengers that are produced by the endocrine glands and carried by the bloodstream to all parts of the body.

● **pituitary gland** A pea-sized gland just beneath the hypothalamus that controls growth and regulates other glands.

● **adrenal glands** Glands at the top of each kidney that are responsible for regulating moods, energy level, and the ability to cope with stress.

● **pancreas** A dual-purpose gland under the stomach that performs both digestive and endocrine functions.

● **ovaries** Sex-related endocrine glands that produce hormones involved in women's sexual development and reproduction.

● **testes** Sex-related endocrine glands in the scrotum that produce hormones involved in men's sexual development and reproduction.

neurons have not been destroyed, brain function often becomes restored over time. There are three ways in which repair of the damaged brain might take place:

- *Collateral sprouting,* the process by which axons of some healthy neurons adjacent to damaged cells grow new branches.
- *Substitution of function,* the process by which the damaged region's function is taken over by another area or areas of the brain.
- *Neurogenesis,* the process by which new neurons are generated.

Researchers have found that neurogenesis occurs in mammals such as mice. Recent research has revealed that exercise increases neurogenesis whereas social isolation decreases it (Creer & others, 2010; Gil-Mohapel & others, 2011; Leasure & Decker, 2009). It is now accepted that neurogenesis can occur in humans (Goritz & Frisén, 2012). However, to date, the presence of new neurons has been documented only in the hippocampus, which is involved in memory, and the olfactory bulb, which is involved in the sense of smell (Xu & others, 2013). And researchers are exploring how the grafting of neural stem cells to various regions of the brain, such as the hypothalamus, might increase neurogenesis (Decimo & others, 2012). If researchers can discover how new neurons are generated, possibly the information can be used to fight degenerative diseases of the brain such as Alzheimer disease and Parkinson disease (Walton & others, 2012).

Brain Tissue Implants

The brain naturally recovers some, but not all, functions that are lost following damage. Recent research has generated excitement about *brain grafts*—implants of healthy tissue into damaged brains (Hattiangady & Shetty, 2012). Brain grafts have greater potential success when the brain tissue used is from the fetal stage—an early stage in prenatal development (M. Thomas & others, 2009). The reason for this advantage is that the fetal neurons are still growing and have a much higher probability of making connections with other neurons than does mature brain tissue. In a number of studies, researchers have damaged part of an adult rat's brain, waited until the animal recovered as much as possible by itself, and assessed its behavioral deficits. They then took the corresponding area of a fetal rat's brain and transplanted it into the damaged brain of the adult rat. In these studies, the rats that received the brain transplants demonstrated considerable behavioral recovery (Shetty, Rao, & Hattiangady, 2008).

Might such brain grafts be successful in humans suffering from brain damage? The research results are promising, but finding donors is a problem (Glaw & others, 2009). Although using brain tissue from aborted fetuses is a possibility, there are ethical concerns about that practice.

Perhaps one of the most heated debates in recent years has concerned the use of human embryonic stem cells in research and treatment (Ideguchi & others, 2010). The human body contains more than 220 different types of cells, but **stem cells** are unique because they are primitive cells that have the capacity to develop into most types of human cells. Stem cells were first harvested from embryos by researchers at the University of Wisconsin, Madison, and Johns Hopkins University in 1998. Because of their amazing plasticity, stem cells might potentially replace damaged cells in the human body, including cells involved in spinal cord injury and brain damage (Rosser & Bachoud-Levi, 2012; Yoo, Kim, & Hwang, 2013).

Typically, researchers have harvested the stem cells from frozen embryos left over from *in vitro fertilization* procedures. In these procedures, a number of eggs, or *ova,* are collected from a woman's ovaries in order to be fertilized in a lab. In successful in vitro fertilization, the ova are brought together with sperm, producing human embryos. Because the procedure is difficult and delicate, doctors typically fertilize a large number of eggs in the hope that some will survive when implanted in the woman's uterus. In the typical procedure, there are leftover embryos. These embryos are in the *blastocyst* stage, which occurs five days after conception. At this stage the embryo has not yet

● **stem cells** Unique primitive cells that have the capacity to develop into most types of human cells.

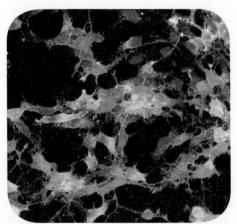

This fluorescent micrograph shows glial stem cells. Like other stem cells, these have the capacity to develop into a wide range of other cells.

attached to the uterus and has no brain, no central nervous system, and no mouth—it is an undifferentiated ball of cells.

Some supporters of stem cell technology—among them the late actor Christopher Reeve (2000)—emphasize that using these cells for research and treatment might relieve a great deal of human suffering. Opponents of abortion disapprove of the use of stem cells in research or treatment on the grounds that the embryos die when the stem cells are removed. (In fact, leftover embryos are likely to be destroyed in any case.) In 2009, President Barack Obama removed restrictions on stem cell research.

6· GENETICS AND BEHAVIOR

In addition to the brain and nervous system, other aspects of our physiology also have consequences for psychological processes. Genes, the focal point of this section, are an essential contributor to these processes (Belk & Maier, 2013). As noted in Chapter 1, the influence of nature (our internal genetic endowment) and nurture (our external experience) on psychological characteristics has long fascinated psychologists. We begin by examining some basic facts about the central internal agent of our human differences: our genes.

Chromosomes, Genes, and DNA

Within the human body are literally trillions of cells. The nucleus of each human cell contains 46 **chromosomes,** threadlike structures that come in 23 pairs, with one member of each pair originating from each biological parent. Chromosomes contain the remarkable substance **deoxyribonucleic acid (DNA),** a complex molecule that carries genetic information. **Genes,** the units of hereditary information, are short chromosome segments composed of DNA. The relationship among cells, chromosomes, genes, and DNA is illustrated in Figure 3.21.

Genes hold the code for creating proteins out of amino acids forming the bases for everything our bodies do. Specifically, genes direct and regulate the production of these

● **chromosomes** In the human cell, threadlike structures that come in 23 pairs, one member of each pair originating from each parent, and that contain the remarkable substance DNA.

● **deoxyribonucleic acid (DNA)** A complex molecule in the cell's chromosomes that carries genetic information.

● **genes** The units of hereditary information, consisting of short segments of chromosomes composed of DNA.

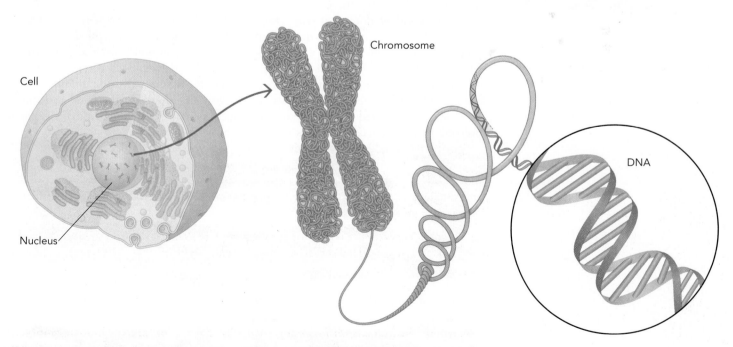

FIGURE 3.21 Cells, Chromosomes, Genes, and DNA (*Left*) The body houses trillions of cells, which are the basic structural units of life. Each cell contains a central structure, the nucleus. (*Middle*) Chromosomes and genes are located in the nucleus of the cell. Chromosomes are made up of threadlike structures composed mainly of DNA molecules. Note that inside the chromosome are the genes. (*Right*) A gene is a segment of DNA that contains the hereditary code. The structure of DNA resembles a spiral ladder.

A positive result from the Human Genome Project. Shortly after Andrew Gobea was born, his cells were genetically altered to prevent his immune system from failing.

● **dominant-recessive genes principle**
The principle that, if one gene of a pair is dominant and one is recessive, the dominant gene overrides the recessive gene. A recessive gene exerts its influence only if both genes of a pair are recessive.

proteins. Although every cell in our body contains a full complement of our genes, different genes are active in each cell. Many genes encode proteins that are unique to a particular cell and give the cell its identity. Will it be a neuron or a bone cell? The activation of our genes holds the key to this question. Some genes are involved in the development of the embryo and then are turned off for the rest of life. Genes do not operate independently but work with one another and in collaboration with hormones and the environment to direct the body's function (Moore, 2013).

An international research program called the Human Genome Project (*genome* refers to an organism's complete genetic material, as discussed below) is dedicated to documenting the human genome. Human beings have approximately 20,500 genes (National Human Genome Research Institute, 2012). When these 20,500 genes from one parent combine at conception with the same number of genes from the other parent, the number of possibilities is staggering. Although scientists are still a long way from unraveling all the mysteries about the way genes work, some aspects of this process are well understood, starting with the fact that multiple genes interact to give rise to observable characteristics.

The Study of Genetics

Historically speaking, genetics is a relatively young science. Its origins go back to the mid-nineteenth century, when an Austrian monk, Gregor Mendel, studied heredity in generations of pea plants. By crossbreeding plants with different characteristics and noting the characteristics of the offspring, Mendel discovered predictable patterns of heredity and thereby laid the foundation for modern genetics.

Mendel noticed that some genes seem to be more likely than others to show up in the physical characteristics of an organism. In some gene pairs, one gene is dominant over the other. If one gene of a pair is dominant and one is recessive, the **dominant-recessive genes principle** applies, meaning that the dominant gene overrides the recessive gene—that is, it prevents the recessive gene from expressing its instructions. The recessive gene exerts its influence only if *both* genes of a pair are recessive. If you inherit a recessive gene from only one biological parent, you may never know you carry the gene.

In the world of dominant-recessive genes, brown eyes, farsightedness, and dimples rule over blue eyes, nearsightedness, and freckles. If, however, you inherit a recessive gene for a trait from *both* of your biological parents, you will show the trait. That is why two brown-haired parents can have a child with red hair: Each parent would have dominant genes for brown hair and recessive genes for red hair. Because dominant genes override recessive genes, the parents have brown hair. However, the child can inherit recessive genes for red hair from each biological parent. With no dominant genes to override them, the recessive genes would make the child's hair red.

Yet the relationship between genes and characteristics is complex. Even simple traits such as eye color and hair color are likely the product of *multiple* genes. Moreover, many different genes probably influence complex human characteristics such as personality and intelligence. Scientists use the term *polygenic inheritance* to describe the influences of multiple genes on behavior.

Present-day researchers continue to apply Mendel's methods, as well as the latest technology, in their quest to expand our knowledge of genetics. We next survey four ways in which scientists investigate our genetic heritage: molecular genetics, selective breeding, genome-wide association method, and behavior genetics.

MOLECULAR GENETICS

The field of *molecular genetics* involves the manipulation of genes using technology to determine their effect on behavior. There is currently a great deal of enthusiasm about the use of molecular genetics to discover the specific locations on genes that determine an individual's susceptibility to many diseases and other aspects of health and well-being (Kendler & others, 2012; Riley & others, 2012).

SELECTIVE BREEDING

Selective breeding is a genetic method in which organisms are chosen for reproduction based on how much of a particular trait they display. Mendel developed this technique in his studies of pea plants. A more recent example involving behavior is the classic selective breeding study conducted by Robert Tryon (1940). He chose to study maze-running ability in rats. After he trained a large number of rats to run a complex maze, he then mated the rats that were the best at maze running ("maze bright") with each other and the ones that were the worst ("maze dull") with each other. He continued this process with 21 generations of rats. As Figure 3.22 shows, after several generations, the maze-bright rats significantly outperformed the maze-dull rats.

Selective breeding studies demonstrate that genes are an important influence on behavior, but that does not mean experience is unimportant. For example, in another study, maze-bright and maze-dull rats were reared in one of two environments: (1) an impoverished environment that consisted of a barren wire-mesh group cage or (2) an enriched environment that contained tunnels, ramps, visual displays, and other stimulating objects (Cooper & Zubeck, 1958). When they reached maturity, only the maze-dull rats that had been reared in an impoverished environment made more maze-learning errors than the maze-bright rats.

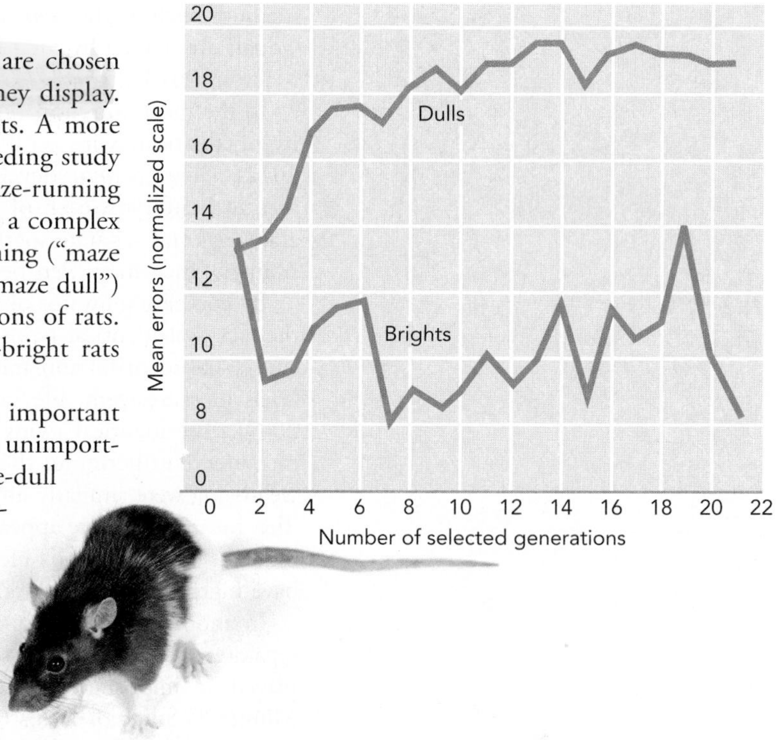

It is unethical to conduct selective breeding studies with human beings. (*Eugenics* refers to the application of selective breeding to humans; Adolf Hitler notoriously espoused this practice in Nazi Germany.) In humans, researchers generally examine the influence of genetics on psychological characteristics by using behavior genetics.

FIGURE 3.22 **Results of Tryon's Selective Breeding Experiment with Maze-Bright and Maze-Dull Rats** These results demonstrate genetic influences on behavior.

GENOME-WIDE ASSOCIATION METHOD

Completion of the Human Genome Project has led to use of the *genome-wide association method* to identify genetic variations linked to a particular disease, such as cancer, cardiovascular disease, or Alzheimer disease (National Human Genome Research Institute, 2012). To conduct a genome-wide association study, researchers obtain DNA from individuals who have the disease under study and from those who do not. Then, each participant's complete set of DNA, or genome, is purified from the blood or cells and scanned on machines to determine markers of genetic variation. If the genetic variations occur more frequently in people who have the disease, the variations point to the region in the human genome where the disease-causing problem exists. Genome-wide association studies have recently been conducted for a variety of diseases and disorders, including Alzheimer disease (Raj & others, 2012), and depression (Major Depressive Disorder Working Group of the Psychiatric GWAS Consortium, 2013).

Genes that are close to one another in our DNA are more likely to be inherited together. This link between genes is used in what is called *linkage analysis*. This analysis may help identify the location of certain genes by referring to those genes whose position is already known, which is a strategy often used to search for genes associated with a disease (Lyon & Wang, 2012). Gene linkage studies are now being conducted on a wide variety of disorders and health issues, including attention deficit hyperactivity disorder (Caylak, 2012), autism (O'Roak & others, 2012), depression (Cohen-Woods, Craig, & McGuffin, 2012), and Alzheimer disease (Bertram & Tanzi, 2012).

BEHAVIOR GENETICS

Behavior genetics is the study of the degree and nature of heredity's influence on behavior. Behavior genetics is less invasive than the other types of genetic investigation. Using methods such as the *twin study*, behavior geneticists examine the extent to which individuals are shaped by their heredity and their environmental experiences (Kaplan, 2012; Maxson, 2013).

In the most common type of twin study, researchers compare the behavioral similarity of identical twins with the behavioral similarity of fraternal twins (Bell & Saffery, 2012). *Identical twins* develop from a single fertilized egg that splits into two genetically identical embryos, each of which becomes a person. *Fraternal twins* develop from separate eggs and separate sperm, and so they are genetically no more similar than non-twin siblings. They may even be of different sexes.

By comparing groups of identical and fraternal twins, behavior geneticists capitalize on the fact that identical twins are more similar genetically than are fraternal twins. In one study, 428 identical and fraternal twin pairs in Italy were compared with respect to their levels of self-esteem, life satisfaction, and optimism for the future (Caprara & others, 2009). The identical twins were much more similar than the fraternal twins on these measures. Furthermore, the researchers found that these various aspects of the person's well-being were similarly affected by genes but differently influenced by the environment. That means that there appeared to be a genetic tendency to have a positive attitude toward different aspects of one's life. In contrast, the environment explained how a person might have high self-esteem but lower life satisfaction (Caprara & others, 2009).

In another type of twin study, researchers evaluate identical twins who were reared in separate environments. If their behavior is similar, the assumption is that heredity has played an important role in shaping their behavior. This strategy is the basis for the Minnesota Study of Twins Reared Apart, directed by Thomas Bouchard and his colleagues (1996). The researchers bring identical twins who have been reared apart to Minneapolis from all over the world to study their behavior. They ask thousands of questions about their family, childhood, interests, and values. Detailed medical histories are obtained, including information about diet, smoking, and exercise habits. This approach has its critics, however, who variously argue that some of the separated twins in the Minnesota study had been together several months prior to their adoption, that some had been reunited prior to testing (in certain cases, for a number of years), that adoption agencies often put identical twins in similar homes, and that even strangers are likely to have some coincidental similarities (Joseph, 2006).

You have probably heard of instances of twins who were separated at birth and who, upon being reunited later in life, found themselves strikingly similar to each other. To think critically about such cases, consider the story of Jim Springer and Jim Lewis in the Psychological Inquiry on page 97.

Genes and the Environment

So far, we have focused a lot on genes, and you are probably getting the picture that genes are a powerful force in an organism. The role of genetics in some characteristics may seem obvious; for instance, how tall you are depends to a large degree on how tall your parents are. However, imagine a person growing up in an environment with poor nutrition, inadequate shelter, little or no medical care, and a mother who had received no prenatal care. This individual may have genes that call for the height of an NBA or a WNBA center, but without environmental support for this genetic capacity, he or she may never reach that genetically programmed height.

The relationship between an individual's genes and the actual person we see before us is not a perfect one-to-one correspondence. Even for a characteristic such as height, genes do not fully determine where a person will stand on this variable. We need to account for the role of nurture, or environmental factors, in the characteristics we see in the fully grown person.

If the environment matters for an apparently simple characteristic such as height, imagine the role it might play in a complex psychological characteristic such as being outgoing or intelligent. For such a trait, genes

Our height depends significantly on the genes we inherit. However, even if we have genes that call for the stature of a basketball center, we may not reach that "genetically programmed" height if we lack good nutrition, adequate shelter, and medical care.

psychological *inquiry*

The Jim Twins

The Jim twins, Jim Springer (*right*) and Jim Lewis, were unaware of each other for 39 years. This pair of twins in the Minnesota Study of Twins Reared Apart was separated at 4 weeks of age and did not see each other again until they were 39 years old.

As adults, the Jims had uncanny similarities. Both worked as part-time deputy sheriffs, had vacationed in Florida, had owned Chevrolets, had dogs named Toy, and had married and divorced women named Betty. Both liked math but not spelling. Both were good at mechanical drawing. Both put on 10 pounds at about the same time in life, and both started suffering headaches at 18 years of age.

Such similarities seem to provide very strong evidence of the power of genes. Do they really? Think critically as you answer these questions.

1. Imagine that you did not see the photo of the two Jims and were simply asked how similar two men of the same ethnicity, age, and first name might be. In what ways might such men be similar?

2. How many dogs might be named Toy, how many women might be named Betty, and how many men own Chevrolets?

3. How common might it be for men in general to like math better than spelling, to be good at mechanical drawing, and to put on 10 pounds at some point in life?

4. Is it possible that some of the similarities between Springer and Lewis are not so surprising after all? Explain.

5. What does this exercise tell you about the power of vivid and unusual cases in the conclusions we reach?

---

are, again, not directly reflected in the characteristics of the person. Indeed, genes cannot tell us exactly what a person will be like. Genes are simply related to some of the characteristics we see in a person.

To account for this gap between genes and actual observable characteristics, scientists distinguish between a genotype and a phenotype. A **genotype** is an individual's genetic heritage, the actual genetic material present in every cell in the person's body. A **phenotype** is the individual's observable characteristics. The relationship between a genotype and phenotype is not always obvious. Recall that some genetic characteristics are dominant and others are recessive. Seeing that a person has brown eyes (his or her phenotype) tells us nothing about whether the person might also have a gene for blue eyes (his or her genotype) hiding out as well. The phenotype is influenced by the genotype but also by environmental factors.

The word *phenotype* applies to both physical *and* psychological characteristics. Consider a trait such as extraversion—the tendency to be outgoing and sociable. Even if we knew the exact genetic recipe for extraversion, we still could not perfectly predict a person's level of (phenotypic) extraversion from his or her genes, because at least some of this trait comes from the person's experience. We will revisit the concepts of genotype and phenotype throughout this book—for example, in Chapter 8 when we look at intelligence, Chapter 9 when we explore human development, and Chapter 12 when we examine personality.

● **genotype** An individual's genetic heritage; his or her actual genetic material.

● **phenotype** An individual's observable characteristics.

test yourself

1. What is the relationship among chromosomes, genes, and DNA?
2. According to the dominant-recessive genes principle, how could two brown-haired parents have a blonde-haired child?
3. What term refers to our genetic makeup, and what term refers to the observable physical expression of that genetic makeup?

● **stress** The responses of individuals to environmental stressors.

● **stressors** Circumstances and events that threaten individuals and tax their coping abilities and that cause physiological changes to ready the body to handle the assault of stress.

Snapshots

"Bridges falling down, killer pumpkin eaters, blind mice with carving knives ... I CAN'T TAKE IT ANYMORE!"

© Jason Love www.CartoonStock.com.

Whether a gene is "turned on"—that is, directing cells to assemble proteins—is a matter of collaboration between hereditary and environmental factors. *Genetic expression,* a term that refers to gene activity that affects the body's cells, is influenced by the genes' environment (Gottlieb, 2007). For example, hormones that circulate in the blood make their way into the cell, where they can turn genes on and off. This flow of hormones can be affected by external environmental conditions, such as light level, day length, nutrition, and behavior.

Numerous studies have shown that external events outside the original cell and the person, as well as events inside the cell, can excite or inhibit gene expression (Gottlieb, 2007). One study, for instance, revealed that an increase in the concentration of stress hormones such as cortisol produced a fivefold increase in DNA damage (Flint & others, 2007). Also, a recent study found that exposure to radiation changed the rate of DNA synthesis in cells (K. Y. Lee & others, 2011). As we will see next, stress can be a powerful factor in health and wellness.

7· PSYCHOLOGY'S BIOLOGICAL FOUNDATIONS AND HEALTH AND WELLNESS

So far, we have explored the structure and function of various aspects of the nervous system. The components of the nervous system play an essential role in our health and wellness.

Stress is the response of individuals to **stressors,** which are the circumstances and events that threaten them and tax their coping abilities. Recall that the sympathetic nervous system jumps into action when we encounter a threat in the environment. When we experience stress, our body readies itself to handle the assault.

You certainly know what stress feels like. Imagine, for example, that you show up for class one morning, and it looks as if everyone else knows that there is a test that day. You hear others talking about how much they have studied, and you nervously ask yourself: "Test? What test?" You might start to sweat, and your heart might thump fast and hard in your chest. Sure enough, the instructor shows up with a stack of exams. You are about to be tested on material you have not even thought about, much less studied.

As we have seen, stress begins with a "fight or flight" response sparked by the sympathetic nervous system. This reaction quickly mobilizes the body's physiological resources to prepare us to deal with threats to survival. An unexpected exam is not literally a threat to your survival, but the human stress response is such that it can occur in reaction to *anything* that threatens personally important motives (Sapolsky, 2004).

Acute stress is the stress that occurs in response to an immediate perceived threat. When the stressful situation ends, so does acute stress. Acute stress is adaptive, because it allows us to do the things we need to do in an emergency. Once the danger passes, the parasympathetic nervous system can calm us down and focus on body maintenance. However, we are not in a live-or-die situation most of the time when we experience stress. Indeed, we can even "stress ourselves out" just by thinking.

Chronic stress—stress that goes on continuously—may lead to persistent autonomic nervous system arousal (Leonard & Myint, 2009). While the sympathetic nervous system is working to meet the demands of whatever is stressing us out, the parasympathetic nervous system is not getting a chance to do its job of maintenance and repair, of digesting food, and of keeping our organs in good working order. Furthermore, in chronic stress, the stress hormones adrenaline and norepinephrine, produced by the endocrine system, are constantly circulated in the body, eventually causing a breakdown of the immune system (Sapolsky, 2004). In other words, over time, chronic autonomic nervous system activity can bring about an immune system collapse (Miller, Chen, & Cole, 2009).

Chronic stress is clearly best avoided. The brain, a structure that is itself powerfully affected by chronic stress, can be our ally in helping us avoid such continuous stress (Xanthopoulos & Daniel, 2013). Consider that when we face a challenging situation, we can exploit the brain's abilities and interpret the experience in a way that is not so stressful. For example, maybe we can approach an upcoming audition for a play not so much as a stressor but as an opportunity to shine. Many cognitive therapists believe that changing the way people think about their life opportunities and experiences can help them live less stressfully (Craighead & others, 2013; Gallo & others, 2013).

At the beginning of this chapter, we considered how changing the way we think leads to physical changes in the brain and its operations. In light of this remarkable capacity, it is reasonable to conclude that we can use our brain's powers to change how we look at life experiences—and maybe even to deploy the brain as a defense against stress.

The biological foundations of psychology are in evidence across the entire nervous system, including the brain, the intricately working neurotransmitters, the endocrine system, and our genes. These physical realities of our body work in concert to produce our behavior, thoughts, and feelings. The activities you perform every day are all signs of the success of this physical system. Your mastery of the material in this chapter is only one reflection of the extraordinary capabilities of this biological achievement.

test yourself

1. Explain what stress and stressors are.
2. What part of the nervous system sets off the "fight or flight" reaction, and how does this reaction affect the body?
3. What is the difference between acute stress and chronic stress?

1. THE NERVOUS SYSTEM

The nervous system is the body's electrochemical communication circuitry. Four important characteristics of the brain and nervous system are complexity, integration, adaptability, and electrochemical transmission. The brain's special ability to adapt and change is called plasticity.

Decision making in the nervous system occurs in specialized pathways of nerve cells. Three of these pathways involve sensory input, motor output, and neural networks.

The nervous system is divided into two main parts: central (CNS) and peripheral (PNS). The CNS consists of the brain and spinal cord. The PNS has two major divisions: somatic and autonomic. The autonomic nervous system consists of two main divisions: sympathetic and parasympathetic. The sympathetic nervous system drives our body's response to threatening circumstances, while the parasympathetic nervous system is involved in maintaining the body, digesting food, and healing wounds.

2. NEURONS

Neurons are cells that specialize in processing information. They make up the communication network of the nervous system. The three main parts of the neuron are the cell body, dendrite (receiving part), and axon (sending part). A myelin sheath encases and insulates most axons and speeds up transmission of neural impulses.

Impulses are sent from a neuron along its axon in the form of brief electrical impulses. Resting potential is the stable, slightly negative charge of an inactive neuron. The brief wave of electrical charge that sweeps down the axon, called the action potential, is an all-or-nothing response. The synapse is the space between neurons. At the synapse,

neurotransmitters are released from the sending neuron, and some of these attach to receptor sites on the receiving neuron, where they stimulate another electrical impulse. Neurotransmitters include acetylcholine, GABA, glutamate, norepinephrine, dopamine, serotonin, endorphins, and oxytocin. Neural networks are clusters of neurons that are interconnected and that develop through experience.

3. STRUCTURES OF THE BRAIN AND THEIR FUNCTIONS

The main techniques used to study the brain are brain lesioning, electrical recording, and brain imaging. These methods have revealed a great deal about the three major divisions of the brain—the hindbrain, midbrain, and forebrain.

The cerebral cortex makes up most of the outer layer of the brain, and it is here that higher mental functions such as thinking and planning take place. The wrinkled surface of the cerebral cortex is divided into hemispheres, each with four lobes: occipital, temporal, frontal, and parietal. There is considerable integration and connection among the brain's lobes.

The brain has two hemispheres. Two areas in the left hemisphere that involve specific language functions are Broca's area (speech) and Wernicke's area (language comprehension). The corpus callosum is a large bundle of fibers that connects the two hemispheres. Research suggests that the left brain is more dominant in processing verbal information (such as language) and the right brain in processing nonverbal information (such as spatial perception, visual recognition, faces, and emotion). Nonetheless, in a person whose corpus callosum is intact, both hemispheres of the cerebral cortex are involved in most complex human functioning.

SUMMARY

4. THE ENDOCRINE SYSTEM

The endocrine glands release hormones directly into the bloodstream for distribution throughout the body. The pituitary gland is the master endocrine gland. The adrenal glands play important roles in moods, energy level, and ability to cope with stress. Other parts of the endocrine system include the pancreas, which produces insulin, and the ovaries and testes, which produce sex hormones.

5. BRAIN DAMAGE, PLASTICITY, AND REPAIR

The human brain has considerable plasticity, although this ability to adapt and change is greater in young children than later in development. Three ways in which a damaged brain might repair itself are collateral sprouting, substitution of function, and neurogenesis. Brain grafts are implants of healthy tissue into damaged brains. Brain grafts are more successful when fetal tissue is used. Stem cell research is a controversial new area of science that may allow for novel treatments for damaged nervous systems.

6. GENETICS AND BEHAVIOR

Chromosomes are threadlike structures that occur in 23 pairs, with one member of each pair coming from each parent. Chromosomes contain the genetic substance deoxyribonucleic acid (DNA). Genes, the units of hereditary information, are short segments of chromosomes composed of DNA. According to the dominant-recessive genes principle, if one gene of a pair is dominant and one is recessive, the dominant gene overrides the recessive gene.

Two important concepts in the study of genetics are the genotype and phenotype. The genotype is an individual's actual genetic material. The phenotype is the observable characteristics of the person.

Different ways of studying heredity's influence are molecular genetics, selective breeding, genome-wide association method, and behavior genetics. Two methods used by behavior geneticists are twin studies and adoption studies.

Both genes and environment play a role in determining the phenotype of an individual. Even for characteristics in which genes play a large role (such as height and eye color), the environment also is a factor.

7. PSYCHOLOGY'S BIOLOGICAL FOUNDATIONS AND HEALTH AND WELLNESS

Stress is the body's response to changes in the environment. Stressors are the agents of those changes—that is, the circumstances and events that threaten the organism. The body's stress response is largely a function of sympathetic nervous system activation that prepares us for action in the face of a threat. The stress response involves slowing down maintenance processes (such as immune function and digestion) in favor of rapid action.

Acute stress is an adaptive response, but chronic stress can have negative consequences for our health. Although stress may be inevitable, our reaction to a stressful event is largely a function of how we think about it.

key terms

apply your *knowledge*

1. Consider the four characteristics of the nervous system discussed in this chapter. Suppose you had to do without one of them. Which would you choose, and what would be the consequences of your decision for your behavior?

2. Do an Internet search for "nutrition" and "the brain." Examine the claims made by one or more of the websites. In light of what you have learned about the nervous system in this chapter, how could nutrition affect brain function? Based on your scientific knowledge, how believable are the claims on the site? Explain.

3. Imagine that you could make one part of your brain twice as big as it is now. Which part would it be, and how do you think your behavior would change as a result? What if you had to make another part of your brain half its current size? Which part would you choose to shrink, and what would the effects be?

4. Search the Internet for information about a humor gene. How would you evaluate research on such a gene, given what you have read so far in this book? What (if anything) would the existence of such a gene mean for your ability to find humor in your life?

5. Do you know anyone who has experienced a brain-damaging event, such as a stroke or head injury? If you feel comfortable doing so, ask the person about the experience and the life changes it may have caused. Based on your interview, which areas of the individual's brain might have been affected?

CHAPTER 4

Sensation and Perception

Our Senses: The World's Greatest Smellers and the World's Worst Smell

For many animals, the sense of smell is crucial for survival. That is how sharks are able to detect a tiny drop of blood more than a mile away. Looking at a snake's rather minimal nose, you might be surprised to learn that snakes have excellent smelling abilities. But snakes do not smell with their noses. They use their tongues. Some birds are outstanding smellers, too. An albatross, soaring above the ocean, swoops down to capture its prey not because it sees that prey but because it smells it.

Consider how we think about the sense of smell. Although someone with a particularly sensitive nose might find a job testing perfumes, in general we do not think of humans as being very strong in the competition for sense of smell. But we might consider entering a contest for creating the world's worst smells! Pamela Dalton, a psychologist who studies sensation, cooked up a concoction that might just take first prize. Dalton created an odor for the U.S. Department of Defense, which was, at the time, considering using odors as nonlethal weapons to fight terrorists. The odor, called "stench soup," pulls together chemicals responsible for the most disgusting smells: "rotting corpses and human excrement" coupled with "a sweet, fruity overtone" (Zitner, 2002).

Like other animals, we use our senses to survive. But we differ from animals in that we also use our noses, tongues, eyes, ears, and skin for many other purposes. The best and the worst aspects of the world around us compete for the title of our favorite (or most detested) smell, flavor, artwork, or song. And, of course, our senses also determine which we prefer—a back rub or a foot rub! ●

PREVIEW

In this chapter we explore sensation and perception, the vital processes by which we connect with and function in the world. We first examine vision, the sense about which scientists know the most. We then investigate the nature of hearing, the skin senses, taste, smell, and the kinesthetic and vestibular senses. Finally, we trace the connections between our senses and health and wellness.

1· HOW WE SENSE AND PERCEIVE THE WORLD

Sensation and perception researchers represent a broad range of specialties, including *ophthalmology,* the study of the eye's structure, function, and diseases; *audiology,* the science concerned with hearing; *neurology/neuroscience,* the scientific study of the nervous system; and many others. Understanding sensation and perception requires comprehending the physical properties of the objects of our perception—light, sound, texture, and so on. The psychological approach to these processes involves understanding the physical structures and functions of the sense organs, as well as the brain's conversion of information from these organs into experience.

The Processes and Purposes of Sensation and Perception

● **sensation** The process of receiving stimulus energies from the external environment and transforming those energies into neural energy.

Our world is alive with stimuli—all the objects and events that surround us. Sensation and perception are the processes through which we detect and understand these various stimuli. We do not actually experience these stimuli directly; rather, our senses allow us to get information about aspects of our environment, and we then take that information and form a perception of the world. **Sensation** is the process of receiving stimulus energies from the external environment and transforming those energies into neural energy. Specialized receptor cells in the sense organs—the eyes, ears, skin, nose, and tongue—detect physical energy, such as light, sound, and heat. When the receptor cells register a stimulus, the energy is converted to an electrochemical impulse or action potential that relays information about the stimulus through the nervous system to the brain (Harris & Attwell, 2012). When it reaches the brain, the information travels to the appropriate area of the cerebral cortex (Swaminathan & Freedman, 2012).

● **perception** The process of organizing and interpreting sensory information so that it makes sense.

The brain gives meaning to sensation through perception. **Perception** is the process of organizing and interpreting sensory information so that it makes sense. Receptor cells in our eyes record—that is, sense—a sleek silver object in the sky, but they do not "see" a jet plane. Recognizing that silver object as a plane is perception. Sensation and perception may seem like the same process as we experience the world, but sensation refers to the raw materials of experience (those energies that form the world) whereas perception is the experience itself (what the brain does with those raw ingredients).

BOTTOM-UP AND TOP-DOWN PROCESSING

● **bottom-up processing** The operation in sensation and perception in which sensory receptors register information about the external environment and send it up to the brain for interpretation.

● **top-down processing** The operation in sensation and perception, launched by cognitive processing at the brain's higher levels, that allows the organism to sense what is happening and to apply that framework to information from the world.

Psychologists distinguish between bottom-up and top-down processing in sensation and perception (Waszak, Pfister, & Kiesel, 2013). In **bottom-up processing,** sensory receptors register information about the external environment and send it up to the brain for interpretation. Bottom-up processing means taking in information and trying to make sense of it (Andersen, Müller, & Martinovic, 2012; McMains & Kastner, 2011). In contrast, **top-down processing** starts with cognitive processing in the brain. In top-down processing we begin with some sense of what is happening (the product of our experiences) and apply that framework to incoming information from the world (Song, Tian, & Liu, 2012; van Gaal & Lamme, 2011).

Top-Down Processing

...that the brain interprets as music.

Thinking about the music...

...creates a preceptual experience in the mind's ear.

Taking in the sounds...

Bottom-Up Processing

FIGURE 4.1   Top-Down and Bottom-Up Processes in Perception When you listen to a song for the first time, bottom-up processing allows you to get a feel for the tune. Once you know the song well, you can create a perceptual experience in your mind's ear, by "playing" it in your head. That's top-down processing.

One way to understand the difference between bottom-up and top-down processing is to think about how you experience a song you have never heard before versus that same song when you have heard it many times (Figure 4.1). The first time you hear the song, you listen carefully to get a "feel" for it. That is bottom-up processing: taking the incoming information of the music and relying on that external experience. Now, once you have a good feel for the song, you listen to it in a different way. You have expectations, and know what comes next. That is top-down processing. You might even sing along with the song when it comes on the radio or at a club. Be careful, though, because top-down expectations are not always accurate, and you might find yourself singing to a remix that differs from what you are used to.

Top-down processing can happen even in the absence of any stimulus at all. You can experience top-down processing by "listening" to your favorite song in your head. As you "hear" the song in your mind's ear, you are engaged in a perceptual experience produced by top-down processing.

Bottom-up and top-down processing work together in sensation and perception to allow us to function accurately and efficiently (K. Meyer, 2011). For example, by themselves our ears provide only incoming information about sound in the environment. Only when we consider both what the ears hear (bottom-up processing) and what the brain interprets (top-down processing) can we fully understand sound perception. In fact, in everyday life, the two processes of sensation and perception are essentially inseparable. For this reason, most psychologists refer to sensation and perception as a unified information-processing system (Goldstein, 2014).

Have you ever begged a friend to listen to your favorite song, only to be disappointed when he or she reacted to it with a shrug? If so, you might note that although all four ears register the same information, perception is a very subjective interpretation of that information. Check out the Psychological Inquiry feature for further perspective on the difference between sensation and perception.

THE PURPOSES OF SENSATION AND PERCEPTION

Why do we perceive the world? From an evolutionary perspective, the purpose of sensation and perception is adaptation that improves a species' chances for survival. An organism must be able to sense and respond quickly and accurately to events in the immediate environment, such as the approach of a predator, the presence of prey, or the appearance of a potential mate.

Not surprisingly, therefore, most animals—from goldfish to gorillas to humans—have eyes and ears, as well as sensitivities to touch and chemicals (smell and taste) (Moss & Carr, 2013). Furthermore, a close comparison of sensory systems in animals reveals that

Most predatory animals have eyes at the front of their face; most animals that are prey have eyes on the sides of their head. Through these adaptations, predators perceive their prey accurately, and prey gain a measure of safety from their panoramic view of their environment.

psychological *inquiry*

Old Woman or Young Woman?

Study the illustration and analyze your perceptions by answering these questions.

1. What do you see? If you see an old woman, can you see a young woman as well? (Hint: The old woman's nose is the young woman's jawline.) If you see a young woman, can you see an old woman as well? (Hint: The young woman's chin is the tip of the old woman's nose.)

2. How many pictures do you sense visually in the illustration? Notice that for each of *two* possible perceptions, just *one image* is sensed.

3. What do you think determined your first response to this picture? Explain.

each species is exquisitely adapted to the habitat in which it evolved (Hoefnagels, 2012; Jacobs, 2013). Animals that are primarily predators generally have their eyes at the front of their face so that they can perceive their prey accurately. In contrast, animals that are more likely to be someone else's lunch have their eyes on the sides of their head, giving them a wide view of their surroundings at all times.

The remarkable smellers we considered at the beginning of this chapter provide excellent examples of this match between an animal's need to survive and its sense organs. Sharks rely so heavily on smell that two-thirds of a shark's brain is wired for smell. The albatross that relies on smells to detect prey under the surface of the water has an especially large nose at the top of its beak for just this purpose, allowing it to capture food even in the dark. Looking in a mirror, you might consider the evidence you find there of the important ways that humans' sense organs are adapted for the world in which we live.

Sensory Receptors and the Brain

● **sensory receptors** Specialized cells that detect stimulus information and transmit it to sensory (afferent) nerves and the brain.

All sensation begins with **sensory receptors,** specialized cells that detect stimulus information and transmit it to sensory (*afferent*) nerves and the brain (Sherwood, Klandorf, & Yancey, 2013). Afferent nerves bring information to the brain from the world. Sensory receptors are the openings through which the brain and nervous system experience the world. Figure 4.2 shows the human sensory receptors for vision, hearing, touch, smell, and taste.

Figure 4.3 depicts the flow of information from the environment to the brain. Sensory receptors take in information from the environment, creating local electrical currents. The receptors trigger action potentials in sensory neurons, which carry that information to the central nervous system. Of course, stimuli in the environment differ in their intensity. Candlelight, for instance, is a great deal dimmer than the beam of a searchlight. How do sensory neurons communicate these differences in intensity to the brain? Because sensory neurons (like all neurons) follow the all-or-nothing principle,

	Vision	Hearing	Touch	Smell	Taste
Sensory Receptor Cells					
Type of Energy Reception	Photoreception: detection of light, perceived as sight	Mechano-reception: detection of vibration, perceived as hearing	Mechano-reception: detection of pressure, perceived as touch	Chemoreception: detection of chemical stimuli, perceived as smell	Chemoreception: detection of chemical stimuli, perceived as taste
Sense Organ	Eyes	Ears	Skin	Nose	Tongue

FIGURE 4.2 **Human Senses: Organs, Energy Stimuli, and Sensory Receptors** The receptor cells for each sense are specialized to receive particular types of energy stimuli.

described in Chapter 3, the intensity of the stimulus, such as that of a dim versus a bright light, cannot be communicated to the brain by changing the strength of the action potential. That strength is the same no matter the intensity of the stimulus. Instead, the receptor varies the *frequency* of action potentials sent to the brain. So, if a stimulus is very intense, like the bright sun on a hot day, the neuron will fire more frequently to let the brain know that the light is, indeed, very, very bright.

Other than frequency, the action potentials of all sensory nerves are alike. This sameness raises an intriguing question: How can an animal distinguish among sight, sound, odor, taste, and touch? The answer is that sensory receptors are selective and have different neural pathways. They are specialized to absorb a particular type of energy—light energy, sound vibrations, or chemical energy, for example—and convert it into an action potential.

Sensation involves detecting and transmitting information about different kinds of energy (Sherwood, 2013). The sense organs and sensory receptors fall into several main classes based on the type of energy that is detected, including

- *Photoreception:* detection of light, perceived as sight
- *Mechanoreception:* detection of pressure, vibration, and movement, perceived as touch, hearing, and equilibrium
- *Chemoreception:* detection of chemical stimuli, perceived as smell and taste

Each of these processes belongs to a particular class of receptors and brain processes. There are rare cases, however, in which the senses can become confused. The term *synaesthesia* describes an experience in which one sense (say, sight) induces an experience in another sense (say, hearing) (Simner, 2012a, 2012b; White & Aimola Davies, 2012). For example, a person might "see" music or "taste" a color. One woman was able to taste sounds, so that a piece of music, to her, tasted like tuna fish (Beeli, Esslen, & Jancke, 2005). Neuroscientists are exploring the neurological bases of synaesthesia, especially in the connections among the various sensory regions of the

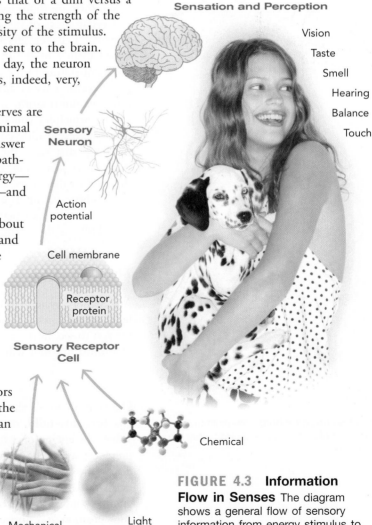

FIGURE 4.3 **Information Flow in Senses** The diagram shows a general flow of sensory information from energy stimulus to sensory receptor cell to sensory neuron to sensation and perception.

cerebral cortex (Chiou, Stelter, & Rich, 2013; Neufeld & others, 2012; Niccolai, Wascher, & Stoerig, 2012).

Phantom limb pain is another example of confused senses. Among individuals who have lost an arm or a leg, as many as 95 percent of them report alarming and puzzling pain in the amputated limb. Although the limb that contains the sensory receptors is gone, the areas of the brain and nervous system that received information from those receptors are still there, causing confusion (Elbert, 2012; Foell & others, 2011).

Amputee veterans of combat in Iraq and Afghanistan have found some relief in an unexpected place: looking in a mirror. In this treatment, individuals place a mirror in front of their existing limb and move the limb around while watching the mirror. So, if a person's left leg has been amputated, the mirror is placed so that the right leg is seen moving in the mirror where the left leg would be if it had not been amputated. This procedure seems to trick the brain into perceiving the missing limb as still there, allowing it to make sense of incoming sensation (Flor & Diers, 2009).

The success of this mirror therapy demonstrates how our senses cooperate to produce experience—how the bottom-up processes (the incoming messages from the missing limb) and the top-down processes (the brain's efforts to make sense of these messages) work together. Although promising, a research review concluded that mirror therapy has mixed results in treating phantom leg syndrome (Subedi & Grossberg, 2011).

In the brain, nearly all sensory signals go through the thalamus, the brain's relay station. From the thalamus, the signals go to the sensory areas of the cerebral cortex, where they are modified and spread throughout a vast network of neurons.

Certain areas of the cerebral cortex are specialized to handle different sensory functions (C. I. Baker, 2013; Kaas, O'Brien, & Hackett, 2013). Visual information is processed mainly in the occipital lobes; hearing in the temporal lobes; and pain, touch, and temperature in the parietal lobes. Keep in mind, however, that the interactions and pathways of sensory information are complex, and the brain often must coordinate extensive information and interpret it (Coren, 2013; van Atteveldt & others, 2010).

The principles you have read about so far apply to all of the senses. The senses are about detecting different energies. They all have specialized receptor cells and areas of the brain that serve their functions. You have probably heard about a "sixth" sense—*extrasensory perception,* or *ESP*. ESP means that a person can detect information from the world without receiving concrete sensory input. Examples of ESP include *telepathy* (the ability to read another person's mind) and *precognition* (the ability to sense future events). Do human beings have a sixth sense? To read more about how psychologists view ESP, see the Critical Controversy on page 109.

Thresholds

Any sensory system must be able to detect varying degrees of energy in the form of light, sound, chemical, or mechanical stimulation. How much of a stimulus is necessary for you to see, hear, taste, smell, or feel something? What is the lowest possible amount of stimulation that will still be detected?

ABSOLUTE THRESHOLD

● **absolute threshold** The minimum amount of stimulus energy that a person can detect.

One way to think about the lowest limits of perception is to assume that there is an **absolute threshold,** or minimum amount of stimulus energy that a person can detect. When the energy of a stimulus falls below this absolute threshold, we cannot detect its presence; when the energy of the stimulus rises above the absolute threshold, we can detect the stimulus (Lim, Kyung, & Kwon, 2012). As an example, find a clock that ticks; put it on a table and walk far enough away that you no longer hear it. Then gradually move toward the clock. At some point, you will begin to hear it ticking. Hold your position and notice that occasionally the ticking fades, and you may have to move forward to reach the threshold; at other times, it may become loud, and you can move backward.

CRITICAL CONTROVERSY

Can We Feel the Future?

Some people report experiences that seem to involve precognition—for instance, "just knowing" that a friend is in trouble and later finding out that he was in a car accident. Such experiences can be fascinating and even spooky, but do they reflect the existence of extrasensory perception (ESP) or is it a simple coincidence?

In truth, the notion that human beings can sense future events challenges the basic principle that cause precedes effect (and not the other way around). Paraphrasing French mathematician Pierre-Simon Laplace, the American astrophysicist Carl Sagan famously observed, "Extraordinary claims require extraordinary evidence." The assertion that ESP exists is an extraordinary claim. Is the evidence for this claim equally extraordinary? For most psychologists, the answer is a definite no (French & others, 2008; R. Hyman, 2010; Wiseman & Watt, 2006).

Social psychologist Daryl Bem (2011) rekindled the ESP debate, publishing nine studies testing for the existence of precognition. In eight of those studies, Bem claimed to show that future events could influence present behavior. For example, in one study, participants saw two pictures of curtains on a computer screen. They were told that one curtain had a picture behind it, and the other did not. Their task was to select the curtain with a picture. Some of the pictures contained erotic images; others showed positive, negative, or neutral images. The computer randomly placed the pictures behind the curtains *after* participants had made their guesses. A staunch believer in ESP, Bem predicted that participants would select the curtain that would eventually show the erotic images at rates greater than chance—and the results did reveal that they had selected that curtain 53.1 percent of the time (higher than the chance rate of 50 percent). Bem concluded that these choices were *caused* by the *future event* of the erotic image being placed behind the curtain.

Bem's findings and their publication in the prestigious *Journal of Personality and Social Psychology* caused an uproar, inspiring articles in the *New York Times* (Carey, 2011b) and *Science* (G. Miller, 2011); a flurry of activity in the blogosphere; and an appearance by Bem himself on the *Colbert Report*. Among other things, critics of Bem's work pointed to inconsistencies across the studies (LeBel & Peters, 2011; Wagenmakers & others, 2011). For instance, in some studies precognition was shown for erotic (but not negative) images; in others for negative (but not erotic) images; in other studies women (but not men) showed precognition; and in other cases only extraverts did.

The statistical tests Bem used are at the heart of the controversy. To understand this issue, reconsider the questions posed above: Do Bem's results reflect ESP—or simple coincidence? Psychologists typically use statistics to determine whether an effect is real or a matter of chance (or coincidence). In the results

© Betsy Streeter. www.CartoonStock.com.

just described, participants were 3.1 percent more likely than chance to select the curtain with the erotic image. Is this difference extraordinary evidence for an extraordinary claim?

Before answering, consider the following situation. Imagine that you are offered $1 million if you can accurately assess whether a coin is rigged (that is, biased to produce more heads than tails). If you flip that coin 100 times and it comes up heads 53 times, should you conclude the coin is biased? How sure are you of your conclusion? How many times will you need to repeat your test to be sure?

The probability of Bem's obtaining his result completely by chance was 1 in 100. But is 1 in 100 convincing enough to support the existence of a phenomenon that challenges the very nature of cause and effect? Many critics answered that question with a resounding no (R. Hyman, 2010; Kruschke, 2011; LeBel & Peters, 2011; G. Miller, 2011; Schimmack, 2013; Wagenmakers & others, 2011; Wetzels & others, 2011). Jeffrey Rouder and Richard Morey (2011) applied a different statistical tool to Bem's studies and concluded that although there might be some evidence in Bem's data for the existence of precognition, it was too slight to overcome the appropriate level of skepticism that scholars require for findings that involve suspending the laws of physics.

Clearly, although an important tool, statistics are not a direct pathway to truth. Statistics are not a substitute for a sound rationale for predictions and conclusions. Raymond Hyman (2010), a longtime critic of research on ESP, argues that in the absence of a theory about why or how precognition exists, along with independently repeatable methods, any evidence for the phenomenon is suspect.

There are many reasons to question the existence of ESP. Think about precognition in the ways we have studied sensation and perception. Sensation involves detecting energy from the environment. If ESP exists, consider this: Which afferent neurons send psychic messages from the future to the brain, and what sort of energy conveys these messages? Scientists who study ESP have not produced answers to these important questions.

The controversy over Bem's paper highlights a tension within science between openness and enthusiasm for ideas (no matter how strange or counterintuitive they might seem) and a deep and intense skepticism. Recognizing this difficult tension between wonder and skepticism, Carl Sagan concluded about science, "This is how deep truths are winnowed from deep nonsense."

WHAT DO YOU THINK

- Do you believe in the phenomenon of ESP? Why or why not?
- What kind of evidence would be necessary for you to change your belief?
- Should research on ESP be held to a higher standard than other research? Explain.

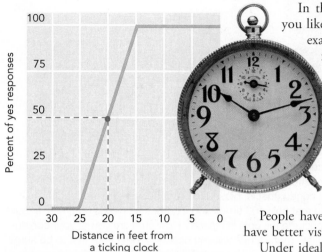

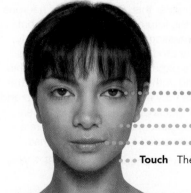

FIGURE 4.4 Measuring Absolute Threshold Absolute threshold is the minimum amount of energy we can detect. To measure absolute threshold, psychologists have arbitrarily decided to use the criterion of detecting the stimulus 50 percent of the time. In this graph, the person's absolute threshold for detecting the ticking clock is at a distance of 20 feet.

● **noise** Irrelevant and competing stimuli—not only sounds but also any distracting stimuli for the senses.

● **difference threshold** The degree of difference that must exist between two stimuli before the difference is detected.

In this experiment, if you measure your absolute threshold several times, you likely will record several different distances for detecting the stimulus. For example, the first time you try it, you might hear the ticking at 25 feet from the clock. However, you probably will not hear it every time at 25 feet. Maybe you hear it only 38 percent of the time at this distance, but you hear it 50 percent of the time at 20 feet away and 65 percent of the time at 15 feet. Figure 4.4 shows one person's measured absolute threshold for detecting a clock's ticking sound. Psychologists have arbitrarily decided that absolute threshold is the point at which the individual detects the stimulus 50 percent of the time—in this case, 20 feet away. Using the same clock, another person might have a measured absolute threshold of 26 feet, and yet another, 18 feet.

People have different thresholds. Some have better hearing than others, and some have better vision. Figure 4.5 lists the approximate absolute thresholds of five senses.

Under ideal circumstances, our senses have very low absolute thresholds, so we can be remarkably good at detecting small amounts of stimulus energy. You might be surprised to learn that the human eye can see a candle flame at 30 miles on a dark, clear night. However, our environment seldom gives us ideal conditions with which to detect stimuli. If the night were cloudy, for example, you would have to be closer to see the candle flame. In addition, other lights on the horizon—car or house lights—would hinder your ability to detect the candle's flicker. **Noise** is the term given to irrelevant and competing stimuli—not just sounds but any distracting stimuli for the senses (Ikeda, Sekiguchi, & Hayashi, 2010).

DIFFERENCE THRESHOLD

Psychologists also investigate the degree of *difference* that must exist between two stimuli before the difference is detected. This is the **difference threshold,** or *just noticeable difference.* An artist might detect the difference between two similar shades of color. A fashion designer might notice a difference in the texture of two fabrics. How different must the colors and textures be for someone to say, "These are different"? Like the absolute threshold, the difference threshold is the smallest difference in stimulation required to discriminate one stimulus from another 50 percent of the time.

What determines whether we can detect the difference between two stimuli? Difference thresholds increase as a stimulus becomes stronger. That means that at very low levels of stimulation, small changes can be detected, but at very high levels, small changes are less noticeable. When music is playing softly, you may notice when your roommate increases the volume by even a small amount. If, however, he or she turns the volume up an equal amount when the music is already playing very loudly, you may not notice. If you are carrying one heavy book in your backpack, you might notice the addition of a smaller volume. But, if you are carrying two heavy books, you might not even notice the additional weight of that slim volume.

Vision A candle flame at 30 miles on a dark, clear night

Hearing A ticking clock at 20 feet under quiet conditions

Smell One drop of perfume diffused throughout three rooms

Taste A teaspoon of sugar in 2 gallons of water

Touch The wing of a fly falling on your neck from a distance of 1 centimeter

FIGURE 4.5 Approximate Absolute Thresholds for Five Senses These thresholds show the amazing power of our senses to detect even very slight variations in the environment.

psychological *inquiry*

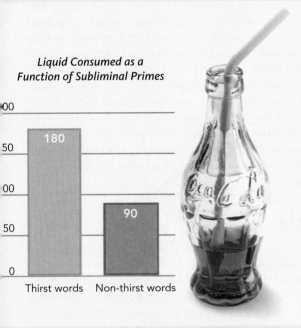

Liquid Consumed as a Function of Subliminal Primes

Thirst words: 180
Non-thirst words: 90

Subliminal Perception: Working Up a Thirst

This graph is adapted from the results of the study by Erin Strahan, Steven Spencer, and Mark Zanna (2002) described in the text. The dependent variable is represented on the vertical, or Y, axis. The columns represent the results of the study for each of the two groups—those who were exposed to "thirst words" and those who saw "non-thirst words." Answer the following questions.

1. What was the independent variable in this study? Explain.
2. Which group would be considered the experimental group? Which is the control group?
3. Why were the participants randomly assigned to conditions?

E. H. Weber made an important discovery about the difference threshold more than 150 years ago. **Weber's law** is the principle that two stimuli must differ by a constant proportion to be perceived as different. For example, we add 1 candle to 20 candles and notice a difference in the brightness of the candles; we add 1 candle to 120 candles and do not notice a difference, but we would notice the difference if we added 6 candles to 120 candles. Weber's law generally holds true (Mohring, Libertus, & Bertin, 2012).

● **Weber's law** The principle that two stimuli must differ by a constant minimum percentage (rather than a constant amount) to be perceived as different.

SUBLIMINAL PERCEPTION

Can sensations that occur below our absolute threshold affect us without our being aware of them? **Subliminal perception** refers to the detection of information below the level of conscious awareness. In 1957, James Vicary, an advertising executive, announced that he was able to increase popcorn and soft drink sales by secretly flashing the words "EAT POPCORN" and "DRINK COKE" on a movie screen in a local theater (Weir, 1984). Vicary's claims were a hoax, but people have continued to wonder whether behavior can be influenced by stimuli that are presented so quickly that we cannot perceive them. Studies have shown that the brain responds to information that is presented below the conscious threshold, and such information can influence behavior (Dupoux, de Gardelle, & Kouider, 2008; Radel, Sarrazin, & Pelletier, 2009; Tsushima, Sasaki, & Watanabe, 2006).

In one study researchers randomly assigned participants to come to the study having not had anything to drink for at least 3 hours prior (Strahan, Spencer, & Zanna, 2002). The participants were shown either words related to being thirsty (such as *dry* and *thirst*) or other words of the same length not related to thirst (such as *won* and *pirate*) flashed on a computer screen for 16 milliseconds while they performed an unrelated task. None of the participants reported actually seeing the flashed words. After this subliminal exposure to thirst or non-thirst words, participants were allowed to drink a beverage. When given a chance to drink afterward, those who had seen thirst-related words drank more. The Psychological Inquiry feature explores the results of the study.

● **subliminal perception** The detection of information below the level of conscious awareness.

The notion that stimuli we do not consciously perceive can influence our behavior challenges the usefulness of the idea of thresholds (Rouder & Morey, 2009). If stimuli that fall below the threshold can have an impact on us, you may be wondering, what do thresholds really tell us?

Further, you might have noticed that the definition of absolute threshold is not very absolute. It refers to the intensity of stimulation detected *50 percent of the time*. How can something absolute change from one trial to the next? If, for example, you tried the ticking clock experiment described earlier, you might have found yourself making judgment calls. Sometimes you felt very sure you could hear the clock, but other times you were uncertain and probably took a guess. Sometimes you guessed right, and other times you were mistaken. Now, imagine that someone offered to pay you $50 for every correct answer you gave—would that incentive change your judgments? Alternatively, what if you were charged $50 for every time you said you heard the clock and it was not ticking? In fact, perception is often about making such judgment calls.

An alternative approach to the question of whether a stimulus is detected acknowledges that saying (or not saying) "Yes, I hear that ticking" is actually a decision. This approach is called *signal detection theory*.

Signal Detection Theory

Signal detection theory focuses on decision making about stimuli under conditions of uncertainty. In signal detection theory, detection of sensory stimuli depends on a variety of factors besides the physical intensity of the stimulus and the sensory abilities of the observer (Haase & Fisk, 2011; Lim & Merfeld, 2012). These factors include individual and contextual variations, such as fatigue, expectations, and the urgency of the moment.

To grasp how signal detection theory works, consider this scenario. Your cousin is getting married in a week, and you are looking for a date for the wedding. While studying at the library, you see a potential candidate, someone with whom you have exchanged glances before. Now you face a decision: Should you proceed to ask this person out? Is the signal (that is, a good date for the wedding) present? You scan your library acquaintance for indications of availability (no wedding or engagement ring) and interest (didn't he or she smile at you as you passed by earlier?). You consider other information as well: Do you find the person attractive? Does he or she seem friendly? Based on these factors, you decide that (1) yes, you will ask the person to the wedding (because you have determined that the signal is present) or (2) no, you will keep looking (the signal is not present). These decisions might be correct or incorrect, leading to four possible outcomes (Figure 4.6):

■ Hit: You ask, and he or she says yes.

■ Miss: He or she would have said yes, but you do not ask.

■ False alarm: You think the individual seemed interested, but your offer is politely declined—ouch.

■ Correct rejection: You do not ask the person out, and he or she would have said no—whew.

● **signal detection theory** An approach to perception that focuses on decision making about stimuli under conditions of uncertainty.

Decision making in signal detection theory has two main components: information acquisition and criterion. *Information acquisition* refers to the gathering of relevant indicators. *Criterion* refers to the standards that will be used to make a decision. In terms of information acquisition, the question applicable to our example is, what information is the person who is your potential wedding date communicating? Is the person available? Attractive? And so on. The criterion component of signal detection theory is the basis for making a judgment from the available information. The criterion is the decision maker's assessment of the stakes involved in each possible outcome. Is a miss (not asking out someone who would have said yes) or a false alarm (getting turned down) a worse outcome? Is

	Observer's Response	
	"Yes, I see the signal."	"No, I don't see the signal."
Signal Present	Hit (correct)	Miss (mistake)
Signal Absent	False alarm (mistake)	Correct rejection (correct)

FIGURE 4.6 Four Outcomes in Signal Detection Signal detection research helps to explain when and how perceptual judgments are correct or mistaken.

getting a "hit" worth surviving some false alarms? So, in addition to relying on the characteristics of your potential wedding date, you might also be feeling desperate, because your family is always giving you a hard time about never having a date. Maybe getting a lot of rejections (false alarms) is not as bad as missing an opportunity to keep them quiet. Alternatively, you may feel that rejections are just too upsetting and prefer to experience "misses" even if it means going stag to your cousin's wedding.

Let's return now to the domain of sensation and perception. Can you see how signal detection theory might provide a way to examine the processes that underlie our judgments about whether we perceive a stimulus or not? By presenting stimuli of varying intensities, as well as trials when no stimulus is presented at all, and by asking a research participant to report on his or her detection of the sound or sight of interest, a researcher can use signal detection theory to understand the results. Importantly, signal detection theory allows us to consider the mistakes a perceiver might make—and the reasons behind those errors (Chaudhuri & Merfeld, 2013).

Perceiving Sensory Stimuli

As we just saw, perception of stimuli is influenced by more than the characteristics of the environmental stimuli themselves. Two important factors in perceiving sensory stimuli are attention and perceptual set.

ATTENTION

Attention is the process of focusing awareness on a narrowed aspect of the environment. The world holds a lot of information to perceive. At this moment you are perceiving the letters and words that make up this sentence. Now gaze around you and fix your eyes on something other than this book. Afterward, curl up the toes on your right foot. In each of these activities, you engaged in **selective attention,** which involves focusing on a specific aspect of experience while ignoring others (Lamy, Leber, & Egeth, 2013; Reel & Hicks, 2012). A familiar example of selective attention is the ability to concentrate on one voice among many in a crowded airline terminal or noisy restaurant. Psychologists call this common occurrence the *cocktail party effect* (Kuyper, 1972).

Highly practiced and familiar stimuli, such as your own name and hometown, often are perceived so automatically that it is almost impossible to ignore them. The *Stroop effect,* named for John Ridley Stroop (1935), who first showed the effect, refers to the way that automatically reading a color name can make it difficult to name the color in which the word is printed. To experience the Stroop effect, see Figure 4.7. Most of the time, the highly practiced and almost automatic perception of word meaning makes

● **attention** The process of focusing awareness on a narrowed aspect of the environment.

● **selective attention** The act of focusing on a specific aspect of experience while ignoring others.

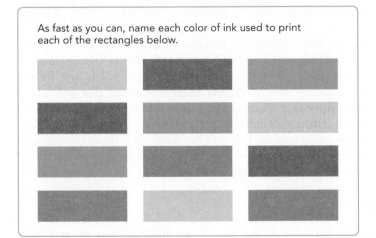

As fast as you can, name each color of ink used to print each of the rectangles below.

Now, as fast as you can, name the color of ink used to print each word shown below, ignoring what each word says.

GREEN   BLUE   RED
RED   GREEN   BLUE
YELLOW   RED   YELLOW
BLUE   YELLOW   GREEN

FIGURE 4.7   The Stroop Effect Before reading further, read the instructions above and complete the tasks. You probably had little or no difficulty naming the colors of the rectangles in the set on the left. However, you likely stumbled more when you were asked to name the color of ink used to print each word in the set on the right. This automaticity in perception is the Stroop effect.

reading easier. However, this automaticity makes it hard to ignore the meaning of the words for colors (such as *blue*) when they are printed in a different color (such as orange). Thus, the Stroop effect represents a failure of selective attention.

Attention not only is selective but also is *shiftable.* For example, you might be paying close attention to your instructor's lecture, but if the person next to you starts texting, you might look to see what is going on over there. The fact that we can attend selectively to one stimulus and shift readily to another indicates that we must be monitoring many things at once.

Certain features of stimuli draw attention to them. *Novel stimuli* (those that are new, different, or unusual) often attract our attention. *Size, color, and movement* also influence our attention; we are more likely to attend to objects that are large, vividly colored, or moving than objects that are small, dull-colored, or stationary. In addition, *emotional stimuli* can influence attention and therefore perception (Stewart & others, 2010).

In the case of emotional stimuli, here is how the process works. An emotionally laden stimulus, such as the word *torture,* captures our attention. As a result, we are often quicker and more accurate at identifying an emotional stimulus than a neutral stimulus. This advantage for emotional stimuli may come at a cost to other stimuli we experience. The term *emotion-induced blindness* refers to the fact that when we encounter an emotionally charged stimulus, we often fail to recognize a stimulus that is presented immediately after it (Bocanegra & Zeelenberg, 2009; Kennedy & Most, 2012; Wang, Kennedy, & Most, 2012). Imagine, for example, that you are driving along a highway, and an ambulance, with sirens screaming and lights flashing, whizzes by. You might not notice the other cars around you or a road sign because you are preoccupied by the ambulance.

Sometimes, especially if our attention is otherwise occupied, we miss even very interesting stimuli. *Inattentional blindness* refers to the failure to detect unexpected events when our attention is engaged by a task (Castel, Vendetti, & Holyoak, 2012). For instance, when we are focusing intently on a task, such as finding a seat in a packed movie theater, we might not detect an unexpected stimulus such as a friend waving to us in the crowd.

Research conducted by Daniel Simons and Christopher Chabris (1999) provides a striking example of inattentional blindness. The researchers asked participants to watch a video of two teams playing basketball. The participants were instructed to closely count the number of passes thrown by each team. During the video, a small woman dressed in a gorilla suit walked through the action and was clearly visible for 5 seconds. Surprisingly, over half of the participants (who were apparently deeply engaged in the counting task) never noticed the "gorilla." When they later saw the video without having to count passes, many of the participants could not believe they had missed a gorilla in their midst (Chabris & Simons, 2010). Inattentional blindness is more likely to occur when a task is difficult (Macdonald & Lavie, 2008) and when the distracting stimulus is very different from stimuli that are relevant to the task at hand (Wiemer, Gerdes, & Pauli, 2012).

Emotion-induced blindness and inattentional blindness have important implications for driving safety (Pammer & Blink, 2013). Engaging in a task such as talking on a cell phone or sending text messages can so occupy attention that little is left over for the important task of piloting a motor vehicle. Recent research revealed that individuals who text message while they drive face 23 times the risk of a crash or near-crash compared to nondistracted drivers (Blanco & others, 2009; Hanowski & others, 2009). In this research, cameras continuously observed drivers for more than 6 million miles of driving. Texting drew the drivers' eyes away from the road long enough for the vehicle to travel the length of a football field at 55 miles an hour.

PERCEPTUAL SET

Place your hand over the playing cards on the right in the illustration on the next page and look at the playing cards on the left. As quickly as you can, count how many aces of spades you see. Then place your hand over the cards on the left and count the number of aces of spades among the cards on the right.

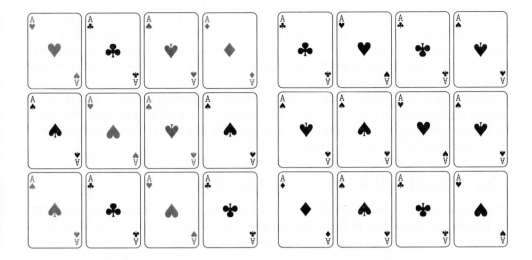

Most people report that they see two or three aces of spades in the set of cards on the left. However, if you look closely, you will see that there are five. Two of the aces of spades are black and three are red. When people look at the set of cards on the right, they are more likely to count five aces of spades. Why do we perceive the two sets of cards differently? We expect the ace of spades to be black because it is always black in a regular deck of cards. We do not expect red spades, so we skip right over the red ones: Expectations influence perceptions.

Psychologists refer to a predisposition or readiness to perceive something in a particular way as a **perceptual set.** Perceptual sets, which reflect top-down influences on perception, act as psychological filters in processing information about the environment (Fei-Fei & others, 2007). Interestingly, young children are more accurate than adults at the task involving the ace of spades. The reason is that they have not built up the perceptual set that the ace of spades is black.

● **perceptual set** A predisposition or readiness to perceive something in a particular way.

Sensory Adaptation

Turning out the lights in your bedroom at night, you stumble across the room to your bed, blind to the objects around you. Gradually the objects reappear and become clearer. The ability of the visual system to adjust to a darkened room is an example of **sensory adaptation**—a change in the responsiveness of the sensory system based on the average level of surrounding stimulation (Iglesias, 2012; Elliott & others, 2009).

You have experienced sensory adaptation countless times in your life. For example, you adjust to the water in an initially "freezing" swimming pool. You turn on your windshield wipers while driving in the rain, and shortly you are unaware of their rhythmic sweeping back and forth. You enter a room and are at first bothered by the air conditioner's hum, but after a while you get used to it. All of these experiences represent sensory adaptation.

In the example of adapting to the dark, when you turn out the lights, everything at first is black. Conversely, when you step out into the bright sunshine after spending time in a dark basement, light floods your eyes and everything appears light. These momentary blips in sensation arise because adaptation takes time.

● **sensory adaptation** A change in the responsiveness of the sensory system based on the average level of surrounding stimulation.

test yourself

1. What are sensation and perception? How are they linked?
2. Compare and contrast top-down and bottom-up processing.
3. What is meant by the terms *absolute threshold* and *difference threshold*? What is *subliminal perception*?

2· THE VISUAL SYSTEM

When Michael May of Davis, California, was 3 years old, an accident left him visually impaired, with only the ability to perceive the difference between night and day. He went on to live a rich, full life, marrying and having children, founding a successful company, and becoming an expert skier. Twenty-five years passed before doctors transplanted stem cells into May's right eye, a procedure that gave him partial sight (Kurson, 2007). May can now see; his right eye is functional and allows him to detect color and negotiate the world without the use of a cane or reliance on his seeing-eye dog. His visual experience remains unusual, however, in that he sees the world as if it is an abstract painting. He can catch a ball thrown to him by his sons, but he cannot recognize his wife's face. Importantly, his brain has to work at interpreting the new information that his right eye is providing.

May's experience highlights the intimate connection between the brain and the sense organs in producing perception. Vision is a remarkable process that involves the brain's interpretation of the visual information sent from the eyes. Let's now explore the physical foundations of the visual system.

The Visual Stimulus and the Eye

When you see the beautiful colors of a fall day, what your eyes and brain are responding to is really the differences in light reflected from the various colorful leaves. Our ability to detect visual stimuli depends on the sensitivity of our eyes to differences in light.

LIGHT

Light is a form of electromagnetic energy that can be described in terms of wavelengths. Light travels through space in waves. The *wavelength* of light is the distance from the peak of one wave to the peak of the next. Wavelengths of visible light range from about 400 to 700 nanometers (a nanometer is 1 billionth of a meter and is abbreviated nm). The wavelength of light that is reflected from a stimulus determines its *hue* or color.

Outside the range of visible light are longer radio and infrared radiation waves and shorter ultraviolet and X rays (Figure 4.8). These other forms of electromagnetic energy continually bombard us, but we do not see them.

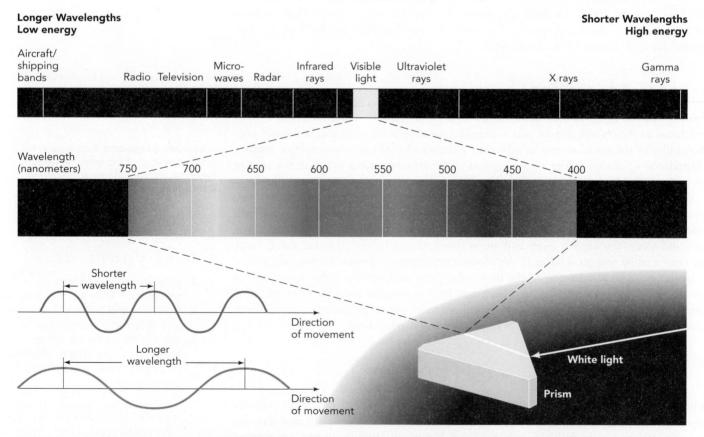

FIGURE 4.8 The Electromagnetic Spectrum and Visible Light (*Top*) Visible light is only a narrow band in the electromagnetic spectrum. Visible light wavelengths range from about 400 to 700 nm. X rays are much shorter; radio waves, much longer. (*Bottom*) The two graphs show how waves vary in length between successive peaks. Shorter wavelengths are higher in frequency, as reflected in blue colors; longer wavelengths are lower in frequency, as reflected in red colors.

We can also describe waves of light in terms of their height, or *amplitude,* which determines the brightness of the stimulus (Figure 4.9). Finally, the *purity* of the wavelengths—whether they are all the same or a mix of waves—determines the perceived *saturation,* or richness, of a visual stimulus. The color tree shown in Figure 4.10 can help you to understand saturation. Colors that are very pure have no white light in them. They are located on the outside of the color tree. Notice how the closer we get to the center of the color tree, the more white light has been added to the single wavelength of a particular color. In other words, the deep colors at the edge fade into pastel colors toward the center.

THE STRUCTURE OF THE EYE

The eye, like a camera, is constructed to get the best possible picture of the world. An accurate picture is in focus, is not too dark or too light, and has good contrast between the dark and light parts. Each of several structures in the eye plays an important role in this process.

If you look closely at your eyes in the mirror, you will notice three parts—the sclera, iris, and pupil (Figure 4.11). The *sclera* is the white, outer part of the eye that helps to maintain the shape of the eye and to protect it from injury. The *iris* is the colored part of the eye, which might be light blue in one individual and dark brown in another. The *pupil,* which appears black, is the opening in the center of the iris. The iris contains muscles that control the size of the pupil and, hence, the amount of light that gets into the eye. To get a good picture of the world, the eye needs to be able to adjust the amount of light that enters. In this sense, the pupil acts like the aperture of a camera, opening to let in more light when it is needed and closing to let in less light when there is too much.

Two structures bring the image into focus: the *cornea,* a clear membrane just in front of the eye, and the *lens,* a transparent and somewhat flexible, disklike structure filled with a gelatinous material. The function of both of these structures is to bend the light falling on the surface of the eye just enough to focus it at the back. The curved surface of the cornea does most of this bending, while the lens fine-tunes things. When you are looking at faraway objects, the lens has a relatively flat shape because the light reaching the eye from faraway objects is parallel, and the bending power of the cornea is sufficient to keep things in focus. However, the light reaching the eye from objects that are close is more scattered, so more bending of the light is required to achieve focus.

Without this ability of the lens to change its curvature, the eye would have a tough time focusing on close objects such as reading material. As we get older, the lens loses its flexibility and hence its ability to change from its normal flattened shape to the rounder shape needed to bring close objects into focus. That is why many people with normal vision throughout their young adult lives require reading glasses as they age.

The parts of the eye we have considered so far work together to give us the sharpest picture of the world. This effort would be useless, however, without a vehicle for recording the images the eyes take of the world—in essence, the film of the camera. Photographic film is made of a material that responds to light. At the back of the eye is the eye's "film," the multilayered **retina,** which is the light-sensitive surface that records electromagnetic energy and converts it to neural impulses for processing in the brain. The analogy between the retina and film goes only so far, however. The retina is amazingly complex and elegantly designed. It is, in fact, the primary mechanism of sight. Even after decades of intense study, the full marvel of this structure is far from understood (Collin & others, 2012; Herberstein & Kemp, 2012).

The human retina has approximately 126 million receptor cells. They turn the electromagnetic energy of light into a form of energy that the nervous system can process. There are two kinds of visual receptor cells: rods and cones. Rods and cones differ both in how they respond to light and in their patterns of distribution on the surface of the retina. **Rods** are the receptors in the retina that are sensitive to light, but they are not

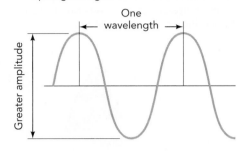

Light waves of greater amplitude make up brighter light.

Greater amplitude

One wavelength

Light waves of smaller amplitude make up dimmer light.

Smaller amplitude

One wavelength

FIGURE 4.9 Light Waves of Varying Amplitude The top graph might suggest a spotlight on a concert stage; the bottom might represent a candlelit dinner.

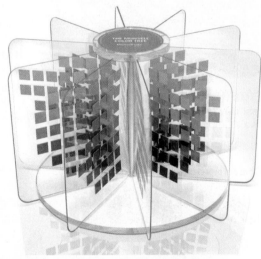

FIGURE 4.10   A Color Tree Showing Color's Three Dimensions: Hue, Saturation, and Brightness Hue is represented around the color tree—saturation horizontally and brightness vertically.

● **retina** The multilayered light-sensitive surface in the eye that records electromagnetic energy and converts it to neural impulses for processing in the brain.

● **rods** The receptor cells in the retina that are sensitive to light but not very useful for color vision.

FIGURE 4.11 Parts of the Eye
Note that the image of the butterfly on the retina is upside down. The brain allows us to see the image right side up.

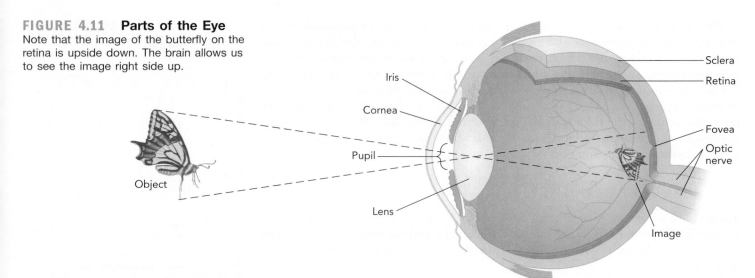

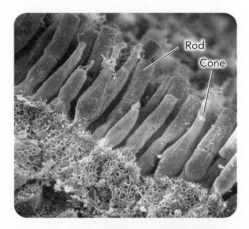

FIGURE 4.12 Rods and Cones In real life, rods and cones look somewhat like stumps and corncobs.

very useful for color vision. Rods function well under low illumination; they are hard at work at night. Humans have about 120 million rods. **Cones** are the receptors that we use for color perception. Like rods, cones are light-sensitive. However, they require a larger amount of light to respond than the rods do, so they operate best in daylight or under high illumination. There are about 6 million cone cells in human eyes. Figure 4.12 shows what rods and cones look like.

The most important part of the retina is the *fovea,* a tiny area in the center of the retina at which vision is at its best (see Figure 4.11). The fovea contains only cones and is vital to many visual tasks. To get a sense of how well the cones in the fovea work, try reading out of the corner of your eye. The task is difficult because the fovea is not getting to "see" the page. Rods are found almost everywhere on the retina except in the fovea. Rods give us the ability to detect fainter spots of light on the peripheral retina than at the fovea. If you want to see a very faint star, you should gaze slightly away from it, to allow your rods to do their work. Figure 4.13 summarizes the characteristics of rods and cones.

Figure 4.14 shows how the rods and cones at the back of the retina convert light into electrochemical impulses. The signal is transmitted to the *bipolar cells* and then moves on to another layer of specialized cells called *ganglion cells* (Lebrun-Julien & others, 2010). The axons of the ganglion cells make up the **optic nerve,** which carries the visual information to the brain for further processing.

One place on the retina contains neither rods nor cones. This area, the *blind spot,* is the place on the retina where the optic nerve leaves the eye on its way to the brain (see Figure 4.14). We cannot see anything that reaches only this part of the retina. To prove to yourself that you have a blind spot, look at Figure 4.15. Once you have seen the yellow pepper disappear, you have probably noticed it took a while to succeed at this task. Now shut one eye and look around. You see a perfectly continuous picture of the world around you; there is no blind spot. This is a great example of top-down processing and a demonstration of the constructive aspect of perception. Your brain fills in the gap for you (the one that ought to be left by your blind spot) with some pretty good guesses about what must be in that spot, like a creative artist painting in the blind spot.

Visual Processing in the Brain

The eyes are just the beginning of visual perception. The next step occurs when neural impulses generated in the retina are dispatched to the brain for analysis and integration (Teismann & others, 2012).

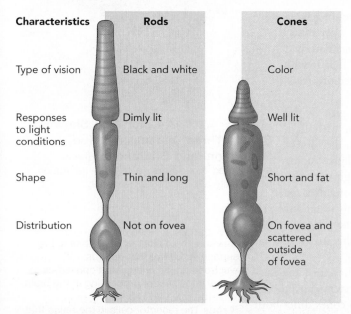

FIGURE 4.13 Characteristics of Rods and Cones
Rods and cones differ in shape, location, and function.

Characteristics	Rods	Cones
Type of vision	Black and white	Color
Responses to light conditions	Dimly lit	Well lit
Shape	Thin and long	Short and fat
Distribution	Not on fovea	On fovea and scattered outside of fovea

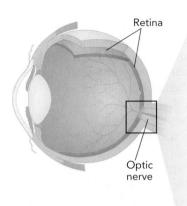

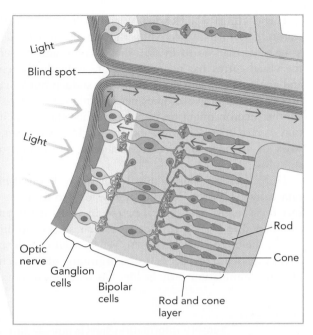

FIGURE 4.14 **Direction of Light in the Retina** After light passes through the cornea, pupil, and lens, it falls on the retina. Three layers of specialized cells in the retina convert the image into a neural signal that can be transmitted to the brain. First, light triggers a reaction in the rods and cones at the back of the retina, transducing light energy into electrochemical neural impulses. The neural impulses activate the bipolar cells, which in turn activate the ganglion cells. Then light information is transmitted to the optic nerve, which conveys it to the brain. The arrows indicate the sequence in which light information moves in the retina.

● **cones** The receptor cells in the retina that allow for color perception.

● **optic nerve** The structure at the back of the eye, made up of axons of the ganglion cells, that carries visual information to the brain for further processing.

● **feature detectors** Neurons in the brain's visual system that respond to particular features of a stimulus.

The optic nerve leaves the eye, carrying information about light toward the brain. Light travels in a straight line; therefore, stimuli in the left visual field are registered in the right half of the retina in both eyes, and stimuli in the right visual field are registered in the left half of the retina in both eyes (Figure 4.16, p. 120). In the brain, at a point called the *optic chiasm,* the optic nerve fibers divide, and approximately half of the nerve fibers cross over the midline of the brain. As a result, the visual information originating in the right halves of the two retinas is transmitted to the right side of the occipital lobe in the cerebral cortex, and the visual information coming from the left halves of the retinas is transmitted to the left side of the occipital lobe. These crossings mean that what we see in the left side of our visual field is registered in the right side of the brain, and what we see in the right visual field is registered in the left side of the brain (see Figure 4.16). Then this information is processed and combined into a recognizable object or scene in the visual cortex.

THE VISUAL CORTEX

The *visual cortex,* located in the occipital lobe at the back of the brain, is the part of the cerebral cortex involved in vision. Most visual information travels to the primary visual cortex, where it is processed, before moving to other visual areas for further analysis (C. I. Baker, 2013).

An important aspect of visual information processing is the specialization of neurons. Like the cells in the retina, many cells in the primary visual cortex are highly specialized (Shushruth & others, 2012). **Feature detectors** are individual neurons or groups of neurons in the brain's visual system that respond to particular features of a stimulus. These neurons might respond to the edges of an object or stimulus, or to its movement.

FIGURE 4.15 **The Eye's Blind Spot** There is a normal blind spot in your eye, a small area where the optic nerve leads to the brain. To find your blind spot, hold this book at arm's length, cover your left eye, and stare at the red pepper on the left with your right eye. Move the book slowly toward you until the yellow pepper disappears. To find the blind spot in your left eye, cover your right eye, stare at the yellow pepper, and adjust the book until the red pepper disappears.

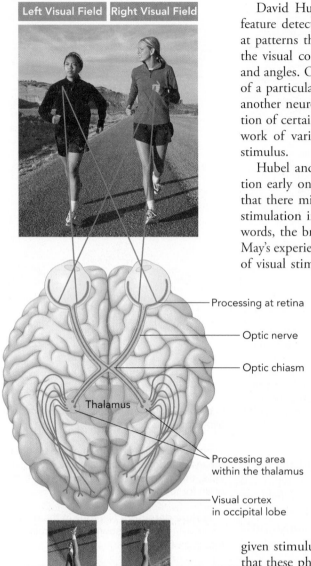

FIGURE 4.16 Visual Pathways to and Through the Brain Light from each side of the visual field falls on the opposite side of each eye's retina. Visual information then travels along the optic nerve to the optic chiasm, where most of the visual information crosses over to the other side of the brain. From there visual information goes to the occipital lobe at the rear of the brain. All these crossings mean that what we see in the left side of our visual field (here, the shorter, dark-haired woman) is registered in the right side of our brain, and what we see in the right visual field (the taller, blonde woman) is registered in the left side of our brain.

● **parallel processing** The simultaneous distribution of information across different neural pathways.

David Hubel and Torsten Wiesel (1963) won a Nobel Prize for their research on feature detectors. By recording the activity of a *single* neuron in a cat while it looked at patterns that varied in size, shape, color, and movement, the researchers found that the visual cortex has neurons that are individually sensitive to different types of lines and angles. One neuron might show a sudden burst of activity when stimulated by lines of a particular angle; another neuron might fire only when moving stimuli appear; yet another neuron might be stimulated when the object in the visual field has a combination of certain angles, sizes, and shapes. In a way, then, seeing a "whole" stimulus is the work of various feature detectors, each responding to the specific aspects of a that stimulus.

Hubel and Wiesel also noted that when deprived of certain types of visual stimulation early on, kittens lost the ability to perceive these patterns. This finding suggested that there might be a critical period in visual development and that the brain requires stimulation in its efforts to delegate its resources to different perceptual tasks. In other words, the brain "learns" to perceive through experience. This process explains Michael May's experience (described at the beginning of this section), whereby his brain, deprived of visual stimulation early in life, has redeployed its resources to other tasks.

PARALLEL PROCESSING

Sensory information travels quickly through the brain because of **parallel processing,** the simultaneous distribution of information across different neural pathways (Nassi & Callaway, 2009). A system designed to process information about sensory qualities serially or consecutively (such as processing first the shapes of images, then their colors, then their movements, and finally their locations) would be too slow to allow us to handle our rapidly changing world. To function in the world, we need to "see" all of these characteristics at once, which is parallel processing. There is some evidence suggesting that parallel processing also occurs for the sensations of touch and hearing (Recanzone & Sutter, 2008).

BINDING

Some neurons respond to color, others to shape, and still others to movement; but note that all of these neurons are involved in responding to a given stimulus—for instance, a toddler running toward us. How does the brain know that these physical features, communicated by different neurons, all belong to the same object of perception?

One of the most exciting topics in visual perception today, **binding** is the bringing together and integration of what is processed by different pathways or cells (Kirt & Bachmann, 2013; Tacca, 2011). Binding involves the coupling of the activity of various cells and pathways. Through binding, you can integrate information about the shape of the toddler's body, his or her smile, and the child's movement into a complete image in the cerebral cortex. How binding occurs is a puzzle that fascinates neuroscientists (McMahon & Olson, 2009).

Researchers have found that all the neurons throughout pathways that are activated by a visual object pulse together at the same frequency (Engel & Singer, 2001). Within the vast network of cells in the cerebral cortex, this set of neurons appears to *bind* together all the features of the objects into a unified perception (Hayworth, 2012).

Color Vision

Imagine how dull a world without color would be. Art museums are filled with paintings that we enjoy in large part for their use of color, and flowers and sunsets would lose much of their beauty if we could not see their rich hues. The process of color perception starts in the retina, the eyes' film. Interestingly, theories about how the retina processes color were developed long before methods existed to study the anatomical and neurophysiological bases of color perception. Instead, psychologists made some extraordinarily accurate guesses about how color vision occurs in the retina by observing how people see. The two main theories proposed were the trichromatic theory and opponent-process theory. Both turned out to be correct.

The **trichromatic theory,** proposed by Thomas Young in 1802 and extended by Hermann von Helmholtz in 1852, states that color perception is produced by three types of cone receptors in the retina that are particularly sensitive to different, but overlapping, ranges of wavelengths. The theory is based on experiments showing that a person with normal vision can match any color in the spectrum by combining three other wavelengths. Young and Helmholtz reasoned that if the combination of any three wavelengths of different intensities is indistinguishable from any single pure wavelength, the visual system must base its perception of color on the relative responses of three receptor systems—cones sensitive to red, blue, and green.

The study of defective color vision, or *colorblindness* (Figure 4.17), provides further support for the trichromatic theory. Complete colorblindness is rare; most colorblind people, the vast majority of whom are men, can see some colors but not others. The nature of colorblindness depends on which of the three kinds of cones (red, blue, or green) is inoperative (Machado, Oliveira, & Fernandes, 2009). In the most common form of colorblindness, the green cone system malfunctions in some way, rendering green indistinguishable from certain combinations of blue and red.

In 1878, the German physiologist Ewald Hering observed that some colors cannot exist together, whereas others can. For example, it is easy to imagine a greenish blue but nearly impossible to imagine a reddish green. Hering also noticed that trichromatic theory could not adequately explain *afterimages,* sensations that remain after a stimulus is removed (Figure 4.18 gives you a chance to experience an afterimage). Color afterimages involve particular pairs of colors. If you look at red long enough, eventually a green afterimage will appear. If you look at yellow long enough, eventually a blue afterimage will appear.

Hering's observations led him to propose that there were not three types of color receptor cones (as proposed by trichromatic theory) but four, organized into complementary pairs: red-green and blue-yellow. Hering's view, **opponent-process theory,** states that cells in the visual system respond to red-green and blue-yellow colors; a given cell might be excited by red and inhibited by green, whereas another cell might be excited by yellow and inhibited by blue. Hering's theory does indeed explain afterimages (Jameson & Hurvich, 1989). If you stare at red, for instance, your red-green system seems to "tire," and when you look away, it rebounds and gives you a green afterimage.

If you have seen The Wizard of Oz, *you might remember that goose bumps moment when Dorothy steps out of her house and the black-and-white of Kansas gives way to the Technicolor glory of Oz.*

● **binding** In the sense of vision, the bringing together and integration of what is processed by different neural pathways or cells.

● **trichromatic theory** Theory stating that color perception is produced by three types of cone receptors in the retina that are particularly sensitive to different, but overlapping, ranges of wavelengths.

● **opponent-process theory** Theory stating that cells in the visual system respond to complementary pairs of red-green and blue-yellow colors; a given cell might be excited by red and inhibited by green, whereas another cell might be excited by yellow and inhibited by blue.

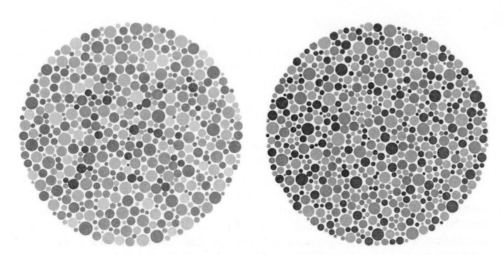

FIGURE 4.17   Examples of Stimuli Used to Test for Colorblindness People with normal vision see the number 16 in the left circle and the number 8 in the right circle. People with red-green colorblindness may see just the 16, just the 8, or neither. A complete colorblindness assessment involves the use of 15 stimuli.

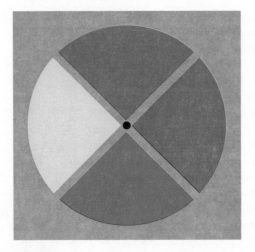

FIGURE 4.18 Negative Afterimage—Complementary Colors If you gaze steadily at the dot in the colored panel on the left for a few moments, then shift your gaze to the gray box on the right, you will see the original hues' complementary colors. The blue appears as yellow, the red as green, the green as red, and the yellow as blue. This pairing of colors has to do with the fact that color receptors in the eye are apparently sensitive as pairs: When one color is turned off (when you stop staring at the panel), the other color in the receptor is briefly turned on. The afterimage effect is especially noticeable with bright colors.

If the trichromatic theory of color perception is valid, and we do, in fact, have three kinds of cone receptors like those predicted by Young and Helmholtz, then how can the opponent-process theory also be accurate? The answer is that the red, blue, and green cones in the retina are connected to retinal ganglion cells in such a way that the three-color code is immediately translated into the opponent-process code (Figure 4.19). For example, a green cone might inhibit and a red cone might excite a particular ganglion cell. Thus, *both* the trichromatic and opponent-process theories are correct—the eye and the brain use both methods to code colors.

● **figure-ground relationship** The principle by which we organize the perceptual field into stimuli that stand out (figure) and those that are left over (ground).

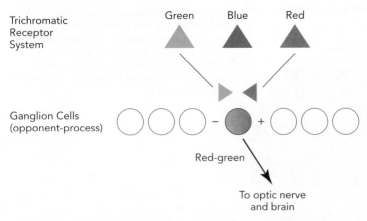

FIGURE 4.19 Trichromatic and Opponent-Process Theories: Transmission of Color Information in the Retina Cones responsive to green, blue, or red light form a trichromatic receptor system in the retina. As information is transmitted to the retina's ganglion cells, opponent-process cells are activated. As shown here, a retinal ganglion cell is inhibited by a green cone (−) and excited by a red cone (+), producing red-green color information.

Perceiving Shape, Depth, Motion, and Constancy

Perceiving visual stimuli means organizing and interpreting the fragments of information that the eye sends to the visual cortex. Information about the dimensions of what we are seeing is critical to this process. Among these dimensions are shape, depth, motion, and constancy.

SHAPE

Think about the visible world and its shapes—buildings against the sky, boats on the horizon, the letters on this page. We see these shapes because they are marked off from the rest of what we see by *contour,* a location at which a sudden change of brightness occurs (Cavina-Pratesi & others, 2010).

Now think about the letters on this page. As you look at the page, you see letters, which are shapes or figures, in a field or background—the white page. The **figure-ground relationship** is the principle by which we organize the perceptual field into stimuli that stand out (*figure*) and those that are left over (*background,* or *ground*). Generally this principle works well for us, but some figure-ground relationships are highly ambiguous, and it may be difficult to tell what is figure and what is ground. Figure 4.20 shows a well-known ambiguous figure-ground relationship. As you look at the figure, your perception is likely to shift from seeing two faces to seeing a single goblet.

The figure-ground relationship is a gestalt principle (Figure 4.21 shows others). *Gestalt* is German for "configuration" or "form," and **gestalt psychology** is a school of thought interested in how people naturally organize their perceptions according to certain patterns. One of gestalt psychology's main principles is that the whole is different from the sum of its parts. For example, when you watch a movie, the motion you see in the film cannot be found in the film itself; if you examine the film, you see only separate frames. When you watch the film, the frames move past a light source at a rate of many per second, and you perceive a whole that is very different from the separate frames that are the film's parts. Similarly, thousands of tiny pixels make up an image (whole) on a computer screen.

DEPTH PERCEPTION

Images appear on our retinas in two-dimensional form, yet remarkably we see a three-dimensional world. **Depth perception** is the ability to perceive objects three-dimensionally. Look around you. You do not see your surroundings as flat. You see some objects farther away, some closer. Some objects overlap each other. The scene and objects that you are looking at have depth. How do you see depth? To perceive a world of depth, we use two kinds of information, or cues—binocular and monocular.

Because we have two eyes, we get two views of the world, one from each eye. **Binocular cues** are depth cues that depend on the combination of the images in the left and right eyes and on the way the two eyes work together. The pictures are slightly different because the eyes are in slightly different positions. Try holding your hand about 10 inches from your face. Alternately close and open your left and right eyes so that only one eye is open at a time. The image of your hand will appear to jump back and forth, because the image is in a slightly different place on the left and right retinas. The *disparity,* or difference, between the images in the two eyes is the binocular cue the brain uses to determine the depth, or distance, of an object. The combination of the two images in the brain, and the disparity between them in the eyes, give us information about the three-dimensionality of the world (Proffitt & Caudek, 2013). Those 3-D glasses that you wear for viewing some movies give you a sense of depth by creating visual disparity. The coloring of the lenses presents a different image to each eye. Your eyes then compete with each other, and your brain makes sense of the conflict by creating the perception of three dimensions.

Convergence is another binocular cue to depth and distance. When we use our two eyes to look at something, they are focused on the same object. If the object is near us, our eyes converge, or move together, almost crossing. If the object is farther away, we can focus on it without pulling our eyes together. The muscle movements involved in convergence provide information about how far away or how deep something is.

In addition to using binocular cues to get an idea of objects' depth, we rely on a number of **monocular cues,** or depth cues, available from the image in one eye, either right or left. Monocular cues are powerful, and under normal circumstances they can provide a

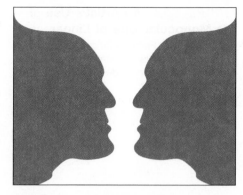

FIGURE 4.20 Reversible Figure-Ground Pattern Do you see the silhouette of a goblet or a pair of faces in profile?

● **gestalt psychology** A school of thought interested in how people naturally organize their perceptions according to certain patterns.

● **depth perception** The ability to perceive objects three-dimensionally.

● **binocular cues** Depth cues that depend on the combination of the images in the left and right eyes and on the way the two eyes work together.

● **convergence** A binocular cue to depth and distance in which the muscle movements in an individual's two eyes provide information about how deep and/or far away something is.

● **monocular cues** Powerful depth cues available from the image in one eye, either the right or the left.

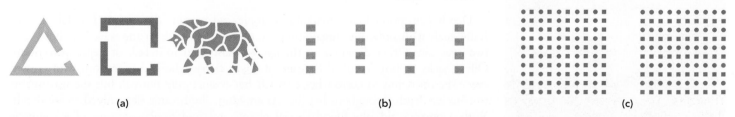

FIGURE 4.21 Gestalt Principles of Closure, Proximity, and Similarity (a) *Closure:* When we see disconnected or incomplete figures, we fill in the spaces and see them as complete figures. (b) *Proximity:* When we see objects that are near each other, they tend to be seen as a unit. You are likely to perceive the grouping as four columns of four squares, not one set of 16 squares. (c) *Similarity:* When we see objects that are similar to each other, they tend to be seen as a unit. Here, you are likely to see vertical columns of circles and squares in the left box but horizontal rows of circles and squares in the right box.

FIGURE 4.22 An Artist's Use of the Monocular Cue of Linear Perspective Famous landscape artist J. M. W. Turner used linear perspective to give the perception of depth in *Rain, Steam, and Speed.*

compelling impression of depth. Try closing one eye—your perception of the world still retains many of its three-dimensional qualities. Examples of monocular cues are

- *Familiar size:* This cue to the depth and distance of objects is based on what we have learned from experience about the standard sizes of objects. We know how large oranges tend to be, so we can tell something about how far away an orange is likely to be by the size of its image on the retina.
- *Height in the field of view:* All other things being equal, objects positioned higher in a picture are seen as farther away.
- *Linear perspective and relative size:* Objects that are farther away take up less space on the retina. So, things that appear smaller are perceived to be farther away. As Figure 4.22 shows, as an object recedes into the distance, parallel lines in the scene appear to converge.
- *Overlap:* We perceive an object that partially conceals or overlaps another object as closer.
- *Shading:* This cue involves changes in perception due to the position of the light and the position of the viewer. Consider an egg under a desk lamp. If you walk around the desk, you will see different shading patterns on the egg.
- *Texture gradient:* Texture becomes denser and finer the farther away it is from the viewer (Figure 4.23).

Depth perception is a remarkably complex adaptation (Proffitt & Caudek, 2013). Individuals with only one functioning eye cannot see depth in the way that those with two eyes can. Other disorders of the eye can also lead to a lack of depth perception. Oliver Sacks (2006) described the case of Susan Barry, who had been born with crossed eyes. The operation to correct her eyes left her cosmetically normal, but she was unable to perceive depth throughout her life. As an adult, she became determined to see depth. With a doctor's aid, she found special glasses and undertook a process of eye muscle exercises to improve her chances of perceiving in three dimensions. It was a difficult and long process, but one day she noticed things starting to "stick out" at her—as you might experience when watching a film in 3-D. Although Barry had successfully adapted to life in a flat visual world, she had come to realize that relying on monocular cues was not the

FIGURE 4.23 Texture Gradient The gradients of texture create an impression of depth on a flat surface.

same as experiencing the rich visual world of binocular vision. She described flowers as suddenly appearing "inflated." She noted how "ordinary things looked extraordinary" as she saw the leaves of a tree, an empty chair, and her office door projecting out from the background. For the first time, she had a sense of being inside the world she was viewing.

MOTION PERCEPTION

Motion perception plays an important role in the lives of many species (Boeddeker & Hemmi, 2010). Indeed, for some animals, motion perception is critical for survival. Both predators and their prey depend on being able to detect motion quickly (Russell, Hertz, & McMillan, 2014). Frogs and some other simple vertebrates may not even see an object unless it is moving. For example, if a dead fly is dangled motionlessly in front of a frog, the frog cannot sense its winged meal. The bug-detecting cells in the frog's retinas are wired only to sense movement.

Whereas the retinas of frogs can detect movement, the retinas of humans and other primates cannot. According to one neuroscientist, "The dumber the animal, the 'smarter' the retina" (Baylor, 2001). In humans the brain takes over the job of analyzing motion through highly specialized pathways (Raudies & Neumann, 2010).

How do humans perceive motion? First, we have neurons that are specialized to detect motion. Second, feedback from our body tells us whether we are moving or whether someone or some object is moving; for example, you move your eye muscles as you watch a ball coming toward you. Third, the environment we see is rich in cues that give us information about movement.

Psychologists are interested in both real movement and **apparent movement,** which occurs when we perceive a stationary object as moving (Zhang, Chen, & Zhou, 2012). You can experience apparent movement at IMAX movie theaters. In watching a film of a climb of Mount Everest, you may find yourself feeling breathless as your visual field floods with startling images. In theaters without seats, viewers of these films are often warned to hold the handrail because perceived movement is so realistic that they might fall.

PERCEPTUAL CONSTANCY

Retinal images change constantly. Yet even though the stimuli that fall on our retinas change as we move closer to or farther away from objects, or as we look at objects from different orientations and in light or dark settings, our perception of them remains stable. **Perceptual constancy** is the recognition that objects are constant and unchanging even though sensory input about them is changing (Kavšek & Granrud, 2012; Lee & Wallraven, 2013).

We experience three types of perceptual constancy—size constancy, shape constancy, and color constancy—as follows:

- *Size constancy* is the recognition that an object remains the same size even though the retinal image of the object changes (Figure 4.24). Experience is important to size perception: No matter how far away you are from your car, you know how large it is.

- *Shape constancy* is the recognition that an object retains the same shape even though its orientation to you changes. Look around. You probably see objects of various shapes— chairs and tables, for example. If you walk around the room, you will see these objects from different sides and angles. Even though the retinal image of the object changes as you walk, you still perceive the objects as having the same shape (Figure 4.25).

- *Color constancy* is the recognition that an object retains the same color even though different amounts of light fall on it. For example, if you are reaching for a green Granny Smith apple, it looks green to you whether you are having it for lunch, in the bright noon sun, or as an evening snack in the pale pink of sunset.

FIGURE 4.24 Size Constancy Even though our retinal images of the hot air balloons vary, we still realize the balloons are approximately the same size. This illustrates the principle of size constancy.

● **apparent movement** The perception that a stationary object is moving.

● **perceptual constancy** The recognition that objects are constant and unchanging even though sensory input about them is changing.

FIGURE 4.25 Shape Constancy The various projected images from an opening door are quite different, yet you perceive a rectangular door.

Ponzo Illusion
The top line looks much longer than the bottom, but they are the same length.

Rotational Illusion
The two rings appear to rotate in different directions when we approach or move away from this figure while fixing our eyes on the center.

Blinking Effect Illusion
Stare at the white circles and notice the intermittent blinking effect. Your eyes make the static figure seem dynamic, attempting to fill in the white circle intersections with the black of the background.

Pattern Recognition
Although the diagram contains no actual triangles, your brain "sees" two overlapping triangles. The explanation is that the notched circles and angled lines merely suggest gaps in which complete objects should be. The brain fills in the missing information.

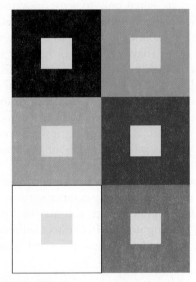

Induction Illusion
The yellow patches are identical, but they look different and seem to take on the characteristics of their surroundings when they appear against different-color backgrounds.

FIGURE 4.26 **Perceptual Illusions** These illusions show how adaptive perceptual cues can lead to errors when taken out of context. These mind-challenging images are definitely fun, but keep in mind that these illusions are based on processes that are quite adaptive in real life.

test yourself

1. What is light? What are some terms scientists use to describe it?
2. What are rods and cones and their functions in the eye?
3. What are the main principles of trichromatic theory? How does this theory explain color vision and colorblindness?

Note that perceptual constancy tells us about the crucial role of interpretation in perception: We *interpret* sensation. That is, we perceive objects as having particular characteristics regardless of the retinal image detected by our eyes. Images may flow across the retina, but experiences are made sensible through perception. The many cues we use to visually perceive the real world can lead to optical illusions when they are taken out of that real-world context, as you can experience for yourself in Figure 4.26.

3· THE AUDITORY SYSTEM

Just as light provides us with information about the environment, so does sound. Sounds tell us about the presence of a person behind us, the approach of an oncoming car, the force of the wind, and the mischief of a 2-year-old. Perhaps most important, sounds allow us to communicate through language and music.

The Nature of Sound and How We Experience It

At a fireworks display, you may feel the loud boom of the explosion in your chest. At a concert, you might have sensed that the air around you was vibrating. Bass instruments are especially effective at creating mechanical pulsations, even causing the floor to vibrate. When the bass is played loudly, we can sense air molecules being pushed forward in waves from the speaker. How does sound generate these sensations?

Sound waves are vibrations in the air that are processed by the *auditory* (hearing) system. Remember that light waves are much like the waves in the ocean moving toward the beach. Sound waves are similar. Sound waves also vary in length. Wavelength determines the sound wave's *frequency*—that is, the number of cycles (full wavelengths) that pass through a point in a given time interval. *Pitch* is the perceptual interpretation of the frequency of a sound. We perceive high-frequency sounds as having a high pitch, and low-frequency sounds as having a low pitch. A soprano voice sounds high-pitched. A bass voice has a low pitch. As with the wavelengths of light, human sensitivity is limited to a range of sound frequencies. It is common knowledge that dogs, for example, can hear higher frequencies than humans can.

Sound waves vary not only in frequency but also, like light waves, in amplitude (see Figure 4.9). A sound wave's *amplitude,* measured in decibels (dB), is the amount of pressure the sound wave produces relative to a standard. The typical standard—0 decibels—is the weakest sound the human ear can detect. *Loudness* is the perception of the sound wave's amplitude. In general, the higher the amplitude of the sound wave, or the higher the decibel level, the louder we perceive the sound to be. In terms of amplitude, the air is pressing more forcibly against you and your ears during loud sounds and more gently during quiet sounds.

So far we have been describing a single sound wave with just one frequency. A single sound wave is similar to the single wavelength of pure colored light, discussed in the context of color matching. Most sounds, including those of speech and music, are *complex sounds,* those in which numerous frequencies of sound blend together. *Timbre* is the tone saturation, or the perceptual quality, of a sound. If two musicians play a note of the same pitch (let's say a high C), even though the pitch is the same, the tones will sound different. Timbre is responsible for this perceptual difference, as well as for the quality differences we hear in human voices. Figure 4.27 illustrates the physical differences in sound waves that produce the different qualities of sounds.

Structures and Functions of the Ear

What happens to sound waves once they reach your ear? How do various structures of the ear transform sound waves into signals that the brain will recognize as sound?

Physical Dimension	Perceptual Dimension	Form of Sound Waves	
Amplitude (intensity)	Loudness	Loud	Soft
Frequency	Pitch	Low	High
Complex sounds	Timbre	(Form of sound wave from a clarinet)	

FIGURE 4.27 Physical Difference in Sound Waves and the Qualities of Sound They Produce Here we can see how the input of sound stimuli requires our ears and brain to attend to varying characteristics of the rich sensory information that is sound.

FIGURE 4.28 **The Outer, Middle, and Inner Ear** On entering the outer, ear, sound waves travel through the auditory canal, where they generate vibrations in the eardrum. These vibrations are transferred via the hammer, anvil, and stirrup to the fluid-filled cochlea in the inner ear. There the mechanical vibrations are converted to an electrochemical signal that the brain will recognize as sound.

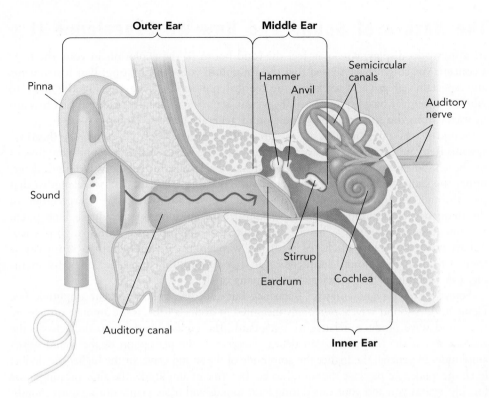

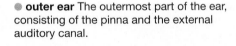

Functionally the ear is analogous to the eye. The ear serves the purpose of transmitting a high-fidelity version of sounds in the world to the brain for analysis and interpretation. Just as an image needs to be in focus and sufficiently bright for the brain to interpret it, a sound needs to be transmitted in a way that preserves information about its location, its frequency (which helps us distinguish the voice of a child from that of an adult), and its timbre (which allows us to identify the voice of a friend on the telephone). The ear is divided into three parts: outer ear, middle ear, and inner ear (Figure 4.28).

OUTER EAR

● **outer ear** The outermost part of the ear, consisting of the pinna and the external auditory canal.

The **outer ear** consists of the pinna and the external auditory canal. The funnel-shaped *pinna* (plural, *pinnae*) is the outer, visible part of the ear. (Elephants have very large pinnae.) The pinna collects sounds and channels them into the interior of the ear. The pinnae of many animals, such as cats, are movable and serve a more important role in sound localization than do the pinnae of humans. Cats turn their ears in the direction of a faint and interesting sound.

MIDDLE EAR

● **middle ear** The part of the ear that channels sound through the eardrum, hammer, anvil, and stirrup to the inner ear.

After passing the pinna, sound waves move through the auditory canal to the middle ear. The **middle ear** channels the sound through the eardrum, hammer, anvil, and stirrup to the inner ear. The *eardrum* or tympanic membrane separates the outer ear from the middle ear and vibrates in response to sound. It is the first structure that sound touches in the middle ear. The *hammer, anvil,* and *stirrup* are an intricately connected chain of the three smallest bones in the human body. When they vibrate, they transmit sound waves to the fluid-filled inner ear. The muscles that operate these tiny bones take the vibration of the eardrum and transmit it to the oval window, the opening of the inner ear.

If you are a swimmer, you know that sound travels far more easily in air than in water. Sound waves entering the ear travel in air until they reach the inner ear. At the border between the middle and the inner ear—which, as we will see below, is a border between air and fluid—sound meets the same kind of resistance, as do shouts directed at an underwater swimmer when the shouts hit the surface of the water. To compensate, the muscles of the middle ear can maneuver the hammer, anvil, and stirrup to amplify the sound waves. Importantly, these muscles, if necessary, can also work to decrease the intensity of sound waves, to protect the inner ear.

INNER EAR

The function of the **inner ear,** which includes the oval window, cochlea, and basilar membrane, is to convert sound waves into neural impulses and send them on to the brain (Gregan, Nelson, & Oxenham, 2011). The stirrup is connected to the membranous *oval window,* which transmits sound waves to the cochlea. The *cochlea* is a tubular, fluid-filled structure that is coiled up like a snail (Figure 4.29). The *basilar membrane* lines the inner wall of the cochlea and runs its entire length. It is narrow and rigid at the base of the cochlea but widens and becomes more flexible at the top. The variation in width and flexibility allows different areas of the basilar membrane to vibrate more intensely when exposed to different sound frequencies (Wojtczak & Oxenham, 2009).

In humans and other mammals, hair cells line the basilar membrane (see Figure 4.29). These *hair cells* are the ear's sensory receptors. They are called hair cells because of the tufts of fine bristles, or *cilia,* that sprout from the top of them. The movement of the hair cells against the *tectorial membrane,* a jellylike flap above them, generates impulses that the brain interprets as sound (Nowotny & Gummer, 2011). Hair cells are so delicate that exposure to loud noise can destroy them, leading to deafness or difficulties in hearing. Once lost, hair cells cannot regenerate.

Cochlear implants are devices that were specifically developed to replace damaged hair cells. A *cochlear implant*—a small electronic device that is surgically implanted in the ear and head—allows deaf or profoundly hard-of-hearing individuals to detect sound (Hassepass & others, 2013; Radulescu & others, 2013). The implant works by using electronic impulses to directly stimulate whatever working auditory nerves the recipient has in his or her cochlea (Zhou, Xu, & Pfingst, 2012). Worldwide, over 200,000 individuals have received cochlear implants (U.S. Food and Drug Administration, 2009).

● **inner ear** The part of the ear that includes the oval window, cochlea, and basilar membrane and whose function is to convert sound waves into neural impulses and send them to the brain.

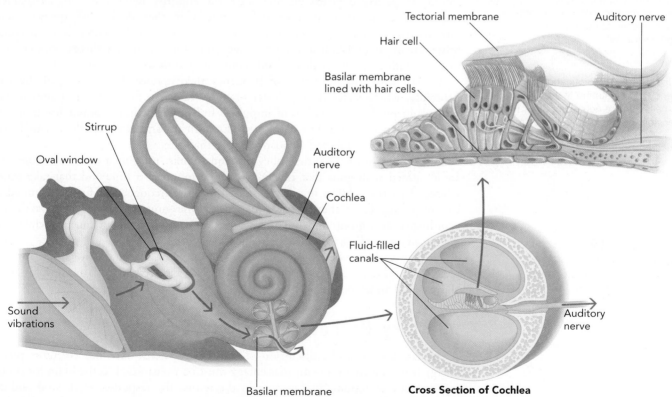

FIGURE 4.29 **The Cochlea** The cochlea is a spiral structure consisting of fluid-filled canals. When the stirrup vibrates against the oval window, the fluid in the canals vibrates. Vibrations along portions of the basilar membrane correspond to different sound frequencies. The vibrations exert pressure on the hair cells (between the basilar and tectorial membranes); the hair cells in turn push against the tectorial membrane, and this pressure bends the hairs. This sequence of events triggers an action potential in the auditory nerve.

Theories of Hearing

One of the auditory system's mysteries is how the inner ear registers the frequency of sound—for example, how we hear a high-pitched piccolo versus the low tones of a cello. Two theories aim to explain this mystery: place theory and frequency theory.

Place theory states that each frequency produces vibrations at a particular spot on the basilar membrane. Georg von Békésy (1960) studied the effects of vibration applied at the oval window on the basilar membrane of human cadavers. Through a microscope, he saw that this stimulation produced a traveling wave on the basilar membrane. A traveling wave is like the ripples that appear in a pond when you throw in a stone. However, because the cochlea is a long tube, the ripples travel in only one direction—from the oval window at one end of the cochlea to the far tip of the cochlea. High-frequency vibrations create traveling waves that maximally displace, or move, the area of the basilar membrane closest to the oval window; low-frequency vibrations maximally displace areas of the membrane closer to the tip of the cochlea. So, the high-pitched tinkle of a little bell stimulates the narrow region of the basilar membrane at the base of the cochlea, whereas the low-pitched tones of a tuba stimulate the wide end.

Place theory adequately explains high-frequency but not low-frequency sounds. A high-frequency sound like the screech of a referee's whistle or the piercing high note of an opera diva, stimulates a precise area on the basilar membrane, just as place theory suggests. However, a low-frequency sound, like the tone of a tuba or the croak of a bullfrog, causes a large part of the basilar membrane to be displaced, making it hard to identify an exact location on the membrane that is associated with hearing this kind of sound. Looking only at the movement of the basilar membrane, you would get the impression that humans are probably not very good at hearing low-frequency sounds, and yet we are. Therefore, some other factors must be at play in low-frequency hearing.

Frequency theory gets at these other influences by stating that the perception of a sound's frequency depends on how *often* the auditory nerve fires. Higher-frequency sounds cause the auditory nerve to fire more often than do lower-frequency sounds. One limitation of frequency theory, however, is that a single neuron has a maximum firing rate of about 1,000 times per second. Therefore, frequency theory does not apply to tones with frequencies that would require a neuron to fire more rapidly.

To deal with this limitation of frequency theory, researchers developed the **volley principle,** which states that a cluster of nerve cells can fire neural impulses in rapid succession, producing a volley of impulses. Individual neurons cannot fire faster than 1,000 times per second, but if the neurons team up and alternate their neural firing, they can attain a combined frequency above that rate.

To get a sense for how the volley principle works, imagine a troop of soldiers who are all armed with guns that can fire only one round at a time and that take time to reload. If all the soldiers fire at the same time, the frequency of firing is limited and cannot go any faster than it takes to reload those guns. If, however, the soldiers are coordinated as a group and fire at different times, some of them can fire while others are reloading, leading to a greater frequency of firing.

Frequency theory better explains the perception of sounds below 1,000 times per second. However, a combination of frequency and place theory is needed for sounds above 1,000 times per second.

Auditory Processing in the Brain

As we considered in the discussion of the visual system, once our receptors pick up energy from the environment, that energy must be transmitted to the brain for processing and interpretation. We saw that in the retina, the responses of the rod and cone receptors feed into ganglion cells and leave the eye via the optic nerve. In the auditory system, information about sound moves from the hair cells of the inner ear to the **auditory nerve,** which carries neural impulses to the brain's auditory areas. Remember that it is the movement of the hair cells that transforms the physical stimulation of sound waves into the action potential of neural impulses.

● **place theory** Theory on how the inner ear registers the frequency of sound, stating that each frequency produces vibrations at a particular spot on the basilar membrane.

● **frequency theory** Theory on how the inner ear registers the frequency of sound, stating that the perception of a sound's frequency depends on how often the auditory nerve fires.

● **volley principle** Modification of frequency theory stating that a cluster of nerve cells can fire neural impulses in rapid succession, producing a volley of impulses.

● **auditory nerve** The nerve structure that receives information about sound from the hair cells of the inner ear and carries these neural impulses to the brain's auditory areas.

Touring the Senses

GOALS OF THE TOUR

1 **Parts of the Eye.** Identify the structures of the human eye and describe their functions.

2 **Visual Pathways.** Identify the pathways for visual stimulation and describe the brain's role in visual information processing.

3 **Parts of the Ear.** Identify the three areas of the ear and describe the key structures of the inner ear.

4 **Parts of the Nose.** Describe how the nose (olfactory sense) processes a smell or odor.

Parts of the Eye and Visual Pathways

1 Identify the structures of the human eye and describe their functions.

2 Identify the pathways for visual stimulation and describe the brain's role in visual information processing.

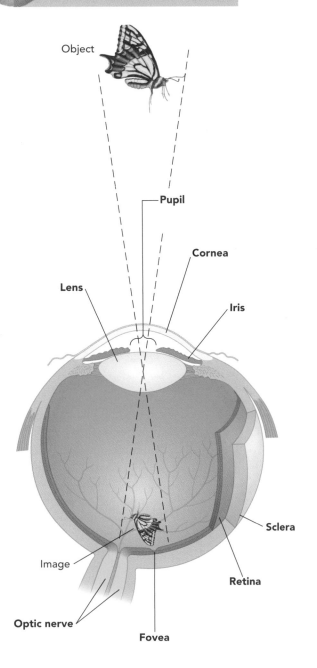

Object

Pupil

Cornea

Lens

Iris

Image

Optic nerve

Fovea

Sclera

Retina

Left visual field

Right visual field

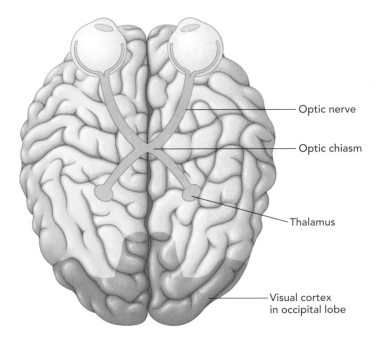

Optic nerve

Optic chiasm

Thalamus

Visual cortex in occipital lobe

Parts of the Ear and Parts of the Nose

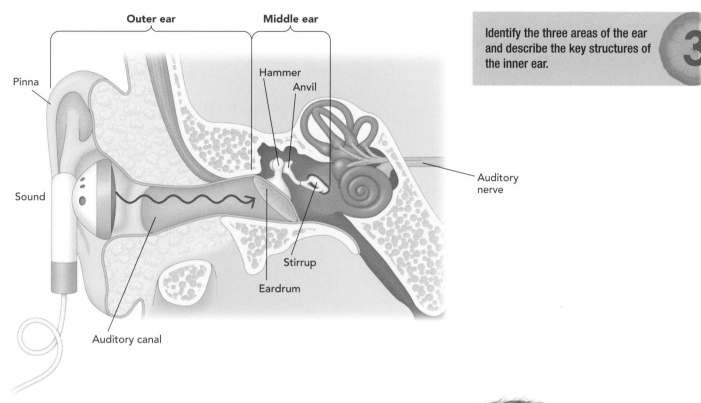

Outer ear

Middle ear

Pinna

Sound

Hammer

Anvil

Auditory nerve

Stirrup

Eardrum

Auditory canal

3 Identify the three areas of the ear and describe the key structures of the inner ear.

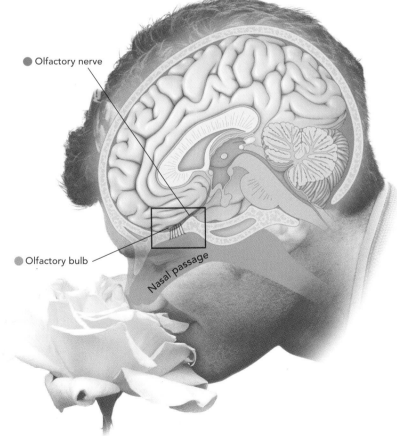

● Olfactory nerve

● Olfactory bulb

Nasal passage

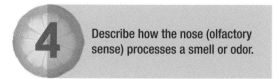

4 Describe how the nose (olfactory sense) processes a smell or odor.

1. PARTS OF THE EYE

The *sclera* is the outer membrane of the eyeball that makes up the white of the eye.

The *retina* is made up of a layer of cells in the interior of the eye that contain the *photoreceptors*, the rods and the cones.

The *cornea* is the transparent membrane in the front of the eye that protects the eye and bends light to provide focus.

The *pupil* is the opening that allows light to enter the eye.

The *iris* is the colored muscle that surrounds the pupil and adjusts the amount of light entering into the eye through the pupil. It dilates (opens) or constricts (closes) in response to the intensity (brightness) of the light. It also dilates in response to certain emotions.

The *lens* focuses the image onto the retinal layer on the back surface of the eye. As in a camera, the image projected by the lens onto the retina is reversed.

The *fovea* is the region of the retina that is directly in line with the pupil and contains mostly cones, which are involved in color perception and visual acuity (sharpness).

The *optic nerve* receives inputs from the photoreceptors and sends information to the brain.

2. VISUAL PATHWAYS

Images of objects in the right visual field are projected to the left half of the retina of each eye, which in turn sends the information first to the thalamus for initial processing and then to the visual cortex in the left hemisphere where perception takes place. Likewise, images of objects in the left visual field are projected to the right half of the retina of each eye, which in turn sends the information to the thalamus and then to the visual cortex in the right hemisphere.

3. PARTS OF THE EAR

The *outer ear* is the visible portion of the ear and the auditory canal (ear canal) that funnels sound waves to the eardrum.

The *middle ear* includes the eardrum and three tiny bones (hammer, anvil, and stirrup) that transmit the eardrum's vibrations to a membrane on the cochlea called the oval window.

The *inner ear* includes the snail-shaped tube called the *cochlea*, which translates sound waves into fluid waves, and the semicircular canals, which sense equilibrium.

4. PARTS OF THE NOSE

Airborne molecules (olfactory chemicals) enter the nasal passages and reach receptor cells located in the olfactory epithelium of the upper nasal passage. The receptors send messages to the brain's olfactory bulb and then onward to the primary smell cortex located in the temporal lobes.

Auditory information moves up the auditory pathway via electrochemical transmission in a more complex manner than does visual information in the visual pathway. Many synapses occur in the ascending auditory pathway, with most fibers crossing over the midline between the hemispheres of the cerebral cortex, although some proceed directly to the hemisphere on the same side as the ear of reception (Lewald & Getzmann, 2011). This means that most of the auditory information from the left ear goes to the right side of the brain, but some also goes to the left side of the brain. The auditory nerve extends from the cochlea to the brain stem, with some fibers crossing over the midline. The cortical destination of most of these fibers is the temporal lobes of the brain (beneath the temples of the head). As in the case of visual information, researchers have found that features are extracted from auditory information and transmitted along parallel pathways in the brain (J. W. Lewis & others, 2012).

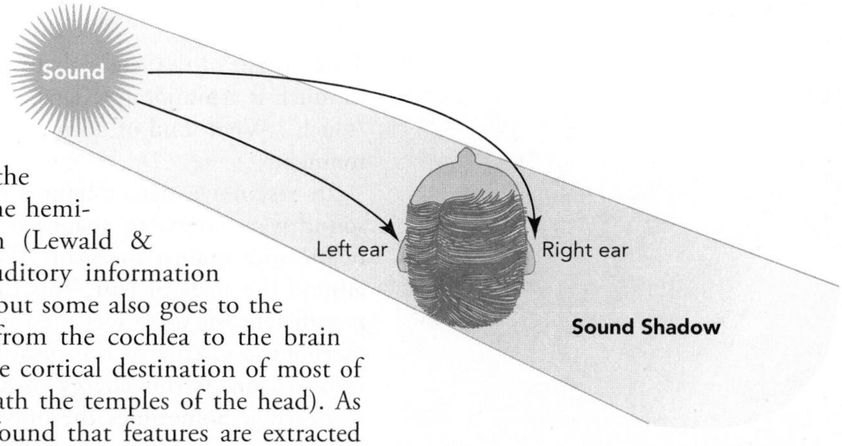

FIGURE 4.30   The Sound Shadow The sound shadow is caused by the listener's head, which forms a barrier that reduces the sound's intensity. Here the sound is to the person's left, so the sound shadow will reduce the intensity of the sound that reaches the right ear.

Localizing Sound

When we hear the siren of a fire engine or the bark of a dog, how do we know where the sound is coming from? The basilar membrane gives us information about the frequency, pitch, and complexity of a sound, but it does not tell us where a sound is located.

Earlier in the chapter we saw that because our two eyes see slightly different images, we can determine how near or far away an object is. Similarly, having two ears helps us to localize a sound because each receives somewhat different stimuli from the sound source. A sound coming from the left has to travel different distances to the two ears, so if a barking dog is to your left, your left ear receives the sound sooner than your right ear. Also, your left ear will receive a slightly more intense sound than your right ear in this case. The sound reaching one ear is more intense than the sound reaching the other ear for two reasons: (1) It has traveled less distance, and (2) the other ear is in what is called the *sound shadow* of the listener's head, which provides a barrier that reduces the sound's intensity (Figure 4.30).

Thus, differences in both the *timing* of the sound and the *intensity* of the sound help us to localize a sound (Salminen & others, 2010). You often have difficulty localizing a sound that is coming from a source that is directly in front of you because it reaches both ears simultaneously. The same is true for sounds directly above your head or directly behind you, because the disparities that provide information about localization are not present.

test yourself

1. When you hear the pitch of a voice or an instrument, what quality of sound are you perceiving? When you hear the loudness of music, what characteristic of sound are you perceiving?
2. When you hear any sound, what vibrates, and how are the vibrations then transferred to the inner ear?
3. What is the pinna? What role does it play in hearing?

4· OTHER SENSES

We turn now to the body's other sensory systems. These include the skin senses and the chemical senses (smell and taste), as well as the kinesthetic and vestibular senses (systems that allow us to stay upright and to coordinate our movements).

The Skin Senses

You know when a friend has a fever by putting your hand to her head; you know how to find your way to the light switch in a darkened room by groping along the wall; and you know whether a pair of shoes is too tight by the way the shoes rub different parts of your feet when you walk. Many of us think of our skin as a painter's canvas: We color it with cosmetics, dyes, and tattoos. In fact, the skin is our largest sensory system, draped over the body with receptors for touch, temperature, and pain (Hollins, 2010). These three kinds of receptors form the *cutaneous senses.*

TOUCH

Touch is one of the senses that we most often take for granted, yet our ability to respond to touch is astounding (Klatzky & Lederman, 2013). What do we detect when we feel "touch"? What kind of energy does our sense of touch pick up from our external environment?

In vision we detect light energy. In hearing we detect the vibrations of air or sound waves pressing against our eardrums. In touch we detect mechanical energy, or pressure against the skin. The lifting of a single hair causes pressure on the skin around the shaft of hair. This tiny bit of mechanical pressure at the base of the hair is sufficient for us to feel the touch of a pencil point. More commonly we detect the mechanical energy of the pressure of a car seat against our buttocks or of a pencil in our hand. Is this energy so different from the kind of energy we detect in vision or hearing? Sometimes the only difference is one of intensity—the sound of a rock band playing softly is an auditory stimulus, but at the high volumes that make a concert hall reverberate, this auditory stimulus is also *felt* as mechanical energy pressing against our skin.

How does information about touch travel from the skin through the nervous system? Sensory fibers arising from receptors in the skin enter the spinal cord. From there the information travels to the brain stem, where most fibers from each side of the body cross over to the opposite side of the brain. Next the information about touch moves on to the thalamus, which serves as a relay station. The thalamus then projects the map of the body's surface onto the somatosensory areas of the parietal lobes in the cerebral cortex (Hirata & Castro-Alamancos, 2010; Hsiao & Gomez-Ramirez, 2013).

Just as the visual system is more sensitive to images on the fovea than to images in the peripheral retina, our sensitivity to touch is not equally good across all areas of the skin. Human toolmakers need excellent touch discrimination in their hands, but they require much less touch discrimination in other parts of the body, such as the torso and legs. The brain devotes more space to analyzing touch signals coming from the hands than from the legs. Consider the following example illustrating the hand's sensitivity. Standing in front of a vending machine, you find you need another nickel. Without looking, you are able to pull out the right coin. That is something that not even the most sophisticated robot can do. Engineers who design robots for use in surgical and other procedures have been unable to match the human hand's amazing sensitivity.

TEMPERATURE

We not only can feel the warmth of a comforting hand on our hand, we also can feel the warmth or coolness of a room. In order to maintain our body temperature, we have to be able to detect temperature. **Thermoreceptors,** sensory nerve endings under the skin, respond to changes in temperature at or near the skin and provide input to keep the body's temperature at 98.6 degrees Fahrenheit. There are two types of thermoreceptors: warm and cold. Warm thermoreceptors respond to the warming of the skin, and cold thermoreceptors respond to the cooling of the skin. When warm and cold receptors that are close to each other in the skin are stimulated simultaneously, we experience the sensation of hotness. Figure 4.31 illustrates this "hot" experience.

PAIN

Pain is the sensation that warns us of damage to the body. When contact with the skin takes the form of a sharp pinch, our sensation of mechanical pressure changes from touch to pain. When a pot handle is so hot that it burns our hand, our sensation of temperature becomes one of pain. Intense stimulation of any one of the senses can produce pain—too much light, very loud sounds, or too many habanero peppers, for example.

● **thermoreceptors** Sensory nerve endings under the skin that respond to changes in temperature at or near the skin and provide input to keep the body's temperature at 98.6 degrees Fahrenheit.

● **pain** The sensation that warns an individual of damage to the body.

Warm water   Cold water

FIGURE 4.31   A "Hot" Experience
When two pipes, one containing cold water and the other warm water, are braided together, a person touching the pipes feels a sensation of "hot." The perceived heat coming from the pipes is so intense that the individual cannot touch them for longer than a couple of seconds.

Our ability to sense pain is vital for our survival as a species. In other words, this ability is adaptive. Individuals who cannot perceive pain often have serious difficulty navigating the world. They might not notice that they need to move away from a danger such as a hot burner on a stove or that they have seriously injured themselves. Pain functions as a quick-acting messenger that tells the brain's motor systems that they must act fast to eliminate or minimize damage.

Pain receptors are dispersed widely throughout the body—in the skin, in the sheath tissue surrounding muscles, in internal organs, and in the membranes around bone. Although all pain receptors are anatomically similar, they differ in the type of physical stimuli to which they most readily react. Mechanical pain receptors respond mainly to pressure, such as when we encounter a sharp object. Heat pain receptors respond primarily to strong heat that is capable of burning the tissue in which the receptors are embedded. Other pain receptors have a mixed function, responding to both types of painful stimuli. Many pain receptors are chemically sensitive and respond to a range of pain-producing substances (Latremoliere & Woolf, 2009; Millecamps & others, 2013).

Pain receptors have a much higher threshold for firing than receptors for temperature and touch (Bloom, Nelson, & Lazerson, 2001). Pain receptors react mainly to physical stimuli that distort them or to chemical stimuli that irritate them into action. Inflamed joints or sore, torn muscles produce *prostaglandins,* which stimulate the receptors and cause the experience of pain. Drugs such as aspirin likely reduce the feeling of pain by reducing prostaglandin production.

Two different neural pathways transmit pain messages to the brain: a fast pathway and a slow pathway (Bloom, Nelson, & Lazerson, 2001). In the *fast pathway,* fibers connect directly with the thalamus and then to the motor and sensory areas of the cerebral cortex. This pathway transmits information about sharp, localized pain, as when you cut your skin. The fast pathway may serve as a warning system, providing immediate information about an injury—it takes less than a second for the information in this pathway to reach the cerebral cortex. In the *slow pathway,* pain information travels through the limbic system, a detour that delays the arrival of information at the cerebral cortex by seconds. The unpleasant, nagging pain that characterizes the slow pathway may function to remind the brain that an injury has occurred and that we need to restrict normal activity and monitor the pain (Gao & Ji, 2010; Linnman & others, 2010).

Many neuroscientists believe that the brain actually generates the experience of pain. There is evidence that turning pain signals on and off is a chemical process that probably involves *endorphins.* Recall from Chapter 3 that endorphins are neurotransmitters that function as natural opiates in producing pleasure and pain (Mirilas & others, 2010; Quang & Schmidt, 2010). Endorphins are believed to be released mainly in the synapses of the slow pathway.

Perception of pain is complex and often varies from one person to the next (H. S. Smith, 2010). Some people rarely feel pain; others seem to be in great pain if they experience a minor bump or bruise. To some degree, these individual variations may be physiological. A person who experiences considerable pain even with a minor injury may have a neurotransmitter system that is deficient in endorphin production. However, perception of pain goes beyond physiology. Although it is true that all sensations are affected by motivation, expectation, and other related decision factors, the perception of pain is especially susceptible to these factors (Watson & others, 2006).

Researchers have reported that women experience more clinical pain than men (Jarrett, 2011). However, a recent research review of studies from 1998 to 2008 of laboratory-induced pain in nonclinical participants found no sex differences in perception of pain intensity and unpleasantness and no sex differences in many types of pain (Racine & others, 2012a, 2012b). An important factor to consider in the realm of gender differences in pain is the important role of cultural expectations. Interestingly, research has shown that men are particularly likely to show high pain tolerance when the experimenter is a woman, and especially if she is an attractive woman (Levine &

De Simone, 1991). Cultural and ethnic contexts also influence the degree to which an individual experiences or reports pain (Jarrett, 2011).

Before we leave the topic of pain, let's revisit the notion that the experience of pain is important: The feeling of pain provides us with information about what is happening to us. This feeling, like all of our other senses, connects us to the external world. A pain-free existence might sound nice, but in fact pain is an important sensation. Consider the situation of Ashlyn Blocker, age 12. She was born without the ability to sense pain. Ashlyn was a baby who did not cry—even when stinging eye drops were put in her eyes, even when she had a terrible diaper rash.

Researchers have studied Ashlyn to understand not only the cause of her condition but the nature of pain itself (Staud & others, 2011). It turns out that Ashlyn has two genetic mutations that short-circuit the pain signals in her brain. Without pain, she has missed some of life's "warning signals," suffering severe burns as well as two broken ankles in her short life. She has had to remind herself that the sight of blood coming from a cut means that something is wrong. Cases like Ashlyn's remind us that although we might wish we could avoid feeling pain altogether, pain plays an important role in allowing us to navigate the world.

The Chemical Senses

The information processed through our senses comes in many diverse forms: electromagnetic energy in vision, sound waves in hearing, and mechanical pressure and temperature in the skin senses. The two senses we now consider, smell and taste, are responsible for processing chemicals in our environment. Through smell, we detect airborne chemicals, and through taste we detect chemicals that have been dissolved in saliva. Smell and taste are frequently stimulated simultaneously. We notice the strong links between the two senses when a nasty cold with lots of nasal congestion takes the pleasure out of eating. Our favorite foods become "tasteless" without their characteristic smells. Despite this link, taste and smell are two distinct systems.

TASTE

Think of your favorite food. Why do you like it? Imagine that food without its flavor. The thought of giving up a favorite taste, such as chocolate, can be depressing. Indeed, eating food we love is a major source of pleasure.

How does taste happen? To get at this question, try this. Take a drink of milk and allow it to coat your tongue. Then go to a mirror, stick out your tongue, and look carefully at its surface. You should be able to see rounded bumps above the surface. Those bumps, called **papillae,** contain *taste buds*, the receptors for taste. Your tongue houses about 10,000 taste buds, which are replaced about every two weeks. As we age, this replacement process is not quite as efficient, and an older individual may have just 5,000 working taste buds at any given moment. As with all of the other sensory systems we have studied, the information picked up by these taste receptors is transmitted to the brain for analysis and, when necessary, for a response (spitting something out, for example) (Di Lorenzo & Youngentob, 2013).

Traditionally, tastes were categorized as sweet, sour, bitter, and salty. However, today, most neuroscientists believe that the breakdown of taste into those four categories far underestimates the complexity of taste (Cauller, 2001). The taste fibers leading from a taste bud to the brain often respond strongly to a range of chemicals spanning *multiple* taste elements, such as salty and sour. The brain processes these somewhat ambiguous incoming signals and integrates them into a perception of taste (Iannilli & others, 2012). So, although people often categorize taste sensations along the four dimensions of sweet, bitter, salty, and sour, our tasting ability goes far beyond these.

Recently, researchers and chefs have been exploring a taste called *umami* (Maruyama & others, 2006). *Umami* is the Japanese word for "delicious" or "yummy." The taste of umami, one that Asian cooks have long recognized, is the flavor of L-glutamate. What is that taste? Umami is a savory flavor that is present in many seafoods as well as soy

● **papillae** Rounded bumps above the tongue's surface that contain the taste buds, the receptors for taste.

sauce, parmesan and mozzarella cheese, anchovies, mushrooms, and hearty meat broths.

Culture certainly influences the experience of taste. Any American who has watched the Japanese version of *Iron Chef* or *Bizarre Foods* on television quickly notices that some people enjoy the flavor of sea urchin or raw meat, while others just do not get the appeal. In some cultures, food that is so spicy as to be practically inedible for the outsider may be viewed as quite delicious. The culture in which we live can influence the foods we are exposed to as well as our sense of what tastes good. In some cultures, very spicy food is introduced slowly into children's diets so that they can learn what is delicious at an early age.

SMELL

Why do we have a sense of smell? One way to appreciate the importance of smell is to think about animals with a more sophisticated sense of smell than our own. A dog, for example, can use smell to find its way back from a long stroll, to distinguish friend from foe, and even (with practice) to detect illegal drugs concealed in a suitcase. In fact, dogs can detect odors in concentrations 100 times lower than those detectable by humans. Given the nasal feats of the average dog, we might be tempted to believe that the sense of smell has outlived its usefulness in humans.

Many animals have a stronger sense of smell than humans do. Dogs have an especially powerful olfactory sense. Watson, a Labrador retriever, reliably paws his owner 45 minutes before her epileptic seizures begin, giving her time to move to a safe place. How does Watson know to do so? The best hypothesis is that the dog smells the chemical changes that precede epileptic seizures.

What do humans use smell for? For one thing, humans need the sense of smell to decide what to eat. We can distinguish rotten food from fresh food and remember (all too well) which foods have made us ill in the past. The smell of a food that has previously made us sick is often by itself enough to make us feel nauseated. Second, although tracking is a function of smell that we often associate only with animals, humans are competent odor trackers. We can follow the odor of gas to a leak, the smell of smoke to a fire, and the aroma of a hot apple pie to a windowsill.

What physical equipment do we use to process odor information? Just as the eyes scan the visual field for objects of interest, the nose is an active instrument. We actively sniff when we are trying to track down the source of a fire or an unfamiliar chemical odor. The **olfactory epithelium** lining the roof of the nasal cavity contains a sheet of receptor cells for smell (Figure 4.32), so sniffing maximizes the chances of detecting an odor. The receptor cells are covered with millions of minute, hairlike antennae that project through the mucus in the top of the nasal cavity and make contact with air on its way to the throat and lungs (Di Lorenzo & Youngentob, 2013; Lapid & others, 2011). Interestingly, unlike the neurons of most sensory systems, the neurons in the olfactory epithelium tend to replace themselves after injury (Vukovic & others, 2009).

● **olfactory epithelium** The lining the roof of the nasal cavity, containing a sheet of receptor cells for smell.

What is the neural pathway for information about smell? Although all other sensory pathways pass through the thalamus, the pathway for smell does not. In smell, the neural pathway first goes to the olfactory areas in the temporal lobes and then projects to various brain regions, especially the limbic system, which is involved in emotion and memory (Huart, Collet, & Rombaux, 2009; Stankewitz & May, 2011). Unlike the other senses, smells take a superhighway to emotion and memory, a phenomenon we will consider in more detail in Chapter 7.

Smell might have a role to play in the chemistry of interpersonal attraction (Hurst, 2009). From an evolutionary perspective, the goal of human mating is to find someone with whom to produce the healthiest offspring (Buss, 2012). Mates with differing sets of genes (known as the *major histocompatibility complex,* or *MHC*) produce healthier offspring with the broadest immune systems (Mueller, 2010). How do we find these people, short of taking a blood test?

Martie Haselton (2006) has conducted studies on interpersonal attraction using the "smelly T-shirt" paradigm. In this research, men are asked to wear a T-shirt to bed every day for a week without washing it. After they have been thoroughly imbued with a

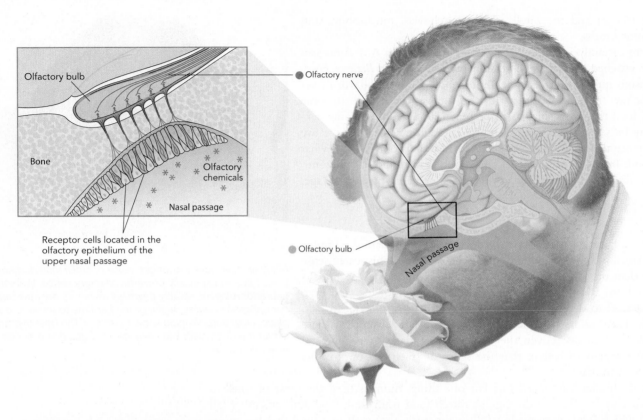

FIGURE 4.32 **The Olfactory Sense** Airborne molecules of an odor reach tiny receptor cells in the roof of the nasal cavity. The receptor cells form a mucus-covered membrane called the olfactory epithelium. Then the olfactory nerve carries information about the odor to the brain for further processing.

male's personal scent, the T-shirts are presented to women to smell and rate for attractiveness. Women reliably rate men whose MHCs are different from their own as more attractive, on the basis of the aroma of the T-shirts. Thus, although the eyes may be the window to the soul, the nose might be the gateway to love. To learn more about how smells relate to our emotions, see the Intersection.

The Kinesthetic and Vestibular Senses

You know the difference between walking and running, and between lying down and sitting up. To perform even the simplest act of motor coordination, such as reaching out to take a book off a shelf or getting up out of a chair, the brain must constantly receive and coordinate information from every part of the body. Your body has two kinds of senses that give you information about your movement and orientation in space, as well as help you to maintain balance. The **kinesthetic senses** provide information about movement, posture, and orientation. The **vestibular sense** provides information about balance and movement.

No specific organ contains the kinesthetic senses. Instead, they are embedded in muscle fibers and joints. As we stretch and move, these receptors signal the state of the muscle. *Kinesthesia* is a sense that you often do not even notice until it is gone. Try walking when your leg is "asleep" or smiling (never mind talking) when you have just come from a dentist's office and are still under the effects of Novocain. The kinesthetic senses are how you are able to touch your nose with your fingertip, even if your eyes are closed, because you feel where your body and body parts are, even without seeing them.

We can appreciate the sophistication of kinesthesis when we think about it in terms of memory. Even a mediocre typist can bang out 20 words per minute—but how many of us could write down the order of the letters on a keyboard without looking? Typing is a skill that relies on very coordinated sensitivity to the orientation, position, and

● **kinesthetic senses** Senses that provide information about movement, posture, and orientation.

● **vestibular sense** Sense that provides information about balance and movement.

Emotion and Sensation: What Do Feelings Smell Like?

For many species, it is adaptive to send out alarms calls to the other members of the group. Such calls do not always involve actual noises; sometimes they are smells. For example, when faced with a hungry predator, a nervous fish might release chemicals that alert members of its school to escape. Recall from the opening of this chapter the shark's amazing sense of smell. A potential shark snack does not have to be bleeding for a shark to notice—the shark can pick up on these alarm signals as well. When a fish sends out chemical warning signals, both members of its school and the potential predator can smell its fear. In nonhuman animals, such "chemosignals" provide a quick way to communicate alarms.

Traditionally, it has been thought that humans do not have chemosignals, that our emotions do not cause us to smell a certain way to others (Wyatt, 2003). However, research has begun to suggest that our emotions may cause our sweat to *smell* different. Consider a study that compared sweat generated by donors who were afraid and sweat generated by those engaged in sports (Zhou & Chen, 2009). Sweat from those who were afraid led to greater caution in the smellers than sweat from physical activity.

In a recent study, Jasper de Groot and his colleagues (2012) examined whether the chemical signals emitted by a person while in a particular emotional state would foster that same emotion in another person who smelled that person's sweat. In the first part of the study, the researchers,

What other feelings might change our body odor?

essentially, collected sweat. Men, seated in a very warm room, watched one of two film clips meant to foster feelings of fear (scenes from the movie *The Shining*) or disgust (scenes from the television show *Jackass*) while absorbent pads were tucked into their armpits. These pads were then frozen so that they could be used later in the study.

In the second part of the study, women smelled the thawed pads (along with some unused "control pads") while various measures were taken. First, the researchers precisely measured facial muscle activity to see if the women's expressions conformed to the emotions the men had experienced when they emitted the sweat. Results showed that women's faces were more likely to show a fear face when smelling the fear sweat and more likely to show a disgust face when smelling the disgust sweat.

Second, the women's heart rate was measured during the task, and it was higher while sniffing the fear sweat. In addition, the emotion associated with the sweat influenced the type of sniffing that occurred. For fear sweat, women were more likely to take a big second whiff of the sweat, but for disgust sweat the second sniff was much smaller. Importantly, the smelling portion of the study was a double-blind procedure, meaning that neither the women nor the researcher running the study knew which pads were which.

When you think about how humans communicate fear, you might immediately think about screaming. But these results suggest that even in humans, letting others know we are afraid might travel through not only auditory or visual channels but also olfactory ones. If we want to appear calm and cool under duress, we might amend the saying, "Never let them see you sweat" to "and don't let them smell your sweat, either!"

movements of our fingers. We say that our fingers "remember" the positions of the keys. Likewise, the complicated movements a pitcher uses to throw a baseball cannot be written down or communicated easily using language. They involve nearly every muscle and joint in the body. Most information about the kinesthetic senses is transmitted from the joints and muscles along the same pathways to the brain as information about touch.

The vestibular sense tells us whether our head (and hence usually our body) is tilted, moving, slowing down, or speeding up. It works in concert with the kinesthetic senses to coordinate *proprioceptive feedback,* which is information about the position of our limbs and body parts in relation to other body parts. Consider the combination of sensory abilities involved in the motion of an ice hockey player skating down the ice, cradling the puck, and pushing it forward with the stick. The hockey player is responding simultaneously to a multitude of sensations, including those produced by the slickness of the ice, the position of the puck, the speed and momentum of the forward progression, and the requirements of the play to turn and to track the other players on the ice.

FIGURE 4.33 The Semicircular Canals and the Vestibular Sense The semicircular canals provide feedback to the gymnast's brain as her head and body tilt in different directions. Any angle of head rotation is registered by hair cells in one or more semicircular canals in both ears. (*Inset*) The semicircular canals.

● **semicircular canals** Three fluid-filled circular tubes in the inner ear containing the sensory receptors that detect head motion caused when an individual tilts or moves the head and/or the body.

test yourself

1. What three kinds of receptors form the cutaneous senses?
2. Describe how and why pain is adaptive.
3. What information about the body do the kinesthetic senses and the vestibular sense provide?

The **semicircular canals** of the inner ear contain the sensory receptors that detect head motion caused when we tilt or move our head and/or body (Figure 4.33). These canals consist of three fluid-filled, circular tubes that lie in the three planes of the body—right-left, front-back, and up-down. We can picture these as three intersecting hula hoops. As you move your head, the fluid of the semicircular canals flows in different directions and at different speeds (depending on the force of the head movement). Our perception of head movement and position is determined by the movements of these receptor cells (Welgampola, Bradshaw, & Halmagyi, 2011).

This ingenious system of using the motion of fluid in tubes to sense head position is similar to the auditory system of the inner ear. However, the fluid movement in the cochlea results from the pressure sound exerts on the oval window, whereas the movements in the semicircular canals reflect physical movements of the head and body. Vestibular sacs in the semicircular canals contain hair cells embedded in a gelatinous mass. Just as the hair cells in the cochlea trigger hearing impulses in the brain, the hair cells in the semicircular canals transmit information about balance and movement.

The brain pathways for the vestibular sense begin in the auditory nerve, which contains both the cochlear nerve (with information about sound) and the vestibular nerve (which has information about balance and movement). Most of the axons of the vestibular nerve connect with the medulla, although some go directly to the cerebellum. There also appear to be vestibular projections to the temporal cortex, but research has not fully charted their specific pathways.

Information from the sense of vision supplements the combination of kinesthetic and vestibular senses. This principle causes a motorist to slam on the brakes in his tiny sports car when the big truck next to him starts to move forward. When everything in our visual field appears to be moving, it is generally because *we* are moving.

5· SENSATION, PERCEPTION, AND HEALTH AND WELLNESS

Our senses are a vital connection to the world and to our experience, and we should not take them for granted. Ensuring the health of our senses means caring for our precious sensory organs—for example, by getting vision and hearing screenings and noting changes that might occur in our sensory experiences (Kolomeyer & others, 2013; McCaslin, 2013).

Taking care of your eyes means avoiding high-fat food, not smoking, and eating a diet rich in vitamins A, E, and C, zinc, and beta carotene. This means consuming a wide variety of fruits and vegetables (including your spinach). It also means reading with appropriate lighting (three times brighter than the rest of the room light) and with your work at eye level—about 16 inches away—and wearing sunglasses that protect your eyes from UVA and UVB, the sun's damaging rays. Some of the common causes of blindness are preventable but also undetectable. A glaucoma test is especially important after the age of 60. Staying active and eating healthy are important for avoiding another cause of blindness: diabetic retinopathy.

With respect to our hearing, perhaps the most dangerous threat comes from loud noise. A special concern is hearing damage that can be caused by loud noise during leisure activities (Beach, Williams, & Gilliver, 2013). Many of us enjoy listening to our favorite tunes on a portable media player. As these devices have become smaller and smaller, they have grown increasingly popular—we use them whenever we desire and wherever we are. These players use earbuds that transmit sound directly into the ear canal. How might this technology affect our hearing?

A study examined the safety of iPods for the hearing of listeners. Cory Portnuff and Brian Fligor (2006) found that a typical person could safely listen to an iPod for nearly 5 hours at 70 percent volume. The researchers concluded that those who like their tunes louder should not listen as long; if you listen at 90 percent volume, for example, keep yourself plugged in for no more than 90 minutes. One important issue is the environment in which the person is listening. Participants in the study were more likely to pump up the volume if they were listening to their iPods in environments that were already noisy. Interestingly, effects on hearing did not depend on the participants' choice of music. So, whether it is Kanye West, Barry Manilow, or Mozart, sensible listening is wise.

Throughout this chapter we have viewed sensation and perception as our connections to the world. How about treating your senses by taking them outside? Few things engage all of our senses like being outside in a natural environment. And experiences with the natural world have been shown to improve overall physical and psychological well-being (Cervinka, Röderer, & Hefler, 2012; Devlin & Arneill, 2003; Nisbet, Zelenski, & Murphy, 2011). Hospital patients recover more quickly if they have a window that looks out onto trees, sky, and plants (Ulrich, 1991). Taking a walk outside is an excellent way to get exercise as well as to open up your senses to the world. While you are walking, remember to stop and smell the flowers—literally. Flowers are visually pleasant and they smell good, so they are a natural mood booster for both men and women (Haviland-Jones & others, 2005).

Our senses allow us to experience the world in all its vibrancy. Sue Berry, who achieved the ability to perceive depth only after a long, arduous effort, described her encounter with nature on a snowy day. "I felt myself within the snow fall, among the snowflakes. . . . I was overcome with a sense of joy. A snow fall can be quite beautiful—especially when you see it for the first time" (quoted in Sacks, 2006, p. 73). Recall the example of Michael May who was able to see after 25 years of blindness. One night, with his seeing-eye dog Josh at his side, he decided to go look at the sky. Lying on the grass in a field, he opened his eyes. He thought he was "seeing stars"—in the metaphorical sense. He thought that the thousands of white lights in the sky could not really be real, but they were. As he remarked in his vision diary: "How sweet it is" (May, 2003; Stein, 2003).

test yourself

1. What are several strategies individuals can use to protect and preserve their vision?
2. What factor poses the most serious threat to hearing?
3. How do portable media players such as iPods impact hearing, and what can consumers do to reduce the potential harm from using them?

1. HOW WE SENSE AND PERCEIVE THE WORLD

Sensation is the process of receiving stimulus energies from the environment. Perception is the process of organizing and interpreting sensory information to give it meaning. Perceiving the world involves both bottom-up and top-down processing. All sensation begins with sensory receptors, specialized cells that detect and transmit information about a stimulus to sensory neurons and the brain. Sensory receptors are selective and have different neural pathways.

Psychologists have explored the limits of our abilities to detect stimuli. Absolute threshold refers to the minimum amount of energy that people can detect. The difference threshold, or just noticeable difference, is the smallest difference in stimulation required to discriminate one stimulus from another 50 percent of the time.

Signal detection theory focuses on decision making about stimuli in the presence of uncertainty. In this theory, detection of sensory stimuli depends on many factors other than the physical properties of the stimuli, and differences in these other factors may lead different people to make different decisions about identical stimuli.

Perception is influenced by attention, beliefs, and expectations. Sensory adaptation is a change in the responsiveness of the sensory system based on the average level of surrounding stimulation, essentially the ways that our senses start to ignore a particular stimulus once it is around long enough.

2. THE VISUAL SYSTEM

Light is the stimulus that is sensed by the visual system. Light can be described in terms of wavelengths. Three characteristics of light waves determine our experience: wavelength (hue), amplitude (brightness), and purity (saturation).

In sensation, light passes through the cornea and lens to the retina, the light-sensitive surface in the back of the eye that houses light receptors called rods (which function in low illumination) and cones (which react to color). The fovea of the retina contains only cones and sharpens detail in an image. The optic nerve transmits neural impulses to the brain. There it diverges at the optic chiasm, so that what we see in the left visual field is registered in the right side of the brain and vice versa. In the occipital lobes of the cerebral cortex, the information is integrated.

The trichromatic theory of color perception holds that three types of color receptors in the retina allow us to perceive three colors (green, red, and blue). The opponent-process theory states that cells in the visual system respond to red-green and blue-yellow colors. Both theories are probably correct—the eye and the brain use both methods to code colors.

Shape perception is the ability to distinguish objects from their background. Depth perception is the ability to perceive objects three-dimensionally and depends on binocular (two-eye) cues and monocular (one-eye) cues. Motion perception by humans depends on specialized neurons, feedback from the body, and environmental cues. Perceptual constancy is the recognition that objects are stable despite changes in the way we see them.

3. THE AUDITORY SYSTEM

Sounds, or sound waves, are vibrations in the air that are processed by the auditory system. These waves vary in important ways that influence what we hear. Pitch (how high or low in tone a sound is) is the

SUMMARY

perceptual interpretation of wavelength frequency. Amplitude of wavelengths, measured in decibels, is perceived as loudness. Complex sounds involve a blending of frequencies. Timbre is the tone saturation, or perceptual quality, of a sound.

The outer ear consists of the pinna and external auditory canal and acts to funnel sound to the middle ear. In the middle ear, the eardrum, hammer, anvil, and stirrup vibrate in response to sound and transfer the vibrations to the inner ear. Important parts of the fluid-filled inner ear are the oval window, cochlea, and basilar membrane. The movement of hair cells between the basilar membrane and the tectorial membrane generates nerve impulses.

Place theory states that each frequency produces vibrations at a particular spot on the basilar membrane. Place theory adequately explains high-frequency sounds but not low-frequency sounds. Frequency theory holds that the perception of a sound's frequency depends on how often the auditory nerve fires. The volley principle states that a cluster of neurons can fire impulses in rapid succession, producing a volley of impulses.

Information about sound moves from the hair cells to the auditory nerve, which carries information to the brain's auditory areas. The cortical destination of most fibers is the temporal lobes of the cerebral cortex. Localizing sound involves both the timing of the sound and the intensity of the sound arriving at each ear.

4. OTHER SENSES

The skin senses include touch, temperature, and pain. Touch is the detection of mechanical energy, or pressure, against the skin. Touch information travels through the spinal cord, brain stem, and thalamus and on to the somatosensory areas of the parietal lobes. Thermoreceptors under the skin respond to increases and decreases in temperature. Pain is the sensation that warns us about damage to the body.

The chemical senses of taste and smell enable us to detect and process chemicals in the environment. Papillae are bumps on the tongue that contain taste buds, the receptors for taste. The olfactory epithelium contains a sheet of receptor cells for smell in the roof of the nose.

The kinesthetic senses provide information about movement, posture, and orientation. The vestibular sense gives us information about balance and movement. Receptors for the kinesthetic senses are embedded in muscle fibers and joints. The semicircular canals in the inner ear contain the sensory receptors that detect head motion.

5. SENSATION, PERCEPTION, AND HEALTH AND WELLNESS

Senses connect us to the world. Taking care of your precious sense organs means adopting healthy practices such as eating a low-fat diet rich in vitamins and beta carotene. Caring for your eyes means wearing protective lenses when you are in the bright sun. Protecting your hearing requires avoiding dangerously loud noises. Noise at 80 decibels or higher, if heard for prolonged periods, can damage hearing. Experiences in nature have been shown to reduce stress and enhance well-being.

key *terms*

sensation, p. 104
perception, p. 104
bottom-up processing, p. 104
top-down processing, p. 104
sensory receptors, p. 106
absolute threshold, p. 108
noise, p. 110
difference threshold, p. 110
Weber's law, p. 111
subliminal perception, p. 111
signal detection theory, p. 112
attention, p. 113

selective attention, p. 113
perceptual set, p. 115
sensory adaptation, p. 115
retina, p. 117
rods, p. 117
cones, p. 118
optic nerve, p. 118
feature detectors, p. 119
parallel processing, p. 120
binding, p. 120
trichromatic theory, p. 121
opponent-process theory, p. 121

figure-ground relationship, p. 122
gestalt psychology, p. 123
depth perception, p. 123
binocular cues, p. 123
convergence, p. 123
monocular cues, p. 123
apparent movement, p. 125
perceptual constancy, p. 125
outer ear, p. 128
middle ear, p. 128
inner ear, p. 129
place theory, p. 130

frequency theory, p. 130
volley principle, p. 130
auditory nerve, p. 130
thermoreceptors, p. 132
pain, p. 132
papillae, p. 134
olfactory epithelium, p. 135
kinesthetic senses, p. 136
vestibular sense, p. 136
semicircular canals, p. 138

apply your *knowledge*

1. Find a partner and test your absolute threshold for sugar. Have your partner set up the following sugar-and-water mixtures. Mix 2 teaspoons of sugar in 4 cups of water. Label this solution ("solution X," for example). Take 2 cups of solution X, add 2 cups of water, and give this solution a second label ("solution D," for example). Then take 2 cups of solution D, add 2 cups of water, and give this a third label ("solution Q"). Continue taking 2 cups from each successive solution until you have a total of eight solutions, making sure to keep track of which solution is which. When you are done, the concentration of the solutions should be equivalent to 1 teaspoon in each of the following amounts of water: 1 pint (2 cups), 1 quart, 1 half-gallon, 1 gallon, 2 gallons, 4 gallons, and 8 gallons. Your partner should place a sample of one of the solutions in a cup and a sample of plain water in another, identical cup. You should taste the solution in each cup and decide which one is the sugar solution. Do this with all of the solutions until you can decide what your absolute threshold is according to the text's definition. Do you think your absolute threshold would vary depending on what you had recently eaten? Why or why not?

2. If you found the example of inattentional blindness in this chapter interesting, check out this website where you will find a video so that you can see for yourself:

   www.theinvisiblegorilla.com

3. It has been said that we taste with our eyes first. Professional chefs give great thought to the presentation of foods. Think about your favorite food and focus not on how it tastes but on how it looks. Now think about how it smells. How do vision, smell, and taste work together to produce the experience of your favorite dish? Would your favorite beef stew be just as appetizing if it were served in a dog food bowl?

4. Create a gestalt moment. You can use the corners of the pages of this book or a notebook. Draw a series of small, simple pictures, sketching one on the lower right-hand corner of each page. How about a stick figure—standing still, and then moving its arm, and then waving? Each successive picture should be as close to the one before it as possible but changing slightly to reflect the movement. Then, using your thumb, quickly allow the pages to flip rapidly in front of you. You have created a cartoon.

5. If you have a few minutes and a strong stomach, give your vestibular system a workout. Spin around quickly and repeatedly for a minute. You can spin in a swivel chair or standing in the center of a room (be careful of sharp edges nearby). When you stop, you will feel dizzy. Here's what is happening. The fluid in the semicircular canals moves slowly and is even slower to change direction. When we spin for a while, the fluid eventually catches up with our rate of motion and starts moving in the same direction. When we stop moving, however, the slow-moving fluid keeps on moving. It tells the hair cells in the vestibular canals (which in turn tell the brain), "We are still spinning"—and we feel as if we are.

6. Jot down all the foods you have eaten today. Search the web for the nutritional information on these—and evaluate how good you have been to your eyes today.

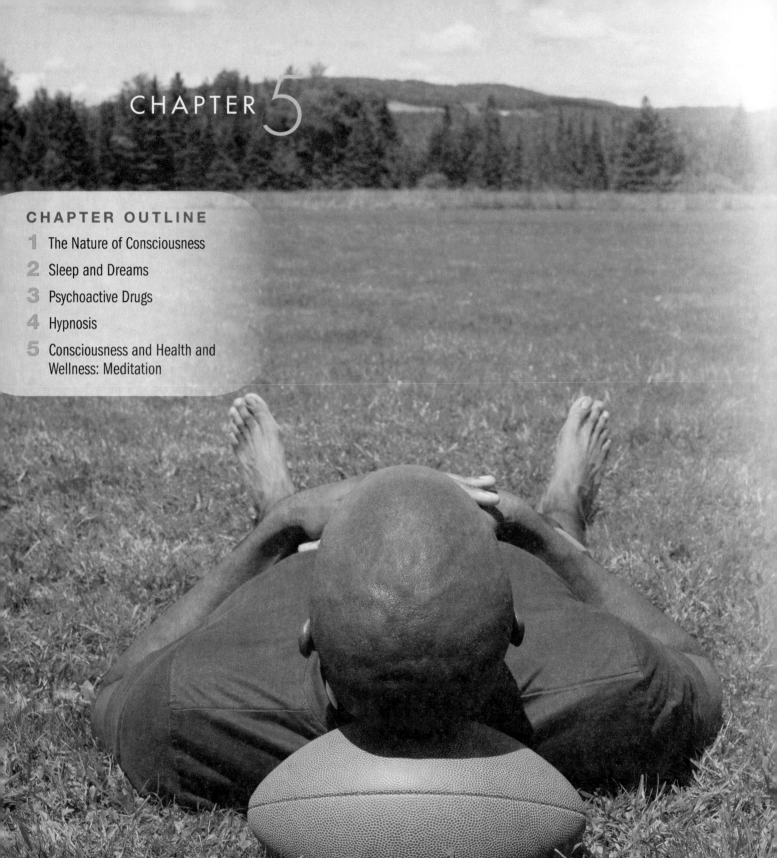

CHAPTER 5

States of Consciousness

When the Mind Is a Buried Treasure

The daily life of Erik Ramsey would seem to be the stuff of nightmares. In 1999, at age 16, he was horribly injured in a car accident. A blood clot in his brain stem caused a stroke, leaving Erik with a rare and permanent condition called *locked-in syndrome* (Foer, 2008). Erik cannot move or speak. He can feel an itch on his face but cannot reach up and scratch it. The only muscles over which he has any control are those that allow him to move his eyes. Erik uses his eye movements to communicate, answering yes (by looking up) or no (by looking down). Asked if he ever wished he had not survived his accident, Erik looks down. For all the limitations in his life, Erik has one important thing left: his mind.

Erik also has a loving family and a team of scientists dedicated to inventing a way for him to communicate. Scientists are working tirelessly to develop computer–brain interfaces that might eventually allow Erik, and individuals like him, to communicate with others using the ability to think (Chorost, 2011). In 2004, doctors used fMRI to pinpoint the brain locations that were active when Erik imagined himself speaking. They implanted electrodes in those areas. Since then, Erik has been laboriously learning to *think* the sounds he cannot make with his voice and to do so in a way that a computer will recognize and then translate them into speech. By 2010, he was able to produce three vowel sounds (Brumberg & Guenther, 2010).

The neurosurgeons, engineers, and computer scientists who are developing the technology hope that Erik will be able to "say" additional vowels, consonants, and perhaps even words and sentences with his mind. They are devoted to this task because the person thinking and feeling inside his eerily still body remains, they believe, Erik. Such is the power of consciousness in human life—that a conscious mind, locked in a body however limited, is still a person very much worth reaching. ●

PREVIEW

In this chapter, we review various states of consciousness, as well as the world of sleep and dreams. We also survey two channels of altered states of consciousness—psychoactive drugs and hypnosis. Finally, we consider the effects of achieving a meditative state of consciousness on health and well-being.

1· THE NATURE OF CONSCIOUSNESS

Consciousness is a crucial part of human experience (Bachmann, 2011; Chica & Bartolomeo, 2012). Our conscious awareness represents that private inner mind where we think, feel, plan, wish, pray, imagine, and quietly relive experiences. Consider that if we did not have private thoughts and feelings, we could not tell a lie.

● **stream of consciousness** Term used by William James to describe the mind as a continuous flow of changing sensations, images, thoughts, and feelings.

In 1890, psychology pioneer William James described the mind as a **stream of consciousness,** a continuous flow of changing sensations, images, thoughts, and feelings (James, 1950). The content of our awareness changes from moment to moment. Information moves rapidly in and out of consciousness. Our minds can race from one topic to the next—from the person approaching us to our physical state today to the café where we will have lunch to our strategy for the test tomorrow.

In his description of the stream of consciousness, James included aspects of our awareness that he described as on the "fringe" of the stream of consciousness. This fringe includes all of the thoughts and feelings that we have *about* our thoughts. We are aware not only of those things that take center stage in our mental life, those shiny fish in the stream of consciousness, but also of all the thoughts and feelings that surround those fish.

Today, psychologists use the term *metacognition* to describe the processes by which we think about thinking (McCormick, Dimmitt, & Sullivan, 2013). This term includes our awareness of the fringe elements of the conscious stream. When we read a text, for instance, the difficulty or ease with which we comprehend what is written can influence how we feel about what we read. When written text is easy to read, we are more likely to think that what we are reading is true and accurate (Petrova, Schwarz, & Song, 2012; Schwarz, Song, & Xu, 2009).

The metacognitive experience of ease can impact our thought processes in surprising ways. Consider the two items below, taken from a questionnaire that measures the experience of meaning in life (Steger & others, 2006). The top one is printed in a difficult-to-read font, the bottom one in a clear, easy-to-read font:

I HAVE FOUND a really significant MEANING IN my life.
I have found a really significant meaning in my life.

A recent study found that participants rated their meaning in life to be lower when the scale used the difficult-to-read font (Trent, Lavelock, & King, 2013).

Other research has shown that when youth experienced metacognitive difficulty in thinking about their life goals, they were less likely to believe they could reach those goals (Oyserman, Elmore, & Smith, 2012). The logic behind such results is that while thinking about his or her life goals, the person might reason, "If it is this hard for me to even imagine myself pursuing these goals, they must not be very possible."

During much of the twentieth century, psychologists focused less on the study of mental processes and more on the study of observable behavior. More recently, the study of consciousness has regained widespread respectability in psychology (Aly & Yonelinas, 2012; Bachmann, 2011). Scientists from many different fields are interested in consciousness (Shkurko, 2013; Silberstein & Chemero, 2012; J. G. Taylor, 2012).

Defining Consciousness

We define consciousness in terms of its two parts: awareness and arousal. **Consciousness** is an individual's awareness of external events and internal sensations under a condition of arousal. *Awareness* includes awareness of the self and thoughts about one's experiences. Consider that on an autumn afternoon, when you see a beautiful tree, vibrant with color, you do not simply perceive the colors; you are also *aware* that you are seeing them.

The second part of consciousness is *arousal*, the physiological state of being engaged with the environment. Thus, a sleeping person is not conscious in the same way that he or she would be while awake.

Consciousness and the Brain

There has been a dramatic increase in theoretical and research interest in determining more specifically how the brain functions to produce consciousness (Demertzi, Soddu, & Laureys, 2013; Northoff, 2013). The two aspects of consciousness, awareness and arousal, are associated with different parts of the brain (de Graaf, Hsieh, & Sack, 2012). Stanilas Dehaene and his colleagues describe *awareness,* the subjective state of being conscious of what is going on, as occurring in a *global brain workspace* that involves a variety of brain areas working in parallel (Dehaene & Changeux, 2011; Dehaene & others, 2006; Del Cul & others, 2009; Faugeras & others, 2012). This wide-reaching brain workspace is an assembly of neurons that are thought to work in cooperation to produce the subjective sense of consciousness.

Areas of the prefrontal cortex appear to be especially involved in the ways that awareness goes beyond the input of sensory information. For instance, these areas of the brain are active when we taste complex flavors, such as umami, and track the subjective pleasure that accompanies rewarding the experiences (Kringelbach, 2005). According to the brain workspace approach to consciousness, the widespread availability of information broadcast throughout the brain is what we experience as conscious awareness (Baars, 2010; Bartolomei & Naccache, 2011; Sergent & Naccache, 2012). However, scientists still do not know many of the details that link consciousness with brain states.

The second part of consciousness, *arousal,* is a physiological state determined by the reticular activating system, a network of structures including the brain stem, medulla, and thalamus. Arousal refers to the ways that awareness is regulated: If we are in danger, we might need to be on "high alert," but if we are in a safe environment with no immediate demands, we can relax, and our arousal may be quite low.

You might think of consciousness as the mind, that part of yourself that contains your private thoughts and feelings. It might seem obvious that other people have private thoughts and feelings as well, but the human ability to recognize the subjective experience of another is a true developmental accomplishment. Developmental psychologists who study children's ideas about mental states use the phrase **theory of mind** to refer to individuals' understanding that they and others think, feel, perceive, and have private experiences (Astington & Hughes, 2013; Wellman, 2011**)**. Although previous research suggested that theory of mind was likely to emerge around the age of 4, more recently studies have shown that if the tasks used to measure theory of mind are simplified, even younger children demonstrate a capacity to understand that other people have their own perspective on things (Rubio-Fernández & Geurts, 2013).

Theory of mind is essential to many valuable social capacities, such as empathy and sympathy (Reniers & others, 2012; Sebastian & others, 2012). Simon Baron-Cohen (1995, 2008, 2011) is an expert on *autism,* a disorder that affects communication and social interaction. He has proposed that the emergence of theory of mind is so central to human functioning that evolution would not leave it up to chance. Baron-Cohen

● **consciousness** An individual's awareness of external events and internal sensations under a condition of arousal, including awareness of the self and thoughts about one's experiences.

● **theory of mind** Individuals' understanding that they and others think, feel, perceive, and have private experiences.

suggests that we are born with a brain mechanism that is ready to develop a theory of mind; he has proposed that autistic individuals lack a well-developed theory of mind, a condition that would explain their unique social deficits.

Levels of Awareness

The flow of sensations, images, thoughts, and feelings that William James spoke of can occur at different levels of awareness. Although we might think of consciousness as either present or not, there are in fact shades of awareness, just as there are shades of perception in signal detection theory, as discussed in Chapter 4. Here we consider five levels of awareness: higher-level consciousness, lower-level consciousness, altered states of consciousness, subconscious awareness, and no awareness (Figure 5.1).

HIGHER-LEVEL CONSCIOUSNESS

● **controlled processes** The most alert states of human consciousness, during which individuals actively focus their efforts toward a goal.

In **controlled processes,** the most alert states of human consciousness, individuals actively focus their efforts toward a goal (de Lange & others, 2011; Diamond, 2013). For example, watch a classmate as he struggles to master the unfamiliar buttons on his new smartphone. He does not hear you humming or notice the intriguing shadow on the wall. His state of focused awareness illustrates the idea of controlled processes. Controlled processes require selective attention (see Chapter 4): the ability to concentrate on a specific aspect of experience while ignoring others (Gazzaley & Nobre, 2012). Controlled processes are slower than automatic processes and are more likely to involve the prefrontal cortex (Gaillard & others, 2009). Often, after we have practiced an activity a great deal, we no longer have to think about it while doing it. It becomes automatic and faster.

● **executive function** Higher-order, complex cognitive processes, including thinking, planning, and problem solving.

A key aspect of controlled processing is executive function. **Executive function** refers to higher-order, complex cognitive processes, including thinking, planning, and problem solving. These cognitive processes are linked to the functioning of the brain's prefrontal cortex (Carlson, Zelazo, & Faja, 2013; Liew, 2012). Executive function is the person's capacity to harness consciousness, to focus in on specific thoughts while ignoring others.

FIGURE 5.1 Levels of Awareness Each level of awareness has its time and place in human life.

Level of Awareness	Description	Examples
Higher-Level Consciousness	Involves controlled processing, in which individuals actively focus their efforts on attaining a goal; the most alert state of consciousness	Doing a math or science problem; preparing for a debate; taking an at-bat in a baseball game
Lower-Level Consciousness	Includes automatic processing that requires little attention, as well as daydreaming	Punching in a number on a cell phone; typing on a keyboard when one is an expert; gazing at a sunset
Altered States of Consciousness	Can be produced by drugs, trauma, fatigue, possibly hypnosis, and sensory deprivation	Feeling the effects of having taken alcohol or psychedelic drugs; undergoing hypnosis to quit smoking or lose weight
Subconscious Awareness	Can occur when people are awake, as well as when they are sleeping and dreaming	Sleeping and dreaming
No Awareness	Freud's belief that some unconscious thoughts are too laden with anxiety and other negative emotions for consciousness to admit them	Having unconscious thoughts; being knocked out by a blow or anesthetized

This aspect of executive function is called *cognitive control;* it is the capacity to maintain attention by reducing interfering thoughts and being cognitively flexible (Diamond, 2013).

Think about all the times you need to engage in cognitive control. Ellen Galinsky, a noted researcher on cognitive development, has suggested these common situations of cognitive control (Galinsky, 2010):

- Making a real effort to stick with a task; avoiding interfering thoughts or environmental events and instead doing what is most effective.

- Stopping and thinking before acting to avoid blurting out something a minute or two later you wished you hadn't said.

- Continuing to work on something that is important but boring when there is something a lot more fun to do. Inhibiting your behavior and doing the boring but important task, saying to yourself, "I have to show the self-discipline to finish this."

LOWER-LEVEL CONSCIOUSNESS

Beneath the level of controlled processes are other levels of conscious awareness. Lower levels of awareness include automatic processes and daydreaming.

Automatic Processes A few weeks after acquiring his smartphone, your classmate sends a text message in the middle of a conversation with you. He does not have to concentrate on the keys and hardly seems aware of the device as he continues to talk to you while finishing his lunch. Using his phone has reached the point of automatic processing.

Automatic processes are states of consciousness that require little attention and do not interfere with other ongoing activities. Automatic processes require less conscious effort than controlled processes (Darling & others, 2012). When we are awake, our automatic behaviors occur at a lower level of awareness than controlled processes, but they are still conscious behaviors. Your classmate pushed the right buttons, so at some level he apparently was aware of what he was doing. This kind of automatic behavior suggests that we can be aware of stimuli on some level without paying attention to them (Schmitz & Wentura, 2012).

Psychologists from a variety of subfields have been interested in studying the interplay of controlled and automatic processes. One area in which there has been a great deal of recent research is in the domain of moral reasoning. Historically, psychologists interested in moral decision making focused on the ways that conscious reasoning influenced moral judgment (Kohlberg, 1981). However, more recently scientists have begun to question the role of conscious reflection in resolving moral dilemmas. To read more about this work, see the Critical Controversy.

● **automatic processes** States of consciousness that require little attention and do not interfere with other ongoing activities.

Daydreaming Another state of consciousness that involves a low level of conscious effort is *daydreaming,* which lies between active consciousness and dreaming while asleep. It is a little like dreaming while we are awake (Domhoff, 2011; Stawarczyk & others, 2012). Daydreams usually begin spontaneously when we are doing something that requires less than our full attention.

Mind wandering is probably the most obvious type of daydreaming (Marchetti, Koster, & De Raedt, 2012; Smallwood & others, 2011). We regularly take brief side trips into our own private kingdoms of imagery and memory while reading, listening, or working. When we daydream, we drift into a world of fantasy. We perhaps imagine ourselves on a date, at a party, on television, in a faraway place, or at another time in our life. Sometimes our daydreams are about everyday events, such as paying the rent, going to the dentist, and meeting with somebody at school or work.

The semiautomatic flow of daydreaming can be useful. As you daydream while ironing a shirt or walking to the store, you may make plans, solve a problem, or come up with a creative idea. Daydreams can remind us of important things ahead. Daydreaming keeps our minds active while helping us to cope, create, and fantasize (Mar, Mason, & Litvack, 2012). When our mind wanders, it often wanders to the future (Baird, Smallwood, & Schooler, 2011; Schooler & others, 2011).

CRITICAL CONTROVERSY

Does Conscious Reflection Matter to Matters of Conscience?

Sam is the captain of a military submarine traveling under an iceberg. An explosion onboard has left the vessel with limited oxygen. One crewmember is mortally injured. He will certainly die. The remaining oxygen onboard is not enough for Sam and his crew to survive. The only way to save his crew is for Sam to shoot dead the injured crewman. Is it okay for Sam to kill him?

As you consider this moral dilemma, see if you can detect the two kinds of processes, automatic and controlled, at work. Your automatic reaction might involve outright horror at the thought of killing the crewman. As you reflect, though, you might consider that killing that crewman makes rational sense: One man will die, but many others will be saved. This conclusion illustrates a *utilitarian* moral stance, one that considers the greatest good for the greatest number.

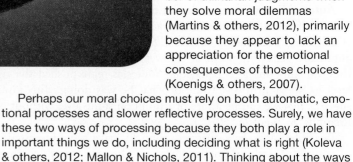

Social psychologist Jon Haidt (2001) proposed a *social-intuitionist* model of moral reasoning. The model claims that we often make moral decisions based on automatic, emotional reactions. From this perspective, conscious thought is used not so much to reach those decisions, but to justify them after the fact. Research using moral dilemmas, like Sam's, has shown that moral judgments often involve emotional processes and automatic reactions, rather than careful conscious thought (Greene & Haidt, 2002). Indeed, the brain regions that are active while individuals resolve personal moral dilemmas (such as the amygdalae) are often those involved in automatic emotional reactions (Sommer & others, 2010; Xue, Wang, & Tang, 2013). Such reactions are more common than utilitarian conclusions, especially when people are stressed (Youssef & others, 2012). Still, many scholars, including Haidt, believe that conscious reflection does play an important role in moral judgments, especially in helping us change our reactions or convincing others of the morally correct course of action (Haidt, 2003; Haidt & Kesebir, 2010; Kluver, Frazier, & Haidt, 2012).

How does conscious reflection influence moral decision making? As you might guess from the example above, when people give the matter careful thought, they are more likely to reach utilitarian conclusions (Paxton, Ungar, & Greene, 2012). Are such decisions more likely to be "morally right"? That is a difficult and complex question.

Consider that individuals who rely *primarily* on utilitarian principles in making moral judgments also tend to possess personality characteristics, like low levels of empathy, associated with *immoral* behavior, such as exploiting other people (Bartels & Pizarro, 2011). In addition, compared to healthy individuals, those who have suffered brain injuries, particularly damage to the ventromedial prefrontal cortex, reach an unusually high number of utilitarian judgments when they solve moral dilemmas (Martins & others, 2012), primarily because they appear to lack an appreciation for the emotional consequences of those choices (Koenigs & others, 2007).

Perhaps our moral choices must rely on both automatic, emotional processes and slower reflective processes. Surely, we have these two ways of processing because they both play a role in important things we do, including deciding what is right (Koleva & others, 2012; Mallon & Nichols, 2011). Thinking about the ways conscious thought influences moral judgments promises to illuminate not only those judgments, but also the very definition of what is morally right.

If you would like to explore and reflect on your own morality, check out www.yourmorals.org, a website created by Haidt and other social psychologists, where you can take self-assessments, participate in surveys, and learn more about how "moral minds" work.

WHAT DO YOU THINK
- What was the last moral dilemma you faced? How did you solve it?
- Why might it be adaptive for humans to have two ways of thinking about moral dilemmas?

ALTERED STATES OF CONSCIOUSNESS

Altered states of consciousness or *awareness* are mental states that are noticeably different from normal awareness (Fields, 2013). Altered states of consciousness can range from losing one's sense of self-consciousness to hallucinating. Such states can be produced by trauma, fever, fatigue, sensory deprivation, meditation, hypnosis, and psychological disorders. Drug use can also induce altered states of consciousness (Fields, 2013), as we will consider later in this chapter.

SUBCONSCIOUS AWARENESS

In Chapter 3, we saw that a great deal of brain activity occurs without that activity impinging on awareness. Right now you are unaware of many things your brain is doing to keep your body functioning or even the many stimuli in the environment to which your brain is responding. Your brain is processing information without you even noticing it. Psychologists are increasingly interested in the subconscious processing of information, which can take place while we are awake or asleep (Gainotti, 2012; Straube, Mothes-Lasch, & Miltner, 2011).

Waking Subconscious Awareness When we are awake, processes are going on just below the surface of our awareness (Almeida & others, 2013; Mealor & Dienes, 2012). For example, while we are grappling with a problem, the solution may pop into our head. Such insights can occur when a subconscious connection between ideas is so strong that it rises into awareness.

"If you ask me, all three of us are in different states of awareness."
© Edward Frascino/The New Yorker Collection. www.cartoonbank.com.

Incubation refers to the subconscious processing that leads to a solution to a problem after a break from conscious thought about the problem. The phenomenon of incubation is interesting because it suggests that even as you have stopped actively thinking about a problem, on some level your brain is still working on finding a solution. Interestingly, successful incubation requires that we first expend effort thinking carefully about the problem (Gonzalez-Vallejo & others, 2008). This suggests that although subconscious processing can ultimately lead to a solution, it requires that the appropriate information be thoughtfully considered to do so.

Recall Chapter 4's discussion of the parallel processing of visual information. Subconscious information processing also can occur simultaneously in a distributed manner along many parallel tracks. For example, when you look at a dog running down the street, you are consciously aware of the event but not of the subconscious processing of the object's identity (a dog), its color (black), and its movement (fast). In contrast, conscious processing occurs in sequence and is slower than much subconscious processing. Note that the various levels of awareness often work together. You rely on controlled processing when memorizing material for class, but later, the answers on a test just pop into your head as a result of automatic or subconscious processing.

Subconscious Awareness During Sleep and Dreams When we sleep and dream, our level of awareness is lower than when we daydream, but sleep and dreams are not best regarded as the absence of consciousness (Hobson & Friston, 2012; Windt & Noreika, 2011). Rather, they are low levels of consciousness.

Researchers have found that when people are asleep, they remain aware of external stimuli to some degree. In sleep laboratories, when people are clearly asleep (as determined by physiological monitoring devices), they are able to respond to faint tones by pressing a handheld button (Ogilvie & Wilkinson, 1988). In one study, the presentation of pure auditory tones to sleeping individuals activated auditory processing regions of the brain, whereas participants' names activated language areas, the amygdala, and the prefrontal cortex (Stickgold, 2001). We return to the topics of sleep and dreams in the next section.

NO AWARENESS

The term *unconscious* generally applies to someone who has been knocked out by a blow or anesthetized, or who has fallen into a deep, prolonged unconscious state (Laureys & Schiff, 2012; Lobo & Schraag, 2011). However, Sigmund Freud (1917) used the term *unconscious* in a very different way. **Unconscious thought,** said Freud, is a reservoir of unacceptable wishes, feelings, and thoughts that are beyond conscious awareness. In other words, Freud's interpretation viewed the unconscious as a storehouse for vile thoughts.

● **unconscious thought** According to Freud, a reservoir of unacceptable wishes, feelings, and thoughts that are beyond conscious awareness.

● **sleep** A natural state of rest for the body and mind that involves the reversible loss of consciousness.

● **biological rhythms** Periodic physiological fluctuations in the body, such as the rise and fall of hormones and accelerated and decelerated cycles of brain activity, that can influence behavior.

● **circadian rhythms** Daily behavioral or physiological cycles that involve the sleep/ wake cycle, body temperature, blood pressure, and blood sugar level.

● **suprachiasmatic nucleus (SCN)** A small brain structure that uses input from the retina to synchronize its own rhythm with the daily cycle of light and dark; the body's way of monitoring the change from day to night.

He believed that some aspects of our experience remain unconscious for good reason, as if we are better off not knowing about them. For example, from Freud's perspective, the human mind is full of disturbing impulses such as a desire to have sex with our parents.

Although Freud's interpretation remains controversial, psychologists now widely accept that unconscious processes do exist (Emmanouil, Burton, & Ro, 2013; Gainotti, 2012). Recently, researchers have found that many mental processes (thoughts, emotions, and perceptions) can occur outside of awareness. These unconscious processes can have a substantial impact on behavior. In Chapter 4, for example, we saw how stimuli presented outside of awareness can influence thoughts and behaviors, and in Chapter 6 we will see that many forms of learning operate without the need for awareness.

2· SLEEP AND DREAMS

By this point in your life, you have had quite a bit of experience with sleep. You already know that sleep involves a decrease in body movement and (typically) having one's eyes closed. What is sleep, more exactly? We can define **sleep** as a natural state of rest for the body and mind that involves the reversible loss of consciousness. Surely, sleep must be important, because it comprises a third of our life, taking up more time than anything else we do. *Why* is sleep so important? Before tackling this question, let's first consider how sleep is linked to our internal biological rhythms.

Biological Rhythms and Sleep

Biological rhythms are periodic physiological fluctuations in the body. We are unaware of most biological rhythms, such as the rise and fall of hormones and accelerated and decelerated cycles of brain activity, but they can influence our behavior. These rhythms are controlled by biological clocks, which include annual or seasonal cycles such as those involving the migration of birds and the hibernation of bears, as well as 24-hour cycles such as the sleep/wake cycle and temperature changes in the human body. Let's further explore the body's 24-hour cycles.

CIRCADIAN RHYTHMS

Circadian rhythms are daily behavioral or physiological cycles. Daily circadian rhythms involve the sleep/wake cycle, body temperature, blood pressure, and blood sugar level (Kujanik & Mikulecky, 2010; Powell & Schlotz, 2012). For example, body temperature fluctuates about 3 degrees Fahrenheit in a 24-hour day, peaking in the afternoon and dropping to its lowest point between 2 A.M. and 5 A.M.

Researchers have discovered that the body monitors the change from day to night by means of the **suprachiasmatic nucleus (SCN),** a small brain structure that uses input from the retina to synchronize its own rhythm with the daily cycle of light and dark (Oliver & others, 2012; Zeman & Herichova, 2013). The SCN sends information to the hypothalamus and pineal gland to regulate daily rhythms such as temperature, hunger, and the release of hormones such as melatonin (Lazar & others, 2013). The SCN also communicates with the reticular formation to regulate daily rhythms of sleep and wakefulness (Figure 5.2). Although a number of biological clocks seem to be involved in regulating circadian rhythms, researchers have found that the SCN is the most important (Han & others, 2012).

Many individuals who are totally blind experience lifelong sleeping problems because their retinas cannot detect light. These people have a kind of permanent jet lag and periodic insomnia because their circadian rhythms often do not follow a 24-hour cycle (Waller, Bendel, & Kaplan, 2008).

DESYNCHRONIZING THE BIOLOGICAL CLOCK

Biological clocks can become *desynchronized*, or thrown off their regular schedules. Among the circumstances of life that can introduce irregularities into our sleep are jet

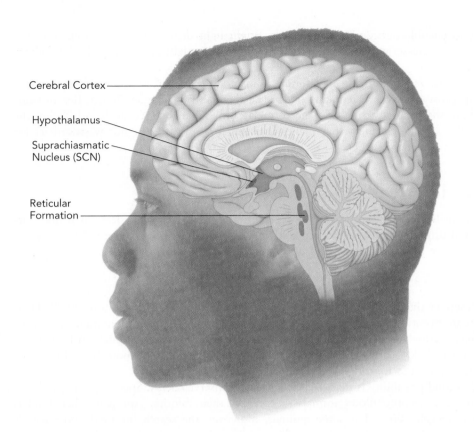

FIGURE 5.2 **Suprachiasmatic Nucleus** The suprachiasmatic nucleus (SCN) plays an important role in keeping our biological clock running on time. The SCN is located in the hypothalamus. It receives information from the retina about light, which is the external stimulus that synchronizes the SCN. Output from the SCN is distributed to the rest of the hypothalamus and to the reticular formation.

Cerebral Cortex

Hypothalamus

Suprachiasmatic Nucleus (SCN)

Reticular Formation

travel, changing work shifts, and insomnia (Lack & Wright, 2012; Vallières & Bastille-Denis, 2012). What effects might such irregularities have on circadian rhythms?

If you fly from Los Angeles to New York and then go to bed at 11 P.M. eastern time, you may have trouble falling asleep because your body is still on West Coast time. Even if you sleep for 8 hours that night, you may have a hard time waking up at 7 A.M. eastern time, because your body thinks it is 4 A.M. If you stay in New York for several days, your body will adjust to this new schedule.

The jet lag you experience when you fly from Los Angeles to New York occurs because your body time is out of phase, or synchronization, with clock time (Paul & others, 2011). Jet lag is the result of two or more body rhythms being out of sync. You usually go to bed when your body temperature begins to drop, but in your new location, you might be trying to go to sleep when it is rising. In the morning, your adrenal glands release large doses of the hormone cortisol to help you wake up. In your new geographic time zone, the glands may be releasing this chemical just as you are getting ready for bed at night.

Circadian rhythms may also become desynchronized when shift workers change their work hours (Kim, Woo, & Kim, 2012; Waage & others, 2012). A number of near accidents in air travel have been associated with pilots who have not yet become synchronized to their new shifts and are not working as efficiently as usual (Powell, Spencer, & Petrie, 2011). Shift-work problems most often affect night-shift workers who never fully adjust to sleeping in the daytime after they get off work. Sometimes these employees fall asleep at work, and they face an increased risk of heart disease, gastrointestinal disorders, and impaired immune system functioning (Haus & Smolensky, 2012; Puttonen, Viltasalo, & Härmä, 2011; Vogel & others, 2012).

RESETTING THE BIOLOGICAL CLOCK

If your biological clock for sleeping and waking becomes desynchronized, how can you reset it? With regard to jet lag, if you take a transoceanic flight and arrive at your destination during the day, it is a good idea to spend as much

Changing to a night-shift job can desynchronize our biological clocks and affect our circadian rhythms and performance.

time as possible outside in the daylight. Bright light during the day, especially in the morning, increases wakefulness, whereas bright light at night delays sleep (Paul & others, 2011).

Researchers are studying melatonin, a hormone that increases at night in humans, for its possible effects in reducing jet lag (Leatherwood & Dragoo, 2012). Recent studies have shown that a small dosage of melatonin can reduce jet lag by advancing the circadian clock—an effect that makes it useful for eastward but not westward jet lag (Herman & others, 2011).

Why Do We Need Sleep?

All animals require sleep. Furthermore, the human body regulates sleep, as it does eating and drinking, and this fact suggests that sleep may be just as essential for survival. Yet why we need sleep remains a bit of a mystery.

THEORIES ON THE NEED FOR SLEEP

A variety of theories have been proposed for the need for sleep (Harrison, 2012). First, from an evolutionary perspective, sleep may have developed because animals needed to protect themselves at night. The idea is that it makes sense for animals to be inactive when it is dark, because nocturnal inactivity helps them to avoid both becoming other animals' prey and injuring themselves due to poor visibility.

A second possibility is that sleep is a way to conserve energy. Spending a large chunk of any day sleeping allows animals to conserve their calories, especially when food is scarce (Siegel, 2005). For some animals, moreover, the search for food and water is easier and safer when the sun is up. When it is dark, it is adaptive for these animals to save their energy. Animals that are likely to serve as someone else's food sleep the least of all. Figure 5.3 illustrates the average amount of sleep per day of various animals.

A third explanation for the need for sleep is that sleep is restorative (Frank, 2006). Scientists have proposed that sleep restores, replenishes, and rebuilds the brain and body, which the day's waking activities can wear out. This idea fits with the feeling of being tired before we go to sleep and restored when we wake up. In support of the theory of a restorative function of sleep, many of the body's cells show increased production and reduced breakdown of proteins during deep sleep (Aton & others, 2009; Vazquez & others, 2008). Protein molecules are the building blocks needed for cell growth and for repair of damage from factors such as stress. One study linked short sleep duration with higher T-cell and lower NK-cell activities, indicating higher stress levels and lower immune system functioning (Fondell & others, 2011). Further, a recent study showed that sleep deprivation influences the immune system in a way that is similar to the effects of stress (Ackermann & others, 2012).

A final explanation for the need for sleep centers on the role of sleep in brain plasticity (Chauvette, Seigneur, & Timofeev, 2012; Tononi & Cirelli, 2011). Recall from Chapter 3 that the plasticity of the brain refers to its capacity to change in response to experience. Sleep has been recognized as playing an important role in the ways that experiences influence the brain. For example, neuroscientists recently have argued that sleep enhances synaptic connections between neurons (Chauvette, Seigneur, & Timofeev, 2012; Timofeev, 2011).

Findings such as these suggest an important role for sleep in the consolidation of memories (P. A. Lewis & others, 2011; M. P. Walker, 2012). A research review concluded that sleep is vital for memory consolidation, whether it is for specific information, for skills, or for emotional experiences (Diekelmann, Wilhelm, & Born, 2009). One possible explanation is that during sleep the cerebral cortex is free to conduct activities that strengthen memory associations, so that memories formed during recent waking hours can be integrated into long-term memory storage. Lost sleep often results in lost memories (Fenn & Hambrick, 2013).

So, if you are thinking about studying all night for your next test, you might want to think again. Sleep can enhance your memory. In a recent study that tracked over

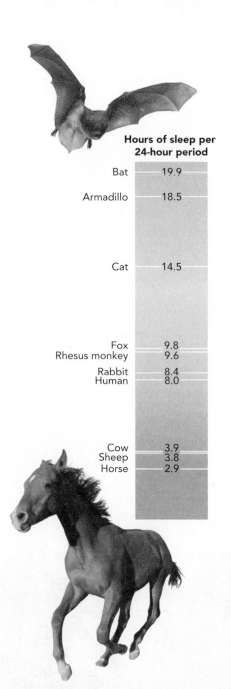

	Hours of sleep per 24-hour period
Bat	19.9
Armadillo	18.5
Cat	14.5
Fox	9.8
Rhesus monkey	9.6
Rabbit	8.4
Human	8.0
Cow	3.9
Sheep	3.8
Horse	2.9

FIGURE 5.3 From Bats to Horses: The Wide Range of Sleep in Animals We might feel envious of bats, which sleep nearly 20 hours a day, and more than a little in awe of horses, still running on just under 3 hours of rest.

500 students throughout their high school years, researchers found that those who sacrificed sleep in order to study had more difficulty learning new material the next day in school and were at greater risk for academic problems over time (Gillen-O'Neel, Huynh, & Fuligni, 2013). These effects were found even for students who set very high academic goals for themselves. Sleep can be as important as studying when it comes to academic achievement.

THE EFFECTS OF CHRONIC SLEEP DEPRIVATION

Most people think of 8 hours of sleep as a good night's rest. And though some research suggests that we do our best when we sleep at least 8 hours a night (Habeck & others, 2004), the basic amount of sleep each person needs may vary from person to person and as a function of age and activities (Matricciani & others, 2012).

Lack of sleep is stressful and has an impact on the body and the brain (Koenis & others, 2013; Monk, 2012). When deprived of sleep, people have trouble paying attention to tasks and solving problems (Jackson & others, 2011). Studies have shown that sleep deprivation decreased brain activity in the thalamus and the prefrontal cortex (Libedinsky & others, 2011) and reduced the complexity of brain activity (Jeong & others, 2001). The tired brain must compensate by using different pathways or alternative neural networks when thinking (Koenis & others, 2013). Sleep deprivation can reduce our ability to make other healthy choices. For instance, sleep deprivation may lead to difficulty in choosing healthy foods (Benedict & others, 2012).

The profound effects of sleep deprivation are vividly evident in a very rare disorder known as *fatal familial insomnia (FFI)*. This disorder, caused by a genetic mutation, involves a progressive inability to sleep. Over time, the person sleeps less and less, becomes agitated, engages in strange motor movements, and is confused. The person may hallucinate and enact dreams (Montagna & others, 2003). FFI has no known cure, and it leads to death, typically about 18 months after symptoms appear. The disorder can be difficult to diagnose and may be mistaken for other neurological disorders such as dementia or psychological disorders that include hallucinations (Moody & others, 2011).

Although few people suffer from FFI, this unusual condition demonstrates the vital restorative power of sleep. In addition, FFI highlights the role of the thalamus in sleep, because in cases of FFI the thalamus shows enormous damage.

Why do Americans get too little sleep? Pressures at work and school, family responsibilities, and social obligations often lead to long hours of wakefulness and irregular sleep/wake schedules (S. Y. Park, 2012). Not having enough hours to do all that we want or need to do in a day, we cheat on our sleep. As a result we may suffer from a "sleep debt," an accumulated level of exhaustion.

Stages of Wakefulness and Sleep

Have you ever awakened from sleep and been totally disoriented? Have you ever awakened in the middle of a dream and then gone right back into the dream as if it were a movie running just below the surface of your consciousness? These two experiences reflect two distinct stages in the sleep cycle.

Stages of sleep correspond to massive electrophysiological changes that occur throughout the brain as the fast, irregular, and low-amplitude electrical activity of wakefulness is replaced by the slow, regular, high-amplitude waves of deep sleep. Using the electroencephalograph (EEG) to monitor the brain's electrical activity, scientists have identified two stages of wakefulness and five stages of sleep.

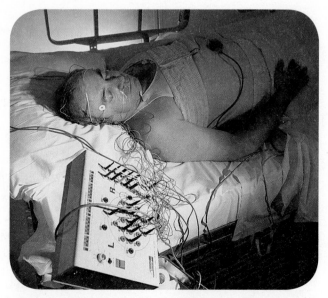

WAKEFULNESS STAGES

When people are awake, their EEG patterns exhibit two types of waves: beta and alpha. *Beta waves* reflect concentration and alertness. These

An individual being monitored by an EEG in a sleep experiment.

waves are the highest in frequency and lowest in amplitude—that is, they go up and down a great deal but do not have very high peaks or very low ebbs. They also are more *desynchronous* than other waves, meaning that they do not form a very consistent pattern. Inconsistent patterning makes sense given the extensive variation in sensory input and activities we experience when we are awake.

When we are relaxed but still awake, our brain waves slow down, increase in amplitude, and become more *synchronous,* or regular. These waves, associated with relaxation or drowsiness, are called *alpha waves.*

Using an EEG, we can differentiate the five stages of sleep by the various wave patterns. Furthermore, the depth of sleep varies from one stage to another, as we now consider.

SLEEP STAGES 1 TO 4

Stage 1 sleep is characterized by drowsy sleep. In this stage, the person may experience sudden muscle movements called *myoclonic jerks.* If you watch someone in your class fighting to stay awake, you might notice his or her head jerking upward. This reaction demonstrates that this first stage of sleep often involves the feeling of falling.

EEGs of individuals in stage 1 sleep are characterized by *theta waves,* which are even slower in frequency and greater in amplitude than alpha waves. The difference between being relaxed and being in stage 1 sleep is gradual. Figure 5.4 shows the EEG pattern of stage 1 sleep, along with the EEG patterns for the other four sleep stages and beta and alpha waves.

FIGURE 5.4 Characteristics and Formats of EEG Recordings During Stages of Sleep Even while you are sleeping, your brain is busy. No wonder you sometimes wake up feeling tired.

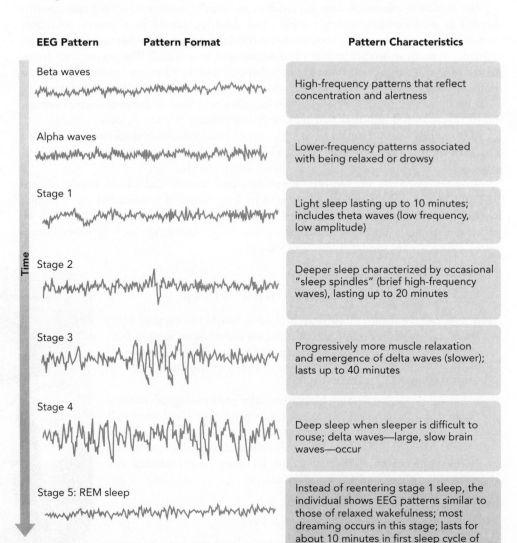

EEG Pattern	Pattern Format	Pattern Characteristics
Beta waves		High-frequency patterns that reflect concentration and alertness
Alpha waves		Lower-frequency patterns associated with being relaxed or drowsy
Stage 1		Light sleep lasting up to 10 minutes; includes theta waves (low frequency, low amplitude)
Stage 2		Deeper sleep characterized by occasional "sleep spindles" (brief high-frequency waves), lasting up to 20 minutes
Stage 3		Progressively more muscle relaxation and emergence of delta waves (slower); lasts up to 40 minutes
Stage 4		Deep sleep when sleeper is difficult to rouse; delta waves—large, slow brain waves—occur
Stage 5: REM sleep		Instead of reentering stage 1 sleep, the individual shows EEG patterns similar to those of relaxed wakefulness; most dreaming occurs in this stage; lasts for about 10 minutes in first sleep cycle of the night and up to 1 hour in the last

In *stage 2 sleep,* muscle activity decreases, and the person is no longer consciously aware of the environment. Theta waves continue but are interspersed with a defining characteristic of stage 2 sleep: *sleep spindles.* These involve a sudden increase in wave frequency (Andrillon & others, 2011). Stages 1 and 2 are both relatively light stages of sleep, and if people awaken during one of these stages, they often report not having been asleep at all.

Stage 3 and *stage 4 sleep* are characterized by *delta waves,* the slowest and highest-amplitude brain waves during sleep. These two stages are often referred to as *delta sleep.* Distinguishing between stage 3 and stage 4 is difficult, although typically stage 3 is characterized by delta waves occurring less than 50 percent of the time and stage 4 by delta waves occurring more than 50 percent of the time. Delta sleep is our deepest sleep, the time when our brain waves are least like our brain waves while we are awake. It is during delta sleep that it is the most difficult to wake sleepers. This is also the stage when bedwetting (in children), sleepwalking, and sleep talking occur. When awakened during this stage, people usually are confused and disoriented.

FIGURE 5.5 **REM Sleep** During REM sleep, your eyes move rapidly.

REM SLEEP

After going through stages 1 to 4, sleepers drift up through the sleep stages toward wakefulness. Instead of reentering stage 1, however, they enter stage 5, a different form of sleep called REM (rapid eye movement) sleep (Colrain & Baker, 2011). **REM sleep** is an active stage of sleep during which the most vivid dreaming occurs (Boeve, 2010). The EEG pattern for REM sleep shows fast waves similar to those of relaxed wakefulness, and the sleeper's eyeballs move up and down and from left to right (Figure 5.5).

Specialists refer to sleep stages 1 to 4 as *non-REM sleep.* Non-REM sleep is characterized by a lack of rapid eye movement and little dreaming. A person who is awakened during REM sleep is more likely to report having dreamed than when awakened at any other stage (Marzano & others, 2011). Even people who claim they rarely dream frequently report dreaming when they are awakened during REM sleep. The longer the period of REM sleep, the more likely the person will report dreaming. Dreams also occur during slow-wave or non-REM sleep, but the frequency of dreams in these stages is relatively low (McNamara, McLaren, & Durso, 2007), and we are less likely to remember these dreams. Reports of dreaming by individuals awakened from REM sleep are typically longer, more vivid, more physically active, more emotionally charged, and less related to waking life than reports by those awakened from non-REM sleep (Hobson, 2004).

● **REM sleep** An active stage of sleep during which dreaming occurs.

SLEEP CYCLING THROUGH THE NIGHT

The five stages of sleep we have considered make up a normal cycle of sleep. One of these cycles lasts about 90 to 100 minutes and recurs several times during the night. The amount of deep sleep (stages 3 and 4) is much greater in the first half of a night's sleep than in the second half. Most REM sleep takes place toward the end of a night's sleep, when the REM stage becomes progressively longer. The night's first REM stage might last for only 10 minutes, but the final REM stage might continue for as long as an hour. During a normal night of sleep, individuals will spend about 60 percent of sleep in light sleep (stages 1 and 2), 20 percent in delta or deep sleep, and 20 percent in REM sleep (Webb, 2000).

SLEEP AND THE BRAIN

The five sleep stages are associated with distinct patterns of neurotransmitter activity initiated in the reticular formation, the core of the brain stem (Peigneux, Urbain, & Schmitz, 2012). In all vertebrates, the reticular formation plays a crucial role in sleep and arousal (see Figure 5.2). As previously noted, damage to the reticular formation can result in coma and death.

Three important neurotransmitters involved in sleep are serotonin, norepinephrine, and acetylcholine (Elmenhorst & others, 2012; Koziorynska & Rodriquez, 2011). As sleep begins, the levels of neurotransmitters sent to the forebrain from the reticular

psychological *inquiry*

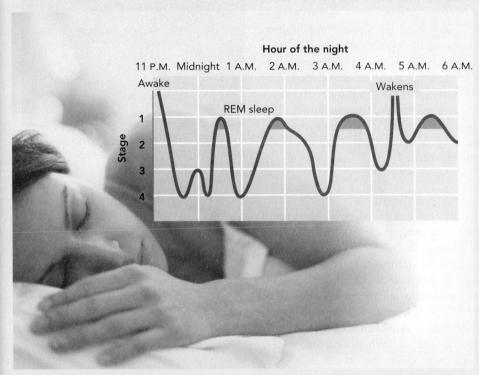

Taking a Ride on the Sleep Cycles

This graph depicts a night's sleep. During nightly sleep, we go through several cycles. Depth of sleep decreases, and REM sleep (shown in light blue) increases as the night progresses. Look carefully at the graph and answer the following questions.

1. How many sleep cycles are presented?

2. What time does the sleeper wake up?

3. If you woke the sleeper up at 2 A.M., would he or she be likely to remember a dream? Explain.

4. How much time is this sleeper spending in slow-wave sleep?

5. Trace the rise and fall of the neurotransmitters acetylcholine, serotonin, and nor-epinephrine in the sleep cycle depicted.

6. Has the sleeper whose night's sleep is illustrated here achieved a good night's rest? Why or why not?

formation start dropping, and they continue to fall until they reach their lowest levels during the deepest sleep stage—stage 4. REM sleep (stage 5) is initiated by a rise in acetylcholine, which activates the cerebral cortex while the rest of the brain remains relatively inactive. REM sleep ends when there is a rise in serotonin and norepinephrine, which increase the level of forebrain activity nearly to the awakened state (Miller & O'Callaghan, 2006). You are most likely to wake up just after a REM period. If you do not wake up then, the level of the neurotransmitters falls again, and you enter another sleep cycle. To review the sleep cycles, complete the Psychological Inquiry exercise above.

Sleep Throughout the Life Span

Getting sufficient sleep is important at every stage of human life. Figure 5.6 shows how total sleep time and time spent in each type of sleep varies over the life span.

Sleep may benefit physical growth and brain development in infants and children. For example, deep sleep coincides with the release of growth hormone in children. Children are more likely to sleep well when they avoid caffeine, experience a regular bedtime routine, are read to before going to bed, and do not have a television in their bedroom (Mindell & others, 2009).

As children age, their sleep patterns change. Many adolescents stay up later at night and sleep longer in the morning than they did when they were children, and these shifting sleep patterns may influence their academic work. During adolescence, the brain, especially the cerebral cortex, is continuing to develop, and the adolescent's need for sleep may be linked to this brain development (Colrain & Baker, 2012; Feinberg & Campbell, 2013).

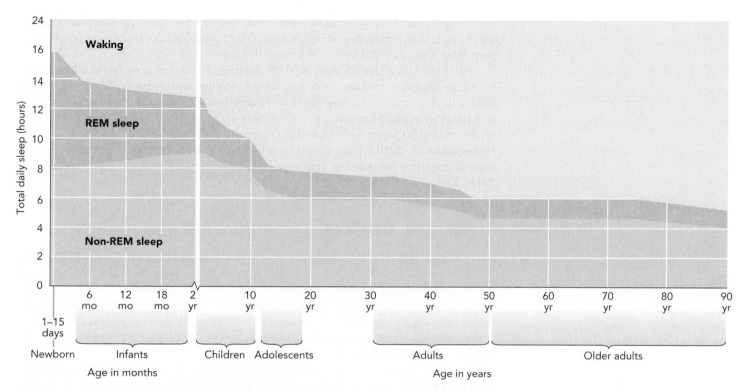

FIGURE 5.6 **Sleep Across the Human Life Span** With age, humans require less sleep.

Mary Carskadon and her colleagues have conducted a number of studies on adolescent sleep patterns (Carskadon, 2006, 2011a, 2011b; Crowley & Carskadon, 2010; Tarokh & Carskadon, 2010). They found that when given the opportunity, adolescents will sleep an average of 9 hours and 25 minutes a night. Most, however, get considerably less than 9 hours of sleep, especially during the week. This shortfall creates a sleep debt that adolescents often attempt to make up on the weekend.

The researchers also found that older adolescents tend to be sleepier during the day than younger adolescents. They theorized that this sleepiness was not due to academic work or social pressures. Rather, their research suggests that adolescents' biological clocks undergo a shift as they get older, delaying their period of wakefulness by about an hour. A delay in the nightly release of the sleep-inducing hormone melatonin seems to underlie this shift. Melatonin is secreted at about 9:30 P.M. in younger adolescents and approximately an hour later in older adolescents (Eckerberg & others, 2012). Based on her research, Carskadon has suggested that early school starting times may cause grogginess, inattention in class, and poor performance on tests. One study revealed that just a 30-minute delay in school start time was linked to improvements in adolescents' sleep, alertness, mood, and health (Owens, Belon, & Moss, 2010).

Do sleep patterns change in emerging adulthood (18–25 years of age)? Research indicates that they do (Galambos, Howard, & Maggs, 2011). In one study, the weekday bedtimes and rise times of first-year college students were approximately 1 hour and 15 minutes later than those of seniors in high school (Lund & others, 2010). However, the first-year college students had later bedtimes and rise times than third- and fourth-year college students, indicating that between 20 and 22 years of age, a reverse in the timing of bedtimes and rise times occurs.

Sleep patterns also change as people age through the middle-adult (40s and 50s) and late-adult (60s and older) years (Malhotra & Desai, 2010; Nakamura & others, 2011; Olbrich & Dittmer, 2011). Many adults in these age spans go to bed earlier at night and wake up earlier in the morning than they did in their younger years. As well, beginning in the 40s, individuals report that they are less likely to sleep through the entire night than when they were younger. Middle-aged adults also spend less time in deep sleep than they did before their middle years.

One study found that changes in sleep duration across five years in middle age were linked to cognitive abilities such as problem solving and memory (Ferrie & others, 2011). In this study, a decrease from 6, 7, or 8 hours of sleep and an increase from 7 or 8 hours were related to lower scores on most cognitive assessments. In late adulthood, approximately 50 percent of older adults complain of having difficulty sleeping (Neikrug & Ancoli-Israel, 2010). Poor sleep can result in earlier death and is linked to a lower level of cognitive functioning (Howrey & others, 2012; Naismith, Lewis, & Rogers, 2011; Tuckman & others, 2011).

Sleep and Disease

Sleep plays a role in a large number of diseases and disorders (S. R. Patel & others, 2012). For example, stroke and asthma attacks are more common during the night and in the early morning, probably because of changes in hormones, heart rate, and other characteristics associated with sleep (Teodorescu & others, 2006). Sleeplessness is also associated with obesity and heart disease (Sabanayagam & Shankar, 2010). Importantly, although lack of sleep is often associated with health problems, sleeping too much may also be a sign of problems (Hale & others, 2013).

Neurons that control sleep interact closely with the immune system (Imeri & Opp, 2009). As anyone who has had the flu knows, infectious diseases make us sleepy. The probable reason is that chemicals called cytokines, produced by the body's cells while we are fighting an infection, are powerfully sleep-inducing (Besedovsky, Lange, & Born, 2012). Sleep may help the body conserve energy and other resources it needs to overcome infection (Irwin & others, 2006).

Sleep problems afflict most people who have psychological disorders, including those with depression (Eidelman & others, 2012; Hidaka, 2012). Individuals with depression often awaken in the early hours of the morning and cannot get back to sleep, and they often spend less time in delta wave or deep sleep than do individuals who are not depressed.

Sleep problems are common in many other disorders as well, including Alzheimer disease, stroke, and cancer (Banthia & others, 2009; Fleming & Davidson, 2012; Gaig & Iranzo, 2012). In some cases, however, these problems may be due not to the disease itself but to the drugs used to treat the disease.

Sleep Disorders

Many individuals suffer from undiagnosed and untreated sleep disorders that leave them feeling unmotivated and exhausted through the day (Edinger & Morin, 2012; Rajaratnam & others, 2011). The major sleep disorders include insomnia, sleepwalking and sleep talking, nightmares and night terrors, narcolepsy, and sleep apnea.

INSOMNIA

A common sleep problem is *insomnia,* the inability to sleep. Insomnia can involve a problem in falling asleep, waking up during the night, or waking up too early (Gehrman, Findley, & Perlis, 2012). In the United States, as many as one in five adults has insomnia (Pearson, Johnson, & Nahin, 2006). Insomnia is more common among women and older adults, as well as among individuals who are thin, stressed, or depressed (National Sleep Foundation, 2007).

For short-term insomnia, most physicians prescribe sleeping pills. However, most sleeping pills stop working after several weeks of taking them nightly, and their long-term use can interfere with good sleep. Mild insomnia often can be reduced by simply practicing good sleep habits, such as always going to bed at the same time, even on weekends, and sleeping in a dark, quiet place. In more serious cases, researchers are experimenting with light therapy, melatonin supplements, and other ways to alter circadian cycles (Cardinali & others, 2012; Lichstein, Vander Wal, & Dillon, 2012; Zeitzer, Friedman, & Yesavage, 2011). Behavioral changes (such as avoiding naps and caffeine and setting an alarm in the morning) can help insomniacs increase their sleep time and awaken less frequently in the night.

SLEEPWALKING AND SLEEP TALKING

Somnambulism is the formal term for sleepwalking, which occurs during the deepest stages of sleep (Umanath, Sarezky, & Finger, 2011). For many years, experts believed that somnambulists were acting out their dreams. However, somnambulism takes place during stages 3 and 4, usually early in the night, when a person is unlikely to be dreaming (Zadra & Pilon, 2012).

SLEEPWALKERS CLUB NIGHT OUT

© Steamy Raimon. www.CartoonStock.com.

The specific causes of sleepwalking have not been identified, but it is more likely to occur when individuals are sleep deprived or when they have been drinking alcohol. There is nothing abnormal about sleepwalking, and despite superstition, it is safe to awaken sleepwalkers. In fact, they probably should be awakened, as they may harm themselves wandering around in the dark (Swanson, 1999).

Another quirky night behavior is sleep talking, or *somniloquy*. If you interrogate sleep talkers, can you find out what they did, for instance, last Thursday night? Probably not. Although sleep talkers will converse with you and make fairly coherent statements, they are soundly asleep. Thus, even if a sleep talker mumbles a response to your question, do not count on its accuracy.

You may have heard of cases of an even rarer sleep behavior—sleep eating. Ambien is a widely prescribed sleep medication for insomnia. Some Ambien users began to notice odd things upon waking up from a much-needed good night's sleep, such as candy wrappers strewn around the room, crumbs in the bed, and food missing from the refrigerator. One woman gained 100 pounds without changing her awake eating or exercise habits. How could this be? Dr. Mark Mahowald, the medical director of the Minnesota Regional Sleep Disorders Center in Minneapolis, has confirmed that sleep eating may be a side effect of using Ambien (CBS News, 2009).

The phenomenon of sleep eating illustrates that even when we feel fast asleep, we may be "half-awake"—and capable of putting together some unusual late-night snacks, including buttered cigarettes, salt sandwiches, and raw bacon. The maker of Ambien has noted this unusual side effect on the label of the drug. Even more alarming than sleep eating is sleep driving (Saul, 2006). Sleep experts agree that sleep driving while taking Ambien is rare and extreme but plausible.

For individuals who are battling persistent insomnia, a drug that provides a good night's rest may be worth the risk of these unusual side effects. Furthermore, no one should abruptly stop taking any medication without consulting a physician.

NIGHTMARES AND NIGHT TERRORS

A *nightmare* is a frightening dream that awakens a dreamer from REM sleep (Germain, 2012). The nightmare's content invariably involves danger—the dreamer is chased, robbed, or thrown off a cliff. Nightmares are common (Schredl, 2010); most of us have had them, especially as young children. Nightmares peak at 3 to 6 years of age and then decline, although the average college student experiences four to eight nightmares a year (Hartmann, 1993). Reported increases in nightmares or worsening nightmares are often associated with an increase in life stressors such as the loss of a job, the death of a loved one, or conflicts with others.

A *night terror* features sudden arousal from sleep and intense fear. Night terrors are accompanied by a number of physiological reactions, such as rapid heart rate and breathing, loud screams, heavy perspiration, and movement (Zadra & Pilon, 2012). Night terrors, which peak at 5 to 7 years of age, are less common than nightmares, and unlike nightmares, they occur during slow-wave stage 4 (non-REM) sleep.

NARCOLEPSY

The disorder *narcolepsy* involves the sudden, overpowering urge to sleep. The urge is so uncontrollable that the person may fall asleep while talking or standing up. Narcoleptics immediately enter REM sleep rather than progressing through the first four sleep stages (Siegel, 2011). Individuals with narcolepsy are often very tired during the day. Narcolepsy can be triggered by extreme emotional reactions, such as surprise, laughter, excitement, or anger. The disorder appears to involve problems with the hypothalamus and amygdala (Brabec & others, 2011). Although narcolepsy usually emerges in adulthood, signs of the problem may be evident in childhood (Nevsimalova, 2009).

SLEEP APNEA

Sleep apnea is a sleep disorder in which individuals stop breathing because the windpipe fails to open or because brain processes involved in respiration fail to work properly. People with sleep apnea experience numerous brief awakenings during the night so that they can breathe better, although they usually are not aware of their awakened state. During the day, these people may feel sleepy because they were deprived of sleep at night. A common sign of sleep apnea is loud snoring, punctuated by silence (the apnea).

Sleep apnea affects approximately 18 million Americans (Ho & Brass, 2011). The disorder is most common among infants and adults over the age of 65. Sleep apnea also occurs more frequently among obese individuals, men, and individuals with large necks and recessed chins (Kotsis & others, 2010; Sinnapah & others, 2013). Untreated sleep apnea can cause high blood pressure, stroke, and sexual dysfunction (Ho & Brass, 2011; Parati, Lombardi, & Narkiewicz, 2007; Vitulano & others, 2013). In addition, the daytime sleepiness caused by sleep apnea can result in accidents, lost productivity, and relationship problems (Hartenbaum & others, 2006). Sleep apnea is commonly treated by weight-loss programs, side sleeping, propping the head on a pillow, or wearing a device (called a CPAP, for *continuous positive airway pressure*) that sends pressurized air through a mask to prevent the airway from collapsing.

Sleep apnea may also be a factor in *sudden infant death syndrome (SIDS),* the unexpected sleep-related death of an infant less than one year old. SIDS is typically confirmed with an autopsy that reveals no specific cause of death (Byard & Krous, 2004; Fifer & Myers, 2002). It is common for infants to have short pauses in their breathing during sleep, but for some infants frequent sleep apnea may be a sign of problems in regulating arousal (Kato & others, 2003). There is evidence that infants who die of SIDS in fact experience multiple episodes of sleep apnea in the days before the fatal event (Kahn & others, 1992). One possible explanation for SIDS is an abnormality in the brain stem areas responsible for arousal (Broadbelt & others, 2012). Such an abnormality may lead to sleep apnea, which in turn might worsen the brain stem damage, ultimately leading to death.

Dreams

Have you ever dreamed that you left your long-term romantic partner for a former lover? If so, did you tell your partner about that dream? Not likely. However, you would have probably wondered about the dream's meaning, and if so you would not be alone. The meaning of dreams has eternally fascinated human beings. As early as 5000 B.C.E., Babylonians recorded and interpreted their dreams on clay tablets. Egyptians built temples in honor of Serapis, the god of dreams. Dreams are described at length in more than 70 passages in the Bible. Psychologists have also examined this intriguing topic.

FREUD'S PSYCHODYNAMIC APPROACH

Sigmund Freud put great stock in dreams as a key to our unconscious minds. He believed that dreams (even nightmares) symbolize unconscious wishes and that analysis of dream symbols could uncover our hidden desires. Freud distinguished between a dream's manifest content and its latent content. **Manifest content** is the dream's surface content, which contains dream symbols that disguise the dream's true meaning; **latent content** is the dream's hidden content, its unconscious—and true—meaning. For example, if a person had a dream about riding on a train and talking with a friend, the train ride would be the dream's manifest content.

Freud thought that this manifest content expresses a wish in disguised form. To get to the latent or true meaning of the dream, the person would have to analyze the dream images. In our example, the dreamer would be asked to think of all the things that come to mind when the person thinks of a train, the friend, and so forth. By following these associations to the objects in the manifest content, the latent content of the dream could be brought to light.

More recently, psychologists have approached dreams not as expressions of unconscious wishes but as mental events that come from various sources. Research has revealed a great deal about the nature of dreams (De Koninck, 2012). A common misconception is that dreams are typically bizarre or strange, but many studies of thousands of dreams, collected from individuals in sleep labs and sleeping at home, have shown that dreams generally are not especially strange. Instead, research shows that dreams are often very similar to waking life (Domhoff, 2007; Schredl, 2009; Schwartz, 2010).

So, *why* do many of us believe that our dreams are very peculiar? The probable reason is that we are likely to remember our most vividly bizarre dreams and to forget those dreams that are more mundane. Thus, we never realize how commonplace most dreams are. Although some aspects of dreams *are* unusual, dreams often are no more bizarre than a typical fairy tale, TV show episode, or movie plot. However, dreams do generally contain more negative emotion than everyday life; and certainly some unlikely characters, including dead people, sometimes show up in dreams.

There is also no evidence that dreams provide opportunities for problem solving or advice about how to handle life's difficulties. We may dream about a problem we are facing, but we typically find the solution while we are awake and thinking about the problem, not during the dream itself (Domhoff, 2007). There is also no evidence that people who remember their dreams are better adjusted psychologically than those who do not (Blagrove & Akehurst, 2000).

So, if the typical dream involves doing ordinary things, what *are* dreams? The most prominent theories that attempt to explain dreams are cognitive theory and activation-synthesis theory.

● **manifest content** According to Freud, the surface content of a dream, containing dream symbols that disguise the dream's true meaning.

● **latent content** According to Freud, a dream's hidden content; its unconscious and true meaning.

COGNITIVE THEORY OF DREAMING

The **cognitive theory of dreaming** proposes that we can understand dreaming by applying the same cognitive concepts we use in studying the waking mind. The theory rests on the idea that dreams are essentially subconscious cognitive processing. Dreaming involves information processing and memory. Indeed, thinking during dreams appears to be very similar to thinking in waking life (De Gennaro & others, 2012; Domhoff, 2011; Kahan & Sullivan, 2012).

In the cognitive theory of dreaming, there is little or no search for the hidden, symbolic content of dreams that Freud sought. Instead, dreams are viewed as dramatizations of general life concerns that are similar to relaxed daydreams. Even very unusual aspects of dreams—such as odd activities, strange images, and sudden scene shifts—can be understood as metaphorically related to a person's preoccupations while awake (Domhoff, 2007, 2011; Zadra & Domhoff, 2011). The cognitive theory also ties the brain activity that occurs during dreams to the activity that occurs during waking life. The term *default network* refers to a collection of neurons that are active during mind wandering and daydreaming, essentially whenever we are not focused on a task. Research suggests that dreaming during sleep may also emerge from the activity of this network (Domhoff, 2011).

The cognitive theory of dreaming strongly argues that dreams should be viewed as a kind of mental simulation that is very similar in content to our everyday waking thoughts. The same themes that occupy us in our waking life occupy our dreams. This perspective on dreams contrasts with activation-synthesis theory of dreaming.

● **cognitive theory of dreaming** Theory proposing that dreaming can be understood by applying the same cognitive concepts used to study the waking mind.

ACTIVATION-SYNTHESIS THEORY OF DREAMING

According to **activation-synthesis theory of dreaming,** dreaming occurs when the cerebral cortex synthesizes neural signals generated from activity in the lower part of the brain. Dreams result from the brain's attempts to find logic in random brain activity that occurs during sleep (Hobson, 1999; Hobson & Friston, 2012; Hobson & Voss, 2011).

When we are awake and alert, our conscious experience tends to be driven by *external* stimuli, all those things we see, hear, and respond to. During sleep, according to activation-synthesis theory, conscious experience is driven predominantly by internally generated stimuli that have no apparent behavioral consequence. A key source of such internal stimulation is spontaneous neural activity in the brain stem (Hobson, 2000). Of course, some of the neural activity that produces dreams comes from external sensory experiences. If a fire truck with sirens blaring drives past your house, you might find yourself dreaming about an emergency. Many of us have had the experience of incorporating the sound of our alarm clock going off in an early morning dream.

Supporters of activation-synthesis theory have suggested that neural networks in other areas of the forebrain play a significant role in dreaming (Hobson, Pace-Schott, & Stickgold, 2000). Specifically, they believe that the same regions of the forebrain that are involved in certain waking behaviors also function in particular aspects of dreaming (Lu & others, 2006). As levels of neurotransmitters rise and fall during the stages of sleep, some neural networks are activated and others shut down.

Random neural firing in various areas of the brain leads to dreams that are the brain's attempts to make sense of the activity. So, firing in the primary motor and sensory areas of the forebrain might be reflected in a dream of running and feeling wind on your face. From the activation-synthesis perspective, our nervous system is cycling through various activities, and our consciousness is simply along for the ride (Hobson, 2004). Dreams are merely a flashy sideshow, not the main event (Hooper & Teresi, 1993). Indeed, one activation-synthesis theorist has referred to dreams as so much "cognitive trash" (Hobson, 2002, p. 23).

Like all dream theories, activation-synthesis theory has its critics. A key criticism is that damage to the brain stem does not necessarily reduce dreaming, suggesting that this area of the brain is not the only starting point for dreaming. Furthermore, life experiences stimulate and shape dreaming more than activation-synthesis theory acknowledges (Domhoff, 2007; Malcolm-Smith & others, 2008).

One of the biggest reasons for the mystery associated with dreams is that dreams, like other contents of our minds, are private. Although we can share our dreams with others by talking about them or creating art that seeks to capture them, they are in some ways only truly available to the dreamer. Recently, scientists have begun examining the possibility of making private dreams public, using brain-imaging techniques. To read about this fascinating research, see the Intersection on page 163.

3· PSYCHOACTIVE DRUGS

One way that people seek to alter their own consciousness is through the use of psychoactive drugs. In fact, illicit drug use is a global problem. According to the United Nations Office on Drugs and Crime (UNODC), more than 200 million people worldwide use drugs each year (UNODC, 2012). Among those, approximately 27 million individuals are characterized as problem drug users—individuals whose drug habit interferes with their ability to engage in work and social relationships (UNODC, 2012).

Drug consumption among youth is a special concern because of its links to problems such as unsafe sex, sexually transmitted infections, unplanned pregnancy, depression, and school-related difficulties (Eaton & others, 2012; UNODC, 2012). The use of drugs among U.S. secondary school students declined in the 1980s but began to increase in the early 1990s (Johnston & others, 2012). Then in the late 1990s and early 2000s, the proportion of secondary school students reporting the use of any illicit drug again declined (Johnston & others, 2012).

● **activation-synthesis theory of dreaming** Theory that dreaming occurs when the cerebral cortex synthesizes neural signals generated from activity in the lower part of the brain and that dreams result from the brain's attempts to find logic in random brain activity that occurs during sleep.

test yourself

1. Describe how the human body monitors the change from day to night.
2. What happens during each of the five stages of sleep?
3. According to researchers, what functions does sleep play in infants and children? What functions does it play in adolescents?

Consciousness and Neuroscience: Can We Tell What the Brain Is Dreaming About?

Have you ever woken up from a vivid dream only to find that, in mere seconds, it is gone, seemingly wiped from your memory? At such times, you might wish that you had a mental DVR so you could replay that dream. Advances in neuroscience and computational technology have allowed scientists to take the first steps toward bringing this desire a little closer to reality.

The logic behind this work is surprisingly straightforward, although the actual research is, as you will see, quite arduous. Essentially, it involves systematically mapping out activity in the brain that is associated with various visual stimuli. Then, researchers plot that brain activity to recreate images of the stimuli.

For instance, in an early study, a team of Japanese scientists led by Yukiyasu Kamitani (Miyawaki & others, 2008) used fMRI to track brain activity in the occipital lobe (where visual stimuli are processed) while individuals were shown various images repeatedly. By recording the precise activity that occurred while participants were looking at different shapes, the researchers were able to develop ways to *work backward* from the brain activity to the image. In this way, they were able to recreate the image a person was seeing using only the brain activity as a guide (Miyawaki & others, 2008). This technology allowed them to create reproductions of the images a person was seeing in

Would you want others to see your dreams?

dreams, based only on his or her brain activity. Might such an approach allow us to "see" another person's dreams?

These researchers explored this question using EEG. Recall that during an EEG a person wears a cap featuring numerous electrodes that measure brain waves. Unlike fMRI, EEG is fast and can be used on subjects not inside a scanner, making it better suited to measuring people's sleeping brain activity (dreaming).

In a recent study, three volunteers wore EEG caps while sleeping (Costandi, 2012). The researchers woke up the participants shortly after they had fallen asleep and asked what they were dreaming about, a procedure that was repeated, multiple times through the night. Participants were awakened 10 times every hour. This very bad night's sleep for the participants provided about 200 different dream reports. Later, those same hardy souls returned to the lab for additional EEG measures taken while they looked at pictures of the things that they had reported had shown up in their dreams. Using this information, the researchers built a model that predicted dream content with surprising accuracy. Focusing on brain activity during the 9 seconds before participants were awakened, they could predict, for instance, whether there was a man in the dream with an accuracy of 75 to 80 percent (Costandi, 2012).

Surely, these results are a far cry from actually watching someone else's dreams, but they do provide a glimpse into the ways our brains dream, and they remind us that even when we are dreaming our brains are hard at work.

Imagine a world where others could see what we are dreaming or thinking. Sounds like science fiction, but the research presented here tells us that this fiction might someday be fact.

Drug use by U.S. high school seniors since 1975 and by U.S. eighth- and tenth-graders since 1991 has been tracked in a national survey called Monitoring the Future (Johnston & others, 2012). This survey is the focus of the Psychological Inquiry feature on page 164. Let's take a look at these trends.

Uses of Psychoactive Drugs

Psychoactive drugs act on the nervous system to alter consciousness, modify perception, and change mood. Some people use psychoactive drugs as a way to deal with life's

● **psychoactive drugs** Drugs that act on the nervous system to alter consciousness, modify perception, and change mood.

psychological *inquiry*

Drug Use by U.S. Teenagers

This graph shows the percentage of U.S. eighth-, tenth-, and twelfth-grade students who reported having taken an illicit drug in the last 12 months from 1991 to 2012 (for eighth- and tenth-graders) and from 1975 to 2012 (for twelfth-graders) (Johnston & others, 2012). The vertical axis shows the percentage of children and adolescents who report using illegal substances. The horizontal axis identifies the year of data collection. The most notable declines in adolescent drug use in the twenty-first century have occurred for marijuana, LSD, Ecstasy, steroids, and cigarettes. As you examine the data, answer these questions.

1. Do some research to find out about the social and cultural climate in each of the decades represented. Who was president at the time, and what historical events occurred? How does adolescent drug use reflect those times?

2. Data were not collected from eighth- and tenth-graders until 1991. Why do you think these two age groups were added?

3. After the mid-1990s, all age groups showed a similar decline in drug use. Why might this pattern have occurred in all three groups?

4. What are the implications of using self-reports from children and adolescents to track their drug use? Do you think each age group is similarly likely to report honestly, to overreport, or to underreport their drug use? Explain.

● **tolerance** The need to take increasing amounts of a drug to get the same effect.

● **physical dependence** The physiological need for a drug that causes unpleasant withdrawal symptoms such as physical pain and a craving for the drug when it is discontinued.

● **psychological dependence** The strong desire to repeat the use of a drug for emotional reasons, such as a feeling of well-being and reduction of stress.

● **addiction** Either a physical or a psychological dependence, or both, on a drug.

● **depressants** Psychoactive drugs that slow down mental and physical activity.

difficulties. Drinking, smoking, and taking drugs reduce tension, relieve boredom and fatigue, and help people to escape from the harsh realities of life. Some people use drugs because they are curious about their effects.

The use of psychoactive drugs, whether it is to cope with problems or just for fun, can carry a high price tag. These include losing track of one's responsibilities, problems in the workplace and in relationships, drug dependence, and increased risk for serious, sometimes fatal diseases (Fields, 2013; Zilney, 2011). For example, drinking alcohol may initially help people relax and forget about their worries. If, however, they turn more and more to alcohol to escape reality, they may develop a dependence that can destroy their relationships, career, and health.

Continued use of psychoactive drugs leads to **tolerance,** the need to take increasing amounts of a drug to get the same effect (Goldberg, 2010). For example, the first time someone takes 5 milligrams of the tranquilizer Valium, the person feels very relaxed. However, after taking the pill every day for six months, the individual may need to consume twice as much to achieve the same calming effect.

Continuing drug use can also result in **physical dependence,** the physiological need for a drug that causes unpleasant withdrawal symptoms such as physical pain and a craving for the drug when it is discontinued. **Psychological dependence** is the strong desire to repeat the use of a drug for emotional reasons, such as a feeling of well-being and reduction of stress. Experts on drug abuse use the term **addiction** to describe either a physical or a psychological dependence, or both, on the drug (Hales, 2011).

How does the brain become addicted? Psychoactive drugs increase dopamine levels in the brain's reward pathways (Espana & Jones, 2013). This reward pathway is located in the *ventral tegmental area* (VTA) and *nucleus accumbens* (NAcc) (Figure 5.7). Only the limbic and prefrontal areas of the brain are directly activated by dopamine, which comes from the VTA (Hnasko & others, 2010). Although different drugs have different mechanisms of action, each drug increases the activity of the reward pathway by increasing dopamine transmission. As we will see throughout this book, the neurotransmitter dopamine plays a vital role in the experience of rewards.

Types of Psychoactive Drugs

Three main categories of psychoactive drugs are depressants, stimulants, and hallucinogens. All have the potential to cause health or behavior problems or both. To evaluate whether you abuse drugs, see Figure 5.8.

DEPRESSANTS

Depressants are psychoactive drugs that slow down mental and physical activity. Among the most widely used depressants are alcohol, barbiturates, tranquilizers, and opiates.

Alcohol Alcohol is a powerful drug. It acts on the body primarily as a depressant and slows down the brain's activities. This effect might seem surprising, as people who tend to be inhibited may begin to talk, dance, and socialize after a few drinks. However, people "loosen up" after a few drinks because the brain areas involved in inhibition and judgment slow down. As people drink more, their inhibitions decrease even further, and their judgment becomes increasingly impaired. Activities that require intellectual functioning and motor skills, such as driving, become harder to perform. Eventually the drinker falls asleep. With extreme intoxication, the person may lapse into a coma and die. Figure 5.9 illustrates alcohol's main effects on the body.

The effects of alcohol vary from person to person. Factors in this variation are body weight, the amount of alcohol consumed, individual differences in the way the body metabolizes alcohol, and the presence or absence of tolerance (Sparling & Redican, 2012). Men and women differ in terms of the intoxicating effects of alcohol. Because of differences in body fat as well as stomach enzymes, women are likely to be more strongly affected by alcohol than men.

How does alcohol affect the brain? Like other psychoactive drugs, alcohol goes to the VTA and the NAcc (Ting-A-Kee & others, 2013). Alcohol also increases the

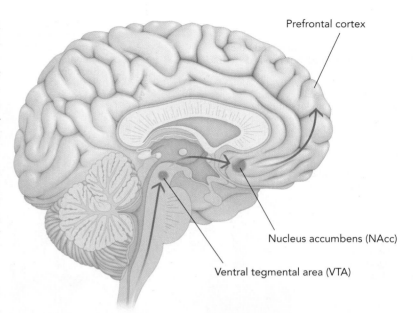

FIGURE 5.7 **The Brain's Reward Pathway for Psychoactive Drugs** The ventral tegmental area (VTA) and nucleus accumbens (NAcc) are important locations in the reward pathway for psychoactive drugs (Russo & others, 2010). Information travels from the VTA to the NAcc and then up to the prefrontal cortex. The VTA is located in the midbrain just above the pons, and the NAcc is located in the forebrain just beneath the prefrontal cortex.

Respond yes or no to the following items:

Yes	No	
☐	☐	I have gotten into problems because of using drugs.
☐	☐	Using alcohol or other drugs has made my college life unhappy at times.
☐	☐	Drinking alcohol or taking other drugs has been a factor in my losing a job.
☐	☐	Drinking alcohol or taking other drugs has interfered with my studying for exams.
☐	☐	Drinking alcohol or taking other drugs has jeopardized my academic performance.
☐	☐	My ambition is not as strong since I've been drinking a lot or taking drugs.
☐	☐	Drinking or taking other drugs has caused me to have difficulty sleeping.
☐	☐	I have felt remorse after drinking or taking drugs.
☐	☐	I crave a drink or other drugs at a definite time of the day.
☐	☐	I want a drink or other drug in the morning.
☐	☐	I have had a complete or partial loss of memory as a result of drinking or using other drugs.
☐	☐	Drinking or using other drugs is affecting my reputation.
☐	☐	I have been in the hospital or another institution because of my drinking or taking drugs.

College students who responded yes to items similar to these on the Rutgers Collegiate Abuse Screening Test were more likely to be substance abusers than those who answered no. If you responded yes to just 1 of the 13 items on this screening test, consider going to your college health or counseling center for further screening.

FIGURE 5.8 **Do You Abuse Drugs?** Take this short quiz to see if your use of drugs and alcohol might be a cause for concern.

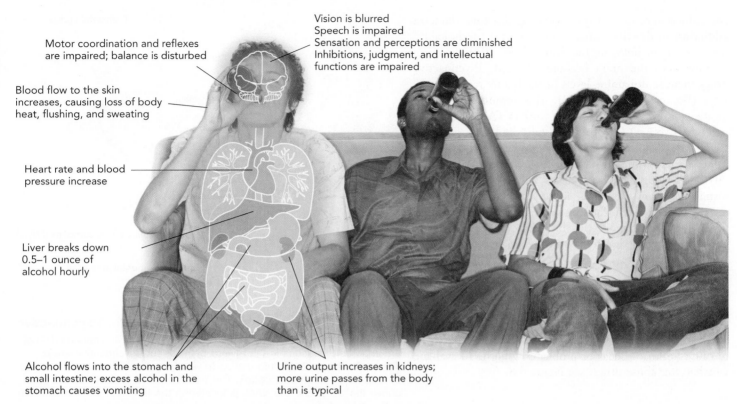

Motor coordination and reflexes are impaired; balance is disturbed

Vision is blurred
Speech is impaired
Sensation and perceptions are diminished
Inhibitions, judgment, and intellectual functions are impaired

Blood flow to the skin increases, causing loss of body heat, flushing, and sweating

Heart rate and blood pressure increase

Liver breaks down 0.5–1 ounce of alcohol hourly

Alcohol flows into the stomach and small intestine; excess alcohol in the stomach causes vomiting

Urine output increases in kidneys; more urine passes from the body than is typical

FIGURE 5.9 **The Physiological and Behavioral Effects of Alcohol** Alcohol has a powerful impact throughout the body. It affects everything from the operation of the nervous, circulatory, and digestive systems to sensation, perception, motor coordination, and intellectual functioning.

concentration of the neurotransmitter gamma aminobutyric acid (GABA), which is widely distributed in many brain areas, including the cerebral cortex, cerebellum, hippocampus, amygdala, and nucleus accumbens (Tateno & Robinson, 2011). Researchers believe that the frontal cortex holds a memory of the pleasure involved in prior alcohol use and contributes to continued drinking. Alcohol consumption also may affect the areas of the frontal cortex involved in judgment and impulse control (Bouchard, Brown, & Nadeau, 2012). It is further believed that the basal ganglia, which are involved in compulsive behaviors, may lead to a greater demand for alcohol, regardless of reason and consequences (Brink, 2001).

After caffeine, alcohol is the most widely used drug in the United States. As many as two-thirds of U.S. adults drink beer, wine, or liquor at least occasionally, and in one survey approximately 30 percent reported drinking more than five drinks at one sitting at least once in the last year (National Center for Health Statistics, 2005). The common use of alcohol is related to other serious problems, including death and injury from driving while drinking (Levinthal, 2010; National Highway Traffic Safety Administration, 2007).

Research has also found a link between alcohol and violence and aggression (Gallagher & Parrott, 2010; Noel & others, 2009). More than 60 percent of homicides involve alcohol use by the offender or the victim, and 65 percent of aggressive sexual acts against women are associated with alcohol consumption by the offender. Two recent studies found that substance use was linked to dating violence in adolescents (Epstein-Ngo & others, 2013; Temple & others, 2013).

A special concern is the high rate of alcohol use by U.S. secondary school and college students (Chen & Jacobson, 2012; Chung & others, 2012). In the Monitoring the Future survey, 40 percent of high school seniors surveyed reported

consuming alcohol in the last 30 days in 2011 (Johnston & others, 2012). The good news: That percentage (40) represents a decline from 54 percent in 1991. In the most recent survey, 25 percent of the high school seniors surveyed had engaged in binge drinking (having five or more drinks in a row) at least once during the previous month, down from 34 percent in 1997.

Binge drinking often increases during the first two years of college, and it can take its toll on students (Littlefield & Sher, 2010). In a national survey of drinking patterns on college campuses, almost half of the binge drinkers reported problems such as missed classes, injuries, trouble with the police, and unprotected sex (Wechsler & others, 2000, 2002). Binge-drinking college students were 11 times more likely to fall behind in school, 10 times more likely to drive after drinking, and 2 times as likely to have unprotected sex as college students who did not binge drink. Many emerging adults, however, decrease their alcohol use as they assume adult responsibilities such as a permanent job, marriage or cohabitation, and parenthood (Chen & Jacobson, 2012).

Alcoholism is a disorder that involves long-term, repeated, uncontrolled, compulsive, and excessive use of alcoholic beverages and that impairs the drinker's health and social relationships. Approximately 18 million people in the United States are alcoholics (MedlinePlus, 2012). A longitudinal study linked early onset of drinking to later alcohol problems. Individuals who began drinking alcohol before 14 years of age were more likely to become alcohol dependent than their counterparts who began drinking alcohol at 21 years of age or older (Hingson, Heeren, & Winter, 2006).

One in nine individuals who drink continues down the path to alcoholism. Those who do are disproportionately related to alcoholics; family studies consistently find a high frequency of alcoholism in the close biological relatives of alcoholics (Buscemi & Turchi, 2011; Sintov & others, 2010). A possible explanation is that the brains of people genetically predisposed to alcoholism may be unable to produce adequate dopamine, the neurotransmitter that can make us feel pleasure (Landgren & others, 2011). For these individuals, alcohol may increase dopamine concentration and resulting pleasure to the point where it leads to addiction (Meyer, Meshul, & Phillips, 2009).

Like other psychological characteristics, though, alcoholism is not all about nature: Nurture matters too. Indeed, research shows that experience plays a role in alcoholism (Kendler, Gardner, & Dick, 2011). Many alcoholics do not have close relatives who are alcoholics (Duncan & others, 2006), a finding that points to environmental influences.

● **alcoholism** A disorder that involves long-term, repeated, uncontrolled, compulsive, and excessive use of alcoholic beverages and that impairs the drinker's health and social relationships.

What does it take to stop alcoholism? About one-third of alcoholics recover whether they are in a treatment program or not. This finding came from a long-term study of 700 individuals (Vaillant, 2003). George Vaillant followed these individuals for over 60 years, and he formulated the so-called one-third rule for alcoholism: By age 65, one-third are dead or in terrible shape; one-third are still trying to beat their addiction; and one-third are abstinent or drinking only socially. In his extensive research, Vaillant found that recovery from alcoholism was predicted by (1) having a strong negative experience with drinking, such as a serious medical emergency; (2) finding a substitute dependency, such as meditation, exercise, or overeating (which has its own adverse health effects); (3) developing new, positive relationships; and (4) joining a support group such as Alcoholics Anonymous.

Barbiturates **Barbiturates,** such as Nembutal and Seconal, are depressant drugs that decrease central nervous system activity. Physicians once widely prescribed barbiturates as sleep aids. In heavy dosages, they can lead to impaired memory and decision making. When combined with alcohol (for example, sleeping pills taken after a night of binge drinking), barbiturates can be lethal. Heavy doses of barbiturates by themselves can cause death. For this reason, barbiturates are the drug most often used in suicide attempts. Abrupt withdrawal can produce seizures. Because of the addictive potential and relative ease of toxic overdose, barbiturates have largely been replaced by tranquilizers in the treatment of insomnia.

● **barbiturates** Depressant drugs, such as Nembutal and Seconal, that decrease central nervous system activity.

● **tranquilizers** Depressant drugs, such as Valium and Xanax, that reduce anxiety and induce relaxation.

● **opiates** Opium and its derivatives; narcotic drugs that depress the central nervous system's activity and eliminate pain.

Tranquilizers **Tranquilizers,** such as Valium and Xanax, are depressant drugs that reduce anxiety and induce relaxation. In small doses tranquilizers can bring on a feeling of calm; higher doses can lead to drowsiness and confusion. Tolerance for tranquilizers can develop within a few weeks of usage, and these drugs are addictive. Widely prescribed in the United States to calm anxious individuals, tranquilizers can produce withdrawal symptoms when use is stopped (Levinthal, 2010). Prescription tranquilizers were part of the lethal cocktail of drugs that ended the life of actor Heath Ledger in 2008.

Opiates Narcotics, or **opiates,** consist of opium and its derivatives; they depress the central nervous system's activity. These drugs are used as powerful painkillers. The most common opiate drugs—morphine and heroin—affect synapses in the brain that use endorphins as their neurotransmitter. When these drugs leave the brain, the affected synapses become understimulated. For several hours after taking an opiate, the person feels euphoric and pain-free and has an increased appetite for food and sex. Opiates are highly addictive, and users experience craving and painful withdrawal when the drug becomes unavailable.

Opiate addiction can also raise the risk of exposure to HIV, the virus that causes AIDS (Nath, 2010). Most heroin addicts inject the drug intravenously. When they share needles without sterilizing them, one infected addict can transmit the virus to others.

STIMULANTS

● **stimulants** Psychoactive drugs—including caffeine, nicotine, amphetamines, and cocaine—that increase the central nervous system's activity.

Stimulants are psychoactive drugs that increase the central nervous system's activity. The most widely used stimulants are caffeine, nicotine, amphetamines, and cocaine.

Caffeine Often overlooked as a drug, caffeine is the world's most widely used psychoactive drug. Caffeine is a stimulant and a natural component of the plants that are the sources of coffee, tea, and cola drinks. Caffeine also is present in chocolate, in many nonprescription medications, and in energy drinks such as Red Bull. People often perceive the stimulating effects of caffeine as beneficial for boosting energy and alertness, but some experience unpleasant side effects.

Caffeinism refers to an overindulgence in caffeine. It is characterized by mood changes, anxiety, and sleep disruption. Caffeinism often develops in people who drink

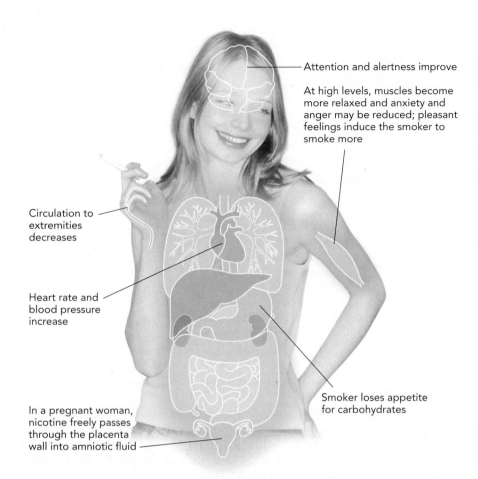

Attention and alertness improve

At high levels, muscles become more relaxed and anxiety and anger may be reduced; pleasant feelings induce the smoker to smoke more

Circulation to extremities decreases

Heart rate and blood pressure increase

In a pregnant woman, nicotine freely passes through the placenta wall into amniotic fluid

Smoker loses appetite for carbohydrates

FIGURE 5.10 The Physiological and Behavioral Effects of Nicotine Smoking has many physiological and behavioral effects. Highly addictive, nicotine delivers pleasant feelings that make the smoker smoke more, but tobacco consumption poses very serious health risks in the individual.

five or more cups of coffee (at least 500 milligrams) each day. Common symptoms are insomnia, irritability, headaches, ringing ears, dry mouth, increased blood pressure, and digestive problems (Hogan, Hornick, & Bouchoux, 2002).

Caffeine affects the brain's pleasure centers, so it is not surprising that it is difficult to kick the caffeine habit. When individuals who regularly consume caffeinated beverages remove caffeine from their diet, they typically experience headaches, lethargy, apathy, and concentration difficulties. These symptoms of withdrawal are usually mild and subside after several days.

Nicotine   Nicotine is the main psychoactive ingredient in all forms of smoking and smokeless tobacco. Even with all the publicity given to the enormous health risks posed by tobacco, we sometimes overlook the highly addictive nature of nicotine. Nicotine stimulates the brain's reward centers by raising dopamine levels (Kovacs, Lajtha, & Sershen, 2010). Behavioral effects of nicotine include improved attention and alertness, reduced anger and anxiety, and pain relief (Levinthal, 2010). Figure 5.10 shows the main effects of nicotine on the body.

Tolerance develops for nicotine both in the long run and on a daily basis, so that cigarettes smoked later in the day have less effect than those smoked earlier. Withdrawal from nicotine often quickly produces strong, unpleasant symptoms such as irritability, craving, inability to focus, sleep disturbance, and increased appetite. Withdrawal symptoms can persist for months or longer.

Tobacco poses a much larger threat to public health than illegal drugs. According to the Centers for Disease Control and Prevention (CDC), tobacco is involved in 1 in every 5 deaths in the United States (CDC, 2012c). That is more than the total number killed by AIDS, alcohol, motor vehicles, homicide, illegal drugs, and suicide combined. Today there are approximately 1 billion smokers globally, and estimates are that by 2030, another 1 billion young people will have started to smoke (United Nations World Youth

FIGURE 5.11 Trends in Cigarette Smoking by U.S. Secondary School Students Cigarette smoking by U.S. high school students is on the decline.

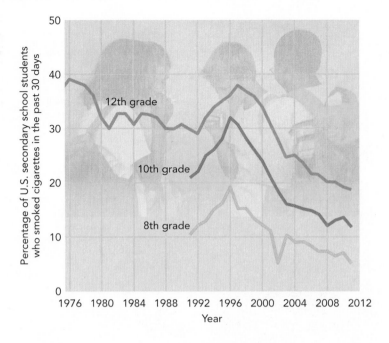

Report, 2005). In 2010, there were approximately 45.3 million adult smokers in the United States (CDC, 2012c).

Cigarette smoking is decreasing among both adolescents and college students. In the national Monitoring the Future survey, the percentage of U.S. adolescents who are current cigarette smokers continued to decline in 2011 (Johnston & others, 2012). Cigarette smoking peaked in 1996 and 1997 and then decreased 13 to 18 percent, depending on grade level, from 1998 to 2011 (Figure 5.11).

The drop in cigarette use by U.S. youth may have several sources, including higher cigarette prices, less tobacco advertising reaching adolescents, more antismoking advertisements, and more negative publicity about the tobacco industry than previously. Increasingly, adolescents report perceiving cigarette smoking as dangerous, disapprove of it, are less accepting of being around smokers, and prefer to date nonsmokers (Johnston & others, 2012). With respect to college students and young adults, smoking has shown a smaller decline than adolescent and adult smoking (Johnston & others, 2012).

In sum, cigarette smoking appears to be generally on the decline. Most smokers recognize the serious health risks of smoking and wish they could quit. Chapter 17 explores the difficulty of giving up smoking and strategies for quitting.

Amphetamines Amphetamines, or uppers, are stimulant drugs that people use to boost energy, stay awake, or lose weight. Often prescribed in the form of diet pills, these drugs increase the release of dopamine, which enhances the user's activity level and pleasurable feelings. Prescription drugs for attention deficit disorder, such as Ritalin, are also stimulants.

Perhaps the most insidious illicit drug for contemporary society is crystal methamphetamine, or crystal meth. Smoked, injected, or swallowed, crystal meth (also called "crank" or "tina") is a synthetic stimulant that causes a powerful feeling of euphoria, particularly the first time it is ingested. Meth is made using household products such as battery acid, cold medicine, drain cleaner, and kitty litter, and its effects have been devastating, notably in rural areas of the United States.

Crystal meth releases enormous amounts of dopamine in the brain, producing intense feelings of pleasure. The drug is highly addictive. The extreme high of crystal meth leads to a severe "come down" experience that is associated with strong cravings. Crystal meth also damages dopamine receptors, so that the crystal meth addict is chasing a high that the person's brain can no longer produce. Because the individual's

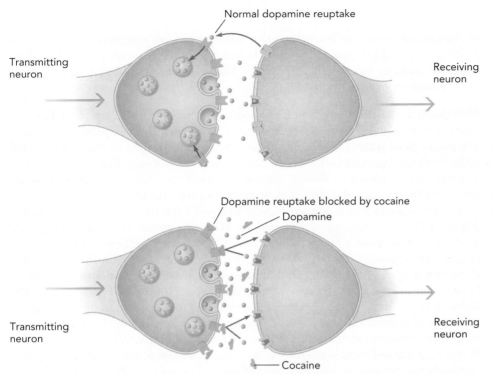

FIGURE 5.12 Cocaine and Neurotransmitters Cocaine concentrates in areas of the brain that are rich in dopamine synapses such as the VTA and the nucleus accumbens (NAcc). (*Top*) What happens in normal reuptake. The transmitting neuron releases dopamine, which stimulates the receiving neuron by binding to its receptor sites. After binding occurs, dopamine is carried back into the transmitting neuron for later release. (*Bottom*) What happens when cocaine is present in the synapse. Cocaine binds to the uptake pumps and prevents them from removing dopamine from the synapse. The result is that more dopamine collects in the synapse, and more dopamine receptors are activated.

very first experience with crystal meth can lead to ruinous consequences, the Drug Enforcement Agency has started a website, designed by and targeted at teenagers, www.justthinktwice.com, to share the hard facts of the horrific effects of this and other illicit substances.

Cocaine   Cocaine is an illegal drug that comes from the coca plant, native to Bolivia and Peru. Cocaine is either snorted or injected in the form of crystals or powder. Used this way, cocaine floods the bloodstream rapidly, producing a rush of euphoric feelings that lasts for about 15 to 30 minutes. Because the rush depletes the brain's supply of the neurotransmitters dopamine, serotonin, and norepinephrine, an agitated, depressed mood usually follows as the drug's effects decline. Figure 5.12 shows how cocaine affects dopamine levels in the brain.

Crack is a potent form of cocaine, consisting of chips of pure cocaine that are usually smoked. Scientists believe that crack is one of the most addictive substances known. Treatment of cocaine addiction is difficult (Ahmadi & others, 2009; Silva de Lima & others, 2010). Cocaine's addictive properties are so strong that, six months after treatment, more than 50 percent of abusers return to the drug, a statistic that highlights the importance of prevention.

MDMA (Ecstasy)   MDMA—called Ecstasy, X, or XTC—is an illegal synthetic drug with both stimulant and hallucinogenic properties (Degenhardt, Bruno, & Topp, 2010). People have called Ecstasy an "empathogen" because under its influence, users tend to feel warm bonds with others. MDMA produces its effects by releasing serotonin, dopamine, and norepinephrine. The effects of the drug on serotonin are particularly problematic. According to the National Institute on Drug Abuse (NIDA), MDMA depletes the brain of this important neurotransmitter, producing lingering feelings of listlessness that often continue for days after use (NIDA, 2009a).

MDMA impairs memory and cognitive processing. Heavy users of Ecstasy show cognitive deficits (Gouzoulis-Mayfrank & Daumann, 2009; Sofuoglu, Sugarman, & Carroll, 2010) that persist even 2 years after they begin to abstain (Rogers & others, 2009). Because MDMA destroys axons that release serotonin (Riezzo & others, 2010), repeated use might lead to susceptibility to depression (Cowan, Roberts, & Joers, 2008).

HALLUCINOGENS

Hallucinogens are psychoactive drugs that modify a person's perceptual experiences and produce visual images that are not real. Hallucinogens are also called *psychedelic* (from the Greek meaning "mind-revealing") drugs. Marijuana has a mild hallucinogenic effect; LSD, a stronger one.

Marijuana   Marijuana is the dried leaves and flowers of the hemp plant *Cannabis sativa,* which originated in Central Asia but is now grown in most parts of the world. The plant's dried resin is known as hashish. The active ingredient in marijuana is THC (delta-9-tetrahydrocannabinol). Unlike other psychoactive drugs, THC does not affect a specific neurotransmitter. Rather, marijuana disrupts the membranes of neurons and affects the functioning of a variety of neurotransmitters and hormones.

The physical effects of marijuana include increased pulse rate and blood pressure, reddening of the eyes, coughing, and dry mouth. Marijuana smoke is more damaging to the lungs than smoke from tobacco (NIDA, 2009b). Psychological effects include a mixture of excitatory, depressive, and mildly hallucinatory characteristics that make it difficult to classify the drug. Marijuana can trigger spontaneous unrelated ideas; distorted perceptions of time and place; increased sensitivity to sounds, tastes, smells, and colors; and erratic verbal behavior. The drug can also impair attention and memory. Recent research indicates a number of negative outcomes for the offspring of mothers who used marijuana during pregnancy, including increased admission to the neonatal intensive care unit (Hayatbakhsh & others, 2012) and lower intelligence at age 6 (Goldschmidt & others, 2008). Long-term marijuana use can lead to addiction and difficulties in quitting (NIDA, 2009b).

Marijuana is the illegal drug most widely used by high school students. In the Monitoring the Future survey, 46 percent of U.S. high school seniors said they had tried marijuana in their lifetime, and 23 percent reported that they had used marijuana in the last 30 days (Johnston & others, 2012). One concern about adolescents' use of marijuana is that the drug might be a gateway to the use of other more serious illicit substances. Although there is a correlational link between using marijuana and using other illicit drugs, evidence for the notion that using marijuana leads to using other drugs is mixed (Tarter & others, 2006).

Marijuana has been considered as a potential treatment for people who suffer from a variety of diseases, including AIDS, cancer, and chronic pain. For such individuals, "medical marijuana" may promote appetite, calm anxiety, stimulate well-being, and relieve pain (P. J. Cohen, 2009; Joy, Watson, & Benson, 1999; Wilsey & others, 2008). Since 1998, 18 U.S. states have legalized medical marijuana, and in 2012 Colorado and Washington legalized the recreational use of the marijuana. However, federal law continues to treat marijuana as an illegal substance.

LSD   LSD (lysergic acid diethylamide) is a hallucinogen that even in low doses produces striking perceptual changes. Objects change shape and glow; colors become kaleidoscopic, and astonishing images unfold. LSD-induced images are sometimes pleasurable and sometimes grotesque. LSD can also influence a user's sense of time so that brief glances at objects are experienced as deep, penetrating, and lengthy examinations, and minutes turn into hours or even days. A bad LSD trip can trigger extreme anxiety, paranoia, and suicidal or homicidal impulses.

LSD's effects on the body can include dizziness, nausea, and tremors. LSD acts primarily on the neurotransmitter serotonin in the brain, although it also can affect dopamine (Gonzalez-Maeso & Sealfon, 2009). Emotional and cognitive effects may include rapid mood swings and impaired attention and memory. The use of LSD peaked in the 1960s and 1970s, and its consumption has been decreasing in the twenty-first century (Johnston & others, 2012). Figure 5.13 summarizes the effects of LSD and a variety of other psychoactive drugs.

test yourself

1. What are psychoactive drugs, and for what reasons do people use them?
2. Describe what stimulants and depressants are, and give three examples of each.
3. What are hallucinogens? What are two common examples of hallucinogens?

4· HYPNOSIS

Fifty-three-year-old Shelley Thomas arrived at a London hospital for a 30-minute pelvic surgery. Before the operation, with her hypnotherapist guiding her, Shelley counted

Drug Classification	Medical Uses	Short-Term Effects	Overdose Effects	Health Risks	Risk of Physical/ Psychological Dependence
Depressants					
Alcohol	Pain relief	Relaxation, depressed brain activity, slowed behavior, reduced inhibitions	Disorientation, loss of consciousness, even death at high blood-alcohol levels	Accidents, brain damage, liver disease, heart disease, ulcers, birth defects	Physical and psychological: moderate
Barbiturates	Sleeping pill	Relaxation, sleep	Breathing difficulty, coma, possible death	Accidents, coma, possible death	Physical and psychological: moderate to high
Tranquilizers	Anxiety reduction	Relaxation, slowed behavior	Breathing difficulty, coma, possible death	Accidents, coma, possible death	Physical: low to moderate Psychological: moderate
Opiates (narcotics)	Pain relief	Euphoric feelings, drowsiness, nausea	Convulsions, coma, possible death	Accidents, infectious diseases such as AIDS	Physical: high Psychological: moderate to high
Stimulants					
Amphetamines	Weight control	Increased alertness, excitability; decreased fatigue, irritability	Extreme irritability, feelings of persecution, convulsions	Insomnia, hypertension, malnutrition, possible death	Physical: possible Psychological: moderate to high
Cocaine	Local anesthetic	Increased alertness, excitability, euphoric feelings; decreased fatigue, irritability	Extreme irritability, feelings of persecution, convulsions, cardiac arrest, possible death	Insomnia, hypertension, malnutrition, possible death	Physical: possible Psychological: moderate (oral) to very high (injected or smoked)
MDMA (Ecstasy)	None	Mild amphetamine and hallucinogenic effects; high body temperature and dehydration; sense of well-being and social connectedness	Brain damage, especially memory and thinking	Cardiovascular problems; death	Physical: possible Psychological: moderate
Caffeine	None	Alertness and sense of well-being followed by fatigue	Nervousness, anxiety, disturbed sleep	Possible cardiovascular problems	Physical and psychological: moderate
Nicotine	None	Stimulation, stress reduction, followed by fatigue, anger	Nervousness, disturbed sleep	Cancer and cardiovascular disease	Physical and psychological: high
Hallucinogens					
LSD	None	Strong hallucinations, distorted time perception	Severe mental disturbance, loss of contact with reality	Accidents	Physical: none Psychological: low
Marijuana*	Treatment of the eye disorder glaucoma	Euphoric feelings, relaxation, mild hallucinations, time distortion, attention and memory impairment	Fatigue, disoriented behavior	Accidents, respiratory disease	Physical: very low Psychological: moderate

FIGURE 5.13 **Categories of Psychoactive Drugs: Depressants, Stimulants, and Hallucinogens** Note that these various drugs have different effects and negative consequences. *Classifying marijuana is difficult, because of its diverse effects.

backward from 100 and entered a hypnotic trance. Her surgery was performed with no anesthesia (Song, 2006); rather, Shelley relied on hypnosis to harness her mind's powers to overcome pain.

You may have seen a hypnotist on TV or in a nightclub, putting a person into a trance and then perhaps making the individual act like a chicken or pretend to be a contestant on *American Idol* or enact some similarly strange behavior. When we observe someone in such a trance, we might be convinced that hypnosis involves a powerful manipulation of another person's consciousness. What is hypnosis, really? The answer to this question is itself the source of some debate.

© Tony Zuvela. www.CartoonStock.com

● **hypnosis** An altered state of consciousness or a psychological state of altered attention and expectation in which the individual is unusually receptive to suggestions.

Some psychologists think of hypnosis as an altered state of consciousness, while others believe that it is simply a product of more mundane processes such as focused attention and expectation (Lee & Pyun, 2012; S. J. Lynn & others, 2012). In fact, both views are reasonable, and we may define **hypnosis** as an altered state of consciousness or as a psychological state of altered attention and expectation in which the individual is unusually receptive to suggestions. People have used basic hypnotic techniques since the beginning of recorded history, in association with religious ceremonies, magic, and the supernatural.

Today, psychology and medicine recognize hypnosis as a legitimate process, although researchers still have much to learn about how it works. In addition, there is continuing debate about whether hypnosis truly is an altered state of consciousness (Lynn & Green, 2011).

The Nature of Hypnosis

When Shelley Thomas was in a hypnotic trance, what exactly was happening in her brain? Patterns of brain activity during the hypnotic state suggest that hypnosis produces a state of consciousness similar to other states of consciousness. For example, individuals in a hypnotic state display a predominance of alpha and beta waves, characteristic of people in a relaxed waking state, when monitored by an EEG (Cavallaro & others, 2010; Williams & Gruzelier, 2001). In a brain-imaging study, widespread areas of the cerebral cortex—including the occipital lobes, parietal lobes, sensorimotor cortex, and prefrontal cortex—were activated when individuals were in a hypnotic state (Faymonville, Boly, & Laureys, 2006). A similar activation pattern is found in individuals in a nonhypnotic waking state who are engaging in mental imagery. In sum, a hypnotic state is not like being asleep. It is more similar to being relaxed and awake. How does the hypnotist lead people into this state of relaxation and imagery?

THE FOUR STEPS IN HYPNOSIS

Hypnosis involves four steps. The hypnotist

1. Minimizes distractions and makes the person to be hypnotized comfortable.
2. Tells the person to concentrate on something specific, such as an imagined scene or the ticking of a watch.
3. Informs the person what to expect in the hypnotic state, such as relaxation or a pleasant floating sensation.
4. Suggests certain events or feelings he or she knows will occur or observes occurring, such as "Your eyes are getting tired." When the suggested effects occur, the person interprets them as being caused by the hypnotist's suggestion and accepts them as an indication that something is happening. This increase in the person's expectations that the hypnotist will make things happen in the future makes the person even more suggestible.

INDIVIDUAL VARIATIONS IN HYPNOSIS

Some people are more easily hypnotized than others, and some are more strongly influenced by hypnotic suggestions. *Hypnotizability* refers to the extent to which a person's responses *are changed* by being hypnotized (Enea & Dafinoiu, 2013; Santarcangelo & others, 2012). There is no easy way to know if a person is hypnotizable without first trying to hypnotize the individual. If you have the capacity to immerse yourself deeply in an imaginative activity—listening to a favorite piece of music or reading a novel, for example—you might be a likely candidate (Spiegel, 2010). Still, the relationship between the ability to become completely absorbed in an experience and hypnotizability is weak (Nash, 2001).

Explaining Hypnosis

How does hypnosis have its effects? Contemporary theorists disagree as to whether hypnosis is a divided state of consciousness or simply a learned social behavior.

A DIVIDED STATE OF CONSCIOUSNESS

Ernest Hilgard (1977, 1992), in his **divided consciousness view of hypnosis,** proposed that hypnosis involves a special divided state of consciousness, a splitting of consciousness into separate components. One component follows the hypnotist's commands, while another component acts as a "hidden observer."

Hilgard placed one hand of hypnotized individuals in a bucket of ice-cold water and told them that they would not feel pain but that a part of their mind—a hidden part that would be aware of what was going on—could signal any true pain by pressing a key with the hand that was not submerged (Figure 5.14). The individuals under hypnosis reported afterward that they had not experienced any pain; yet while their hand had been submerged in the ice-cold water, they had pressed the key with their non-submerged hand, and they had pressed it more frequently the longer their hand was in the cold water. Thus, in Hilgard's view, in hypnosis, consciousness has a hidden part that stays in contact with reality and feels pain while another part of consciousness feels no pain.

Critics of Hilgard's view suggest that the hidden observer simply demonstrates that the hypnotized person is not in an altered state of consciousness at all. From this perspective, the hidden observer is simply the person himself or herself, having been given permission to admit to the pain that he or she was always feeling (Green & others, 2005). This argument is part of the social cognitive behavior view of hypnosis.

SOCIAL COGNITIVE BEHAVIOR

Some experts are skeptical that hypnosis is an altered state of consciousness (Chaves, 2000; Lynn & Green, 2011; S. J. Lynn & others, 2012). In the **social cognitive behavior view of hypnosis,** hypnosis is a normal state in which the hypnotized person behaves the way he or she believes that a hypnotized person should behave. The social cognitive perspective frames the important questions about hypnosis around cognitive factors—the attitudes, expectations, and beliefs of good hypnotic participants—and around the powerful social context in which hypnosis occurs (Lynn & Green, 2011). Individuals being hypnotized surrender their responsibility to the hypnotist and follow the hypnotist's suggestions; and they have expectations about what hypnosis is supposed to be like.

Experts have continued to debate whether hypnosis is indeed an altered state of consciousness (Kihlstrom, 2005) or simply a reaction to a special social situation (S. J. Lynn & others, 2012). Although there may be no consensus about what hypnosis is, scientists use hypnosis to explore the brain and its functions, and health professionals have begun to apply this powerful technique to a number of problems.

Uses of Hypnosis

As psychologists' interest in studying consciousness has grown, hypnosis has emerged as a useful tool (Tomé-Pires & Miró, 2012). Some researchers employ hypnosis in a way similar to transcranial magnetic stimulation (described in Chapter 3), to experimentally dampen brain processes (Cox & Bryant, 2008). Combining hypnosis with brain imaging allows researchers to understand both the effects of hypnosis itself and the brain's functioning (Oakley & Halligan, 2011).

Beyond its role in basic research, hypnosis has been applied to a variety of problems. In the United States, practitioners of hypnosis use the technique to treat alcoholism, somnambulism, depression, suicidal tendencies, post-traumatic stress disorder, overeating, diabetes, smoking, and various types of pain, including migraine headaches and pain in labor and childbirth (Abdeshahi & others, 2013; Madden & others, 2012; Tahiri & others, 2012). Whether hypnosis actually works for these diverse problems remains debatable (D. Brown, 2007). Individuals in these treatment programs rarely achieve dramatic results unless they are already motivated to change. Hypnosis is most effective when combined with psychotherapy (Rossi, 2009). Psychotherapy, a major focus in Chapter 16, is a form of nonmedical treatment in which a professional seeks to help someone overcome life difficulties.

A long history of research and practice has clearly demonstrated that hypnosis can reduce the experience of pain (Elkins, Johnson, & Fisher, 2012). A fascinating study

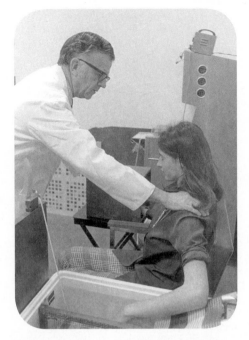

FIGURE 5.14 Hilgard's Divided Consciousness Experiment Ernest Hilgard tests a participant in the study in which he had individuals place one hand in ice-cold water.

● **divided consciousness view of hypnosis** Hilgard's view that hypnosis involves a splitting of consciousness into two separate components, one that follows the hypnotist's commands and the other that acts as a "hidden observer."

● **social cognitive behavior view of hypnosis** The perspective that hypnosis is a normal state in which the hypnotized person behaves the way he or she believes that a hypnotized person should behave.

examined the pain perceptions of hypnotized individuals, with the goal of changing their pain threshold. In that study, the brains of participants were monitored while they received painful electrical shocks (rated 8 or higher on a 1 to 10 pain scale) (Schulz-Stubner & others, 2004). Those who were hypnotized to find the shocks less painful did rate them as lower in pain (giving them a 3 or less). The brain-scanning results were most interesting: The subcortical brain areas (the brain stem and midbrain) of the hypnotized patients responded the same as those of the patients who were not hypnotized, suggesting that these brain structures recognized the painful stimulation. However, the sensory cortex was not activated in the hypnotized patients, suggesting that although they sensed pain on some level, they were never conscious of it. In essence, the "ouch" signal never made it to awareness.

In summary, although the nature of hypnosis remains a mystery, evidence is increasing that hypnosis can play a role in a variety of health contexts, and it can influence the brain in fascinating ways (Del Casale & others, 2012). For psychologists, part of the ambiguity about the definition of hypnosis comes from the fact that it has been studied in specific social contexts, involving a hypnotist. It is also possible, however, to experience altered states of consciousness without these special circumstances, as we next consider.

5· CONSCIOUSNESS AND HEALTH AND WELLNESS: MEDITATION

The altered consciousness of hypnosis can also be achieved through meditation. **Meditation** involves attaining a peaceful state of mind in which thoughts are not occupied by worry. The meditator is mindfully present to his or her thoughts and feelings but is not consumed by them. Let's look at how meditation can enhance well-being and examine further what it is.

Mindfulness Meditation

Melissa Munroe, a Canadian woman diagnosed with Hodgkin lymphoma (a cancer of the immune system), was tormented by excruciating pain (Wijesiri, 2005). Seeking ways to cope with the agony, Munroe enrolled in a meditation program. She was skeptical at first. "What I didn't realize," she said, "is that if people have ever found themselves taking a walk in the countryside or in the forest or on a nice pleasant autumn day . . . and find themselves in a contemplative state, that's a form of meditation." Munroe worked hard to use meditation to control her pain. Interestingly, the way she harnessed the power of her mind to overcome pain was by concentrating her thoughts on the pain—not by trying to avoid it.

Using *mindfulness meditation,* a technique practiced by yoga enthusiasts and Buddhist monks, Munroe focused on her pain. By doing so, she was able to isolate the pain from her emotional response to it and to her cancer diagnosis. She grew to see her physical discomfort as bearable. Munroe's success shows that contrary to what a non-meditator might think, meditation is not about avoiding one's thoughts. Indeed, the effort involved in avoidance steers the person away from the contemplative state. Munroe described her thoughts as like people striding by her on the street, walking in the other direction; she explained, "They come closer and closer, then they pass you by."

A number of studies have supported the role of mindfulness meditation in enhancing psychological well-being (Eberth & Sedlmeier, 2012). Meditation has been found to enhance attention (Moore & others, 2012), to aid in refueling mental energy even after strenuous tasks (Friese, Messner, & Schaffner, 2012), and to help individuals lose weight (Sojcher, Fogerite, & Perlman, 2012). Recently, some have recommended incorporating mindfulness meditation training in schools and using age-appropriate activities to increase students' reflection on moment-to-moment experiences that can improve focused attention and self-control (Roeser & Zelazo, 2012; Zelazo & Lyons, 2012).

test yourself

1. What is hypnosis?
2. What are the four steps in hypnosis?
3. Name and describe two different theories about hypnosis.

● **meditation** The attainment of a peaceful state of mind in which thoughts are not occupied by worry; the meditator is mindfully present to his or her thoughts and feelings but is not consumed by them.

Among those practicing meditation are Zen monks who explore the Buddha-nature at the center of their being.

Jon Kabat-Zinn (2006, 2009) has pioneered the use of meditation techniques in medical settings. Research by Kabat-Zinn and colleagues has demonstrated the beneficial effects of mindfulness meditation for a variety of conditions, including depression, panic attacks, and anxiety (Miller, Fletcher, & Kabat-Zinn, 1995), chronic pain (Kabat-Zinn, Lipworth, & Burney, 1985), and stress and the skin condition psoriasis (Kabat-Zinn & others, 1998). Many of these effects have also been shown to be long-lasting.

Richard Davidson and colleagues (including Jon Kabat-Zinn) studied the brain and immune system changes that might underlie the health and wellness effects of meditation (Davidson & others, 2003). They performed MRIs on the brains of individuals who were in a standard eight-week meditation-training program. After the training program and as compared to a control group, those in the meditation program reported reduced anxiety and fewer negative emotions. Furthermore, brain scans revealed that these individuals showed increased activation in the left hemisphere. In addition, the meditators showed better immune system response to a flu vaccine (Davidson & others, 2003; Kabat-Zinn & Davidson, 2012). These results suggest that our conscious minds may have a role to play in enhancing our psychological and physical health (Davidson & Begley, 2012; Kabat-Zinn & Davidson, 2012).

The Meditative State of Mind

What actually is the meditative state of mind? As a physiological state, meditation shows qualities of sleep *and* wakefulness, yet it is distinct from both. You may have experienced a state called *hypnagogic reverie*—an overwhelming feeling of wellness right before you fall asleep, the sense that everything is going to work out. Meditation has been compared to this relaxed sense that all is well (Friedman, Myers, & Benson, 1998).

In a study of Zen meditators, researchers examined what happens when people switch from their normal waking state to a meditative state (Ritskes & others, 2003). Using fMRI, the experimenters obtained images of the brain before and after the participants entered the meditative state. They found that the switch to meditation involved initial increases in activation in the basal ganglia and prefrontal cortex (the now familiar area that is often activated during consciousness). However, and interestingly, they also found that these initial activations led to decreases in the anterior cingulate, the brain area associated with conscious awareness and acts of will.

These results provide a picture of the physical events of the brain that are connected with the somewhat paradoxical state of meditation—controlling one's thoughts in order to let go of the need to control. Research is also beginning to explore the role of neurotransmitters in meditation (Edwards & others, 2012).

Getting Started with Meditation

Would you like to experience the meditative state? If so, you can probably reach that state by following some simple instructions:

- Find a quiet place and a comfortable chair.
- Sit upright in the chair, rest your chin comfortably on your chest, and place your arms in your lap. Close your eyes.
- Now focus on your breathing. Every time you inhale and every time you exhale, pay attention to the sensations of air flowing through your body, the feeling of your lungs filling and emptying.
- After you have focused on several breaths, begin to repeat silently to yourself a single word every time you breathe out. You can make a word up, use the word *one*, or try a word associated with an emotion you want to produce, such as *trust, love, patience,* or *happy.* Experiment with several different words to see which one works best for you.
- If you find that thoughts are intruding and you are no longer attending to your breathing, refocus on your breathing and say your chosen word each time you exhale.

Regular mediations can help you to clarify your goals and purpose in life, strengthen your values, and improve your outlook.

test yourself

1. What does the meditator experience during meditation?
2. What changes in the brain and immune system did Davidson and his colleagues discover that might explain meditation's benefits for health and wellness?
3. On what body process does a meditator focus, and how is that focus maintained?

After you have practiced this exercise for 10 to 15 minutes, twice a day, every day for two weeks, you will be ready for a shortened version. If you notice that you are experiencing stressful thoughts or circumstances, simply meditate, on the spot, for several minutes. If you are in public, you do not have to close your eyes; just fix your gaze on a nearby object, attend to your breathing, and say your word silently every time you exhale.

Meditation is an age-old practice. Without explicitly mentioning meditation, some religions advocate related practices such as daily prayer and peaceful introspection. Whether the practice involves praying over rosary beads, chanting before a Buddhist shrine, or taking a moment to commune with nature, a contemplative state clearly has broad appeal and conveys many benefits (Kabat-Zinn & Davidson, 2012; Travis & Shear, 2010). Current research on the contemplative state suggests that there are good reasons why human beings have been harnessing its beneficial powers for thousands of years.

1. THE NATURE OF CONSCIOUSNESS

Consciousness is the awareness of external events and internal sensations, including awareness of the self and thoughts about experiences. Most experts agree that consciousness is likely distributed across the brain. A global brain workspace that includes the association areas and prefrontal lobes is believed to play an important role in consciousness.

William James described the mind as a stream of consciousness. Consciousness occurs at different levels of awareness that include higher-level awareness (controlled processes and selective attention), lower-level awareness (automatic processes and daydreaming), altered states of consciousness (produced by drugs, trauma, fatigue, and other factors), subconscious awareness (waking subconscious awareness, sleep, and dreams), and no awareness (unconscious thought).

Psychologists refer to our understanding of other people's consciousness as theory of mind. Theory of mind is important to social capacities such as empathy, and some experts believe that deficits in theory of mind functioning are related to autism.

2. SLEEP AND DREAMS

The biological rhythm that regulates the daily sleep/wake cycle is the circadian rhythm. The part of the brain that keeps our biological clocks synchronized is the suprachiasmatic nucleus, a small structure in the hypothalamus that registers light. Biological clocks can become desynchronized by jet travel and work shifts; however, there are some helpful strategies for resetting the biological clock.

We need sleep for physical restoration, adaptation, growth, and memory. Research studies increasingly reveal that people do not function optimally when they are sleep-deprived.

Stages of sleep correspond to massive electrophysiological changes that occur in the brain and that can be assessed by an EEG. Humans go through four stages of non-REM sleep and one stage of REM (rapid eye movement) sleep. Most dreaming occurs during REM sleep. A sleep cycle of five stages lasts about 90 to 100 minutes and recurs several times during the night. The REM stage lasts longer toward the end of a night's sleep.

The sleep stages are associated with distinct patterns of neurotransmitter activity. Levels of the neurotransmitters serotonin, norepinephrine, and acetylcholine decrease as the sleep cycle progresses from stage 1 through stage 4. Stage 5, REM sleep, begins when the reticular formation raises the level of acetylcholine.

Sleep plays a role in a large number of diseases and disorders. Neurons that control sleep interact closely with the immune system, and when our body is fighting infection, our cells produce a substance that makes us sleepy. Individuals with depression often have sleep problems.

Many Americans suffer from chronic, long-term sleep disorders that can impair normal daily functioning. These include insomnia, sleepwalking and sleep talking, nightmares and night terrors, narcolepsy, and sleep apnea.

Contrary to popular belief, most dreams are not bizarre or strange. Freud thought that dreams express unconscious wishes in disguise. Cognitive theory attempts to explain dreaming in terms of the same concepts that are used in studying the waking mind. According to activation-synthesis theory, dreaming occurs when the cerebral cortex synthesizes neural signals emanating from activity in the lower part of the brain. In this view, the rising level of acetylcholine during REM sleep plays a role in neural activity in the brain stem that the cerebral cortex tries to make sense of.

3. PSYCHOACTIVE DRUGS

Psychoactive drugs act on the nervous system to alter states of consciousness, modify perceptions, and change moods. Some people are attracted to these drugs because they seem to help them deal with difficult life situations.

Addictive drugs activate the brain's reward system by increasing dopamine concentration. The reward pathway involves the ventral tegmental area and nucleus accumbens. The abuse of psychoactive drugs can lead to tolerance, psychological and physical dependence, and addiction—a pattern of behavior characterized by a preoccupation with using a drug and securing its supply.

Depressants slow down mental and physical activity. Among the most widely used depressants are alcohol, barbiturates, tranquilizers, and opiates.

After caffeine, alcohol is the most widely used drug in the United States. The high rate of alcohol abuse by high school and college students is especially alarming. Alcoholism is a disorder that involves long-term, repeated, uncontrolled, compulsive, and excessive use of alcoholic beverages that impairs the drinker's health and work and social relationships.

Stimulants increase the central nervous system's activity and include caffeine, nicotine, amphetamines, cocaine, and MDMA (Ecstasy). Hallucinogens modify a person's perceptual experiences and produce visual images that are not real. Marijuana has a mild hallucinogenic effect; LSD has a strong one.

4. HYPNOSIS

Hypnosis is a psychological state or possibly altered attention and awareness in which the individual is unusually receptive to suggestions. The hypnotic state is different from a sleep state, as EEG recordings confirm. Inducing hypnosis involves four basic steps, beginning with minimizing distractions and making the person feel comfortable and ending with the hypnotist's suggesting certain events or feelings that he or she knows will occur or observes occurring.

There are substantial individual variations in people's susceptibility to hypnosis. Two theories have been proposed to explain hypnosis. In Hilgard's divided consciousness view, hypnosis involves a divided state of consciousness, a splitting of consciousness into separate components. One component follows the hypnotist's commands; the other acts as a hidden observer. In the social cognitive behavior view, hypnotized individuals behave the way they believe hypnotized individuals are expected to behave.

5. CONSCIOUSNESS AND HEALTH AND WELLNESS: MEDITATION

Meditation refers to a state of quiet reflection; the practice has benefits for a wide range of psychological and physical illnesses. Meditation can also benefit the body's immune system. Research using fMRI suggests that meditation allows an individual to control his or her thoughts in order to "let go" of the need to control.

Mindfulness meditation is a powerful tool for managing life's problems. How we think about our lives and experiences plays a role in determining whether we feel stressed and worried or challenged and excited about life. Seeking times of quiet contemplation can have a positive impact on our ability to cope with life's ups and downs.

key *terms*

stream of consciousness, p. 144
consciousness, p. 145
theory of mind, p. 145
controlled processes, p. 146
executive function, p. 146
automatic processes, p. 147
unconscious thought, p. 149
sleep, p. 150
biological rhythms, p. 150
circadian rhythms, p. 150

suprachiasmatic nucleus (SCN), p. 150
REM sleep, p. 155
manifest content, p. 161
latent content, p. 161
cognitive theory of dreaming, p. 161
activation-synthesis theory of dreaming, p. 162
psychoactive drugs, p. 163

tolerance, p. 164
physical dependence, p. 164
psychological dependence, p. 164
addiction, p. 165
depressants, p. 165
alcoholism, p. 167
barbiturates, p. 168
tranquilizers, p. 168
opiates, p. 168

stimulants, p. 168
hallucinogens, p. 172
hypnosis, p. 174
divided consciousness view of hypnosis, p. 175
social cognitive behavior view of hypnosis, p. 175
meditation, p. 176

apply your *knowledge*

1. Take 20 minutes and document your stream of consciousness. Just write whatever comes into your mind for this period. When you have finished, take a close look at what your stream of consciousness reveals. What topics came up that surprised you? Are the thoughts and feelings you wrote down reflective of your daily life? Your important goals and values? What is *not* mentioned in your stream of consciousness that is surprising to you?

2. Keep a sleep journal for several nights. Compare your sleep patterns with those described in the text. Do you have a sleep debt? If so, which stages of sleep are you most likely missing? Does a good night's sleep affect your behavior? Keep a record of your mood and energy levels after a short night's sleep and then after you have had at least 8 hours of sleep in one night. What changes do you notice, and how do they compare with the changes predicted by research on sleep deprivation described in the chapter?

3. Keep a dream diary for a few days. When you wake up in the morning, immediately write down all that you can remember about your dreams. Have you had many bizarre or unusual dreams? Are there themes in your dreams that reflect the concerns of your daily life? Compare the content of your dream diary with the stream-of-consciousness document you produced for question 1, above. Are there similarities in the content of your relaxed, waking mind and your dreams?

4. Go on a caffeine hunt. Check out the ingredients for the beverages, painkillers, and snacks you typically consume. Which contain caffeine? Are you surprised how much caffeine you ingest regularly?

5. Try out mindfulness meditation. Following the guidelines on pages 177–178, meditate once a day for a week. Keep track of your mood, health, and behaviors over the course of the week. How did mindfulness meditation work for you?

CHAPTER 6

Learning

Service Dogs: Using Learning to Save Lives

Gracie, Celeste, and Kira have two things in common: They have all saved the lives of their dearest friends, and they are all dogs. These three dogs are specially trained to "alert" when, based on scent, they detect that their owners, all of whom have diabetes, are suffering from dangerously low levels of blood glucose.

Many individuals with diabetes, which involves problems in regulating insulin and glucose in the blood, are not aware when their glucose levels are too low. Dogs can be trained to use their amazing sense of smell to sound an alarm when blood glucose levels drop to a dangerous point. When her owner, an 8-year-old girl, shows signs of low blood glucose, Gracie, a British Labrador, alerts the girl's mom by ringing a bell (Linebaugh, 2012). When she detects a problem, Celeste, a 60-pound yellow lab, nudges the mother of her charge, a 15-year-old boy. Kira, a golden retriever, saved her owner's life one night in early 2013. While her owner, Jeff Hoffmeister, slept, Kira whined, pawed, and tried her best to wake him up. Finally, she lay on top of Jeff, licking his face. Roused from sleep, Jeff checked his blood sugar level, which was at a life-threatening low. Kira had saved his life ("Diabetes service dog saves man's life," 2013).

Gracie, Celeste, and Kira are just three of the estimated 30,000 assistance dogs working in the United States (Linebaugh, 2012). Service dogs are trained to aid people with a variety of disabilities. Their skills are amazing. They provide sound discrimination for the hearing impaired, assist with mobility, retrieve items, and locate people, bathrooms, elevators, and even lost cell phones. They open and close doors, help people dress and undress, flush toilets, and even put clothes in a washer and dryer.

Truly, service dogs are highly skilled professionals. Anyone who has a lazy mutt at home might wonder how it is possible for dogs to acquire these skills. Service dogs are trained to perform these complex acts using the principles that psychologists have uncovered in studying the processes that underlie learning, the focus of this chapter. ●

PREVIEW

This chapter begins by defining learning and sketching out its main types: associative learning and observational learning. We then turn attention to two types of associative learning—classical conditioning and operant conditioning—followed by a close look at observational learning. Next, we consider the role of cognitive processes in learning before finally examining biological, cultural, and psychological constraints on learning. The close of the chapter looks at the role of learning in human health and wellness.

1· TYPES OF LEARNING

Learning anything new involves change. Once you learned the alphabet, it did not leave you; it became part of a "new you" who had been changed through the process of learning. Similarly, once you learn how to drive a car, you do not have to go through the process again at a later time. When you first arrived on campus at your school, you might have spent a lot of time lost. But once you got the lay of the land, you were able to navigate just fine. And perhaps you have a particular food that you know to avoid, because you once ate it, and it made you sick.

By way of experience, too, you may have learned that you have to study to do well on a test, that there usually is an opening act at a rock concert, and that a field goal in U.S. football adds 3 points to the score. Putting these pieces together, we arrive at a definition of **learning:** a systematic, relatively permanent change in behavior that occurs through experience.

If someone were to ask you what you learned in class today, you might mention new ideas you heard about, lists you memorized, or concepts you mastered. However, how would you define learning if you could not refer to unobservable mental processes? You might follow the lead of behavioral psychologists. **Behaviorism** is a theory of learning that focuses solely on observable behaviors, discounting the importance of mental activity such as thinking, wishing, and hoping. Psychologists who examine learning from a behavioral perspective define learning as relatively stable, observable changes in behavior. The behavioral approach has emphasized general laws that guide behavior change and make sense of some of the puzzling aspects of human life (Miltenberger, 2012).

Behaviorism maintains that the principles of learning are the same whether we are talking about animals or humans. Because of the influence of behaviorism, psychologists' understanding of learning started with studies of rats, cats, pigeons, and even raccoons. A century of research on learning in animals and in humans suggests that many of the principles generated initially in research on animals also apply to humans (Dewsbury, 2013; Domjan, 2010).

In this chapter we look at two types of learning: associative learning and observational learning. **Associative learning** occurs when an organism makes a connection, or an association, between two events. *Conditioning* is the process of learning these associations (Leahey, 2013). There are two types of conditioning—classical and operant—both of which have been studied by behaviorists.

In *classical conditioning,* organisms learn the association between two stimuli. As a result of this association, organisms learn to anticipate events. For example, lightning is associated with thunder and regularly precedes it. Thus, when we see lightning, we anticipate that we will hear thunder soon afterward. In *operant conditioning,* organisms learn the association between a behavior and a consequence, such as a reward. As a result of this association, organisms learn to increase behaviors that are followed by rewards and to decrease behaviors that are followed by punishment. For example, children are likely to repeat their good manners if their parents reward them with candy after they have shown good manners. Also, if children's bad manners provoke scolding

● **learning** A systematic, relatively permanent change in behavior that occurs through experience.

● **behaviorism** A theory of learning that focuses solely on observable behaviors, discounting the importance of mental activity such as thinking, wishing, and hoping.

● **associative learning** Learning that occurs when an organism makes a connection, or an association, between two events.

Classical Conditioning

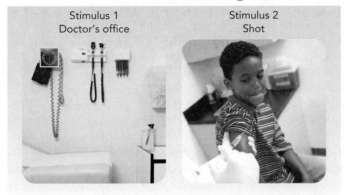

| Stimulus 1 Doctor's office | Stimulus 2 Shot |

Operant Conditioning

| Behavior | Consequences |

FIGURE 6.1 **Associative Learning: Comparing Classical and Operant Conditioning** (*Left*) In this example of classical conditioning, a child associates a doctor's office (stimulus 1) with getting a painful injection (stimulus 2). (*Right*) In this example of operant conditioning, performing well in a swimming competition (behavior) becomes associated with getting awards (consequences).

words and harsh glances by parents, the children are less likely to repeat the bad manners. Figure 6.1 compares classical and operant conditioning.

Much of what we learn, however, is not a result of direct consequences but rather of exposure to models performing a behavior or skill (Meltzoff & Williamson, 2013). For instance, as you watch someone shoot baskets, you get a sense of how the shots are made. The learning that takes place when a person observes and imitates another's behavior is called **observational learning.** Observational learning is a common way that people learn in educational and other settings. Observational learning is different from the associative learning described by behaviorism because it relies on mental processes: The learner has to pay attention, remember, and reproduce what the model did. Observational learning is especially important to human beings. In fact, watching other people is another way in which human infants acquire skills.

Human infants differ from baby monkeys in their strong reliance on imitation (Bandura, 2010a, 2011). After watching an adult model perform a task, a baby monkey will figure out its own way to do it, but a human infant will do exactly what the model did. Imitation may be the human baby's way to solve the huge problem it faces: To learn the vast amount of cultural knowledge that is part of human life. Many of our behaviors are rather arbitrary. Why do we clap to show approval or wave "hello" or "bye-bye"? The human infant has a lot to learn and may be well served to follow the old adage, "When in Rome, do as the Romans do."

Learning applies to many areas of acquiring new behaviors, skills, and knowledge (Bjork, Dunlosky, & Kornell, 2013). Our focus in this chapter is on the two types of associative learning—classical conditioning and operant conditioning—and on observational learning.

● **observational learning** Learning that occurs through observing and imitating another's behavior.

test yourself

1. What is associative learning?
2. What is conditioning? What two types of conditioning have behavioral psychologists studied?
3. What is observational learning? Give two examples of it.

2· CLASSICAL CONDITIONING

Early one morning, Bob is in the shower. While he showers, his wife enters the bathroom and flushes the toilet. Scalding hot water suddenly bursts down on Bob, causing him to yell in pain. The next day, Bob is back for his morning shower, and once again his wife enters the bathroom and flushes the toilet. Panicked by the sound of the toilet flushing, Bob yelps in fear and jumps out of the shower stream. Bob's panic at the sound of the toilet illustrates the learning process of **classical conditioning,** in which a neutral stimulus (the sound of a toilet flushing) becomes associated with an innately meaningful stimulus (the pain of scalding hot water) and acquires the capacity to elicit a similar response (panic).

● **classical conditioning** Learning process in which a neutral stimulus becomes associated with an innately meaningful stimulus and acquires the capacity to elicit a similar response.

Pavlov's Studies

Even before beginning this course, you might have heard about Pavlov's dogs. The work of the Russian physiologist Ivan Pavlov is well known. Still, it is easy to take its true significance for granted. Importantly, Pavlov demonstrated that neutral aspects of the environment can attain the capacity to evoke responses through pairing with other stimuli and that bodily processes can be influenced by environmental cues.

In the early 1900s, Pavlov was interested in the way the body digests food. In his experiments, he routinely placed meat powder in a dog's mouth, causing the dog to salivate. By accident, Pavlov noticed that the meat powder was not the only stimulus that caused the dog to drool. The dog salivated in response to a number of stimuli associated with the food, such as the sight of the food dish, the sight of the individual who brought the food into the room, and the sound of the door closing when the food arrived. Pavlov recognized that the dog's association of these sights and sounds with the food was an important type of learning, which came to be called *classical conditioning.*

Pavlov wanted to know *why* the dog salivated in reaction to various sights and sounds before eating the meat powder. He observed that the dog's behavior included both unlearned and learned components. The unlearned part of classical conditioning is based on the fact that some stimuli automatically produce certain responses apart from any prior learning; in other words, they are inborn (innate). *Reflexes* are such automatic stimulus–response connections. They include salivation in response to food, nausea in response to spoiled food, shivering in response to low temperature, coughing in response to throat congestion, pupil constriction in response to light, and withdrawal in response to pain.

An **unconditioned stimulus (US)** is a stimulus that produces a response without prior learning; food was the US in Pavlov's experiments. An **unconditioned response (UR)** is an unlearned reaction that is automatically elicited by the US. Unconditioned responses are involuntary; they happen in response to a stimulus without conscious effort. In Pavlov's experiment, drooling in response to food was the UR. In the case of Bob and the flushing toilet, Bob's learning and experience did not cause him to shriek when the hot water hit his body. His cry of pain was unlearned and occurred automatically. The hot water was the US, and Bob's panic was the UR.

In classical conditioning, a **conditioned stimulus (CS)** is a previously neutral stimulus that eventually elicits a conditioned response after being paired with the unconditioned stimulus. The **conditioned response (CR)** is the learned response to the conditioned stimulus that occurs after CS–US pairing (Pavlov, 1927). Sometimes conditioned responses are quite similar to unconditioned responses, but typically they are not as strong.

● **unconditioned stimulus (US)** A stimulus that produces a response without prior learning.

● **unconditioned response (UR)** An unlearned reaction that is automatically elicited by the unconditioned stimulus.

● **conditioned stimulus (CS)** A previously neutral stimulus that eventually elicits a conditioned response after being paired with the unconditioned stimulus.

● **conditioned response (CR)** The learned response to the conditioned stimulus that occurs after conditioned stimulus–unconditioned stimulus pairing.

Pavlov (the white-bearded gentleman in the center) is shown demonstrating the nature of classical conditioning to students at the Military Medical Academy in Russia.

In studying a dog's response to various stimuli associated with meat powder, Pavlov rang a bell before giving meat powder to the dog. Until then, ringing the bell did not have a particular effect on the dog, except perhaps to wake the dog from a nap. The bell was a *neutral* stimulus, meaning that in the dog's world, this stimulus did not have any signal value at all. Prior to being paired with the meat powder, the bell was meaningless. However, the dog began to associate the sound of the bell with the food and salivated when it heard the bell. The bell had become a conditioned (learned) stimulus (CS), and salivation was now a conditioned response (CR). In the case of Bob's interrupted shower, the sound of the toilet flushing was the CS, and panicking was the CR after the scalding water (US) and the flushing sound (CS) were paired. Figure 6.2 summarizes how classical conditioning works.

Researchers have shown that salivation can be used as a conditioned response not only in dogs and humans but also in, of all things, cockroaches (Watanabe & Mizunami, 2007). These researchers paired the smell of peppermint (the CS, which was applied to the cockroaches' antennae) with sugary water (the US). Cockroaches naturally salivate (the UR) in response to sugary foods, and after repeated pairings between peppermint smell and sugary water, the cockroaches salivated in response to the smell of peppermint (the CR). When they collected and measured the cockroach saliva, the researchers found that the cockroaches had slobbered over that smell for 2 minutes.

ACQUISITION

Whether it is human beings, dogs, or cockroaches, the first part of classical conditioning is called acquisition. **Acquisition** is the initial learning of the connection between the US and CS when these two stimuli are paired (as with the smell of peppermint and the sugary water). During acquisition, the CS is repeatedly presented followed by the US. Eventually, the CS will produce a response. Note that classical conditioning is a type of learning that occurs without awareness or effort, based on the presentation of

● **acquisition** The initial learning of the connection between the unconditioned stimulus and the conditioned stimulus when these two stimuli are paired.

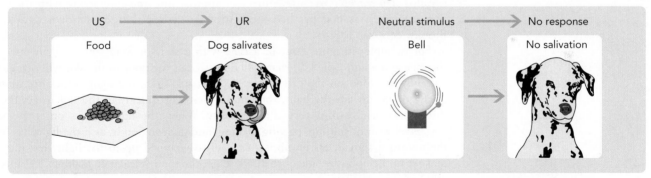
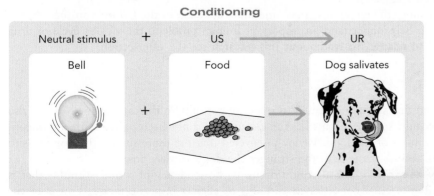
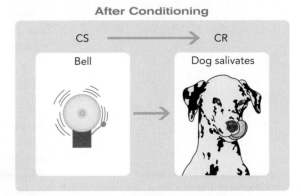

FIGURE 6.2 **Pavlov's Classical Conditioning** In one experiment, Pavlov presented a neutral stimulus (bell) just before an unconditioned stimulus (food). The neutral stimulus became a conditioned stimulus by being paired with the unconditioned stimulus. Subsequently, the conditioned stimulus (bell) by itself was able to elicit the dog's salivation.

© Harley Schwadron. www.CartoonStock.com.

two stimuli together. For this pairing to work, however, two important factors must be present: contiguity and contingency.

Contiguity simply means that the CS and US are presented very close together in time—even a mere fraction of a second (Wheeler & Miller, 2008). In Pavlov's work, if the bell had rung 20 minutes before the presentation of the food, the dog probably would not have associated the bell with the food. However, pairing the CS and US close together in time is not all that is needed for conditioning to occur.

Contingency means that the CS must not only precede the US closely in time, it must also serve as a reliable indicator that the US is on its way (Rescorla, 1966, 1988, 2009). To get a sense of the importance of contingency, imagine that the dog in Pavlov's experiment is exposed to a ringing bell at random times all day long. Whenever the dog receives food, the delivery of the food always immediately follows a bell ring. However, in this situation, the dog will not associate the bell with the food, because the bell is not a reliable signal that food is coming: It rings a lot when no food is on the way. Whereas contiguity refers to the fact that the CS and US occur close together in time, contingency refers to the information value of the CS relative to the US. When contingency is present, the CS provides a systematic signal that the US is on its way.

Note that once the association between the CS and the US has been formed, the *meaning* of the CS changes. What was once simply an arbitrary object in the environment becomes, instead, motivationally important, a reliable signal that something significant is going to happen. After being paired with a desired stimulus (the US), like a magnet, the CS signals that something good is on the way (Berridge, 1996). This change influences the animal's behavior, indicating that sometimes the CS is treated as if it *is* the US. For example, Pavlov noted that dogs in his study would sometimes respond to the sound of the bell as if it were the food itself, licking at the air as if "to eat the sound" (Pavlov, 1932, p. 95).

In fact, animal learning studies show that sometimes the attraction of the CS can be even more powerful than the draw of the US it signals. Some animals show a pattern of behavior indicating an unusually high level of attachment to the CS. This tendency is called *sign tracking* because it involves approaching and interacting with the CS (the sign or signal), as if it has become a strongly desired thing in its own right (Tomie, Brooks, & Zito, 1989).

For example, imagine a rat in a cage with a slot for food (the US) on one side of the cage and a light (the CS) that, when lit, signals the door to the slot will open shortly, revealing the food on the other side of the cage. When the light comes on, many rats briefly orient toward the light, then make their way quickly to the slot to get the food. But others behave in a very different way. When the light comes on, they become entranced with it: sniffing, pawing, licking, and gnawing on it, as if the light has become the reward it signals. Such animals can get so wrapped up in the light that they never make it to the opposite side of the cage to get the food (Hearst & Jenkins, 1974; Killeen, 2003; Zener, 1937).

Sign tracking, the tendency to become more attached to the CS than to the US, has been used to help understand an important human problem: the vicious cycle of drug addiction and relapse. To read about this research see the Intersection.

GENERALIZATION AND DISCRIMINATION

Pavlov found that the dog salivated in response not only to the tone of the bell but also to other sounds, such as a whistle. These sounds had not been paired with the unconditioned stimulus of the food. Pavlov discovered that the more similar the noise was to the original sound of the bell, the stronger the dog's salivary flow.

Generalization in classical conditioning is the tendency of a new stimulus that is similar to the original conditioned stimulus to elicit a response that is similar to the conditioned response (Harris, Andrew, & Livesey, 2012). Generalization has value in preventing learning from being tied to specific stimuli. Once we learn the association between a given CS (say, flashing police lights behind our car) and a particular US

● **generalization (in classical conditioning)** The tendency of a new stimulus that is similar to the original conditioned stimulus to elicit a response that is similar to the conditioned response.

Learning and Clinical Psychology: Can Classical Conditioning Help Us Understand Drug Abuse?

Addiction is heartbreaking—for both the addict and for those who love the person. Even after individuals have seemingly broken free from the lock of addiction, many people still relapse. How can addicts come to value their next high more than the people who love them, more than their job, more than their own health and well-being? Research using the principles of classical conditioning is uncovering the processes that underlie these tragic patterns, offering hope for permanently breaking the habit.

One of the great dilemmas of addiction recovery is the very high frequency of relapse. After being diagnosed with an addiction disorder, 90 percent of individuals relapse, going back to the drug that has caused them so many problems (DeJong, 1994). Psychologists believe that environmental cues—such as the people, places, and drug paraphernalia involved in drug use, all of which are conditioned stimuli (CS) that have been paired repeatedly with drug use—play an important role in this relapse. These signals (CS) become powerful cues in people's lives, prompting craving and the use of drugs. They are very difficult for addicts to ignore (Flagel, Akil, & Robinson, 2009). How can we come to understand the immense power of conditioned stimuli in the lives of addicts?

Psychologists have used sign tracking to help illuminate this process. Perhaps the power of environmental cues in

How might sign tracking explain other human behaviors? Can you recognize sign tracking in your own behavior?

the lives of addicts can be understood as a kind of sign tracking, suggesting that individuals who are addicted to drugs may be drawn into relapse by these powerfully attractive cues. So, for addicts, the cues associated with the use of drugs take on very strong motivational appeal.

Even more disturbing, research has shown that some drugs of abuse, such as nicotine and cocaine, also promote particularly strong attachments to conditioned

stimuli, due to their neurological effects (Palmatier & others, 2013; Uslaner & others, 2006). This means that addictive drugs may predispose the individuals who use them to sign tracking, as if these drugs possess a built-in capacity to promote not only addiction but relapse. The research suggests that these drugs set the stage for very strong associations to the situational factors present when they are used, laying a path of psychological magnets to tempt the recovering addict.

This study illuminates the difficulties involved in drug addiction. By examining the genetic, neurological, and psychological factors that may predispose individuals to sign tracking, researchers aim to illuminate the factors that may predispose individuals to addictions and offer innovative treatment directions (Tomie, Grimes, & Pohorecky, 2008).

(the dread associated with being pulled over), we do not have to learn it all over again when a similar stimulus presents itself (a police car with its siren howling as it cruises directly behind our car).

Stimulus generalization is not always beneficial. For example, the cat that generalizes from a harmless minnow to a dangerous piranha has a major problem; therefore, it is important to also discriminate among stimuli. **Discrimination** in classical conditioning is the process of learning to respond to certain stimuli and not others. To produce discrimination, Pavlov gave food to the dog only after ringing the bell and not after any other sounds. In this way, the dog learned to distinguish between the bell and other sounds.

● **discrimination (in classical conditioning)** The process of learning to respond to certain stimuli and not others.

psychological *inquiry*

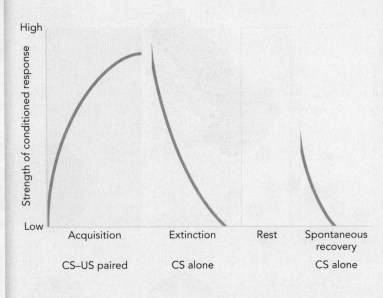

From Acquisition to Extinction (to Spontaneous Recovery)

The figure illustrates the strength of a conditioned response (CR), shown on the Y or vertical axis, across the stages from acquisition, to extinction, to a rest period, and finally to spontaneous recovery. Using the graphs, answer the following questions.

1. What happens to the unconditioned stimulus (US) and the conditioned stimulus (CS) during acquisition, and how does this influence the conditioned response (CR)?

2. When is the CR strongest and when is it weakest?

3. What happens to the US and CS during extinction, and how does this influence the CR?

4. Notice that spontaneous recovery occurs after a rest period. Why is this rest necessary?

5. In your own life, what are some conditioned stimuli that are attached to conditioned responses for you? Trace them through these steps.

EXTINCTION AND SPONTANEOUS RECOVERY

● **extinction (in classical conditioning)** The weakening of the conditioned response when the unconditioned stimulus is absent.

After conditioning the dog to salivate at the sound of a bell, Pavlov rang the bell repeatedly in a single session and did not give the dog any food. Eventually the dog stopped salivating. This result is **extinction,** which in classical conditioning is the weakening of the conditioned response when the unconditioned stimulus is absent (Moustafa & others, 2013). Without continued association with the unconditioned stimulus (US), the conditioned stimulus (CS) loses its power to produce the conditioned response (CR).

Extinction is not always the end of a conditioned response (Martin-Fardon & Weiss, 2013). The day after Pavlov extinguished the conditioned salivation to the sound of a bell, he took the dog to the laboratory and rang the bell but still did not give the dog any meat powder. The dog salivated, indicating that an extinguished response can spontaneously recur. **Spontaneous recovery** is the process in classical conditioning by which a conditioned response can recur after a time delay, without further conditioning (Martin-Fardon & Weiss, 2013; Rescorla, 2005).

● **spontaneous recovery** The process in classical conditioning by which a conditioned response can recur after a time delay, without further conditioning.

Consider an example of spontaneous recovery you may have experienced: You thought that you had forgotten about (extinguished) an old girlfriend or boyfriend, but then you found yourself in a particular context (perhaps the restaurant where you used to dine together), and you suddenly got a mental image of your ex, accompanied by an emotional reaction to him or her from the past (spontaneous recovery).

The steps in classical conditioning are reviewed in the Psychological Inquiry above. The figure in the feature shows the sequence of acquisition, extinction, and spontaneous recovery. Spontaneous recovery can occur several times, but as long as the conditioned stimulus is presented alone (that is, without the unconditioned stimulus), spontaneous recovery becomes weaker and eventually ceases.

● **renewal** The recovery of the conditioned response when the organism is placed in a novel context.

Extinction is not always the end of a conditioned response. **Renewal** refers to the recovery of the conditioned response when the organism is placed in a novel context (Miquez, Cham, & Miller, 2012). Renewal can be a powerful problem to overcome—as it is when a person leaves a drug treatment facility to return to his or her previous living situation (Stasiewicz, Brandon, & Bradizza, 2007).

Classical Conditioning in Humans

Classical conditioning has a great deal of survival value for human beings (Chance, 2014). Here we review examples of classical conditioning at work in human life.

EXPLAINING FEARS

Classical conditioning provides an explanation of fears (Mazur, 2013). John B. Watson (who coined the term *behaviorism*) and Rosalie Rayner (1920) demonstrated classical conditioning's role in the development of fears with an infant named Albert. They showed Albert a white laboratory rat to see whether he was afraid of it. He was not (so the rat is a neutral stimulus or CS). As Albert played with the rat, the researchers sounded a loud noise behind his head (the bell is then the US). The noise caused little Albert to cry (the UR). After only seven pairings of the loud noise with the white rat, Albert began to fear the rat even when the noise was not sounded (the CR). Albert's fear was generalized to a rabbit, a dog, and a sealskin coat.

Today, Watson and Rayner's (1920) study would violate the ethical guidelines of the American Psychological Association. In any case, Watson correctly concluded that we learn many of our fears through classical conditioning. We might develop fear of the dentist because of a painful experience, fear of driving after having been in a car crash, and fear of dogs after having been bitten by one.

If we can learn fears through classical conditioning, we also can possibly unlearn them through that process (Craighead & others, 2013; Powell & Honey, 2013). In Chapter 16, for example, we will examine the application of classical conditioning to therapies for treating phobias.

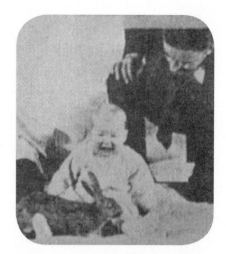

Watson and Rayner conditioned 11-month-old Albert to fear a white rat by pairing the rat with a loud noise. When little Albert was later presented with other stimuli similar to the white rat, such as the rabbit shown here with Albert, he was afraid of them too. This study illustrates stimulus generalization in classical conditioning.

BREAKING HABITS

Counterconditioning is a classical conditioning procedure for changing the relationship between a conditioned stimulus and its conditioned response. Therapists have used counterconditioning to break apart the association between certain stimuli and positive feelings (Kerkhof & others, 2011). **Aversive conditioning** is a form of treatment that consists of repeated pairings of a stimulus with a very unpleasant stimulus. Electric shocks and nausea-inducing substances are examples of noxious stimuli that are used in aversive conditioning (A. R. Brown & others, 2011).

To reduce drinking, for example, every time a person drinks an alcoholic beverage, he or she also consumes a mixture that induces nausea. In classical conditioning terminology, the alcoholic beverage is the conditioned stimulus, and the nausea-inducing agent is the unconditioned stimulus. Through a repeated pairing of alcohol with the nausea-inducing agent, alcohol becomes the conditioned stimulus that elicits nausea, the conditioned response. As a consequence, alcohol no longer is associated with something pleasant but rather something highly unpleasant. Antabuse, a drug treatment for alcoholism since the late 1940s, is based on this association (Ullman, 1952). When someone takes this drug, ingesting even the smallest amount of alcohol will make the person quite ill, even if the exposure to the alcohol is through mouthwash or cologne. Antabuse continues to be used in the treatment of alcoholism today (Bell & others, 2012; Rezvani & others, 2012).

● **counterconditioning** A classical conditioning procedure for changing the relationship between a conditioned stimulus and its conditioned response.

● **aversive conditioning** A form of treatment that consists of repeated pairings of a stimulus with a very unpleasant stimulus.

CLASSICAL CONDITIONING AND THE PLACEBO EFFECT

Chapter 2 defined the *placebo effect* as the effect of a substance (such as taking a pill orally) or a procedure (such as using a syringe to inject a substance) that researchers use as a control to identify the actual effects of a treatment. Placebo effects are observable changes (such as a drop in pain) that cannot be explained by the effects of an actual treatment. The principles of classical conditioning can help to explain some of these effects (Hyland, 2011). In this case, the pill or syringe serves as a CS, and the actual drug is the US. After the experience of pain relief following the consumption of a drug, for instance, the pill or syringe might lead to a CR of lowered pain even in the absence of an actual painkiller. The strongest evidence for the role of classical conditioning on placebo effects comes from research on the immune system and the endocrine system.

CLASSICAL CONDITIONING AND THE IMMUNE AND ENDOCRINE SYSTEMS

Even the human body's internal organ systems can be classically conditioned. The immune system is the body's natural defense against disease. Robert Ader and Nicholas Cohen have conducted a number of studies that reveal that classical conditioning can produce *immunosuppression,* a decrease in the production of antibodies, which can lower a person's ability to fight disease (Ader, 2000; Ader & Cohen, 1975, 2000).

The initial discovery of this link between classical conditioning and immunosuppression came as a surprise. In studying classical conditioning, Ader (1974) was examining how long a conditioned response would last in some laboratory rats. He paired a conditioned stimulus (saccharin solution) with an unconditioned stimulus, a drug called Cytoxan, which induces nausea. Afterward, while giving the rats saccharin-laced water without the accompanying Cytoxan, Ader watched to see how long it would take the rats to forget the association between the two.

Unexpectedly, in the second month of the study, the rats developed a disease and began to die off. In analyzing this unforeseen result, Ader looked into the properties of the nausea-inducing drug he had used. He discovered that one of its side effects was suppressed immune system functioning. It turned out that the rats had been classically conditioned to associate sweet water not only with nausea but also with the shutdown of the immune system. The sweet water apparently had become a conditioned stimulus for immunosuppression.

Researchers have found that conditioned immune responses also occur in humans (Olness & Ader, 1992, Schedlowski & Pacheco-Lopez, 2010; Wirth & others, 2011). For example, in one study, patients with multiple sclerosis were given a flavored drink prior to receiving a drug that suppressed the immune system. After this pairing, the flavored drink by itself lowered immune functioning, similarly to the drug (Giang & others, 1996).

Similar results have been found for the endocrine system. Recall from Chapter 3 that the endocrine system is a loosely organized set of glands that produce and circulate hormones. Research has shown that placebo pills can influence the secretion of hormones if patients had previous experiences with pills containing actual drugs that affected hormone secretion (Benedetti & others, 2003). Studies have revealed that the sympathetic nervous system (the part of the autonomic nervous systems that responds to stress) plays an important role in the learned associations between conditioned stimuli and immune and endocrine functioning (Saurer & others, 2008).

TASTE AVERSION LEARNING

Consider this scenario. Mike goes out for sushi with some friends and eats tekka maki (tuna roll), his favorite dish. He then proceeds to a jazz concert. Several hours later, he becomes very ill with stomach pains and nausea. A few weeks later, he tries to eat tekka maki again but cannot stand it. Importantly, Mike does not experience an aversion to jazz, even though he attended the jazz concert that night before getting sick. Mike's experience exemplifies *taste aversion:* a special kind of classical conditioning involving the learned association between a particular taste and nausea (Garcia & Koelling 1966; Kwok & Boakes, 2012; Mickley & others, 2013).

Taste aversion is special because it typically requires only one pairing of a neutral stimulus (a taste) with the unconditioned response of nausea to seal that connection, often for a very long time. As we consider later, it is highly adaptive to learn taste aversion in only one trial. An animal that required multiple pairings of taste with poison would likely not survive the acquisition phase. It is notable, though, that taste aversion can occur even if the "taste" had nothing to do with getting sick—perhaps, in Mike's case, he was simply coming down with a stomach bug. Taste aversion can even occur when a person has been sickened by a completely separate event, such as being spun around in a chair (Klosterhalfen & others, 2000).

Although taste aversion is often considered an exception to the rules of learning, Michael Domjan (2010) has suggested that this form of learning demonstrates how classical conditioning works in the natural world, where associations matter to survival. Remember, in taste aversion, the taste or flavor is the CS; the agent that made the person sick (it could be a roller-coaster ride or salmonella, for example) is the US; nausea or vomiting is the UR; and taste aversion is the CR.

Taste aversion learning is particularly important in the context of the traditional treatment of some cancers. Radiation and chemotherapy for cancer often produce nausea in patients, with the result that individuals sometimes develop strong aversions to many foods that they ingest prior to treatment (Holmes, 1993; Jacobsen & others, 1993). Consequently, they may experience a general tendency to be turned off by food, a situation that can lead to nutritional deficits (Mahmoud & others, 2011).

Researchers have used classical conditioning principles to combat these taste aversions, especially in children, for whom antinausea medication is often ineffective (Skolin & others, 2006) and for whom aversions to protein-rich food is particularly problematic (Ikeda & others, 2006). Early studies demonstrated that giving children a "scapegoat" conditioned stimulus prior to chemotherapy would help contain the taste aversion to only one specific type of food or flavor (Broberg & Bernstein, 1987). For example, children might be given a particular flavor of Lifesaver candy or ice cream before receiving treatment. For these children, the nausea would be more strongly associated with the Lifesaver or ice cream flavor than with the foods they needed to eat for good nutrition. These results show discrimination in classical conditioning—the kids developed aversions only to the specific scapegoat flavors.

The U.S. Fish and Wildlife Service is trying out taste aversion as a tool to prevent Mexican gray wolves from preying on cattle. To instill taste aversion for beef, the agency is deploying bait made of beef and cowhide but that also contains odorless and flavorless substances that induce nausea (Bryan, 2012). The hope is that wolves that are sickened by the bait will no longer prey on cattle and might even rear their pups to enjoy alternative meals.

CLASSICAL CONDITIONING AND ADVERTISING

Classical conditioning provides the foundation for many of the commercials that we are bombarded with daily. (Appropriately, when John Watson, whom you will recall from the baby Albert study, left the field of psychology, he went into advertising.) Think about it: Advertising involves creating an association between a product and pleasant feelings (buy that Grande Misto and be happy). TV advertisers cunningly apply classical conditioning principles to consumers by showing ads that pair something positive—such as a beautiful woman (the US) producing pleasant feelings (the UR)—with a product (the CS) in hopes that you, the viewer, will experience those positive feelings toward the product (the CR). You might have seen that talking baby (US) trying to get viewers to sign up and buy stocks through E*TRADE (CS).

Even when commercials are not involved, advertisers exploit classical conditioning principles—for instance, through the technique of product placement, or what is known as *embedded marketing*. For example, suppose that while viewing a TV show or movie, you notice that a character is drinking a particular brand of soft drink or eating a particular type of cereal. By placing their products in the context of a show or movie you like, advertisers are hoping that your positive feelings about the show, movie plot, or a character (the UR) rub off on their product (the CS). It may seem like a long shot, but all they need to do is enhance the chances that, say, navigating through a car dealership or a grocery store, you will feel attracted to their product.

DRUG HABITUATION

Chapter 5 noted how, over time, a person might develop a tolerance for a psychoactive drug and need a higher and higher dose of the substance to get the same effect. Classical conditioning helps to explain **habituation**, which refers to the decreased responsiveness to a stimulus after repeated presentations. A mind-altering drug is an unconditioned stimulus: It naturally produces a response in the person's body. As

● **habituation** Decreased responsiveness to a stimulus after repeated presentations.

FIGURE 6.3 **Drug Habituation** The figure illustrates how classical conditioning is involved in drug habituation. As a result of conditioning, the drug user will need to take more of the drug to get the same effect as the person did before the conditioning. Moreover, if the user takes the drug without the usual conditioned stimulus or stimuli—represented in the middle panel by the bathroom and the drug tablets—overdosing is likely.

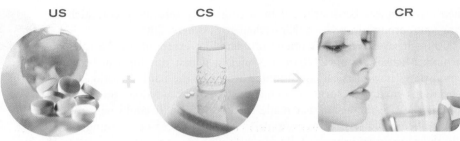

US

The psychoactive drug is an unconditioned stimulus (US) because it naturally produces a response in a person's body.

CS

Appearance of the drug tablets and the room where the person takes the drug are conditioned stimuli (CS) that are paired with the drug (US).

CR

The body prepares to receive the drug in the room. Repeated pairings of the US and CS have produced a conditioned response (CR).

described in the Intersection, this unconditioned stimulus is often paired systematically with a previously neutral stimulus (CS). For instance, the physical appearance of the drug in a pill or syringe, and the room where the person takes the drugs, are conditioned stimuli that are paired with the unconditioned stimulus of the drug. These repeated pairings should produce a conditioned response, and they do—but it is different from those we have considered so far.

The conditioned response to a drug can be the body's way of *preparing* for the effects of a drug (Rachlin & Green, 2009). In this case, the body braces itself for the effects of the drug with a CR that is the opposite of the UR. For instance, if the drug (the US) leads to an increase in heart rate (the UR), the CR might be a drop in heart rate. The CS serves as a warning that the drug is coming, and the conditioned response in this case is the body's compensation for the drug's effects (Figure 6.3). In this situation the conditioned response works to decrease the effects of the US, making the drug experience less intense. Some drug users try to prevent habituation by varying the physical location of where they take the drug.

This aspect of drug use can play a role in deaths caused by drug overdoses. How is classical conditioning involved? A user typically takes a drug in a particular setting, such as a bathroom, and acquires a conditioned response to this location (Siegel, 1988). Because of classical conditioning, as soon as the drug user walks into the bathroom, the person's body begins to prepare for and anticipate the drug dose in order to lessen the effect of the drug. However, if the user takes the drug in a location other than the usual one, such as at a rock concert, the drug's effect is greater because no conditioned responses have built up in the new setting, and therefore the body is not prepared for the drug.

In cases in which heroin causes death, researchers often have found that the individuals took the drug under unusual circumstances, at a different time, or in a different place relative to the context in which they usually took the drug (Marlow, 1999). In these cases, with no CS signal, the body is unprepared for (and tragically overwhelmed by) the drug's effects.

3· OPERANT CONDITIONING

Recall from early in the chapter that classical conditioning and operant conditioning are forms of associative learning, which involves learning that two events are connected. In classical conditioning, organisms learn the association between two stimuli (US and CS). Classical conditioning is a form of *respondent behavior,* behavior that occurs in automatic response to a stimulus such as a nausea-producing drug, and later to a conditioned stimulus such as sweet water that was paired with the drug.

Classical conditioning explains how neutral stimuli become associated with unlearned, *involuntary responses.* Classical conditioning is not as effective, however, in explaining *voluntary behaviors* such as a student's studying hard for a test, a gambler's playing slot machines in Las Vegas, or a service dog fetching his owner's cell phone on command.

test yourself

1. What is meant by an unconditioned stimulus (US) and an unconditioned response (UR)? In Pavlov's experiments with dogs, what were the US and the UR?
2. What is meant by a conditioned stimulus (CS) and a conditioned response (CR)? In Pavlov's experiments with dogs, what were the CS and the CR?
3. What learning principle does the Watson and Rayner study with baby Albert illustrate?

Operant conditioning is usually much better than classical conditioning at explaining such voluntary behaviors. Whereas classical conditioning focuses on the association between stimuli, operant conditioning focuses on the association between behaviors and the stimuli that follow them.

Defining Operant Conditioning

Operant conditioning or **instrumental conditioning** is a form of associative learning in which the consequences of a behavior change the probability of the behavior's occurrence. The American psychologist B. F. Skinner (1938) chose the term *operant* to describe the behavior of the organism. An operant behavior occurs spontaneously. According to Skinner, the consequences that follow such spontaneous behaviors determine whether the behavior will be repeated.

Imagine, for example, that you spontaneously decide to take a different route while driving to campus one day. You are more likely to repeat that route on another day if you have a pleasant experience—for instance, arriving at school faster or finding a new coffee place to try—than if you have a lousy experience such as getting stuck in traffic. In either case, the consequences of your spontaneous act influence whether that behavior happens again.

Recall that *contingency* is an important aspect of classical conditioning in which the occurrence of one stimulus can be predicted from the presence of another one. Contingency also plays a key role in operant conditioning. For example, when a rat pushes a lever (behavior) that delivers food, the delivery of food (consequence) is contingent on that behavior. This principle of contingency helps explain why passersby should never praise, pet, or feed a service dog while he is working (at least without asking first). Providing rewards during such times might interfere with the dog's training.

● **operant conditioning or instrumental conditioning** A form of associative learning in which the consequences of a behavior change the probability of the behavior's occurrence.

Thorndike's Law of Effect

Although Skinner emerged as the primary figure in operant conditioning, the experiments of E. L. Thorndike (1898) established the power of consequences in determining voluntary behavior. At about the same time that Pavlov was conducting classical conditioning experiments with salivating dogs, Thorndike, another American psychologist, was studying cats in puzzle boxes. Thorndike put a hungry cat inside a box and placed a piece of fish outside. To escape from the box and obtain the food, the cat had to learn to open the latch inside the box. At first the cat made a number of ineffective responses. It clawed or bit at the bars and thrust its paw through the openings. Eventually the cat accidentally stepped on the lever that released the door bolt. When the cat returned to the box, it went through the same random activity until it stepped on the lever once more. On subsequent trials, the cat made fewer and fewer random movements until finally it immediately stepped on the lever to open the door (Figure 6.4). Thorndike's resulting **law of effect** states that behaviors followed by pleasant outcomes are strengthened and that behaviors followed by unpleasant outcomes are weakened (Brown & Jenkins, 2009).

● **law of effect** Thorndike's law stating that behaviors followed by positive outcomes are strengthened and that behaviors followed by negative outcomes are weakened.

The law of effect is profoundly important because it presents the basic idea that the consequences of a behavior influence the likelihood of that behavior's recurrence (Olson & Hergenhahn, 2013). Quite simply, a behavior can be followed by something good or something bad, and the probability of a behavior's being repeated depends on these outcomes. As we now explore, Skinner's operant conditioning model expands on this basic idea.

Skinner's Approach to Operant Conditioning

Skinner believed that the mechanisms of learning are the same for all species. This conviction led him to study animals in the hope that he could discover the components of learning with organisms simpler than humans, including pigeons. During World War II,

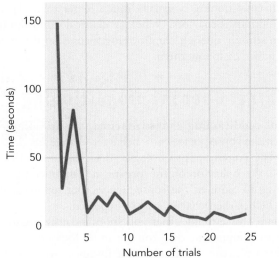

FIGURE 6.4 **Thorndike's Puzzle Box and the Law of Effect** (*Left*) A box typical of the puzzle boxes Thorndike used in his experiments with cats to study the law of effect. Stepping on the treadle released the door bolt; a weight attached to the door then pulled the door open and allowed the cat to escape. After accidentally pressing the treadle as it tried to get to the food, the cat learned to press the treadle when it wanted to escape the box. (*Right*) One cat's learning curve over 24 separate trials. Notice that the cat escaped much more quickly after about five trials. It had learned the consequences of its behavior.

Skinner trained pigeons to pilot missiles. Naval officials just could not accept pigeons piloting their missiles in a war, but Skinner congratulated himself on the degree of control he was able to exercise over the pigeons (Figure 6.5).

Skinner and other behaviorists made every effort to study organisms under precisely controlled conditions so that they could examine the connection between the operant behavior and the specific consequences in minute detail (Dewsbury, 2013). One of Skinner's creations in the 1930s to control experimental conditions was the Skinner box (Figure 6.6). A device in the box delivered food pellets into a tray at random. After a rat became accustomed to the box, Skinner installed a lever and observed the rat's behavior. As the hungry rat explored the box, it occasionally pressed the lever, and a food pellet was dispensed. Soon the rat learned that the consequences of pressing the lever were positive: It would be fed. Skinner achieved further control by soundproofing the box to ensure that the experimenter was the only influence on the organism. In many of the experiments, the responses were mechanically recorded, and the food (the consequence) was dispensed automatically. These precautions were aimed to prevent human error.

● **shaping** Rewarding successive approximations of a desired behavior.

Shaping

Imagine trying to teach even a really smart dog how to signal that her owner's blood glucose level is low—or how to turn on the lights or do the laundry. These challenges might seem insurmountable, as it is unlikely that a dog will spontaneously perform any of these behaviors. You could wait a very long time for such feats to occur. Nevertheless, it *is* possible to train a dog or another animal to perform highly complex tasks through shaping.

Shaping refers to rewarding successive approximations of a desired behavior (Chance, 2014; Slater & Dymond, 2011). For example, shaping can be used to train a rat to press a bar to obtain food. When a rat is first placed in a Skinner box, it rarely presses the bar. Thus, the experimenter may start off by giving the rat a food pellet if it is in the same half of the cage as the bar. Then the experimenter might reward the rat's

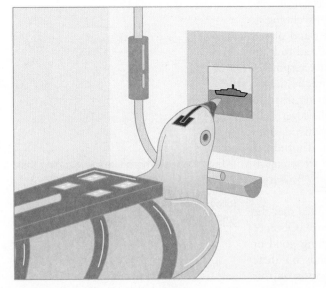

FIGURE 6.5 **Skinner's Pigeon-Guided Missile** Skinner wanted to help the military during World War II by using pigeons' tracking behavior. A gold electrode covered the tip of the pigeon's beaks. Contact with the screen on which the image of the target was projected sent a signal informing the missile's control mechanism of the target's location. A few grains of food occasionally given to the pigeons maintained their tracking behavior.

behavior only when it is within 2 inches of the bar, then only when it touches the bar, and finally only when it presses the bar.

Returning to the service dog example, rather than waiting for the dog spontaneously to put the clothes in the washing machine, we might reward the dog for carrying the clothes to the laundry room and for bringing them closer and closer to the washing machine. Finally, we might reward the dog only when it gets the clothes inside the washer. Indeed, trainers use this type of shaping technique extensively in teaching animals to perform tricks. A dolphin that jumps through a hoop held high above the water has been trained to perform this behavior through shaping.

Principles of Reinforcement

We noted earlier that a behavior can be followed by something pleasant or something unpleasant. When behaviors are followed by a desirable outcome, the behaviors are likely to be repeated. When behaviors are followed by an undesirable outcome, they are less likely to occur. Now we can put some labels on these different patterns.

Reinforcement is the process by which a stimulus or event (a *reinforcer*) following a particular behavior increases the probability that the behavior will happen again. These desirable (or rewarding) consequences of a behavior fall into two types, called *positive reinforcement* and *negative reinforcement*. Both of these types of consequences are experienced as pleasant, and both increase the frequency of a behavior.

POSITIVE AND NEGATIVE REINFORCEMENT

In **positive reinforcement,** the frequency of a behavior increases because it is followed by a desirable stimulus. For example, if someone you meet smiles at you after you say, "Hello, how are you?" and you keep talking, the smile has reinforced your talking. The same principle of positive reinforcement is at work when you teach a dog to "shake hands" by giving it a piece of food when it lifts its paw.

In contrast, in **negative reinforcement,** the frequency of a behavior increases because it is followed by *the removal* of something undesirable. For example, if your father nagged you to clean out the garage and kept nagging until you cleaned out the garage, your response (cleaning out the garage) removed the unpleasant stimulus (your dad's nagging). Taking an aspirin when you have a headache works the same way: A reduction of pain reinforces the act of taking an aspirin. Similarly, if your TV is making an irritating buzzing sound, you might give it a good smack on the side, and if the buzzing stops, you are more likely to smack the set again if the buzzing resumes. Ending the buzzing sound rewards the TV-smacking.

Notice that both positive and negative reinforcement involve rewarding behavior—but they do so in different ways. Positive reinforcement means following a behavior with the addition of something pleasant, and negative reinforcement means following a behavior with the removal of something unpleasant. So, in this case "positive" and "negative" have nothing to do with "good" and "bad." Rather, they refer to processes in which something is given (positive reinforcement) or removed (negative reinforcement).

Whether it is positive or negative, reinforcement is about increasing a behavior. Figure 6.7 provides further examples to help you understand the distinction between positive and negative reinforcement.

A special kind of response to negative reinforcement is avoidance learning. **Avoidance learning** occurs when the organism learns that by making a particular response, a negative stimulus can be altogether avoided. For instance, a student who receives one bad grade might thereafter always study hard in order to avoid the negative outcome of bad grades in the future. Even when the bad grade is no longer present, the pattern of behavior sticks. Avoidance learning is very powerful in the sense that the behavior is maintained even in the absence of any aversive stimulus. For example, animals that have

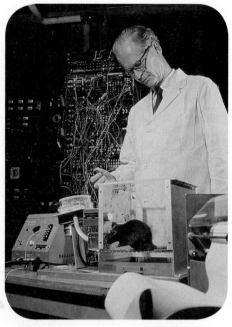

FIGURE 6.6 The Skinner Box
B. F. Skinner conducting an operant conditioning study in his behavioral laboratory. The rat being studied is in an operant conditioning chamber, sometimes referred to as a Skinner box.

Through shaping, animals can learn to do amazing things—even ride a wave, like this alpaca shown with its trainer, Peruvian surfer Domingo Pianezzi.

● **reinforcement** The process by which a stimulus or event (a reinforcer) following a particular behavior increases the probability that the behavior will happen again.

● **positive reinforcement** The presentation of a stimulus following a given behavior in order to increase the frequency of that behavior.

● **negative reinforcement** The removal of a stimulus following a given behavior in order to increase the frequency of that behavior.

● **avoidance learning** An organism's learning that it can altogether avoid a negative stimulus by making a particular response.

Positive Reinforcement

Behavior	Rewarding Stimulus Provided	Future Behavior
You turn in homework on time.	Teacher praises your performance.	You increasingly turn in homework on time.
You wax your skis.	The skis go faster.	You wax your skis the next time you go skiing.
You randomly press a button on the dashboard of a friend's car.	Great music begins to play.	You deliberately press the button again the next time you get into the car.

Negative Reinforcement

Behavior	Stimulus Removed	Future Behavior
You turn in homework on time.	Teacher stops criticizing late homework.	You increasingly turn in homework on time.
You wax your skis.	People stop zooming by you on the slopes.	You wax your skis the next time you go skiing.
You randomly press a button on the dashboard of a friend's car.	An annoying song shuts off.	You deliberately press the button again the next time the annoying song is on.

FIGURE 6.7 **Positive and Negative Reinforcement** Positive reinforcers involve adding something (generally something rewarding). Negative reinforcers involve taking away something (generally something aversive).

● **learned helplessness** An organism's learning through experience with negative stimuli that it has no control over negative outcomes.

been trained to avoid a negative stimulus, such as an electrical shock, by jumping into a safe area may always thereafter gravitate toward the safe area, even when the shock is no longer presented.

Experience with unavoidable negative stimuli can lead to a particular deficit in avoidance learning called learned helplessness. In **learned helplessness,** the organism has learned that it has no control over negative outcomes. Learned helplessness was first identified by Martin Seligman and his colleagues (Altenor, Volpicelli, & Seligman, 1979; Hannum, Rossellini, & Seligman, 1976). Seligman and his associates found that dogs that were first exposed to inescapable shocks were later unable to learn to avoid those shocks, even when they could avoid them (Seligman & Maier, 1967). This inability to learn to escape was persistent: The dogs would suffer painful shocks hours, days, and even weeks later and never attempt to escape.

Exposure to unavoidable negative circumstances may also set the stage for humans' inability to learn avoidance, such as with the experience of depression and despair (Pryce & others, 2011). Learned helplessness has aided psychologists in understanding a variety of perplexing issues, such as why some victims of domestic violence fail to escape their terrible situation and why some students respond to failure at school by giving up trying.

TYPES OF REINFORCERS

● **primary reinforcer** A reinforcer that is innately satisfying; one that does not take any learning on the organism's part to make it pleasurable.

● **secondary reinforcer** A reinforcer that acquires its positive value through an organism's experience; a secondary reinforcer is a learned or conditioned reinforcer.

Psychologists classify positive reinforcers as primary or secondary based on whether the rewarding quality of the consequence is innate or learned. A **primary reinforcer** is innately satisfying; that is, a primary reinforcer does not take any learning on the organism's part to make it pleasurable. Food, water, and sexual satisfaction are primary reinforcers.

A **secondary reinforcer** acquires its positive value through an organism's experience; a secondary reinforcer is a learned or conditioned reinforcer. Secondary reinforcers can be linked to primary reinforcers through classical conditioning. For instance, if someone wanted to train a cat to do tricks, the person might first repeatedly pair the sound of a whistle with food. Once the cat associates the whistle with food, the whistle can be used in training.

We encounter hundreds of secondary reinforcers in our lives, such as getting an *A* on a test and a paycheck for a job. Although we might think of these as positive outcomes, they are not innately positive. We learn through experience that *A*'s and paychecks are good. Secondary reinforcers can be used in a system called a *token economy*. In a token economy behaviors are rewarded with tokens (such as poker chips or stars on a chart) that can be exchanged later for desired rewards (such as candy or money).

GENERALIZATION, DISCRIMINATION, AND EXTINCTION

Not only are generalization, discrimination, and extinction important in classical conditioning, they also are key principles in operant conditioning.

Generalization   In operant conditioning, **generalization** means performing a reinforced behavior in a different situation. For example, in one study pigeons were reinforced for pecking at a disk of a particular color (Guttman & Kalish, 1956). To assess stimulus generalization, researchers presented the pigeons with disks of varying colors. As Figure 6.8 shows, the pigeons were most likely to peck at disks closest in color to the original. When a student who gets excellent grades in a calculus class by studying the course material every night starts to study psychology and history every night as well, generalization is at work.

Discrimination   In operant conditioning, **discrimination** means responding appropriately to stimuli that signal that a behavior will or will not be reinforced (Chance, 2014). For example, you go to a restaurant that has a "University Student Discount" sign in the front window, and you enthusiastically flash your student ID with the expectation of getting the reward of a reduced-price meal. Without the sign, showing your ID might get you only a puzzled look, not cheap food.

The principle of discrimination helps to explain how a service dog "knows" when she is working. Typically, the dog wears a training harness while on duty but not at other times. Thus, when a service dog is wearing her harness, it is important to treat her like the professional that she is. Similarly, an important aspect of the training of service dogs is the need for selective disobedience. Selective disobedience means that in addition to obeying commands from her human partner, the service dog must at times override such commands if the context provides cues that obedience is not the appropriate response. So, if a guide dog is standing at the corner with her visually impaired human, and the human commands her to move forward, the dog might refuse if she sees the "Don't Walk" sign flashing. Stimuli in the environment serve as cues, informing the organism if a particular reinforcement contingency is in effect.

Extinction   In operant conditioning, **extinction** occurs when a behavior is no longer reinforced and decreases in frequency (Mazur, 2013). If, for example, a soda machine that you frequently use starts "eating" your coins without dispensing soda, you quickly stop inserting more coins. Several weeks later, you might try to use the machine again, hoping that it has been fixed. Such behavior illustrates spontaneous recovery in operant conditioning.

CONTINUOUS REINFORCEMENT, PARTIAL REINFORCEMENT, AND SCHEDULES OF REINFORCEMENT

Most of the examples of reinforcement we have considered so far involve *continuous reinforcement,* in which a behavior is reinforced every time it occurs. When continuous reinforcement takes place, organisms learn rapidly. However, when reinforcement stops, extinction takes place quickly.

A variety of conditioning procedures have been developed that are particularly resistant to extinction. These involve *partial reinforcement,* in which a reinforcer follows a

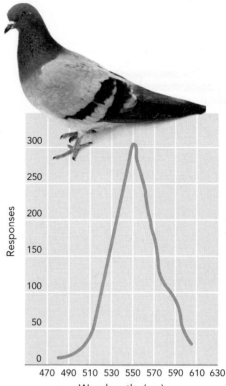

FIGURE 6.8 Stimulus Generalization In the experiment by Norman Guttman and Harry Kalish (1956), pigeons initially pecked a disk of a particular color (In this graph, a color with a wavelength of 550 nm) after they had been reinforced for this wavelength. Subsequently, when the pigeons were presented disks of colors with varying wavelengths, they were likelier to peck those that were similar to the original disk.

● **generalization (in operant conditioning)**
Performing a reinforced behavior in a different situation.

● **discrimination (in operant conditioning)**
Responding appropriately to stimuli that signal that a behavior will or will not be reinforced.

● **extinction (in operant conditioning)**
Decreases in the frequency of a behavior when the behavior is no longer reinforced.

behavior only a portion of the time (Mitchell & others, 2010). Partial reinforcement characterizes most life experiences. For instance, a golfer does not win every tournament she enters; a chess whiz does not win every match he plays; a student does not get a pat on the back each time she solves a problem.

Schedules of reinforcement are specific patterns that determine when a behavior will be reinforced (Bermúdez, Bruner, & Lattal, 2013; Orduña, García, & Hong, 2010). There are four main schedules of partial reinforcement: fixed ratio, variable ratio, fixed interval, and variable interval. With respect to these, *ratio schedules* involve the number of behaviors that must be performed prior to reward, and *interval schedules* refer to the amount of time that must pass before a behavior is rewarded. In a fixed schedule, the number of behaviors or the amount of time is always the same. In a variable schedule, the required number of behaviors or the amount of time that must pass changes and is unpredictable from the perspective of the learner. Let's look concretely at how each of these schedules of reinforcement influences behavior.

A *fixed-ratio schedule* reinforces a behavior after a set number of behaviors. For example, a child might receive a piece of candy or an hour of video game play not *every* time he practices his piano, but after five days of practicing, at least an hour a day. A mail carrier must deliver mail to a fixed number of houses each day before he or she can head home. The business world often uses fixed-ratio schedules to increase production. For instance, a factory might require a line worker to produce a certain number of items in order to get paid a particular amount. As you can imagine, fixed-ratio schedules are not very mysterious, especially to human learners.

Consider, for instance, if you were playing the slot machines in Atlantic City, and they were on a fixed-ratio schedule, providing a $5 win every 20th time you put money in the machine. It would not take long to figure out that if you watched someone else play the machine 18 or 19 times, not get any money back, and then walk away, you should step up, insert your coin, and get back $5. Of course, if the reward schedule for a slot machine were that easy to figure out, casinos would not be so successful.

What makes gambling so tantalizing is the unpredictability of wins (and losses). Slot machines are on a *variable-ratio schedule,* a timetable in which behaviors are rewarded an average number of times but on an unpredictable basis. For example, a slot machine might pay off at *an average* of every 20th time, but the gambler does not know when this payoff will be. The slot machine might pay off twice in a row and then not again until after 58 coins have been inserted. This averages out to a reward for every 20 behavioral acts, but *when* the reward will be given is unpredictable.

Variable-ratio schedules produce high, steady rates of behavior that are more resistant to extinction than the other three schedules. Clearly, slot machines can make quite a profit. This is because not only are the rewards unpredictable, but they require behavior on the part of the person playing. One cannot simply wait around and then put in a coin after hours of not playing, hoping for a win. The machine requires that a certain *number* of behaviors occur; that is what makes it a *ratio* schedule.

In contrast to ratio schedules of reinforcement, *interval* reinforcement schedules are determined by the *time elapsed* since the last behavior was rewarded. A *fixed-interval schedule* reinforces the first behavior after a fixed amount of time has passed. If you take a class that has four scheduled exams, you might procrastinate most of the semester and cram just before each test. Fixed-interval schedules of reinforcement are also responsible for the fact that pets seem to be able to "tell time," eagerly sidling up to their food dish at 5 P.M. in anticipation of dinner. On a fixed-interval schedule, the rate of a behavior increases rapidly as the time approaches when the behavior likely will be reinforced. For example, as you put a tray of delectable cookies into the oven you might set a timer. But before the timer goes off, you find yourself checking them, over and over.

A *variable-interval schedule* is a timetable in which a behavior is reinforced after a variable amount of time has elapsed. Pop quizzes occur on a variable-interval schedule. Random drug testing follows a variable-interval schedule as well. So does fishing—you do not know if the fish will bite in the next minute, in a half hour, in an hour, or ever. Because it is difficult to predict when a reward will come, behavior is *slow and consistent* on a variable-interval schedule (Staddon, Chelaru, & Higa, 2002). This is why pop

● **schedules of reinforcement** Specific patterns that determine when a behavior will be reinforced.

Slot machines are on a variable-ratio schedule of reinforcement.

psychological *inquiry*

Schedules of Reinforcement and Different Patterns of Responding

This figure shows how the different schedules of reinforcement result in different rates of responding. The X or horizontal axis represents time. The Y or vertical axis represents the cumulative responses. That means that as the line goes up, the total number of responses are building and building. In the figure, each hash mark indicates the delivery of reinforcement. That is, each of those little ticks indicates that a reward is being given.

Look closely at the pattern of responses over time for each schedule of reinforcement. On the fixed-ratio schedule, notice the dropoff in responding after each response; on the variable-ratio schedule, note the high, steady rate of responding. On the fixed-interval schedule, notice the immediate dropoff in responding after reinforcement and the increase in responding just before reinforcement (resulting in a scalloped curve); and on the variable-interval schedule, note the slow, steady rate of responding.

1. Which schedule of reinforcement represents the "most bang for the buck"? That is, which one is associated with the most responses for the least amount of reward?
2. Which schedule of reinforcement is most like pop quizzes?
3. Which is most like regular tests on a course syllabus?
4. Which schedule of reinforcement would be best if you have very little time for training?
5. Which schedule of reinforcement do you think is most common in your own life? Why?

quizzes lead to more consistent levels of studying compared to the cramming that might be seen with scheduled tests.

Let's take a closer look at the responses associated with each schedule of reinforcement in the Psychological Inquiry feature, above.

PUNISHMENT

We began this section by noting that behaviors can be followed by something good or something bad. So far, we have explored only the good things—reinforcers that are meant to increase behaviors. Sometimes, however, the goal is to decrease a behavior, and in such cases the behavior might be followed by something unpleasant. **Punishment** is a consequence that decreases the likelihood that a behavior will occur. For instance, a child plays with matches and gets burned when he lights one; the child consequently is less likely to play with matches in the future. As another example, a student interrupts the instructor, and the instructor scolds the student. This consequence—the teacher's verbal reprimand—makes the student less likely to interrupt in the future. In punishment, a response decreases because of its unpleasant consequences.

● **punishment** A consequence that decreases the likelihood that a behavior will occur.

● **positive punishment** The presentation of a stimulus following a given behavior in order to decrease the frequency of that behavior.

● **negative punishment** The removal of a stimulus following a given behavior in order to decrease the frequency of that behavior.

Just as the positive–negative distinction applies to reinforcement, it can also apply to punishment. As was the case for reinforcement, "positive" means adding something, and "negative" means taking something away. Thus, in **positive punishment** a behavior decreases when it is followed by the presentation of a stimulus, whereas in **negative punishment** a behavior decreases when a stimulus is removed. Examples of positive punishment include spanking a misbehaving child and scolding a spouse who forgot to call when she was running late at the office; the coach who makes his team run wind sprints after a lackadaisical practice is also using positive punishment. *Time-out* is a form of negative punishment in which a child is removed from a positive reinforcer, such as her toys. Getting grounded is also a form of negative punishment as it involves taking a teenager away from the fun things in his life. Figure 6.9 compares positive reinforcement, negative reinforcement, positive punishment, and negative punishment.

TIMING, REINFORCEMENT, AND PUNISHMENTS

How does the timing of reinforcement and punishment influence behavior? And does it matter whether the reinforcement is small or large?

Immediate Versus Delayed Reinforcement   As is the case in classical conditioning, in operant conditioning learning is more efficient when the interval between a behavior and its reinforcer is a few seconds rather than minutes or hours, especially in lower animals (Freestone & Church, 2010). If a food reward is delayed for more than 30 seconds after a rat presses a bar, it is virtually ineffective as reinforcement. Humans, however, have the ability to respond to delayed reinforcers (Holland, 1996).

Sometimes important life decisions involve whether to seek and enjoy a small, immediate reinforcer or to wait for a delayed but more highly valued reinforcer (Martin & Pear, 2011). For example, you might spend your money now on clothes, concert tickets, and the latest smartphone, or you might save your money and buy a car later. You might choose to enjoy yourself now in return for immediate small reinforcers, or you

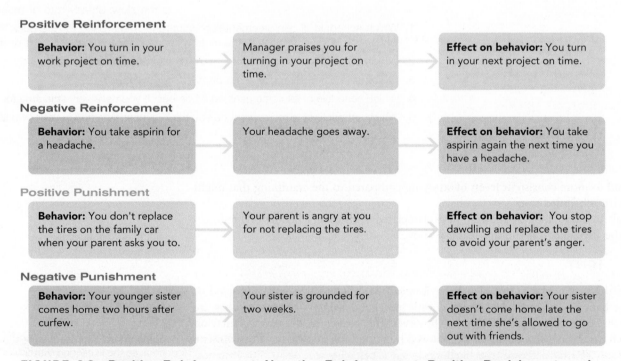

Positive Reinforcement

| **Behavior:** You turn in your work project on time. | Manager praises you for turning in your project on time. | **Effect on behavior:** You turn in your next project on time. |

Negative Reinforcement

| **Behavior:** You take aspirin for a headache. | Your headache goes away. | **Effect on behavior:** You take aspirin again the next time you have a headache. |

Positive Punishment

| **Behavior:** You don't replace the tires on the family car when your parent asks you to. | Your parent is angry at you for not replacing the tires. | **Effect on behavior:** You stop dawdling and replace the tires to avoid your parent's anger. |

Negative Punishment

| **Behavior:** Your younger sister comes home two hours after curfew. | Your sister is grounded for two weeks. | **Effect on behavior:** Your sister doesn't come home late the next time she's allowed to go out with friends. |

FIGURE 6.9 **Positive Reinforcement, Negative Reinforcement, Positive Punishment, and Negative Punishment** The fine distinctions here can sometimes be confusing. With respect to reinforcement, note that both types of reinforcement are intended to increase behavior, either by presenting a stimulus (in positive reinforcement) or by taking away a stimulus (in negative reinforcement). Punishment is meant to decrease a behavior either by presenting something (in positive punishment) or by taking away something (in negative punishment). The words *positive* and *negative* mean the same things in both cases.

might opt to study hard in return for delayed stronger reinforcers such as good grades, a scholarship to graduate school, and a better job.

Immediate Versus Delayed Punishment As with reinforcement, in most instances of research with lower animals, immediate punishment is more effective than delayed punishment in decreasing the occurrence of a behavior. However, also as with reinforcement, delayed punishment can have an effect on human behavior. Not studying at the beginning of a semester can lead to poor grades much later, and humans have the capacity to notice that this early behavior contributed to the negative outcome.

Immediate Versus Delayed Reinforcement and Punishment Many daily behaviors revolve around rewards and punishments, both immediate and delayed. We might put off going to the dentist to avoid a small punisher (such as the discomfort that comes with getting a cavity filled). However, this procrastination might contribute to greater pain later (such as the pain of having a tooth pulled). Sometimes life is about enduring a little pain now to avoid a lot of pain later.

How does receiving immediate small reinforcement versus delayed strong punishment affect human behavior (Martin & Pear, 2011)? One reason that obesity is such a major health problem is that eating is a behavior with immediate positive consequences—food tastes great and quickly provides a pleasurable, satisfied feeling. Although the potential delayed consequences of overeating are negative (obesity and other possible health risks), the immediate consequences are difficult to override. When the delayed consequences of behavior are punishing and the immediate consequences are reinforcing, the immediate consequences usually win, even when the immediate consequences are minor reinforcers and the delayed consequences are major punishers.

Smoking and drinking follow a similar pattern. The immediate consequences of smoking are reinforcing for most smokers—the powerful combination of positive reinforcement (enhanced attention, energy boost) and negative reinforcement (tension relief, removal of craving). The primarily long-term effects of smoking are punishing and include shortness of breath, a chronic sore throat and/or coughing, chronic obstructive pulmonary disease (COPD), heart disease, and cancer. Likewise, the immediate pleasurable consequences of drinking override the delayed consequences of a hangover or even alcoholism and liver disease.

Now think about the following situations. Why are some of us so reluctant to take up a new sport, try a new dance step, run for office on campus or in local government, or do almost anything different? One reason is that learning new skills often involves minor punishing consequences, such as initially looking and feeling stupid, not knowing what to do, and having to put up with sarcastic comments from others. In these circumstances, reinforcing consequences are often delayed. For example, it may take a long time to become a good enough golfer or a good enough dancer to enjoy these activities, but persevering through the rough patches just might be worth it.

Applied Behavior Analysis

Some thinkers have criticized behavioral approaches for ignoring mental processes and focusing only on observable behavior. Nevertheless, these approaches do provide an optimistic perspective for individuals interested in changing their behaviors. That is, rather than concentrating on factors such as the type of person you are, behavioral approaches imply that you can modify even longstanding habits by changing the reward contingencies that maintain those habits (Craighead & others, 2013; Miltenberger, 2012).

One real-world application of operant conditioning principles to promote better functioning is applied behavior analysis. **Applied behavior analysis** (also called **behavior modification**) is the use of operant conditioning principles to change human behavior. In applied behavior analysis, the rewards and punishers that exist in a particular setting are carefully analyzed and manipulated to change behaviors (Alberto & Troutman,

● **applied behavior analysis or behavior modification** The use of operant conditioning principles to change human behavior.

2012). Applied behavior analysis seeks to identify the rewards that might be maintaining unwanted behaviors and to enhance the rewards of more appropriate behaviors. From this perspective, we can understand all human behavior as being influenced by rewards and punishments. If we can figure out what rewards and punishers are controlling a person's behavior, we can change them—and eventually the behavior itself.

A manager who rewards staff members with a casual-dress day or a half-day off if they meet a particular work goal is employing applied behavior analysis. So are a therapist and a client when they establish clear consequences of the client's behavior in order to reinforce more adaptive actions and discourage less adaptive ones (Chance, 2014). A teacher who notices that a troublesome student seems to enjoy the attention he receives—even when that attention is scolding—might use applied behavior analysis by changing her responses to the child's behavior, ignoring it instead (an example of negative punishment).

These examples show how attending to the consequences of behavior can be used to improve performance in settings such as the workplace and a classroom. Advocates of applied behavior analysis believe that many emotional and behavioral problems stem from inadequate or inappropriate consequences (Alberto & Troutman, 2012).

Applied behavior analysis has been effective in a wide range of situations. Practitioners have used it, for example, to train individuals with autism (Frazier, 2012; Klintwall & Eikeseth, 2012), children and adolescents with psychological problems (Miltenberger, 2012), and residents of mental health facilities (Phillips & Mudford, 2008); to instruct individuals in effective parenting (Phaneuf & McIntyre, 2007); to enhance environmentally conscious behaviors such as recycling and not littering (Geller, 2002); to get people to wear seatbelts (Streff & Geller, 1986); and to promote workplace safety (Geller, 2006). Applied behavior analysis can help people improve their self-control in many aspects of mental and physical health (Levy, 2013; Mazur, 2013).

4· OBSERVATIONAL LEARNING

Would it make sense to teach a 15-year-old boy how to drive with either classical conditioning or operant conditioning procedures? Driving a car is a voluntary behavior, so classical conditioning would not apply. In terms of operant conditioning, we could ask him to try to drive down the road and then reward his positive behaviors. Not many of us would want to be on the road, though, when he makes mistakes.

Albert Bandura (2010a, 2011) believes that if all our learning were conducted in such a trial-and-error fashion, learning would be exceedingly tedious and at times hazardous. Instead, he says, many complex behaviors are the result of exposure to competent models. By observing other people, we can acquire knowledge, skills, rules, strategies, beliefs, and attitudes (Meltzoff & Williamson, 2013; Schunk, 2012). The capacity to learn by observation eliminates trial-and-error learning, and often such learning takes less time than operant conditioning.

Bandura's *observational learning*, also called *imitation* or *modeling*, is learning that occurs when a person observes and imitates behavior. Perhaps the most famous example of observational learning is the Bobo doll study (Bandura, Ross, & Ross, 1961). Bandura and his colleagues randomly assigned some children to watch an adult model aggressive behavior and other children to watch an adult behaving nonaggressively. In the experimental condition, children saw the model hit an inflated Bobo doll with a mallet, kick it in the air, punch it, and throw it, all the while hollering aggressive phrases such as "Hit him!" "Punch him in the nose!" and "Pow!" In the control condition, the model played with Tinkertoys and ignored the Bobo doll. Children who watched the aggressive model were much more likely to engage in aggressive behavior when left alone with Bobo (Bandura, Ross, & Ross, 1961).

Bandura (1986) described four main processes that are involved in observational learning: attention, retention, motor reproduction, and reinforcement. The first process that must occur is *attention* (which we considered in Chapter 4 due to its crucial role in perception). To reproduce a model's actions, you must attend to what the model is saying or doing. You might not hear what a friend says if music is blaring, and you might miss

test yourself

1. What is operant conditioning?
2. Define shaping and give two examples of it.
3. What is the difference between positive reinforcement and negative reinforcement? Between positive punishment and negative punishment?

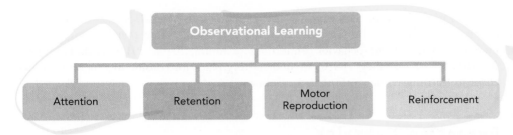

FIGURE 6.10 **Bandura's Model of Observational Learning** In terms of Bandura's model, if you are learning to ski, you need to attend to the Instructor's words and demonstrations. You need to remember what the instructor did and his or her tips for avoiding disasters. You also need the motor abilities to reproduce what the instructor has shown you. Praise from the Instructor after you have completed a few moves on the slopes should improve your motivation to continue skilling.

your instructor's analysis of a problem if you are admiring someone sitting in the next row. As a further example, imagine that you decide to take a class to improve your drawing skills. To succeed, you need to attend to the instructor's words and hand movements. Characteristics of the model can influence attention to the model. Warm, powerful, atypical people, for example, command more attention than do cold, weak, typical people.

Retention is the second process required for observational learning to occur. To reproduce a model's actions, you must encode the information and keep it in memory so that you can retrieve it. A simple verbal description, or a vivid image of what the model did, assists retention. (Memory is such an important cognitive process that Chapter 7 is devoted exclusively to it.) In the example of taking a class to sharpen your drawing skills, you will need to remember what the instructor said and did in modeling good drawing skills.

Motor reproduction, a third element of observational learning, is the process of imitating the model's actions. People might pay attention to a model and encode what they have seen, but limitations in motor development might make it difficult for them to reproduce the model's action. Thirteen-year-olds might see a professional basketball player do a reverse two-handed dunk but be unable to reproduce the pro's play. Similarly, in your drawing class, if you lack fine motor reproduction skills, you might be unable to follow the instructor's example.

Reinforcement is a final component of observational learning. In this case, the question is whether the model's behavior is followed by a consequence. Seeing a model attain a reward for an activity increases the chances that an observer will repeat the behavior—a process called *vicarious reinforcement.* On the other hand, seeing the model punished makes the observer less likely to repeat the behavior—a process called *vicarious punishment.* Unfortunately, vicarious reinforcement and vicarious punishment are often absent in, for example, media portrayals of violence and aggression.

Observational learning has been studied in a variety of contexts. Researchers have explored observational learning, for example, as a means by which gorillas learn from one another about motor skills (Byrne, Hobaiter, & Klailova, 2011). They have also studied it as a process by which people learn whether stimuli are likely to be painful (Helsen & others, 2011) and as a tool individuals use to make economic decisions (Feri & others, 2011). Researchers are also interested in comparing learning from *experience* with learning through *observation* (Nicolle, Symmonds, & Dolan, 2011).

Observational learning can be an important factor in the functioning of role models in inspiring people and changing their perceptions. Whether a model is similar to us can influence that model's effectiveness in modifying our behavior. The shortage of role models for women and minorities in science and engineering has often been suggested as a reason for the lack of women and minorities in these fields. After the election of Barack Obama as president of the United States, many commentators noted that for the first time, African American children could see concretely they might also attain the nation's highest office someday. Figure 6.10 summarizes Bandura's model of observational learning.

5· COGNITIVE FACTORS IN LEARNING

In learning about learning, we have looked at cognitive processes only as they apply in observational learning. Skinner's operant conditioning perspective and Pavlov's classical conditioning approach focus on the environment and observable behavior, not what is

test yourself

1. What are the four processes involved in observational learning?
2. What are two other names for observational learning?
3. What are vicarious reinforcement and vicarious punishment?

going on in the head of the learner. Many contemporary psychologists, including some behaviorists, recognize the importance of cognition and believe that learning involves more than environment–behavior connections (Bandura, 2010a, 2011; Bjork, Dunlosky, & Kornell, 2013; Leahey, 2013). A good starting place for considering cognitive influences in learning is the work of E. C. Tolman.

Purposive Behavior

E. C. Tolman (1932) emphasized the *purposiveness* of behavior—the idea that much of behavior is goal-directed. Tolman believed that it is necessary to study entire behavioral sequences in order to understand why people engage in particular actions. For example, high school students whose goal is to attend a leading college or university study hard in their classes. If we focused only on their studying, we would miss the purpose of their behavior. The students do not always study hard because they have been reinforced for studying in the past. Rather, studying is a means to intermediate goals (learning, high grades) that in turn improve their likelihood of getting into the college or university of their choice (Schunk, 2012).

We can see Tolman's legacy today in the extensive interest in the role of goal setting in human behavior (Carlson, Zelazo, & Faja, 2013; Schunk & Zimmerman, 2013). Researchers are especially curious about how people self-regulate and self-monitor their behavior to reach a goal (Anderman, Gray, & Chang, 2013).

EXPECTANCY LEARNING AND INFORMATION

In studying the purposiveness of behavior, Tolman went beyond the stimuli and responses of Pavlov and Skinner to focus on cognitive mechanisms. Tolman said that when classical conditioning and operant conditioning occur, the organism acquires certain expectations. In classical conditioning, the young boy fears the rabbit because he expects it will hurt him. In operant conditioning, a woman works hard all week because she expects a paycheck on Friday. Expectancies are acquired from people's experiences with their environment. Expectancies influence a variety of human experiences. We set the goals we do because we believe that we can reach them.

Expectancies also play a role in the placebo effect, described earlier. Many painkillers have been shown to be more effective in reducing pain if patients can see the intravenous injection sites (Price, Finniss, & Benedetti, 2008). If patients can observe that they are getting a drug, they can harness their own expectations for pain reduction.

Tolman (1932) emphasized that the information value of the conditioned stimulus is important as a signal or an expectation that an unconditioned stimulus will follow. Anticipating contemporary thinking, Tolman believed that the information that the CS provides is the key to understanding classical conditioning.

One contemporary view of classical conditioning describes an organism as an information seeker, using logical and perceptual relations among events, along with preconceptions, to form a representation of the world (Rescorla, 2003, 2004, 2005, 2006a, 2006b, 2006c, 2009).

A classic experiment conducted by Leon Kamin (1968) illustrates the importance of an organism's history and the information provided by a conditioned stimulus in classical conditioning. Kamin conditioned a rat by repeatedly pairing a tone (CS) and a shock (US) until the tone alone produced fear (CR). Then he continued to pair the tone with the shock, but he turned on a light (a second CS) each time the tone sounded. Even though he repeatedly paired the light (CS) and the shock (US), the rat showed no conditioning to the light (the light by itself produced no CR). Conditioning to the light was blocked, almost as if the rat had not paid attention. The rat apparently used the tone as a signal to predict that a shock would be coming; information about the light's pairing with the shock was redundant with the information already learned about the tone's pairing with the shock.

In this experiment, conditioning was governed not by the contiguity of the CS and US but instead by the rat's history and the information it received. Contemporary classical conditioning researchers are further exploring the role of information in an organism's learning (Kluge & others, 2011; Y. X. Xue & others, 2012).

LATENT LEARNING

Experiments on latent learning provide other evidence to support the role of cognition in learning. **Latent learning** or **implicit learning** is unreinforced learning that is not immediately reflected in behavior.

In one study, researchers put two groups of hungry rats in a maze and required them to find their way from a starting point to an end point (Tolman & Honzik, 1930). The first group found food (a reinforcer) at the end point; the second group found nothing there. In the operant conditioning view, the first group should learn the maze better than the second group, which is exactly what happened. However, when the researchers subsequently took some of the rats from the nonreinforced group and gave them food at the end point of the maze, they quickly began to run the maze as effectively as the reinforced group. The nonreinforced rats apparently had learned a great deal about the maze as they roamed around and explored it. However, their learning was *latent,* stored cognitively in their memories but not yet expressed behaviorally. When these rats were given a good reason (reinforcement with food) to run the maze speedily, they called on their latent learning to help them reach the end of the maze more quickly.

Outside a laboratory, latent learning is evident when you walk around a new setting to get "the lay of the land." The first time you visited your college campus, you may have wandered about without a specific destination in mind. Exploring the environment made you better prepared when the time came to find that 8 A.M. class.

● **latent learning or implicit learning** Unreinforced learning that is not immediately reflected in behavior.

Insight Learning

Like Tolman, the German gestalt psychologist Wolfgang Köhler believed that cognitive factors play a significant role in learning. Köhler spent four months in the Canary Islands during World War I observing the behavior of apes. There he conducted two fascinating experiments—the stick problem and the box problem. Although these two experiments are basically the same, the solutions to the problems are different. In both situations, the ape discovers that it cannot reach an alluring piece of fruit, either because the fruit is too high or because it is outside of the ape's cage and beyond reach. To solve the stick problem, the ape has to insert a small stick inside a larger stick to reach the fruit. To master the box problem, the ape must stack several boxes to reach the fruit (Figure 6.11).

According to Köhler (1925), solving these problems does not involve trial and error or simple connections between stimuli and responses. Rather, when the ape realizes that its customary actions are not going to help it get the fruit, it often sits for a period of time and appears to ponder how to solve the problem. Then it quickly rises, as if it has had a sudden flash of insight, piles the boxes on top of one another, and gets the fruit. **Insight learning** is a form of problem solving in which the organism develops a sudden insight into or understanding of a problem's solution.

The idea that insight learning is essentially different from learning through trial and error or through conditioning has always been controversial (Spence, 1938). Insight learning appears to entail both gradual and sudden processes, and understanding how these lead to problem solving continues to fascinate psychologists (Chu & MacGregor, 2011).

Research has documented that nonhuman primates are capable of remarkable learning that certainly appears to be insightful (Manrique, Völter, & Call, 2013). In one study, researchers observed orangutans trying to figure out a way to get a tempting

● **insight learning** A form of problem solving in which the organism develops a sudden insight into or understanding of a problem's solution.

FIGURE 6.11 **Insight Learning** Sultan, one of Köhler's brightest chimps, was faced with the problem of reaching a cluster of bananas overhead. He solved the problem by stacking boxes on top of one another to reach the bananas. Köhler called this type of problem solving "insight learning."

test yourself

1. What did Tolman mean by the purposiveness of behavior?
2. How do expectancies develop through classical and operant conditioning?
3. Define latent learning and insight learning and give an example of each.

peanut out of a clear plastic tube (Mendes, Hanus, & Call, 2007). The primates wandered about their enclosures, experimenting with various strategies. Typically, they paused for a moment before finally landing on a solution: Little by little they filled the tube with water that they transferred by mouth from their water dishes to the tube. Once the peanut floated to the top, the clever orangutans had their snack. More recent research shows that chimps can solve the floating peanut task through observational learning (Tennie, Call, & Tomasello, 2010).

Insight learning requires that we think "outside the box," setting aside previous expectations and assumptions. One way to enhance insight learning and creativity in human beings is through multicultural experiences (Leung & others, 2008). Correlational studies have shown that time spent living abroad is associated with higher insight learning performance among MBA students (Maddux & Galinsky, 2007). Experimental studies have also demonstrated this effect. In one study, U.S. college students were randomly assigned to view one of two slide shows—one about Chinese and U.S. culture and the other about a control topic. Those who saw the multicultural slide show scored higher on measures of creativity and insight, and these changes persisted for a week (Leung & others, 2008).

Importantly, we can gain the benefits of multicultural exposure even without travel abroad or particular slide shows. One of the most dramatic changes in U.S. higher education is the increasing diversity of the student body ("Forecast for growth on campuses: More women, minorities," 2011). Might this growing diversity benefit students? Research suggests that it does. For instance, in a study of over 53,000 undergraduates at 124 colleges and universities, students' reported interactions with individuals from other racial and ethnic backgrounds predicted a variety of positive outcomes, including academic achievement, intellectual growth, and social competence (Hu & Kuh, 2003).

Many universities recognize that as U.S. society becomes more multiculturally diverse, students must be prepared to interact in a diverse community as they enter the job market. Participation in diversity courses in college is related to cognitive development (Bowman, 2010) and civic involvement (Gurin & others, 2002), with outcomes especially positive for non-Latino White students (Hu & Kuh, 2003). Diverse groups provide broader knowledge and more varied perspectives than do homogeneous groups, to the positive benefit of all group members. As university communities become more diverse, they offer students an ever-greater opportunity to share and to benefit from those differences.

6· BIOLOGICAL, CULTURAL, AND PSYCHOLOGICAL FACTORS IN LEARNING

Albert Einstein had many special talents. He combined enormous creativity with keen analytic ability to develop some of the twentieth century's most important insights into the nature of matter and the universe. Genes obviously endowed Einstein with extraordinary intellectual skills that enabled him to think and reason on a very high plane, but cultural factors also contributed to his genius. Einstein received an excellent, rigorous European education, and later in the United States he experienced the freedom and support believed to be important in creative exploration. Would Einstein have been able to develop his skills fully and to make such brilliant insights if he had grown up in a less advantageous environment? It is unlikely. Clearly, both biological *and* cultural factors contribute to learning.

Biological Constraints

Human beings cannot breathe under water, fish cannot ski, and cows cannot solve math problems. The structure of an organism's body permits certain kinds of learning and inhibits others (Chance, 2014). For example, chimpanzees cannot learn to speak human languages because they lack the necessary vocal equipment. In animals, various aspects of their physical makeup can influence what they can learn. Sometimes, species-typical behaviors (or instincts) can override even the best reinforcers, as we now consider.

INSTINCTIVE DRIFT

Keller and Marion Breland (1961), students of B. F. Skinner, used operant conditioning to train animals to perform at fairs and conventions and in television advertisements. They applied Skinner's techniques to teach pigs to cart large wooden nickels to a piggy bank and deposit them. They also trained raccoons to pick up a coin and drop it into a metal tray.

Although the pigs and raccoons, as well as chickens and other animals, performed most of the tasks well (raccoons became adept basketball players, for example—see Figure 6.12), some of the animals began acting strangely. Instead of picking up the large wooden nickels and carrying them to the piggy bank, the pigs dropped the nickels on the ground, shoved them with their snouts, tossed them in the air, and then repeated these actions. The raccoons began to hold on to their coins rather than dropping them into the metal tray. When two coins were introduced, the raccoons rubbed them together in a miserly fashion. Somehow these behaviors overwhelmed the strength of the reinforcement. This example of biological influences on learning illustrates **instinctive drift,** the tendency of animals to revert to instinctive behavior that interferes with learning.

Why were the pigs and the raccoons misbehaving? The pigs were rooting, an instinct that is used to uncover edible roots. The raccoons were engaging in an instinctive food-washing response. Their instinctive drift interfered with learning.

PREPAREDNESS

Some animals learn readily in one situation but have difficulty learning in slightly different circumstances (Garcia & Koelling, 1966, 2009). The difficulty might result not from some aspect of the learning situation but from the organism's biological predisposition (Seligman,

● **instinctive drift** The tendency of animals to revert to instinctive behavior that interferes with learning.

FIGURE 6.12   Instinctive Drift This raccoon's skill in using its hands made it an excellent basketball player, but because of instinctive drift, the raccoon had a much more difficult time dropping coins into a tray.

● **preparedness** The species-specific biological predisposition to learn in certain ways but not others.

1970). **Preparedness** is the species-specific biological predisposition to learn in certain ways but not others.

Much of the evidence for preparedness comes from research on taste aversion (Garcia, 1989; Garcia & Koelling, 2009). Recall that taste aversion involves a single trial of learning the association between a particular taste and nausea. Rats that experience low levels of radiation after eating show a strong aversion to the food they were eating when the radiation made them ill. This aversion can last for as long as 32 days. Such long-term effects cannot be accounted for by classical conditioning, which would argue that a single pairing of the conditioned and unconditioned stimuli would not last that long (Garcia, Ervin, & Koelling, 1966). Taste aversion learning occurs in animals, including humans, that choose their food based on taste and smell. Other species are prepared to learn rapid associations between, for instance, colors of foods and illness.

Another example of preparedness comes from research on conditioning humans and monkeys to associate snakes with fear. Susan Mineka and Arne Ohman have investigated the fascinating natural power of snakes to evoke fear in many mammals (Mineka & Ohman, 2002; Ohman & Mineka, 2003). Many monkeys and humans fear snakes, and both monkeys and humans are very quick to learn the association between snakes and fear. In classical conditioning studies, when pictures of snakes (CS) are paired with electrical shocks (US), the snakes are likely to quickly and strongly evoke fear (CR). Interestingly, pairing pictures of, say, flowers (CS) with electrical shocks produces much weaker associations (Mineka & Ohman, 2002; Ohman & Soares, 1998). More significantly, pictures of snakes can serve as conditioned stimuli for fearful responses, even when the pictures are presented so rapidly that they cannot be consciously perceived (Ohman & Mineka, 2001).

The link between snakes and fear has been demonstrated not only in classical conditioning paradigms. Monkeys that have been raised in the lab and that have never seen a snake rapidly learn to fear snakes, even entirely by observational learning. Lab monkeys that see a videotape of a monkey expressing fear toward a snake learn to be afraid of snakes faster than monkeys seeing the same fear video spliced so that the feared object is a rabbit, a flower, or a mushroom (Ohman & Mineka, 2003).

Mineka and Ohman (2002) suggest that these results demonstrate preparedness among mammals to associate snakes with fear and aversive stimuli. They suggest that this association is related to the amygdala (the part of the limbic system that is related to emotion) and is difficult to modify. These researchers suggest that this preparedness for fear of snakes has emerged out of the threat that reptiles likely posed to our evolutionary ancestors.

Cultural Influences

Traditionally, interest in the cultural context of human learning has been limited, partly because the organisms in those contexts typically were animals. The question arises, how might culture influence human learning? Most psychologists agree that the principles of classical conditioning, operant conditioning, and observational learning are universal and are powerful learning processes in every culture. However, culture can influence the *degree* to which these learning processes are used (Matsumoto & Juang, 2013). For example, Mexican American students may learn more through observational learning, while non-Latino White students may be more accustomed to learn through direct instruction (Mejia-Arauz, Rogoff, & Paradise, 2005).

In addition, culture can determine the *content* of learning (Mistry, Contreras, & Dutta, 2013; Zhang & Sternberg, 2013). We cannot learn about something we do not experience. The 4-year-old who grows up among the Bushmen of the Kalahari Desert is unlikely to learn about taking baths and eating with a knife and fork. Similarly, a child growing up in Chicago is unlikely to be skilled at tracking animals and finding water-bearing roots in the desert. Learning often requires practice, and certain behaviors are practiced more often in some cultures than in others. In Bali, many children are

On the Indonesian island of Bali, young children learn traditional dances, whereas in Norway children commonly learn to ski early in life. As cultures vary, so does the content of learning.

skilled dancers by the age of 6, whereas Norwegian children are much more likely to be good skiers and skaters by that age.

Psychological Constraints

Are there psychological constraints on learning? For animals, the answer is probably no. For humans, the answer may well be yes. This section opened with the claim that fish cannot ski. The truth of this statement is clear. Biological circumstances make it impossible. If we put biological considerations aside, we might ask ourselves about times in our lives when we feel like a fish trying to ski—when we feel that we just do not have what it takes to learn a skill or master a task. Some people believe that humans have particular learning styles that make it easier for them to learn in some ways but not others. To read about this possibility, see the Critical Controversy.

Carol Dweck (2006, 2013) uses the term *mindset* to describe the way our beliefs about ability dictate what goals we set for ourselves, what we think we *can* learn, and ultimately what we *do* learn. Individuals have one of two mindsets: a *fixed mindset,* in which they believe that their qualities are carved in stone and cannot change; or a *growth mindset,* in which they believe their qualities can change and improve through their effort. These two mindsets have implications for the meaning of failure. From a fixed mindset, failure means lack of ability. From a growth mindset, however, failure tells the person what he or she still needs to learn. Your mindset influences whether you will be optimistic or pessimistic, what your goals will be, how hard you will strive to reach those goals, and how successful you are in college and after.

Dweck (2006) studied first-year pre-med majors taking their first chemistry class in college. Students with a growth mindset got higher grades than those with a fixed mindset. Even when they did not do well on a test, the growth-mindset students bounced back on the next test. Fixed-mindset students typically read and re-read the text and class notes or tried to memorize everything verbatim. The fixed-mindset students who did poorly on tests concluded that chemistry and maybe pre-med were not for them. By contrast, growth-mindset students took charge of their motivation and learning, searching for themes and principles in the course and going over mistakes until they understood why they made them. In Dweck's analysis (2006, p. 61), "They were studying to learn, not just ace the test. And, actually, this is why they got higher grades—not because they were smarter or had a better background in science."

Dweck and her colleagues recently incorporated information about the brain's plasticity into their effort to improve students' motivation to achieve and succeed (Blackwell & Dweck, 2008; Blackwell, Trzesniewski, & Dweck, 2007; Dweck, 2013; Dweck & Master, 2009). In one study, they assigned two groups of students to eight sessions of either (1) study skills instruction or (2) study skills instruction plus information about the importance of developing a growth mindset (called *incremental theory* in the research) (Blackwell, Trzesniewski, & Dweck, 2007).

One of the exercises in the growth-mindset group was titled "You Can Grow Your Brain," and it emphasized that the brain is like a muscle that can change and grow as it gets exercised and develops new connections. Students were informed that the more they challenged their brain to learn, the more their brain cells would grow. Prior to the intervention, both groups had a pattern of declining math scores. Following the intervention, the group that received only the study skills instruction continued to decline, but the group that received the study skills instruction *plus* the growth-mindset emphasis reversed the downward trend and improved their math achievement.

In other work, Dweck has created a computer-based workshop, "Brainology," to teach students that their intelligence can change (Blackwell & Dweck, 2008). Students experience six modules about how the brain works and how they can make their brain

CRITICAL CONTROVERSY

Do Learning Styles Matter to Learning?

Learning styles refers to the idea that people differ in terms of the method of instruction that will be most effective for them. You may have heard, for example, that someone can be a visual learner (he or she learns by seeing), an aural learner (the person learns by listening), or a kinesthetic learner (the individual learns through hands-on experience).

The notion that people have different learning styles is extremely popular. Many educational training programs and school districts advise teachers to take such differences into account in the classroom, tailoring their methods to fit students' learning styles. This advice is, of course, based on the assumption that individuals will learn better when instructions are targeted to their particular learning style. Is there sound evidence for this assumption? Does tailoring instruction to different learning styles improve learning? To answer this question, a number of experts have examined research on this question (Pashler & others, 2008; Rohrer & Pashler, 2012), and their answer might surprise you. The scientific evidence shows that although children and adults report consistent preferences for particular learning styles, there is no evidence that tailoring instructional methods to "visual," "auditory," or "kinesthetic" learners produces better learning (Pashler & others, 2008).

Consider one study, in which researchers first measured whether participants were verbal or visual learners and then had them study a list of words presented verbally or visually. This study period was followed by a memory test. Results showed that all participants did better in the visual condition, and there was no relationship between preferred learning styles and memory for the material (Constantinidou & Baker, 2002).

In another series of studies, participants who identified themselves as visual or verbal learners were given the option to use visual or verbal help materials as they completed a computer-based learning unit. Although learning styles predicted the kind of materials participants preferred, the match between a person's learning style and the mode of instruction was unrelated to learning (Massa & Mayer, 2006). The investigators concluded that there was no evidence that different instructional methods should be used for different learners

(Massa & Mayer, 2006). Based on these and other studies, Harold Pashler, an expert on human learning, and his colleagues concluded that the disconnect between the popularity of the learning styles approach within education and the lack of credible evidence for its usefulness was both "striking and disturbing" (2008, p. 117).

The notion of learning styles is appealing at least in part because it reflects something we know to be true: People learn differently. However, the different ways humans learn do not seem to be well captured by learning styles (Willingham, 2011). The effectiveness of particular methods of teaching may depend more on the material to be covered, a student's prior knowledge, motivation, and other factors. Coming at any topic from many different angles may improve student learning. Teachers may reach more students more effectively when they try different ways of approaching material—for instance, coming up with a hands-on tool to demonstrate a problem—but that is just good instruction, not instruction that is tailored to particular styles. Our senses work together to connect us to the external world. The brain and our sensory organs are not specialized to learn in specific ways.

Is there any harm in our trying to determine our preferred learning style? Perhaps, if the outcome constrains learning—if we assume, for example, that our personal learning style tells us what we cannot do or should not try. Sometimes the most meaningful learning experiences are those that push us beyond our comfort zone. Teachers and topics that challenge us to put in extra effort, to see the world and ourselves in different ways, may be the key to meaningful learning. Sometimes the easiest path is not the one most likely to lead to life-changing learning.

WHAT DO YOU THINK

- Do you think that you have a particular learning style? If so, how does it influence your learning?

- Even if evidence supported the effectiveness of tailoring teaching methods to specific types of learning styles, how would we implement a program based on these ideas?

improve. After the recent testing of the modules in 20 New York City schools, students strongly endorsed the value of the computer-based brain modules. One student said, "I will try harder because I know that the more you try, the more your brain knows" (Dweck & Master, 2009, p. 137).

Following are some effective strategies for developing a growth mindset (Dweck, 2006):

- *Understand that your intelligence and thinking skills are not fixed but can change.* Even if you are extremely bright, with effort you can increase your intelligence.
- *Become passionate about learning and stretch your mind in challenging situations.* It is easy to withdraw into a fixed mindset when the going gets tough. However, as you bump up against obstacles, keep growing, work harder, stay the course, and improve your strategies; you will become a more successful person.
- *Think about the growth mindsets of people you admire.* Possibly you have a hero, someone who has achieved something extraordinary. You may have thought his or her accomplishments came easily because the person is so talented. If you find out more about this person, though, you likely will discover that hard work and effort over a long period of time were responsible for his or her achievements.
- *Begin now.* If you have a fixed mindset, commit to changing now. Think about when, where, and how you will begin using your new growth mindset.

Dweck's work challenges us to consider the limits we place on our own learning. Our beliefs about ability profoundly influence what we try to learn. As any 7-year-old with a growth mindset would tell you, you never know what you can do until you try.

test yourself

1. What are two biological constraints on learning?
2. How does culture influence learning?
3. What is the difference between a fixed mindset and a growth mindset?

7· LEARNING AND HEALTH AND WELLNESS

In this chapter, we have examined the main psychological approaches to learning. In this final section, we consider specific ways that research on learning has shed light on human health and wellness. We examine in particular the factors that animal learning models have identified as playing an important role in the experience of stress—which, as you will recall from Chapter 3, is the organism's response to a threat in the environment. A great deal of research in learning has relied primarily on models of animals, such as rats, to examine the principles that underlie human learning. Research on the stress response in rats provides useful insights into how we humans can deal with stress.

STRESS AND PREDICTABILITY

One very powerful aspect of potentially stressful experiences is their predictability. For a rat, predictability might depend on getting a warning buzzer before receiving a shock. Although the rat still experiences the shock, a buzzer-preceded shock causes less stress than a shock that is received with no warning (Abbott, Schoen, & Badia, 1984). Even having *good* experiences on a predictable schedule is less stressful than having good things happen at random times. For example, a rat might do very well receiving its daily chow at specific times during the day, but if the timing is random, the rat experiences stress. Similarly, when you receive a gift on your birthday or a holiday, the experience feels good. However, if someone surprises you with a present out of the blue, you might feel some stress as you wonder, "What is this person up to?"

Also relevant is classic research by Judith Rodin and her colleagues, which demonstrated that nursing home residents showed better adjustment if they experienced a

given number of visits at predictable times rather than the same number of visits at random times (Langer & Rodin, 1976).

STRESS AND CONTROL

Feeling in control may be a key to avoiding feelings of stress over difficulties (Carver & Scheier, 2013). Specifically, once you have experienced control over negative events, you may be "protected" from stress, even during trying times.

Returning to an animal model, suppose that a rat has been trained to avoid a shock by pressing a lever. Over time, even when the lever is no longer related to the shock, the rat presses it during the shock—and experiences less stress. We might imagine the rat thinking, "Gee, it would be really worse if I weren't pressing this lever!" Researchers have also found links between having control and experiencing stress in humans. For example, nursing home residents are more likely to thrive if they receive visits at times they personally choose. In addition, simply having a plant to take care of is associated with living longer for nursing home residents (Langer & Rodin, 1976).

A lack of control over aversive stimuli can be particularly stressful. For example, individuals exposed to uncontrollable loud blasts of noise show lowered immune system function (Sieber & others, 1992). One result of exposure to uncontrollable negative events is *learned helplessness,* which we examined earlier in this chapter. In learned helplessness, the organism has learned through experience that outcomes are not controllable. As a result, the organism stops trying to exert control.

Research has shown that, to break the lock of learned helplessness, dogs and rats have to be forcibly moved to escape an aversive shock (Seligman, Rosellini, & Kozak, 1975). From such animal studies, we can appreciate how difficult it may be for individuals who find themselves in situations in which they have little control—for example, women who are victims of domestic violence (L. E. A. Walker, 2009)—to take action. We can also appreciate the helplessness sometimes experienced by students with learning difficulties who withdraw from their coursework because they feel unable to influence outcomes in school (Gwernan-Jones & Burden, 2010).

STRESS AND IMPROVEMENT

Imagine that you have two mice, both of which are receiving mild electrical shocks. One of them, Jerry, receives 50 shocks every hour, and the other, Chuck-E, receives 10 shocks every hour. The next day both rats are switched to 25 shocks every hour. Which one is more stressed out at the end of the second day? The answer is that even though Jerry has experienced more shocks in general, Chuck-E is more likely to show the wear and tear of stress. In Jerry's world, even with 25 shocks an hour, *things are better*. The perception of improvement, even in a situation that is objectively worse than another, is related to lowered stress (Sapolsky, 2004).

OUTLETS FOR FRUSTRATION

When things are not going well for us, it often feels good to seek out an outlet, such as going for a run or, perhaps even better, taking a kickboxing class. Likewise, for a rat, having an outlet for life's frustrations is related to lowered stress symptoms. Rats that have a wooden post to gnaw on or even a furry little friend to complain to are less stressed out in response to negative circumstances.

Although studies using rats and dogs may seem far afield of our everyday experiences, researchers' observations provide important clues for avoiding stress. When we cultivate predictable environments and take control of circumstances, stress decreases. Further, when we can see improvement, even in difficult times, stress is likely to diminish. Finally, when we have an outlet for our frustrations in life—whether it is physical exercise, writing, or art—we can relieve our stress. When it comes to stress, humans have a lot to learn from rats.

test yourself

1. Based on research involving animal models, what are four ways in which human beings can reduce stress?
2. What is the main effect of learned helplessness on an organism?
3. Why do individuals who are experiencing domestic violence often have difficulty in overcoming their troubles?

1. TYPES OF LEARNING

Learning is a systematic, relatively permanent change in behavior that occurs through experience. Associative learning involves learning by making a connection between two events. Observational learning is learning by watching what other people do. Conditioning is the process by which associative learning occurs. In classical conditioning, organisms learn the association between two stimuli. In operant conditioning, they learn the association between behavior and a consequence.

2. CLASSICAL CONDITIONING

Classical conditioning occurs when a neutral stimulus becomes associated with a meaningful stimulus and comes to elicit a similar response. Pavlov discovered that an organism learns the association between an unconditioned stimulus (US) and a conditioned stimulus (CS). The US automatically produces the unconditioned response (UR). After conditioning (CS–US pairing), the CS elicits the conditioned response (CR) by itself. Acquisition in classical conditioning is the initial linking of stimuli and responses, which involves a neutral stimulus being associated with the US so that the CS comes to elicit the CR. Two important aspects of acquisition are contiguity and contingency.

Generalization in classical conditioning is the tendency of a new stimulus that is similar to the original conditioned stimulus to elicit a response that is similar to the conditioned response. Discrimination is the process of learning to respond to certain stimuli and not to others. Extinction is the weakening of the CR in the absence of the US. Spontaneous recovery is the recurrence of a CR after a time delay without further conditioning. Renewal is the occurrence of the CR (even after extinction) when the CS is presented in a novel environment.

In humans, classical conditioning has been applied to eliminating fears, treating addiction, understanding taste aversion, and explaining different experiences such as pleasant emotions and drug overdose.

3. OPERANT CONDITIONING

Operant conditioning is a form of learning in which the consequences of behavior produce changes in the probability of the behavior's occurrence. Skinner described the behavior of the organism as operant: The behavior operates on the environment, and the environment in turn operates on the organism. Whereas classical conditioning involves respondent behavior, operant conditioning involves operant behavior. In most instances, operant conditioning is better at explaining voluntary behavior than is classical conditioning.

Thorndike's law of effect states that behaviors followed by pleasant outcomes are strengthened, whereas behaviors followed by unpleasant outcomes are weakened. Skinner built on this idea to develop the notion of operant conditioning.

Shaping is the process of rewarding approximations of desired behavior in order to shorten the learning process. Principles of reinforcement include the distinction between positive reinforcement (the frequency of a behavior increases because it is followed by a rewarding stimulus) and negative reinforcement (the frequency of behavior increases because it is followed by the removal of an aversive, or unpleasant, stimulus). Positive reinforcement can be classified as primary reinforcement (using reinforcers that are innately satisfying) and secondary reinforcement (using reinforcers that acquire positive value through experience).

Reinforcement can also be continuous (a behavior is reinforced every time) or partial (a behavior is reinforced only a portion of the time). Schedules of reinforcement—fixed ratio, variable ratio, fixed interval, and variable interval—determine when a behavior will be reinforced.

Operant, or instrumental, conditioning involves generalization (giving the same response to similar stimuli), discrimination (responding to stimuli that signal that a behavior will or will not be reinforced), and extinction (a decreasing tendency to perform a previously reinforced behavior when reinforcement is stopped).

Punishment is a consequence that decreases the likelihood that a behavior will occur. In positive punishment, a behavior decreases when it is followed by a (typically unpleasant) stimulus. In negative punishment, a behavior decreases when a positive stimulus is removed from it.

Applied behavior analysis, or behavior modification, involves the application of operant conditioning principles to a variety of real-life behaviors.

4. OBSERVATIONAL LEARNING

Observational learning occurs when a person observes and imitates someone else's behavior. Bandura identified four main processes in observational learning: attention (paying heed to what someone is saying or doing), retention (encoding that information and keeping it in memory so that you can retrieve it), motor reproduction (imitating the actions of the person being observed), and reinforcement (seeing the person attain a reward for the activity).

5. COGNITIVE FACTORS IN LEARNING

Tolman emphasized the purposiveness of behavior. His belief was that much of behavior is goal-directed. In studying purposiveness, Tolman went beyond stimuli and responses to discuss cognitive mechanisms; he believed that expectancies, acquired through experiences with the environment, are an important cognitive mechanism in learning.

Latent learning is unreinforced learning that is not immediately reflected in behavior. Latent learning may occur when a rat or a person roams a particular location and shows knowledge of the area when that knowledge is rewarded.

Köhler developed the concept of insight learning, a form of problem solving in which the organism develops a sudden insight into or understanding of a problem's solution.

6. BIOLOGICAL, CULTURAL, AND PSYCHOLOGICAL FACTORS IN LEARNING

Biology restricts what an organism can learn from experience. These constraints include instinctive drift (the tendency of animals to revert to instinctive behavior that interferes with learned behavior), preparedness (the species-specific biological predisposition to learn in certain ways but not in others), and taste aversion (the biological predisposition to avoid foods that have caused sickness in the past).

Although most psychologists agree that the principles of classical conditioning, operant conditioning, and observational learning are universal, cultural customs can influence the degree to which these learning processes are used. Culture also often determines the content of learning.

In addition, what we learn is determined in part by what we believe we can learn. Dweck emphasizes that individuals benefit enormously from having a growth mindset rather than a fixed mindset.

7. LEARNING AND HEALTH AND WELLNESS

Research using rats and other animals has demonstrated four important variables involved in the human stress response: predictability, perceived control, perceptions of improvement, and outlets for frustration.

key *terms*

learning, p. 182

behaviorism, p. 182

associative learning, p. 182

observational learning, p. 183

classical conditioning, p. 183

unconditioned stimulus (US), p. 184

unconditioned response (UR), p. 184

conditioned stimulus (CS), p. 184

conditioned response (CR), p. 184

acquisition, p. 185

generalization (in classical conditioning), p. 186

discrimination (in classical conditioning), p. 187

extinction (in classical conditioning), p. 188

spontaneous recovery, p. 188

renewal, p. 188

counterconditioning, p. 189

aversive conditioning, p. 189

habituation, p. 191

operant conditioning or instrumental conditioning, p. 193

law of effect, p. 193

shaping, p. 194

reinforcement, p. 195

positive reinforcement, p. 195

negative reinforcement, p. 195

avoidance learning, p. 195

learned helplessness, p. 196

primary reinforcer, p. 196

secondary reinforcer, p. 196

generalization (in operant conditioning), p. 197

discrimination (in operant conditioning), p. 197

extinction (in operant conditioning), p. 197

schedules of reinforcement, p. 198

punishment, p. 199

positive punishment, p. 200

negative punishment, p. 200

applied behavior analysis or behavior modification, p. 201

latent learning or implicit learning, p. 205

insight learning, p. 205

instinctive drift, p. 207

preparedness, p. 208

apply your *knowledge*

1. Enlist some of your classmates to play this mind game on your professor. Every time your instructor moves to the right side of the room during lecture, be more attentive, smile, and nod. Start out by shaping—every time he or she moves even a little to the right, give a smile or nod. See how far you can get the instructor to go using this simple reward. In one introductory psychology class, students got their professor to move all the way to the right wall of the classroom, where she leaned, completely clueless.

2. The next time you are alone with a friend, try your best to use shaping and the principles of operant conditioning to get the person to touch the tip of his or her nose. Can you do it?

3. Demonstrate Pavlov's work with your friends. First buy some lemons and slice them. Then gather a group of friends to watch something on TV together, maybe the Academy Awards or the Super Bowl. Pick a conditioned stimulus that you know will come up a lot on the show—for example, someone saying "thank you" during

the Oscars or a soft drink or beer ad during the Super Bowl. For the first half hour, everyone has to suck on a lemon slice (the US) when the CS is presented. After the first half hour, take the lemons away. Have everyone report on their salivation levels (the CR) whenever the CS is presented later in the show. What happens?

4. Positive reinforcement and negative reinforcement can be difficult concepts to grasp. The real-world examples and accompanying practice exercises on the following website should help to clarify the distinction:

http://psych.athabascau.ca/html/prtut/reinpair.htm

5. Imagine that you are about to begin an internship in an organization where you would like to have a permanent position someday. Use the processes of observational learning to describe your strategy for making the most of your internship.

CHAPTER 7

CHAPTER OUTLINE

Memory

Photographs, Souvenirs, and Mementos: Memory and Meaning

On May 20, 2013, Moore, Oklahoma was struck by a tornado that killed 23 people and damaged over one thousand homes. Among the many things lost to survivors of the storm were photographs of their lives. Photos from Moore were found as far away as Tulsa, over 100 miles away, carried by the tornado's 210 mph winds.

Those photos, mementoes of the past, became a source of hope for Moore residents whose lives were turned upside down by the storm. As one survivor noted, "We may lose our home, we lost our vehicles, but that would be okay if we can save our pictures," she says. "I just hope they're still there" (Miller, 2013). Another woman lovingly paged through the family photo albums that made it through the storm, "These are memories. They're priceless," she said (Miller, 2013). Multiple social media resources were set up to link the photos and mementoes found in the debris with their owners.

Human beings naturally tend to collect concrete evidence to support their memories. When something important happens, we take a picture. On vacation, we might pick up souvenirs: a T-shirt, a coffee mug, or a postcard. The preciousness of this material evidence of where we have been, with whom, and what we did reveals two important truths about memory: There are some things we want to remember forever, and we are not sure that memory itself will suffice. Certainly, memory provides crucial support for many mundane activities—for example, it allows us to know what we were looking for when we opened the fridge, where we left our running shoes, and when we need to mail Aunt Lucy's birthday card. But our memories are also precious because they represent a lasting imprint of our experiences, moments from the past that give our lives meaning. ●

PREVIEW

Through memory, we weave the past into the present and establish a foundation for the future. In this chapter, we explore key processes of memory, including how information gets into our memory and how it is stored, retrieved, and sometimes forgotten. We also probe what the science of memory can teach us about the best way to study and retain course material. In the final section, we look at autobiographical memory and what it may reveal about how individuals function and discover life meaning, and we also consider strategies by which to keep memory sharp as we age.

1· THE NATURE OF MEMORY

The stars are shining and the moon is full. A beautiful evening is coming to a close. You look at your significant other and think, "I'll never forget this night." How is it possible that in fact you never do forget it? Years from now, you might tell your children about that one special night so many years ago, even if you had not thought about it in the years since. How does one perfect night become a part of your enduring life memory?

Psychologists define **memory** as the retention of information or experience over time. Memory occurs through three important processes: encoding, storage, and retrieval. For memory to work, we have to take in information (encode the sights and sounds of that night), store it or represent it in some manner (retain it in some mental storehouse), and then retrieve it for a later purpose (recall it when someone asks, "So, how did you two end up together?"). In the three main sections that follow, we focus on these phases of memory: encoding, storage, and retrieval (Figure 7.1).

Except for the occasional annoying moment when your memory fails or the upsetting situation in which someone you know experiences memory loss, you probably do not often consider how much everything you do or say depends on the smooth operation of your memory system (Schacter & Wagner, 2011). Consider a restaurant server. He has to attend to the orders he receives—who is asking for what and how would the person like it prepared. To do so, he must encode the information about each customer and each order. He might look at each customer and associate the person's face with the menu items requested. Without writing anything down, he must retain the information, at least until he gets the orders to the kitchen or onto the computer. He might rehearse the orders in his mind as he walks to the back of the restaurant. When delivering the food to the table, he must accurately retrieve the information about who ordered what. Human memory systems truly are remarkable when we consider how much information we put into our memories and how much we must retrieve to perform life's activities (Kahana, 2012; Lieberman, 2012).

Encoding

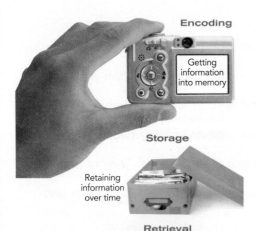

Getting information into memory

Storage

Retaining information over time

Retrieval

Taking information out of storage

FIGURE 7.1 Processing Information in Memory As you read about the many aspects of memory in this chapter, think about the organization of memory in terms of these three main activities.

test yourself

1. How do psychologists define memory?
2. What three important processes play key roles in memory?
3. Which memory process is centrally involved when we recall information?

2· MEMORY ENCODING

The first step in memory is **encoding,** the process by which information gets into memory storage. When you are listening to a lecture, watching a play, reading a book, or talking with a friend, you are encoding information into memory. Some information gets into memory virtually automatically, whereas encoding other information takes effort. Here we examine some of the encoding processes that require effort. These include paying attention, processing deeply, elaborating, and using mental imagery.

Attention

To begin the process of memory encoding, we have to pay attention to information (Maddox & others, 2012). Recall from Chapter 4 that *selective attention* involves focusing on a specific aspect of experience while ignoring others. Attention is selective because the brain's resources are limited—they cannot attend to everything (Lamy, Leber, & Egeth, 2013). These limitations mean that we have to attend selectively to some things in our environment and ignore others (Ernst, Palmer, & Boynton, 2012; Majerus & others, 2012). So, on that special night with your romantic partner, you never noticed the bus that roared by or the people whom you passed as you strolled along the street. Those aspects of that night did not make it into your enduring memory.

In addition to selective attention, psychologists have described two other ways that attention may be allocated: divided attention and sustained attention (McAvinue & others, 2012). **Divided attention** involves concentrating on more than one activity at the same time. If you are listening to music or the television while you are reading this chapter, you are engaging in divided attention. **Sustained attention** (also called **vigilance**) is the ability to maintain attention to a selected stimulus for a prolonged period of time. For example, paying close attention to your notes while studying for an exam is a good application of sustained attention.

Divided attention can be especially detrimental to encoding. *Multitasking,* which in some cases involves dividing attention not just between two activities but among three or more (Lisman & Sternberg, 2013), may be the ultimate in divided attention. It is not unusual for high school and college students to divide their attention among homework, instant messaging, web surfing, and looking at an iTunes playlist, simultaneously. Multitaskers are often very confident in their multitasking skills (Pattillo, 2010).

However, a recent study revealed that heavy media multitaskers performed worse on a test of task-switching ability, apparently because of their decreased ability to filter out interference from an irrelevant task (Ophir, Nass, & Wagner, 2009). Such research indicates that trying to listen to a lecture in class while simultaneously texting or playing a game on your smartphone is likely to impede your ability to pay adequate attention to the lecture (Glenn, 2010). Indeed, one study showed that students' texting during class was related to less learning of course material (Wei, Wang, & Klausner, 2012). Heavy multitasking may have negative effects on more than academic outcomes. A recent study revealed that media multitasking was associated with symptoms of depression and social anxiety (Becker, Alzahabi, & Hopwood, 2013).

Levels of Processing

Another factor that influences memory is whether we engage with information superficially or really get into it. Fergus Craik and Robert Lockhart (1972) first suggested that encoding can be influenced by levels of processing. The term **levels of processing** refers to a continuum from shallow to intermediate to deep.

Imagine that you are asked to memorize a list of words, including the word *mom.* Shallow processing includes noting the physical features of a stimulus, such as the shapes of the letters in the word *mom.* Intermediate processing involves giving the stimulus a label, as in reading the word *mom.* The deepest level of processing entails thinking about the meaning of a stimulus—for instance, thinking about the meaning of the word *mom* and about your own mother, her face, and her special qualities.

The more deeply we process, the better the memory (Howes, 2006; Rose & Craik, 2012) (Figure 7.2). For example, researchers have found that if we encode something meaningful about a face and make associations with it, we are more likely to remember the face (Harris & Kay, 1995). One study showed that when students deeply processed

● **memory** The retention of information or experience over time as the result of three key processes: encoding, storage, and retrieval.

● **encoding** The first step in memory; the process by which information gets into memory storage.

● **divided attention** Concentrating on more than one activity at the same time.

● **sustained attention or vigilance** The ability to maintain attention to a selected stimulus for a prolonged period of time.

● **levels of processing** A continuum of memory processing from shallow to intermediate to deep, with deeper processing producing better memory.

FIGURE 7.2   **Depth of Processing**
According to the levels of processing principle, deeper processing of stimuli produces better memory of them.

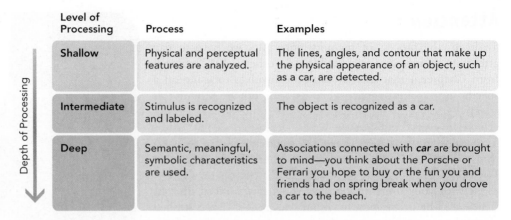

Level of Processing	Process	Examples
Shallow	Physical and perceptual features are analyzed.	The lines, angles, and contour that make up the physical appearance of an object, such as a car, are detected.
Intermediate	Stimulus is recognized and labeled.	The object is recognized as a car.
Deep	Semantic, meaningful, symbolic characteristics are used.	Associations connected with *car* are brought to mind—you think about the Porsche or Ferrari you hope to buy or the fun you and friends had on spring break when you drove a car to the beach.

Depth of Processing ↓

information on an academic advising website, they were more likely to make good use of the information (Boatright-Horowitz, Langley, & Gunnip, 2009). In an fMRI study of emotional memory formation, the brain's prefrontal cortex was involved in deep processing, and the amygdala was mainly at work in shallow processing (Ritchey, LaBar, & Cabeza, 2011).

Elaboration

Effective encoding of a memory depends on more than just depth of processing. Within deep processing, the more extensive the processing, the better the memory (Terry, 2009). **Elaboration** refers to the formation of a number of different connections around a stimulus at any given level of memory encoding.

● **elaboration** The formation of a number of different connections around a stimulus at any given level of memory encoding.

Elaboration is like creating a huge spider web of links between some new information and everything one already knows, and it can occur at any level of processing. In the case of the word *mom,* a person can elaborate on *mom* even at a shallow level—for example, by thinking of the shapes of the letters and how they relate to the shapes of other letters, say, how an *m* looks like two *n's.* At a deeper level of processing, a person might elaborate by thinking about various mothers he or she knows, images of mothers in art, and portrayals of mothers on television and in film. Generally speaking, the more elaborate the processing, the better memory will be. Deep, elaborate processing is a powerful way to remember (Kroneisen, Erdfelder, & Buchner, 2013).

When we elaborate on material, we memorize without trying to memorize. For example, you might use the process of elaboration in remembering the definition of *memory.* You might weave a complex spider web around the concept of memory by coming up with a real-world example of how information enters your mind, how it is stored, and how you can retrieve it. Thinking of concrete examples of a concept is a good way to understand it. *Self-reference*—relating material to your own experience—is another effective way to elaborate deeply on information, drawing mental links between aspects of your own life and new information (Hunt & Ellis, 2004) (Figure 7.3).

The process of elaboration is evident in the physical activity of the brain. Neuroscience research has shown a link between elaboration during encoding and brain activity (Han & others, 2012a; Holland, Addis, & Kensinger, 2011). In one study, researchers placed individuals in magnetic resonance imaging (MRI) machines (see Chapter 3) and flashed one word every 2 seconds on a screen inside (Wagner & others, 1998). Initially, the individuals simply noted whether the words were in uppercase or lowercase letters. As the study progressed, they were asked to determine whether each word was concrete, such as *chair* or *book,* or abstract, such as *love* or *democracy.* In this

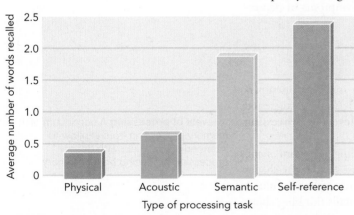

FIGURE 7.3   **Memory Improves When Self-Reference is Used** In one study, researchers asked participants to remember lists of words according to the words' physical, acoustics (sound), semantic (meaning), or self-referent characteristics. As the figure illustrates, when individuals generated self-references for the words, they remembered them better.

study, the participants showed more neural activity in the left frontal lobe of the brain during the concrete/abstract task than they did when they were asked merely to state whether the words were in uppercase or lowercase letters. Further, they demonstrated better memory in the concrete/abstract task. The researchers concluded that greater elaboration of information is linked with neural activity, especially in the brain's left frontal lobe, and with improved memory. Research also indicates that the hippocampus is activated when individuals use elaboration during encoding (Staresina, Gray, & Davachi, 2009).

Imagery

One of the most powerful ways to remember is to use mental imagery (Dennis, Astell, & Dritschel, 2012). Consider, for instance, Akira Haraguchi, who in 2005 recited the digits of pi to the first 83,431 decimal places ("Japanese breaks pi memory record," 2005). Think about memorizing a list of over 80,000 numbers. How would you go about it? One way would be to use mental imagery to create a rich visual walk through the digits. To memorize the first eight digits of pi (3.1415926), one might say, "3 is a chubby fellow who walks with a cane (1), up to a take-out window (4), and orders 15 hamburgers. The cook (9), who has very large biceps (2), slips on his way to deliver the burgers (6)." Imagery functions as a powerful encoding tool for all of us (Reed, 2010), certainly including the memory record holders shown in Figure 7.4.

Mental imagery can come in handy in everyday life. A restaurant server might remember who ordered what by imagining each person eating his or her food. A student might remember last night's reading material by associating it with a figure or photo on the page. You might remember someone's name by imagining how the name relates to the person's face.

Classic studies by Allan Paivio (1971, 1986, 2007) have documented how imagery can improve memory. Paivio argues that memory is stored in one of two ways: as a verbal code (a word or a label) or an image code. Paivio thinks that the image code, which is highly detailed and distinctive, produces better memory than the verbal code. His *dual-code hypothesis* claims that memory for pictures is better than memory for words because pictures—at least those that can be named—are stored as both image codes and verbal codes (Paivio & Sadoski, 2011). Thus, when we use imagery to remember, we have two potential avenues by which we can retrieve information.

test yourself

1. What four encoding processes do not happen automatically but instead require effort?
2. How does divided attention differ from selective attention?
3. Explain the process of elaboration and its importance.

Memorization of...	Record Holder	Country	Year	Record
Written numbers in 1 minute, no errors	Gunther Karsten	Germany	2007	102 numbers
Random words in 15 minutes*	Simon Reinhard	Germany	2010	300 words
Speed to recall a single deck of 52 shuffled playing cards, no errors	Simon Reinhard	Germany	2011	21.19 seconds
Historic dates in 5 minutes	Johannes Mallow	Germany	2010	120 dates
Abstract images in 15 minutes	Johannes Mallow	Germany	2012	434 images

*Participants view random words in columns of 25 words. Scoring is tabulated by column: one point for each word. One mistake reduces the score for that column by half, and the second mistake reduces the score for that column to zero.

FIGURE 7.4 World Champions of Memory For memorization wizards such as these world record holders, imagery is a powerful encoding tool. SOURCE: www.recordholders.org/en/list/memory.html

FIGURE 7.5 Atkinson and Shiffrin's Theory of Memory In this model, sensory input goes into sensory memory. Through the process of attention, information moves into short-term memory, where it remains for 30 seconds or less unless it is rehearsed. When the information goes into long-term memory storage, it can be retrieved over a lifetime.

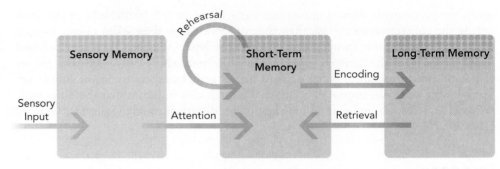

3· MEMORY STORAGE

● **storage** The retention of information over time and how this information is represented in memory.

● **Atkinson-Shiffrin theory** Theory stating that memory storage involves three separate systems: sensory memory, short-term memory, and long-term memory.

● **sensory memory** Memory system that involves holding information from the world in its original sensory form for only an instant, not much longer than the brief time it is exposed to the visual, auditory, and other senses.

The quality of encoding does not alone determine the quality of memory. A memory also needs to be stored properly after it is encoded (Eysenck & Keane, 2010). **Storage** encompasses how information is retained over time and how it is represented in memory.

We remember some information for less than a second, some for half a minute, and some for minutes, hours, years, or even a lifetime. Richard Atkinson and Richard Shiffrin (1968) formulated an early popular theory of memory that acknowledged the varying life span of memories (Figure 7.5). The **Atkinson-Shiffrin theory** states that memory storage involves three separate systems:

■ *Sensory memory:* time frames of a fraction of a second to several seconds
■ *Short-term memory:* time frames up to 30 seconds
■ *Long-term memory:* time frames up to a lifetime

As you read about these three memory storage systems, you will find that time frame is not the only thing that makes them different from one another. Each type of memory also operates in a distinctive way and has a special purpose.

Sensory Memory

Sensory memory holds information from the world in its original sensory form for only an instant, not much longer than the brief time it is exposed to the visual, auditory, and other senses. Sensory memory is very rich and detailed, but we lose the information in it quickly unless we use certain strategies that transfer it into short-term or long-term memory.

Think about the sights and sounds you encounter as you walk to class on a typical morning. Literally thousands of stimuli come into your field of vision and hearing—cracks in the sidewalk, chirping birds, a noisy motorcycle, the blue sky, faces and voices of hundreds of people. You do not process all of these stimuli, but you do process a number of them. In general, you process many more stimuli at the sensory level than you consciously notice. Sensory memory retains this information from your senses, including a large portion of what you think you ignore. However, sensory memory does not retain the information very long.

Echoic memory (from the word *echo*) refers to auditory sensory memory, which is retained for up to several seconds. Imagine standing in an elevator with a friend who suddenly asks, "What was that song?" about the piped-in tune that just ended. If your friend asks his question quickly enough, you just might have a trace of the song left on your sensory registers.

Iconic memory (from the word *icon,* which means "image") refers to visual sensory memory, which is retained only for about ¼ of a second (Figure 7.6). Visual sensory memory is responsible for our ability to "write" in the air using a sparkler on the Fourth of July—the residual iconic memory is what makes a

Type of Sensory Register

Auditory	Visual
Up to several seconds	About ¼ second

FIGURE 7.6 Auditory and Visual Sensory Memory If you hear this bird's call while walking through the woods, your auditory sensory memory holds the information for several seconds. If you see the bird, your visual sensory memory holds the information for only about ¼ of a second.

moving point of light appear to be a line. The sensory memory for other senses, such as smell and touch, has received little attention in research studies.

The first scientific research on sensory memory focused on iconic memory. In George Sperling's (1960) classic study, participants viewed patterns of stimuli such as those in Figure 7.7. As you look at the letters, you have no trouble recognizing them. However, Sperling flashed the letters on a screen for very brief intervals, about 1/20 of a second. Afterward, the participants could report only four or five letters. With such a short exposure, reporting all nine letters was impossible.

Some participants in Sperling's study reported feeling that for an instant, they could see all nine letters within a briefly flashed pattern. They ran into trouble when they tried to name all the letters they had initially seen. One hypothesis to explain this experience is that all nine letters were initially processed as far as the iconic sensory memory level. This is why all nine letters were seen. However, forgetting from iconic memory occurred so rapidly that the participants did not have time to transfer all the letters to short-term memory, where they could be named.

Sperling reasoned that if all nine letters are actually processed in sensory memory, they should all be available for a brief time. To test this possibility, Sperling sounded a low, medium, or high tone just after a pattern of letters was shown. The participants were told that the tone was a signal to report only the letters from the bottom, middle, or top row. Under these conditions, the participants performed much better, and this outcome suggests a brief memory for most or all of the letters in the display.

To appreciate Sperling's discovery, glance at a page of this book for only a second. All the letters are present in your sensory memory for an instant, creating a mental image that exists in its entirety for just a moment. By giving the participants the signal, Sperling helped them to quickly scan their mental image (like the one you created by glancing at a page) so that they could find specific pieces of the information that it contained in various places. Their ability to do so demonstrates that all the material was actually there.

FIGURE 7.7   Sperling's Sensory Memory Experiment This array of stimuli is similar to those flashed for about 1/20 of a second to the participants in Sperling's study.

Short-Term Memory

Much information goes no further than the stage of auditory and visual sensory memory. We retain this information for only a brief instant. However, some information, especially that to which we pay attention, proceeds into short-term memory. **Short-term memory** is a limited-capacity memory system in which information is usually retained for only as long as 30 seconds unless we use strategies to retain it longer. Compared with sensory memory, short-term memory is limited in capacity, but it can store information for a longer time.

George Miller examined the limited capacity of short-term memory in the classic paper "The Magical Number Seven, Plus or Minus Two" (G. A. Miller, 1956). Miller pointed out that on many tasks, individuals are limited in how much information they can keep track of without external aids. Usually the limit is in the range of 7 ± 2 items. If you think of important numbers in your life (such as phone numbers, student ID numbers, and your Social Security number), you will probably find that they fit into the 7 ± 2 range. The most widely cited example of this phenomenon involves *memory span,* the number of digits an individual can report back in order after a single presentation of them. Most college students can remember eight or nine digits without making errors (think about how easy it is to remember a phone number). Longer lists pose problems because they exceed short-term memory capacity. If you rely on simple short-term memory to retain longer lists, you probably will make errors.

● **short-term memory** Limited-capacity memory system in which information is usually retained for only as long as 30 seconds unless the individual uses strategies to retain it longer.

CHUNKING AND REHEARSAL

Two ways to improve short-term memory are chunking and rehearsal. *Chunking* involves grouping or "packing" information that exceeds the 7 ± 2 memory span into higher-order units that can be remembered as single units. Chunking works by making large amounts of information more manageable (Gobet & Clarkson, 2004).

To get a sense of chunking, consider this list: *hot, city, book, forget, tomorrow,* and *smile.* Hold these words in memory for a moment; then write them down. If you recalled the words, you succeeded in holding 30 letters, grouped into six chunks, in memory. Now hold the following list in memory and then write it down:

| O | LDH | ARO | LDAN | DYO | UNGB | EN |

How did you do? Do not feel bad if you did poorly. This string of letters is very difficult to remember, even though it is arranged in chunks. The problem is that the chunks lack meaning. If you re-chunk the letters to form the meaningful words "Old Harold and Young Ben," they become much easier to remember.

Another way to improve short-term memory involves *rehearsal,* the conscious repetition of information (Theeuwes, Belopolsky, & Olivers, 2009). You are likely very familiar with rehearsal already. It simply means repeating the information over and over in your head to keep it in memory. Information stored in short-term memory lasts half a minute or less without rehearsal. However, if rehearsal is not interrupted, information can be retained indefinitely. Rehearsal is often verbal, giving the impression of an inner voice, but it can also be visual or spatial, giving the impression of a private inner eye (Kaiser & others, 2010; Ramsoy & others, 2009).

Rehearsal works best when we must briefly remember a list of numbers or items such as entrées from a dinner menu. When we need to remember information for longer periods of time, as when we are studying for a test coming up next week or even an hour from now, other strategies usually work better. A main reason rehearsal does not work well for retaining information over the long term is that rehearsal often involves just mechanically repeating information, without imparting meaning to it. The fact that, over the long term, we remember information best when we add meaning to it demonstrates the importance of deep, elaborate processing.

WORKING MEMORY

Though useful, Atkinson and Shiffrin's theory of the three time-linked memory systems fails to capture the dynamic way short-term memory functions (Baddeley, 2008, 2012). We do not simply store information in short-term memory: We attend to it, manipulate it, and use it to solve problems (Bui, Maddox, & Balota, 2013; N. Cowan & others, 2011). How can we understand these processes?

One way psychologists have addressed this question is though the concept of working memory. **Working memory** refers to a combination of components that include short-term memory and attention that allow us to hold information temporarily as we perform cognitive tasks (N. Cowan, 2008; N. Cowan & others, 2012).

Working memory is not the same thing as short-term memory. Short-term memory is a *passive* storehouse with shelves to store information until it moves to long-term memory. Working memory, in contrast, is an *active* memory system. For instance, a person can hold a list of words in short-term memory by rehearsing them over and over. But we cannot solve a problem while we are rehearsing information using short-term memory, and we cannot rehearse information (requiring effort and attention) while we are trying to solve a problem.

Working memory capacity is separable from short-term memory capacity. Because short-term memory capacity can rely on rehearsal, 7 ± 2 chunks are generally manageable. However, in working memory, if the chunks are relatively complex, most young adults can only remember 4 ± 1, that is 3 to 5 chunks (N. Cowan, 2010). This might explain why measures of short-term memory capacity are not strongly related to cognitive aptitudes, such as intelligence, whereas working memory capacity is (N. Cowan, 2008).

Working memory can be thought of as a mental blackboard, a place where we can imagine and visualize. In this sense, working memory is the context for conscious thought (see Chapter 5). In working memory, the brain manipulates (works with) and assembles information to help us understand, make decisions, and solve problems. If, say, all of the information on the hard drive of your computer is like long-term memory,

● **working memory** A combination of components, including short-term memory and attention, that allow individuals to hold information temporarily as they perform cognitive tasks; a kind of mental workbench on which the brain manipulates and assembles information to guide understanding, decision making, and problem solving.

then working memory is comparable to what you actually have open and active at any given moment. Working memory has a limited capacity, and, to take the computer metaphor further, the capacity of the working memory is like RAM.

Essentially, working memory is the mental place where thinking occurs. Anthropologists, archaeologists, and psychologists are interested in understanding how working memory evolved. Some commentators have suggested that working memory lays the foundation for creative culture. Prehistoric tools (Haidle, 2010) and works of art (Wynn, Coolidge, & Bright, 2009) reveal how (and when) early humans were thinking. Recently, working memory has been proposed as a key aspect of explaining the difference between Neanderthals and *Homo sapiens* (Wynn & Coolidge, 2010). Consider the "Lion Man," an ivory sculpture archaeologists found in a cave in Germany. The 28-cm figurine, with the head of a lion and the body of a man, is believed to have been created 32,000 years ago (Balter, 2010). This ancient work of art must have been the product of an individual who had the capacity to see two things and, *in working memory,* ask something like, "What would they look like if I combined them?"

Working memory also has served as a helpful framework for addressing practical problems outside the laboratory (Baddeley, 2012). For example, advances in the understanding of working memory have allowed researchers successfully to identify students at risk for academic underachievement and to improve their memory (Dumontheil & Klingberg, 2012; Gathercole & Alloway, 2008; G. Roberts & others, 2011). Working memory also has been beneficial in the early detection of Alzheimer disease (Crawford & others, 2013; Foley & others, 2011; Kaschel & others, 2009). How does working memory work?

British psychologist Alan Baddeley (1993, 1998, 2003, 2008, 2012) has proposed an influential model of working memory featuring a three-part system that allows us to hold information temporarily "in mind" as we perform cognitive tasks. The three components of Baddeley's model are the phonological loop, the visuo-spatial sketchpad, and the central executive. You can think of them as two assistants (the phonological loop and the visuo-spatial sketchpad) who work for the same boss (the central executive). Let's take a closer look at these components:

1. The *phonological loop* is specialized to briefly store speech-based information about the sounds of language. The phonological loop contains two separate components: an acoustic code (the sounds we heard), which decays in a few seconds, and rehearsal, which allows us to repeat the words in the phonological store.

2. The *visuo-spatial sketchpad* stores visual and spatial information, including visual imagery. As in the case of the phonological loop, the capacity of the visuo-spatial sketchpad is limited. If we try to put too many items in the visuo-spatial sketchpad, we cannot represent them accurately enough to retrieve them successfully. The phonological loop and the visuo-spatial sketchpad function independently. We can rehearse numbers in the phonological loop while making spatial arrangements of letters in the visuo-spatial sketchpad.

3. The *central executive* integrates information not only from the phonological loop and the visuo-spatial sketchpad but also from long-term memory. In Baddeley's (2010, 2012) view, the central executive plays important roles in attention, planning, and organizing. The central executive acts like a supervisor who monitors which information deserves our attention and which we should ignore. It also selects which strategies to use to process information and solve problems. Like the phonological loop and the visuospatial sketchpad, the central executive has a limited capacity. If working memory is like the files you have open on your computer, the central executive is *you.* You pull up information you need, close out other things, and so forth.

Though it is compelling, Baddeley's notion of working memory is just a conceptual model describing processes in memory. Neuroscientists have only just begun to search for brain areas and activity that might be responsible for these processes (Rissman & Wagner, 2012). Still, Baddeley's working memory model is useful. Take a closer look at it in the Psychological Inquiry.

Consider the "Lion Man," an ivory sculpture archaeologists found in a cave in Germany. The 28-cm figurine, with the head of a lion and the body of a man, is believed to have been created 32,000 years ago.

psychological *inquiry*

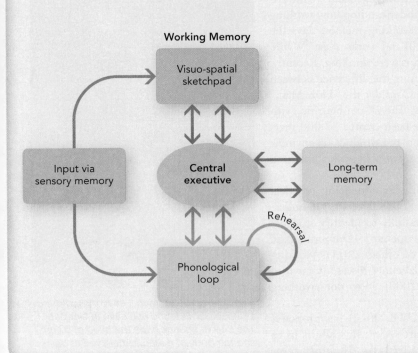

Working Memory

Visuo-spatial sketchpad

Input via sensory memory

Central executive

Long-term memory

Rehearsal

Phonological loop

The Inner Workings of Working Memory

This figure represents Baddeley's working memory model. Although the diagram might seem complicated, take a moment to answer the following questions, and it will all start to make sense.

1. What is the central executive, and why is it in the center of the figure?

2. Can you see where rehearsal takes place? Why would rehearsal fit there?

3. Notice the number of double-headed arrows in this figure. They signify that information flows in both directions. Now look for the single-headed arrows (there are three). Why does that information flow in only one direction?

4. Imagine that you have met a very attractive person whom you would like to get to know better. The individual has just given you his or her phone number. Trace that information along the steps of this figure. How does it flow, and where does it end up? When and how will you take it out and put it to use?

Long-Term Memory

● **long-term memory** A relatively permanent type of memory that stores huge amounts of information for a long time.

Long-term memory is a relatively permanent type of memory that stores huge amounts of information for a long time. The capacity of long-term memory is staggering. John von Neumann (1958), a distinguished mathematician, put the size at 2.8×10^{20} (280 quintillion) bits, which in practical terms means that our storage capacity is virtually unlimited. Von Neumann assumed that we never forget anything; but even considering that we do forget things, we can hold several billion times more information than a large computer.

An interesting question is how the availability of information on the Internet has influenced memory. If we know we can look something up on the web, why bother storing it in our own heads? A series of studies by Betsy Sparrow and colleagues (Sparrow, Liu, & Wegner, 2011) demonstrated that in the face of difficult memory tasks, people are likely to think immediately of using their computer to find the answer, rather than doing the hard work of remembering.

COMPONENTS OF LONG-TERM MEMORY

Long-term memory is complex, as Figure 7.8 shows. At the top level, it is divided into substructures of explicit memory and implicit memory (Kuper & others, 2012). Explicit memory can be further subdivided into episodic and semantic memory. Implicit memory includes the systems involved in procedural memory, classical conditioning, and priming.

In simple terms, explicit memory has to do with remembering who, what, where, when, and why; implicit memory has to do with remembering how. To explore the distinction, let's look at the case of a person known as H. M. Afflicted with severe epilepsy, H. M. underwent surgery in 1953 that involved removing the hippocampus and a portion of the temporal lobes of both hemispheres in his brain. (We examined the location and

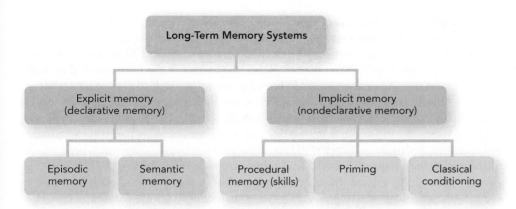

Long-Term Memory Systems

Explicit memory (declarative memory)

Implicit memory (nondeclarative memory)

Episodic memory

Semantic memory

Procedural memory (skills)

Priming

Classical conditioning

FIGURE 7.8 Systems of Long-Term Memory Long-term memory stores huge amounts of information for long periods of time, much like a computer's hard drive. The hierarchy in the figure shows the division of long-term memory at the top level into explicit memory and implicit memory. Explicit memory can be further divided into episodic and semantic memory; implicit memory includes procedural memory, priming, and classical conditioning.

functions of these brain areas in Chapter 3.) H. M.'s epilepsy improved, but something devastating happened to his memory. Most dramatically, he developed an inability to form new memories that outlive working memory. H. M.'s memory time frame was only a few minutes at most, so he lived, until his death in 2007, in a perpetual present and could not remember past events (explicit memory). In contrast, his memory of *how* to do things (implicit memory) was less affected. For example, he could learn new physical tasks, even though he had no memory of how or when he learned them.

H. M.'s situation demonstrates a distinction between explicit memory, which was dramatically impaired in his case, and implicit memory, which was less influenced by his surgery. Let's explore the subsystems of explicit and implicit memory more thoroughly.

Explicit Memory   **Explicit memory** (also called **declarative memory**) is the conscious recollection of information, such as specific facts and events and, at least in humans, information that can be verbally communicated (Tulving, 2000). Examples of using explicit or declarative memory include recounting the events in a movie you have seen and recalling the names of the people in the president's cabinet.

How long does explicit memory last? Explicit memory includes things you are learning in your classes even now. Will it stay with you? Research by Harry Bahrick has examined this very question. Ohio Wesleyan University, where Bahrick is a professor of psychology, is a small (about 1,800 students) liberal arts school that boasts very loyal alumni who faithfully return to campus for reunions and other events. Bahrick (1984, 2000) took advantage of this situation to conduct an ingenious study on the retention of course material over time. He gave vocabulary tests to individuals who had taken Spanish in college as well as to a control group of college students who had not taken Spanish in college. The individuals chosen for the study had used Spanish very little since their college courses. Some individuals were tested at the end of an academic year (just after having taken the courses), but others were tested years after graduation—as many as 50 years later. When Bahrick assessed how much the participants had forgotten, he found a striking pattern (Figure 7.9): Forgetting tended to occur in the first 3 years after taking the classes and then leveled off, so that adults maintained considerable knowledge of Spanish vocabulary words up to 50 years later.

Bahrick (1984) assessed not only how long ago adults studied Spanish but also how well they did in Spanish during college. Those who got an *A* in their courses 50 years earlier remembered more Spanish than adults who got a *C* grade when taking Spanish only 1 year earlier. Thus, how well students initially learned the material was even more important than how long ago they studied it.

Bahrick calls information that is retained for such a long time "permastore" content (Bahrick, 2000, 2005; Bahrick, Hall, & Da Costa, 2008). *Permastore memory* represents that portion of original learning that

● **explicit memory or declarative memory** The conscious recollection of information, such as specific facts or events and, at least in humans, information that can be verbally communicated.

Your explicit memory system is activated when you describe events in a movie you have seen.

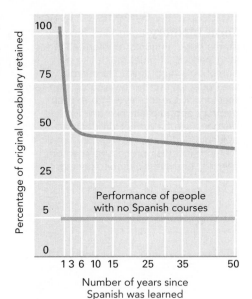

FIGURE 7.9 Memory for Spanish as a Function of Age Since Spanish Was Learned An initial steep drop over about a 3-year period in remembering the vocabulary learned in Spanish classes occurred. However, there was little dropoff in memory for Spanish vocabulary from 3 years after taking Spanish classes to 50 years after taking them. Even 50 years after taking Spanish classes, individuals still remembered almost 50 percent of the vocabulary.

● **episodic memory** The retention of information about the where, when, and what of life's happenings—that is, how individuals remember life's episodes.

● **semantic memory** A person's knowledge about the world, including his or her areas of expertise; general knowledge, such as of things learned in school, and everyday knowledge.

● **implicit memory or nondeclarative memory** Memory in which behavior is affected by prior experience without a conscious recollection of that experience.

Characteristic	Episodic Memory	Semantic Memory
Units	Events, episodes	Facts, ideas, concepts
Organization	Time	Concepts
Emotion	More important	Less important
Retrieval process	Deliberate (effortful)	Automatic
Retrieval report	"I remember"	"I know"
Education	Irrelevant	Relevant
Intelligence	Irrelevant	Relevant
Legal testimony	Admissible in court	Inadmissible in court

FIGURE 7.10 Some Differences Between Episodic and Semantic Memory These characteristics have been proposed as the main ways to differentiate episodic from semantic memory.

appears destined to be with the person virtually forever, even without rehearsal. In addition to focusing on course material, Bahrick and colleagues (1974) have probed adults' memories for the faces and names of their high school classmates. Thirty-five years after graduation, the participants visually recognized 90 percent of the portraits of their high school classmates, with name recognition being almost as high. These results held up even in relatively large classes (the average class size in the study was 294).

Canadian cognitive psychologist Endel Tulving (1972, 1989, 2000) has been the foremost advocate of distinguishing between two subtypes of explicit memory: episodic and semantic. **Episodic memory** is the retention of information about the where, when, and what of life's happenings—basically, how we remember life's episodes. Episodic memory is autobiographical (Marsh & Roediger, 2013). For example, episodic memory includes the details of where you were when your younger brother or sister was born, what happened on your first date, and what you ate for breakfast this morning.

Episodic memory, then, is essentially about the episodes or stories we collect in our lives. Intriguing research has shown that there are cultural differences in episodic memory. To learn about this work, see the Intersection.

Semantic memory is a type of explicit memory pertaining to a person's knowledge about the world. It includes your areas of expertise, general knowledge of the sort you are learning in school, and everyday knowledge about the meanings of words, famous individuals, important places, and common things (McNamara, 2013). For example, semantic memory is involved in a person's knowledge of chess, of geometry, and of who the Dalai Lama, LeBron James, and Lady Gaga are. An important aspect of semantic memory is that it appears to be independent of an individual's personal identity with the past. You can access a fact—such as the detail that Lima is the capital of Peru—and not have the foggiest notion of when and where you learned it. Your memory of your first day on campus involves episodic memory. If you take a history class, your memory of the information you need to know to do well on the next test involves semantic memory.

The difference between episodic and semantic memory is also demonstrated in certain cases of amnesia (memory loss). A person with amnesia might forget entirely who she is—her name, family, career, and all other vital information about herself—yet still be able to talk, know what words mean, and have general knowledge about the world, such as what day it is or who currently holds the office of U.S. president (Vo & Wolfe, 2013). In such cases, episodic memory is impaired, but semantic memory remains.

Figure 7.10 summarizes some aspects of the episodic/semantic distinction. The differences that are listed are controversial. One criticism is that many cases of explicit, or declarative, memory are neither purely episodic nor purely semantic but fall in a gray area in between. Consider your memory for what you studied last night. You probably added knowledge to your semantic memory—that was, after all, the reason you were studying. You probably remember where you were studying, as well as about when you started and when you stopped. You probably also can remember some minor occurrences, such as a burst of loud laughter from the room next door or the coffee you spilled on the desk. Is episodic or semantic memory involved here? Tulving (1983, 2000) argues that semantic and episodic systems often work together in forming new memories. In such cases, the memory that ultimately forms might consist of an autobiographical episode *and* semantic information.

Implicit Memory In addition to explicit memory, there is a type of long-term memory that is related to nonconsciously remembering skills and sensory perceptions rather than consciously remembering facts (Geyer & others, 2013). **Implicit memory** (also called **nondeclarative memory**) is memory in which behavior is affected by prior experience without a conscious recollection of that experience. Implicit memory comes into play, for example, in the skills of playing tennis and snowboarding, as well as in the physical act of text messaging.

Cognitive and Cultural Psychology: How Does Culture Influence Episodic Memory?

If you asked five people the question, "What did you do last night?" you would probably get five very different answers, described in five very different ways. One might regale you with his exciting adventure at a party, while another who attended the very same shindig might simply answer, "I went to a party."

Episodic memories can be specific or quite general. Cultural differences have been observed in the vividness and detail included in episodic memory. Westerners tend to have very specific episodic memories compared to East Asians and Asian Americans (Dritschel & others, 2011; Wang, 2009a, 2009b). These differences apply to the ways individuals imagine future episodes (Wang & others, 2011) and to episodic memory in children from these different cultures (Wang, 2006; Wang & others, 2011).

Interestingly, research shows that these cultural differences in episodic memory reflect differences throughout the process of memory, including encoding and recall. For example, in one study, U.S. college students of European and Asian descent kept a diary for a week. Each night they were asked to write down all of the events that happened to them that day. The re-

What did you do last night? How does your culture influence how you answer that question?

sults showed that the European American students actually reported having more events happen to them than the Asian American students (Wang, 2009b). The two groups differed in the sheer number of experiences they attended to and encoded each day. When they were later asked to recall those episodes, the European American students remembered more of the events as well.

Another study showed that the way European American and Asian American students think about episodes differs. In that study, all of the students were asked to read a diary entry and cut it up into the individual episodes that happened in the story described. The European American students segmented the story into more substories than the Asian American students (Wang, 2009b). This difference suggests that the European American students saw more "little stories" inside the larger one that all the students read.

What might explain these differences? One possibility is that Westerners, who tend to be more individualistic, are more likely to view their memories as important aspects of identity (Wang, 2009b). From this perspective, Westerners view episodic memory as an important part of their unique sense of self. In contrast, East Asians are more collectivistic and may view memory as tied to social contexts and roles. They may be less motivated to view themselves as unique. For these individuals episodic memory may serve as a source of identity that makes them more similar to others, not more different.

Cultural values and customs have an influence on an important context of social interaction: conversations (Matsumoto & Juang, 2013; Mistry, Contreras, & Dutta, 2013). In many ways, our conversations reveal what our culture finds interesting, what topics are important to share, and what kinds of social goals we are trying to accomplish. It is no surprise then that culture would influence the ways we remember the episodes of our lives. We walk around our social world gathering up episodic memories to share, and we encode those experiences in ways that fit our culture's expectations. We all have the capacity to think episodically, but culture may shape the way we use this capacity.

Another example of implicit memory is the repetition in your mind of a song you heard in the supermarket, even though you did not notice the song playing. Implicit memory explains why you might find yourself knowing all the words to a song you hate. You have heard it so many times that you have memorized it without even trying.

Three subsystems of implicit memory are procedural memory, classical conditioning, and priming. All of these subsystems refer to memories that you are not aware of but that influence behavior (Slotnick & Schacter, 2006).

Procedural memory is an implicit memory process that involves memory for skills (Crossley, Madsen, & Ashby, 2012; A. Johnson, 2013). For example (assuming that you are an expert typist), as you type a paper, you are not conscious of where the keys are

● **procedural memory** Memory for skills.

for the various letters, but your well-learned, unconscious typing skill allows you to hit the right keys. Similarly, once you have learned to drive a car, you remember how to go about it: You do not have to remember consciously how to drive the car as you put the key in the ignition, turn the steering wheel, depress the gas pedal, and step on the brake pedal. To grasp the distinction between explicit memory and procedural memory, imagine trying to describe to someone in words exactly how to tie a shoe—something you can do successfully in just a few seconds—without having a shoe around.

Another type of implicit memory involves *classical conditioning,* a form of learning discussed in Chapter 6. Recall that classical conditioning involves the automatic learning of associations between stimuli, so that one comes to evoke the same response as the other. Classically conditioned associations such as this involve non-conscious, implicit memory (L. R. Johnson & others, 2012). So without realizing it, you might start to like the person who sits next to you in your favorite class, because she is around while you are feeling good.

A final type of implicit memory process is priming. **Priming** is the activation of information that people already have in storage to help them remember new information better and faster (McNamara, 2013; Schmitz & Wentura, 2012). In a common demonstration of priming, individuals study a list of words (such as *hope, walk,* and *cake*). Then they are given a standard recognition task to assess explicit memory. They must select all of the words that appeared in the list—for example, "Did you see the word *hope*? Did you see the word *form*?" Then participants perform a stem-completion task, which assesses implicit memory. In this task, they view a list of incomplete words (for example, *ho__, wa__, ca__*), called word stems, and must fill in the blanks with whatever word comes to mind. The results show that individuals more often fill in the blanks with the previously studied words than would be expected if they were filling in the blanks randomly. For example, they are more likely to complete the stem *ho__* with *hope* than with *hole*. This result occurs even when individuals do not recognize the words on the earlier recognition task. Because priming takes place even when explicit memory for previous information is not required, it is assumed to be an involuntary and unconscious process (Johnson & Halpern, 2012).

Priming occurs when something in the environment evokes a response in memory—such as the activation of a particular concept. Priming a term or concept makes it more available in memory (Thomson & Milliken, 2012) and can influence behavior (A. Johnson, 2013). For example, social cognitive psychologist John Bargh and colleagues (2001) asked students to perform a word-search puzzle. Embedded in the puzzle were either neutral words (*shampoo, robin*) or achievement-related words (*compete, win, achieve*). Participants who were exposed to the achievement-related words did better on a later puzzle task, finding an average of 26 words in other puzzles, whereas those with the neutral primes found only 21.5. Other research has shown that individuals primed with words like *professor* and *intelligent* performed better at a game of Trivial Pursuit than those primed with words like *stupid* and *hooligan* (Dijksterhuis & Van Knippenberg, 1998). These effects occur without awareness, with no participants reporting suspicion about the effects of the primes on their behavior.

HOW MEMORY IS ORGANIZED

Explaining the forms of long-term memory does not address the question of how the different types of memory are organized for storage. The word *organized* is important: Memories are not haphazardly stored but instead are carefully sorted.

Here is a demonstration. Recall the 12 months of the year as quickly as you can. How long did it take you? What was the order of your recall? Chances are, you listed them within a few seconds in chronological order (January, February, March, and so on). Now try to remember the months in alphabetical order. How long did it take you? Did you make any errors? It should be obvious that your memory for the months of the year is organized in a particular way. Indeed, one of memory's most distinctive features is its organization.

Researchers have found that if people are encouraged to organize material simply, their memories of the material improve even if they receive no warning that their

● **priming** The activation of information that people already have in storage to help them remember new information better and faster.

memories will be tested (Mandler, 1980). Psychologists have developed a variety of theories of how long-term memory is organized. Let's consider two of these more closely: schemas and connectionist networks.

Schemas   You and a friend have taken a long drive to a new town where neither of you has ever been before. You stop at the local diner, have a seat, and look over the menu. You have never been in this diner before, but you know exactly what is going to happen. Why? Because you have a schema for what happens in a restaurant. When we store information in memory, we often fit it into the collection of information that already exists, as you do even in a new experience with a diner. A **schema** is a preexisting mental concept or framework that helps people to organize and interpret information. Schemas from prior encounters with the environment influence the way we handle information— how we encode it, the inferences we make about it, and how we retrieve it.

Each of us has a schema for what happens in a restaurant.

Schemas can also be at work when we recall information. Schema theory holds that long-term memory is not very exact. We seldom find precisely the memory that we want, or at least not all of what we want; hence, we have to *reconstruct* the rest. Our schemas support the reconstruction process, helping us fill in gaps between our fragmented memories.

We have schemas for lots of situations and experiences—for scenes and spatial layouts (a beach, a bathroom), as well as for common events (playing football, writing a term paper). A **script** is a schema for an event (Schank & Abelson, 1977). Scripts often have information about physical features, people, and typical occurrences. This kind of information is helpful when people need to figure out what is happening around them. For example, if you are enjoying your after-dinner coffee in an upscale restaurant and a man in a tuxedo comes over and puts a piece of paper on the table, your script tells you that the man probably is a waiter who has just given you the check. Scripts help to organize our storage of memories about events.

Connectionist Networks   Schema theory has little or nothing to say about the role of the physical brain in memory. Thus, a new theory based on brain research has generated a wave of excitement among psychologists. **Connectionism,** also called **parallel distributed processing (PDP),** is the theory that memory is stored throughout the brain in connections among neurons, several of which may work together to process a single memory (McClelland, 2011). We initially considered the concept of neural networks in Chapter 3 and the idea of parallel sensory processing pathways in Chapter 4. These concepts also apply to memory.

In the connectionist view, memories are not large knowledge structures (as in schema theories). Instead, memories are more like electrical impulses, organized only to the extent that neurons, the connections among them, and their activity are organized. Any piece of knowledge—such as your dog's name—is embedded in the strengths of hundreds or thousands of connections among neurons and is not limited to a single location.

How does the connectionist process work? A neural activity involving memory, such as remembering your dog's name, is spread across a number of areas of the cerebral cortex. The locations of neural activity, called *nodes,* are interconnected. When a node reaches a critical level of activation, it can affect another node across synapses. We know that the human cerebral cortex contains millions of neurons that are richly interconnected through hundreds of millions of synapses. Because of these synaptic connections, the activity of one neuron can be influenced by many other neurons. Owing to these simple reactions, the connectionist view argues that changes in the strength of synaptic connections are the fundamental bases of memory (McClelland & others, 2010). From

● **schema** A preexisting mental concept or framework that helps people to organize and interpret information. Schemas from prior encounters with the environment influence the way individuals encode, make inferences about, and retrieve information.

● **script** A schema for an event, often containing information about physical features, people, and typical occurrences.

● **connectionism or parallel distributed processing (PDP)** The theory that memory is stored throughout the brain in connections among neurons, several of which may work together to process a single memory.

the connectionist network perspective, memories are organized sets of neurons that are routinely activated together.

Part of the appeal of the connectionist view is that it is consistent with what we know about brain function and allows psychologists to simulate human memory studies using computers (Marcus, 2001). Connectionist approaches also help to explain how priming a concept (achievement) can influence behavior (performance). Furthermore, insights from this connectionist view support brain research undertaken to determine where memories are stored (Laszlo & Plaut, 2012), another fascinating and complex topic.

Indeed, so far we have examined the many ways cognitive psychologists think about how information is stored. The question remains, *where?* The puzzle of the physical location of memories has long fascinated psychologists. Although memory may seem to be a mysterious phenomenon, it, like all psychological processes, must occur in a physical place: the brain.

WHERE MEMORIES ARE STORED

Karl Lashley (1950) spent a lifetime looking for a location in the brain in which memories are stored. He trained rats to discover the correct pathway in a maze and then cut out various portions of the animals' brains and retested their memory of the maze pathway. Experiments with thousands of rats showed that the loss of various cortical areas did not affect rats' ability to remember the pathway, leading Lashley to conclude that memories are not stored in a specific location in the brain. Other researchers, continuing Lashley's quest, agreed that memory storage is diffuse, but they developed additional insights. Canadian psychologist Donald Hebb (1949, 1980) suggested that assemblies of cells, distributed over large areas of the cerebral cortex, work together to represent information, just as the connectionist network perspective would predict.

Neurons and Memory Today many neuroscientists believe that memory is located in specific sets or circuits of neurons. Brain researcher Larry Squire, for example, says that most memories are probably clustered in groups of about 1,000 neurons (1990, 2004, 2007). At the same time, single neurons are also at work in memory (Braun & others, 2012; Squire, 2007). Researchers who measure the electrical activity of single cells have found that some respond to faces and others to eye or hair color, for example. Still, in order for you to recognize your Uncle Albert, individual neurons that provide information about hair color, size, and other characteristics must act together.

Researchers also believe that brain chemicals may be the ink with which memories are written. Remember that neurotransmitters are the chemicals that allow neurons to communicate across the synapse. These chemicals play a crucial role in forging the connections that represent memory.

Ironically, some of the answers to complex questions about the neural mechanics of memory come from studies on a very simple experimental animal—the inelegant sea slug. Eric Kandel and James Schwartz (1982) chose this large snail-without-a-shell because of the simple architecture of its nervous system, which consists of only about 10,000 neurons. (You might recall from Chapter 3 that the human brain has about 100 billion neurons.)

The sea slug is hardly a quick learner or an animal with a good memory, but it is equipped with a reliable reflex. When anything touches the gill on its back, it quickly withdraws it. First the researchers accustomed the sea slug to having its gill prodded. After a while, the animal ignored the prod and stopped withdrawing its gill. Next the researchers applied an electric shock to its tail when they touched the gill. After many rounds of the shock-accompanied prod, the sea slug violently withdrew its gill at the slightest touch. The researchers found that the sea slug remembered this message for hours or even weeks. They also determined that shocking the sea slug's gill releases the neurotransmitter serotonin at the synapses of its nervous system, and this chemical release basically provides a reminder that the gill was shocked. This "memory" informs the nerve cell to send out chemical commands to retract the gill the next time it is touched. If nature builds complexity out of simplicity, then the mechanism used by the sea slug may work in the human brain as well.

Species of sea slug similar to that studied by Kandel and Schwartz (1982).

Researchers have proposed the concept of *long-term potentiation* to explain how memory functions at the neuron level. In line with connectionist theory, this concept states that if two neurons are activated at the same time, the connection between them—and thus the memory—may be strengthened (Grigoryan, Korkotian, & Segal, 2012). Long-term potentiation has been demonstrated experimentally by administering a drug that increases the flow of information from one neuron to another across the synapse, raising the possibility of someday improving memory through drugs that increase neural connections (Zorumski & Izumi, 2012). Imagine that what you experience as a memory is really a collection of well-worn pathways in your brain.

Brain Structures and Memory Functions
Whereas some neuroscientists are unveiling the cellular basis of memory, others are examining its broad-scale architecture in the brain. Many different parts of the brain and nervous system are involved in the rich, complex process that is memory (Rissman & Wagner, 2012). Although there is no one memory center in the brain, researchers have demonstrated that specific brain structures are involved in particular aspects of memory.

Figure 7.11 shows the location of brain structures active in different types of long-term memory. Note that implicit and explicit memory appear to involve different locations in the brain.

- *Explicit memory:* Neuroscientists have found that the hippocampus, the temporal lobes in the cerebral cortex, and other areas of the limbic system play a role in explicit memory (Koski, Olson, & Newcombe, 2013; Rugg & Vilberg, 2013). In many aspects of explicit memory, information is transmitted from the hippocampus to the frontal lobes, which are involved in both *retrospective memory* (remembering things from the past) and *prospective memory* (remembering things that you need to do in the future) (Poppenk & others, 2010). The left frontal lobe is especially active when we encode new information into memory; the right frontal lobe is more active when we subsequently retrieve it (Babiloni & others, 2006). In addition, the amygdala, which is part of the limbic system, is involved in emotional memories (Ries & others, 2012).

- *Implicit memory:* The cerebellum (the structure at the back and toward the bottom of the brain) is active in the implicit memory required to perform skills (Bussy & others, 2011). Various areas of the cerebral cortex, such as the temporal lobes and hippocampus, function in priming (H. Kim, 2011).

Neuroscientists studying memory have benefited greatly from the use of fMRI, which allows them to track neural activity during cognitive tasks (Khare & others, 2012; Nett & others, 2012). For instance, brain activity can be used to distinguish between individuals who have actually forgotten something from those who are pretending to have forgotten it. Fake forgetting is more likely to be associated with activity in the right hemisphere (Liang & others, 2012).

Brain imaging has allowed researchers to investigate how the brain responds to personally familiar stimuli (such as photos of family members) compared to the kinds of stimuli usually used in memory tasks. Activation in the left prefrontal cortex is especially strong for personally familiar stimuli (Detour & others, 2011). Research has shown that the greater the activation in both prefrontal lobes and a particular region of the hippocampus during viewing, the better people remember (Brewer & others, 1998; Rugg & Vilberg, 2013).

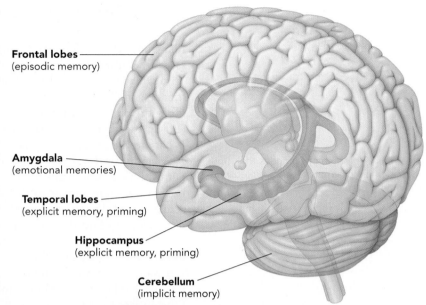

Frontal lobes
(episodic memory)

Amygdala
(emotional memories)

Temporal lobes
(explicit memory, priming)

Hippocampus
(explicit memory, priming)

Cerebellum
(implicit memory)

FIGURE 7.11 Structures of the Brian Involved in Different Aspects of Long-Term Memory Note that explicit memory and implicit memory appear to involve different locations in the brain.

test yourself

1. How do sensory memory and short-term memory differ in terms of their duration?
2. What two kinds of memory are at the top level of long-term memory, and how is each defined?
3. How do the schema theory of memory and the connectionist network theory of memory differ in terms of their explanation of memories?

4· MEMORY RETRIEVAL

Remember that unforgettable night of shining stars with your romantic partner? Let's say the evening has indeed been encoded deeply and elaborately in your memory. Through the years you have thought about the night a great deal and told your best friends about it. The story of that night has become part of the longer story of your life with your significant other. Fifty years later, your grandson asks, "How did you two end up together?" You share that story you have been saving for just such a question. What are the retrieval processes that allow you to do so?

● **retrieval** The memory process that occurs when information that was retained in memory comes out of storage.

Memory **retrieval** takes place when information that was retained in memory comes out of storage. You might think of long-term memory as a library. You retrieve information in a fashion similar to the process you use to locate and check out a book in an actual library. To retrieve something from your mental data bank, you search your store of memory to find the relevant information.

The efficiency with which you retrieve information from memory is impressive. It usually takes only a moment to search through a vast storehouse to find the information you want. When were you born? What was the name of your first date? Who developed the first psychology laboratory? You can, of course, answer all of these questions instantly. (The answer to that last one is Wilhelm Wundt.) Yet retrieval of memory is a complex and sometimes imperfect process (Robertson, 2012).

Before examining ways that retrieval may fall short, let's look at some basic concepts and variables that are known to affect the likelihood that information will be accurately encoded, stored, and ultimately retrieved. As we will see, retrieval depends heavily on the circumstances under which a memory was encoded and the way it was retained (Pierce & Gallo, 2011; Ritchey & others, 2013).

Serial Position Effect

● **serial position effect** The tendency to recall the items at the beginning and end of a list more readily than those in the middle.

The **serial position effect** is the tendency to recall the items at the beginning and end of a list more readily than those in the middle. If you are a reality TV fan, you might notice that you always seem to remember the first person to get voted off and the last few survivors. All those people in the middle, however, are a blur. The *primacy effect* refers to better recall for items at the beginning of a list; the *recency effect* refers to better recall for items at the end. Together with the relatively low recall of items from the middle of the list, this pattern makes up the serial position effect (Laming, 2010). You can sharpen your understanding of the serial position effect by completing the exercise in the Psychological Inquiry.

Psychologists explain these effects using principles of encoding. With respect to the primacy effect, the first few items in the list are easily remembered because they are rehearsed more or because they receive more elaborative processing than do words later in the list (Atkinson & Shiffrin, 1968; Craik & Tulving, 1975). Working memory is relatively empty when the items enter, so there is little competition for rehearsal time. Moreover, because the items get more rehearsal, they stay in working memory longer and are more likely to be encoded successfully into long-term memory. In contrast, many items from the middle of the list drop out of working memory before being encoded into long-term memory.

As for the recency effect, the last several items are remembered for different reasons. First, when these items are recalled, they might still be in working memory. Second, even if these items are not in working memory, the fact that they were just encountered makes them easier to recall.

Interestingly, both primacy and recency can influence how we feel about stimuli as well. In one study, wine tasters were more likely to prefer the first wine they sipped, an outcome demonstrating primacy (Mantonakis & others, 2009). In another study, participants felt that the best was saved for last when they evaluated paintings and *American Idol* audition tapes, an outcome demonstrating recency (Li & Epley, 2009). Of course, not every bit of information that is in the middle is likely to be forgotten! If information is extremely vivid or unusual, it will be remembered.

off the mark.com   by Mark Parisi

LOOK, I KNOW YOU TOLD ME YOUR NAME BUT I FORGOT TO SAVE IT...

offthemark.com   ©2006 MARK PARISI DIST. BY UFS INC.

psychological *inquiry*

The Serial Position Effect: Lost in Midstream

This figure shows typical serial position effects. The vertical axis is the probability of an individual's remembering a particular item in a list. Notice the highest value on this axis is 1.0, meaning that the chance of remembering the item is 100 percent. The horizontal axis is the position of the items from first to last (in this case the 20th item). Examine the figure to answer the following questions:

1. What is the probability that the item presented in the 15th position will be remembered? What about the item that was presented first?

2. In this figure, which is stronger—primacy or recency? Explain.

3. When it is time for final exams, which information from your class do you think it would be best to brush up on, and why?

4. Suppose you are going for a job interview, and there are several other candidates there that day for interviews. If you want to make a memorable impression, which position in the sequence of interviews would you prefer, and why?

Probability of Recall

Primacy effects

Recency effects

Serial position of items

Retrieval Cues and the Retrieval Task

Two other factors are involved in retrieval: the nature of the cues that can prompt your memory and the retrieval task that you set for yourself. We consider each in turn.

If effective cues for what you are trying to remember do not seem to be available, you need to create them—a process that takes place in working memory (Rummel, 2010). For example, if you have a block about remembering a new friend's name, you might go through the alphabet, generating names that begin with each letter. If you manage to stumble across the right name, you will probably recognize it.

We can learn to generate retrieval cues. One good strategy is to use different subcategories. For example, write down the names of as many of your classmates from middle or junior high school as you can remember. When you run out of names, think about the activities you were involved in during those school years, such as math class, student council, lunch, drill team, and so on. Does this set of cues help you to remember more of your classmates?

Although cues help, your success in retrieving information also depends on the retrieval task you set for yourself. For instance, if you are simply trying to decide whether something seems familiar, retrieval is probably a snap. Let's say that you see a short, dark-haired woman walking toward you. You quickly decide that she is someone who shops at the same supermarket as you do. However, remembering her name or a precise detail, such as when you met her, can be harder. Such distinctions have implications for police investigations: A witness might be certain she has previously seen a face, yet she might have a hard time deciding whether it was at the scene of the crime or in a mug shot.

RECALL AND RECOGNITION

The presence or absence of good cues and the retrieval task required are factors in an important memory distinction: recall versus recognition. *Recall* is a memory task in which the individual has to retrieve previously learned information, as on essay tests. *Recognition* is a memory task in which the individual only has to identify (recognize) learned items, as on multiple-choice tests. Recall tests such as essay tests have poor retrieval cues. You are told to try to recall a certain class of information ("Discuss the factors that caused World War I"). In recognition tests such as multiple-choice tests, you merely judge whether a stimulus is familiar (such as that Archduke Franz Ferdinand was assassinated in 1914).

You probably have heard some people say that they never forget a face. However, recognizing a face is far simpler than recalling a face "from scratch," as law enforcement officers know. In some cases, police bring in an artist to draw a suspect's face from witnesses' descriptions (Figure 7.12). Recalling faces is difficult, and artists' sketches of suspects are frequently not detailed or accurate enough to result in apprehension.

ENCODING SPECIFICITY

Another consideration in understanding retrieval is the *encoding specificity principle,* which states that information present at the time of encoding or learning tends to be effective as a retrieval cue (Unsworth, Brewer, & Spillers, 2011). For example, you know your instructors when they are in the classroom setting—you see them there all the time. If, however, you run into one of them in an unexpected setting and in more casual attire, such as at the gym in workout clothes, the person's name might escape you. Your memory might fail because the cues you encoded are not available for use.

CONTEXT AT ENCODING AND RETRIEVAL

An important consequence of encoding specificity is that a change in context between encoding and retrieval can cause memory to fail (Boywitt & Meiser, 2012). In many instances, people remember better when they attempt to recall information in the same context in which they learned it—a process referred to as *context-dependent memory.* This better recollection is believed to occur because they have encoded features of the

FIGURE 7.12 Remembering Faces (*Left*) The FBI artist's sketch of Ted Kaczynski. Kaczynski, also known as the Unabomber, is a serial killer who conducted a sequence of mail bombings targeting universities and airlines beginning in the late 1970s. (*Right*) A photograph of Kaczynski. The FBI widely circulated the artist's sketch, which was based on bits and pieces of observations people had made of the infamous Unabomber, in the hope that someone would recognize him. Would you have been able to recognize Kaczynski from the artist's sketch? Probably not. Although most people say they are good at remembering faces, they usually are not as good as they think they are.

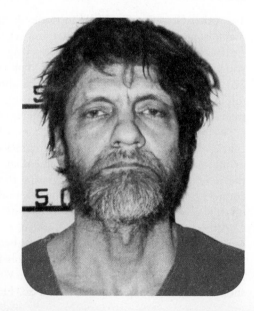

context in which they learned the information along with the actual information. Such features can later act as retrieval cues (Bridge, Chiao, & Paller, 2010).

In one study, scuba divers learned information on land and under water (Godden & Baddeley, 1975). Later they were asked to recall the information when they were either on land or under water. The divers' recall was much better when the encoding and retrieval contexts were the same (both on land or both under water).

Special Cases of Retrieval

We began this discussion by likening memory retrieval to looking for and finding a book in the library. However, the process of retrieving information from long-term memory is not as precise as the library analogy suggests. When we search through our long-term memory storehouse, we do not always find the exact "book" we want—or we might find the book but discover that several pages are missing. We have to fill in these gaps somehow.

Our memories are affected by a number of factors, including the pattern of information we remember, schemas and scripts, the situations we associate with memories, and the personal or emotional context. Certainly, everyone has had the experience of remembering a shared situation with a particular individual, only to have him or her remind us, "Oh, that wasn't me!" Such moments provide convincing evidence that memory may well be best understood as "reconstructive." This subjective quality of memory certainly has implications for important day-to-day procedures such as eyewitness testimony (Garrett, 2011; Houston & others, 2013).

Although the factors that we have discussed so far relate to the retrieval of generic information, various kinds of special memory retrieval also have generated a great deal of research. These memories have special significance because of their relevance to the self, to their emotional or traumatic character, or because they show unusually high levels of apparent accuracy (Piolino & others, 2006). Researchers in cognitive psychology have debated whether these memories rely on processes that are different from those already described or are simply extreme cases of typical memory processes (Lane & Schooler, 2004; Schooler & Eich, 2000). We now turn to these special cases of memory.

RETRIEVAL OF AUTOBIOGRAPHICAL MEMORIES

Autobiographical memory, a special form of episodic memory, is a person's recollections of his or her life experiences (Marsh & Roediger, 2013). An intriguing discovery about autobiographical memory is the *reminiscence bump*—the effect that adults remember more events from the second and third decades of life than from other decades (Copeland, Radvansky, & Goodwin, 2009). This reminiscence bump may occur because it is during our teens and 20s that we are forging a sense of identity. On the other hand, it may be that these are simply the times in our life when a lot of important events happen (Berntsen & Rubin, 2002). In fact, when children describe what they think will happen to them in the future, they anticipate that they will have significant experiences in their early adult years (Bohn & Berntsen, 2011). So, it may be that the reminiscence bump is really simply a life event bump.

Autobiographical memories are complex and seem to contain unending strings of stories and snapshots, but researchers have found that they can be categorized (Marsh & Roediger, 2013). For example, based on their research, Martin Conway and David Rubin (1993) sketched a structure of autobiographical memory that has three levels (Figure 7.13). The most abstract level consists of *life time periods;* for example, you might remember something about your life in high school. The middle level in the hierarchy is made up of *general events,* such as a trip you took with your friends after you graduated from high school. The

● **autobiographical memory** A special form of episodic memory, consisting of a person's recollections of his or her life experiences.

Level	Label	Description
Level 1	Life time periods	Long segments of time measured in years and even decades
Level 2	General events	Extended composite episodes measured in days, weeks, or months
Level 3	Event-specific knowledge	Individual episodes measured in seconds, minutes, or hours.

FIGURE 7.13 **The Three-Level Hierarchical Structure of Autobiographical Memory** When people relate their life stories, all three levels of information are typically present and intertwined.

most concrete level in the hierarchy is composed of *event-specific knowledge;* for example, from your postgraduation trip, you might remember the exhilarating experience you had the first time you jet-skied. When people tell their life stories, all three levels of information are usually present and intertwined.

Most autobiographical memories include some reality and some myth. Personality psychologist Dan McAdams (2001, 2006, 2013) argues that autobiographical memories are less about facts and more about meanings. They provide a reconstructed, embellished telling of the past that connects the past to the present. We will explore McAdams's approach to autobiographical memory in more detail in Chapter 12.

RETRIEVAL OF EMOTIONAL MEMORIES

When we remember our life experiences, the memories are often wrapped in emotion. Emotion affects the encoding and storage of memories and thus shapes the details that are retrieved (Rimmele, Davachi, & Phelps, 2012; Todd & others, 2012). The role that emotion plays in memory is of considerable interest to contemporary researchers and has echoes in public life.

● **flashbulb memory** The memory of emotionally significant events that people often recall with more accuracy and vivid imagery than everyday events.

Flashbulb memory is the memory of emotionally significant events that people often recall with more accuracy and vivid imagery than everyday events (Lanciano & others, 2013). Previous generations of Americans might have discussed flashbulb memories for the assassination of President John F. Kennedy. More recently, individuals might have experienced flashbulb memories for the terrorist attacks on the United States on September 11, 2001, the killing of Osama bin Laden on May 2, 2011, or the mass killing at Sandy Hook Elementary School in Connecticut on December 14, 2012.

An intriguing dimension of flashbulb memories is that several decades later, people often remember where they were and what was going on in their lives at the time of such an emotionally charged event. These memories seem to be part of an adaptive system that fixes in memory the details that accompany important events so that they can be interpreted at a later time.

Most people express confidence about the accuracy of their flashbulb memories. However, flashbulb memories probably are not as precisely etched in our brain as we think. One way to gauge the exactness of flashbulb memories is to look at the consistency of the details of these memories over time. Research on memories for the 9/11 terrorist attack shows that the physical proximity of individuals to the event affected the accuracy of memory. For instance, individuals in New York showed greater accuracy than those in Hawaii (Pezdek, 2003).

In another study, Canadian students' memories for 9/11 were tested at 1 week and again at 6 months following the tragedy. Results showed that 6 months after the events, students were better at remembering details about their own experience of hearing about the event than they were at remembering details about the event itself (Smith, Bibi, & Sheard, 2003). These results reflect our subjective experience of flashbulb memories. We might say, "I will never forget where I was when I heard about" some important event. Such a statement fits with research showing that we may be more likely to remember our own personal experiences of an event, rather than details of the event itself.

Still, on the whole, flashbulb memories do seem more durable and accurate than memories of day-to-day happenings (Davidson, Cook, & Glisky, 2006). One possible explanation is that flashbulb memories are quite likely to be rehearsed in the days following the event. However, it is not just the discussion and rehearsal of information that make flashbulb memories so long-lasting. The emotions triggered by flashbulb events also figure in their durability.

Although we have focused on negative news events as typical of flashbulb memories, such memories can also occur for positive

Many people have flashbulb memories of where they were and what they were doing when the shooter attacked Sandy Hook Elementary School in Connecticut on December 14, 2012.

events. An individual's wedding day and the birth of a child are events that may become milestones in personal history and are always remembered.

MEMORY FOR TRAUMATIC EVENTS

In 1890, the American psychologist and philosopher William James said that an experience can be so emotionally arousing that it almost leaves a scar on the brain. Personal traumas are candidates for such emotionally stirring experiences. Are traumatic events more or less likely to be remembered accurately? Some psychologists argue that memories of emotionally traumatic events are precisely retained, possibly forever, in considerable detail (J. J. Langer, 1991).

There is good evidence that memory for traumatic events is usually more accurate than memory for ordinary events (Boals & Rubin, 2011; Rubin, 2011; Schooler & Eich, 2000). Stress-related hormones likely play a role in memories that involve personal trauma. The release of stress-related hormones, signaled by the amygdala (see Figure 7.11), likely accounts for some of the extraordinary durability and vividness of traumatic memories (Bucherelli & others, 2006; Goosens, 2011). Nevertheless, even traumatic memories can contain errors (Laney & Loftus, 2009; Moore & Zoellner, 2012). Distortions in traumatic memories may arise in the details of the traumatic episode.

REPRESSED MEMORIES

Can an individual forget, and later recover, memories of traumatic events? There is a great deal of debate surrounding this question (Bruck & Ceci, 2012; Klemfuss & Ceci, 2012a, 2012b; Kuehnle & Connell, 2013)? *Repression* is a defense mechanism by which a person is so traumatized by an event that he or she forgets it and then forgets the act of forgetting. According to psychodynamic theory, repression's main function is to protect the individual from threatening information.

The prevalence of repression is a matter of controversy. Most studies of traumatic memory indicate that a traumatic life event such as childhood sexual abuse is very likely to be remembered. However, there is evidence that childhood sexual abuse may not be remembered. Linda Williams and her colleagues have conducted a number of investigations of memories of childhood abuse (Banyard & Williams, 2007; Liang, Williams, & Siegel, 2006; L. M. Williams, 2003, 2004). One study involved 129 women for whom hospital emergency room records indicated a childhood abuse experience (L. M. Williams, 1995). Seventeen years after the abuse incident, the researchers contacted the women and asked (among other things) whether they had ever been the victim of childhood sexual abuse. Of the 129 women, most reported remembering and never having forgotten the experience. Ten percent of the participants reported having forgotten about the abuse at least for some portion of their lives.

If it does exist, repression can be considered a special case of **motivated forgetting,** which occurs when individuals forget something because it is so painful or anxiety-laden that remembering is intolerable (Fujiwara, Levine, & Anderson, 2008). This type of forgetting may be a consequence of the emotional trauma experienced by victims of rape or physical abuse, war veterans, and survivors of earthquakes, plane crashes, and other terrifying events. These emotional traumas may haunt people for many years unless they can put the details out of mind. Even when people have not experienced trauma, they may use motivated forgetting to protect themselves from memories of painful, stressful, or otherwise unpleasant circumstances (Shu, Gino, & Bazerman, 2011).

Cognitive psychologist Jonathan Schooler suggested that recovered memories are better termed *discovered memories* because, regardless of their accuracy, individuals do experience them as real (Geraerts & others, 2009; Schooler, 2002). Schooler and his colleagues (1997) were able to identify cases in which the perpetrator or some third party could verify a discovered memory. The existence of such cases suggests that it is inappropriate to reject all claims by adults that they were victims of long-forgotten childhood sexual abuse.

● **motivated forgetting** Forgetting that occurs when something is so painful or anxiety-laden that remembering it is intolerable.

How do psychologists consider these cases? Generally, there is consensus around a few key issues (Knapp & VandeCreek, 2000). First, all agree that child sexual abuse is an important and egregious problem that has been unacknowledged historically. Second, psychologists widely believe that most individuals who were sexually abused as children remember all or part of what happened to them and that these continuous memories are likely to be accurate. Third, there is broad agreement that it is possible for someone who was abused to forget those memories for a long time, and it is also possible to construct memories that are false but that feel very real to an individual. Finally, it is highly difficult to separate accurate from inaccurate memories, especially if methods such as hypnosis have been used in the "recovery" of memories.

We might think that a great deal of mystery would be removed if only cases of abuses were reported immediately rather than many years later. In such cases, very often children's accounts of their memories for the abuse serve as a crucial piece of evidence. Are their memories likely to be accurate?

Over the last 30 years, Gail Goodman, a cognitive developmental psychologist with expertise in legal issues, has pioneered psychological research examining whether children are easily coerced and whether they are likely to make false claims (Block & others, 2012; Chae & others, 2011; Cordon & others, 2013; Goodman, 1991, 2005, 2006; Goodman & others, 1997). Her studies have used research models in which children undergo relatively traumatic events (for instance, getting vaccinated) or embarrassing experiences (for instance, having a genital exam as part of a physical at the doctor's office) and in which the kids are then interviewed about their experiences. The interviews follow procedures that mimic those in legal settings, including the use of anatomically correct dolls, leading questions (such as, "Did the doctor touch you here?"), and even criminal lineups where the children are asked to identify the perpetrator of the "crime" ("Who gave you the shot?"). The results of these studies demonstrate that children over the age of 4 are very unlikely to falsely report genital touching; only about 8 percent of children gave such false reports.

Although Goodman's research suggests that very few children spontaneously (and falsely) report genital touching, consider that even the low rate of 8 percent could lead to false accusations. Importantly, children's mistaken memories are only problematic if the fact finders in a case (police, investigators, prosecutors, and jurors) are unable to determine whether children's recollections are true or false. *Can* adults determine if a child's memory is accurate or inaccurate? To read about research on addressing this question, see the Critical Controversy.

EYEWITNESS TESTIMONY

By now, you should realize that memory is not a perfect reflection of reality. Understanding the distortions of memory is particularly important when people are called on to report what they saw or heard in relation to a crime. Eyewitness testimonies, like other sorts of memories, may contain errors (Houston & others, 2013; Wells & Loftus, 2013), and faulty memory in criminal matters has especially serious consequences. When eyewitness testimony is inaccurate, the wrong person might go to jail or even be put to death, or the perpetrator of the crime might not be prosecuted. It is important to note that witnessing a crime is often traumatic for the individual, and so this type of memory typically fits in the larger category of memory for highly emotional events.

Much of the interest in eyewitness testimony focuses on distortion, bias, and inaccuracy in memory (Frenda, Nichols, & Loftus, 2011; Wells & Loftus, 2013). One reason for distortion is that, quite simply, memory fades with time. Furthermore, unlike a video, memory can be altered by new information (Simons & Chabris, 2011). In one study, researchers showed students a film of an automobile accident and then asked them how fast the white sports car was going when it passed a barn (Loftus, 1975). Although there was no barn in the film, 17 percent of the students mentioned the barn in their answer.

CRITICAL CONTROVERSY

Can Adults Tell If Children's Memories Are Accurate?

On June 22, 2012, former Penn State University assistant football coach Jerry Sandusky was convicted on multiple charges of sexual abuse of boys participating in a program for troubled youth. Testimony suggested that some of the children had recounted their abuse to adults at the time, but these accounts were not taken as seriously as they should have been. Those adults simply could not believe what the children were telling them about a respected member of the community. Clearly, in the Sandusky case, a great deal of harm could have been avoided if the adults had believed the children. Can adults tell when children's memory reports are accurate?

A recent study probed this key question. Gail Goodman and her colleagues showed adults videos in which children were interviewed about memories for positive events (for instance, getting a new toy, going to Disneyland) and negative events (being punished for throwing a rock through a window, having another child pull the child's pants down in front a store) (Block & others, 2012). None of the children were told to lie, but some spontaneously claimed that they had experienced events that they had not, and some denied experiencing events that they had (based on the parents' reports). The researchers found that adults did a fairly good job of recognizing true reports and rejecting false reports (Block & others, 2012). However, they also discovered that adults were likely to believe children who made *false denials*: If a child (falsely) said that an event had not happened, adults generally thought the child was telling the truth.

This finding is especially troubling in light of research showing that false denials may be a common feature of child sexual abuse claims. Indeed, one study found that even in cases in which there was substantial evidence of abuse—for example, medical evidence, a perpetrator's confession, or multiple victim complaints against the accused—20 percent of children denied at some point during the investigation that abuse had occurred (Malloy, Lyon, & Quas, 2007).

Are children's memories reliable? How does stress influence memory accuracy? Are children especially susceptible to coercion and suggestion? Can adults differentiate truth from falsehood when listening to children's accounts? These are all important topics of research in psychology. The answers remain controversial in both the scientific literature and the courtroom (Bruck & Ceci, 2012; Klemfuss & Ceci, 2012a, 2012b).

WHAT DO YOU THINK

- If a child told you about an experience of sexual abuse, what would you do? Why?
- Should children's accounts of sexual abuse be believed more often than not? Explain.
- Do you think adults are better or worse at judging the accuracy of memories conveyed by adults compared to those conveyed by children? Why?

Bias is also a factor in faulty memory (Brigham & others, 2007). Studies have shown that people of one ethnic group are less likely to recognize individual differences among people of another ethnic group (Horry, Wright, & Tredoux, 2010). In one experiment, a mugging was shown on a television news program (Loftus, 1993). Immediately after, a lineup of six suspects was broadcast, and viewers were asked to phone in and identify which one of the six individuals they thought had committed the robbery. Of the 2,000 callers, more than 1,800 identified the wrong person. In addition, even though the robber was a non-Latino White male, one-third of the viewers identified an African American or a Latino suspect as the criminal.

Hundreds of individuals have been harmed by witnesses who have made a mistake (Frenda, Nichols, & Loftus, 2011;). In his book *Convicting the Innocent*, law professor Brandon Garrett (2011) traced the first 250 cases in the United States in which a convicted individual was exonerated—proved to be not guilty—by DNA evidence. Of those cases, 190 (or *76 percent*) involved mistaken eyewitness identification of the accused.

Every year, more than 75,000 individuals are asked to identify suspects, and estimates are that these identifications are wrong one-third of the time (Pezdek, 2012). *CSI* and other TV crime dramas might give the impression that DNA evidence is widely available to protect innocent people from false accusations. However, estimates are that less than 5 percent of legal cases involving eyewitness identifications include biological evidence to potentially exonerate mistakenly identified convicts (Wells, Steblay, & Dysart, 2011). So, for many crimes, eyewitness identification remains an important piece of evidence—and improving the validity of these identifications is a crucial goal (Smalarz & Wells, 2013).

To reduce the chances that innocent individuals will be accused of crimes, law enforcement officials are applying psychological research findings to improve the way they conduct criminal lineups. In such lineups, a witness views a group of individuals in real time, or looks at photos of individuals, one of whom is the suspect. The witness is asked to identify the perpetrator of the crime if he or she is among those shown.

Psychological research has influenced these procedures in two ways. First, research strongly supports the use of *double-blind* procedures (Brewer & Wells, 2011). Recall that in a double-blind study, neither the participants nor the experimenter knows what condition the participants are in, to reduce the effects of bias on the results. For police lineups this means that no one directly involved in administering the lineup has any knowledge of the case or of which individual is suspected of the crime, removing any bias. Second, research shows that presenting suspects (either their pictures or in person) sequentially (that is, one at a time) is less likely to produce erroneous identifications than presenting them all at one time (Steblay, Dysart, & Wells, 2011). A large-scale field study examined the effectiveness of double-blind sequential and simultaneous lineups in four different jurisdictions in the United States in actual criminal investigations and found that such procedures decreased witness errors (Wells, Steblay, & Dysart, 2011).

Faulty memory is not just about accusing the wrong person. For example, faulty memories were evident in descriptions of the suspects' vehicle in the sniper attacks in 2002 that killed 10 people in and around Washington, DC. Witnesses reported seeing a white truck or van fleeing several of the crime scenes. It appears that a white van may have been near one of the first shootings; media repetition of this information contaminated the memories of witnesses to later attacks, making them more likely to remember a white truck or van. When caught, the sniper suspects were driving a blue car.

Faulty memories complicated the search for the perpetrators in the sniper attacks that killed 10 people in and around Washington, DC, in 2002. Police released photos of the type of white truck or van that witnesses said they saw fleeing some of the crime scenes (left). In the end, however, the suspects were driving a blue car when law enforcement officials apprehended them (above).

Before police even arrive at a crime scene, witnesses talk among themselves, and this dialogue can contaminate memories. This is why, during the DC sniper attacks, law enforcement officials advised any persons who might witness the next attack to write down immediately what they had seen—even on their hands if they did not have a piece of paper.

5· FORGETTING

test yourself

1. What are the primacy effect and the recency effect, and how do psychologists explain each?
2. What is the difference between recall and recognition?
3. Explain autobiographical memory and the "reminiscence bump."

Human memory has its imperfections, as we have all experienced. It is not unusual for two people to argue about whether something did or did not happen, each supremely confident that his or her memory is accurate and the other person's is faulty. We all have had the frustrating experience of trying to remember the name of a person or a place but not quite being able to retrieve it. Missed appointments, misplaced keys, the failure to recall the name of a familiar face, and the inability to recall your password for Internet access are everyday examples of forgetting. Why do we forget?

One of psychology's pioneers, Hermann Ebbinghaus (1850–1909), was the first person to conduct scientific research on forgetting. In 1885, he made up and memorized a list of 13 nonsense syllables and then assessed how many of them he could remember as time passed. (*Nonsense syllables* are meaningless combinations of letters that are unlikely to have been learned already, such as *zeq, xid, lek,* and *riy.*) Even just an hour later, Ebbinghaus could recall only a few of the nonsense syllables he had memorized. Figure 7.14 shows Ebbinghaus's learning curve for nonsense syllables. Based on his research, Ebbinghaus concluded that most forgetting takes place soon after we learn something.

If we forget so quickly, why put effort into learning something? Fortunately, researchers have demonstrated that forgetting is not as extensive as Ebbinghaus envisioned (Averell & Heathcote, 2011; Harris, Sutton, & Barnier, 2010). Ebbinghaus studied meaningless nonsense syllables. When we memorize more meaningful material—such as poetry, history, or the content of this text—forgetting is neither so rapid nor so extensive. Following are some of the factors that influence how well we can retrieve information from long-term memory.

Encoding Failure

Sometimes when people say they have forgotten something, they have not really forgotten it; rather, they never encoded the information in the first place. *Encoding failure* occurs when the information was never entered into long-term memory.

As an example of encoding failure, think about what the U.S. penny looks like. In one study, researchers showed 15 versions of the penny to participants and asked them which one was correct (Nickerson & Adams, 1979). Look at the pennies in Figure 7.15 (but do not read the caption yet) and see whether you can tell which is the real penny. Most people do not do well on this task. Unless you are a coin collector, you probably have not encoded a lot of specific details about pennies. You may have encoded just enough information to distinguish them from other coins (pennies are copper-colored, dimes and nickels are silver-colored; pennies fall between the sizes of dimes and quarters).

The penny exercise illustrates that we encode and enter into long-term memory only a small portion of our life experiences. In a sense, then, encoding failures really are not cases of forgetting; they are cases of not remembering.

Hermann Ebbinghaus (1850–1909)
Ebbinghaus was the first psychologist to conduct scientific research on forgetting.

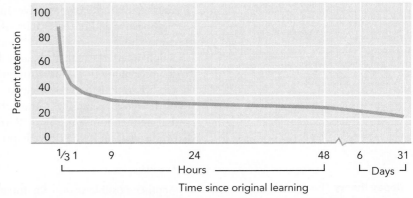

FIGURE 7.14 Ebbinghaus's Forgetting Curve The figure illustrates Ebbinghaus's conclusion that most forgetting occurs soon after we learn something.

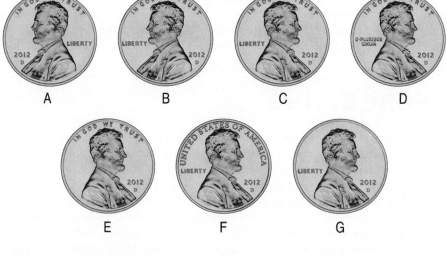

FIGURE 7.15 Which Is a Real U.S. Penny? In the original experiment, participants viewed 15 versions of pennies; only one version was an actual U.S. penny. This figure shows only 7 of the 15 versions, and as you likely can tell, the task is still very difficult. Why? By the way, the actual U.S. penny is (c).

Retrieval Failure

Problems in retrieving information from memory are clearly examples of forgetting (Law & others, 2012; Ortega-Castro & Vadillo, 2013). Psychologists have theorized that the causes of retrieval failure include problems with the information in storage, the effects of time, personal reasons for remembering or forgetting, and the brain's condition (Barrouillet, De Paepe, & Langerock, 2012; García-Bajos & Migueles, 2013).

INTERFERENCE

● **interference theory** The theory that people forget not because memories are lost from storage but because other information gets in the way of what they want to remember.

Interference is one reason that people forget (Malmberg & others, 2012). According to **interference theory,** people forget not because memories are lost from storage but because other information gets in the way of what they want to remember. In other words, memory for one thing fails because memory for something else gets in the way.

● **proactive interference** Situation in which material that was learned earlier disrupts the recall of material that was learned later.

There are two kinds of interference: proactive and retroactive. **Proactive interference** occurs when material that was learned earlier disrupts the recall of material learned later (Yi & Friedman, 2011). Remember that *pro* means "forward in time." For example, suppose you had a good friend 10 years ago named Prudence and that last night you met someone named Patience. You might find yourself calling your new friend Prudence because the old information (Prudence) interferes with retrieval of new information (Patience).

● **retroactive interference** Situation in which material that was learned later disrupts the retrieval of information that was learned earlier.

Retroactive interference occurs when material learned later disrupts the retrieval of information learned earlier (Solesio-Jofre & others, 2011). Remember that *retro* means "backward in time." Suppose you have lately become friends with Ralph. In sending a note to your old friend Raul, you might mistakenly address it to Ralph because the new information (Ralph) interferes with the old information (Raul). Figure 7.16 depicts another example of proactive and retroactive interference.

Proactive and retroactive interference might both be explained as problems with retrieval cues. The reason the name Prudence interferes with the name Patience and the name Ralph interferes with the name Raul might be that the cue you are using to remember the one name does not distinguish between the two memories. For example, if the cue you are using is "my good friend," it might evoke both names. The result might be retrieval of the wrong name or a kind of blocking in which each name interferes with the other and neither comes to mind. Retrieval cues (such as "friend" in our example) can become overloaded, and when that happens we are likely to forget or to retrieve incorrectly.

DECAY

● **decay theory** Theory stating that when an individual learns something new, a neurochemical memory trace forms, but over time this trace disintegrates; suggests that the passage of time always increases forgetting.

Another possible reason for forgetting is the passage of time. According to **decay theory,** when we learn something new, a neurochemical memory trace forms, but over time this trace disintegrates. Decay theory suggests that the passage of time always increases forgetting.

Memories often do fade with the passage of time, but decay alone cannot explain forgetting. For example, under the right retrieval conditions, we can recover memories

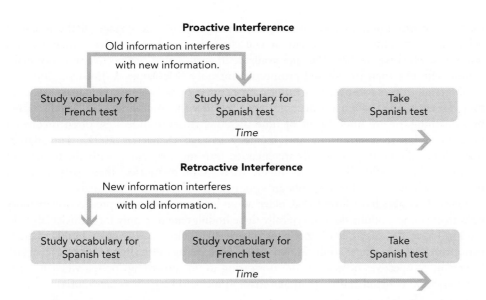

Proactive Interference

Old information interferes
with new information.

| Study vocabulary for French test | Study vocabulary for Spanish test | Take Spanish test |

Time

Retroactive Interference

New information interferes
with old information.

| Study vocabulary for Spanish test | Study vocabulary for French test | Take Spanish test |

Time

FIGURE 7.16 Proactive and Retroactive Interference *Pro* means "forward"; in proactive interference, old information has a forward influence by getting in the way of new material learned. Retro means "backward"; in retroactive interference, new information has a backward influence by getting in the way of material learned earlier.

that we seem to have forgotten (Brown & Lewandowsky, 2010). You might have forgotten the name of someone in your high school class, for instance, but when you return to the setting where you knew the person, the name pops back into your head. Similarly, you may not have thought about someone from your past for a very long time, but when the person "friends" you on Facebook, you may remember experiences you shared.

TIP-OF-THE-TONGUE PHENOMENON

We are all familiar with the retrieval glitch called **tip-of-the-tongue (TOT) phenomenon**— a type of "effortful retrieval" that occurs when we are confident that we know something but cannot quite pull it out of memory (A. S. Brown, 2012). In a TOT state we usually can successfully retrieve characteristics of the word, such as the first letter and the number of syllables, but not the word itself. The TOT phenomenon arises when we can retrieve some of the desired information but not all of it (Schwartz & Metcalfe, 2011).

The TOT phenomenon reveals some interesting aspects of memory. For one thing, it demonstrates that we do not store all of the information about a particular topic or experience in one way. If you have ever struggled to think of a specific word, you probably came up with various words that mean the same thing as the word you were looking for, but you still had a nagging feeling that none was quite right. Sometimes you might find the solution in an unexpected way. For example, imagine that you are doing a crossword puzzle with the clue "Colorful scarf" for a seven-letter word. You have a feeling you know this word. If you have not thought of the answer yet, say the following word aloud: *bandage.* If you were experiencing the TOT phenomenon when doing the crossword, thinking of *bandage* might have helped you come up with the correct answer, *bandana.* Although the meaning of *bandage* is unrelated to that of *bandana,* the fact that these words start with the same sounds (and therefore are linked in verbal memory) can lead you to the word *bandana* (Abrams & Rodriguez, 2005). Research on TOT has shown that the sounds of words are linked in memory even if their meanings are not (Antón-Méndez & others, 2012; Buján & others, 2012).

PROSPECTIVE MEMORY

The main focus of this chapter has been on **retrospective memory,** which is remembering the past. **Prospective memory** involves remembering information about doing something in the future; it includes memory for intentions (Barrouillet, De Paepe, & Langerock, 2012; Lee & McDaniel, 2013). Prospective memory includes both *timing*— when we have to do something—and *content*—what we have to do.

We can make a distinction between time-based and event-based prospective memory. *Time-based* prospective memory is our intention to engage in a given behavior after a specified amount of time has gone by, such as an intention to make a phone call to

- **tip-of-the-tongue (TOT) phenomenon** A type of effortful retrieval associated with a person's feeling that he or she knows something (say, a word or a name) but cannot quite pull it out of memory.

- **retrospective memory** Remembering information from the past.

- **prospective memory** Remembering information about doing something in the future; includes memory for intentions.

"This amnesia of yours . . . can you remember how long you've had it?"

© Kes. www.CartoonStock.com

● **amnesia** The loss of memory.

● **anterograde amnesia** A memory disorder that affects the retention of new information and events.

● **retrograde amnesia** Memory loss for a segment of the past but not for new events.

test yourself

1. What is the term for the failure of information to enter long-term memory?
2. Name four factors that, according to psychologists, may be the cause of retrieval failure.
3. What is the tip-of-the-tongue (TOT) phenomenon, and what does it reveal about how we store information?

someone in one hour. In *event-based* prospective memory, we engage in the intended behavior when some external event or cue elicits it, as when we give a message to a roommate when we see her. The cues available in event-based prospective memory make it more effective than time-based prospective memory (McDaniel & Einstein, 2007).

Some failures in prospective memory are referred to as "absentmindedness." We are more absentminded when we become preoccupied with something else, are distracted by something, or are under a lot of time pressure. Absentmindedness often involves a breakdown between attention and memory storage (Schacter, 2001). Fortunately, research has shown that our goals are encoded into memory along with the features of situations that would allow us to pursue them. Our memories, then, prepare us to recognize when a situation presents an opportunity to achieve those goals.

Researchers also have found that older adults perform worse on prospective memory tasks than younger adults do, but typically these findings are true only for artificial lab tasks (Smith, Horn, & Bayen, 2012; Zollig & others, 2012). In real life, older adults generally perform as well as younger adults in terms of prospective memory (Rendell & Craik, 2000). Generally, prospective memory failure (forgetting to do something) occurs when retrieval is a conscious, effortful (rather than automatic) process (Henry & others, 2004).

AMNESIA

Recall the case of H. M. in the discussion of explicit and implicit memory. In H. M.'s surgery, the part of his brain responsible for laying down new memories was damaged beyond repair. The result was **amnesia,** the loss of memory.

H. M. suffered from **anterograde amnesia,** a memory disorder that affects the retention of new information and events (*antero* indicates amnesia that moves forward in time) (Ward, 2010). What he learned before the surgery (and thus before the onset of amnesia) was not affected. For example, H. M. could identify his friends, recall their names, and even tell stories about them—*if* he had known them before the surgery. People who met H. M. after the surgery remained strangers, even if they spent thousands of hours with him. H. M.'s postsurgical experiences were rarely encoded in his long-term memory.

Whereas anterograde amnesia involves the inability to make new memories, **retrograde amnesia** involves memory loss for a segment of the past events (*retro* indicates amnesia that moves back in time) (Abbate & others, 2012). In contrast to anterograde amnesia, in retrograde amnesia the forgotten information is *old*—it occurred prior to the event that caused the amnesia—and the ability to acquire new memories is not affected. Retrograde amnesia is much more common than anterograde amnesia and frequently occurs when the brain is assaulted by an electrical shock or a physical blow such as a head injury to a football player. Sometimes individuals have both anterograde and retrograde amnesia.

6· STUDY TIPS FROM THE SCIENCE OF MEMORY

How can you apply your new knowledge of memory processes to improving your academic performance? No matter what model of memory you use, you can sharpen your memory by thinking deeply about the "material" of life and connecting the information to other things you know. The most connected node or most elaborate schema to which you can link new information is the self—what you know and think about yourself. To make something meaningful and to secure its place in memory, you must make it matter to you.

If you think about memory as a physical event in the brain, you can see that memorizing material is like training a muscle. Repeated recruitment of sets of neurons creates the connection you want available not only at exam time but throughout life.

ORGANIZE

Before you engage the powerful process of memory, the first step in improving your academic performance is to make sure that the information you are studying is accurate and well organized.

Tips for Organizing

■ *Review your course notes routinely and catch potential errors and ambiguities early.* There is no sense in memorizing inaccurate or incomplete information.

■ *Organize the material in a way that will allow you to commit it to memory effectively.* Arrange information, rework material, and give it a structure that will help you to remember it.

■ *Experiment with different organizational techniques.* One approach is to use a hierarchy such as an outline. You might create analogies (such as the earlier comparison of retrieval from long-term memory to finding a book in the library) that take advantage of your preexisting schemas. As you begin to organize the information, you might explore possible mnemonics to help you memorize.

ENCODE

Once you ensure that the material to be remembered is accurate and well organized, it is time to memorize. Although some types of information are encoded automatically, academic learning usually requires considerable effort (Bruning & others, 2004).

Tips for Encoding

■ *Pay attention.* Remember that staying focused on one thing is crucial. In other words, no divided attention.

■ *Process information at an appropriate level.* Think about the material meaningfully and process it deeply.

■ *Elaborate on the points to be remembered.* Make associations to your life and to other aspects of the material you want to remember.

■ *Use imagery.* Devising images to help you remember (such as the mental picture of a computer screen to help you recall the concept of working memory) allows you to "double-encode" the information.

■ *Use chunking.* Breaking up the material into chunks will help you get it into memory.

■ *Understand that encoding is not simply something that you should do before a test.* Rather, encode early and often. During class, while reading, or in discussing issues, take advantage of opportunities to create associations to your course material.

REHEARSE

While learning material initially, relate it to your life and attend to examples that help you do so. After class, rehearse the course material over time to solidify it in memory.

Tips for Rehearsing

■ *Rewrite, type, or retype your notes.* Some students find this exercise a good form of rehearsal.

■ *Talk to people about what you have learned and how it is important to real life in order to reinforce memory.* You are more likely to remember information over the long term if you understand it and relate it to your world than if you just mechanically rehearse and memorize it. Rehearsal works well for information in short-term memory, but when you need to encode, store, and then retrieve information from long-term memory, it is much less efficient. Thus, for most information, understand it, give it meaning, elaborate on it, and personalize it.

■ *Test yourself.* It is not enough to look at your notes and think, "Oh, yes, I know this." Sometimes recognition instills a false sense of knowing. If you have developed mnemonics for material, test your ability to use them effectively. It is not enough to simply know that you have memorized, "Pete LoVeS CatE" to remember the components of Baddeley's model of working memory. You must be able to produce the produce the concepts this mnemonic stands for: Phonological Loop, Visuo-spatial Sketchpad, and Central Executive. If you look at a definition, and it seems so familiar that you are certain you know it, challenge yourself. What happens when you close the book and try to reconstruct the definition? Check your personal definition with the technical one in the book. How did you do?

- *While reading and studying, ask yourself questions.* Ask things such as, "What is the meaning of what I just read?" "Why is this important?" and "What is an example of the concept I just read about?" When you make a concerted effort to ask yourself questions about what you have read or about an activity in class, you expand the number of associations you make with the information you will need to retrieve later.

- *Treat your brain kindly.* If you are genuinely seeking to improve your memory performance, keep in mind that the brain is a physical organ. Perhaps the best way to promote effective memory storage is to make sure that your brain is able to function at maximum capacity. That means resting it, nourishing it by eating well, and keeping it free of mind-altering substances. A key way we can take care of our memory capacity is to get sufficient sleep.

RETRIEVE

So, you have studied not just hard but deeply, elaborating on important concepts and committing lists to memory. You have slept well and eaten a nutritious breakfast, and now it is exam time. How can you best retrieve the essential information?

Tips for Retrieving

- *Use retrieval cues.* Sit in the same seat where you learned the material. Remember that the exam is full of questions about topics that you have thoughtfully encoded. Some of the questions on the test might help jog your memory for the answers to others.

- *Sit comfortably, take a deep breath, and stay calm.* Bolster your confidence by recalling that research on long-term memory has shown that material that has been committed to memory is there for a very long time—even among those who may experience a moment of panic when the test is handed out.

Memory is crucial for learning and academic success, but it also serves many other purposes. As we now consider, these include contributing to healthy functioning as we age and giving our life a sense of meaning.

7· MEMORY AND HEALTH AND WELLNESS

Autobiographical memory may be one of the most important aspects of human life (Fivush, 2011; Marsh & Roediger, 2013). For instance, one of the many functions that autobiographical memory serves is to allow us to learn from our experiences (Pillemer, 1998). In autobiographical memory, we store the lessons we have learned from life. These memories become a resource to which we can turn when faced with life's difficulties.

Autobiographical memory also allows us to understand ourselves and provides us with a source of identity. In his studies of self-defining autobiographical memories, Jefferson Singer and his colleagues maintain that these internalized stories of personal experience serve as signs of the meaning we have created out of our life events and give our lives coherence (Baddeley & Singer, 2010; Singer & Blagov, 2004; Singer & Conway, 2011; Singer, Singer, & Berry, 2013).

According to Dan McAdams (2006, 2009, 2013), autobiographical memories form the core of our personal identity. A number of studies have now shown that the stories we tell about our lives have important implications. For instance, McAdams and his colleagues have demonstrated that individuals who describe important life experiences that go from bad to better (*redemptive stories*) are more *generative*—that is, they are the kind of people who make a contribution to future generations, people who leave a legacy that will outlive them (Bauer, McAdams, & Sakaeda, 2005). These individuals are also better adjusted than those whose self-defining memories go from good to bad (*contamination stories*). A recent study showed that individuals in Alcoholics Anonymous

test yourself

1. What steps can you take to ensure that your course information is well organized?
2. Give at least three tips for encoding information and at least three tips for rehearsing information.
3. What strategies can help you retrieve essential information when taking an examination?

who told stories about their last drink that were characterized by redemption were more likely to abstain from alcohol (Dunlop & Tracy, 2013). Clearly, the construction and reconstruction of autobiographical memory may reveal important aspects of how individuals function, grow, and discover meaning in their lives (Cox & McAdams, 2012; King & Hicks, 2007; McAdams, 2013).

Memory matters to us in social ways as well. We apologize if we have forgotten someone's name, even if that forgetting is unintentional. Remembering details such as names is a way we demonstrate that we matter to one another (King & Geise, 2011).

Keeping Memory Sharp—and Preserving Brain Function

As a process rooted in the brain, memory is also an indicator of brain functioning. Preserving memory is of vital importance as we age. A strong message from research on aging and memory is that, as for many things in life, the phrase "Use it or lose it" applies to memory.

Consider the case of Richard Wetherill, a retired lecturer and an uncommonly good chess player (Melton, 2005). Wetherill was so skilled that he was able to think eight moves ahead in a chess match. At one point, he noticed that he was having trouble playing chess—he could anticipate only five moves ahead. He was sure that something was seriously wrong with him, despite his wife's assurances that she noticed no changes. A battery of cognitive tests revealed no abnormalities, and a brain scan was similarly reassuring. Two years later, Wetherill was dead, and the autopsy showed a brain ravaged by Alzheimer disease, a progressive, irreversible brain disorder that is characterized by gradual deterioration of memory, reasoning, language, and eventually physical functioning. Brain damage of this sort should indicate a person who was incapable of coherent thought. Wetherill's symptoms, however, had been limited to a small decline in his skill at playing chess.

Wetherill's case is surprising but also typical. Individuals who lead active intellectual lives seem to be protected against the mental decline generally associated with age. Indeed, research has shown that individuals who are educated, have high IQs, and remain mentally engaged in complex tasks tend to cope better with a variety of assaults to the brain, including Alzheimer disease, stroke, head injury, and even poisoning with neurotoxins (Melton, 2005). Some research has suggested that an active mental life leads to the accumulation of a "cognitive store"—an emergency stash of mental capacity that allows individuals to avoid the negative effects of harm to the brain.

Yaakov Stern found that among a group of individuals with Alzheimer disease who appeared to be equal in terms of their outward symptoms, those who were more educated were actually suffering from much worse brain damage—yet they were functioning at a level similar to others with relatively less damage (Stern & others, 1992). Stern and his colleagues (2004) have also shown that intellectual pursuits such as playing chess and reading reduce the severity of Alzheimer symptoms. However, more recent research demonstrates that although maintaining an active mental life can reduce the speed of cognitive decline associated with Alzheimer disease, it can also be related to more rapid decline once a person is diagnosed (Wilson & others, 2010).

Apparently, a lifetime of mental activity and engagement produces this cognitive reserve that allows the brain to maintain its ability to recruit new neural networks that compensate for damage. These brains are better able to move to a backup plan to maintain the individual's level of functioning (Andel & others, 2005). The clear message from these studies is the importance of building up a cognitive reserve by staying mentally active throughout life. In addition to educational achievement, staying physically active also seems to play a role in maintaining a sharp mind (Diamond, 2013; Guiney & Machado, 2013; Sattler & others, 2012).

Memory and the Shaping of Meaningful Experiences

Before we leave the science of memory, let's consider the role of memory in shaping meaningful experiences in daily life. Think of the most meaningful event of your life. Clearly, that event is one that you remember, among *all* the things you have experienced in your life.

Engaging in an intellectually challenging activity such as playing chess seems to offer some protection against the mental decline associated with aging.

We all have certain particularly vivid autobiographical memories that stand out as indicators of meaning, such as those studied by Jefferson Singer that we reviewed above. In fact, however, everyday life is filled with potentially remarkable moments—a beautiful sunrise, a delicious meal prepared just for you, an unexpected telephone call from an old friend. Experiencing the richness of everyday life requires us to be attentive and engaged. Sometimes daily chores and problems lead us to feel that we are just going through the motions. This sort of mindless living may be a way to survive, but it is unlikely to be a way to thrive.

The processes of attention and encoding that we have explored in this chapter suggest that actively engaging in life—investing ourselves in the events of the day (Cantor & Sanderson, 1999)—is the way we can be assured that our life stories are rich and nuanced. That way, when someone asks, "So, tell me about yourself," we have a story to tell.

test yourself

1. What crucial functions does autobiographical memory serve?
2. What did McAdams mean when he described certain individuals as "generative"?
3. What factors are involved in keeping memory sharp as we age?

SUMMARY

1. THE NATURE OF MEMORY

Memory is the retention of information over time. The three processes involved in memory are encoding (getting information into storage), storage (retaining information over time), and retrieval (taking information out of storage).

2. MEMORY ENCODING

Encoding requires attention, but the attention must be selective. Memory is negatively influenced by divided attention.

According to the theory of levels of processing, information is processed on a continuum from shallow (sensory or physical features are encoded) to intermediate (labels are attached to stimuli) to deep (the meanings of stimuli and their associations with other stimuli are processed). Deeper processing produces better memory. Elaboration, the extensiveness of processing at any given level of memory encoding, improves memory. Using imagery, or mental pictures, as a context for information can improve memory.

3. MEMORY STORAGE

The Atkinson-Shiffrin theory describes memory as a three-stage process: sensory memory, short-term memory, and long-term memory.

Sensory memory holds perceptions of the world for only an instant. Visual sensory memory (iconic memory) retains information for about ¼ of a second; auditory sensory memory (echoic memory) preserves information for several seconds.

Short-term memory is a limited-capacity memory system in which information is usually retained for as long as 30 seconds. Short-term memory's limitation is 7 ± 2 bits of information. Chunking and rehearsal can benefit short-term memory. Working memory is a combination of short-term memory and attention, a mental workspace where we hold information in mind and solve problems. Because it cannot rely on rehearsal, working memory capacity is estimated to be 4 ± 1 chunks of information. Baddeley's model of working memory has three components: a central executive and two assistants (phonological loop and visuo-spatial sketchpad).

Long-term memory is a relatively permanent type of memory that holds huge amounts of information for a long time. Long-term memory has two main subtypes: explicit and implicit memory. Explicit memory is the conscious recollection of information, such as specific facts or events. Implicit memory affects behavior through prior experiences that are not consciously recollected.

Explicit memory has two dimensions. One dimension includes episodic memory and semantic memory. The other dimension includes retrospective memory and prospective memory. Implicit memory is multidimensional too and includes systems for procedural memory, priming, and classical conditioning.

4. MEMORY RETRIEVAL

The serial position effect is the tendency to recall items at the beginning and the end of a list better than the middle items. The primacy effect is the tendency to recall items at the beginning of the list better than the middle items. The recency effect is the tendency to remember the items at the end of a list better than the middle items.

Retrieval is easier when effective cues are present. Another factor in effective retrieval is the nature of the retrieval task. Simple recognition of previously remembered information in the presence of cues is generally easier than recall of the information.

According to the encoding specificity principle, information present at the time of encoding or learning tends to be effective as a retrieval cue, a process referred to as context-dependent memory. Retrieval also benefits from priming, which activates particular connections or associations in memory. The tip-of-the-tongue phenomenon occurs when we cannot quite pull something out of memory.

Special cases of retrieval include autobiographical memory, emotional memory, memory for trauma, repressed memory, and eyewitness testimony. Autobiographical memory is a person's recollections of his or her life experiences. The reminiscence bump refers to the fact that most people have more autobiographical memories for the second and third decades of life. Autobiographical memory has three levels: life time periods, general events, and event-specific knowledge. Biographies of the self connect the past and the present to form our identity.

Emotional memories may be especially vivid and enduring. Particularly significant emotional memories, or flashbulb memories, capture emotionally profound events that people often recall accurately and vividly. Memory for personal trauma also is usually more accurate than memory for ordinary events, but it too is subject to distortion and inaccuracy. People tend to remember the core information about a personal trauma but might distort some of the details. Personal trauma can cause individuals to repress emotionally laden information so that it is not accessible to consciousness.

Repression means forgetting a particularly troubling experience because it would be too upsetting to remember it. Eyewitness testimony may contain errors due to memory decay or bias.

5. FORGETTING

Encoding failure is forgetting information that was never entered into long-term memory. Retrieval failure can occur for at least four reasons.

First, interference theory stresses that we forget not because memories are lost from storage but because other information gets in the way of what we want to remember. Interference can be proactive (as occurs when material learned earlier disrupts the recall of material learned later) or retroactive (as occurs when material learned later disrupts the retrieval of information learned earlier).

The second reason for retrieval failure is explained by decay theory, which states that when we learn something new, a neurochemical memory trace forms, but over time this chemical trail disintegrates.

Third, motivated forgetting occurs when we want to forget something. It is common when a memory becomes painful or anxiety-laden, as in the case of emotional traumas such as rape and physical abuse.

Finally, amnesia, the physiologically based loss of memory, can cause retrieval failure. Anterograde amnesia affects the retention of new information or events. Retrograde amnesia affects memories of the past but not memories of new events. Amnesia can be a combination of both types.

6. STUDY TIPS FROM THE SCIENCE OF MEMORY

Effective encoding strategies when studying include paying attention and minimizing distraction, understanding the material rather than relying on rote memorization, asking yourself questions, and taking good notes. Research on memory suggests that the best way to remember course material is to relate it to many different aspects of your life.

7. MEMORY AND HEALTH AND WELLNESS

Autobiographical memories, particularly self-defining memories, provide a unique source of identity, and sharing those memories with others plays a role in social bonding.

Taking on challenging cognitive tasks throughout life can stave off the effects of age on memory and lessen the effects of Alzheimer disease.

Engaging in everyday life means living memorably. Mindfulness to life events provides a rich reservoir of experiences upon which to build a storehouse of autobiographical memories.

key *terms*

memory, p. 218
encoding, p. 218
divided attention, p. 219
sustained attention or vigilance, p. 219
levels of processing, p. 219
elaboration, p. 220
storage, p. 222
Atkinson-Shiffrin theory, p. 222
sensory memory, p. 222
short-term memory, p. 223

working memory, p. 224
long-term memory, p. 226
explicit memory or declarative memory, p. 227
episodic memory, p. 228
semantic memory, p. 228
implicit memory or nondeclarative memory, p. 228
procedural memory, p. 229
priming, p. 230
schema, p. 231

script, p. 231
connectionism or parallel distributed processing (PDP), p. 231
retrieval, p. 234
serial position effect, p. 234
autobiographical memory, p. 237
flashbulb memory, p. 238
motivated forgetting, p. 239
interference theory, p. 244
proactive interference, p. 244

retroactive interference, p. 244
decay theory, p. 244
tip-of-the-tongue (TOT) phenomenon, p. 245
retrospective memory, p. 245
prospective memory, p. 245
amnesia, p. 246
anterograde amnesia, p. 246
retrograde amnesia, p. 246

apply your *knowledge*

1. Write down a memory that you feel has been especially important in making you who you are. What are some characteristics of this self-defining memory? What do you think the memory says about you? How does it relate to your current goals and aspirations? Do you think of the memory often? You might find that this part of your life story can be inspiring when things are going poorly or when you are feeling down.

2. Become a memory detective and explore the accuracy of your own memory for major events. Think about an event for which you might have a flashbulb memory. You might choose from a major event in recent history, such as the 9/11 attacks, Hurricane Sandy, or the earthquake in Haiti. Then ask yourself some easily verifiable questions about it, such as what day of the week did it happen? What time of day? What were the date and year? How many people were involved? When you have done your best to answer these questions, check your facts online. Were your memories accurate?

3. It is sometimes difficult to believe that our memories are not as accurate as we think. To test your ability to be a good eyewitness, visit one of the following websites:

www.pbs.org/wgbh/pages/frontline/shows/dna/

www.psychology.iastate.edu/~glwells/theeyewitnesstest.html

Did this exercise change your opinion of the accuracy of eyewitness testimony? Explain.

CHAPTER 8

Thinking, Intelligence, and Language

The Value of a Really Good Idea

We are surrounded by evidence of people's really great ideas. From the alarm clock to the computer, human ingenuity touches us at every turn. These inventions happened because somebody noticed a problem and came up with a solution.

Having a really good idea is the beginning of a long journey—one that can be difficult and costly. A relatively new resource to assist individuals in that journey is *crowdfunding,* the raising of money, via the Internet, to support the creative initiatives of people and groups. Kickstarter.com is a place where creative people can apply to receive startup funds to put their really good ideas into action (Pogue, 2012). Would-be inventors post descriptions of their projects, which can range from artistic (cutting a CD) to technological (building a new gadget), and propose a budget for their venture. If visitors to the site pledge enough funds to cover the anticipated costs, the posters get the money to bring their big dreams to reality. Most interesting is that those who pledge funds to the projects are not typical investors. In fact, they are not investors at all. They receive nothing (except a T-shirt or trinket) in return for their money; they donate money based solely on their own enthusiasm for a really good idea.

Some proposals are surprisingly successful. A proposal for a puppet-show version of Romeo and Juliet received over three times its requested budget (Kickstarter.com, 2013).

Why would everyday people give their hard-earned cash to an idea? Some cannot resist the appeal of the human capacity to recognize a problem and to devise a creative solution. ●

PREVIEW

Cognitive psychology is the study of mental processes. This chapter investigates the basic cognitive processes of thinking, intelligence, and language. We first define cognition and look at the cognitive revolution that led to new understanding about the workings of the human mind. Thinking refers to the process of cognition itself. We examine types of thinking, including problem solving, reasoning, critical thinking, and creativity. We then examine the quality of mental processes, focusing on a central indicator of cognitive ability, intelligence. We next explore the way that thoughts are typically expressed as we focus on the unique contribution of language to mental processes. Finally, we close by considering the role of thinking in health and wellness.

1- THE COGNITIVE REVOLUTION IN PSYCHOLOGY

● **cognition** The way in which information is processed and manipulated in remembering, thinking, and knowing.

Artificial intelligence (AI) researchers are currently exploring frontiers that were once the context for sci-fi movie plots. ASIMO ("Advanced Step in Innovative Mobility") is a humanoid robot designed by Honda. ASIMO can open doors, walk with fluid movement, climb stairs, and kick a soccer ball while balancing on one foot. With cameras for eyes, ASIMO navigates and can even address people by name if the information is stored in its database. After 20 years of development, in 2011 Honda unveiled ASIMO at the FIRST ("For Inspiration in Science and Technology") Championships in St. Louis, Missouri.

Cognitive psychologists study **cognition**—the way in which information is processed and manipulated in remembering, thinking, and knowing. Cognitive psychology is a relatively young field, scarcely more than a half-century old. We begin by tracing its history.

After the first decade of the twentieth century, behaviorism (which we examined in Chapter 6) dominated the thinking of experimental psychologists. Behaviorists such as B. F. Skinner believed that the human mind is a black box best left to philosophers, and they considered observable behavior to be psychologists' proper focus. The behaviorist perspective had little use for the mental processes occurring in that dark place between your ears.

In the 1950s, psychologists' views began to change. The advent of computers provided a new way to think about the workings of the human mind. If we could "see" what computers were doing internally, maybe we could use our observations to study human mental processes, scientists reasoned. Indeed, computer science was a key motivator in the birth of the study of human cognition. The first modern computer, developed by mathematician John von Neumann in the late 1940s, showed that machines could perform logical operations. In the 1950s, researchers speculated that computers might model some mental operations, and they believed that such modeling might shed light on how the human mind works (Marcus, 2001).

Cognitive psychologists often use the computer as an analogy to help explain the relationship between cognition and the brain (Forsythe, Bernard, & Goldsmith, 2006). They describe the physical brain as the computer's hardware, and cognition as its software. Herbert Simon (1969) was among the pioneers in comparing the human mind to computer processing systems. In this analogy, the sensory and perceptual systems provide an "input channel," similar to the way data are entered into the computer (Figure 8.1). As input (information) comes into the mind, mental processes, or operations, act on it, just as the computer's software acts on the data. The transformed input generates information that remains in memory much in the way a computer stores what it has worked on. Finally, the information is retrieved from memory and "printed out" or "displayed" (so to speak) as an observable response.

Computers provide a logical and concrete, but oversimplified, model of human information processing. Inanimate computers and human brains function quite differently in some respects. For example, most computers receive information from a human who has already coded the information and removed much of its ambiguity. In contrast, each brain cell, or neuron, can respond to ambiguous information transmitted through sensory receptors such as the eyes and ears.

Computers can do some things better than humans. For instance, computers can perform complex numerical calculations much faster and more accurately than humans could ever hope to (Liu & others, 2012). Computers can also apply and follow rules

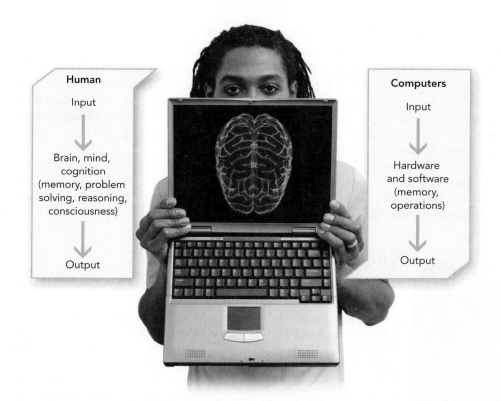

FIGURE 8.1 **Computers and Human Cognition** An analogy is commonly drawn between human cognition and the way computers work. The brain is analogous to a computer's hardware, and cognition is analogous to a computer's software.

more consistently and with fewer errors than humans and can represent complex mathematical patterns better than humans.

Still, the brain's extraordinary capabilities will probably not be mimicked completely by computers any time in the near future. Attempts to use computers to process visual information or spoken language have achieved only limited success in specific situations. The human brain also has an incredible ability to learn new rules, relationships, concepts, and patterns that it can generalize to novel situations. In comparison, computers are quite limited in their ability to learn and generalize. Although a computer can improve its ability to recognize patterns or use rules of thumb to make decisions, it does not have the means to develop new learning goals.

Furthermore, the human mind is aware of itself; the computer is not. Indeed, no computer is likely to approach the richness of human consciousness (Agnati & others, 2012; Nunez, 2012).

Nonetheless, the computer's role in cognitive psychology continues to increase. An entire scientific field called **artificial intelligence (AI)** focuses on creating machines capable of performing activities that require intelligence when people do them. AI is especially helpful in tasks requiring speed, persistence, and a vast memory (Goel & Davies, 2011; Hermundstad & others, 2011). AI systems also assist in diagnosing medical illnesses and prescribing treatment, examining equipment failures, evaluating loan applicants, and advising students about which courses to take (A. C. Chang, 2012). Computer scientists continue to develop computers that more closely approximate human thinking (Fleuret & others, 2011).

By the late 1950s the cognitive revolution was in full swing, and it peaked in the 1980s. The term *cognitive psychology* became a label for approaches that sought to explain observable behavior by investigating mental processes and structures that we cannot directly observe (Leahey, 2013; Robinson-Riegler & Robinson-Riegler, 2012; Sternberg, 2013a). Cognitive psychology is a broad field that includes the study of consciousness (Chapter 5), memory (Chapter 7), as well as cognitive neuroscience (Chapter 3). In this chapter we delve into three additional important aspects of cognition—thinking, intelligence, and language. We begin by examining the processes of problem solving, decision making, and critical thinking.

● **artificial intelligence (AI)** A scientific field that focuses on creating machines capable of performing activities that require intelligence when they are done by people.

test yourself

1. On what did behaviorists believe that psychology should properly focus?
2. What technological development gave psychologists a new way to look at the human mind?
3. How is the human mind superior to computers?

● **thinking** The process of manipulating information mentally by forming concepts, solving problems, making decisions, and reflecting critically or creatively.

● **concepts** Mental categories that are used to group objects, events, and characteristics.

● **prototype model** A model emphasizing that when people evaluate whether a given item reflects a certain concept, they compare the item with the most typical item(s) in that category and look for a "family resemblance" with that item's properties.

2· THINKING

When you save a file you have completed on a computer, you hear a sound from inside, and you know the computer is processing the work you have just done. Unlike a computer, the brain does not make noise to let us know it is working. Rather, the brain's processing is the silent operation of thinking. Formally defined, **thinking** involves manipulating information mentally by forming concepts, solving problems, making decisions, and reflecting in a critical or creative manner.

In this section we probe the nature of concepts—the basic components of thinking. We then explore the cognitive processes of problem solving, reasoning, and decision making. We also examine two capacities related to enhanced problem solving: critical thinking and creativity.

Concepts

A fundamental aspect of thinking is the notion of concepts. **Concepts** are mental categories that are used to group objects, events, and characteristics. Humans have a special ability for creating categories to help us make sense of information in our world (Goldstone, Kersten, & Carvalho, 2013; Rips, Smith, & Medin, 2012). We know that apples and oranges are both fruits. We know that poodles and collies are both dogs and that cockroaches and ladybugs are both insects. These items differ from one another in various ways, and yet we recognize that they belong together because we have concepts for fruits, dogs, and insects.

Concepts are important for four reasons. First, concepts allow us to generalize. If we did not have concepts, each object and event in our world would be unique and brand new to us each time we encountered it. Second, concepts allow us to associate experiences and objects. Basketball, ice hockey, and track are sports. The concept *sport* gives us a way to compare these activities. Third, concepts aid memory by making it more efficient so that we do not have to reinvent the wheel each time we come across a piece of information. Imagine having to think about how to sit in a chair every time we find ourselves in front of one. Fourth, concepts provide clues about how to react to a particular object or experience. Perhaps you have had the experience of trying an exotic new cuisine and feeling puzzled as you consider the contents of your plate. If a friend tells you reassuringly, "That's food!" you know that given the concept *food,* it is okay to dig in.

Psychologists have developed a variety of ways to understand the structure and function of concepts. One of these is known as the prototype model. The **prototype model** emphasizes that when people evaluate whether a given item reflects a certain concept, they compare the item with the most typical item(s) in that category and look for a "family resemblance" with that item's properties. Birds generally fly, sing, and build nests, so we know that robins and sparrows are both birds. We recognize exceptions to these properties, however—we know that a penguin is still a bird even though it does not fly, sing, and build a nest. The prototype model maintains that people use characteristic properties to create a representation of the average or ideal member—the prototype—for each concept. Comparing individual cases to our mental prototypes may be a good way to decide quickly whether something fits a particular category. As we will see later in this chapter, concepts can have particularly negative effects when they are applied to *people* rather than to objects.

Although it has a ducklike bill and lays eggs, the platypus is nevertheless a mammal like the tiger, as platypus females produce milk with which they feed their young. The prototypical birdlike characteristics of the platypus can lead us to think mistakenly that the platypus is a bird. Its atypical properties place the platypus on the extreme of the concept mammal.

Problem Solving

Concepts tell us *what* we think about but not *why* we think (Patalano, Wengrovitz, & Sharpes, 2009). *Why* do we bother to engage in the mental effort of thinking? Consider Levi Hutchins, an ambitious young man who sought to wake up at 4 A.M. every morning. Levi had a specific goal—he wanted to beat the sun up every day. To solve this problem (and achieve his goal), he invented the alarm clock in 1787. **Problem solving** means finding an appropriate way to attain a goal when the goal is not readily available (Bassok & Novick, 2012; Leighton & Sternberg, 2013). Problem solving entails following several steps and overcoming mental obstacles.

● **problem solving** The mental process of finding an appropriate way to attain a goal when the goal is not readily available.

FOLLOWING THE STEPS IN PROBLEM SOLVING

Psychological research points to four steps in the problem-solving process.

1. Find and Frame Problems   Recognizing a problem is the first step toward a solution (Mayer, 2000). Finding and framing problems involves asking questions in creative ways and "seeing" what others do not.

The ability to recognize and frame a problem is difficult to learn. Furthermore, many real-world problems are ill defined or vague and have no clear-cut solutions (Schunk, 2012). The visionaries who developed the many inventions that influence our daily lives—such as the computer, telephone, and light bulb—all saw problems that everyone else was content to live with. Recognizing problems involves being aware of and open to experiences (two mental habits we will examine later). It also means listening carefully to that voice in your head that occasionally sighs, "There must be a better way."

2. Develop Good Problem-Solving Strategies   Once we find a problem and clearly define it, we need to develop strategies for solving it. Among the effective strategies are subgoals, algorithms, and heuristics.

Subgoals are intermediate goals or intermediate problems that we devise to put us in a better position for reaching a final goal or solution. Imagine that you are writing a paper for a psychology class. What are some subgoaling strategies for approaching this task? One might be locating the right books and research journals on your chosen topic. At the same time that you are searching for the right publications, you will likely benefit from establishing some subgoals within your time frame for completing the project. If the paper is due in two months, you might set a subgoal of a first draft of the paper two weeks before it is due, another subgoal of completing your reading for the paper one month before it is due, and still another subgoal of starting your library research tomorrow. Notice that in establishing the subgoals for meeting the deadline, you worked backward. Working backward in establishing subgoals is a good strategy. You first create the subgoal that is closest to the final goal and then work backward to the subgoal that is closest to the beginning of the problem-solving effort.

● **subgoals** Intermediate goals or intermediate problems devised to put the individual in a better position for reaching the final goal or solution.

Algorithms are strategies that guarantee a solution to a problem. Algorithms come in different forms, such as formulas, instructions, and the testing of all possible solutions (Liu & Er, 2012; Mandal & Sairam, 2012). We use algorithms in cooking (by following a recipe) and driving (by following directions to an address). What all of these strategies have in common is that they lead to a single answer: The right one.

● **algorithms** Strategies—including formulas, instructions, and the testing of all possible solutions—that guarantee a solution to a problem.

An algorithmic strategy might take a long time. Staring at a rack of letters during a game of Scrabble, for example, you might find yourself moving the tiles around and trying all possible combinations to make a high-scoring word. Instead of using an algorithm to solve your Scrabble problem, however, you might rely on some rules of thumb about words and language. You know that if you have a Q, you are going to need a U. If you have an X and a T, the T is probably not going to come right before the X. So, in this example, rather than using an algorithm, you are using some quick rules that provide possible solutions to the problem. These shortcuts are called heuristics.

Heuristics are shortcut strategies or guidelines that suggest a solution to a problem but do not guarantee an answer (Bednark & others, 2013; Marewski & Schooler, 2011). In the real world, we are more likely to solve the types of problems we face by heuristics than by algorithms. Heuristics help us to narrow down the possible solutions and to find one

● **heuristics** Shortcut strategies or guidelines that suggest a solution to a problem but do not guarantee an answer.

quickly that works. Heuristics are different from algorithms because they are fast, can lead to different answers to a given problem, and do not always lead to a clear right answer.

3. Evaluate Solutions Once we think we have solved a problem, we will not know how effective our solution is until we find out if it works. It helps to have in mind a clear criterion, or standard against which to judge the effectiveness of the solution. For example, what will your criterion be for judging the effectiveness of your solution to the assignment of writing a psychology paper? Will you judge your solution to be effective if you simply complete the paper? If you get an *A*? If the instructor says that it is one of the best papers a student ever turned in on the topic?

4. Rethink and Redefine Problems and Solutions over Time An important final step in problem solving is to rethink and redefine problems continually. Good problem solvers tend to be more motivated than the average person to improve on their past performances and to make original contributions. Can we make the computer faster and more powerful? Can we make the iPod Shuffle even smaller?

AN OBSTACLE TO PROBLEM SOLVING: BECOMING FIXATED

A key ingredient of being a good problem solver is to acknowledge that you do not know everything—that your strategies and conclusions are always open to revision. Optimal problem solving may require a certain amount of humility, or the ability to admit that you are not perfect and that there may be better ways to solve life's problems. It is easy to fall into the trap of becoming fixated on a particular strategy for solving a problem.

● fixation Using a prior strategy and failing to look at a problem from a fresh new perspective.

● functional fixedness Failing to solve a problem as a result of fixation on a thing's usual functions.

Fixation involves using a prior strategy and failing to look at a problem from a fresh new perspective. **Functional fixedness** occurs when individuals fail to solve a problem because they are fixated on a thing's usual functions. Imagine having to hammer a nail but lacking a hammer. What to do? The functionally fixed person is stuck. If you have ever used a shoe to hammer a nail, you have overcome functional fixedness to solve a problem.

An example of a problem that requires overcoming functional fixedness is the Maier string problem, depicted in Figure 8.2 (Maier, 1931). The problem is to figure out how to tie two strings together when you must stand in one spot and cannot reach both at the same time. It seems as though you are stuck. However, there is a pair of pliers on a table. Can you solve the problem?

The solution is to use the pliers as a weight, tying them to the end of one string (Figure 8.3). Swing this string back and forth like a pendulum and grasp the stationary

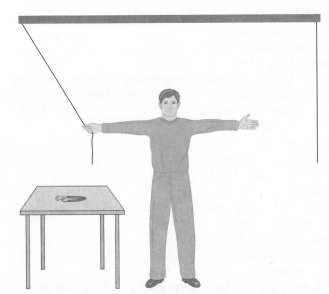

FIGURE 8.2 **Maier String Problem** How can you tie the two strings together if you cannot reach them both at the same time?

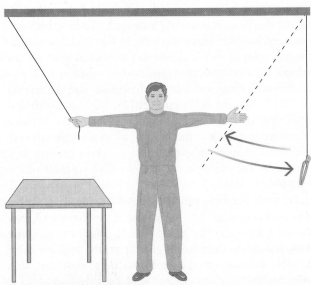

FIGURE 8.3 **Solution to the Maier String Problem** Use the pliers as a weight to create a pendulum motion that brings the second string closer.

psychological *inquiry*

The Candle Problem

How would you mount a candle on a wall so that it won't drip wax on a table or a floor while it is burning?

The Nine-Dot Problem

Take out a piece of paper and copy the arrangement of dots shown below. Without lifting your pencil, connect the dots using only four straight lines.

The Six-Matchstick Problem

Arrange six matchsticks of equal length to make four equilateral triangles, the sides of which are one matchstick long.

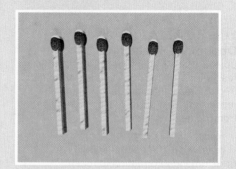

Thinking Outside the Box

The figure presents examples of how fixation impedes problem solving. These tasks help psychologists measure creative problem solving.

Each of the problems calls for a special kind of thinking—breaking out of your usual assumptions and looking at objects in a different way. Try your hand at solving each one and then answer the questions. Solutions to the problems are on page 285.

1. Which of the problems was most difficult to solve? Why?

2. Do you think these problems capture an important ability, or are they more like trick questions? Why?

3. Are these problems best solved by effortful thinking or by just going with your hunches? Explain.

string. Your past experience with pliers and your fixation on their usual function make this a difficult problem to solve. To do so, you need to find an unusual use for the pliers—in this case, as a weight to create a pendulum.

Effective problem solving often necessitates trying something new, or thinking outside the box—that is, exploring novel ways of approaching tasks and challenges and finding solutions. This way of thinking might require admitting that your past strategies were not ideal or do not readily translate to a particular situation. Students who are used to succeeding in high school by cramming for tests and relying on parental pressure to get homework done may find that in college these strategies are no longer viable ways to succeed.

Sometimes successful problem solving means being *cognitively flexible*—recognizing that options are available and adapting to the situation. To explore how fixation might play a role in your own problem solving, try out the questions in the Psychological Inquiry.

Reasoning and Decision Making

In addition to forming concepts and solving problems, thinking includes the higher-order mental processes of reasoning and decision making. These activities require rich connections among neurons and the ability to apply judgment. The end result of this type of thinking is an evaluation, a conclusion, or a decision.

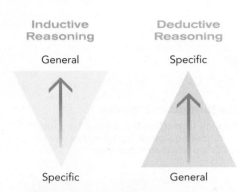

FIGURE 8.4 **Inductive and Deductive Reasoning** (*Left*) The upside-down pyramid represents inductive reasoning—going from specific to general. (*Right*) The right-side-up pyramid represents deductive reasoning—going from general to specific.

● **reasoning** The mental activity of transforming information to reach conclusions.

● **inductive reasoning** Reasoning from specific observations to make generalizations.

● **deductive reasoning** Reasoning from a general case that is known to be true to a specific instance.

● **decision making** The mental activity of evaluating alternatives and choosing among them.

REASONING

Reasoning is the mental activity of transforming information to reach a conclusion. This type of thinking uses *reason*—weighing arguments, applying rules of logic, and coming up with sound conclusions. Reasoning is involved in problem solving and decision making. It is also a skill closely tied to critical thinking (Hahn & Oaksford, 2012; Leighton & Sternberg, 2013). Reasoning can be either inductive or deductive (Figure 8.4).

Inductive reasoning involves reasoning from specific observations to make generalizations. You can think of inductive reasoning as "bottom-up processing" that we discussed in Chapter 4, when talking about perception. Inductive reasoning means starting with incoming information and then drawing conclusions. Inductive reasoning is an important way that we form beliefs about the world. For instance, having turned on your cell phone many times without having it explode, you have every reason to believe that it will not explode the next time you turn it on. From your prior experiences with the phone, you form the general belief that it is not likely to become a dangerous object.

A great deal of scientific knowledge is the product of inductive reasoning. We know, for instance, that men and women are genetically different, with women having two X chromosomes and men having an X and a Y chromosome, though no one has actually tested every single human being's chromosomes to verify this generalization. Inductive reasoning is always involved when we make generalizations. Psychological research is often inductive as well, studying a sample of participants in order to yield conclusions about the population from which the sample is drawn.

In contrast, **deductive reasoning** is reasoning from a general principle that we know to be true to a specific instance (Markovits, Forgues, & Brunet, 2012). Using deductive reasoning, we draw conclusions based on facts. For example, we might start with the general premise that all Texans love the Dallas Cowboys. Thus, if John is a Texan, we logically might surmise that John loves the Dallas Cowboys. Notice, however, that the logic of this deductive reasoning requires that the first statement be true; if all Texans do not love the Cowboys, John just might be a Philadelphia Eagles fan.

When psychologists and other scientists use theories to make predictions and then evaluate their predictions by making further observations, deductive reasoning is at work. When psychologists develop a hypothesis from a theory, they are using a form of deductive reasoning, because the hypothesis is a specific, logical extension of the general theory. If the theory is true, then the hypothesis will be true as well.

DECISION MAKING

Think of all the decisions, large and small, that you have to make in life. Should you major in biology, psychology, or business? Should you go to graduate school right after college or get a job first? Should you establish yourself in a career before settling down to have a family? Do you want fries with that? **Decision making** involves evaluating alternatives and choosing among them (LeBoeuf & Shafir, 2012).

Decision making differs from reasoning. Reasoning involves following established rules to reach a sound conclusion. In decision making, such rules may not exist, and we may not know the consequences of the decisions (Diederich & Busemeyer, 2013; Molet & others, 2012). Some of the information might be missing, and we might not trust all of the information we have. In this sense, decision making is less certain than reasoning. Making decisions means weighing information and coming to some conclusion that we feel will maximize our outcome: Yes, we will be able to see the movie from this row in the theater; no, we will not run that red light to get to class on time.

TWO SYSTEMS OF REASONING AND DECISION MAKING

Recall from Chapter 5 the idea of automatic and controlled processes in consciousness. Many psychologists similarly divide reasoning and decision making into two levels—one that is automatic (often referred to as *system 1*) and one that is controlled (*system 2*) (Evans & Stanovich, 2013). The automatic system involves processing that is rapid, heuristic, associative, and intuitive; it entails following one's hunches about a particular decision or problem (Halberstadt, 2010; Kahneman & Klein, 2009). Intuitive judgment means knowing that something feels right even if the reason why is unknown (Topolinski & Strack, 2009). In contrast, the controlled system is slower, effortful, and analytical. It involves conscious reflection. This is the kind of thinking that might be required to solve a difficult math problem, for example.

Although conscious effortful thinking is invaluable for solving many problems, research has shown that intuitive processing may also have an important role to play in decision making (Dijksterhuis & Nordgren, 2006; Halberstadt, 2010; Hicks & others, 2010; Morewedge & Kahneman, 2010). No doubt you have had the experience of consciously grappling with a problem and spending a good deal of time trying to solve it, with no success. Then you take a break to listen to music or go for a run, and suddenly the solution pops into your head.

Research by Ap Dijksterhuis and colleagues (2006) might ring a bell for you. In a series of laboratory studies, the experimenters presented participants with a number of pieces of information relevant to a decision, such as which apartment to pick out a variety of possibilities. After seeing the information, half of the participants were distracted while the other half had time to think consciously about the decision. The results showed that the distracted participants were more likely to pick the best option among the many choices. Similar results have been found for the accuracy of predictions about sporting events (Dijksterhuis & others, 2009; Halberstadt, 2010). Sometimes, following your gut feelings can be a good way to reach an optimal choice (Nordgren & Dijksterhuis, 2009; Topolinski & Strack, 2008).

The popular media sometimes portray intuitive hunches as sort of magical. However, these gut feelings do not emerge out of thin air. Rather, they are the product of learned associations such as those described in Chapter 6 (Kahneman & Klein, 2009; Unkelbach, 2007); of overlearned automatic processes like those explored in Chapter 5 (Halberstadt, 2010); and of implicit memory, as described in Chapter 7 (Cheng & Huang, 2011). Your gut feelings about the right answer on a test are certainly more likely to be accurate if you have put in the requisite hours of conscious effortful study. The accuracy of intuitive judgments, then, may depend on the hours of conscious effort, even if the judgment feels like a gut feeling.

Keep in mind that system 1 processes are as rapid as they are because they often rely on heuristics. As noted above, unlike algorithms, heuristics do not guarantee a right answer. Although following these quick rules of thumb can often lead to a satisfying decision, it can also lead to mistakes (Bednark & others, 2013; D. Griffin, 2012; Kahneman, Lovallo, & Sibony, 2011), as we now consider.

BIASES AND HEURISTICS

In many cases, our decision-making strategies are well adapted to deal with a variety of problems (Nisbett & Ross, 1980; Tversky & Kahneman, 1974). However, at times, reliance on heuristics can lead to biased decisions and outright errors. Here we look at a few biases and heuristic errors, summarized in Figure 8.5.

Confirmation bias is the tendency to search for and use information that supports our ideas rather than refutes them (N. W. Jackson, 2012; Mendel & others, 2011). Our decisions can also become further biased because we tend to seek out and listen to people whose views confirm our own while we avoid those with dissenting views.

Confirmation bias is sometimes also referred to as "myside bias," as it involves seeking out and believing information that supports one's own beliefs. For instance, during the 2012 U.S. presidential elections, many polling experts agreed that President Obama would win reelection. Nevertheless, pundits who supported former Governor Mitt Romney argued forcefully that the polls were wrong and were quite surprised by the outcome. Members of Romney's staff were described as "utterly 'shellshocked'" (Firestone, 2012). Avoiding confirmation bias means seeking out disconfirming information and applying the same rigorous analysis to both sides of an argument, even when the information seems to point in a direction we dread.

Hindsight bias is our tendency to report falsely, after the fact, that we accurately predicted an outcome. It is sometimes referred to as the "I knew it all along effect." With this

● **confirmation bias** The tendency to search for and use information that supports one's ideas rather than refutes them.

● **hindsight bias** The tendency to report falsely, after the fact, that one has accurately predicted an outcome.

Confirmation Bias

Description

Tendency to search for and use information that supports rather than refutes one's ideas

Example: A politician accepts news that supports his views and dismisses evidence that runs counter to these views.

Base Rate Neglect

Description

Tendency to ignore information about general principles in favor of very specific but vivid information

Example: You read a study showing that the majority of owners of a TV you are intending to buy are very satisfied with it, but you decide not to buy it when a friend tells you about a bad experience with that model.

Hindsight Bias

Description

Tendency to report falsely, after the fact, that one accurately predicted an outcome

Example: You read about the results of a particular psychological study and say, "I always knew that," though in fact you have little knowledge about the issues examined in the study.

Representativeness Heuristic

Description

Tendency to make judgments about group membership based on physical appearances or one's stereotype of a group rather than available base rate information

Example: The victim of a holdup, you view police photos of possible perpetrators. The suspects look very similar, but you choose the individual whose hair and clothing look dirtiest and most disheveled.

Availability Heuristic

Description

Prediction about the probability of an event based on the ease of recalling or imagining similar events

Example: A girl from an extended family in which no family member ever attended college tells her mother that she wants to be a doctor. Her mother cannot imagine her daughter in such a career and suggests that she become a home health-care aide.

FIGURE 8.5 Decision-Making Problems: Biases and Heuristics Biases and heuristics (rules of thumb) affect the quality of many of the decisions we make.

type of bias, people tend to view events that have happened as more predictable than they were and to represent themselves as being more accurate in their predictions than they actually were (Yopchick & Kim, 2012). For instance, at the end of a long baseball season, fans might say they knew all along that a particular team would win the World Series.

Although the hindsight bias might sound self-serving in the sense that it means remembering ourselves as having known more than we really did know, cognitive psychologists recognize that this bias may be based on new learning and on updating our knowledge about the world (Nestler, Blank, & Egloff, 2010; Pezzo, 2011). One reason for hindsight bias is that actual events are more vivid in our minds than all those things that failed to happen, an effect called the availability heuristic.

● **availability heuristic** A prediction about the probability of an event based on the ease of recalling or imagining similar events.

The **availability heuristic** refers to a prediction about the probability of an event based on the ease of recalling or imagining similar events (McDermott, 2009). Essentially, this heuristic means we think that events that are *cognitively available* are more likely to happen. Have you ever experienced a sudden fear of flying right after hearing about an airplane crash? Shocking events such as plane crashes stick in our minds, making it seem as if such disasters are common. The chance of dying in a plane crash in a given year, however, is tiny (1 in 400,000) compared to the chance of dying in a car accident (1 in 6,500). Because car accidents are less newsworthy, they are less likely to catch our attention and remain in our awareness.

The availability heuristic can reinforce generalizations about other people (Chou & Edge, 2012). Imagine, for instance, that Elvedina, a Mexican American girl, tells her mother that she wants to be a doctor. Her mother, who has never seen a Latina doctor, finds it hard to conceive of her daughter's pursuing such a career and might suggest that she try nursing instead.

● **base rate neglect** The tendency to ignore information about general principles in favor of very specific but vivid information.

Also reflective of the impact of vivid cases on decision making is **base rate neglect**, the tendency to ignore information about general principles in favor of very specific but vivid information. Let's say that as a prospective car buyer, you read *Consumer Reports* and find that a panel of experts rates a particular vehicle exceptionally well. You might still be swayed in your purchasing decision, however, if a friend tells you about her bad experiences with that car. Similarly, imagine being told that the average exam score for a test in your psychology class was 75 percent. If you were asked to guess a random student's score, 75 percent would be a good answer—the mean tells us the central tendency of any distribution. Yet if the student provided just a little bit of information, such as how many hours he studied, you might give too much weight to that specific information, losing sight of the valuable base rate information you have, namely, the class mean.

To experience another heuristic in action, consider the following example. Your psychology professor tells you she has assembled 100 men, all in their 20s, in the hallway outside your classroom. The group consists of 5 members of the U.S. National Swim Team and 95 engineers. She is going to randomly select one man and bring him into the room, and you can win $100 if you accurately guess whether he is an engineer or an Olympic-caliber swimmer. The man stands before you. Tall and lanky, he is wearing a tight T-shirt, jeans, and flip-flops. He has sunglasses perched on his clean-shaven head. Is he an engineer or an elite swimmer? If you guessed Olympic swimmer, you have just fallen victim to the representativeness heuristic.

The **representativeness heuristic** is the tendency to make judgments about group membership based on physical appearances or the match between a person and one's stereotype of a group rather than on available base rate information (Nilsson, Juslin, & Olsson, 2008). Essentially, a stereotype is the use of concepts to make generalizations about a group of people. We will examine stereotypes in some detail in Chapter 13. In the example just described, the base rate information tells you that, 95 times out of 100, the man in your class is likely to be an engineer. The optimal approach to winning the $100 is simply to shut your eyes and guess engineer, no matter what the man looks like.

The representativeness heuristic can be particularly damaging in the context of social judgments. Consider a scenario where a particular engineering corporation seeks to hire a new chief executive officer (CEO). Lori, a top-notch candidate with an undergraduate engineering degree and an MBA from an outstanding business school, applies. If there are few women in upper management at the firm, the company's board of directors might inaccurately view Lori as "not fitting" their view of the prototypical CEO—and miss the chance to hire an exceptional candidate.

Heuristics help us make decisions rapidly, but to solve problems accurately and make the best decisions, we must sometimes override these shortcuts and think more deeply, critically, and creatively. Now that you have learned about heuristics and their potential to lead to biased and inaccurate conclusions, you might be wondering if this learning will pay off. Will you be less likely to be influenced by such biases in the future? Some people seem more likely to use heuristics whereas others are more likely to apply careful thought to decisions, overriding the influence of these shortcuts. Intelligence, interest in thinking through complex problems carefully, and maintaining an open mind are associated with less susceptibility to the biases promoted by heuristics (Chiesi, Primi, & Morsanyi, 2011; Toplak, West, & Stanovich, 2011).

However, even very smart deep thinkers may not recognize their own vulnerability to cognitive biases, what is called the *bias blind spot*. To read about recent research addressing this issue, see the Intersection.

● **representativeness heuristic** The tendency to make judgments about group membership based on physical appearances or the match between a person and one's stereotype of a group rather than on available base rate information.

Thinking Critically and Creatively

Problem solving and decision making are basic cognitive processes that we use multiple times each day. Certain strategies lead to better solutions and choices than others, and some people are particularly good at these cognitive exercises. In this section we examine two skills associated with superior problem solving: critical thinking and creativity.

CRITICAL THINKING

Critical thinking means thinking reflectively and productively and evaluating the evidence. Recall from Chapter 1 that scientists are critical thinkers. Critical thinkers grasp

Cognitive Psychology and Personality: Do Sophisticated Thinkers Avoid the Bias Blind Spot?

The *bias blind spot* refers to the tendency to recognize when others engage in biased processing but fail to see the same biases when they influence our own thought processes (Pronin, 2007). The bias blind spot has been studied widely in terms of social judgments and the ways that we might miss our own biases in judging other people (Pronin & Kugler, 2007), demonstrating that we may be good at recognizing racial prejudice or sexism in other people but miss these biases in ourselves. Certainly, it makes sense that we would not want to think of ourselves as biased against others. But does this blind spot exist even for the kinds of cognitive biases we have discussed in this chapter? Furthermore, would people who are especially high in cognitive ability avoid this blind spot?

To address these questions, Richard West and his colleagues conducted two studies, one with 482 college students and the other with 265 nonstudent adults (West, Meserve, & Stanovich, 2012). All of the participants completed measures of cognitive ability and traits related to careful thinking. The investigators then gave the participants information about a number of different heuristics and biases, including base rate neglect and myside bias. After reading each description, the participants in both studies estimated the likelihood that they themselves would commit these mistakes, and then they made the same estimate for the average person. The results showed the bias blind spot: Participants felt that they were less likely to fall prey to these biases compared to average people. Further, those who scored the highest on the measures of cognitive ability in both groups of participants showed the largest bias blind spot.

Now, you might be thinking, maybe those participants were actually correct. After all, they are sophisticated thinkers. Perhaps they would be less biased by these heuristics.

Importantly, the researchers took this research one step further. At the end of the studies, participants were asked to complete a variety of tasks that involved the very heuristics that had been described for them at the beginning. The results showed that even those who had high scores on cognitive ability demonstrated the biases promoted by the heuristics, the very biases they had claimed they would not fall prey to, compared to others. More intelligent individuals were *not* less biased, and they exhibited little insight into their own biases.

> *How have heuristics led to errors in your own life?*

Why are these heuristics so powerful? The researchers suggest that these basic heuristics may be a formidable part of system 1 processing, one that is very difficult override (Evans & Stanovich, 2013; West, Meserve, & Stanovich, 2012).

This blind spot is thought to be rooted in two processes, both related to the desire to see ourselves in a positive light. The first is naive realism—the belief that one perceives and responds to the world objectively. Because we like to view ourselves as objective, we tend to miss our own biases.

The second factor in the bias blind spot is the tendency to rely too much on introspection as a way to judge ourselves. When we judge other people, we tend to focus on their behavior, but when we judge ourselves we focus instead on our thoughts. We might reflect on our thought processes and conclude that we did not engage in biased processing. Although it probably makes us feel good to think that we are less biased than others, these feelings may come at a cost, because we may be missing opportunities for insight (Chance & others, 2011).

These results tell us that no one is immune to biases and that even very bright people can be caught asleep at the wheel of information processing. No matter how smart we are, it is always wise to take a moment and think about not only our thoughts but our behaviors.

the deeper meaning of ideas, question assumptions, and decide for themselves what to believe or do (Bonney & Sternberg, 2011; Fairweather & Cramond, 2011). Critical thinking requires maintaining a sense of humility about what we know (and what we do not know). It means being motivated to see past the obvious.

Critical thinking is vital to effective problem solving. However, few schools teach students to think critically and to develop a deep understanding of concepts (Brooks & Brooks, 2001; McCombs, 2013). Instead, especially in light of pressures to maximize students' scores on standardized tests, teachers concentrate on getting students to give a single correct answer in an imitative way rather than on encouraging new ideas (Bransford & others, 2006). Further, many people are inclined to stay on the surface of problems rather than to stretch their minds. The cultivation of two mental habits is essential to critical thinking: mindfulness and open-mindedness.

Mindfulness means being alert and mentally present for one's everyday activities. The mindful person maintains an active awareness of the circumstances of his or her life (Roeser & Zelazo, 2012). When we are mindful, we are engaged mentally in what is happening to us. According to Ellen Langer (1997, 2000, 2005), mindfulness is a key to critical thinking. Langer distinguishes *mindful* behavior from *mindless* behaviors—automatic activities we perform without thought.

● **mindfulness** The state of being alert and mentally present for one's everyday activities.

In a classic study, Langer found that people (as many as 90 percent) would mindlessly give up their place in line for a copy machine when someone asked, "Can I go first? I need to make copies" as compared to when the same person simply said, "Can I go first?" (just 60 percent) (Langer, Blank, & Chanowitz, 1978). For the mindless persons in the study, even a completely meaningless justification—after all, everyone in line was there to make copies—was reason enough to step aside. A mindless person engages in automatic behavior without careful thinking. In contrast, a mindful person is engaged with the environment, responding in a thoughtful way to various experiences.

Open-mindedness means being receptive to other ways of looking at things. People often do not even know that there is another side to an issue or evidence contrary to what they believe. Simple openness to other viewpoints can help to keep individuals from jumping to conclusions. As Socrates once said, knowing what it is you do not know is the first step to true wisdom. *Actively open-minded thinking* refers to thinking that is flexible and open to questioning; it is not dogmatic or categorical (West, Toplak, & Stanovich, 2008). Individuals who engage in active open-minded thinking tend to be less susceptible to biases in their conclusions (West, Meserve, & Stanovich, 2012).

● **open-mindedness** The state of being receptive to other ways of looking at things.

Being mindful and maintaining an open mind may be more difficult than the alternative of going through life on automatic pilot. Critical thinking is valuable, however, because it allows us to make better predictions about the future, to evaluate situations objectively, and to effect appropriate changes. In some sense, critical thinking requires courage. When we expose ourselves to a broad range of perspectives, we risk finding out that our assumptions might be wrong. When we engage our critical minds, we may discover problems, but we are also more likely to have opportunities to make positive changes.

CREATIVE THINKING

In addition to thinking critically, coming up with the best solution to a problem may involve thinking creatively. The word *creative* can apply to an activity or a person, and creativity as a process may be open even to people who do not think of themselves as creative. When we talk about **creativity** as a characteristic of a person, we are referring to the ability to think about something in novel and unusual ways and to devise unconventional solutions to problems (Kaufman & Sternberg, 2013).

● **creativity** The ability to think about something in novel and unusual ways and to devise unconventional solutions to problems.

We can look at the thinking of creative people in terms of divergent and convergent thinking. **Divergent thinking** produces many solutions to the same problem. **Convergent thinking** produces the single best solution to a problem. Perhaps you can see how these two types of thinking might work together in creativity. Divergent thinking occurs during *brainstorming,* which happens when a people openly throw out a range of possible solutions to a problem, even some that might seem crazy. Having a lot of possible solutions, however, still requires that they come up with the solution that is best. That is where convergent thinking comes in. Convergent thinking means taking all of those possibilities and finding the right one for the job. Convergent thinking is best when a problem has only one right answer.

● **divergent thinking** Thinking that produces many solutions to the same problem.

● **convergent thinking** Thinking that produces the single best solution to a problem.

CRITICAL CONTROVERSY

Is There a Link Between Creative Genius and Psychopathology?

In her book *The Insanity Hoax: Exposing the Myth of the Mad Genius,* Judith Schlesinger (2012) sharply criticizes the idea that creative geniuses are prone to psychological disorders. Among other things, she points out that research based on relatively small samples should not be used to paint creative people with broad strokes.

According to Schlesinger, the notion that there is an association between creativity and psychological disorders is, itself, the result of a particular cognitive bias called an *illusory correlation.* An illusory correlation refers to the tendency for two vivid stimuli, when they occur together, to become linked erroneously in memory. Highly creative individuals are unusual, and so are those with psychological disorders. When we hear about these two things co-occurring in the same person, we conclude that they are related to each other.

For example, when we think of an outstanding jazz artist, like Billie Holiday, we might note that she was an amazingly talented woman, but she was also a troubled drug addict who died too young at just 44. We might conclude that jazz genius is associated with psychological problems. But, how would that conclusion fit with the life of jazz great Dave Brubeck who died in 2012, just a day shy of his 92nd birthday, survived by his wife of 70 years?

Schlesinger points out that the notion that creative geniuses suffer for that genius is essentially a stereotype. She argues that creativity does not imply torment but rather is a source of joy. Supporting Schlesinger's argument are studies showing that, in fact, severe psychological disorders are associated with *less* creativity (Ghadirian, Gregoire, & Kosmidis, 2001; Rybakowski &

Klonowska, 2011) and that creativity itself is associated with enhanced psychological well-being (Park, Peterson, & Seligman, 2004; Ryan & Deci, 2000).

Still, other scholars have suggested that there may be a (small) kernel of truth to the stereotype. Both creative genius and psychological disorders are, of course, very complex human experiences. These experiences may share some features (Eysenck, 1995).

For example, both creative genius and psychological disorders are related to looking at the world in unconventional ways (DeYoung, Grazioplene, & Peterson, 2012). Creative geniuses pay attention to things that others take for granted, noticing things that others miss. The creative genius may recognize the relevance of information that someone else finds irrelevant. Similarly, some psychological disorders include the tendency to see things differently and to ascribe relevance to information that others dismiss. For these individuals, though, these insights are not rooted in reality and may often feel confusing rather than inspiring. So, high levels of intellectual or creative ability may be linked to unconventional ways of seeing the world, which are, paradoxically, also symptomatic of some psychological disorders (DeYoung, Grazioplene, & Peterson, 2012).

Consider too the motivation required to be a creative genius—not simply to see what others do not, but to pursue one's passions, sometimes in the face of enormous obstacles. Pursuing one's goals so doggedly can come at a price. Those who are motivated by obsessive passion may, essentially, forget their other life goals (Bélanger & others, 2013). So, if you are the spouse of a creative genius who is motivated in this single-minded way, you might expect him or her to miss your birthday or anniversary every now and then. One review of the literature on scientific geniuses concluded that, in general, they were, "autonomous, introverted, open to new experiences, norm-doubting, self-confident, self-accepting, driven, ambitious, dominant, hostile, and impulsive" (Feist, 1998, p. 299). As eminent psychologist Dean Simonton noted, creative geniuses "may not be the kinds of folks you would prefer as lovers, friends, in-laws, co-workers, or neighbors" (2010, p. 218).

Finally, sometimes the world can be less than kind to individuals whose insights challenge what everyone knows. Galileo, the Italian physicist, saw the world for what it was, a planet in a solar system, revolving around the sun. Being right about this aspect of the world did not make his life any easier.

WHAT DO YOU THINK

- Who is the most creative person you know? How would you describe his or her psychological health?

- If genius is not linked to psychological disorders, what are some factors that might promote the belief that it is?

- Do you think that society places too much or too little emphasis on creative achievement and why?

Individuals who think creatively also show the following characteristics (Perkins, 1994):

- *Flexibility and playful thinking:* Creative thinkers are flexible and play with problems. This trait gives rise to the paradox that, although creativity takes hard work, the work goes more smoothly if it is taken lightly. In a way, humor greases the wheels of creativity (Goleman, Kaufman, & Ray, 1993). When you are joking around, you are more likely to consider any possibility and to ignore the inner censor who can condemn your ideas as off base.

- *Inner motivation:* Creative people often are motivated by the joy of creating. They tend to be less motivated by grades, money, or favorable feedback from others. Thus, creative people are inspired more internally than externally (Hennessey, 2011).

- *Willingness to face risk:* Creative people make more mistakes than their less imaginative counterparts because they come up with more ideas and more possibilities. They win some; they lose some. Creative thinkers know that being wrong is not a failure—it simply means that they have discovered that one possible solution does not work.

- *Objective evaluation of work:* Most creative thinkers strive to evaluate their work objectively. They may use established criteria to make judgments or rely on the judgments of respected, trusted others. In this manner, they can determine whether further creative thinking will improve their work.

So far we have explored creativity as a positive force in human life. However, history is filled with examples of creative geniuses who suffered from psychological disorders. From painters (Vincent van Gogh) to authors (William Faulkner) to gifted musicians (Amy Winehouse), it seems that creative geniuses tend to be tortured, psychologically. Some scholars have suggested that there is, in fact, a link between creativity and psychological disorders (Andreason, 1987; Jamison, 2009; Ludwig, 1995), but others strongly disagree. To read about this provocative topic, see the Critical Controversy on page 266.

3· INTELLIGENCE

Like *creative,* the word *intelligent* can apply to a behavior or a person. We might say that someone who decides to quit smoking has made an intelligent choice. When we apply the word to a person, however, defining *intelligent* can be trickier.

Cultures vary in the ways they define intelligence (Zhang & Sternberg, 2013). Most non-Latino White Americans think of intelligence in terms of reasoning and thinking skills, but people in Kenya consider responsible participation in family and social life an integral part of intelligence. An intelligent person in Uganda is someone who knows what to do and follows through with appropriate action. Intelligence to the Iatmul people of Papua New Guinea involves the ability to remember the names of 10,000 to 20,000 clans. The residents of the widely dispersed Caroline Islands incorporate the talent of navigating by the stars into their definition of intelligence (Figure 8.6).

In the United States, we generally define **intelligence** as an all-purpose ability to do well on cognitive tasks, to solve problems, and to learn from experience. Consider the ways we have described thinking—as problem solving, reasoning, decision making, critical analysis, and creativity. Intelligence refers to *how well* a person is able to perform these various cognitive activities.

The idea that intelligence captures a common general ability that is reflected in performance on various cognitive tests was introduced in 1904 by Charles Spearman. Spearman noted that schoolchildren who did well in math also did well in reading, and he came up with the idea that intelligence is a general ability, which he called *g.* This view of intelligence suggests that general intelligence underlies performance in a variety of areas, whether it is mathematics, verbal ability, or abstract reasoning. Spearman's *g* essentially assumes that the intelligent person is a jack-of-all-cognitive-trades.

test yourself

1. What are four reasons why concepts are important?
2. Name and explain the key steps in solving a problem.
3. Name at least two biases and two heuristics that affect the quality of our decisions, and give an example of each.

● **intelligence** All-purpose ability to do well on cognitive tasks, to solve problems, and to learn from experience.

FIGURE 8.6 **Iatmul and Caroline Island Intelligence** The intelligence of the Iatmul people of Papua New Guinea involves the ability to remember the names of many clans. For the residents of the 680 Caroline Islands in the Pacific Ocean east of the Philippines, intelligence includes the ability to navigate by the stars.

Measuring Intelligence

Psychologists measure intelligence using tests that produce a score known as the person's *intelligence quotient* (*IQ*). To understand how IQ is derived and what it means, let's first examine the criteria for a good intelligence test: validity, reliability, and standardization.

In the realm of testing, **validity** refers to the extent to which a test measures what it is intended to measure. If a test is supposed to measure intelligence, then it should measure intelligence, not some other characteristic, such as anxiety. One of the most important indicators of validity is the degree to which it predicts an individual's performance when that performance is assessed by *other measures*, or criteria, of the attribute (Neukrug & Fawcett, 2010). For example, if an intelligence test is valid, we might expect it to predict other variables, such as grades in school or work performance. When the scores on a measure relate to important outcomes, we say the test has high *criterion validity*.

Reliability is the extent to which a test yields a consistent, reproducible measure of performance. That is, a reliable test is one that produces the same score over time and repeated testing. Reliability and validity are related, but they are not the same thing. If we think that the characteristic a test measures is stable, then for a test of that characteristic to be valid, it must be reliable. However, a test can be quite reliable but not valid. A person can get the same score on a test, over and over, and yet those scores may wrong, each and every time. Imagine that someone proposes that eye color is a good measure of intelligence. Certainly, a person's eye color is not likely to change so this measure will be very reliable. The question for validity, though, is whether eye color bears any relationship to intelligence. It does not. So, we have a reliable measure that is not valid. To keep these important terms clear, remember that *reliability* refers only to the stability of scores on a test over time. *Validity,* in contrast, refers to the extent to which a scale measures what it purports to measure.

Good intelligence tests are not only reliable and valid but also standardized (Salvia, Ysseldyke, & Bolt, 2010). **Standardization** involves developing uniform procedures for administering and scoring a test, as well as creating *norms,* or performance standards, for the test. Uniform testing procedures require that the testing environment be as similar as possible for all individuals. Norms are created by giving the test to a large group of people who are representative of the population for whom the test is intended. Norms tell us which scores are considered high, low, or average. Many tests of intelligence are designed for individuals from diverse groups. So that the tests are applicable to such different groups, they may have different norms for individuals of different ages, socioeconomic statuses, and ethnic groups (Urbina, 2011). Figure 8.7 summarizes the criteria for test construction and evaluation.

● **validity** The extent to which a test measures what it is intended to measure.

● **reliability** The extent to which a test yields a consistent, reproducible measure of performance.

● **standardization** The development of uniform procedures for administering and scoring a test, and the creation of norms (performance standards) for the test.

Validity

Does the test measure what it purports to measure?

Reliability

Is test performance consistent?

Standardization

Are uniform procedures for administering and scoring the test used?

FIGURE 8.7 **Test Construction and Evaluation** Tests are a tool for measuring important abilities such as intelligence. Good tests show high reliability and validity and are standardized so that people's scores can be compared.

IQ TESTS

In 1904, the French Ministry of Education asked psychologist Alfred Binet to devise a method that would determine which students did not learn effectively from regular classroom instruction. School officials wanted to reduce overcrowding by placing such students in special schools. Binet and a student (Theophile Simon) developed an intelligence test to meet this request. Test items ranged from the ability to touch one's nose or ear on command to the ability to draw designs from memory and to define abstract concepts. To measure intelligence, Binet came up with the idea of comparing a person's mental abilities to the mental abilities that are typical for a particular age group.

Binet developed the concept of **mental age (MA),** which is an individual's level of mental development relative to that of others. Binet reasoned that, because cognitive ability increases with age, we might expect a child with an intellectual disability to perform like a normally developing child *of a younger age.* To think about a person's level of intelligence, then, we might compare the person's mental age (MA) to his or her chronological age (CA), or age from birth. A very bright child has an MA considerably above CA; a less bright child has an MA considerably below CA.

The German psychologist William Stern devised the term **intelligence quotient (IQ)** in 1912. IQ consists of an individual's mental age divided by chronological age multiplied by 100:

$$IQ = (MA/CA) \times 100$$

If mental age is the same as chronological age, then the individual's IQ is 100 (average); if mental age is above chronological age, the IQ is more than 100 (above average); if mental age is below chronological age, the IQ is less than 100 (below average). For example, a 6-year-old child with a mental age of 8 has an IQ of 133, whereas a 6-year-old child with a mental age of 5 has an IQ of 83.

In childhood, mental age increases as the child ages, but once the child reaches about age 16, the concept of mental age loses its meaning. That is why many experts today prefer to examine IQ scores in terms of how unusual a person's score is when compared to the scores of other adults. For this purpose, researchers and testers use standardized norms that they have identified in the many people who have been tested.

In fact, over the years, the Binet test has been given to thousands of children and adults of different ages selected at random from different parts of the United States. Now called the *Stanford-Binet* (the name reflects the fact that the revisions were completed at Stanford University), it continues to be one of the most widely used individual tests of intelligence. Individuals from the age of 2 through adulthood take the current Stanford-Binet test. It includes a wide variety of items, some requiring verbal responses, others nonverbal responses. For example, items that characterize a 6-year-old's performance on the test include the verbal ability to define at least six words, such as *orange* and *envelope,* and the nonverbal ability to trace a path through a maze. Items that reflect the average adult's intelligence include defining words such as *disproportionate* and *regard,* explaining a proverb, and comparing idleness and laziness.

Currently, there are a number of intelligence tests in wide usage. The most popular of these are the Wechsler Adult Intelligence Scale (the WAIS) and the Wechsler Intelligence Scale for Children (the WISC). Originally developed by David Wechsler (1939), these scales provide scores on various subscales rather than a single IQ score. In addition, items were designed specifically for adults or for children.

An important feature of intelligence tests is their distribution. The *distribution* refers to the frequencies of various scores on a scale—basically, how many people receive each of the possible scores. Scores on intelligence tests approximate a normal distribution. A **normal distribution** is a symmetrical, bell-shaped curve, with a majority of the scores falling in the middle of the possible range and few scores appearing toward the extremes of the range. To master the important idea of the normal distribution, complete the Psychological Inquiry on page 270.

Alfred Binet (1857–1911) Binet Constructed the first intelligence test after being asked to create a measure to determine which children would benefit from instruction in France's schools.

● **mental age (MA)** An individual's level of mental development relative to that of others.

● **intelligence quotient (IQ)** An individual's mental age divided by chronological age multiplied by 100.

● **normal distribution** A symmetrical, bell-shaped curve, with a majority of the scores falling in the middle of the possible range and few scores appearing toward the extremes of the range.

psychological *inquiry*

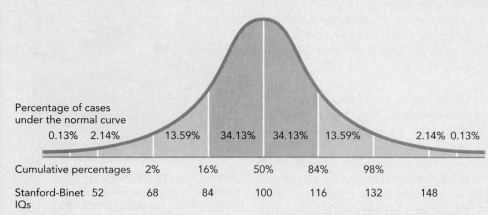

Percentage of cases
under the normal curve

0.13%   2.14%   13.59%   34.13%   34.13%   13.59%   2.14% 0.13%

Cumulative percentages	2%		16%		50%		84%		98%		
Stanford-Binet IQs	52	68		84		100		116		132	148

The Normal Curve

This figure shows the normal curve and Stanford-Binet IQ scores. The distribution of IQ scores approximates a normal distribution. Answer the following questions, keeping in mind that the area under the curve represents the number of people who obtain a given score on the test.

1. Do most people fall in the low, medium, or high range? How do you know?

2. If someone scored a 132 on the test, how many people scored below that person's score?

3. What is the mean or average on the IQ test? Where does the mean fall on the bell-shaped curve?

4. Notice that in a normal distribution, extremely high and extremely low scores are rare. What other human characteristics might follow this pattern?

CULTURAL BIAS IN TESTING

Many early intelligence tests were culturally biased, favoring people who were from urban rather than rural environments, of middle rather than low socioeconomic status, and non-Latino White rather than African American (Provenzo, 2002). For example, a question on an early test asked what one should do if one finds a 3-year-old child in the street. The correct answer was "call the police." However, children from inner-city families who perceive the police as scary are unlikely to choose this answer. Similarly, children from rural areas might not choose this answer if there is no police force nearby. Such questions clearly do not measure the knowledge necessary to adapt to one's environment or to be "intelligent" in an inner-city or a rural neighborhood (Scarr, 1984). In addition, members of minority groups may not speak English or may speak nonstandard English. Consequently, they may be at a disadvantage in trying to understand verbal questions that are framed in standard English, even if the content of the test is appropriate (Cathers-Shiffman & Thompson, 2007).

The experience of Gregory Ochoa illustrates the impact of cultural bias in intelligence tests. As a high school student, Gregory and his classmates took an IQ test. Looking at the test questions, Gregory understood only a few words because he did not speak English well and spoke Spanish at home. Several weeks later, Gregory was placed in a special class for intellectually disabled students. Many of the students in the class, it turns out, had last names such as Ramirez and Gonzales. Gregory lost interest in school, dropped out, and eventually joined the navy, where he took high school courses and earned enough credits to attend college when he was discharged. He graduated from San Jose City College as an honor student, continued his education, and became a professor of social work at the University of Washington in Seattle.

As a result of such cases, researchers have sought to develop tests that accurately reflect a person's intelligence, regardless of cultural background (Reynolds, Livingston, & Willson, 2006). **Culture-fair tests** are intelligence tests that are intended to be culturally unbiased. One type of culture-fair test includes questions that are

● **culture-fair tests** Intelligence tests that are intended to be culturally unbiased.

familiar to people from all socioeconomic and ethnic backgrounds. A second type contains no verbal questions. Figure 8.8 shows a sample question from the Raven Progressive Matrices Test. Even though tests such as the Raven are designed to be culture-fair, people with more education still score higher than do those with less education.

Why is it so hard to create culture-fair tests? Just as the definition of intelligence may vary by culture, most tests of intelligence reflect what is important to the dominant culture. If tests have time limits, the test will be biased against groups not concerned with time. If languages differ, the same words might have different meanings for different language groups. Even pictures can produce bias, because some cultures have less experience with drawings and photographs (Urbina, 2011). Because of such difficulties, Robert Sternberg and his colleagues conclude that there are no culture-fair tests, only *culture-reduced tests* (Sternberg, 2012a; Zhang & Sternberg, 2013).

Moreover, within the same culture, different groups can have different attitudes, values, and motivation, and these variations can affect their performance on intelligence tests (Ang & van Dyne, 2009; Sternberg, 2012a). Questions about railroads, furnaces, seasons of the year, distances between cities, and so on can be biased against groups who have less experience than others with these contexts. One explanation for the effects of education on IQ test scores is that education (and other environmental factors) may influence intelligence, a possibility to which we now turn.

Genetic and Environmental Influences on Intelligence

There is no doubt that genes influence intelligence, but understanding how and how much they do so has proved challenging (Chabris & others, 2012). Indeed, recently psychologists have come to recognize that we may not know as much as we thought we did about the influence of genes on intelligence, as a result of our growing understanding of genes themselves.

In Chapter 3 we described the concepts of genotype and phenotype. Genotype refers to an organism's genetic material. Phenotype refers to the actual characteristics the organism possesses. When we are talking about genetic influences on intelligence, we are interested in understanding how differences at the level of the genotype predict differences in the phenotype of intelligence.

For quite some time, scientists relied on a statistic called heritability to describe the extent to which the observable differences among people in a group (the phenotype) can be explained by the genetic differences of the group's members (the genotype). **Heritability** is the proportion of observable differences in a group that can be explained by differences in the genes of the group's members. For intelligence, that means that heritability tells us how much of the differences we observe in intelligence is attributable to differences in genes. Because heritability is a proportion, the highest degree of heritability is 100 percent. Research on heritability has typically involved comparing the similarity of the phenotypes of identical or monozygotic twins to that of fraternal or dizygotic twins. Assuming that identical twins share 100 percent of their genetic material, and fraternal twins 50 percent of theirs, scientists estimated the heritability of intelligence to be about 75 percent, reflecting a strong genetic influence (Neisser & others, 1996).

However, this conclusion, and others based on heritability estimates, has recently been called into question (Charney, 2012; Crusio, 2012). A key assumption of the heritability estimate, that twins share a specific amount of genetic material, is, it turns out, not completely accurate. Research suggests that the human genome possesses some degree of *plasticity*. Essentially, after conception, our genes can change. Identical twins might have identical DNA at the moment of conception, but DNA can move around prenatally (Xing & others, 2009) and postnatally, especially in the brain (Baillie & others, 2011).

Such findings have led some to call for heritability to be discarded as a measure of genetic influence on behaviors (Charney, 2012; Crusio, 2012). Other researchers have

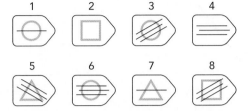

FIGURE 8.8   Sample Item from the Raven Progressive Matrices Test For this item, the respondent must choose which of the numbered figures would come next in the order. Can you explain why the right answer is number 6? SOURCE: Simulated item similar to those found in the *Raven's Progressive Matrices* (Standard, Sets A-E). Copyright © 1976, 1958, 1938 NCS Pearson, Inc. Reproduced with permission. All rights reserved. "Raven's Progressive Matrices" is a trademark, in the US and/or other countries, of Pearson Education, Inc. or its affiliate(s).

● **heritability** The proportion of observable differences in a group that can be explained by differences in the genes of the group's members.

suggested that these discoveries may simply help to explain some of the errors in heritability estimates (Battaglia, 2012); or that they do not justify complete dismissal of heritability studies (Miller, DeYoung, & McGue, 2012; Vilarroya, 2012); or that the frequency of genetic change is not so great as to call into question the validity of heritability estimates (MacDonald & LaFreniere, 2012). At the very least, we might be wise to consider that 75 percent heritability estimate for intelligence with some skepticism.

Even if we believe that 75 percent estimate to be a reasonably good indicator of the amount of variability in intelligence that is explained by genetics, there are some important points to keep in mind. First and most important, heritability is a statistic that provides information about a group, not a single individual (Sesardic, 2006). This means that finding out that heritability for intelligence is 75 percent tells us nothing at all about the source of an individual person's intelligence. We cannot dissect your intelligence and determine that you got 75 percent of it from your parents and 25 percent from your schooling. Heritability has no meaning when applied to a single case. Recall from Chapter 2 that group statistics do not apply in a single given case. That is, *statistics describe groups*, not individuals.

Certainly, heritability estimates can change over time and across different groups (Nisbett & others, 2012; Turkheimer & others, 2003). If a group of individuals lives in the same advantageous setting (with good nutrition, supportive parents, great schools, stable neighborhoods, and plenty of opportunities), heritability estimates for intelligence might be quite high, as this optimal environment allows genetic characteristics to flourish to their highest potential. However, if a group of individuals lives in a highly variable environment (with some individuals experiencing rich, nurturing environments full of opportunity and others experiencing less supportive contexts), genetic characteristics may be less predictive of differences in intelligence in that group, relative to environmental factors.

Finally, even if the heritability of a characteristic is very high, the environment still matters. Take height, for example. Heritability estimates suggest that more than 90 percent of the variation in height is explained by genetic variation. Generally speaking, humans continue to get taller and taller, however, and this trend demonstrates that environmental factors such as nutrition have an impact. Similarly, in the case of intelligence, most researchers agree that for most people, modifications in environment can change their IQ scores considerably (Esposito, Grigorenko, & Sternberg, 2012; Nisbett & others, 2012).

Enriching an environment can improve school achievement and develop crucial workplace skills. A research analysis by Richard Nisbett and his colleagues revealed a 12- to 18-point increase in IQ when children from low-income backgrounds were adopted by parents from middle-income backgrounds (Nisbett & others, 2012). Although genetics may influence intellectual ability, environmental factors and opportunities make a difference (Nisbett, 2009; Sternberg, 2013a).

Researchers are increasingly interested in manipulating the early environment of children who are at risk for impoverished intelligence (Phillips & Lowenstein, 2011). Programs that educate parents to be more sensitive caregivers and that train them to be better teachers can make a difference in a child's intellectual development, as can support services such as high-quality child-care programs (Morrison, 2012).

One effect of education on intelligence is evident in rapidly increasing IQ test scores around the world, a phenomenon called the *Flynn effect* (Flynn, 1999, 2006, 2013). Scores on these tests have been rising so fast that a high percentage of people regarded as having average intelligence in 1932 would be regarded as having below-average intelligence today (Figure 8.9). Because the increase has taken place in a relatively short period of time, it cannot be due to heredity but rather may be due to rising levels of education attained by a much greater percentage of the world's population or to other environmental factors, such as the explosion of information to which people are now exposed.

Environmental influences are complex (Grusec, 2011; R. H. Wright & others, 2012). Growing up with all the advantages does not guarantee success. Children from wealthy families may have easy access to excellent schools, books, tutors, and travel, but they

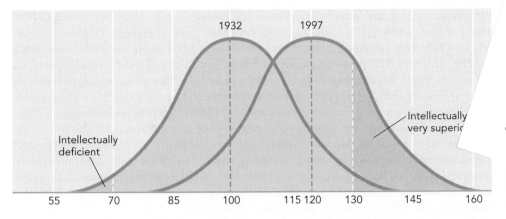

Intellectually deficient

1932 1997

Intellectually very superi[...]

55   70   85   100   115 120   130   145   160

[...]
the "very [...]
suggest that IQ [...]
norms to continue to be [...]

may take such opportunities for granted and not be motivated to learn and to achieve. Alternatively, poor or disadvantaged children may be highly motivated and successful. Caregivers who themselves lacked educational opportunities may instill a strong sense of the value of learning and achievement in their children.

Let's return to the idea that the word *intelligent* describes not only people but also behaviors. Mastering skills, thinking about life actively, and making decisions thoughtfully are intelligent behaviors in which people can engage regardless of the numerical intelligence quotient on their permanent record. Intelligent behavior is always an option, no matter one's IQ score. As we saw in Chapter 6, our beliefs about cognitive ability, specifically whether it is fixed or changeable, have important implications for the goals we set for learning new skills (Dweck, 2006, 2013). We never know what we might accomplish if we try, and no one is doomed because of a number, no matter how powerful that number may seem.

Extremes of Intelligence

Intelligence, then, appears to emerge from a combination of genetic heritage and environmental factors. As we have seen, scores on IQ tests generally conform to the bell-shaped normal curve. We now examine the implications of falling on either tail of that curve.

GIFTEDNESS

There are people whose abilities and accomplishments outshine those of others—the *A+* student, the star athlete, the natural musician. People who are **gifted** have high intelligence (an IQ of 130 or higher) and/or superior talent in a particular area. Lewis Terman (1925) conducted a study of 1,500 children whose Stanford-Binet IQs averaged 150, a score that placed them in the top 1 percent. A popular myth is that gifted children are maladjusted, but Terman found that his participants ("Termites") were not only academically gifted but also socially well adjusted. Many of them later became successful doctors, lawyers, professors, and scientists. Do gifted children grow into gifted and highly creative adults? In Terman's research, gifted children typically did become experts in a well-established domain, such as medicine, law, or business; but the Termites did not become major creators or innovators (Winner, 2000, 2006).

In light of the sweeping social and economic changes of the digital age, are today's gifted children perhaps better able than the Termites to use their

● **gifted** Possessing high intelligence (an IQ of 130 or higher) and/or superior talent in a particular area.

gifts in innovative and important ways in adulthood? The results from a longitudinal study of profoundly gifted children begun by Julian Stanley at Johns Hopkins University in 1971 seem to indicate just that. The Study of Mathematically Precocious Youth (SMPY) includes 320 participants whom researchers recruited before age 13 based on IQ scores, with the group's average IQ estimated at 180. This group is said to represent the top 1 in 10,000 IQ scores (Lubinski & others, 2001).

Following up on these individuals in their 20s, David Lubinski and colleagues (2006) found that these strikingly gifted young people were doing remarkable things. At age 23, they were pursuing doctoral degrees at a rate 50 times higher than the average. Some reported achievements such as receiving creative writing awards, creating original art and music, publishing in scholarly journals, and developing commercially viable software and video games. Thus, unlike the Termites, this group has been quite creative and innovative (Wai, Lubinski, & Benbow, 2005).

Interestingly, the Flynn effect appears to apply to even those with very high IQs. Studies of individuals at the very highest level of intelligence show that their scores are also getting higher (Wai, Putallaz, & Makel, 2012). For this reason, newer studies similar to the SMPY research have begun to incorporate cognitive ability measures that have more "headroom." In other words, the tests are even more challenging (often designed for older youth or adults) to allow extraordinarily intelligent children to show their stuff (Wai & others, 2010).

Like intelligence itself, giftedness is likely a product of both heredity and environment. Experts who study giftedness point out that gifted individuals recall showing signs of high ability in a particular area at a very young age, prior to or at the beginning of formal training (Howe & others, 1995). This result suggests the importance of innate ability in giftedness. However, researchers also have found that the individuals who enjoy world-class status in the arts, mathematics, science, and sports all report strong family support and years of training and practice (Bloom, 1985). Deliberate practice is an important characteristic of individuals who become experts in a particular domain (Ericsson & Moxley, 2012).

An increasing number of experts argue that typical U.S. classrooms often do not meet the educational needs of gifted children (Olszewski-Kubilius & Thomson, 2013). Some educators conclude that the problem of inadequate education of gifted adolescents has been compounded by the federal government's No Child Left Behind policy, which seeks to raise the achievement level of students who are not doing well in school at the expense of enriching the education of gifted children (Clark, 2008; Cloud, 2008). Ellen Winner (1996, 2006) recommends that children and adolescents who are not sufficiently challenged be allowed to attend advanced classes in their domain of exceptional ability, as did Bill Gates, Microsoft's founder, who took college math classes at 13, and famed cellist Yo-Yo Ma, who graduated from high school at 15 and then attended the Juilliard School of Music.

INTELLECTUAL DISABILITY

Just as some individuals are at the high extreme of intelligence, others are at the lower end. **Intellectual disability** (or **intellectual developmental disorder**) is a condition of limited mental ability that affects functioning in three domains:

- *Conceptual skills,* including language, reading, writing, math, reasoning, and memory
- *Social skills,* including empathy, social judgment, interpersonal communication, and the ability to make friends
- *Practical skills,* including self-management of personal care, job responsibilities, money management, recreation, and organizing school and work tasks

Assessment of capacities in these areas can be used to determine the amount of care the person requires for daily living—not as a function of IQ but as a gauge of the person's ability to negotiate life's challenges.

Intellectual disability may have an organic cause, or it may be cultural and social in origin (Hallahan, Kauffman, & Pullen, 2012). *Organic intellectual disability* is caused

● **intellectual disability or intellectual developmental disorder** A condition of limited mental ability that affects an individual's functioning in everyday life.

by a genetic disorder or brain damage; *organic* refers to the tissues or organs of the body, so there is some physical damage in organic retardation. Down syndrome, one form of organic intellectual disability, occurs when an extra chromosome is present in the individual's genetic makeup. Most people who suffer from organic retardation have an IQ between 0 and 50.

Cultural-familial intellectual disability is a mental deficit with no evidence of organic brain damage. Individuals with this type of disability have an IQ between 55 and 70. Psychologists suspect that such mental deficits result at least in part from growing up in a below-average intellectual environment. As children, individuals with this disability can be identified in school, where they often fail, need tangible rewards (candy rather than grades, for example), and are highly sensitive to what peers and adults expect of them (Vaughn, Bos, & Schumm, 2003). As adults, however, these individuals usually go unnoticed, perhaps because adult settings do not tax their cognitive skills as much. It may also be that the intelligence of such individuals increases as they move toward adulthood.

There are several classifications of intellectual disability (Hodapp & others, 2011). In one classification system, disability ranges from mild, to moderate, to severe or profound, according to the person's IQ (Heward, 2013). The large majority of individuals diagnosed with intellectual disability fall in the mild category. Most school systems still use this system. However, these categories, based on IQ ranges, are not perfect predictors of functioning. Indeed, it is not unusual to find clear *functional* differences between two people who have the same low IQ. For example, looking at two individuals with a similarly low IQ, we might find that one of them is married, employed, and involved in the community while the other requires constant supervision in an institution. Such differences in social competence have led psychologists to include deficits in adaptive behavior in their definition of intellectual disability (Turnbull & others, 2013).

A person with Down syndrome may never accomplish the amazing academic feats of gifted individuals. However, he or she may be capable of building close, warm relations with others, serving as an inspiration to loved ones, and bringing smiles into an otherwise gloomy day (Van Riper, 2007). Moreover, individuals with Down syndrome might possess different kinds of intelligence, even if they are low on general cognitive ability. The possibility that other intelligences exist alongside cognitive ability (or disability) has inspired some psychologists to suggest that we need more than one concept of intelligence.

Individuals with Down syndrome may excel in sensitivity toward others. The possibility that other strengths or intelligences coexist with cognitive ability (or disability) has led some psychologists to propose the need for expanding the concept of intelligence.

Theories of Multiple Intelligences

Is it more appropriate to think of an individual's intelligence as a general ability or as a number of specific abilities? Traditionally, most psychologists have viewed intelligence as a general, all-purpose problem-solving ability, termed *g* by Spearman (1904). Others have proposed that we think about different kinds of intelligence, such as *emotional intelligence,* the ability to perceive emotions in oneself and others accurately (Brackett, Rivers, & Salovey, 2011; Mayer & others, 2011). Robert Sternberg and Howard Gardner have developed influential theories presenting the viewpoint that there are *multiple intelligences.*

STERNBERG'S TRIARCHIC THEORY AND GARDNER'S MULTIPLE INTELLIGENCES

Robert J. Sternberg developed the **triarchic theory of intelligence,** which says that intelligence comes in multiple (specifically, three) forms (2011, 2012c, 2013a, 2013b). These forms are

- *Analytical intelligence:* The ability to analyze, judge, evaluate, compare, and contrast.
- *Creative intelligence:* The ability to create, design, invent, originate, and imagine.
- *Practical intelligence:* The ability to use, apply, implement, and put ideas into practice.

● **triarchic theory of intelligence** Sternberg's theory that intelligence comes in three forms: analytical, creative, and practical.

Howard Gardner suggests there are nine types of intelligence, or "frames of mind" (1983, 1993, 2002). These are described here, with examples of the types of vocations in which they are reflected as strengths (Campbell, Campbell, & Dickinson, 2004):

- *Verbal:* The ability to think in words and use language to express meaning. Occupations: author, journalist, speaker.
- *Mathematical:* The ability to carry out mathematical operations. Occupations: scientist, engineer, accountant.
- *Spatial:* The ability to think three-dimensionally. Occupations: architect, artist, sailor.
- *Bodily-kinesthetic:* The ability to manipulate objects and to be physically adept. Occupations: surgeon, craftsperson, dancer, athlete.
- *Musical:* The ability to be sensitive to pitch, melody, rhythm, and tone. Occupations: composer, musician.
- *Interpersonal:* The ability to understand and interact effectively with others. Occupations: teacher, mental health professional.
- *Intrapersonal:* The ability to understand oneself. Occupations: theologian, psychologist.
- *Naturalist:* The ability to observe patterns in nature and understand natural and human-made systems. Occupations: farmer, botanist, ecologist, landscaper.
- *Existentialist:* The ability to grapple with the big questions of human existence, such as the meaning of life and death, with special sensitivity to issues of spirituality. Gardner has not identified an occupation for existential intelligence, but one career path would likely be philosopher.

According to Gardner, everyone has all of these intelligences to varying degrees. As a result, we prefer to learn and process information in different ways. People learn best when they can do so in a way that uses their stronger intelligences.

EVALUATING THE MULTIPLE-INTELLIGENCES APPROACHES

Sternberg's and Gardner's approaches have stimulated teachers to think broadly about what makes up children's competencies. They have motivated educators to develop programs that instruct students in multiple domains. These theories have also contributed to interest in assessing intelligence and classroom learning in innovative ways, such as by evaluating student portfolios (Woolfolk, 2013).

Doubts about multiple intelligences persist, however. A number of psychologists think that the proponents of multiple intelligences have taken the concept of specific intelligences too far (Reeve & Charles, 2008). Some critics argue that a research base to support the three intelligences of Sternberg or the nine intelligences of Gardner has not yet emerged. One expert on intelligence, Nathan Brody (2007), observes that people who excel at one type of intellectual task are likely to excel at others. Thus, individuals who do well at memorizing lists of digits are also likely to be good at solving verbal problems and spatial layout problems. Other critics ask, if musical skill, for example, reflects a distinct type of intelligence, why not also label the skills of outstanding chess players, prizefighters, painters, and poets as types of intelligence? In sum, controversy still characterizes whether it is more accurate to conceptualize intelligence as a general ability, specific abilities, or both (Brody, 2007; Nisbett & others, 2012; Sternberg, 2013a, 2013b).

One question that remains is whether and how we can enhance our cognitive abilities. Susanne Jaeggi and colleagues (2008) found that undertaking complex cognitive tasks led to enhanced reasoning ability. In this work, the participants engaged in a complicated memory game similar to the card game Concentration, in which all the cards are placed face down and players have to remember where each one is in order to find matches. After training for a half hour a day for several days, participants increased their scores on reasoning ability, compared to a control group who did not complete the training. The more the participants trained, the smarter they got. Researchers have begun to explore the neural correlates of these changes in cognitive ability (Buschkuehl, Jaeggi, & Jonides, 2012).

One aspect of this study is particularly interesting. The researchers designed the memory game so that as participants mastered it, it became harder and harder. In short, getting smarter is not just a matter of mastering a skill and then resting on our laurels. Reasoning ability can increase, but for that to happen, we have to keep challenging ourselves to think about things in increasingly new, and sometimes difficult, ways.

Our examination of cognitive abilities has highlighted how individuals differ in the quality of their thinking and how thoughts may differ from one another. Some thoughts reflect critical thinking, creativity, or intelligence. Other thoughts are perhaps less inspired. One thing thoughts have in common is that they usually involve language. Even when we talk to ourselves, we do so with words. The central role of language in cognitive activity is the topic to which we now turn.

test yourself

1. With respect to testing, what do validity, reliability, and standardization mean?
2. What two terms respectively define individuals at the high end and at the low end of intelligence?
3. How does Spearman's *g* compare to multiple-intelligences approaches?

4· LANGUAGE

Language is a form of communication—whether spoken, written, or signed—that is based on a system of symbols. We need language to speak with others, listen to others, read, and write (Butcher & Kintsch, 2013; Clifton & others, 2013; Rayner, Pollatsek, & Schotter, 2013). In this section we first examine the fundamental characteristics of language and then trace the links between language and cognition.

● **language** A form of communication—whether spoken, written, or signed—that is based on a system of symbols.

The Basic Properties of Language

All human languages have *infinite generativity,* the ability to produce an endless number of meaningful sentences. This superb flexibility comes from five basic rule systems:

- **Phonology:** a language's sound system. Language is made up of basic sounds, or *phonemes.* Phonological rules ensure that certain sound sequences occur (for example, *sp, ba,* or *ar*) and others do not (for example, *zx* or *qp*) (Kuhl & Demasio, 2012). A good example of a phoneme in the English language is /*k*/, the sound represented by the letter *k* in the word *ski* and the letter *c* in the word *cat.* Although the /*k*/ sound is slightly different in these two words, the /*k*/ sound is described as a single phoneme in English.

● **phonology** A language's sound system.

- **Morphology:** a language's rules for word formation. Every word in the English language is made up of one or more morphemes. A morpheme is the smallest unit of language that carries meaning. Some words consist of a single morpheme—for example, *help.* Others are made up of more than one; for example, *helper* has two morphemes, *help + er.* The morpheme *-er* means "one who"—in this case, "one who helps." As you can see, not all morphemes are words; for example, *pre-, -tion,* and *-ing* are morphemes. Just as the rules that govern phonemes ensure that certain sound sequences occur, the rules that govern morphemes ensure that certain strings of sounds occur in particular sequences (D. Brown, 2013; Croft, 2012).

● **morphology** A language's rules for word formation.

- **Syntax:** a language's rules for combining words to form acceptable phrases and sentences (de Villiers & de Villiers, 2013; Dixon, 2012). If someone says, "John kissed Emily" or "Emily was kissed by John," you know who did the kissing and who was kissed in each case because you share that person's understanding of sentence structure. You also understand that the sentence "You didn't stay, did you?" is a grammatical sentence but that "You didn't stay, didn't you?" is unacceptable.

● **syntax** A language's rules for combining words to form acceptable phrases and sentences.

- **Semantics:** the meaning of words and sentences in a particular language. Every word has a unique set of semantic features (Pan & Uccelli, 2009). *Girl* and *woman,* for example, share many semantic features (for instance, both signify a female human being), but they differ semantically in regard to age. Words have semantic restrictions on how they can be used in sentences. The sentence "The bicycle talked the boy into buying a candy bar" is syntactically correct but semantically incorrect. The sentence violates our semantic knowledge that bicycles do not talk.

● **semantics** The meaning of words and sentences in a particular language.

● **pragmatics** The useful character of language and the ability of language to communicate even more meaning than is verbalized.

■ **Pragmatics:** the useful character of language and the ability of language to communicate even more meaning than is said (Al-Wer, 2014; Bryant, 2012). The pragmatic aspect of language allows us to use words to get the things we want. If you ever find yourself in a country in which you know only a little of the language, you will certainly take advantage of pragmatics. Wandering the streets of, say, Madrid, you might approach a stranger and ask, simply, "Autobus?" (the Spanish word for *bus*). You know that given your inflection and perhaps your desperate facial expression, the person will understand that you are looking for the bus stop.

With this basic understanding of language in place, we can examine the connections between language and cognition.

Whorf's view is that our cultural experiences with a particular concept shape a catalog of names that can be either rich or poor. Consider how rich your mental library of names for camel might be if you had extensive experience with camels in a desert world, and how poor your mental library of names for snow might be if you lived in a tropical world of palm trees and parrots. Despite its intriguing appeal, Whorf's view likely overstates the role of language in shaping thought.

Language and Cognition

Language is a vast system of symbols capable of expressing most thoughts; it is the vehicle for communicating most of our thoughts to one another. Although we do not always think in words, our thinking would be greatly impoverished without words.

The connection between language and thought has been of considerable interest to psychologists. Some have even argued that we cannot think without language. This proposition has produced heated controversy. Is thought dependent on language, or is language dependent on thought?

THE ROLE OF LANGUAGE IN COGNITION

Recall from Chapter 7 that memory is stored not only in the form of sounds and images but also in words. Language helps us think, make inferences, tackle difficult decisions, and solve problems (Gleitman & Papafragou, 2012; Goldin-Meadow & Cook, 2012). It is also a tool for representing ideas (Kovacs, 2009).

Today, most psychologists would accept these points. However, linguist Benjamin Whorf (1956) went a step further: He argued that language determines the way we think, a view that has been called the *linguistic relativity hypothesis*. Whorf and his student Edward Sapir were specialists in Native American languages, and they were fascinated by the possibility that people might perceive the world differently as the result of the different languages they speak. The Inuit people in Alaska, for instance, have a dozen or more words to describe the various textures, colors, and physical states of snow. In contrast, English has relatively few words to describe snow, and thus, according to Whorf's view, English speakers *cannot see* the different kinds of snow because they have no words for them.

Whorf's bold claim appealed to many scholars. Some even tried to apply Whorf's view to gender differences in color perception. Asked to describe the colors of two sweaters, a woman might say, "One is mauve and the other is magenta," while a man might say, "They're both pink." Whorf's view of the influence of language on perceptual ability might suggest that women are able to see more colors than men simply because they have a richer color vocabulary (Hepting & Solle, 1973). It turns out, however, that men can learn to discriminate among the various hues that women use, and this outcome suggests that Whorf's view is not quite accurate.

Indeed, critics of Whorf's ideas say that words merely reflect, rather than cause, the way we think. The Inuits' adaptability and livelihood in Alaska depend on their capacity to recognize various conditions of snow and ice. A skier or snowboarder who is not Inuit might also know numerous words for snow, far more than the average person, and a person who does not know the words for the different types of snow might still be able to perceive these differences. Interestingly, research has shown that Whorf might have been accurate for information that is presented to the left hemisphere of the brain. That is, when colors were presented in the right visual field (and therefore went to the left brain), having names for the colors enhanced perception of and discrimination among those colors (Gilbert & others, 2006).

Although the strongest form of Whorf's hypothesis—that language determines perception—seems doubtful, research has continued to demonstrate the influence of language on how we think, even about something as fundamental as our own personalities. For example, in a series of studies, researchers interviewed bilingual individuals (that is, people who fluently speak two languages, in this case Spanish and English) (Ramirez-Esparza & others, 2006). Each person rated his or her own personality characteristics, once in Spanish and once in English. Across all studies, and regardless of whether the individuals lived in a Spanish-speaking or an English-speaking country, respondents reported themselves as more outgoing, nicer, and more responsible when responding to the survey in English.

THE ROLE OF COGNITION IN LANGUAGE

Clearly, then, language can influence cognition. Researchers also study the possibility that cognition is an important foundation for language (Jackendoff, 2012).

One feature of human language that separates it from animal communication is the capacity to talk about objects that are not currently present (Hockett, 1960). A study comparing 12-month-old infants (who had not yet begun to talk) to chimpanzees suggests that this cognitive skill may underlie eventual language (Liszkowski & others, 2009). In this study, infants were more likely to communicate their desire for a toy by pointing to the place where the toy used to be. For many infants, this was the first thing they did to get their point across to another person who was present. In contrast, chimpanzees rarely pointed to where their desired object (food) had been, except as they desperately started pointing all over the place. So, even before they can talk, humans are communicating with others about what they want. Sometimes that communication demonstrates an appreciation of shared knowledge even about objects that are no longer present.

If language is a reflection of cognition in general, we would expect to find a close link between language ability and general intellectual ability. In particular, we would expect that problems in cognition are paralleled by problems in language. We would anticipate, for example, that general intellectual disability is accompanied by lowered language abilities. It is often but not always the case that individuals with intellectual disability have a reduced language proficiency. For instance, individuals with Williams syndrome—a genetic disorder that affects about 1 in 20,000 births—tend to show extraordinary verbal, social, and musical abilities while having an extremely low IQ and difficulty with motor tasks and numbers (Asada & Itakura, 2012). Williams syndrome demonstrates that intellectual disability is not always accompanied by poor language skills.

In summary, although thought influences language and language influences thought, there is increasing evidence that language and thought are not part of a single system. Instead, they seem to have evolved as separate but related components of the mind.

Biological and Environmental Influences on Language

Everyone who uses language in some way "knows" its rules and has the ability to create an infinite number of words and sentences. Is this knowledge the product of biology, or is language learned and influenced by experiences in the environment?

Noam Chomsky (b. 1928) MIT linguist Noam Chomsky was one of the early architects of the view that children's language development cannot be explained by environmental input. In Chomsky's opinion, language has strong biological underpinnings, with children biologically prewired to learn language at a certain time and in a certain way.

BIOLOGICAL INFLUENCES

Scientists believe that humans acquired language about 100,000 years ago. In evolutionary time, then, language is a very recent human ability. A number of biological systems are required for language, including the brain, nervous system, and vocal apparatus. Physically equipped to do so, *Homo sapiens* went beyond grunting and shrieking to develop abstract speech. This sophisticated language ability gave humans an enormous edge over other animals and increased their chances of survival (Arbib, 2012).

Language Universals   American linguist Noam Chomsky (1975) has argued that humans come into the world biologically prewired to learn language at a certain time and in a certain way. According to Chomsky and many other language experts, the strongest evidence for language's biological basis is the fact that children all over the world reach language milestones at about the same time and in about the same order, despite vast variations in the language input they receive from their environment. For example, in some cultures, such as some Samoan tribes (Schieffelin & Ochs, 1986), parents snuggle their babies but rarely talk to infants under 1 year of age, yet these infants still acquire language (Sterponi, 2010).

In Chomsky's view, children cannot possibly learn the full rules and structure of languages by only imitating what they hear. Rather, nature must provide children with a biological, prewired, universal grammar, allowing them to understand the basic rules of all languages and to apply these rules to the speech they hear. They learn language without an awareness of its underlying logic. Think about it: The terms we used above to define the characteristics of language—*phonology, morphology, semantics,* and so forth—may be new to you, but on some level you have mastered these principles. This mastery is demonstrated by your reading of this book, writing a paper for class, and talking with a friend. Like all other humans, you are engaged in the use of a rule-based language system even without knowing that you know those rules.

Language and the Brain   There is strong evidence to back up experts who believe language has a biological foundation. Neuroscience research has shown that the brain contains particular regions that are predisposed to language use (Griffiths & others, 2013; Price, 2012). As we saw in Chapter 3, accumulating evidence suggests that language processing, such as speech and grammar, mainly occurs in the brain's left hemisphere (McGettigan & others, 2012). Recall the importance of Broca's area, which contributes to speech production, and Wernicke's area, which is involved in language comprehension.

Using brain-imaging techniques such as PET scans, researchers have found that when an infant is about 9 months old, the hippocampus, the part of the brain that stores and indexes many kinds of memory, becomes fully functional (Bauer, 2009, 2013). This is also the time at which infants appear to be able to attach meaning to words, for instance to look at the ball if someone says "ball"—suggesting links among language, cognition, and the development of the brain.

ENVIRONMENTAL INFLUENCES

Decades ago, behaviorists opposed Chomsky's hypothesis and argued that language represents nothing more than chains of responses acquired through reinforcement (Skinner, 1957). A baby happens to babble "ma-ma," mama rewards the baby with hugs and smiles, the baby says "mama" more and more. Bit by bit, said the behaviorists, the baby's language is built up. According to behaviorists, language is a complex learned skill, much like playing the piano or dancing.

Such a view of language development is simply not tenable, however, given the rapid way children learn language, as well as the lack of evidence that social environments carefully reinforce language skills (R. Brown, 1973). This is not to say the environment has no role in language development. Many language experts argue that a child's experiences, the particular language to be learned, and the context in which learning takes place can strongly influence language acquisition (Hirsh-Pasek & Golinkoff, 2013; Tamis-LeMonda & Song, 2013).

Evidence for the important role of the environment in language development comes from case histories of children who have lacked exposure to language. In 1970, a California social worker made a routine visit to the home of a partially blind woman who had applied for public assistance. The social worker discovered that the woman and her husband had kept their 13-year-old daughter, Genie, locked away in almost total isolation during her childhood. Genie could not speak or stand erect. She had spent every day bound naked to a child's potty seat. She could move only her hands and feet. At night, she had been placed in a kind of straightjacket and caged in a crib with wire mesh sides and a cover. Whenever Genie had made a noise, her father had beaten her. He had never communicated with her in words; he had growled and barked at her instead (Rymer, 1993).

After she was rescued from her parents, Genie spent a number of years in extensive rehabilitation programs, including speech and physical therapy (Curtiss, 1977). She eventually learned to walk, although with a jerky motion, and to use the toilet. Genie also learned to recognize many words and to speak in rudimentary sentences. Gradually, she was able to string together two-word combinations such as "big teeth," "little marble," and "two hand" and then three-word combinations such as "small two cup." As far as we know, unlike normal children, Genie did not learn to ask questions and did not develop a language system that allowed her to understand English grammar. As an adult, she speaks in short, mangled phrases such as "father hit leg," "big wood," and "Genie hurt."

Children who, like Genie, are abused and lack exposure to language for many years rarely speak normally. Some language experts have argued that these cases support the idea that there is a critical period for language development, a special time in a child's life (usually the preschool years) during which language must develop or it never will. Because these children also suffer severe emotional trauma and possible neurological deficits, however, the issue is still far from clear. Whether or not these cases suggest such a critical period, they certainly support the idea that the environment is crucial for the development of language.

Clearly, most humans do not learn language in a social vacuum. Most children are bathed in language from a very early age (Kuhl, 2012). The support and involvement of caregivers and teachers greatly facilitate a child's language learning (Hirsh-Pasek & Golinkoff, 2013). For example, one study showed that when mothers immediately smiled and touched their 8-month-old infants after they had babbled, the infants subsequently made more complex speechlike sounds than when mothers responded to their infants in a random manner (Goldstein, King, & West, 2003) (Figure 8.10).

In another study, researchers observed the language environments of children from two different backgrounds: families of middle-income professionals and families living on welfare (Hart & Risley, 1995; Risley & Hart, 2006). Then they examined the children's language development. All of the children developed normally in terms of learning to talk and acquiring the basic rules of English and a fundamental vocabulary. However, the researchers found enormous differences in the sheer amount of language to which the children were exposed and in the level of the children's language development. For example, in a typical hour, the middle-income professional parents spent almost twice as much time communicating with their children as did the parents in the lower socioeconomic families. The children from the middle-income professional families heard about 2,100 words an hour; the children in the poorer families heard only 600 words an hour. The researchers estimated that by 4 years of age, the average child

FIGURE 8.10 The Power of Smile and Touch
Research has shown that when mothers immediately smiled and touched their 8-month-old infants after they babbled, the infants subsequently made more complex speechlike sounds than when mothers responded randomly to their infants.

from the poorer family group would have 13 million fewer words of cumulative language experience than the average child from the middle-income professional family group. Amazingly, some of the 3-year-old children from middle-class professional families had a recorded vocabulary that exceeded the recorded vocabulary of some of the parents from the poorer families.

Research findings about environmental influences on language learning complicate the understanding of its foundations. In the real world of language learning, children appear to be neither exclusively biologically programmed linguists nor exclusively socially driven language experts. We have to look at how biology and environment interact when children learn language (Wagner & Hoff, 2013). That is, children are biologically prepared to learn language but benefit enormously from being immersed in a competent language environment from an early age (Gunning, 2013).

FIGURE 8.11 Language Milestones All children are different and acquire language at varying rates, but these milestones provide a general sense of how language emerges in human life. NOTE: This list is meant not to be exhaustive but rather to highlight some of the main language milestones. Also keep in mind that there is a great deal of variation in the ages at which children can reach these milestones and still be considered within the normal range of language development.

Age	Milestones
0–6 Months	Cooing Discrimination of vowels Babbling present by 6 months
6–12 Months	Babbling expands to include sounds of spoken language Gestures used to communicate about objects First words spoken 10–13 months
12–18 Months	Understands 50+ words on average
18–24 Months	Vocabulary increases to an average of 200 words Two-word combinations
2 Years	Vocabulary rapidly increases Correct use of plurals Use of past tense Use of some prepositions
3–4 Years	Mean length of utterances increases to 3–4 morphemes in a sentence Use of yes and no questions, wh- questions Use of negatives and imperatives Increased awareness of pragmatics
5–6 Years	Vocabulary reaches an average of about 10,000 words Coordination of simple sentences
6–8 Years	Vocabulary continues to increase rapidly More skilled use of syntactical rules Conversational skills improve
9–11 Years	Word definitions include synonyms Conversational strategies continue to improve
11–14 Years	Vocabulary increases with addition of more abstract words Understanding of complex grammar forms Increased understanding of function a word plays in a sentence Understands metaphor and satire
15–20 Years	Understands adult literary works

Language Development over the Life Span

Most individuals develop a clear understanding of their language's structure, as well as a large vocabulary, during childhood. Most adults in the United States have acquired a vocabulary of nearly 50,000 words. Researchers have taken a great interest in the process by which these aspects of language develop (Parrish-Morris, Golinkoff, & Hirsh-Pasek, 2013). Their many studies have provided an understanding of the milestones of language development (Figure 8.11).

Language researchers are fascinated by babies' speech even before the little ones say their first words (Goldin-Meadow & Alibali, 2013). *Babbling*—endlessly repeating sounds and syllables, such as "bababa" or "dadada"—begins at the age of about 4 to 6 months and is determined by biological readiness, not by the amount of reinforcement or the ability to hear (Menn & Stoel-Gammon, 2009). Even babies that are deaf babble for a time (Lenneberg, Rebelsky, & Nichols, 1965). Babbling probably allows babies to exercise their vocal cords and helps develop the ability to articulate different sounds.

Patricia Kuhl's research reveals that long before they begin to learn words, infants can sort through a number of spoken sounds in search of the ones that have meaning for their culture (1993, 2000, 2011, 2012). Kuhl argues that from birth to about 6 months of age, children are "universal linguists" who are capable of distinguishing each of the sounds that make up the various different human languages. By about 6 months of age, they have started to specialize in the speech sounds (or phonology) of their native language (Figure 8.12).

A child's first words, uttered at the age of 10 to 13 months, name important people ("dada," "mama"), familiar animals ("kitty"), vehicles ("car"), toys ("ball"), food ("milk"), body parts ("eye"), clothes ("hat"), household items ("clock"), and greetings ("bye"). These were babies' first words a century ago, and they are babies' first words still (Bloom, 2004).

By the time children reach the age of 18 to 24 months, they usually utter two-word statements. They quickly grasp the importance of expressing concepts and the role that language plays in communicating with others (Sachs, 2009). To convey meaning in two-word statements, the child relies heavily on gesture, tone, and context. Although these two-word sentences omit many parts of speech, they are remarkably effective in conveying many messages. When a toddler demands, "Pet doggie!" parents know he means, "May I please pet the doggie?" Very young children learn that language is a good way to get what they want, suggesting that they grasp another aspect of language—its pragmatics.

Although childhood is an important time for language learning, we continue to learn language (new words, new skills) throughout life (Obler, 2009). For many years, it was claimed that if individuals did not learn a second language prior to puberty, they would never reach native-language learners' levels in the second language (Johnson & Newport, 1991). However, recent research indicates a more complex conclusion: Sensitive periods likely vary across different

FIGURE 8.12 From Universal Linguist to Language-Specific Listener A baby is shown in Patricia Kuhl's research laboratory. In this research, babies listen to recorded voices that repeat syllables. When the sounds of the syllables change, the babies quickly learn to look at the bear. Using this technique, Kuhl has demonstrated that babies are universal linguists until about 6 months of age but in the next 6 months become language-specific listeners.

Around the world, young children learn to speak in two-word utterances at 18 to 24 months of age.

language systems (Thomas & Johnson, 2008). Thus, for late second-language learners, such as adolescents and adults, new vocabulary is easier to learn than new sounds or new grammar (Neville, 2006). For example, children's ability to pronounce words with a native-like accent in a second language typically decreases with age, with an especially sharp drop occurring after about 10 to 12 years of age.

For adults, learning a new language requires a special kind of cognitive exercise. As we have seen, a great deal of language learning in infancy and childhood involves recognizing the sounds that are part of one's native tongue. This process also entails learning to ignore sounds that are *not* important to one's first language. For instance, in Japanese, the phonemes /l/ and /r/ are not distinguished from each other, so that, for a Japanese adult, the word *lion* is not distinguishable from the name *Ryan*. Recent research suggests that mastering a new language in adulthood may involve overriding such learned habits and learning to listen to sounds that one previously ignored. Indeed, adults can learn to hear and discriminate sounds that are part of a new language, and this learning can contribute to speech fluency and language skill (Evans & Iverson, 2007). Thus, learning a new language in adulthood involves cognitively stretching ourselves away from our assumptions.

5. THINKING, PROBLEM SOLVING, AND HEALTH AND WELLNESS

The way we think about life events can have a profound impact on our experience of stress. Recall that stress refers to our response to changes in the environment and that stressors are those changes. Consider the stressors in your life. They can be anything from losing irreplaceable notes from a class, to being yelled at by a friend, to failing a test, to being in a car wreck. Although everyone's body may have a similar response to stressors, not everyone perceives the same events as stressful, as we consider in this final section.

Cognitive Appraisal and Stress

Whether an experience "stresses us out" depends on how we think about that experience. For example, you may perceive an upcoming job interview as a threatening obligation, whereas your roommate may perceive it as a challenging opportunity. He or she might feel some anxiety but see the experience as a chance to shine. You might view a *D* on a paper as threatening; your roommate may view the same grade as an incentive to work harder. To some degree, then, what is stressful depends on how we think about events—what psychologists call cognitive appraisal (Schwarzer & Luszczynska, 2013).

Cognitive appraisal refers to a person's interpretation of a situation. This appraisal includes whether the event or situation is viewed as harmful and threatening, or as challenging, and the person's determination of whether he or she has the resources to cope effectively with the events. Is moving to a new apartment stressful? It depends on how you look at it and whether you have the resources you need to handle the challenge effectively.

Coping is essentially a kind of problem solving. It involves managing taxing circumstances, expending effort to solve life's problems, and seeking to master or reduce stress (Xanthopoulos & Daniel, 2013). Richard Lazarus (1993, 2000) most clearly articulated the importance of cognitive appraisal to stress and coping. In Lazarus's view, people appraise events in two steps: primary appraisal and secondary appraisal.

In *primary appraisal,* individuals interpret whether an event involves *harm* or loss that has already occurred, a *threat* of some future danger, or a *challenge* to be overcome.

test yourself

1. What are the terms for a language's sound system, its rules for combining words to form acceptable sentences, and the meanings of its words and sentences?
2. State Whorf's linguistic relativity hypothesis and explain why some scholars have criticized it.
3. What evidence has neuroscience research provided for a biological foundation of language?

● **cognitive appraisal** Interpreting the events and experiences in one's life as harmful and threatening, or as challenging, and determining whether one has the resources to cope effectively.

● **coping** Managing taxing circumstances, expending effort to solve life's problems, and seeking to master or reduce stress.

Lazarus believed that perceiving a stressor as a challenge to be overcome, rather than as a threat, is a good strategy for reducing stress. To understand Lazarus's concept of primary appraisal, consider two students, each of whom has a failing grade in a psychology class at midterm. Sam is almost frozen by the stress of the low grade and looks at the rest of the term as a threatening prospect. In contrast, Pam does not become overwhelmed by the harm already done and the threat of future failures. She looks at the low grade as a challenge that she can address and overcome. This initial appraisal of an event as threatening or challenging can have profound impact on health and wellness (Seery, 2011). For example, a recent study showed that threat appraisals were associated with more rapid cellular aging (O'Donovan & others, 2012).

In *secondary appraisal,* individuals evaluate their resources and determine how effectively they can be used to cope with the event (Slattery & others, 2013). This appraisal is secondary because it both comes after primary appraisal and depends on the degree to which the event is appraised as harmful/threatening or challenging. For example, Sam might have some helpful resources for coping with his low midterm grade, but he views the stressful circumstance as so harmful and threatening that he does not take stock of and use his resources. Pam, in contrast, evaluates the resources she can call on to improve her grade during the second half of the term. These include asking the instructor for suggestions about how to study better for the tests in the course, setting up a time management program to include more study hours, and consulting with several high-achieving classmates about their strategies. Importantly, *rethinking* our appraisals of potential stressors can influence health and wellness.

Cognitive Reappraisal

Once an event or experience has been appraised, it need not be set in stone. Indeed, one way of dealing with potentially stressful situations is to reappraise the event actively and come up with a new way of thinking about it.

Cognitive reappraisal involves regulating our feelings about an experience by reinterpreting it or thinking about it in a different way or from a different angle (Roseman & Smith, 2009). Research has shown that reappraising an event can change not only the way people feel about it (Urry, 2010), but also the brain activity linked to the experience. For example, in one brain-imaging study, participants were shown images that were likely to produce negative feelings (McRae & others, 2010). To examine the effects of cognitive reappraisal, the researchers told participants to look at the pictures and think about them in a way that would reduce their negative feelings. Results showed

● **cognitive reappraisal** Regulating one's feelings about an experience by reinterpreting that experience or thinking about it in a different way or from a different angle.

The Candle Problem	**The Nine-Dot Problem**	**The Six-Matchstick Problem**
The solution requires a unique perception of the function of the box in which the matches came. It can become a candleholder when tacked to the wall.	Most people have difficulty with this problem because they try to draw the lines within the boundaries of the dots. Notice that by extending the lines beyond the dots, the problem can be solved.	Nothing in the instructions said that the solution had to be two-dimensional.
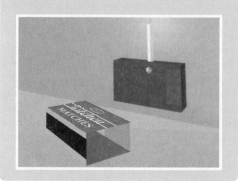	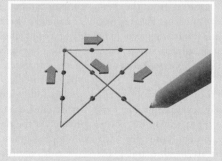	

Solutions to problems from the Psychological Inquiry feature on page 259.

that reappraising the stimuli resulted in decreased negative feelings, decreased activation in the amygdala, and increased activation in prefrontal regions.

Reappraising negative life events can involve a process called *benefit finding*. Benefit finding means looking at a stressful life event in a particular way, focusing on the good that has arisen in one's life as a result. Finding benefits in negative life events can be a way to make meaning out of those experiences (Mock & Boerner, 2010; C. L. Park, 2010, 2012). Finding benefits in negative life events has been related to better physical health (Bower, Moskowitz, & Epel, 2009) and better functioning in the context of a variety of illnesses (C. L. Park, 2010, 2012; C. L. Park & others, 2009).

It may be challenging to think of negative life events as opportunities. However, the capacity to think about such events differently—to engage creatively with the notion that even objectively negative life events have helped us to become more compassionate, wiser, or better able to meet the challenges of the future—can be a powerful tool for staving off stress (King & Hicks, 2007).

test yourself

1. What is cognitive appraisal?
2. What is cognitive reappraisal?
3. How does benefit finding relate to physical health and to body function in a variety of illnesses?

SUMMARY

1. THE COGNITIVE REVOLUTION IN PSYCHOLOGY

Cognition is the way in which information is processed and manipulated in remembering, thinking, and knowing. The advent of the computer in the mid-twentieth century spurred a cognitive revolution in which psychologists took on the challenge of understanding human information processing. Artificial intelligence (AI), the science of creating machines capable of performing activities that require intelligence when people do them, is a byproduct of the cognitive revolution.

2. THINKING

Concepts are mental categories used to group objects, events, and characteristics. Concepts help us to generalize; they improve our memories; and they keep us from having to learn new things with every new instance or example of a concept. The prototype model suggests that members of a concept vary in terms of their similarity to the most typical item.

Problem solving is an attempt to find a way to attain a goal when the goal is not readily available. The four steps in problem solving are to (1) find and frame the problem, (2) develop good problem-solving strategies, (3) evaluate solutions, and (4) rethink and redefine problems and solutions over time. Among effective strategies for solving problems are setting subgoals (intermediate goals that put us in a better position to reach our goal), devising algorithms (strategies that guarantee a solution), and using heuristics (shortcuts that suggest, but do not guarantee, a solution to a problem).

Reasoning is the mental activity of transforming information to reach conclusions. Inductive reasoning is reasoning from the specific to the general. Deductive reasoning is reasoning from the general to the specific. Decision making involves evaluating alternatives and making choices among them. Biases and heuristics that may lead to problematic decision making include confirmation bias, hindsight bias, the availability heuristic, and the representativeness heuristic.

Critical thinking and creativity improve problem solving. Critical thinking involves thinking productively, evaluating the evidence, being mindful, and keeping an open mind. Creativity is the ability to think in novel and unusual ways and to come up with unconventional solutions. Creative thinkers are flexible and playful, self-motivated, willing to face risk, and objective in evaluating their work.

3. INTELLIGENCE

Intelligence consists of the ability to solve problems and to adapt to and learn from everyday experiences. Traditionally, intelligence has been measured by tests designed to compare people's performance on cognitive tasks.

A good test of intelligence meets three criteria: validity, reliability, and standardization. Validity is the extent to which a test measures what it is intended to measure. Reliability is how consistently an individual performs on a test. Standardization focuses on uniform procedures for administering and scoring a test and establishing norms.

Binet developed the first intelligence test. Individuals from age 2 through adulthood take the current Stanford-Binet test. Some intelligence tests are unfair to individuals from different cultures. Culture-fair tests are intelligence tests that are intended to be culturally unbiased.

Genes are clearly involved in intelligence. The proportion of differences in intelligence that is explained by genetic variation (or heritability) is substantial, although recently critics have questioned the heritability estimate. Environmental influences on intelligence have also been demonstrated. The fact that intelligence test scores have risen considerably around the world in recent decades—called the Flynn effect—supports the role of environment in intelligence.

At the extreme ends of intelligence are giftedness and intellectual disability. People who are gifted have high intelligence (IQ of 130 or higher) and/or superior talent for a particular domain. Research has shown that individuals who are gifted are likely to make important and creative contributions. Intellectual disability (or intellectual learning disorder) is a condition of limited mental ability affecting a person's daily functioning. Intellectual disability can have an organic cause or can be cultural and social in origin.

Instead of focusing on intelligence as a single, broad cognitive ability, some psychologists view intelligence as a variety of life skills. Sternberg's triarchic theory states there are three main types of intelligence: analytical, creative, and practical. Gardner identifies nine types of intelligence, involving skills that are verbal, mathematical, spatial, bodily-kinesthetic, musical, interpersonal, intrapersonal, naturalist, and existential. The multiple-intelligences approaches have broadened the definition of intelligence and motivated educators to develop programs that instruct students in different domains.

Critics maintain that multiple-intelligences theories include factors that really are not part of intelligence, such as musical skills, and that people who are highly intelligent are likely to excel in many different areas, not just one. Skeptics also argue that there is not enough research to support the concept of multiple intelligences.

4. LANGUAGE

Language is a form of communication that is based on a system of symbols. All human languages have common aspects, including infinite generativity and organizational rules about structure. Also, all languages have five characteristics: phonology, the sound system of a language; morphology, the rules for combining morphemes (which are meaningful strings of sounds that contain no smaller meaningful parts); syntax, the ways words are combined to form acceptable phrases and sentences; semantics, the meaning of words and sentences; and pragmatics, the uses of language.

Although language and thought influence each other, there is increasing evidence that they evolved as separate, modular, biologically prepared components of the mind. Evolution shaped humans into linguistic creatures. Chomsky said that humans are biologically prewired to learn language at a certain time and in a certain way. In addition, there is strong evidence that particular regions in the left hemisphere of the brain are predisposed to be used for language. Experience is also crucial to language development. It is important for children to interact with language-skilled people. Children are biologically prepared to learn language but benefit enormously from being in a competent language environment from early in development.

Although we often think of language, thinking, and intelligence as fixed when we are adults, research shows that we can continue to master skills and even increase intelligence by engaging in challenging mental tasks.

5. THINKING, PROBLEM SOLVING, AND HEALTH AND WELLNESS

The way individuals think about life events determines whether they experience them as stressful. Cognitive appraisal is individuals' interpretation of the events in their lives as either threatening (and stressful) or challenging (and not stressful). Coping refers to people's attempts to handle situations that they perceive as stressful. Cognitive reappraisal can be a powerful tool for coping with negative life events. One type of reappraisal, benefit finding, relates to enhanced psychological and physical health.

key *terms*

cognition, p. 254
artificial intelligence (AI), p. 255
thinking, p. 256
concepts, p. 256
prototype model, p. 256
problem solving, p. 256
subgoals, p. 257
algorithms, p. 257
heuristics, p. 257
fixation, p. 258
functional fixedness, p. 258
reasoning, p. 260
inductive reasoning, p. 260

deductive reasoning, p. 260
decision making, p. 260
confirmation bias, p. 262
hindsight bias, p. 262
availability heuristic, p. 262
base rate neglect, p. 262
representativeness
    heuristic, p. 263
mindfulness, p. 265
open-mindedness, p. 265
creativity, p. 265
divergent thinking, p. 265
convergent thinking, p. 265

intelligence, p. 267
validity, p. 268
reliability, p. 268
standardization, p. 268
mental age (MA), p. 269
intelligence quotient (IQ), p. 269
normal distribution, p. 269
culture-fair tests, p. 270
heritability, p. 271
gifted, p. 273
intellectual disability or
    intellectual developmental
    disorder, p. 274

triarchic theory of
    intelligence, p. 275
language, p. 277
phonology, p. 277
morphology, p. 277
syntax, p. 277
semantics, p. 277
pragmatics, p. 278
cognitive appraisal, p. 284
coping, p. 284
cognitive reappraisal,
    p. 285

apply your *knowledge*

1. To get a sense of the roles of divergent and convergent thinking in creativity, try the following exercise. First take 10 minutes and jot down all of the uses that you can think of for a cardboard box. Don't hold back—include every possibility that comes to mind. That list represents divergent thinking. Now look over the list. Which of the possible uses are most unusual or most likely to be worthwhile? That is convergent thinking.

2. Ask a few friends to define the term *intelligent*. Do they mostly describe intelligent people or intelligent behaviors? Do their definitions focus on cognitive ability or other abilities?

3. Many different intelligence tests are available online, such as www. iqtest.com/. Give this one a try and then do a web search for intelligence tests and see if you get the same results when you take a different test. Do the websites tell you how reliable the tests are? Do they provide information on standardization or validity? If your scores on the two tests are very different, what might account for this difference?

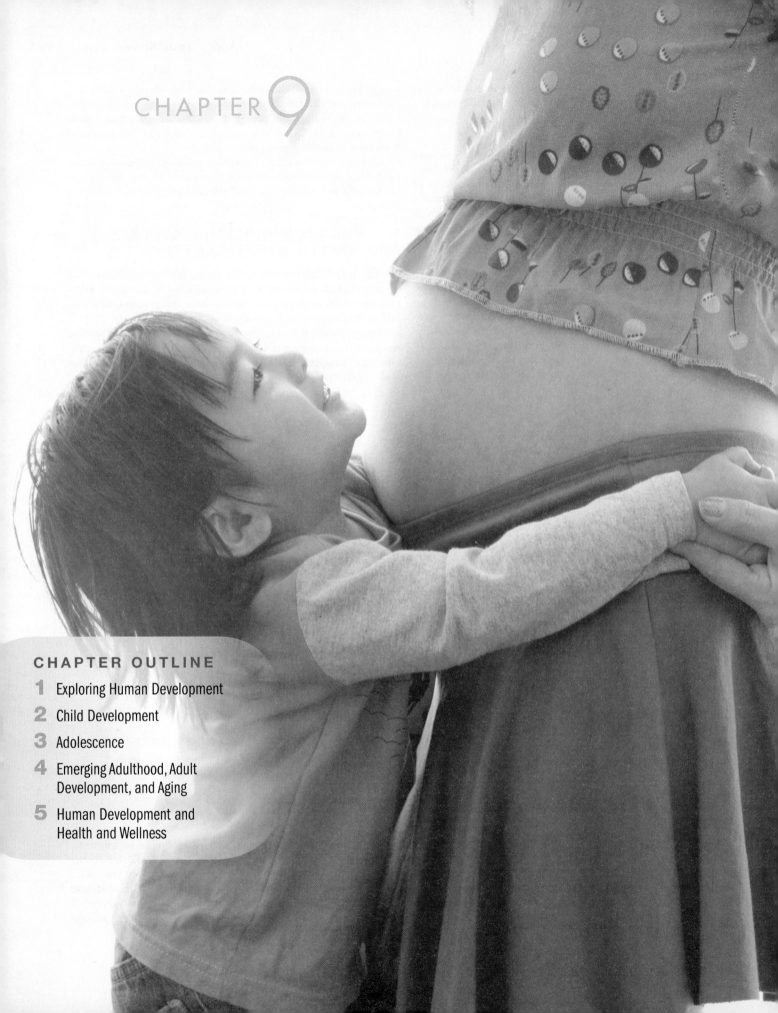

CHAPTER 9

Human Development

The Time Machine That Is a Human Life

Have you ever been called upon to help a parent (or grandparent) navigate a social media account or figure out a new smartphone? New technology is often viewed as the domain of the younger generation. For instance, in the earliest days of the web, young adults were commonly the only bloggers. This has changed, however; older individuals now typically dominate the blogosphere (Lenhart & others, 2010).

Arizona resident Bernando LaPallo is, by some estimates, the world's oldest blogger. Born in Brazil in 1901, Bernando blogs at www.agelesslivemorestore.com/. Sure, blogging may be increasingly viewed as hopelessly uncool by the young, but consider for a moment what it means for someone who is 111 years old to blog. Bernando lived in a world without many of the things we take for granted, and certainly without computers and the Internet. For most of his life, contacting someone meant finding a landline to call or writing a letter (on paper) to drop in the snail mail. When Bernando was young, women could not vote, and cars were not commonplace. Isn't it astonishing to think of someone from that world now posting his thoughts on the web?

The range of experiences that can be part of one human life span is amazing. We can see Bernando's life as a kind of time machine—but not in the science-fiction sense of going back in time to see dinosaurs or ahead to witness flying cars or moving sidewalks. Every human life is like a time machine. From the moment our lives begin, we are on a journey into the future. If you were born in the early 1990s, you have on average over 75 years to fill up with experiences. Maybe you will be lucky like Bernando and ride this time machine of life well into the 22nd century. Imagine what the world might hold for you then. ●

PREVIEW

Developmental psychologists are interested in all the ways a person grows and changes throughout the time travel that is life, from its beginning to its inevitable end. We begin this chapter by examining the meaning of development and exploring key questions in the field. We then trace the processes of physical, cognitive, and socioemotional development throughout the life span: prenatally (before birth), during childhood, and in adolescence and adulthood. We round off our tour of the human life span with a look at development and wellness.

1· EXPLORING HUMAN DEVELOPMENT

● **development** The pattern of continuity and change in human capabilities that occurs throughout life, involving both growth and decline.

Development refers to the pattern of continuity and change in human capabilities that occurs throughout the course of life. Most development involves growth, although it also is concerned with decline (for example, physical abilities may decline with age). Developmental psychology is interested in how people change—physically and psychologically as they age. These changes occur on three different levels:

- *Physical processes* involve changes in an individual's biological nature. Genes inherited from parents; the hormonal changes of puberty and menopause; and changes throughout life in the brain, height and weight, and motor skills—all of these reflect the developmental role of biological processes. Such biological growth processes are called *maturation*.

- *Cognitive processes* involve changes in an individual's thought, intelligence, and language. Observing a colorful mobile as it swings above a crib, constructing a sentence about the future, imagining oneself as a movie star, memorizing a new telephone number—these activities reflect the role of cognitive processes in development.

- *Socioemotional processes* involve changes in an individual's relationships with other people, in emotions, and in personality. An infant's smile in response to her mother's touch, a girl's development of assertiveness, an adolescent's joy at the senior prom, a young man's aggressiveness in sport, and an older couple's affection for each other all reflect the role of socioemotional processes.

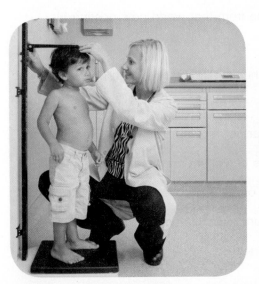

Human development is complex because it is the product of several processes. A child's growth in height and weight, a phone user's tapping out a friend's number from memory, and a young couple's joy on the occasion of their prom reflect physical, cognitive, and socioemotional processes, respectively.

These physical, cognitive, and socioemotional processes are intricately interwoven. As you read this chapter, remember that you are studying the development of an integrated human being, in whom body, mind, and emotion are interdependent.

Researchers in developmental psychology are interested in the ways that these three processes—physical, cognitive, and socioemotional—change over the human life span. Their work centrally probes how a person's *age* relates to different aspects of his or her physical, cognitive, and socioemotional characteristics. Because age is a variable that cannot be experimentally manipulated, studies on the relationship between age and other characteristics are by definition correlational in nature. This aspect of developmental research carries important implications for research design, as we now consider.

Research Methods in Developmental Psychology

Human development is about the changes that occur with age. To know what age-related differences mean, however, we must consider the kind of research presented.

In *cross-sectional studies,* a number of people of different ages are assessed at one point in time, and differences are noted. By examining how the ages of these individuals relate to the characteristics measured, researchers can find out whether younger individuals differ from older ones. Age differences, however, are not the same as developmental change.

One problem in cross-sectional studies is cohort effects. A cohort is a generational group, people born in the same time period. *Cohort effects* are differences between individuals that stem not necessarily from their ages but from the historical and social time period in which they were born and developed (Schaie, 2009, 2010, 2012). For instance, individuals who were born in the 1940s might be less likely to have attended college than those born in the 1990s. Differences observed between these groups might be due not to their age but rather to these differing experiences.

In contrast to a cross-sectional study, a *longitudinal study,* as described in Chapter 2, assesses the same participants multiple times over a lengthy period. A longitudinal study can find out not only whether age groups differ but also whether the same individuals change with respect to a particular characteristic as they age (Reznick, 2013).

To appreciate the difference between a cross-sectional and a longitudinal design, consider a cross-sectional study of approximately 28,000 individuals ages 18 to 88 indicating that happiness increases with age (Yang, 2008). About 33 percent of the participants were very happy at 88 years of age, compared to only about 24 percent of those in their late teens and early 20s. From this work we *might* conclude that people become happier as they age, but this conclusion is limited by the cross-sectional nature of the design used. We cannot know if the happy 88-year-olds were less happy when they were in their 20s. It may be that these individuals were very happy even in their 20s. Perhaps the explanation is that relatively more happy people survive into their senior years.

Clearly, many conclusions about developmental changes in psychological characteristics require longitudinal designs (Lindenberger & others, 2011). Using these and other methods, human development researchers have grappled with three big questions that are relevant to all of psychology, as we consider next.

How Do Nature and Nurture Influence Development?

Developmental psychologists seek to understand how nature and nurture influence development. **Nature** refers to a person's biological inheritance, especially his or her genes; **nurture** refers to the individual's environmental and social experiences. In Chapter 3 we considered the concept of a *genotype* (the individual's genetic heritage—his or her actual genetic material). We also examined the idea of a *phenotype* (the person's observable characteristics). The phenotype shows the contributions of both nature (genetic heritage) and nurture (environment). The genotype may be expressed in various ways, depending on both the environment and characteristics of the genotype itself.

● **nature** An individual's biological inheritance, especially his or her genes.

● **nurture** An individual's environmental and social experiences.

Researchers often rely on twins to measure the influence of nature or genetics on development. Keep in mind that even among twins, the nurture, or experience, matters.

Recall, for example, that a recessive gene, though part of the genotype, will not show up in the phenotype at all if it is paired with a dominant gene.

An illustration of the role of environmental influences in genetic expression is a condition called *phenylketonuria* (PKU). Caused by two recessive genes, PKU results in an inability to metabolize the amino acid phenylalanine (a major component of the artificial sweetener aspartame, used in many soft drinks and other products). Decades ago, it was thought that the genotype for PKU led to a specific phenotype: irreversible brain damage, developmental disabilities, and seizures. However, we now know that as long as those with the PKU genotype stick to a diet that is very low in phenylalanine, these phenotypic characteristics can be avoided (Cotugno & others, 2011; Giovannini & others, 2012). Thus, environmental precautions can change the phenotype associated with this genotype.

PKU demonstrates that a person's observable and measurable characteristics (phenotype) might not reflect his or her genetic heritage (genotype) very precisely because of experience. Instead, for each genotype, a *range* of phenotypes may be expressed, depending on environmental factors. An individual can inherit the genetic potential to grow very tall, but good nutrition, an environmental factor, is important for achieving that potential. The person whom we see before us emerges through the interplay of genetic and environmental experiences. Development is the product of nature, nurture, and the complex interaction of the two (Moore, 2013).

One of the factors that must be taken into account in the development process is the developer himself or herself, as we consider next.

What Is the Developer's Role in Development?

Nature and nurture have at least one thing in common. Because we cannot pick our genes or our parents, each of us would seem to be stuck with the genes and environment we got at birth. However, importantly, the developing human being also has a role to play in development (Turkheimer, 2011). Although you might think of nature and nurture as the raw ingredients of yourself as a person, the fact is that you take those ingredients and make them into the person you are.

Indeed, some psychologists believe that we can develop beyond what our genetic inheritance and our environment give us. They argue that a key aspect of development involves seeking optimal experiences in life (Armor, Massey, & Sackett, 2008). They cite examples of individuals who go beyond what life has given them to achieve extraordinary things. These individuals build and shape their own lives, authoring a unique developmental path, and sometimes transforming apparent weaknesses into real strengths.

In our efforts to experience our lives in optimal ways, we develop *life themes* that involve activities, social relationships, and life goals (Frensch, Pratt, & Norris, 2007; Rathunde, 2010). Some individuals are especially successful at constructing optimal life experiences. For example, Martin Luther King, Jr., Mother Teresa, Nelson Mandela, Bill and Melinda Gates, and Oprah Winfrey looked for and found meaningful life themes as they developed. Their lives were not restricted to biological survival or to settling for their particular life situations. Many of them, in fact, faced hardships early in life and yet managed to contribute to the world in meaningful ways. A developmental question that naturally flows from this discussion is whether early or later life experiences are more important to a person's development over the life span.

Microsoft founder Bill Gates and his wife, Melinda, have quested after—and carved out—meaningful life experiences as they have progressed through their development.

Are Early or Later Life Experiences More Important in Development?

A key question in developmental psychology centers on the extent to which childhood experiences (nurture) determine aspects of later life. If early experiences provide the foundation for later development, does that mean that childhood experiences are likely to influence (and limit or damage) us for the rest of our lives?

Developmental psychologists debate whether early experiences or later experiences are more important (Dixon & others, 2013; Kagan, 2013). Some believe that unless infants receive warm, nurturing caregiving in their first year or so of life, they will not develop to their full potential (Cassidy & others, 2011). Other psychologists emphasize the power of later experience, arguing that important development occurs later on in life as well (Antonucci, Birditt, & Ajrouch, 2013).

Life-span developmentalists, who study both children and adults, stress that researchers have given too little attention to adult development and aging. They argue that although early experiences contribute powerfully to development, they are not necessarily more influential than later experiences (Hershfield & others, 2013; Park & McDonough, 2013). These experts say that both early and later experiences make significant contributions to development, and thus no one is doomed to be a prisoner of his or her childhood.

A key concept in understanding the role of negative early experiences in later development is resilience. **Resilience** is a person's ability to recover from or adapt to difficult times. Resilience means that even in the face of adversity, a person shows signs of positive functioning (Tol, Song, & Jordans, 2013; Wolfe, 2013). Resilience can refer to factors that compensate for difficulties, buffering the individual from the effects of these, or to the fact that moderate difficulties may themselves help to promote development (Ager, 2013).

Despite undergoing hardship time and time again, resilient children grow up to be capable adults. Researchers have found that resilient children have one or more advantages—such as strong intellectual functioning or a close, supportive relationship with a parent or other adult—that help them to overcome their disadvantages (Masten, 2009, 2011, 2013). Although often studied as an aspect of childhood and adolescence, resilience can also characterize development in adulthood and old age (Gooding & others, 2012; Jeste & others, 2013).

Having a supportive relationship with a parent or a competent adult outside the home can contribute to childhood resilience.

● **resilience** A person's ability to recover from or adapt to difficult times.

2· CHILD DEVELOPMENT

In this section we focus on the three fundamental developmental processes—physical, cognitive, and socioemotional—of childhood. To understand childhood in all its dimensions, we must begin before it even starts, with prenatal development.

Prenatal Development

Prenatal development is a time of astonishing change, beginning with conception. *Conception* occurs when a single sperm cell from the male merges with the female's ovum (egg) to produce a *zygote,* a single cell with 23 chromosomes from the mother and 23 from the father.

THE COURSE OF PRENATAL DEVELOPMENT

Development from zygote to fetus is divided into three periods:

- *Germinal period—weeks 1 and 2:* The germinal period begins with conception. After 1 week and many cell divisions, the zygote is made up of 100 to 150 cells. By the end of 2 weeks, the mass of cells has attached to the uterine wall.

- *Embryonic period—weeks 3 through 8:* The rate of cell differentiation intensifies, support systems for the cells develop, and the beginnings of organs appear (Figure 9.1a). In the third week, the neural tube, which eventually becomes the spinal cord, starts to take shape. Within the first 28 days after conception, the neural tube is formed and closes, encased inside the embryo. By the end of the embryonic period, the heart begins to beat, the arms and legs become more differentiated, the face starts to form, and the intestinal tract appears (Figure 9.1b).

test yourself

1. What three broad processes of change do developmental psychologists study?
2. Why are longitudinal studies commonly used to investigate developmental questions? What are the limitations of cross-sectional studies with respect to studying such questions?
3. In what ways can the developing individual play a role in his or her own development?

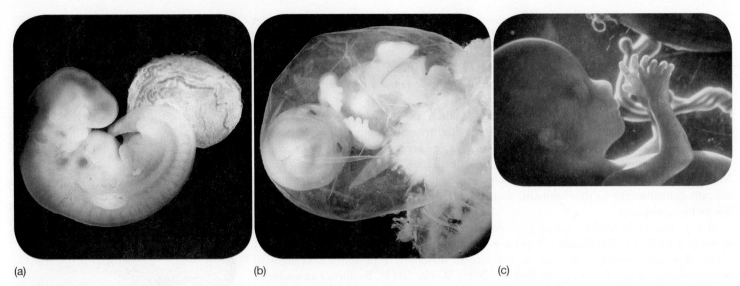

(a)   (b)   (c)

FIGURE 9.1 **From Embryo to Fetus** (a) At about 4 weeks, an embryo is about 0.2 inch (less than 1 centimeter) long. The head, eyes, and ears begin to show; the head and neck are half the length of the body; the shoulders will be located where the whitish arm buds are attached. (b) At 8 weeks, the developing individual is about 1.6 inches (4 centimeters) long and has reached the end of its embryonic phase. It has become a fetus. Everything that will be found in the fully developed human being has now begun to form. The fetal stage is a period of growth and perfection of detail. The heart has been beating for a month, and the muscles have just begun their first exercises. (c) At 4½ months, the fetus is just over 7 inches (about 18 centimeters) long. When the thumb comes close to the mouth, the head may turn, and the lips and tongue begin their sucking motions—a reflex for survival.

■ *Fetal period—months 2 through 9:* At 2 months, the fetus is the size of a kidney bean and has started to move around. At 4 months, the fetus is 5 inches long and weighs about 5 ounces (Figure 9.1c). At 6 months, the fetus has grown to a pound and a half. The last 3 months of pregnancy are the time when organ functioning increases, and the fetus puts on considerable weight and size, adding baby fat.

Although it floats in a well-protected womb, the fetus is not immune to the larger environment surrounding the mother (Dunkel Schetter, 2011). Sometimes, normal development is disrupted by environmental insults.

THREATS TO THE FETUS

A *teratogen* is any agent that causes a birth defect. Teratogens include chemical substances ingested by the mother (such as nicotine if the mother smokes and alcohol if she drinks) and certain illnesses (such as rubella, or German measles). Substances that are ingested by the mother can lead to serious birth defects (Hutson & others, 2013; Matlow & others, 2013).

For example, *fetal alcohol spectrum disorders (FASD)* are a cluster of abnormalities and problems that appear in the offspring of mothers who drink alcohol heavily during pregnancy (Yang & others, 2012). These abnormalities include a small head, defects in the limbs and heart, and below-average intelligence (Arnold & others, 2013). Heavy drinking is linked to FASD, but even moderate drinking can lead to serious problems (Cannon & others, 2012). The best advice for a woman who is pregnant or thinking of becoming pregnant is to avoid alcohol.

The effects of chemical teratogens depend on the timing of exposure. The body part or organ system that is developing when the fetus encounters the teratogen is most vulnerable (Hyoun, Obican, & Scialli, 2012). Genetic characteristics may buffer or worsen the effects of a teratogen. Perhaps most importantly, the environment the child encounters *after birth* can influence the ultimate effects of prenatal insults.

Sexually transmitted infections (STIs) also threaten the fetus. Some STIs, such as gonorrhea, can be transferred to the baby during delivery. Others, including syphilis and the human immunodeficiency virus (HIV), the virus that causes AIDS, can also infect the fetus while it is in the womb. Besides transmission of infections to the fetus and newborns, STI exposure enhances the risk of stillbirth, as well as a number of other problems, such as eye infections and blindness (in the case of gonorrhea). Many STIs also increase the risk of preterm birth.

A *preterm infant,* one who is born prior to 37 weeks after conception, may also be at risk for developmental difficulties. Whether a preterm infant will have developmental problems is a complex issue, however. Preterm infants who grow up in poverty are more likely to have problems than are those who live in better socioeconomic conditions (Madan & others, 2006). Postnatal experience plays a crucial role in determining the ultimate effects of preterm birth. For example, research has shown that massage can improve developmental outcomes for premature infants (Field, Diego, & Hernandez-Reif, 2011; Wang, He, & Zhang, 2013).

Physical Development in Infancy and Childhood

Human infants are the world's most helpless newborns. One reason for their helplessness is that they are born not quite finished. Our enormous brain sets humans apart from other animals. Getting that big brain out of the relatively small birth canal is a challenge that nature has met by sending human babies out of the womb before the brain has fully developed. The first months and years of life allow the developing human (and the environment) to put the finishing touches on that important organ.

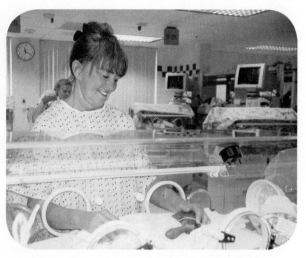

The photograph shows Tiffany Field massaging a newborn infant. Field's research has demonstrated the power of massage in improving the developmental outcome of at-risk infants. Under her direction, the Touch Research Institute in Miami, Florida, investigates the role of touch in a number of domains of health and well-being.

REFLEXES

Newborns come into the world equipped with several genetically wired reflexes that are crucial for survival. Babies are born with the ability to suck and swallow. If they are dropped in water, they will naturally hold their breath, contract their throats to keep water out, and move their arms and legs to stay afloat at least briefly. Some reflexes persist throughout life—coughing, blinking, and yawning, for example. Others, such as automatically grasping something that touches the fingers, disappear in the months following birth, as higher brain functions mature and infants develop voluntary control over many behaviors. Figure 9.2 shows some examples of reflexes.

Rooting

What provokes the response? Stroking of the infant's cheek

What the infant does Head turns in the direction of the touch, and the infant opens his or her mouth for feeding.

Gripping

What provokes the response? Something that is placed in the infant's hand

What the infant does The infant grasps the item and can hold on very well— almost enough to support his or her own weight.

Toe Curling

What provokes the response? Stroking of the inner or outer sole of the infant's foot

What the infant does If the inner sole is stroked, the infant curls his or her toes. If the outer sole is stroked, the toes spread out.

Moro or Startle

What provokes the response? Sudden noise or movement

What the infant does The infant throws his or her head back and arms and legs out (and then cries).

Galant

What provokes the response? Stroking of the infant's lower back, next to the spinal cord

What the infant does The infant curves toward the side that was stroked— and looks like a fencer when doing so.

FIGURE 9.2 **Some Infant Reflexes** Infants are born with a number of reflexes to get them through life, and they are incredibly cute when they perform them. These reflexes disappear as infants mature.

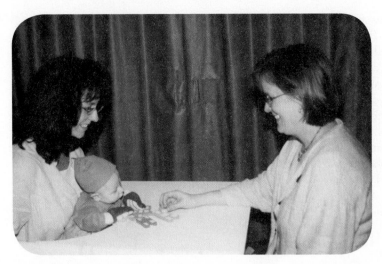

FIGURE 9.3 **Infants' Use of "Sticky Mittens" to Explore Objects** Amy Needham and her colleagues (2002) found that "sticky mittens" enhance young infants' object exploration skills.

● **preferential looking** A research technique that involves giving an infant a choice of what object to look at.

MOTOR AND PERCEPTUAL SKILLS

Relative to the rest of the body, a newborn's head is gigantic, and it flops around uncontrollably. Within 12 months, the infant becomes capable of sitting upright, standing, stooping, climbing, and often walking. During the second year, growth decelerates, but rapid gains occur in such activities as running and climbing. Researchers used to think that motor milestones—such as sitting up, crawling, and walking—unfolded as part of a genetic plan. However, psychologists now recognize that motor development is not the consequence of nature or nurture alone.

Experiences play a role in motor development (Keen, 2011). In one study, 3-month-old infants participated in play sessions wearing "sticky mittens"—mittens with palms that stick to the edges of toys and allow the infants to pick up the toys (Needham, Barrett, & Peterman, 2002) (Figure 9.3). Infants who participated in sessions with the mittens grasped and manipulated objects earlier in their development than a control group of infants who did not have the "mitten" experience. The experienced infants looked at the objects longer, swatted at them, and were more likely to put the objects in their mouths.

Infants are active developers, and their motor and perceptual skills develop together and mutually promote each other. Because a baby can see a new toy, she wants to reach out for it, and her motivation to do so may foster the development of her motor abilities. Babies are continually coordinating their movements with information they perceive through their senses to learn how to maintain their balance, reach for objects in space, and move across various surfaces and terrains (Adolph & Berger, 2013; Adolph & Robinson, 2013). Moving from place to place in the environment teaches babies how objects and people look from different perspectives and whether surfaces will support their weight (Gibson, 2001).

Psychologists face a daunting challenge in studying infant perception. Infants cannot talk, so how can scientists tell what they can see, hear, or feel? Researchers who study infants have no choice but to become very clever methodologists, relying on what infants can do to understand what they know (Atkinson & Braddick, 2013; S. P. Johnson, 2012, 2013). One thing infants can do is look. The **preferential looking** technique involves giving an infant a choice of what object to look at. If an infant shows a reliable preference for one stimulus (say, a picture of a face) over another (a scrambled picture of a face) when these are repeatedly presented in differing locations, we can infer that the infant can tell the two images apart.

Using this technique, researchers have found that as early as *7 days old*, infants are already engaged in organized perception of faces and are able to put together sights and sounds. If presented with two faces with mouths moving, infants will watch the face whose mouth matches the sounds they are hearing (K. Lee & others, 2013b; Lewkowicz & Hansen-Tift, 2012). At 3 months, infants prefer real faces to scrambled faces, and their mother's face to a stranger's (Slater, Field, & Hernandez-Reif, 2007).

The most important recent advance in measuring infant perceptual development is the use of sophisticated eye-tracking equipment. Figure 9.4 shows an infant wearing eye-tracking headgear in recent research on visually guided motor behavior and social interaction. Eye tracking also is being used to study development in many other areas as well, including attention, memory, and face processing (Bulf & Valenza, 2013; Pel & others, 2013; Rueda & Posner, 2013).

Such techniques have provided a great deal of information about infants' remarkable abilities, but they are also limited. Research using brain imaging suggests that infants may know more than even these clever strategies reveal.

FIGURE 9.4 **What Are You Looking At?** Eye-tracking technology allows infant perception researchers to identify exactly what infants are looking at.

THE BRAIN

As an infant plays, crawls, shakes a rattle, smiles, and frowns, the baby's brain is changing dramatically. At birth and in early infancy, the brain's 100 billion neurons have only

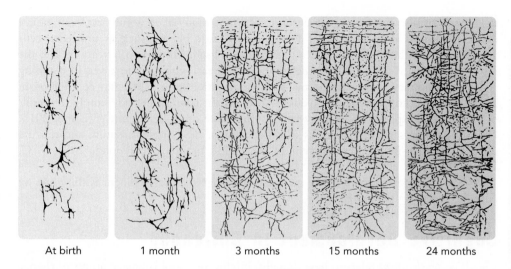

FIGURE 9.5 **Dendritic Spreading**
Note the increase among neurons over the course of the first 2 years of life.
Reprinted by permission of the publisher from *The Postnatal Development of the Human Cerebral Cortex*, Volumes I–VIII, by Jesse LeRoy Conel, Cambridge, MA.: Harvard University Press, Copyright © 1939, 1941, 1947, 1951, 1955, 1959, 1963, 1967 by the President and Fellows of Harvard College. Copyright © renewed 1967, 1969, 1975, 1979, 1983, 1987, 1991.

minimal connections. The infant brain literally is ready and waiting for the experiences that will create these connections (Markant & Thomas, 2013; Sharma, Classen, & Cohen, 2013). During the first 2 years of life, the dendrites of the neurons branch out, and the neurons become far more interconnected (Figure 9.5). Myelination, the process of encasing axons with fat cells (the myelin sheath described in Chapter 3), begins prenatally and continues after birth well into adolescence and young adulthood (Buttermore, Thaxton, & Bhat, 2013).

During childhood, *synaptic connections* increase dramatically (R. E. Watson & others, 2006). Recall from Chapter 3 that a *synapse* is a gap between neurons that is bridged by chemical neurotransmitters. Nearly twice as many synapses are available as will ever be used (Huttenlocher, 1999). The connections that are made become stronger and will survive; the unused ones will be replaced by other neural pathways or disappear. In the language of neuroscience, these unused connections are "pruned." Figure 9.6 illustrates the steep growth and later pruning of synapses during infancy in specific areas of the brain.

Brain-imaging studies demonstrate that children's brains also undergo remarkable anatomical changes (Zelazo, 2013). Repeated brain scans of the same children for up

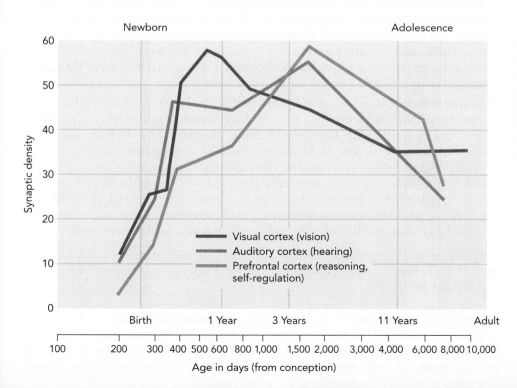

FIGURE 9.6 **Synaptic Density in the Human Brain from Infancy to Adulthood** The graph shows the dramatic increase and then pruning in synaptic density in three regions of the brain: visual cortex, auditory cortex, and prefrontal cortex. Synaptic density is believed to be an important indication of the extent of connectivity between neurons.

Jean Piaget (1896–1980) Piaget, the famous Swiss developmental psychologist, changed the way we think about the development of children's minds.

● **assimilation** An individual's incorporation of new information into existing knowledge.

● **accommodation** An individual's adjustment of his or her schemas to new information.

● **sensorimotor stage** Piaget's first stage of cognitive development, lasting from birth to about 2 years of age, during which infants construct an understanding of the world by coordinating sensory experiences with motor (physical) actions.

to 4 years of age show that the amount of brain material in some areas can nearly double within as little as a year, followed by a drastic loss of tissue as unneeded cells are purged and the brain continues to reorganize itself. From 3 to 6 years of age, the most rapid growth takes place in the frontal lobe areas, which are involved in planning and organizing new actions and in maintaining attention to tasks (Gogtay & Thompson, 2010; P. M. Thompson & others, 2000). These brain changes are not simply the result of nature; new experiences in the world also promote brain development (Lamb, 2013; Narvaez & others, 2013). Thus, as in other areas of development, nature and nurture operate together in the development of the child's brain (A. Diamond, 2013; S. C. Levine & others, 2012).

As the brain develops, thinking matures. This cognitive development is the topic we consider next.

Cognitive Development in Childhood

Cognitive development refers to how thought, intelligence, and language processes change as people mature. *Cognition* refers to the way individuals think and also to their cognitive skills and abilities. In this section we review one of the most important theories in psychology—that proposed by Jean Piaget (1896–1980), the famous Swiss developmental psychologist. In addition, we consider alternatives to Piaget's view and more recent information-processing approaches to cognitive development.

PIAGET'S THEORY OF COGNITIVE DEVELOPMENT

Piaget believed that children *actively construct* their cognitive world as they go through a series of stages. In Piaget's view, children use schemas to make sense of their experience.

Recall from Chapter 7 that a *schema* is a mental concept or framework that organizes and provides a structure for interpreting information. Schemas are expressed as various behaviors and skills that the child can exercise in relation to objects or situations. For example, sucking is a simple early schema. More complex schemas that occur later in childhood include licking, blowing, and crawling. In adulthood, schemas represent more complex expectations and beliefs about the world.

Piaget (1952) described two processes responsible for how schemas develop:

■ **Assimilation** occurs when individuals incorporate new information into existing knowledge: Faced with a new experience, the person applies old ways of doing things. An infant who sucks on whatever new thing he encounters, an adolescent who applies skills learned playing video games to driving a car, and an adult who uses the same strategies to resolve conflict with a spouse that worked in the past with previous romantic partners are all using assimilation.

■ **Accommodation** occurs when individuals adjust their schemas to new information: Rather than using one's old ways of doing things, a new experience promotes new ways of dealing with experience. Existing schemas can be changed, and new schemas can be developed. An infant who has been sticking everything in her mouth might begin to accommodate the sucking schema by being more selective with it. An adolescent who has typically gone with the flow of social pressure might develop a new way of dealing with such pressure by standing up for his beliefs. For an adult, accommodation may mean rethinking old strategies for problem solving when a new challenge, such as the loss of a job, presents itself.

According to Piaget, we go through four stages in understanding the world (Figure 9.7). Each stage involves a qualitatively different way of making sense of the world than the one before it.

Sensorimotor Stage   Piaget's first stage, the **sensorimotor stage,** lasts from birth to about 2 years of age. In this stage, infants construct an understanding of the world by coordinating sensory experiences (such as seeing and hearing) with motor (physical) actions—hence the term *sensorimotor.* As newborns they have little more than reflexive

Sensorimotor Stage	Preoperational Stage	Concrete Operational Stage	Formal Operational Stage
The infant constructs an understanding of the world by coordinating sensory experiences with physical actions. An infant progresses from reflexive, instinctual action at birth to the beginning of symbolic thought toward the end of the stage.	The child begins to represent the world with words and images. These words and images reflect increased symbolic thinking and go beyond the connection of sensory information and physical action.	The child can now reason logically about concrete events and classify objects into different sets.	The adolescent reasons in more abstract, idealistic, and logical ways.
Birth to 2 Years of Age	**2 to 7 Years of Age**	**7 to 11 Years of Age**	**11 Years of Age Through Adulthood**

FIGURE 9.7 Piaget's Four Stages of Cognitive Development Jean Piaget described how human beings, through development, become ever more sophisticated thinkers about the world.

patterns with which to work. By the end of this stage, 2-year-olds show complex sensorimotor patterns and are beginning to use symbols or words in their thinking.

Object permanence is Piaget's term for the crucial accomplishment of understanding that objects and events continue to exist even when they cannot directly be seen, heard, or touched. Piaget believed that "out of sight" literally was "out of mind" for very young infants. Object permanence is an enormous developmental milestone. Once the infant knows that objects still exist even if she cannot see them, the infant can think about future events. Piaget studied object permanence by showing an infant an interesting toy and then covering the toy with a blanket. Piaget reasoned that if the baby understood that the toy still existed, the infant would try to uncover it (see the Psychological Inquiry feature).

● **object permanence** Piaget's term for the crucial accomplishment of understanding that objects and events continue to exist even when they cannot directly be seen, heard, or touched.

Preoperational Stage Piaget's second stage of cognitive development, the **preoperational stage,** lasts from approximately 2 to 7 years of age. Preoperational thought is more symbolic than sensorimotor thought. In preschool years, children begin to represent their world with words, images, and drawings.

The type of symbolic thinking that children are able to accomplish during this stage is limited. They still cannot perform what Piaget called *operations,* by which he meant mental representations that are reversible. Preoperational children have difficulty understanding that reversing an action may restore the original conditions from which the action began.

A well-known test of whether a child can think "operationally" is to present a child with two identical beakers, A and B, filled with liquid to the same height (Figure 9.8). Next to them is a third beaker, C. Beaker C is tall and thin, whereas beakers A and B are short and wide. The liquid is poured from B into C, and the child is asked whether the amounts in A and C are the same. The 4-year-old child invariably says that the amount of liquid in the tall, thin beaker (C) is greater than that in the short, wide beaker (A). The 8-year-old child consistently says the amounts are the same. The

● **preoperational stage** Piaget's second stage of cognitive development, lasting from about 2 to 7 years of age, during which thought is more symbolic than sensorimotor thought.

FIGURE 9.8 Piaget's Conservation Task The beaker test determines whether a child can think operationally—that is, can mentally reverse action and understand conservation of the substance. (a) Two identical beakers are presented to the child, each containing the same amount of liquid. As the child watches, the experimenter pours the liquid from B into C, which is taller and thinner than A and B. (b) The experimenter then asks the child whether beakers A and C have the same amount of liquid. The preoperational child says no. When asked to point to the beaker that has more liquid, the child points to the tall, thin one.

4-year-old child, a preoperational thinker, cannot mentally reverse the pouring action; that is, she cannot imagine the liquid going back from container C to container B. Piaget said that such a child has not grasped the concept of *conservation,* a belief in the permanence of certain attributes of objects despite superficial changes.

To sharpen your sense of preoperational thought, consider the following example. Babysitting for two thirsty 4-year-olds, you might give them each the same amount of apple juice poured into two different cups, one tall and thin and the other short and wide. Try as you might to explain to them that the amounts are the same, they will fight over the tall, thin cup because *it looks like more.* Now, in the same situation, older children—who are operational thinkers—would not bat an eye, because they understand that the amounts are equal.

Children's thought in the preoperational stage is egocentric because preoperational children cannot put themselves in someone else's shoes. Preoperational thinking is also intuitive, meaning that preoperational children make judgments based on gut feelings rather than logic. In reaching a basic level of operational understanding, children progress to the third of Piaget's cognitive stages.

● **concrete operational stage** Piaget's third stage of cognitive development, lasting from about 7 to 11 years of age, during which the individual uses operations and replaces intuitive reasoning with logical reasoning in concrete situations.

Concrete Operational Stage Piaget's **concrete operational stage** (7 to 11 years of age) involves using operations and replacing intuitive reasoning with logical reasoning in concrete situations. Children in the concrete operational stage can successfully complete the beaker task described above. They are able to imagine the operation of reversing the pouring of the liquid back into the wide beaker. Many of the concrete operations identified by Piaget are related to the properties of objects. For instance, when playing with Play-doh, the child in the concrete operational stage realizes that *changing its shape does not change the amount of Play-doh.*

One important skill at this stage of reasoning is the ability to classify things into different sets or subsets and to consider their interrelations. Children in the concrete operational stage might enjoy playing games that involve sorting objects into types and identifying objects that do not fit with a group. (You might remember the childhood song that goes, "One of these things is not like the others," which aimed to coax you into concrete operations.)

Concrete operational thought involves logical reasoning in concrete but not hypothetical contexts. According to Piaget, this kind of abstract, logical reasoning occurs in the fourth, and final, cognitive stage.

● **formal operational stage** Piaget's fourth stage of cognitive development, which begins at 11 to 15 years of age and continues through the adult years; it features thinking about things that are not concrete, making predictions, and using logic to come up with hypotheses about the future.

Formal Operational Stage Individuals enter the **formal operational stage** of cognitive development at 11 to 15 years of age. This stage continues through the adult years. Formal operational thought is more abstract and logical than concrete operational thought. Most important, formal operational thinking includes thinking about things that are not concrete, making predictions, and using logic to come up with hypotheses about the future.

Unlike elementary schoolchildren, adolescents can conceive of hypothetical, purely abstract possibilities. This type of thinking is called *idealistic* because it involves comparing how things are to how they might be. Adolescents also think more logically. They begin to think more as a scientist thinks, devising plans to solve problems and systematically testing solutions. Piaget called this type of problem solving *hypothetical-deductive reasoning*. The term denotes adolescents' ability to develop hypotheses, or best hunches, about ways to solve a problem such as an algebraic equation. It also denotes their ability to systematically deduce, or come to a conclusion about, the best path for solving the problem. In contrast, before adolescence, children are more likely to solve problems by trial and error.

In summary, over the course of Piaget's four developmental stages, a person progresses from sensorimotor cognition to abstract, idealistic, and logical thought. Let's consider the current thinking about Piaget's theories of cognitive development.

EVALUATING PIAGET'S THEORY

Piaget opened up a new way of looking at how the human mind develops (P. H. Miller, 2011). We owe him for a long list of masterful concepts that have enduring power and fascination. We also owe Piaget for the currently accepted vision of children as active, constructive thinkers who play a role in their own development.

Nevertheless, just as other psychological theories have been criticized and amended, so have Piaget's. First, Piaget may have overestimated the cognitive acumen of adolescents and adults. Formal operational thought does not emerge as consistently and universally in early adolescence as Piaget envisioned (Kuhn, 2009). Many adolescents and adults do not reason as logically as Piaget proposed. Second, Piaget likely underestimated the cognitive capacities of very young children. As methods have improved for assessing infants and children, researchers have found that many cognitive abilities emerge earlier than Piaget envisioned (Bauer, Larkina, & Deocampo, 2011; de Hevia & Spelke, 2010; Meltzoff, 2011; Quinn, 2011).

Piaget's object permanence task has been criticized for not giving infants a chance to show their stuff. To get a sense of the limitations of Piaget's task, check out the Psychological Inquiry.

BAILLARGEON: A NATIVIST APPROACH TO INFANT COGNITION

Renée Baillargeon has documented that infants as young as 3 months of age know that objects continue to exist even when hidden, and even these very young infants have expectations about objects in the world that seem quite a bit more sophisticated than Piaget imagined (Baillargeon, 2014; Baillargeon, Scott, & He, 2010; Baillargeon & others, 2012; Luo, Kaufman, & Baillargeon, 2009).

In one study, researchers presented 3-month-old infants a puppet show featuring Minnie Mouse (Luo & Baillargeon, 2005). In the center of the stage was a flat cardboard cutout of a castle. Minnie entered stage right and proceeded toward the castle, disappearing behind it. When Minnie went behind the castle wall from one side, the infants looked for her to appear in the doorway and to come out on the other side, suggesting that even though Minnie was out of sight, she was not out of mind. Not only did these 3-month-olds realize that Minnie still existed, but they also *had expectations* about where she was heading.

Such findings have led many developmental psychologists to assert that we must expand our appreciation for the perceptual and cognitive tools that are available to infants with very little experience (Baillargeon, 2014; Scott & Baillargeon, 2013; Spelke, Bernier, & Snedeker, 2013). From this perspective, sometimes called the *nativist* approach, infants possess primitive expectancies about events and objects in the world

psychological *inquiry*

Thinking Critically About Object Permanence

Let's revisit the classic object permanence task developed by Piaget to consider how the aspects of this task might have led Piaget to underestimate infants' abilities. Remember that from Piaget's perspective, "proving" object permanence meant that the child must search for the hidden toy, reach out, and retrieve it.

Let's assume that the child does believe that the toy exists even if he or she cannot see it. What skills must the child possess in order to enact the behaviors that Piaget thought would indicate object permanence? Answer the following questions to sharpen your understanding of this measure of object permanence.

1. Look at the two photos. Assuming that the child does understand that the toy still exists behind the board, what behavior must the baby exhibit to indicate that understanding?

2. What motor and perceptual skills are required for the child to enact those behaviors?

3. What motivational states (or goals) are required for the child to enact them?

4. If the baby does not reach out for the toy even though he knows it still exists, what might the failure mean?

5. Why do you think it took over 50 years for psychologists to question the appropriateness of Piaget's methods?

that are less dependent upon experience than Piaget imagined. In a sense, babies possess a very simple sense of physics, an architecture that appears to be present as early as scientists have been able to measure it (Hespos & van Marle, 2012; Kinzler, Dupoux, & Spelke, 2013). Nativist thinkers recognize later experience as important but see it as building on this architecture (Spelke & Kinzler, 2007).

The *nativist* approach contrasts with the *empiricist* approach. The empiricist approach emphasizes the role of experience in the world as the central driver of cognitive and perceptual development (Newcombe, 2002). The empiricist perspective points out that even if very young infants show an understanding of object permanence, that capacity might still originate in (very early) experience (Spencer & others, 2009). Of course, those very young infants would still have learned object permanence much earlier than Piaget asserted.

VYGOTSKY'S SOCIOCULTURAL COGNITIVE THEORY

Piaget did not think that culture and education play important roles in children's cognitive development. For Piaget, the child's active interaction with the physical world was all that was needed to go through these stages. The Russian psychologist Lev Vygotsky (1962) took a different approach, recognizing that cognitive development is very much an interpersonal process that happens in a cultural context (Gauvain & Parke, 2010).

Vygotsky thought of children as apprentice thinkers who develop as they interact in dialogue with more knowledgeable others, such as parents and teachers (Daniels, 2011; Holzman, 2009). Vygotsky theorized that these expert thinkers spur cognitive development by interacting with a child in a way that is just above the level of sophistication the child has mastered. In effect, these interactions provide scaffolding that allows the child's cognitive abilities to be built higher and higher.

Teachers and parents, then, provide a framework for thinking that is always just at a level the child can strive to attain. Furthermore, in Vygotsky's view, the goal of cognitive development is to learn the skills that will allow the individual to be competent in his or her particular culture. Expert thinkers are not simply guiding a child into a level of cognitive sophistication but also, along the way, sharing with the child important aspects of culture, such as language and customs. For Vygotsky, a child is not simply learning to think about the world—he or she is learning to think about *his or her own world*.

INFORMATION-PROCESSING THEORY

The *information-processing theory* of development focuses on how individuals encode information, manipulate it, monitor it, and create strategies for handling it (R. S. Siegler, 2012; R. S. Siegler & others, 2013). In contrast to Piaget's emphasis on broad stages of cognitive development, information-processing theory focuses on specific cognitive processes, such as memory, as we have reviewed in previous chapters.

For instance, researchers have studied the emergence of autobiographical memory as children come to mentally represent the events that make up their life stories (Bauer, 2013; Fivush, 2011). *Working memory*, that mental workspace that is used for problem solving (Chapter 7), is linked to many aspects of children's development (Baddeley, 2012; Grunewaldt & others, 2013; Myatchin & Lagae, 2013; Reznick, 2013). Children who have better working memory are more advanced in reading comprehension, math skills, and problem solving than their counterparts with less effective working memory (Kroesbergen, van't Noordende, & Kolkman, 2013; Nevo & Breznitz, 2013). One study found that working memory in kindergarten predicted math achievement at the end of the first grade (Monette, Bigras, & Guay, 2011).

A particularly important aspect of cognitive development in childhood is executive function. Recall that *executive function* refers to higher-order, complex cognitive processes, including thinking, planning, and problem solving. Executive function involves managing one's thoughts to engage in goal-directed behavior and to exercise self-control (Carlson, Zelazo, & Faja, 2013; A. Diamond, 2013). In preschoolers, executive function involves cognitive skills such as holding back on one's automatic impulses, being cognitively flexible, setting goals, and the ability to forgo an immediate pleasure or reward for a more desirable one later (Bell & Cuevas, 2013; Carlson & White, 2011; Vuontela & others, 2013; Zelazo & Muller, 2011). To be successful in school, one must be able to sit still, wait in line, raise one's hand, and so forth. These simple tasks require self-control and the capacity to inhibit one's automatic responses (Diamond & Lee, 2011). It is not surprising then that executive function during the preschool years is linked to school readiness (Ursache, Blair, & Raver, 2012), perhaps even more strongly than general IQ (Blair & Razza, 2007).

A large longitudinal study showed that aspects of executive function assessed in early childhood predict less risk-taking, decreased drop-out rates, and less drug use in adolescence, as well as better physical and psychological health, better earnings, and less criminal behavior in adulthood (some 30 years later) (Moffitt & others, 2011). Clearly, then, executive function is important. Can it be fostered by experience?

Parents and teachers play important roles in the development of executive function. Parents who model executive function and self-control can serve as scaffolds for these skills (Herbers & others, 2011; Masten, 2013; Masten & others, 2008). A variety of activities increase children's executive function, such as computerized training that uses games to improve working memory (CogMed, 2013), aerobic exercise (Y. K. Chang & others, 2012), and mindfulness training (Zelazo & Lyons, 2012).

Specific experiences can facilitate executive function, as well. In one study, 3-year-olds were read one of two stories, either *Planet Opposite* (a fantasy book in which everything is turned upside down) or *Fun Town* (a reality-oriented fiction book) (Carlson & White, 2011). The two stories

presented different cognitive experiences. In *Planet Opposite*, the children learned about a topsy-turvy imaginary world. Might such an experience allow them to be more cognitively flexible?

To examine this question, after being read one of the books, the kids were asked to complete the Less Is More Task. In this task, they were shown two trays of candy—one with 5 pieces, the other with 2—and told that the tray they picked would be given to the stuffed animal seated at the table. This simple task is difficult for 3-year-olds. They have a very hard time not immediately picking the tray they want *for themselves*. So, their first inclination is to pick the tray with more candy (only to have it handed over to a stuffed animal). The results showed that 60 percent of the 3-year-olds who heard *Planet Opposite* managed to select the tray with the smaller number of candies (keeping the 5 pieces for themselves) compared to only 20 percent of the children who heard the other story (Carlson & White, 2011). Stretching their thinking using imagination led the children to be better able to think through the Less Is More Task, overriding the urge to pick the tray with more candy.

Socioemotional Development in Infancy and Childhood

When we observe the newborns behind the window of a hospital nursery, one thing is clear: Humans differ from one another in terms of their emotional demeanor from the very beginning of life. Some are easygoing, and some are prone to distress. Furthermore, in the earliest days of life, infants encounter a social network that will play an important role as they develop their sense of self and the world. To begin our exploration of the socioemotional aspects of development, we focus first on these raw ingredients of emotional and social characteristics that are present early in life—infant temperament and attachment.

TEMPERAMENT

● **temperament** An individual's behavioral style and characteristic ways of responding.

Temperament refers to an individual's behavioral style and characteristic way of responding. There are a number of ways to think about infant temperament. For example, psychiatrists Alexander Chess and Stella Thomas (1977, 1996) identified three basic types of temperament in children:

■ *The easy child* generally is in a positive mood, quickly establishes regular routines in infancy, and easily adapts to new experiences.

■ *The difficult child* tends to react negatively and to cry frequently, engages in irregular daily routines, and is slow to accept new experiences.

■ *The slow-to-warm-up child* has a low activity level, is somewhat negative, is inflexible, and is very cautious in the face of new experiences.

Other researchers suggest that infant temperament also includes other dimensions, such as *effortful control* or *self-regulation* (controlling arousal and not being easily agitated), *inhibition* (being shy and showing distress in an unfamiliar situation), and *negative affectivity* (tending to be frustrated or sad) (Kagan, 2013; Rothbart & Gartstein, 2008). The emotional characteristics that a child brings into the world are thought to serve as a foundation for later personality (Casalin & others, 2012; Shiner & DeYoung, 2013). Similarly, the child's earliest social bonds might set the stage for later social relationships.

ATTACHMENT

Just as infants require nutrition and shelter, they need warm social interaction to survive and develop. A classic study by Harry Harlow (1958) demonstrates the essential importance of warm contact. Harlow separated infant monkeys from their mothers at birth and placed them in cages with two artificial "mothers." One of the mothers was a

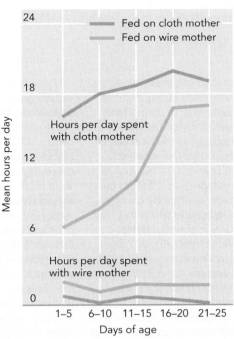

FIGURE 9.9 **Contact Time with Wire and Cloth Surrogate Mothers** Regardless of whether the infant monkeys were fed by a wire or a cloth mother, they overwhelmingly preferred to spend contact time with the cloth mother.

physically cold wire mother; the other was a warm, fuzzy cloth mother (the "contact comfort" mother). Each mother could be outfitted with a feeding mechanism. Half of the infant monkeys were fed by the wire mother, half by the cloth mother. The infant monkeys nestled close to the cloth mother and spent little time on the wire one, even if it was the wire mother that gave them milk (Figure 9.9). When afraid, the infant monkeys ran to the comfy mom.

Harlow's work is important because it demonstrates that contact comfort, not feeding, is crucial to an infant's attachment to its caregiver. This work set the stage for our modern understanding of the vital role of warm physical contact between caregivers and infants.

Infant attachment is the close emotional bond between an infant and its caregiver. British psychiatrist John Bowlby (1969, 1989) theorized that the infant and the mother instinctively form an attachment. For Bowlby, the newborn comes into the world equipped to stimulate the caregiver to respond; it cries, clings, smiles, and coos. Bowlby thought that this early relationship with our primary caregiver was internalized so that it served as our schema for our sense of self and the social world. Many developmental psychologists concur that such attachment during the first year provides an important foundation for later development (Bretherton, 2012; Brisch, 2012; Sroufe, Coffino, & Carlson, 2010).

Mary Ainsworth devised the *strange situation test* to measure children's attachment (Ainsworth, 1979; Ainsworth & others, 1978). In this procedure, caregivers leave infants alone with a stranger and then return. Children's responses to this situation are used to classify them into one of three attachment styles. **Secure attachment** means infants use the caregiver, usually the mother, as a secure base from which to explore the environment. In the strange situation, the secure infant is upset when the mother leaves, but calms down and appears happy to see her when she returns (Behrens, Parker, & Haltigan, 2011). The securely attached infant moves freely away from the mother but also keeps tabs on her by periodically glancing at her.

In contrast, there are two types of insecure attachments, *avoidant* and *anxious/ambivalent*. In the strange situation, the avoidant infant might not even notice the mother has gone. The anxious/ambivalent infant responds with intense distress, only to rage at the mother when she returns.

One criticism of attachment theory is that it does not adequately account for cultural variations (van IJzendoorn & Bakermans-Kranenburg, 2010). For example, in some cultures infants show strong attachments to many people, not just to their primary caregiver (Rothbaum & others, 2000, 2007). In addition, attachment theory does not account for temperamental differences among infants that might color the attachment

● **infant attachment** The close emotional bond between an infant and its caregiver.

● **secure attachment** The ways that infants use their caregiver, usually their mother, as a secure base from which to explore the environment.

Developmental and Social Psychology: Is Attachment an Enduring Aspect of Life?

Social psychologists interested in studying close relationships have found Bowlby's observations about infant attachment to be an extraordinarily useful way to understand adult relationships. Relationships with romantic partners differ from those with parents, but romantic partners fulfill some of the same needs for adults as parents do for their children (Nosko & others, 2011; Mikulincer & Shaver, 2013a). Just as securely attached infants use their caregiver as a secure base from which to explore the environment, adults may count on their romantic partners to be a secure base to which they can return and obtain comfort and security in stressful times.

How is attachment security defined in adulthood? Securely attached adults have positive views of relationships, find it easy to get close to others, and are not overly concerned with or stressed out about their romantic relationships. Insecure attachment is divided into two types: avoidant and anxious. Avoidant individuals are hesitant about getting involved in romantic relationships and once in a relationship tend to distance themselves from their partner. Anxiously attached individuals demand closeness, are less trusting, more emotional, jealous, and possessive.

Measuring attachment styles is considerably easier with adults than with infants. Unlike infants, adults can answer questionnaires and interviews. Studies using such measures show that the majority of adults (about 60 to 80 percent) describe themselves as securely attached (Zeifman & Hazan, 2008).

Research with adults shows that securely attached individuals report more positive romantic relationships (Holland & Roisman, 2010). Anxiously attached individuals show strong ambivalence toward a romantic partner (Mikulincer & others, 2010) and to their relationship commitment (Joel, MacDonald, & Shimotomai, 2011). A national survey indicated that insecurely attached (avoidant and anxious) adults were more likely to develop diseases and chronic illnesses, especially cardiovascular problems such as high blood pressure, heart attack, and stroke (McWilliams & Bailey, 2010).

A key question, of course, is whether adult romantic attachment styles are linked to infant attachment. Do infants who respond to the strange situation in a way that indicates secure attachment actually become adults who are more securely attached in their romantic relationships? To answer this question, we would need to measure infant attachment using the strange situation and then follow up on those same individuals, many years later, when they are in romantic relationships. Sounds next to impossible, but Everett Waters and his colleagues (2000) conducted just such a study.

How do your adult relationships reflect your childhood relationship with your parents?

These researchers administered romantic attachment style interviews with 60 young adults who, 20 years earlier, had participated in a study measuring their attachment style using the strange situation. The results? In terms of classifying participants as secure or insecure, infant attachment style matched with adulthood romantic attachment style for 72 percent of these individuals. Considering that these classifications were based on very different assessment instruments and were separated by 20 years, this level of agreement is striking. For those participants who had changed in attachment style, most typically from secure to insecure, Waters and his colleagues (2000) identified traumatic or stressful events as a potential reason.

If you have an insecure attachment style, are you stuck with it? Attachment styles show some stability in adulthood (Fraley & others, 2011), but adults have the capacity to change their attachment thinking and behavior; our working models of relationships are open to revision by our close relationships themselves (Mikulincer & Shaver, 2013a). Keep in mind, as well, that although it might seem like a no brainer that everyone would want to be securely attached, the differences that exist among us are often exactly what make our lives rich and our relationships rewarding (Ein-Dor & others, 2010). In the context of satisfying close relationships, partners can find something to love, even in our faults.

relationship. Finally, caregivers and infants likely share genetic characteristics, and it might be that the attachment relationship is really a product of these shared genes (Gervai, 2009). Despite such criticisms, there is ample evidence that secure attachment is important to development (R. A. Thompson, 2013a, 2013b, 2013c).

From Bowlby's perspective, an infant's experiences lay the groundwork for expectations about what human relationships will be like, setting the stage for future relationships, including our romantic relationships as adults. Do such early experiences provide a stable template of relationships we carry with us throughout life? To answer this question, see the Intersection.

Given these raw ingredients of temperament and attachment, how does a human being develop in the socioemotional domain? Erik Erikson, who devised a theory of what he called *psychosocial development,* addressed this question. Like Piaget's theory of cognitive development, Erikson's theory has guided thinking about how human beings' social and emotional capacities develop throughout the life span.

ERIKSON'S THEORY OF SOCIOEMOTIONAL DEVELOPMENT

Erik Erikson (1902–1994) Erikson generated one of the most important developmental theories of the twentieth century.

Erik Erikson (1902–1994) proposed eight psychosocial stages of development from infancy through old age. In Erikson's (1968) view, the first four stages take place in childhood; the last four, in adolescence and adulthood (Figure 9.10).

Erikson's theory is important because he viewed socioemotional development as a *lifelong* process, marked by important developmental milestones in young and middle adulthood and into old age. Each of Erikson's stages represents a developmental task that the individual must master at a particular place in the life span.

Erikson's developmental tasks are represented by two possible outcomes—one, greater strength and competence; the other, greater weakness and vulnerability. Which outcome occurs depends on whether the person's needs at each stage are well met or frustrated. Using Erikson's stages as a guide, let's consider the various ways that human beings develop in terms of their capacities for interpersonal relationships and emotional well-being in infancy and childhood.

SOCIOEMOTIONAL DEVELOPMENT IN INFANCY AND CHILDHOOD: FROM TRUST TO INDUSTRY

We examine Erikson's adolescence and adult stages later in this chapter. His four childhood stages are:

- *Trust versus mistrust:* Trust is built in infancy (birth to 18 months) when a baby's basic needs—such as comfort, food, and warmth—are met by responsive, sensitive caregivers. At this stage, the helpless infant depends on caregivers to establish a sense that the world is a predictable and friendly place. Once trust is established, toddlers begin to see themselves as independent agents in the world.

- *Autonomy versus shame and doubt:* During toddlerhood (18 months through 3 years), children can develop either a positive sense of independence and autonomy or negative feelings of shame and doubt. In seeking autonomy, they are likely to develop a strong sense of independence. A toddler who is experiencing toilet training is learning the beginnings of self-control. The toddler's growing independence is evident in the child's insistence that no matter how difficult the task, "I can do it myself!" Similarly common is the toddler's assertion of autonomy with a simple two-letter word: "No!"

- *Initiative versus guilt:* In early childhood (3 to 5 years), preschoolers experience what it is like to forge their own interests and friendships and to take on responsibilities. If you have ever spent time with a 3-year-old, you know how often the child wants to help with whatever an adult is doing. When they experience a sense of taking on responsibility, preschoolers develop initiative. Otherwise, according to Erikson, they may feel guilty or anxious.

- *Industry versus inferiority:* Children in middle and late childhood (6 years to puberty) can achieve industry by mastering knowledge and intellectual skills. When they do not, they can feel inferior. At the end of early childhood, children

Trust Versus Mistrust	**Autonomy Versus Shame and Doubt**	**Initiative Versus Guilt**	**Industry Versus Inferiority**
Developmental period: Infancy (birth to 1½ years)	**Developmental period:** Toddlerhood (1½ to 3 years)	**Developmental period:** Early childhood (preschool years, ages 3–5)	**Developmental period:** Middle and late childhood (elementary school years, 6 years–puberty)
Characteristics: A sense of trust requires a feeling of physical comfort and minimal amount of fear about the future. Infants' basic needs are met by responsive, sensitive caregivers.	**Characteristics:** After gaining trust in their caregivers, infants start to discover that they have a will of their own. They assert their sense of autonomy, or independence. They realize their will. If infants are restrained too much or punished too harshly, they are likely to develop a sense of shame and doubt.	**Characteristics:** As preschool children encounter a widening social world, they are challenged more and need to develop more purposeful behavior to cope with these challenges. Children are now asked to assume more responsibility. Uncomfortable guilt feelings may arise, though, if the children are irresponsible and are made to feel too anxious.	**Characteristics:** At no other time are children more enthusiastic than at the end of early childhood's period of expansive imagination. As children move into the elementary school years, they direct their energy toward mastering knowledge and intellectual skills. The danger at this stage involves feeling incompetent and unproductive.

FIGURE 9.10 Erikson's Eight Stages of Psychosocial Development Erikson changed the way psychologists think about development by tracing the process of growth over the entire life span.

are ready to turn their energy to learning academic skills. If they do not, they can develop a sense of being incompetent and unproductive. During the beginnings of elementary school, children learn the value of what Erikson called *industry,* gaining competence in academic skills and acquiring the ability to engage in self-discipline and hard work.

From Erikson's perspective, then, children should grow toward greater levels of autonomy and self-confidence as they progress from infancy to school age and beyond. At each stage, Erikson said, parents can facilitate the child's growth, or they can thwart it by being overly protective or neglectful.

EVALUATING ERIKSON'S THEORY

Like Piaget's theory, Erikson's conclusions have had their critics (Kroger, 2007). Erikson mainly practiced case study research, which some reject as the sole research foundation for his approach. Critics also argue that Erikson's attempt to capture each developmental stage with a single concept leaves out other important developmental tasks. For example, as we will see, Erikson said that the main task for young adults is to resolve a conflict between intimacy and isolation, yet another important developmental task at this life stage revolves around careers and work.

PARENTING AND CHILDHOOD SOCIOEMOTIONAL DEVELOPMENT

Various researchers have tried to identify styles of parenting associated with positive developmental outcomes. Diana Baumrind (1991, 1993, 2012) described four basic styles of interaction between parents and their children:

● **authoritarian parenting** A restrictive, punitive style in which the parent exhorts the child to follow the parent's directions.

■ **Authoritarian parenting** is a strict punitive style. The authoritarian parent firmly limits and controls the child with little verbal exchange. In a difference of opinion about how to do something, for example, the authoritarian parent might say, "You do it my way or else." Children of authoritarian parents sometimes lack social skills, show poor initiative, and compare themselves with others.

Identity Versus Identity Confusion	**Intimacy Versus Isolation**	**Generativity Versus Stagnation**	**Integrity Versus Despair**
Developmental period: Adolescence (10–20 years)	**Developmental period:** Eary adulthood (20s, 30s)	**Developmental period:** Middle adulthood (40s, 50s)	**Developmental period:** Late adulthood (60s–)
Characteristics: Individuals are faced with finding out who they are, what they are all about, and where they are going in life. An important dimension is the exploration of alternative solutions to roles. Career exploration is important.	**Characteristics:** Individuals face the developmental task of forming intimate relationships with others. Erikson described intimacy as finding oneself yet losing oneself in another person.	**Characteristics:** A chief concern is to assist the younger generation in developing and leading useful lives.	**Characteristics:** Individuals look back and evaluate what they have done with their lives. The retrospective glances can be either positive (integrity) or negative (despair).

Importantly, culture influences the effects of authoritarian parenting. In one study (Rudy & Grusec, 2006), collectivist mothers (in this case Iranian, Indian, Egyptian, and Pakistani) described themselves as more authoritarian but did not express negative attitudes about their children, and the children did not show these more negative outcomes. For Latino families, some psychologists have suggested that authoritarian parenting may express culturally valued childrearing goals such as family, respect, and education and that this parenting style must be understood in the context of these cultural ideals (Halgunseth, Ispa, & Rudy, 2006).

- **Authoritative parenting** encourages the child to be independent but still places limits and controls on behavior. This parenting style is more collaborative. Extensive verbal give-and-take is allowed, and parents are warm and nurturing toward the child. An authoritative father might put his arm around the child in a comforting way and say, "You know you should not have done that; let's talk about how you can handle the situation better next time." Children whose parents are authoritative tend to be socially competent, self-reliant, and socially responsible.

- **Neglectful parenting** is distinguished by a lack of parental involvement in the child's life. Children of neglectful parents might develop a sense that other aspects of their parents' lives are more important than they are. Children whose parents are neglectful tend to be less competent socially, to handle independence poorly, and (especially) to show poor self-control.

- **Permissive parenting** involves placing few limits on the child's behavior. A permissive parent lets the child do what he or she wants. Some parents deliberately rear their children this way because they believe that the combination of warm involvement and few limits will produce a creative, confident child. However, children with very permissive parents typically rate poorly in social competence. They often fail to learn respect for others, expect to get their own way, and have difficulty controlling their behavior. Recall that socioemotional development involves becoming increasingly adept at controlling and regulating one's emotions and behaviors (Vazsonyi & Huang, 2010). Children may require structure from their caregivers in order to acquire these skills.

● **authoritative parenting** A parenting style that encourages the child to be independent but that still places limits and controls on behavior.

● **neglectful parenting** A parenting style characterized by a lack of parental involvement in the child's life.

● **permissive parenting** A parenting style characterized by the placement of few limits on the child's behavior.

Lawrence Kohlberg (1927–1987)
Kohlberg created a provocative theory of moral development. In his view, "Moral development consists of a sequence of qualitative changes in the way an individual thinks."

Moral Development in Childhood

Another aspect of social development that psychologists study is how an individual becomes a person of character—someone who behaves morally. This aspect of development features yet another classic theory in developmental psychology, that of Lawrence Kohlberg (1927–1987). Moral development involves changes with age in thoughts, feelings, and behaviors regarding the principles and values that guide what people should do.

KOHLBERG'S THEORY

Kohlberg (1958) began his study of moral thinking by creating a series of stories and asking children, adolescents, and adults questions about the stories. One of the stories goes something like this. A man, Heinz, whose wife is dying of cancer, knows about a drug that might save her life. He approaches the pharmacist who has the drug, but the pharmacist refuses to give it to him without being paid a very high price. Heinz is unable to scrape together the money and eventually decides to steal the drug.

After reading the story, each person interviewed was asked a series of questions about the moral dilemma. Should Heinz have stolen the drug? Kohlberg was less interested in the answer to this question than he was to the next one: Why? Based on the reasons people gave for their answers, Kohlberg (1986) evaluated their level of moral development. Kohlberg's stages of moral development consist of three general levels:

1. *Preconventional:* The individual's moral reasoning is based primarily on the consequences of behavior and punishments and rewards from the external world. Moral reasoning is guided by not wanting Heinz to go to jail or concern for the druggists' profits.

2. *Conventional:* The individual abides by standards learned from parents or society's laws. At this level the person might reason that Heinz should act in accord with expectations or his role as a good husband or reason that Heinz should follow the law no matter what.

3. *Postconventional:* The individual recognizes alternative moral courses, explores the options, and then develops an increasingly personal moral code. At this level, the person might reason that saving Heinz's wife is more important than a law.

Kohlberg believed that moral development advances because of the maturation of thought, the availability of opportunities for role taking, and the chance to discuss moral issues with a person who reasons at a stage just above one's own.

Kohlberg studied with Piaget, and Kohlberg's approach to moral reasoning emphasized the individual's capacity to reason in a sophisticated way, as did Piaget's theory. As we will see, subsequent theories of moral development have focused on its social and emotional components. For Kohlberg, a sense of justice was at the heart of moral reasoning, which he believed laid the foundation for moral behavior.

EVALUATING KOHLBERG'S THEORY

Kohlberg's ideas have stimulated considerable research about how people think about moral issues (Lapsley, 2013; Lapsley & Yaeger, 2013; Narvaez, 2013; Nucci, 2013; L. J. Walker, 2013). At the same time, his theory has numerous critics.

One criticism is that moral *reasoning* does not necessarily mean moral *behavior.* When people are asked about their moral reasoning, what they say might fit into Kohlberg's advanced stages, but their actual behavior might involve cheating, lying, and stealing. The cheaters, liars, and thieves might know what is right but still do what is wrong.

Another criticism is that Kohlberg's view does not adequately reflect concern for other people and social bonds (Hardy & Carlo, 2011). Kohlberg's theory is called a *justice perspective* because it focuses on the rights of the individual as the key to sound moral reasoning. In contrast, the *care perspective,* which lies at the heart of Carol Gilligan's (1982) approach to moral development, views people in terms of their connectedness with others and emphasizes interpersonal communication, relationships, and concern for others. From Gilligan's perspective, this weakness in Kohlberg's approach explains why, using his measures, women generally score lower than men on moral development.

Similarly, culture can influence whether a person approaches a moral dilemma from the perspective of justice or care (Gibbs, 2010; J. Miller, 2013; Tappan, 2013; Wainryb, 2013). In Western cultures, where people generally tend toward an individualistic sense of self and are therefore inclined to take a justice perspective, individuals might score higher in Kohlberg's scheme than their counterparts in collectivistic Asian cultures, where people have a sense of the self as part of a larger group.

One final criticism of Kohlberg centers on his overestimation of the role of logical reasoning in moral judgments. Contemporary research suggests that Kohlberg missed the very large role of emotion and intuition in moral decision making (Greene & Haidt, 2002).

CURRENT RESEARCH ON MORAL DEVELOPMENT

Researchers interested in moral development have increasingly studied **prosocial behavior,** behavior that is intended to benefit other people (Eisenberg, Spinrad, & Morris, 2013). For example, researchers are probing how, when, and why children engage in everyday acts of kindness toward others (Carlo & others, 2011). Studies have found that supportive parenting and parental monitoring relate to increased helping and comforting of others (Dodge, Coie, & Lynam, 2006). Furthermore, research suggests that the capacities to empathize with others and engage in prosocial behavior are linked with the ability to engage in self-control more generally (Eisenberg, Spinrad, & Morris, 2013).

Other recent research has focused on when a child first shows signs of possessing a conscience (Kochanska & others, 2008). Having a conscience means hearing that voice in our head that tells us that something is morally good or bad. Deborah Laible and Ross Thompson (2000, 2002, 2007) have examined the conversations between mothers and toddlers at times when the child did something well or got into trouble. They have found that by 3 years of age, children begin to show signs of early conscience development. Parent–child interactions that are clear, elaborate, and rich with emotional content and that include shared positive emotion foster this development. Childhood characteristics are important because longitudinal research shows that kind, moral children are more likely to be kind, moral adults (Eisenberg, Fabes, & Spinrad, 2006).

How can parents successfully rear a kind, helpful, and moral child? Research shows that warm and supportive parenting, rather than overly punishing and rigid parenting, is the key; this parenting involves children in decision making and models moral behavior, thereby promoting prosocial behavior in children (Eisenberg & Murphy, 1995; Eisenberg & Valiente, 2002; Eisenberg & others, 2009).

Carol Gilligan (b. 1936) Gilligan argues that Kohlberg's approach does not give adequate attention to relationships. In Gilligan's view, "Many girls seem to fear, most of all, being alone—without friends, family, and relationships."

● **prosocial behavior** Behavior that is intended to benefit other people.

test yourself

1. What are teratogens? Give several examples of them.
2. According to Piaget, what two processes are responsible for how people use and adapt their schemas, and what is involved in each process? What are some key aspects of Vygotsky's theory and information-processing theory?
3. What are Erikson's four childhood stages of development, and with what is each centrally concerned?

3· ADOLESCENCE

Adolescence is the developmental period of transition from childhood to adulthood, beginning around ages 10 to 12 and ending at 18 to 21. Adolescents are not all the same. Variations in ethnicity, culture, history, gender, socioeconomic status, and lifestyle characterize their life trajectories (Diamond & Savin-Williams, 2013). In this section we examine the changes that occur in adolescence in the domains of physical, cognitive, and socioemotional development.

Physical Development in Adolescence

Dramatic physical changes characterize adolescence, especially early adolescence. Among the major physical changes of adolescence are those involving puberty and the brain.

PUBERTAL CHANGE

● **puberty** A period of rapid skeletal and sexual maturation that occurs mainly in early adolescence.

● **androgens** The class of sex hormones that predominate in males, produced by the testes in males and by the adrenal glands in both males and females.

● **estrogens** The class of sex hormones that predominate in females, produced mainly by the ovaries.

The signature physical change in adolescence is **puberty,** a period of rapid skeletal and sexual maturation that occurs mainly in early adolescence. We will look at these developments more specifically in Chapter 11.

Hormonal changes lie at the core of pubertal development. The concentrations of certain hormones increase dramatically during puberty (Susman & Dorn, 2013). *Testosterone*—an **androgen,** which is the class of sex hormones that predominate in males—is associated in boys with the development of genitals, an increase in height, and voice change. *Estradiol*—an **estrogen,** the class of sex hormones that predominate in females—is associated in girls with breast, uterine, and skeletal development. Developmental psychologists believe that hormonal changes account for at least some of the emotional ups and downs of adolescence, but hormones are not alone responsible for adolescent behavior (Graber, 2007; Negriff, Susman, & Trickett, 2011).

Remember that physical and socioemotional development are intertwined. Nowhere is this link more apparent than in the timing of puberty. Boys who mature earlier than their peers tend to show more positive socioemotional outcomes, such as being popular with their peers and having higher self-esteem (Graber, Brooks-Gunn, & Warren, 2006). Longitudinal studies have shown that boys who matured early in adolescence were more successful and less likely to drink alcohol, smoke cigarettes, or engage in delinquent behaviors than late-maturing boys (Taga, Markey, & Friedman, 2006; van der Geest, Blokland, & Bijleveld, 2009). In contrast, girls who are early bloomers tend to be less outgoing and less popular, and they are more likely to smoke, use drugs, become sexually active, and engage less in academic pursuits (Blumenthal & others, 2011; Sontag-Padilla & others, 2012).

THE ADOLESCENT BRAIN

Brain-imaging studies show important changes in the brain during adolescence (Blakemore & Mills, 2014; Kar, Vijay, & Mishra, 2013; Steinberg, 2013). These changes focus on the earlier development of the amygdala, which involves emotion, and the later development of the prefrontal cortex, which is concerned with reasoning and decision making (Figure 9.11).

These changes in the brain may help to explain why adolescents often display very strong emotions but cannot yet control these passions. It is as if the adolescent brain does not have the brakes to slow down emotions. Because of the relatively slow development of the prefrontal cortex, which continues to mature into early adulthood, adolescents may lack the cognitive skills to control their impulses effectively. This developmental disjunction may account for increased risk taking and other problems in adolescence (Steinberg, 2012, 2013).

Biological changes in the brain are linked with experiences (Lerner, Boyd, & Du, 2008). For instance, one study of adolescents found that resisting peer pressure was correlated with prefrontal cortex thickening and more brain connections (Paus & others, 2008). This correlational study cannot tell us if the brain changes promoted peer-pressure resistance or if this resistance promoted changes in the brain, but it does highlight the nature–nurture question that permeates the study of development.

Prefrontal Cortex
Involved in higher-order cognitive functioning, such as decision making

Amygdala
Involved in processing information about emotion

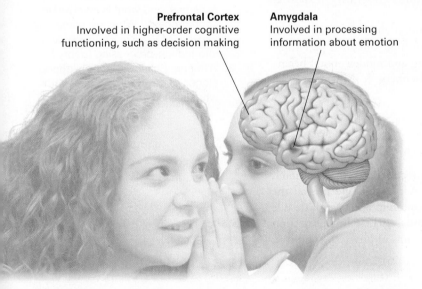

FIGURE 9.11 **Developmental Changes in the Adolescent's Brain** The amygdala, which is responsible for processing information about emotion, matures earlier than the prefrontal cortex, which is responsible for making decisions and other higher-order cognitive functions.

Cognitive Development in Adolescence

As they advance into Piaget's formal operational thinking, adolescents undergo other significant cognitive changes (Byrnes, 2012; Kuhn, 2009, 2011). One characteristic of adolescent thinking, especially in early adolescence, is egocentrism. Although children are also considered egocentric, *adolescent egocentrism* has a different focus; it involves the belief that others are as preoccupied with the adolescent as he or she is and that the individual is both unique and invincible (that is, incapable of being harmed) (Albert & Steinberg, 2011). Egocentric adolescents perceive others as observing them more than actually is the case—think of the eighth-grade boy who senses that everyone has noticed the small pimple on his face.

However, research is calling into question whether adolescents believe they are invincible. In one study, 12- to 18-year-olds were asked about their chance of dying in the next year and before age 20; these respondents greatly overestimated this dire outcome (Fischhoff & others, 2010).

Socioemotional Development in Adolescence

Among the key aspects of adolescent development are identity exploration and the roles that parents and peers play in adolescent development.

IDENTITY

Recall from Figure 9.10 that Erikson (1968) viewed the key challenge of adolescence (his fifth stage) as *identity versus identity confusion.* Erikson's approach to the formation of identity during adolescence is one of his most important contributions (Kroger, 2012; Syed, 2013). In seeking an identity, adolescents face the challenges of finding out who they are, what they are all about, and where they are going in life. Adolescents are confronted with many new roles and adult statuses—from jobs and careers to friendships and romantic relationships. If they do not adequately explore their identity during this stage, they end up confused about who they are. Erikson argued that parents should allow adolescents to explore many different roles and many paths within a particular role.

Adolescents who spend this time in their lives exploring alternatives can reach some resolution of the identity crisis and emerge with a new sense of self. Those who do not successfully resolve the crisis suffer what Erikson calls *identity confusion,* which is expressed in one of two ways: The individual either withdraws, becoming isolated from peers and family, or the person loses himself or herself in the crowd.

Marcia's Theory on Identity Status Building on Erikson's ideas, James Marcia proposed the concept of *identity status* to describe a person's position in the development of an identity (Kroger, Martinussen, & Marcia, 2010; Marcia, 1980, 2002). In Marcia's view, two dimensions of identity, exploration and commitment, are important. *Exploration* refers to a person's investigating various options for a career and for personal values. *Commitment* involves making a decision about which identity path to follow and making a personal investment in attaining that identity. Various combinations of exploration and commitment give rise to one of four identity statuses.

Marcia's approach focuses on identity as an active construction, an outcome of a process of thinking about and trying on different identities (Klimstra & others, 2009, 2010). To master Marcia's approach, check out the Psychological Inquiry.

Ethnic Identity Developing an identity in adolescence can be especially challenging for individuals from ethnic minority groups (Schwartz & others, 2012, 2013; Syed, 2013). As they mature cognitively, many adolescents become acutely aware of how the majority culture views their ethnic group. In addition, an increasing number of minority adolescents face the challenge of *biculturalism*—identifying in some ways with their ethnic minority group and in other ways with the majority culture (Marks, Patton, & Coll, 2011).

Research has shown that for ethnic minority youth, feeling both a positive attachment to their minority group and an attachment to the larger culture is related to more positive

off the mark .com　by Mark Parisi

RELAX, DAD! THEY'RE NOT **REAL** PIERCINGS, THEY'RE TATTOOS OF PIERCINGS...

Copyright by Mark Parisi, www.offthemark.com.

psychological
inquiry

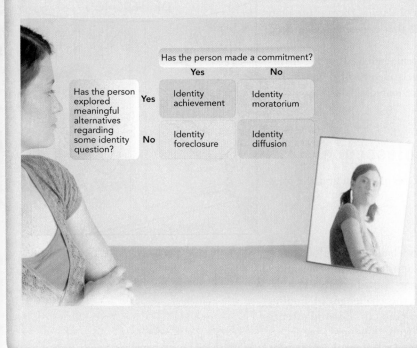

Looking at Identity Exploration

This figure summarizes Marcia's conceptualization of identity development. Notice that the different quadrants of the square represent the crossings of the two factors of commitment and exploration and that every possible combination of the two is represented. Answer the following questions.

1. Imagine a young woman who comes from a family in which no one ever attended college. What sorts of experiences might influence her journey to identity? How might her background influence her identity exploration?

2. Find yourself in this figure. That is, in which quadrant is your own identity located? Do you feel that you fully explored your potential identities? Why or why not?

3. Which path to identity do you believe is most common in young people today? Why?

4. Finding one's path in life is a common theme in popular books, TV, and film. Can you identify a book or movie that depicts the combination of exploration and resolution? Why do you think this theme is so popular?

---

academic and emotional outcomes (Iturbide, Raffaelli, & Carlo, 2009; Umaña-Taylor, Updegraff, & Gonzales-Bracken, 2011; Umaña-Taylor & others, 2012; Yip, Kiang, & Fuligni, 2008). Although it might seem that being a member of an ethnic minority would make life more stressful, studies have indicated that having a strong ethnic identity can buffer adolescents from the effects of discrimination (Iturbide, Raffaelli, & Carlo, 2009; Sellers & others, 2006). For both minority and majority adolescents, developing a positive identity is an important life theme (Kort-Butler & Hegewen, 2011; Oyserman & others, 2003; Umaña-Taylor, Updegraff, & Gonzales-Bracken, 2011).

In addition to ethnic identity, adolescence can be a time when other aspects of one's identity come to the fore, such as sexual orientation and gender role. We discuss these issues in depth in Chapter 11.

PARENT AND PEER INFLUENCES

Parents and peers play important roles in adolescent development, including helping adolescents explore and answer the central questions of identity, "Who am I, and who do I hope to become?" (Bornstein, Jager, & Steinberg, 2013).

Parenting As in childhood, the preferred parenting style for most adolescents is authoritative, being associated with positive outcomes (Baumrind, 2012). To help adolescents reach their full potential, a key parental role is to be an effective manager—one who locates information, makes contacts, helps to structure offsprings' choices, and provides guidance. By assuming this managerial role, parents help adolescents to avoid pitfalls and to work their way through the decisions they face (Simpkins & others, 2009).

Although adolescence is a time of establishing independence, a crucial aspect of the managerial role of parenting is effective monitoring (Branstetter & Furman, 2013; Racz & McMahon, 2011). Monitoring includes supervising the adolescent's choice of social settings, activities, and friends, as well as his or her academic efforts. A research review concluded that when African American parents monitored their sons' academic achievement—by ensuring that they completed homework; by restricting the time spent on activities like video games and TV; and by participating in a consistent, positive dialogue with teachers—their sons' academic achievement benefited (Mandara, 2006).

How competent the adolescent will become often depends on access to legitimate opportunities for growth, such as a quality education, community and societal support for achievement and involvement, and good jobs. Especially important in adolescent development is long-term, deeply caring support from adults (Lerner & others, 2013). Successfully parenting adolescents means allowing adolescents to explore their own identity and handle increasing levels of autonomy in a positive manner, while also remaining an involved parent (Smetana & others, 2009).

Peer Relations   During adolescence, individuals spend more time with peers than they did in childhood. These peer influences can be positive or negative (Wentzel, 2013). A significant aspect of positive peer relations is having one or more close friends. Adolescents can learn to be skilled and sensitive partners in intimate relationships by forging close friendships with selected peers (Tucker & others, 2012). However, some peers and friends can negatively impact adolescents' development. Researchers have found that hanging out with delinquent peers in adolescence can be a strong predictor of substance abuse, delinquent behavior, and depression (Laursen & others, 2012).

The managerial role of parenting involves effective monitoring of the adolescent's friends, social activities, and academic efforts.

4· EMERGING ADULTHOOD, ADULT DEVELOPMENT, AND AGING

Development continues throughout adulthood. Developmental psychologists identify three approximate periods in adult development: early adulthood (20s and 30s), middle adulthood (40s and 50s), and late adulthood (60s until death). Each phase features distinctive physical, cognitive, and socioemotional changes.

Erikson believed that once the issues of identity are resolved, the young adult turns to the important domain of intimate relationships. However, more recently, scholars have noted that during the life stage after adolescence, many young people are putting off the commitments to marriage, family, and career that are traditionally associated with adult life. Jeffrey Arnett introduced the concept of *emerging adulthood* to describe this transitional period, which is partly an extended adolescence and partly a "trying on" of adult roles (Arnett, 2004, 2007, 2010, 2012). If you are a traditional-age college student, you are at this point in the life span. We begin our survey of postadolescent development by briefly examining this transitional life stage.

Emerging Adulthood

Emerging adulthood is the transitional period from adolescence to adulthood (Arnett, 2004, 2006, 2007, 2012). The age range for emerging adulthood is approximately 18 to 25 years of age. Experimentation and exploration characterize the emerging adult. At this point in their development, many individuals are still exploring which career path they want to follow, what they want their identity to be, and what kinds of close relationships they will have.

Jeffrey Arnett (2006, 2010, 2012) identified five main features of emerging adulthood:

- *Identity exploration, especially in love and work:* Emerging adulthood is the time of significant changes in identity for many individuals.
- *Instability:* Residential changes peak during emerging adulthood, a time during which there also is often instability in love, work, and education.
- *Self-focus:* Emerging adults "are self-focused in the sense that they have little in the way of social obligations, [and] little in the way of duties and commitments to others, which leaves them with a great deal of autonomy in running their own lives" (Arnett, 2006, p. 10).

test yourself

1. What characteristics of the adolescent brain help to explain why adolescents often display strong emotions that they cannot control?
2. According to Erikson, what challenges do adolescents face in trying to establish an identity, and what happens if they do not successfully resolve this crisis?
3. In what ways do parents and peers contribute to adolescent development?

● **emerging adulthood** The transitional period from adolescence to adulthood, spanning approximately 18 to 25 years of age.

■ *Feeling "in between":* Many emerging adults consider themselves neither adolescents nor full-fledged adults.

■ *Age of possibilities, a time when individuals have an opportunity to transform their life:* Arnett (2006) describes two ways in which emerging adulthood is the age of possibilities: (1) Many emerging adults are optimistic about their future, and (2) for emerging adults who have experienced difficult times while growing up, emerging adulthood presents an opportunity to guide their lives in a positive direction.

Physical Development in Adulthood

Like other developmental periods, our bodies change during adulthood. Most of the changes that occur following adolescence involve declines in physical and perceptual abilities, as we now consider.

PHYSICAL CHANGES IN EARLY ADULTHOOD

Most adults reach their peak physical development during their 20s and are the healthiest then. Early adulthood, however, is also the time when many physical skills begin to decline. The decline in strength and speed often is noticeable in the 30s. Perceptual abilities also decline. Hearing loss is very common with age. In fact, starting at about age 18, hearing begins a gradual decline, though it is so slow that most people do not notice it until the age of 50 or so.

PHYSICAL CHANGES IN MIDDLE AND LATE ADULTHOOD

By the 40s or 50s, the skin has begun to wrinkle and sag because of the loss of fat and collagen in underlying tissues. Small, localized areas of pigmentation in the skin produce age spots, especially in areas exposed to sunlight such as the hands and face (McCullough & Kelly, 2006). Hair becomes thinner and grayer due to a lower replacement rate and a decline in melanin production. Individuals lose height in middle age, and many gain weight (Landsberg & others, 2013). Once individuals hit their 40s, age-related vision changes usually become apparent, especially difficulty in seeing things up close and after dark.

For women, entering middle age means that menopause will soon occur. Usually in the late 40s or early 50s, a woman's menstrual periods cease completely. With menopause comes a dramatic decline in the ovaries' production of estrogen. Estrogen decline can produce uncomfortable symptoms such as *hot flashes* (sudden, brief flushing of the skin and a feeling of elevated body temperature), nausea, fatigue, and rapid heartbeat. Menopause does not produce serious psychological or physical problems for most women (Henderson, 2011; Judd, Hickey, & Bryant, 2011).

For both men and women, a variety of bodily systems are likely to show the effects of wear and tear as the body becomes less and less able to repair damage and regenerate itself (Parr, Coffey, & Hawley, 2013). Physical strength declines and motor speed slows, and bones may become more brittle (especially for women). Nearly every bodily system may change with age.

Significantly, however, even as age is associated with some inevitable decline, important aspects of successful aging are within the person's control (Bertrand, Graham, & Lachman, 2013; I. C. Siegler & others, 2013a, 2013b). For instance, a healthy diet and regular exercise can help to slow the effects of age (Vissers & others, 2013). Regular physical activity can have wide-reaching benefits not only for physical health but for cognitive functioning as well (Morikawa & others, 2013).

One way older adults navigate the physical changes associated with age is through a process of changing their goals and developing new ways to engage in desired activities. Psychologists refer to this process as *selective optimization with compensation,* which means that older adults match their goals with their current abilities and compensate for declines by finding other ways to do the things they enjoy (Freund, Nikitin, & Riediger, 2013; Hutchinson & Nimrod, 2012). A 75-year-old who can no longer drive because of cataracts might become an expert on her city's train and bus system, for example.

On the island of Okinawa (part of Japan), individuals live longer than anywhere else in the world, and Okinawa has the world's highest prevalence of *centenarians*—individuals who live to 100 years or beyond. Examination of Okinawans' lives provides insights into their longevity. Specific factors are diet (they eat nutritious foods such as grains, fish, and vegetables); lifestyle (they are easygoing and experience low stress); community (Okinawans look out for one another and do not isolate or ignore older adults); activity (they lead active lifestyles, and many older adults continue to work); and spirituality (they find a sense of purpose in spiritual matters) (Willcox & others, 2008). Just as physical changes are interwoven with socioemotional processes in childhood and adolescence, so they are as human beings enter the later stages of life.

BIOLOGICAL THEORIES OF AGING

Of the many proposed biological theories of aging, three especially merit attention: cellular-clock theory, free-radical theory, and hormonal stress theory.

Cellular-Clock Theory   Leonard Hayflick's (1977) *cellular-clock theory* is that cells can divide a maximum of about 100 times and that, as we age, our cells become less capable of dividing. Hayflick found that cells extracted from adults in their 50s to 70s had divided fewer than 100 times. The total number of cell divisions was roughly related to the individual's age. Based on the way cells divide, Hayflick places the human life span's upper limit at about 120 years.

Recently, scientists have been examining why cells lose their ability to divide (Broer & others, 2013). The answer may lie at the tips of chromosomes. Each time a cell divides, the *telomeres* protecting the ends of chromosomes shorten. After about 100 replications, the telomeres are dramatically reduced, and the cell no longer can reproduce (Prescott & others, 2011).

It is not surprising then that scientists are interested in discovering ways to maintain high levels of the telomere-extending enzyme—telomerase. Some have examined how genetic manipulation of telomerase activators might influence levels of telomerase (C. Harrison, 2012). Meditation, described in Chapter 5, might also help to enhance telomerase activity. One study found that individuals who participated in a 3-month meditation retreat showed greater telomerase activity relative to a control group (Jacobs & others, 2011).

Free-Radical Theory   A second biological theory of aging is the *free-radical theory.* This theory states that people age because unstable oxygen molecules known as *free radicals* are produced inside their cells. These molecules damage DNA and other cellular structures (Bachschmid & others, 2013; Brandes & others, 2013). The damage done by free radicals may lead to a range of disorders, including cancer and arthritis (Eckert, Schmitt, & Gotz, 2011).

Keep in mind, however, that although free radicals sound like the enemy of a healthy body, these cells are themselves important to the body's survival. Immune cells will attack invading bacteria with free radicals to annihilate them. You have probably seen fruit juices and other foods labeled as rich in antioxidants. The notion that foods high in antioxidants are good for health and longevity rests on the free-radical theory of cellular aging, though the actual benefits of antioxidant supplements have not been borne out by research (Moyer, 2013).

Hormonal Stress Theory   A third theory of aging, *hormonal stress theory,* argues that aging in the body's hormonal system can lower resistance to stress and increase the likelihood of disease. As individuals age, the hormones stimulated by stress stay in the bloodstream longer than is the case for younger people (Finch, 2011). These prolonged, elevated levels of stress hormones are linked to increased risks for many diseases, including cardiovascular disease, cancer, and diabetes (Gems & Partridge, 2013). Recently, the hormonal stress theory of aging has focused on the role of chronic stress in reducing immune system functioning (Naumova & others, 2013).

AGING AND THE BRAIN

Just as the aging body has a greater capacity for renewal than previously thought, so does the aging brain (Lövdén & others, 2013; Park & McDonough, 2013). For decades,

FIGURE 9.12 The Brains of the Mankato Nuns At 95 years old, Nun Study participant Sister Nicolette Welter remains an active contributing member of her community of sisters. (*Inset*) A neuroscientist holds a brain donated by one of the Mankato Nun Study participants.

scientists believed that no new brain cells are generated past early childhood. However, researchers have recently discovered that adults can grow new brain cells throughout life (Curtis, Kam, & Faull, 2011; Kazanis, 2013), although the evidence is limited to the hippocampus and the olfactory bulb (H. Xu & others, 2013). Researchers currently are studying factors that might inhibit and promote neurogenesis, including various drugs, stress, and exercise (Shin & others, 2013; Vega-Rivera & others, 2013). They also are examining how grafting neural stem cells to various brain regions, such as the hippocampus, might increase neurogenesis (Arber & Li, 2013; Hattiangany & Shetty, 2012; Taghipour & Razmkon, 2012).

Research from the Nun Study (described in Chapter 2) provides evidence for the role of experience in maintaining the brain. Recall that this study involves nearly 700 nuns in a convent in Mankato, Minnesota (Snowdon, 2003, 2007) (Figure 9.12). Although in Chapter 2 we surveyed the aspects of the study related to happiness, this research has also investigated brain functioning. By examining the nuns' donated brains as well as those of others, neuroscientists have documented the aging brain's remarkable ability to grow and change. Even the oldest Mankato nuns lead intellectually challenging lives, and neuroscientists believe that stimulating mental activities increase dendritic branching. Keeping the brain actively engaged in challenging activities can help to slow the effects of age.

Even in late adulthood, the brain has remarkable repair capability (Dunnett, 2013; Greenberg & Jin, 2013). Stanley Rapaport (1994) compared the brains of younger and older adults when they were engaged in the same tasks. The older adults' brains literally rewired themselves to compensate for losses. If one neuron was not up to the job, neighboring neurons helped to pick up the slack. Rapaport concluded that as brains age, they can shift responsibilities for a given task from one region to another.

Changes in lateralization may provide one type of adaptation in aging adults (Angel & others, 2013; Zhu, Zacks, & Slade, 2010). *Lateralization* is the specialization of function in one hemisphere of the brain or the other. Using neuroimaging techniques, researchers have found that brain activity in the prefrontal cortex is lateralized less in older adults than in younger adults when they are engaging in mental tasks (Cabeza, 2002; Cabeza, Nyberg, & Park, 2005; Raw & others, 2012). For example, when younger adults are given the task of recognizing words they have previously seen, they process the information primarily in the right hemisphere, whereas older adults are more likely to use both hemispheres (Madden & others, 1999). The decrease in lateralization in older adults might play a compensatory role in the aging brain (Angel & others, 2011). That is, using both hemispheres may help to maintain the mental abilities of older adults.

Cognitive Development in Adulthood

Recall that for Piaget, each stage of cognitive development entails a way of thinking that is *qualitatively different* from the stage before. From Piaget's perspective, meaningful cognitive development ceases after the individual reaches the formal operational stage. Subsequent research has examined not qualitative differences in thinking over time, but the ebb and flow of cognitive abilities as a function of age. What kind of cognitive changes occur in adults?

COGNITION IN EARLY ADULTHOOD

Just as physical abilities peak in early adulthood, might intellectual skills also peak during this time in life (Kitchener, King, & DeLuca, 2006)? Some experts on cognitive development argue that the typical idealism of Piaget's formal operational stage is replaced in young adulthood by more realistic, pragmatic thinking (Labouvie-Vief, 1986). Gisela Labouvie-Vief (2006) proposed that the increasing complexity of cultures in the past century has generated a greater need for reflective, more complex thinking that takes into account the changing nature of knowledge and the kinds of challenges contemporary thinkers face. She emphasizes that key aspects of cognitive development for young adults include deciding on a particular worldview, recognizing that the worldview is subjective, and understanding that diverse worldviews should be acknowledged. In her perspective, only some individuals attain the highest level of thinking.

COGNITION IN MIDDLE ADULTHOOD

What happens to cognitive skills in middle adulthood? Although some cross-sectional studies indicate that middle adulthood is a time of cognitive decline, longitudinal evidence presents a different picture. K. Warner Schaie is conducting an extensive longitudinal study by repeatedly measuring a host of different intellectual abilities in adults, starting in 1956 (Schaie, 1994, 2007, 2010, 2012). The highest level of functioning for four of the six intellectual abilities occurred in middle adulthood (Schaie, 2006, 2010, 2012). Only two of the six abilities declined in middle age. Based on the longitudinal data he has collected so far, Schaie concludes that middle (not early) adulthood is the period when many people reach their peak for a range of intellectual skills.

COGNITION IN LATE ADULTHOOD

Many contemporary psychologists conclude that some dimensions of intelligence decline in late adulthood, whereas others are maintained or may even increase (Dixon & others, 2013). One of the most consistent findings is that when the speed of processing information is involved, older adults do not perform as well as their younger counterparts (Figure 9.13). This decline in speed of processing is apparent in middle-aged adults and becomes more pronounced in older adults (Salthouse, 2012).

Older adults also tend to not do as well as younger adults in most, but not all, aspects of memory (Brockmole & Logie, 2013). In the area of memory involving knowledge of the world (for instance, the capital of Peru), older adults usually take longer than younger adults to remember the information, but they often are able to retrieve it (Singh-Manoux & others, 2012). In the important area of memory in which individuals manipulate and assemble information to solve problems and make decisions, decline occurs in older adults as well.

Some aspects of cognition might improve with age. One such area is **wisdom,** expert knowledge about the practical aspects of life (Ferrari & Westrate, 2013; Staudinger & Gluck, 2011). Wisdom may increase with age because of the buildup of life experiences, but individual variations characterize people throughout their lives (Grossman & others, 2010). Thus, not every older person has wisdom, and some young people are wise beyond their years.

Some factors can lessen the decline in cognitive ability among older adults. Training these adults to use specific strategies can enhance their memory, and there is increasing evidence that physical fitness sharpens the thinking skills of older adults (Mortimer & others, 2012). When older adults continue to increase their engagement in cognitive and physical activities, they are better able to maintain their cognitive functioning in late adulthood (C. L. Brown & others, 2013; Lindwall & others, 2013; Mitchell & others, 2013). Still, many experts conclude that older adults are less able to adapt than younger adults and thus are limited in how much they can improve their cognitive skills (Finch, 2009; Salthouse, 2012).

Socioemotional Development in Adulthood

In the physical and the cognitive domains, the developmental story is generally one of rapid growth during childhood, with continuing gains in adolescence, followed by steady decline with age. Does a similar pattern hold for socioemotional development? Let's consider the changes that characterize adult socioemotional development, first returning to Erikson's stage theory of life-span development and then looking at what current research has to say.

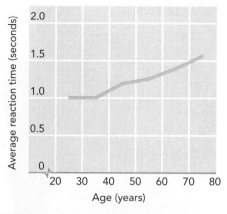

FIGURE 9.13   The Relationship Between Age and Reaction Time In one study, the average reaction time slowed in the 40s, and this decline accelerated in the 60s and 70s (Salthouse, 1994). The task used to assess reaction time required individuals to match numbers with symbols on a computer screen.

● **wisdom** Expert knowledge about the practical aspects of life.

Copyright by Mark Parisi, www.offthemark.com.

"We only live once. Hop in."

© Joseph Farris. www.CartoonStock.com.

SOCIOEMOTIONAL DEVELOPMENT IN EARLY ADULTHOOD

According to Erikson (1968), during early adulthood, people face a developmental dilemma involving *intimacy versus isolation* (see Figure 9.10). At this stage, individuals either form intimate relationships with others or become socially isolated. If the young adult develops healthy friendships and an intimate relationship with a partner, intimacy will likely be achieved. One key way that a young adult achieves intimacy is through a long-term relationship with a romantic partner, often in the form of marriage.

Just as the notion of emerging adulthood would indicate, men and women have been waiting longer to marry in the last few decades. In 2011, the average age for a first marriage in the United States climbed to 28.7 years for men and 26.5 years for women, higher than at any other point in history (Cohn, 2011). In 1980, the average age for a first marriage in the United States was 24 years for men and 21 years for women. This trend may be good news, because a woman's age at her first marriage is related to the ultimate survival of the marriage. Approximately 6 in 10 marriages in which the wife is younger than 18 end in divorce within 15 years, compared with almost 4 in 10 of marriages in which the woman is 20 or older (Center for Family and Demographic Research, 2002).

What makes a marriage successful? John Gottman has been studying married couples' lives since the early 1970s (Gottman, 1994, 2006; Gottman & Gottman, 2009; Gottman, Gottman, & Declaire, 2006; Gottman & Silver, 1999). He interviews couples, films them interacting with each other, and even takes measures of their heart rate and blood pressure during their interactions (Gottman, Swanson, & Swanson, 2002; Madhyastha, Hamaker, & Gottman, 2011). He also checks back with the couples every year to see how their marriages are faring. Gottman and his colleagues continue to follow married couples, as well as same-sex partners, to try to understand what makes relationships thrive. Gottman (2006) has identified four principles at work in successful marriages:

- *Nurturing fondness and admiration:* Partners sing each other's praises. When couples put a positive spin on their talk with and about each other, marriages tend to work.
- *Turning toward each other as friends:* Partners see each other as friends and turn toward each other for support in times of stress and difficulty.
- *Giving up some power:* Bad marriages often involve one partner who is a power-monger. Abuse of power is more common in husbands, but some wives have the problem as well.
- *Solving conflicts together:* Couples work to solve problems, regulate their emotion during times of conflict, and compromise to accommodate each other.

SOCIOEMOTIONAL DEVELOPMENT IN MIDDLE ADULTHOOD

According to Erikson, following the resolution of the intimacy versus isolation dilemma, the adult turns to concerns about *generativity versus stagnation* (see Figure 9.10). *Generativity* means making a contribution to the next generation. The feeling that one has made a lasting and memorable contribution to the world is related to higher levels of psychological well-being (Busch & Hofer, 2012; Cox & others, 2010).

Although Erikson did not think that parenting alone was a guarantee of generativity, he did believe that parenting could be a way to experience this important developmental accomplishment. So, we might expect parenthood to be a personally fulfilling experience that enhances well-being. Yet, how parenthood relates to the well-being of parents is a matter of some debate in psychology. To learn more about this topic, see the Critical Controversy.

SOCIOEMOTIONAL DEVELOPMENT AND AGING

From Erikson's perspective, the person who has entered the later years of life is engaged in looking back—evaluating his or her life and seeking meaning. Erikson called this stage of life *integrity versus despair* (see Figure 9.10). Through this process of life review and reminiscence, the older adult comes to a sense of meaning or despair, Erikson theorized. The individual is also occupied with coming to terms with his or her own death, according to Erikson. If the individual has a well-established sense of integrity, experiencing life as a meaningful and coherent whole, he or she faces the later years with a strong sense of meaning and low fear of death. In the absence of integrity, the older adult is filled with despair and fear.

RESEARCH ON ADULT SOCIOEMOTIONAL DEVELOPMENT

Research on socioemotional development and aging reveals that Erikson was correct in his view that meaning is a central concern for older adults. However, he may have overlooked that this meaning derives not only from the past but also from the present. Let's conclude our look at socioemotional development in adulthood by considering recent research findings about how adults' lives change socially and emotionally over time.

In terms of social relationships, older adults may become more selective about their social networks (Carstensen, 2006, 2008, 2010; Carstensen & others, 2011). At the same time, older adults report greater happiness than their younger counterparts (Carstensen & others, 2011; Mroczek & Spiro, 2005; Ram & others, 2008; Stanley & Isaacowitz, 2012; Wrzus & others, 2012) and that satisfaction with life increases with age. One study showed that happiness increased through the 80s (Stone & others, 2010).

Laura Carstensen developed *socioemotional selectivity theory* to address the narrowing of social contacts and the increase in positive emotion that occur with age (Carstensen, 2006, 2011). The theory states that older adults tend to be selective in their social interactions in order to maximize positive, meaningful experiences. Although younger adults may gain a sense of meaning in life from long-term goals, older adults gain a sense of meaning by focusing on satisfying relationships and activities in the *present*. Unlike younger adults, who may be preoccupied with the future, older adults embrace the present moment with increasing vitality (Hicks & others, 2012; Kotter-Grühn & Smith, 2011; Lachman & others, 2008).

Socioemotional selectivity theory posits that it is not old age itself that spurs people to maximize positive meaning in the present but, rather, limited time. Young adults who are asked to imagine having limited time (for instance, because they are about to go on a long trip) show the same pattern of maximizing time they spend with a narrow set of important friends and family members (Carstensen, 2011).

With age, engagement in one's *present life* can be a vital source of meaning. The more active and involved older people are, the more satisfied they are and the more likely they are to stay healthy (Hendricks & Hatch, 2006). Older people who go to church, attend meetings, take trips, and exercise are happier than those who sit at home (George, 2006).

The capacity to regulate emotions, maximizing positive experiences, appears to be a central feature of aging (Sullivan, Mikels, & Carstensen, 2010). Researchers have found that across diverse samples—Norwegians, Catholic nuns, African Americans, Chinese Americans, and non-Latino White Americans—older adults report better control of their emotions than younger adults (Charles & Carstensen, 2010).

Emotion regulation benefits may have far-reaching consequences. In one study, adults who had expressed positive attitudes about aging some 20 years previously, lived, on average, 7½ years longer than those with more negative attitudes about aging (Levy, Slade, & Kasl, 2002). An important factor in the link between attitudes and longevity was a person's belief that life was full, hopeful, and worthwhile.

test yourself

1. What are the five main features of emerging adulthood?
2. What is brain lateralization, and how might a decrease in lateralization in older adults play a role in the aging brain?
3. What do longitudinal studies indicate about intellectual abilities in middle adulthood?

Is Parenthood Associated with Happiness?

Are parents happier than those who are not parents? Do parents experience greater happiness when spending time with their children compared to when they are doing other things? Research addressing these questions has produced mixed results.

Some studies have shown that having children is associated with lowered well-being (Evenson & Simon, 2005; McLanahan & Adams, 1987; Ross & Van Willigen, 1996), while others find no relationship or that parenting is associated with higher well-being (Keizer, Dykstra, & Poortman, 2010).

Studies that examine the same individuals before and after the birth of a child show that life satisfaction decreases in the months following the birth (Luhmann & others, 2012). One study showed that mothers in Texas enjoyed shopping and watching television more than they enjoyed the parenting (Kahneman & others, 2004). Is it possible that parenthood, despite its importance, takes a serious toll on happiness?

Recently, a team of researchers led by Katherine Nelson examined this issue in a series of studies (S. K. Nelson & others, 2013). The first study examined a nationally representative U.S. sample of almost 7,000 parents and nonparents. Compared to childless adults, parents reported being happier. In addition, among parents, having *more* children was associated with greater happiness.

Because the data were correlational, the researchers then examined the role of potential third variables in these results, including the sex of the participant, marital status, and age. With regard to sex, they found that parenthood was an especially strong predictor of happiness for men but not for women. With regard to marital status, they found that married couples with children were no different from married couples without children, but single parents were less happy than single people without children. Finally, compared to their childless peers, younger parents (those ages 17 to 25) reported less happiness, but older parents (ages 26 to 62) reported greater happiness.

Next, the researchers examined the daily experience of happiness among more than 300 adults. In this study, an electronic pager beeped the participants five times a day for a week. When beeped, participants filled out a survey that measured their experience of positive and negative emotions. The results? Parents experienced more positive emotion than nonparents. Once again differences were especially strong for fathers.

These first two studies challenge the notion that parenthood is negatively associated with happiness. Still, as with all correlational studies, these conclusions might be open to an alternative explanation—namely, that happier people are more likely to *become* parents. Does parenting lead to happiness, or were those individuals always happier, even before they had kids?

To address this issue, the researchers looked at parenting activity in a sample of almost 200 parents. Participants reconstructed their daily activities, and for each activity rated their levels of enjoyment and meaning. Parents reported experiencing more positive emotion and meaning while engaged in child care compared to all the other activities of the day.

In sum, these studies show that parenthood and parenting are associated with greater happiness. Of course, parenting is a complex activity. As Nelson and her colleagues acknowledge, having the resources and psychological maturity to balance parenting with other life demands likely plays an important role in the relationship between having children and happiness.

Perhaps the question should not be whether parenting influences happiness. Instead, we might ask how other factors in people's lives may make this crucially important experience rewarding—not only for parents but for their children too.

WHAT DO YOU THINK
- Why might parenting be more strongly related to happiness for fathers but not mothers?
- How does this research affect your view of parenting and why?

5· HUMAN DEVELOPMENT AND HEALTH AND WELLNESS

Compared to childhood, development in adulthood is more likely to be a conscious process and therefore a truer mark of an individual's accomplishment (King & Hicks, 2007; Levenson & Crumpler, 1996). In this concluding section we consider the active developer as the individual meets the challenges of adulthood, and we seek to understand how adults "grow" themselves.

Coping and Adult Development

One way that adults develop is through coping with life's difficulties. Psychologist Carolyn Aldwin and her colleagues have suggested that stress and coping play a role in development (Aldwin, 2007; Aldwin, Levenson, & Kelly, 2009; Aldwin, Spiro, & Park, 2006; Aldwin, Yancura, & Boeninger, 2007; Boeninger & others, 2009). To understand how, consider that Piaget's ideas of assimilation and accommodation in childhood cognitive development may be applied to adult development as well (Block, 1982).

Volunteering our time and talents and working with younger people can contribute to our well-being and life satisfaction as we age.

Recall that in assimilation, existing cognitive structures are used to make sense out of the current environment. Assimilation allows the person to enjoy a feeling of meaning because experiences fit into his or her preexisting schemas (King & Hicks, 2007). However, life does not always conform to our expectations. When experience conflicts with existing schemas, it is necessary to modify current ways of thinking. Accommodation is the process whereby existing schemas are modified or new structures are developed. Accommodation helps us to change so that we can make sense of life's previously incomprehensible events. When we encounter a negative life circumstance, such as an illness or a loss, we have the opportunity to change—to develop and to mature (Bauer, Schwab, & McAdams, 2011; Caserta & others, 2009; Davis & others, 2007; Gunty & others, 2011; LoSavio & others, 2011). Indeed, research suggests that individuals who are faced with difficulties in life are more likely to come to a rich, complex view of themselves and the world (King & Hicks, 2007; Wrosch, Amir, & Miller, 2011).

Life Themes and Life-Span Development

A life theme involves a person's efforts to cultivate meaningful optimal experiences (Massimini & Delle Fave, 2000; Rathunde & Csikszentmihalyi, 2006). Consider someone who has spent much of his or her adult life pursuing wealth and career success and who turns to selfless pursuits in middle age. To contribute to the well-being of the next generation, the individual devotes more energy and resources to helping others—for example, by volunteering or working with young people. This reorientation can ease the individual into a positive and meaningful old age.

These motivations are demonstrated by numerous individuals who use their successes for the betterment of the world. Actor George Clooney, for example, has dedicated himself to a variety of humanitarian causes. Clooney cofounded the organization Not On Our Watch to end the genocide in Sudan as well as to stop atrocities elsewhere. However, one need not be middle-aged to attend to the motivations to make the world a better place. For instance, Facebook founder Mark Zuckerberg donated $100 million to public schools in Newark, New Jersey.

As children, our psychological development occurs in concert with physical development. As we become strong and skilled enough to walk, the horizons of our world open up to new discoveries. In adulthood, we get many of our developmental cues from ourselves—where do we go, once we have managed the many tasks we faced in childhood and adolescence? Development, then, is a lifelong process—as we encounter opportunities to grow, to change, and to make a mark in the world in which we live. Every morning when we wake up, we step out of the amazing time machine of human life into a whole new world of possibilities.

test yourself

1. How does Piaget's idea of assimilation apply to adult development?
2. How does accommodation, in Piaget's sense of the term, help adults to cope with life's difficulties?
3. What is involved when an individual pursues a life theme?

1. EXPLORING HUMAN DEVELOPMENT

Development is the pattern of change in human capabilities that begins at birth and continues throughout the life span. Research on human development can be cross-sectional, which demonstrates age differences, or longitudinal, which demonstrates age-related change. To make strong conclusions about development, longitudinal data are necessary.

Both nature (biological inheritance) and nurture (environmental experience) extensively influence development. However, people are not at the mercy of either their genes or their environment when they actively construct optimal experiences. Resilience refers to the capacity of individuals to thrive during difficulties at every stage of development.

2. CHILD DEVELOPMENT

Prenatal development progresses through the germinal, embryonic, and fetal periods. Particular drugs, such as alcohol and nicotine, as well as certain illnesses, can adversely affect the fetus. These environmental threats are called teratogens. Preterm birth is another potential problem, especially if the infant is very small or grows up in an adverse environment.

The infant's physical development is dramatic in the first year, and a number of motor milestones are reached in infancy. Extensive changes in the brain, including denser connections between synapses, take place in infancy and childhood.

With regard to cognitive development, in Piaget's view, children use schemas to actively construct their world, either assimilating new information into existing schemas or adjusting schemas to accommodate that information. Piaget identified four stages of cognitive development: the sensorimotor stage, the preoperational stage, the concrete operational stage, and the formal operational stage. Two other theoretical views of children's cognitive development are Vygotsky's sociocultural cognitive theory and information-processing theory. Key aspects of information-processing theory are focusing on detailed aspects of cognitive processes, especially attention, memory, and executive function.

Socioemotional development in childhood includes consideration of Erikson's psychosocial stages as well as moral development. Erikson presented a major, eight-stage psychosocial view of life-span development; its first four stages occur in childhood. In each stage, the individual seeks to resolve a particular socioemotional conflict. Kohlberg proposed a cognitive theory of moral development with three levels (preconventional, conventional, and postconventional). More recent research has focused on the development of prosocial behavior and the influence of socioemotional factors in putting moral reasoning into action.

3. ADOLESCENCE

Puberty is a period of rapid skeletal and sexual maturation that occurs mainly in early adolescence. Its onset occurs about 2 years earlier in girls than in boys. Hormonal changes trigger pubertal development.

According to Piaget, cognitive development in adolescence is characterized by the appearance of formal operational thought, the final stage in his theory. This stage involves abstract, idealistic, and logical thought.

One of the most important aspects of socioemotional development in adolescence is identity. Erikson's fifth stage of psychosocial development is identity versus identity confusion. Marcia proposed four statuses of identity based on crisis and commitment. A special concern is the development of ethnic identity. Despite great differences among adolescents, the majority of them develop competently.

4. EMERGING ADULTHOOD, ADULT DEVELOPMENT, AND AGING

Psychologists refer to the period between adolescence and adulthood as emerging adulthood. This period is characterized by the exploration of identity through work and relationships, instability, and self-focus.

Most adults reach their peak physical performance during their 20s and are healthiest then. Physical skills begin to decline during the 30s. The cellular-clock, free-radical, and hormonal stress theories are three important biological explanations for aging. Even in late adulthood, the brain has remarkable repair capacity and plasticity.

Piaget argued that no new cognitive changes occur in adulthood. However, some psychologists have proposed that the idealistic thinking of adolescents is replaced by the more realistic, pragmatic thinking of young adults. Longitudinal research on intelligence shows that many cognitive skills peak in middle age. Overall, older adults do not do as well on memory and other cognitive tasks and are slower to process information than younger adults. However, older adults may have greater wisdom than younger adults.

Erikson's three stages of socioemotional development in adulthood are intimacy versus isolation (early adulthood), generativity versus stagnation (middle adulthood), and integrity versus despair (late adulthood). A special concern, beginning when individuals are in their 50s, is the challenge of understanding life's meaning. Researchers have found that remaining active increases the likelihood that older adults will be happy and healthy. They also have found that older adults often reduce their general social affiliations and instead are motivated to spend more time with close friends and family members. Older adults also experience more positive emotion, are happier, and are more satisfied with their lives than younger adults.

Until recently, the positive dimensions of aging were largely ignored. Developmentalists now recognize that many adults can sustain or even improve their functioning as they age. Researchers today widely view adult development as a self-motivated process limited only by the individual's imagination.

5. HUMAN DEVELOPMENT AND HEALTH AND WELLNESS

Though often associated with childhood, psychological development can continue throughout life. Psychologists have suggested that coping with life's difficulties is one way in which adults may develop. For adults, taking an active approach to developing oneself may be an important motivator in development. Piaget's concepts of assimilation and accommodation have been applied to the process of developing through difficult times. An individual may experience meaning in life by applying his or her current understanding of the world (assimilation). In contrast, the individual may find that some experiences require a revision of that understanding (accommodation). In adulthood, people have the opportunity to pursue new goals that represent important life themes, such as leaving a legacy for the future.

SUMMARY

key *terms*

apply your *knowledge*

1. Consider the style of parenting with which you were raised. It might help to think of specific situations or moments when your parents put limits on your behavior (or did not). If you have one or more siblings, ask for their opinion, too. Do you agree with one another about your parents' style? Now give these definitions to your parents, and ask which, if any, describes them. Sometimes there are as many different views of a family as there are members of that family.

2. A major part of any child's life is playing—and when kids are playing, they are often playing with toys. Using the information on perceptual and cognitive development reviewed in this chapter, design a toy that you think is a perfect fit for a child of 2 months, 2 years, and 10 years old. With respect to the child's development, what features of the toy are especially good for the child of each age group?

3. Go online and Google "parenting discussion boards." Click on one or two of the many sites that come up, and see what parents are talking about. What issues seem to concern them most? Do these parents appear to have a sense of the issues addressed by developmental psychologists? Does the advice that parents share with one another seem to be based on the science of psychology?

4. Set aside 15 minutes to write a brief essay as follows. Think about your life in the future, when you are 70 or 80 years old. Imagine that everything has gone as well as it possibly could, and you have achieved your life dreams. What is your life like at this stage? What things about you are the same as they are for you now as a student of psychology? What things have changed? What is your best possible older adult self? How have aspects of your life today contributed to this happily-older-after?

5. You might have heard the statement that "40 is the new 30" or "50 is the new 40." What trend do these statements reflect? What might explain this trend? What might it mean for our understanding of adult development?

Motivation and Emotion

What Makes Us Do the Things We Do?

On February 20, 2013, Vice President Joe Biden choked up as he presented the Medal of Valor to 18 public safety officers for exceptional courage in the line of duty. One of the recipients was Reeshemah Taylor, a corrections officer at Florida's Osceola County Jail. She earned the recognition for her heroic actions when she encountered an inmate, a gang member serving three life sentences, who had taken a fellow officer hostage. The inmate had changed into that officer's uniform, taking the guard's fully loaded semiautomatic handgun. When Taylor confronted the would-be escapee, he pointed the weapon directly at her head. In an instant, she knocked the gun from the man's hand. She thrust her knee into the inmate's groin and threw herself on top of him, pinning his legs with her own. With her free hand, she radioed for help.

Taylor's heroism is amazing and a bit of a puzzle. Considering how frightening the situation would be, the sense of panic it might instill in even the most courageous, it is hard to understand her quick-thinking determination. As Vice President Biden commented about all of the heroes receiving the Medal of Valor that day, "you all share a selflessness that's not easy to explain, a commitment to your fellow man that's rare, a bravery that inspires. . . . I still grapple with what makes you do what you do?" (Curtis, 2013; Lederman, 2013).

Why do they do it? Why do any of us do the big and small things we do in our everyday lives? How do our feelings influence that behavior, and how is it that we can sometimes override those feelings in the service of our goals? These are the questions we will address in this chapter.

The terms *motivation* and *emotion* come from the Latin word *movere,* which means "to move." Motivation and emotion are the "go" of human life, propelling us as we pursue our goals. Our emotions often provide a sense of the meaning of life events. We feel joy, pride, sorrow, or frustration depending on how those events influence our most cherished life dreams. ●

PREVIEW

This chapter examines the ways psychologists study motivation and emotion. We first review some general approaches to motivation and consider one important physiological source of motivation: hunger. We then examine motivation as it applies to everyday life. Next, we explore the rich topic of emotion. To close, we consider the ways that motivation and emotion intertwine in the pursuit of happiness.

1· THEORIES OF MOTIVATION

● **motivation** The force that moves people to behave, think, and feel the way they do.

Motivation is the force that moves people to behave, think, and feel the way they do. Motivated behavior is energized, directed, and sustained. Psychologists have proposed a variety of theories about why organisms are motivated to do what they do. In this section we explore some of the main theoretical approaches to motivation.

The Evolutionary Approach

● **instinct** An innate (unlearned) biological pattern of behavior that is assumed to be universal throughout a species.

Early evolutionary accounts of motivation emphasized the role of instincts. An **instinct** is an innate (unlearned) biological pattern of behavior that is assumed to be universal throughout a species. Generally, an instinct is set in motion by a *sign stimulus*—something in the environment that turns on a fixed pattern of behavior. Instincts may explain a great deal of nonhuman animal behavior. In addition, some human behavior is instinctive. Recall, for example, the discussion of infant reflexes in Chapter 9. Babies do not have to learn to suck; they instinctively do it when something is placed in their mouth. So, for infants, an object touching the lips is a sign stimulus. After infancy, though, it is hard to think of specific behaviors that all human beings engage in when presented with a particular stimulus.

More recently, evolutionary psychologists emphasize how human motivation is rooted in our evolutionary past (Bolhuis & others, 2011; Buss, 2012). Because evolutionary approaches emphasize the passing on of one's genes, these theories focus on domains of life that are especially relevant to reproduction, such as sexual behavior and behaviors relevant to competition among members of a species, such as aggression and achievement.

In general, even these behaviors are far too complex to be explained on the basis of instinct. Indeed, it would hardly seem adaptive for humans to have a fixed action pattern that is invariably set in motion by a particular signal in the environment. To understand human behavior, psychologists have developed a variety of other approaches, as we now consider.

Drive Reduction Theory

● **drive** An aroused state that occurs because of a physiological need.

● **need** A deprivation that energizes the drive to eliminate or reduce the deprivation.

Another way to think about motivation is through the constructs of drive and need. A **drive** is an aroused state of tension that occurs because of a physiological need. You can think of a drive as a psychological itch that requires scratching. A **need** is a deprivation that energizes the drive to eliminate or reduce the deprivation. Generally, psychologists think of needs as underlying our drives. You may have a need for water; the drive that accompanies that need is your feeling of being thirsty. Drive pertains to a psychological state, whereas need involves a physiological one.

Usually but not always, needs and drives are closely associated. Drives do not always follow from needs. For example, if you are deprived of oxygen because of a gas leak, you have a need for oxygen. You may feel lightheaded but may never experience the drive for oxygen that might lead you to open a window. Moreover, drives sometimes seem to come out of nowhere. Having eaten a fine meal and feeling full to the point of not wanting another single bite, you might nevertheless feel ready to tackle the double chocolate oblivion when the waiter wheels over the dessert cart.

Drive reduction theory explains that as a drive becomes stronger, we are motivated to reduce it. The goal of drive reduction is **homeostasis,** the body's tendency to maintain an equilibrium, or a steady state or balance. Hundreds of biological states in the body must be maintained within a certain range; these include temperature, blood sugar level, potassium and sodium levels, and oxygenation. When you dive into an icy swimming pool, your body uses energy to maintain its normal temperature. When you step into the heat of a summer day, your body releases excess heat by sweating. These physiological changes occur automatically to keep your body in an optimal state of functioning.

Most psychologists conclude that drive reduction theory does not provide a comprehensive framework for understanding motivation because people often behave in ways that increase rather than reduce a drive. Many things we do involve increasing (not decreasing) tensions—for example, taking a challenging course in school, raising a family, and working at a difficult job.

Optimum Arousal Theory

When psychologists talk about arousal, they are generally referring to a person's feelings of being alert and engaged. When we are very excited, our arousal levels are high. When we are bored, they are low. Optimal arousal theory suggests that there should be a level of arousal that is ideal for facilitating goal attainment.

You have probably noticed that motivation influences arousal levels. Sometimes you can want something (for example, to do well on a test) so much that you can become overly motivated and anxious. On the other hand, you might be so unmotivated for a task (such as doing the dishes) that you can hardly force yourself to complete it. Sometimes, to do well, you need to have an arousal level that is "just right" (Keeley, Zayac, & Correia, 2008).

Early in the twentieth century, two psychologists described how arousal can influence performance. According to their formulation, known as the **Yerkes-Dodson law,** performance is best under conditions of moderate arousal rather than either low or high arousal. At the low end of arousal, you may be too lethargic to perform tasks well; at the high end, you may not be able to concentrate. To master the Yerkes-Dodson law, check out the Psychological Inquiry.

The link between arousal and performance is one reason that individuals in many professions are trained to overlearn important procedures. **Overlearning** means learning to perform a task so well that it becomes automatic. Recall Reeshemah Taylor, the heroic corrections officer who disarmed the threatening inmate, or consider the Navy SEALS who conducted the raid on Osama bin Laden's compound in Pakistan in 2011. For individuals who must perform at their best in a crisis, success depends on knowing what to do so well that it requires little or no thought. With this extra learning, when these individuals are under conditions of high arousal, they can rely on automatic pilot to do what needs to be done.

2· HUNGER, OBESITY, AND EATING DISORDERS

Part of the power of motivation in life is tied to physiological needs. We experience strong motivational forces, for example, when we are hungry or thirsty. Furthermore, the physiological state of being hungry has often been used as a path toward understanding a variety of human motivations. We use words about hunger in contexts that are not physiological, such as when we say that someone is "craving" attention or "starving" for affection. In this section we examine the basic motivational processes underlying hunger and eating, including the related topic of eating disorders.

Performance under high-arousal conditions, such as those faced by Osceola County Department of Corrections Officer Reeshema Taylor when she confronted the would-be prison escapee, requires being trained to the point of overlearning.

● **homeostasis** The body's tendency to maintain an equilibrium, or steady state or balance.

● **Yerkes-Dodson law** The psychological principle stating that performance is best under conditions of moderate arousal rather than either low or high arousal.

● **overlearning** Learning to perform a task so well that it becomes automatic.

test yourself

1. What is motivation?
2. What are three theoretical approaches to motivation?
3. What is overlearning, and how can it help an individual who must perform at his or her best?

psychological *inquiry*

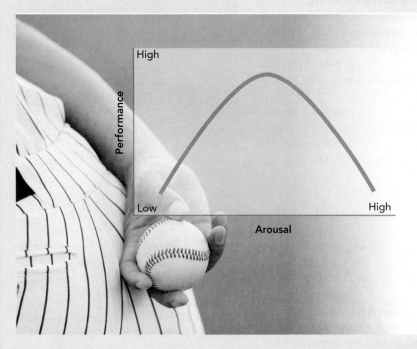

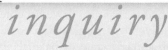

Obeying the (Yerkes-Dodson) Law

The graph displays the relationship between arousal (shown on the X, or horizontal, axis) and performance (shown on the Y, or vertical, axis). Note that the curve is in the form of an inverted *U*. Using the figure as a reference, answer the questions below.

1. What was your arousal level the last time you took an exam? If you were very nervous, your arousal level would be considered high. If you were excited and engaged but not too worried, your level would be in the medium range. If you were feeling sluggish, your arousal level would be low.

2. How did you actually do on that test? Plot your performance on the graph. Does it fit with the Yerkes-Dodson prediction?

3. Now think about performance in sports or the arts. Imagine your favorite athlete, musician, or actor. How might that person feel when he or she is on the spot, trying to sink a winning free throw, strike out the last batter, or impress an audience? How might arousal influence performance in those cases?

4. In many professions, individuals are forced to perform under conditions of very high arousal. These include EMTs, lifeguards, and emergency room staff. (Name some others.) How might such individuals train themselves to perform even under conditions of extreme arousal?

The Biology of Hunger

You know you are hungry when your stomach growls and you feel hunger pangs. What role do such signals play in hunger?

GASTRIC SIGNALS

In 1912, Walter Cannon and A. L. Washburn conducted an experiment that revealed a close association between stomach contractions and hunger (Figure 10.1). In one step of the procedure, a partially inflated balloon was passed through a tube inserted in Washburn's mouth and pushed down into his stomach. A machine that measures air pressure was connected to the balloon to monitor Washburn's stomach contractions. Every time Washburn reported hunger pangs, his stomach was also contracting.

Sure enough, a growling stomach needs food. The stomach tells the brain not only how full it is but also how much nutrient is present. That is why rich foods stop hunger faster than the same amount of water. The hormone cholecystokinin (CCK) helps start the digestion of food, travels to the brain through the bloodstream, and signals us to stop eating (Moss & others, 2012). Hunger involves a lot more than an empty stomach, however.

BLOOD CHEMISTRY

Three key chemical substances play a role in hunger, eating, and *satiety* (the state of feeling full): glucose, insulin, and leptin.

Glucose (blood sugar) is an important factor in hunger, probably because the brain critically depends on sugar for energy. One set of sugar receptors, located in the brain, triggers hunger when sugar levels fall too low. Another set of sugar receptors is in the liver, which stores excess sugar and releases it into the blood when needed. The sugar receptors in the liver signal the brain when its sugar supply falls, and this signal also can make you hungry.

The hormone *insulin* also plays a role in glucose control (Hansen & others, 2012; Tsiotra & others, 2013). When we eat complex carbohydrates such as bread and pasta, insulin levels go up and fall off gradually. When we consume simple sugars such as candy, insulin levels rise and then fall sharply—the all-too-familiar "sugar low" (Rodin, 1984). This difference explains why we are more likely to eat again within the next several hours after eating simple sugars than after eating complex carbohydrates.

Released by fat cells, the chemical *leptin* (from the Greek word *leptos,* meaning "thin") decreases food intake and increases energy expenditure or metabolism (Vasselli & others, 2013). Leptin's functions were discovered in a strain of genetically obese mice, called *ob mice* (Pelleymounter & others, 1995). Because of a genetic mutation, the fat cells of ob mice cannot produce leptin. The ob mouse has a low metabolism, overeats, and gets extremely fat. Leptin appears to act as an anti-obesity hormone (Procaccini, Jirillo, & Matarese, 2012). If ob mice are given daily injections of leptin, their metabolic rate increases, and they become more active, eat less, and lose weight. Figure 10.2 shows an untreated ob mouse and an ob mouse that has received injections of leptin.

In humans, high concentrations of leptin have been linked with lower weight, less body fat, and weight loss in response to dieting (Lee & Bishop, 2011; Lopez & Knudson, 2012). Scientists continue to explore the possibility that disorders in the production and uptake of leptin may explain human obesity (Carnell & others, 2012; Dougkas & others, 2013; Kissileff & others, 2013).

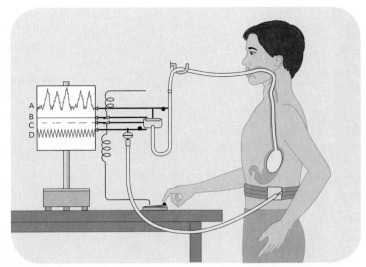

FIGURE 10.1   Cannon and Washburn's Classic Experiment on Hunger In this experiment, the researchers demonstrated that stomach contractions, which were detected by the stomach balloon, accompany a person's hunger feelings, which were indicated by pressing the key. Line A in the chart records increases and decreases in the volume of the balloon in the participant's stomach. Line B records the passage of time. Line C records the participant's manual signals of feelings of hunger. Line D records a reading from the belt around the participant's waist to detect movements of the abdominal wall and ensure that such movements are not the cause of changes in stomach volume.

BRAIN PROCESSES

Chapter 3 described the central role of the hypothalamus in regulating important body functions, including hunger. More specifically, activity in two areas of the hypothalamus plays a role in hunger. The *lateral hypothalamus* (located on the outer portions) is involved in stimulating eating. When this area is electrically stimulated in a well-fed animal, the animal begins to eat. If this part of the hypothalamus is destroyed, even a starving animal will show no interest in food. The *ventromedial hypothalamus* (located more in the middle) is involved in reducing hunger and restricting eating. When this area of an animal's brain is stimulated, the animal stops eating. When the area is destroyed, the animal eats profusely and quickly becomes obese.

It might be confusing that these regions of the hypothalamus have very different functions but very similar names. Remember that *lateral* here refers to the outer sides (and you might *go out* to eat when hungry), whereas *ventromedial* refers to the inner portions (and you might *stay in* if you are already full).

Although the lateral and ventromedial hypothalamuses both influence hunger, there is much more to the brain's role in determining hunger than these on/off centers in the hypothalamus. Neurotransmitters (the chemical messengers

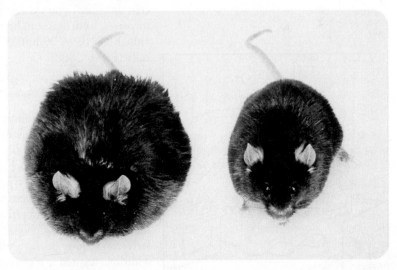

FIGURE 10.2 Leptin and Obesity The ob mouse on the left is untreated; the one on the right has been given injections of leptin.

that convey information from neuron to neuron) and neural circuits (clusters of neurons that often involve different parts of the brain) also function in hunger (Marston & others, 2011). Leptin influences eating by inhibiting the production of a neurotransmitter in the hypothalamus that induces eating. The neurotransmitter serotonin is partly responsible for the satiating effect of CCK, and serotonin antagonists have been used to treat obesity in humans (Ellis & others, 2013; Zhao, Goldberg, & Vaccarino, 2012).

Obesity

Given that the brain and body are so elegantly wired to regulate eating behavior, why do so many people in the United States overeat and suffer the effects of this behavior? According to the Centers for Disease Control and Prevention (CDC), 60 percent of Americans are overweight, and one-third of those are considered obese (dangerously overweight) (CDC, 2009). The National Health and Nutrition Examination Survey (NHANES) projected that 86 percent of Americans will be overweight or obese by 2030 if current weight trends continue (Beydoun & Wang, 2009). An international comparison of 33 developed countries revealed that the United States had the highest percentage of obese adults (OECD, 2010).

Obesity and overweight raise one's risk for a host of health problems, including cardiovascular disease and type 2 diabetes (Malhotra & others, 2013; Oliveras & Schmieder, 2013). Currently, the number of people considered overweight around the world is 20 percent higher than the number suffering from hunger. Overweight and obesity are global health problems.

Why so many people overeat to the point of becoming obese is a motivational puzzle, because it involves eating when one is not in need of nutrition. As is the case with much behavior, biological, psychological, and sociocultural factors interact in diverse ways to produce eating and overeating.

THE BIOLOGY OF OBESITY

Obesity clearly has a genetic component (Knoll & others, 2013). After the discovery of an ob gene in mice, researchers found a similar gene in humans. Only 10 percent of children who do not have obese parents become obese themselves, whereas 40 percent of children who have one obese parent become obese, and 70 percent of children who have two obese parents become obese.

● **set point** The weight maintained when the individual makes no effort to gain or lose weight.

Another factor in weight is **set point,** the weight maintained when the individual makes no effort to gain or lose weight. Set point is determined in part by the number of *adipose cells,* or fat cells, stored in the body (Speakman & others, 2011). When these cells are filled, you do not get hungry. When people gain weight, their fat cell number increases, and they might not be able to get rid of extra ones. A normal-weight individual has 10 to 20 billion fat cells. An obese individual can have up to 100 billion fat cells (Fried, 2008). Consequently, an obese individual has to eat more to feel satisfied.

PSYCHOLOGICAL FACTORS IN EATING AND OBESITY

Psychologists used to think that obesity stemmed from factors such as unhappiness and external food cues. These ideas make some sense; drowning one's sorrows in chocolate or eating some cookies just because they are there seems common enough to explain overeating. However, many psychological factors affect what, when, and how much we eat.

From an evolutionary perspective, human taste preferences developed at a time when reliable food sources were scarce. Our earliest ancestors needed a lot of calories to survive in challenging circumstances. They likely developed a preference for sweet and fatty foods. Today, many people still have a taste for such foods although modern sweet and fatty foods provide far more calories than we need with far less nutritional value. In addition, learned associations of food with a particular time and place are characteristic of many organisms (Jaeger & others, 2011), including humans. If it is noon, we eat lunch; in a movie theater, we eat popcorn.

Of particular concern in the battle over obesity is *how much* people eat. Indeed, growing portion sizes have been implicated in the alarming rates of obesity in the United States (Ledikwe, Ello-Martin, & Rolls, 2005). It is puzzling, though, that portion sizes should matter. After all, a person does not have to eat all of the food on the plate. Interestingly, research shows that smaller portions of snacks can be just as satisfying as larger portions (van Kleef, Shimizu, & Wansink, 2013). So, why do people eat an entire portion of food when just a bit of it might have led to the same feeling of fullness?

Of course, parents often teach their children to "finish what's on your plate." Many people eat automatically and rely not on a feeling of fullness but rather on the sight of an empty plate or bowl as the cue to stop eating (Wansink, 2013; Wansink, Painter, & North, 2005). Increasingly, however, cleaning one's plate has involved eating more and more food. Why might this be the case?

A fascinating body of research by Brian Wansink (2005, 2013) and his colleagues has examined the factors that influence how much food people eat. One surprising factor that influences portion sizes is plate size. Since 1900, the width of the average plate has increased from about 9½ inches to nearly a foot (Van Ittersum & Wansink, 2012). Larger plates often lead to larger portions and more eating (Wansink & Cheney, 2005). A study at an ice cream social found that larger bowls led even experts in nutrition to serve larger portions and to eat more (Wansink, Van Ittersum, & Painter, 2006).

What steps can be taken to reduce mindless eating? One possibility is to segment food in a way that alerts eaters to how much they are eating. In one study, participants ate tubes of stacked potato chips while watching a movie. The control group ate regular chips. The experimental group was given tubes of chips in which a potato chip that had been dyed red appeared every 7th chip. Participants who encountered the red chips (which were otherwise identical to the other chips) ate less than half the number of chips and were more accurate in their estimates of how much they had eaten compared to the control group (Geier, Wansink, & Rozin, 2012). The red chips allowed eaters to be less mindless in their consumption. Dieting is a continuing U.S. obsession (Dulloo, Jacquet, & Montani, 2012). However, some people trying to lose weight are doing so not to improve their health but because they have an eating disorder, the topic we turn to next.

Disordered Eating

For some people, concerns about weight and body image become a serious, debilitating disorder (Stice, Marti, & Rohde, 2013; Wilson & Zandberg, 2012). For such individuals, the very act of eating is an arena where a variety of complex biological, psychological, and cultural issues are played out, often with tragic consequences.

A number of famous people have coped with eating disorders, including Paula Abdul, Mary-Kate Olsen, Kelly Clarkson, and Demi Lovato. Eating disorders are characterized by extreme disturbances in eating behavior—from eating very, very little to eating a great deal. In this section we examine three eating disorders—anorexia nervosa, bulimia nervosa, and binge eating disorder.

ANOREXIA NERVOSA

Anorexia nervosa is an eating disorder that involves the relentless pursuit of thinness through starvation. According to the National Institute of Mental Health (NIMH), anorexia nervosa is much more common in girls and women than boys and men and affects between 0.5 and 3.7 percent of young women (NIMH, 2011). The American Psychiatric Association (2013a) lists these main characteristics of anorexia nervosa:

- Weight less than 85 percent of what is considered normal for age and height, and refusal to maintain weight at a healthy level.
- An intense fear of gaining weight that does not decrease with weight loss.
- Persistent behavior to prevent weight gain.
- A distorted body image (Stewart & others, 2012). Even when individuals with anorexia nervosa are extremely thin, they never think they are thin enough.

● **anorexia nervosa** An eating disorder that involves the relentless pursuit of thinness through starvation.

Uruguayan model Eliana Ramos posed for the camera in her native country. Tragically, the super-thin Eliana died at age 18 in February 2007, two years after this picture was taken, reportedly from health problems associated with anorexia nervosa.

● **bulimia nervosa** An eating disorder in which the individual (typically female) consistently follows a binge-and-purge eating pattern.

Over time, anorexia nervosa can lead to physical changes, such as the growth of fine hair all over the body, thinning of bones and hair, severe constipation, and low blood pressure (NIMH, 2011). Dangerous and even life-threatening complications of anorexia nervosa include damage to the heart and thyroid. Anorexia nervosa is said to have the highest mortality rate (about 5.6 percent of individuals with anorexia nervosa die within 10 years of diagnosis) of any psychological disorder (Hoek, 2006; NIMH, 2011).

Anorexia nervosa typically begins in the teenage years, often following an episode of dieting and some type of life stress (Fitzpatrick, 2012). Most individuals with anorexia nervosa are non-Latino White female adolescents or young adults from well-educated middle- and upper-income families (Darcy, 2012; Dodge, 2012). They are often high-achieving perfectionists (Forbush, Heatherton, & Keel, 2007). In addition to perfectionism, obsessive thinking about weight and compulsive exercise are related to anorexia nervosa (Hildebrant & others, 2012; Simpson & others, 2013).

BULIMIA NERVOSA

Bulimia nervosa is an eating disorder in which an individual (typically female) consistently follows a binge-and-purge eating pattern. The individual goes on an eating binge and then purges by self-induced vomiting or the use of laxatives. Most people with bulimia nervosa are preoccupied with food, have a strong fear of becoming overweight, and are depressed or anxious (Birgegård, Norring, & Clinton, 2012). Because bulimia nervosa occurs within a normal weight range, the disorder is often difficult to detect. A person with bulimia nervosa usually keeps the disorder a secret and experiences a great deal of self-disgust and shame.

Bulimia nervosa can lead to complications such as a chronic sore throat, kidney problems, dehydration, and gastrointestinal disorders (NIMH, 2011). The disorder is also related to dental problems, as persistent exposure to the stomach acids in vomit can wear away tooth enamel.

Bulimia nervosa typically begins in late adolescence or early adulthood (Uher & Rutter, 2012). The disorder affects between 1 and 4 percent of young women (NIMH, 2011). Many young women who develop bulimia nervosa are highly perfectionistic (Lampard & others, 2012). At the same time, they tend to have low levels of self-efficacy (Bardone-Cone & others, 2006). In other words, these are young women with very high standards but very low confidence that they can achieve their goals. Impulsivity, negative emotion, and childhood obsessive-compulsive tendencies (see Chapter 15) are also related to bulimia (Roncero, Perpina, & Garcia-Soriano, 2011; Tchanturia & others, 2004; Vervaet, van Heeringen, & Audenaert, 2004). Bulimia nervosa is associated, too, with sexual and physical abuse in childhood (Lo Sauro & others, 2008).

ANOREXIA NERVOSA AND BULIMIA NERVOSA: CAUSES AND TREATMENTS

What is the etiology (cause) of anorexia nervosa and bulimia nervosa? For many years researchers thought that sociocultural factors, such as media images of very thin women and family pressures, were the central determinant of these disorders (Le Grange & others, 2010). Media images that glorify extreme thinness can influence women's body image, and emphasis on the thin ideal is related to anorexia nervosa and bulimia nervosa (Carr & Peebles, 2012).

However, as powerful as these media messages might be, relatively few females develop eating disorders of the countless number exposed to them. Many young women embark on diets, but comparatively few develop eating disorders.

Furthermore, eating disorders occur in cultures that do not emphasize the ideal of thinness, although the disorders may differ from Western descriptions (Carr & Peebles, 2012). For instance, in Eastern cultures, individuals can show the symptoms of anorexia nervosa, but they lack the fear of getting fat that is common in North Americans with the disorder (Pike, Yamamiya, & Konishi, 2011).

Since the 1980s, researchers have moved beyond a sole focus on sociocultural factors and have increasingly probed the potential biological underpinnings of these disorders.

This research has examined the interplay of social and biological factors in eating disorders. Genes play a substantial role in both anorexia nervosa and bulimia nervosa (Lock, 2012; Mas & others, 2013). In fact, genes influence many psychological characteristics (for example, perfectionism, impulsivity, obsessive-compulsive tendencies, thinness drive) and behaviors (restrained eating, binge eating, self-induced vomiting) that are associated with anorexia nervosa and bulimia nervosa (Slof-Op't Landt & others, 2013; Schur, Heckbert, & Goldberg, 2010). These genes are also factors in the regulation of serotonin, and problems in regulating serotonin are related to both anorexia nervosa and bulimia nervosa (Capasso, Putrella, & Milano, 2009).

Keep in mind that even as biological factors play a role in the emergence of eating disorders, eating disorders themselves affect the body, including the brain (Kaye & others, 2013). Most psychologists believe that although social factors and experiences may play a role in triggering dieting, the physical effects of dieting, bingeing, and purging may change the neural networks that then sustain the disordered pattern, in a kind of vicious cycle (Lock, 2012). In terms of social factors, problems in family functioning are increasingly thought to be involved in the appearance of eating disorders in adolescence (Stiles-Shields & others, 2012).

Although anorexia and bulimia nervosa are serious disorders, recovery is possible (Fitzpatrick, 2012; Treasure, Claudino, & Zucker, 2010). Anorexia nervosa may require hospitalization. The first target of intervention is promoting weight gain, in extreme cases through the use of a feeding tube. A common obstacle in the treatment of anorexia nervosa is that individuals with the disorder deny that anything is wrong (Wilson, Grilo, & Vitousek, 2007). Psychotherapy, family therapy, and drug treatments have been shown to be effective in treating anorexia nervosa and bulimia nervosa (Couturier, Kimber, & Szatmari, 2013; Hagman & Frank, 2012; Wilson & Zandberg, 2012).

BINGE EATING DISORDER

Binge eating disorder (BED) is characterized by recurrent episodes of eating more food in a short period of time than most people would eat, during which the person feels a lack of control over eating (Birgegård, Norring, & Clinton, 2012; Schag & others, 2013). Most individuals with BED are overweight or obese (Carrard, der Linden, & Golay, 2012).

Individuals with BED frequently eat alone because of embarrassment or guilt, and they feel ashamed and disgusted with themselves after bingeing. The most common of all eating disorders, BED affects men, women, and ethnic groups within the United States more similarly than anorexia nervosa or bulimia nervosa (Azarbad & others, 2010). An estimated 2 to 5 percent of Americans will suffer from BED in their lifetime (NIMH, 2011).

Binge eating disorder is thought to characterize approximately 8 percent of individuals who are obese. Unlike obese individuals who do not suffer from BED, binge eaters are more likely to place great value on their physical appearance, weight, and body shape (Grilo, Masheb, & White, 2010). The complications of BED are those of obesity more generally, including diabetes, hypertension, and cardiovascular disease.

BINGE EATING DISORDER: CAUSES AND TREATMENTS

Researchers are examining the role of biological and psychological factors in BED (Tanofsky-Kraff & others, 2013). Genes play a role (Akkermann & others, 2012), as does dopamine, the neurotransmitter related to reward pathways in the brain (C. Davis & others, 2010). The fact that binge eating often occurs after stressful events suggests that binge eaters use food to regulate their emotions (Wilson, Grilo, & Vitousek, 2007). The areas of the brain and endocrine system that respond to stress are overactive in individuals with BED (Lo Sauro & others, 2008). Individuals with BED may be more likely to perceive events as stressful and then seek to manage that stress by binge eating. A recent fMRI study also

● **binge eating disorder (BED)** An eating disorder characterized by recurrent episodes of eating more food in a short period of time than most people would eat, during which the person feels a lack of control over eating.

Unlike individuals with anorexia nervosa or bulimia nervosa, most people with binge eating disorder (BED) are overweight or obese.

found that the areas of the brain involved in self-regulation and impulse control, especially the prefrontal cortex, showed diminished activity in individuals with binge eating disorder (Balodis & others, 2013).

Little research has examined the sociocultural factors in binge eating disorder. One study examined whether exposure to U.S. culture might increase the risk of developing BED (Swanson & others, 2012). With the research controlled for a variety of factors, the results showed that Mexicans who immigrated to the United States and Mexican Americans were more likely to develop BED than were Mexicans who lived in Mexico (Swanson & others, 2012).

Just as treatment for anorexia nervosa first focuses on weight gain, some believe that treatment for BED should first target weight loss (De Angelis, 2002). Others argue that individuals with BED must be treated for disordered eating per se, and they insist that if the underlying psychological issues are not addressed, weight loss will not be successful or permanent (de Zwaan & others, 2005; Hay & others, 2009). Recent research indicates that drugs targeting the functioning of neurotransmitters serotonin and norepinephrine show some promise in treating BED (Marazziti & others, 2012).

Food is unquestionably necessary for survival. Individuals struggling with disordered eating must change their relationship with this vital resource in order to survive and, eventually, thrive. Clearly, though, thriving involves more than food. We next turn to the broader implications of motivation in everyday life.

3. APPROACHES TO MOTIVATION IN EVERYDAY LIFE

Think about the wide range of human actions and achievements, such as Reeshemah Taylor's heroism from the opening of this chapter. Such behaviors are not easily explained by motivational approaches that focus on physiological needs. Increasingly, psychologists are recognizing the role of goals that people set for themselves in motivation. In this section, we explore the ways that psychologists have come to understand the processes that underlie everyday human behavior.

Maslow's Hierarchy of Human Needs

Humanistic theorist Abraham Maslow (1954, 1971) proposed a **hierarchy of needs** that must be satisfied in the following sequence: physiological needs, safety, love and belongingness, esteem, and self-actualization (Figure 10.3). The strongest needs are at the base of the hierarchy (physiological), and the weakest are at the top (self-actualization).

According to this hierarchy, people are motivated to satisfy their need for food first and to fulfill their need for safety before their need for love. If we think of our needs as calls for action, hunger and safety needs shout loudly, whereas the need for self-actualization beckons with a whisper. Maslow asserted that each lower need in the hierarchy comes from a deficiency—such as being hungry, afraid, or lonely—and that we can only see the higher-level needs in a person who is relatively satisfied in these most basic needs. Such an individual can then turn his or her attention to the fulfillment of a higher calling.

Self-actualization, the highest and most elusive of Maslow's needs, is the motivation to develop one's full potential as a human being. According to Maslow, self-actualization is possible only after the other needs in the hierarchy are met. Maslow cautions that most people stop moving up the hierarchy after they have developed a high level of esteem and do not become self-actualized.

The idea that human motives are hierarchically arranged is appealing; however, Maslow's ordering of the needs is debatable (Kenrick & others, 2010). Some people, for example, might seek greatness in a career to achieve self-esteem, while putting on hold their needs for love and belongingness. Certainly history is full of examples of individuals who, in the most difficult circumstances, were still able to engage in acts of kindness that seem to come from higher-level needs. Often, the individuals with the least financial resources are most likely to give generously to others.

Perhaps Maslow's greatest contribution to our understanding of motivation is that he asked the key question about motivation for modern people: How can we explain what humans do, once their bellies are full? That is, how do we explain the "why" of human behavior when survival is not the most pressing need? This is the kind of questioning that inspired *self-determination theory* (Deci & Ryan, 2002; Ryan & Deci, 2009; Weinstein, Deci, & Ryan, 2011).

Self-Determination Theory

Psychologists Edward Deci and Richard Ryan have explored the role of motivation in optimal human functioning from a perspective that emphasizes particular kinds of needs as factors in psychological and physical well-being (Deci & Ryan, 2000; Ryan & Deci, 2009). Their **self-determination theory** asserts that there are three basic organismic needs: competence, relatedness, and autonomy. The word *organismic* here means that these psychological needs are innate and exist in every person. They are basic to human growth and functioning, just as water, soil, and sunshine are necessary for plant growth. This metaphor is especially apt, because once we plant a seed, all it requires to thrive and grow is a supportive environment. Similarly, self-determination theory holds that we all have the capacity for growth and fulfillment in us, ready to emerge if given the right context.

Importantly, from the perspective of self-determination theory, these organismic needs do not arise from deficits. Self-determination theory is not a drive reduction theory. Deci and Ryan (2000) argue that these needs concern personal growth, not the filling of deficiencies. Let's examine each of these needs in depth.

The first organismic need described by self-determination theory, *competence,* is met when we feel that we are able to bring about desired outcomes (Reis & others, 2000). Competence motivation involves *self-efficacy* (the belief that you have the competence to accomplish a given goal or task) and *mastery* (the sense that you can gain skills and overcome obstacles). One domain in which competence needs may be met is in the realm of achievement. Some individuals are highly motivated to succeed and spend considerable effort striving to excel.

The second organismic need described by self-determination theory is *relatedness*— the need to engage in warm relations with other people. The need for relatedness is reflected in the importance of parents nurturing children's development, the intimate moments of sharing private thoughts in friendship, the uncomfortable feelings we have when we are lonely, and the powerful attraction we experience when we are in love.

The critical role of social bonds is also demonstrated in research examining the effects of being socially excluded (Hess & Pickett, 2010; K. D. Williams, 2007). When people are left out, they tend to engage in a variety of self-defeating behaviors, such as overeating and drinking to excess (Twenge, 2008). Research has shown that even when the exclusion is unintentional (for instance, when someone is ignored, though not purposely), it can lead to distress and the feeling that one's life is meaningless (K. D. Williams, 2012).

The third need proposed by self-determination theory is *autonomy*—the sense that we are in control of our own life. Autonomy means feeling that one's behavior is self-motivated and emerging from genuine interest (Weinstein, Deci, & Ryan, 2011). Of course, many of the behaviors we engage in may feel like things we are forced to do, but a sense of autonomy is strongly related to well-being (Sheldon & others, 2005).

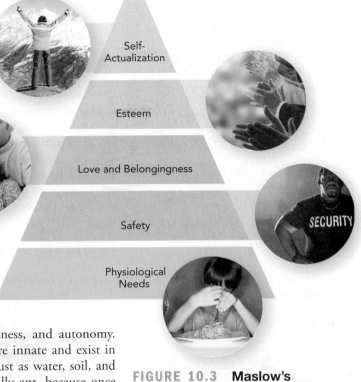

FIGURE 10.3 Maslow's Hierarchy of Needs Abraham Maslow developed the hierarchy of human needs to show that we have to satisfy basic physiological needs before we can satisfy other, higher needs.

REMEMBER YOU ARE NOT INDISPENSABLE

WORK OR DIE!

THERE ARE PLENTY OF PEOPLE WHO'D DO YOUR JOB FOR LESS!

"Mr. Frimley, sir, can I have a word about the motivational artwork . . ."

© Clive Goddard. www.CartoonStock.com.

● **intrinsic motivation** Motivation based on internal factors such as organismic needs (competence, relatedness, and autonomy), as well as curiosity, challenge, and fun.

● **extrinsic motivation** Motivation that involves external incentives such as rewards and punishments.

● **self-regulation** The process by which an organism effortfully controls behavior in order to pursue important objectives.

off the mark.com   by Mark Parisi

MAYBE YOU SHOULD SET SPECIFIC GOALS... I'M NOT SURE IT'S REALISTIC TO WANT TO GET INTO EVERYTHING...

© Mark Parisi. www.offthemark.com.

Research supports the idea that progress on goals that serve the three organismic needs is strongly related to well-being (Sheldon, 2013). Further, valuing more extrinsic qualities—such as money, prestige, and physical appearance—over these organismic concerns is associated with lowered well-being, lowered self-actualization, and physical illness (Kasser & Ryan, 1996; Kasser & others, 2004).

Self-determination theory maintains that one of the most important aspects of healthy motivation is the sense that we do the things we do because we have freely chosen to do them. When we can choose our behaviors and feel ownership over those choices, we are likely to experience heightened fulfillment (Koestner & others, 2012).

From the self-determination theory perspective, when our behaviors serve the needs for competence, autonomy, and relatedness, we experience intrinsic motivation. When our behavior, instead, serves needs for other values—such as prestige, money, or approval—our behavior is extrinsically motivated (Ryan & Deci, 2009). We examine this important distinction between intrinsic and extrinsic motivation next.

Intrinsic Versus Extrinsic Motivation

One way psychologists understand the "why" of our goals is by distinguishing between intrinsic and extrinsic motivation. **Intrinsic motivation** is based on internal factors such as organismic needs (competence, relatedness, and autonomy), as well as curiosity, challenge, and fun. When we are intrinsically motivated, we engage in a behavior because we enjoy it. **Extrinsic motivation** involves external incentives such as rewards and punishers. When we are extrinsically motivated, we engage in a behavior for some external payoff or to avoid an external punishment.

Some students study hard because they are internally motivated to put forth considerable effort and achieve high quality in their work (intrinsic motivation). Other students study hard because they want to make good grades or avoid parental disapproval (extrinsic motivation). Many psychologists believe that intrinsic motivation leads to more positive outcomes than extrinsic motivation (Blumenfeld, Kempler, & Krajcik, 2006; Patell, Cooper, & Robinson, 2008; Ryan & Deci, 2009). They argue that intrinsic motivation is more likely to produce competent behavior and mastery.

Have you ever had the experience of doing something because you liked it only to have that enjoyment be completely ruined when you started doing it for pay? This experience is not unusual but also presents a motivational puzzle. Why should getting a reward ruin a feeling of intrinsic motivation? To read more about this puzzle, check out the Critical Controversy.

Many very successful individuals are both intrinsically motivated (they have high personal standards of achievement and emphasize personal effort) and extrinsically motivated (they are strongly competitive) (Ciani & Sheldon, 2010; Schunk, 2012). Indeed, many of us might think of the ideal occupation as one in which we get paid (an extrinsic reward) for doing something we love to do (intrinsic motivation).

Self-Regulation: The Successful Pursuit of Goals

Today many psychologists approach motivation in the way that you yourself might—by asking about the goals a person is trying to accomplish in everyday life (Anderman, Gray, & Chang, 2013).

Goal approaches to motivation include the concept of self-regulation (Schunk & Zimmerman, 2013). **Self-regulation** is the process by which an organism effortfully controls behavior in order to pursue important objectives (Carver & Scheier, 2013). A key aspect of self-regulation is getting feedback about how we are doing in our goal pursuits. Our daily mood has been proposed as a way that we may receive this feedback—that is, we feel good or bad depending on how we are doing in the areas of life we value. Note that the role of mood in self-regulation means that we cannot be happy

CRITICAL CONTROVERSY

Do Extrinsic Rewards Undermine Intrinsic Motivation?

A longstanding debate in the psychology of motivation is whether extrinsic rewards reduce intrinsic motivation. Indeed, two comprehensive reviews of research on rewards and intrinsic motivation reached opposite conclusions (Cameron, Banko, & Pierce, 2001; Deci, Koestner, & Ryan, 1999). Edward Deci and his colleagues (1999) analyzed 128 studies and concluded that external rewards restrict self-determination and interfere with intrinsic motivation. Just 2 years later, an analysis of 145 studies by Judy Cameron and her colleagues yielded mixed results (Cameron, Banko, & Pierce, 2001). Cameron's group found that extrinsic rewards sometimes negatively affected intrinsic motivation but at other times had a positive effect or no effect at all. Cameron and her colleagues proposed that extrinsic motivation has no overall effect on intrinsic motivation.

The basic principles of operant conditioning tell us that rewarding a behavior should increase the likelihood that it will happen again, right? Yet, research on extrinsic rewards seems to indicate just the opposite: Rewarding a behavior will *reduce* the performance of that behavior, as well as the enjoyment associated with it. How can we make sense of this apparent contradiction?

According to Cameron and her colleagues, a prime issue is *which behavior,* exactly, is rewarded (Cameron & Pierce, 2002; Cameron & others, 2005). When extrinsic rewards are given for the quality and creativity of a behavior, they actually enhance that behavior (Eisenberger & Aselage, 2009). Furthermore, when extrinsic rewards are provided for mastering skills, intrinsic motivation itself increases (Cameron & others, 2005).

In daily life, people often do things that are not intrinsically motivating, such as, perhaps, mowing the lawn and studying mathematics. Without external rewards, they may simply lose interest in performing those tasks. In such cases, extrinsic motivation may help foster intrinsic motivation. For example, a creative mathematics teacher might use rewards such as extra credit, math games, and verbal praise as a way to instill a lifelong love of mathematics. Similarly, if an employee is producing shoddy work, seems bored, or has a negative attitude, offering an external incentive may improve motivation. There are times, though, when external rewards can diminish intrinsic motivation. The problem with using a reward as an incentive is that individuals may perceive that the reward rather than their own motivation caused their achievement behavior.

A richer understanding of intrinsic and extrinsic motivation might allow for more accurate predictions of when extrinsic motivation will reduce, increase, or not affect intrinsic motivation. It might then be possible for employers and teachers to help employees and students develop the deep intrinsic motivation that most experts agree is indispensable to well-being.

WHAT DO YOU THINK

- What are some instances in your own life in which your intrinsic motivation was *reduced* by external rewards? What are some instances in which your intrinsic motivation was *increased* by external rewards?

- What other factors might determine whether extrinsic rewards influence intrinsic motivation?

---

all the time. In order to effectively pursue our goals, we have to be open to the bad news that might occasionally come our way (King, 2008).

Putting our personal goals into action is a potentially complex process that involves setting goals, planning for their implementation, and monitoring our progress. Individuals' success improves when they set goals that are specific and moderately challenging (Bandura, 1997; Schunk, 2012). A fuzzy, nonspecific goal is "I want to be successful." A concrete, specific goal is "I want to have a 3.5 average at the end of the semester."

Accomplishing long-term goals is facilitated by the pursuit of short-term goals. When you set long-term goals, such as "I want to be a clinical psychologist," make sure that you also create short-term goals as steps along the way, such as "I want to get an *A* on my next psychology test." Planning how to reach a goal and monitoring progress toward the goal are critical aspects of achievement (Schunk & Zimmerman, 2013). Make commitments in manageable chunks. High-achieving individuals monitor their own learning and systematically evaluate their progress toward their goals more than do low-achieving individuals (Schunk, 2012).

Even as we keep our nose to the grindstone in pursuing short-term goals, it is also important to have a sense of the big picture. Dedication to a long-term dream or personal mission can enhance one's sense of purpose in life. Although short-term goals can provide a feeling of accomplishment, attaching these goals to a future dream can allow individuals to experience a sense of meaning and to maintain their efforts in the face of short-term failure (Houser-Marko & Sheldon, 2008).

A key concept in understanding how individuals successfully pursue goals is *delay of gratification*—putting off a pleasurable experience in the interest of some larger but later reward. Successful delay of gratification is evident in the student who does not go out with friends but instead stays in and studies for an upcoming test, perhaps thinking, "There will be plenty of time to party after this test is over." Delay of gratification is challenging. Think about it—future payoffs are simply much less certain than current rewards. If an organism is in a situation where rewards are few and far between, it might make sense to eat or drink or be merry based on whatever is around right now (Logue, 1995).

Walter Mischel and his colleagues examined how children managed to delay gratification, in what have become known as the Stanford Marshmallow Experiments (Mischel, Cantor, & Feldman, 1996; Mischel & Moore, 1980). They placed children in a difficult situation—alone in a room with a very tempting marshmallow in their reach. The children were told that if they wanted to, at any time they could ring a bell and eat the marshmallow. Otherwise, they could wait until the experimenter returned, and then they would get two marshmallows. The children were then left alone to face this self-control dilemma. In truth, the experimenter was not coming back. The researchers were interested in measuring how long the children could wait before giving in to temptation and eating the marshmallow.

There were a variety of responses to this unusual situation. Some children sat dead still, focused on the tempting marshmallow. Some stared the marshmallow down. Some smelled the marshmallow. Others turned away, sang songs, picked their noses, or did anything but pay attention to the marshmallow.

How did the children who were able to resist temptation do it? Mischel and colleagues found that the kids who were able to distract themselves from the marshmallow by focusing on "cool thoughts" (that is, non-marshmallow-related things) were better able to delay gratification. In contrast, children who remained focused on the marshmallow and all its delightful qualities—what Mischel called "hot thoughts"—ate the marshmallow sooner (Metcalfe & Mischel, 1999).

These findings have implications for self-control. Imagine that you are in a long-term romantic relationship that you wish to continue, and you meet an appealing new person to whom you are physically attracted. Should you cultivate a friendship with him or her? Maybe not, if you want to avoid temptation and preserve your current relationship. Think about all the current and potential "marshmallows" in your life—those things that have the power to distract you from achieving your long-term plans. Mischel's research with children demonstrates that avoiding these hot issues might be a good way to see a long-term plan through to its completion.

Interestingly, Mischel and his colleagues continued to study those children for many years. They found that the amount of time the children were able to delay gratification predicted their academic performance in high school and college (Mischel, 2004) and even their self-regulation skills in their 40s (Casey & others, 2011; Mischel & others, 2011).

4· EMOTION

The concept of self-regulation suggests that motivation and emotion are closely linked. We feel happy or sad depending on how events influence the likelihood of our getting the things we want in life. Our emotions tell us what really matters to us. We might think, for instance, that we have lost interest in a romantic partner until that person initiates a breakup. Suddenly, we realize how much the person really meant to us.

test yourself

1. What is Maslow's theory of a hierarchy of needs? Explain.
2. What is self-actualization, according to Maslow, and on what does it depend?
3. How do intrinsic motivation and extrinsic motivation differ?

Emotions are complex. The body, the mind, and the face play key roles in emotion, although psychologists debate which of these components is most significant in emotion and how they mix to produce emotional experiences (Christenfeld & Mandler, 2013; Davidson, Scherer, & Goldsmith, 2002; Kalat & Shiota, 2012). For our purposes, **emotion** is feeling, or affect, that can involve physiological arousal (such as a fast heartbeat), conscious experience (feeling joy), and behavioral expression (a smile).

● **emotion** Feeling, or affect, that can involve physiological arousal (such as a fast heartbeat), conscious experience (thinking about being in love with someone), and behavioral expression (a smile or grimace).

Biological Factors in Emotion

A friend whom you have been counseling about a life problem texts you, "r u home? On my way over." You get nervous. What could be going on? You feel burdened—you have a lot of work to do, and you do not have time for a talk session. When she arrives with a gift-wrapped package and a big smile, your nerves give way to relief. She announces, "Here's a present to say thanks for all your help." Your heart warms, and you feel a strong sense of your enduring bond with her. As you moved through the emotions of worry, relief, and joy, your body changed. Indeed, the body is a crucial part of our emotional experience.

THE AUTONOMIC NERVOUS SYSTEM

Recall from Chapter 3 that the *autonomic nervous system (ANS)* takes messages to and from the body's internal organs, monitoring such processes as breathing, heart rate, and digestion. The ANS is divided into the sympathetic and the parasympathetic nervous systems (Figure 10.4). The *sympathetic nervous system (SNS)* is responsible for rapid reactions to threats. SNS arousal causes increased blood pressure, faster heart rate, more rapid breathing, and more efficient blood flow to the brain and major muscle groups. These changes prepare us for action, the "fight or flight" response. In contrast, the *parasympathetic nervous system (PNS)* calms the body, promoting processes of maintenance and healing. When the PNS is activated, blood pressure drops, heart rate and breathing slow, and food digestion increases, which is the "rest and digest" response.

FIGURE 10.4   The Autonomic Nervous System and Its Role in Arousing and Calming the Body The two parts of the autonomic nervous system work in different ways. The sympathetic nervous system arouses the body in reaction to a stressor, evoking the "fight or flight" response. In contrast, the parasympathetic nervous system calms the body, promoting relaxation and healing. Remember, the latter system functions to "rest and digest."

Sympathetic Nervous System		Parasympathetic Nervous System
Increases	Blood flow to brain	Decreases
Dilate	Pupils of eyes	Constrict
Increases	Skin perspiration	Decreases
Faster	Heartbeat	Slower
Faster	Breathing rate	Slower
Increases; stress hormones released	Adrenal gland activity	Decreases; stress hormones inhibited
Decreases	Digestive activity	Increases

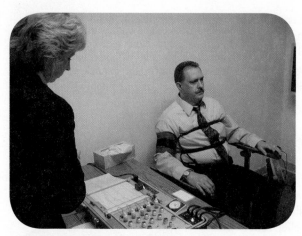

Examiners use a polygraph to tell whether someone is lying. A polygraph monitors changes in the body believed to be influenced by emotional states. Controversy has swirled about the polygraph's use because it is unreliable.

● **polygraph** A machine, commonly called a lie detector, that monitors changes in the body, used to try to determine whether someone is lying.

● **James-Lange theory** The theory that emotion results from physiological states triggered by stimuli in the environment.

The sympathetic and parasympathetic nervous systems evolved to improve the human species' likelihood for survival. It does not take a life-threatening situation to activate the SNS response. *Emotions* are associated with SNS arousal as well, suggesting that such arousal plays a role in emotional experience.

MEASURING ANS ACTIVITY

Clearly, when the SNS is active, the body jumps to action. How might we measure these changes? One way psychologists have measured this arousal is *skin conductance level (SCL),* a rise in the skin's electrical conductivity when sweat gland activity increases. A sweaty palm conducts electricity better than a dry one. This difference provides the basis for SCL as a measure of autonomic arousal.

Another measure of arousal is the **polygraph** or lie detector, a machine examiners use to try to determine whether someone is lying. The polygraph monitors changes in the body—heart rate, breathing, and SCL—thought to be influenced by emotional states. In a typical polygraph test, the examiner asks the individual a number of neutral questions and several key, less neutral questions. If the individual's heart rate, breathing, and SCL responses increase substantially when the key questions are asked, the individual is assumed to be lying (Grubin, 2010).

How accurate is the lie detector? Experts argue that the polygraph errs just under 50 percent of the time (Iacono & Lykken, 1997; Lykken, 1987, 2001; Seymour & others, 2000). The problem with the polygraph is that heart rate, breathing, and SCL can increase for reasons other than lying—for instance, because a person is *nervous* (not necessarily guilty). For this reason, the Employee Polygraph Protection Act of 1988 restricts polygraph testing outside of government agencies, and most courts do not accept the results of polygraph testing.

THEORIES OF EMOTION

Imagine that you and your date are enjoying a picnic in the country. Suddenly, a bull runs across the field toward you. Why are you afraid? Two well-known theories of emotion that involve physiological processes provide answers to this question.

Common sense tells you that you are trembling and running away from the bull because you are afraid, but William James (1950) and Carl Lange (pronounced "Long-uh") (1922) said emotion works in the opposite way. According to the **James-Lange theory,** emotion results from physiological states triggered by stimuli in the environment: Emotion occurs *after* physiological reactions. This perspective holds that emotions are not mental events that lead to reactions but rather that those physiological reactions are what lead to emotional states. Lange especially emphasized that each emotion—from anger to rapture—has a distinct set of physiological changes, evident in changes in heart rate, breathing patterns, sweating, and other responses.

Let's apply the James-Lange theory to the situation with the bull. You see the bull scratching its hoof on the ground, and you begin to run away. Your aroused body then sends sensory messages to your brain, at which point emotion is perceived. According to this theory, you do not run away because you are afraid; rather, you are afraid because you are running away. You perceive a stimulus in the environment, your body responds, and you interpret the body's reaction as emotion.

Walter Cannon (1927) rejected the idea that each emotional experience has its own particular set of physiological changes. He argued that different emotions could not be associated with specific physiological changes because autonomic nervous system responses are too diffuse and slow to account for rapid and differentiated emotional responses.

To understand Cannon's view, imagine the bull and the picnic once again. Seeing the bull scratching its hoof causes the thalamus of your brain to do two things simultaneously: First, it stimulates your autonomic nervous system to produce the physiological changes involved in emotion (increased heart rate, rapid breathing); second, it sends messages to

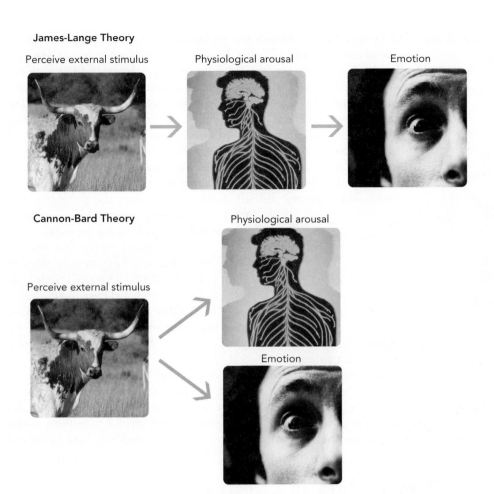

James-Lange Theory

Perceive external stimulus   Physiological arousal   Emotion

Cannon-Bard Theory

Physiological arousal

Perceive external stimulus

Emotion

FIGURE 10.5   James-Lange and Cannon-Bard Theories From the James-Lange perspective, the experience of fear is an outcome of physiological arousal. In the Cannon-Bard view, fear occurs at the same time as the physiological response.

your cerebral cortex, where the experience of emotion is perceived. Philip Bard (1934) supported this analysis, and so the theory became known as the **Cannon-Bard theory**— the proposition that emotion and physiological reactions occur *simultaneously*.

Unlike the James-Lange theory, which proposes that the physical reactions come first, in the Cannon-Bard theory, the body plays a less important role. Figure 10.5 shows how the James-Lange and Cannon-Bard theories differ. Whether emotions involve discrete autonomic nervous system responses, as Lange expected, continues to be debated (Barrett, 2011).

● **Cannon-Bard theory** The proposition that emotion and physiological reactions occur simultaneously.

NEUROTRANSMITTERS AND NEURAL CIRCUITS

Contemporary researchers are keenly interested in discovering the role of neurotransmitters and charting the neural circuitry of emotions. Research suggests the involvement of neurotransmitters in emotional experience (Amano & others, 2011; Lovheim, 2012). For instance, dopamine and endorphins are linked to positive emotions, such as happiness (Koepp & others, 2009), and norepinephrine functions in regulating arousal and anxiety (Berridge & Kringelbach, 2008; Greeson & others, 2009).

With regard to the brain structures involved in emotional experience, research has focused on the limbic system and especially the amygdalae, the almond-shaped structures in the limbic system that we considered in Chapter 3. The limbic system, including the amygdalae, is involved in the experience of positive emotions (Hurleman & others, 2010; Koepp & others, 2009; Ritchey, LaBar, & Cabeza, 2011). However, most research has focused on the important role of the amygdalae in the experience of negative emotion, particularly fear.

Research by Joseph LeDoux and his colleagues demonstrates that the amygdala plays a central role in fear (Johansen & others, 2012; LeDoux, 2009, 2012, 2013). When the amygdala determines that danger is present, it shifts into high gear, marshaling the

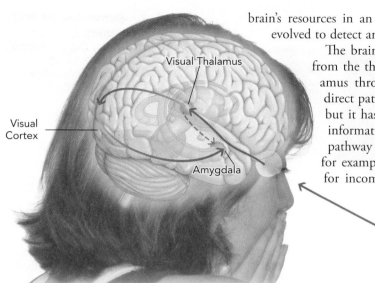

FIGURE 10.6 Direct and Indirect Brain Pathways in the Emotion of Fear Information about fear can follow two pathways in the brain when an individual sees a snake. The direct pathway (*broken arrow*) conveys information rapidly from the thalamus to the amygdala. The indirect pathway (*solid arrows*) transmits information more slowly from the thalamus to the sensory cortex (here, the visual cortex) and then to the amygdala.

● **two-factor theory of emotion** Schachter and Singer's theory that emotion is determined by two factors: physiological arousal and cognitive labeling.

brain's resources in an effort to protect the organism from harm. This fear system evolved to detect and respond to natural dangers that threaten survival or territory. The brain circuitry for fear can follow two pathways: a direct pathway from the thalamus to the amygdala or an indirect pathway from the thalamus through the sensory cortex to the amygdala (Figure 10.6). The direct pathway does not convey detailed information about the stimulus, but it has the advantage of speed—and speed is a vital characteristic of information for an organism facing a threat to its survival. The indirect pathway carries nerve impulses from the sensory organs (eyes and ears, for example) to the thalamus (recall that the thalamus is a relay station for incoming sensory stimuli); from the thalamus, the nerve impulses travel to the sensory cortex, which then sends appropriate signals to the amygdala.

The amygdala retains fear associations for a very long time (Debiec & LeDoux, 2006; Duvarci, Nader, & LeDoux, 2008; LeDoux, 2009, 2012, 2013). This quality is useful, because once we learn that something is dangerous, we do not have to relearn it. However, we pay a penalty for this ability. Once acquired, fears may be quite difficult to unlearn.

Part of the reason fears are so difficult to change is that the amygdala is well connected to the cerebral cortex, in which thinking and decision making primarily occur (Linnman & others, 2012). The amygdala is in a much better position to influence the cerebral cortex than the other way around, because it sends more connections to the cerebral cortex than it gets back. This may explain why it is sometimes hard to control our emotions, and why, once fear is learned, it is hard to erase.

Cognitive Factors in Emotion

Does emotion depend on the tides of the mind? Are we happy only when we think we are happy? Cognitive theories of emotion center on the premise that emotion always has a cognitive component (Derryberry & Reed, 2002; Frijda, 2007; Johnson-Laird, Mancini, & Gangemi, 2006). Thinking is said to be responsible for feelings of love and hate, joy and sadness. Although cognitive theorists do recognize the role of the brain and body in emotion, they give cognitive processes the main credit for these responses.

THE TWO-FACTOR THEORY OF EMOTION

In the **two-factor theory of emotion** developed by Stanley Schachter and Jerome Singer (1962), emotion is determined by two factors: physiological arousal and cognitive labeling (Figure 10.7). Schachter and Singer argued that we look to the external world for an explanation of *why* we are aroused. We interpret external cues and label the emotion. For example, if you feel good after someone has made a pleasant comment to you, you might label the emotion "happy." If you feel bad after you have done something wrong, you may label the feeling "guilty."

To test their theory of emotion, Schachter and Singer (1962) injected volunteer participants with epinephrine, a drug that produces high arousal. After participants received the drug, they observed someone else behave in either a euphoric way (shooting papers at a wastebasket) or an angry way (stomping out of the room). As predicted, the euphoric and angry behavior influenced the participants' cognitive interpretation of their own arousal. When they were with a happy person, they rated themselves as happy; when they were with an angry person, they said they were angry. This effect occurred, however, only when the participants were not told about the true effects of the injection. When they were told that the drug would increase their heart rate and make them jittery, they said the reason for their own arousal was the drug, not the other person's behavior.

The two-factor theory of emotion tells us that often our bodies send us ambiguous messages about what is going on in the world. We take those messages and look for

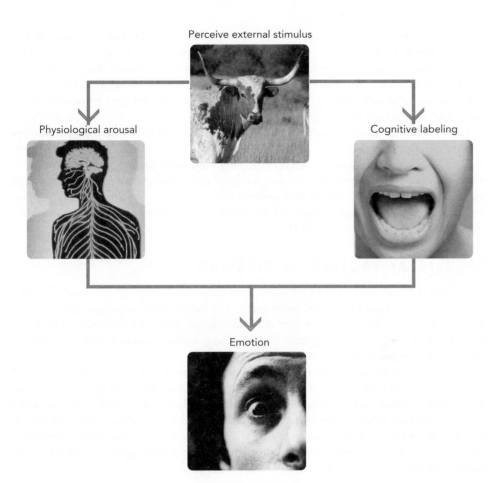

Perceive external stimulus

Physiological arousal

Cognitive labeling

Emotion

FIGURE 10.7 **Schachter and Singer's Two-Factor Theory of Emotion** The two-factor theory includes not only arousal but also cognitive labeling: You feel afraid of the bull because you label your physiological response "fear."

explanations in our immediate circumstances, and that is what produces emotions. Imagine that you are late for class on an important exam day. You sprint across campus as fast as you can, arriving just in time for the test. As you look over the questions, your heart is racing, your breathing is fast, and you feel sweaty. Are you nervous about the test or just recovering from your run to the classroom? The two-factor theory suggests that you just might mistake your bodily sensations as indications that you are scared of the test.

THE PRIMACY DEBATE: COGNITION OR EMOTION?

Which comes first, thinking or feeling? Fans of vintage episodes of TV's *Star Trek* may recognize this theme from the frequent arguments between Mr. Spock, the logical Vulcan, and Dr. McCoy, the emotional doctor on the *Enterprise*. In the 1980s and 1990s, two eminent psychologists, Richard Lazarus and Robert Zajonc, debated which was more central—cognition or emotion?

Recall from Chapter 8 that Lazarus said that we cognitively appraise ourselves and our circumstances and that these appraisals determine how we feel about events and experiences. For Lazarus (1991), then, thinking is primary—he believed cognitive activity causes our feelings. Our appraisals—which are guided by values, goals, beliefs, and expectations—determine our emotions (Urry, 2010; Wilkowski & Robinson, 2010). Consider a student who fails a test. This event would seem to be negative to everyone. But Lazarus would say that the emotions that follow depend on appraisal. If the class is important to the student's goals, she might feel distress, but if she had been looking for a reason to change her major, she might feel relief.

Zajonc (1984) disagreed with Lazarus. Emotions are primary, he said, and our thoughts are a result of them. Zajonc famously argued that "preferences need no inferences," meaning that the way we feel about something requires no thought.

Vintage Star Trek *episodes explored the question, what comes first—thinking or feeling?*

Which of the two psychologists is right? *Both* are likely correct. Lazarus talked mainly about a cluster of related events that occur over a period of time, whereas Zajonc described single events or a preference for one stimulus over another. Lazarus was concerned with love over the course of months and years, a sense of value to the community, and plans for retirement; Zajonc spoke about a car accident, an encounter with a snake, and a penchant for ice cream over spinach.

Some of our emotional reactions are virtually instantaneous and probably do not involve cognitive appraisal, such as shrieking upon detecting a snake (Young & Claypool, 2010). Other emotional circumstances, especially long-term feelings such as a depressed mood or anger toward a friend, are more likely to involve cognitive appraisal (Smith & Kirby, 2009). Indeed, the direct and indirect brain pathways described earlier support the idea that some of our emotional reactions do not involve deliberate thinking, whereas others do (LeDoux, 20012).

Behavioral Factors in Emotion

Remember that our definition of emotion includes not only physiological and cognitive components but also a behavioral component. The behavioral component can be verbal or nonverbal. Verbally, a person might show love for someone by professing it in words or might display anger by saying nasty things. Nonverbally, a person might smile, frown, show a fearful expression, or slouch.

The most interest in the behavioral dimension of emotion has focused on the nonverbal behavior of facial expressions (Hasegawa & Unuma, 2010; Sacco & Hugenberg, 2009; Todd & others, 2011). Emotion researchers have been intrigued by people's ability to detect emotion from a person's facial expression (Perkins & others, 2012; Tanaka & others, 2012). In a typical research study, participants, when shown photographs like those in Figure 10.8, are usually able to identify six emotions: happiness, anger, sadness, surprise, disgust, and fear (Ekman & O'Sullivan, 1991).

FIGURE 10.8 Recognizing Emotions in Facial Expressions Look at the six photographs and determine the emotion reflected in each of the six faces: (*top*) happiness, anger, sadness; (*bottom*) surprise, disgust, fear.

Emotion and Health Psychology: Can a Smile Protect Against Stress?

If you think about the last time you were seriously stressed out, you probably remember that you felt your heart racing. Indeed, stress can take a toll on the cardiovascular system. If smiling can improve an individual's mood, might it also help us cope with stressful experiences, potentially assisting the cardiovascular system in recovering from the effects of stress?

In a recent study, Tara Kraft and Sarah Pressman (2012) set out to answer this question. These researchers designed an experiment in which heart rate was monitored while participants, who were posing different facial expressions, engaged in challenging tasks. All of the participants were asked to hold chopsticks in their mouths to get them to pose one of three different facial expressions:

- The control group held the chopsticks in their mouth, closing their lips lightly, so that the sticks stuck straight out—a procedure that produced a neutral expression.
- The first experimental group held the chopsticks between their teeth, pulling their lips back, so that the sticks, again, stuck straight out. This pose produced a standard smile, but one that did not involve the muscles around the eyes.
- The second experimental group held the chopsticks crosswise between their teeth, with their lips pulled back, so that the sticks were in a horizontal position. This procedure produced a Duchenne smile, the genuine smile that involves the muscles around the eyes as well as those around the mouth.

While posing these expressions, participants engaged in two difficult tasks. In the first task, participants traced a star as many time as possible in 2 minutes, using their nondominant hand. The researchers increased the task difficulty by allowing participants to see their hand and the star only in mirror images. Further, participants were told that the average person could trace 8 stars with fewer than 25 errors in 2 minutes. If participants could do better than that, they would receive a reward of chocolate. In fact, this goal was impossible. Participants averaged just 2 tracings with more than 25 errors. For the second task, participants submerged their hands in ice water for 1 minute. This task, called the "cold pressor" task, has been used in many studies, and it can be quite painful.

In between the tasks, participants were given rest periods in which their heart rate was recorded. The results showed that during those rest periods, the participants who were posing both types of smiles showed faster heart rate recovery compared to those in the control condition. Those who were posing a Duchenne smile showed especially quick recovery.

What might these results mean for coping with stress? First, it is important to keep in mind that faking facial expressions can be taxing itself (Goldberg & Grandey, 2007). So smiling all the time, even when you are feeling down, might not be a great strategy. But, during acute stressful moments, such as the next time you get a flu shot, wearing a grin just might do the trick.

Have you ever tried to just "grin and bear it"? Did it work?

Might our facial expressions not only reflect our emotions but also influence them? According to the **facial feedback hypothesis,** facial expressions can influence emotions as well as reflect them (Davis, Senghas, & Ochsner, 2009). In this view, facial muscles send signals to the brain that help us to recognize the emotion we are experiencing (Keillor & others, 2002). For example, we feel happier when we smile and sadder when we frown.

The facial feedback hypothesis provides support for the James-Lange theory of emotion discussed earlier—namely, that emotional experiences can be generated by changes in and awareness of our own bodily states. The influence of facial expressions on emotional experiences has been explored in the context of coping with stress, as we review in the Intersection above.

● **facial feedback hypothesis** The idea that facial expressions can influence emotions as well as reflect them.

FIGURE 10.9 **Emotional Expressions in the United States and New Guinea** (*Top*) Two women from the United States. (*Bottom*) Two men from the Fore tribe in New Guinea. Notice the similarity in their expressions of disgust and happiness. Psychologists believe that the facial expression of emotion is virtually the same in all cultures.

● **display rules** Sociocultural standards that determine when, where, and how emotions should be expressed.

In the Middle Eastern country of Yemen, male-to-male kissing is commonplace, but in the United States it is less common.

Sociocultural Factors in Emotion

Are the facial expressions that are associated with different emotions largely innate, or do they vary across cultures? Answering this question requires a look at research findings on sociocultural influences in emotions.

CULTURE AND THE EXPRESSION OF EMOTION

In 1872 Charles Darwin stated in *The Expression of the Emotions in Man and Animals* that the facial expressions of human beings are innate, not learned; are the same in all cultures around the world; and have evolved from the emotions of animals (Darwin, 1965). Many psychologists still believe that emotions, especially facial expressions of emotion, have strong biological ties (Gelder & others, 2006; Peleg & others, 2006). For example, children who are blind from birth and have never observed the smile or frown on another person's face smile or frown in the same way that children with normal vision do (Shariff & Tracy, 2011). If emotions and the facial expressions that go with them are unlearned, then they should be the same the world over. Are they?

Extensive research has examined the universality of facial expressions and the ability of people from different cultures accurately to label the emotion that lies behind facial expressions (Sauter & others, 2010). Paul Ekman's careful observations reveal that the many faces of emotion do not differ significantly from one culture to another (Ekman, 1980, 1996, 2003). For example, Ekman and Wallace Friesen photographed people expressing emotions such as happiness, fear, surprise, disgust, and grief. When they showed the photographs to people from the United States, Chile, Japan, Brazil, and Borneo (an Indonesian island in the western Pacific), the participants recognized the emotions the faces were meant to show, across the various cultures (Ekman & Friesen, 1969). Similarly, in another study, members of the Fore tribe, an isolated Stone Age culture in New Guinea, were able to match descriptions of emotional situations with photographs of faces expressing fear, happiness, anger, and surprise (Ekman & Friesen, 1971). Figure 10.9 shows the similarity of facial expressions of emotions by persons in New Guinea and the United States.

Not all psychologists believe that facial expressions of basic emotions are universal (Barrett, 2011), but all would certainly agree that cultures have different norms that govern the expression of emotion (Fischer, 2006; Fok & others, 2008; Matsumoto & others, 2008). **Display rules** are sociocultural standards that determine when, where, and how emotions should be expressed. For example, although happiness is a universally expressed emotion, when, where, and how people display it may vary from one culture to another (Engelmann & Pogosyan, 2013; Sauter & others, 2010). The same is true for other emotions, such as fear, sadness, and anger. The importance of display rules is especially evident when we evaluate the emotional expression of another. Does that grieving husband on a morning talk show seem appropriately distraught over his wife's murder? Or might he be a suspect?

Many nonverbal signals of emotion vary from one culture to another (Mesquita, 2002). For example, male-to-male kissing is commonplace in Yemen but uncommon in the United States. The "thumbs up" sign, which in most cultures means either that everything is okay or that one wants to hitch a ride, is an insult in Greece, similar to a raised third finger in the United States—a cultural difference to keep in mind if you find yourself backpacking through Greece.

EMOTIONAL EXPRESSION IN COMPUTER COMMUNICATIONS

A fairly recent area of interest to psychologists is the expression of emotion in computer-mediated communications, including e-mails, blogs, and instant messages. Emoticons are used to express a variety of feelings, from joy **:D** to sadness **:-(** to silliness **;P** to great shock and dismay **: - O.**

Emoticons allow us to compensate for the loss of information from other expressive channels, such as vocal tone and facial expression (Derks, Bos, & von Grumbkow, 2008; Lo, 2008). People use emoticons as they do other displays of emotion, such as laughter, often at the end of the statement they are trying to clarify (Provine, Spencer, & Mandell, 2007).

Just as culture influences emotional expressions, it influences emoticons. For instance, East Asian emoticons are less likely to be presented sideways, so that a Japanese student might convey her level of exhaustion with **(-.-)Zzzzz** rather than **l-)Zzzzz.** Even with emoticons, display rules can be important. A Japanese student expressing a thumbs up **d(^_^)b** might encounter an American who thinks he is saying he has big ears.

Emoticons reveal a potentially unique aspect of computer-mediated communication. Consider that back when people often communicated by writing letters (an art that would seem to share the limitations of e-mail and texting), emoticons were not used. Looking at the letters of great writers, we do not find smileys and frownies explaining their feelings. Computer-mediated communication such as instant messaging might be considered a mixture of spoken conversation and the written word (Tagliamonte & Denis, 2008). Emoticons certainly demonstrate how crucial emotions are to our communications.

"...close with 'Yours truly, Phil' — and could you sprinkle a few appropriate emoticons around?"

© Chris Wildt. www.CartoonStock.com.

Classifying Emotions

There are more than 200 words for emotions in the English language, indicating the complexity and variety of emotions. Not surprisingly, psychologists have created ways to classify emotions—to summarize these many emotions along various dimensions (Izard, 2009), including their valence, arousal, and motivational quality.

VALENCE

The *valence* of an emotion refers to whether it feels pleasant or unpleasant. You probably are not surprised to know that happiness, joy, pleasure, and contentment are positively valenced emotions. In contrast, sadness, anger, and worry are negatively valenced emotions. Research has shown that emotions tend to go together based on their valence, so that if someone is sad, he or she is also likely to be angry or worried, and if a person is happy, he is or she is also likely to be feeling confident, joyful, and content (Watson, 2001).

● **negative affect** Negative emotions such as anger, guilt, and sadness.

● **positive affect** Positive emotions such as joy, happiness, and interest.

We can classify many emotional states on the basis of valence. Indeed, according to some experts in emotion (Watson, 2001), there are two broad dimensions of emotional experience: negative affect and positive affect. **Negative affect** refers to emotions such as anger, guilt, and sadness. **Positive affect** refers to emotions such as joy, happiness, and interest.

Although it seems essential to consider the valence of emotions as a way to classify them, valence does not fully capture all that we need to know about emotional states. The joy a person experiences at the birth of a child and the mild high at finding a $5 bill are both positive states, but they clearly differ. One way in which they differ is in their level of arousal.

AROUSAL LEVEL

The *arousal level* of an emotion (sometimes called *activation level*) is the degree to which the emotion is reflected in an individual's being active,

psychological *inquiry*

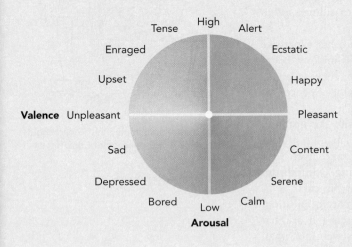

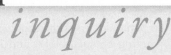

The Full Circle of Emotions

The figure shows a commonly used representation of human emotions—the circumplex model. Note that the circle is created by two independent dimensions: valence and arousal. Emotions that are similar are closer together, and those that differ are farther apart. Using the figure as a reference, answer the following questions.

1. Locate the emotions "upset" and "sad" on the circumplex. According to the circumplex, these two feelings differ primarily in terms of their arousal. Which is higher in arousal? Do you agree with this placement of these emotions? Explain.

2. According to the model, which emotion is the exact opposite of "serene"?

3. Where would you place the following feelings on the circle: worried, proud, angry, embarrassed?

engaged, or excited versus passive, disengaged, or calm. Positive and negative emotions can be high or low in arousal. Ecstasy and excitement are examples of high-arousal positive emotions, whereas contentment and tranquility are low-arousal positive emotions. Examples of high-arousal negative emotions are rage, fury, and panic, whereas irritation and boredom represent low-arousal negative emotions.

Valence and arousal level are independent dimensions that together describe a vast number of emotional states. Using these dimensions, psychologists have created a wheel of mood states that they call a *circumplex model of mood* (Posner, Russell, & Peterson, 2005). A circumplex is a graph that creates a circle from two independent dimensions. Using the dimensions of valence and arousal level, we can arrange emotional states in an organized fashion. To view the circumplex model and grasp its usefulness, see the Psychological Inquiry.

THE MOTIVATIONAL QUALITY OF EMOTIONS

The notion that emotions can motivate action has been recognized since Darwin, who proposed that emotional expressions are themselves remnants of the actions an emotion would provoke. You can probably think of actions that are associated with emotions, even if you do not engage in those actions literally. For instance, anger might engender the behavior of striking out at another person. Joy might move us to seek out other people (in a friendlier manner). Fear might tell us to run away from whatever is making us afraid.

Recently, psychologists have begun to classify emotions based on their relevance to motivations—as either emotions to *avoid* punishers or to *approach* rewards (Carver & Harmon-Jones, 2009). Fear, for instance, is thought of as an avoidance-motivating emotion because it tells us to escape the threatening stimulus. In contrast, anger is thought to be an approach-related emotion because it directs our behavior outward. Moreover, anger is concerned with rewards: When we feel angry or frustrated, it is because something (or someone) is blocking us from what we want. Studies have shown that viewing pictures of fearful facial expressions foster behaviors that suggest avoidance and pictures of angry faces foster approach behaviors (Wilkowski & Meier, 2010).

Thinking about emotions in this way can lead to unexpected predictions. For instance, consider the emotions anger and joy. Clearly, these emotions differ in their valence, but in terms of their motivational pull, both involve approach motivation and rewards. Interestingly, research suggests that positive emotions and anger share an approach motivational tendency (Pettersson & Turkheimer, 2013). When we think about emotions in a motivational context, even very different feelings can be linked together.

The Adaptive Functions of Emotions

In considering the functions of emotions, it is fairly easy to come up with a good reason for us to have emotions such as fear and anger. Negative emotions carry direct and immediate adaptive benefits in situations that threaten survival. Negative emotions indicate clearly that something is wrong and that we must take action. Positive emotions do not signal a problem. So, what is the adaptive function of positive emotions?

According to Fredrickson's broaden-and-build model, a good mood paves the way for building resources such as close friends and health-promoting activities.

Confronting this question, Barbara Fredrickson proposed the **broaden-and-build model** of positive emotion (Fredrickson, 1998, 2001, 2006, 2009, 2013b). This model states that the function of positive emotions is to broaden the scope of attention and foster the building of resources.

The model begins with the influence of positive emotion on attention. Positive moods, such as contentment and humor, have been shown to broaden our attentional focus; they allow us to see the forest for the trees. As a result, when in a good mood, we may be more disposed to think outside the box—to see unusual possibilities that escaped us before. The "building" part of the model comes in as positive mood signals that there is no immediate threat in the environment and we can explore without concern. We can take the time to make friends, to exercise to promote our health, to branch out in new ways. These activities allow us to build up strengths that we can use when we encounter life's difficulties (Kok, Catalino, & Fredrickson, 2008; Papousek & others, 2010). For example, joy creates the urge to play, push the limits, and be creative. Interest creates the motivation to explore, absorb new information and experiences, and expand the self (Csikszentmihalyi, 1990; Ryan & Deci, 2000).

The adaptive function of positive emotions can be seen in the quality of *resilience*. Recall from Chapter 9 that resilience is the ability to bounce back from negative experiences, to be flexible and adaptable when things are not going well. Resilient individuals might be thought of as tall trees with the ability to bend but not break in response to strong winds. In contrast, people who lack resilience might be characterized as more brittle—more likely to snap or break in the face of adversity (Block & Kremen, 1996).

Positive emotions play an important role in the ability of resilient individuals to cope successfully with life's challenges. Resilient individuals are zestful, optimistic, and energetic in their approach to life (Block & Kremen, 1996). They cultivate positive emotion through the use of humor (Segerstrom, 2006). Michelle Tugade, Barbara Fredrickson, and Lisa Feldman Barrett (2004) found that the superior coping of resilient individuals came from their ability to use positive emotions to bounce back from negative emotional experiences. Using measures of cardiovascular activity, the researchers found that resilient individuals were better able to regulate their responses to stressful situations (for instance, being told they were about to give an important speech) by strategically experiencing positive emotion.

Resilient individuals seem to show a kind of emotional wisdom; they capitalize on the power of positive emotions to reverse the stress of negative feelings. This skill was demonstrated in a study of responses to the terrorist attacks of September 11, 2001. Resilient individuals were found to be less likely to fall prey to depression after 9/11, and this capacity to flourish in the face of the crisis was a result of their attention to positive emotions (Fredrickson & others, 2003).

● **broaden-and-build model** Fredrickson's model of positive emotion, stating that the function of positive emotions lies in their effects on an individual's attention and ability to build resources.

test yourself

1. What are the key differences between the James-Lange theory and the Cannon-Bard theory of emotion?
2. What is the facial feedback hypothesis, and how has it been supported experimentally?
3. What is meant by the *valence* of an emotion and by the terms *positive affect* and *negative affect*?

5· MOTIVATION, EMOTION, AND HEALTH AND WELLNESS: THE PURSUIT OF HAPPINESS

Motivation is about what people want, and a quick scan of the bestseller list or the self-help section of any bookstore would seem to indicate that one thing people want very much is to be happy—or happier.

There might be good reasons to pursue happiness. The experience of negative emotions, such anger and sadness is related to reports of pain, disease (Giesser & others, 2000), heart attack, and death (Cohen, Janicki-Deverts, & Miller, 2007; Hemingway & Marmot, 1999). In contrast, the experience of positive emotions has been linked to lower levels of pain and disease (Pressman & Cohen, 2005) as well as improved disease survival (Moskowitz, 2003) and longer lives (Chida & Steptoe, 2008; Diener & Chan, 2011). A recent study, examining individuals from 42 countries, showed that self-reported health was strongly related to both negative and positive emotional experiences, even in developing nations (Pressman, Gallagher, & Lopez, 2013).

So, perhaps becoming happier is a worthwhile goal. Can people become happier? Let's consider the evidence.

Biological Factors in Happiness

As we have seen, the brain is certainly at work in the experience of positive emotions. Genes also play a role. For instance, research on the heritability of well-being has tended to show that a substantial proportion of well-being differences among people can be explained by genetics. The heritability estimates for happiness range from 50 to 80 percent (Lykken, 1999). Remember from Chapter 8 that heritability is a statistic that describes characteristics of a group, that heritability estimates can vary across groups and over time, and that even highly heritable characteristics can be influenced by experience. Thus, a person is not necessarily doomed to an unhappy life, even if the person has particularly miserable parents.

Recall the concept of *set point* in our discussion of weight. As it happens, there may also be a happiness set point—a person's basic level of happiness when the individual is not intentionally trying to increase his or her happiness (Sheldon & Lyubomirsky, 2007, 2012). Like weight, the happiness level may fluctuate around this set point. In investigating how to increase happiness, we must consider the role of this powerful starting spot, which is likely the result of genetic factors and personal disposition.

Other factors also complicate the pursuit of happiness. As we shall see, these include getting caught up on the hedonic treadmill and making happiness itself the direct goal.

Obstacles in the Pursuit of Happiness

The first key challenge individuals encounter in trying to increase their happiness is the hedonic (meaning "related to pleasure") treadmill (Brickman & Campbell, 1971; Fredrick & Loewenstein, 1999). The term *hedonic treadmill* captures the idea that any aspect of life that enhances one's positive feelings is likely to do so for only a short time, because individuals generally adapt to any life change that would presumably influence their happiness. Winning the lottery, moving into a dream home, or falling in love may lead to temporary gains in the experience of joy, but eventually people go back to their baseline (Schkade & Kahneman, 1998). What a person first experiences as a life-changing improvement eventually fades to a routine (but still necessary) aspect of life, all too soon to be taken for granted. How can individuals increase their happiness if such pleasure enhancers lose their power?

A second obstacle in the goal of enhancing happiness is that pursuing happiness for its own sake is rarely a good way to get happy or happier. When happiness is the goal,

Well, you could try being happy for a while and if it doesn't work you can go back to being miserable.

the pursuit is likely to backfire (Schooler, Ariely, & Loewenstein, 2003). Indeed, those who explicitly link the pursuit of their everyday goals to happiness fare quite poorly (McIntosh, Harlow, & Martin, 1995).

In light of this difficult path, how can we enhance our happiness without having any new capacity for joy become ho-hum? How might we achieve happiness *without trying to* pursue it?

Happiness Activities and Goal Striving

Sonja Lyubomirsky and her colleagues have suggested a promising approach to enhancing happiness (Lyubomirsky, 2011, 2013; Sheldon & Lyubomirsky, 2007, 2012; Sin & Lyubomirsky, 2009). Lyubomirsky proposes beginning with intentional activities. For example, she notes that physical activity, kindness, and positive self-reflection all enhance positive affect (Lyubomirsky & others, 2011a, 2011b; Sheldon & Lyubomirsky, 2007). Engaging in altruistic behavior—habitually helping others, especially through a wide range of acts of service—is another powerful way to enhance happiness, according to Lyubomirsky (2008, 2013).

One technique for engaging in positive self-reflection is to keep a gratitude journal. Studies by Robert Emmons and Michael McCullough (2004) have demonstrated the ways that being grateful can lead to enhanced happiness and psychological well-being. In one study, they asked individuals to keep a diary in which the participants counted their blessings every day. Those who counted their blessings were better off on various measures of well-being. Although some individuals seem to be naturally more grateful than others, experimental evidence indicates that even people who are not naturally grateful can benefit from taking a moment to count their blessings (Emmons & McCullough, 2003).

Another potentially useful approach to enhancing happiness is to commit to the pursuit of personally meaningful goals. Stop for a minute and write down the things you are typically trying to accomplish in your everyday behavior. You might identify a goal such as "to get better grades" or "to be a good friend (or partner or parent)." Such everyday goals and the pursuit of them have been shown to relate strongly to subjective well-being (Brunstein, 1993; Sheldon, 2002). Goal pursuit provides the glue that meaningfully relates a chain of life events, endowing life with beginnings, middles, and ends (King, 2008).

The scientific literature on goal investment offers a variety of ideas about the types of goals that are likely to enhance happiness. To optimize the happiness payoffs of goal pursuit, one ought to set goals that are important and personally valuable and that reflect the intrinsic needs of relatedness, competence, and autonomy (Sheldon, 2002). These goals also should be moderately challenging and should share an instrumental relationship with each other—so that the pursuit of one goal facilitates the accomplishment of another (Emmons & King, 1988).

With regard to the hedonic treadmill, goal pursuit has a tremendous advantage over many other ways of trying to enhance happiness. Goals change and are changed by life experience. As a result, goal pursuit may be less susceptible to the dreaded hedonic treadmill over time. Goals accentuate the positive but do not necessarily eliminate the negative. When we fail to reach our goals, we may experience momentary increases in unhappiness (Pomerantz, Saxon, & Oishi, 2000), which can be a very good thing. Because goals can make us happy and unhappy, they keep life emotionally interesting, and their influence on happiness does not wear off over time.

Overall, goal pursuit may lead to a happier life. Goals keep the positive possible and interesting. The conclusion to be drawn from the evidence, assuming that you want to enhance your happiness, is to strive mightily for the goals that you value. You may fail now and then, but missing the mark will only make your successes all the sweeter.

test yourself

1. Explain the term *hedonic treadmill* and give some real-world examples of it.
2. According to Lyubomirsky, how can individuals cultivate positive emotion?
3. How does committing oneself to personally meaningful goals relate to well-being?

S U M M A R Y

1. THEORIES OF MOTIVATION

Motivated behavior is energized, directed, and sustained. Early evolutionary theorists considered motivation to be based on instinct—the innate biological pattern of behavior.

A drive is an aroused state that occurs because of a physiological need or deprivation. Drive reduction theory was proposed as an explanation of motivation, with the goal of drive reduction being homeostasis: the body's tendency to maintain equilibrium.

Optimum arousal theory focuses on the Yerkes-Dodson law, which states that performance is best under conditions of moderate rather than low or high arousal. Moderate arousal often serves us best, but there are times when low or high arousal is linked with better performance.

2. HUNGER, OBESITY, AND EATING DISORDERS

Stomach signals are one factor in hunger. Glucose (blood sugar) and insulin both play an important role in hunger. Glucose is needed for the brain to function, and low levels of glucose increase hunger. Insulin can cause a rise in hunger.

Leptin, a protein secreted by fat cells, decreases food intake and increases energy expenditure. The hypothalamus plays an important role in regulating hunger. The lateral hypothalamus is involved in stimulating eating; the ventromedial hypothalamus, in restricting eating.

Obesity is a serious problem in the United States. Heredity, basal metabolism, set point, and fat cells are biological factors involved in obesity. Time and place affect eating. Our early ancestors ate fruits to satisfy nutritional needs, but today we fill up on the empty calories in sweets.

Three eating disorders are anorexia nervosa, bulimia nervosa, and binge eating disorder. Anorexia nervosa is characterized by extreme underweight and starvation. Anorexia nervosa is related to perfectionism and obsessive-compulsive tendencies. Bulimia nervosa involves a pattern of binge eating followed by purging through self-induced vomiting or laxatives. Binge eating disorder involves binge eating without purging.

Anorexia nervosa and bulimia nervosa are much more common in women than men, but there is no gender difference in binge eating disorder. Although sociocultural factors were once thought to be primary in explaining eating disorders, more recent evidence points to the role of biological factors.

3. APPROACHES TO MOTIVATION IN EVERYDAY LIFE

According to Maslow's hierarchy of needs, our main needs are satisfied in this sequence: physiological needs, safety, love and belongingness, esteem, and self-actualization. Maslow gave the most attention to self-actualization: the motivation to develop to one's full potential.

Self-determination theory states that intrinsic motivation occurs when individuals are engaged in the pursuit of organismic needs that are innate and universal. These needs include competence, relatedness, and autonomy. Intrinsic motivation is based on internal factors. Extrinsic motivation is based on external factors, such as rewards and punishments.

Self-regulation involves setting goals, monitoring progress, and making adjustments in behavior to attain desired outcomes. Research suggests that setting intermediate goals on the path toward a long-term goal is a good strategy.

4. EMOTION

Emotion is feeling, or affect, that has three components: physiological arousal, conscious experience, and behavioral expression. The biology of emotion focuses on physiological arousal involving the autonomic nervous system and its two subsystems. Skin conductance level and the polygraph have been used to measure emotional arousal.

The James-Lange theory states that emotion results from physiological states triggered by environmental stimuli: Emotion follows physiological reactions. The Cannon-Bard theory states that emotion and physiological reactions occur simultaneously. Contemporary biological views of emotion increasingly highlight neural circuitry and neurotransmitters. LeDoux has charted the neural circuitry of fear, which focuses on the amygdala and consists of two pathways, one direct and the other indirect. It is likely that positive and negative emotions use different neural circuitry and neurotransmitters.

Schachter and Singer's two-factor theory states that emotion is the result of both physiological arousal and cognitive labeling. Lazarus believed that cognition always directs emotion, but Zajonc argued that emotion directs cognition. Both probably were right.

Research on the behavioral component of emotion focuses on facial expressions. The facial feedback hypothesis states that facial expressions can influence emotions, as well as reflect them.

Many psychologists believe that facial expressions of basic emotions are the same across cultures. However, display rules—nonverbal signals of body movement, posture, and gesture—vary across cultures. Differences in emoticons across cultures reinforce the idea that display rules are culture-dependent.

Emotions can be classified based on valence (pleasant or unpleasant) and arousal (high or low). Using the dimensions of valence and arousal, emotions can be arranged in a circle, or circumplex model. Emotions may also be classified in terms of whether they suggest approach or avoidance motivation.

Positive emotions may play a role in well-being by broadening our focus and allowing us to build resources. Resilience is an individual's capacity to thrive even during difficult times. Research has shown that one way resilient individuals thrive is by experiencing positive emotions.

5. MOTIVATION, EMOTION, AND HEALTH AND WELLNESS: THE PURSUIT OF HAPPINESS

Happiness is highly heritable, and there is reason to consider each person as having a happiness set point. Still, many people would like to increase their level of happiness. One obstacle to changing happiness is the hedonic treadmill: the idea that we quickly adapt to changes that might enhance happiness. Another obstacle is that pursuing happiness for its own sake often backfires.

Ways to enhance happiness include engaging in physical activity, helping others, and engaging in positive self-reflection and experiencing meaning (such as by keeping a gratitude journal). Another way to enhance happiness is to pursue personally valued goals passionately.

key *terms*

motivation, p. 328
instinct, p. 328
drive, p. 328
need, p. 328
homeostasis, p. 329
Yerkes-Dodson law, p. 329
overlearning, p. 329
set point, p. 332

anorexia nervosa, p. 333
bulimia nervosa, p. 334
binge eating disorder
    (BED), p. 335
hierarchy of needs, p. 336
self-actualization, p. 336
self-determination theory, p. 337
intrinsic motivation, p. 338

extrinsic motivation, p. 338
self-regulation, p. 338
emotion, p. 341
polygraph, p. 342
James-Lange theory, p. 342
Cannon-Bard theory, p. 343
two-factor theory of
    emotion, p. 344

facial feedback hypothesis, p. 347
display rules, p. 348
negative affect, p. 349
positive affect, p. 349
broaden-and-build
    model, p. 351

apply your *knowledge*

1. Ask your friends and your parents to define the word *motivation*. Compare your friends' and parents' definitions with the way psychologists define and approach motivation. What are the similarities? What are the differences? How do the definitions of your friends differ from those of your parents? Why do you think all of these variations exist?

2. To explore your own goals and sense of purpose, try the following activity. First list the top 5 or 10 goals that you are trying to accomplish in your everyday behavior. Then write your responses to the following questions that William Damon used in his interviews (Damon, 2008, p. 135):

   • Do you have any long-term goals?
   • What does it mean to have a good life?
   • What does it mean to be a good person?
   • If you were looking back on your life now, how would you like to be remembered?

   Finally, consider: Are your everyday goals leading to the fulfillment of your long-term dream? How are you working in your everyday behavior to achieve your grander purposes?

3. Some psychologists believe that the ability to identify and regulate one's emotions is a kind of intelligence. Emotionally intelligent people are also thought to be better at reading the emotional expressions of others. Do a web search for "emotional intelligence tests" and take some online quizzes, or try the one at http://testyourself.psychtests.com/testid/3038. Do you think you are emotionally intelligent? Does your performance on the test seem to reflect your actual experience? What is your opinion of the test you tried? Is there information on the site showing its validity and reliability?

4. This chapter reviewed the use of autonomic nervous system activity in the detection of deception. Psychologists have devised various ways to detect lying. Go online and search for information on detecting deception and lies. Is there a good way to tell if someone is being truthful? Explain.

CHAPTER 11

Gender, Sex, and Sexuality

Is Military Combat Women's Work?

In 2013, the U.S. Department of Defense lifted the ban on women serving in combat. For many women, this landmark decision meant the rules, at last, fit the reality of their lives. Over 280,000 American women have served in the wars in Iraq and Afghanistan. Technically, they have held *noncombat* roles—military police, medics, intelligence officers, or photographers—attached to, but not part of, all-male combat units. War, though, does not abide by technicalities: Nearly 1,000 women have been injured or killed in combat since 2001.

In Iraq, Air Force Staff Sergeant Stacy Pearsall was temporarily attached to an Army unit when it was ambushed. As the men of the unit responded, Pearsall jumped into an armed carrier, opening fire. Spotting an injured man, she crawled out to him. Though he was twice her size, she dragged him back to the vehicle. A medic arrived and asked if she was a medic. "No," she replied, "I'm the photographer" (Dao, 2013).

The idea of women in combat can stir concerns—rooted not only in the physical differences between the sexes but in cultural norms and beliefs. Should mothers and daughters be engaged in acts of war or exposed to the dangers of combat? What about military goals and the principle of equal opportunity? Importantly, prior to lifting the ban, commanders could not assign the best person for a job, if the best person was a woman. The ban had also excluded women from promotion to ranks requiring combat service. Defense Secretary Leon Panetta concluded, "Not everyone is going to be able to be a combat soldier. But everyone is entitled to a chance" (Brennan, 2013).

PREVIEW

Women in combat is just one of a host of contemporary issues involving gender, sex, and sexuality. In this chapter we will explore what psychology brings to these provocative topics. We begin by defining key terms related to gender, sex, and sexuality. Next, we consider the major theoretical approaches to gender development, followed by a review of the psychology of gender differences. We then explore sexual orientation and examine sexual practices and behaviors. A look at several sexual variations and disorders follows, and we close by taking stock of the important place of sexuality in health and wellness.

1· DEFINING SEX AND GENDER

Let's start by defining the two terms we will use throughout this chapter. You have no doubt heard and used the words *sex* and *gender* frequently in your life. Their technical definitions are key to understanding how scientists study these concepts.

Sex and Its Biological Components

● **sex** The properties of a person that determine his or her classification as male or female.

● **sex chromosomes** In humans, the pair of genes that differs between the sexes and determines a person's sex as male or female.

● **gonads** Glands that produce sex hormones and generate ova (eggs) in females and sperm in males; collectively called gametes, the ova and sperm are the cells that eventually will be used in reproduction.

Sex refers to the properties of a person that determine his or her classification as male or female. In this section we review five physical characteristics used to classify sex, including chromosomes, gonads, hormones, genitalia, and secondary sex characteristics.

Chromosomes are the packages of DNA that carry our genes. Human beings have 23 pairs of chromosomes, with one of each pair being provided by each parent. The 23rd pair differs across the sexes. Scientists call this differing pair of genes the **sex chromosomes** because the pair determines a person's genetic sex. In females, both sex chromosomes are similar and are called X chromosomes. Males have one X and one Y chromosome—the latter so named because it looks like an upside-down Y (Figure 11.1).

Another set of physical structures used to classify us as male or female is our gonads, a part of the endocrine system. **Gonads** are glands that produce sex hormones and generate ova (eggs) in females and sperm in males, the cells that eventually will be used in reproduction. Female gonads are the *ovaries* (located on either side of the abdomen). Male gonads are the *testes* (located in the *scrotum*, the pouch of skin that hangs below the penis).

Sex may also be classified by the hormones that these gonads produce. Hormones are chemicals produced by endocrine glands. No hormones are unique to one sex, but the levels of hormones vary by sex. As we discussed in Chapter 9, the hormones *estrogen* and *progesterone* are higher in women than in men, and the hormones called *androgens*

FIGURE 11.1 **The Genetic Difference Between Males and Females** The chromosome structures of a male (*left*) and female (*right*). The 23rd pair is shown at bottom right. Notice that the male's Y chromosome is smaller than his X chromosome. To obtain pictures of chromosomes, a cell is removed from a person's body, usually from inside the mouth, and the chromosomes are photographed under magnification.

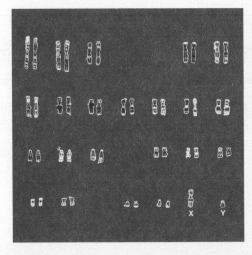

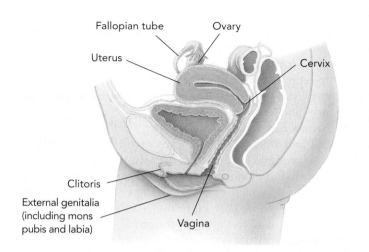

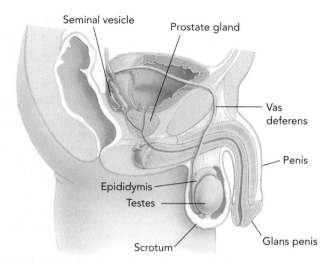

FIGURE 11.2   Female and Male Internal Sex Organs and External Genitalia These figures show the female (*left*) and male (*right*) Internal sex organs and external genitalia.

(the most common being *testosterone*) are higher in men than in women. In women, androgens are produced by the adrenal glands, and in men some of the androgens that are produced by the testes are converted into estrogens.

These hormones play a role in the development of internal reproductive structures, external genitalia, and the secondary sex characteristics that are also used in classifying us as male or female. Figure 11.2 shows the internal reproductive structures of females and males. In women, these organs allow the ovum to travel from the ovaries to the uterus, and they play roles in sexual functioning, the menstrual cycle, and pregnancy. In men, the internal sex organs include the structures involved in the production and storage of sperm, as well as those that play a role in sexual arousal and orgasm.

The external genitalia of males and females are found between their legs (see Figure 11.2). The external genitalia of females, collectively called the *vulva*, include the *mons pubis* (a fleshy area just above the vagina), the *labia* (the lips surrounding the vaginal opening), and the *clitoris* (a small sensory organ at the top where the labia meet). For males, the external genitalia include the *penis* and *scrotum*.

Recall from Chapter 9 that puberty is a period of rapid maturation that occurs mainly in early adolescence (Figure 11.3). Hormones produced during puberty drive the development of **secondary sex characteristics,** traits that differ between the two sexes but are not part of the reproductive system (Susman & Dorn, 2013). Breasts in females and facial hair in males are secondary sex characteristics.

These many physical attributes may play a role in classifying a person as male or female. However, as we will see, physical characteristics may or may not match a person's psychological experience of himself or herself as male or female—that is, the person's gender.

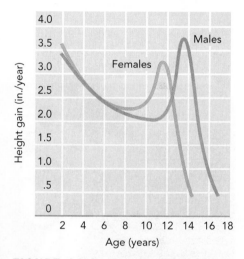

FIGURE 11.3   Pubertal Growth Spurt On average, the pubertal growth spurt begins and peaks about 2 years earlier for girls (starts at 9, peaks at 11½) than for boys (starts at 11½, peaks at 13½). From J. M. Tanner et al., in *Archives of Diseases in Childhood, 41,* 1966. Reproduced with permission from the BMJ Publishing Group.

● **secondary sex characteristics** Traits that differ between the two sexes but are not part of the reproductive system; they include breasts in females and facial hair in males.

● **gender** The social and psychological aspects of being female or male; gender goes beyond biological sex to include an individual's personal understanding of the meaning of being male or female.

● **gender identity** An individual's multifaceted sense of belonging to the male or female sex.

Gender

Gender refers to the social and psychological aspects of being female or male. Gender goes beyond biological sex to include a person's understanding of the *meaning* of being male or female. Although checking off "male" or "female" on a questionnaire may seem like a simple choice, gender is a complex variable influenced by biological factors, as well as socialization and experience.

Gender identity is an individual's sense of belonging to the male or female sex. Gender identity is multifaceted, and individuals vary in their experience of it. For example, for some people, gender identity is central to their sense of self; some are more comfortable than others with their gender category; and some feel socially encouraged to conform to a particular gender identity (Leaper, 2013).

In describing a person's gender identity, we might talk about attributes such as masculinity and femininity. Technically speaking, these words mean, respectively, "being like a man" and "being like a woman." Psychologists have studied these gender-related characteristics using the terms *instrumentality* (for more masculine traits) and *expressiveness* (for more feminine traits) to represent these broad dimensions. Instrumental attributes include being assertive, brave, independent, and dominant. Expressive traits include being nurturing, warm, gentle, and sensitive to others.

Although there are differences between men and women on these traits, with men scoring as more instrumental and women as more expressive (Fink & others, 2007; Lippa, 2008), they are not as strong as you might expect (Carothers & Reis, 2013). Indeed, the degree of instrumentality or expressiveness a person feels may depend on the social context and the activity in which he or she is engaged (Leszczynski, 2009). A father playing with his toddler may feel quite expressive; a WNBA guard running up the basketball court on a fast break may feel quite instrumental.

Instrumentality and expressiveness are not systematically related to each other, so every possible combination of these characteristics is possible. We might call someone who is highly instrumental but not very expressive "masculine," and someone else who is highly expressive but not very instrumental "feminine." **Androgynous** means that a person is high on both instrumental and expressive qualities, having attributes that we typically associate with both genders (Bem, 1993). Individuals who are *low* on both dimensions are referred to as undifferentiated. Individuals who are *not* strongly gender-typed according to these scales tend to have better psychological adjustment and resilience than those rated as extremely masculine or feminine (Lam & McBride-Chang, 2007). In fact, a balance between instrumentality and expressiveness relates to a variety of positive outcomes in many cultures (Cheng, 2005; Helgeson, 1994; Mosher & Danoff-Burg, 2008).

● **androgynous** Having attributes that are typically associated with both genders.

It is tempting to think of *sex* as the term for biologically based differences between males and females, and *gender* as the word for differences that are a product of environment or socialization. Many psychologists distinguish sex and gender in this way (Caplan & Caplan, 2005). However, others argue that sex and gender are so strongly intertwined that separating them encourages an artificial boundary (Fausto-Sterling, Garcia Coll, & Lamarre, 2012; Jordan-Young & Rumiati, 2012). Distinguishing between sex as biological and gender as psychosocial would seem to ignore the very strong relationship between the body and mind that we have emphasized throughout this text. Let's take a close look at the processes that connect sex and gender.

Genes, Sex, and Gender

In the first few weeks after conception, male and female embryos look alike. With regard to sex organs, female fetuses essentially stay the same, whereas male fetuses change from this default status. The raw materials of male and female genitals and gonads are fundamentally the same. The penis and clitoris take shape from the same embryonic structures, as do the testes (in males) and ovaries (in females), and the scrotum (in males) and the labia (in females).

What causes the development of male sexual features? A particular gene on the Y chromosome, the *SRY gene* (the sex-determining region of the Y chromosome), is activated early in the first 3 months of pregnancy (Hines, 2013). Of course, only males have a Y chromosome, so only male fetuses are exposed to the effects of the SRY gene, which causes the development of embryonic testes. The testes, then, begin to manufacture androgens that spread throughout the developing embryo,

Some successful entertainers, among them Adam Lambert and Lady Gaga, challenge common notions of gender.

influencing the growing body and brain. Through this process, the XY embryo essentially *turns itself* into a male. Low levels of androgen in a female embryo allow for the development of the female body and brain.

These early processes might seem to set the stage for sex and, potentially, gender. Prenatal hormones, for instance, play a role in brain development (Berenbaum, Blakemore, & Beltz, 2011; Hines, 2013), and we might assume then that these biological processes provide a firm foundation for our sense of ourselves as male or female. However, the roles of nature (biological factors) and nurture (experience) in gender development are complex, as is illustrated by our next topics, disorders of sexual development and transgender experience.

Disorders of Sexual Development

Genes and prenatal hormones play crucial roles in the development of the genitals, which in turn are generally used to identify a child's sex, through a prenatal ultrasound or at birth. Typically a baby's sex is straightforward, but in rare cases the external genitalia are ambiguous. Prenatal hormone exposure, chromosomal abnormalities, and environmental factors (such as exposure to radiation, chemicals, or some medications) can lead to genitals that are not clearly male or female, such as a very small penis, an enlarged clitoris, or genitals that appear to include both a penis and vaginal labia. Formerly called *intersex conditions* (or *hermaphroditism*), these conditions are termed **disorders of sexual development (DSD)** (Hughes & others, 2006), defined as congenital conditions in which the development of chromosomal, gonadal, or anatomical sex is atypical (P. A. Lee & others, 2006).

Imagine being the parent of a child born with ambiguous genitalia, not clearly male or female. How would you feel? What would you do? Professionals continue to debate the best way to handle such cases (Hines, 2013; Karkazis, Tamar-Mattis, & Kon, 2010). Experts long believed that immediate surgery and sex assignment were crucial for both parents and children (Money, Hampson, & Hampson, 1955, 1957). This plan of action rested on two assumptions (Berenbaum, 2006; Meyer-Bahlburg, 1998):

● **disorders of sexual development (DSD)** Congenital conditions in which the development of chromosomal, gonadal, or anatomical sex is atypical; formerly called intersex conditions or hermaphroditism.

- Children cannot develop normally with ambiguous genitalia.
- Gender identity is entirely determined by socialization (nurture), not biological factors (nature).

Ironically, these assumptions were tested originally by a case in which a child was born with *unambiguously* male genitalia. John Money, a well-known sex researcher, believed strongly that socialization was the main determinant of gender. In the 1960s, he tested his theory in the famous "John/Joan" case. The case involved one member of a pair of twin boys. A few months after birth, the boy's penis was destroyed during circumcision. Money persuaded the boy's parents to allow him to transform surgically the injured male genitals into female genitals and to agree to treat the child as a girl. Reared as a girl, according to Money, the former boy essentially became a girl (Money & Tucker, 1975). The case became famous as an example of nurture's triumph over nature.

Milton Diamond, a biologist and strong critic of Money's theory, followed up on "John/Joan" (Diamond & Sigmundson, 1997). Diamond found that over time, "Joan" became less and less interested in being a girl, eventually refusing to continue the process of feminization that Money had devised. We now know that "Joan" was really David Reimer, whose biography, *As Nature Made Him* (Colapinto, 2000), revealed the difficulties of his life as a boy, then a girl, then a boy, and finally a man. David struggled with traumatic gender-related experiences and depression. He committed suicide in 2004.

David's story seems to suggest that biological factors powerfully guide gender identity development. Yet this one case may not represent the full picture. Remember from Chapter 2 that it is difficult to make generalizations based on a single case study. This tragic case does not close the door on the possibility that socialization can significantly shape gender development.

Research on samples of individuals born with genitalia that conflict with their genetic sex points to a different conclusion—namely, that socialization is powerfully (but not perfectly) related to eventual gender identity (Berenbaum, 2006; Meyer-Bahlburg, 2005; Zucker, 1999). For example, one study showed that among genetic males born without a penis (due to a birth defect) and reared as females, 78 percent lived their adult lives as women. Of those who were reared as male, 100 percent of them were living as male (Meyer-Bahlburg, 2005).

In considering the discrepancy between those percentages, we might assume that all of these individuals would have experienced more stable gender identity if they had been reared in their genetic sex. However, this conclusion misses the complexity of the decision facing parents and doctors in these cases. Surgical procedures to construct a penis are difficult, costly, and not always successful. The stability of sex assignment may depend on genetic and hormonal factors, as well as parental reactions (Reiner, 2011). And, of course, we might ask whether stability is the most important issue for the child. Indeed, the person whose opinion matters most to this decision—the child him- or herself—has not been consulted at all.

Experts agree that these decisions should be made based on the child's well-being, not parental distress (Consortium on the Management of Disorders of Sexual Development, 2006; Hines, 2013; Schönbucher & others, 2012).

● **transgender** Experiencing one's psychological gender as different from one's physical sex, as in the cases of biological males who identify as female, and biological females who identify as male.

When Genetic Sex and Gender Conflict: Transgender Experience

Transgender refers to experiencing one's psychological gender as different from one's biological sex. Transgender individuals can be biological males who identify as female, or biological females who identify as male.

Portrayals of transgender experience, especially among young people, have become more common on shows like *Glee* and *Degrassi*. Real-life cases of transgender individuals have also drawn attention to this phenomenon. Chastity Bono, the daughter of pop singers Sonny and Cher, came out as transgender and changed her name to Chaz.

In addition, the media has covered cases of children experiencing themselves as transgender (Talbot, 2013). Jazz Jennings was born a boy but has insisted even as a preschooler that she is a girl (Goldberg & Adriano, 2008). At first her parents humored their son, allowing him to play with girls' toys and to dress like a girl at home. Eventually, Jazz's parents decided to allow her to be herself, to dress and to act like a girl everywhere she went, and she entered kindergarten as a girl. Coy Mathis was born a boy, but has lived as a girl since kindergarten. Her parents filed suit in Colorado when her grade school announced that she would no longer be permitted to use the girls' restroom at school (Payne & Fantz, 2013).

How do psychologists understand transgender experience? Until recently, *gender identity disorder* was a diagnosis applied to such individuals. Now, individuals who experience distress over their biological sex may be diagnosed with *gender dysphoria*, the term the American Psychiatric Association (APA) uses (APA, 2013b); however, there is considerable controversy over whether such individuals should be considered as having a disorder at all (Byne & others, 2012).

Generally, the treatment for transgender individuals involves gradual stages that move from reversible treatments to permanent ones (Coleman & others, 2011). The first stage may involve dressing and living as their preferred gender identity. Then the person might receive hormones that support that identity, followed by surgery to remove secondary sex characteristics (such as breasts), and potentially culminating in *sex reassignment surgery*. This surgery involves the surgical reconstruction of the genitals. The surgical challenges that female-to-male

Chaz Bono, who completed the transition from female to male, is an activist for the lesbian, gay, bisexual, and transgender communities.

(FTM) transgender individuals face are more complicated and much more expensive (about $100,000) than those for male-to-female (MTF) transgender people, involving costs of about $15,000 (Talbot, 2013). Increasingly, mental health professionals are called upon not to treat these individuals but to provide evaluations of their suitability for various treatments (Byne & others, 2012).

Among youth who identify as the opposite of their biological sex, the majority will ultimately adopt the gender identity of their biological sex; however, some will continue to identify as transgender (Byne & others, 2012). Because it is difficult to distinguish these two groups during childhood, some advocate offering medications to delay puberty so that the youth can have a "time-out" from sexual development. This time-out prevents the permanent bodily changes spurred by puberty, giving the individual and his or her parents the opportunity to fully contemplate the path ahead (Ehrensaft, 2013).

Many transgender individuals do not desire sex reassignment surgery (Cohen-Kettenis & Pfafflin, 2010). Some opt for hormone treatment only. Still others prefer to think of their gender identity in an alternative, broader way: They embrace their identity as a quality that challenges the notion of sexual identity as one of two opposing categories. For such individuals, being transgender means living according to the belief that a person can be a man who happens to have a vagina or a woman who has a penis (Lev, 2007)—as an individual who occupies a different but valid gender territory (Meyer-Bahlburg, 2010; Pfafflin, 2010). In many ways, transgender experience reflects and informs a growing recognition that gender identity is enormously complex.

test yourself

1. Explain the difference between sex and gender.
2. Discuss the causes of the differentiation of the sexes.
3. What is gender dysphoria? What is the only treatment for gender dysphoria that has been evaluated by research?

2· THEORIES OF GENDER DEVELOPMENT

For most people, genetic sex and psychological gender are experienced as a reasonably good fit. Nevertheless, we might wonder how a person who is XX or XY comes to think of him- or herself as female or male. Various theories of gender development have addressed this question. In this section we examine the major theoretical approaches to gender development.

Biological Approaches

We have seen that a number of biological factors—including genes, gonads, and hormones—identify a person as male or female. Biological approaches to gender draw links between these aspects of the person's biological sex and his or her eventual psychological feelings of gender. Individuals who study biological factors in gender development focus on variables such as genes, prenatal hormones, and brain structures and functions, as these differ between males and females and potentially account for the experiences of ourselves in those sexes. Importantly, research on the biological bases of gender does not simply focus on how biological factors (genes, hormones, and so on) *determine* gender development but also on how such factors contribute to gender development in interaction with experience (Berenbaum, Blakemore, & Beltz, 2011; Leaper, 2013).

Biologically based research has looked at differences between the sexes in infancy, searching for clues to gender-related characteristics in the earliest days of life. In infancy, boys are larger and more active than girls (Fausto-Sterling, Garcia Coll, & Lamarre, 2012). In one study, 1-day-old infants were shown two stimuli: a human face and a mobile made out of a picture of that face (Connellan & others, 2000). The researchers found that the baby girls spent more time looking at the human face, while the baby boys were more interested

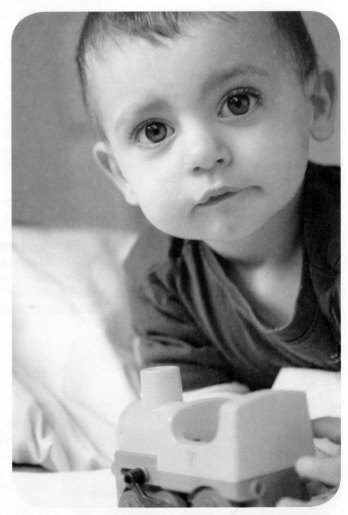

Research on infants from 3 to 8 months of age found that males spent more time looking at boy toys, such as trucks and machines, than other toys.

in the mobile. Similarly, research on infants from 3 to 8 months of age found that males spent more time looking at typical boy toys, including trucks and machines, and females spent more time looking at typical girl toys, such as dolls (Alexander, Wilcox, & Woods, 2009). Nonhuman primates exhibit similar differences (Alexander & Hines, 2002; Hassett, Siebert, & Wallen, 2008). In humans, such differences are thought to be biologically, not socially, based because very young infants have not yet had social experiences that might influence gender development.

Evolutionary Psychology

The evolutionary psychology approach to gender views the differences between the sexes through the lens of natural selection and adaptation. From this perspective, the factors that produce gender are the product of millions of years of natural selection.

Recall from Chapter 1 that, according to Charles Darwin's theory of evolution, a species' characteristics reflect natural selection, the process by which the environment determines the adaptiveness of particular genetic characteristics. Organisms with the fittest genes are most likely to survive and reproduce. This slow process is responsible for creating the typical characteristics of any species. Applying these ideas to gender, evolutionary psychologists assert that the differences we see between contemporary men and women can be explained by the *selection pressures,* or environmental challenges, that confronted our distant human ancestors (Buss, 2012; Cosmides & Tooby, 2013). To understand the potential role of selection pressures on gender, evolutionary psychologists focus on sexual selection and the differing reproductive challenges faced by men and women.

SEXUAL SELECTION

Differences between male and female members of the same species abound in nature. For instance, the beautiful peacock with the colorful tail and the cardinal with brilliant red feathers are both males, while the female members of those species are duller in appearance. What accounts for these sex differences within species? Darwin (1871) proposed that many sex differences that occur within species have evolved through sexual selection. **Sexual selection** means that the male and female members of a species differ from each other because of differences in competition and choice. *Competition* occurs among members of the same sex as they vie for the opportunity to mate with members of the opposite sex. Members of that opposite sex in turn exercise *choice,* selecting the lucky one (or ones) with whom they will mate. In peacocks, males use their amazing plumage to compete with one another for females, and females select the prettiest male with whom to reproduce.

Who chooses and who competes? Generally, the sex that invests the most in producing offspring is the one that chooses, and the other sex is the one that competes (Andersson & Simmons, 2006; Bateman, 1948; Clutton-Brock, 2007, 2010). Applying these ideas to humans, evolutionary psychologists believe that differences between women and men are evidence that sexual selection has occurred in our species. Women are the sex that gives birth, and as such they ought to do the choosing. Men, on the other hand, show characteristics that are thought to be well suited for competing. For example, men are physically larger and stronger than women. Evolutionary psychologists explain human males' physical size as an adaptation that helps men to compete against one another for female mates.

Sexual selection is more complicated in human beings than in other species. Specifically, because human infants are so helpless, it makes sense from a survival standpoint for men to invest in their offspring—so sometimes men get to be the choosers, and women are the competitors vying for those men who are likely to invest in their children (Andersson & Simmons, 2006; Halpern & others, 2007). This aspect of sexual selection is of particular interest in humans because of the different challenges men and women face in reproducing.

● **sexual selection** According to Darwin's theory of evolution, the differentiation between the male and female members of a species because of the differences between the two in competition and choice.

This male peacock uses his beautiful plumage to attract female mates.

REPRODUCTIVE CHALLENGES FOR MEN AND WOMEN

Men and women share the same evolutionary goal—to reproduce—but accomplishing that objective presents different challenges to each sex. Women experience pregnancy and childbirth. They can reproduce only about once per year and have a limited time of fertility. Thus, evolutionary psychologists believe that women must be choosy in selecting sexual partners, putting a premium on high *quality*—seeking sexual partners who have adequate resources to invest in a family.

Men do not bear the obligation of childbearing, and they are generally fertile from puberty onward. Therefore, say evolutionary theorists, they can focus on *quantity,* reproducing as often as possible. Evolutionary psychologists suggest that men should be less selective than women about sexual behavior (Buss, 2012; Geary, 2010). A sticking point for this strategy, though, is that as noted above, babies are so helpless that it is adaptive for men to invest in their offspring.

Further, men have an additional problem. Because the moment when the egg is fertilized by the sperm is a mystery for the parties involved, a man cannot be certain whether the child in whom he is investing his resources is genetically *his* child. Evolutionarily speaking, for a man, the worst-case scenario is to invest his resources to ensure the survival of someone else's offspring.

How might men avoid this dreaded outcome? Evolutionary psychologists point out that across cultures, men are likely to prefer women who are younger than they are (Buss, 2012). This preference for younger women may be a way for a man to minimize the chances that his betrothed is already pregnant with someone else's offspring.

Sex differences that emerge shortly after birth, as well as cross-cultural similarities in mate preferences, would seem to support biological and evolutionary theories of gender development. But, let's stop and think about the potential role of the social environment in the emergence of gender. Family and friends begin to buy pink and blue baby clothes before a child is even born. That child is introduced to a social network with strong expectations about gender-appropriate behavior. If a little boy shows even a slight preference for playing with a truck, we might smile and conclude, "He's *all boy*." If the same child expresses interest in trying on a dress or playing with a doll, we might respond quite differently. Do these different social responses influence the child's developing sense of self?

Consider too that the male preference for younger sexual partners may reflect social expectations or the power differences that exist between men and women in many cultures. These considerations reflect concerns that are represented in two additional views of gender development: social cognitive approaches and social role theory.

Social Cognitive Approaches

Social cognitive theories of gender development focus on how children *learn* about gender and how they come to occupy a particular gender identity. These approaches emphasize both the way that children internalize information about gender (Bem, 1983, 1993) and the way the environment reinforces gender-related behavior (Bussey & Bandura, 2004).

From this perspective, gender behavior is learned through reward and punishment, observational learning, and modeling (Bandura & Bussey, 2004; Bussey & Bandura, 2004), processes we examined in Chapter 6. According to Albert Bandura, modeling is an especially potent mechanism

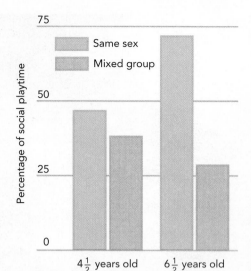

FIGURE 11.4 Developmental Changes in Percentage of Time Spent in Same-Sex and Mixed-Group Settings Observations of children show that they are more likely to play in same-sex than mixed-sex groups. This tendency increases between 4 and 6 years of age.

● **social role theory** Eagly's theory of gender development that acknowledges the physical differences between the sexes that have historically influenced different tasks performed by men and women; points out the ways that these differences color social expectations and create social structures that limit opportunities for both sexes.

for transmitting values (Bandura, 1986; Bussey & Bandura, 2004). Children gain information about gender from models of each sex. Who leaves for work every day? Who does the housekeeping? When children see their parents and other adults engaging in behavior (and as they observe whether and how these behaviors are reinforced), they learn about how *men* and *women* behave.

In subtle ways, children may be rewarded for engaging in gender-conforming behavior and punished for engaging in behavior that does not fit with expectations for their sex, what is called *gender-nonconforming behavior*. Examples of gender-conforming behavior include playing with dolls (for girls) and playing with trucks (for boys). Examples of gender-nonconforming behavior are a girl's playing with a train set and a boy's playing dress-up or house. The social environment responds to behaviors in various ways, coloring the child's perception of their appropriateness. A girl might learn that pretending to be a professional football player is not a way to please her parents. A boy might pick up on his mother's subtle frown when he announces that he wants to try on her high-heeled shoes (Fagot, 1978).

Peers play an important role in gender development. Especially after age 6, peer groups often segregate into boy groups and girl groups (Maccoby, 2002) (Figure 11.4). Peers are stricter than most parents in rewarding gender-conforming behavior and punishing gender-nonconforming behavior, especially for boys (Pasterski, Golombok, & Hines, 2011).

Through these varied experiences, children learn that gender is an important organizing principle in social life, and they come to recognize that boys and girls, and men and women, are different in ways that matter (Leaper, 2013). Children develop a *gender schema*—a mental framework for understanding what is considered appropriate behavior for females and males in their culture (Martin & Ruble, 2010). This gender schema then serves as a cognitive framework by which children interpret further experiences related to gender.

Although acknowledging biological differences between males and females, social cognitive psychologists believe that social and cultural factors have a much stronger influence on eventual gender identity (Bandura & Bussey, 2004). From this perspective, differences in men's and women's career and life choices can be explained by differences in the availability of role models and beliefs about self-efficacy and personal control. Social cognitive practitioners would say, for example, that men and women differ in their career choices primarily because they have different beliefs about both their ability to achieve their career goals and the extent to which success is in their control.

Social Role Theory

Alice Eagly has proposed that to understand gender, we must recognize the larger social and cultural institutions surrounding the psychological phenomenon of gender identity (Eagly, 1987, 2009, 2010, 2012). **Social role theory,** introduced by Eagly, is a theory of gender development that acknowledges that there are physical differences between the sexes that, historically, led men and women to perform different tasks, but points out the ways that these differences color social expectations and create and support social structures that limit opportunities for both sexes. Like evolutionary theory, social role theory begins by acknowledging that women are more innately and directly involved in reproduction than men, and men are larger and stronger than women. Eagly proposed that these differences resulted in a division of labor between the sexes, with women being more involved in the home and with childrearing, and men being more likely to work outside the home.

Eagly points out that this division of labor can lead to important beliefs about what it means to be a woman or a man. The activities and occupations we see men and women performing give rise to expectations and beliefs about what it means to be male or female, what a male or female person *ought* to do, and what we believe that person *can* do. In this way, the division of labor spawns the social construct of **gender roles,** expectations for how females and males should think, act, and feel (Eagly, 2009, 2010, 2012).

Gender roles are related to **gender stereotypes**—overly general beliefs and expectations about what women and men are like. Gender stereotypes might suggest that women are warm, caring, and emotional and that men are strong, dominant, and rational. Social role theory asserts that each of us internalizes these roles and stereotypes and comes to evaluate our own behavior and choices according to their gender typicality (Chalabaev & others, 2013; Deaux & LaFrance, 1998).

For example, gender roles and gender stereotypes might influence our life goals (Diekman & Eagly, 2008; Evans & Diekman, 2009). If a particular occupation (say, an engineer or a nurse) conflicts with our perceived gender role, we may view it as less desirable and less likely to bring us success. Notably, when men and women make choices that are guided by gender roles and gender stereotypes, they tend to become more and more different from each other in their behaviors, attitudes, and aspirations, with each sex engaging in more stereotypical pursuits (Eagly, Wood, & Johannesen-Schmidt, 2004). In turn, these sex-based differences, driven by gender roles and stereotypes, maintain the social structure (Eagly, 1987; Eagly & Wood, 2010).

Social role theory recognizes the institutional structures and patterns of opportunity that perpetuate gender differences (Eagly & Wood, 2010; Wood & Eagly, 2010). Differences between men and women in access to education and in the treatment they receive from teachers, for instance, helps to explain differences in career choices (Weisgram, Dinella & Fulcher, 2011).

One prediction from social role theory is that as social structures change, gender differences should decrease—and this prediction has been borne out (Carothers & Reis, 2013; Eagly & Diekman, 2003). For example, in cultures in which women have greater access to economic opportunities, education, and careers, women are less likely to prefer men with resources as suggested by the evolutionary perspective (Eagly & Wood, 2010; Kasser & Sharma, 1999).

Importantly, social role theory asserts that thinking about men and women simply in terms of their sex misses big differences among people within each group. Indeed, in Eagly's view, lumping people together according to their sex (assuming that biological sex means the same thing as gender) is essentially engaging in gender stereotyping.

The consequences of using sex as a way to categorize men and women has been a particular concern in research on brain differences between the sexes. To read about this work, see the Intersection.

Traditional gender roles and gender stereotypes often (but not always, as the photo shows) shape individuals' life goals and career choices.

● **gender roles** Roles that reflect the individual's expectation for how females and males should think, act and feel.

● **gender stereotypes** Overly general beliefs and expectations about what women and men are like.

Evaluating the Theoretical Approaches to Gender

In summary, scholars think about gender and its origins in a number of persuasive ways, including biological, evolutionary, social cognitive, and social role perspectives. These theories are not mutually exclusive, and a comprehensive understanding of gender might well take all of them into account.

Biology alone would not seem to offer a sufficient explanation for gender. Indeed, wide variations occur within each sex, for there are certainly girls and women who are assertive and dominant, as well as boys and men who are submissive and subordinate (Hyde, 2014). Yet biological differences between the sexes are likely more significant than the social cognitive approach acknowledges: Just ask the parents whose daughter insists on playing with dolls instead of trucks or who witness their son turning a stuffed bunny into a weapon.

Similarities in patterns of gender differences across different cultures support evolutionary psychology approaches. However, the application of sexual selection to human behavior has been strongly criticized. Some suggest that gender differences can be better explained by social factors, such as group cooperation, than by natural selection (Hyde & Else-Quest, 2013; Roughgarden, Oishi, & Akçay, 2006).

Gender and Neuroscience: Are There His and Hers Brains (and Should We Even Ask That Question)?

Prenatal androgens powerfully influence the developing XY embryo. Could these hormones create "his" and "hers" brains?

Some research would seem to support the role of brain differences in gender differences. For example, compared to men's brains, women's brains have more *gray matter* (Goldstein & others, 2001), and research has linked the greater gray matter to greater social concern (Yamasue & others, 2008). Some research has shown that male brains show more connections to the right hemisphere, whereas female brains show greater connectivity to the left hemisphere (Tomasi & Volkow, 2012), which might seem to fit with the stereotype of women being more verbally skilled than men. How does learning about these brain differences influence your thoughts on gender? Do brain differences seem, perhaps, more foundational or *more real* than other differences between the sexes?

The controversy over comparing the brains of men and women is not so much about whether differences exist as it is about where these differences come from and what they are thought to mean. From a strong biological perspective, prenatal exposure to androgens *sets the stage* for a brain that is oriented toward things, rather than people (Beltz, Swanson, & Berenbaum, 2011; Berenbaum, Bryk, & Beltz, 2012). However, setting the stage is not the same thing as producing the actual play, and this is where the experience of the brain is especially important to consider.

Examining this issue, Rebecca Jordan-Young and Raffaella Rumiati (2012) compared the effects of prenatal androgen exposure on two very different organs—the genitals and the brain. There is no question that prenatal hormone exposure permanently changes the genitals. Penises and vulva are anatomical structures that remain consistent across the life span. In the absence of unusual circumstances, these structures are not changed by experience. If you were given photographs of male and female genitalia and no other information about the individuals to whom they belong, you could likely sort them into male and female with 100 percent accuracy.

Why are people so often fascinated by brain differences between the sexes?

Now, consider the brain. Obviously, given the same sorts of photos of brains, even a skilled neuroscientist could not categorize these individually by sex. Differences that have been found are small, and they are only perceptible at the group level: On average, the brains of men and women differ, but there is considerable variation within groups (Jordan-Young & Rumiati, 2012). As we have seen throughout our exploration of psychology, the brain is uniquely adaptable: It is changed by experience. Even in nonhuman animals, early hormone exposure does not have permanent effects on the brain.

Media reports of research on sex differences in the brain have been criticized because they can lead people to assume that such differences are, in a way, *hardwired*—that is, genetically or innately determined rather than learned through experience (Fine, 2010; Jordan-Young & Rumiati, 2012). As we have seen, it is simply not accurate to describe the brain as "hardwired" and certainly not in terms of gender.

Media sound bites rarely capture the nuances of research conclusions. To the general public, brain differences might appear to suggest *innate* differences between the sexes, implying that fighting against sexism and improving opportunities for men and women are pointless or even damaging—a conclusion that has no scientific basis.

Certainly, having role models is a factor in the attitudes that men and women form about their choices of life goals, as the social cognitive view suggests. Further, there is no question that social roles are also important. Indeed, it is shocking to think that although we live in a world where in some nations a woman can serve as national leader, in other countries a girl is not permitted even to go to school, and a woman cannot leave home without an escort.

Biological, evolutionary, social cognitive, and social role theorists approach gender development from different levels of analysis, and each approach poses different research questions to answer (Figure 11.5). Throughout the rest of this chapter, we often will refer to these broad perspectives to see how each one applies with regard to the specific

Theoretical Approach	Summary	Research Questions
Biological	Focuses on the various biological processes that underlie differences between men and women. Researchers from this perspective examine variables such as genes, hormones, and brain structures and functions to identify the biological underpinnings of gender.	• How does prenatal hormone exposure relate to later sex-typed behavior? • How do genetic factors influence the development of gender identity?
Evolutionary	Focuses on the ways that differences between men and women can be understood as serving adaptive functions for our distant ancestors. Sexual selection is used to explain gender differences in behavior, and sex differences in reproductive challenges are thought to underlie differences in sexual behavior.	• How do men and women differ in terms of engaging in casual sex? • Do sex differences in nonhuman primates show the same patterns as those found in humans?
Social Cognitive	Focuses on how processes such as learning (including modeling and rewards and punishers) and the development of cognitive schemas associated with sex lead to conceptions of male and female.	• When do children learn that a person's sex makes a difference in how he or she is treated by others? • How do peer groups react to children who behave in gender-atypical ways?
Social Role	Focuses on the ways that the division of labor between the sexes leads to expectations about what is appropriate behavior for members of each sex. The division of labor leads to the construction of gender roles and stereotypes that influence the opportunities and aspirations of men and women.	• Do women seek out different opportunities in cultures that have more egalitarian attitudes toward the sexes? • Do gender differences we see in one culture translate to another?

FIGURE 11.5 **Summary of Major Theoretical Approaches to Gender and Gender Development** Note how each approach focuses on a different aspect of human life, ranging from genetic and hormonal influences to relationships, psychological processes, and social structures.

topics and issues addressed. Each of these theories, for example, has something to say about whether and how the sexes should differ from each other on various attributes, our next topic.

3· THE PSYCHOLOGY OF GENDER DIFFERENCES

To think about gender differences, let's start with a game we will call "Who are more _____ ?" For each adjective below, answer as quickly as you can with either "Men" or "Women."

Who are more . . .		
	Assertive	Rational
	Emotional	Aggressive
	Strong	Sexually adventurous
	Creative	Reserved
	Verbal	Active

Now, for each of those descriptors, think of someone you know who is of the opposite sex to your answer and who is very high on the quality described. What does this game tell you about gender stereotypes? Might it suggest that even though you may have ready stereotypes for gender differences, in fact men and women vary widely with respect to a number of qualities?

In this section we will review the research on gender differences in four main areas:

- Emotion, empathy, and helping
- Cognitive ability
- Aggression
- Sexuality

Keep in mind that because gender cannot be manipulated, research comparing men and women is by definition correlational, so causal claims are not justified.

test yourself

1. What are four major theoretical approaches to gender development? What is the main idea behind each?
2. Explain sexual selection, a key concept of the evolutionary psychology approach.
3. What are gender roles and gender stereotypes? What does social role theory say about them?

Emotion, Empathy, and Helping

Unless you have been isolated on a mountaintop, you probably know the stereotype about gender and emotion: She is emotional; he is not. This stereotype is a powerful and pervasive image across cultures (Schirmer, 2013) and is one rationale given for not allowing women to serve in combat. However, researchers have found that men and women are often more alike in the way they experience emotion than the stereotype would lead us to believe (Carothers & Reis, 2013).

Women and men often use the same facial expressions, adopt the same language, and describe their emotional experiences similarly when they keep diaries about their experiences. For many emotional experiences, researchers do not find gender differences (Hyde, 2014). Where differences do emerge, they suggest that women report more feelings of sadness and anxiety than men do, and men report more anger and irritability than women do (Schirmer, 2013). Neuroimaging studies suggest that the responsiveness of the amygdalae to emotion-arousing stimuli varies according to gender, with women being more responsive to negative stimuli and men being more responsive to positive stimuli (Stevens & Hamann, 2012).

Understanding these differences requires consideration of gender-related beliefs about emotion and the contexts in which emotions are experienced (Brannon, 1999; Brody, 1999; Shields, 1991). Females may be judged harshly for expressions of anger, and males might be evaluated as weak if they express worry or sadness. Both women and men are certainly aware of the gender-specific expectations for emotional behavior (Blakemore, Berenbaum, & Liben, 2009; Schirmer, 2013). Indeed, men who embrace a stereotypically masculine gender identity are more likely to report themselves as less emotional (Jakupcak & others, 2003). Gender differences in emotion are much more tied to social context than to biological sex (Derntl & others, 2012).

Empathy is a person's feeling of oneness with the emotional state of another person. When we feel empathy for someone, we feel what that person is feeling. Women do report themselves as more empathic than men (Carothers & Reis, 2013). Empathy requires an appreciation of another person's mental states, suggesting the important role of theory of mind in this capacity. Theory of mind, as noted in Chapter 5, is the ability to understand the inner life of another person. Comparing the sexes on measures of theory of mind, where differences are found, women tend to show an advantage (Baron-Cohen & others, 2001; Hall & Matsumoto, 2004; Ibanez & others, 2013; Voracek & Dressler, 2006).

Gender differences in empathy and theory of mind have been a focus of research on *autism spectrum disorders (ASD)*, a cluster of neurodevelopmental disorders affecting communication and social interaction. Individuals with ASD exhibit delayed or impaired language development, have narrow interests, and perform repetitive actions. They also show impairments on theory of mind tasks (Baron-Cohen & others, 2001).

Simon Baron-Cohen (1995, 2008, 2011), an autism expert, has proposed that ASD is centrally characterized by theory of mind deficits. In fact, Baron-Cohen suggests that we can understand ASD by thinking about gender differences more generally. Boys are four to five times more likely than girls to be diagnosed with ASD (Rivet & Matson, 2011). Might this big difference suggest a link between ASD and gender? To read about this provocative idea, see the Critical Controversy.

Empathy is a strong predictor of an individual's willingness to help another in need. If women are more empathic than men, are they also more helpful? The answer to this question is, it depends (Best, 2010; Eisenberg, Spinrad, & Morris, 2013). Women are more likely than men to help when doing so does not involve risks to personal safety. For instance, women donate more to charitable causes (Leslie, Snyder, & Glomb, 2013). In contrast, men are more likely than women to help in situations in which a perceived danger is present (for instance, picking up a hitchhiker) and in which they feel competent to help (as in assisting someone with a flat tire) (Eagly & Crowley, 1986).

● **empathy** A feeling of oneness with the emotional state of another person.

CRITICAL CONTROVERSY

Does Autism Spectrum Disorder Represent an Extreme Male Brain?

Could gender differences hold the key to understanding autism spectrum disorders (ASD)? Simon Baron-Cohen thinks so.

Baron-Cohen (2011) developed two ways to think about human motivation: systematizing and empathizing. *Systematizing* is the drive to analyze situations to uncover their structure and fascination with creating systems. *Empathizing* is the drive to understand other people. Baron-Cohen proposes that the balance between these two motivational tendencies is different for the genders: Men are likely to be higher in systematizing than empathizing; women are likely to be higher in empathizing than systematizing. These motivational differences, Baron-Cohen claims, help to explain why there are more men than women in systematizing occupations (such as engineering).

Moreover, Baron-Cohen draws a link between the male tendency to systematize versus empathize and the tendency of individuals with ASD to exhibit limited interest and have poor performance on theory of mind tasks. To him, these tendencies are characteristic of men in general. Thus, he suggests, ASD might be viewed as representing an extreme male brain (Baron-Cohen, 2002).

This provocative approach to ASD has been criticized as drawing very broad conclusions based on very little direct evidence (Fausto-Sterling, Garcia Coll, & Lamarre, 2012). Nevertheless, by drawing attention to the gender difference in ASD diagnoses and proposing the extreme male brain theory of ASD,

Baron-Cohen's work has led researchers to notice things they otherwise might not have.

Perhaps most interestingly, the gender difference in ASD diagnoses *only* appears in samples of children with relatively high IQ. Among individuals with ASD who are intellectually disabled, the number of boys and girls is more balanced (Fombonne, 2005; Rivet & Matson, 2011). Such findings suggest potential biases in diagnoses. Rather than showing that autism reflects an extreme male brain, the gender differences we see in diagnoses may reflect the readiness of practitioners to label boys (rather than girls) with ASD. Alternatively, girls who have ASD but have higher IQs may be overlooked in diagnostic standards and may miss out on resources and aid as a result.

In some ways, the controversy over the extreme male brain approach to autism demonstrates how even an idea that might be wrong can lead to research that uncovers important and innovative insights. Inspired by a controversial claim, researchers can uncover essential information they did not even know they were looking for.

WHAT DO YOU THINK
- How does the extreme male brain theory of autism influence your view of men, in general?
- If you had a child who was diagnosed with ASD, how would you feel about the extreme male brain hypothesis?
- What assumptions underlie Baron-Cohen's approach, and do you think they are valid?

Cognitive Ability

A gender difference that is a source of interest for many researchers, as well as for the general public, is the underrepresentation of women in math and science careers. This issue has been a focal point at many conferences.

At such a gathering in January 2005, Larry Summers, then president of Harvard University, sparked a major controversy. Summers commented that he believed that a key determinant of the underrepresentation of women was gender differences in innate ability in math and science—specifically, women's lack of natural cognitive ability relevant to careers in math and science. Summers's words set off a firestorm of criticism. Some were shocked and dismayed that he would suggest such a thing, and others felt that he was a victim of political correctness.

What do the data tell us about cognitive differences between men and women? To summarize the evidence on gender differences, Janet Shibley Hyde (2005) reviewed the meta-analyses that had been conducted on gender differences over a wide range of characteristics. Recall that meta-analysis is a statistical technique that allows researchers to pull together findings from a variety of studies that all address the same questions, so that they can determine whether differences from one study represent real differences in the world and can estimate the size of those differences. In relying only on meta-analyses, Hyde was, in a sense, using the most solid data available. With regard to cognitive factors, Hyde found that where differences did emerge, they were quite small, with girls scoring higher on some measures of verbal ability and boys scoring higher on spatial tasks.

As an example of girls' superior performance on verbal tasks, one study examined the verbal performance of fourth-graders in 33 different countries (Mullis & others, 2003; Ogle & others, 2003). In every country, the average performance of girls on verbal tasks was higher than the average performance of boys. In turn, research has revealed that, at least by preschool age, boys show greater accuracy in performing tasks requiring mental rotation of objects in space (Levine & others, 1999; Loring-Meier & Halpern, 1999).

As children age, these differences are most likely to show up on tasks requiring the person to imagine objects moving in space—for instance, to state when two objects will crash (Liu & Huang, 1999). Sex differences have been observed in research using eye-tracking equipment to gauge infants' capacities to visually track objects. Although younger infants (for instance, 4-month-olds) show no differences, by around 9 to 10 months, boys perform better than girls (Wilcox & others, 2012).

What might explain these differences? Biological theorists have looked to genetic or hormonal differences, although aptitude for science is similarly predicted by genes for both males and females (Haworth, Dale, & Plomin, 2009). From an evolutionary perspective, the differences are thought to be tied to females' important roles in socializing offspring and negotiating the interpersonal landscape and to ancestral males' need to traverse the landscape for food and to find their way home again (Geary, 2010).

Social cognitive and social role theorists might say that these differences reflect differences in experience. Interactions with parents, which are likely influenced by parents' beliefs, can magnify small differences over time (Fausto-Sterling, Garcia Coll, & Lamarre, 2012). In fact, research revealed that with as little as 10 hours of training (playing an action-oriented video game), the sex difference in spatial cognition declined considerably (Feng, Spence, & Pratt, 2007).

Overall, in her analysis, Hyde found strong support for what she called the **gender similarities hypothesis**—the idea that men and women (and boys and girls) are much more similar than they are different (Hyde, 2005, 2006, 2007, 2014). This conclusion suggests that the very large gender difference in the pursuit of careers in math and science is unlikely to result from these small cognitive differences between males and females.

To explain the shortage of women in math and science, we might therefore consider the *multiple* factors that lead an individual to pursue a particular career. That choice is likely to be a product of many interrelated factors, including what the person feels he or she is especially good at and likes to do, the role models encountered, the social support from family and friends, and the likelihood that a particular career path will ultimately lead to the life the person envisions for himself or herself in the future (Halpern, 2012).

Aggression

Aggression is behavior that is intended to harm another person (Crick & Grotpeter, 1995). Are men or women more aggressive? The answer depends on the particular *type* of aggression we are talking about.

Overt aggression refers to physically or verbally harming another person directly. Males tend to be higher on overt aggression than females. As children, boys are more likely than girls to get in fights in which they are physically aggressive toward one another (Bukowski, Brendgen, & Vitaro, 2007). As adolescents, males are more likely to join gangs and to commit violent acts (Dodge, Coie, & Lynam, 2006). As adults, men are more likely than women to be chronically hostile and to commit violent crimes (White & Frabutt, 2006).

Women's smaller physical size may be one reason they are less likely to engage in overt aggression. To understand aggressive tendencies in girls and women, researchers have focused instead on **relational aggression**, behavior that is meant to harm the social standing of another person through activities such as gossiping and spreading rumors (Crick & Grotpeter, 1995; Kawabata & others, 2013; Zimmer-Gembeck & others, 2013).

● **gender similarities hypothesis** Hyde's proposition that men and women (and boys and girls) are much more similar than they are different.

● **aggression** Behavior that is intended to harm another person.

● **overt aggression** Physically or verbally harming another person directly.

● **relational aggression** Behavior that is meant to harm the social standing of another person.

Relational aggression differs from overt aggression in that it requires that the aggressor have a considerable level of social and cognitive skill. To be relationally aggressive, an individual must have a good understanding of social circumstances and be motivated to plant rumors that are likely to damage the intended party. Relational aggression is more subtle than overt aggression, and the relationally aggressive individual may not seem to be aggressive to others, as the aggressive acts typically are committed secretly.

Mixed findings have characterized research on whether girls show more relational aggression than boys, but one consistent finding is that relational aggression comprises a greater percentage of girls' overall aggression than it does for boys (Underwood, 2011). One research review revealed that girls engage in more relational aggression than boys in adolescence but not in childhood (Smith, Rose, & Schwartz-Mette, 2010).

Although relational aggression does not lead to the physical injury that might result from overt aggression, it can be extremely painful nevertheless. In 2010, Phoebe Prince, a 15-year-old who had recently moved from Ireland to the United States with her family, became the target of unrelenting rumors and harassment from a group of popular girls at her high school after she had a brief relationship with a popular senior boy. Prince became so distraught that she hanged herself after school one day. Even after her suicide, the girls who had harassed her posted rumors about her on the Facebook page that was set up as a memorial (Cullen, 2010).

The various theoretical approaches we reviewed earlier would explain these gender differences in aggression in different ways. With regard to the overt aggression of boys and men, biological researchers might focus on the role of a hormone such as testosterone, which circulates at higher levels in men than women (van Bokhoven & others, 2006). The evolutionary psychologist would view the overt aggression of males as an outgrowth of ancestral male competition for females with whom to mate (Buss, 2012). From this perspective, the propensity for relational aggression derives from females' need to compete for male partners with resources.

From a social cognitive perspective, gender differences in styles of aggression would reflect differences in boys' and girls' socialization, with girls being taught early on that overt aggression is inappropriate (Archer, 2004). Similarly, social role theory would see these differences as emerging out of gender roles, and responses to these forms of aggression would reflect stereotypes of male and female (Eagly, 2012).

Phoebe Prince's family buried her in her native Ireland because "they wanted an ocean between her and the people who hounded her to the grave" (Cullen, 2010).

Sexuality

Broadly speaking, **sexuality** refers to the ways people experience and express themselves as sexual beings. Sexuality involves activity that is associated with sexual pleasure. Although stereotypes might point to very strong gender differences in sexuality, with men being more preoccupied with sex than women, research has shown that differences are smaller and less consistent than those stereotypes might suggest (Carothers & Reis, 2013). In some cases, it is clear that social expectations influence people's responses to questions about their sexual behavior. For instance, men often report having more sex partners than women do. In a study using a fake lie detector test (called the *bogus pipeline*), however, this difference disappeared when men and women thought that the researchers could tell if they were lying (Alexander & Fisher, 2003).

Do men at least *think about* having sex more often than women do? In one study, undergraduate participants kept tallies of how many times they thought about sex, food, and sleep for a week (Fisher, Moore, & Pittenger, 2012). Men did report thinking about sex more than women did. However, men also thought about food and sleep more than women did as well. The researchers concluded that men may be more focused than women on their own physical needs.

Stereotypes and evolutionary psychology tell us that men and women differ in their partner preferences, with men valuing physical attractiveness and women valuing resources. In one study, Paul Eastwick and Eli Finkel (2008) set up a series of speed-dating events to examine these differences. Although before-the-event ratings of desirable characteristics in romantic partners followed the stereotypical patterns, men and women valued appearance and status *equally* in their selections in the actual speed-dating events.

● **sexuality** The ways people experience and express themselves as sexual beings.

A meta-analysis of research examining gender differences in sexuality found differences on the following: Men engaged in more masturbation, viewed more pornography, engaged in more casual sex, and had more permissive attitudes about casual sex than did women (Petersen & Hyde, 2010).

The evolutionary perspective on gender strongly predicts gender differences in sexual behavior—specifically, that women should be more selective, and men less so, when it comes to casual sex (Buss, 2012). To test this prediction, Russell Clark and Elaine Hatfield (1989) sent five men and five women experimenters to a college campus with a mission. They were to approach members of the opposite sex whom they found quite attractive and say, "I have been noticing you around campus. I find you very attractive." Then they were to ask one of three questions:

- "Would you like to go out with me?"
- "Would you like to go to my apartment with me?"
- "Would you like to go to bed with me?"

The independent variables in this study were the sex of the person approached and the type of question asked. The dependent variable was whether that person said yes or no to the question. The results showed no differences between men and women in their answers to the "going out" question—about half of each sex said yes. However, dramatic sex differences emerged for the other two questions: The large majority of men said yes to the "apartment" question (most women said no) and to the "bed" question (all of the women said no). The Psychological Inquiry shows the results.

psychological *inquiry*

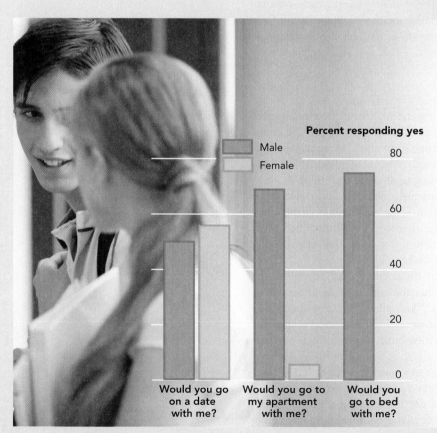

Percent responding yes

Would you go on a date with me? | Would you go to my apartment with me? | Would you go to bed with me?

Sex and Casual Sex

The figure shows the results of the Clark and Hatfield study (1989). Recall that the experimenters approached men and women on a college campus and asked one of three questions. Review the details of the study and answer the following questions.

1. This study was an experiment. What are the independent and dependent variables?

2. Why do you think that men were more likely to say yes to the "bed" question than they were to the "date" question?

3. Recall that in this study, the experimenters were judged to range from slightly unattractive to moderately attractive and were told to approach people whom they found to be quite attractive. How might these circumstances have influenced the results?

4. Perhaps the most striking aspect of this experiment's results is the big gender difference on the "bed" question. Most men said yes, and not a single woman did. What is another question that might have produced such a stunning gender difference?

5. Imagine that you strongly favor the social role theory of gender development. How would you explain these results from that perspective?

Interestingly, men who said no to the "bed" question felt the need to explain themselves with statements like "I have a girlfriend" or "I'm married." In contrast, women who were asked if they would like to go to bed with a male experimenter were more likely to give responses such as "You've got to be kidding" and "What is wrong with you? Leave me alone" (Clark & Hatfield, 1989, p. 52). For many years, this study was recognized as supporting the predictions that men are more interested in casual sex compared to women and that women are choosier than men.

If you think about this study long enough you might see that there is a *confound* or a *third variable* in the study design. As described in Chapter 2, a confound in an experiment is a variable, other than the independent variable, that systematically differs across the groups and that might explain the results. Terri Conley noted that although men and women in the study differed in their willingness to say yes to a proposal for casual sex, they were responding to proposers who systematically differed in terms of their sex as well: Women were always approached *by men,* and men were always approached *by women* (Conley, 2011). Isn't it possible, Conley asked, that the sex of the person doing the asking might have influenced whether those who were approached said yes to the proposal?

In a series of studies, Conley showed that the proposer's characteristics influence whether the approached person accepts or rejects a proposal for casual sex (Conley, 2011). For instance, she found that both men and women rated a male stranger as potentially more dangerous than a female stranger. Would women be so choosy if a familiar person rather than a stranger approached them? Conley discovered that women were more likely to report that they would say yes to casual sex if it was offered by a familiar person, such as an attractive friend, or by a celebrity, such as Johnny Depp. She also found that bisexual women were more likely to say they would engage in casual sex with a female, but not a male, who approached them.

Men and women differ sexually in other ways. Compared to men, women tend to show more changes in their sexual patterns and sexual desires over their lifetime (Baumeister, 2000; L. M. Diamond, 2008a; Knight & Morales Hope, 2012; Mock & Eibach, 2011). Women are more likely than men, for instance, to have had sexual experiences with same- and opposite-sex partners, even if they identify strongly as heterosexual or lesbian. Women are more likely than men to identify as bisexual (Gates, 2011).

In contrast, male sexuality may be more limited to particular targets of attraction. One study compared the sexual arousal of heterosexual women, lesbian women, heterosexual men, and homosexual men while they watched erotic films of various sexual acts featuring male and female actors or bonobo apes (Chivers, Seto, & Blanchard, 2007). The films included scenes of sexual activity between same- and opposite-sex human partners and between opposite-sex bonobos, and scenes of men and women masturbating alone or engaging in aerobic exercise while naked. Physiological measures of sexual arousal showed that both heterosexual women and lesbian women were aroused by all of the films showing sexual activity (including those featuring the bonobos). However, gay men were aroused only by the films that included men, and heterosexual men were aroused only by the films that included women.

How would the various theoretical approaches interpret gender differences in sexuality? From the biological perspective, differences in sexuality can be explained by genetic and hormonal differences between men and women. The evolutionary psychology approach would see these differences as supporting the role of sexual selection in human evolution. Social cognitive theories would focus on the ways that boys and girls learn about what is considered appropriate sexual behavior for each gender. Finally, social role theory would assert that these gender differences reflect the differing gender roles, stereotypes, and opportunities that cultures construct for men and women. In some cultures, for example, women cover their heads and faces when they are out in public. Their husbands are the only men who ever see them uncovered. Clearly, biological explanations are not needed to explain why these women would not be likely to engage in casual sex.

● **sexual orientation** The direction of an individual's erotic interests.

● **heterosexual** Referring to a sexual orientation in which the individual is generally sexually attracted to members of the opposite sex.

● **homosexual** Referring to a sexual orientation in which the individual is generally sexually attracted to members of the same sex.

● **bisexual** Referring to a sexual orientation in which the individual is sexually attracted to people of both sexes.

Evaluating the Evidence for Gender Differences

It is safe to say that in talking about gender differences, people can be prone to extremes. For instance, a bestselling book suggested that men and women are so different that they must have come from different planets, with men hailing from warlike, competitive Mars and women from the love planet, Venus (Gray, 2004). Clearly, our survey of gender differences does not support such a radical view.

With regard to emotion, empathy, and helping, women show some advantage in reading emotions in others, but gender differences in these domains require us to consider the social context. Gender differences appear to be strongest in the areas of aggression and are weaker in the domains of cognitive ability and sexuality. On the whole, we can state with certainty that men and women are indeed both from planet Earth (Carothers & Reis, 2013).

One way in which men and women clearly differ is that men generally are sexually attracted to women, whereas women typically are sexually attracted to men. Of course, these patterns of attraction are not always the case, as human beings differ from one another in their sexual orientation, our next topic.

4· SEXUAL ORIENTATION

An individual's **sexual orientation** is the direction of his or her erotic interests. Sexual orientation does not mean simply sexual behavior. A man who has sex with other men while in prison may not think of himself as homosexual, and once released from prison he may never engage in such behavior again. A woman might always find herself sexually attracted to other women but never act on those feelings. When we talk about sexual orientation, we mean a *whole range* of human experiences that interest psychologists, including not only behaviors but also desires, feelings, fantasies, and a person's sense of identity.

Defining Sexual Orientation

An individual who self-identifies as **heterosexual** is generally sexually attracted to members of the opposite sex. An individual who self-identifies as **homosexual** is generally sexually attracted to members of the same sex. Today, sexual orientation is commonly viewed as a continuum from exclusive male–female relations to exclusive same-sex relations (B. M. King, 2005). Some individuals self-identify as **bisexual,** meaning that they are sexually attracted to people of both sexes.

Despite the widespread use of labels such as "homosexual," "gay," "lesbian," and "bisexual," some researchers argue that they are misleading. Instead, erotic attractions may be fluid, and these categories ignore the potential flexibility of human sexual attraction and behavior (L. M. Diamond, 2008a, 2009).

In some cultures, engaging in same-sex sexual activity is not viewed as an indication of the person's identity (Nanda, 2008), but in Western societies, there is a strong belief that sexual orientation is a stable personal attribute. Stability of sexual orientation might also depend on the orientation. Longitudinal studies have shown very high stability for heterosexuality over time (Kinnish, Strassberg, & Turner, 2005; Mock & Eibach, 2011). Non-heterosexual individuals may be more likely to shift their erotic interests, especially in adolescence (Diamond & Savin-Williams, 2013).

Related to this issue is the very definition of bisexuality. Some people think that bisexuality is simply a steppingstone to homosexuality, whereas others view it as a sexual orientation itself or as an indicator of sexual fluidity. Evidence supports the notion that bisexuality is a stable orientation that involves attraction to both sexes (Lippa, 2013; Mock & Eibach, 2011). In a decade-long longitudinal study of non-heterosexual women, Lisa Diamond (2008b) found evidence for the existence of a stable bisexual identity. Among women who identified themselves as lesbian or bisexual in 1995, change was more likely to occur in the direction of lesbian women moving toward bisexuality rather than bisexual women changing to a lesbian or heterosexual orientation. Demonstrating the difference between orientation and behavior, Diamond found that although bisexual orientation was unlikely to change, sexual behavior did. Women who self-identified as bisexual were more likely, over time, to engage in exclusively homosexual or heterosexual behavior, because many of them had settled into a long-term relationship with one partner by the end of the study (Diamond, 2008b).

Occurrence of the Different Sexual Orientations

Homosexual behavior is relatively common in nature, having been observed in 1,500 different species, including rats, nonhuman primates, giraffes, ostriches, guppies, cats, bison, dolphins, and fruit flies (Sommer & Vasey, 2006). Long-term same-sex partnerships occur in nonhuman species. In 2004, the *New York Times* reported the story of Roy and Silo, two male penguins who appeared to share a long-term monogamous sexual relationship at the Central Park Zoo, even raising their adopted daughter Tango (they have since broken up) (D. Smith, 2004). In humans, homosexuality is present in all cultures, regardless of whether a culture is tolerant or not. Obviously, the majority of people, regardless of culture, are heterosexual.

It is difficult to know precisely how many gays, lesbians, and bisexuals there are in the world, partly because fears of discrimination may prevent individuals from answering honestly on surveys. Estimates of the frequency of homosexuality range from 2 percent to 10 percent of the population (Zietsch & others, 2008). Demographer Gary Gates (2011) summarized the available U.S. data and concluded that approximately 3.8 percent or 9 million Americans are gay, lesbian, or bisexual, which is essentially the population of New Jersey.

Roy and Silo, same-sex partners who raised their adopted daughter Tango, are chinstrap penguins like these.

Origins of Sexual Orientation: A Scientific Puzzle

What is the source of sexual orientation? Scientists have speculated extensively about this question (Rahman, 2005; M. Rosenthal, 2013). Charles Darwin (1862) himself commented, "We do not even in the least know the final cause of sexuality. The whole subject is hidden in darkness."

Since Darwin's time, scientists have learned something about factors that *do not* predict sexual orientation. First, being reared by a gay parent *does not* increase the chances of being gay (Golombok & Tasker, 1996; Patterson & Farr, 2010; Patterson & Wainright, 2010). In fact, the vast majority of gay individuals have heterosexual parents, so it does not seem that observational learning or modeling play a role in the development of sexual orientation. Nor does a particular parenting style relate to the emergence of sexual orientation (Bell, Weinberg, & Hammersmith, 1981). Given the many different ways in which parents interact with their children and the fact that the vast majority of people are heterosexual, it seems highly unlikely that heterosexuality is explained by particular parenting strategies. Finally, same-sex sexual experience or experimentation in childhood does not predict eventual adult homosexuality (Bailey, 2003; Bogaert, 2000).

So, what factors might account for sexual orientation? Before we probe this question, let's pause to consider some key issues in the science behind sexual orientation.

THINKING CRITICALLY ABOUT SEXUAL ORIENTATION

Scientists approach the puzzle of sexual orientation with an openness to the different potential answers empirical data might suggest. Before exploring the current evidence for various explanations of sexual orientation, it may be helpful to review five important issues for critical thinkers.

■ *Unlikelihood of a single cause:* For any psychological characteristic, it is unlikely that a single cause can be identified, and sexual orientation is no exception. As we consider the accumulated data on this topic, keep in mind that it is very probable that many factors work together to foster sexual orientation and that factors that have not even been considered will likely emerge in the future.

- *Within-group variation:* There is a great deal of variation within any group of people who share the same sexual orientation. All heterosexual men are sexually attracted to women, but that attraction may be the only thing that any two heterosexual men have in common. Similarly, all gay men share a sexual attraction to men, but any two gay men may have little else in common.

- *Research challenges:* Comparing individuals from different sexual orientations presents research design challenges. One such challenge is representativeness, for in some studies the heterosexual and homosexual participants are recruited in very different ways. Gay and lesbian participants are sometimes recruited only from gay pride events, for example, and so they may not be representative of all homosexual and bisexual individuals. Similarly, small sample size can be an issue because of the difficulty involved in recruiting gay participants. Indeed, in a study reported in 2000, just 6 gay men were compared to 256 "non-gay" men (Lippa, 2000). Recall that studies using larger samples are more likely to yield generalizable results.

- *The meaning of cross-sex similarities:* In presenting research on the origins of sexual orientation, the popular media often emphasize similarities between gay men and heterosexual women and between lesbian women and heterosexual men. Regardless of their sexual orientation, gay men are men, and lesbian women are women.

- *Explaining sexual orientation does not mean explaining only homosexuality:* Finally, and perhaps most importantly, any good theory of sexual orientation should explain how *any of us* (gay or straight) becomes sexually oriented toward individuals of a particular sex. As scientists, we want to explain the sexual orientations of men and women who are attracted to men or women or both.

With these cautions in mind, let's look at the evidence concerning sexual orientation.

GENETIC INFLUENCES

Researchers have examined genes as a factor in sexual orientation by using twins to estimate the heritability of sexual orientation. Recall from Chapter 8 that heritability is a statistic that tells us the extent to which we can explain observed differences in a given characteristic based on differences in genes. A study of nearly 4,000 twins in Sweden demonstrated that the heritability of same-sex sexual behavior was about 35 percent in men and 19 percent in women (Langstrom & others, 2010). These heritability estimates suggest that although genes play a role, they are not as strong an influence on sexual orientation as they are for other characteristics, such as intelligence.

Of course, genes do not impact psychological characteristics as directly as they do a physical characteristic like eye color. We therefore need to consider other factors that might provide the bridge between genes and the psychological experience of sexual orientation.

PRENATAL HORMONES AND BRAIN DIFFERENCES

One way in which genes might influence sexual orientation is through their effect on brain development. Recall that prenatal androgens play a crucial role in the development of sexual characteristics (Hines, 2013). Might these hormones also influence whether the brain develops into one that is sexually attracted to females?

Because prenatal androgen levels can vary for female embryos, we can examine whether females who were exposed to prenatal androgens are more likely to be bisexual or lesbian rather than heterosexual. Researchers have tested this possibility in a variety of ways (Meyer-Bahlburg & others, 2008). One strategy for examining the link between prenatal hormones and sexual orientation is to identify physical features that are associated with prenatal testosterone. The idea is that once we identify the effects of prenatal testosterone on various physical features of the body, we can look at those features and see whether they differ in adults who are either gay or straight (McFadden, 2008; Rahman, 2005; Rahman, Clarke, & Morera, 2009).

The best known of these features is the ratio between the second and fourth digits on the hand (the pointer and the ring finger), called the *2D:4D ratio*. Men tend to have a ring finger that is longer than their pointer, whereas for women the two fingers are nearly the same length (Manning, 2002; Medland & Loehlin, 2008). Thus, women tend to have larger 2D:4D ratios than men. This ratio is influenced by prenatal testosterone (Lutchmaya & others, 2004; McFadden & others, 2005). If prenatal testosterone exposure is related to developing a brain that is attracted to females, we might expect lesbian women to show a pattern more similar to heterosexual men—that is, a smaller 2D:4D ratio. Evidence for such differences is mixed (Kraemer & others, 2006; McFadden & Shubel, 2002; Rahman & Wilson, 2003; Voracek & others, 2011).

In addition to examining the 2D:4D ratio, researchers have examined whether sexual orientation is associated with brain differences. Two particular types of brain differences have garnered the most attention among researchers: the thickness of the corpus callosum (the bundle of fibers that connects the two hemispheres) and the symmetry between the brain's two hemispheres. Evidence from brain-imaging studies suggests that gay men may have thicker corpus callosa than heterosexual men (Witelson & others, 2008). In terms of hemispheric symmetry, a brain-imaging study found that heterosexual women and gay men show a similar pattern in which the two hemispheres are alike, whereas heterosexual men and lesbian women display a similar pattern of having a larger right hemisphere relative to left (Savic & Lindström, 2008).

Where do these brain differences come from? Differences in the corpus callosum are thought to have a genetic basis because the corpus callosum's size is strongly heritable (Witelson & others, 2008). Differences in hemispheric symmetry are believed to emerge from prenatal hormone exposure (Savic & Lindström, 2008). A word of caution, however: In trying to interpret these brain characteristics, we must keep in mind that habitual patterns of *behavior* can also influence brain structure and function—and we must consider that these cross-sex similarities may therefore be explained by behavioral similarities between heterosexual women and gay men, as well as between heterosexual men and lesbian women.

SOCIAL FACTORS

What about social experience? We have seen that there is no evidence that specific parenting styles "cause" sexual orientation. Still, some scientists have attempted to explain sexual orientation as a function of early childhood experience. Gender-nonconforming behaviors, activities that run counter to gender stereotypes, have received particular focus (Bem, 1996; Rieger, Linsenmeier, & Bailey, 2009; Rieger & others, 2008). Research shows that homosexual adults are more likely than heterosexual adults to remember themselves as having engaged in gender-nonconforming behaviors (Bailey & Zucker, 1995; Lippa, 2008). Moreover, some evidence suggests that in videos of their childhood activities, gay and lesbian adults pursued more gender-atypical activities as children (Rieger & others, 2008).

For boys, gender-nonconforming behavior may be related to eventual sexual development, but the picture is not clear-cut. For example, one study compared 66 extremely gender-nonconforming boys to 56 gender-conforming boys (Green, 1987). Among the nonconforming boys, 75 percent were either bisexual or homosexual at a follow-up during adolescence or young adulthood. Among the gender-conforming boys, 96 percent were heterosexual at follow-up.

Although this study is sometimes used as evidence of the role of gender-nonconforming behavior in the development of sexual orientation (Bem, 1996), take a good look at those percentages. Although gender-nonconforming boys were more likely to be homosexual or bisexual, note that the percentage of boys in the gender-*conforming* group who eventually emerged as gay or bisexual falls within the typical percentages found in the general population. Thus, boys who are quite gender typical in their behavior can certainly turn out to be gay (or bisexual or straight).

Studies of childhood behavior and sexual orientation are correlational. One challenge of correlational research is the potential for a third variable to explain the relationship between the variables of interest. In thinking about an individual's gender-nonconforming behavior in childhood and his or her eventual sexual orientation, you might note that factors such as genes and prenatal hormone exposure might explain both of these variables (Cohen-Bendahan, van de Beek, & Berenbaum, 2005).

Consider, too, that gender-nonconforming boys may experience a very different social response than gender-nonconforming girls. In fact, many women report having been tomboys (Peplau & others, 1999). Girls who engage in boyish activities are frequently popular among their peers, and the vast majority of tomboys turn out to be heterosexual (Peplau & others, 1999). Social responses to gender-nonconforming boys may be more negative (Lee & Troop-Gordon, 2011) and may play a role in eventual gender identity and sexual orientation. Parents and peers may label a gender-nonconforming boy as homosexual, and that labeling may influence the boy's sense of self and his emerging identity (Hegarty, 2009).

AN UNSOLVED PUZZLE

Clearly, scientists have devised a number of clever ways to identify factors associated with sexual orientation. However, as we have seen, many questions remain (Crooks & Baur, 2014). Although we may not still be in the "darkness" described by Darwin, it is fair to say that the room remains not very well lit.

Similar to many other psychological characteristics, an individual's sexual orientation most likely depends on a combination of genetic, hormonal, cognitive, and environmental factors (Langstrom & others, 2010). Most experts on sexual orientation believe that no one factor alone causes sexual orientation and that the relative weight of each factor can vary within people of the same orientation.

We know that whether heterosexual, homosexual, or bisexual, a person cannot be talked out of his or her sexual orientation. Indeed, Qazi Rahman, a researcher who studies the neurobiology of sexual orientation, asserted that "there is no argument anymore—if you are gay, you are born gay" (quoted in Nicholson, 2008). Whether one is homosexual, heterosexual, or bisexual, sexual orientation is not a choice but an integral part of the functioning human being and his or her sense of self (Katz, 1995; Worthington & others, 2008).

Gay and Lesbian Functioning

We may not know definitively why individuals are gay or lesbian, but research has uncovered some interesting things about gay people. Here we briefly review selected findings as they relate to individual adjustment and well-being, gay and lesbian relationships, and gay and lesbian families.

INDIVIDUAL ADJUSTMENT AND WELL-BEING

Research shows that gay and lesbian individuals are similar to their heterosexual counterparts in many ways (L. M. Diamond, 2013a, 2013b; Fingerhut & Peplau, 2013; Savin-Williams, 2013). Researchers typically find no differences among lesbians, gays, bisexuals, and heterosexuals in a wide range of attitudes and behaviors, as well as in psychological adjustment (Hyde & DeLamater, 2011). Gay men and lesbian women are likely to differ from heterosexuals in terms of the gender typicality of their hobbies, activities, and occupations (Lippa, 2000). Note, however, that if gay men and women live in households that are headed by two men or two women, they will inevitably engage in gender-atypical behavior (for instance, women doing the yard work or men cooking and cleaning) simply because someone has to do those tasks.

One factor in the well-being of gays and lesbians is coping with prejudice and discrimination. Among gay men and lesbians polled in one survey, 90 percent reported that discrimination against homosexuals remains a serious problem (Page, 2012). Still, about the same number reported that the people around them had become more accepting in recent years.

Indeed, attitudes toward gays and lesbians have become increasingly more positive in U.S. society (Page, 2012). Since 2011, national polls have consistently found that over half of Americans support marriage equality for same-sex couples (Murray, 2013; Newport, 2011; Page, 2012). In a 2013 survey, 63 percent felt the federal government should recognize same-sex marriage in the states that offer it (Murray, 2013). Younger Americans are particularly likely to support gay rights. In a 2012 poll, among those ages 18 to 29, 73 percent supported marriage equality (Page, 2012).

This increased acceptance likely stems in part from the greater openness of gay people about their lives. Individuals who know someone who is gay or lesbian are less likely to report prejudicial attitudes toward gays and lesbians (Smith, Axelton, & Saucier, 2009). Polls have shown a steady increase in the number of Americans who know a gay person. In a 2013 poll, 79 percent of respondents reporting knowing someone who is gay (Murray, 2013)—a large increase from a 1984 survey in which only 24 percent reported knowing a gay or bisexual person (Harris Interactive, 2006).

For gays, lesbians, and bisexuals, being open about their sexual orientation is a strong predictor of psychological and physical health (Savin-Williams, 2013), although the benefits of coming out may depend on the social reaction (Legate, Ryan, & Weinstein, 2012). For gay men and lesbian women, living in accord with their sexual orientation is a matter of living authentically, and being "out" to the people around them is part of being true to themselves (King, Burton, & Geise, 2009).

GAY AND LESBIAN RELATIONSHIPS

Research consistently shows that gay men and lesbian women report themselves as more satisfied in their relationships compared to heterosexual couples (Balsam & others, 2008; Kurdek, 2004; MacIntosh, Reissing, & Androff, 2010). What might explain this higher relationship satisfaction? One possibility is that heterosexual individuals may feel more pressure to get married and stay married, regardless of their personal choices, and they may be supported to stay in unsatisfying relationships (Green, Bettinger, & Zacks, 1996).

John Gottman and his colleagues (2003) conducted a longitudinal study of gay, lesbian, and heterosexual couples that included video-recorded interactions over 12 years. Gottman's team found that compared to heterosexual couples, gay and lesbian partners were better able to manage conflicts. They were more likely to use humor and affection in dealing with conflicts, took a more positive attitude toward negative feedback from their partners, and let conflicts go once they were resolved (Gottman & others, 2003).

Despite the fact that gay couples tend to report higher satisfaction with their relationships, research shows that gay couples are also more likely to end their relationships compared to heterosexual married couples, especially heterosexual couples with children (Kurdek, 2004; Lau, 2012). A possible reason for this difference is that heterosexual couples may be more likely to stay in unsatisfying relationships out of concern for their children's welfare, and heterosexual couples are more likely than gay couples to have children. Another possible reason is that the legal status of marriage promotes relationship stability (Shulman, Gotta, & Green, 2012), and divorce makes dissolving relationships more difficult.

In 2000, the state of Vermont legally recognized same-sex civil unions, allowing for a test of this possibility. A study compared three samples of couples: gay and lesbian couples who had been united in a civil union; gay and lesbian couples who had not had a civil union; and heterosexual married couples (Balsam & others, 2008). Three years later, gay and lesbian couples who had not been joined in a civil union were more likely to have broken up—or to be on the brink of breaking up—than either gay couples who were in a civil union or heterosexual married couples. These results suggest that the legal tie of marriage is associated with relationship stability.

GAY AND LESBIAN FAMILIES

Although gay and lesbian couples may be less likely than heterosexual couples to have children, increasingly gay families do include kids. Available evidence suggests that approximately 1 in 4 of gay and lesbian households includes children (O'Barr, 2006). Children reared by gay men and lesbian women tend to be as well-adjusted as those from heterosexual households and are no less likely to be accepted by their peers (Chan,

Lesbian women and gay men are similar to heterosexual women and heterosexual men in many respects.

Raboy, & Patterson, 1998; Farr & Patterson, 2013; Goldberg, 2010; Golombok & others, 2003; Patterson & Farr, 2010; Patterson & Wainright, 2010). A study comparing adolescents who had two mothers with adolescents who had opposite-sex parents revealed no differences in self-reported or peer-reported functioning. For both sets of adolescents, what mattered was their close, warm relationship with their parents (Wainright & Patterson, 2008).

Around the world, same-sex marriages are recognized in 16 nations, including Argentina, Belgium, Brazil, Canada, Denmark, France, Iceland, Ireland, the Netherlands, New Zealand, Norway, Portugal, Uruguay, South Africa, Spain, and Sweden. At this writing, in the United States, same-sex marriage is legal in 13 states and the District of Columbia.

In 2013, the American Psychological Association joined a number of professional societies—including the American Psychiatric Association, the American Academy of Pediatrics, and the American Bar Association—in filing a brief in support of striking down the Defense of Marriage Act, which forbids the federal government from recognizing same-sex marriages in states where they are legal. This endorsement of marriage equality was based on research demonstrating the many benefits of close relationships, the harmful effects of discrimination, and the studies demonstrating that the well-being of children is not threatened by having gay parents and is supported by family stability. In July, 2013, the Supreme Court struck down key portions of the Defense of Marriage Act.

test yourself

1. Name various factors that might influence sexual orientation.
2. What is gender-nonconforming behavior? What is the evidence for the role of gender-nonconforming behavior in the development of sexual orientation?
3. What are some factors associated with gay and lesbian well-being?

5· SEXUAL BEHAVIORS AND PRACTICES

Talking about sexual behaviors can sometimes be uncomfortable or embarrassing. It can also be interesting, enlightening, and exhilarating. In this section, we take up these hot topics and explore the ways that research has addressed them.

Sexual Behaviors

What constitutes sexual behavior—what we commonly refer to as "sex"? When President Bill Clinton was asked whether he had engaged in sex with White House intern Monica Lewinsky, he was widely ridiculed for replying that "it depends" on what sex is. Yet Clinton may have been representing a more general confusion. What counts as sex? Most people might answer that question with "vaginal intercourse," but what about other sexual behaviors, such as anal sex and oral sex? If someone has engaged in these practices, is he or she still a "virgin"? If your significant other reported to you that he or she had recently engaged in oral sex with another person, would you consider that sexual infidelity? What if he or she spent an hour sexting an attractive friend? These are the kinds of questions that come up in trying to define sexual behavior.

One possibility is to define sex as activities that are involved in reproduction. By this interpretation, many gay men and women are virgins, as are adolescents who engage exclusively in, say, oral sex. Further, masturbation would not be a sexual behavior within this definition.

Another approach is to define sexual behavior by the arousal and sexual response that occur when the behavior is performed. Though broader, this definition still might leave out people who could say that they are engaged in sexual behavior. For instance, if a person is unable to experience sexual arousal but performs oral sex on a partner, has that person "had sex"? Alternatively, we might broaden the definition a great deal and define sexual behaviors to include behaviors that are specific to each individual and that are pleasurable in a particular way—one that is unusually intimate and personal.

Confusion over what counts as sex can lead to potentially risky behavior. For example, for many adolescents, oral sex appears to be a recreational activity, and because many individuals under age 20 do not view the practice as sex, they believe that it is a safe alternative to intercourse (Fava & Bay-Cheng, 2012; Song & Halpern-Felsher, 2010). Engaging in oral sex, of course, does not increase the risk of pregnancy, and a recent study suggests that among adolescents girls, those who reported having oral sex prior to vaginal sex were nearly four times less likely to experience teen pregnancy (Reese & others, 2013). As we will consider later in this chapter, however, oral sex exposes individuals to the risk of contracting sexually transmitted infections.

Sexual Practices

When people in the United States engage in sexual behavior, what do they do, and how often? Alfred Kinsey and his colleagues conducted the earliest research on this topic in 1948. Kinsey is widely recognized as the father of sexology, a pioneer who brought scientific attention to sexual behavior. Kinsey collected data wherever he could find it, interviewing anyone willing to discuss the intimate details of his or her sex life.

The Kinsey Reports, published in two volumes, presented his findings for men (Kinsey, Pomeroy, & Martin, 1948) and women (Kinsey, Martin, & Pomeroy, 1953). Among the findings that shocked his readers were Kinsey's estimates of the frequency of bisexuality in men (nearly 12 percent) and women (7 percent) and his estimate that at least 50 percent of married men had been sexually unfaithful. Although acknowledged for initiating the scientific study of sexual behavior, Kinsey's work was limited by the lack of representative samples.

Not until 1994 were more accurate data obtained from a well-designed, comprehensive study of U.S. sexual patterns. Robert Michael and his colleagues (1994) interviewed nearly 3,500 randomly selected people from 18 to 50 years of age. Although 17 percent of the men and 3 percent of the women said they had had sex with at least 21 partners, the overall impression from the survey was that for most Americans, marriage and monogamy rule sexual behavior. Married couples reported having sex most often and were the most likely to have orgasms when they did.

The Psychological Inquiry shows the frequency of sex for married and noncohabiting individuals in the year before the survey was taken. Nearly 75 percent of the married

psychological
inquiry

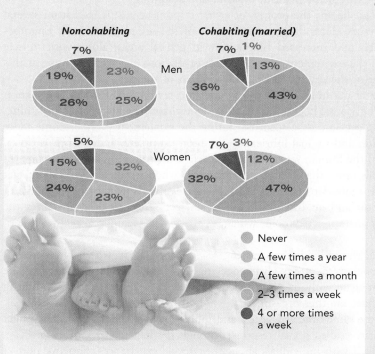

Noncohabiting

Men

7% · 23% · 19% · 26% · 25%

Women

5% · 32% · 15% · 24% · 23%

Cohabiting (married)

Men

7% · 1% · 13% · 36% · 43%

Women

7% · 3% · 12% · 32% · 47%

- Never
- A few times a year
- A few times a month
- 2–3 times a week
- 4 or more times a week

Sex in America

These pie charts show the responses of noncohabiting and cohabiting (married) men and women to the question "How often have you had sex in the past year?" (Michael & others, 1994). Notice that for this type of graph, the area of the pie that is taken up by a response is proportional to the percentage of people giving that response. After studying the charts, answer these questions:

1. Overall, who reported having the most and the least sex?

2. The graphs separate those who are married from those who are not. For which gender did being married matter most in terms of frequency of sex?

3. When the respondents reported on having had sex, what behaviors do you think they included? Do you think these behaviors were the same for men and women? Explain.

4. Do you think that self-report is a good way to find out about sexual behavior? What other methods might researchers use to measure this variable?

men and 85 percent of the married women indicated that they had never been unfaithful. More recent surveys have shown similar results. For instance, in 2004 ABC polled a nationally representative sample and found that individuals in committed relationships had more sex than singles, and the vast majority reported themselves as sexually faithful (ABC News, 2004).

What exactly are people doing when they say they are having sex, and how often are they doing it? In 2002, the Centers for Disease Control conducted a study of sexual behaviors in the United States (Mosher, Chandra, & Jones, 2005). The findings were that among people ages 15 to 44, 10 percent of men and 8 percent of women had never had sex, including vaginal intercourse, oral sex, and anal sex. Among adults ages 25 to 44 years, 97 percent had had vaginal intercourse, and 90 percent had had oral sex. Among men, 40 percent had had anal sex, and among women 35 percent had done so.

A study of a representative sample of nearly 3,000 Swedes examined the frequency of different sexual behaviors (including vaginal intercourse, masturbation, oral sex, and anal sex) in the previous month (Brody & Costa, 2009). Results showed that on average, men reported having vaginal intercourse 5 times and masturbating 4.5 times in the previous month. On average, women reported having vaginal intercourse about 5 times but masturbated less than 2 times during the previous month. For both men and women, oral sex occurred approximately 2 times and anal sex less than once (Brody & Costa, 2009).

What do gay men and lesbian women do when they "have sex"? Research is limited but suggests that among gay men, mutual masturbation, oral sex, and anal sex are common, although as many as a third of gay men report never having engaged in anal sex (Reisner & others, 2009). Among lesbian women, practices include genital-to-genital contact (body rubbing), mutual fondling and masturbation, penetration with the hands or other objects, and oral sex (Marrazzo, Coffey, & Bingham, 2005; Mercer & others, 2007).

The Human Sexual Response Pattern

Regardless of the specific behavior, similar physical processes are involved in sexual responses. To examine the physiological processes involved in sexual activity, William Masters and Virginia Johnson (1966) carefully observed and measured the physiological responses of 382 female and 312 male volunteers as they masturbated or had vaginal intercourse. Masters and Johnson identified a **human sexual response pattern** consisting of four phases—excitement, plateau, orgasm, and resolution.

● **human sexual response pattern**
Masters and Johnson's model of human sexual response, consisting of four phases—excitement, plateau, orgasm, and resolution.

The *excitement phase* begins the process of erotic responsiveness; it lasts from several minutes to several hours, depending on the nature of the sex play involved. Engorgement of blood vessels and increased blood flow in genital areas, along with muscle tension, characterize the excitement phase. The most obvious signs of response in this phase are lubrication of the vagina and partial erection of the penis.

The second phase of the human sexual response, the *plateau phase,* is a continuation and heightening of the arousal begun in the excitement phase. The increases in breathing, pulse rate, and blood pressure that occurred during the excitement phase become more intense, penile erection and vaginal lubrication are more complete, and orgasm is closer.

The third phase of the human sexual response cycle is *orgasm.* How long does orgasm last? Some individuals sense that time is standing still when it takes place, but in fact orgasm lasts for only about 3 to 15 seconds. Orgasm involves an explosive discharge of neuromuscular tension and an intensely pleasurable feeling. With orgasm comes the release of the neurotransmitter oxytocin, which, as we saw in Chapter 3, plays a role in social bonding.

Following orgasm, the individual enters the *resolution phase,* in which blood vessels return to their normal state. A sex difference in this phase is that females may be stimulated to orgasm again without delay, whereas males enter a *refractory period* during which they cannot have another orgasm.

Working around the same time as Masters and Johnson was sex therapist Helen Singer Kaplan (1974). Kaplan studied sexual response through the lens of her clinical practice, during which she talked with individuals about their sexual experiences. Kaplan's view of the sexual response differed from Masters and Johnson's in that she added a key initial stage: *desire*. Kaplan discovered that for many of her clients, sexual desire was sometimes lacking. Kaplan's work highlighted the very important role of motivation in sexual activity. Clearly, she argued, without the desire to have sex, the stages described by Masters and Johnson may never get started. We will return to the human sexual response and the issue of desire later in this chapter when we survey sexual disorders.

Cognition and Other Factors in Sexual Behavior

Sexual behavior is influenced by a variety of factors, ranging from sensation and perception to the ways we think about sexuality (Crooks & Baur, 2014). Finding someone sexually attractive may involve seeing the person, getting to know him or her, and feeling emotionally attached. Certainly, our thoughts play an important role in our sexuality (Kelly, 2006). We might be sexually attracted to someone but understand that we must inhibit our sexual urges until the relationship has time to develop. We have the cognitive capacity to respect our partners and not take sexual advantage of them. We also have the cognitive resources to generate sexual images—to become sexually aroused just by thinking about something erotic.

Recall from Chapter 7 that scripts are mental schemas for events. Sexuality is influenced by *sexual scripts,* patterns of expectancies for how people should behave sexually (Stulhofer, Busko, & Landripet, 2010). We carry these scripts with us in our memories, and men and women have different sexual scripts (McCabe, Tanner, & Heiman, 2010). For men, sex may center more on the genitals, with orgasm being a crucial aspect; for women, sex may be more an expression of intimacy, with orgasm an optional feature (van Lankveld, 2008).

Cognitive interpretation of sexual activity also involves our perceptions of the individual with whom we are having sex, and his or her perceptions of us (Miller, Perlman, & Brehm, 2009). Is this sexual encounter a symbol of a more enduring relationship or just a hookup?

THE INFLUENCE OF CULTURE

The influence of culture on sexuality was demonstrated dramatically in a classic analysis by John Messenger (1971) of the people living on the small island of Inis Beag off the coast of Ireland. They knew nothing about tongue kissing or hand stimulation of the penis, and they detested nudity. For both females and males, premarital sex was out of the question. Men avoided most sexual experiences because they believed that sexual intercourse reduced their energy level and was bad for their health. In this group, sexual intercourse occurred only at night, taking place as quickly as possible. As you might suspect, female orgasm was rare in this culture (Messenger, 1971).

In contrast, around the same time that Messenger was studying the people of Inis Beag, Donald Marshall (1971) studied the Mangaian culture in the South Pacific. In Mangaia, young boys were taught about masturbation and were encouraged to engage in it as much as they liked. At age 13, the boys underwent a ritual initiating them into sexual manhood. First, their elders instructed them about sexual strategies, including how to aid their female partner in having orgasms. Two weeks later, the boy had intercourse with an experienced woman who helped him hold back from ejaculation until she experienced orgasm with him. By the end of adolescence, Mangaians had sex pretty much every day. Mangaian women reported a high frequency of orgasm.

Donald Marshall's work focused on the sexual practices of the people of the South Pacific island of Mangaia.

Few cultures are as isolated and homogeneous as those of Inis Beag and Mangaia. In the United States, sexual behaviors and attitudes reflect the country's diverse multicultural population, falling somewhere in the middle of a continuum going from repressive to open.

SEX EDUCATION

One way that societies teach youth about sex and sexuality is through formal education. Although many topics associated with sex and sexuality spur controversy, most people concerned with sex education share two simple and relatively uncontroversial goals: to encourage the very young to delay sexual activity and to reduce teen pregnancy and sexually transmitted infections. However, there are many different opinions on *how* to achieve these goals.

Comprehensive sex education involves providing students with comprehensive knowledge about sexual behavior, birth control, and the use of condoms in protecting against sexually transmitted infections, while encouraging them to delay sexual activity and practice abstinence. Another form of sex education is the *abstinence-only* approach, which has become increasingly common in the United States. According to federal guidelines (Family and Youth Services Bureau, 2004), abstinence-only educational programs must emphasize that any sexual behavior outside of marriage is harmful to individuals of any age. Instructors can present contraceptives and condoms only in terms of their failure rates. Abstinence-only sex education promotes the notion that abstinence is the only effective way to avoid pregnancy and sexually transmitted infections (Family and Youth Services Bureau, 2004).

Which approach to sex education most effectively delays sexual activity and prevents teen pregnancy? Research strongly indicates that comprehensive sex education outstrips abstinence-only programs in achieving these goals. Two research reviews found that abstinence-only programs do not delay the initiation of sexual intercourse and do not reduce HIV-risk behaviors (Kirby, 2008; Kirby, Laris, & Rolleri, 2007; Underhill, Montgomery, & Operario, 2007). Further, a study revealed that adolescents who experienced comprehensive sex education were less likely to report adolescent pregnancies than those who received abstinence-only sex education or no sex education (Kohler, Manhart, & Lafferty, 2008). A number of leading experts on adolescent sexuality now conclude that sex education programs that emphasize contraceptive knowledge do not increase the incidence of sexual intercourse and are more likely to reduce the risk of adolescent pregnancy and sexually transmitted infections than abstinence-only programs (Constantine, 2008; M. E. Eisenberg & others, 2008; Hampton, 2008; Hyde & DeLamater, 2011).

In many communities in the United States, educational practices have not caught up with the research findings. A recent study of more than 350 middle and high school sex educators found that many felt they were limited in the breadth of information they could share with students, concerning topics such as communicating about sex, teen parenting, abortion, and sexual orientation (M. E. Eisenberg & others, 2013). Perhaps in part due to such issues, the United States has the highest rate of adolescent pregnancy and childbearing in the developed world, though there are encouraging trends. In 2010, the U.S. birth rate for 15- to 19-year-olds was 34.3 births per 1,000 females, the lowest rate ever recorded, which represents a 42 percent decrease from 1991 (Hamilton, Martin, & Ventura, 2012).

test yourself

1. What are some different ways that people define sexual behavior, or "sex"?
2. What do studies indicate about the frequency of sex among married partners and among people in committed relationships versus single people?
3. What are two kinds of sex education, and how effective is each?

6· SEXUAL VARIATIONS AND DISORDERS

If we think of sexual behavior as any behavior that involves sexual pleasure, then we can say that there are many different kinds of sexual behavior. When it comes to sexual pleasure, in fact, variation is the norm. In this section we consider some variant sexual behaviors and draw a contrast between behavior that is pleasurable but not harmful versus behavior that is harmful. We also consider some common disorders of sexual response and desire.

Fetishes

People are sexually aroused by different activities. A man might be sexually stimulated by wearing women's clothing. A woman might be turned on by wearing a necktie. A **fetish** is an object or activity that arouses sexual interest and desire. Fetishes include erotic materials (such as pornographic images and films), clothing, and other physical objects (Gijs, 2008). A person with a *transvestic fetish* (who may be heterosexual or homosexual) gets sexual pleasure from wearing clothing of the opposite sex. *Sadomasochism,* one person (the sadistic partner) gains sexual pleasure from dominating another person (the masochist), who in turn enjoys being dominated.

These behaviors may be unusual, but they are not generally considered abnormal. Indeed, unusual sexual practices are typically considered harmless variations as long as these principles are not violated: The individuals are consenting adults; they do not experience personal distress; and they are not putting themselves in danger of physical harm or death as a result of their activities (Gijs, 2008). When a variation in sexual behavior violates one or more of these principles, however, it may qualify as a *paraphilic disorder,* considered next.

● **fetish** An object or activity that arouses sexual interest and desire.

Paraphilic Disorders

The American Psychiatric Association (2013a) defines **paraphilic disorders** as psychological disorders that involve

- Sexual interests that cause personal distress (beyond that simply resulting from societal disapproval).
- Sexual desires or behaviors that involve another persons' psychological distress, injury, or death.
- Desire for sexual behavior involving unwilling persons or those who cannot give legal consent.

Figure 11.6 lists the various paraphilic disorders that the American Psychiatric Association recognizes.

What causes paraphilic disorders? There is no one answer to this question. Each disorder may have its own origin. Some experts have suggested that principles of classical

● **paraphilic disorders** Sexual disorders that feature recurrent sexually arousing fantasies, urges, or behaviors involving nonhuman objects; the suffering or humiliation of oneself or one's partner; or children or other nonconsenting individuals.

Paraphilic Disorder	Focus
Exhibitionistic Disorder	Exposing one's genitals to a stranger
Fetishistic Disorder	Using nonliving objects for sexual pleasure
Frotteuristic Disorder	Touching and rubbing against a person who has not given consent— for instance, in a crowded subway car
Pedophilic Disorder	Sexual activity with a prepubescent child
Sexual Masochism Disorder	Acts in which the individual derives sexual excitement from being humiliated, beaten, bound, or otherwise made to suffer
Sexual Sadism Disorder	Acts in which the individual derives sexual excitement from the psychological or physical suffering of the victim
Transvestic Disorder	Cross-dressing by a man or woman that causes distress or interferes with daily functioning
Voyeuristic Disorder	Observing unsuspecting individuals, usually strangers, who are naked or in the process of disrobing or engaging in sexual activity

FIGURE 11.6 Types of Paraphilic Disorders Recall that sexual variations are considered harmless if (1) they do not cause a person distress or physical harm; and (2) they do not violate another person. For some of the paraphilic disorders listed here, the issue is one of consent; for others the variations may only qualify as a disorder if they cause the person distress or interfere with daily living. Can you identify which of these principles apply to each?

conditioning can explain the emergence of some paraphilic disorders (Gijs, 2008; Pfaus & others, 2012). Recall that in classical conditioning, a conditioned stimulus (CS) is paired with another stimulus, the unconditioned stimulus (US), which provokes an unconditioned response (UR). After frequent pairings, the CS comes to evoke the response even in the absence of the US. Using this framework, we might say that a man with a shoe fetish might have been around shoes when he masturbated as a boy and that these experiences led to the fetish. For other paraphilic disorders, however, it is likely that more than associative learning is involved.

Pedophilic Disorder

● **pedophilic disorder** A paraphilic disorder in which an adult or an older adolescent sexually fantasizes about or engages in sexual behavior with individuals who have not reached puberty.

Pedophilic disorder is a psychological disorder in which an adult or an older adolescent sexually fantasizes about or engages in sexual behavior with individuals who have not reached puberty. Pedophilic disorder is more common in men than women (Seto, 2009).

The causes of pedophilic disorder are not well understood. Although it was once thought that most individuals who sexually abuse children were themselves sexually abused as children, this explanation has not held up to the evidence (U.S. General Accounting Office, 1996). Adults who sexually abuse children are more likely than other sex offenders to report themselves as having experienced sexual abuse in childhood (Jesperson, Lalumiere, & Seto, 2009), but the vast majority of individuals who have been sexually molested as children do not themselves go on to molest others.

Pedophilic disorder is associated with low self-esteem, poor social skills, low IQ (Hall & Hall, 2007), and a history of head injuries (causing unconsciousness) in childhood (Seto, 2009). The disorder is related to a pattern of cognitive distortions, including minimizing the harm of pedophilic activities, believing that sexual impulses are uncontrollable, and thinking that sexual relationships with children are consensual (Hall & Hall, 2007). Brain-imaging studies suggest that individuals who are sexually attracted to children show a pervasive pattern of brain dysfunction, related to connections between brain regions (Cantor & Blanchard, 2012; Cantor & others, 2008).

Given the potential damage that pedophilic behavior can inflict on its victims, identifying strategies for treatment and prevention is paramount. Therapies have targeted the learned associations between children and sexual arousal or have focused on training offenders in skills needed to recognize and avoid risky situations, such as being around children. Unfortunately, these treatments have not been effective (Marques & others, 2005; Seto, 2009).

In recent years, castration (either surgically, through removal of the testes, or chemically, through drugs that reduce testosterone) has been used to treat sex offenders who victimize children. Hundreds of surgical castrations of sex offenders have been performed throughout Europe, and nine U.S. states have laws that *require* chemical or surgical castration for sex offenders who commit crimes against children as a condition of parole (Seto, 2009). It is difficult to evaluate the effectiveness of castration, however, because individuals are not randomly assigned to the treatment, and those who undergo the procedure may be particularly motivated to change their behavior (Seto, 2009). Furthermore, some critics have suggested that castration is used primarily to punish, not to treat, and as such is unethical (Malón, 2012; Spaulding, 1998; R. G. Wright, 2008).

Acknowledging the difficulties in treating pedophilic disorder, Michael Seto (2009), an expert on the disorder, concluded that efforts should focus on preventing the disorder and implementing interventions aimed at child-victims. With respect to preventing pedophilic disorder, Seto argues that, given the evidence for a neurodevelopmental basis to the problem, enhanced prenatal care and early parenting interventions might be helpful in reducing the occurrence of pedophilic disorder. With respect to preventing abuse and protecting children, Seto advocates educating children to distinguish appropriate and inappropriate touch and empowering them to share their feelings with a trusted adult if someone is making them uncomfortable.

Disorders of Sexual Desire and Sexual Response

Paraphilic disorders are unusual. More common disorders of sexuality involve problems either in sexual desire or in the physical sexual response described by Masters and Johnson.

With regard to sexual desire disorders, studies suggest that up to a quarter of men and nearly half of women report sometimes being troubled with a general lack of interest in sex (Laumann & others, 2005; van Lankveld, 2008). Lack of sexual desire in both men and women can stem from low levels of androgen, stress, anxiety and depression, physical illnesses, and various medications (Hackett, 2008; van Lankveld, 2008). Treatments for lack of sexual desire include drug therapies, psychological therapies, and relationship counseling.

In terms of disorders related to sexual response, two common disorders in men are *erectile dysfunction,* the failure of the penis to become erect, and *premature ejaculation,* the experience of orgasm before the person wishes it. As we have seen, the male genitalia are complex, and the male sexual response involves a number of physiological reactions, from erection to ejaculation. It is not surprising that, at times, this elegant machinery does not function optimally.

In most cases, erectile dysfunction involves a combination of psychological and physical factors (Heidelbaugh, 2010; Lewis, Yuan, & Wang, 2008). Erectile dysfunction may be a symptom of an underlying physical illness, such as diabetes, and is more likely to occur with age. Treatment typically involves medications, such as Viagra, that allow the individual to experience erection (Althof & others, 2010; Claes, 2010).

Premature ejaculation is the most common sexual complaint among men under the age of 40 (Rowland & McMahon, 2008). Psychological, physical, and relationship factors can play a role in premature ejaculation. The problem may be treated with drugs or therapy and may also involve working together with one's sexual partner to develop greater mastery over the sexual response.

Women can also suffer from disorders of sexual response, including problems in sexual arousal and in the experience of orgasm. For some women, dysfunction in arousal is explained by problems in the autonomic nervous system that disrupt the engorgement of the labia and lubrication of the vagina; for other women, the subjective feeling of arousal is absent even when these physical changes occur (Meston, Seal, & Hamilton, 2008). Disorders of sexual orgasm in women involve delayed or absent orgasm during sexual activity. Both of these types of disorders can be related to the experience of childhood sexual abuse, as well as to strict religious beliefs and negative sexual attitudes (van Lankveld, 2008). These disorders of sexual response may be treated with androgens or through psychotherapy. Addressing underlying physical causes can also sometimes improve sexual function.

The occasional occurrence of erectile dysfunction or premature ejaculation in males, and problems with arousal and orgasm in females, are common and normal. It is when these problems cause distress for the individual or difficulties in important relationships that they are considered disorders in need of treatment.

Variations, Disorders, and the Meaning of Normality

A theme throughout this discussion has been whether variations in sexual behavior are problems that require professional help or whether they represent harmless differences that simply reflect human diversity. The difficulties people have in talking about sexuality only perpetuate anxiety, shame, and concern about sex. People are not ashamed to admit that they like certain foods and dislike others. Imagine if we treated sexual tastes in a similarly open way.

test yourself

1. What three principles must not be violated for a variation in sexual behavior to be considered harmless?
2. Why is it difficult to determine the effectiveness of surgical or chemical castration as a treatment for pedophilia?
3. Give examples of sexual response disorders experienced by men, as well as examples of such disorders experienced by women.

7. SEXUALITY AND HEALTH AND WELLNESS

Many of us would agree that healthy sexual activity is an important component of the good life. Yet, for a variety of reasons, we often do not talk about this aspect of our behavior. In this concluding section, we consider two aspects of the intersection of sexuality with health and wellness—first, its implications for physical health; and second, its role in psychological well-being.

Sexual Behavior and Physical Health

● **sexually transmitted infection (STI)** An infection that is contracted primarily through sexual activity—vaginal intercourse as well as oral and anal sex.

A key consideration in any discussion of sexual health is sexually transmitted infections. A **sexually transmitted infection (STI)** is an infection that is contracted primarily through sexual activity—vaginal intercourse as well as oral and anal sex. According to the U.S. Centers for Disease Control, the United States is experiencing an STI "epidemic" (Alexander, 2013).

TYPES AND CAUSES OF SEXUALLY TRANSMITTED INFECTIONS

Some STIs are bacterial in origin, as are gonorrhea and syphilis. Others are caused by viruses, as in the case of genital herpes and HIV. STIs are a top health concern because they can have implications for a person's future fertility, risk of cancer, and life expectancy.

● **acquired immune deficiency syndrome (AIDS)** A sexually transmitted infection, caused by the human immunodeficiency virus (HIV), that destroys the body's immune system.

No single STI has had a greater impact on sexual behavior in the past decades than HIV. **Acquired immune deficiency syndrome (AIDS)** is caused by the *human immunodeficiency virus (HIV),* a sexually transmitted infection that destroys the body's immune system. Without treatment, most people who contract HIV are vulnerable to germs that a healthy immune system can destroy.

Recent improvements in drug therapies have given rise to the view that HIV is a chronic rather than a terminal condition. Because of increased education and the development of more effective drug therapies, deaths due to AIDS have declined in the United States (CDC, 2013b). There are no solid estimates for the life expectancy of someone who is HIV positive, because the existing treatments have been around for only about a decade. Even in this era of improved treatments, however, HIV remains an incurable infection that can lead to early death. Many individuals who are HIV positive are not in treatment, and over 20 percent of those who are HIV positive do not know that they are (CDC, 2013b).

PRACTICING SAFE SEX

Anyone who is sexually active is at risk of contracting HIV and other STIs. The only 100 percent safe behavior is abstinence from sex, which most individuals do not view as an option. Sensual activities such as kissing, French kissing, cuddling, massage, and mutual masturbation (that does not involve the exchange of bodily fluids) involve no risk of an STI. Sexual activities that involve penetration, including vaginal and anal intercourse as well as oral sex, are riskier behaviors that can be made less risky with the use of proper protection.

Generally, condoms are key in the prevention of STIs. In your own sexual experience, it may be difficult to gauge the accuracy of a partner's estimates of risk and his or her status with respect to having an STI. The wisest course of action is always to protect yourself by using a latex condom. When correctly used, latex condoms help to prevent or significantly reduce the risk of transmission of many STIs (Wald, Langenberg, & Krantz, 2005; Winer & others, 2006).

Research has shown that programs to promote safe sex are especially effective if they include the eroticization of condom use—that is, making condoms a part of the sensual experience of foreplay (Scott-Sheldon & Johnson, 2006). Analyses of HIV

This couple probably had no trouble talking openly about their preferences and safety concerns before embarking on this bike ride. Shouldn't sex be like that too?

prevention programs (including over 350 intervention groups and 100 control groups) by Delores Albarracin and her colleagues have produced important recommendations for the best ways to influence behavior (Albarracin, Durantini, & Earl, 2006; Albarracin & others, 2005; Durantini & others, 2006). The studies have found that fear tactics are relatively less effective and that programs emphasizing active skill building (for example, role playing the use of condoms), self-efficacy, and positive attitudes about condom use are effective with most groups. Making safe sex sexy is a great way to practice safe sex.

Sexual Behavior and Psychological Well-Being

Researchers have been particularly interested in people's motives for having sex. Lynne Cooper and her colleagues (Cooper, Shapiro, & Powers, 1998; Cooper & others, 2011) examined the sex motives of a sample of adolescents and young adults whom they followed longitudinally over several years. The researchers examined the reasons these individuals gave for having sex. The participants' reported motives included the following: to connect intimately with someone, to enhance their own self-esteem, to gain a partner's and peers' approval, and to avoid feeling distressed or lonely. Engaging in sex as a form of intimacy with another person was related to having fewer sex partners overall and to practicing less risky sex (Cooper, Shapiro, & Powers, 1998). Conversely, individuals who had sex to cope with negative feelings were less likely to have stable long-term relationships and tended to engage in more unsafe sex. Subsequent research has shown that having sex in order to be close to another person is related to enhanced well-being, but engaging in sex to avoid bad feelings is linked with decreases in well-being (Impett, Peplau, & Gable, 2005).

Research has solidly supported the role of sexual activity in well-being (Brody & Costa, 2009). Furthermore, although the frequency of sexual behavior may decline with age, sexuality remains a significant part of human identity and relationships throughout life (DeLamater & Moorman, 2007; Lindau & Gavrilova, 2010). Importantly, partnered sexual activity is a strong predictor of satisfaction in relationships even when those activities do not include vaginal intercourse (DeLamater & Moorman, 2007; Kennedy, Haque, & Zarankow, 1997). Throughout the life span, then, sexual activities remain a source of pleasure and an avenue for the experience of intimacy with another (Inelmen & others, 2012; Mroczek & others, 2013).

test yourself

1. What is a sexually transmitted infection (STI)?

2. What contraceptive device is key in efforts to protect individuals from contracting STIs? Against what does it offer the most protection?

3. What motives for having sex are associated with increased well-being? With decreased well-being?

SUMMARY

1. DEFINING SEX AND GENDER

Sex refers to biological aspects of the person that are used to classify him or her as male or female. Biological features that serve in this capacity include genes, gonads, hormones, genitals, and secondary sexual characteristics. *Gender* refers to the person's psychological sense of himself or herself as male or female. Gender is sometimes described in terms of a person's level of instrumentality or expressiveness.

Disorders of sexual development are conditions in which a person's genetic, genital, or gonadal sex is atypical. In these cases, the sex in which the child was raised is the most consistent predictor of eventual gender identity.

Individuals who feel trapped in the wrong biological sex are referred to as *transgender*. Transgender individuals are sometimes considered to be suffering from gender dysphoria, which involves intense distress over one's birth sex. Treatment for transgender individuals generally involves steps from reversible interventions to irreversible changes, such as sex reassignment surgery.

2. THEORIES OF GENDER DEVELOPMENT

Perspectives on gender development include biological, evolutionary psychology, social cognitive, and social role theories. Biological approaches focus on the ways that genes, hormones, and brain structures relate to gender differences. Evolutionary psychology views gender through the lens of Darwinian natural selection and states that human beings have evolved through a process of sexual selection in which males compete for mates and females choose their male partners. Social cognitive approaches to gender emphasize how learning, modeling, and cognitive schemas influence the development of gender. Social role theory states that a division of labor between the sexes that is based on male–female physical differences can lead to the social construction of gender roles and gender stereotypes. Social role theory predicts that as social structures change, gender differences should decline.

3. THE PSYCHOLOGY OF GENDER DIFFERENCES

Stereotypes tells us women are more emotional than men, but research suggests this difference may be due to social expectations. Women tend to perform better than men in tasks requiring theory of mind ability. In addition, women are more likely than men to help if helping involves safety, while men are more likely than women to help if helping involves risk. With regard to cognition, girls are better at verbal tasks, and boys are better at spatial tasks, though these differences are relatively small. In terms of aggression, males tend to be more overtly aggressive than females. Females are more relationally than overtly aggressive.

Sexuality refers to the ways people experience and express themselves as sexual beings. Many stereotypes about gender differences in sexuality have not been supported by research. Men do report more frequent sexual arousal and are more likely than women to masturbate. They have more permissive attitudes about casual premarital sex as well. Women are more likely than men to show fluidity in their sexual attractions.

4. SEXUAL ORIENTATION

Sexual orientation refers to the direction of a person's erotic interest and includes heterosexuality, homosexuality, and bisexuality. Sexual orientation is generally measured using questionnaires. The vast majority of people are heterosexual; the number of homosexual or bisexual individuals is between 2 and 10 percent of the population.

Possible explanations for sexual orientation include genetic factors, prenatal hormone exposure, and brain differences. Genes explain a relatively small amount of the variation we see in sexual orientation. Some research indicates that gay men have thicker corpus callosa than heterosexual men. Other research suggests that lesbian women may be more similar to heterosexual men in terms of brain hemisphere asymmetry. Social factors do not seem to play a large role in sexual orientation.

Gay men and lesbian women are similar to their heterosexual counterparts in many ways, but they do show higher levels of relationship satisfaction and are more likely to break up than heterosexual married couples. Gay men and lesbian women in civil unions are less likely to break up than those without such unions. Children with gay parents tend to be as well-adjusted as children with heterosexual parents.

5. SEXUAL BEHAVIORS AND PRACTICES

Research suggests that married couples have sex more often than unmarried couples and singles. Vaginal intercourse is the most common sexual practice for men and women. Both men and women report engaging in oral sex more than anal sex. Regardless of the particular sexual activity, the human sexual response pattern is characterized by four stages—excitement, plateau, orgasm, and resolution.

Sexual desire is a key element in sexual behavior. Sensation, perception, and cognition are all important components of sexual activity. Culture plays a role in sexuality as well.

Some people worry that providing adolescents with comprehensive sex education will lead to premature sexual activity. However, research strongly suggests that education is crucial to preventing unwanted pregnancy.

6. SEXUAL VARIATIONS AND DISORDERS

With regard to sexual tastes and activities, variation is the norm. A fetish is an object that a person finds sexually arousing.

Paraphilic disorders are sexual disorders featuring recurrent sexually arousing fantasies, urges, or behaviors involving nonhuman objects; the suffering or humiliation of oneself or one's partner; or children or other nonconsenting individuals. Pedophilic disorder is a particularly harmful paraphilic disorder involving sexual attraction to children. It is very difficult to treat.

Disorders of sexual desire and sexual response are relatively common. Two common disorders of sexual response in men are erectile dysfunction and premature ejaculation. In women, common sexual response disorders include problems in arousal and in experiencing orgasm.

7. SEXUALITY AND HEALTH AND WELLNESS

Sexually transmitted infections (STIs) are infections that can be spread through sexual contact, including vaginal, anal, and oral sex. When used properly and consistently, latex condoms offer excellent protection against many STIs, including AIDS.

The relationship between sexual behavior and psychological wellness depends on the reasons people have sex. Those who engage in sexual activity based on intimacy motives have fewer overall sex partners and are more likely to practice safe sex. Those who engage in sex to win a partner's approval or to cope with negative feelings tend to show decreases in well-being and to engage in more sexual risk taking. Sexuality is an important aspect of psychological well-being throughout the life span.

key *terms*

sex, p. 358

sex chromosomes, p. 358

gonads, p. 358

secondary sex characteristics, p. 359

gender, p. 359

gender identity, p. 359

androgynous, p. 360

disorders of sexual development (DSD), p. 361

transgender, p. 362

sexual selection, p. 364

social role theory, p. 366

gender roles, p. 367

gender stereotypes, p. 367

empathy, p. 370

gender similarities hypothesis, p. 372

aggression, p. 372

overt aggression, p. 372

relational aggression, p. 372

sexuality, p. 373

sexual orientation, p. 376

heterosexual, p. 376

homosexual, p. 376

bisexual, p. 376

human sexual response pattern, p. 384

fetish, p. 387

paraphilic disorders, p. 387

pedophilic disorder, p. 388

sexually transmitted infection (STI), p. 390

acquired immune deficiency syndrome (AIDS), p. 390

apply your *knowledge*

1. Ask your parents about your gender-related behavior as a child and about their views on how their parenting influenced your gender development. Do their recollections ring true with your memories? What factors do you think played a role in your gender development?

2. Set aside a day and keep a gender-awareness diary. Try to notice every time you have an experience in which your gender matters to your life. From the moment you get up in the morning until you go to bed at night, if you are man, ask yourself, "Would I be doing this if I were a woman?" If you are a woman, ask yourself, "Would I be doing this if I were a man?" When you see a woman performing an activity, ask yourself, "Would this seem appropriate to me if a man were doing it?" Write down your thoughts and feelings about these activities, and reflect on the role of gender in your daily life.

3. The evolutionary psychology approach to gender suggests that men are more likely to seek women who are younger than they are and that women are more likely to seek older men with resources. Check the personal ads from a local paper or on Craigslist and examine those placed by men and women. Does the ads' content support predictions about what men and women look for?

4. States differ in terms of their laws regarding gay and lesbian marriage, adoption rights, and employment protections. Research your own state's legal policies toward the rights of gay men and women. Summarize those rights. Does your state also have laws about the protection of transgender rights?

5. Conduct web searches for "transgender experience" and "gender identity disorder." How do the sites you find differ in terms of their discussion of a person who feels trapped in the wrong sex?

CHAPTER 12

Personality

Picking Up Where They Left Off, 76 Years Ago

Thanks to social media, keeping track of long-lost friends is easier than it used to be. Looking at Facebook posts from someone you knew in first grade, you probably recognize that person as the friend you had from long ago.

Friendships are like that. Margot Slodzina and Renée Duering were best friends as children in Cologne, Germany, in the 1930s. They met in a Jewish girl scout troop and became best friends. When they were 13 years old in 1934, Hitler's rise to power divided the girls. Margot's family fled to Spain and Renée's father was arrested. Years later, Renee and her husband were sent to Auschwitz concentration camp. Both girls survived, and through the work of their children and grandchildren (and some help from the Internet), they were reunited in 2000. In San Francisco airport, they saw each other for the first time in 76 years, at the ages of 88 and 89. Overjoyed, the two women quickly began to talk as if those 76 years had never happened. "We are picking up where we left off," declared Renée (Palevsky, 2000).

How is it possible to feel that way, after nearly eight decades? Surely, for Margot and Renée many things had changed, but something about each of them remained the same. There is something about each person that makes that person who he or she is—that makes the person recognizable as those who "knew them when," whether from the first day of school, at summer camp, or in college. Age and life experiences can change us, but something about us endures throughout life. That "something" is personality, the focus of this chapter. ●

PREVIEW

Personality psychology explores the psychological attributes that underlie who we really are—the unified and enduring core characteristics that account for our existence as one and the same person throughout the life span. In this chapter, we survey the field of personality from a variety of perspectives. We begin with classic theories from psychodynamic and humanistic thinkers and then examine more contemporary approaches, including the trait, life story, social cognitive, and biological perspectives. We then look at personality assessment. Finally, we consider the role of personality in health and wellness.

1. PSYCHODYNAMIC PERSPECTIVES

● **personality** A pattern of enduring, distinctive thoughts, emotions, and behaviors that characterize the way an individual adapts to the world.

● **psychodynamic perspectives** Theoretical views emphasizing that personality is primarily unconscious (beyond awareness).

Personality is a pattern of enduring, distinctive thoughts, emotions, and behaviors that characterize the way an individual adapts to the world. Psychologists have approached these enduring characteristics in a variety of ways, focusing on different aspects of the person.

Psychodynamic perspectives on personality emphasize that personality is primarily unconscious. According to this viewpoint, the enduring patterns that make up personality are largely unavailable to our conscious awareness, and they powerfully shape our behaviors in ways that we cannot readily comprehend (Bornstein, Denckla, & Chung, 2013). Psychodynamic theorists use the word *unconscious* differently from how other psychologists do. From the psychodynamic perspective, aspects of our personality are unconscious because they *must* be: These mysterious, unconscious forces are simply too frightening to be part of our awareness.

Psychodynamic theorists believe that behavior is only a surface characteristic and that to truly understand someone's personality, we have to explore the symbolic meanings of that behavior and the deep inner workings of the mind (C. Levin, 2010; Westen, Gabbard, & Soto, 2008). Psychodynamic theorists also stress that early childhood experience shapes adult personality. The psychodynamic view of personality was introduced by Sigmund Freud.

Freud's Psychoanalytic Theory

Sigmund Freud, one of the most influential thinkers of the twentieth century, was born in Freiberg, Moravia (today part of the Czech Republic), in 1856 and died in London at the age of 83. Freud spent most of his life in Vienna, leaving that city near the end of his career to escape the Holocaust.

Freud has had such a phenomenal impact that just about everyone has an opinion about him, even those who have never studied his work. If you ask others what they think of Freud, you will likely get a variety of interesting answers. Some might comment that Freud was a cocaine addict. Freud did use cocaine early in his career, but he stopped using the drug when he learned of its harmful effects. Others might claim that Freud hated women. As we will see, Freud's theory of development did include the notion that women are morally inferior to men. However, Freud was never satisfied with his approach to the psychology of women. He welcomed women interested in pursuing careers in psychoanalysis, and many of his earliest followers were women. Finally, people might declare that Freud thought everything was about sex. That claim, it turns out, is true, except by *sex* Freud did not mean sexual activity in the usual sense. Freud defined sex as organ pleasure. *Anything* that is pleasurable is sex, according to Freud.

For Freud, the sexual drive was the most important motivator in human life. Freud thought that the human sex drive was the main determinant of personality development, and he felt that psychological disorders, dreams, and all human behavior represent the conflict between unconscious sexual drive and the demands of civilized human society.

Sigmund Freud (1856–1939)
Freud's theories have strongly influenced how people in Western cultures view themselves and the world.

Freud developed *psychoanalysis,* his approach to personality, through his work with patients suffering from hysteria. *Hysteria* refers to physical symptoms that have no physical cause. For instance, a person might be unable to see, even with perfectly healthy eyes, or unable to walk, despite having no physical injury.

In Freud's day (the Victorian era, a time marked by strict rules regarding sex), many young women suffered from hysterical symptoms, physical problems that could not be explained by actual physical illness. In his practice, Freud spent long hours listening to these women talk about their symptoms. Freud came to understand that the hysterical symptoms stemmed from unconscious conflicts, centered on experiences in which the person's drive for pleasure was thwarted by the social pressures of Victorian society. Moreover, the particular symptoms were related symbolically to these underlying conflicts.

For instance, one of Freud's patients, Fraulein Elisabeth Von R., suffered from leg pains that prevented her from standing or walking. Through analysis, Freud discovered that Fraulein Elisabeth had had a number of experiences in which she wanted nothing more than to take a walk but had been prevented from doing so by her duty to her ill father. Fraulein Elisabeth's symptoms were not due to a single experience, but rather to *many repeated* experiences, all related to walking.

Based on such observations, Freud concluded that hysterical symptoms were *overdetermined,* meaning that those symptoms had *many* causes in the unconscious. Eventually, Freud came to use hysterical symptoms as his metaphor for understanding dreams, slips of the tongue, and all human behavior. Everything we do, he said, has a multitude of unconscious causes.

Drawing from his analyses of patients (as well as himself), Freud developed a model of human personality. He saw personality as like an iceberg, existing mostly below the level of awareness, just as the massive part of an iceberg lies beneath the surface of the water. Figure 12.1 illustrates this analogy and depicts the extensiveness of the unconscious part of our mind, in Freud's view.

FIGURE 12.1   The Conscious and Unconscious Mind: The Iceberg Analogy The Iceberg analogy illustrates how much of the mind is unconscious in Freud's theory. The conscious mind is the part of the iceberg above water; the unconscious mind, the part below water. Notice that the id is totally unconscious, whereas the ego and the superego can operate at either the conscious or the unconscious level.

STRUCTURES OF PERSONALITY

The three parts of the iceberg in Figure 12.1 reflect the three structures of personality described by Freud. Freud (1917) called these structures the id, the ego, and the superego. You can get a better feel for these Latin labels by considering their English translations: The id is literally the "it," the ego is the "I," and the superego is the "above-I."

The **id** consists of unconscious drives and is the individual's reservoir of sexual energy. This "it" is a pool of amoral and often vile urges pressing for expression. In Freud's view, the id has no contact with reality. The id works according to the *pleasure principle,* the Freudian concept that the id seeks immediate gratification.

> ● **id** The Freudian structure of personality consisting of unconscious drives; the individual's reservoir of sexual energy.

The world would be pretty scary if personalities were all id. As young children mature, they learn that they cannot act on every impulse: They cannot snatch every candy or slug other children. They must negotiate with others to get the things they want. As children experience the constraints of reality, a new element of personality is formed—the **ego,** the Freudian structure of personality that deals with the demands of reality. According to Freud, the ego abides by the *reality principle.* It tries to get the id what it wants within the norms of society. Whereas the id is completely unconscious, the ego is partly conscious. It houses our higher mental functions—reasoning, problem solving, and decision making, for example.

> ● **ego** The Freudian structure of personality that deals with the demands of reality.

The id and ego do not consider whether something is right or wrong. Rather, the **superego** is the harsh internal judge of our behavior. The superego is reflected in what we often call conscience and evaluates the morality of our behavior.

The ego acts as a mediator between the conflicting demands of the id and the superego, as well as the real world. Your ego might say, for example, "I will have sex only in

> ● **superego** The Freudian structure of personality that serves as the harsh internal judge of our behavior; what we often call conscience.

a committed relationship and always practice safe sex." Your id, however, screams, "Sex! Now!" and your superego commands, "Sex? Don't even think about it."

DEFENSE MECHANISMS

The conflicts that erupt among the demands of the id, the superego, and reality create a great deal of anxiety for the ego. The ego has strategies for dealing with this anxiety, called defense mechanisms. **Defense mechanisms** are tactics the ego uses to *reduce* anxiety by unconsciously *distorting* reality. For example, imagine that Jason's id is pressing to express an unconscious desire to have sex with his mother. Clearly, acting on this impulse would not please the superego or society at large. If he became aware of this impulse, Jason might recoil in horror. Instead, Jason's ego might use a defense mechanism of *displacement*. Displacement means directing unacceptable impulses at a less threatening target. So, Jason might develop a relationship with a girlfriend who looks and acts like his mother. Through displacement, the ego allows Jason to express his id impulse in a way that will not land him in trouble. Of course, Jason's friends might chuckle at the resemblance between his mother and his girlfriend, but you can bet that Jason will never notice.

Figure 12.2 describes several defense mechanisms, many of which were introduced and developed by Freud's daughter Anna, who followed in her father's career footsteps. All defense mechanisms reduce anxiety by distorting reality. Defense mechanisms are unconscious; we are not aware that we are calling on them.

Repression is the most powerful and pervasive defense mechanism. To reduce the anxiety caused by unacceptable id impulses, repression pushes these impulses back into the unconscious. Freud said, for example, that our early childhood experiences, many of which he believed were sexually laden, are too threatening for us to deal with consciously, so we reduce the anxiety of childhood conflict through repression.

Anna Freud (1895–1982) The youngest of Freud's six children, Anna Freud not only did influential work on defense mechanisms but also pioneered in the theory and practice of child psychoanalysis.

● **defense mechanisms** The Freudian term for tactics the ego uses to reduce anxiety by unconsciously distorting reality.

Defense Mechanism	How It Works	Example
Repression	The master defense mechanism; the ego pushes unacceptable impulses out of awareness, back into the unconscious mind.	A young girl was sexually abused by her uncle. As an adult, she can't remember anything about the traumatic experience.
Rationalization	The ego replaces a less acceptable motive with a more acceptable one.	A college student does not get into the fraternity of his choice. He tells himself that the fraternity is very exclusive and that a lot of students could not get in.
Displacement	The ego shifts feelings toward an unacceptable object to another, more acceptable object.	A woman can't take her anger out on her boss, so she goes home and takes it out on her husband.
Sublimation	The ego replaces an unacceptable impulse with a socially acceptable one.	A man with strong sexual urges becomes an artist who paints nudes.
Projection	The ego attributes personal shortcomings, problems, and faults to others.	A man who has a strong desire to have an extramarital affair accuses his wife of flirting with other men.
Reaction Formation	The ego transforms an unacceptable motive into its opposite.	A woman who fears her sexual urges becomes a religious zealot.
Denial	The ego refuses to acknowledge anxiety-producing realities.	A man won't acknowledge that he has cancer even though a team of doctors has diagnosed his cancer.
Regression	The ego seeks the security of an earlier developmental period in the face of stress.	A woman returns home to mother every time she and her husband have a big argument.

FIGURE 12.2 **Defense Mechanisms** Defense mechanisms reduce anxiety in various ways, in all instances by distorting reality.

CRITICAL CONTROVERSY

Do Defense Mechanisms Underlie Homophobia?

Have you noticed that sex scandals seem to erupt around people who have been staunch advocates of traditional sexual mores? Minister Ted Haggard, for example, was outspoken in his attacks on gay rights only to be revealed to be engaging in a secret sexual relationship with a male prostitute. Why would a person who experiences same-sex attraction be such a vocal opponent of gay rights?

The defense mechanism of reaction formation can explain such apparent hypocrisy. *Reaction formation* means that a person's conscious experience is the exact opposite of his or her unconscious feelings (see Figure 12.2). In reaction formation, unconscious attraction to members of one's sex is experienced as homophobia (prejudice against homosexual people). The idea that conscious negative feelings toward gay people are related to unconscious feelings of same-sex attraction was supported by a study showing that men who expressed a strong homophobia also showed higher sexual arousal to same-sex erotic material (Adams, Wright, & Lohr, 1996).

A more recent series of studies by Netta Weinstein and colleagues (2012) explored the relationship between unconscious same-sex feelings and homophobia. The researchers measured sexual orientation in two ways. One measure was thought to tap unconscious (or implicit) feelings, and the other assessed conscious (or explicit) feelings. Note that a participant's implicit and explicit sexual orientation could match up—or not. In a variety of studies, participants whose implicit and explicit sexual orientations matched reported lower homophobia compared to those

Minister Ted Haggard and his wife.

whose implicit sexual orientation revealed homosexual feelings while their self-report did not.

A key factor in these studies was the participants' perceived autonomy support by parents. *Autonomy support* means allowing a person the freedom to explore and identify his or her own needs, feelings, and desires. Individuals who reported high levels of parental autonomy support showed a stronger match between implicit and explicit sexual orientation, as well as less homophobia. Conversely, participants who reported lower parental autonomy support were more likely to show a discrepancy between their implicit and explicit sexual orientation and high levels of homophobia.

The researchers concluded that individuals who experience same-sex attraction may shut out this aspect of themselves due to their deep fears of parental rejection. According to this research, strident negative attitudes may be a way for such individuals to protect a fragile sense of self. The fragility of that sense of self is evidenced in scandals like the one that surrounded Ted Haggard.

WHAT DO YOU THINK

- Do you know someone who is prejudiced against a group of people because of their race, ethnicity, or sexual orientation? How do defense mechanisms apply to that person's attitudes?
- Can you recognize defense mechanisms at work in your own life? How?
- Do you agree that homophobia is explained by reaction formation? Why or why not?

Defense mechanisms have been used to explain prejudice—that is, holding negative attitudes toward a group of people because of their race, ethnicity, or other characteristic. The defense mechanism of *projection* involves seeing the impulses a person fears in him- or herself in others. We might say that prejudicial attitudes involve projecting one's own impulses onto others.

Recent research has sought to link another form of prejudice, homophobia (prejudice against individuals based on their sexual orientation), to another defense mechanism, *reaction formation*. To read about this work, see the Critical Controversy.

PSYCHOSEXUAL STAGES OF PERSONALITY DEVELOPMENT

Freud believed that human beings go through universal stages of personality development and that at each developmental stage we experience sexual pleasure in one part of the body more than in others. Each stage is named for the location of sexual pleasure at that stage. *Erogenous zones* are parts of the body that have especially strong pleasure-giving qualities at particular stages of development.

■ *Oral stage (first 18 months):* The infant's pleasure centers on the mouth. Sucking, chewing, and biting are the chief sources of pleasure that reduce tension in the infant.

■ *Anal stage (18 to 36 months):* During a time when most children are experiencing toilet training, the child's greatest pleasure involves the anus and urethra and their functions. Freud recognized that there is pleasure in "going" and "holding it" as well as in the experience of control over one's parents in deciding when to do either.

■ *Phallic stage (3 to 6 years):* The name of Freud's third stage comes from the Latin word *phallus,* which means "penis." Pleasure focuses on the genitals as the child discovers that self-stimulation is enjoyable.

In Freud's view, the phallic stage has a special importance in personality development because it triggers the Oedipus complex. This name comes from the Greek tragedy in which Oedipus unknowingly kills his father and marries his mother. The **Oedipus complex** is the boy's intense desire to replace his father and enjoy the affections of his mother. Eventually, the boy recognizes that his father might punish him for these incestuous wishes, specifically by cutting off the boy's penis. *Castration anxiety* refers to the boy's intense fear of being mutilated by his father. To reduce this conflict, the boy identifies with his father, adopting the male gender role. The intense castration anxiety is repressed into the unconscious and serves as the foundation for the development of the superego.

Freud recognized differences between boys and girls in the phallic stage. Because a girl does not have a penis, she cannot experience castration anxiety, Freud reasoned. Instead, she compares herself to boys and realizes that she is missing something—a penis—and thus experiences not castration anxiety but "castration completed," resulting in *penis envy*—the intense desire to obtain a penis by eventually marrying and bearing a son. Without castration anxiety, a girl cannot develop a superego in the same sense that boys do. In this way, for Freud, anatomy is destiny: The physical fact that girls lack a penis means they cannot develop a superego. Thus, Freud concluded, women are morally inferior to men.

Although noting that his views ran counter to the feminist thinkers of his time, Freud stood firm that the sexes are not equal in every way. He considered women to be somewhat childlike in their development and thought it was good that fathers, and eventually husbands, should guide them through life. He asserted that the only hope for women's moral development is education.

■ *Latency period (6 years to puberty):* This phase is not a developmental stage but rather a kind of psychic time-out. After the drama of the phallic stage, the child sets aside all interest in sexuality.

■ *Genital stage (adolescence and adulthood):* The genital stage is the time of sexual reawakening, a point when the source of sexual pleasure shifts to someone outside the family. Freud believed that in adulthood, individuals become capable of the two hallmarks of maturity: love and work. However, Freud felt that human beings are inevitably subject to intense conflict, reasoning that everyone, no matter how well adjusted, still has an id pressing for expression. Adulthood, even in the best of circumstances, still involves reliving the unconscious conflicts of childhood.

Freud argued that the individual may become stuck in any of these developmental stages if he or she is overdisciplined or overindulged at a given stage. For example, a parent might wean a child too early (or not early enough) or be too strict (or too lax) in toilet training. *Fixation* occurs when a particular psychosexual stage colors an individual's adult personality. For instance, an *anal retentive* person (someone who is obsessively neat and organized) is fixated at the anal stage. The construct of fixation thus explains how, according to Freud, childhood experiences can have an enormous impact

● **Oedipus complex** According to Freud, a boy's intense desire to replace his father and enjoy the affections of his mother.

Stage	Adult Extensions (Fixations)	Sublimations	Reaction Formations
Oral	Smoking, eating, kissing, oral hygiene, drinking, chewing gum	Seeking knowledge, humor, wit, sarcasm, being a food or wine expert	Speech purist, food faddist, prohibitionist, dislike of milk
Anal	Notable interest in one's bowel movements, love of bathroom humor, extreme messiness; or, alternatively, extreme cleanliness, stubbornness, and a strong desire for simplicity and structure	Interest in painting or sculpture, being overly giving, great interest in statistics	Extreme disgust with feces, fear of dirt, prudishness, irritability
Phallic	Heavy reliance on masturbation, flirtatiousness, expressions of virility	Interest in poetry, love of love, interest in acting, striving for success	Puritanical attitude toward sex, excessive modesty

FIGURE 12.3 Defense Mechanisms and Freudian Stages If a person is fixated at a psychosexual stage, the fixation can color his or her personality in many ways, including the defense mechanisms the person might use to cope with anxiety.

on adult personality. Figure 12.3 illustrates possible links between adult personality characteristics and fixation at the oral, anal, and phallic stages.

Psychodynamic Critics and Revisionists

Because Freud was among the first theorists to explore personality, some of his ideas have needed updating and revision over time, while others have been tossed out altogether. In particular, Freud's critics have said that his ideas about sexuality, early experience, social factors, and the unconscious mind were misguided (Adler, 1927; Erikson, 1968; Fromm, 1947; Horney, 1945; Jung, 1917; Kohut, 1977; Rapaport, 1967; Sullivan, 1953). They stress the following points:

- Sexuality is not the pervasive force that Freud believed it to be. Furthermore, the Oedipus complex is not as universal as Freud maintained. Freud's concepts were heavily influenced by the setting in which he lived—turn-of-the-century Vienna, a society that, compared with contemporary society, was sexually repressed and male-dominated.

- The first five years of life are not as powerful in shaping adult personality as Freud thought. Later experiences warrant attention.

- The ego and conscious thought processes play a larger role in personality than Freud believed. Achievement, thinking, and reasoning are not always tied to sexual impulses.

- Sociocultural factors are much more important than Freud believed. In stressing the id's dominance, Freud placed more emphasis on the biological basis of personality. More contemporary psychodynamic scholars have especially emphasized the interpersonal setting of the family and the role of early social relationships in personality development (Bornstein, Denckla, & Chung, 2013).

A number of dissenters and revisionists to Freud's theory have been influential in the development of psychodynamic theories. Erik Erikson, whose psychosocial stages we examined in Chapter 9, is among these. Here we briefly consider three other thinkers—Karen Horney, Carl Jung, and Alfred Adler—who made notable revisions to Freud's approach.

HORNEY'S SOCIOCULTURAL APPROACH

Karen Horney (1885–1952) rejected the notion that anatomy is destiny. She argued that sociocultural influences on personality development should be investigated as well (Schultz & Schultz, 2012). Consider Freud's concept of penis envy. Horney pointed out that women might envy the penis not because of unconscious issues but because of the status that society bestows on those who have one. Further, she suggested that both

Karen Horney (1885–1952)
Horney developed the first feminist criticism of Freud's theory. Horney's view emphasizes women's positive qualities and self-evaluation.

Carl Jung (1875–1961) Swiss psychoanalytic theorist Jung developed the concepts of the collective unconscious and archetypes.

● **collective unconscious** Jung's term for the impersonal, deepest layer of the unconscious mind, shared by all human beings because of their common ancestral past.

● **archetypes** Jung's term for emotionally laden ideas and images in the collective unconscious that have rich and symbolic meaning for all people.

● **individual psychology** Adler's view that people are motivated by purposes and goals and that perfection, not pleasure, is thus the key motivator in human life.

sexes envy the attributes of the other, with men coveting women's reproductive capacities (Horney, 1967).

Horney believed that the need for security, not sex, is the prime motive in human existence. She reasoned that an individual whose needs for security are met should be able to develop his or her capacities to the fullest extent. She viewed psychological health as allowing the person to express talents and abilities freely and spontaneously.

JUNG'S ANALYTICAL THEORY

Freud's contemporary Carl Jung (1875–1961) shared Freud's interest in the unconscious, but he believed that Freud underplayed the role of the unconscious mind in personality. In fact, Jung believed that the roots of personality go back to the dawn of humanity. The **collective unconscious** is Jung's term for the impersonal, deepest layer of the unconscious mind, shared by all human beings because of their common ancestral past. Describing the collective unconscious as "impersonal" emphasizes that it is the same, across all humanity. In Jung's theory, the experiences of a common past have made a deep, permanent impression on the human mind (Hunt, 2012).

Jung posited that the collective unconscious contains **archetypes,** emotionally laden ideas and images that have symbolic meaning for all people. Jung concluded that these archetypes emerge in art, literature, religion, and dreams (Dourley, 2011; Faber & Mayer, 2009; Morgan, 2012). Archetypes are essentially predispositions to respond to the environment in particular ways.

Jung used the terms *anima* and *animus* to identify two common archetypes. He believed each of us has a passive feminine side—the anima—and an assertive masculine side—the animus. The *persona* is another archetype; Jung thought that the persona represents the public mask that we all wear during social interactions; he believed that it is an essential archetype because the persona allows us always to keep some secret part of ourselves hidden from others.

ADLER'S INDIVIDUAL PSYCHOLOGY

Alfred Adler (1870–1937) was one of Freud's earliest followers, although his relationship with Freud was quite brief and his approach to personality was drastically different. In Adler's **individual psychology,** people are motivated by purposes and goals—thus, perfection, not pleasure, is the key motivator in human life. Adler argued that people have the ability to take their genetic inheritance and their environmental experiences and act upon them creatively to become the person they want to be.

Adler thought that everyone strives for superiority by seeking to adapt, improve, and master the environment (Del Corso, Rehfuss, & Galvin, 2011). Striving for superiority is our response to the uncomfortable feelings of inferiority that we experience as infants and young children when we interact with bigger, more powerful people. *Compensation* is Adler's term for the individual's attempt to overcome imagined or real inferiorities or weaknesses by developing one's own abilities. Adler believed that compensation is normal, and he said that we often make up for a weakness in one ability by excelling in a different one. For example, a person of small stature and limited physical abilities (like Adler himself) might compensate by excelling in academics.

Adler believed that birth order could influence how successfully a person would strive for superiority (Khodarahimi & Ogletree, 2011). He viewed firstborn children to be in a particularly vulnerable state given that they begin life as the center of attention but then are knocked off their pedestal by their siblings. Adler believed that the firstborn are more likely to suffer from psychological disorders and to engage in criminal behavior. Youngest children, however, also are potentially in trouble because they are most likely to be spoiled.

The healthiest birth order? According to Adler, those (including Adler) who are middle-born are in a particularly advantageous situation because they have older siblings as built-in inspiration for superiority striving. Importantly, though, Adler did not believe that anyone is doomed by birth order. Rather, sensitive parents could help children in any position in the family to negotiate their needs for superiority.

Evaluating the Psychodynamic Perspectives

Although psychodynamic theories have diverged from Freud's original psycho-analytic version, they share some core principles:

- Personality is determined both by current experiences *and* by early life experiences.
- Personality can be better understood by examining it developmentally—as a series of stages that unfold with the individual's physical, cognitive, and socioemotional development.
- We mentally transform our experiences, giving them meaning that shapes our personality.
- The mind is not all conscious; unconscious motives lie behind some of our puzzling behavior.
- The individual's inner world often conflicts with the outer demands of reality, creating anxiety that is not easy to resolve.
- Personality and adjustment are important topics of psychological inquiry.

Psychodynamic perspectives have come under fire for a variety of reasons. Some critics say that psychodynamic theorists overemphasize the influence of early family experiences on personality and do not acknowledge that people retain the capacity for change and adaptation throughout life. Moreover, some psychologists believe that Freud and Jung put too much faith in the unconscious mind's ability to control behavior. Others complain that Freud placed too much importance on sexuality in explaining personality.

Some have argued, too, that psychoanalysis is not a theory that researchers can test through empirical studies. However, numerous empirical studies on concepts such as defense mechanisms and the unconscious have proved this criticism to be unfounded (Cramer, 2008a, 2008b, 2009a, 2009b; Weinstein & others, 2012). At the same time, another version of this argument may be accurate. Although it is certainly possible to test hypotheses derived from psychoanalytic theory through research, the question remains whether psychoanalytically oriented individuals who believe strongly in Freud's ideas would be open to research results that call for serious changes in the theory.

In light of these criticisms, it may be hard to appreciate why Freud continues to have an impact on psychology. It is useful to keep in mind that Freud made a number of important contributions, including being the first to propose that childhood is crucial to later functioning, that development might be understood in terms of stages, and that unconscious processes might play a significant role in human life (Cervone & Pervin, 2013).

test yourself

1. What three structures of personality did Freud describe, and how did he define each?
2. What are Freud's psychosexual stages of personality development?
3. What criticisms have been leveled at psychodynamic theories of personality?

2· HUMANISTIC PERSPECTIVES

Humanistic perspectives stress a person's capacity for personal growth and positive human qualities. Humanistic psychologists believe that we all have the ability to control our lives and to achieve what we desire.

Such perspectives contrast with both psychodynamic perspectives and behaviorism, discussed in Chapter 6. Humanistic theorists sought to move beyond Freudian psycho-analysis and behaviorism to a theory that might capture the rich and potentially positive aspects of human nature.

● **humanistic perspectives** Theoretical views stressing a person's capacity for personal growth and positive human qualities.

Maslow's Approach

A leading architect of the humanistic movement was Abraham Maslow (1908–1970), whose hierarchy of needs we considered in Chapter 10. Maslow believed that we can learn the most about human personality by focusing on the very best examples of human beings—self-actualizers.

Recall that at the top of Maslow's (1954, 1971) hierarchy was the need for self-actualization. Self-actualization is the motivation to develop one's full potential as a human being. Maslow described self-actualizers as spontaneous, creative, and possessing a childlike capacity for awe. According to Maslow, a person at this optimal level of existence would be tolerant of others, have a gentle sense of humor, and be likely to pursue the greater good. Self-actualizers also maintain a capacity for "peak experiences," or breathtaking moments of spiritual insight. As examples of self-actualized individuals, Maslow included Pablo Casals (cellist), Albert Einstein (physicist), Ralph Waldo Emerson (writer), William James (psychologist), Thomas Jefferson (politician), Eleanor Roosevelt (humanitarian, diplomat), and Albert Schweitzer (humanitarian).

Created more than 40 years ago, Maslow's list of self-actualizers is limited. Because he concentrated on people who were successful in a particular historical context, Maslow's self-actualizers include only those who had opportunities for success in that setting. Maslow listed considerably more men than women, and mostly individuals from Western cultures and of European ancestry. Today, we might add to Maslow's list individuals such as Nobel Peace Prize winners the Dalai Lama (Tenzin Gyatso), Tibetan spiritual and political leader; and Ellen Johnson Sirleaf, Leymah Gbowee, and Tawakkol Karman, three women who received the coveted 2011 prize "for their nonviolent struggle for the safety of women and for women's rights to full participation in peace-building work."

Rogers's Approach

The other key figure in the development of humanistic psychology, Carl Rogers (1902–1987), began his career as a psychotherapist struggling to understand the unhappiness of the individuals he encountered in therapy. Rogers's work established the foundations for more contemporary studies of personal growth and self-determination.

Like Freud, Rogers began his inquiry into human nature with troubled people. Based on his clinical observations, Rogers (1961) devised his own approach to personality. He believed that we are all born with the raw ingredients of a fulfilling life. We simply need the right conditions to thrive. Just as a sunflower seed, once planted in rich soil and given water and sunshine, will grow into a strong and healthy flower, all humans will flourish in the appropriate environment.

This analogy is particularly apt and reveals the differences between Rogers's view of human nature and Freud's. A sunflower seed does not have to be shaped away from its dark natural tendencies by social constraints, nor does it have to reach a difficult compromise between its vile true impulses and reality. Instead, given the appropriate environment, it will grow into a beautiful flower. Rogers believed that, similarly, each person is born with natural capacities for growth and fulfillment. We are also endowed with an innate sense—a gut feeling—that allows us to evaluate whether an experience is good or bad for us. Finally, we are all born with a need for positive regard from others. We need to be loved, liked, or accepted by people around us. As children interacting with our parents, we learn early on to value the feeling that they value us, and we gain a sense of self-worth.

EXPLAINING UNHAPPINESS

If we have innate tendencies toward growth and fulfillment, why are so many people so unhappy? The problem arises when our need for positive regard from others is not met *unconditionally*. **Unconditional positive regard** means being accepted, valued, and treated positively regardless of one's behavior. Rogers noted that often others value us only when we behave in particular ways that meet particular standards. **Conditions of worth** are the standards we must live up to in order to receive positive regard. For instance, parents might give their son positive regard only when he achieves in school or chooses a profession that they themselves value. According to Rogers, as we grow up, people who are central to our lives condition us to move away from our genuine feelings, to earn their love by pursuing those goals that they value, even if those goals do not reflect our deepest wishes.

Carl Rogers (1902–1987) Rogers was a pioneer in the development of the humanistic perspective.

● **unconditional positive regard** Rogers's construct referring to the individual's need to be accepted, valued, and treated positively regardless of his or her behavior.

● **conditions of worth** The standards that the individual must live up to in order to receive positive regard from others.

Rogers's theory includes the idea that we develop a *self-concept,* our conscious representation of who we are and who we wish to become, during childhood. This idea is quite different from Freud's ego. For Rogers, the self-concept is the hub of human functioning. Optimally, this self-concept reflects our genuine, innate desires. However, conditions of worth can become part of the self-concept. As a result, we can become alienated from our real feelings and strive to actualize a self that does not represent our authentic desires. A person who dedicates himself or herself to such goals might be very successful by outward appearances but might feel utterly unfilled. Such an individual might be able to check off all the important boxes in life's to-do lists and complete all that he or she is "supposed to do," but never feel truly happy.

PROMOTING OPTIMAL FUNCTIONING

To remedy this situation, Rogers believed that the person must reconnect with his or her true feelings and desires. He proposed that to achieve this reconnection, the individual must experience a relationship that includes three essential qualities: unconditional positive regard, empathy, and genuineness. We consider each in turn.

First, Rogers said that regardless of what they do, people need unconditional positive regard. Although an individual might lack unconditional positive regard in childhood, he or she can experience this unconditional acceptance from others later, in friendships and/or romantic relationships or during sessions with a therapist. Even when a person's behavior is inappropriate, obnoxious, or unacceptable, he or she still needs the respect, comfort, and love of others (Ryckman, 2013). Research supports the notion that an enduring, stable sense of self-esteem is more likely to emerge if we feel good about ourselves, without having to live up to external standards (Crocker & Park, 2012; DiDonato & Krueger, 2010).

Second, Rogers said that individuals can become more fulfilled by interacting with people who are empathic toward them. Empathy involves being a sensitive listener and understanding another's true feelings.

Genuineness is a third requirement in the individual's path to become fully functioning. Being genuine means being open with one's feelings and dropping all pretenses and facades. The importance that Rogers placed on the therapist's acting genuinely in the therapeutic relationship demonstrates his strong belief in the positive character of human nature. For Rogers, we can help others simply by being present for them as the authentic individuals we really are. Research on being genuine or authentic supports Rogers's assertion that being true to ourselves is associated with stable self-esteem (Jordan & Zeigler-Hill, 2013; Kernis, 2003) and well-being more generally (Schlegel, Hirsch, & Smith, 2013; Schlegel & others, 2013).

Thus, according to Rogers, unconditional positive regard, empathy, and genuineness are three essential ingredients of healthy human relations. Anyone—a manager, teacher, counselor, member of the clergy—who is interested in promoting optimal human functioning can apply these principles.

Evaluating the Humanistic Perspectives

The humanistic perspectives emphasize that the way we perceive ourselves and the world around us is an essential element of personality. Humanistic psychologists also stress that we need to consider the whole person and the positive side of human nature (Schneider, 2009; Schultz & Schultz, 2012). Their emphasis on conscious experience has given us the view that personality contains a well of potential that can be developed to its fullest (Hill, 2000).

Some critics believe that humanistic psychologists are too optimistic about human nature. Others argue that humanistic approaches do not hold individuals accountable for their behaviors, if all negative human behavior is seen as emerging out of negative situations.

Self-determination theory, which we considered in Chapter 10, demonstrates the way that psychologists have studied humanistic ideas (Kusurkar & others, 2013; Standage & others, 2012). Their work bears witness to the enduring impact of humanistic perspectives on contemporary personality psychology.

test yourself

1. What do the humanistic perspectives on personality emphasize?
2. What name did Maslow give to the motivation to develop one's full human potential?
3. According to Rogers, what three qualities do individuals need in order to connect with their feelings and desires? How did Rogers define each?

3· TRAIT PERSPECTIVES

If you are setting up a friend on a blind date, you are likely to describe the person in terms of his or her *traits,* or lasting personality characteristics. Trait perspectives on personality have been the dominant approach for the past three decades.

Trait Theories

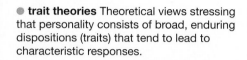

● **trait theories** Theoretical views stressing that personality consists of broad, enduring dispositions (traits) that tend to lead to characteristic responses.

According to **trait theories,** personality consists of broad, enduring dispositions that tend to lead to characteristic responses. These enduring dispositions are called *traits.* In other words, we can describe people in terms of the ways they behave, such as whether they are outgoing, friendly, private, or hostile. People who have a strong tendency to behave in certain ways are referred to as "high" on the traits; those with a weak tendency to behave in these ways are "low" on the traits. Although trait theorists differ about which traits make up personality, they agree that traits are the fundamental building blocks of personality (De Pauw & Mervielde, 2010; McCrae & Sutin, 2009; Miserandino, 2012).

Gordon Allport (1897–1967), sometimes referred to as the father of American personality psychology, was particularly bothered by the negative view of humanity that psychoanalysis portrayed. He rejected the notion that the unconscious was central to an understanding of personality and believed that to understand healthy people, we must focus on their lives *in the present,* not on their childhood experiences. In defining personality, Allport (1961) stressed each person's uniqueness and capacity to adapt to the environment. He was dedicated to the idea that psychology should have relevance to issues facing modern society, and his scholarship has influenced not only personality psychology but also the psychology of religion and prejudice (1954).

Allport believed that personality psychology should focus on understanding healthy, well-adjusted individuals (1961). He described the healthy mature person as having

"Gerry's downloading a personality."
© Rob Murray. www.CartoonStock.com

- A positive but objective sense of self and others
- Interest in issues beyond their own experience
- A sense of humor
- Common sense
- A unifying philosophy of life—typically but not always provided by religious faith

Allport asserted that traits were the optimal way to understand personality. He defined traits as mental structures that make different situations the same for the person. For instance, if Carly is sociable, she is likely to behave in an outgoing fashion whether she is at a party or in a group study session. Allport's definition implies that behavior should be consistent across different situations.

We get a sense of the down-to-earth quality of Allport's approach to personality by looking at his study of traits. In the late 1930s, Allport and his colleague H. S. Odbert (1936) sat down with two big unabridged dictionaries and pulled out all the words that could be used to describe a person—a method called the *lexical approach.* This approach reflects the idea that if a trait is important to people in real life, it ought to be represented in the natural language people use to talk about one another. Allport and Odbert started with 18,000 words and gradually pared down that list to 4,500.

Clearly, 4,500 traits would make for a very long questionnaire. Do we really need them all? Imagine that you are asked to rate a person, Ignacio, on some traits. You use a scale from 1 to 5, with 1 meaning "not at all" and 5 meaning "very much." If you give Ignacio a 5 on "outgoing," what do you think you might give him on "shy"? So, we may not need 4,500 traits to summarize the way we describe personality. Still, how might we whittle down these descriptors further without losing something important?

With advances in statistical methods and the advent of computers, the lexical approach became considerably less cumbersome. Researchers began to analyze trait words to look for underlying structures that might explain their overlap. Specifically, a statistical procedure called *factor analysis* allowed researchers to identify the traits that go together. Factor analysis essentially tells us what items on a scale people are responding to as if they mean the same thing. For example, if Ignacio got a 5 on "outgoing," he probably would get a 5 on "talkative" and a 1 or 2 on "shy." Factor analysis involves taking the various ratings and reducing them down to a few underlying factors that explain their overlap.

One important characteristic of factor analysis is that it relies on the scientist to interpret the meaning of the factors, and the researcher must make some decisions about how many factors are enough to explain the data (Goldberg & Digman, 1994). In 1963, W. T. Norman reanalyzed the Allport and Odbert traits and concluded that only five factors were needed to summarize these traits. Norman's research set the stage for the dominant approach in personality psychology today: the five-factor model (Digman, 1990).

The Five-Factor Model of Personality

Pick a friend and jot down 10 of that person's most notable personality traits. Did you perhaps list "reserved" or "a good leader"? "Responsible" or "unreliable"? "Sweet," "kind," or "friendly"? Maybe "creative"? Researchers in personality psychology have found that there are essentially five broad personality dimensions that are represented in the natural language; these dimensions also summarize the various ways psychologists have studied traits (Costa & McCrae, 2006, 2013; Crede & others, 2012; McCrae, Gaines, & Wellington, 2013).

The **big five factors of personality**—the broad traits that are thought to describe the main dimensions of personality—are neuroticism (the tendency to worry and experience negative emotions and is sometimes identified by its opposite, emotional stability), extraversion, openness to experience, agreeableness, and conscientiousness. Openness to experience is often the most difficult to understand. Although it sounds like it involves being open to trying new things, this trait refers to a tendency to enjoy intellectual pursuits, an interest in art and culture, and creative pursuits. Today it is most commonly labeled "openness to experience," but it was previously termed "intellect" and "culture." Personality psychologists typically refer to the traits as N, E, O, A, and C. If you create an anagram from these first letters of the trait names, you get the word *OCEAN*.

Figure 12.4 more fully defines the big five traits. To find out where you stand on these traits, see the Psychological Inquiry.

Each of the big five traits has been the topic of extensive research (Costa & McCrae, 2013; Karsten & others, 2012; King & Trent, 2013; Ozer & Benet-Martinez, 2006). The following is a just a sampling of the interesting work that the five-factor model has inspired:

- *Neuroticism* is related to feeling negative emotion more often than positive emotion in one's daily life (Widiger, 2009). Neuroticism predicts health complaints (Carver & Connor-Smith, 2010) and coronary heart disease risk (Koelsch, Enge, & Jentschke, 2012). In a longitudinal study tracking older individuals for nearly 7 years, neuroticism predicted dying during the study (Fry & Debats, 2009).

- Individuals high in *extraversion* are more likely than others to engage in social activities (Emmons & Diener, 1986) and to experience gratitude (McCullough, Emmons, & Tsang, 2002) and a strong sense of meaning in life (King & others, 2006).

● **big five factors of personality** The five broad traits that are thought to describe the main dimensions of personality: neuroticism (emotional instability), extraversion, openness to experience, agreeableness, and conscientiousness.

Openness	**C**onscientiousness	**E**xtraversion	**A**greeableness	**N**euroticism (emotional instability)
• Imaginative or practical	• Organized or disorganized	• Sociable or retiring	• Softhearted or ruthless	• Calm or anxious
• Interested in variety or routine	• Careful or careless	• Fun-loving or somber	• Trusting or suspicious	• Secure or insecure
• Independent or conforming	• Disciplined or impulsive	• Energetic or reserved	• Helpful or uncooperative	• Self-satisfied or self-pitying

FIGURE 12.4 **The Big Five Factors of Personality** Each of the broad traits encompasses more narrow traits and characteristics. Use the acronym *OCEAN* to remember the big five personality factors: openness, conscientiousness, extraversion, agreeableness, and neuroticism.

psychological *inquiry*

Your Personality Traits: Who Are You?

Use the following scale to rate yourself on the trait items listed below. Next to each item, write the number from the scale that best corresponds to how you rate yourself with respect to that trait.

Disagree strongly	Disagree moderately	Disagree a little	Neither agree nor disagree	Agree a little	Agree moderately	Agree strongly
1	**2**	**3**	**4**	**5**	**6**	**7**

I see myself as:

1. _____ extraverted, enthusiastic.
2. _____ critical, quarrelsome.
3. _____ dependable, self-disciplined.
4. _____ anxious, easily upset.
5. _____ open to new experiences, complex.
6. _____ reserved, quiet.
7. _____ sympathetic, warm.
8. _____ disorganized, careless.
9. _____ calm, emotionally stable.
10. _____ conventional, uncreative.

You have just completed the Ten-Item Personality Inventory, or TIPI (Gosling, Rentfrow, & Swann, 2003), a measure of the big five traits. All of the even-numbered items are *reverse-scored*, meaning your ratings should be reversed for these. (Reverse items are included in scales to fully identify a characteristic and to make sure that respondents are reading items carefully.) So, if you gave item number 2 a rating of 7, it should be a 1; a rating of 6 should be a 2, and so on. The first step in calculating your scores is to reverse your scores on these even-numbered items. Then average together your ratings for the following items for each trait, using the steps in the table below.

Trait	Items	Sum of Your Ratings	Your Score (divide the sum by 2)	Low Score	Medium Score	High Score
Emotional Stability (the opposite of neuroticism)	4, 9	_____	_____	3.41	4.83	6.25
Extraversion	1, 6	_____	_____	2.99	4.44	5.89
Openness to Experience	5, 10	_____	_____	4.13	5.38	6.45
Agreeableness	2, 7	_____	_____	4.12	5.23	6.34
Conscientiousness	3, 8	_____	_____	4.08	5.40	6.72

The last three columns provide information about what those scores mean. The "medium scores" reflect the mean score found in a sample of more than 1,800 participants. The "low scores" are that mean minus one standard deviation. The "high scores" are the mean plus one standard deviation. Now answer the following questions.

1. Do your scores reflect your sense of who you really are? Explain.
2. Why do you think the researchers included one reverse-scored item for each scale?
3. The guides for low, medium, and high scores were provided by data from a sample of college students at the University of Texas. Do you think these norms might differ at your school? Why or why not?
4. Although this is a very short assessment, scores on this short scale are highly correlated with scores on longer scales measuring the same traits (Ehrhart & others, 2009). What does it mean to say that the scores are highly correlated?

In addition, extraverts are more forgiving (Thompson & others, 2005). People rate extraverts as smiling, standing energetically, and dressing stylishly (Naumann & others, 2009). One study found that extraverted salespeople sold more cars, especially if they were also good at picking up interpersonal cues (Blickle, Wendel, & Ferris, 2010).

- *Openness to experience* is related to liberal values, open-mindedness, tolerance (McCrae & Sutin, 2009), and creativity (Silvia & others, 2009). Openness is also associated with superior cognitive functioning and IQ across the life span (Sharp & others, 2010). Individuals who rate themselves as open to experience are more likely to dress distinctively (Naumann & others, 2009), to pursue entrepreneurial goals (for instance, starting their own business), and to experience success in those pursuits (Zhao, Seibert, & Lumpkin, 2010). Individuals high on openness to experience are more likely to use social media (Correa, Hinsley, & de Zuniga, 2010). Moreover, a recent meta-analysis found that openness to experience was linked to living longer (Ferguson & Bibby, 2012).

- *Agreeableness* is related to generosity, altruism (Caprara & others, 2010), religious faith (Haber, Koenig, & Jacob, 2011), and more satisfying romantic relationships (Donnellan, Larsen-Rife, & Conger, 2005). There are also links between agreeable people viewing other people more positively (Wood, Harms, & Vazire, 2010). In online dating profiles, agreeableness is negatively related to lying about oneself (J. A. Hall & others, 2010).

- *Conscientiousness* is a key factor in a variety of life domains. A recent meta-analysis found that a higher level of conscientiousness was linked to higher college grade-point averages (McAbee & Oswald, 2013). Conscientiousness also predicts better work performance (S. D. Brown & others, 2011). Conscientiousness is associated with dressing neatly, especially among men (Naumann & others, 2009), and, like openness, is related to entrepreneurial success (Zhao, Seibert, & Lumpkin, 2010). Conscientiousness relates to better-quality friendships (Jensen-Campbell & Malcolm, 2007) and higher levels of religious faith (Saroglou, 2010). Low levels of conscientiousness are linked with criminal behavior (Wiebe, 2004) and substance abuse (Walton & Roberts, 2004).

Keep in mind that because the five factors are theoretically independent of one another, a person can be any combination of them. Do you know a neurotic extravert or an agreeable introvert, for example? Reading about the correlates of personality traits can sometimes be dissatisfying. If you are low in conscientiousness, are you doomed to an unsuccessful career?

In many ways, the role of personality traits in our life depends on the situations in which we find ourselves. Traits can be strengths or weaknesses, depending on the types of situations we encounter and the kinds of situations we seek out for ourselves (King & Trent, 2013). Even a trait like agreeableness may be a liability when the situation calls for confrontational behavior. For instance, a woman whose marriage is breaking up might wish for a divorce lawyer who treats her kindly but might prefer one who is less than agreeable at the bargaining table. Eminent psychologist Lee Cronbach (1957, p. 679) once said, "If for each environment there is a best organism, for every organism there must be a best environment." If our personalities are not particularly well suited to a situation, we can change that situation or create one that fits better (King & Trent, 2013).

The notion that we must consider the fit between a person and situational factors is a theme that has emerged in research examining the relationship between personality traits and obesity (van Reedt Dortland & others, 2012). To read about this work, see the Intersection.

TRAITS AND PERSONALITY DEVELOPMENT

Although it is an assumption of the trait approach that these aspects of personality are relatively stable (Costa & McCrae, 2006; McCrae & Costa, 2006), studies have shown that meaningful personality change continues throughout life.

Personality and Health Psychology: Are Traits Linked to Obesity?

Obesity is a major worldwide health crisis (Hahn, Payne, & Lucas, 2013; Thompson, Manore, & Vaughan, 2013). Overweight and obesity are second only to smoking in terms of controllable causes of death (Mokdad & others, 2004). Controllable means that these unhealthy conditions can be influenced by behavior, specifically by eating patterns and physical activity levels. If personality traits predict typical patterns of behavior, might they provide a way to understand preferences in eating and activity? Do personality traits predict weight gain and obesity?

A longitudinal study followed nearly 2,000 people over the course of 50 years. Conducted by Angelina Sutin and her colleagues (2011), the study involved measuring the big five traits and weighing participants at each testing occasion. Looking at the data cross-sectionally, the researchers found that neuroticism and extraversion were positively related to body weight. In contrast, conscientiousness was negatively related to body weight. These relationships were most strongly explained by *impulsivity*, a trait that involves acting without planning. Impulsivity has been conceptualized as a dimension of neuroticism and extraversion, and it is negatively related to conscientiousness. How strongly was impulsivity related to weight? On average, those scoring in the top 10 percent on impulsivity weighed *24 pounds more* than those scoring in the bottom 10 percent.

Although in general people gained weight gradually over the 50-year span, certain traits related to how quickly they gained over time. Conscientiousness was strongly negatively related to rate of weight gain. Neuroticism was associated with gaining weight more quickly.

Although this study might suggest that personality can make a person fat (depressing news for those low on conscientiousness!), several facts are important to keep in mind. First, even in a longitudinal study, third variables, such as genetics, cannot be ruled out as an explanation for the link between personality and body weight. Second, personality does not directly add inches to one's waistline; rather, it is proposed to do so through *behavior.* So, Sutin and her colleagues suggest that information about personality traits might be useful in tailoring interventions to help individuals control their weight. Personality traits relate to one's typical behavior patterns. If losing weight means stepping outside those patterns, interventions can perhaps pinpoint behavioral strategies that a person might not otherwise use. Individuals high on impulsivity (or low on conscientiousness) might benefit, for example, by engaging in active planning of meals and exercise routines. For extraverts, support groups might work best, while for introverts self-directed programs or one-on-one interventions might be most successful in bringing about weight loss.

How do your personality traits relate to your health behaviors? Could changing your health behaviors improve your personality?

Consider too that as with any correlational study, the causal arrow might run in the other direction: Engaging in healthy behavior might lead to a healthier *personality.* This intriguing possibility is supported by a recent longitudinal study on smoking and personality. In that study, college students who reduced their smoking behavior were more likely to show decreases in both neuroticism and impulsivity, and these changes were especially strong between the ages of 18 and 25 (Littlefield & Sher, 2012).

These results highlight the remarkable and complex links between mind and body. They also remind us that healthy behavior can have benefits for our entire being.

For example, in a meta-analysis, Brent Roberts and his colleagues analyzed 92 different longitudinal studies that included thousands of participants ranging from ages 12 to over 80 years old and that measured aspects of the big five across the life course (Roberts, Walton, & Viechtbauer, 2006). They found consistent evidence for trait changes throughout life, even into adulthood. Social dominance (a facet of extraversion), conscientiousness, and emotional stability (the opposite of neuroticism) were found to increase especially between the ages of 20 and 40. Social vitality, another facet of extraversion, and openness to experience increased most during adolescence but then declined in old age. Agreeableness showed a steady rise over the life course.

Research has shown that especially between ages 17 and 24, individuals are likely to become more responsible and less distressed (Blonigen & others, 2008; Klimstra & others, 2009). In general, changes in personality traits across adulthood occur in a direction suggesting that people become more socially mature with time (Roberts & Mroczek, 2008). Personality psychologists have increasingly come to treat these age-related changes in the big five traits as reflecting personality development (Roberts, Donnellan, & Hill, 2013).

CROSS-CULTURAL STUDIES ON THE BIG FIVE

Some research on the big five factors addresses the extent to which the factors appear in personality profiles in different cultures (Lingjaerde, Foreland, & Engvik, 2001; Miacic & Goldberg, 2007; Pukrop, Sass, & Steinmeyer, 2000). The question is, do the big five show up in the assessment of personality in cultures around the world? Many studies suggest that they do: A version of the five factors appears in people in countries as diverse as Canada, Finland, Poland, China, and Japan (Paunonen & others, 1992; X. Zhou & others, 2009). Among the big five, the factors most likely to emerge across cultures and languages are extraversion, agreeableness, and conscientiousness (De Raad & others, 2010).

ANIMAL STUDIES ON THE BIG FIVE

Researchers have found evidence for at least some of the big five personality traits in animals, including domestic dogs (Gosling, 2008; Gosling, Kwan, & John, 2003) and hyenas (Gosling & John, 1999). In addition, studies have turned up evidence for general personality traits (such as overall outgoingness) in orangutans, geese, lizards (Weinstein, Capitanio, & Gosling, 2008), fish (McGhee & Travis, 2010; Wilson & Godin, 2010), cockatiels (Fox & Millam, 2010), and squid (Sinn, Gosling, & Moltschaniwskyj, 2008); although some researchers have found that squid "personality" may be more a function of environmental factors than stable individual differences (Sinn & others, 2010).

Sam Gosling, a professor at the University of Texas, is a personality psychologist who has conducted research on animal personality as well as the ways that we express our traits through websites, dorm room decoration, and other contexts.

Evaluating the Trait Perspectives

As already noted, the trait approach is the dominant perspective on personality psychology today. The emergence of the five-factor model has provided personality psychologists with a common language and a set of tools for understanding a host of important topics, including the prediction of behavior, psychological well-being, psychological disorders, and health and illness (George, Helson, & John, 2011; Leary & Hoyle, 2009a; Turiano & others, 2012).

Despite strong evidence for the big five, some personality researchers say that these traits might not end up being the ultimate list of broad traits; they argue that more specific traits are better predictors of behavior (Moskowitz, 2010). One alternative, the HEXACO model, incorporates a sixth dimension, honesty/humility, to capture the moral dimensions of personality (Ashton & Lee, 2008; K. Lee & others, 2013a).

The trait approach has been faulted for missing the importance of *situational* factors in personality and behavior (Engler, 2014; Kammrath & Scholer, 2013; Leary & Hoyle, 2009b). For example, a person might rate herself as introverted among new people but very outgoing with family and friends. Further, some have criticized the trait perspective for painting an individual's personality with very broad strokes. They say that although traits can tell us much about someone whom we have never met, they reveal little about the nuances of an individual's personality.

4· PERSONOLOGICAL AND LIFE STORY PERSPECTIVES

If two people have the same levels of the big five traits, do they essentially have the same personality? Researchers who approach personality from the personological and life story perspectives do not think so (McAdams & Olson, 2010). One of the goals of personality psychology is to understand how each of us is unique.

test yourself

1. How do trait theorists define personality?
2. What kind of work did the lexical approach of Allport and Odbert involve, and what key idea about personality traits did it reflect?
3. What traits are included in the big five factors of personality? Define them.

Henry Murray's psychological profile of Adolf Hitler, developed in 1943 during World War II, serves as a model for criminal profiling today.

● **personological and life story perspectives** Theoretical views stressing that the way to understand the person is to focus on his or her life history and life story.

Personological and life story perspectives stress that the way to understand the uniqueness of each person is to focus on his or her life history and life story.

Murray's Personological Approach

Henry Murray (1893–1988) was a young biochemistry graduate student when he became interested in the psychology of personality after meeting Carl Jung and reading his work. Murray went on to become the director of the Psychological Clinic at Harvard at the same time that Gordon Allport was a member of that faculty. Murray and Allport saw personality very differently. Whereas Allport was most comfortable focusing on conscious experience and traits, Murray embraced the psychodynamic notion of unconscious motivation.

Murray coined the word *personology* to refer to the study of the whole person. He believed that to understand a person, we have to know that person's history, including the physical, psychological, and sociological aspects of the person's life. Murray applied his insights into personality during World War II, when he was called upon by the Office of Strategic Services (a precursor to the CIA) to develop a psychological profile of Adolf Hitler. That document, produced in 1943, accurately predicted that Hitler would commit suicide rather than be taken alive. Murray's analysis of Hitler was the first "offender profile," and it has served as a model for modern criminal profiling.

The aspect of Murray's research that has had the most impact on contemporary personality psychology is his approach to motivation. Murray believed that our motives are largely unknown to us. This circumstance complicates the study of motivation: Researchers cannot simply ask people to say what it is they want. To address the issue, Murray, along with Christiana Morgan, developed the Thematic Apperception Test (TAT), to which we return later in this chapter (Morgan & Murray, 1935).

For the TAT, a person looks at an ambiguous picture and writes or tells a story about what is going on in the scene. A variety of scoring procedures have been devised for analyzing the unconscious motives that are revealed in imaginative stories (C. P. Smith, 1992). These scoring procedures involve *content analysis,* a procedure in which a psychologist takes the person's story and codes it for different images, words, and so forth. Although Murray posited 22 different unconscious needs, three have been the focus of most current research:

■ *Need for achievement:* an enduring concern for attaining excellence and overcoming obstacles
■ *Need for affiliation:* an enduring concern for establishing and maintaining interpersonal connections
■ *Need for power:* an enduring concern for having impact on the social world

David Winter (2005) analyzed the motives revealed in inaugural addresses of U.S. presidents. He found that certain needs revealed in these speeches corresponded to later events during the person's presidency. For instance, presidents who scored high on need for achievement (such as Jimmy Carter) were less successful during their terms. Note that the need for achievement is about striving for personal excellence and may have little to do with playing politics, negotiating interpersonal relationships, or delegating responsibility. Presidents who scored high on need for power tended to be judged as more successful (John F. Kennedy, Ronald Reagan), and presidents whose addresses suggested a high need for affiliation tended to experience scandal during their presidencies (Richard M. Nixon).

The Life Story Approach to Identity

Following in the Murray tradition, Dan McAdams developed the *life story approach* to identity (McAdams, 2001, 2006, 2011, 2012; McAdams & Olson, 2010). His work centers on the idea that each of us has a unique life story, representing our memories of what makes us who we are. This life story is a constantly changing narrative that provides us with a sense of coherence. For McAdams, our life story is our very identity.

McAdams (1989) also introduced the concept of intimacy motivation. The *intimacy motive* is an enduring concern for warm interpersonal encounters for their own sake. Intimacy motivation is revealed in the warm, positive interpersonal imagery in the stories people tell. Intimacy motive has been shown to relate to positive outcomes. For instance, college men who were high on intimacy motivation showed heightened levels of happiness and lowered work strain some 30 years later (McAdams & Bryant, 1987). A study of the coming-out stories of gay men and lesbians demonstrated that intimacy-related imagery (for example, experiencing falling in love or warm acceptance from others) was associated with well-being and personality development (King & Smith, 2005).

Research by David Winter (2005) has analyzed presidential motives in inaugural addresses such as those delivered by Richard M. Nixon (left) and John F. Kennedy (right). Winter found that certain needs revealed in these speeches corresponded to later events during these individual's terms in office.

Other personality psychologists have relied on narrative accounts of experiences as a means of understanding how individuals create meaning in life events (King & others, 2000). In one study, parents of children with Down syndrome wrote down the story of how they found out about their child's diagnosis. Parents whose stories ended happily scored higher on measures of happiness, life meaning, and personal growth than others. Parents who told stories about struggling to make sense of the experience tended to mature psychologically over time (King & others, 2000). By using narratives, personal documents (such as diaries), and even letters and speeches, personality psychologists search for the deeper meaning that cannot be revealed through tests that ask people directly about whether specific items capture their personality traits.

Finally, some personality psychologists use the life story approach to understand individual lives. *Psychobiography* is a type of inquiry in which personality psychologists attempt to apply personality theory to a one person's life (Runyon, 2007; W. T. Schultz, 2005). Erik Erikson's study of Gandhi's life, described in Chapter 2, is an example of a psychobiography. Psychobiographies have been written about a diverse array of figures, including Sigmund Freud, Gordon Allport, George W. Bush, Osama bin Laden, and Elvis Presley (W. T. Schultz, 2005).

Evaluating the Personological and Life Story Perspectives

Studying individuals through narratives and personal interviews provides an extraordinarily rich opportunity for the researcher. Imagine having the choice of reading someone's diary versus seeing that person's scores on a questionnaire measuring traits. Not many would pass up the chance to read the diary.

However, such studies are difficult and time-consuming. Personologist Robert W. White (1992) referred to the study of narratives as exploring personality "the long way." Collecting interviews and narratives is often just the first step. Turning these personal stories into scientific data means transforming them into numbers, and that process involves extensive coding and content analysis. Further, for narrative studies to be worthwhile, they must tell us something we could not have found out in a much easier way (King, 2003). Moreover, psychobiographical inquiries are prone to the biases of the scholars who conduct them and may not serve the scientific goal of generalizability.

test yourself

1. What did Murray mean by *personology*, and what did he believe was essential to understanding who a person really is?
2. On what does McAdams say our identities are dependent?
3. What is the intimacy motive? What has research revealed about it?

5· SOCIAL COGNITIVE PERSPECTIVES

● **social cognitive perspectives**
Theoretical views emphasizing conscious
awareness, beliefs, expectations, and goals.

Social cognitive perspectives on personality emphasize conscious awareness, beliefs, expectations, and goals. While incorporating principles from behaviorism (see Chapter 6), social cognitive psychologists explore the person's ability to reason; to think about the past, present, and future; and to reflect on the self. They emphasize the person's individual interpretation of situations and thus focus on the uniqueness of each person by examining how behavior is tailored to the diversity of situations in which people find themselves.

Social cognitive theorists are not interested in broad traits such as the big five. Rather, they investigate how more specific factors, such as beliefs, relate to behavior and performance. In this section we consider the two major social cognitive approaches, developed respectively by Albert Bandura and Walter Mischel.

Bandura's Social Cognitive Theory

In his social cognitive approach to learning, Albert Bandura took the basic tenets of behaviorism (Chapter 6) and added a recognition of the role of mental processes in determining behavior (Bandura, 1986, 2012a). Applying these principles to personality, Bandura's social cognitive theory states that behavior, environment, and person/cognitive factors are *all* important in understanding personality.

Bandura coined the term *reciprocal determinism* to describe the way behavior, environment, and person/cognitive factors interact to create personality (Figure 12.5). Reciprocal determinism means that the relationships among the person, his or her behavior, and the environment are all two-way streets. The environment can determine a person's behavior, but the person can act to change the environment. Similarly, person/cognitive factors can both influence behavior and be influenced by behavior. Our behavior, for instance, doing well on a test, can influence our beliefs about ourselves and in turn influence future behaviors.

From Bandura's perspective, then, behavior is a product of a variety of forces—some of which come from the situation and some of which the person brings to the situation. We now review the important processes and variables Bandura used to understand personality.

OBSERVATIONAL LEARNING

Recall from Chapter 6 Bandura's belief that observational learning is a key aspect of how we learn. By observing how others behave and noticing the consequences of their actions, we might come to adopt the behavior ourselves. For example, a boy might observe that his mother's hostile exchanges with other people are an effective way to get what she wants. Later, when the boy is with his peers, he might adopt the same strategy. Social cognitive theorists believe that we acquire a wide range of behaviors, thoughts, and feelings by watching others' behavior and that our observations strongly shape our personality (Bandura, 2010a, 2012a).

PERSONAL CONTROL

Social cognitive theorists emphasize that we can regulate and control our own behavior despite our changing environment (Bandura, 2012a; Mischel, 2004; Schunk & Zimmerman, 2013). For example, a young executive who observes her boss behave in an overbearing and sarcastic manner toward his subordinates may find the behavior distasteful and go out of her way to encourage and support her own staff. Psychologists commonly describe a sense of behavioral control as coming from inside the person (an *internal locus of control*) or outside the person (an *external locus of control*). When we feel that we ourselves are controlling our choices and behaviors, the locus of control is internal, but when other influences are controlling them, the locus of control is external.

Albert Bandura (b. 1925) Bandura's practical, problem-solving social cognitive approach has made a lasting mark on personality theory and therapy.

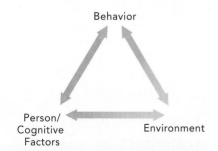

FIGURE 12.5 **Bandura's Social Cognitive Theory** Bandura's social cognitive theory emphasizes reciprocal influences of behavior, environment, and person/cognitive factors. Notice that from Bandura's perspective, all of those arrows are double-headed, meaning that causation goes in both directions.

Consider the question of whether you will perform well on your next test. With an internal locus of control, you believe that you are in command of your choices and behaviors, and your answer will depend on what you can realistically do (for example, study hard or attend a special review session). With an external locus of control, however, you might say that you cannot predict how things will go because so many outside factors influence performance, such as whether the test is difficult, how the curve is set in the course, and whether the instructor is fair. Feeling a strong sense of personal control is vital to many aspects of performance, behavior, and well-being (Bertrand, Graham, & Lachman, 2013; Morrison, Ponitz, & McClelland, 2010; Tigani & others, 2012).

SELF-EFFICACY

Self-efficacy is the belief that one has the competence to accomplish a given goal or task and produce positive change. Bandura and others have shown that self-efficacy is related to a number of positive developments in people's lives, including solving problems and becoming more sociable (Bandura, 2012a; Schunk, 2012).

● **self-efficacy** The belief that one can accomplish a given goal or task and produce positive change.

Self-efficacy influences whether people even try to develop healthy habits, as well as how much effort they expend in coping with stress, how long they persist in the face of obstacles, and how much stress and pain they experience (Becker, Kang, & Stuifbergen, 2012; Schaubroeck & others, 2011). We will return to the topics of personal control and self-efficacy at the end of this chapter.

Mischel's Contributions

Like Bandura, Walter Mischel is a social cognitive psychologist who has explored how personality influences behavior. Mischel has left his mark on the field of personality in two notable ways. First, his critique of the idea of consistency in behavior ignited a flurry of controversy. Second, he proposed the CAPS model, a new way of thinking about personality.

MISCHEL'S CRITIQUE OF CONSISTENCY

Whether we are talking about unconscious sexual conflicts, traits, or motives, all of the approaches we have considered so far maintain that these various personality characteristics are an enduring influence on behavior. This shared assumption was attacked in 1968 with the publication of Walter Mischel's *Personality and Assessment,* a book that nearly ended the psychological study of personality.

To understand Mischel's argument, recall Gordon Allport's definition of a trait as a characteristic that ought to make different situations equivalent for a given person. This quality of traits suggests that a person should behave consistently in different situations—in other words, the individual should exhibit *cross-situational consistency.* For example, an outgoing person should act highly sociably whether she is at a party or in the library. However, Mischel looked at the research compiled on trait prediction of behavior and found it to be lacking. He concluded that there was no evidence for cross-situational consistency in behavior—and thus no evidence for the existence of personality as it had been previously conceptualized.

Rather than understanding personality as consisting of broad, internal traits that produce consistent behavior across situations, Mischel said that personality often changes according to a given situation. Mischel asserted that behavior is discriminative; that is, a person looks at each situation and responds accordingly. Mischel's view is called *situationism,* the idea that personality and behavior often vary considerably from one context to another.

Personality psychologists responded to Mischel's situationist attack in various ways (Donnellan, Lucas, & Fleeson, 2009; Funder, 2009; Hogan, 2009). Researchers showed that it is not a matter of *whether* personality predicts behavior but *when and how* it does so, often in combination with situational factors (Sherman, Nave, & Funder, 2010). The research findings were that

- The narrower and more limited a trait is, the more likely it will predict behavior.

- Some people are consistent on some traits, and other people are consistent on other traits.

- Personality traits exert a stronger influence on an individual's behavior when situational influences are less powerful. A very powerful situation is one that contains many clear cues about how a person is supposed to behave. For example, even a highly talkative person typically sits quietly during a class lecture. In weaker situations, however, such as during leisure time, the person may spend most of the time talking.

Moreover, individuals select the situations they are in. Consequently, even if situations determine behavior, traits play a role by influencing which situations people choose—such as going to a party or staying home to study (Emmons & Diener, 1986).

Interestingly, a recent study showed that people *do* behave in a consistent fashion across different interpersonal situations. In that research, participants were videotaped as they interacted with different partners (Leikas, Lönnqvist, & Verkasalo, 2012). The partners were trained actors who served as confederates. The confederates were instructed to behave in different ways toward the participants across four different interactions; they were either friendly or quarrelsome and were either dominant or submissive. The way participants behaved in response to these different partners was coded afterward, based on the tapes.

The results showed that many of the participants' behaviors during the interactions were rather consistent, especially being talkative, using gestures, and expressing emotion (Leikas, Lönnqvist, & Verkasalo, 2012). Indeed, even when the type of treatment they received influenced their behavior, participants maintained a high level of cross-situational consistency in their *rank order*. This means that although an extraverted person might be less talkative than usual when interacting with a dominant partner, he or she was still more talkative than an introvert in the same situation.

Interestingly, the judges—who rated the big five traits of the participants based on the videotapes—agreed with the participants' self-reports of the traits. This means that even when observing a person in different situations, observers recognize whether that the person is extraverted, agreeable, conscientious, neurotic, or open to experience.

Let's pause and reflect on what it means to be consistent. You might believe that being consistent is part of being a genuine, honest person and that tailoring behavior to different situations means being fake. On the other hand, consider that a person who never changes his or her behavior to fit a situation might be unpleasant to have around. For example, think about someone who cannot put aside his competitive drive even when playing checkers with a 4-year-old. Clearly, adaptive behavior might involve sometimes being consistent and sometimes tailoring behavior to the situation.

Over time, Mischel (2004, 2009) has developed an approach to personality that he feels is better suited to capturing the nuances of the relationship between the individual and situations in producing behavior. Imagine trying to study personality without using traits or broad motives. What would you focus on? Mischel's answer to this dilemma is his CAPS theory.

CAPS THEORY

Recall Mischel's work on delay of gratification from Chapter 10 (Mischel, Cantor, & Feldman, 1996; Mischel & Moore, 1980; Mischel & others, 2011). In that work, children were left in a room with a tempting marshmallow. Mischel measured the amount of time the kids were able to delay eating the marshmallow, and he and his colleagues continued to study those children for many years. They found that the amount of time the children were able to delay gratification predicted their academic performance in high school and even college (Mischel, 2004). These results indicate remarkable stability in personality over time (Casey & others, 2011).

Mischel's approach to personality is concerned with just such stability (or coherence) in the pattern of behavior *over time*, not with consistency across differing situations.

That is, Mischel and his colleagues have studied how behaviors in very different situations have a coherent pattern, such as a child's waiting to eat the marshmallow and that same individual's (as a grown college student) deciding to stay home and study instead of going out to party.

In keeping with the social cognitive emphasis on the person's cognitive abilities and mental states, Mischel conceptualizes personality as a set of interconnected **cognitive affective processing systems (CAPS)** (Kross, Mischel, & Shoda, 2010; Mischel, 2004; Mischel & Ayduk, 2011; Mischel & Shoda, 1999). This label captures how the CAPS approach understands personality: It involves information processing (cognitive) and emotional experience (affective) interacting to systematically determine behavior, as the person encounters different situations. According to this approach, our thoughts and emotions about ourselves and the world affect our behavior and become linked in ways that matter to behavior (Kammrath & Scholer, 2013).

Personal control and self-efficacy are psychological connections that a person has made among situations, beliefs, and behaviors. For example, Raoul may be excited by the challenge of a new assignment from his boss and think about all the possible strategies to complete the project and get down to work immediately. Yet this go-getter may respond differently to other challenges, depending on who gives the assignment, what it is, or whether he feels he can do a good job.

From the CAPS perspective, it makes no sense to ask a person "How extraverted are you?" because the answer is always, "It depends." A person may be outgoing in one situation (on the first day of class) and not so in another (right before an exam), and that unique pattern of flexibility is what personality is all about.

Not surprisingly, CAPS theory focuses on how people behave in different situations and how they uniquely interpret situational features. Research using the CAPS approach generally involves observing individuals behaving in a variety of contexts in order to identify the patterns of associations that exist among beliefs, emotions, and behavior for each person across different situations (Romero-Canyas & others, 2010).

● **cognitive affective processing systems (CAPS)** Mischel's theoretical model for describing that individuals' thoughts and emotions about themselves and the world affect their behavior and become linked in ways that matter to that behavior.

Evaluating the Social Cognitive Perspectives

Social cognitive theory focuses on the interactions of individuals with their environments. The social cognitive approach has fostered a scientific climate for understanding personality that highlights the observation of behavior. Social cognitive theory emphasizes the influence of cognitive processes in explaining personality and suggests that people have the ability to control their environment (Ryckman, 2013).

Critics of the social cognitive perspective on personality take issue with one or more aspects of the theory. For example, they charge that

- The social cognitive approach is too concerned with change and situational influences on personality. It does not pay adequate tribute to the enduring qualities of personality.
- Social cognitive theory ignores the role biology plays in personality.
- In its attempt to incorporate both the situation and the person into its view of personality, social cognitive psychology tends to lead to very specific predictions for each person in any given situation, making generalizations impossible.

test yourself

1. In what ways did Bandura react to and modify Skinner's approach to understanding human functioning?
2. What is self-efficacy, and to what kinds of positive life developments has research linked it?
3. With what is Mischel's cognitive affective processing systems (CAPS) approach centrally concerned?

6· BIOLOGICAL PERSPECTIVES

The notion that physiological processes influence personality has been around since ancient times. Around 400 B.C.E., Hippocrates, the father of medicine, described human beings as having one of four basic personalities based on levels of particular bodily fluids (called *humours*). For Hippocrates, a "sanguine" personality was a happy, optimistic individual who happened to have an abundance of blood. A "choleric" person was quick-tempered with too much yellow bile. A "phlegmatic" personality referred to a placid, sluggish individual with too much phlegm, and a "melancholic" pessimist had too much black bile.

Hippocrates' ideas about bodily fluids have fallen by the wayside, but personality psychologists have long acknowledged that personality involves the brain and biological processes. Psychologists' beliefs about these interacting processes in personality, though, were based on assumptions, not direct study. For instance, Freud's psychosexual stages demonstrate his strong belief in the connection between the mind (personality) and the body; Allport defined traits as "*neuro*psychic" structures, and personality as a "*psycho-physical*" system; and Murray once declared, "No brain, no personality." More recently, with advances in method and theory, biological perspectives on personality have become more prominent (South & others, 2013; Zuckerman, 2013).

Personality and the Brain

The brain is clearly important in personality as in other psychological phenomena. Recall the case of Phineas Gage, described in Chapter 3. A key effect of Gage's horrific accident was that it changed his personality. He went from being gentle, kind, and reliable to being angry, hostile, and untrustworthy.

A great deal of research is currently addressing the ways in which brain activity is associated with various personality traits (Adelstein & others, 2011; DeYoung & others, 2010; Xu & Potenza, 2012). For example, research has shown that an extraverted person's left prefrontal cortex is more responsive to positive stimuli and that the same area in neurotic individuals is more responsive to negative stimuli (Canli, 2008a, 2008b; Haas & others, 2007; Schmidtke & Heller, 2004). Hans Eysenck and Jeffrey Gray have proposed two theoretical approaches to the biology of personality.

EYSENCK'S RETICULAR ACTIVATION SYSTEM THEORY

British psychologist Hans Eysenck (1967) was among the first to describe the role of a particular brain system in personality. He developed an approach to extraversion/introversion based on the role of arousal in personality and behavior. In Chapter 5, we discussed the meaning of arousal as a state of engagement with the environment. In Chapter 3, we noted that reticular formation is located in the brain stem and plays a role in wakefulness or arousal. Eysenck focused on the *reticular activation system (RAS),* which is the name given to the reticular formation and its connections.

Eysenck posited that all of us share an optimal arousal level, a level at which we feel comfortably engaged with the world. However, Eysenck proposed, the RAS of extraverts and introverts differs with respect to the baseline level of arousal. You know that an extravert tends to be outgoing, sociable, and dominant and that an introvert is quieter and more reserved and passive. According to Eysenck, these behavioral differences reflect different arousal regulation strategies (Figure 12.6). Extraverts wake up in the morning under-aroused, *below* the optimal level, whereas introverts start out *above* the optimal level.

If *you* were feeling under-engaged with life, what might you do? You might listen to loud music or hang out with friends—in other words, behave like an extravert. If, on the other hand, you were feeling over-aroused or too stimulated, what would you do? You might spend time alone, keep distractions to a minimum, maybe sit quietly and

FIGURE 12.6 Eysenck's Reticular Activation System Theory Eysenck viewed introversion and extraversion as characteristic behavioral patterns that aim to regulate arousal around the individual's baseline level.

Introversion		Extraversion
Quiet, reserved, passive	**Personality Characteristics**	Outgoing, social, dominant
Above optimal level	**Level of Arousal**	Below optimal level
Keeping distractions to a minimum Being alone Reading quietly	**Typical Activities**	Seeking out distractions Spending time with friends Listening to loud music

read a book—in other words, you might act like an introvert. Thus, from Eysenck's perspective, we can understand the continuum of extraversion/introversion as demonstrating patterns of behavior aimed at regulating arousal around our baseline.

Research has not shown that extraverts and introverts differ in terms of baseline arousal. Instead, a process similar to Eysenck's model has been found—not involving the activation of RAS, but rather blood flow in the striatum, a part of the basal ganglia—that plays a role in dopamine levels (Hermes & others, 2011). Recall that dopamine is the neurotransmitter linked with the experience of reward. From this approach, introverts have higher baseline blood flow and extraverts have lower baseline blood flow to this region of the brain. Because extraverts are motivated to bring those dopamine levels up, they are more likely to seek out pleasurable experiences and thus behave in extraverted ways.

GRAY'S REINFORCEMENT SENSITIVITY THEORY

Jeffrey Gray proposed a neuropsychology of personality, called *reinforcement sensitivity theory*, that has been the subject of much research (Gray, 1987; Gray & McNaughton, 2000; Smillie & others, 2012). On the basis of animal learning principles, Gray posited that two neurological systems—the *behavioral activation system (BAS)* and the *behavioral inhibition system (BIS)*—could be viewed as underlying personality, as Figure 12.7 shows.

According to Gray, these systems explain differences in an organism's attention to rewards and punishers in the environment. An organism sensitive to rewards is more likely to learn associations between behaviors and rewards and therefore to show a characteristic pattern of seeking out rewarding opportunities. In contrast, an organism with a heightened sensitivity to punishers in the environment is more likely to learn associations between behaviors and negative consequences. Such an organism shows a characteristic pattern of avoiding such consequences.

In Gray's theory, the BAS is sensitive to rewards in the environment, predisposes one to feelings of positive emotion, and underlies the trait of extraversion. In contrast, the BIS is sensitive to punishments and is involved in avoidance learning; it predisposes the individual to feelings of fear and underlies the trait of neuroticism (Berkman, Lieberman, & Gable, 2009; Corr, 2008; Gray & McNaughton, 2000). Psychologists often measure the BAS and BIS in humans by using questionnaires that assess a person's attention to rewarding or punishing outcomes (Schmeichel, Harmon-Jones, & Harmon-Jones, 2010).

Gray's conceptual model of reinforcement sensitivity proposed interacting brain systems as primarily responsible for the behavioral manifestations of the BAS and BIS. Research has provided some evidence for the biological underpinnings of these systems. The amygdala, the prefrontal cortex, and the anterior cingulated cortex appear to serve together as a system for affective style (Davidson, 2005; McNaughton & Corr, 2008) and are particularly implicated in the BAS or extraversion (Pickering & Smillie, 2008; Smillie & others, 2012).

THE ROLE OF NEUROTRANSMITTERS

Neurotransmitters have also been implicated in personality in ways that fit Gray's model. As noted above, the neurotransmitter dopamine functions in the experience of reward. Dopamine is vital to learning that certain behaviors are rewarding, sending the message, "do it again!" Research has shown that dopamine is a factor in BAS or extraversion (Munafo & others, 2008; Wacker & others, 2012), suggesting that the dopaminergic system in extraverts is well prepared to learn associations between environmental cues and rewards (Depue & Collins, 1999).

Even stronger than the link between dopamine and extraversion is the relationship between the neurotransmitter serotonin and neuroticism (Brummett & others, 2008; Middeldorp & others, 2007). In this case, neuroticism is associated with low levels of circulating serotonin. Neuroticism is especially related to a certain serotonin transporter gene and to the binding of serotonin in the thalamus (Gonda & others, 2009; Harro & others, 2009; Vinberg & others, 2010). Individuals who have less circulating serotonin are prone to negative mood; giving them drugs that inhibit the reuptake of serotonin tends to decrease negative mood and enhance feelings of sociability (Hart, Ksir, & Ray, 2011). Interestingly, the influence of this gene on personality may depend

Behavioral Activation System

Sensitive to
Environmental reward

Behavior
Seek positive
consequences/rewards

Character of emotion
Positive

Personality trait
Extraversion

Behavioral Inhibition System

Sensitive to
Environmental punishment

Behavior
Avoid negative
consequences/punishments

Character of emotion
Negative

Personality trait
Neuroticism

FIGURE 12.7 Gray's Reinforcement Sensitivity Theory Gray theorized that two neurological systems, the BAS and the BIS, explain differences in an organism's attention to environmental rewards and punishments and in this way shape personality.

● **behavioral genetics** The study of the inherited underpinnings of behavioral characteristics.

on experience. Whether individuals who have this genetic characteristic actually develop into worriers depends on their social experiences (Pluess & others, 2010).

Keep in mind that finding associations between neurotransmitters and personality does not tell us about the potential causal pathways between these variables. Behavior can influence brain processes, and patterns of behavior can determine brain activity. One thing that behavior cannot influence, at least not yet, is genes, another important biological factor in personality.

Personality and Behavioral Genetics

Behavioral genetics is the study of the inherited underpinnings of behavioral characteristics. A great deal of research in behavioral genetics has involved twin studies, and the hub of this work is, appropriately, the University of Minnesota, Twin Cities.

Twin studies show that genetic factors explain a substantial amount of the observed differences in each of the big five traits. Remember that to conduct these studies, researchers compare identical twins, who share 100 percent of their genes, with fraternal twins, who share just 50 percent. All of the participants complete questionnaires measuring their traits. Then the researchers see if the identical twins are more similar to each other than the fraternal twins. Heritability estimates for the five factors are about 50 percent (Bouchard & Loehlin, 2001; Jang, Livesley, & Vernon, 1996; South & Krueger, 2008; Veselka & others, 2009). As noted in Chapter 8, heritability statistics have come into question (Charney, 2012; Crusio, 2012), and as such these estimates are likely higher than reality. Still, they suggest a substantial role of genes in explaining differences between people on personality traits.

Even aspects of personality that are not traits reveal genetic influence. For example, autobiographical memories about one's childhood and early family experiences (the kind of data that the personologist might find interesting) are influenced by genetics. Robert Krueger and his colleagues examined retrospective reports on the quality of family environments in a sample of twins who were reared apart (Krueger, Markon, & Bouchard, 2003). Participants rated their adoptive families on a variety of characteristics such as parental warmth, feelings of being wanted, and the strictness of their parents. These twins, though obviously sharing genetics, were reared by different families, so they were describing different experiences. Yet their recollections of their early family experiences were similar, and the heritability estimate for family cohesion ranged from 40 to 60 percent.

Understanding the role of genetic factors in personality is enormously complex. Research on non-twin samples often suggests much lower heritability, for reasons that are not well understood (South & Krueger, 2008). Furthermore, because genes and environment are often intertwined, it is very difficult to tease apart whether, and how, genes or experience explains enduring patterns of behavior. For instance, a little girl who is genetically predisposed to disruptive behavior may often find herself in a time-out or involved in arguments with parents or teachers. When that child emerges as an adult with a "fighting spirit" or lots of "spunk," are those adult traits the product of genes, experiences, or both? Finally, most traits are probably influenced by multiple genes (Costa & others, 2010), making the task of identifying specific molecular links very challenging.

Evaluating the Biological Perspectives

Exploring the biological aspects of personality is a vital continuing goal in personality psychology (South & others, 2013; Zuckerman, 2013). This work ties the field of personality to animal learning models, advances in brain imaging, and evolutionary theory (Revelle, 2008). However, a few cautions are necessary in thinking about biological variables and their place in personality.

As we considered above, biology can be the effect, not the cause, of personality. To be sure that you grasp this idea, first recall that personality is the individual's characteristic pattern of behavior, thoughts, and feelings. Then recall from previous chapters that behavior, thoughts, and feelings are physical events in the body and brain. If traits predispose individuals to particular and consistent behaviors, thoughts, and emotional responses, traits may play a role in forging particular habitually used pathways in the brain. Recall, too, from Chapter 7 that memory may be thought of as patterns of activation among neurons. The autobiographical memories that interest personologists, then, might be viewed as well-worn patterns of activation. To the extent that personality represents a person's characteristic pattern of thought or the accumulation of memories over the life span, personality may not only be influenced by the brain—it may also play a role in the brain's very structure and functions.

7· PERSONALITY ASSESSMENT

One of the great contributions of personality psychology is its development of rigorous methods for measuring mental processes. Psychologists use a number of scientifically developed methods to evaluate personality. They assess personality for different reasons—from clinical evaluation to career counseling and job selection (Huprich & Hopwood, 2013; Lowmaster & Morey, 2012; Makransky, Mortensen, & Glas, 2013; Slavin-Mulford & others, 2013).

Self-Report Tests

The most commonly used method of measuring personality characteristics is the **self-report test** (also called an *objective test* or an *inventory*), which directly asks people whether specific items describe their personality traits. Self-report personality tests include items such as

- I am easily embarrassed.
- I love to go to parties.
- I like to watch cartoons on TV.

Respondents choose from a limited number of answers (yes or no, true or false, agree or disagree).

One problem with self-report tests is *social desirability.* To grasp the idea of social desirability, imagine answering the item "I am lazy at times." This statement is probably true for everyone, but would you feel comfortable admitting it? When motivated by social desirability, individuals say what they think will make them look better. One way to measure the influence of social desirability is to give individuals a questionnaire that is designed to tap into this tendency. Such scales typically contain universally true but threatening items ("I like to gossip at times," "I have never said anything intentionally to hurt someone's feelings"). If scores on a trait item correlate with this measure of social desirability, we know that the test takers were probably not being straightforward on their trait ratings.

Another way to get around social desirability issues is to design scales so that it is virtually impossible for the respondent to know what the researcher is trying to measure. One means of accomplishing this goal is to use an **empirically keyed test,** a type of self-report test that is created by first identifying two groups that are known to be different. The researcher would give these two groups a large number of questionnaire items and then see which items show the biggest differences between the groups. Those items would become part of the scale to measure the group difference. For instance, a researcher might want to develop a test that distinguishes between individuals with a history of substance abuse and those with no such history. The researcher might generate a long list of true/false items asking about a variety of topics but not mentioning substance abuse. These questions would be presented to the members of the two groups, and on the basis of the responses, the researcher can then select the items that best discriminate between the members of the differing groups.

Note that an empirically keyed test avoids the issue of social desirability because the items that distinguish between the two groups are not related in any obvious way to the

test yourself

1. According to Eysenck, what part of the brain influences whether a person is an introvert or an extravert?
2. How does Gray's reinforcement sensitivity theory of personality explain extraversion and neuroticism?
3. What is behavioral genetics, and what kind of study is commonly used in research in this area?

● **self-report test** A method of measuring personality characteristics that directly asks people whether specific items describe their personality traits; also called an objective test or an inventory.

● **empirically keyed test** A type of self-report test that presents many questionnaire items to two groups that are known to be different in some central way.

"I like the way I look, but I hate my personality."

actual purpose of the test. For instance, those without a substance abuse history might typically respond "true" to the item "I enjoy taking long walks," whereas those with a history of substance abuse might respond "false"; but this item does not mention substance use, and there is no clear reason why it should distinguish between these groups.

Indeed, an important consideration with respect to empirically keyed tests is that researchers often do *not* know why a given test item distinguishes between two groups. Imagine, for example, that an empirically keyed test of achievement motivation includes an item such as "On TV, I prefer to watch sports, not romantic movies." A researcher might find that this item does a good job of distinguishing between higher-paid versus lower-paid managers in a work setting. However, does this item measure achievement motivation or, instead, simply the respondents' gender?

MMPI

● **Minnesota Multiphasic Personality Inventory (MMPI)** The most widely used and researched empirically keyed self-report personality test.

The **Minnesota Multiphasic Personality Inventory (MMPI)** is the most widely used and researched empirically keyed self-report personality test. The MMPI was initially constructed in the 1940s to assess "abnormal" personality tendencies. The most recent version of the inventory, the MMPI-2, is still widely used around the world to assess personality and predict outcomes (Butcher & others, 2011; Goodwin, Sellborn, & Arbisi, 2013; K. Han & others, 2013). The scale features 567 items and provides information on a variety of personality characteristics. The MMPI also includes items meant to assess whether the respondent is lying or trying to make a good impression (social desirability). The MMPI is used to assess mental health (Greene, 2011), as a tool in hiring decisions (Caillouet & others, 2010), and in forensic settings, assessing criminal risk (Bow, Flens, & Gould, 2010; Sellbom & others, 2010).

ASSESSMENT OF THE BIG FIVE FACTORS

● **face validity** The extent to which a test item appears to fit the particular trait it is measuring.

● **projective test** A personality assessment test that presents individuals with an ambiguous stimulus and asks them to describe it or tell a story about it—to project their own meaning onto the stimulus.

Paul Costa and Robert McCrae (1992) constructed the Neuroticism Extraversion Openness Personality Inventory—Revised (or NEO-PI-R, for short), a self-report test assessing the five-factor model: neuroticism, extraversion, openness, agreeableness, and conscientiousness. Other measures of the big five traits have relied on the lexical approach and offer the advantage of being available without a fee.

Unlike empirically keyed tests, measures of the big five generally contain straightforward items; for instance, the trait "talkative" might show up on an extraversion scale. These items have what psychologists call **face validity,** which means that the items seem on the surface to be testing the characteristic in question. Measures of the big five typically involve items that are obvious in terms of what they measure, but not all self-report assessments have this quality.

It is likely that you could give a reasonably good assessment of your own levels of traits such as neuroticism and extraversion. What about the more mysterious aspects of yourself and others? If you are like most people, you think of psychological assessments as tools to find out things you do not already know about yourself. For that objective, psychologists might turn to projective tests.

Projective Tests

I don't know... they **ALL** look like cows to me.

© Dan Reynolds. www.CartoonStock.com.

A **projective test** presents individuals with an ambiguous stimulus and asks them to describe it or tell a story about it—in other words, to *project* their own meaning onto the stimulus. Projective tests are based on the assumption that the ambiguity of the stimulus allows individuals to interpret it based on their feelings, desires, needs, and attitudes. Based on the defense mechanism of projection, projective tests are especially designed to elicit the individual's unconscious feelings and conflicts, providing an assessment that goes deeper than the surface of personality (Sahly & others, 2011).

Projective tests attempt to get inside the mind to discover how the test taker really feels and thinks; that is, they aim to go beyond the way the individual overtly presents himself or herself. Projective tests are theoretically aligned with psychodynamic perspectives on personality, which give more weight to the unconscious than do other perspectives.

Projective techniques require content analysis. The examiner must code the responses for the underlying motivations revealed in the story.

Perhaps the most famous projective test is the **Rorschach inkblot test,** developed in 1921 by Swiss psychiatrist Hermann Rorschach. The test consists of 10 cards, half in black-and-white and half in color, which the individual views one at a time (Figure 12.8). The test taker is asked to describe what he or she sees in each of the inkblots. The individual may say, for example, "I see two fairies having a tea party" or "This is a picture of the female reproductive organs." These responses are scored based on indications of various underlying psychological characteristics (Bornstein, 2012).

The Rorschach's usefulness in research is controversial. The test's reliability and validity have both been criticized (Garb & others, 2001; Hunsley & Bailey, 2001; Weiner, 2004). If the Rorschach were reliable, two different scorers would agree on the personality characteristics of the individual being tested. If the Rorschach were valid, it would predict behavior outside of the testing situation; that is, it would predict, for example, whether an individual will attempt suicide, become severely depressed, cope successfully with stress, or get along well with others. Research shows that the Rorschach does not meet these criteria of reliability and validity (Lilienfeld, Wood, & Garb, 2000).

Although still administered in clinical circles (Huprich, 2013; Krishnamurthy, Archer, & Groth-Marnat, 2011) and applied settings (Del Giudice, 2010), the Rorschach is not commonly used in personality research. However, the projective method itself remains a tool for studying personality, especially in the form of the Thematic Apperception Test (TAT).

The **Thematic Apperception Test (TAT),** developed by Henry Murray and Christiana Morgan in the 1930s, is designed to elicit stories that reveal something about an individual's personality. The TAT consists of a series of pictures like the one in Figure 12.9, each on an individual card or slide. The TAT test taker is asked to tell a story about each of the pictures, including events leading up to the situation described, the characters' thoughts and feelings, and the way the situation turns out.

In addition to being administered as a projective test in clinical practice, the TAT is used in research on people's need for achievement, affiliation, power, intimacy, and a variety of other needs (Brunstein & Maier, 2005; Schultheiss & Brunstein, 2005); unconscious defense mechanisms (Cramer, 2008a, 2008b; Cramer & Jones, 2007); and cognitive styles (Woike, 2008; Woike & Matic, 2004). In contrast to the Rorschach, TAT measures have shown reliability and validity (Woike, 2001).

Other Assessment Methods

Self-report questionnaires and projective techniques are just two of the multitude of assessment methods developed and used by personality psychologists. Many personality psychologists incorporate interviews as well as friend or peer ratings of individuals' traits or other characteristics. Personality psychologists also measure behavior directly, by observing a person either live or in a video (Kelly & Agnew, 2012). In addition, cognitive assessments have become more common in personality psychology, as researchers investigate topics such as the relation between personality and processes of attention and memory. Personality psychologists also use a host of psychophysiological measures, such as heart rate and skin conductance. Increasingly, personality psychologists are incorporating brain imaging as well.

Whether personality assessments are being used by clinical psychologists, psychological researchers, or other practitioners, the choice of assessment instrument depends greatly on the researcher's theoretical perspective. Figure 12.10 summarizes which methods are associated with each of the theoretical perspectives. The figure also summarizes each approach, including its major assumptions, and gives a sample research question addressed by each. Personality psychology is a diverse field, unified by a shared interest in understanding those aspects of the person that make the individual who he or she really is.

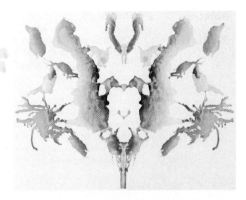

FIGURE 12.8 Type of Stimulus Used in the Rorschach Inkblot Test What do you see in this figure? Do you see two green seahorses? Or a pair of blue spiders? A psychologist who relies on the Rorschach test would examine your responses to find out who you are.

● **Rorschach inkblot test** A famous projective test that uses an individual's perception of inkblots to determine his or her personality.

● **Thematic Apperception Test (TAT)** A projective test that is designed to elicit stories that reveal something about an individual's personality.

FIGURE 12.9 Picture from the Thematic Apperception Test (TAT) What are this man and woman thinking and feeling? How did they come to this situation, and what will happen next? A psychologist who uses the TAT would analyze your story to find out your unconscious motives. Reprinted by permission of the publishers from *Thematic Apperception Test* by Henry A. Murray, Card 12F, Cambridge, MA: Harvard University Press. Copyright © 1943 by the President and the Fellows of Harvard College. Copyright © 1971 by Henry A. Murray.

Approach	Summary	Assumptions	Typical Methods	Sample Research Question
Psychodynamic	Personality is characterized by unconscious processes. Childhood experiences are of great importance to adult personality.	The most important aspects of personality are unconscious.	Case studies, projective techniques.	How do unconscious conflicts lead to dysfunctional behavior?
Humanistic	Personality evolves out of the person's innate, organismic motives to grow and actualize the self. These healthy tendencies can be undermined by social pressure.	Human nature is basically good. By getting in touch with who we are and what we really want, we can lead happier, healthier lives.	Questionnaires, interviews, observation.	Can situations be changed to support individuals' organismic values and enhance their well-being?
Trait	Personality is characterized by five general traits that are represented in the natural language that people use to describe themselves and others.	Traits are relatively stable over time. Traits predict behavior.	Questionnaires, observer reports.	Are the five factors universal across cultures?
Personological and Life Story	To understand personality, we must understand the whole person. We all have unique life experiences, and the stories we tell about those experiences make up our identities.	The life story provides a unique opportunity to examine the personality processes associated with behavior, development, and well-being.	Written narratives, TAT stories, autobiographical memories, interviews, and psychobiography.	How do narrative accounts of life experiences relate to happiness?
Social Cognitive	Personality is the pattern of coherence that characterizes a person's interactions with the situations he or she encounters in life. The individual's beliefs and expectations, rather than global traits, are the central variables of interest.	Behavior is best understood as changing across situations. To understand personality, we must understand what each situation means for a given person.	Multiple observations over different situations; video-recorded behaviors rated by coders; questionnaires.	When and why do individuals respond to challenging tasks with fear versus excitement?
Biological	Personality characteristics reflect underlying biological processes such as those carried out by the brain, neurotransmitters, and genes. Differences in behaviors, thoughts, and feelings depend on these processes.	Biological differences among individuals can explain differences in their personalities.	Brain imaging, twin studies, molecular genetic studies.	Do genes explain individual differences in extraversion?

FIGURE 12.10 **Approaches to Personality Psychology** This figure summarizes the broad approaches to personality described in this chapter. Many researchers in personality do not stick with just one approach but apply the various theories and methods that are most relevant to their research questions.

test yourself

1. What is an empirically keyed test?
2. What is a common problem with self-report tests?
3. What technique does the Thematic Apperception Test (TAT) involve?

8· PERSONALITY AND HEALTH AND WELLNESS

Personality comprises a set of enduring characteristics that influence behavior. As such, personality affects many behaviors that impact physical health and psychological wellness, as we consider in this final section.

Personality and Physical Health

We first survey personality characteristics that are linked, respectively, to health and to illness.

CONSCIENTIOUSNESS

Conscientiousness is not the sexiest personality trait, but it might well be the most important of the big five when it comes to longevity and healthy living (Hampson & others, 2013; Roberts & Mroczek, 2008; B. W. Roberts & others, 2009). The capacity to follow a sensible plan may be just what it takes to do the mundane tasks required to live a long, healthy life.

A variety of studies show that conscientious people tend to do all the things that they are told are good for their health, such as getting regular exercise, avoiding drinking and smoking, wearing seatbelts, and checking smoke detectors (O'Connor & others, 2009; Rush, Becker, & Curry, 2009; Turiano & others, 2012). Conscientiousness is correlated with better health and lower stress (Gartland, O'Connor, & Lawton, 2012; Murphy, Miller, & Wrosch, 2013; Takahashi, Roberts, & Hoshino, 2012). Research has shown that conscientious individuals are less likely to die than their counterparts who are less conscientious (Fry & Debats, 2009; Iwassa & others, 2008, 2009; Kern & Friedman, 2008; R. S. Wilson & others, 2004). In a longitudinal study of more than 1,200 individuals across seven decades, conscientiousness predicted a lower mortality risk from childhood through late adulthood (Martin, Friedman, & Schwartz, 2007).

PERSONAL CONTROL

Another personality characteristic associated with taking the right steps toward a long, healthy life is personal control (Baumeister & Alquist, 2009; Griffin & others, 2012). Feeling in control can reduce stress during difficult times and can lead to the development of problem-solving strategies to deal with hardship (S. E. Taylor, 2012; S. C. Thompson, 2001). Personal control has been linked to lower risk of cancer and cardiovascular disease (Sturmer, Hasselbach, & Amelang, 2006). Personal control has been related to emotional well-being, successful coping with a stressful event, healthy behavior change, and good health (Bertrand, Graham, & Lachman, 2013; Hughes, Berg, & Wiebe, 2012; Little, Snyder, & Wehmeyer, 2006; Sproesser & others, 2011).

SELF-EFFICACY

Self-efficacy is related to success in a wide variety of positive life changes, including achieving weight loss (Byrne, Barry, & Petry, 2012), exercising regularly (Lippke & Plotnikoff, 2006), quitting smoking (Berndt & others, 2012), reducing substance abuse (Goldsmith & others, 2012), practicing safe sex (Buhi & others, 2011), and adopting a healthy lifestyle (Axelsson & others, 2012). Evidence shows a strong link between self-efficacy and cardiovascular functioning following heart failure. Individuals high in self-efficacy are not only less likely to suffer a second hospitalization due to heart failure but also likely to live longer (Maeda & others, 2012; Sarkar, Ali, & Whooley, 2009).

If there is a problem to be fixed, self-efficacy—having a can-do attitude—is related to finding a solution. In one study, smokers were randomly assigned to one of three conditions. In the *self-efficacy condition,* individuals were told they had been chosen for the study because they had great potential to quit smoking (Warnecke & others, 2001). Then they participated in a 14-week program on smoking cessation. In the *treatment-alone condition,* individuals participated in the 14-week smoking cessation program but were told that they had been randomly selected for it. In the *no-treatment control condition,* individuals did not participate in the smoking cessation program. At the end of the 14 weeks, individuals in the self-efficacy condition were more likely to have quit smoking than their counterparts in the other two conditions. The Psychological Inquiry shows the results.

OPTIMISM

A factor that is often linked to positive functioning and adjustment is optimism (Carver & Connor-Smith, 2010; Peterson & Seligman, 2003). Researchers have found that optimism is associated with taking proactive steps to protect one's health (Carver, Scheier, & Segerstrom, 2010; Ramirez-Maestre, Esteve, & Lopez, 2012).

Optimism has been studied in two different ways. First, some scientists, including Martin Seligman (1990), focus on how optimists and pessimists explain the causes of events in their lives. From this perspective, optimists explain the causes of bad events as external, unstable, and specific, whereas pessimists explain them as internal, stable, and global. Studies have associated explaining life events optimistically with a variety of positive outcomes (Jowsey & others, 2012; Reivich & Gillham, 2003).

Martin Seligman (b. 1942) Seligman went from pessimist to optimist and believes that others can, too. Seligman (1990) provided the details in his book *Learned Optimism.*

psychological *inquiry*

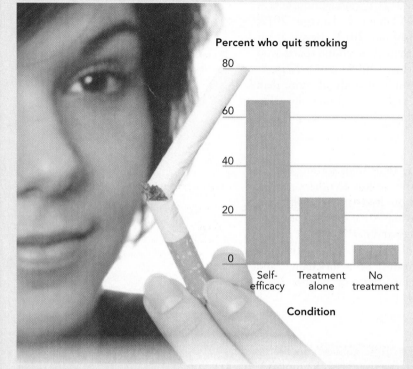

Percent who quit smoking

Condition (X-axis): Self-efficacy, Treatment alone, No treatment

A Can-Do Attitude Means You Can Quit Smoking

The figure shows the results of the study on self-efficacy and smoking cessation (Warnecke & others, 2001). Smokers were randomly assigned to one of three conditions—self-efficacy, treatment alone, and no treatment. Notice that the Y, or vertical, axis shows the dependent variable, the percentage of participants who quit smoking. The X, or horizontal, axis shows the independent variable, the groups to which participants were assigned. Try your hand at the following questions.

1. Why were participants randomly assigned to groups?

2. If the researchers concluded that the self-efficacy manipulation caused these differences, would their conclusion be justified? Explain.

3. How might the results of this study be generalized to groups who wish to change other behaviors?

4. How would you design a correlational study that would examine the relationship between self-efficacy and smoking cessation?

A second approach to optimism focuses on optimism as having the general expectation that good things are more likely than bad things to occur in the future (Carver & Connor-Smith, 2010; Carver & Scheier, 2009). Numerous studies reveal that those who hold these positive expectancies for the future are physically and mentally healthier than pessimists (Boehm & Kubzansky, 2012; Gallagher, Lopez, & Pressman, 2013; Tindle & others, 2012). Optimism is related to effective immune system functioning (O'Donovan & others, 2009, 2012; Segerstrom & Sephton, 2010). A recent study found that a higher level of optimism predicted fewer adverse clinical events among patients with coronary heart disease 12 months later (Hevey, McGee, & Horgan, 2013). Another study of people ages 100 or more showed a relationship between an optimistic outlook and physical health (Tigani & others, 2012).

As you think about the traits we have examined—conscientiousness, personal control, self-efficacy, and optimism—and their relationship to good health, keep in mind that you can *cultivate* these qualities. Studies show that even conscientiousness, the most stable of these characteristics, can increase, especially in young adulthood. Although these characteristics are generally associated with wellness, other aspects of personality are linked to health problems, as we now consider.

PERSONALITY TYPES: THE TYPE A/TYPE B AND TYPE D BEHAVIOR PATTERNS

In the late 1950s, a secretary for two cardiologists, Meyer Friedman and Ray Rosenman, observed that the chairs in their waiting rooms were tattered and worn, but only on the front edges. The cardiologists themselves had noticed the impatience of their cardiac patients, who often arrived exactly on time and were in a great hurry to leave. Intrigued by this consistency, they conducted a study of 3,000 healthy men between the ages of 35 and 59 over 8 years to find out whether people with certain behavioral characteristics might be prone to heart problems (Friedman & Rosenman, 1974). During the 8 years, one group of men had twice as many heart attacks or other forms of heart disease as the other men.

Friedman and Rosenman described the common personality characteristics of the men who developed coronary disease as the **Type A behavior pattern,** a cluster of characteristics—being excessively competitive, hard-driven, impatient, and hostile. Rosenman and Friedman labeled the behavior of the healthier group, who were more relaxed and easygoing, the **Type B behavior pattern.**

Subsequent research showed that the link between Type A behavior and coronary disease is not as strong as Friedman and Rosenman believed (Suls & Swain, 1998; R. B. Williams, 2001, 2002). However, certain components of Type A are linked with coronary risk (Spielberger, 2004), especially hostility (Mwendwa & others, 2013). People who are hostile are more likely to develop heart disease than their less angry counterparts (Eng & others, 2003; K. A. Matthews & others, 2004). People with hostile feelings tend to have strong physiological reactions to stress: Their heart races, their breathing quickens, and their muscles tense up (K. King, 2012; Vella & others, 2012).

There has been increased interest in the **Type D behavior pattern,** which describes individuals who are generally distressed, frequently experience negative emotions, and are socially inhibited (Beutel & others, 2012; Cosci, 2012; Molloy & others, 2012). Even after adjustment for depression, Type D individuals face a threefold increased risk of adverse cardiovascular outcomes (Denollet & Conraads, 2011). A meta-analysis found that Type D individuals with cardiovascular disease are at a higher risk for major adverse cardiac events and have a lower health-related quality of life (O'Dell & others, 2011).

Personality and Psychological Well-Being

Among the most consistent findings in personality research is the strong association between personality traits and psychological well-being. Specifically, neuroticism is strongly related to lower levels of well-being, whereas extraversion is related to higher levels (Ni Mhaolain & others, 2012: Otonari & others, 2012; Wilt & Revelle, 2009). The links between these two traits and well-being have even been found in orangutans (Weiss, King, & Perkins, 2006). What explains these connections?

As defined by psychologists, **subjective well-being** is a person's assessment of his or her level of positive affect and negative affect, and an evaluation of his or her life in general (Diener, 2012a). This definition provides a clue as to why the traits of neuroticism and extraversion are so strongly related to well-being. Neurotic individuals experience more negative affect than others, and their moods are more changeable. David Watson, a personality and clinical psychologist who specializes in the study of mood, has suggested that negative emotion is at the very core of the trait of neuroticism (Miller, Vachon, & Lynam, 2009; Watson & Clark, 1997).

Interestingly, however, research has shown that neurotics can be happy—especially if they are also extraverted (Hotard & others, 1989). Indeed, Watson suggests that positive emotion is the core of the trait of extraversion (Watson & Naragon, 2009). Research has shown that extraverts are happier than introverts even when they are alone (Lucas, 2008). In fact, research has supported the conclusion that extraverts are happier regardless of what they are doing or with whom they are doing it (Lucas, 2007; McNiel, Lowman, & Fleeson, 2010).

If you are not very conscientious, or you are a pessimist with an external locus of control, or you are hostile, or neurotic, or an introvert—or a hostile, neurotic introvert—you may be feeling your mood deflating. If personality is stable, what good is it to find out that your personality—who you really are—might put you at risk for illness and make you miserable?

A positive way to think about these issues is to focus on the difference between traits and states (Marine & others, 2006). Recall that traits are enduring characteristics—the way you generally are. In contrast, states (such as positive or negative moods) are briefer experiences. Having a trait, such as neuroticism, that predisposes you to feelings of worry (a state) does not mean that your overall well-being must suffer.

● **Type A behavior pattern** A cluster of characteristics—including being excessively competitive, hard-driven, impatient, and hostile—related to a higher incidence of heart disease.

● **Type B behavior pattern** A cluster of characteristics—including being relaxed and easygoing—related to a lower incidence of heart disease.

● **Type D behavior pattern** A cluster of characteristics—including being generally distressed, having negative emotions, and being socially inhibited—related to adverse cardiovascular outcomes.

● **subjective well-being** A person's assessment of his or her own level of positive affect relative to negative affect, and an evaluation of his or her life in general.

test yourself

1. What are four personality characteristics that are associated with positive functioning and positive life changes?
2. How have various researchers defined optimism?
3. What is the Type A behavior pattern, and what specific aspect of it is most often linked to coronary disease?

Instead, recognizing that you tend to be neurotic may be an important step in noting when your negative moods are potentially being fed by this trait and are not necessarily the result of objective events. Finding out that you have a personality style associated with higher levels of stress or lower levels of happiness does not mean that you are doomed. Rather, you can use this information to cultivate good habits and to make the most of your unique qualities.

Remember, too, that personality characteristics influence health through their relationships to behaviors and the experience of stress. Even a person very low in conscientiousness can engage in healthy behaviors. Consider that characteristics such as locus of control and self-efficacy are about your beliefs about the world, and these aspects of personality are changeable. Recall that in the Psychological Inquiry on page 426 self-efficacy was manipulated by simply telling people they had high potential to change. Believing in *your own* potential may be the first step to enhancing your health and wellness.

1. PSYCHODYNAMIC PERSPECTIVES

Freud developed psychoanalysis through his work with patients suffering from hysterical symptoms (physical symptoms with no physical cause). Freud viewed these symptoms as representing conflicts between sexual drive and duty. Freud believed that most personality—which, in his theory, includes the id, ego, and superego—is unconscious. The ego uses various defense mechanisms, Freud said, to reduce anxiety.

A number of theorists criticized and revised Freud's approach. Horney said that the need for security, not sex or aggression, is our most important need. Jung developed the concept of the collective unconscious, a storehouse of archetypes. Adler's individual psychology stresses that people are striving toward perfection.

Weaknesses of the psychodynamic perspectives include overreliance on reports from the past and overemphasis of the unconscious mind. Strengths of psychodynamic approaches include recognizing the importance of childhood, conceptualizing development through stages, and calling attention to the role of unconscious processes in behavior.

2. HUMANISTIC PERSPECTIVES

Humanistic perspectives stress a person's capacity for personal growth and positive human qualities. Maslow developed the concept of a hierarchy of needs, with self-actualization being the highest human need. In Rogers's approach, each of us is born with a tendency toward growth, a sense of what is good and bad for us, and a need for unconditional positive regard. Because we are often denied unconditional positive regard, we may become alienated from our innate growth tendencies. In order to reconnect with these innate tendencies, Rogers felt, a person required a relationship that included unconditional positive regard, empathy, and genuineness.

The humanistic perspectives recognize positive human capacities, but critics suggest the approach is too optimistic and may downplay personal responsibility.

3. TRAIT PERSPECTIVES

Trait theories emphasize that personality consists of traits—broad, enduring dispositions that lead to characteristic responses. Allport stated that traits should produce consistent behavior in different situations, and he used the lexical approach to personality traits, which involves using all the words in the natural language that could describe a person as a basis for understanding the traits of personality.

The current dominant perspective in personality psychology is the five-factor model. The big five traits include openness to experience, conscientiousness, extraversion, agreeableness, and neuroticism. Studying people in terms of their traits has value, but trait approaches are criticized for focusing on broad dimensions and not attending to each person's uniqueness.

4. PERSONOLOGICAL AND LIFE STORY PERSPECTIVES

Murray described personology as the study of the whole person. Contemporary followers of Murray study personality through narrative accounts and interviews. McAdams introduced the life story approach to identity, which views identity as a constantly changing story with a beginning, a middle, and an end. Psychobiography is a form of personological investigation that applies personality theory to one person's life. Life story approaches to personality reveal the richness of each person's unique life story, but it is difficult to carry out and is time-consuming.

5. SOCIAL COGNITIVE PERSPECTIVES

Social cognitive theory states that behavior, environment, and person/cognitive factors are important in understanding personality. In Bandura's view, these factors reciprocally interact.

Two important concepts in social cognitive theory are self-efficacy and personal control. Self-efficacy is the belief that one can master a situation and produce positive outcomes. Personal control refers to individuals' beliefs about whether the outcomes of their actions depend on their own acts (internal) or on events outside of their control (external).

Mischel's controversial book *Personality and Assessment* stressed that people do not behave consistently across different situations but rather tailor their behavior to suit particular situations. Personality psychologists countered that personality does predict behavior for some people some of the time. Mischel developed a revised approach to personality centered on cognitive affective processing systems (CAPS). According to CAPS, personality is best understood as a person's habitual emotional and cognitive reaction to specific situations.

A particular strength of social cognitive theory is its focus on cognitive processes. However, social cognitive approaches have not given adequate attention to enduring individual differences, to biological factors, and to personality as a whole.

6. BIOLOGICAL PERSPECTIVES

Eysenck suggested that introversion/extraversion can be understood as reflecting differences in arousal regulation. Gray developed a reinforcement sensitivity theory of personality, suggesting that extraversion and neuroticism can be understood as two neurological systems that respond to rewards (the behavioral activation system, or BAS) and punishments (the behavioral inhibition system, or BIS) in the environment.

Research has found that dopamine is associated with behavioral approach (extraversion) and serotonin with behavioral avoidance (neuroticism). Behavioral genetic studies have shown that the heritability of personality traits is approximately 50 percent. Studies of biological processes in personality are valuable but can overestimate the causal role of biological factors.

7. PERSONALITY ASSESSMENT

Self-report tests assess personality by asking participants about their preferences and behaviors. One problem in self-report research is the tendency for individuals to respond in socially desirable ways. Empirically keyed tests avoid social desirability problems by using items that distinguish between groups even if we do not know why the items do so.

The Minnesota Multiphasic Personality Inventory (MMPI) is the most widely used empirically keyed personality test. The most popular test for assessing the big five traits is the NEO-PI-R, which uses self-report items to measure each of the traits.

Projective tests, designed to assess unconscious aspects of personality, present individuals with an ambiguous stimulus, such as an inkblot or a picture, and ask them to tell a story about it. Projective tests are based on the assumption that individuals will project their personalities onto these stimuli. The Thematic Apperception Test (TAT) is a projective test that has been used in personality research. Other assessment methods include behavioral observation, reports from peers, and psychophysiological and neuropsychological measures.

8. PERSONALITY AND HEALTH AND WELLNESS

Conscientiousness and personal control relate to health and longevity through their association with healthy lifestyle choices. Self-efficacy is also related to the ability to make positive changes in lifestyle. Optimism is another personality characteristic that is related to better health.

The Type A behavior pattern is a set of characteristics including hostility, time urgency, and competitiveness. Type B behavior, in contrast, refers to a more easygoing style. With regard to predicting cardiovascular disease, the crucial aspect of Type A appears to be hostility. The Type D personality is prone to distress, and this type has been linked to poorer health outcomes.

Personality traits that are related to health and wellness can also be thought of as states. Thus, even if you are low on these wellness traits, you can still benefit by seeking out states that foster positive attributes.

key *terms*

personality, p. 396

psychodynamic perspectives, p. 396

id, p. 397

ego, p. 397

superego, p. 397

defense mechanisms, p. 398

Oedipus complex, p. 400

collective unconscious, p. 402

archetypes, p. 402

individual psychology, p. 402

humanistic perspectives, p. 403

unconditional positive regard, p. 404

conditions of worth, p. 404

trait theories, p. 406

big five factors of personality, p. 407

personological and life story perspectives, p. 412

social cognitive perspectives, p. 414

self-efficacy, p. 415

cognitive affective processing systems (CAPS), p. 417

behavioral genetics, p. 420

self-report test, p. 421

empirically keyed test, p. 421

Minnesota Multiphasic Personality Inventory (MMPI), p. 422

face validity, p. 422

projective test, p. 422

Rorschach inkblot test, p. 423

Thematic Apperception Test (TAT), p. 423

Type A behavior pattern, p. 427

Type B behavior pattern, p. 427

Type D behavior pattern, p. 427

subjective well-being, p. 427

apply your *knowledge*

1. Consider a facet of your personality that you might want to change. From the perspective of Freud's psychoanalytic theory and Rogers's humanistic theory, could you change this aspect of your personality? If so, how?

2. How important has your childhood been in the development of your adult personality? Choose an experience or series of experiences in childhood and describe how they are represented in your current personality.

3. If you are a fan of reality television, try your hand at identifying the personality characteristics of the individuals involved. Are any of the folks from *Real Housewives* or *Survivor* particularly neurotic or conscientious? If you prefer fictional shows, consider your favorite characters: What are the traits these individuals express?

4. Look at your own social networking profile. Do you think you are expressing the "real you"? If so, how?

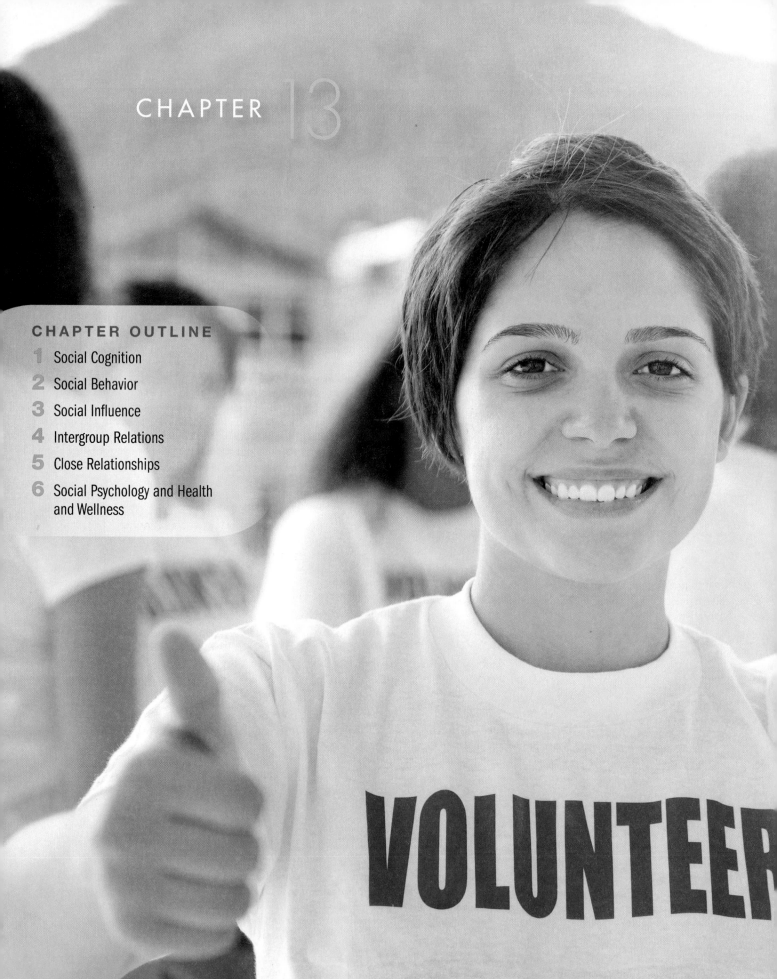

CHAPTER 13

VOLUNTEER

Social Psychology

Feeding 200 Children

Imagine trying to feed 200 children. How would you do it? In the United States, some 17 million children do not have access to adequate food (Coleman-Jensen & others, 2012). Hunger can have far-reaching consequences for children's development and school progress. Because poor families may rely on schools to provide meals for children, hunger can be especially problematic when schools are on break.

In 2011, 10 high school students in San Diego decided to combat hunger in their community. Partnering with a local nonprofit agency, they created the FULL program, with the goal of feeding needy children during school breaks. Canvassing local neighborhoods for donations of food and money, those 10 students ultimately raised more than $10,000 and provided 3,750 meals to over 200 children (Stayclassy.org, 2011).

Sometimes, solving problems requires that people come together and do more than any one person could ever accomplish alone. The ways that people come together—to solve problems, interact, and form bonds with one another—is the essence of social psychology. ●

PREVIEW

We begin our study of social psychology by examining social cognition and then exploring social behavior, including altruism and aggression. We next look at conformity, obedience, and social influence before considering how the groups to which we belong shape our interactions with other groups. We probe the world of close relationships, including attraction and love. Finally, we consider the vital role of social connections in health and wellness.

1· SOCIAL COGNITION

● **social psychology** The study of how people think about, influence, and relate to other people.

Social psychology is the study of how people think about, influence, and relate to other people. As you will see, social psychologists take many of the topics we have covered so far—including perception, cognition, and emotion—and examine them in a social context. Social psychologists are especially interested in the ways that social situations influence behavior.

Social cognition is the area of social psychology that explores how people select, interpret, remember, and use social information (Carlston, 2013; Forgas, Fiedler, & Sedikides, 2012). Essentially, it is the way in which individuals think in social situations (Eiser, 2012; Hamilton & Carlston, 2013; Koerner, 2012).

Person Perception

Person perception refers to the processes by which we use social stimuli to form impressions of others (Semin & Garrido, 2012). One important social cue is the face (Hugenberg & Wilson, 2013; Waenke, Samochowiecz, & Landwehr, 2012). Research shows that we automatically process information about trustworthiness and dominance conveyed in faces, without conscious effort (Stewart & others, 2012).

Alexander Todorov and his colleagues (2005) examined how perception of faces can influence political elections. They asked people to rate the competence of individuals from photographs of their faces. The faces were of candidates in the 2000, 2002, and 2004 U.S. House and Senate elections. Respondents' ratings accurately predicted the outcome for about *70 percent* of the elections. Those faces gave away information about the candidates that was meaningful to the perceivers, including how competent the perceivers felt each office-seeker would be (Mattes & others, 2010). Other aspects of faces can also have important implications for social perception, as we now consider.

PHYSICAL ATTRACTIVENESS AND OTHER PERCEPTUAL CUES

Physical attractiveness has been recognized as a powerful social cue (Harter, 2012). Judith Langlois and her colleagues found that even infants as young as 3 to 6 months of age showed a preference for looking at attractive faces versus unattractive faces, as rated by adults (Hoss & Langlois, 2003; Ramsey & others, 2004). Attractive individuals are generally assumed to have a variety of other positive characteristics, including being better adjusted, socially skilled, friendly, likable, extraverted, and likely to achieve superior job performance (Langlois & others, 2000). These positive expectations for physically attractive individuals have been referred to as the "beautiful is good" stereotype.

● **stereotype** A generalization about a group's characteristics that does not consider any variations from one individual to another.

A **stereotype** is a generalization about a group's characteristics that does not consider any variations from one individual to another. Stereotypes are a natural extension of the limits on human cognitive processing and our reliance on concepts in cognitive processing (Gaines, 2012). We simplify the task of understanding people by classifying them as members of groups or categories with which we are familiar. It takes more mental effort to consider a person's individual characteristics than it does to label him or her as a member of a particular group or category. In this sense, stereotypes are heuristics, those mental shortcuts we reviewed in Chapter 8.

Is there any truth to the "beautiful is good" stereotype? Attractive people may indeed possess a number of positive characteristics (Langlois & others, 2000). Does that mean that attractiveness is naturally related to, for example, better social skills? Not necessarily.

One way that stereotypes can influence individuals is through *self-fulfilling prophecy*. In a self-fulfilling prophecy, expectations cause individuals to act in ways that serve to make the expectations come true. Robert Rosenthal and Lenore Jacobsen conducted the classic self-fulfilling prophecy study in 1968. The researchers told grade-school teachers that five students were likely to be "late bloomers"—that these students had high levels of ability that would likely shine forth over time. In reality, however, the researchers had randomly selected the students. Nonetheless, a year later, the researchers found that teachers' expectations for the "late bloomers" were reflected in student performance—the academic performance of these five was beyond that of other students. Self-fulfilling prophecy shows the potential power of stereotypes and other sources of expectations on human behavior.

Let's apply self-fulfilling prophecy to physically attractive individuals. Attractive people may receive differential treatment from others throughout their lives. This special treatment increases the likelihood that the attractive individuals might well develop enhanced social skills and be more self-confident than others.

Another relevant question is, what makes a face attractive? *People* magazine's "50 Most Beautiful People" issue might lead you to conclude that attractiveness is about being exceptional in some physical way. Consider Beyoncé's radiant smile or Ryan Gosling's icy blue eyes. It turns out, though, that very attractive faces are actually *average*.

Using computer technology that allowed them to digitally "average" the faces of a large group of individuals of varying attractiveness, Langlois and her colleagues (1994) created composite faces. A large sample of college students then rated the individual faces and the composites. The results showed that individual faces were less attractive than faces that were created by averaging 8, 16, or 32 other faces. These researchers concluded that attractive faces are "just average." Although "averageness" is not the only predictor of attractiveness, Langlois and her colleagues suggest that being average is an essential component (along with variables such as symmetry and youthfulness) of facial attractiveness.

What makes a face attractive? Research has found that "averageness" is an essential component.

FIRST IMPRESSIONS

When we first meet someone, typically the new acquaintance quickly makes an impression. That first impression can have lasting effects (North & Fiske, 2012; Uleman & Kressel, 2013). Why are they so powerful? One possibility is the primacy effect (Chapter 7): the tendency to attend to and remember what they learned first (N. H. Anderson, 1965). How quickly do we make these initial impressions of others? In one study, individuals needed just a 100-millisecond exposure time to unfamiliar faces to form an impression (Willis & Todorov, 2006).

Are first impressions correct? A number of studies have shown that they can be. Based on photographs or very brief interactions or video clips, people are able to accurately discern a person's romantic interest in them (Place & others, 2012), propensity for violence (Fowler, Lilienfeld, & Patrick, 2009; Stillman, Maner, & Baumeister, 2010), and sexual orientation (Ambady, Hallahan, & Conner, 1999; Stern & others, 2013b).

In addition, a large body of evidence suggests that even in cases where two people are only slightly acquainted, ratings of personality traits can be surprisingly accurate. In one study, participants watched video clips of a group of target individuals, and they rated the targets on various traits. After just *5 seconds*, those ratings related very well to the targets' self-reports for extraversion, conscientiousness, and intelligence. Neuroticism, openness to experience, and agreeableness took a little longer, but within 1 minute judges were reasonably good at producing ratings that agreed with the targets' self-ratings (Carney, Colvin, & Hall, 2007).

Of course, once you become acquainted with someone, you have a lot more information to use to form an opinion of the person. The process by which we come to understand the causes of others' behavior and form an impression of them as individuals is called *attribution*.

Attribution

Attributions are explanations of the causes of behavior (Reeder, 2013). We can observe someone's actions, such as a friend giving money to a homeless person. To determine the underlying cause of that behavior, what it means about that friend, we often have to make inferences. Making inferences means taking the information we have and coming up with a good guess about who someone is and what the person is likely to do in the future (Manusov, 2012; Todorov, 2013). The results of those inferences are our attributions. What factors play a role in the attributions we make about behaviors? This question is addressed by attribution theory.

● **attribution theory** The view that people are motivated to discover the underlying causes of behavior as part of their effort to make sense of the behavior.

Attribution theory views people as motivated to discover the underlying causes of behavior as part of their effort to make sense of the behavior (Heider, 1958; Kelley, 1973; Weiner, 2006). Attributions vary along three dimensions:

- *Internal/external causes:* Internal attributions are causes inside and specific to the person, such as his or her traits and abilities. External attributions are causes outside the person, such as social pressure, aspects of the social situation, the weather, and luck. Did Beth get an *A* on the test because she is smart or because the test was easy?

- *Stable/unstable causes:* Whether the cause of behavior is relatively enduring and permanent or temporary influences attributions. Did Aaron blow up at his girlfriend because he is a hostile guy or because he was in a bad mood that day?

- *Controllable/uncontrollable causes:* We perceive that people have power over some causes (for instance, by preparing delicious food for a picnic) but not others (rain on picnic day). So, if a rainstorm spoils Henry's picnic, we would not hold that against him.

● **fundamental attribution error** Observers' overestimation of the importance of internal traits and underestimation of the importance of external situations when they seek explanations of an actor's behavior.

ATTRIBUTIONAL ERRORS

In attribution theory, the person who produces the behavior to be explained is called the *actor.* The person who offers a causal explanation of the actor's behavior is called the *observer.* Actors often explain their own behavior in terms of external causes. In contrast, observers frequently explain the actor's behavior in terms of internal causes. Taylor might explain that she honked at a car that was slow to move when the light turned green because she was in a hurry to get to the hospital to see her ill father, but the other driver might think she was rude.

● **false consensus effect** People's overestimation of the degree to which everybody else thinks or acts the way they themselves do.

The **fundamental attribution error** refers to the tendency of observers to overestimate the importance of internal traits and underestimate the importance of external factors when they explain an actor's behavior (Jones & Harris, 1967; Kressel & Uleman, 2010; Ramsey & de C. Hamilton, 2010) (Figure 13.1).

Although it is called the *fundamental* attribution error, this error is not universal. Cross-cultural studies show that Westerners tend to attribute causes of behavior to the person. In contrast, those from collectivistic cultures are more likely to look to the situation to explain the behavior of others (Imada, 2012; Morris & Peng, 1994; Rips, 2011).

Observer Tends to give internal, trait explanations of actor's behavior

"She's late with her report because she can't concentrate on her own responsibilities."

HEURISTICS IN SOCIAL INFORMATION PROCESSING

When we make attributions, we are engaging in social information processing. Just as heuristics are useful in general information processing, they can play a role in *social* information processing (Gigerenzer & Gaissmaier, 2011; McDonald & others, 2011). Heuristics can be helpful tools for navigating the complex social landscape, but they can lead to mistakes.

Actor Tends to give external, situational explanations of own behavior

"I'm late with my report because other people keep asking me to help them with their projects."

One common heuristic is the false consensus effect. The **false consensus effect** means overestimating the degree to which everybody else thinks or acts the way we do. Ask yourself: "How many students at your school support the death penalty?" The false consensus effect tells us that your answer is likely to depend on whether *you* support the death penalty.

FIGURE 13.1 **The Fundamental Attribution Error** In this situation, the supervisor is the observer, and the employee is the actor.

The fundamental attribution error and the false consensus effect are both related to the special significance of our own thoughts and circumstances. Both of these effects reflect the vast amount of information we have about ourselves relative to the more limited information we have about other people, and they suggest the special place of the self in social information processing.

The Self as a Social Object

Each of us carries around mental representations of ourselves. We can think of the self as our schema, as described in Chapter 7, for who we are, what we are like (and not like), and how we feel about these perceptions. The self is different from other social objects because we know so much more about ourselves than we do about others (Hoyle, 2013).

The self is special as well because we value ourselves. One of the most important self-related variables is *self-esteem*, the degree to which we have positive or negative feelings about ourselves (Harter, 2013; Kernis, 2013). In general, research has shown that it is good to feel good about oneself (Koch, 2013; O'Brien, Bartoletti, & Leitzel, 2013; Solomon, 2013).

Individuals with high self-esteem often possess a variety of **positive illusions**—rosy views of themselves that are not necessarily rooted in reality (Hansen & Pronin, 2012). Indeed, research shows that many of us think of ourselves as "above average" on valued characteristics, including how trustworthy, objective, and capable we are (Gregg & Sedikides, 2010; Hepper & Sedikides, 2012; Hepper, Sedikides, & Cai, 2013; Sedikides, 2009; Sedikides & Skowronski, 2009, 2012).

Shelley Taylor and her colleagues have demonstrated that those who hold positive illusions about themselves are psychologically healthier and more likely to be judged positively by others (S. E. Taylor, 2011c, 2013; Taylor & Sherman, 2008; Taylor & others, 2003a, 2003b, 2007).

Self-serving bias refers to the tendency to take credit for our successes and to deny responsibility for our failures when we make attributions about our own behavior. Think about taking an exam. If you do well, you are likely to take credit for that success ("I'm smart"); you tend to make internal attributions. If you do poorly, however, you are more likely to blame situational factors ("The test was too hard"); you tend to make external attributions.

SELF-OBJECTIFICATION

Self-objectification refers to the tendency to see oneself as an object in others' eyes. Researchers have focused on how women have been socialized to think of themselves and their bodies as objects in the social world (Fredrickson & Roberts, 1997). Making women aware of their status as sexual objects can induce body image concerns, shame, and restricted eating (Moradi & Huang, 2008). Chronic feelings of objectification are associated with lower self-esteem and higher levels of depression (Miner-Rubino, Twenge, & Fredrickson, 2002). Women who feel objectified are less likely to reject sexism and less likely to engage in social activism (Calogero, 2013).

Self-objectification can interfere with task performance. For example, in a series of studies, men and women were asked first to try on either a sweater or a swimsuit and then to complete a math test. After trying on a swimsuit, women performed much more poorly on the math test. The researchers surmised that trying on the swimsuit heightened women's experience of self-objectification and body shame, reducing their mental resources for completing the math test (Fredrickson & others, 1998).

Self-objectification research suggests that reminding women of the fact that they are often judged based on their appearance has important implications for their feelings and behavior. A similar process has been found for members of stereotyped groups.

● **positive illusions** Favorable views of the self that are not necessarily rooted in reality.

● **self-serving bias** The tendency to take credit for one's successes and to deny responsibility for one's failures.

● **self-objectification** The tendency to see oneself primarily as an object in the eyes of others.

STEREOTYPE THREAT

● **stereotype threat** An individual's fast-acting, self-fulfilling fear of being judged based on a negative stereotype about his or her group.

Stereotype threat is an individual's fast-acting, self-fulfilling fear of being judged based on a negative stereotype about his or her group. A person who experiences stereotype threat is well aware of stereotypical expectations for him or her as a member of a group. In stereotype-relevant situations, the individual experiences anxiety about living "down" to expectations and consequently underperforms (Aronson & others, 2013; Hartley & Sutton, 2013; Weger & others, 2012). Claude Steele and Eliot Aronson (1995, 2004) have shown that when a test is presented to African American and European American students who have first simply checked a box indicating their ethnicity, the African Americans perform more poorly. When attention is not drawn to ethnicity, no differences in performance emerged.

Stereotype threat affects performance on math tests by women compared to men, even when both groups have equally strong math training (Spencer, Steele, & Quinn, 1999). European American men, too, can fall prey to stereotype threat; in a study of golf ability, European American men performed more poorly than African American men when they were told the test measured "natural athletic ability" (Stone, 2002).

What factors might may help prevent the consequences of stereotype threat? In one study, African American schoolchildren who were asked their race prior to a math test did not perform as well unless the test was presented to them as a challenge, not as a threat (Alter & others, 2010). In addition, self-esteem may help buffer the effects of stereotype threat in women, especially if women are reminded of another aspect of the self (for instance, "college student") that is positively associated with math performance (Rydell & Boucher, 2010).

SOCIAL COMPARISON

● **social comparison** The process by which individuals evaluate their thoughts, feelings, behaviors, and abilities in relation to others.

Have you ever felt great about getting a *B* on a test, only to feel deflated after finding out a friend got an *A*? Comparing ourselves to other people is one way we come to understand our own behavior. **Social comparison** is the process by which we evaluate our thoughts, feelings, behaviors, and abilities in relation to others. Social comparison tells us what our distinctive characteristics are and aids us in building an identity.

Sixty years ago, Leon Festinger (1954) proposed a theory of social comparison. The theory states that when no objective means are available to evaluate our opinions and abilities, we compare ourselves with others. Extended and modified over the years, Festinger's theory continues to provide an important rationale for how individuals come to know themselves (Brakel, Dijkstra, & Buunk, 2012). Contemporary researchers have focused on *downward* social comparisons, that is, individuals' comparisons with people whom they consider inferior to themselves. People under threat (from negative feedback or low self-esteem, for example) try to feel better by comparing themselves with others who are less fortunate (Caricati, 2012).

Attitudes

● **attitudes** An individual's opinions and beliefs about people, objects, and ideas—how the person feels about the world.

Attitudes are our opinions and beliefs about people, objects, and ideas—how we feel about the world. Social psychologists are interested in how attitudes relate to behavior and in whether and how attitudes can change (Arpan, Rhodes, & Roskos-Ewoldsen, 2012; Briñol & Petty, 2012; Wegener & Petty, 2013).

CAN ATTITUDES PREDICT BEHAVIOR?

People sometimes say one thing but do another. On a survey, you might report positive attitudes about recycling but still pitch an aluminum soda can in the trash. Studies over the past half-century indicate some of the conditions under which attitudes guide actions (Briñol & Petty, 2012):

■ *When the person's attitudes are strong* (Ajzen, 2001): If you are very passionate about recycling, you are less likely to pitch that soda can in the trash compared to someone who has only a weak attitude.

■ *When the person shows a strong awareness of an attitude and rehearses and practices it* (Fazio & Olsen, 2007; Fazio & others, 1982): For example, a person who has been asked to give a speech about the benefits of recycling is more likely to recycle than is an individual with the same attitude about recycling who has not done so.

■ *When the person has a vested interest* (Sivacek & Crano, 1982): People are more likely to act on attitudes when the issue at stake is something that will affect them personally. A classic study examined whether students would show up for a rally protesting a change that would raise the legal drinking age from 18 to 21 (Sivacek & Crano, 1982). Although generally students were against the change, only those in the critical age group (from 18 to 20) were likely to show up to protest.

CAN BEHAVIOR PREDICT ATTITUDES?

Does the link between attitudes and behaviors run in both directions? Social psychologists offer two main explanations for how behavior influences attitudes: cognitive dissonance theory and self-perception theory.

Cognitive Dissonance Theory   **Cognitive dissonance,** another concept introduced by Festinger (1957), is the psychological discomfort (*dissonance*) caused by two inconsistent thoughts. According to the theory, we feel uneasy when we notice an inconsistency between what we believe and what we do. In a classic study, Festinger and J. Merrill Carlsmith (1959) asked college students to engage in a series of very boring tasks, such as sorting spools into trays and turning wooden pegs. These participants were later asked to persuade another student (who was in fact a confederate) to participate in the study by telling him that the task was actually interesting and enjoyable. Half of the participants were randomly assigned to be paid $1 for telling this white lie, and the other half received $20. Afterward, all of the participants rated how interesting and enjoyable the task really was.

● **cognitive dissonance** An individual's psychological discomfort (dissonance) caused by two inconsistent thoughts.

Those who were paid only $1 to tell the lie rated the task as significantly more enjoyable than those who were paid $20. Festinger and Carlsmith reasoned that those paid $20 to tell the lie could attribute their behavior to the high value of the money they received. On the other hand, those who were paid $1 experienced cognitive dissonance: "How could I *lie* for just $1? If I said I liked the task, I must have really liked it." The inconsistency between what they *did* (tell a lie) and what they *were paid for it* (just $1) moved these individuals to change their attitudes about the task.

When attitudes and behavior conflict, we can reduce cognitive dissonance in one of two ways: change our behavior to fit our attitudes or change our attitudes to fit our behavior. In the classic study above, participants changed their attitudes about the task to match their behavior. If you pitched that soda can, for example, you might feel dissonance ("Wait, I believe in recycling, yet I just pitched that can") and relieve that dissonance by telling yourself, "Recycling is not really *that* important." Through cognitive dissonance, your behavior changed your attitude.

One type of dissonance reduction is called effort justification. *Effort justification* means coming up with a rationale for the amount of work we put into getting something, typically by increasing the value associated with things that are difficult to attain. Effort justification explains the strong group loyalty that emerges after enduring difficult experiences to get into groups, such as initiation rites for Greek organizations, boot camp in the Marines, and the rigors of medical school en route to becoming a physician. From a cognitive dissonance perspective, individuals in these situations are likely to think, "If it's this tough to get into, it must be worth it." Working hard to get into a group can change our attitudes about that group. In the 2012 U.S. presidential elections, many voters waited in line for hours to cast their votes. You can imagine that many of them felt that the right to vote was extraordinarily important to them, after the long wait.

Working hard to get into a group inspires loyalty through cognitive dissonance.

● **self-perception theory** Bem's theory on how behaviors influence attitudes, stating that individuals make inferences about their attitudes by perceiving their behavior.

Self-Perception Theory   **Self-perception theory** is Daryl Bem's (1967) take on how behavior influences attitudes. According to self-perception theory, individuals make inferences about their attitudes by observing their behavior. That is, behaviors can cause attitudes, because when we are questioned about our attitudes, we think back on our behaviors for information. If someone asked about your attitude toward sushi, for example, you might think, "Well, I rarely eat it, so I must not like it." Your behavior has led you to recognize something about yourself that you had not noticed before. According to Bem, we are especially likely to look to our behavior to determine our attitudes when those attitudes are unclear.

Figure 13.2 compares cognitive dissonance theory and self-perception theory. Both theories have merit in explaining the connection between attitudes and behavior, and these opposing views bring to light the complexity that may exist in this connection. Both theories suggest that behavior can change attitudes. Another route to attitude change is persuasion.

PERSUASION

Persuasion involves trying to change someone's attitude—and often his or her behavior as well (Briñol & Petty, 2012; Perrin & others, 2010; Prislin & Crano, 2012). Teachers, lawyers, and sales representatives study techniques that will help them sway their audiences (children, juries, and buyers). Presidential candidates have arsenals of speechwriters and image consultants to help ensure that their words are persuasive. Advertisers are skilled persuaders, who draw on a full array of techniques to sell everything from cornflakes to carpets to cars.

Carl Hovland and his colleagues originally identified the various elements of persuasion (Hovland, Janis, & Kelley, 1953; Janis & Hovland, 1959):

■ *The communicator (source):* A key factor in persuasion is the person doing the persuading. Is the person delivering the message (or the source of the message) viewed as credible (or believable)? Trustworthiness, expertise, power, attractiveness, likability, and similarity are all credibility characteristics that help a communicator change people's attitudes or convince them to act. When a source has a vested interest in the message, attempts at persuasion may be more difficult (Harrison & Michelson, 2012).

FIGURE 13.2   Two Theories of the Connections Between Attitudes and Behavior Although we often think of attitudes as causing behavior, behavior can change attitudes, through either dissonance reduction or self-perception.

Festinger Cognitive Dissonance Theory

We are motivated toward consistency between attitudes and behavior and away from inconsistency.

Example: "I hate my job. I need to develop a better attitude toward it or else quit."

Bem Self-Perception Theory

We make inferences about our attitudes by perceiving and examining our behavior and the context in which it occurs, which might involve inducements to behave in certain ways.

Example: "I am spending all of my time thinking about how much I hate my job. I really must not like it."

■ *The medium:* Another persuasion factor is the medium or technology used to get the message across. Is the message presented in print, on TV, on twitter, or YouTube? Because it presents live images, television is generally a more powerful medium than print sources for changing attitudes. Of course, the effects of the medium of a message may depend on who is receiving it. When Missouri Senator Claire McCaskill announced her support for same-sex marriage, she did so on Tumblr, perhaps suggesting the age group she was trying to reach.

■ *The target (audience):* The audience or target of a message can play a role in message persuasiveness. Younger people are more likely to change their attitudes than older ones. And individuals with weak attitudes are more easily persuaded than those with strong ones.

■ *The message:* The final aspect of persuasion is the message itself. What kind of message is persuasive? Some messages involve strong logical arguments, and others focus on exciting emotions such as fear and anger in the audience. Which is more likely to work and when? The elaboration likelihood model addresses this question.

The **elaboration likelihood model** identifies two pathways of persuasion: a central route and a peripheral route (Briñol & Petty, 2012; DeMarree & Petty, 2007; Petty & Briñol, 2008; Petty & Cacioppo, 1986). The *central route* works by engaging the audience thoughtfully with a sound, logical argument. The *peripheral route* involves factors such as the source's attractiveness or the emotional power of an appeal. The peripheral route is effective when people are not paying close attention or lack the time or energy to think about the message (Brewer, Barnes, & Sauer, 2011). As you might guess, television advertisers often use the peripheral route to persuasion on the assumption that during the commercials you are probably not paying full attention to the screen. However, the central route is more persuasive when people have the ability and the motivation to pay attention (Sparks & Areni, 2008).

● **elaboration likelihood model** Theory identifying two ways to persuade: a central route and a peripheral route.

Successful Persuasion

Sooner or later, nearly everyone will be in a position of selling someone something. Social psychologists have studied ways in which social psychological principles influence whether a salesperson makes that sale (Cialdini, 1993).

One strategy is called the *foot-in-the-door* technique (Freedman & Fraser, 1966). The foot-in-the-door strategy involves making a smaller request ("Would you be interested in a three-month trial subscription to a magazine?") at the beginning, saving the biggest demand ("How about a full year?") for last. The foot-in-the-door strategy relies on the notion that in agreeing to the smaller offer, the customer has created a relationship with the seller, expressing a level of trust.

A different strategy is called the *door-in-the-face* technique (Cialdini & others, 1975). The door-in-the-face technique involves making the biggest pitch first ("Would you be interested in a full-year subscription?"), which the customer probably will reject, and then making a smaller, "concessionary" demand ("Okay, then, how about a three-month trial?"). This technique relies on the fact that the customer feels a sense of obligation: You let him off the hook with that big request, maybe he should be nice and take the smaller offer.

During her term as Secretary of State, Hillary Rodham Clinton was called upon to use persuasion, as she did here during the Beghazi hearings.

Resisting Persuasion

Advertisers and salespeople work their hardest to persuade us to buy their products. How do we resist their appeals? According to William McGuire, one way to resist persuasion is through *inoculation* (McGuire, 2003; McGuire & Papageorgis, 1961). McGuire proposed that just as administering a vaccine inoculates individuals from a virus by introducing a weakened or dead version of that virus to the immune system, giving people a weak version of a persuasive message and allowing them time to argue against it can help individuals avoid persuasion.

Such "inoculation" helps college students resist plagiarism (Compton & Pfau, 2008) as well as credit card marketing appeals (Compton & Pfau, 2004). When individuals are warned that they are going to be hit with persuasive appeals and are given arguments to help them resist these pitches, they are able to do so.

test yourself

1. What do psychologists mean by a stereotype, and how do they define a stereotype threat?
2. What is involved in making a fundamental attribution error? Give an example of such an error.
3. Identify and briefly explain the four elements of persuasion.

2· SOCIAL BEHAVIOR

We do not just think socially; we also behave in social ways. Two particular types of behavior that have interested psychologists represent the extremes of human social activity: altruism and aggression.

Altruism

High school junior Meghan Vogel was running the 3,200-meter race in the 2012 Ohio Division III State Track Championships. Ahead of her was Arden McMath, a sophomore from another school. With just 20 meters to go, Arden collapsed, and then something amazing happened. Instead of passing her, Meghan stopped and helped. Putting Arden's arm around her own neck, Meghan supported her to the finish line, ensuring that Arden crossed the line before she did (Binder, 2012). This simple act of kindness gained widespread praise, though for Meghan it was nothing special.

In everyday life, we witness and perform "random acts of kindness"—maybe adding a quarter to someone's expired parking meter or giving up our seat on a bus to someone in need. All of these acts are *prosocial behaviors*—they all involve helping another person (Burks & Kobus, 2012; Eisenberg, Spinrad, & Morris, 2013). Such acts of kindness bear the markings of altruism. **Altruism** means giving to another person with the ultimate goal of benefiting that person, even if it incurs a cost to oneself. Are acts of kindness truly altruistic?

Psychologists debate whether human behavior is ever truly altruistic. Altruistic motives contrast with selfish or egoistic motives (Cialdini, 1991; Maner & others, 2002). **Egoism** means helping another person for personal gain, such as to feel good, or avoid guilt. Kindness might also serve selfish purposes by ensuring *reciprocity*, meaning that we help another person to increase the chances that the person will return the favor.

Altruism has presented a puzzle for evolutionary psychologists (Andre & Morin, 2011; Van Doorn & Taborsky, 2012). How can behavior that rewards others, and not oneself, be adaptive? Evolutionary theorists note that helping is especially likely to occur among family members, because helping a relative also means promoting the survival of the family's genes (Buss, 2012; Leigh, 2010). Evolutionary theorists believe that reciprocity in relationships with nonfamily members is essentially the mistaken application of a heuristic that made sense in human evolutionary history—to engage in selfless acts of kindness to one's own family (Nowak, Page, & Sigmund, 2000).

Acts of kindness seem to have one powerful payoff for those who do them: Helping others strongly and consistently leads to increased positive mood (Dunn, Aknin, & Norton, 2008; Omoto & Snyder, 1995; Schaller & Cialdini, 1988; Williamson & Clark, 1989). Prosocial spending, or spending money on others rather than oneself, is linked to greater well-being, potentially universally (Aknin & others, 2013). Does the fact that behaving prosocially leads to feelings of pleasure mean that such behavior is always selfish?

Feelings of pleasure are linked with adaptive behaviors, those things we need to do to survive and reproduce. We enjoy eating. We enjoy sex. Is it possible that the strong link between pleasure and kindness demonstrates that prosocial behavior is an important adaptation for humans who depend on one another for survival (Chudek & Henrich, 2011)? Interestingly, kindness is not exclusive to humans. Ethology—the study of animal behavior—has examined whether acts of kindness occur in nonhuman animals. Ethologists have found that nonhuman primates show altruistic acts of kindness (de Waal, Leimgruber, & Greenberg, 2008).

Setting aside the question of whether such acts are altruistic, in this section we review biological, psychological, and sociocultural factors that predict prosocial behavior. As you read, consider whether you think altruism is a problem to be solved or a natural aspect of human life.

BIOLOGICAL FACTORS IN PROSOCIAL BEHAVIOR

Research has shown that genetics play a role in prosocial behavior. Genetic factors explain between 30 and 53 percent of the differences we see in the tendency to engage

---

● **altruism** Unselfish interest in helping another person.

● **egoism** Giving to another person to ensure reciprocity; to gain self-esteem; to present oneself as powerful, competent, or caring; or to avoid censure from oneself and others for failing to live up to society's expectations.

in kind acts (Knafo, Israel, & Ebstein, 2011). These genetic factors, in turn, are related to neurotransmitters in the brain. High levels of serotonin are associated with prosocial behavior (Crockett, 2009). Dopamine receptors in the brain are also associated with prosocial behavior (Knafo, Israel, & Ebstein, 2011). Finally, the neurohormone oxytocin, which plays a role in social bonding, is associated with enhanced prosocial behavior (Kogan & others, 2011; Poulin, Holman, & Buffone, 2012). Experiments with humans show that administering oxytocin increases trust, cooperation, and generosity (Baumgartner & others, 2008; Declerck, Boone, & Kiyonari, 2010).

In terms of brain structures, research suggests that when we feel compassion for another person, areas of the midbrain associated with the perception of pain are likely to be active (Simon-Thomas & others, 2012). These same areas are associated with nurturing parental behaviors, suggesting that neural factors associated with the parent–child relationship are involved in kindness toward others.

PSYCHOLOGICAL FACTORS IN PROSOCIAL BEHAVIOR

Among the psychological factors thought to play a role in prosocial behavior are empathy, personality, and mood.

Empathy   As we discussed in Chapter 11, *empathy* is a person's feeling of oneness with the emotional state of another. When we feel empathy for someone, we feel what that person is feeling. Empathy allows us to put ourselves in another person's shoes (Eisenberg, Spinrad, & Sadovsky, 2013). We can feel empathy even for those we do not particularly like, as demonstrated by the playing of "Sweet Caroline" (a tradition of the Boston Red Sox) at Yankee Stadium during the game with their archrivals following the Boston Marathon bombing in 2013.

Daniel Batson has spent the better part of his career searching for proof that true altruism does exist, and he argues that empathy is the key to altruism (Batson, 2002, 2006, 2012; Batson & others, 2007). When we are feeling empathy for someone else's plight, we are moved to action—not to make ourselves feel better but out of genuine concern for the other person.

Personality   Agreeableness (see Chapter 12) is the personality trait most strongly associated with prosocial behaviors (Caprara & others, 2010). The association between agreeableness and brain structures helps to illuminate its role in acts of kindness. Agreeableness is related to greater volume in the posterior cingulate cortex (DeYoung & others, 2010), a brain area associated with understanding other people's beliefs and with empathy (Saxe & Powell, 2006).

Mood   Our mood can determine whether or not we engage in kind behaviors. The research literature strongly concludes that happy people are more likely than unhappy people to help others (Snyder & Lopez, 2007). Does it then follow that being in a bad mood makes people less helpful? Not necessarily, because adults (especially) generally understand that doing good for another person can be a mood booster. When people are in a bad mood, they might be likely to help if they think that doing so will improve their mood.

SOCIOCULTURAL FACTORS IN PROSOCIAL BEHAVIOR

Three sociocultural factors that influence prosocial behavior are socioeconomic status, the presence of bystanders, and the media.

Socioeconomic Status   Socioeconomic status is a sociocultural factor in prosocial behavior. Although they have less, those of lower socioeconomic status tend to be more likely to help than those who have more (Piff & others, 2010). Compared to wealthier individuals, those from poorer backgrounds tend be more attuned to the suffering of others (Stellar & others, 2012). It may be that relative wealth promotes a focus on maintaining one's standing in the world to the detriment of reaching out to help those in need (Kraus & others, 2012).

The Bystander Effect   In 1964, a young woman named Kitty Genovese was brutally murdered in New York City. She was attacked at about 3 A.M. in a courtyard surrounded by apartment buildings. It took the slayer approximately 30 minutes to kill Genovese. Thirty-eight neighbors watched the gory scene from their windows and heard Genovese's screams. Media reports declared that no one helped or called the police.

Those reports turned out to be erroneous (Manning, Levine, & Collins, 2007). Nevertheless, inspired by this case, John Darley and Bibb Latané (1968) conducted a number of studies on the bystander effect. The **bystander effect** is the tendency for an individual to be less likely to help in an emergency when other people are present. Most bystander studies show that when alone, a person will help 75 percent of the time, but when another bystander is present, the figure drops to 50 percent. Apparently the difference is due to diffusion of responsibility among witnesses and the tendency to look to the behavior of others for cues about what to do.

The bystander effect is still with us. In 2009, in Richmond, California, a 15-year-old high school girl was raped and beaten by as many as 10 people outside a homecoming dance (Walter, 2010). More than 20 people watched the assault. No one called for help.

● **bystander effect** The tendency of an individual who observes an emergency to help less when other people are present than when the observer is alone.

Media Influences   Media—including music, TV, film, and video games—can influence prosocial behavior. Listening to music with prosocial lyrics can promote kindness (Greitemeyer, 2009). Watching television shows with positive content predicts prosocial behavior (Hearold, 1986). Playing prosocial video games enhances prosocial thoughts (Greitemeyer & Osswald, 2011) and acts of kindness (Whitaker & Bushman, 2012).

A series of studies showed that participants who played a video game such as Lemmings, in which the player tries to save the hapless creatures from a variety of disasters, were more likely than those who played either a neutral or a violent game to help an experimenter pick up a cup of spilled pencils (Greitemeyer & Osswald, 2010). Playing a prosocial video game also led participants to be more likely to intervene when a confederate posing as the experimenter's ex-boyfriend began to harass her (Greitemeyer & Osswald, 2010).

The human ability to engage in kindness sits alongside the capacity to cause others harm. Some evolutionary scientists have suggested that altruism, especially when it is directed at the members of one's own group, may coexist with hostile actions toward other groups (Arrow, 2007). A soldier may perform selfless acts of altruism for his or her country, but for a person on the other side of the combat, that behavior is harmful. Thus, altruism within a group may be linked to aggression.

Aggression

Aggression refers to social behavior with the objective of harming someone, either physically or verbally. Ethologists note aggression in nonhuman animals (Lorenz, 1965; Tinbergen, 1969). However, in the animal kingdom, most hostile encounters do not escalate to killing or even severe harm. Much of the fighting is ritualistic and involves threat displays—for example, a cat arching its back, baring its teeth, and hissing.

Evolutionary theorists believe that human beings are not much different from other animals. A basic theme of their theory is the survival of the fittest (Barber, 2009; Cosmides, 2011; Wrangham & Glowacki, 2012). Thus, they conclude that early in human evolution the survivors were probably aggressive individuals. In this section we will review biological, psychological, and sociocultural influences on aggression.

● **aggression** Social behavior with the objective of harming someone, either physically or verbally.

In the animal world, aggression often is ritualistic and typically involves threat displays such as a cat's arching its back, baring its teeth, and hissing.

BIOLOGICAL INFLUENCES IN AGGRESSION

Researchers who approach aggression from a biological viewpoint examine the influence of genetics and neurobiological factors.

Genes   Genes are important in explaining the biological basis of aggression (Butovskaya & others, 2012). The selective breeding of animals provides evidence for genetic influences in aggression. After a number of breedings among only aggressive animals and among only docile animals, vicious and timid strains of animals emerge. The vicious strains attack nearly anything in sight; the timid strains rarely fight, even when attacked.

The genetic basis for aggression is more difficult to demonstrate in humans than animals and may depend on the type of aggression studied (L. A. Baker & others, 2008; Brendgen & others, 2008). Specifically, twin studies have shown that physical aggression that is proactive in nature (that is, unprovoked aggression) may be more influenced by genes, but more reactive aggression may be more susceptible to environmental effects.

Neurobiological Factors   Although humans do not have a specific aggression center in the brain, aggressive behavior often results when areas such as the limbic system are stimulated by electric currents (Herbert, 1988; Wood & Liossi, 2006). The frontal lobes of the brain—the areas most involved in executive functions such as planning and self-control—have also been implicated in aggression. Research has examined the brains of individuals who have committed the ultimate act of violence: murder (Nordstrom & others, 2011; Raine, 2008; Yang, Glen, & Raine, 2008). The results indicate that murderers may differ from others in deficits in the functioning of these areas of the brain.

Neurotransmitters—particularly, lower levels of serotonin—have been linked to aggressive behavior (Neumann, Veenema, & Beiderbeck, 2010; Rosell & others, 2010). However, a recent meta-analysis of 175 independent samples of more than 6,500 participants revealed that the link between low serotonin and aggression is very small (Duke & others, 2013).

Hormones are another biological factor that may play a role in aggression, as noted in Chapter 11. The hormone that is typically implicated in aggressive behavior is testosterone. Research on rats and other animals has shown that testosterone relates to aggression (Cunningham & McGinnis, 2007), but results with humans have been less consistent (van Bokhoven & others, 2006).

PSYCHOLOGICAL INFLUENCES IN AGGRESSION

Psychological influences on aggression include personality characteristics, frustrating circumstances, and cognitive and learning factors.

Personality   Some people are more likely to behave aggressively than others. Not surprisingly, low levels of agreeableness are associated with more aggressive behavior (Muris, Meesters, & Timmermans, 2013). In addition, a constellation of traits—including low agreeableness, low conscientiousness, and high levels of neuroticism—is associated with aggression (Settles & others, 2012). A meta-analysis showed that individuals who are high on hostility and irritability are more likely to behave aggressively, whether provoked or not (Bettencourt & others, 2006). Other personality characteristics are associated with greater aggressive behavior only when individuals are provoked. For instance, individuals who ruminate over interpersonal slights are more likely to aggress when provoked (Bettencourt & others, 2006).

Frustrating and Aversive Circumstances   Many years ago, John Dollard and his colleagues (1939) proposed that *frustration,* the blocking of an individual's attempts to reach a goal, triggers aggression. The *frustration-aggression hypothesis* states that frustration always leads to aggression. Soon, however, psychologists found that aggression is not the only possible response to frustration. Some individuals who experience frustration become passive, for example (N. E. Miller, 1941).

Psychologists later recognized that, besides frustration, a broad range of aversive experiences can cause aggression. They include physical pain, personal insults, crowding, and unpleasant events. Aversive circumstances also include factors in the physical environment, such as the weather. Murder, rape, and assault increase when temperatures are the highest, as well as in the hottest years and the hottest cities (Anderson & Bushman, 2002).

Cognitive Determinants   Aspects of the environment may prime us to behave aggressively (Englander, 2006). Recall from Chapter 7 that priming can involve making

Aversive circumstances that might stimulate aggression include factors in the physical environment such as noise and crowding.

something salient to a person, even subliminally or without the person's awareness. Research by Leonard Berkowitz and others has shown that the mere presence of a weapon (such as a gun) may prime hostile thoughts and produce aggression (Anderson, Benjamin, & Bartholow, 1998; Berkowitz, 1990; Berkowitz & LePage, 1996). The tendency for the presence of firearms to enhance aggression is known as the *weapons effect*. In support of Berkowitz's ideas, a well-known study found that individuals who lived in a household with a gun were 2.7 times more likely to be murdered than those dwelling in a household without a gun (Kellerman & others, 1993).

Observational Learning   Social cognitive theorists believe that individuals learn aggression through reinforcement and observational learning (Englander, 2006). Watching others engage in aggressive actions can evoke aggression, as you might recall from the classic Bobo doll study described in Chapter 6 (Bandura, Ross, & Ross, 1961). One of the strongest predictors of aggression is witnessing aggression in one's own family (Ferguson & others, 2008). Watching television provides a ready opportunity to observe aggression in our culture, which we consider further in the discussion below on media violence.

SOCIOCULTURAL INFLUENCES IN AGGRESSION

Aggression and violence are more common in some cultures than others (Kitayama, 2011; Kitayama & Cohen, 2007). In this section, we review sociocultural influences on aggression including the "culture of honor" and media influences.

The Culture of Honor   Dov Cohen has examined how cultural norms about masculine pride and family honor may foster aggressive behavior (Cohen, 2001; Vandello & Cohen, 2004, 2008; Vandello & others, 2009). In cultures of honor, a man's reputation is thought to be an essential aspect of his economic survival. Such cultures see insults to a man's honor as diminishing his reputation and view violence as a way to compensate for that loss.

In these cultures, family pride might lead to so-called honor killings in which, for example, a female rape victim is slain by her male family members so that they, in turn, are not "contaminated" by the rape. In April 2009, a Jordanian man confessed to stabbing his pregnant sister with a meat cleaver because she had left her husband, and he believed she was seeing other men. He felt that he had to kill her to protect his family honor (Gavlak, 2009).

Cohen has examined how, in the United States, southerners are more likely than northerners to be aggressive when honor is at stake. In one study, Cohen and his colleagues (1996) had men who were from either the North or the South take part in an experiment that required them to walk down a hallway. A member of the study passed all the men, bumping against them and quietly calling them a derogatory name. The southerners were more likely than the northerners to think their masculine reputation was threatened, to become physiologically aroused by the insult, and to engage in actual aggressive or dominant acts. In contrast, the northerners were less likely to perceive a random insult as "fightin' words."

Media   Images of violence pervade the U.S. popular media: newscasts, television shows, sports broadcasts, movies, video games, Internet videos, and song lyrics. Do portrayals of violence lead to aggression?

Although some critics reject the conclusion that TV violence causes aggression (Savage & Yancey, 2008), many scholars insist that TV violence can prompt aggressive or antisocial behavior in children (Brown & Tierney, 2011; Bushman & Huesmann, 2012; Comstock, 2012). Of course, television violence is not the only cause of aggression in children or adults. Like all social behaviors, aggression has multiple determinants (Matos, Ferreira, & Haase, 2012). The link between TV violence and aggression in children is influenced by children's personality traits and attitudes toward violence.

Another type of media that has interested psychologists is violent pornography. Violent pornography includes films, videos, websites, and magazines portraying the degradation of women in a sexual context. Do such media foster violence toward women? Based on several meta-analyses and on research of their own, Neil Malamuth and his colleagues concluded that pornography consumption does have a small effect on male sexual aggression and is related to more tolerance of violence toward women (Hald, Malamuth, & Yuen, 2010; Malamuth, Addison, & Koss, 2000). Yet Malamuth and his colleagues caution that pornography is only one of a number of factors that may lead to sexual violence against women (Hald, Malamuth, & Yuen, 2010; Vega & Malamuth, 2007). The most problematic materials are those that depict women enjoying being the victims of male sexual violence (Hald, Malamuth, & Yuen, 2010). Such violent pornography reinforces the *rape myth*—the false belief that women desire coercive sex.

As we discussed earlier, research shows that prosocial video games foster prosocial behavior. Do violent video games foster aggression? Experimental evidence shows that playing a violent video game can lead to more aggressive thoughts and behaviors in children (Saleem, Anderson, & Gentile, 2012) and adults (Hasan, Bègue, & Bushman, 2013). Correlational studies demonstrate an association between playing violent video games and a number of negative outcomes. A meta-analysis concluded that children and adolescents who play violent video games extensively are more aggressive, less sensitive to real-life violence, and more likely to engage in delinquent acts than their counterparts who spend less time playing the games or do not play them at all (C. A. Anderson & others, 2010).

Critics of the conclusion that violent video game exposure leads to aggression have pointed out that the acts of aggression studied in the laboratory are not generalizable to real-world criminal violence (Ritter & Elsea, 2005; Savage, 2008; Savage & Yancey, 2008). Operationalizing aggression in the laboratory is challenging. Researchers might provide participants the opportunity to "aggress" against another, for instance, by subjecting the individual to a blast of loud noise, dispensing a mild electrical shock, or administering a large dose of Tabasco to swallow. Whether these operational definitions of aggression are applicable to real-life violence is a matter of much debate (Savage & Yancey, 2008).

Finally, critics of research showing a link between violent video games and aggression stress that many studies have not consistently measured important third variables, such as family violence, in predicting both video game use and aggression (Ferguson & Kilburn, 2010; Ferguson & others, 2008).

Social psychologists sometimes ask the participants in a study to assign the amount of hot sauce a person must drink as a measure of aggression. Do you think that is a good operational definition of aggression?

test yourself

1. What is the difference between altruism and egoism?
2. Explain the bystander effect and give an example.
3. What have researchers found about the influence of prosocially oriented video games? What have they learned about the effects of violent video games?

3· SOCIAL INFLUENCE

Another topic of interest to social psychologists is how our behavior is influenced by other individuals and groups. This section explores key aspects of social influence: conformity, obedience, and group influence.

Conformity and Obedience

Research on conformity and obedience started in earnest after World War II. Psychologists sought answers to the disturbing question of how ordinary people could be influenced to commit the sort of atrocities inflicted on Jews, Gypsies, and other minorities during the Holocaust. Researchers wanted to understand the processes by which people change their behavior to conform to the behavior of others or to the demands of an authority figure.

CONFORMITY

● **conformity** A change in a person's behavior to coincide more closely with a group standard.

Conformity is a change in a person's behavior to coincide more closely with a group standard. Conformity takes many forms and affects many aspects of people's lives, in positive and negative ways. Conformity is at work when we obey the rules and regulations that allow society to run smoothly. Consider how chaotic it would be if people did not conform to social norms such as stopping at a red light, driving on the correct side of the road, and not punching others in the face. Conformity can also be a powerful way to increase group cohesion. Even something as simple as marching in step together or singing a song along with a group can lead to enhanced cooperation among group members (Wiltermuth & Heath, 2009).

Conformity can also be destructive. Conformity is at work, for example, when a person comes to college and starts to drink heavily at parties, even though he or she might have never consumed alcohol before. Conformity is a powerful social force. You can feel the pressure of conformity for yourself if, the next time you get on an elevator with other people, you do not turn around to face the door. We begin our exploration of conformity by considering a classic study by Solomon Asch.

Asch's Experiment Put yourself in this situation: You are taken into a room where you see five other people seated along a table. A person in a white lab coat enters the room and announces that you are about to participate in an experiment on perceptual accuracy. The group is shown two cards—the first having only a single vertical line on it and the second having three vertical lines of varying length. You are told that the task is to determine which of the three lines on the second card is the same length as the line on the first card. You look at the cards and think, "What a snap. It's so obvious which is the same."

What you do not know is that the other people in the room are confederates who are working with the experimenter. On the first several trials, everyone agrees about which line matches the standard. Then on the fourth trial, each of the others picks the same *incorrect* line. As the last person to make a choice, you have the dilemma of responding as your eyes tell you or conforming to what the others before you said. How would you answer?

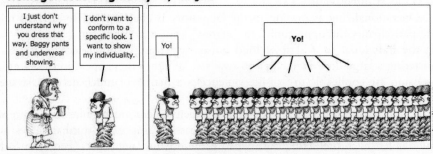

Homogeneous Originality by CIAgent

I just don't understand why you dress that way. Baggy pants and underwear showing.

I don't want to conform to a specific look. I want to show my individuality.

Yo!

Yo!

Solomon Asch conducted this classic experiment on conformity in 1951. Asch instructed the confederates to give incorrect responses on 12 of 18 trials. To his surprise, Asch (1951) found that participants conformed to the incorrect answers 35 percent of the time.

Why would people go along with a group even when they have clear-cut information disputing the others, such as the lines in the Asch experiment? Next we review biological, psychological, cultural answers to this question.

Biological Factors in Conformity   Research on how the brain responds to moments when we do not fit in with a group suggest that the brain may actually "feel better" when we fit in. Using fMRI, one study examined what happens in the brain when people find out that their opinions conflict with those of others (Klucharev & others, 2009). Women were asked to rate a variety of female faces for attractiveness, and their brains were scanned while they received feedback about whether their ratings agreed with those of the other group members. When participants were told that their ratings differed from the group's ratings, they showed enhanced activation in the brain area typically associated with monitoring for errors. In other words, the brain responded to judgments that differed from the group's as if they were mistakes.

Further, when their ratings differed from the group's, women experienced less activation in the nucleus accumbens and the ventral tegmental area, the brain's reward centers. The greater the degree to which women's brains responded to being different as an error and as not rewarding, the more they tended to conform when given a chance to re-rate the faces at the end of the study.

Another biological factor in conformity is oxytocin, the neurotransmitter and hormone associated with social bonding. In a recent double-blind experiment, participants were randomly assigned to receive oxytocin or a placebo and were then placed in groups to make ratings about the attractiveness of various symbols. Those who were given oxytocin were more likely produce preferences that matched the ratings of members of their groups—that is, to conform (Stallen & others, 2012).

Psychological Factors in Conformity   Two main psychological factors have been identified as contributing to conformity: informational social influence and normative social influence.

Informational social influence refers to the influence other people have on us because we want to be right. The social group can provide us with information that we did not know or may help us see things in ways that had not occurred to us. As a result, we may conform because we have come to agree with the group. The tendency to conform based on informational social influence depends especially on two factors: how confident we are in our own judgment and how well informed we perceive the group to be. Basically, informational social influence means that sometimes we go along with the crowd to be right. For example, if you know little about computers and three of your acquaintances who are IT geeks tell you not to buy a particular brand of computer, you are likely to conform to their recommendation.

● **informational social influence** The influence other people have on us because we want to be right.

In contrast, **normative social influence** is the influence others have on us because we want them to like us. Whether the group is an inner-city gang or members of a profession such as medicine or law, if a particular group is important to us, we might adopt a clothing style that people in the group wear or use the same slang words, and we might assume the attitudes that characterize the group's members (Hewlin, 2009). Normative social influence means we go along with the crowd to be liked.

● **normative social influence** The influence others have on us because we want them to like us.

Cultural Factors in Conformity   As we have reviewed previously, individualistic cultures value independence and individual accomplishments and emphasize differences and uniqueness. Collectivistic cultures value the group, emphasize group harmony, and believe that accomplishments depend on individuals' carrying out their roles in the larger social network. It is not surprising, then, that collectivism has been associated with greater levels of conformity. One research review, summarizing 133 experiments following Asch's design, found that individualism within cultures was negatively correlated with conformity (Bond & Smith, 1996).

Social Psychology and Cross-Cultural Psychology: Why Are Some Nations More Conforming Than Others?

Researchers have sought to identify the origins of cultural differences in conformity in an unusual place—germs. That's right. Scholars have suggested that one factor that might influence cultural characteristics and help explain the origins of cultural difference is the prevalence of *pathogens*—agents, such as viruses and bacteria, which cause infectious disease—in particular locales.

If a geographical location has relatively more pathogens floating around, might that fact influence norms for social behaviors? Surviving in a world in which infectious agents are an ever-present threat might mean curtailing social behaviors through which diseases are more likely to spread. Strong cultural norms for conformity might be a way that groups control the spread of infectious diseases (Murray & Schaller, 2010). Might pathogen prevalence help to explain the origins of cultural differences in conformity?

In a provocative study, Damian Murray and his colleagues examined how pathogen prevalence in a host of nations related to four indicators of conformity (Murray, Trudeau, &

Schaller, 2011). Among these conformity indicators were:

- Behavior of individuals in various nations in Asch-style conformity studies
- The percentage of people in each nation prioritizing the value of obedience
- The percentage of adults reporting themselves as left-handed

What other cultural norms might be related to germs? How do you think the prevalence of pathogens influences your own behavior?

This last indicator might seem surprising. To this day, in some countries children who show a preference for left-handedness are trained away from this inclination, sometimes being forced to use their right hand while learning to write and perform other tasks. Murray and his colleagues predicted that nations with a low tolerance for nonconformists would be more likely to pressure lefties to conform to the right-handed way of doing things.

Results showed that pathogen prevalence was positively related to higher levels of conformity in laboratory settings, to more endorsement of the value of obedience, and to a lower percentage of lefties in the adult population.

Many factors beyond pathogens play a role in the emergence of cultural traditions, of course. But probing the connections between these traditions and the natural world is a promising step toward understanding the kinds of problems that culture solves, as well as the functions that cultural norms serve in survival.

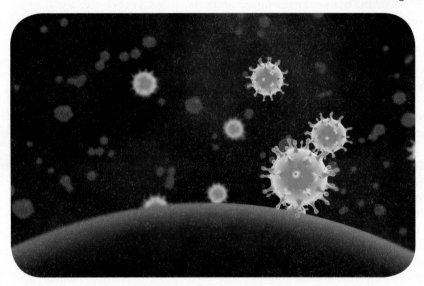

An intriguing question is *why* people who live in different geographic locations have developed and preserved different cultural traditions. One important set of factors is characteristics of the natural environment in which cultures exist, such as the terrain, the weather, and whether the environment facilitates farming or hunting (Kitayama & Bowman, 2010; Murray & Schaller, 2010). These aspects of the natural world determine what a group must do to survive. To read about how another aspect of the natural environment helps to explain cultural differences in conformity, check out the Intersection.

OBEDIENCE

Obedience is behavior that complies with the explicit demands of the individual in authority. We are obedient when an authority figure demands that we do something, and we do it. Note that in conformity, people change their thinking or behavior so that it will be more like that of others, while in obedience, there is an explicit demand to comply.

● **obedience** Behavior that complies with the explicit demands of the individual in authority.

Obedient behavior sometimes can be distressingly cruel. One of the most infamous examples of the destructive nature of obedience is the Nazi crimes against Jews and others during World War II. More recent examples include the obedience of radical Muslims instructed to participate in suicide attacks against Israelis and Westerners (McCauley & Segal, 2009) and that of U.S. military personnel at Abu Ghraib prison in Iraq, who justified their horrendous abuse of detainees by asserting that they were "just following orders" (A. G. Miller, 2004).

Millions of people throughout history have obeyed commands to commit terrible acts. Two classic experiments provide insight into obedience.

Milgram's Experiment

A classic series of experiments by Stanley Milgram (1965, 1974) demonstrated the profound effect of obedience. Imagine that, as part of a psychology experiment on the effects of punishment on memory, you are asked to deliver a series of electric shocks to another person. Your role is to be the "teacher" and to punish the mistakes made by the "learner." Each time the learner makes a mistake, you are to increase the intensity of the shock.

You are introduced to the learner, a nice 50-year-old man who mumbles something about having a heart condition. Strapped to a chair in the next room, he communicates with you through an intercom. The apparatus in front of you has 30 switches, ranging from 15 volts (slight) to 450 volts (marked as beyond dangerous, "XXX").

As the trials proceed, the learner quickly runs into trouble and is unable to give the correct answers. As you increase the intensity of the shock, the learner says that he is in pain. At 150 volts, he demands to have the experiment stopped. At 180 volts, he cries out that he cannot stand it anymore. At 300 volts, he yells about his heart condition and pleads to be released. If you hesitate in shocking the learner, however, the experimenter tells you, "You must go on. The experiment requires that you continue."

Eventually the learner stops responding altogether, and the experimenter tells you that not responding is the same as a wrong answer. The learner is unresponsive. He might be injured or even dead. Would you keep going? Do you think most people would? As shown in Figure 13.3, when Milgram conducted this study, the majority of the teachers obeyed the experimenter: Almost two-thirds delivered the full 450 volts. By the way, the 50-year-old man was a confederate and was not being shocked at all. Of course, the teachers were unaware that the learner was only pretending to be shocked.

"You must go on. The experiment requires that you continue." Imagine that with those simple statements the experimenter was able to calmly command people (as far as they knew) to shock a man to unconsciousness and possibly death. Such is the power of obedience to authority.

Milgram's studies have been an ethical controversy since they began. Under today's ethical guidelines, it is unlikely that these experiments would have been approved. Nonetheless, we are still learning from Milgram's data. A meta-analysis of his experiments suggested that the critical decision was at the 150-volt level, when the learner first requested that the experiment be halted. At that point, 80 percent of those who were going to stop did so (Packer, 2008). Apparently, individuals who were going to disobey were those who responded not to the later anguished cries of pain but to the learner's first request to be set free.

You might wonder whether Milgram's results would apply today. To examine this question, Jerry Burger (2009) recreated Milgram's study. His study was very similar to Milgram's with a key exception: Burger's participants were never allowed to go higher than 150 volts. At 150 volts, the confederate asked to

I DON'T CARE IF YOU DO THINK I'M "DISSING" YOU I WANT YOU IN THE STORY CORNER **NOW**!

© Fran. www.CartoonStock.com.

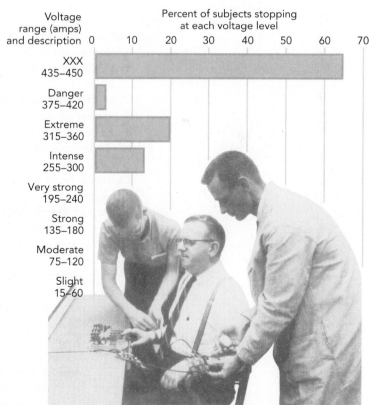

FIGURE 13.3   **Milgram Obedience Study** A 50-year-old man, the "learner," is strapped into a chair. The experimenter makes it look as if a shock generator is being connected to his body through several electrodes. The chart shows the percentage of "teachers" who stopped shocking the learner at each voltage level.

Adapted from Stanley Milgram, "Behavioral Study of Obedience" in *Journal of Abnormal and Social Psychology*, 67: 371–378, 1963.

psychological
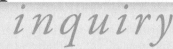
inquiry

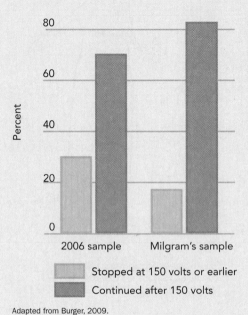

Stopped at 150 volts or earlier

Continued after 150 volts

Adapted from Burger, 2009.

Obedience Then and Now

The figure shows the results of Burger's obedience study, conducted in 2006 and published in 2009, and the results of one of Milgram's studies. The vertical, or Y axis, shows the percent of participants who stopped or continued shocking the learner after that individual first expressed a desire to end the study. Try out the following questions.

1. Does this comparison surprise you? Why or why not?

2. Burger did not allow participants who knew of Milgram's study to take part in his study. How might the results have differed if these individuals had been permitted to participate?

3. If you had been a "teacher" in this study, what do you think you would have done?

end the study, and immediately after participants decided whether to continue, the experiment was ended. Surprisingly, Burger's participants were only slightly less likely to obey than Milgram's had been. The Psychological Inquiry probes the results of Burger's study.

The Stanford Prison Experiment Another controversial demonstration of the power of obedience is provided by the famous Stanford prison experiment, conducted by Philip Zimbardo in 1971. This study illustrates the potentially horrific effects of obedience, not only on those who obey but on those who wield authority.

Zimbardo and his students created a simulated prison in the basement of a Stanford University building (Haney, Banks, & Zimbardo, 1973; Zimbardo, 1972, 1973, 2007). Newspaper ads recruited men for a 2-week study of prison life that would pay $15 per day (about $85 today). After undergoing screening to ensure they were psychologically healthy, 24 men began the study. Each was assigned to the role of either "prisoner" or "guard."

The prisoners were "arrested" at their homes, booked and fingerprinted at the local police station, and brought to the prison. They were strip-searched and given uncomfortable uniforms. They were assigned three to a cell, where they were to spend most of their time, night and day. The guards wore uniforms and mirrored sunglasses (to prevent eye contact with prisoners) and wielded wooden batons. They could leave the prison between their 8-hour shifts. Zimbardo, acting as the prison superintendent, told the guards that they had all the power in the prison (Zimbardo, 1989). He informed the guards that they would be taking away each prisoner's individuality.

The course of the study surprised even Zimbardo. Things got ugly very quickly. During the first 2 days, one prisoner had to be released when he started raging uncontrollably, and a group of prisoners blockaded themselves in their cells. Additional guards were brought in to control the uprising. Some guards attacked prisoners with fire extinguishers while not being watched by the research staff. One-third of the guards behaved in extremely sadistic ways, forcing prisoners to stand naked in their cells or allowing them only a bucket in which to urinate and defecate. The study was cut short after just 6 days, prompted by a graduate student's concern for participant safety (Zimbardo, Maslach, & Haney, 2000).

Zimbardo concluded that situational factors powerfully affect human behavior. To explain why prisoners did not quit the study, he argued that they had internalized their roles. To explain the guards' cruelty, Zimbardo reasoned that when an authority figure removes personal responsibility, when other people are dehumanized, and when norms support otherwise horrifying behavior, true evil can emerge. The conclusions drawn from this work are similar to those of the Milgram obedience studies: Anyone would do vile things if put in the same situation, and good people will do evil things to other good people if the situation supports those deeds (Zimbardo, Maslach, & Haney, 2000).

Scholars have questioned whether Zimbardo's study provides evidence of human nature's potential for shocking and inhumane behavior (Haslam & Reicher, 2003). For instance, recall that Zimbardo recruited participants with an ad that mentioned "prison life." Thomas Carnahan and Sam McFarland (2007) placed two ads in a newspaper, one that mentioned prison life and one that did not. Individuals who answered the first ad differed from those who answered the second: They were higher on characteristics such as aggression and exploitativeness and lower in altruism and empathy.

Like Milgram's studies, the Stanford prison experiment has been criticized on ethical grounds (De Vos, 2010; Fromm, 1973; Savin, 1973). Participants in the experiment (and Milgram's studies, for that matter) did not express regret and felt the study was worthwhile (Zimbardo, 2007). Perhaps you can see how cognitive dissonance might explain such responses. Still, the Stanford prison experiment is an influential study in social psychology. It continues to inform our understanding of human behavior in prison contexts (Zimbardo, 1971, 2007) and to inspire controversy (McAdams, 2007).

EXERTING PERSONAL CONTROL

After reading about these classic studies by Asch, Milgram, and Zimbardo, you may be questioning the value of conformity and obedience and wondering what it might take for people to stand up to group pressure or against the demands of an authority figure. It can be difficult to go against the crowd and risk being wrong or rejected. When people believe that they have control over their own actions, they are less likely to conform (Alquist, Ainsworth, & Baumeister, 2013).

Reactance refers to the motivation to reject attempts to control us (Brehm, 2000). Reactance occurs when a person feels that someone or something is taking away his or her choices. Sometimes when authority figures overreach, reactance propels people to defy those authorities. Reactance might explain the high levels of voter turnout in the 2012 presidential election in places where authorities had attempted to limit voting.

Daily life requires some amount of conformity and obedience, but there are times when all of us must exert personal control over our actions. Although it may not be easy to resist the group or authority, living with the knowledge that you compromised your own moral integrity may be more difficult in the long run.

Group Influence

On November 19, 2011, a frantic 911 call reported that a member of Florida A&M University's famous Marching 100 had lost consciousness in the band's bus. The injured man, 26-year-old drum major Robert Champion, died that day as a result of an alleged hazing. To gain membership in an elite percussion group in the band, Champion had walked down the aisle of the charter bus that had taken the band to an away game. That passageway became a gauntlet of punches from band mates that Champion's body could not withstand. None of the band members disliked Champion. Certainly, none would have ever hit him or behaved aggressively toward him in any way in their daily interactions. Yet in the context of that bus on that fateful day, members of the group to which Champion, by all accounts, was wholly devoted, had beaten him to death.

Why do individuals who would never perform destructive, even murderous, acts when alone perpetrate them when in a group? This central question has driven research in the social psychology of group influence.

Why do individuals who would never perform destructive acts when alone perpetrate them when in a group?

● **deindividuation** The reduction in personal identity and erosion of the sense of personal responsibility when one is part of a group.

DEINDIVIDUATION

One process that sheds light on the behavior of individuals in groups is **deindividuation,** which occurs when being part of a group reduces personal identity and erodes the sense of personal responsibility (Levine, Cassidy, & Jentzsch, 2010; Zimbardo, 2007). An example of the effects of deindividuation is the wild street celebrations that erupt after a team's victory in the World Series or Super Bowl.

One explanation for the effects of deindividuation is that groups give us anonymity. When we are part of a group, we may act in an uninhibited way because we believe that no one will be able to identify us. The Ku Klux Klan demonstrates a variety of ways that human beings can deindividuate: acting in groups, often under cover of darkness, and wearing white hoods to conceal identity.

SOCIAL CONTAGION

● **social contagion** Imitative behavior involving the spread of actions, emotions, and ideas.

Have you ever noticed that a movie you watched in a crowded theater seemed funnier than it did when you watched it alone at home? People laugh more when others are laughing. Babies cry when other babies are crying. The effects of others on our behavior can take the form of **social contagion,** imitative behavior involving the spread of actions, emotions, and ideas (Gino, Ayal, & Ariely, 2009; Kiuru & others, 2012; Poirier & Cobb, 2012). Social contagion effects can be observed in such varied phenomena as social fads, the popularity of dog breeds (Herzog, 2006), the spread of unhealthy behaviors such as smoking and drinking among adolescents (Rodgers, 2007), and symptoms of eating disorders among young women (Crandall, 2004; Forman-Hoffman & Cunningham, 2008).

One way to observe social contagion is to sit in a quiet but crowded library and start coughing. You will soon notice others doing the same thing. Similarly, imagine that you are walking down the sidewalk and come upon a group of people who are all looking up. How likely is it that you can avoid the temptation of looking up to see what is so interesting?

GROUP PERFORMANCE

Are two or three heads better than one? Some studies reveal that we do better in groups; others show that we are more productive when we work alone (Mojzisch & Schulz-Hardt, 2010). We can make sense out of these contradictory findings by looking closely at the circumstances in which performance is being analyzed (Nijstad, 2009).

Social Facilitation If you have ever given a presentation in a class, you might have noticed that you did a much better job standing in front of your classmates than during any of your practice runs. **Social facilitation** occurs when an individual's performance improves because of the presence of others (Mendes, 2007). Robert Zajonc (1965) argued that the presence of other individuals arouses us. The arousal produces energy and facilitates our performance in groups. If our arousal is too high, however, we are unable to learn new or difficult tasks efficiently. Social facilitation, then, improves our performance on well-learned tasks. For new or difficult tasks, we might be best advised to work things out on our own before trying them in a group.

● **social facilitation** Improvement in an individual's performance because of the presence of others.

Social Loafing   Another factor in group performance is the degree to which one's behavior is monitored. **Social loafing** refers to each person's tendency to exert less effort in a group because of reduced accountability for individual effort. The effect of social loafing is lowered group performance (Latané, 1981). The larger the group, the more likely it is that an individual can loaf without detection.

Researchers have identified ways to decrease social loafing. They include making individuals' contributions more identifiable and unique, simplifying the evaluation of these contributions, and making the group's task more attractive (Karau & Williams, 1993).

● **social loafing** Each person's tendency to exert less effort in a group because of reduced accountability for individual effort.

GROUP DECISION MAKING

Many of the decisions we make take place in groups—juries, teams, families, clubs, school boards, and the U.S. Senate, for example. What happens when people put their minds to the task of making a group decision? How do they decide whether a criminal is guilty, whether a country should attack another, where a family should go on vacation, or whether sex education should be part of a school curriculum? Three aspects of group decision making bear special mention: risky shift and group polarization; groupthink; and majority and minority influence.

Risky Shift and Group Polarization   Imagine that you have a friend, Ann, who works as an accountant. All her life Ann has longed to be a writer. In fact, she believes that she has the next great American novel in her head; she just needs time and energy to devote to writing it. Would you advise Ann to quit her job and go for it? What if you knew beforehand that her chances of success were 50-50? How about 60-40? How much risk would you advise Ann to take?

In one investigation, participants were presented with fictitious dilemmas like this one and were asked how much risk the characters in the scenarios should take (Stoner, 1961). When the individuals discussed the dilemmas as a group, they endorsed riskier decisions than when they were queried alone. The so-called **risky shift** is the tendency for a group decision to be riskier than the average decision made by the individual group members (Goethals & Demorest, 1995).

● **risky shift** The tendency for a group decision to be riskier than the average decision made by the individual group members.

However, people do not always make riskier decisions in a group than when alone. Instead, a group discussion can move individuals more strongly in the direction of the position they initially held (Moscovici, 1985). The **group polarization effect** is the solidification and further strengthening of an individual's position as a consequence of a group discussion or interaction. For example, in 2013, a YouTube clip surfaced of (now former) Rutgers men's basketball coach Mike Rice abusing players during a practice. Administrators had seen the video months earlier and had decided that a fine, suspension, and anger management courses would be appropriate consequences. However, after the wider public saw and discussed the clip, it became clear that a more extreme punishment was required, and Rice was fired.

● **group polarization effect** The solidification and further strengthening of an individual's position as a consequence of a group discussion or interaction.

Why would conversation lead to more extreme opinions? First, during the discussion, new, more persuasive arguments can strengthen an original position. Second, social comparison can have influence. The administrators at Rutgers certainly wanted to see themselves as standing up for what was right, and in this case the group conversation revealed they needed to do more to achieve that goal.

Groupthink: Getting Along but Being Very Wrong   **Groupthink** refers to the impaired group decision making that occurs when making the right decision is less important than maintaining group harmony. Instead of engaging in an open discussion

● **groupthink** The impaired group decision making that occurs when making the right decision is less important than maintaining group harmony.

of all the available information, in groupthink, members of a group place the highest value on conformity and unanimity. Members are encouraged to "get with the program." Those who dissent are met with very strong disapproval.

Groupthink can result in disastrous decisions. Irving Janis (1972) introduced the concept of groupthink to explain a number of enormous decision-making errors throughout history. Such errors include the lack of U.S. preparation for the Japanese bombing of Pearl Harbor during World War II, the escalation of the Vietnam War in the 1960s, the Watergate coverup in 1974, and the *Challenger* space shuttle disaster in 1986.

After the 9/11 terrorist attacks, some suggested the possibility that groupthink interfered with the proper implementation of intelligence. Whistleblower Colleen Rowley, an FBI special agent, revealed that the FBI power hierarchy had been unresponsive to information that might have helped prevent the attacks. Many criticized President George W. Bush and his cabinet for not listening to dissenting voices in the days leading up to the Iraq War. Groupthink might also help explain the unresponsiveness of officials to allegations that former assistant football coach Jerry Sandusky of Penn State University engaged in many acts of child abuse.

Symptoms of groupthink include overestimating the power and morality of one's group, close-mindedness and unwillingness to hear all sides of an argument, and pressure for uniformity (Post & Panis, 2011). Groupthink can occur whenever groups value conformity over accuracy (Degnin, 2009).

Groupthink can be prevented if groups avoid isolation, allow the airing of all sides of an argument, have an impartial leader, include outside experts in the debate, and encourage members who are strongly identified with the group to speak out in dissent (Packer, 2009). The decision in 2011 for the Navy SEALS to conduct an assassination raid on Osama bin Laden's compound involved an open discussion. Although most of President Obama's advisors hedged their bets, Vice President Biden specifically advised against the raid, whereas then–CIA Director Leon Panetta explicitly recommended going in (Landler, 2012).

Majority and Minority Influence Most groups make decisions by voting, and, even in the absence of groupthink, the majority usually wins. The majority exerts influence on group decision making through both informational influence (they have greater opportunity to share their views) and normative influence (they set group norms). Those who do not go along may be ignored or even given the boot.

Prospects might seem dim for minority opinion holders, but they *can* make a difference. Because it is outnumbered, the minority cannot win through normative pressure. Instead, it must do its work through informational pressure. If the minority presents its views consistently and confidently, then the majority is more likely to listen to the minority's perspectives. A powerful way that minority opinion holders can have influence is by winning over former majority members to their points of view.

4· INTERGROUP RELATIONS

Conflicts between groups, especially ethnic and cultural groups, are rampant around the world (Dovidio, Newheiser, & Leyens, 2012; Gelfand & others, 2012; Holbrook & Fessler, 2013). The terrorist organization al Qaeda attacks the United States and other countries that its members perceive to be too secular and materialistic. The wronged nations retaliate. Israelis and Palestinians fight over territory in the Middle East, each claiming religious and historical rights to the disputed land. In countries across Africa, tribal chiefs try to craft a new social order favorable to their own rule. A variety of concepts introduced by social psychologists can help us understand the intensity of such cultural and ethnic conflicts and can provide insight into how to reduce them (Maoz, 2012; Reynolds, Haslam, & Turner, 2012).

Group Identity

Think about the groups of which you are a member—your religious and social organizations, your ethnic group, your nationality. When someone asks you to identify yourself,

test yourself

1. Compare and contrast informational social influence and normative social influence.
2. What is the difference between conformity and obedience?
3. What do the concepts of risky shift and group polarization have to say about decision making in a group context?

Social psychologists understand ethnic conflict in the context of group processes and social identity.

how often do you respond by mentioning these group memberships? And how much does it matter whether the people you associate with are members of the same groups as you?

SOCIAL IDENTITY

Social identity refers to the way we define ourselves in terms of our group membership. In contrast to personal identity, which can be highly individualized, social identity assumes some commonalities with others (Biernat & Deaux, 2012; Haslam, Reicher, & Reynolds, 2012). A person's social identity might include identifying with a religious group, a country, a social organization, a political party, and many other groups (M. Becker & others, 2012; Fleischmann, Phalat, & Klein, 2011; Vaes, Heflick, & Goldenberg, 2010). These diverse forms of social identity reflect the numerous ways people connect to groups and social categories (Hogg, 2012; Jaspal & Cinnirella, 2012). Social psychologist Kay Deaux (2001) identified five distinct types of social identity: ethnicity and religion, personal relationships, vocations and avocations, political affiliations, and stigmatized groups (Figure 13.4).

For many people, ethnic identity and religious identity are central to their social identity (King, Ramos, & Clardy, 2012; Rivas-Drake, 2012). Ethnic identity can be a source of pride (Umaña-Taylor & Guimond, 2010). In the United States, special events celebrate the rich cultural contributions of many different groups to the society. Such experiences may provide individuals with an important resource in coping with biases

● **social identity** The way individuals define themselves in terms of their group membership.

Ethnicity & Religion	Relationships	Vocations & Avocations	Political Affiliation	Stigmatized Identities
Jewish Asian American Southern Baptist West Indian	Parent Mother Son Widow	Artist Athlete Psychologist Military veteran	Environmentalist Feminist Republican	Overweight person Person with AIDS Homeless person Alcoholic

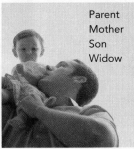

FIGURE 13.4   Types of Identity When we identify ourselves, we draw on a host of different characteristics associated with the various social groups to which we belong.

they encounter (Crocker, Major, & Steele, 1998). Feeling connected to one's ethnic group may buffer individuals from the stressful effects of injustice (Torres, Yzaga, & Moore, 2011; Tynes & others, 2012).

Social psychologist Henry Tajfel (1978), a Holocaust survivor, wanted to explain the extreme violence and prejudice that his religious group (Jews) experienced. Tajfel's **social identity theory** states that our social identities are a crucial part of our self-image and a valuable source of positive feelings about ourselves. To feel good about ourselves, we need to feel good about the groups to which we belong. For this reason, individuals invariably think of the group to which they belong as an *in-group,* a group that has special value in comparison with other groups, called *out-groups.* To improve our self-image, we continually compare our in-groups with out-groups (M. R. Parks, 2007). In the process, we often focus more on the differences between the two groups than on their similarities.

Research by Tajfel (and many others who have used his theory) shows how easy it is to lead people to think in terms of "us" and "them" (Tajfel, 1978). In one experiment, Tajfel had participants look at a screen featuring a huge number of dots and estimate how many dots were displayed. He then assigned the participants to groups based on an arbitrary situation—whether they overestimated or underestimated the number of dots. Once assigned to one of the two groups, the participants were asked to award money to other participants. Taifel found that individuals awarded money to members of their in-group, not to participants in the out-group, even though the group assignment had been essentially arbitrary. If we favor the members of a group that was formed on such a trivial basis, it is no wonder that we show intense in-group favoritism when differences are not so trivial.

ETHNOCENTRISM

Ethnocentrism is the tendency to favor one's own ethnic group over other groups. Ethnocentrism is not simply taking pride in one's group; it involves asserting the group's superiority over other groups. As such, ethnocentrism encourages in-group/out-group or we/they thinking (Dovidio & others, 2012). Consequently, ethnocentrism implies that ethnic out-groups are not just different; they are worse than one's group. Hence, ethnocentrism may underlie prejudice.

PREJUDICE

Prejudice is an unjustified negative attitude toward an individual based on the individual's membership in a particular group. The group can be made up of people of a specific ethnicity, sex, age, religion—essentially, people who are different in some way from a prejudiced person (Billig, 2012; Monteith, Woodcock, & Lybarger, 2013). Prejudice as a worldwide phenomenon can be seen in many eruptions of hatred in human history. In the Balkan Peninsula of eastern Europe, the Serbs' prejudice against Bosnians prompted

social identity theory Tajfel's theory that social identity is a crucial part of self-image and a valuable source of positive feelings about oneself.

ethnocentrism The tendency to favor one's own ethnic group over other groups.

prejudice An unjustified negative attitude toward an individual based on the individual's membership in a group.

Ethnic identity evokes ethnic pride. Here, Italian American soccer fans in Boston's North End rejoice at the Italian soccer team's World Cup win; Chinese American children touch the "lion" in the streets of New York City's Chinatown on the day of Chinese New Year, in hopes of receiving good luck and prosperity; and children and adults dance during a Kwanzaa celebration at Philadelphia's Canaan Baptist Church to strengthen their ties to their African heritage.

the Serb policy of "ethnic cleansing." The prejudice of the Hutus against the Tutsis in Rwanda led them to go on a murderous rampage, attacking the Tutsis with machetes.

A powerful example of destructive prejudice within U.S. society is racial prejudice against African Americans. When Africans were brought to colonial America as slaves, they were considered property and treated inhumanely. In the first half of the twentieth century, most African Americans still lived in the South and remained largely segregated based on skin color; restaurants, movie theaters, and buses had separate areas for Whites and Blacks.

It is useful at this point to note that talking openly about race and ethnicity can be awkward. Even coming up with labels to use to describe different groups of people can be difficult. In the United States, typical labels have changed from Black and White to African American and European American. But even these labels are not without problem. Many times labels are based not on information about the person's origins, but solely on the color of the person's skin. Nelson Mandela, for instance, is not African American. He is African. How do we distinguish between Mandela and F. W. de Klerk, the former South African president who shared the Nobel Peace Prize with Mandela in 1993 for abolishing apartheid?

Typically today, we rely simply on the person's own assessment of his or her group membership to identify race. President Barack Obama embodies the complex issues of race in America. His mother was European American, his father African, and he labels himself African American. In our discussion here, we will use the terms *Black* and *White* when in a particular study the actual ethnic background of targets of social judgment is not specified. In these instances, the only cue to the person's background, or anything else about that person, is skin color. Unfortunately, skin color can have a remarkably negative effect on how people are treated.

Despite progress over the years, there remain notable racial disparities among Americans, in terms of poverty, employment, education, and healthcare. Research continues to demonstrate the influence of race in U.S. life. In one study, researchers sent out 5,000 résumés in response to 1,200 job ads placed in newspapers in Chicago and Boston. The résumés were identical in qualifications. They differed only in whether the candidates' names were stereotypically White or Black. "White" names included Meredith, Emily, Brad, and Greg. "Black" names included Tamika, Lakisha, Darnell, and Kareem. The researchers found that even with identical qualifications, the applicants with White-sounding names were 50 percent more likely to be called for an interview (Bertrand & Mullainathan, 2004).

Another study examined the way race influenced the advice that bankruptcy attorneys gave to clients. During the recent financial crisis, many Americans resorted to bankruptcy. Declaring bankruptcy means that a person is admitting that he or she is unable to repay debts. This legal claim can allow people to start the arduous process of regaining financial solvency. The two ways of declaring bankruptcy are Chapter 7 and Chapter 13. Chapter 7 bankruptcy is less expensive and often less burdensome than Chapter 13. An analysis of bankruptcy cases across the United States showed that African Americans were more likely than Whites to file Chapter 13 rather than Chapter 7 bankruptcy (Braucher, Cohen, & Lawless, 2012).

Why would a group of individuals choose the more difficult and expensive form of bankruptcy? Could attorneys be steering African Americans toward this more burdensome path? To address this question, the researchers conducted an experiment involving a random sample of bankruptcy lawyers. Participants read scenarios in which potential clients were identified as either "Reggie and Latisha" or "Todd and Alison." Even when all other aspects of the cases were identical, lawyers were more likely to recommend that Todd and Alison declare Chapter 7 and that Reggie and Latisha pursue Chapter 13 (Braucher, Cohen, & Lawless, 2012).

Results such as these are troubling. It is important to keep in mind that these responses to Black-sounding names might not reflect intentional biases but instead subtle and potentially unconscious racial biases. The possibly unconscious nature of racism in modern life is a challenge for researchers interested in understanding and reducing prejudice.

Because racial prejudice is socially unacceptable, few people today would readily admit to racist or prejudicial views. Today, prejudiced individuals are more likely than before to appear unprejudiced on the surface while nevertheless holding racist views at a deeper level (Sears, 2008). Indeed, individuals may not be consciously aware of their own racial (or gender or age) biases.

To confront this problem, social psychologists examine prejudicial attitudes on two levels—explicit racism and implicit racism. *Explicit racism* is a person's conscious and openly shared attitude, which might be measured using a questionnaire. *Implicit racism* refers to attitudes that exist on a deeper, hidden level. Implicit attitudes must be measured with a method that does not require awareness (Trawaiter & Shapiro, 2010). For example, implicit racism is sometimes measured using the Implicit Associations Test (IAT), a computerized survey that assesses the ease with which a person can associate a Black or White person with good things (for example, flowers) or bad things (for example, misery) (Greenwald & others, 2009; Nosek & Banaji, 2007; Sriram & Greenwald, 2009). This test is based on the idea that preexisting biases may make it easier to associate some social stimuli with positive rather than negative items. Although the IAT is widely used, scholars have raised concerns about its validity (Blanton & others, 2009).

Implicit prejudice can influence behavior. In one study, White college students completed measures of explicit and implicit attitudes toward Black people using an implicit measure similar to the IAT (Dovidio, Kawakami, & Gaertner, 2002). The students then interacted with a Black student partner. Explicit prejudice predicted what people said to a person of a different race—that is, White students who said they were not prejudiced were unlikely to say overtly racist things. However, implicit prejudice related to nonverbal aspects of the interaction, such as White students' facial expressions and how close they sat to their partners.

Why do people develop prejudice? Social psychologists have explored a number of possible reasons. Competition between groups, especially when resources are scarce, can contribute to prejudice. For example, immigrants often compete with established low-income members of a society for jobs—a situation that can lead to persistent conflict between the two groups. Cultural learning is also clearly involved. Children can adopt the prejudicial attitudes of their families and friends before they even meet a person from an out-group. In addition, when people feel bad about themselves, they might bolster their self-esteem by demeaning out-group members.

A final factor that might underlie prejudice comes from the limits on our information-processing abilities. As already noted, individuals have a limited capacity for effortful thought, but we face a complex social environment. To simplify the challenge of understanding others' behavior, people use categories or stereotypes. Stereotypes can be a powerful force in developing and maintaining prejudicial attitudes.

STEREOTYPING AND PREJUDICE

Recall that stereotypes are generalizations about a group that deny variations within the group. Researchers have found that we are less likely to detect variations among individuals who belong to "other" groups than among individuals who belong to "our" group. So, we might see the people in our in-group as varied, unique individuals while viewing the members of out-groups as "all the same" (Amodio & Mendoza, 2010). At the root of prejudice is a particular kind of stereotype: a negative generalization about a group that is applied to all members of that group (Stangor, 2009; Wetherell, 2012).

In Chapter 8 we considered heuristics in cognitive processing. If individuals are prone to behave in an automatic fashion, we might expect them to be more likely to rely on stereotypes in judging others and, in that sense, to be more prejudiced. Conversely, we might expect those who are more mindful and prone to thinking critically to be less likely to use stereotypes and less prejudiced. The notion that cognitive abilities might play a role in prejudice has been the subject of much recent research. To read about this provocative work, read the Critical Controversy.

DISCRIMINATION

● **discrimination** An unjustified negative or harmful action toward a member of a group simply because the person belongs to that group.

Discrimination is an unjustified negative or harmful action toward a member of a group simply because the person belongs to that group. Discrimination occurs when negative emotional reactions combine with prejudicial beliefs and are translated into

CRITICAL CONTROVERSY

Is Intelligence Related to Prejudice and Political Beliefs?

Most research on racism has focused on the motivational or emotional side of this problematic attitude. Researchers have begun to explore the link between cognitive ability and prejudicial attitudes. This work has generally shown that intelligence is negatively correlated with prejudice (Piber-Dabrowska, Sedek, & Kofta, 2010). In other words, the more intelligent people are, the less likely they are to be prejudiced, and vice versa.

In one study, Gordon Hodson and Michael Busseri (2012) examined two representative samples in the United Kingdom including nearly 16,000 people. Intelligence was measured when the participants were 10 or 11 years old, and racial attitudes were assessed when they were in their early 30s. Prejudicial attitudes were assessed with items like "I wouldn't mind working with people from other races" (for such an item, a high rating would indicate low racism). Results showed that lower intelligence in childhood predicted greater racism in adulthood, even when differences in education levels and socioeconomic status were taken into account.

The researchers then boldly took these questions a step further. Beyond measuring intelligence and racism, Hodson and Busseri measured *social conservatism,* by asking individuals about their positions on such matters as valuing traditional roles for men and women and supporting harsh sentences for criminals. The results indicated that individuals who were lower in cognitive ability were more likely to endorse traditional views on these matters. The researchers argued that this endorsement explained the respondents' tendency to report more prejudicial attitudes.

When these results spread across the Internet, headlines clearly revealed the biases of bloggers in responding to the controversial findings. "Conservatives scientifically proven as stupid and racist" declared a liberal blog. "Low IQ and liberal beliefs linked to poor research?" posed a conservative blog.

To sort out what these controversial findings can—and cannot—tell us about potential associations between cognitive ability, prejudice, and political orientation, let's consider the research methods used. First, the measure of political orientation was very limited: Conservatism was defined in *narrow terms* and did not address many aspects of conservatism. Second, the measure of racism relied on *self-reports.* Consider that brighter individuals might know better than to admit to undesirable negative racial attitudes. Third, this research was *correlational,* meaning that causation cannot be assumed between the factors studied (for example, we cannot conclude that being less intelligent caused individuals to be more socially conservative). Fourth, group-level results *cannot be generalized* to specific individuals. As Hodson and Busseri noted, there are certainly very intelligent conservatives in the world, and not-so-bright liberals as well. Further, all social conservatives are not prejudiced, and all prejudiced individuals are not social conservatives.

Holding either extreme right-wing or extreme left-wing views may be a way for those with lower cognitive ability to find easy answers in a difficult world. Thinking critically and mindfully about the social world may be a more difficult but worthwhile alternative. Thinking critically and mindfully about provocative research is similarly worthwhile.

WHAT DO YOU THINK

- Intelligence has been rising around the world (recall the Flynn effect from Chapter 8). Do you think this increase in intelligence is reflected in decreases in prejudice? Why or why not?
- What other childhood factors might likely be stronger predictors of prejudice in adulthood than intelligence?
- Do you know someone who is prejudiced? How do these results apply?

---

behavior (Bergman & others, 2012: D. R. Williams & others, 2012). Many forms of discrimination are illegal in the U.S. workplace. Since the Civil Rights Act of 1964 (revised in 1991), it has been unlawful to deny someone employment on the basis of gender or ethnicity (Parker, 2006).

Ways to Improve Intergroup Relations

Martin Luther King, Jr., said, "I have a dream that my four little children will one day live in a nation where they will not be judged by the color of their skin but by the content of their character." How might we attain the world that King envisioned?

One way might be for people to come to know one another better so that they can get along. However, in daily life many people interact with individuals from other ethnic groups, and this contact does not necessarily lead to tolerance or warm relations. Indeed, researchers have consistently found that contact by itself—attending the same school or working in the same company—does not necessarily improve relations among people of different ethnic backgrounds. So, rather than focusing on contact per se, researchers have examined how *various features* of a contact situation may be optimal for reducing prejudice and promoting intergroup harmony (Stott, Drury, & Reicher, 2012: Vezzali & others, 2011).

Gordon Allport (1954), whose contributions to personality psychology we examined in Chapter 12, theorized that particular aspects of the contact between groups could help to reduce prejudice. According to Allport, intergroup contact is likely to reduce prejudice when group members

- Think that they are of equal status
- Feel that an authority figure sanctions their positive relationships
- Believe that friendship might emerge from the interaction
- Engage in cooperative tasks in which everyone has something to contribute

Research supports many of Allport's ideas (Pettigrew & Tropp, 2006). In particular, studies have examined the role of *task-oriented cooperation*—working together on a shared goal—in reducing tensions between groups. Two examples of the power of task-oriented cooperation are Sherif's Robbers Cave Study and Aronson's jigsaw classroom.

It may be hard to imagine in our post-*Survivor* era, but even before Jeff Probst started handing out color-coded "buffs" on the TV show *Survivor,* Muzafer Sherif and his colleagues (1961) had the idea of exploring group processes by assigning 11-year-old boys to two competitive groups (the "Rattlers" and the "Eagles") in a summer camp called Robbers Cave (see the Psychological Inquiry). Sherif, disguised as a janitor so that he could observe the boys, arranged for the two groups to compete in baseball, touch football, and tug-of-war. If you have watched reality television, you have some idea how this experiment went. In short order, relations between the groups deteriorated. Members of each group expressed negative opinions of members of the other group, and the Rattlers and Eagles became battling factions.

psychological *inquiry*

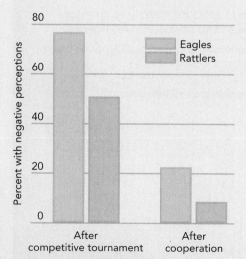

Improving Group Relations Through Cooperative Activities

The figure illustrates the results of Sherif's (1961) Robbers Cave Study. The graph shows the negative feelings expressed by members of the Eagles and Rattlers toward the other group (the out-group) after a competitive tournament and after cooperative activity. Try your hand at these questions.

1. When did hostility between the groups peak? When did it drop?

2. What is up with the Eagles? What are some reasons why they might be more negative about the Rattlers?

3. In your own life, are there examples of holding particular attitudes toward a group different from your own? How have your attitudes changed and what events preceded these changes?

What would bring these clashing groups together? Sherif created tasks that required the joint efforts of both groups, such as working together to repair the camp's only water supply. When the groups were required to work cooperatively to solve problems, the Rattlers and Eagles developed more positive relationships.

Sherif's idea was later tested in the real world in Austin, Texas, when ethnic tensions increased and violence erupted among African Americans, Mexican Americans, and European Americans in desegregated schools. Social psychologist Eliot Aronson was asked to help address the problem, and he devised the *jigsaw classroom* (1986), where all of the students had to pull together to get the "big picture."

Let's say an ethnically diverse class consists of 30 students. The academic goal for all students is to learn about the life of Rosa Parks. The class might be broken up into five study groups of six students each, with the groups being as equal as possible in ethnic composition and academic achievement level. Learning about Parks's life becomes a class project divided into six parts, with one part given to each member of the six-person group. The components might be various books about Parks or information about different aspects of her life. The parts are like the pieces of a jigsaw puzzle: They have to be put together to form the complete puzzle.

U.S. classrooms have used the jigsaw approach, and it is has been associated with increased self-esteem, better academic performance, friendships among classmates, and improved interethnic perceptions (Slavin, 2006).

test yourself

1. What does social identity theory say about groups?
2. What is prejudice? Give two real-world examples, either historical or contemporary.
3. According to Allport, what particular aspects of the contact between groups could help to reduce prejudice?

5· CLOSE RELATIONSHIPS

Along with good health and happiness, close relationships figure prominently in most people's notions of a good life. Every day we see commercials lauding the ability of various online matchmaking sites to link us up with the love of our life. Online dating services represent a $2.1 billion industry (Dating Sites Reviews, 2013).

Because close romantic relationships are so crucial for most of us, it is no wonder that social psychologists are interested in studying this vital part of human existence. A vast literature has accumulated in social psychology, examining attraction, love, and intimacy.

Attraction

At the beginning of this chapter, we discussed one key factor in interpersonal attraction, namely, physical attractiveness. Research on interpersonal attraction has illuminated a variety of other factors that play a role in the dynamic of attraction.

PROXIMITY AND SIMILARITY

Even in the age of Internet dating, it is very unlikely that you are going to become attracted to someone without meeting the person. *Proximity,* or physical closeness, is a strong predictor of attraction. You are more likely to become attracted to someone you pass in the hall every day than to a person you rarely see. One potential mechanism for the role of proximity in attraction is the mere exposure effect (Zajonc, 1968, 2001). The **mere exposure effect** is the phenomenon that the more we encounter someone or something (a person, a word, an image), the more probable it is that we will start liking the person or thing even if we do not realize we have seen it before.

In addition to proximity, similarity plays an important role in attraction (Qian, 2009). We have all heard that opposites attract, but what is true of magnets is not usually true of human beings. We like to associate with people who are similar to us (Berscheid, 2000). Our friends and lovers are much more like us than unlike us. We share similar attitudes, behavior patterns, taste in clothes, intelligence, personality, other friends, values, lifestyle, and physical attractiveness.

The concept of *consensual validation* explains why people are attracted to others who are similar to them. Our own attitudes and behavior are supported when someone else's attitudes and behavior are familiar—their attitudes and behavior validate ours. Another reason that similarity matters is that we tend to shy away from the unknown. Similarity

© Ralph Hagen. www.CartoonStock.com.

● **mere exposure effect** The phenomenon that the more individuals encounter someone or something, the more probable it is that they will start liking the person or thing even if they do not realize they have seen it before.

As love matures, passionate love tends to give way to affectionate love.

● **romantic or passionate love** Love with strong components of sexuality and infatuation, often dominant in the early part of a love relationship.

● **affectionate or companionate love** Love that occurs when individuals desire to have another person near and have a deep, caring affection for the person.

● **social exchange theory** The view of social relationships as involving an exchange of goods, the objective of which is to minimize costs and maximize benefits.

implies that we will enjoy doing things with another person who has comparable tastes and attitudes.

Love

Some relationships never progress much beyond the attraction stage. Others deepen to friendship and perhaps even to love. Social psychologists have long puzzled over exactly what love is (Berscheid, 2006, 2010; Sternberg, 2013c). One way to think about love is to consider the types of love that characterize different human relationships—for instance, friendships versus romantic relationships (Hendrick & Hendrick, 2009; Rawlins & Russell, 2013). Here we consider two types of love: romantic love and affectionate love.

Poets, playwrights, and musicians through the ages have celebrated the fiery passion of romantic love—and lamented the searing pain when it fails. Think about songs and books that hit the top of the charts. Chances are, they are about romantic love. **Romantic love,** also called **passionate love,** is love with strong components of sexuality and infatuation, and it often predominates in the early part of a love relationship (Hendrick & Hendrick, 2006). This is the kind of sexually charged feeling we usually mean when we talk about being "in love" (Berscheid, 1988).

Love is more than just passion, however (Fitness & Williams, 2013; Prager & others, 2013). **Affectionate love,** also called **companionate love,** is the type of love that occurs when individuals desire to have the other person near and have a deep, caring affection for the person. There is a growing belief that the early stages of love have more romantic ingredients and that as love matures, passion tends to give way to affection (Berscheid & Regan, 2005).

Models of Close Relationships

What makes long-term romantic relationships last? Two theoretical approaches to this sometimes bewildering question include social exchange theory and the investment model.

SOCIAL EXCHANGE THEORY

The social exchange approach to close relationships focuses on the costs and benefits of one's romantic partner. **Social exchange theory** is based on the notion of social relationships as involving an exchange of goods, the objective of which is to minimize costs and maximize benefits. This theory looks at human relations as an exchange of rewards between actors.

From the social exchange perspective, the most important predictor of a relationship's success is *equity*—a feeling on the part of the individuals in the relationship that each is doing his or her "fair share." Essentially, social exchange theory asserts that the partners keep a mental balance sheet, tallying the pluses and minuses associated with each other—what they put in ("I paid for our last date") and what they get out ("He brought me flowers").

As relationships progress, equity may no longer apply. In fact, research shows that over time, this kind of accounting not only is less likely to explain what happens in a relationship but also becomes distasteful to the partners. Happily married couples are less likely to keep track of "what I get versus what I give," and they avoid thinking about the costs and benefits of their relationships (Buunk & Van Yperen, 1991; Clark & Chrisman, 1994). Surely we can all think of long-term relationships in which one partner remains committed even when the benefits are hard for the outsider to see—as in the case where the person's romantic partner is gravely ill for a long time.

THE INVESTMENT MODEL

Another way to think about long-term romantic relationships is to focus on the underlying factors that characterize stable, happy relationships compared to others. The

investment model examines the ways that commitment, investment, and the availability of attractive alternative partners predict satisfaction and stability in relationships (Rusbult, Agnew, & Arriaga, 2012).

From the investment model perspective, long-term relationships are likely to continue when both partners are committed to the relationship and both have invested a great deal; in addition, relationships are more enduring when there are few tempting alternatives for the partners. For example, college students who are committed to their romantic partners are less likely to cheat on them sexually during spring break (Drigotas, Safstrom, & Gentilia, 1999).

Commitment to a relationship also predicts a willingness to sacrifice for a romantic partner. In one study, individuals were given a chance to climb up and down a short staircase, over and over, to spare their partner from having to do so. Those who were more committed to their partner worked harder climbing up and down to spare their loved one the burden (Van Lange & others, 1997). When two partners are deeply invested in a relationship, they can also bring the best out in each other, mutually helping themselves grow into their best possible selves (Rusbult, Finkel, & Kumashiro, 2009).

6· SOCIAL PSYCHOLOGY AND HEALTH AND WELLNESS

The principles of social psychology have provided a strong foundation for ongoing research in the areas of health and wellness (Kok & de Vries, 2006; S. E. Taylor, 2012, 2013). In this concluding section, we glimpse some of the significant connections that researchers have uncovered among social contacts, physical health, and psychological wellness.

A long list of studies has shown that social ties are an important, if not the *most* important, variable in predicting health. For example, in a landmark study, social isolation had six times the effect on mortality rates that cigarette smoking had (House, Landis, & Umberson, 1988). In another study involving 1,234 heart attack patients, those living alone were nearly twice as likely to have a second heart attack (Case & others, 1992). Further, in a study of leukemia patients, of those who said that they had little support prior to undergoing a bone marrow transplant, only 20 percent were alive 2 years later, compared to 54 percent who reported that they felt strong support (Colón & others, 1991). Loneliness is linked with impaired physical health (Hawkley, Preacher, & Cacioppo, 2010; Hawkley, Thisted, & Cacioppo, 2009). Chronic loneliness can lead to an early death (Cornwell & Waite, 2009; Cuijpers, 2001). Without a doubt, being connected to others is crucial to human survival.

Having many different social ties may be especially important during difficult times (Hawkley & Cacioppo, 2009; S. E. Taylor, 2012). Individuals who participate in more diverse social networks—for example, having a close relationship with a partner; interacting with family members, friends, neighbors, and fellow workers; and belonging to social and religious groups—live longer than those with a narrower range of social relationships (Vogt & others, 1992). One study investigated the effects of diverse social ties on the susceptibility to getting a common cold (S. Cohen & others, 1998). Individuals reported the extent of their participation in 12 types of social ties. Then they were given nasal drops containing a cold virus and monitored for the appearance of a cold. Individuals with more diverse social ties were less likely to get a cold than their counterparts with less diverse social networks.

Each of us has times in our life when we feel lonely, particularly when we are going through major life transitions. For example, when individuals leave the familiar world of their hometown and family to begin college, they can feel especially lonely. Indeed, experiencing loneliness at the beginning of one's college career is quite common and normal (Cutrona, 1982).

● **investment model** A model of long-term relationships that examines the ways that commitment, investment, and the availability of attractive alternative partners predict satisfaction and stability in relationships.

test yourself

1. Explain the concept of consensual validation.
2. What is the difference between romantic love and affectionate love, and what is another name for each?
3. What does social exchange theory say about happy romantic relationships?

test yourself

1. What are some physical illnesses in which social isolation plays a significant role, according to researchers?

2. What kinds of social networks are especially important in times of trouble?

3. If a friend were struggling with loneliness, what strategy would you recommend for coping with it?

If you are lonely, there are strategies you can use to become better connected with others. You might consider joining activities, such as volunteering your time for a cause in which you believe. When interacting with others, you will improve your chances of developing enduring relationships if you are considerate, honest, trustworthy, and cooperative. If you cannot get rid of your loneliness on your own, you might want to contact the counseling services at your college.

Having completed this chapter's survey of social psychology, you may be surprised to learn that we have barely scratched the surface of this broad and deep field: The branch of psychology that focuses on the ways human beings relate to one another is a rich, intriguing area of study. In the next few days, think about the stories that are making the headlines and that you are talking about with your friends. Reflecting back on this chapter, you might notice that social psychology would have something to say about most of these topics.

SUMMARY

1. SOCIAL COGNITION

The face conveys information to social perceivers, including attractiveness. Self-fulfilling prophecy means that our expectations of others can have a powerful impact on their behavior.

Attributions are our thoughts about why people behave as they do and about who or what is responsible for the outcome of events. Attribution theory views people as motivated to discover the causes of behavior as part of their effort to make sense of it. The dimensions used to make sense of the causes of human behavior include internal/external, stable/unstable, and controllable/uncontrollable.

The fundamental attribution error is observers' tendency to overestimate traits and to underestimate situations when they explain an actor's behavior. Self-serving bias means attributing our successes to internal causes and blaming our failures on external causes. Heuristics are used as shortcuts in social information processing. One such heuristic is a stereotype—a generalization about a group's characteristics that does not consider any variations among individuals in the group.

The self is our mental representation of our own characteristics. Self-esteem refers to the attitude we take toward ourselves. Stereotype threat is an individual's fast-acting, self-fulfilling fear of being judged based on a negative stereotype about his or her group. In order to understand ourselves better, we might engage in social comparison, evaluating ourselves by comparison with others.

Attitudes are our feelings—about people, objects, and ideas. Attitudes predict behavior when an individual's attitudes are strong, when the person is aware of his or her attitudes and expresses them often, and when the person has a vested interest in the attitude. Sometimes changes in behavior precede changes in attitude.

According to cognitive dissonance theory, our strong need for cognitive consistency causes us to change our behavior to fit our attitudes or to change our attitudes to fit our behavior. Self-perception theory stresses the importance of making inferences about attitudes by observing our own behavior, especially when our attitudes are not clear.

2. SOCIAL BEHAVIOR

Altruism is an unselfish interest in helping someone else. Reciprocity often is involved in altruism. Genes play a role in prosocial behavior, along with neurotransmitters serotonin, dopamine, and oxytocin. The experience of empathy is linked to helping as is the personality trait of agreeableness. Individuals who are in a good mood are more helpful. The bystander effect means that individuals who observe an emergency are less likely to help when someone else is present than when they are alone.

Aggression is behavior meant to harm another person. Evidence for genetic and neurobiological factors are mixed and generally less clear-cut than that suggested by research with animals. Psychological factors in aggression include frustrating and aversive circumstances. Sociocultural factors include cross-cultural variation, the culture of honor, and violence in the media.

3. SOCIAL INFLUENCE

Conformity involves a change in behavior to coincide with a group. Factors that influence conformity include informational social influence (going along to be right) and normative social influence (going along to be liked).

Obedience is behavior that complies with the explicit demands of an authority. Milgram's experiments demonstrated the power of obedience. Another such demonstration is the Stanford prison experiment, illustrating the potential effects of obedience not only on individuals who obey but also on those who exercise authority.

People often change in their behavior when they are in a group. Deindividuation refers to the lack of inhibition and diffusion of responsibility that can occur in groups. Social contagion refers to imitative behaviors involving the spread of behavior, emotions, and ideas. Our performance in groups can be improved through social facilitation and lowered because of social loafing.

Risky shift refers to the tendency for a group decision to be riskier than the average decision made by the individual group members. The group polarization effect is the solidification and further strengthening of a position as a consequence of group discussion or interaction. Groupthink involves impaired decision making resulting from valuing group harmony over accuracy.

4. INTERGROUP RELATIONS

Social identity is our definition of ourselves in terms of our group memberships. Social identity theory states that when individuals are assigned to a group, they invariably think of it as the in-group. Identifying with the group allows the person to have a positive self-image. Ethnocentrism is the tendency to favor one's own ethnic group over others.

Prejudice is an unjustified negative attitude toward an individual based on membership in a group. The underlying reasons for prejudice include competition between groups over scarce resources, a person's motivation to enhance his or her self-esteem, cognitive processes that tend to categorize and stereotype others, and cultural learning. Prejudice is also based on stereotypes. The cognitive process of stereotyping can lead to discrimination, an unjustified negative or harmful action toward a member of a group simply because he or she belongs to that group. Discrimination results when negative emotional reactions combine with prejudicial beliefs and are translated into behavior.

An effective strategy for enhancing the effects of intergroup contact is to set up task-oriented cooperation among individuals from different groups.

5. CLOSE RELATIONSHIPS

We tend to be attracted to people whom we see often and who are similar to us. Romantic love (passionate love) includes feelings of infatuation and sexual attraction. Affectionate love (companionate love) is more akin to friendship and includes deep, caring feelings for another.

Social exchange theory states that a relationship is likely to be successful if individuals feel that they get out of the relationship what they put in. The investment model focuses on commitment, investment, and the availability of attractive alternatives in predicting relationship success.

6. SOCIAL PSYCHOLOGY AND HEALTH AND WELLNESS

Social isolation is a strong risk factor for a range of physical illnesses. Loneliness relates to a number of negative health outcomes, including impaired physical health and early death. Individuals who participate in more diverse social networks live longer than those with a narrower range of social relationships. Loneliness often emerges when people make life transitions, so it is not surprising that loneliness is common among college freshmen. Strategies that can help to reduce loneliness include participating in activities with others and taking the initiative to meet new people.

key *terms*

social psychology, p. 432

stereotype, p. 432

attribution theory, p. 434

fundamental attribution
    error, p. 434

false consensus effect, p. 434

positive illusions, p. 435

self-serving bias, p. 435

self-objectification, p. 435

stereotype threat, p. 436

social comparison, p. 436

attitudes, p. 436

cognitive dissonance, p. 437

self-perception
    theory, p. 438

elaboration likelihood
    model, p. 439

altruism, p. 440

egoism, p. 440

bystander effect, p. 442

aggression, p. 442

conformity, p. 446

informational social
    influence, p. 447

normative social influence, p. 447

obedience, p. 448

deindividuation, p. 452

social contagion, p. 452

social facilitation, p. 453

social loafing, p. 453

risky shift, p. 453

group polarization effect, p. 453

groupthink, p. 453

social identity, p. 455

social identity theory, p. 456

ethnocentrism, p. 456

prejudice, p. 456

discrimination, p. 458

mere exposure effect, p. 461

romantic or passionate love, p. 462

affectionate or companionate
    love, p. 462

social exchange theory, p. 462

investment model, p. 463

apply your *knowledge*

1. Check out this website to see how the averaging of faces works: www.faceresearch.org/demos/average. Pick some faces you consider unattractive. What happens when you average them together? If you have a digital photograph of yourself and some friends, see what happens when you average those faces. Do you agree that average faces are more attractive than any single face?

2. Many people are surprised by the results of the IAT when they take this implicit measure. Try it out at https://implicit.harvard.edu/implicit. Do you think your results are valid? Explain.

3. We are often unaware of how many attributions we make about the behavior of others. To demonstrate this point to yourself, spend some time in a crowded area observing the interactions of others (alternatively, watch some scenes in television shows or movies). Take careful notes about the social behaviors that occur and then document your impression of why the individuals behaved as they did. What cues did you use in making your attributions about their behavior? Did your knowledge of the fundamental attribution error influence your attributions? Why or why not?

4. Take a day and engage in altruistic behavior. Act as kindly toward others as you can, without telling anyone what you are up to. Keep track of your thoughts and feelings as you experience this day of kindness. How does it influence your feelings about altruism?

5. Interview the happiest couple you know. Ask the partners individually about the things that they think help make their relationship work. Then examine your notes. How do the characteristics of your "ideal" couple's relationship compare with the findings of research on close relationships?

CHAPTER 14

Industrial and Organizational Psychology

Would You Work Even If You Didn't Have To?

For many people a job is a means to an end. We work to make money. Looking at how some of the world's wealthiest people spend their time, though, it is clear that these individuals work hard and work a lot—even though they have more than enough money to never work again. Tycoons in business and technology—such as Warren Buffett, Bill Gates, and Mark Zuckerberg—maintain long workdays, as do enormously successful writers, musicians, actors, and athletes. Zuckerberg, not yet 30 years old, has an estimated personal worth of $13.3 billion. Even spending $10,000 a day, he would need to live over *3,600 years* to spend it all. Why do people with sufficient wealth to never work at all still devote long hours and great effort to work?

Work is more than a way to earn money. It is an opportunity to use our skills and abilities and to feel successful and effective. It offers a context for meaningful relationships with others. And, work provides us with a sense of identity and purpose. ●

PREVIEW

In this chapter we first examine the origins of industrial-organizational (I-O) psychology. We then investigate each of the two major domains of this approach—the "I" or industrial psychology side, concerned with personnel selection, and the "O" or organizational psychology side, including the topics of management style, workers' attitudes and behavior, and leadership. We pay special attention to one aspect of the "O" side, organizational culture. Finally, we complete our survey of the I-O field by exploring the crucial role of work in health and well-being.

1· ORIGINS OF INDUSTRIAL AND ORGANIZATIONAL PSYCHOLOGY

● **industrial and organizational (I-O) psychology** The field of psychology that applies the science of human behavior to work and the workplace.

Industrial and organizational (I-O) psychology applies the science of psychology to work and the workplace. In I-O psychology, researchers are interested in a broad range of topics related to the work environment, including the selection of the right person for a job, the influence of attitudes on job performance, and the ways people work together in groups (Highhouse & Schmitt, 2013; Kozlowski & Bell, 2013; Ryan & Ployhart, 2014). Many of these topics are also the subject of psychological research in other areas, such as cognition, personality, motivation, and social psychology (Diederich & Busemeyer, 2013; Friedman, 2014; Godsil & Fanselow, 2013; Maio, Olson, & Cheung, 2013). I-O psychology is unique, however, in that it examines these topics in the important real-world context of work.

The notion that the principles of science should be applied to work settings has been around for only about 100 years. Contemporary I-O psychology has roots in the history of industry and the twentieth century's two world wars. Here we review three important influences on the development of I-O psychology: scientific management, ergonomics, and the human relations approach to management.

Scientific Management

● **scientific management** The managerial philosophy that emphasizes the worker as a well-oiled machine and the determination of the most efficient methods for performing any work-related task.

The pioneers in applying scientific methods to the workplace were not psychologists but engineers. They focused on **scientific management**—the managerial philosophy that emphasizes the worker as a well-oiled machine and the determination of the most efficient methods for performing any work-related task. Yet these engineers sounded like psychologists at times. Among them was Frederick Winslow Taylor, the mastermind of the idea of scientific management. Taylor (1911) suggested the following guidelines, which have continuing influence today:

■ Jobs should be carefully analyzed to identify the best way to perform them.

■ Employees should be hired according to the characteristics associated with success at a task. Identify such characteristics by examining individuals who are already successful at a job.

■ Employees should be trained at the job they will perform.

■ Employees should be rewarded for productivity, to encourage high levels of performance.

The advent of the assembly line demonstrates the spirit of scientific management and its emphasis on efficiency. Before the twentieth century, individuals or teams created an entire single product, putting each and every piece together from beginning to end, whether the product was a clock, a car, or a pair of shoes. In 1901, Ransom E. Olds invented the *assembly line*, which revolutionized the automobile industry: Each individual laborer assembled one (and only one) part of a car. Henry Ford, founder of

Ford Motor Company, added a motorized conveyor belt, so that the car being assembled automatically moved along, and workers stayed in the same place. Ford brought in Frederick Taylor to conduct *time and motion studies,* which involved examining the precise movements required to complete a task and identifying and eliminating unnecessary movements. In 1913, the first moving assembly line in history was complete. It was a boon to productivity and efficiency. Indeed, by 1916, Ford Motor Company produced twice as many cars as all of its competitors combined.

With the outbreak of World War I in 1914, psychologists played a growing role in the application of science to the workplace, particularly in the military. Psychologists were called upon to help address the crucial concerns of recruitment, selection, and morale (Bryan & Vinchur, 2013). Between the two world wars, the field that would become known as I-O psychology expanded beyond the military into a variety of settings, including private industry, as it became ever more apparent that applying scientific research to the work environment would help employers improve efficiency (Bryan & Vinchur, 2013).

Ergonomics: Where Psychology Meets Engineering

Many occupations involve the interaction of human beings with tools. Whether these tools are computers or hand-press drills, vast numbers of people earn a living by working with the help of machines. Understanding and enhancing the safety and efficiency of the human–machine interaction is the central focus of **ergonomics,** also called **human factors,** a field that combines engineering and psychology to improve the fit between tools and the human body (Grote, 2013; Moore & Barnard, 2012). Desks, chairs, switches, buttons—all of the objects people use every day are the product of design decisions aimed at promoting a worker's efficiency and safety on the job.

Ergonomic specialists represent a range of expertise, from perception, attention, and cognition (individuals who have good ideas about the placement of buttons on a control panel or the preferred coloring of those buttons), to learning (individuals who design training programs for the use of machines), to social and environmental psychologists (individuals who address issues such as living in a constrained environment like that of the space shuttle). To appreciate the role of ergonomics in daily life, see Figure 14.1, which shows how the design of something as common as the computer mouse reflects expert attention to the human–machine relationship.

Scientific management and ergonomics focus on efficiency and safety. However, from the late 1920s to the present day, a third—and very different—approach has shaped thinking about the workplace. This third influence on I-O psychology—the historic Hawthorne studies—drew attention to the larger context of the workplace as a social environment, as well as to the worker as a human being with feelings, motivations, and attitudes.

The Hawthorne Studies and the Human Relations Approach to Management

A defining moment in I-O history occurred after the end of World War I. A series of studies was conducted at the Western Electric Hawthorne Works, a plant outside Chicago, from 1927 to 1932 under the leadership of psychologist and sociologist Elton Mayo. In what became known as the Hawthorne studies, Mayo and his colleagues were initially interested in examining how various work conditions (for example, room lighting, humidity, breaks, work hours, and management style) could influence productivity. What they found surprised them: Essentially, *any change* at all could increase productivity. Just being studied led workers to work harder and harder. These results led to the coining of the term **Hawthorne effect,** which refers to the tendency of individuals to perform better simply because of being singled out and made to feel important.

FIGURE 14.1   Building a Better Mouse The figure shows the evolution of the computer mouse from its wooden-box beginnings (*top*) to its later, sleeker forms (*middle photos*). The evolution has continued with the development of the touchpad or trackpad (*bottom*)–a built-in mouse substitute in laptop computers. The mouse and the touchpad are tools that many of us take for granted, but they are the product of design decisions that have improved their utility and efficiency.

● **ergonomics or human factors** A field that combines engineering and psychology and that focuses on understanding and enhancing the safety and efficiency of the human–machine interaction.

● **Hawthorne effect** The tendency of individuals to perform better simply because of being singled out and made to feel important.

Year	Employer	Location	Type	Number of Employees*	Sampling of Perks and Benefits
2013	Google	California	Software/Internet services	34,311 33% Women 36% Minorities	Roller hockey rink; 7-acre sports complex; free massages
2012	Google	California	Software/Internet services	34,300 33% Women 36% Minorities	25 cafes with free food; bowling alley; revenue sharing
2011	SAS	North Carolina	Software	5,629 45% Women 16% Minorities	Onsite health care; summer day camp stipend
2010	SAS	North Carolina	Software	5,487 45% Women 16% Minorities	Unlimited sick days; child care
2009	NetApp	California	Network storage/software	5,014 24% Women 34% Minorities	Over $10,000 in adoption aid; 5 paid days for volunteering
2008	Google	California	Software/Internet services	8,134 33% Women 36% Minorities	Onsite fitness center; child care; stock options; free cappuccino
2007	Google	California	Online software/Internet services	5,063 36% Women 31% Minorities	Tuition reimbursement; onsite doctors and dentists
2006	Genentech	California	Biotechnology, pharmaceuticals	8,121 50% Women 43% Minorities	3 weeks' vacation per year
2005	Wegmans Food Markets	New York	Food/grocery	30,128 54% Women 15% Minorities	Company motto: "Employees first. Customers second."
2004	J. M. Smucker Company	Ohio	Manufacturing (jam, jelly, and other food products)	2,585 42% Women 20% Minorities	Gimmick-free management, stressing integrity

*Number of employees in the year in which the firm was named the best place to work.

FIGURE 14.2 **The Number 1 Best Places to Work in the United States, 2004–2013** These are the best places to work, according to *Fortune* magazine. Note the various locations and types of companies that are represented by these top-rated employers.

Though later analyses have suggested that the Hawthorne results might have resulted from a variety of factors, including the beginning of the Great Depression (Franke & Kaul, 1978), or the fact that workers received feedback about their performance (Chiesa & Hobbs, 2008; Parsons, 1974), the Hawthorne studies are landmark. They persuasively demonstrated that the workplace is a social system populated by human beings. When workers felt that what they did mattered to someone, they performed better.

Mayo was especially critical of management's obsession with efficiency and its effect on the human side of business. Emphasizing the time-and-motion aspects of a job, Mayo said, takes away from both the experience of craftsmanship and the capacity of workers to identify with the products they are creating. He believed that traditional approaches to the science of work erroneously assumed that what was good for business was good for the employee. Mayo's Hawthorne studies moved researchers away from scientific management toward an emphasis on a human relations approach to management.

The **human relations approach** emphasizes the psychological characteristics of workers and managers and stresses the significance of factors such as morale, attitudes,

● **human relations approach** A management approach emphasizing the psychological characteristics of workers and managers, stressing the importance of factors such as morale, attitudes, values, and humane treatment of workers.

values, and humane treatment of workers (Dalton, Hoyle, & Watts, 2011; Schmidt, Beck, & Gillespie, 2013). The human relations view focuses on the workplace as an important social system, emphasizing positive interpersonal relations among coworkers, teamwork, leadership, job attitudes, and the social skills of managers. Human relations methods stress that fulfilling work meets other important human needs beyond purely economic ones (Dalal, 2013; Lamberton & Minor-Evans, 2010; Reece, Brandt, & Howie, 2011).

Scientific management, ergonomics, and the human relations approach have a continuing influence on I-O psychology today. Although we examine each side of industrial and organizational psychology in separate sections below, the two areas overlap a great deal, and some topics, such as motivation, are a focal point in both areas. Although the emphasis of the two approaches may be different—with the "I" side more concerned with maximizing efficiency, safety, and cost effectiveness, and the "O" side more targeted at the human relations processes that contribute to feelings of fulfillment—both sides seek to apply scientific methods to understanding the complex processes associated with people at work. I-O psychologists are interested in what makes organizations successful, whether success is measured in terms of profits or the satisfaction and engagement of the workforce.

Each year, the Great Place to Work Institute conducts a survey to identify the best workplaces in the United States, which are then announced in *Fortune* magazine. Today, the best places to work are characterized as flexible, diverse, learning-oriented, and open in communication. In 2013, Google was ranked the number 1 best place to work in the United States. Second place went to SAS, a producer of statistical software used by many psychologists. CHG Healthcare Services, a Salt Lake City medical staffing firm, was third, and the Boston Consulting Group, an elite management consulting company, was fourth ("100 best companies to work for," 2013).

Figure 14.2 provides an overview of the best places to work in the United States in the last 10 years. What makes these firms so great? In the following sections, as we survey the topics of interest to I-O psychologists, let's see if we can answer that question, including how it applies to Google and other successful companies.

2· INDUSTRIAL PSYCHOLOGY

Industrial psychology is the older of the two sides of I-O psychology. Industrial psychology focuses on increasing efficiency and productivity through the appropriate use of a firm's personnel, or employees—its *human resources* (Bryan & Vinchur, 2013). The field of industrial psychology has a four-pronged emphasis:

- *Job analysis:* Organizing and describing the tasks involved in a job.
- *Employee selection:* Matching the best person to each job.
- *Training:* Bringing new employees up to speed on the details of the position.
- *Performance appraisal:* Evaluating whether the person is doing a good job.

In this section we explore each of these dimensions of the field.

Job Analysis

Job analysis is the process of generating a description of what a job involves, including the knowledge and skills that are necessary to carry out the job's functions (Colquitt, LePine, & Wesson, 2011; Sackett, Walmsley, & Laczo, 2013).

An effective job analysis includes three essential elements (Brannick & Levine, 2002). First, the analysis must follow a systematic procedure that is set up in advance. Second, it must break down the job into small units so that each aspect can be easily understood. Third, the analysis should lead to an employee manual that accurately characterizes the job.

His landmark Hawthorne studies led Elton Mayo (1880–1949) to challenge the conventional thinking that what was good for business was good for employees.

test yourself

1. What does the managerial philosophy known as scientific management emphasize?
2. What is ergonomics, and with what aspects of the workplace is it concerned?
3. Why are the Hawthorne studies important?

● **job analysis** The process of generating a description of what a job involves, including the knowledge and skills that are necessary to carry out the job's functions.

Enthusiasm can be an important job qualification. Patagonia seeks to hire people who are passionate climbers and hikers.

● **KSAOs or KSAs** Common elements in a person-oriented job analysis; an acronym for **k**nowledge, **s**kills, **a**bilities, and **o**ther characteristics.

A job analysis can focus on the job itself or on the characteristics of the person who is suited for the job (Mondy, 2010; Sackett, Walmsley, & Laczo, 2013). A job-oriented analysis outlines what the job entails (say, analyzing scientific data) and what it requires (for instance, expertise with both basic computer programs and statistics software). A person-oriented job analysis involves what are sometimes called **KSAOs** (or **KSAs**). The acronym stands for **k**nowledge, **s**kills, **a**bilities, and **o**ther characteristics. Knowledge, of course, refers to what the person needs to know to function in the job. Skills are what the individual must be able to do. Abilities include the person's capacity to learn the job and to gain new skills. Other characteristics may also be important. For a child-care worker, for instance, the ability to handle frequent diaper changes and to chase energetic toddlers may be required.

Increasingly, employers focus on the *competencies* that are central to a job. Competencies refer to a person's capacity to put the KSAOs into action and apply them effectively in the workplace. Competencies refer not only to what a person *can do,* but to what he or she *will do* on the job (Cortina & Luchman, 2013).

Creating a job analysis typically involves collecting information from a variety of informants, including job analysts, individuals who already have the job, supervisors, and trained observers (Nkomo, Fottler, & McAfee, 2011). These individuals may be asked to complete a questionnaire about the importance of various skills to a job, or they might be directed to describe the essential elements of the job in an interview.

Job analyses establish a foundation for other aspects of personnel decision making. A thorough job analysis can provide information that directs hiring decisions and performance evaluations. Quite simply, a manager cannot select the right person for the job or evaluate job performance without knowing what the job formally requires. In addition, job analyses can guide training and provide information to I-O researchers who are interested in examining how aspects of jobs relate to outcomes, such as productivity, absenteeism, and work stress.

A final area where job analysis is important is the legal realm. The KSAOs mentioned in a job analysis must be clearly relevant to the specific job. Some job attributes have caused controversy—for example, should height and physical fitness be considered job-relevant characteristics for police officers? The requirement of such attributes historically has excluded some women and others of shorter stature from police duty, and the courts have struck down many such requirements.

A thorough job analysis should accurately describe the essential and nonessential functions of a job. *Essential functions* are the fundamental, necessary tasks and duties of a job as defined by the employer, usually in writing. For example, a child-care worker must be capable of being physically active, and a data analyst must be able to utilize and apply advanced statistical techniques. *Nonessential functions* are aspects of the job that are desirable but not necessary. For example, a pizza delivery person must have a valid driver's license, but driving is not essential for a kitchen worker at the pizza shop.

The Americans with Disabilities Act (ADA) of 1990 (provisions of which are shown in Figure 14.3) made it illegal to refuse employment or a promotion to someone with a disability that prevents the person from performing only nonessential functions (Colella & Bruyère, 2010). The ADA defines a person with a disability as qualified for a position if he or she is able to perform the essential job functions, with or without reasonable accommodations. Accommodations may include changes in facilities, equipment, or policies that permit an otherwise qualified individual with disabilities to

No (employer) shall discriminate against a qualified individual with a disability because of the disability of such individual in regard to job application procedures, the hiring, advancement, or discharge of employees, employee compensation, job training, and other terms, conditions, and privileges of employment.

. . . [T]he term "discriminate" includes

1. limiting, segregating, or classifying a job applicant or employee in a way that adversely affects the opportunities or status of such applicant or employee because of (his or her) disability . . . ;

2. utilizing standards, criteria, or methods of administration that have the effect of discrimination on the basis of disability; or that perpetuate the discrimination of others . . . ;

3. excluding or otherwise denying equal jobs or benefits to a qualified individual because of the known disability of an individual with whom the qualified individual is known to have a relationship or association;

4. not making reasonable accommodations to the known physical or mental limitations of an otherwise qualified individual with a disability who is an applicant or employee, unless such (employer) can demonstrate that the accommodation would impose an undue hardship . . . ;

5. using qualification standards, employment tests or other selection criteria that screen out or tend to screen out an individual with a disability . . . unless the standard, test or other selection criteria, as used by the covered entity, is shown to be job-related for the position in question and is consistent with business necessity; and

6. failing to select and administer tests concerning employment in the most effective manner to ensure that, when such test is administered to a job applicant or employee who has a disability that impairs sensory, manual, or speaking skills, such test results accurately reflect the skills, aptitude, or whatever other factor of such applicant or employee that such test purports to measure, rather than reflecting the impaired sensory, manual, or speaking skills of (the individual). . . .

The term "qualified individual with a disability" means an individual with a disability who, with or without reasonable accommodation, can perform the essential functions of the employment position that such individual holds or desires. . . . [I]f an employer has prepared a written description before advertising or interviewing applicants for the job, this description shall be considered evidence of the essential functions of the job.

FIGURE 14.3   Excerpts from the Americans with Disabilities Act of 1990, Title I Passed in 1990, the Americans with Disabilities Act forbids discrimination in the workplace based on disability or illness.

perform the essential functions of a job. An accommodation is considered reasonable—and is required—if it effectively allows the person to perform the essential job tasks while not placing an undue hardship on the employer. Although at times such regulations may seem burdensome for employers, they promote fairness and kindness (Aguinis, 2010) and help to diversify the workforce, bringing many unique perspectives to bear on an organization's goals (Colella & Bruyère, 2010).

An accurate job analysis increases the likelihood that individuals will feel that they have been treated fairly in hiring and promotion decisions (Mitchell, Alliger, & Morfopoulos, 1997; Truxillo & Bauer, 2010). If a job analysis is done well, it can clarify the reasons for such decisions. For example, an employee who is very shy may understand being turned down for a promotion if the job analysis for the position clearly indicates that it requires an active leadership style.

A job analysis is more formal and exact than a job description, which is generally of interest to job seekers. Job descriptions allow people to evaluate their interest in a particular occupation. The U.S. Department of Labor (2013) has produced an enormous database called O*NET (www.onetonline.org/) that compiles job descriptions for thousands of occupations. The descriptions are based on authoritative ratings and interviews with experts in the various occupations, and new occupations are added frequently. The site can be searched for jobs by various categories and requirements, such as whether they are "green" occupations and what their growth rate is expected to be in the coming years. Figure 14.4 presents the descriptions from the U.S. Department of Labor for the jobs of actor, predatory-animal hunter, and personal shopper.

Are you good at memorization? Does "removing designated parts" of an animal sound interesting to you? How about "escorting a customer through a store"? Job descriptions

TITLE: Actor

Portrays role in dramatic production to interpret character or present characterization to audience: Rehearses part to learn lines and cues as directed. Interprets serious or comic role by speech, gesture, and body movement to entertain or inform audience for stage, motion picture, television, radio, or other media production. May write or adapt own material. May dance and sing. May direct self and others in production. May read from script or book, utilizing minimum number of stage properties and relying mainly on changes of voice and inflection to hold audience's attention and be designated Dramatic Reader.

TITLE: Predatory-Animal Hunter

Hunts, traps, and kills predatory animals to collect bounty: Hunts quarry using dogs, and shoots animals. Traps or poisons animals depending on environs and habits of animals sought. Removes designated parts, such as ears or tail from slain animals, using knife, to present as evidence of kill for bounty. May skin animals and treat pelts for marketing. May train dogs for hunting. May be designated according to animal hunted as Cougar Hunter; Coyote Hunter; Wolf Hunter.

TITLE: Personal Shopper

Selects and purchases merchandise for department store customers, according to mail or telephone requests. Visits wholesale establishments or other department stores to purchase merchandise which is out-of-stock or which store does not carry. Records and processes mail orders and merchandise returned for exchange. May escort customer through store.

FIGURE 14.4 **Sample Job Descriptions** Do you aspire to a career as an actor, a predatory-animal hunter, or a personal shopper? If so, the description reproduced here from the U.S. Department of Labor's *Dictionary of Occupational Titles* will give you a distinct flavor of the job and its day-to-day responsibilities.

may be a first step for job seekers interested in finding a good match to their interests and skills.

According to the Bureau of Labor Statistics' *Occupational Outlook Handbook, 2012–2013,* the occupations in the United States that are expected to grow fastest through 2020 are personal care aides, home health aides, and biomedical engineers. The Psychological Inquiry shows the relevant data and the percentage increase in other fast-growing jobs.

Employee Selection

Once a position is defined, the task for managers is to select the best from among the pool of recruits (Breaugh, 2013). That pool can be huge. Google gets 20,000 job applicants *a week.*

Where do qualified applicants come from? An analysis of 36 different companies in 2012 identified how those companies found their new hires. Figure 14.5 shows some of the results. *Referrals* were the most popular way that candidates ended up landing jobs (Crispin & Mehler, 2012). A referral means that a potential candidate for an opening was identified through current or former employees' social networks. If the candidate is ultimately hired, the referring employee may receive a bonus.

psychological
inquiry

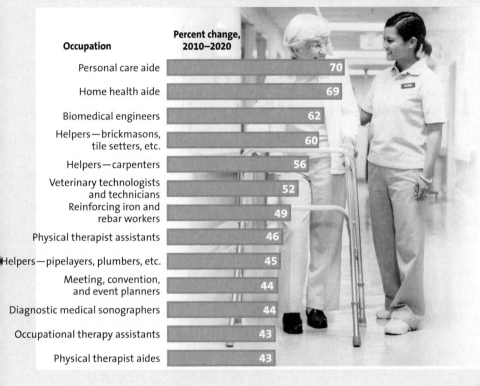

Occupation	Percent change, 2010–2020
Personal care aide	70
Home health aide	69
Biomedical engineers	62
Helpers—brickmasons, tile setters, etc.	60
Helpers—carpenters	56
Veterinary technologists and technicians	52
Reinforcing iron and rebar workers	49
Physical therapist assistants	46
Helpers—pipelayers, plumbers, etc.	45
Meeting, convention, and event planners	44
Diagnostic medical sonographers	44
Occupational therapy assistants	43
Physical therapist aides	43

The Fastest-Growing Jobs in the United States

This figure presents the projected percentage change in demand for the fastest-growing jobs in the United States, from 2010 to 2020. The jobs listed have various training and/or educational requirements. For example, an associate's degree is required to be a physical therapist's aide, and a bachelor's degree is necessary to be a biomedical engineer. Try your hand at the questions below.

1. Which of the listed occupations have the lowest projected growth?

2. Considering the training that is described above for each of these occupations, do you think the training is appropriate? Why or why not?

3. Imagine how this list might differ from similar lists compiled 20 years ago. Which careers do you think are the newest arrivals? Why?

4. What do these data tell you about U.S. society today and in the coming years?

How powerful are referrals in leading to hires? Referred candidates had a one in five chance of being hired—pretty good odds in a tough job market. The power of referrals is clear in the best places to work. Wegmans Food Markets is regularly listed as a best place to work (ranking fifth in 2013), and one in five of its employees are family members. At Edward Jones, a St. Louis-based securities firm ranked the eighth best place to work in 2013, 44 percent of the new hires are employee referrals.

In addition to referrals, employers use *job boards* to recruit new hires. These are websites that employers use to advertise openings. Another way the web has influenced job recruiting is through sites like Monster.com and Indeed.com (Darnold & Rynes, 2013).

Industrial psychologists have played a significant role in developing techniques for selecting individuals and placing them in positions that match their strengths (Bernardin, 2010; Ryan & Ployhart, 2014). Based on a job analysis, the KSAOs necessary for a particular job should be clear. The next step is to measure the KSAOs of the recruits in order to evaluate their appropriateness for a position. These measures include testing and interviews, as well as work samples and exercises.

TESTING

Managers or human resource personnel may administer tests to prospective candidates to ascertain whether they are good matches for the position (Cascio & Aguinis, 2011; Cortina & Luchman, 2013; Darnold & Rynes, 2013). Some firms employ cognitive ability tests, such as intelligence tests.

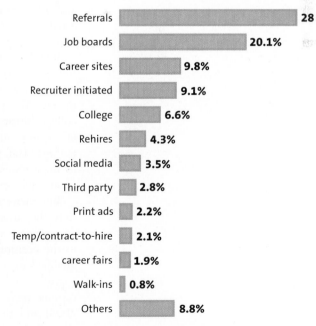

Referrals	28
Job boards	20.1%
Career sites	9.8%
Recruiter initiated	9.1%
College	6.6%
Rehires	4.3%
Social media	3.5%
Third party	2.8%
Print ads	2.2%
Temp/contract-to-hire	2.1%
career fairs	1.9%
Walk-ins	0.8%
Others	8.8%

FIGURE 14.5 How Did New Hires Get Their Foot in the Door? This figure shows the results of a 2012 survey of 36 companies reporting where their new hires came from. How might these figures influence your next job search? Adapted from Crispin & Mehler, 2012.

● **integrity test** A type of job-screening examination that is designed to assess whether a candidate will be honest on the job.

Other organizations use psychological tests that assess factors such as personality traits and motivation. An **integrity test,** another type of examination sometimes used in personnel screening, is designed to assess whether the candidate is likely to be honest on the job. An *overt integrity test* contains items that ask the individual to give his or her attitude about lying. A sample item might be "It's okay to lie if you know you won't get caught."

Not surprisingly, most employers hope to hire conscientious employees who will treat others in the organization with respect and be highly motivated to excel at work. Employers also want workers who will be honest, not steal from the workplace, or engage in cheating. A key drawback, though, with the use of tests to screen individuals for these characteristics is that people can fake a good impression. A number of strategies have been devised to overcome this problem (Cortina & Luchman, 2013; Hough & Johnson, 2013).

Many employers are increasingly interested in a person's adaptability (Cortina & Luchman, 2013). Someone who is adaptable is an effective, creative problem solver even when unanticipated obstacles arise. Employers want to hire people who are flexible and able to handle change. Adaptable workers are able to work with people who are different from them and to work effectively in changing contexts, handling emergencies and crises (Sonnentag & Frese, 2013).

How do employers assess a candidate's adaptability? One method for doing so might be situational judgment tests. A **situational judgment test** presents a job candidate with realistic, hypothetical scenarios and asks the individual to identify the most appropriate response (Weekley & Ployhart, 2005). Situational judgment tests are one way to assess not simply knowledge and skill but competencies, or how the applicant uses these knowledge and skills effectively. These tests can involve forced choices or open-ended responses. Situational judgment tests are less obvious than some other methods of testing and therefore may be less susceptible to faking.

● **situational judgment test** A type of job-screening examination that presents job candidates with realistic, hypothetical scenarios and asks them to identify the most appropriate response.

INTERVIEWS

Perhaps the most common way that job candidates are evaluated is through an interview. An interview is, of course, a conversation between two (or more) people. Interviewers and interviewees have different goals. The interviewer wants to find the best person for a particular position. The interviewee wants to get the job. Balancing these two goals is one of the reasons effective interviewing can be a challenge.

Imagine interviewing for your dream job—to be a high school English teacher. During the interview, the school principal asks if you might also be able to teach history or coach the volleyball team. If you really want the job, it might not seem like a stretch to say, "Yes, I might be able to do those things" (if only you had taken even a single college history class or paid better attention to last summer's Olympic Games). Certainly, job candidates try to put their best foot forward and refrain from revealing their failings (Tsai, Chen, & Chiu, 2005; Weiss & Feldman, 2006). *Interviewer illusion* refers to interviewers' mistaken tendency to believe in their own ability to discern the truth from a job applicant (Nisbett, 1987).

Interviewers are not only challenged by the candidate's efforts to make a good impression; they must also separate irrelevant factors from those that matter to the job. During an interview, a person may display a lot of different qualities, not all of which are relevant to the position in question. For instance, interviews reveal not only whether a person is qualified for a job but also aspects of his or her personality, interview skills, and general cognitive ability (Cortina & Luchman, 2013). Research shows that interviewers are susceptible to factors such as whether the person has a firm handshake (Stewart & others, 2008) and the ease with which the candidate establishes rapport with the interviewer (Barrick, Swider, & Stewart, 2010). Although social skills are important in life in general, they are not necessarily important for every job. Certainly, for interviews to serve their purpose, they must be about more than simply whether the interviewer likes the candidate. The interviewer must hone in on those qualities that are directly related to the job.

It shall be an unlawful employment practice for an employer:

1. to fail or refuse to hire or to discharge any individual, or otherwise to discriminate against any individual with respect to his compensation, terms, conditions, or privileges of employment, because of such individual's race, color, religion, sex, or national origin;

or

2. to limit, segregate, or classify his employees or applicants for employment in any way which would deprive or tend to deprive any individual of employment opportunities or otherwise adversely affect his status as an employee, because of such individual's race, color, religion, sex, or national origin.

It shall be an unlawful employment practice for an employment agency to fail or refuse to refer for employment, or otherwise to discriminate against, any individual because of his race, color, religion, sex, or national origin, or to classify or refer for employment any individual on the basis of his race, color, religion, sex, or national origin.

It shall be an unlawful employment practice for any employer, labor organization, or joint labor-management committee controlling apprenticeship or other training or retraining, including on-the-job training programs, to discriminate against any individual because of his race, color, religion, sex, or national origin in admission to, or employment in, any program established to provide apprenticeship or other training.

FIGURE 14.6 Excerpts from the Civil Rights Act of 1964, Title VII (revised, 1991) The Civil Rights Act forbids discrimination based on race, national origin, sex, or religious affiliation.

As we saw in Chapter 13, first impressions can be made very rapidly. This immediate first impression may have nothing to do with a person's ability, for example, to program a computer or to develop a new drug. First impressions can also be subject to gender and ethnic biases, and since the Civil Rights Act of 1964 (revised in 1991), it has been illegal in the United States to deny someone employment on the basis of gender or ethnicity (Parker, 2006). Figure 14.6 lists the provisions of the Civil Rights Act that set the standards for fair personnel decisions in the United States.

Interviewers can improve the quality of the information they obtain by asking the same specific questions of all candidates. In a **structured interview,** candidates are asked specific questions that methodically seek to obtain truly useful information for the interviewer. Rather than posing the question "Do you get along with others?" the interviewer might ask the candidate, "Can you tell me about a time when you had a conflict with someone at work and how you resolved it?"

When conducting a structured interview, interviewers must take notes or record the interviews in order to avoid memory biases (Middendorf & Macan, 2002). Structured interviews are far superior to unstructured interviews in terms of predicting eventual job performance (Blackman, 2008; Cortina & Luchman, 2013; Huffcutt & Culbertson, 2010). Interestingly, structured interviews also facilitate the *job candidate's* performance during the interview (Maurer, Solamon, & Lippstreu, 2008). Unlike unstructured interviews, structured interviews put all of the candidates on equal footing and give them all the same chance to show their stuff.

● **structured interview** A kind of interview in which candidates are asked specific questions that methodically seek to obtain truly useful information for the interviewer.

MOTHER GOOSE & GRIMM © 2009 Grimmy, Inc. King Features Syndicate.

Applying for a job in fields such as graphic design and photography often requires showing a portfolio of work samples.

● **orientation** A program by which an organization introduces newly hired employees to the organization's goals, familiarizes them with its rules and regulations, and lets them know how to get things done.

● **training** Teaching a new employee the essential requirements to do the job well.

WORK SAMPLES AND EXERCISES

Another technique for pinpointing the best-suited candidate for a particular job is requiring an applicant to submit work samples. For a job such as photographer, copywriter, or graphic designer, for example, the candidate typically must present samples.

An additional evaluation method is to require candidates to complete mock job-related tasks that allow the direct assessment of their skills. Seeing applicants handle unexpected situations or think on their feet gives potential employers a sense of the candidates' fit for the job (Ployhart & MacKenzie, 2010). These activities might include an "in-basket" exercise in which candidates must organize and prioritize a pile of potential assignments and a "leaderless group" exercise in which each prospective employee is observed in a group problem-solving task.

Training

You got the job! Now, what was that job again? Once a new employee is hired, the challenge facing the organization (and the new recruit) is to learn all that is necessary to carry out the job effectively. Three aspects of training are orientation, formal training, and mentoring.

ORIENTATION

Learning the ropes of a new job and workplace can be difficult for new hires (Nelson & Quick, 2011; Noe & others, 2007). To help them overcome the hurdles, most firms have a program of **orientation,** which generally involves introducing newly hired employees to the organization's goals, familiarizing them with its rules and regulations, and letting them know how to get things done. Studies suggest that orientation programs do work, especially with regard to instilling an understanding of organizational values and philosophies and socializing the new employee (Aguinis & Kraiger, 2009).

Some organizations have turned to computer-based orientation programs in order to cut expenses. One study examined the implications of using computer-based versus in-person orientation programs (Wesson & Gogus, 2005). Although both methods provided new employees with information, the computer-based orientation fell short on social factors. Employees who received a computer-based orientation might have learned how to work the copy machine or get a computer repaired, but they probably did not come away with a list of their acquaintances from their orientation or a good sense of the social culture of their new workplace.

FORMAL TRAINING

Training involves teaching the new employee the essential requirements to do the job well (Aguinis & Kraiger, 2009; Brown & Sitzmann, 2010). Training needs vary by occupation. The engineers who join Google probably need only an orientation and a sign pointing to the computers (and perhaps another directing them to the free cappuccino). The position of home health aide requires only basic on-the-job training. In contrast, other positions, such as airline pilot, require extensive training.

The foundation of any training program is to establish the goals of the training and a sense for how the trainer will know that the person is ready. An assumption of training is that whatever the employee learns in training will generalize to the real world when he or she starts work. Training is an important part of eventual job performance and mastery of the technical skills required for a job (Aguinis & Kraiger, 2009). Although fewer studies have examined the effects of training on organizational profits, the findings support the idea that sound training does positively impact the bottom line (Arthur & others, 2003).

Organizations vary with respect to the value they place on training (Juntunen & Bailey, 2013). This difference is shown, for example, by the degree of training observed from company to company for similar jobs. Consider that trainees at the Container Store get 241 hours of training, as compared with the 7 hours of training that is the retail industry average.

Although we have considered training primarily as it relates to beginning a new job, employee learning and the expansion of employee skills (what is called *employee development* or *management training*) are important throughout a career, for employees and firms alike. Even individuals with a great deal of expertise can benefit from development programs (Brown & Sitzmann, 2010). I-O psychologists, in consultation with the organization, often develop these programs.

MENTORING

Mentoring is a relationship between an experienced employee and a novice in which the more experienced employee—the *mentor*—serves as an advisor, a sounding board, and a source of support for the newer employee (Eby, 2010; Saver, 2013). Mentoring may benefit both the employee and the organization, as mentors guide new employees through the beginning of their career and help them achieve their goals within the organization, as well as provide a strong interpersonal bond.

Some organizations assign individuals to mentors (Raabe & Beehr, 2003). Assigned mentors may not be as effective as those that emerge naturally—and an incompetent mentor may be worse than having no mentor at all (Ragins, Cotton, & Miller, 2000). "Natural" mentoring relationships, however, may be based on common interests and other similarities and as such may be less likely to develop for women and for members of ethnic minorities in fields that are dominated by non-Latino White males. In such situations, assigned mentors who are sensitive and open and who have time to devote to new protégés are all the more important. At minimum, coworkers who differ in every other way share one common bond: the organization.

"This call may be monitored for training purposes or just to keep our staff amused."

© Aaron Bacall. www.CartoonStock.com.

● **mentoring** A relationship between an experienced employee—a mentor—and a novice, in which the more experienced employee serves as an advisor, a sounding board, and a source of support for the newer employee.

Performance Appraisal

Industrial psychologists are also interested in **performance appraisal,** the evaluation of a person's success at meeting his or her organization's goals (Grant & Wrzesniewski, 2010; Motowidlo & Kell, 2013).

Performance appraisal is important for a variety of reasons. It allows employees to get feedback and make appropriate changes in their work habits. It also helps guide decisions about promotions and raises, as well as terminations or firings (Ivancevich & Konopaske, 2011). Within the U.S. government, for example, firing must be performance based. This requirement means that before a government employer can terminate someone, there must be documented evidence of poor performance. In Canada, this regulation applies to private businesses as well. Regular performance appraisals provide a paper trail that serves to justify promotion and termination decisions.

In some occupations, objective measures can be used to gauge performance. These might include the number of products a factory worker is able to make per hour, the dollar amount of sales by a sales representative, the number of days late to work, the number of legal cases won, and the number of surgical operations performed. Of course, not all jobs provide such measurable output (Tannenbaum, 2006). In addition, it may not be clear what a "high number" is: How high would the number have to be to be "good"? Simple counts, taken out of context, may not be informative. For example, consider a sales agent with a very challenging territory who sets a selling record even though her sales fall below the average of other representatives who are assigned to less difficult areas.

Finally, focusing on objective counts may miss the quality of the person's work. For these reasons, many performance evaluations, while including an assessment of objective numbers, also entail subjective ratings made by a supervisor or panel of experts. These

● **performance appraisal** The evaluation of a person's success at meeting his or her organization's goals.

ratings typically involve multiple items that are meant to assess different aspects of performance, such as work quality and efficiency.

FACTORS PREDICTING PERFORMANCE APPRAISALS

A great deal of research in I-O psychology examines the predictors of performance appraisals. Work performance is related to deep knowledge and experience at a job, but the strongest predictor of work performance among the many different qualities studied is general cognitive ability (Drasgow, 2013; Schmidt, Beck, & Gillespie, 2013). One meta-analysis summarizing 22,000 studies showed that general cognitive ability predicted job performance across a variety of jobs, situations, and organizations (Ones, Viswesvaran, & Dilchert, 2005).

Other psychological characteristics that have been examined as predictors of job performance are called *psychological capital* (Luthans, Youssef, & Avolio, 2007; Schaubroeck & others, 2011). Psychological capital includes positive qualities such as self-efficacy, optimism, hope, and resilience that serve as important resources in the workplace. These attributes predict increased employee performance (Luthans & others, 2006) and decreased work absences (Avey, Patera, & West, 2006). This research supports the notion that these various psychological qualities are strengths at work. The psychological capital approach has been applied in various organizational settings including manufacturing, education, and the military.

Recall from Chapter 12 that self-efficacy is the belief that one has the ability to take on a particular task or goal and see it through. A great deal of research supports the relationship between self-efficacy and success in a variety of settings (de Haan & others, 2013; Fu & others, 2010; Laguna, 2013; Tay, Ang, Van Dyne, 2006). Self-efficacy is thought to enhance effort and activity that are needed to achieve difficult goals in the workplace (Schmidt, Beck, & Gillespie, 2013; Wood & Bandura, 1989).

It is hard to imagine that having a "can do" attitude would ever be a bad thing, but some research in I-O psychology has suggested that self-efficacy can lead to lower effort and even poor performance. To read about this provocative work, see the Critical Controversy.

SOURCES OF BIAS IN PERFORMANCE APPRAISALS

● **halo effect** A bias, common in performance appraisals, that occurs when a rater gives an employee the same rating on all of the items being evaluated, even though the individual varies across the dimensions being assessed.

As subjective judgments, performance appraisals may be prone to biases and errors (Aguinis, 2009; Austin & Crespin, 2006). One error is the **halo effect,** common in performance appraisals, that occurs when a rater gives an employee the same rating on all of the items being evaluated, even though the individual varies across the dimensions being assessed. In making halo effect errors, the rater allows his or her general impression of the person to guide the ratings. So, for example, the supervisor might give someone a 9 on a 1-to-10 scale for all assessment items, even though the employee's work quality was a 9, but his efficiency was more like a 5.

Factors other than work quality can influence a performance evaluation. Supervisors are human, and in evaluating the work of others, they are engaged in a social process. They have expectancies and look for confirming information.

360-DEGREE FEEDBACK

● **360-degree feedback** A method of performance appraisal whereby an employee's performance is rated by a variety of individuals, including himself or herself, a peer, a supervisor, a subordinate, and perhaps a customer or client.

One way to improve the quality of the information used in a performance evaluation is to collect feedback from a variety of sources (Wildman & others, 2010). To this end, appraisers use a method called 360-degree feedback (Baldwin & Padgett, 1993). In **360-degree feedback,** an employee's performance is rated by a variety of individuals, including himself or herself, a peer, a supervisor, a subordinate, and perhaps a customer or client. Although there is some agreement among the different raters using the 360-degree feedback process, there is also more likely to be variability, suggesting that ratings are indeed about the person's performance and not a general impression (Maurer, Mitchell, & Barbeite, 2002; Wildman & others, 2010).

CRITICAL CONTROVERSY

Does Self-Efficacy Always Lead to Better Performance?

I-O psychologist Jeffrey Vancouver (2005, 2012) argues that there are times when self-efficacy might lead to reduced effort and thus to poor performance. To understand Vancouver's perspective, consider the variety of goals you are trying to accomplish in your everyday life. Perhaps you are striving to achieve excellence in your courses, do well at work, be kind to others, develop your athletic abilities, and be a supportive friend, romantic partner, son, daughter, or parent. You might view accomplishing some goals in this diverse array to be a cinch. Others you recognize as requiring more effort.

Vancouver reasons that among all the goals a person is trying to accomplish, the easy ones, the ones for which a person is likely to feel a great deal of self-efficacy, should be the ones for which the person expends little effort. Instead, it is the goals about which a person has lower self-efficacy that should require more effort. And, indeed, Vancouver and his colleagues have shown that when we consider goals in such a context, it is the case that high self-efficacy predicts lower levels of effort (Vancouver, More, & Yoder, 2008). For instance, students studied fewer hours for tests in classes about which they had very high self-efficacy (Vancouver & Kendall, 2006). Even in these studies, however, overall self-efficacy related to better performance (Vancouver, 2012).

How, then, might self-efficacy lead to poor performance? Answering this question requires that we think about the accuracy of self-efficacy beliefs. Human beings are not always correct when we assess how difficult a task will be. If your boss asks you if you can finish a project in a week, saying yes might seem realistic at the time. But once you dig in, things might start looking quite a bit thornier than you first imagined. Perhaps you can recall a time when you walked into an exam believing it would be easy, only to find it much harder than you expected. Or, imagine a salesperson who views a customer as an "easy mark," fails to give that customer the required level of attention, and does not make the sale. Vancouver points out that when self-efficacy beliefs are inaccurate, we may not put in the effort required to

succeed, and so we do not end up performing as well as we had expected. Research has shown that self-efficacy can lead to reduced preparation, less effort, and poorer performance (Vancouver, Thompson, & Williams, 2001: Vancouver & others, 2002).

Albert Bandura (2012b; Bandura & Locke, 2003) has harshly criticized this work and Vancouver's conclusions, passionately defending the importance of self-efficacy in human functioning. He has expressed grave concerns that Vancouver's work might lead to the mistaken conclusion that self-efficacy is not a strength but a potentially debilitating condition. Would Vancouver suggest, asked Bandura, that teachers, bosses, and coaches strive to *lower* self-efficacy to get students, workers, and athletes to work harder?

Bandura notes that for people to succeed at difficult goals, they must be able to invest themselves and their efforts when circumstances are uncertain. In the face of high uncertainty, extreme difficulty, or daunting challenges, a strong and durable sense of self-efficacy can separate successful individuals from those who never even try (Bandura & Locke, 2003).

Applying these arguments to your own life, you might decide that both sides make sense. On the one hand, in balancing multiple goals over time, you may devote effort to goals depending on how much you think they require for success. At the same time, it might be that to take on big challenges, self-efficacy is indispensable.

At least, this debate over how beliefs shape effort clearly shows that even psychological qualities that seem to be wholly positive may be more complicated than they appear.

WHAT DO YOU THINK

- Can you think of a time when self-efficacy had a positive effect in your goal pursuit? What about a negative effect?

- Which perspective—Vancouver's or Bandura's—rings most true to your own experience and why?

- What are some possible reasons for inaccurate self-efficacy beliefs?

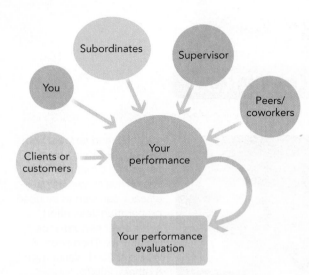

FIGURE 14.7 360-Degree Feedback
360-degree feedback means that everyone who is affected by your work has some input in evaluating your performance.

● **organizational citizenship behavior (OCB)** Discretionary actions on the part of an employee that promote organizational effectiveness but are not included in the person's formal responsibilities.

Web-based evaluation systems have simplified the logistics of the 360-degree feedback approach, illustrated in Figure 14.7. Recently, in response to a variety of scandals in its highest ranks, the U.S. military adopted the 360-degree feedback approach, incorporating lower level officers in evaluations of high-ranking individuals.

THE IMPORTANCE OF FAIRNESS

A performance appraisal can be stressful for both the evaluator(s) and the evaluated employee. Few people relish telling someone that her work has been rated poorly, and the temptation might be to send off the evaluation by e-mail. Talking about the evaluation face-to-face is vital to perceptions of fair treatment. Allowing the individual to sit down with the supervisor and openly discuss the evaluation enhances feelings of fairness in the process, even when the ratings are negative (Truxillo & Bauer, 2010).

Just as hiring decisions cannot be based on ethnicity or gender, performance evaluation systems must not discriminate. In order to enhance the legal defensibility of a termination decision, a job analysis should define the dimensions that will be used in the performance appraisal; the raters should be trained; employees should have an opportunity to appeal the ratings; and the organization should meticulously document performance (Barrett & Kernan, 1987). Organizations might also offer counseling or developmental opportunities to poorly performing employees.

The experience of being fired from a job can be both economically and emotionally devastating (Lucas & others, 2004), and people who feel they have been treated unfairly may take legal action. The use of multiple raters in performance evaluations is associated with greater success in defending firing decisions in court (Werner & Bolino, 1997).

ORGANIZATIONAL CITIZENSHIP BEHAVIOR

One type of behavior that may find its way into a performance evaluation is **organizational citizenship behavior (OCB)**—discretionary actions on an employee's part that promote organizational effectiveness but are not included in the person's formal responsibilities (Organ, Podsakoff, & Podsakoff, 2010). OCB includes behaviors such as coming in early, staying late, and helping a colleague with an assignment. Conscientiousness is associated with higher levels of OCB, yet even those low on conscientiousness engage in OCB when they are especially happy at their jobs (Bowling, 2010).

OCB is thought to influence organizations in two ways. First, it may directly impact productivity and economic success (MacKenzie, Podsakoff, & Ahearne, 1998). Second, OCB may have a more general influence on the social system of the workplace, making fellow employees feel more positive about their jobs (Organ, Podsakoff, & Podsakoff, 2010; Regts & Molleman, 2013). As such, OCB occupies the middle ground in I-O psychology, influencing both the efficiency and profitability of business (the "I" side) and the wider social climate of the organization (the "O" side).

Although OCB is certainly associated with many positive outcomes, it is important to note that it may have its drawbacks (Bolino & others, 2013). Although OCB may appear to be altruistic, it might be engaged in as a way to compete with others or to get ahead in an organization. Also, if OCB interferes with completing one's actual job duties, it can take a toll on performance and organizational success. Finally, individuals who engage in OCB may find themselves spread too thin.

One thing that influences the effects of OCB is the wider social context of the organization. Is showing up for work early every day an example of OCB, or is it simply "kissing up" (Eastman, 1994) or playing office politics (Snell & Wong, 2007)? Did your coworker text you that reminder at 5 A.M. to be helpful or to point out that she was at her desk working while you were still asleep?

Research shows that responses to OCB can depend on the quality of a supervisor in a given organization (Schyns & Schilling, 2013; Tepper & others, 2004). When a supervisor is prone to hostile behaviors, emotional outbursts, public criticism, or sarcastic comments, even apparently kind behavior can have a negative effect on the job satisfaction of coworkers. With a hostile supervisor, OCB might raise suspicions among coworkers, suggesting that the meaning of a behavior may differ depending on its organizational context. That context is the domain of organizational psychology.

3· ORGANIZATIONAL PSYCHOLOGY

As we have seen, industrial psychology, the "I" in I-O, introduced the idea of human resources. We turn now to its "O" counterpart, organizational psychology, in which the main interest is research and practice involving human relations (Kozlowski & Bell, 2013; Schmidt, Beck, & Gillespie, 2013).

Organizational psychology emphasizes the psychological experience of the worker. It examines how the relationships among people at work influence their job satisfaction and commitment, as well as their efficiency and productivity. Although it may seem reasonable that companies should concentrate on "the bottom line," focusing exclusively on the economic results of work may not always be the best way to do business. As the following discussion reveals, other important factors also matter, including management approaches, job satisfaction, employee commitment, the meaning of work, and leadership styles (Avolio, Sosik, & Berson, 2013; Griffin & Moorhead, 2010).

Approaches to Management

Managers are in a position of power in an organization. They make decisions about personnel, direct activities, and ensure that the staff does the work correctly and on time. A manager's approach to this role can have widespread impact on organizational success as well as on employees' lives (Bateman & Snell, 2011; Connolly, Ordonez, & Barker, 2013). To appreciate the importance of management styles to business, we begin by considering the historic contrast between American and Japanese automakers.

THE "JAPANESE" MANAGEMENT STYLE

In the 1980s, as the U.S. automobile industry took note of the emerging dominance of Japanese car brands in the U.S. market, Japanese management principles became popular. At this time, U.S. automakers also adopted the so-called Japanese principles of quality control and worker participation in organizational decision making. Interestingly, an American engineer and statistician, W. Edwards Deming, originally suggested these principles.

In the 1940s, Deming developed ideas about management that focused on quality; indeed, he has been called the father of the quality revolution. His philosophy of management was not well received in the United States, however, as American industry was wedded to scientific management with its emphases on efficiency and the bottom line. After World War II, Deming played a large role in the successful rebuilding of the Japanese economy, particularly the automobile industry.

Deming had a lot to say about management. One of his key points was that industry must embrace innovation and plan for the future, not remain narrowly focused on economic results. He compared the results-oriented management of the typical U.S. factory to driving a car with our eyes fixed on the rearview mirror (Deming, 1986). Results, he stressed, tell us about past performance—how we did. What concerned Deming, however, was what we going to do *next*. Deming called upon industry to make a long-term commitment to having an eye always trained on the future. He emphasized innovation and a managerial style that takes risks, makes decisions based on quality, and fosters strong relationships with suppliers, employees, and customers.

The contrast between Frederick Taylor's approach to scientific management and Deming's innovation-oriented thinking can also be seen in other psychological approaches to management styles, as we now consider.

test yourself

1. What are the four prongs that the field of industrial psychology emphasizes?
2. Name and discuss some useful functions of job analyses.
3. Identify and define the three key aspects of job training.

So great were the contributions of American statistician W. Edwards Deming (1900–1993) in the recovery of the Japanese economy after World War II that the prime minister of Japan, on behalf of Emperor Hirohito, honored him with the Order of the Sacred Treasures, second class, in 1960.

THEORY X AND THEORY Y

- **Theory X managers** Managers who assume that work is innately unpleasant and that people have a strong desire to avoid it; such managers believe that employees need direction, dislike responsibility, and must be kept in line.

- **Theory Y managers** Managers who assume that engaging in effortful behavior is natural to human beings; they recognize that people seek out responsibility and that motivation can come from allowing employees to suggest creative and meaningful solutions.

- **strengths-based management** A management style emphasizing that maximizing an employee's existing strengths is much easier than trying to build such attributes from the ground up.

In his book *The Human Side of Enterprise,* Douglas McGregor (1960) identified two general approaches to management, which he termed Theory X and Theory Y. **Theory X managers** assume that work is innately unpleasant and that people have a strong desire to avoid it. Such managers believe that employees need direction, dislike responsibility, and must be kept in line. Theory X managers motivate performance by exerting control and threatening punishment.

In contrast, **Theory Y managers,** those with the outlook that McGregor advocated, assume that engaging in effortful behavior is natural to human beings—that even at play, people often work hard. Theory Y managers recognize that people seek out responsibility and that motivation can come from allowing them to suggest creative and meaningful solutions to problems. These managers assume that people have untapped creative and intellectual potential that can benefit the organization.

Although over 50 years have passed since his book was published, McGregor's distinctions between the two managerial styles remain a source of inspiration, particularly for practitioners in I-O psychology who consult with organizations to enhance managerial effectiveness (Carson, 2005; Robinson, 2008).

STRENGTHS-BASED MANAGEMENT

Donald Clifton, a former CEO of the Gallup polling organization, emphasized the vast potential of employees. In keeping with the view of Theory Y managers, Clifton stressed that managers need to identify and make use of their employees' strengths. Clifton's **strengths-based management** emphasized that maximizing an employee's existing strengths is a much easier proposition than trying to build such attributes from the ground up. By "strength" Clifton meant the consistent ability to attain a near-perfect performance on a given task (Clifton & Nelson, 1992; Hodges & Clifton, 2004). To develop worker strengths, a manager must recognize that each person has unique talents and that discovering these and putting them to use is crucial not only to an effective organization but also to the worker's sense of fulfillment (Bateman & Snell, 2011).

Focusing on employee strengths can have a powerful influence on profits. A study of 65 organizations found only 4 were taking a strengths-based approach (Clifton & Harter, 2003). Compared to the other 61, those 4 showed an increase in productivity equal to $1,000 per employee. In real-money terms, that translates into about $5.4 million for the average company. The various management styles are summarized in Figure 14.8.

Approach	Theorist	Manager's Mission	Manager's Problem-Solving Strategy	Manager's Focus When Things Are Going Well
"Japanese" style	Deming	Focus on the future, always seeking innovation and high quality. Forge strong relationships with people in every aspect of the organization.	Take risks, think about the future, and try something new.	Keep looking to the future, to potential innovation, and to risks.
Theory X	McGregor	Control employees, enforce rules, and make sure everyone is working hard. Keep the ship afloat.	Punish employees who fail.	Reward employees who succeed, and don't rock the boat.
Theory Y	McGregor	Challenge employees with responsibility; let them apply their talents, insights, and abilities.	Look to employees for input; harness their wisdom and insight to solve the problem.	Talk to employees about their insights into success and what to do next.
Strengths-based	Clifton	Identify employee strengths and match employees with jobs that will maximize these.	Reexamine the fit between employee strengths and assigned tasks.	Continue to build on employee strengths.

FIGURE 14.8 **Approaches to Management** Different approaches to management can have different consequences for employees and companies. Managers vary not only in general philosophy but also in problem-solving strategies and responses to success.

One reason managers are important is that they have profound influence on how people feel while at work. Someone might find her dream job ruined by a really lousy manager. Or a great manager might be able to make a boring job seem important and worthwhile. How people feel about their occupations is another topic that interests I-O psychologists.

Job Satisfaction

I-O psychologists are keenly interested in people's attitudes about their jobs. **Job satisfaction** is the extent to which an individual is content in his or her job. Job satisfaction is a relatively recent idea. In the past, many people simply did whatever their parents did to earn a living. However, economic conditions and social change have allowed more individuals access to education and employment, so the question has become not only whether a job puts money in the bank and food on the table but whether an individual feels fulfilled by his or her occupation.

Job satisfaction matters to organizations. It is related to lower job turnover and absenteeism (Crampton & Wagner, 1994), higher organizational citizenship (Organ & Ryan, 1995), and performance (Judge & others, 2001). The most common way to measure job satisfaction is with employee rating scales. Job satisfaction can be assessed globally, as with an item such as "How happy are you with your job, overall?" or in terms of more specific factors such as pay, work responsibilities, variety of tasks, promotional opportunities, and coworkers.

One factor that is not as strongly related to job satisfaction as you might expect is pay (Dalal, 2013; Judge & others, 2010). Among those who are making the minimum wage, some people are quite satisfied with their jobs. And among those who are earning a six-figure salary, some are dissatisfied. One study found that job satisfaction did not depend on the amount of money per se but rather on the person's perception that his or her pay was fair (Cohen-Charash & Spector, 2001).

Possibly it is the person, rather than the job, that matters most for job satisfaction. A 50-year longitudinal study revealed that a worker's emotional disposition was linked to job satisfaction 50 years later (Staw, Bell, & Clausen, 1986). Some individuals may simply be predisposed to be more satisfied than others. There may not be one perfect job but rather a very good but different job for each of us. Research demonstrates that the fit between the person and the job is the most important aspect of job satisfaction (Kristof-Brown & Guay, 2010; Verquer, Beehr, & Wagner, 2003).

Job satisfaction is just one of the attitudes that I-O psychologists have probed. Another fertile area of research focuses on worker commitment, as we now consider.

● **job satisfaction** The extent to which a person is content in his or her job.

"Flexible hours sounds good. Put me down for any shift you're NOT here."
© 1999 by Carol Simpson Productions.

Employee Commitment

By the time an employee has completed training, the organization has already dedicated a great deal of resources to the person. Clearly, it is in the organization's interest to keep the employee around. Especially during times of organizational change, understanding employee commitment is important to industry and psychologists.

I-O psychologists have examined work commitment as a key determinant of work-related outcomes (Cooper-Hakim & Viswesvaran, 2005). A highly influential framework emphasizes three types of commitment—affective, continuance, and

● **affective commitment** A kind of job commitment deriving from the employee's emotional attachment to the workplace.

● **continuance commitment** A kind of job commitment deriving from the employee's perception that leaving the organization would be too costly, both economically and socially.

● **normative commitment** A kind of job commitment deriving from the employee's sense of obligation to the organization for the investment it has made in the individual's personal and professional development.

normative—that are essential to understanding an employee's level of dedication to the workplace (Meyer, Becker, & Vandenberghe, 2004; Van Dick, Becker, & Meyer, 2006):

■ **Affective commitment** refers to the person's emotional attachment to the workplace. A person with a strong affective commitment identifies closely with the goals of the organization and wants to be a part of it. Affective commitment is associated with feelings of "we-ness," of identifying with the group that is one's workplace (Johnson & Chang, 2006). Individuals with strong affective commitment feel loyalty to the organization because they want to. Affective commitment is thought to result in better job performance because those high in affective commitment are likely to work harder (Riketta, 2002).

■ **Continuance commitment** derives from the employee's perception that leaving the organization would be too costly, both economically and socially. The person may dread the hassle of relocation or the effort that a new job search would entail. Such individuals might remain with an organization because of the feeling that they "have to." Continuance commitment has been shown to be either unrelated or negatively related to job performance and citizenship behaviors (Meyer & others, 2002).

■ **Normative commitment** is the sense of obligation an employee feels toward the organization because of the investment the organization has made in the person's personal and professional development. If an organization has subsidized a person's education, for example, the employee might feel that she owes it to her boss to stick around. Normative commitment means being committed because one feels one "ought to."

The Meaning of Work

Occupations define people in fundamental ways (Blustein, 2013; Hellriegel & Slocum, 2011; Parker, 2014; Prilleltensky & Stead, 2013). People identify with their work, and the work shapes many aspects of their lives. Work is an important influence on their financial standing, leisure activities, home location, friendships, and health. One of the strongest predictors of job satisfaction is feeling that one is engaged in something meaningful or significant. In one study, individuals who were asked about the meaning associated with their work reported that contributing to the economic maintenance of one's family, having a job that allowed them to have a positive impact on the organization, and work as self-expression were important ways their work had meaning for them (Wrzesniewski, Dutton, & Debebe, 2003).

A trend in in the U.S. workforce that is detrimental to job satisfaction and the meaningfulness of work is the disappearing long-term career for an increasing number of adults, especially men in private-sector jobs (Greenhaus & Callanan, 2013). Among the reasons for the disappearance of many long-term jobs is the dramatic rise in technology and companies' use of cheaper labor in other countries. More and more workers, both young and older adults, are working at a series of jobs, and many work in short-term jobs. Early careers are especially unstable as some young workers move from "survival jobs" to "career jobs" as they seek one that matches their personal interests and goals (Greenhaus & Callanan, 2013; J. T. Mortimer, 2012).

Individuals' perspectives on their work and its place in their lives can have an impact on their job performance, their workplace, and their lives in general (Jones & George, 2007). I-O psychologist Amy Wrzesniewski and her colleagues (1997) studied 300 workers and found that their perceptions of their occupation had a substantial impact on important aspects of their work and well-being. Some described the occupation as a "job," one that involved no training and allowed no personal control and little freedom. These individuals tended to focus on the material benefits of work. Another group of participants identified their occupation as a "career." They saw their occupation as a steppingstone to greater advancement and accordingly focused on the attainment of better pay, promotions, and moving up the organizational ladder. A final group of participants viewed their occupation as a "calling." They perceived the occupation as requiring a great deal of training and as involving personal control and freedom. For these individuals, work was not a means to financial ends but rather a valuable endeavor in and of itself. Indeed, some saw their occupation as their "mission in life." Importantly, all of these individuals were describing the same job—that of hospital maintenance worker. Other research has uncovered similar results for administrative assistants, with about equal numbers having each work orientation (Wrzesniewski, 2003).

Individuals who view their occupation as a calling are more likely to experience work as meaningful and fulfilling. They show higher levels of life satisfaction and job satisfaction. These individuals are more likely to engage in organizational citizenship behaviors, to devote more time to work, and to miss work less often (Bartel, Wrzesniewski, & Wiesenfeld, 2007; Wrzesniewski, 2003). Those with a calling orientation also derive more satisfaction from the work domain than from hobbies or leisure activities.

You might think that those who view their work as a calling must have just gotten lucky and found the right job for themselves. Wrzesniewski (2003) argues, however, that the ability to view one's occupation as a calling is a "portable" resource that a person can take from one context to another. She uses the term **job crafting** to refer to the physical and cognitive changes individuals can make within the constraints of a task to make the work "their own."

For example, one hospital maintenance worker took it upon himself to start rotating the artwork on the walls of the hospital rooms as he cleaned them. Doing so was not part of his written job description—it was his idea for improving the quality of life for patients facing long hospital stays. Job crafting means taking advantage of the freedom one has to bring fulfillment to an occupation (Berg, Grant, & Johnson, 2010; Berg, Wrzesniewski, & Dutton, 2010).

● **job crafting** The physical and cognitive changes individuals can make within the constraints of a task to make the work "their own."

Leadership

Just about every organization has a leader. In a business it may be a CEO, on a jury it is the foreperson, and on a team it is the captain or coach. I-O psychologists are especially interested in understanding what makes an effective leader and what effect leadership characteristics have on organizations (Avolio, Sosik, & Berson, 2013).

Leaders are not necessarily the same as managers (Bateman & Snell, 2011; Bridgman, 2007). Even in informal groups at work, someone may be perceived as a leader regardless of his or her formal title. Furthermore, not all managers are effective leaders. A leader is a person who influences others, motivates them, and enables them to succeed (Barling, Christie, & Hoption, 2010; Beeler, 2010).

In terms of personality, a meta-analysis summarizing 94 studies of effective leadership showed that conscientiousness, extraversion, and openness to experience were the strongest personality predictors of effective leadership (Judge & others, 2002). What leaders do, for better or worse, matters a great deal to organizational outcomes (Hess & Cameron, 2006). Leadership may be especially crucial during an internal crisis, such as when two organizations merge or when the organization reduces its workforce (Tikhomirov & Spangler, 2010). Two major types of leadership are transactional leadership and transformational leadership.

TRANSACTIONAL LEADERSHIP

Sometimes a leader is simply "the person in charge." That is, as a leader she sees herself as responsible for running operations

I-O psychologists study the qualities of effective leaders such as Glenn "Doc" Rivers, here during one of his seasons with the Boston Celtics.

● **transactional leader** An individual in a leadership capacity who emphasizes the exchange relationship between the worker and the leader and who applies the principle that a good job should be rewarded.

but not changing things. A **transactional leader** is an individual who emphasizes the exchange relationship between the worker and the leader (Bass, 1985), applying the principle "You do a good job and I will reward you."

Like a Theory X manager, a transactional leader believes that people are motivated by the rewards (or punishers) they receive for their work, and such a leader gives clear and structured directions to followers. The transactional leader works within the goals of the existing organizational system ("that's how we do it around here") and may exhibit management by exception—stepping in only when a problem arises. With regard to personality traits, transactional leaders tend to be characterized by low conscientiousness and low agreeableness (Zopiatis & Constanti, 2012).

TRANSFORMATIONAL LEADERSHIP

While a transactional leader primarily concentrates on keeping the ship sailing, a different type of leader focuses on defining the direction of the ship. An individual with this leadership style dedicates thought to the meaning of leadership itself and to the impact she might have in improving an organization. A **transformational leader** is a dynamic individual who brings charisma, passion, and vision to the position (Mumford, Scott, & Hunter, 2006). A transformational leader is concerned not with enforcing the rules but with changing them.

● **transformational leader** An individual in a leadership capacity who is dynamic and who brings charisma, passion, and vision to the position.

What are transformational leaders like? Research shows that transformational leaders tend to rate themselves high on conscientiousness, extraversion, and openness to experience (Zopiatis & Constanti, 2012). Four elements of transformational leadership have been described (Harms & Crede, 2010; Simola, Barling, & Turner, 2010):

- Transformation leaders exert idealized influence. They do what they believe is right and serve as a role model for employees.
- Transformational leaders motivate by inspiring others to do their very best.
- Transformational leaders are devoted to intellectually stimulating their employees. They make it clear that they need input from employees because they themselves do not have all the answers.
- Transformational leaders provide individualized consideration to their employees, showing a sincere concern for each person's well-being.

Transformational leaders can help people do more than they believed possible. In one study, elite UK Royal Marine recruits were more likely to make it through the challenges of boot camp if they had a transformational leader (Hardy & others, 2010). Transformational leaders can be especially inspiring for workers whose jobs do not involve a great deal of personal autonomy and freedom (Den Hartog & Belschak, 2012). One reason transformational leaders improve worker satisfaction and job attitudes is that they create opportunities for workers to fulfill the central human needs of relatedness, autonomy, and competence (Kovjanic & others, 2012).

Transformational leadership is associated with positive organizational outcomes in a wide variety of settings, from sports teams (Charbonneau, Barling, & Kelloway, 2001) to profit-oriented businesses (Barling, Weber, & Kelloway, 1996; Tikhomirov & Spangler, 2010) to the military (Hardy & others, 2010). Transformational leaders strive to foster trust in the organization, to persuade employees about the meaningfulness of their work, and finally to strengthen employees' **organizational identity**—their feelings of oneness with the organization and its goals (Sivanathan & others, 2004).

● **organizational identity** Employees' feelings of oneness with the organization and its goals.

I-O psychologists recognize that leadership is experienced in a social relationship (Bono, Hooper, & Yoon, 2012). To understand how leadership works, we have to consider not only leaders but followers. A transformational leader must not only have vision but followers who buy into that vision. Indeed, being a transformational leader is not just about the leader's behavior but about the perceptions of that behavior by followers.

I-O Psychology and Personality Psychology: Are Transformational Leaders in the Eye of the Beholder?

If you have ever watched a TED talk on the recommendation of a friend, you might note that one person's inspiring guru can be another person's bloviating bore. One employee might find a boss to be a truly charismatic visionary, and another might view the very same boss as an overly enthusiastic pain in the neck. Are some followers more likely to find their leaders transformational?

Followers who have personality traits that are similar to those of transformational leaders are more likely to view their leaders as transformational. That means that followers who are high in extraversion (Bono, Hooper, & Yoon, 2012; Schyns & Sanders, 2007), conscientious, and openness to experience (Bono, Hooper, & Yoon, 2012) are more likely to view their supervisors as transformational leaders. In addition, in followers, agreeableness is related to viewing one's boss as transformational (Bono, Hooper, Yoon, 2012).

How does your personality affect your views of the leaders in your life?

An interesting series of studies showed that the relationship between follower traits and leader ratings may depend on the organizational context itself. In an accounting firm, for example, conscientiousness predicted follower ratings of leaders as transformational, whereas in a hospital and at a telecommunications company, agreeable employees were more likely to view their supervisors as transformational leaders (Schyns & Sanders, 2007).

What does it mean to find out that follower personalities play a role in perceptions of their leaders? On the one hand it should not be surprising that employees respond to the same leader in different ways, depending on their personalities. The workplace is, of course, a social setting, and the relationship between leaders and followers is as complex as any social relationship (Felfe & Schyns, 2006). On the other hand, these results also tell us that being a truly effective leader, an agent of change in an organization, may be even more challenging than it seems. Being a truly transformational leader who implements a vision in an organization may involve the challenge of winning over individuals whose very personalities render them reluctant to get on board.

Many studies ask employees to rate the transformational leadership of their supervisors (Bass, 1985; Bass & Avolio, 1995). These are the types of characteristics employees are asked to assess:

- Helps me develop my strengths
- Talks about his or her most important values and beliefs
- Instills pride in me for being associated with him or her
- Seeks differing perspectives when solving problems

With these ratings, subordinates are making subjective judgments based on their impressions and memories. Some of those ratings might reflect not so much the behavior of the leader as the employee's personality. To read about this possibility, see the Intersection.

One notable difference between transactional and transformational leaders lies in their approach to the workplace culture. Transactional leaders *work within* the context of that culture, whereas transformational leaders seek to *define and redefine* it (Ostroff, Kinicki, & Muhammad, 2013; Schneider, Ehrhart, & Macey, 2013). Industry analysts widely consider the dynamic culture of organizations such as Google to be their biggest selling point. What does it mean to talk about organizational culture? In the next section we probe this fascinating topic.

test yourself

1. With what is the field of organizational psychology primarily concerned?
2. How do Theory X and Theory Y managers differ?
3. Define transactional and transformational leadership. How do these styles differ?

4· ORGANIZATIONAL CULTURE

● **organizational culture** An organization's shared values, beliefs, norms, and customs.

Organizational culture refers to an organization's shared values, beliefs, norms, and customs. How do people dress? Do they socialize? Is it okay to decorate cubicles with personal items? Can the employees talk to the CEO? These are the kinds of questions a new employee might ask, and the answers reveal the formality, warmth, and status consciousness of the workplace culture. Organizational culture describes the "flavor" of an organization—the "way we get things done around here" (Deal & Kennedy, 1982).

Even unspoken aspects of organizational culture can influence the everyday behavior of individuals within an organization (Griffin & Moorhead, 2010). Recall the phenomenon of groupthink from Chapter 13. Groupthink occurs when individuals in a group squelch dissent and seek consensus above all else. A more open climate may produce greater conflict, but conflict over important matters may be a good thing. An open climate characterizes the Harley-Davidson Motor Company. Because many Harley-Davidson employees are themselves motorcycle enthusiasts, their ideas are welcome at any time. In Harley's open-door policy, everyone can talk to everyone else. This free exchange is valued because the company's success relies on passion for motorcycles. Such openness reveals a strong level of respect for the contributions of individuals across the organization.

Positive Organizational Culture

Positive organizational culture stems from a variety of factors, including active leadership, explicit policies, and less tangible aspects such as the "feel" of an organization. Creating a positive organizational culture can be as simple as giving employees constructive reinforcement for good work (Wiegand & Geller, 2004). Leaders who reward outstanding performance and acknowledge the contributions that employees make to an organization may foster achievement motivation and promote success. Similarly, a positive climate can be nurtured by leaders who incorporate fairness and safety into the cultural climate as part of a well-functioning workplace, rather than treating these concerns as hassles that must be endured (Aguinis, 2010).

Positive organizational cultures are compassionate (Kanov & others, 2006). Compassion can be expressed in creative and humane corporate policies. For example, the Boston Consulting Group values work–life balance and issues a "red zone report" when individuals are working too many long weeks. Workers can also receive $10,000 for volunteering at a nonprofit. At another best place to work—NetApp, a data storage company in Sunnyvale, California—a top executive asks managers to notify him if they catch someone doing something right. He then calls 10 to 20 employees *every day* to thank them.

● **downsizing** A dramatic cutting of the workforce that has become a popular business strategy to enhance profitability.

Sometimes business seems to require a lack of compassion. For example, downsizing is an increasingly popular U.S. corporate strategy to enhance profitability. **Downsizing** refers to dramatically cutting the workforce, especially during difficult economic times, such as the financial crisis that began in 2007. By downsizing, companies often intend to send the message to stockholders that they are taking profit seriously. Certainly downsizing has human costs for those who are laid off (Cameron, 2003, 2005). Does sacrificing staff members pay off economically? Perhaps not. I-O psychologist Kim Cameron (2003) analyzed companies that downsized and found that less than 10 percent reported improvements in product quality, innovation, and organizational climate. In fact, a majority of firms that downsized lagged behind in stock value even 3 years later (Cameron, 2003).

Related to compassion is virtue, or moral goodness. Employees who believe that their organization is committed to doing the right thing may be able to cope with difficult times and circumstances.

Cameron (2003) also examined the role of organizational virtue in response to downsizing. In eight downsized companies, he found that organizations in which the top leaders were perceived as fostering a culture of virtuousness showed higher productivity and higher-quality output, as well as less turnover, after downsizing.

Toxic Factors in the Workplace

Unfortunately, not all work settings are positive. *Workplace incivility* refers to rude or disrespectful behaviors that reveal a lack of regard for others, such as spreading rumors, sending inflammatory e-mails, and sabotaging the work of fellow employees. Such incivility can spiral into a variety of other negative behaviors (Trevino, 2014). Here we focus on two extreme cases of such incivility: sexual harassment and workplace aggression and violence.

SEXUAL HARASSMENT

Sexual harassment is unwelcome behavior or conduct of a sexual nature that offends, humiliates, or intimidates another person. In the workplace, sexual harassment includes unwanted sexual advances, requests for sexual favors, and other verbal or physical conduct of a sexual nature (Berdahl & Raver, 2010; Elias, Gibson, & Barney, 2013).

In the United States, sexual harassment is an illegal form of sexual discrimination that violates Title VII of the Civil Rights Act of 1964. The victim of sexual harassment can be a man or woman and need not be the opposite sex of the perpetrator. The victim does not necessarily have to be the person harassed; it can be anyone affected by the offensive conduct. For example, a man who works in a setting in which women are routinely demeaned may find his workplace toxic. A woman who is offended by sexual comments made to other women or among men at her workplace may also be the victim of sexual harassment. The harasser can be a coworker, supervisor, or even someone who is not an employee.

Many people meet their romantic partners at work, of course. Sexual conduct is unlawful only when it is unwelcome. On average, over 14,000 cases of sexual harassment per year have been reported to the U.S. Equal Employment Opportunity Commission (EEOC) since 2000, with 11,364 cases reported in 2011 (EEOC, 2012). Women file approximately 84 percent of the complaints. Estimates of the frequency of sexual harassment in the workplace vary from 40 to 75 percent for women and 13 to 31 percent for men (McDonald, 2012). Sexual harassment is more likely in organizations with poor social ties among workers and poor relationships between employees and management (Snyder, Scherer, & Fisher, 2012).

Sexual harassment is related to reduced job satisfaction and well-being and heightened distress and intentions to leave a job (Dionisi, Barling, & Dupré, 2012; Nielsen & Einarsen, 2012). Experiences of harassment are linked to depression, anxiety, and feelings of hopelessness, humiliation, and helplessness (McDonald, 2012).

Sexual harassment is also costly to organizations. It is associated with lower productivity, poor time management (Snyder, Scherer, & Fisher, 2012), and higher levels of worker turnover (McDonald, 2012). Monetary benefits (not including those awarded from litigation) paid out for sexual harassment cases amount to about $50 million per year (EEOC, 2012).

Sexual harassment has two related forms: quid pro quo and hostile work environment. *Quid pro quo sexual harassment* refers to unwelcome sexual advances, requests for sexual favors, and verbal or physical conduct of a sexual nature in which submission is made either explicitly or implicitly a condition of the victim's employment. That is, the harassed individual is expected to tolerate the behavior or submit to sexual demands in order to be hired or to keep his or her job. Quid pro quo sexual harassment can also occur if rejection of the inappropriate conduct becomes the basis for employment decisions affecting the victim. For example, a woman who rejects her boss's advances may be denied a promotion or may receive a negative performance evaluation. *Hostile work environment sexual harassment* refers to unwelcome sexual behavior when this conduct

"I got downsized after the king subscribed to that online joke service!"

© Harley Schwadron. www.CartoonStock.com.

● **sexual harassment** Unwelcome behavior or conduct of a sexual nature that offends, humiliates, or intimidates another person.

What to Do If You Think You Are Being Sexually Harassed

1. Keep careful records. Write down times, dates, places, and names of individuals who have witnessed the behavior.

2. Build a paper trail related to the harassment. If someone has sent you offensive or troubling e-mails, letters, or phone messages, keep them. Information that is documented may be helpful in pursuing a complaint.

3. Talk to a trusted friend, counselor, or therapist who will keep the information confidential. An objective third party may have suggestions for resolving the problem. If the harassment is occurring at work, consult with the human resources department. If it is taking place at school, talk to someone at your college's counseling center.

4. Write a letter to the individual you believe is harassing you. If you feel uncomfortable talking to the harasser in person, a letter may be a good alternative. The letter should include not only a description of specific examples of the behavior and your feelings about it, but also a statement of what you would like to happen next. Keep a copy of the letter for yourself.

5. If you have concerns about your safety or have been assaulted, immediately call the police. Most students do not report sexual harassment but wish they could (AAUW, 2006). Reporting sexual harassment can be a challenge, but it is important. Sexual harassment is likely to be repeated if the perpetrator does not get feedback about the problem behavior.

FIGURE 14.9 **Coping with Sexual Harassment**
A serious problem on college campuses, sexual harassment can crop up in relations between students, students and their professors, and members of the university staff. If you feel that you are being sexually harassed, first consider that someone can sexually harass you without meaning to and that the solution can be as simple as informing the individual that his or her behavior makes you uncomfortable. If talking to the person alone is uncomfortable, take someone with you for moral support. If you feel that confronting the person might be dangerous, there are other steps you can take, as described in the figure.

has the purpose or effect of interfering with an individual's work performance or creating an intimidating or offensive work environment. Behaviors that might produce a hostile environment include sexually graphic humor, suggestive remarks, ridiculing someone's body, and touching individuals inappropriately.

Victim distress can be compounded when organizations fail to respond effectively to sexual harassment claims (Fitzgerald, 2003). Research examining over 6,000 sexual harassment victims in the U.S. military demonstrated that an organization's tendency to minimize the negative effects of harassment, to retaliate against the victim, and to seek to remedy the situation in unsatisfactory ways is a strong predictor of victim distress (Bergman & others, 2002).

Sexual harassment is a serious problem. No one has to tolerate inappropriate sexual conduct at work. For information on how to cope with sexual harassment, see Figure 14.9.

WORKPLACE AGGRESSION AND VIOLENCE

Aggression involves engaging in behavior meant to harm another person. Aggression in the workplace includes verbal abusiveness, intimidating behavior, and bullying (Barling, Dupré, & Kelloway, 2009). Such behavior can have negative effects on workers. Longitudinal research has found that individuals who have experienced mean-spirited teasing from coworkers show increases in psychological health problems (Hogh, Henriksson, & Burr, 2005). Nonsexual aggression shares a strong negative relationship with job satisfaction (Lapierre, Spector, & Leck, 2005).

At the extreme end of such aggression is workplace violence, which includes physical assault and even homicide (Barclay & Aquino, 2010; Dillon, 2012). Although sexual harassment is recognized as a form of sex-based discrimination, workplace violence falls within the realm of workplace safety. According to the Occupational Safety and Health Act, an employer is required to "furnish each of his employees employment and a place of employment which are free from recognized hazards that are causing or are likely to cause death or serious physical harm to his employees" (Occupational Safety and Health Administration, 2002).

High-profile cases of workplace violence often grab the headlines. For example, on Christmas night in 2000, Michael McDermott, a software tester for Edgewater Technology in Wakefield, Massachusetts, went to his workplace and stashed two-dozen boxes of ammunition, two rifles, a shotgun, a pistol, and a bayonet. On the day after Christmas, after a morning spent at work and chatting with coworkers about video games, he strode into the human resources department and, within a few minutes, killed seven people. McDermott was convicted of seven counts of murder in 2002 (Blades, 2006).

According to the U.S. Department of Labor (2006), as many as half of U.S. employers with more than 1,000 employees reported at least 1 incident of workplace violence in 2005. Importantly, over 70 percent of U.S. workplaces have no formal policy addressing workplace violence. Understanding and preventing workplace violence is a concern for both employers and I-O psychologists (Barclay & Aquino, 2010; Dillon, 2012).

Workplace violence may occur between coworkers, but it also includes violence perpetrated by outsiders such as customers, clients, or patients (Foley & Rauser, 2012). Consider a store clerk confronted by a robber, a teacher faced with a hostile high school student in the classroom, or a nurse dealing with a physically abusive patient—all are in a position in which they might become a victim of violence. Employers are expected to anticipate and take action to prevent victimization in such circumstances.

Although no organization can identify every potential problem, companies can take steps to prevent workplace violence (Bowen, Privitera, & Bowie, 2011; Hess & Hess, 2013). Examples of strategies include:

- Create a humane environment in which employees feel they are being treated fairly. Individuals who perceive that they have been treated unfairly are more likely to aggress, verbally and physically.
- Strive for an open approach to resolving conflicts. Commitment to solving problems head-on can defuse potentially difficult situations before they escalate to violence.
- Establish zero-tolerance policies toward violent behavior, and ensure that the policy covers not just employees but clients, customers, patients, visitors, and anyone else who may come into the organization.

test yourself

1. What is meant by organizational culture?
2. Name some key factors in a positive organizational culture?
3. What is sexual harassment? Discuss its two forms.

5. I-O PSYCHOLOGY AND HEALTH AND WELLNESS

Given the significant place of work in human life, it is no surprise that work affects health and wellness (Jex, Swanson, & Grubb, 2013). In this final section we review the relationship between unemployment and well-being, the experience of stress at work, and ways to cope with work stress.

Unemployment

The importance of work in our life is never more apparent than when individuals lose their job. Unemployment is related to physical problems (such as heart attack, stroke, obesity, and diabetes), psychological disorders (such as anxiety and depression), marital and family troubles, and homicide and other crimes (Gallo & others, 2006; Kilicarslan & others, 2006; Patten & others, 2006).

Individuals who are employed full-time have lower stress, lower depression, and report better health behaviors, including healthier eating and physical activity, compared to those who are unemployed (Rosenthal & others, 2012). A 15-year longitudinal study of 24,000 people living in Germany found that unemployment had a devastating effect on well-being (Lucas & others, 2004). Although individuals recovered much of the happiness they had enjoyed prior to becoming unemployed, many failed to return fully to those levels. One research review concluded that unemployment was associated with an increased mortality risk especially for individuals in the early and middle stages of their careers (Roelfs & others, 2011).

In difficult economic times, people are more likely to experience repeated spells of unemployment. A recent study found that among those who had experienced repeated unemployment, those who were employed even temporarily between bouts of unemployment were better able to cope (Booker & Sacker, 2012). These results suggest that the experience of work itself can serve as a buffer against the effects of unemployment. Yet that work can also be a source of considerable stress and conflict.

Stress at Work

Job stress refers to the experience of stress on the job (Griffin & Clarke, 2010; Sonnentag & Frese, 2013). A key source of job stress is role conflict. **Role conflict** may occur when a person tries to meet the demands of more than one important life role, such as worker and mother (Allen, 2013; Richardson & Schaeffer, 2013). Because work may compete with other valued activities for our time and energy, it can be difficult to resolve the demands of our various valued roles: Should I stay at work and finish this project, or head home to have dinner with my family?

● **job stress** The experience of stress on the job and in the workplace setting.

● **role conflict** The kind of stress that arises when a person tries to meet the demands of more than one important life role, such as worker and mother.

Some jobs are more stressful than others. Four particular characteristics of work settings are linked with employee stress and health problems (Matthews, Bulger, & Barnes-Farrell, 2010; Moos, 1986; Wirtz & others, 2010):

- High job demands such as having a heavy workload and time pressure
- Inadequate opportunities to participate in decision making
- A high level of supervisor control
- A lack of clarity about the criteria for competent performance

● **burnout** A distressed psychological state in which a person experiences emotional exhaustion and little motivation for work.

When work stress becomes chronic, individuals may fall victim to **burnout,** a distressed psychological state in which a person experiences emotional exhaustion and little motivation for work. Burnout may include feelings of being overworked and underappreciated and can feature depersonalization, confusion, worry, and resentment (Ahola & others, 2006). Symptoms can be physical (exhaustion, headaches, gastrointestinal problems, suppressed immune function, sleep disturbance), behavioral (increased use of alcohol, drugs, caffeine; absenteeism; and social withdrawal), and emotional (increased cynicism and negativity, hopelessness, irritability, emotional distancing, depression, and anxiety). Coworker support and clear job requirements are related to lower levels of stress (Matthews, Bulger, & Barnes-Farrell, 2010).

Managing Job Stress

● **leisure** The pleasant times before or after work when individuals are free to pursue activities and interests of their own choosing, such as hobbies, sports, and reading.

Stress at work does not always lead to burnout, especially if individuals develop enjoyable leisure activities. Indeed, an important aspect of life, beyond being competent at and enjoying one's work, is to relax and enjoy leisure (Ahmed & others, 2005). **Leisure** refers to the pleasant times before or after work when individuals are free to pursue activities and interests of their own choosing—hobbies, sports, and reading, for example. In a research study on regret, U.S. adults placed "not engaging in more leisure activities" as one of the top six regrets (Roese & Summerville, 2005). Using our leisure time to help others can be a particularly good way to recover from work-related stress (Mojza & others, 2010).

Might taking regular vacations also help individuals to combat work stress? Vacations increase well-being for most people (de Bloom & others, 2011; Dolnicar, Yanamandram, & Cliff, 2012). One study found that in the days and weeks at work just after a vacation, individuals reported that they were less exhausted, had fewer health complaints, and were putting forth more efficient effort than in the week at work prior to the vacation (Fritz & Sonnentag, 2006). Check out the Psychological Inquiry for the results of that study.

Taking vacations can also be associated with living longer. In a longitudinal study, 12,338 men 35 to 57 years of age were assessed each year for 5 years on the question of whether they took vacations (Gump & Matthews, 2000). Then the researchers examined the medical and death records over 9 years for men who lived for at least a year after the last vacation survey. Compared with those who never took vacations, men who went on annual vacations were 21 percent less likely to die over the 9 years and 32 percent less likely to die of coronary heart disease. The same concerns that lead men to skip a vacation—such as not trusting anyone to fill in for them and fearing that they will get behind in their work and someone will replace them—tend to promote heart disease. Such apprehensions are characteristic of the Type A behavioral pattern we examined in Chapter 12.

The benefits of time away are often short-lived (de Bloom, Geurts, & Kompier, 2012). Why do vacations wear off so quickly? One contributing factor is that often workload right after vacation is very heavy (Kühnel & Sonnentag, 2011). Some vacations may be better than others, in terms of relieving stress and doing so with a more enduring effect. Vacations that allow the people to fully detach from work and enjoy themselves are more likely to continue to influence well-being down the line (de Bloom, Geurts, & Kompier, 2012).

psychological *inquiry*

You Need a Vacation!

This graph shows the results of a study examining employees' health complaints before and after they took a vacation. The Y axis (vertical) is the self-rated score on health complaints, and the X axis (horizontal) represents time. Employees rated their health complaints on 12 items (for example, "Have you slept less because of worries?"). The 4-point scale ranged from 1 (not at all) to 4 (much more than normal). Consider these questions:

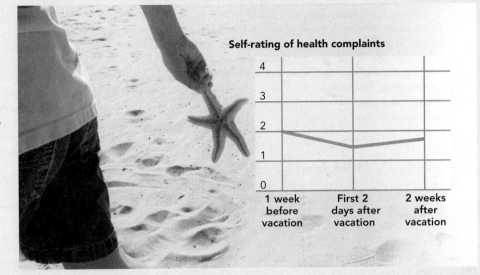

1. When were health complaints at their lowest and highest?

2. If the researchers had measured the employees' level of satisfaction with life, do you think the pattern would look the same? Explain.

3. Was this a correlational study or an experiment? What does your answer mean for the conclusions that can be drawn from this study?

4. In this study, participants completed self-report measures of their health. Was that a wise research decision—or not? Explain.

In addition to developing enjoyable leisure activities and taking regular vacations, what else can you do to cope with work stress? Dealing with job stress in a healthy way involves taking care of your body as well as your mind (Fahey, Insel, & Roth, 2013). Meet your physical needs by eating right, exercising, and getting enough sleep (Schiff, 2013; Sparling & Redican, 2012).

Because work stress, like all stress, is about our perception of experience, it makes sense to hone your coping skills and periodically to monitor your patterns of behavior and well-being (Donatelle, 2013). Have you set realistic goals at work? Are you taking work-related issues too personally? It may be helpful to remind yourself of the goals of Donald Clifton's strengths-based approach to management, described earlier in the chapter. What are your strengths, and how can you use them to do what you do best?

We might at times think of work as a four-letter word. We might view working hard as just that—hard. However, it is vital to keep in mind that work can be a vital part of living a fulfilling life. Indeed, Mihalyi Csikszentmihalyi (1990) found that while working, we are 10 times more likely to experience **flow**—the optimal experience of a match between our skills and the challenge of a task—even though, ironically, we are also 6 times more likely to wish we were somewhere else when on the job.

When we think of work as a calling, we might find ourselves listening for that call with an open mind and heart. Remember, though, that a calling orientation to work is not just about waiting and listening. It is about the active way we craft any job, finding a way to place a personal stamp on the workplace. Transforming a job into a calling is a decision that we make about our work situation.

At the beginning of this chapter, we considered the question, why do people, like Mark Zuckerberg, keep working even if they do not have to? Given the central role of work in human life, perhaps we should rethink that question. Imagine that you, like Zuckerberg, had enough money to keep you more than comfortable for over 3,600 years. What kind of job would you want then?

● **flow** The optimal experience of a match between one's skills and the challenge of a task.

test yourself

1. What role conflicts do you—or does someone you know well—experience?

2. Define burnout and name some physical, behavioral, and emotional symptoms of burnout.

3. What have researchers discovered about the benefits of taking a vacation?

1. ORIGINS OF INDUSTRIAL AND ORGANIZATIONAL PSYCHOLOGY

Industrial and organizational (I-O) psychology applies the science of psychology to work and the workplace. Scientific management views workers as well-oiled machines and seeks to maximize efficiency. Ergonomics, or human factors, is a field of study concerned with the relationship between human beings and the tools or machines they use in their work. Ergonomics is focused on promoting safety and efficiency. The Hawthorne studies, conducted by Mayo and his colleagues, showed that just being made to feel special could increase productivity. This work gave rise to the human relations approach to management that stresses the importance of the psychological characteristics of workers and managers.

2. INDUSTRIAL PSYCHOLOGY

Job analysis involves the systematic description of the knowledge and skills necessary to carry out a job. Some procedures involved in personnel selection include testing, interviews, work samples, and other exercises. Training individuals for their jobs is a key goal for industrial psychologists. Dimensions of training include orientation, formal training, and mentoring, as well as ongoing employee development.

Performance appraisal is an important source of feedback for employees and guides decisions about promotions, raises, and termination. One strategy to avoid errors in performance appraisal is 360-degree feedback, which involves rating a worker through the input of a range of individuals, including coworkers, managers, and customers. Organizational citizenship behavior refers to discretionary behaviors that a person engages in that are not part of the specific job description.

3. ORGANIZATIONAL PSYCHOLOGY

The way managers approach their jobs is an important focus of research in organizational psychology. Deming, an American, developed the "Japanese" management style, stressing innovation, future orientation, and quality. McGregor introduced Theory X and Theory Y management styles. Theory X describes managers who assume that work is unpleasant to workers and who believe that a manager's main role is to keep workers in line. Theory Y managers assume that workers crave and value responsibility and represent important sources of creativity. Strengths-based management, developed by Clifton, asserts that the best approach to management is one that matches individuals' strengths with their jobs.

Job satisfaction is a person's attitude toward his or her occupation. Job satisfaction is not strongly associated with wages and may relate in important ways to the personality characteristics of the worker and the fit between the person and the job.

Employee commitment is an individual's feeling of loyalty to his or her workplace. Three types of commitment are affective commitment (a person's emotional attachment to a job), continuance commitment (a person's perception that leaving a job would be too costly or difficult), and normative commitment (a person's feeling that he or she should stick with a job because of obligation).

Because our jobs define us in many ways, the way we think about work influences our lives more generally. Research has shown that people can perceive the same position as a job, a career, or a calling. Those who perceive their work as a calling show numerous positive benefits.

A transactional leader is one who emphasizes the exchange relationship between the boss and employees. This leader is likely to take action only in reaction to events. In contrast, a transformational leader is a dynamic individual who brings charisma, passion, and vision to the position.

4. ORGANIZATIONAL CULTURE

Organizational culture refers to an organization's shared beliefs, values, customs, and norms. Positive organizational culture can be nurtured through positive reinforcement, as well as genuine concern for the safety of workers. Compassion and virtue also promote positive organizational culture.

Factors such as sexual harassment and workplace violence represent the negative side of organizational culture. Sexual harassment is illegal and may take the form of either quid pro quo (the demand for sexual favors in return for employment or continued employment) or hostile workplace environment. Workplace violence is a growing concern for employers and I-O psychologists. Employers are obligated to create a safe environment for workers, including doing all that they can to foresee and prevent possible violence.

5. I-O PSYCHOLOGY AND HEALTH AND WELLNESS

Unemployment can take a toll on psychological and physical health. Job stress is stress experienced at the workplace. Role conflict, a key source of such stress, results from trying to meet multiple demands in a limited amount of time. Sources of job stress include high demands, inadequate opportunity to participate in decision making, high levels of supervisor control, and unclear criteria for performance. At the extreme, work stress can lead to burnout.

One way to manage job stress is to enrich one's life while not at work. Engaging in satisfying leisure activities can promote workplace wellness. Enjoying time off can have benefits for individuals when they are back on the job.

SUMMARY

key *terms*

industrial and organizational (I-O) psychology, p. 468	human relations approach, p. 470	orientation, p. 478	organizational citizenship behavior (OCB), p. 482
scientific management, p. 468	job analysis, p. 471	training, p. 478	Theory X managers, p. 484
ergonomics or human factors, p. 469	KSAOs or KSAs, p. 472	mentoring, p. 479	Theory Y managers, p. 484
Hawthorne effect, p. 469	integrity test, p. 476	performance appraisal, p. 479	strengths-based management, p. 484
	situational judgment test, p. 476	halo effect, p. 480	
	structured interview, p. 477	360-degree feedback, p. 480	

apply your *knowledge*

1. You might be interested in discovering your personal strengths so that you can identify the occupations that might be best for you. A variety of measures assess vocational abilities, and you can visit your campus career center to check these out. In addition, positive psychologists have developed an assessment tool that measures strengths of character such as achievement motivation, loyalty, sense of humor, capacity to love and be loved, and integrity. To determine your character strengths, visit the Values in Action website at www.viastrengths.org.

2. Browse the *Wall Street Journal* and read the latest news about the corporate world. Can you detect principles of scientific management or human relations approaches in the corporations documented in the stories? What types of corporate leadership do the articles describe?

3. Ask some friends and family members to describe their jobs to you. Where do the descriptions fall with respect to the distinctions between job, career, and calling discussed in this chapter? In light of what you know about your respondents, how much do you think this distinction reflects the job itself and how much reflects the person?

4. Pick someone you know who shows the qualities of a good leader. Interview the individual about times he or she has been in a leadership role. How did the individual manage challenges? How did the person view the people he or she led? What perspective did the person bring to the position of leader? Do you think your candidate fits the Theory X or Theory Y management profile? Is the individual a transactional or transformational leader? Explain your conclusions.

5. If you are interested in exploring possible careers, check out the *Occupational Outlook Handbook* at www.bls.gov/oco/. You might be surprised at some of the jobs that are out there.

Psychological Disorders

When a Family Member Has a Psychological Disorder

When a person is diagnosed with a psychological disorder, family members often want to understand the condition.

Brothers, sisters, and children might pursue careers in fields like psychiatry or psychology, inspired by their own experiences.

Having a family member with a psychological disorder is related to vocational pursuits in another, more surprising way, according to a recent study. Benjamin Campbell and Sam Wang (2012) examined the relationship between having a family member with a mental illness and the intellectual interests of over 1,000 first-year college students. They found that students who had a sibling with autism spectrum disorder were much more likely to pursue math and science majors. In contrast, students who had a family member with depression were more likely to be interested in humanities majors (such as English literature, philosophy, or history). The researchers suggest that these relationships may reflect the shared genetic and environmental experiences of individuals from the same family. They argue that it makes sense that siblings share interests—even if, for one, those interests are reflected in a disorder, and, for another, they influence the person's choice of academic major. Those with autism and those who are interested in math and science, for instance, share an interest in analyzing and systematizing. Deep thought might be a common feature of individuals with depression *and* individuals who pursue a major in the humanities.

These links also tell us something else: Individuals with psychological disorders are not so different from everyone else. This study reminds us that people with psychological disorders are brothers, sisters, grandparents, uncles, aunts, and parents, classmates, and coworkers. Psychological disorders may make their lives more difficult and our relationships with them more challenging, but they cannot take away the ties that bind them to us. ●

PREVIEW

This chapter surveys psychological disorders. We first explore the meaning of the word *abnormal* and examine approaches to understanding abnormal behavior. We then survey a number of disorders. In the concluding section, we consider the influence of the stigma associated with psychological disorders on the health and wellness of those who experience with them.

1· DEFINING AND EXPLAINING ABNORMAL BEHAVIOR

What makes behavior normal or abnormal? Abnormal behavior is certainly statistically unusual or atypical. Alicia Keys, Peyton Manning, and Steven Spielberg are atypical—but we do not categorize them as abnormal. Three criteria help distinguish normal from abnormal behavior. **Abnormal behavior** is behavior that is deviant, maladaptive, or personally distressful over a relatively long period of time. Let's examine each of the three criteria more closely:

- Abnormal behavior is *deviant*. Deviant means that a behavior does not conform to accepted social standards. When atypical behavior deviates from what is acceptable in a culture, it often is considered abnormal. A woman who washes her hands four times an hour and takes seven showers a day is abnormal because her behavior deviates from what we consider acceptable. The *context* of a behavior may determine whether it is deviant. If the woman who washes her hands three or four times an hour and takes repeated showers works in a sterile lab with live viruses or radioactive material, her behavior might be quite acceptable.

- Abnormal behavior is *maladaptive*. Maladaptive behavior interferes with a person's ability to function effectively in the world. A man who believes that he can endanger other people through his breathing may go to great lengths to avoid people, isolating himself from others, for what he believes is their own good. His belief separates him from society and prevents his everyday functioning; thus, his behavior is maladaptive. Importantly, behavior that presents a danger to the person or to those around him or her would be considered maladaptive (and abnormal).

- Abnormal behavior involves *personal distress* over a long period of time. The person engaging in the behavior finds it troubling. A woman who secretly makes herself vomit after every meal may never be seen by others as deviant (because they do not know about it), but this pattern of behavior may cause her to feel intense shame and guilt.

● **abnormal behavior** Behavior that is deviant, maladaptive, or personally distressful over a relatively long period of time.

Accomplished people—such as singer-songwriter Alicia Keys, NFL superstar Peyton Manning, and award-winning film director Steven Spielberg—are atypical but not abnormal. However, when atypical behavior deviates from cultural norms, it often is considered abnormal.

Only one of the three criteria described above needs to be present for behavior to be labeled "abnormal," but typically two or all three may be present. When abnormal behavior persists, it may lead to the diagnosis of a psychological disorder.

Theoretical Approaches to Psychological Disorders

What causes people to develop a psychological disorder, that is, to behave in deviant, maladaptive, and personally distressful ways? Theorists have suggested various approaches to this question.

THE BIOLOGICAL APPROACH

The biological approach attributes psychological disorders to organic, internal causes. This approach primarily focuses on the brain, genetic factors, and neurotransmitter functioning as the sources of abnormality. The American Psychiatric Association (2001, 2006) defines abnormal behavior in medical terms—as a mental illness that affects or is manifested in a person's brain and can affect the way the individual thinks, behaves, and interacts with others. This approach is part of the **medical model,** which describes psychological disorders as medical diseases with a biological origin.

● **medical model** The view that psychological disorders are medical diseases with a biological origin.

THE PSYCHOLOGICAL APPROACH

The psychological approach emphasizes the contributions of experiences, thoughts, emotions, and personality characteristics in explaining psychological disorders. Psychologists might focus, for example, on the influence of childhood experiences or personality traits in the development and course of psychological disorders. Behavioral psychologists probe the rewards and punishers in the environment that determine abnormal behavior, whereas social cognitive psychologists focus on observational learning, cognitions, and beliefs as factors that foster or maintain abnormal behavior.

THE SOCIOCULTURAL APPROACH

The sociocultural approach emphasizes the social contexts in which a person lives, including the individual's culture. Using the criterion of deviance to describe a behavior as abnormal suggests the important role of sociocultural factors in psychological disorders. Cultures establish the norms by which people evaluate behavior, telling us whether it is socially acceptable (Agorastos, Haasen, & Huber, 2012). In evaluating behavior as deviant, culture matters in complex ways (Sue & others, 2013, 2014).

Importantly, cultural norms can be mistaken. Such norms can be limiting, oppressive, and prejudicial (Leong & others, 2013; Potter, 2012). Individuals who fight to change the established social order sometimes face being labeled "deviant" or even "mentally ill." In the late nineteenth and early twentieth centuries, for instance, women in Britain who demonstrated for women's right to vote were widely considered mentally ill. When individuals' behavior challenges social expectations, we must be open to the possibility that such actions are an adaptive response to injustice. Challenging what everyone thinks is true and expressing ideas that seem strange, they may make others feel uncomfortable. However, justifiable demands for social change ought not to be labeled abnormal.

Further, definitions of normal change as societal norms change. One just has to watch an episode of *Mad Men* to recognize that cigarette smoking was not only an acceptable habit in the 1960s but was also promoted as a healthy way to relax.

Cultural variation in what it means to be normal or abnormal makes it very difficult to compare different psychological disorders across different cultures. Many of the diagnostic categories we trace in this chapter primarily reflect Western (and often U.S.) notions of normality, and applying these to other cultures can be inappropriate (Agorastos, Haasen, & Huber, 2012). As individuals move from one culture to another, evaluations of their behavior must take into account the norms in their culture of origin (Bourque & others, 2012; Lee, Choi, & Matejkowski, 2013). Historically, people entering the United States from other countries were examined at Ellis Island, and many were judged to be mentally impaired simply because of differences in their language and customs.

Disorder	Culture	Description/Characteristics
Amok	Malaysia, Philippines, Africa	This disorder involves sudden, uncontrolled outbursts of anger in which the person may injure or kill someone. Amok is often found in males who are emotionally withdrawn before the onset of the disorder. After the attack on someone, the individual feels exhausted and depressed and does not remember the rage and attack.
Anorexia Nervosa	Western cultures, especially the United States	This eating disorder involves a relentless pursuit of thinness through starvation and can eventually lead to death.
Koro	China and Southeast Asia	This disorder in China and Southeast Asia involves the terrifying belief that one's genitalia are retracting into one's abdomen.

FIGURE 15.1 **Some Culture-Related Disorders** Although many psychological disorders are universal, some are associated with specific cultures, as this figure illustrates.

The sociocultural perspective stresses the ways that cultures influence the understanding and treatment of psychological disorders. The frequency and intensity of psychological disorders vary and depend on social, economic, technological, and religious aspects of cultures (Alegría, 2011; Sue & others, 2014). Some disorders are culture-related, as indicated in Figure 15.1.

In addition to recognizing the role of culture in definitions of normality, sociocultural researchers stress the role of social factors—such as gender, ethnicity, socioeconomic status, and family relationships—on psychological disorders. For instance, poverty creates stressful circumstances that can contribute to the development of a psychological disorder (British Psychological Society, 2011; Chen & Miller, 2013; Jeon, Eom, & Min, 2013; Washington & others, 2013).

THE BIOPSYCHOSOCIAL MODEL

Abnormal behavior can be influenced by biological factors (such as genes), psychological factors (such as childhood experiences), and sociocultural factors (such as gender). These factors can operate alone, but they often act in combination with one another (Hooley, Maher, & Maher, 2013; Scheid & Brown, 2010). From the biopsychosocial perspective, none of the factors considered is necessarily viewed as more important than another; rather, biological, psychological, and social factors are *all* significant ingredients in producing both normal and abnormal behavior. Furthermore, these ingredients may combine in unique ways, so that one depressed person might differ from another in terms of the key factors associated with the development of the disorder.

Why do we need to consider these multiple factors? As you will see throughout this chapter, generally speaking, there is no one gene or experience that leads inevitably to the development of a psychological disorder. Two people can share the same gene—one develops a disorder, but another does not. Similarly two people might have the same experience, such as childhood neglect, and one might develop a disorder, but the other does not. Thus, to understand the development of psychological disorders, we must consider a variety of *interacting* factors from each of the domains of experience.

An important concept that has helped psychologists understand the ways different factors influence the development of psychological disorders is the **vulnerability-stress hypothesis** (also called the **diathesis-stress model**). The vulnerability-stress hypothesis suggests that preexisting conditions (such as genetic characteristics, personality dispositions, or experiences) may put a person at risk of developing a psychological disorder. This vulnerability in combination with stressful experiences can lead to a psychological disorder.

One way that psychologists study these processes is by examining the interactions between genetic characteristics and environmental circumstances or gene × environment (G × E) interactions (Moore, 2013). Scientists continue to probe the ways genetic characteristics might produce a vulnerability to psychological disorders in the face of difficult life experiences (Lickliter, 2013; Pilecki, Arentoft, & McKay, 2011).

● **vulnerability-stress hypothesis or diathesis-stress model** Theory suggesting that preexisting conditions (such as genetic characteristics, personality dispositions, or experiences) may put a person at risk of developing a psychological disorder.

Classifying Abnormal Behavior

To understand, prevent, and treat abnormal behavior, psychiatrists and psychologists have devised systems classifying those behaviors into specific psychological disorders. Classifying psychological disorders provides a common basis for communicating. If one psychologist says that her client is experiencing depression, another psychologist understands that a particular pattern of abnormal behavior has led to this diagnosis. A classification system can also help clinicians make predictions about the likelihood of a particular disorder's occurrence, which individuals would be most susceptible to it, and what the best treatment might be (Blashfield, 2014; Halter, Rolin-Kenny, & Grund, 2013). Further, a classification system may benefit the person suffering from psychological symptoms. The fact that an individual's disorder has a name can be a comforting signal that the person may reasonably expect relief.

On the other hand, officially labeling a problem can also have serious negative implications because of the potential for creating *stigma,* a mark of shame that may cause others to avoid or to act negatively toward a person (Pescosolido & others, 2013). Indeed, being diagnosed with a psychological disorder can profoundly influence a person's life because of what the diagnosis means to the person, his or her family, and the larger social world. We return to the important issue of stigma at the end of this chapter.

THE *DSM* CLASSIFICATION SYSTEM

In 1952, the American Psychiatric Association (APA) published the first major classification of psychological disorders in the United States, the *Diagnostic and Statistical Manual of Mental Disorders.* Its current version, **DSM-5,** was approved in 2013. Throughout the history of the *DSM,* the number of diagnosable disorders has increased dramatically. For example, *DSM-5* includes new diagnoses such as binge eating disorder and gambling addiction.

The *DSM* is not the only diagnostic system. The World Health Organization devised the *International Classification of Diseases and Related Health Problems (ICD-10),* which includes a chapter on mental and behavioral disorders. One of the goals of *DSM-5* was to bring diagnoses closer to the *ICD-10* though the two manuals remain different in important ways.

● **DSM-5** The fifth edition of the *Diagnostic and Statistical Manual of Mental Disorders;* the major classification of psychological disorders in the United States.

CRITIQUES OF THE *DSM*

Even before it was published, *DSM-5* was criticized on a number of bases (British Psychological Society, 2011; Skodol, 2012a, 2012b; Spiegel & others, 2013; Widiger & Crego, 2013). A central criticism that applies to all versions of the *DSM* is that it treats psychological disorders as if they are medical illnesses, taking an overly biological view of conditions that may have their roots in social experience (Blashfield, 2014). Even as research has shed light on the complex interaction of genetic, neurobiological, cognitive, social, and environmental factors in psychological disorders, *DSM-5* continues to reflect the medical model (British Psychological Society, 2011), neglecting factors such as poverty, unemployment, and trauma.

Another general criticism of the *DSM* is that it focuses strictly on problems. Critics argue that emphasizing *strengths* as well as weaknesses might help to destigmatize psychological disorders (Roten, 2007). Other criticisms of *DSM-5* include:

■ It relies too much on social norms and subjective judgments.

■ Too many new categories of disorders have been added, some of which do not yet have consistent research support and would lead to a significant increase in the number of people being labeled as having a mental disorder.

■ Loosening the standards for some existing diagnoses will add to the already very high rates of these.

In thinking about critiques of the *DSM,* you might be wondering what all the fuss is about. One reason for these concerns is that generally U.S. insurance companies will only reimburse for treatments of diagnoses that appear in *DSM-5.* Another key reason for concern is that part of the medical model is the assumption that, optimally, disorders would be treated through medical means. Generally, that means prescribing medications. If diagnostic criteria are loosened, many more individuals might be given powerful psychoactive drugs, perhaps unnecessarily. Thus, it is imperative that the *DSM* get it right, and many critics argue that it falls short in this high-stakes context (Andrews, 2014; Blashfield, 2014; Paris, 2012; D. Watson & others, 2013).

Disorder	Changes	Sources of Concern
Major Depressive Disorder	In the past, those experiencing grief due to the loss of a loved one generally have not been considered depressed. This grief exclusion has been dropped.	This change may result in those experiencing normal grief to be labeled with depression.
Attention-Deficit/ Hyperactivity Disorder (ADHD)	Some of the diagnostic requirements have been loosened, and the age of diagnosis has been changed.	Overdiagnosis of ADHD is already a concern, as is the proliferation of drugs used to treat the condition.
Autism Spectrum Disorder	The diagnosis of Asperger syndrome, which was given to high-functioning individuals with autistic characteristics, has been dropped.	Those who were previously diagnosed with Asperger's may not be diagnosed at all and may not receive treatment.
Post-Traumatic Stress Disorder (PTSD)	Previously, a person had to have experienced or witnessed a trauma. Now, PTSD can be diagnosed even for those who only hear about a trauma.	The change may lead to a huge increase in those with this disorder.
Disruptive Mood Regulation Disorder	This is a new diagnosis for children with wild mood swings.	Adding diagnoses targeting children is concerning.
Mild Neurocognitive Impairment	This new diagnosis is for adults experiencing cognitive decline.	Many adults experience mild cognitive decline with age, and this diagnosis may pathologize normal aging.

FIGURE 15.2   **Sample of Changes in *DSM-5***

Figure 15.2 shows some of the changes that are part of the newest formulation of the *DSM*. As you can see, concerns are likely to erupt especially around disorders that pertain to children. One of these is autism spectrum disorder, which we reviewed previously in Chapters 5 and 11.

Autism spectrum disorder refers to a range of neurodevelopmental disorders involving impaired social interaction and communication, repetitive behavior, and restricted interests. Like many other neurodevelopmental conditions, autism spectrum disorder refers to a *range* of symptoms, and there is no single identified cause for the disorder. Those on the autism spectrum are a diverse group, and their level of disability can be relatively mild to quite severe.

It is likely that the disabilities shared by these individuals have numerous complex causes, including genetic and neurological factors (T. Thompson, 2013). Some previously considered causes of this disorder have been discounted thoroughly, including cold or rejecting parents (Rimland, 1964) and childhood vaccinations (Committee to Review Adverse Effects of Vaccines, 2011).

In the United States, estimates are that autism spectrum disorder characterizes 1 in 88 children born in 2000 (Baio, 2012). This estimate suggests higher prevalence than in earlier times. The increase is likely due to greater awareness by parents and healthcare providers and wider availability of reliable diagnostic tests (T. Thompson, 2013). Such awareness is important, as early interventions are particularly helpful in treating children on the autism spectrum.

Another disorder commonly diagnosed in childhood that has seen diagnoses increase dramatically is **attention-deficit/hyperactivity disorder (ADHD).** To read more, see the Critical Controversy.

● **attention-deficit/hyperactivity disorder (ADHD)** A common psychological disorder in which the individual exhibits one or more of the following: inattention, hyperactivity, and impulsivity.

CRITICAL CONTROVERSY

Does Everyone *Have ADHD?*

Chances are you know someone who suffers from ADHD. You might have been diagnosed with it yourself. ADHD involves inattention, hyperactivity, and impulsivity. ADHD diagnoses have skyrocketed. In 1988 just 500,000 cases of ADHD were diagnosed. In 2010, fully 10.4 million children were diagnosed with ADHD (Garfield & others, 2012). Experts previously thought that most children "grow out" of ADHD. However, evidence shows that as many as 70 percent of adolescents (Sibley & others, 2012) and 66 percent of adults (Asherson & others, 2010) diagnosed as children continue to experience ADHD symptoms; as a result, *DSM-5* recognizes ADHD in adults.

The sheer number of ADHD diagnoses has prompted speculation that psychiatrists, parents, and teachers are labeling normal childhood behavior as psychopathology (Mash & Wolfe, 2013; Molina & Pelham, 2014; Morrow & others, 2012). Scholars argue that the spread of ADHD is primarily a function of *over-pathologizing* normal behavior, confusing ADHD for other disorders, and aggressive marketing by pharmaceutical companies (Moncrieff & Timimi, 2010).

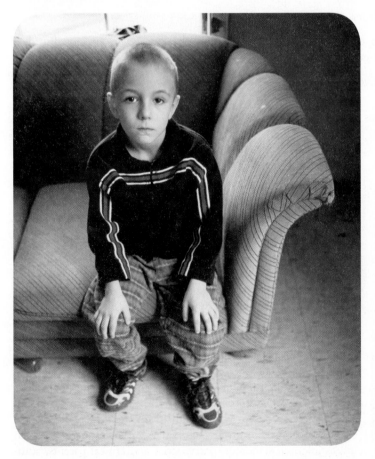

One reason for concern about overdiagnosing ADHD is that the treatment in most cases is drugs such as Ritalin and Adderall (Garfield & others, 2012). Animal research shows that in the absence of ADHD, exposure to such stimulants can predispose the brain to later addiction problems (Leo, 2005). Moreover, as more and more young adults are diagnosed, the availability of these drugs has become widespread. A special concern is that college students provide one another with these drugs, not as a treatment, but to boost academic performance (Schwarz, 2013). These individuals may not realize that supplying others with these drugs is, in fact, a felony.

Is ADHD overdiagnosed? In one study, child psychologists, psychiatrists, and social workers were sent case descriptions of children and were asked to diagnose the children described (Brüchmiller, Margraf, & Schneider, 2012). Some of the descriptions fit the diagnostic criteria for ADHD, but others lacked key features of the disorder. In addition, in the case descriptions the researchers varied whether the child was identified as male or female. The dependent variable was whether these professionals gave a case an ADHD diagnosis. The results? Participants overdiagnosed ADHD, giving an ADHD diagnosis to cases that specifically lacked important aspects of the disorder about 17 percent of the time. Further, regardless of symptoms, boys were twice as likely as girls to receive such a diagnosis.

Untreated, ADHD makes adjustment difficult, so it is critical that diagnoses of the disorder be accurate (Molina & Pelham, 2014). Children with ADHD are at heightened risk of dropping out of school, teen pregnancy, and antisocial behavior (Barkley & others, 2002; von Polier, Vloet, & Herpertz-Dahlmann, 2012). Adolescents and adults with ADHD symptoms are more likely to experience difficulties at work, in driving a car, and in interpersonal relationships; they are also more likely to have substance abuse problems (Chang, Lichtenstein, & Larsson, 2012; Molina & Pelham, 2014; Sibley & others, 2012).

ADHD is not the only controversial diagnosis, nor is it the only one given a great deal of attention by pharmaceutical companies (Mash & Wolfe, 2013). Drug companies commonly fund research that focuses on a disease model of psychological disorders. The controversy over ADHD is a reminder of the important role of research in clarifying and defining diagnostic categories. Nobody wants to label inappropriately, to misdiagnose, or to mistreat people who are already suffering.

WHAT DO YOU THINK

- Would ADHD be as controversial if the treatment did not involve drugs? Why or why not?

- Do you think ADHD would be diagnosed as often as it is if drugs were not readily available for its treatment?

- If a teacher suggested that your child be tested for ADHD, what would you do?

test yourself

1. What three main criteria distinguish abnormal behavior from normal behavior?
2. Why is it important to have formal systems for classifying abnormal behavior into specific psychological disorders?
3. What are some criticisms of *DSM-5*?

● **anxiety disorders** Disabling (uncontrollable and disruptive) psychological disorders that feature motor tension, hyperactivity, and apprehensive expectations and thoughts.

Before we begin our survey of the various psychological disorders, consider this caution. It is very common for individuals who are learning about psychological disorders to recognize the symptoms and behaviors of disorders in themselves or in people around them. Only trained professionals can diagnose a psychological disorder.

2· ANXIETY AND ANXIETY-RELATED DISORDERS

Think about how you felt before a make-or-break exam or a big presentation—or perhaps as you noticed police lights flashing behind your speeding car. Did you feel jittery and nervous and experience tightness in your stomach? These are moments of anxiety, an unpleasant feeling of fear and dread.

Individuals with high levels of anxiety worry a lot, but their anxiety does not necessarily impair their ability to function. In contrast, **anxiety disorders** involve fears that are uncontrollable, disproportionate to the actual danger the person might be in, and disruptive of ordinary life (Andrews, 2014; Gallo & others, 2013). They feature motor tension (jumpiness, trembling), hyperactivity (dizziness, a racing heart), and apprehensive expectations and thoughts.

DSM-5 recognizes 12 types of anxiety disorders. In this section, we survey four of the most common anxiety disorders:

- Generalized anxiety disorder
- Panic disorder
- Specific phobia
- Social anxiety disorder

We also consider two disorders that are not classified by *DSM-5* as anxiety disorders but are related to the experience of anxiety:

- Obsessive-compulsive disorder (categorized under obsessive-compulsive and related disorders)
- Post-traumatic stress disorder (categorized under trauma- and stressor-related disorders)

Generalized Anxiety Disorder

● **generalized anxiety disorder** Anxiety disorder marked by persistent anxiety for at least 6 months, and in which the individual is unable to specify the reasons for the anxiety.

When you are worrying about getting a speeding ticket, you know why you are anxious; there is a specific cause. **Generalized anxiety disorder** is different from such everyday feelings of anxiety in that sufferers experience persistent anxiety for at least 6 months and are unable to specify the reasons for the anxiety (Fisher, Granger, & Newman, 2010; Freeman & Freeman, 2012). People with generalized anxiety disorder are nervous most of the time and worry a great deal. That worry can take a physical toll, so that individuals with generalized anxiety disorder may suffer from fatigue, muscle tension, stomach problems, and difficulty sleeping.

What biopsychosocial factors play a role in generalized anxiety disorder? Among the biological factors are genetic predisposition, deficiency in the neurotransmitter GABA (the brain's brake pedal), and respiratory system abnormalities (Boschen, 2012). The psychological and sociocultural factors include having harsh (or even impossible) self-standards, overly strict and critical parents, automatic negative thoughts when feeling stressed, and a history of uncontrollable traumas or stressors (such as an abusive parent) (Fergusson, McLeod, & Horwood, 2013).

Sleep disturbance is a common problem for people with generalized anxiety disorder.

Panic Disorder

Much like everyone else, you might have a specific experience that sends you into a panic. For example, you work all night on a paper, only to have your computer crash before you save your last changes, or you are just about to dash across a street when you see a large truck coming right at you. Your heart races, your hands shake, and you might break into a sweat. In these situations, you know why you are experiencing feelings of panic.

In **panic disorder,** however, a person experiences recurrent, sudden onsets of intense terror, often without warning and with no specific cause. Panic attacks can produce severe palpitations, extreme shortness of breath, chest pains, trembling, sweating, dizziness, and a feeling of helplessness (Oral & others, 2012). People with panic disorder may feel that they are having a heart attack.

Charles Darwin, the scientist who proposed the theory of evolution, suffered from intense panic disorder (Barloon & Noyes, 1997), as has former NFL running back Earl Campbell.

What factors underlie panic disorder? In terms of biological factors, individuals may have a genetic predisposition to the disorder (Bayoglu & others, 2012; Reif & others, 2013). Of particular interest to researchers are genes that direct the action of neurotransmitters such as norepinephrine (Buttenschøn & others, 2011), GABA (Thoeringer & others, 2009), and serotonin (Graeff, 2012). Another brain chemical, lactate, which plays a role in brain metabolism, is elevated in individuals with panic disorder (Maddock & others, 2009). Further, experimental research has shown that increasing lactate levels can produce panic attacks (Reiman & others 1989).

Other research points to the involvement of a wider range of genes and bodily systems, implicating genes involved in hormone regulation (Wilson, Markie, & Fitches, 2012) and responses to stress (Esler & others, 2009). Panic disorder appears to share biological characteristics with physical illnesses, such as asthma (Domschke & others, 2011) and hypertension (Esler & others, 2009).

Many experts interpret Edvard Munch's painting The Scream *as an expression of the terror brought on by a panic attack.*

● **panic disorder** Anxiety disorder in which the individual experiences recurrent, sudden onsets of intense terror, often without warning and with no specific cause.

With respect to psychological influences, learning processes, as described in Chapter 6, are one factor that has been considered in panic disorder. Classical conditioning research has shown that learned associations between bodily cues of respiration and fear can play a role in panic attacks (Acheson, Forsyth, & Moses, 2012). Interestingly, in humans carbon dioxide (CO_2) is a very strong conditioned stimulus for fear (Feinstein & others, 2013), suggesting that humans may be biologically prepared to learn an association between high concentrations of CO_2 and fear (Acheson, Forsyth, & Moses, 2012; De Cort & others, 2012). Thus, some learning researchers have suggested that at the heart of panic attacks are such learned associations (De Cort & others, 2012).

In addition, the learning concept of *generalization* may apply to panic attack. Recall that in classical conditioning, generalization means showing a conditioned response (in this case, fear) to stimuli other than the particular one used in learning. Individuals who suffer from panic attacks are more likely to display overgeneralization of fear learning (Lissek & others, 2010). Why might those who suffer from panic attacks be more likely to show stronger and more generalized fear associations? It may be that genetic characteristics predispose individuals to develop such associations when they encounter particularly stressful life events, especially involving separation (Choe & others, 2013). Such an explanation represents a vulnerability-stress prediction.

In terms of sociocultural factors in the United States, women are twice as likely as men to have panic attacks (Altemus, 2006). Possible reasons for this difference include biological differences in hormones and neurotransmitters (Fodor & Epstein, 2002) as well as the different ways men and women cope with anxiety-provoking situations (Schmidt & Koselka, 2000).

Specific Phobia

● **specific phobia** Anxiety disorder in which the individual experiences an irrational, overwhelming, persistent fear of a particular object or situation.

Many people are afraid of spiders and snakes; indeed, thinking about letting a tarantula crawl over one's face is likely to give anyone the willies. It is not uncommon to be afraid of particular objects or specific environments such as extreme heights. For most of us, these fears do not interfere with daily life. A fear becomes a phobia when a situation is so dreaded that an individual goes to almost any length to avoid it. A fear of snakes that keeps a city-dweller from leaving his apartment is clearly disproportionate to the actual chance of encountering a snake. **Specific phobia** is an anxiety disorder in which an individual has an irrational, overwhelming, persistent fear of a particular object or situation.

Specific phobias come in many forms as shown in Figure 15.3. John Madden—former NFL coach, football commentator, and video game consultant—is also known for a fear of flying that led him to take a bus to the games that he broadcast.

Where do specific phobias come from? Answering this question typically involves first acknowledging that fear plays an important role in adaptive behavior. Fear tells us when we are in danger and need to take to action. The importance of this function suggests that fears should be relatively quickly learned, because learning to fear things that will hurt us keeps us out of harm's way. Specific phobias might be viewed, then, as an extreme and unfortunate variant on this adaptive process (Coelho & Purkis, 2009; Muris & Merckelbach, 2012).

Many explanations of specific phobias view these as based on experiences, memories, and learned associations (Veale & others, 2013). Perhaps, for example, the individual with a fear of heights experienced a fall from a high place earlier in life and therefore associates heights with pain (a classical conditioning explanation). Alternatively, he or she may have heard about or watched others who demonstrated terror of high places (an observational learning explanation), as when a little girl develops a fear of heights after sitting next to her terrified mother and observing her clutch the handrails, white-knuckled, as the roller coaster creeps steeply uphill.

Not all people who have a specific phobia can easily identify experiences that explain them, so other factors may also be at play (Coelho & Purkis, 2009). Each specific phobia may have its own neural correlates (Lueken, 2011), and some people may be especially prone to phobias (Burstein & others, 2012).

Social Anxiety Disorder

Imagine how you might feel just before you first meet the parents of the person you hope to marry. You might dread the thought of making some awful gaffe, ruining their first impression of you. Or imagine getting ready to give a big speech before a crowd

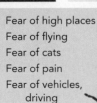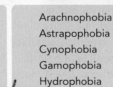

Acrophobia	Fear of high places		Arachnophobia	Fear of spiders		Mysophobia	Fear of dirt
Aerophobia	Fear of flying		Astrapophobia	Fear of lightning		Nyctophobia	Fear of darkness
Ailurophobia	Fear of cats		Cynophobia	Fear of dogs		Ophidiophobia	Fear of nonpoisonous snakes
Algophobia	Fear of pain		Gamophobia	Fear of marriage			
Amaxophobia	Fear of vehicles, driving		Hydrophobia	Fear of water		Thanatophobia	Fear of death
			Melissophobia	Fear of bees		Xenophobia	Fear of strangers

FIGURE 15.3 **Specific Phobia** This figure features examples of specific phobias—psychological disorders characterized by irrational, overwhelming, and persistent fear of a particular object or situation.

and suddenly realizing you have forgotten your notes. **Social anxiety disorder** (also called **social phobia**) is an intense fear of being humiliated or embarrassed in social situations (Lampe & Sunderland, 2013; Morrison & Heimberg, 2013).

Where does social anxiety disorder come from? Genes appear to play a role (Sakolsky, McCracken, & Nurmi, 2012), along with neural circuitry involving the thalamus, amygdala, and cerebral cortex (Damsa, Kosel, & Moussally, 2009). Also, a number of neurotransmitters may be involved, especially serotonin (Christensen & others, 2010). Social anxiety disorder may involve vulnerabilities, such as genetic characteristics or overprotective or rejecting parenting, that lay a foundation of risk, combined with learning experiences in a social context (Higa-McMillan & Ebesutani, 2011t; Pejic & others, 2013).

In *DSM-5*, generalized anxiety disorder, panic disorder, specific phobia, and social anxiety disorder are all classified as anxiety disorders (Andrews, 2014; Gallo & others, 2013). Our next two topics, obsessive-compulsive disorder and post-traumatic stress disorder, are not included under the umbrella of anxiety disorders. Instead, these disorders have their own separate categories. Nonetheless, as we will see, anxiety is relevant to both of these disorders.

● **social anxiety disorder or social phobia** Anxiety disorder in which the individual has an intense fear of being humiliated or embarrassed in social situations.

Obsessive-Compulsive Disorder

Just before leaving on a long road trip, you find yourself checking to be sure you locked the front door. Going to bed the night before an early flight, you check your alarm clock a few times to be sure it will wake you for your 8 A.M. plane. This kind of checking behavior is a normal part of worrying.

In contrast, **obsessive-compulsive disorder (OCD)** involves anxiety-provoking thoughts that will not go away and/or urges to perform repetitive, ritualistic behaviors to prevent or produce some future situation. *Obsessions* are recurrent thoughts, and *compulsions* are recurrent behaviors. Individuals with OCD dwell on normal doubts and repeat their behavioral routines sometimes hundreds of times a day.

The most common compulsions are excessive checking, cleansing, and counting. An individual with OCD might believe that she has to touch the doorway with her left hand whenever she enters a room and count her steps as she walks across the room. If she does not complete this ritual, she may be overcome with fear that something terrible will happen. Indeed, most individuals feel extraordinarily anxious if they do not act out their compulsions (Yap, Mogan, & Kyrios, 2012). Reality show host Howie Mandel has coped with OCD.

● **obsessive-compulsive disorder (OCD)** Psychological disorder in which the individual has anxiety-provoking thoughts that will not go away and/or urges to perform repetitive, ritualistic behaviors to prevent or produce some future situation.

FACTORS CONTRIBUTING TO OCD

Among the theories about the causes of OCD, most researchers agree that there seems to be a genetic component (Alonso & others, 2012, 2013; Mathews & others, 2012). Research also points to low levels of the neurotransmitters serotonin and dopamine (Goljevscek & Carvalho, 2011; D. L. Murphy & others, 2013; Soomro, 2012) and high levels of glutamate (S. E. Stewart & others, 2013) in the brain pathways linked with OCD.

Brain-imaging and EEG studies suggest neurological links for OCD (Millet & others, 2013). Research shows that the brain seems to engage in a hyperactive monitoring of behavior in those with OCD (Endrass & others, 2011, 2013), and brain activation during learning may predispose individuals with OCD to a chronic feeling that something is not quite right (Gehring, Himle, & Nisenson, 2000). One interpretation of these data is that the frontal cortex or basal ganglia are so active in OCD that numerous impulses reach the thalamus, generating obsessive thoughts or compulsive actions (Rotge & others, 2009).

Learning processes are also implicated in OCD (Endrass & others, 2013). A person who engages in compulsive behaviors often feels like doing so is an important way to fend off some dreaded outcome. For instance, consider a woman who feels compelled to check the locks on her apartment door 10 times so that she

"*Since you have a complete record of my life, could you tell me if I remembered to turn the stove off?*"

© Mike Baldwin. www.CartoonStock.com.

knows she has not put herself in danger by leaving the door unlocked. Having locked the door once, she is, of course, safe from this feared result. But she checks 9 more times just to be sure.

Can you see the vicious cycle of her compulsion? Over and over again, she performs the ritual and nothing bad happens. As long as she performs this ritual, she will never discover that the terrible outcome would not have happened anyway. This example suggests that *avoidance learning* might be an important contributor to the maintenance of compulsive symptoms. Recall that avoidance learning is a particularly powerful form of negative reinforcement that occurs when the organism learns that by making a particular response, an unpleasant or aversive stimulus can be avoided completely. That response is maintained even in the absence of any aversive stimulus. The unpleasant stimulus is no longer around, but the avoiding organism will never discover that fact.

If avoidance learning relates to OCD, might those with this disorder perform better than others at avoidance learning tasks? One study showed that individuals with OCD were especially adept at learning which stimulus to avoid compared to healthy control participants (Endrass & others, 2011). The notion that those with OCD may get "stuck" in the vicious circle of avoidance learning is supported by studies showing that OCD is associated with reduced flexibility in picking up on changes in the rules of learning tasks (Bradbury, Cassin, & Rector, 2011).

Not surprisingly, individuals with OCD show a cognitive bias associated with overestimating threats, particularly when those threats are personally relevant (Moritz & others, 2011). According to the cognitive perspective, individuals with OCD show an inability to turn off negative, intrusive thoughts by ignoring or effectively dismissing them (Leahy, Holland, & McGinn, 2012; C. Williams, 2012).

Thus, the science of OCD suggests that these individuals are preoccupied with avoiding a dreaded outcome, are prone to see that outcome as worse and more likely than it actually is, and are likely to be bothered by lingering doubts about whether they have actually avoided it. Once they find a way to fend off the feared result, they are likely to have difficulty unlearning that strategy. Some psychologists propose that, fundamentally, OCD symptoms reflect intolerance of uncertainty (Boelen & Carleton, 2012; Frost & others, 2011; Mathews & others, 2012).

OCD-RELATED DISORDERS

DSM-5 expanded the disorders that are thought to be related to OCD (Abramowitz & Jacoby, 2014). All of these disorders involve repetitive behavior and, often, anxiety. Some of the new additions are listed here:

- *Hoarding disorder* involves compulsive collecting, poor organization skills, and difficulty discarding, but also cognitive deficits in information-processing speed, decision making, and procrastination (Frost, Steketee, & Tolin, 2012). Individuals with hoarding disorder find it difficult to throw things away, troubled by the feeling that they might need, for instance, old newspapers, at a later time (Dimauro & others, 2013).

- *Excoriation* (or skin picking) refers to particular compulsion, picking at one's skin, sometimes to the point of injury. Skin picking is more common among women than men and is seen as a symptom of autism spectrum disorder.

- *Trichotillomania* (hair pulling) is a disorder in which the person compulsively pulls at his or her hair, from the scalp, eyebrows, and other body areas (Walther & others, 2013). Hair pulling from the scalp can lead to patches of baldness that the person may go to great lengths to disguise.

- *Body dysmorphic disorder* involves a distressing preoccupation with imagined or slight flaws in one's physical appearance (Kaplan & others, 2013). Individuals with the disorder cannot stop thinking about their appearance, comparing their appearance to others, checking themselves in the mirror, and so forth. Occurring about equally in men and women, this disorder can involve maladaptive behaviors such as compulsive exercise and bodybuilding and repeated cosmetic surgery.

Post-Traumatic Stress Disorder

If you have ever been in even a minor car accident, you may have had a nightmare or two about it. You might have even found yourself reliving the experience for some time. This normal recovery process takes on a particularly devastating character in post-traumatic stress disorder. **Post-traumatic stress disorder (PTSD)** is a disorder that develops through exposure to a traumatic event that has overwhelmed the person's abilities to cope (Bisson, 2013).

In a controversial move, *DSM-5* expanded the experiences that might foster PTSD, recognizing that PTSD can occur not only in those who directly experience a trauma but also in those who witness it and those who only *hear* about it (APA, 2013a). The symptoms of PTSD vary but include:

Prior to deployment, troops receive stress-management training aimed at helping to prevent PTSD and other disorders that might be triggered by the high-stress conditions of war.

- Flashbacks in which the individual relives the event as if it is happening all over again. A flashback can make the person lose touch with reality and reenact the event for seconds, hours, or (very rarely) days.

- Avoidance of emotional experiences and of talking about emotions with others as well as emotional numbing.

- Feelings of anxiety, nervousness, excessive arousal, and an inability to sleep.

- Difficulties with memory and concentration.

- Impulsive behavior.

● **post-traumatic stress disorder (PTSD)** Psychological disorder that develops through exposure to a traumatic event, a severely oppressive situation, cruel abuse, or a natural or an unnatural disaster.

PTSD symptoms can follow a trauma immediately or can occur after months or years (Solomon & others, 2012). Most individuals who are exposed to a traumatic event experience some of the symptoms in the days and weeks following exposure (National Center for PTSD, 2013).

Clearly, one cause of PTSD is the traumatic event itself (Risbrough & Stein, 2012). However, not every individual exposed to the same event develops PTSD (Brewin & others, 2012; Whitman & others, 2013). Therefore, other factors must influence a person's vulnerability to the disorder (Gabert-Quillen & others, 2012). These include a history of previous traumatic events and conditions, such as abuse and psychological disorders (Canton-Cortes, Canton, & Cortes, 2012), cultural background (Hinton & others, 2012), and genetic predisposition (Mehta & Binder, 2012; Skelton & others, 2012). These preexisting conditions make individuals more vulnerable to PTSD when they are combined with stressful events.

3· DISORDERS INVOLVING EMOTION AND MOOD

Imagine that you have studied hard for a notoriously difficult class. With an *A* on the final, you will ace the course. If you end up with a *C* on the final, you might feel sad or disappointed. If you get an *A+*, you might feel ecstatic. Our emotions tell us how we are doing in life. We feel good or bad depending on our progress on important goals. For some individuals, the link between life experiences and emotions is off-kilter. They may feel sad for no reason at all or a sense of elation in the absence of any great accomplishment. Many psychological disorders involve this kind of dysregulation in a person's emotional life. In this section we examine two such disorders: depressive disorders and bipolar disorders.

Depressive Disorders

Everyone feels blue sometimes. A romantic breakup, the death of a loved one, or a personal failure can cast a dark cloud over life. Sometimes, however, a person might feel unhappy and not know why. **Depressive disorders** are disorders in which the individual suffers from *depression*—an unrelenting lack of pleasure in life.

test yourself

1. Define four anxiety disorders.
2. What are the central features of obsessive-compulsive disorder?
3. Describe the symptoms of post-traumatic stress disorder (PTSD).

● **depressive disorders** Psychological disorders in which the individual suffers from depression—an unrelenting lack of pleasure in life.

This painting by Vincent Van Gogh, Portrait of Dr. Gachet, *reflects the extreme melancholy that characterizes the depressive disorders.*

● **major depressive disorder (MDD)**
Psychological disorder involving a significant depressive episode and depressed characteristics, such as lethargy and hopelessness, for at least 2 weeks.

Depressive disorders are common. A representative U.S. survey including individuals ages 13 and up found that approximately 30 percent reported a depressive episode or diagnosis in the last 12 months (Kessler & others, 2012). A number of successful individuals have been diagnosed with depression, including musicians Sheryl Crow, Eric Clapton, and Peter Gabriel; actors Drew Barrymore and Jim Carrey; and artist Pablo Picasso, photographer Diane Arbus, astronaut Buzz Aldrin (the second man to walk on the moon), famed architect Frank Lloyd Wright, and J. K. Rowling, the author of the *Harry Potter* series.

Major depressive disorder (MDD) involves a significant depressive episode and depressed characteristics, such as lethargy and hopelessness, for at least 2 weeks. MDD impairs daily functioning, and it has been called the leading cause of disability in the United States (NIMH, 2008). The symptoms of major depressive disorder may include:

- Depressed mood most of the day
- Reduced interest or pleasure in activities that were once enjoyable
- Significant weight loss or gain or significant decrease or increase in appetite
- Trouble sleeping or sleeping too much
- Fatigue or loss of energy
- Feeling worthless or guilty in an excessive or inappropriate manner
- Problems in thinking, concentrating, or making decisions
- Recurrent thoughts of death and suicide
- No history of manic episodes (periods of euphoric mood)

Individuals who experience less extreme depressive mood for over 2 months may be diagnosed with *persistent depressive disorder*. This disorder includes symptoms such as hopelessness, lack of energy, poor concentration, and sleep problems. A variety of biological, psychological, and sociocultural factors have been implicated in the development of depressive disorders.

BIOLOGICAL FACTORS

The biological factors implicated in depressive disorders include genes, brain structure and function, and neurotransmitters. Genes appear to play a role in depression (Chou & others, 2013; Goenjian & others, 2012), but they may do so in conjunction with experiences, again suggesting a vulnerability-stress association. For instance, depression has been linked to particular features of the serotonin transporter gene, called the 5-HTTLPR (Brummett & others, 2008; Middeldorp & others, 2007; Vinberg & others, 2010). Importantly, research shows that these features do not inevitably lead to depression. Rather, they are associated with depression only if the person's social environment is stressful (Petersen & others, 2012; Way & Gurbaxani, 2008; Zannas & others, 2012). In fact, individuals who possess these features are at a *decreased* risk for depression if they are also in a warm, positive social environment (Eley & others, 2004).

In addition, specific brain structures are involved in depression. For example, depressed individuals show lower levels of brain activity in a section of the prefrontal cortex that is involved in generating actions (Duman & others, 2012) and in regions of the brain associated with the perception of rewards in the environment (Howland, 2012). A depressed person's brain may not recognize opportunities for pleasurable experiences.

Depression also likely involves problems in neurotransmitter regulation. Individuals with depressive disorder appear to have too few receptors for the neurotransmitters serotonin and norepinephrine (Hamon & Blier, 2013; Houston & others, 2012).

PSYCHOLOGICAL FACTORS

Psychological explanations of depression have drawn on behavioral learning theories and cognitive theories. One behavioral view of depression focuses on learned helplessness (see Chapter 6), an individual's feelings of powerlessness following exposure to aversive circumstances, such as prolonged stress, over which the individual has no control. When people cannot control negative circumstances, they may feel helpless and stop trying to change their situation. This helplessness spirals into a feeling of hopelessness (Becker-Weidman & others, 2009).

Cognitive explanations of depression focus on thoughts and beliefs that can contribute to this sense of hopelessness (Fiske, Wetherell, & Gatz, 2009; Vilhauer & others, 2013). From this perspective, automatic negative thoughts reflect illogical self-defeating beliefs that shape the experiences of individuals who are depressed (Beck, 1967; Beck & Haigh, 2014). These habitual negative thoughts magnify negative experiences (de Graaf & others, 2010). For example, a person who is depressed might overgeneralize about a minor occurrence—say, turning in a work assignment late—and think that he or she is worthless. The accumulation of cognitive distortions can lead to depression (Gibbons & others, 2010).

The course of depression can be influenced by not only what people think but also *how* they think (Mathew & others, 2010). Depressed individuals may ruminate on negative experiences and negative feelings, playing them over and over again in their mind (Aldao, Nolen-Hoeksema, & Schweizer, 2010; Nolen-Hoeksema, 2011; Waller & Rose, 2013). This tendency to ruminate is associated with the development of depression (Aldao, Nolen-Hoeksema, & Schweizer, 2010).

Another cognitive view of depression focuses on the *attributions* people make—their attempts to explain what caused something to happen (Sanjuan, Arranz, & Castro, 2013; Seidel & others, 2012; Wong, Kim, & Tran, 2010). Many researchers believe that depression is related to a pessimistic attributional style. In this approach, individuals regularly explain negative events as having internal causes ("It is my fault I failed the exam"), stable causes ("I'm going to fail again and again"), and global causes ("Failing this exam shows that I won't do well in any of my courses"). Pessimistic attributional style means blaming oneself for negative events and expecting the negative events to recur in the future (Abramson, Seligman, & Teasdale, 1978).

This pessimistic attributional style can be contrasted with an optimistic attributional style. Optimists make external attributions for bad things that happen ("I did badly on the test because it's hard to know what a professor wants on the first exam"). They also recognize that these causes can change ("I'll do better on the next one") and that they are specific ("It was only one test"). Optimistic attributional style has been related to lowered depression and decreased suicide risk in a variety of samples (Rasmussen & Wingate, 2011; Tindle & others, 2012).

Combining the cognitive perspective with research on the brain, we might say that individuals with depression have a brain that is wired for attention to negative information and that their habitual patterns of thought and attributions produce well-worn neurological pathways for maintaining that unhappiness (De Raedt & Koster, 2010).

SOCIOCULTURAL FACTORS

Individuals with a low socioeconomic status (SES), especially people living in poverty, are more likely to develop depression than their higher-SES counterparts (Bryant-Davis & others, 2010; Groffen & others, 2013). Depression increases as standards of living and employment circumstances worsen (Lorant & others, 2007). Studies have found very high rates of depression in Native American groups, among whom poverty, hopelessness, and alcoholism are widespread (LaFromboise, Albright, & Harris, 2010; Teesson & Vogl, 2006).

Women are nearly twice as likely as men to be diagnosed with depression (Yuan & others, 2009). This gender difference

The incidence of depression is high among people living in poverty, as well as single women who are the heads of households.

psychological *inquiry*

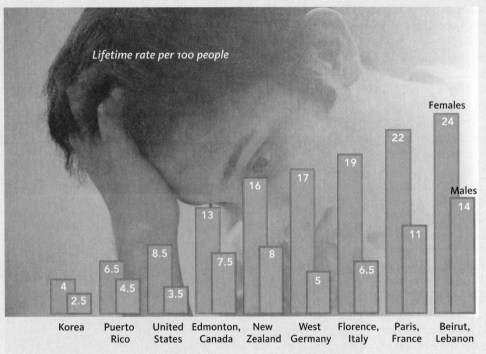

Lifetime rate per 100 people

Females 24
22
19
17
16
13
Males 14
11
8.5
8
7.5
6.5
6.5
6.5
5
4.5
4
3.5
2.5

Korea | Puerto Rico | United States | Edmonton, Canada | New Zealand | West Germany | Florence, Italy | Paris, France | Beirut, Lebanon

Depression Among Women and Men Across Cultures

The graph shows the rates of depression for women and men in nine different cultures (Weissman & Olfson, 1995). The rates represent the number of diagnosed cases per 100 people.

1. Which cultures have the highest and lowest levels of depression overall? What might account for these differences?

2. Which places have the biggest gender difference in depression? What might account for these differences?

3. In order to be diagnosed with depression, a person has to seek treatment for the disorder. How might gender influence a person's willingness to seek treatment?

4. How does your answer to question 3 influence the conclusions you would draw from the data illustrated in the graph?

occurs in many countries (Inaba & others, 2005; Nolen-Hoeksema, 2011). The Psychological Inquiry provides a closer look at gender differences in depression.

Bipolar Disorder

Just as we all have down times, there are times when things seem to be going phenomenally well. For individuals with bipolar disorder, the ups and downs of life take on an extreme and often harmful tone. **Bipolar disorder** is characterized by extreme mood swings that include one or more episodes of *mania,* an overexcited, unrealistically optimistic state. During a manic episode the person feels euphoric and energetic and might sleep very little. A manic state also features an impulsivity that can lead to trouble, such as spending one's life savings on a foolish business venture.

The severity of manic episodes is used to distinguish between two types of bipolar disorder. *Bipolar I disorder* refers to individuals who have extreme manic episodes during which they may experience hallucinations—that is, seeing or hearing things that are not there. *Bipolar II disorder* refers to the milder version in which the individual may experience a less extreme level of euphoria.

Most individuals with bipolar disorder experience multiple cycles of depression interspersed with mania (Hammen & Keenan-Miller, 2013). These people can have manic and depressive episodes four or more times a year, but they usually are separated by 6 months to a year. Bipolar disorder is equally common in women and men. Academy Award–winning actor Catherine Zeta-Jones, famed dancer and choreographer Alvin Ailey, and actor Carrie Fisher (Princess Leia in *Star Wars*) have been diagnosed with bipolar disorder.

What factors play a role in the development of bipolar disorder? Genetic influences are stronger predictors of bipolar disorder than of depressive disorder (Craddock & Forty, 2006; Pirooznia & others, 2012). An individual with an identical twin who has bipolar disorder has about a 70 percent probability of also having the disorder, and a fraternal twin has a more than 10 percent probability (Figure 15.4). Researchers

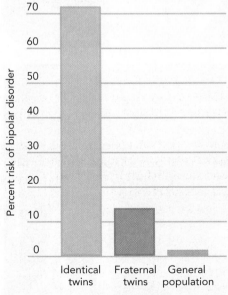

FIGURE 15.4 Risk of Bipolar Disorder in Identical and Fraternal Twins If One Twin Has the Disorder, and in the General Population Notice how much stronger the similarity of bipolar disorder is in identical twins, compared with fraternal twins and the general population. These statistics suggest a strong genetic role in the disorder.

continue to work toward identifying specific genetic under-pinnings of bipolar disorder (Crisafulli & others, 2013; Frey & others, 2013; Rybakowski, 2013).

Other biological processes are also a factor. Bipolar disorder is associated with differences in brain activity. Figure 15.5 shows the metabolic activity in the cerebral cortex of an individual cycling through depressive and manic phases. Notice the decrease in metabolic activity in the brain during depression and the increase in metabolic activity during mania (Baxter & others, 1995). In addition to high levels of norepinephrine and low levels of serotonin, studies link high levels of the neurotransmitter glutamate to bipolar disorder (Dhillon, 2012; Fountoulakis, 2012: Singh & others, 2010; Sourial-Bassillious & others, 2009).

Recently, mental health professionals have noted cases of children who appear to suffer from bipolar disorder (Cosgrove, Roybal, & Chang, 2013; Defilippis & Wagner, 2013). A key dilemma is that treating bipolar disorder in adults involves psychoactive drugs, and these medications have not been approved for use in children. The potential side effects of these drugs could put children's health and development at risk. To address this issue, *DSM-5* included a new diagnosis, *disruptive mood dysregulation disorder*, which is considered a depressive disorder in children who show persistent irritability and recurrent episodes of out-of-control behavior (APA, 2013a). This decision is not without controversy. As we saw with ADHD, it is not clear that children who are prone to wild mood swings are not, simply, children.

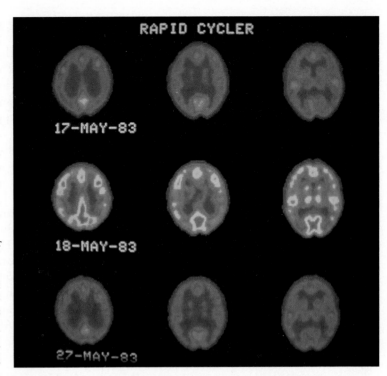

FIGURE 15.5 **Brain Metabolism in Mania and Depression** PET scans of an individual with bipolar disorder, who is described as a rapid cycler because of how quickly severe mood changes occurred (*Top and bottom*) The person's brain in a depressed state (*Middle*) A manic state. The PET scans reveal how the brain's energy consumption falls in depression and rises in mania. The red areas in the middle row reflect rapid consumption of glucose.

4- DISSOCIATIVE DISORDERS

Have you ever been on a long car ride and completely lost track of time, so that you could not even remember a stretch of miles along the road? Have you been so caught up in a daydream that you were unaware of the passage of time? These are examples of normal dissociation. *Dissociation* refers to psychological states in which the person feels disconnected from immediate experience.

At the extreme of dissociation are individuals who feel a sense of disconnection *persistently*. **Dissociative disorders** are psychological disorders that involve a sudden loss of memory or change in identity. Under extreme stress or shock, the individual's conscious awareness becomes *dissociated* (separated or split) from previous memories and thoughts (Espirito-Santo & Pio-Abreu, 2009; Spiegel & others, 2013).

Psychologists believe that dissociation is an individual's way of dealing with extreme stress (Spiegel & others, 2013). Through dissociation the individual mentally protects his or her conscious self from the traumatic event. Dissociative disorders often occur in individuals who also show signs of PTSD (Lanius & others, 2012). Both of these disorders are thought to be rooted, in part, in extremely traumatic life events (Foote & others, 2006). The notion that dissociative disorders are related to problems in pulling together emotional memories is supported by findings showing lower volume in the hippocampus and amygdala in individuals with dissociative disorders (Vermetten & others, 2006). The hippocampus is especially involved in consolidating memory and organizing life experience into a coherent whole (Sar, Akyuz, & Dogan, 2007; Spiegel, 2006). Two kinds of dissociative disorders are dissociative amnesia and dissociative identity disorder.

test yourself

1. What are the features of major depressive disorder (MDD)?
2. Give at least two biological, two psychological, and two sociocultural factors in depression.
3. What are the essential characteristics of bipolar disorder, and how are they different in bipolar I versus bipolar II?

● **bipolar disorder** Psychological disorder characterized by extreme mood swings that include one or more episodes of mania, an overexcited, unrealistically optimistic state.

● **dissociative disorders** Psychological disorders that involve a sudden loss of memory or change in identity due to the dissociation (separation) of the individual's conscious awareness from previous memories and thoughts.

Dissociative Amnesia

● **dissociative amnesia** Dissociative disorder characterized by extreme memory loss that is caused by extensive psychological stress.

Recall from Chapter 7 that *amnesia* is the inability to recall important events (Markowitsch & Staniloiu, 2012). **Dissociative amnesia** is a type of amnesia characterized by extreme memory loss that stems from extensive psychological stress (Dell, 2013). A person experiencing dissociative amnesia still remembers things like how to hail a cab or use a phone. Only aspects of their own identity and autobiographical experiences are forgotten.

Sometimes individuals suffering from dissociative amnesia will unexpectedly travel away from home, even assuming a new identity. For instance, on August 28, 2008, Hannah Upp, a 23-year-old middle schoolteacher in New York City, disappeared while out for a run (Marx & Didziulis, 2009). She had no wallet, identification, cell phone, or money. Her family and friends posted flyers around the city and messages on the Internet. As days went by, they became increasingly concerned that something terrible had happened. Finally, Hannah was found floating face down in the New York harbor on September 16, sunburned and dehydrated but alive. She remembered nothing of her experiences. To her, it felt like she had gone out for a run and 10 minutes later was being pulled from the harbor. To this day, she does not know what event might have led to her dissociative amnesia nor does she remember how she survived during her 2-week disappearance. At one point while she was missing, someone approached her and asked if she was the Hannah everyone was looking for. She answered no.

Dissociative Identity Disorder

● **dissociative identity disorder (DID)** Dissociative disorder in which the individual has two or more distinct personalities or selves, each with its own memories, behaviors, and relationships; formerly called multiple personality disorder.

Dissociative identity disorder (DID), formerly called *multiple personality disorder,* is the most dramatic, least common, and most controversial dissociative disorder. Individuals with this disorder have two or more distinct personalities or identities (Belli & others, 2012). Each identity has its own memories, behaviors, and relationships. One identity dominates at one time; another takes over at another time.

A famous real-life example of dissociative identity disorder (DID) is the "three faces of Eve" case, based on the life of a woman named Chris Sizemore (Thigpen & Cleckley, 1957) (Figure 15.6). Eve White was the original dominant personality. She had no knowledge of her second personality, Eve Black, although Eve Black had been alternating with Eve White for a number of years. Eve White was quiet and serious, Eve Black was carefree and mischievous. Eve Black would emerge at the most inappropriate times, leaving Eve White with hangovers, bills, and a reputation in local bars that she could not explain. During treatment, Jane, a third personality, emerged.

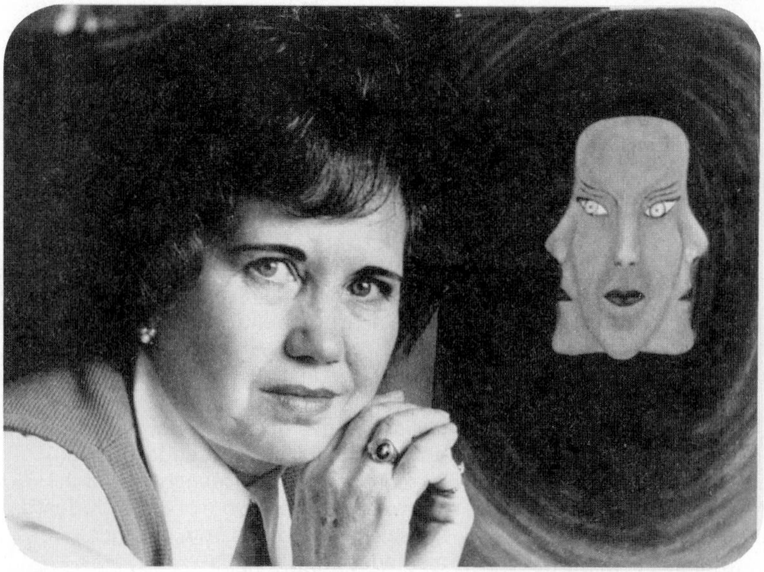

The factors that contribute to DID remain something of a mystery (Boysen & VanBergen, 2013). Research suggests that a high rate of extraordinarily severe sexual or physical abuse during early childhood is related to the condition (Ross & Ness, 2010). Some psychologists believe that a child can cope with intense trauma by dissociating from the experience and developing alternate selves as protectors. Sexual abuse has been reported in as many as 70 percent or more of DID cases (Foote & others, 2006); however, the majority of individuals who have been sexually abused do not develop DID. The vast majority of individuals with DID are women.

Dissociative identity disorder is a controversial diagnosis (Freeland & others, 1993; Sar, Akyuz, & Dogan, 2007; Spiegel, 2006). Until the 1980s, only about 300 cases of DID had ever been reported, but in the years since hundreds more have been diagnosed (Gentile, Dillon, & Gillig, 2013). Between 2000 and 2010, some 1,171 new cases were identified (Boysen & VanBergen, 2013).

FIGURE 15.6   The Three Faces of Eve Chris Sizemore, the subject of the 1950s book and film *The Three Faces of Eve,* is shown here with a work she painted titled *Three Faces in One.*

Social cognitive theorists point out that DID has tended to increase whenever the popular media present a case, such as the film *The Three Faces of Eve*, the miniseries *Sybil*, or the Showtime drama *The United States of Tara*. From this perspective, after exposure to these examples, people may be more likely to view multiple identities as a real condition and develop the disorder through a process of social contagion (as described in Chapter 13). However, research comparing China (a culture in which DID is not widely publicized) and Canada (where it is) shows that dissociative experiences (and traumatic events) were similar across both groups (Ross & others, 2008), casting some doubt on the notion that dissociative experiences are entirely a product of social contagion.

Some experts believe that dissociative identity disorder is a *social construction*—that it represents a category some people adopt to make sense out of their experiences (Spanos, 1996). Rather than being a single person with many conflicting feelings, wishes, and potentially awful experiences, the individual compartmentalizes different aspects of the self into independent identities. In some cases, therapists have been accused of creating alternate personalities. Encountering an individual who appears to have a fragmented sense of self, the therapist may begin to treat each fragment as its own "personality" (Spiegel, 2006).

5· SCHIZOPHRENIA

Have you had the experience of watching a movie and suddenly noticing that the film bears an uncanny resemblance to your life? Have you ever listened to a radio talk show and realized that the host was saying exactly what you were just thinking? Do these moments mean something special about you, or are they coincidences? For individuals with severe psychological disorders, such random experiences take on special and personal meaning.

Psychosis refers to a state in which a person's perceptions and thoughts are fundamentally removed from reality. *DSM-5* recognizes a class of disorders called "schizophrenia spectrum and other psychotic disorders." Within this group is one of the most debilitating psychological disorders and our focus in this section: schizophrenia.

Schizophrenia is a severe psychological disorder that is characterized by highly disordered thought processes. Individuals with schizophrenia may see things that are not there, hear voices inside their heads, and live in a terrifying world of twisted logic. They may say odd things, show inappropriate emotion, and move their bodies in peculiar ways. Often, they are socially withdrawn and isolated.

Schizophrenia is usually diagnosed in early adulthood, around age 18 for men and 25 for women. The suicide risk for individuals with schizophrenia is eight times that for the general population (Pompili & others, 2007).

Symptoms of Schizophrenia

Psychologists classify the symptoms of schizophrenia into positive symptoms, negative symptoms, and cognitive deficits (NIMH, 2008).

POSITIVE SYMPTOMS

Positive symptoms involve a distortion or an excess of normal function. They are "positive" because they reflect something added above and beyond normal behavior. Positive symptoms of schizophrenia include hallucinations, delusions, thought disorders, and movement disorders.

Hallucinations are sensory experiences that occur in the absence of real stimuli. Hallucinations are usually auditory—the person might complain of hearing voices—or visual, and much less commonly they take the form of smells or tastes (Bhatia & others, 2009). Visual hallucinations involve seeing things that are not there. For example, at the age of 21, while serving in Vietnam as a medical corpsman for the Marines,

test yourself

1. What are the main characteristics of dissociative disorders? What does the word *dissociative* mean in reference to them?
2. Identify the characteristics of dissociative amnesia.
3. What explanations have experts given for the development of dissociative identity disorder (DID) in individuals?

● **psychosis** Psychological state in which a person's perceptions and thoughts are fundamentally removed from reality.

● **schizophrenia** Severe psychological disorder characterized by highly disordered thought processes; individuals suffering from schizophrenia may be referred to as psychotic because they are so far removed from reality.

● **hallucinations** Sensory experiences that occur in the absence of real stimuli.

● **delusions** False, unusual, and sometimes magical beliefs that are not part of an individual's culture.

● **thought disorder** The unusual, sometimes bizarre thought processes that are characteristic positive symptoms of schizophrenia.

● **referential thinking** Ascribing personal meaning to completely random events.

● **movement disorders** The unusual mannerisms, body movements, and facial expressions that are characteristic positive symptoms of schizophrenia.

● **catatonia** State of immobility and unresponsiveness lasting for long periods of time.

● **flat affect** The display of little or no emotion—a common negative symptom of schizophrenia.

FIGURE 15.7 Disorders of Movement in Schizophrenia Unusual motor behaviors are positive symptoms of schizophrenia. Individuals may cease to move altogether (a state called catatonia), sometimes holding bizarre postures.

Moe Armstrong experienced a psychotic break. Dead Vietcong soldiers appeared to talk to him, beg him for help, and did not seem to realize that they were dead. Armstrong, now a successful businessman and a sought-after public speaker who holds two master's degrees, relies on medication to keep such experiences at bay (Bonfatti, 2005).

Delusions are false, unusual, and sometimes magical beliefs that are not part of an individual's culture. A delusional person might think that he is Jesus Christ or Muhammad; another might imagine that her thoughts are being broadcast over the radio. Delusions can be difficult to change.

For individuals with schizophrenia, delusional beliefs that might seem completely illogical to the outsider are experienced as all too real. At one point in his life, Bill Garrett, a college student with schizophrenia, was convinced that a blister on his hand was a sign of gangrene. So strong was his belief that he tried to cut off his hand with a knife, before being stopped by his family (M. Park, 2009).

Thought disorder refers to the unusual, sometimes bizarre thought processes that are characteristic positive symptoms of schizophrenia. The thoughts of persons with schizophrenia can be disorganized and confused. Often individuals with schizophrenia do not make sense when they talk or write. For example, someone with schizophrenia might say, "Well, Rocky, babe, happening, but where, when, up, top, side, over, you know, out of the way, that's it. Sign off." Such speech has no meaning for the listener. The individual might also make up new words (*neologisms*) (Kerns & others, 1999). In addition, a person with schizophrenia can show **referential thinking,** which means ascribing personal meaning to completely random events. For instance, the individual might believe that a dead bird on the sidewalk is a sign from God or that a person walking nearby is an agent from the government.

Movement disorders are a final positive symptom of schizophrenia, involving unusual mannerisms, body movements, and facial expressions. The individual may repeat certain motions over and over or, in extreme cases, may become catatonic. **Catatonia** is a state of immobility and unresponsiveness that lasts for long periods of time (Figure 15.7).

NEGATIVE SYMPTOMS

Whereas schizophrenia's positive symptoms are characterized by a distortion or an excess of normal functions, schizophrenia's *negative symptoms* reflect social withdrawal, behavioral deficits, and the loss or decrease of normal functions. One negative symptom is **flat affect,** which means the display of little or no emotion (Alvino & others, 2007; Lepage & others, 2011). Individuals with schizophrenia also may be lacking in the ability to read the emotions of others (Chambon, Baudouin, & Franck, 2006). They may show a deficient ability to plan, initiate, and engage in goal-directed behavior.

COGNITIVE SYMPTOMS

Cognitive symptoms of schizophrenia include deficits in executive functioning (Kluwe-Schiavon & others, 2013), including difficulty sustaining attention, problems holding information in memory, and inability to interpret information and make decisions (Harvey & Bowie, 2013; Kerns, 2007; Sitnikova, Goff, & Kuperberg, 2009).

Causes of Schizophrenia

A great deal of research has investigated schizophrenia's causes, including biological, psychological, and sociocultural factors.

BIOLOGICAL FACTORS

Research provides strong support for biological explanations of schizophrenia. Particularly compelling is the evidence for a genetic predisposition (Tao & others, 2012), but structural brain abnormalities and problems with neurotransmitter regulation also are linked to this disorder (Perez-Costas & others, 2012; Sugranyes & others, 2012).

psychological *inquiry*

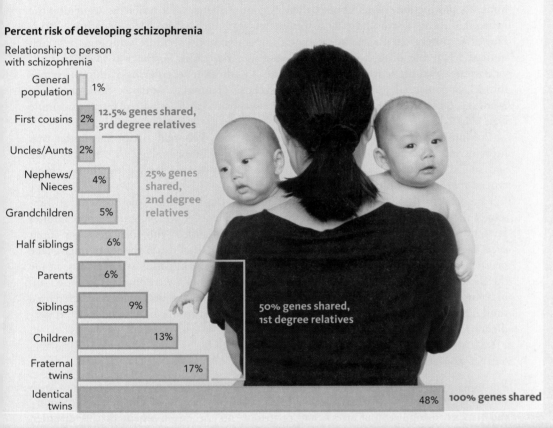

Percent risk of developing schizophrenia

Relationship to person with schizophrenia

General population	1%
First cousins	2%
Uncles/Aunts	2%
Nephews/ Nieces	4%
Grandchildren	5%
Half siblings	6%
Parents	6%
Siblings	9%
Children	13%
Fraternal twins	17%
Identical twins	48%

12.5% genes shared, 3rd degree relatives

25% genes shared, 2nd degree relatives

50% genes shared, 1st degree relatives

100% genes shared

The Association of Genes with Schizophrenia

This figure shows that as genetic relatedness to an individual with schizophrenia increases, so does the lifetime risk of developing schizophrenia. Using the graph, answer these questions:

1. Which familial relations have the lowest and highest level of genetic overlap (shared genes)?

2. What is the difference in genetic overlap between identical twins and non-twin siblings?

3. What is the difference in risk of schizophrenia between identical twins and non-twin siblings of individuals with schizophrenia?

4. What do you think accounts for the differences in your answers to questions 2 and 3?

Genes Research supports the notion that schizophrenia is at least partially explained by genetic factors (Aberg & others, 2013; Paul-Samojedny & others, 2010; Vasco, Cardinale, & Polonia, 2012). Researchers are seeking to pinpoint the chromosomal location of genes involved in susceptibility to schizophrenia (Réthelyi, Benkovits, & Bitter, 2013; Tsang & others, 2013). The Psychological Inquiry shows the results of research examining the role of genetics in schizophrenia.

Structural Brain Abnormalities Studies have found structural brain abnormalities in people with schizophrenia, specifically enlarged ventricles (Acer & others, 2010; Killgore & others, 2009; Rais & others, 2012). Ventricles are fluid-filled spaces, and enlargement of the ventricles indicates deterioration in other brain tissue.

Individuals with schizophrenia also have a smaller prefrontal cortex and lower activity in this area of the brain than healthy individuals (Smieskova & others, 2010). The prefrontal cortex is the region where thinking, planning, and decision making take place. Recall from Chapter 9 that the prefrontal cortex continues to develop throughout adolescence and into early adulthood. It may be telling that the emergence of symptoms of schizophrenia, which typically occurs in young adulthood, happens during the time when the prefrontal cortex becomes fully connected.

Still, differences between the brains of healthy individuals and those with schizophrenia are small (NIMH, 2008). Microscopic studies of brain tissue after death reveal small changes in the distribution or characteristics of brain cells in persons with schizophrenia.

Many of these changes seem to have occurred prenatally because they are not accompanied by glial cells, which are always present when a brain injury occurs after birth (Vuillermot & others, 2010). Problems in prenatal development may predispose a brain to developing schizophrenic symptoms later in life (Fatemi & Folsom, 2009).

Neurotransmitter Regulation Whether it is differences in amount of dopamine, its production, or its uptake, there is good evidence that problems regulating the neurotransmitter dopamine play a role in schizophrenia (Brito-Melo & others, 2012: Howes & others, 2012). A link between dopamine and psychotic symptoms was first noticed when the drug L-dopa (which increases dopamine levels) was given to individuals as a treatment for Parkinson disease. In addition to relieving Parkinson symptoms, L-dopa caused some to experience psychosis (Janowsky, Addario, & Risch, 1987; Madras, 2013). Further, drugs that reduce psychotic symptoms often block dopamine (van Os & Kapur, 2009).

Previously we have encountered dopamine as the "feel good" neurotransmitter that helps us recognize rewarding stimuli in the environment and relates to being outgoing and sociable. How can a neurotransmitter that is associated with good things play a crucial role in schizophrenia?

One way to think about this puzzle is to view dopamine as a neurochemical messenger that shouts out, "Hey! This is important!" whenever we encounter opportunities for reward. Imagine what it might be like to be bombarded with such messages about even the smallest details of life (Rosier & others, 2010). Private thoughts might take on such dramatic proportions that they sound like someone else's voice talking inside the person's head. Fleeting ideas, such as "The traffic lights are turning red *because* I am in a hurry," suddenly seem not silly but true. Hallucinations, delusions, and referential thinking may be expressions of the individual's attempts to make sense of such extraordinary feelings (Kapur, 2003).

PSYCHOLOGICAL FACTORS

Psychologists used to explain schizophrenia as rooted in childhood experiences with unresponsive parents. Such explanations have fallen by the wayside. Contemporary theorists do recognize that stress may contribute to the development of this disorder. Experiences are now viewed through the lens of the vulnerability-stress hypothesis, suggesting that individual with schizophrenia may have biological risk factors that interact with experience to produce the disorder.

SOCIOCULTURAL FACTORS

Sociocultural background is not considered a *cause* of schizophrenia, but sociocultural factors do appear to affect the *course* of the disorder, or how it progresses. Across cultures, individuals with schizophrenia in developing, nonindustrialized nations tend to have better outcomes than those in developed, industrialized nations (Jablensky, 2000; Myers, 2010). This difference may be due to the fact that in developing nations, family and friends are more accepting and supportive of individuals with schizophrenia. In Western samples, marriage, warm supportive friends (Jablensky & others, 1992; Wiersma & others, 1998), and employment are related to better outcomes for individuals diagnosed with schizophrenia (Rosen & Garety, 2005).

Some experts have called for a focus on preventing schizophrenia by identifying those at risk and then intervening early to reduce the level of disability they experience (Addington & others, 2011; Walder & others, 2013). Early intervention can be important because a strong predictor of relapse (that is, having symptoms again after treatment) is the amount of time a person spends in a psychotic state without treatment (ten Velden Hegelstad & others, 2012).

Is there a way to know who might be at risk for schizophrenia? A recent study showed that among those with a family history of schizophrenia, lower levels of *social* functioning distinguished those who went on to develop schizophrenia from others (Cornblatt & others, 2012).

test yourself

1. What is schizophrenia?
2. What are some positive and negative symptoms of schizophrenia?
3. How is dopamine thought to be involved in schizophrenia?

6· PERSONALITY DISORDERS

Are there aspects of your personality that you would like to change? Maybe you worry too much or fall in love too easily. Imagine that your very personality—who you really are—is the core of your life difficulties. **Personality disorders** are chronic, maladaptive cognitive-behavioral patterns that are thoroughly integrated into an individual's personality. Personality disorders affect a person's sense of self and capacity for relationships with others (Trull, Carpenter, & Widiger, 2013). Such disorders are relatively common. In a study of a representative U.S. sample, researchers found that 15 percent had a personality disorder (Grant & others, 2004).

DSM-5 lists 10 personality disorders (Figure 15.8). Below, we survey the two personality disorders that have been studied most extensively: antisocial personality disorder and borderline personality disorder. As we review below, both of these disorders are associated with dire consequences.

● **personality disorders** Chronic, maladaptive cognitive-behavioral patterns that are thoroughly integrated into an individual's personality.

Antisocial Personality Disorder

Antisocial personality disorder (ASPD) is characterized by guiltlessness, law-breaking, exploitation of others, irresponsibility, and deceit. Those with this disorder are aggressive

● **antisocial personality disorder (ASPD)** Psychological disorder characterized by guiltlessness, law-breaking, exploitation of others, irresponsibility, and deceit.

Personality Disorder	Description
Paranoid Personality Disorder	Paranoia, suspiciousness, and deep distrust of others. People with this disorder are always on the lookout for danger and the slightest social mistreatment. They may be socially isolated.
Schizoid Personality Disorder	Extreme lack of interest in interpersonal relationships. People with this disorder are emotionally cold and apathetic, and they are generally detached from interpersonal life.
Schizotypal Personality Disorder	Socially isolated and prone to odd thinking. People with this disorder often have elaborate and strange belief systems and attribute unusual meanings to life events and experiences.
Antisocial Personality Disorder	Manipulative, deceitful, and amoral. People with this disorder lack empathy for others, are egocentric, and are willing to use others for their own personal gain.
Borderline Personality Disorder	Emotionally volatile and unstable sense of self. These individuals are prone to mood swings, excessive self-criticism, extreme judgments of others, and are preoccupied with being abandoned.
Histrionic Personality Disorder	Attention-seeking, dramatic, lively, and flirtatious. These individuals are inappropriately seductive in their interactions with others.
Narcissistic Personality Disorder	Self-aggrandizing yet overly dependent on the evaluations of others. People with this disorder view themselves as entitled and better than others. They show deficits in empathy and in understanding the feelings of others.
Avoidant Personality Disorder	Socially inhibited and prone to feelings of inadequacy, anxiety, and shame. These individuals feel inadequate and hold back in social situations. They have unrealistic standards for their own behavior and avoid setting goals, taking personal risks, or pursuing new activities.
Dependent Personality Disorder	Dependent on others for emotional and physical needs. People with this disorder perceive others as powerful and competent and themselves as childlike and helpless.
Obsessive-Compulsive Personality Disorder	Conforming rigidly to rules. These individuals show an excessive attachment to moral codes and are excessively orderly in daily life.

FIGURE 15.8 **The 10 Personality Disorders Included in *DSM-5*** Diagnoses of these disorders require that the person be over the age of 18, and all involve pervasive aspects of the person that color their cognition, emotion, and behavior. Note that some of the labels are potentially confusing. Schizoid and schizotypal personality disorders are not the same thing as schizophrenia (though schizotypal personality disorder may proceed to schizophrenia). Further, obsessive-compulsive personality disorder is not the same thing as obsessive-compulsive disorder.

(Lobbestael, Cima, & Arntz, 2013) and potentially violent (Yiend & others, 2013). ASPD is far more common in men than in women (Cale & Lilienfeld, 2002).

ASPD is characterized by:

- Failure to conform to social norms or obey the law
- Deceitfulness, lying, or conning others for personal profit or pleasure
- Impulsivity
- Irritability and aggressiveness, getting into physical fights or perpetrating assaults
- Reckless disregard for the safety of self or others
- Consistent irresponsibility, inconsistent work behavior, not paying bills
- Lack of remorse, showing indifference to the pain of others, or rationalizing, having hurt or mistreated another

ASPD is related to criminal behavior, but not all individuals with ASPD engage in crime, and not all criminals suffer from ASPD. Individuals with ASPD can be successful. There are antisocial physicians, clergy, journalists, law enforcement officers, and just about any other occupation. Still, such individuals tend to exploit others, lack empathy, and break the rules.

A number of factors intertwine to produce ASPD. Research has linked ASPD to low levels of activation in the prefrontal cortex and has related these brain differences to poor decision making and problems in learning (Yang & Raine, 2009). Both genetic factors (L. F. Garcia & others, 2010) and childhood abuse are associated with ASPD, but there is evidence that genetic differences may distinguish abused children who go on to commit violent acts from those who do not (Caspi & others, 2002; Lynam & others, 2007).

Individuals with ASPD show lower levels of autonomic nervous system arousal and are less stressed than others by aversive circumstances, including punishment (Fung & others, 2005). They have the ability to keep their cool while engaging in deception (Verschuere & others, 2005), suggesting that those with ASPD might be able to fool a polygraph. The underaroused autonomic nervous system may be a key difference between adolescents who become antisocial adults and those whose behavior improves during adulthood (Raine, Venables, & Williams, 1990).

Psychopaths are one subgroup of individuals with ASPD (Strickland & others, 2013). They are remorseless predators who engage in violence to get what they want. Examples include serial killers John Wayne Gacy (who murdered 33 boys and young men) and Ted Bundy (who confessed to murdering at least 30 young women).

Research on prison inmates with ASPD (all of whom committed violent offenses) shows that those who are classified as psychopaths have lower levels of gray matter than those who are not (Decety, Skelly, & Kiehl, 2013; Gregory & others, 2012). Recall from Chapter 11 that gray matter is thought to be associated with empathy. Not surprisingly, psychopaths show deficits in theory of mind (Shamay-Tsoory & others, 2010).

A key challenge in treating individuals with ASPD, including psychopaths, is their ability to con even sophisticated mental health professionals. Those with ASPD may resist engaging in a therapeutic relationship because it involves giving up a sense of power or control (McRae, 2013). Many never seek therapy, and others end up in prison, where treatment is rarely an option.

Psychopathy refers to a set of personality traits that are often separated into two types: antisocial/impulsive (being callous, risk-taking, shameless, showing poor self-control) and fearless dominance (being dominant, bold, and daring) (Hare, 2003). Although many aspects of psychopathy are undeniably bad, recently researchers have begun to note that parts of psychopathy might have benefits not only for the person but for society. Consider that being a good leader might require that a person show fearless dominance, forcefulness, boldness, and maybe even a little cold-bloodedness. Might those aspects of psychopathy indicating fearless dominance have payoffs for leadership? A recent study examined this question in an interesting group of leaders: presidents of the United States. To read about this intriguing work, see the Intersection.

John Wayne Gacy (top) and Ted Bundy (bottom) exemplify the subgroup of people with ASPD who are also psychopathic.

Clinical Psychology and Personality Psychology: Are Aspects of Psychopathy Related to Leadership Success?

Scott Lilienfeld and his colleagues (2012) gathered a host of information about each of the U.S. presidents up to and including George W. Bush. Historians who were experts on each president made ratings of his personality. Those ratings were used as measures of psychopathy, including antisocial/impulsiveness and fearless dominance. The researchers collected evidence about each man's presidency, such as the amount of legislation passed, foreign policy accomplishments, willingness to take risks, and ability to avoid crucial mistakes, as well as surveys among historians about presidential effectiveness.

Overall, being antisocial and impulsive was unrelated to presidential performance, but fearless dominance predicted many indicators of success. Presidents who scored higher on fearless dominance had higher overall performance ratings and were higher in public persuasiveness, crisis management, leadership, and agenda setting (Lilienfeld & others, 2012).

Which presidents were highest on fearless dominance? These are the rankings for the top five as well as all the living presidents:

1. Theodore Roosevelt
2. John F. Kennedy
3. Franklin D. Roosevelt
4. Ronald Reagan
5. Rutherford B. Hayes
7. Bill Clinton
10. George W. Bush
18. Jimmy Carter
30. George H. W. Bush

Certainly, this work does *not* indicate that any U.S. presidents were psychopaths. Rather, it suggests that aspects of personality indicating boldness related to especially high levels of presidential success. Lilienfeld and his colleagues suggest that fearless dominance, although part of a very undesirable constellation of traits, may be important for individuals who are engaged in extremely high-stakes decision making in the uppermost positions of authority. In such contexts, characteristics related to psychopathy may serve a functional role.

Can you recognize fearless dominance in the leaders in your life?

These results are controversial, and some have argued that if fearless dominance predicts functional outcomes, then it cannot really be part of psychopathy (Lynam & Miller, 2012). Others argue that psychopathy *is* just that complex: It involves some traits that allow psychopaths to be charming, to woo vulnerable individuals, and to take advantage of others (Lilienfeld & others, 2012). After all, if psychopaths were only characterized by their most maladaptive traits, they would not be such a dangerous puzzle for the social world.

President Theodore Roosevelt (left) and President Bill Clinton (right).

Borderline Personality Disorder

Borderline personality disorder (BPD) is a pervasive pattern of instability in interpersonal relationships, self-image, and emotions. Individuals with BPD are impulsive, insecure, and emotional. BPD is related to self-harming behaviors, such as cutting (Gratz & others, 2012) and suicide (D. L. Turnbull & others, 2013).

At the very core of borderline personality disorder is profound instability—in mood, in sense of self, in relationships. Four essential features characterize BPD (Trull & Brown, 2013):

- Unstable affect
- Unstable sense of self and identity, including self-destructive impulsive behavior and chronic feelings of emptiness

● **borderline personality disorder (BPD)** Psychological disorder characterized by a pervasive pattern of instability in interpersonal relationships, self-image, and emotions, and of marked impulsivity beginning by early adulthood and present in a variety of contexts.

Impulsivity of the type that can lead to self-harm can be a symptom of borderline personality disorder.

test yourself

1. How are personality disorders defined?
2. To what sorts of behaviors is antisocial personality disorder related?
3. How is borderline personality disorder defined, and what are four features that characterize it?

■ Negative interpersonal relationships, which are unstable, intense, and characterized by extreme shifts between idealization and devaluation

■ Self-harm, including recurrent suicidal behavior, gestures, or threats or self-mutilating behavior

To cope with their unstable emotional lives, individuals with BPD may engage in a variety of maladaptive behaviors, among them drinking alcohol and using illicit substances (Compton & others, 2013; Jahng & others, 2011). BPD is more common in women than men, among those in low-income brackets, and among those younger than 30 (Tomko & others, 2013). A renowned expert on BPD, Marsha Linehan revealed that she herself has struggled with the disorder (Carey, 2011a).

The potential causes of BPD are complex and likely include biological factors and childhood experiences. The role of genes in BPD has been demonstrated in a variety of studies and across cultures (Distel & others, 2008, 2012; Mulder, 2012). Many individuals with BPD report experiences of childhood sexual abuse, physical abuse, and neglect (De Fruyt & De Clercq, 2012; Lobbestael & Arntz, 2010). It is not clear, however, whether abuse is a primary cause of the disorder (Trull, Carpenter, & Widiger, 2013). Rather, childhood abuse experiences may combine with genetic factors in promoting BPD.

Cognitive factors associated with BPD include a tendency to hold the irrational beliefs that one is powerless and innately unacceptable (Leahy & McGinn, 2012) and that other people are dangerous and hostile (Arntz, 2005). Individuals with BPD also display *hypervigilance:* the tendency to be constantly on the alert, looking for threatening information in the environment (Sieswerda & others, 2007).

Individuals with BPD are very sensitive to how others treat them. They tend to see the world in either-or terms, a thinking style called *splitting.* For example, they typically view other people as either hated enemies with no positive qualities or as beloved, idealized friends who can do no wrong.

Up until about 20 years ago, experts thought that BPD was untreatable, but evidence suggests that many individuals with BPD show improvement over time. As many as 50 percent of individuals with BPD improve within 2 years, and once improved they are not likely to relapse (Gunderson, 2008). One key aspect of improvement appears to be reductions in social stress, such as leaving an abusive romantic partner or establishing a sense of trust in a therapist (Gunderson & others, 2003).

7· SUICIDE

Thinking about suicide is not necessarily abnormal, but attempting or completing the act of suicide is. Sadly, many individuals who, to the outside eye, seem to be leading successful lives have ended their lives through suicide. Examples include poet Sylvia Plath, novelist Ernest Hemingway, and grunge icon Kurt Cobain.

According to the Centers for Disease Control and Prevention (CDC), in 2010, 38,364 people in the United States committed suicide, and suicide was the 10th-leading cause of death in the country for all ages (CDC, 2012a). There are twice as many suicide as homicides in the United States, and the suicide rate increased 13 percent from 1999 to 2010 (Schmitz & others, 2012). Suicide is the third-leading cause of death today in U.S. adolescents ages 13 through 19 (Murphy, Xu, & Kochanek, 2012) and children ages 10 to 14 (NIMH, 2010).

Given these grim statistics, psychologists work with individuals to reduce the frequency and intensity of suicidal impulses. You can do your part. Figure 15.9 provides good advice on what to do and what not to do if you encounter someone who is threatening suicide.

What might prompt an individual to end his or her own life? Biological, psychological, and sociocultural circumstances can be contributing factors.

Suicide tends to run in families. Five suicides occurred in different generations of the Hemingway family, including author Ernest (left) and his granddaughter Margaux (right).

Biological Factors

Genetic factors appear to play a role in suicide, which tends to run in families (Althoff & others, 2012; Peñas-Liedó, Naranjo, & Lierena, 2013). One famous family that has been plagued by suicide is the Hemingways. Five members of that family, spread across generations, committed suicide, including the writer Ernest Hemingway and his granddaughter Margaux, a model and actor. Similarly, in 2009, Nicholas Hughes—a successful marine biologist and the son of Sylvia Plath, a poet who had killed herself—tragically hanged himself. In considering these examples, you might note that Margaux Hemingway and Nicholas Hughes had experienced the suicide of a family member and might therefore have been more likely than most people to view suicide as a way to cope with life's difficulties.

A number of studies link suicide with low levels of serotonin and serotonin-linked genes (Enoch & others, 2013; Lyddon & others, 2013). Poor physical health, especially when it is chronic, is another risk factor for suicide (Webb & others, 2012). Ernest Hemingway had been in failing health for a number of years when he committed suicide.

Psychological Factors

Psychological factors that can contribute to suicide include psychological disorders and traumatic experiences (A. B. Miller & others, 2013; Wanner & others, 2012). Approximately 90 percent of individuals who commit suicide are estimated to have a diagnosable mental disorder (NIMH, 2008). The most common disorders among individuals who commit suicide are depression and anxiety (Blanco & others, 2012; Nauta & others, 2012; Parra Uribe & others, 2013). An immediate and highly stressful circumstance—such as the loss of a loved one, losing one's job, flunking out of school, or an unwanted pregnancy—can lead people to threaten and/or to commit suicide (Kumar & George, 2013; Videtic & others, 2009). In addition, substance abuse is linked with suicide (Conner & others, 2012).

An expert on suicide, Thomas Joiner (2005) has proposed a comprehensive theory of the phenomenon. His *interpersonal theory of suicide* states that suicide involves two factors (Hames, Hagan, & Joiner, 2013; Joiner, 2005; Joiner & Ribeiro, 2011; A. R. Smith & others, 2013):

- A desire to die
- The acquired capability for suicide.

The desire to die, from this perspective, emerges when a person's social needs are not met. Individuals who feel they do not belong,

What to Do

1. Ask direct, straightforward questions in a calm manner. For example, "Are you thinking about hurting yourself?"

2. Be a good listener and be supportive. Emphasize that unbearable pain can be survived.

3. Take the suicide threat very seriously. Ask questions about the person's feelings, relationships, and thoughts about the type of method to be used. If a gun, pills, rope, or other means is mentioned and a specific plan has been developed, the situation is dangerous. Stay with the person until help arrives.

4. Encourage the person to get professional help and assist him or her in getting help. If the person is willing, take the person to a mental health facility or hospital.

What Not to Do

1. Don't ignore the warning signs.

2. Don't refuse to talk about suicide if the person wants to talk about it.

3. Don't react with horror, disapproval, or repulsion.

4. Don't offer false reassurances ("Everything will be all right") or make judgments ("You should be thankful for . . .").

5. Don't abandon the person after the crisis seems to have passed or after professional counseling has begun.

FIGURE 15.9   When Someone is Threatening Suicide Do not ignore the warning signs if you think someone you know is considering suicide. Talk to a counselor if you are reluctant to say anything to the person yourself.

are chronically lonely, and who perceive themselves to be a burden on others are more likely to experience a desire to die (Hames, Hagan, & Joiner, 2013; Van Orden & others, 2008).

Even among those with a desire to die, however, a key variable is the person's acquired capability to complete a suicide attempt. For most people, a fear of death and a strong desire to avoid feeling pain prevent us from suicide. Research suggests that one way individuals might overcome these natural motivations is to develop a tolerance for pain through previous experiences of injury (Joiner, Ribeiro, & Silva, 2012). Through past experiences, then, the interpersonal theory asserts that individuals are able to extinguish the fear response, allowing them to complete the horrific act of suicide.

Sociocultural Factors

Suicide rates vary worldwide; the lowest rates occur in countries with cultural and religious norms against ending one's own life. According to the World Health Organization (WHO), among the nations with the highest suicide rates are several eastern European nations—including Belarus, Bulgaria, and Russia—along with Japan and South Korea. Among the nations with the lowest rates are Haiti, Antigua and Barbuda, Egypt, and Iran (WHO, 2009). Of the 104 nations ranked by the WHO, the United States ranks 40th.

Within cultures, economic conditions and ethnic contexts may contribute to suicide risk. Chronic economic hardship can be a factor in suicide (Ferretti & Coluccia, 2009; Rojas & Stenberg, 2010). In the United States, adolescents' suicide attempts vary across ethnic groups. Native American and Alaskan native adolescents have particularly high suicide attempt rates (more than 20 percent), and suicide accounts for 20 percent of the deaths among these young people (Goldston & others, 2008), who experience high levels of poverty and substance use.

Research has also linked suicide to the culture of honor. Recall that in honor cultures, individuals are more likely to interpret insults as fighting words and to defend their personal honor with aggression. One set of studies examined suicide and depression in the United States, comparing geographic regions that are considered to have a culture of honor (for example, southern states) with other areas. Even accounting for a host of other factors, suicide rates were found to be higher in states with a culture of honor (Osterman & Brown, 2011).

There are gender differences in suicide as well (Sarma & Kola, 2010). Women are three times more likely to attempt suicide than men, but men are four times more likely to complete suicide than women (Kochanek & others, 2004). Men are also more likely to use a firearm in a suicide attempt (Maris, 1998).

test yourself

1. What are the two requirements for suicide as described by the interpersonal theory of suicide?
2. Give at least two biological, two psychological, and two sociocultural factors in suicide.
3. From the perspective of the three criteria for abnormal behavior, how does *thinking* about suicide compare to *attempting* suicide?

8· PSYCHOLOGICAL DISORDERS AND HEALTH AND WELLNESS

Putting a label on a person with a psychological disorder can make the disorder seem like something that happens only to other people. The truth is that psychological disorders are not just about *other* people; they are about people, period. Over 26 percent of Americans ages 18 and older suffer from a diagnosable psychological disorder in a given year—an estimated 57.7 million U.S. adults (Kessler & others, 2005; NIMH, 2008); that is about the same as the combined populations of the states of California and New York. Chances are that you or someone you know will experience a psychological disorder. Figure 15.10 shows how common many psychological disorders are in the United States.

Psychological disorders present a challenge to living a healthy, fulfilling life. For the many individuals who are diagnosed with one or more such disorders, a significant obstacle in the pursuit of that life is the fear of stigma, stereotypes, prejudice, and discrimination.

To appreciate the power of the labels that are attached to individuals with psychological disorders, consider a classic and controversial study by David Rosenhan (1973). He recruited eight adults (including a stay-at-home mother, a psychology graduate student, a pediatrician, and some psychiatrists), none with a psychological disorder, to see a psychiatrist at various hospitals. These "pseudo-patients" were instructed to act in a normal way except to complain about hearing voices that said things like "empty" and "thud." All eight expressed an interest in leaving the hospital and behaved cooperatively. Nevertheless, all eight were labeled with schizophrenia and kept in the hospital from 3 to 52 days. None of the mental health professionals they encountered ever questioned the diagnosis that had been given to these individuals, and all were discharged with the label "schizophrenia in remission." The label "schizophrenia" had stuck to the pseudo-patients and caused the professionals around them to interpret their quite normal behavior as abnormal. Once a person has been labeled with a psychological disorder, that label colors how others perceive everything else he or she does.

If a person is diagnosed with a psychological disorder, can he or she still be a good friend? A good parent? A competent worker? A significant concern for individuals with psychological disorders is the negative attitudes that others might have about people struggling with mental illness (Phelan & Basow, 2007). Stigma can be a significant barrier for individuals coping with a psychological disorder and for their families and loved ones (Corrigan, 2007; Hinshaw, 2007). Fear of stigma can prevent individuals from seeking treatment and from talking about their problems with family and friends. To test your own attitudes about people with psychological disorders, complete the exercise in Figure 15.11.

	Number of U.S. adults in a given year (millions)	Percentage of U.S. adults
Anxiety and anxiety-related disorders		
General anxiety disorder	6.8	3.1%
Panic disorder	6.0	2.7%
Specific phobia	19.2	8.7%
PTSD	7.7	3.5%
Emotion and Mood Disorders		
Major depressive disorder	14.8	6.7%
Bipolar disorder	5.7	2.6%
Schizophrenia	2.4	1.1%

FIGURE 15.10 **The 12-Month Prevalence of the Most Common Psychological Disorders** If you add up the numbers in this figure, you will see then the totals are higher than the numbers given in the text. The explanation is that people are frequently diagnosed with more than one psychological disorder. An individual who has both a depressive and an anxiety disorder would be counted in both of those categories.

Consequences of Stigma

The stigma attached to psychological disorders can provoke prejudice and discrimination toward individuals who are struggling with these problems, complicating an already difficult situation (Pescosolido & others, 2013). Having a disorder and experiencing the stigma associated with it can also negatively affect the physical health of such individuals.

PREJUDICE AND DISCRIMINATION

Labels of psychological disorders can be damaging because they may lead to negative stereotypes, which, as reviewed in Chapter 13, play a role in prejudice. For example, the label "schizophrenic" often has negative connotations such as "frightening" and "dangerous."

Vivid cases of extremely harmful behavior by individuals with psychological disorders can perpetuate the stereotype that people with such disorders are violent. You have probably heard of such cases. In 2007, Cho Seung-Hui, a college student, murdered 32 students and faculty at Virginia Tech University before killing himself. In December 2012, Adam Lanza killed his mother and then killed 20 children and 6 adults at Sandy Hook Elementary School in Newtown, Connecticut, before killing himself. James Eagan Holmes is alleged to have committed a mass shooting in an Aurora, Colorado, movie theater in July 2012, leaving 12 dead and 58 injured.

Rate the following items using a scale of 1–5, with 1 indicating that you completely *disagree* with the statement and 5 indicating that you completely *agree* with the statement.

1=completely disagree 2=slightly agree
3=moderately agree 4=strongly agree
5=completely agree

_____ 1. I would rather not live next door to a person with a psychological disorder.

_____ 2. A person with a psychological disorder is unfit to raise children.

_____ 3. I would be afraid to be around a person with a psychological disorder.

_____ 4. I would not want to live in the same neighborhood as a group home for persons with psychological disorders.

_____ 5. A person with a psychological disorder cannot hold a job.

_____ 6. A person with a psychological disorder is dangerous or potentially violent.

Total _____

Add up your score and divide by 6. If your score is 3 or higher, you may want to rethink your attitudes about individuals with psychological disorders.

It may be revealing to ask yourself how you would respond to these statements if the words "person with a psychological disorder" were replaced with "woman," "African American," or "gay man or lesbian." Sometimes even individuals who would not think of themselves as being prejudiced against other groups find themselves biased against the mentally ill.

FIGURE 15.11 Test Your Attitudes About People with Psychological Disorders Take the survey to discover and evaluate your own attitudes.

Aside from having committed (or alleged to have committed) these notorious acts of violence, these three individuals have something else in common: They all have been described as having a history of psychological disorders. For Cho, it was depression and anxiety; for Lanza, it was a type of autism spectrum disorder; Holmes has been reported to suffer from schizophrenia or a personality disorder. Such vivid cases may give the erroneous impression that individuals who suffer from psychological disorders are prone to violence. That impression is called an *illusory correlation*, because it is an illusion. Consider that these young men share other qualities as well. For instance, they were all young men. They are no more representative of people with psychological disorders than they are representative of young men.

Consider, too, that after the Sandy Hook killings, many commentators noted that to do such a thing, one *must* have a psychological disorder, by definition (Estes, 2013; Solomon, 2012). Whether or not one believes that statement is true, it leads to at least two unfortunate potential inferences. First, it suggests that individuals who commit acts that are widely condemned cannot be held responsible for those acts, because their behaviors are, by definition, symptoms of a disorder. Second, it suggests that such acts are something that people with psychological disorders do. This conclusion is not true. The fact is people with psychological disorders (especially those in treatment) are no more likely to commit violent acts than the general population. Individuals with psychological disorders are more likely to be the victims of violence than the perpetrators (Appleby & others, 2001; Corrigan & others, 2002).

Individuals with psychological disorders are often aware of the stigma attached to these conditions (Brohan & others, 2010; Moses, 2010). They themselves may have previously held such negative attitudes. People with psychological disorders need help, but seeking that assistance may involve sacrificing their status as mentally healthy for a new, stigmatized identity (Thornicroft & others, 2009; Yen & others, 2009).

Among the most feared aspects of stigma is discrimination. As we saw in Chapter 13, discrimination means acting prejudicially toward a person who is a member of a stigmatized group. In the workplace, discrimination against a person with a psychological disorder is illegal. The Americans with Disabilities Act (ADA) of 1990 forbids employers from refusing employment or a promotion to someone with a psychological disorder when the person's condition does not prevent performance of the job's essential functions (Cleveland, Barnes-Farrell, & Ratz, 1997). A person's appearance or behavior may be unusual or irritating, but as long as that individual is able to complete the duties required of a position, he or she cannot be denied employment or promotion.

PHYSICAL HEALTH

Compared to their psychologically healthy counterparts, individuals with psychological disorders are more likely to be physically ill (Gittelman, 2008), to be obese, to smoke, to drink excessively, and to lead sedentary lives (Beard, Weisberg, & Keller, 2010; Chou & others, 2013; H.-Y. Lin & others, 2013).

You might be thinking that these physical health issues are the least of their worries. If people with schizophrenia want to smoke, why not let them? This type of thinking reveals the subtle way that prejudice toward those with psychological disorders can affect their lives. It sells short the capacity of treatments to help those with psychological disorders, and, more importantly, it fails to acknowledge that individuals with serious mental disorders can lead healthy, meaningful lives.

Research has shown that health-promotion programs can work for individuals with a psychological disorder (Bartels & Desilets, 2012; Gierisch & others, 2013; Robson & others, 2013). When we disregard the potential of physical health interventions for people with psychological disorders to make positive life changes, we reveal our own biases.

Overcoming Stigma

How can we effectively combat the stigma of psychological disorders? One obstacle to changing people's attitudes toward individuals with psychological disorders is that mental illness is often invisible. That is, sometimes a person can have a disorder without others ever knowing. Indeed, we may be unaware of *many* courageous lives around us that are being lived within the challenging context of psychological disorders, because worries about being stigmatized keep the affected individuals from "coming out." Thus, stigma leads to a catch-22: Positive examples of individuals coping with psychological disorders are often missing from our experience because those who are doing well shun public disclosure of their disorders.

A critical step toward eliminating stigma is to resist thinking of people with disorders as limited individuals whose disorder colors everything they do. Instead, it is vital to recognize their strengths—both in confronting their disorder and in carrying on despite their problems—and their achievements. By creating a positive environment for people with disorders, we encourage more of them to become visible and empower them to be positive role models for others.

After reading this chapter, you know that many admired individuals have dealt with psychological disorders. Their diagnoses do not detract from their accomplishments. To the contrary, their accomplishments are all the more remarkable in the context of the challenges they have faced.

test yourself

1. What did the classic study by Rosenhan reveal about the power of labels that are applied to individuals?
2. What social and physical effects can result from the stigma with which some people view psychological disorders?
3. What are some critical considerations in efforts to eliminate stigma toward individuals with psychological disorders?

SUMMARY

1. DEFINING AND EXPLAINING ABNORMAL BEHAVIOR

Abnormal behavior is deviant, maladaptive, or personally distressful. Theoretical perspectives on the causes of psychological disorders include biological, psychological, sociocultural, and biopsychosocial approaches.

Biological approaches to disorders view psychological disorders as diseases with origins in neurological, biochemical, and genetic factors. Psychological approaches include the behavioral, social cognitive, and trait perspectives. Sociocultural approaches place emphasis on the larger social and cultural context and factors such as marriage, socioeconomic status, ethnicity, gender, and culture. Biopsychosocial approaches view the interactions among biological, psychological, and social factors as significant forces in producing both normal and abnormal behavior. The vulnerability-stress hypothesis (or the diathesis-stress model) suggests that some factors may predispose a person to developing a psychological disorder in response to stressful experiences.

Classifying disorders facilitates communication, allowing clinicians to make predictions and decide on treatment. The *Diagnostic and Statistical Manual of Mental Disorders (DSM)* is the classification system clinicians use to diagnose psychological disorders. Some psychologists contend that *DSM-5* perpetuates the medical model of psychological disorders, that it labels everyday problems as psychological disorders, and that it fails to address strengths.

2. ANXIETY AND ANXIETY-RELATED DISORDERS

Anxiety disorders involve unrealistic and debilitating high levels of anxiety. Generalized anxiety disorder involves a high level of anxiety with no specific reason for the anxiety. Panic disorder involves attacks marked by the sudden onset of intense terror. Specific phobia is irrational, overwhelming fear of a particular object, such as snakes, or a situation, such as flying. Social anxiety disorder refers to the intense fear that one will do something embarrassing or humiliating in public.

Obsessive-compulsive disorder involves anxiety-provoking thoughts that will not go away (obsession) and/or urges to perform repetitive, ritualistic behaviors to prevent or produce some future situation (compulsion). Post-traumatic stress disorder (PTSD) is a disorder that develops through exposure to traumatic events. Symptoms include flashbacks, emotional avoidance, emotional numbing, and excessive arousal.

3. DISORDERS INVOLVING EMOTION AND MOOD

In depressive disorder, the individual experiences a serious depressive episode and depressed characteristics such as lethargy and hopelessness. Biological explanations of depressive disorders focus on heredity, neurophysiological abnormalities, and neurotransmitter deregulation.

Psychological explanations include behavioral and cognitive perspectives. Sociocultural explanations emphasize socioeconomic and ethnic factors, as well as gender.

Bipolar disorder is characterized by extreme mood swings that include one or more episodes of mania (an overexcited, unrealistic, optimistic state). Individuals with bipolar I disorder have more extreme manic episodes, while those with bipolar II disorder have less extreme episodes.

4. DISSOCIATIVE DISORDERS

Dissociative amnesia involves memory loss caused by extensive psychological stress. In dissociative identity disorder, formerly called multiple personality disorder, two or more distinct personalities are present in the same individual; this disorder is rare.

5. SCHIZOPHRENIA

Schizophrenia is a severe psychological disorder characterized by highly disordered thought processes. Positive symptoms of schizophrenia are behaviors and experiences that are present in individuals with schizophrenia but absent in healthy people; they include hallucinations, delusions, thought disorder, and disorders of movement. Negative symptoms are behaviors and experiences that are part of healthy human life that are absent for those with this disorder; they include flat affect and an inability to plan or engage in goal-directed behavior.

Biological, psychological, and sociocultural factors may be involved in schizophrenia. Biological factors include genes and the neurotransmitter dopamine. Psychological and sociocultural factors are not viewed as stand-alone causes of schizophrenia, but they are related to the course of the disorder.

6. PERSONALITY DISORDERS

Personality disorders are chronic, maladaptive cognitive-behavioral patterns that are thoroughly integrated into an individual's personal-

ity. Antisocial personality disorder (ASPD) is characterized by guiltlessness, law-breaking, exploitation of others, irresponsibility, and deceit. Individuals with this disorder often lead a life of crime and violence. Psychopaths—remorseless predators who engage in violence to get what they want—are a subgroup of individuals with ASPD. Biological factors for ASPD include genetic, brain, and autonomic nervous system differences.

Borderline personality disorder is a pervasive pattern of instability in interpersonal relationships, self-image, and emotions. This disorder is related to self-harming behaviors such as cutting and suicide. The potential causes of BPD are complex and include biological and cognitive factors and childhood experiences.

7. SUICIDE

Severe depression and other psychological disorders can cause individuals to want to end their lives. Theorists have proposed biological, psychological, and sociocultural explanations of suicide. The interpersonal theory of suicide suggests that it requires the desire to die and the acquired capability to kill oneself.

8. PSYCHOLOGICAL DISORDERS AND HEALTH AND WELLNESS

Stigma can create a significant barrier for people coping with a psychological disorder, and for their loved ones. Fear of being labeled can prevent individuals from getting treatment and from talking about their problems with family and friends. In addition, the stigma attached to psychological disorders can lead to prejudice and discrimination toward individuals who are struggling with these problems.

We can help to combat stigma by acknowledging the strengths and the achievements of individuals coping with psychological disorders. By creating a positive environment for people with disorders, we encourage them to be open about their struggles and to thrive, with the result that they can become positive role models for others.

key *terms*

abnormal behavior, p. 500

medical model, p. 501

vulnerability-stress hypothesis or diathesis-stress model, p. 502

DSM-5, p. 503

attention-deficit/hyperactivity disorder (ADHD), p. 504

anxiety disorders, p. 506

generalized anxiety disorder, p. 506

panic disorder, p. 507

specific phobia, p. 508

social anxiety disorder or social phobia, p. 509

obsessive-compulsive disorder (OCD), p. 509

post-traumatic stress disorder (PTSD), p. 511

depressive disorders, p. 511

major depressive disorder (MDD), p. 512

bipolar disorder, p. 514

dissociative disorders, p. 515

dissociative amnesia, p. 516

dissociative identity disorder (DID), p. 516

psychosis, p. 517

schizophrenia, p. 517

hallucinations, p. 517

delusions, p. 518

thought disorder, p. 518

referential thinking, p. 518

movement disorders, p. 518

catatonia, p. 518

flat affect, p. 518

personality disorders, p. 521

antisocial personality disorder (ASPD), p. 521

borderline personality disorder (BPD), p. 523

apply your *knowledge*

1. Spend 15 to 20 minutes observing an area with a large number of people, such as a mall, a cafeteria, or a stadium during a game. Identify and make a list of behaviors you would classify as abnormal. How does your list of behaviors compare with the definition of *abnormal* provided above? What would change in the list if you were in a different setting, such as a church, a bar, or a library? What does this exercise tell you about the meaning of *abnormal*?

2. If you have never encountered anyone with schizophrenia, meet Moe Armstrong by checking out this YouTube video: www.youtube.com/watch?v=p-_j1ZNKzsg

3. Although we might think of people who contend with psychological disorders as troubled and downtrodden, they (like all people) have the capacity to be astonishingly creative. Check out the website maintained by the National Art Exhibitions of the Mentally Ill (NAEMI) to experience some amazing creations of artists who suffer from mental illness. Go to www.naemi.org and click on "Enter" to view each artist's work. How does your exploration of this artwork influence your feelings about mental illness?

4. Go online and search for message boards where individuals with different psychological disorders share with each other. How do the discussion boards reflect what you have learned about these disorders?

CHAPTER 16

Therapies

Recognizing Cries for Help on Social Media

Imagine checking your Facebook newsfeed to find that a friend has posted that she is "giving up on life." Is it just another instance of everyday Facebook angst or something more serious?

Increasingly, experts are looking at social media posts for signs of real need for psychological help (Norcross & others, 2013). One study examining the Facebook status updates of 200 college students found that 25 percent showed depressive symptoms (Moreno & others, 2011). Recognizing that amid the trivia shared on the site some individuals might be expressing genuine deep distress, Facebook provides users an option to report posts that may indicate suicidal thoughts of suicide. After verifying a troubling post, Facebook sends a link to the National Suicide Prevention Lifeline and an online counselor. Yet even with such resources in place, friends and parents might not know how to separate real need from the drama of everyday life.

On her Facebook wall, one mother saw the following posted by her 18-year-old daughter: "I just did something stupid, mom. Help me." The mother asked relatives nearby to check on her daughter, who had in fact taken an overdose, and the young woman was brought to the ER (Hoffman, 2012). A dormitory resident advisor at the University of Wisconsin makes it a policy to "friend" the students on her floor. For any Facebook updates of concern, she checks in with the students in person, explaining, "If they say something alarming on Facebook, they know it's public and they want someone to respond" (Hoffman, 2012).

Social media can be an immediate outlet for our thoughts and feelings. They also provide a way to reach out to friends in need. At the end of a lousy day, it might be common to vent on Facebook. When the bad days start piling up, however, it might be time to seek help, not just from friends and family but also from a trained mental health professional. ●

PREVIEW

The science of psychology has led to the development of various treatments to help relieve psychological suffering. These different forms of therapy are the focus of this chapter. We first consider psychological and biological approaches to treating disorders. Then we turn to a consideration of psychotherapy, including effectiveness and the numerous approaches to psychotherapy devised by psychologists. Next we examine biological, and sociocultural approaches to therapy. Finally, we consider the broad array of benefits that therapy offers for physical health and psychological wellness.

1· APPROACHES TO TREATING PSYCHOLOGICAL DISORDERS

● **clinical psychology** The area of psychology that integrates science and theory to prevent and treat psychological disorders.

● **psychotherapy** A nonmedical process that helps individuals with psychological disorders recognize and overcome their problems.

● **biological therapies or biomedical therapies** Treatments that reduce or eliminate the symptoms of psychological disorders by altering aspects of body functioning.

Clinical psychology is the area of psychology that integrates science and theory to prevent and treat psychological disorders. To treat psychological disorders, clinical psychologists use psychotherapy. **Psychotherapy** is a nonmedical process that helps individuals with psychological disorders recognize and overcome their problems. Psychotherapists employ a number of strategies including talking, interpreting, listening, rewarding, and modeling (Gelo, Pritz, & Rieken, 2014; Prochaska & Norcross, 2010).

As we saw in Chapter 15, the medical model views psychological disorders as akin to diseases requiring specific treatments, typically medications. Such **biological therapies**, also called **biomedical therapies,** are treatments that reduce or eliminate the symptoms of psychological disorders by altering aspects of bodily functioning.

Both psychotherapy and biological therapies share the goal of relieving the suffering of individuals with psychological disorders, but they differ in their focus and in the types of professionals who are able to deliver them, as we now consider.

The Psychological Approach to Therapy

Psychotherapy is practiced by a variety of mental health professionals, including clinical psychologists, counselors, and social workers. Figure 16.1 lists the main types of mental health professionals, their degrees, the years of education required, and the nature of their training.

Licensing and certification are two ways in which society retains control over psychotherapy practitioners (Hall & Altmaier, 2013). Laws at the state level are used to license or certify such professionals. These laws specify the training individuals must have and provide for some assessment of an applicant's skill through formal examination.

During graduate school, those seeking a PhD in clinical psychology begin to see clients under the supervision of a licensed clinical psychologist. In addition to completing their graduate work, these individuals complete a clinical internship—one year spent providing supervised therapy in an accredited site—to hone their therapeutic skills. Psychotherapy may be given alone or in conjunction with medication, which as we review below, is administered by psychiatrists and other medical doctors.

The Biological Approach to Therapy

Generally speaking, those who administer biological therapies are required to have completed the training to become a medical doctor (that is, an MD). *Psychiatrists* are medical doctors who specialize in treating psychological disorders. In the United States, psychiatrists complete medical school and then spend an additional 4 years in a psychiatric residency program. During their residency, these individuals continue training in diagnosing disorders, understanding the effects of drug therapies on disorders, and

Professional Type	Degree	Education Beyond Bachelor's Degree	Nature of Training
Clinical Psychologist	PhD or PsyD	5–7 years	Requires both clinical and research training. Includes a 1-year internship in a psychiatric hospital or mental health facility. Some universities have developed PsyD programs, which have a stronger clinical than research emphasis. The PsyD training program takes as long as the clinical psychology PhD program and also requires the equivalent of a 1-year internship.
Psychiatrist	MD	7–9 years	Four years of medical school, plus an internship and residency in psychiatry, is required. A psychiatry residency involves supervision in therapies, including psychotherapy and biomedical therapy.
Counseling Psychologist	MA, PhD, PsyD, or EdD	3–7 years	Similar to clinical psychologist but with emphasis on counseling and therapy. Some counseling psychologists specialize in vocational counseling. Some counselors complete master's degree training, others PhD or EdD training, in graduate schools of psychology or education.
School Psychologist	MA, PhD, PsyD, or EdD	3–7 years	Training in graduate programs of education or psychology. Emphasis on psychological assessment and counseling practices involving students' school-related problems. Training is at the master's or doctoral level.
Social Worker	MS W/DSW or PhD	2–5 years	Graduate work in a school of social work that includes specialized clinical training in mental health facilities.
Psychiatric Nurse	RN, MA, or PhD	0–5 years	Graduate work in a school of nursing with special emphasis on care of mentally disturbed individuals in hospital settings and mental health facilities.
Occupational Therapist	BS, MA, or PhD	0–5 years	Emphasis on occupational training with focus on physically or psychologically handicapped individuals. Stresses getting individuals back into the mainstream of work.
Pastoral Counselor	None to PhD or DD (Doctor of Divinity)	0–5 years	Requires ministerial background and training in psychology. An internship in a mental health facility as a chaplain is recommended.
Counselor	MA or MEd	2 years	Graduate work in a department of psychology or department of education with specialized training in counseling techniques.

FIGURE 16.1 **Main Types of Mental Health Professionals** A wide range of professionals with varying levels of training has taken on the challenge of helping people with psychological disorders.

practicing psychotherapy. For licensing in the United States, psychiatrists are required to demonstrate proficiency in different approaches to psychotherapy that we will review later in this chapter. Although psychologists and psychiatrists can both administer psychotherapy, for the most part, only psychiatrists can prescribe medications. When a psychotherapist believes that a client would benefit from medication, he or she might refer that client to a trusted psychiatrist to obtain a prescription.

For a number of years, psychologists have sought to obtain the right to prescribe drug treatments to their clients. Currently, the only states that permit psychologists to prescribe drugs are New Mexico and Louisiana. In these states, clinical psychologists complete additional training in medicine to qualify for prescription privileges. Other states have also considered granting psychologists these privileges, often in response to a lack of psychiatrists to treat those with psychological disorders in many areas.

Those who support the idea that psychologists ought to have prescription privileges argue that this change in regulations would make treatment more efficient for those with psychological disorders. In addition, they note that a psychologist's likely first impulse is to treat with psychotherapy, rather than medication, reducing the potential overuse of strong drugs when they are not needed. Those who oppose such a change note that psychoactive drugs are powerful and affect many bodily systems. They feel that additional training simply cannot replace the level of expertise required to prescribe and monitor these medicines. Further, those with psychological disorders may also have physical illnesses that psychologists would not be trained to diagnose or treat.

test yourself

1. Define psychotherapy and biological therapy.
2. What are the differences between a clinical psychologist and a psychiatrist in training and the types of treatment provided?
3. Describe two arguments from both sides regarding whether psychologists should be allowed to prescribe drug treatment.

2· PSYCHOTHERAPY

Although there are different types of psychotherapy, they all involve a trained professional engaging in an interpersonal relationship with someone who is suffering. Later in this section, we will review the specific types of psychotherapies that have been developed from broad theoretical approaches in psychology. Before we do so, let's consider some general issues that are common to all forms of psychotherapy.

Central Issues in Psychotherapy

Psychotherapy can be a very desirable type of treatment. One study showed that 90 percent of those surveyed report that they would prefer to talk to someone than to take medicines for their problems (Duncan & others, 2010). Still, a person seeking psychotherapy might wonder whether it works, whether some therapies work better than others, what factors influence a therapy's effectiveness, and how forms of therapy differ. In this section, we address these questions.

DOES PSYCHOTHERAPY WORK?

There are many debates in psychology, but the effectiveness of psychotherapy in treating psychological disorders is *not* one of them. Many studies have been conducted to answer the question "Does psychotherapy work?" and the answer is a resounding yes (American Psychological Association, 2012). A large body of research and multiple meta-analyses support this conclusion (Beck, 2005; Butler & others, 2006; Clemens, 2010; Duncan & Reese, 2013; Lambert, 2001; Lipsey & Wilson, 1993; Luborsky & others, 2002; Wampold, 2001). Individuals who experience 12 to 14 sessions of psychotherapy are more likely to improve compared to those who receive a placebo treatment or no treatment at all and are likely to maintain these improvements for 2 to 3 years, provided that the treatment they receive is based on sound psychological theory (Lambert, 2013). The Psychological Inquiry shows the results of an analysis of treatment outcomes.

DOES ONE THERAPY WORK BETTER THAN OTHERS?

People who are contemplating seeing a psychotherapist do not just want to know *whether* psychotherapy in general works, but also *which form* of psychotherapy is most effective. In some ways, this question pits the different brands of psychotherapy against each other in a kind of horserace. It is important to bear in mind that it is human nature for psychologists to have allegiances or loyalties to the brand of psychotherapy they use and in which they were trained. The results of many studies addressing the "which therapy is the best" question show that, although there is strong research supporting the notion that therapy is effective, no one therapy has been shown to be significantly more effective than the others, overall (Duncan & Reese, 2013; Gelo, Pritz, & Rieken, 2014; Lambert, 2001; Luborsky & others, 2002; Wampold, 2001; Werbart & others, 2013).

Indeed, the answer to the question which type of therapy works best may be, "It depends on the person's diagnosis." That is, some therapies might be more effective than others for particular psychological disorders (Cukrowicz & others, 2011; Gould, Coulson, & Howard, 2012; Nasser, 2013; S. Reynolds & others, 2012). Some psychologists believe that, to move forward, therapies must be tailored to particular disorders, and therapists should rely on proven treatments for those disorders (Chambless, 2002). This perspective, called **empirically supported treatment,** means that for any given psychological disorder, treatment decisions should be based on the body of research that has been conducted showing which type of therapy works best (Duncan & Reese, 2013). Proponents of empirically supported treatment say that, ideally, each disorder would be treated using the particular type of therapy that has been shown by research to work best for that disorder (Christopherson & VanScoyoc, 2013).

● **empirically supported treatment** An approach to treating psychological disorders that advocates making treatment decisions based on the body of research that has shown which type of therapy works best.

psychological *inquiry*

Percent improved

(Bar graph with Y-axis "Percent improved" ranging from 0 to 80, and X-axis groups: Psychotherapy, Placebo, No treatment)

Does Therapy Work?

This figure provides a summary of numerous studies and reviews of research in which clients were randomly assigned to a no-treatment control group, a placebo control group, or a psychotherapy treatment (Lambert, 2001). Note that the group to which individuals were assigned is indicated on the X (horizontal) axis, and the percent of individuals who improved is shown on the Y (vertical) axis. Use the graph to answer the following questions:

1. Which group improved most and which improved least?

2. Why might those in the "no treatment" group have improved?

3. What does the difference between the psychotherapy group and the placebo group indicate?

4. Do these results allow us to infer causal relationships between therapy and improvement? Explain.

Other psychologists argue that targeting particular disorders with specific treatments amounts to taking an overly medical approach (Horvath, 2013; S. D. Miller & others, 2013). In medicine, drugs (like antibiotics) are specifically prescribed to treat particular illnesses (like strep throat). Critics of empirically supported treatment note that psychotherapies are not like drugs or medicines that target a particular disease. They stress that psychotherapies are best understood as promoting better functioning through common characteristics that lead to benefits. These psychologists are concerned that closely dictating what therapists should do takes away the flexibility that potentially might be vital for improvement.

Relying on empirical research in making treatment decisions is challenging because the evidence is not always clear-cut: For instance, research is not always conducted on appropriate samples (that is, people who are actually diagnosed with particular disorders), or the samples may not be representative of the people clinicians see in practice (Wampold, 2013). A key challenge in relying on empirical evidence to guide treatment decisions is that such evidence is limited or nonexistent for many disorders. Moreover, relying on research to direct decisions leaves the clinician in the dark when research-recommended treatments do not work for a particular client.

A special task force appointed by the president of the American Psychological Association reached a compromise between these two positions. The task force endorsed evidence-based practice. **Evidence-based practice** means that decisions about treatment are made using the best available research and considering the therapist's clinical judgment and client characteristics, culture, and preferences (APA Presidential Task Force on Evidence-Based Practice, 2006; Barlow & others, 2013; Duncan & Reese, 2013). Although evidence-based practice recognizes the importance of scientific evidence, it also permits flexibility for clinicians to consider a broad range of factors in deciding on a course of therapy.

● **evidence-based practice** Integration of the best available research with clinical expertise in the context of client characteristics, culture, and preferences.

- Participates actively
- Draws on personal strengths, abilities, skills, and motivation
- Develops confidence and trust in therapist
- Becomes more hopeful and less alienated

- Participates actively
- Provides genuine support
- Monitors quality of relationship with client

FIGURE 16.2 Factors in Effective Psychotherapy This figure emphasizes the qualities and behaviors of therapists and clients that are essential to a successful therapeutic alliance and effective psychotherapy.

● **therapeutic alliance** The relationship between the therapist and client—an important element of successful psychotherapy.

FACTORS IN EFFECTIVE PSYCHOTHERAPY

Research has also addressed the factors that play an important role in determining the effectiveness of psychotherapy. Here we review three such factors: the therapeutic alliance, the therapist, and the client (Figure 16.2).

The Therapeutic Alliance The **therapeutic alliance** is the relationship between the therapist and client. When therapists and clients feel they are engaged in a real working relationship characterized by trust, respect, and cooperation, the therapeutic alliance is strong. This alliance is an important element of successful psychotherapy (Prochaska & Norcross, 2010; Strupp, 1995).

It important for therapists to monitor the quality of the relationship with each client. Clients of therapists who did not assess the quality of the alliance were two times more likely to drop out of therapy (Hubble & Miller, 2004). Among those who completed therapy, clients of therapists who failed to assess their alliance were three to four times more likely to have a negative outcome (Hubble & Miller, 2004).

The Therapist Whether psychotherapy works or not depends more on the particular therapist than on the type of therapy used (Beutler & others, 2012). Therapists differ in their level of expertise, their deep knowledge about psychological problems, and their treatment (S. D. Miller & others, 2013). Therapists with high expertise are those who not only possess a great deal of knowledge but those who continue to learn, to monitor client progress, and to make changes when necessary.

Research has also shown that the match between a therapist's style and client personality can influence whether therapy is effective. For example, if a client has a strong resistance to changing, a therapist who is more laid back and less directive may have greater success than one who engages directly with the client (Beutler & others, 2012).

The Client Another major factor in therapeutic outcomes is the person seeking treatment. Indeed, meta-analyses suggest that the quality of the client's participation is the most important determinant of whether therapy is successful (Bohart & Tallman, 2010; McKay, Imel, & Wampold, 2006; Wampold, 2001). Even though individuals often seek therapy due to difficulties and problems in their life, it is their strengths, abilities, skills, and motivation that account for therapeutic success (Hubble & Miller, 2004; Wampold & Brown, 2005). A review of the extensive evidence on therapeutic efficacy concluded: "The data make abundantly clear that therapy does not make clients work, but rather clients make therapy work" (Hubble & Miller, 2004, p. 347).

HOW DO PSYCHOTHERAPIES DIFFER?

All psychotherapies involve therapists and clients interacting together in a relationship, but each type of psychotherapy provides a different approach that guides the type of interaction that occurs during treatment. There are two ways to differentiate the types of therapy: (1) the extent to which they focus on insights versus immediate symptoms and skills, and (2) and whether they are directive or not (Beutler & others, 2012; O'Leary, 2013):

- *Insight versus symptoms and skill development:* Some treatments focus on gaining insight into the deeper causes of a problem; others focus on the person's immediate symptoms and on helping the person develop specific skills to manage those symptoms.

- *Directive versus nondirective:* Some treatments call upon the therapist to be quite outspoken in giving advice to the client; these treatments also tend to encourage the therapist to play an active role in the client's life. In contrast, other treatments prompt the client to drive the interaction, with the therapist taking a less active role in treatment.

The remainder of this section focuses on four main approaches to psychotherapy: psychodynamic, humanistic, behavioral, and cognitive therapy, as well as eclectic approaches to therapy that combine many different techniques.

Psychodynamic Therapies

The **psychodynamic therapies** stress the importance of the unconscious mind, extensive interpretation by the therapist, and the role of early childhood experiences in the development of an individual's problems. The goal of psychodynamic therapies is to help individuals gain insight into the unconscious conflicts that underlie their problems (Cabaniss & others, 2013). Many psychodynamic approaches grew out of Freud's psychoanalytic theory of personality.

Psychoanalysis is Freud's therapeutic technique for analyzing an individual's unconscious thoughts. Freud believed that a person's current problems could be traced to childhood experiences, many of which involved unconscious sexual conflicts. To free the person from these unconscious conflicts, the psychoanalyst interprets aspects of what the person shares about his or her life (Dougherty, 2010). A psychoanalyst may ask a person to simply say aloud whatever comes to mind in response to, for instance, the symptoms that have brought him or her to treatment. This process is called *free association*.

The analyst might also ask the person to share his or her dreams. **Dream analysis** is a psychoanalytic technique for interpreting a person's dreams. Psychoanalysts believe that dreams contain information about unconscious thoughts, wishes, and conflicts (Freud, 1911). From this perspective, dreams give us an outlet to express symbolically our unconscious wishes, a mental theater in which our deepest and most secret desires can be played out (Meghnagi, 2011). According to Freud, every dream, even our worst nightmare, contains a hidden, disguised wish. The sheer horror we feel during a nightmare might itself disguise that unconscious wish.

The key aspect of the therapeutic alliance from a psychodynamic perspective is transference. **Transference** is the psychoanalytic term for the client's relating to the analyst in ways that reproduce or relive important relationships in the individual's life. A person might interact with an analyst as if the analyst were a parent or lover, for example. According to Freud, transference is a necessary part of the psychoanalytic relationship, as it models the way that individuals relate to important people in their lives (Faimberg, 2012).

Contemporary psychodynamic therapies differ from Freudian psychoanalysis in many ways. However, these approaches still probe unconscious thoughts about early childhood experiences to gain insight into their clients' current problems (Josephs & Weinberger, 2013; Messer & Abbass, 2010). Contemporary psychoanalysts accord more power to the conscious mind and to a person's current relationships, and they generally place less emphasis on sex (Wallerstein, 2012). The focus of such treatment may involve helping the individual develop the story of his or her experience—putting words on experiences that lack labels (Rosenbaum & others, 2012).

- **psychodynamic therapies** Treatments that stress the importance of the unconscious mind, extensive interpretation by the therapist, and the role of early childhood experiences in the development of an individual's problems.

- **psychoanalysis** Freud's therapeutic technique for analyzing an individual's unconscious thoughts.

- **dream analysis** A psychoanalytic technique for interpreting a person's dreams.

- **transference** A client's relating to the psychoanalyst in ways that reproduce or relive important relationships in the individual's life.

I HAD THAT FLYING DREAM AGAIN.

MOTHER GOOSE & GRIMM © 2010 Grimmy, Inc. King Features Syndicate.

● **humanistic therapies** Treatments, unique in their emphasis on people's self-healing capacities, that encourage clients to understand themselves and to grow personally.

● **client-centered therapy** A form of humanistic therapy, developed by Rogers, in which the therapist provides a warm, supportive atmosphere to improve the client's self-concept and to encourage the client to gain insight into problems; also called Rogerian therapy or nondirective therapy.

● **reflective speech** A technique in which the therapist mirrors the client's own feelings back to the client.

"I see. So what you're saying is that you woke up this morning and your woman had done left you."

© Clive Goddard. www.CartoonStock.com.

● **behavior therapies** Treatments, based on the behavioral and social cognitive theories of learning, that use principles of learning to reduce or eliminate maladaptive behavior.

Like other forms of psychotherapy, psychodynamic therapies can be effective in alleviating symptoms; however, this form of treatment generally takes longer than other approaches (Lambert, 2013).

Humanistic Therapies

The underlying philosophy of humanistic therapies is captured by the metaphor of how an acorn, if provided with appropriate conditions, will grow, pushing naturally toward its actualization as an oak (Schneider, 2002). In **humanistic therapies,** people are encouraged toward self-understanding and personal growth. The humanistic therapies are unique in their emphasis on the person's self-healing capacities. In contrast to psychodynamic therapies, humanistic therapies emphasize conscious rather than unconscious thoughts, the present rather than the past, and self-fulfillment rather than illness (Dulmus & Nisbet, 2013; Greenberg & others, 2013).

Client-centered therapy (also called *Rogerian therapy* or *nondirective therapy*) is a form of humanistic therapy, developed by Carl Rogers, in which the therapist provides a warm, supportive atmosphere to improve the client's self-concept and to encourage the person to gain insight into problems (Rogers, 1961, 1980). The goal of client-centered therapy is to help clients identify and understand their own genuine feelings and become more *congruent,* bringing their actual self closer to their ideal self (Hazler, 2007).

One way to achieve this goal is through active listening and **reflective speech,** a technique in which the therapist mirrors the client's own feelings back to the client. For example, as a woman is describing her grief over the traumatic loss of her husband in a drunk-driving accident, the therapist might suggest "You sound angry" to help her identify her feelings.

As noted in Chapter 12, Rogers believed that humans require three essential elements to grow: unconditional positive regard, empathy, and genuineness. These three elements are reflected in his approach to therapy:

■ *Unconditional positive regard:* The therapist constantly recognizes the inherent value of the client, providing a context for personal growth and self-acceptance.

■ *Empathy:* The therapist strives to put himself or herself in the client's shoes—to feel the emotions the client is feeling.

■ *Genuineness:* The therapist is a real person in his or her relationship with the client, sharing feelings and not hiding behind a facade.

For genuineness to coexist with unconditional positive regard, that regard must be a sincere expression of the therapist's true feelings. The therapist may distinguish between the person's behavior and the person himself or herself. Although the person is acknowledged as a valuable human being, the client's behavior can be evaluated negatively: "You are a good person but your actions are not." Rogers's positive view of humanity extended to his view of therapists. He believed that by being genuine with the client, the therapist could help the client improve.

Behavior Therapies

Psychodynamic and humanistic approaches are called *insight therapies* because they encourage self-awareness as the key to psychological health. We now turn to therapies that take a different approach. In behavior therapies, insight is irrelevant to the goal of treatment. Instead, behavior therapies offer action-oriented strategies to help people change *behavior,* not underlying thoughts or emotions (Craighead & others, 2013).

Behavior therapies use principles of learning to reduce or eliminate maladaptive behavior. Behavior therapies are based on the behavioral and social cognitive theories of learning. Behavior therapists assume that overt symptoms are the central problem and that even if clients discover why they are depressed, that does not mean the depression will cease. To alleviate anxiety or depression, then, behavior therapists focus on eliminating the problematic symptoms or behaviors rather than on helping individuals understand why they are depressed (Miltenberger, 2012; Mineka, 2014; Yamanishi & others, 2009).

Although initially based almost exclusively on the learning principles of classical and operant conditioning, behavior therapies have diversified in recent years. As social cognitive theory grew in popularity, behavior therapists increasingly included observational learning, cognitive factors (Freedy & others, 2012), and self-instruction (encouraging people to change what they say to themselves) in their treatments.

CLASSICAL CONDITIONING TECHNIQUES

Classical conditioning has been used in treating phobias. Recall that phobias are irrational fears that interfere with an individual's life, such as fear of heights, dogs, flying, or public speaking. **Systematic desensitization** is a method of behavior therapy that treats anxiety by teaching the client to associate deep relaxation with increasingly intense anxiety-producing situations (Donahue, Odlaug, & Grant, 2011; Wolpe, 1990).

Desensitization involves exposing someone to a feared situation in a real or an imagined way (Head & Gross, 2009). A therapist might first ask the client which aspects of the feared situation are the most and least frightening. The therapist then arranges these circumstances in order from most to least frightening. The next step is to teach the individual to relax. The client learns to recognize the presence of muscular contractions or tension in various parts of the body and then to tighten and relax different muscles. Once the individual is relaxed, the therapist asks the person to imagine the least feared stimulus in the hierarchy. Subsequently, the therapist moves up the list of items, from least to most feared, while the client remains relaxed. Eventually, the client can imagine the scariest circumstance without fear.

In systematic desensitization, if you are afraid of, say, spiders, the therapist might initially have you watch someone handle a spider and then ask you to engage in increasingly more feared behaviors. You might first go into the same room with a spider, next approach the spider, and then touch the spider. Eventually, you might play with the spider. Figure 16.3 shows an example of a desensitization hierarchy.

Recall from Chapter 6 that aversive conditioning consists of repeated pairings of an undesirable behavior with aversive stimuli to decrease the behavior's positive associations. Through aversive conditioning, people can learn to avoid behaviors such as smoking, overeating, and drinking alcohol. Electric shocks, nausea-inducing substances, and verbal insults are some of the noxious stimuli used in aversive conditioning (Sommer & others, 2006). The Psychological Inquiry illustrates conditioning principles in practice.

OPERANT CONDITIONING TECHNIQUES

The idea behind using operant conditioning as a therapy approach is that just as maladaptive behavior patterns are learned, they can be unlearned. Using operant conditioning, unhealthy behaviors are replaced with healthy ones. Therapy involves conducting a careful analysis of the person's environment to determine which factors need modification. Especially important is changing the consequences of the person's behavior to ensure that healthy, adaptive replacement behaviors are followed by positive reinforcement.

Applied behavior analysis, described in Chapter 6, involves establishing positive reinforcement connections between behaviors and rewards so that individuals engage in appropriate behavior and extinguish inappropriate behavior. It may strike you as unusual that behavioral approaches do not emphasize gaining insight and self-awareness. However, for the very reason that they do not stress these goals, such treatments may be particularly useful in individuals whose cognitive abilities are limited, such as adults with developmental disabilities or children.

Applied behavior analysis has proven effective in treating individuals with autism (T. Thompson, 2013). Based on the assumption that children with autism have the

● **systematic desensitization** A method of behavior therapy that treats anxiety by teaching the client to associate deep relaxation with increasingly intense anxiety-producing situations.

1 A month before an examination
2 Two weeks before an examination
3 A week before an examination
4 Five days before an examination
5 Four days before an examination
6 Three days before an examination
7 Two days before an examination
8 One day before an examination
9 The night before an examination
10 On the way to the university on the day of an examination
11 Before the unopened doors of the examination room
12 Awaiting distribution of examination papers
13 The examination paper lies facedown before her
14 In the process of answering an examination paper

FIGURE 16.3 A Desensitization Hierarchy Involving Test Anxiety In this hierarchy, the individual begins with her least feared circumstance (a month before the exam) and moves through each of the circumstances until reaching her most feared circumstance (being in the process of answering the exam questions). At each step of the way, the person replaces fear with deep relaxation and successful visualization.

psychological *inquiry*

Classical Conditioning: The Backbone of Aversive Conditioning

This figure demonstrates how classical conditioning principles underlie the process of aversive conditioning. It specifically shows how classical conditioning can provide a conditional aversion to alcohol. In studying the figure, recall the abbreviations US (unconditioned stimulus), UR (unconditioned response), CS (conditioned stimulus), and CR (conditioned response). Try your hand at the questions below.

Before Aversive Conditioning

US $\longrightarrow$ UR

Nausea-inducing drug $\longrightarrow$ Nausea

During Aversive Conditioning

Neutral stimulus + US $\longrightarrow$ UR

Alcohol + Nausea-inducing drug $\longrightarrow$ Nausea

After Aversive Conditioning

CS $\longrightarrow$ CR

Alcohol $\longrightarrow$ Nausea

1. In the example illustrated in the figure, what is the conditioned stimulus?

2. What is the likely effect of alcohol *prior to* aversion therapy? Is this effect learned (that is, a conditioned response) or not (an unconditioned response)?

3. What role, if any, does the person's motivation play in the process of conditioning?

4. Looking over the steps in aversive conditioning, how do you think classical conditioning might be applied to prevent psychological problems?

capacity to learn (Løvaas, 1987), behavioral approaches to treatment have become the standard treatment for autism spectrum disorders (Woo & Leon, 2013). Prior to the application of behavioral therapies, estimates were that only 1 to 2 percent of individuals with autism spectrum disorders would improve.

Today, more than half of children receiving early and intense behavioral treatment go on to mainstream classrooms (McEachin, Smith, & Løvaas, 1993; T. Thompson, 2013). How intense is the treatment? Typically, it involves over 20 hours of behavioral intervention per week for 1 to 3 years, incorporating the learning concepts of reinforcement, shaping, and discrimination (T. Thompson, 2013). Researchers are continuing to integrate innovative methods to applied behavior analysis to treat autism (Woo & Leon, 2013).

Cognitive Therapies

● **cognitive therapies** Treatments emphasizing that cognitions (thoughts) are the main source of psychological problems and that attempt to change the individual's feelings and behaviors by changing cognitions.

Cognitive therapies emphasize that cognitions, or thoughts, are the main source of psychological problems; these therapies attempt to change the individual's feelings and behaviors by changing cognitions.

Cognitive therapies differ from psychoanalytic therapies by focusing on symptoms and skill development rather than insight. Compared with humanistic therapies, cognitive therapies are more directive. Cognitive therapists guide individuals in identifying their irrational and self-defeating thoughts. Then they use various techniques to get clients to challenge these thoughts and to consider different, more positive ways of thinking (Hammen & Keenan-Miller, 2013; Hofmann, Asmundson, & Beck, 2013).

FOUNDATIONS OF COGNITIVE THERAPIES

All cognitive therapies involve these basic assumptions: Human beings have control over their feelings, and how individuals feel about something depends on how they think about it (Beck, 2006; Ellis, 2005). Cognitive therapy involves getting people to recognize these connections and helping them use thinking to change their feelings (Germer, Siegel, & Fulton, 2013). *Cognitive restructuring,* a general concept for changing a pattern of thought that is presumed to be causing maladaptive behavior or emotion, is central to cognitive therapies.

Unfortunately, thoughts that lead to emotions can happen so rapidly that we are not even aware of them. Thus, the first goal of therapy is to bring these automatic thoughts into awareness so that they can be changed. The therapist helps clients to identify their own automatic thoughts and to keep records of their thought content and emotional reactions.

With the therapist's assistance, clients learn to recognize logical errors in their thinking and to challenge the accuracy of these automatic thoughts. Logical errors in thinking can lead individuals to the following erroneous beliefs (Carson, Butcher, & Mineka, 1996):

- Perceiving the world as harmful while ignoring evidence to the contrary—for example, when a young woman still feels worthless after a friend has just told her how much other people genuinely like her.
- Overgeneralizing on the basis of limited examples—such as a man's seeing himself as worthless because one person stopped dating him.
- Magnifying the importance of undesirable events—such as one failure as the end of the world.
- Engaging in absolutist thinking—such as exaggerating the importance of someone's mildly critical comment and perceiving it as proof of total inadequacy.

Figure 16.4 describes some of the most widely used cognitive therapy techniques.

COGNITIVE-BEHAVIOR THERAPY

Cognitive-behavior therapy (CBT) is a combination of cognitive therapy, with its emphasis on reducing self-defeating thoughts, and behavior therapy, with its emphasis on changing behavior. In CBT, the therapist takes a directive role, engaging in a dialogue to help the client identify automatic thoughts and the feelings they produce and working with the client to change those thoughts while also focusing on changing behavior (Dobson, 2013; Kanter, 2013). In CBT, the client may be given homework assignments directed at these behavioral changes.

Self-instructional methods are cognitive-behavior techniques aimed at teaching individuals to modify their own behavior (Watson & Tharp, 2014). Using self-instructional techniques, cognitive-behavior therapists prompt clients to change what they say to themselves. The therapist gives the client examples of constructive statements, known as *reinforcing self-statements,* which the client can repeat in order to take positive steps to cope with stress or meet a goal. The therapist also encourages the client to practice the statements through role playing and strengthens the client's newly acquired skills through reinforcement.

An important aspect of cognitive-behavior therapy is *self-efficacy,* the belief that one can master a situation and produce positive outcomes (Bandura, 2001, 2009, 2010b, 2012b). At each step of the therapy process, clients need to bolster their confidence by telling themselves messages such as "I'm going to master my problem," "I can do it," "I'm improving," and "I'm getting better." As they gain confidence and engage in

● **cognitive-behavior therapy** A therapy that combines cognitive therapy and behavior therapy with the goal of developing self-efficacy.

Cognitive Therapy Technique	Description	Example
Challenge Idiosyncratic Meanings	Explore personal meaning attached to the client's words and ask the client to consider alternatives.	When a client says he will be "devastated" by his spouse leaving, ask just how he would be devastated and ways he could avoid being devastated.
Question the Evidence	Systematically examine the evidence for the client's beliefs or assertions.	When a client says she can't live without her spouse, explore how she lived without the spouse before she was married.
Reattribution	Help the client distribute responsibility for events appropriately.	When a client says that his son's failure in school must be his fault, explore other possibilities, such as the quality of the school.
Examine Options and Alternatives	Help the client generate alternative actions to maladaptive ones.	If a client considers leaving school, explore whether tutoring or going part-time to school are good alternatives.
Decatastrophize	Help the client evaluate whether he is overestimating the nature of a situation.	If a client states that failure in a course means he or she must give up the dream of medical school, question whether this is a necessary conclusion.
Fantasize Consequences	Explore fantasies of a feared situation: if unrealistic, the client may recognize this; if realistic, work on effective coping strategies.	Help a client who fantasizes "falling apart" when asking the boss for a raise to role-play the situation and develop effective skills for making the request.
Examine Advantages and Disadvantages	Examine advantages and disadvantages of an issue, to instill a broader perspective.	If a client says he "was just born depressed and will always be that way," explore the advantages and disadvantages of holding that perspective versus other perspectives.
Turn Adversity to Advantage	Explore ways that difficult situations can be transformed into opportunities.	If a client has just been laid off, explore whether this is an opportunity for her to return to school.
Guided Association	Help the client see connections between different thoughts or ideas.	Draw the connections between a client's anger at his wife for going on a business trip and his fear of being alone.
Scaling	Ask the client to rate her emotions or thoughts on scales to help gain perspective.	If a client says she was overwhelmed by an emotion, ask her to rate it on a scale from 0 (not at all present) to 100 (I fell down in a faint).
Thought Stopping	Provide the client with ways of stopping a cascade of negative thoughts.	Teach an anxious client to picture a stop sign or hear a bell when anxious thoughts begin to snowball.
Distraction	Help the client find benign or positive distractions to take attention away from negative thoughts or emotions temporarily.	Have a client count to 200 by 13s when he feels himself becoming anxious.
Labeling of Distortions	Provide labels for specific types of distorted thinking to help the client gain more distance and perspective.	Have a client keep a record of the number of times a day she engages in all-or-nothing thinking—seeing things as all bad or all good.

FIGURE 16.4 **Cognitive Therapy Techniques** Cognitive therapists develop strategies to help change the way people think.

adaptive behavior, the successes become intrinsically motivating. Before long, individuals persist (with considerable effort) in their attempts to solve personal problems because of the positive outcomes that were set in motion by self-efficacy.

CBT is the most common form of therapy used today, and it has proved effective in treating a host of disorders (Craighead & others, 2013; Gould, Coulson, & Howard, 2012; Olatunji & others, 2012; Rector, 2013). Cognitive therapy has successfully treated anxiety disorders (Donegan & Dugas, 2012; K. P. Gallo & others, 2013); mood disorders (Hammen & Keenan-Miller, 2013; Sado & others, 2009); schizophrenia, in combination with drug treatments (Christopher Frueh & others, 2009; Harvey & Bowie, 2013); and personality disorders (McMain & Pos, 2007; Trull, Carpenter, & Widiger, 2013).

	Cause of Problem	Therapy Emphasis	Nature of Therapy and Techniques
Psychodynamic Therapies	Client's problems are symptoms of deep-seated, unresolved unconscious conflicts.	Discover underlying unconscious conflicts and work with client to develop insight.	Psychoanalysis, including free association and dream analysis: therapist interprets heavily.
Humanistic Therapies	Client is not functioning at an optimal level of development.	Develop awareness of inherent potential for growth.	Person-centered therapy, including unconditional positive regard, genuineness, accurate empathy, and active listening; self-appreciation emphasized.
Behavior Therapies	Client has learned maladaptive behavior patterns.	Learn adaptive behavior patterns through changes in the environment and rewards and punishers.	Observation of behavior and its controlling conditions; therapies based on classical conditioning, operant conditioning.
Cognitive Therapies	Client has developed inappropriate thoughts.	Change feelings and behaviors by changing cognitions.	Conversation with client designed to get him or her to change irrational and self-defeating beliefs.

FIGURE 16.5 **Therapy Comparisons** Different therapies address the same problems in very different ways. Many therapists use the tools that seem right for any given client and his or her problems.

The four psychotherapies—psychodynamic, humanistic, behavior, and cognitive—are compared in Figure 16.5.

Therapy Integrations

Many psychotherapists identify themselves as not adhering to one particular method. Rather, they refer to themselves as "eclectic" or "integrative." **Integrative therapy** is a combination of techniques from different therapies based on the therapist's judgment of which particular methods will provide the greatest benefit for the client (Clarkin, 2012; Gold & Stricker, 2013). For example, a therapist might use a behavioral approach to treat an individual with panic disorder and a cognitive approach to treat a client with depressive disorder.

Because clients present a wide range of problems, it makes sense for therapists to use the best tools in each case rather than to adopt a "one size fits all" program. Sometimes a given psychological disorder is so difficult to treat that it requires the therapist to bring all of his or her tools to bear. For example, borderline personality disorder (see Chapter 15) involves emotional instability, impulsivity, and self-harming behaviors, and this disorder responds to a therapy called *dialectical behavior therapy*, or *DBT* (Bedics & others, 2012; Harned, Tkachuck, & Youngberg, 2013).

Like psychodynamic approaches, DBT assumes that early childhood experiences are important to the development of borderline personality disorder. However, DBT employs a variety of techniques, including homework assignments, cognitive interventions, intensive individual therapy, and group sessions involving others with the disorder. Group sessions focus on mindfulness training as well as emotional and interpersonal skills training (Boyd-Franklin & others, 2013).

At their best, integrative therapies are effective, systematic uses of a variety of therapeutic approaches (Prochaska & Norcross, 2010). However, one worry about integrative therapies is that their increased use will result in an unsystematic, haphazard use of therapeutic techniques that some therapists say would be no better than a narrow, dogmatic approach (Lazarus, Beutler, & Norcross, 1992).

Another integrative method is to combine psychotherapy with drug therapy (Michalopoulou & others, 2013). Combined cognitive therapy and drug therapy has been effective in treating anxiety and depressive disorders (Dunner, 2001), eating disorders (Wilson, Grilo, & Vitousek, 2007), and schizophrenia (M. Fisher & others, 2013; Rector & Beck, 2001). A mental health team that includes a psychiatrist and a clinical psychologist might conduct this integrative therapy. The use of medication to treat psychological disorders is a type of biological approach to therapy, our next topic.

● **integrative therapy** Use of a combination of techniques from different therapies based on the therapist's judgment of which particular methods will provide the greatest benefit for the client.

test yourself

1. Describe what psychotherapy is, and identify four psychotherapeutic approaches.
2. What specific behavior therapy technique is used to treat phobias? How does it work?
3. What is cognitive-behavior therapy?
4. What is integrative therapy?

3· BIOLOGICAL THERAPIES

Biological therapies, typically administered by psychiatrists or other medical doctors, involve altering aspects of bodily functioning to treat psychological disorders. Drug therapy is the most common form of biomedical therapy. Electroconvulsive therapy and psychosurgery are much less widely used biomedical therapies.

Drug Therapy

Although people have long used medicine and herbs to alleviate symptoms of emotional distress, it was not until the twentieth century that drug treatments revolutionized mental healthcare. Psychotherapeutic drugs are used to treat many disorders. In this section we explore the effectiveness of drugs for various disorders—including anxiety disorders, depressive disorders, bipolar disorder, and schizophrenia. As you read about these various treatments, you will note that the reasons why a particular drug works for a particular problem are not always understood. Rather, these drugs are used because they work—and research continues to explore the reasons for their effectiveness.

ANTIANXIETY DRUGS

● **antianxiety drugs** Drugs that reduce anxiety by making the individual calmer and less excitable; commonly known as tranquilizers.

Antianxiety drugs, commonly known as tranquilizers, make individuals calmer and less excitable. Benzodiazepines are the antianxiety drugs that generally offer the greatest relief for anxiety symptoms. They work by binding to the receptor sites of neurotransmitters that become overactive during anxiety (Diaper & others, 2012). The most frequently prescribed benzodiazepines include Xanax, Valium, and Librium (Bernardy & others, 2012).

Benzodiazepines are relatively fast-acting, taking effect within hours. Side effects of benzodiazepines include drowsiness, loss of coordination, fatigue, and mental slowing (Fields, 2013). These effects can be hazardous when a person is driving or operating machinery, especially when the individual first starts taking the medication.

Benzodiazepines also have been linked to abnormalities in babies born to mothers who took them during pregnancy (Hudak & others, 2012). Further, the combination of benzodiazepines with alcohol and with other medications can lead to problems such as depression (Dell'Osso & Lader, 2012).

Antianxiety medications are best used only temporarily for symptomatic relief. Too often, they are overused and can become addictive (Lader, 2012; Marazziti, Carlini, & Dell'Osso, 2012).

ANTIDEPRESSANT DRUGS

● **antidepressant drugs** Drugs that regulate mood.

Antidepressant drugs regulate mood. The four main classes of antidepressant drugs are tricyclics, such as Elavil; tetracyclics, such as Avanza; monoamine oxidase (MAO) inhibitors, such as Nardil; and selective serotonin reuptake inhibitors, such as Prozac, Paxil, and Zoloft. These antidepressants are all thought to help alleviate depressed mood through their effects on neurotransmitters in the brain. In different ways, they all allow the person's brain to increase or maintain its level of important neurotransmitters. Let's take a close look at each of these types of antidepressants.

Tricyclics, so-called because of their three-ringed molecular structure, are believed to work by increasing the level of certain neurotransmitters, especially norepinephrine and serotonin (Duric & Duman, 2013; Racagni & Popoli, 2010). You might recall the role of low serotonin levels in negative mood (Chapter 12) and aggression (Chapter 13). The tricyclics reduce the symptoms of depression in approximately 60 to 70 percent of cases, usually taking 2 to 4 weeks to improve mood. Adverse side effects may include restlessness, faintness, trembling, sleepiness, and memory difficulties. A recent meta-analysis of 30 years of studies concluded that the older antidepressant drugs, such as the tricyclics, reduced depression more effectively than the newer antidepressant drugs (Undurraga & Baldessarini, 2012).

People have used medicinal herbs to treat emotional distress since ancient times.

Related to the tricyclics are *tetracyclic* antidepressants (named for their four-ringed structure). Tetracyclics are also called *noradrenergic and specific serotonergic antidepressants,* or NaSSAs. These drugs increase the levels of both norepinephrine and serotonin in the brain.

MAO inhibitors are thought to work because they block monoamine oxidase, an enzyme that breaks down serotonin and norepinephrine in the brain (Meyer, 2012). Scientists believe that the blocking action of MAO inhibitors allows these neurotransmitters to remain in the brain's synapses and help regulate mood. MAO inhibitors are not as widely used as the tricyclics because they are more potentially harmful to the body. However, some individuals who do not respond to the tricyclics do respond to MAO inhibitors. MAO inhibitors may be especially risky because of their potential interactions with certain fermented foods (such as cheese) and other drugs, leading to high blood pressure and risk of stroke (Nishida & others, 2009).

Psychiatrists and general practitioners increasingly are prescribing a type of antidepressant called *selective serotonin reuptake inhibitors* (SSRIs). SSRIs target serotonin and work mainly by interfering only with the reabsorption of serotonin in the brain (Fooladi, Bell, & Davis, 2012; Kocsis, 2013). Figure 16.6 shows how this process works.

The increased use of SSRIs reflects their effectiveness in reducing depressive symptoms with fewer side effects than other antidepressants (Amsterdam, Luo, & Shults, 2013). Still, they can have negative effects, including insomnia, anxiety, headache, and diarrhea (Keeton, Kolos, & Walkup, 2009). They also can impair sexual functioning and produce severe withdrawal symptoms if the individual abruptly stops taking them (Kurose & others, 2012).

A large-scale U.S. study revealed that the number of individuals taking antidepressants rose nearly 400 percent among all ages between 1988 and 2008, with 11 percent of individuals 12 years and older taking an antidepressant in 2008 (Pratt, Brody, & Gu, 2011). More than 60 percent of those surveyed reported that they had been taking antidepressants for 2 years or longer, and 14 percent for 10 years or longer.

In addition to depressive disorder, antidepressant drugs are often prescribed for anxiety disorders, as well as obsessive-compulsive disorder, post-traumatic stress disorder, and some eating and sleep disorders (Camenisch & Hilt, 2013; Milano & others, 2012). Antidepressants are also prescribed for other problems, like sleeplessness and chronic pain. In fact, in 2005, less than half of the individuals in the United States who had taken prescribed antidepressants were doing so for depression (Olfson & Marcus, 2009).

The use of antidepressant drugs to treat depression in children is contentious. To read more about this issue, see the Critical Controversy.

FIGURE 16.6 How the Antidepressant Prozac Works Secreted by a transmitting neuron, serotonin moves across the synaptic gap and binds to receptors in a receiving neuron. Excess serotonin in the synaptic gap is normally reabsorbed by the transmitting neuron. The antidepressant Prozac blocks this reuptake of serotonin by the transmitting neuron, however, leaving excess serotonin in the synaptic gap. The excess serotonin is transmitted to the receiving neuron and circulated through the brain. The result is a reduction of the serotonin deficit found in individuals with depression.

MEDICATION FOR BIPOLAR DISORDER

Lithium is widely used to treat bipolar disorder. Lithium is the lightest of the solid elements in the periodic table of elements. Lithium is thought to stabilize moods by influencing norepinephrine and serotonin, but the exact mechanism of its effect is unknown (Ago & others, 2012). The amount of lithium that circulates in the bloodstream must be carefully monitored because the effective dosage is precariously close to toxic levels. Kidney and thyroid gland complications as well as weight gain can arise as a consequence of lithium therapy (Bauer & others, 2007). Lithium may be combined with antidepressant drugs during depressive episodes.

● **lithium** The lightest of the solid elements in the periodic table of elements, widely used to treat bipolar disorder.

ANTIPSYCHOTIC DRUGS

Antipsychotic drugs are powerful drugs that diminish agitated behavior, reduce tension, decrease hallucinations, improve social behavior, and produce better sleep patterns in individuals who have a severe psychological disorder, especially schizophrenia (Guo & others, 2012). Antipsychotic drugs do not cure schizophrenia. They treat only the

● **antipsychotic drugs** Powerful drugs that diminish agitated behavior, reduce tension, decrease hallucinations, improve social behavior, and produce better sleep patterns in individuals with a severe psychological disorder, especially schizophrenia.

CRITICAL CONTROVERSY

Do Antidepressants Increase Suicide Risk in Children?

In 2000, Caitlin McIntosh, a 12-year-old straight-*A* student, artist, and musician, hanged herself with her shoelaces. Caitlin had been struggling with depression and had begun taking antidepressants shortly before her suicide. Tragic cases such as Caitlin's stirred deep concerns among parents and mental health professionals. Could the very drugs prescribed to alleviate depression be causing children to become suicidal?

In response to these concerns, the FDA in 2004 reviewed clinical trials of antidepressant use with children (Hammad, Laughren, Racoosin, 2006). None of the children in the studies attempted or committed suicide, and there were no differences between the antidepressant and placebo groups on ratings of suicidal thoughts and behaviors. However, children who received antidepressants were two times more likely than those in the placebo groups to spontaneously mention thoughts of suicide, as noted by parents or doctors (the rate of such events was 4 percent in the antidepressant group versus 2 percent for the placebo group).

Based on this difference, the FDA began requiring prescription antidepressants to carry the severest "black box" warning, describing the potential of antidepressants to be associated with suicidal thoughts and behaviors in children and adolescents (FDA, 2004). The warning, which was widely publicized, had a chilling effect: Between March 2004 and June 2005, the number of prescriptions fell 20 percent compared to the same time frame the year before (Rosack, 2007).

Since the advent of the black box warning, a number of studies have shown no link between antidepressants and suicidal thoughts or behavior among youth (Gibbons & others, 2012; Sharmila, 2012). Some observers have noted that in the months after the warning took effect, suicide rates among youth increased after having steadily declined for a decade (Bridge & others, 2008; Gibbons & others, 2007). An analysis of data from annual national surveys of youth found that among those who were depressed, reports of delinquent behaviors and illicit drug use increased while grade point average declined in the years after the warning, compared to their levels in the years before (Busch, Golberstein, & Meara, 2011). Such findings might suggest that the black box warning had unexpected consequences on youth struggling with depression.

Perhaps most troubling, there is no strong evidence that depressed adolescents were more likely to receive psychotherapy after the warning took effect (Busch & others, 2010). Such findings are especially disappointing because drug therapy may not be the first-choice treatment for depressed children. Many children and adolescents have uncomplicated depression that responds well to psychotherapy alone (Morris, 2012).

This controversy highlights issues we have addressed throughout this book. How do we weigh dramatic case study evidence against less vivid scientific data that do not bear out those cases? Are special considerations required when professionals suggest drug therapy in children? How can we best balance the potential benefits and risks of drug treatment? Throughout this debate, the tragedy of suicide has loomed, and professionals have been moved to change their thinking and practices with regard to treating depression in youth.

WHAT DO YOU THINK
- Have antidepressants helped anyone you know? If so, were you aware of negative side effects? Positive side effects? What was the nature of these effects?
- What other events might explain the changes in academic and other outcomes from depressed youth after the black box warning took effect?
- What do you think of the common practice of treating depression with medication first?

---

symptoms of the disorder, not its causes. If an individual with schizophrenia stops taking the medication, the symptoms return. Because schizophrenia is a chronic disorder, many individuals take these medicines for decades (Domino & Swartz, 2008).

Two types of antipsychotic drugs used to treat schizophrenia are neuroleptics and atypical antipsychotic medication. *Neuroleptics* (also called *first-generation antipsychotics*), including Haldol (haloperidol), Loxitane (loxapine), and Thorazine (chlorpromazine), are thought to block dopamine's action in the brain (Zhai, Miller, & Sammis, 2012). *Atypical antipsychotic medications* (also called *second-generation antipsychotics*), including

Clozaril (clozapine) and Risperdal (risperidone), appear to influence dopamine as well as serotonin (Germann, Kurylo, & Han, 2012).

Both neuroleptics and atypical antipsychotic medications have shown some effectiveness in reducing schizophrenia's symptoms (Lieberman & others, 2005; E. J. Park & others, 2013). These types of medications differ, however, in terms of their side effects.

Two serious side effects of antipsychotic medication are tardive dyskinesia and metabolic syndrome. *Tardive dyskinesia* is a neurological disorder characterized by involuntary random movements of the facial muscles, tongue, and mouth, as well as twitching of the neck, arms, and legs (Alexander & Bickerstaff, 2013). *Metabolic syndrome* is a condition associated with obesity and risk for diabetes and heart disease. Neuroleptics carry a higher risk of tardive dyskinesia, and atypical antipsychotic medications carry a higher risk of metabolic syndrome (Stoklosa & Öngür, 2011).

These side effects can influence patient compliance with treatment. When selecting treatments for patients, then, psychiatrists must weigh these risks as well as patient factors that might make them vulnerable to these side effects. Finally, along with medication, individuals with schizophrenia may need training in vocational, family, and social skills.

AND THEN THEY GAVE ME THIS NEW DRUG AND I THOUGHT WHAT THE HECK, WHY NOT, I'VE TAKEN EVERYTHING ELSE ...

LAB RAT REHAB

© Mike Shiell. www.CartoonStock.com.

Figure 16.7 summarizes the drugs used to treat various psychological disorders, the disorders they target, their effectiveness, and their side effects. Notice that for some types of anxiety disorders, such as agoraphobia, MAO inhibitors (antidepressant drugs) might be used rather than antianxiety drugs.

Psychological Disorder	Drug	Effectiveness	Side Effects
Everyday anxiety	Antianxiety drugs; antidepressant drugs	Substantial improvement short term	Antianxiety drugs: less powerful the longer people take them; may be addictive Antidepressant drugs: see below under depressive disorders
Generalized anxiety disorder	Antianxiety drugs	Not very effective	Less powerful the longer people take them; may be addictive
Panic disorder	Antianxiety drugs	About half show improvement	Less powerful the longer people take them; may be addictive
Agoraphobia	Tricyclic drugs and MAO inhibitors	Majority show improvement	Tricyclics: restlessness, fainting, and trembling MAO inhibitors: toxicity
Specific phobias	Antianxiety drugs	Not very effective	Less powerful the longer people take them; may be addictive
Depressive disorders	Tricyclic drugs, MAO inhibitors, SSRI drugs, and tetracyclic drugs	Majority show moderate improvement	Tricyclics: cardiac problems, mania, confusion, memory loss, fatigue MAO inhibitors: toxicity SSRI drugs: nausea, nervousness, insomnia, and in a few cases, suicidal thoughts Tetracyclics: drowsiness, increased appetite, weight gain
Bipolar disorder	Lithium	Large majority show substantial improvement	Toxicity
Schizophrenia	Neuroleptics; atypical antipsychotic medications	Majority show partial improvement	Neuroleptics: irregular heartbeat, low blood pressure, uncontrolled fidgeting, tardive dyskinesia, and immobility of face Atypical antipsychotic medications: metabolic syndrome; less extensive side effects than with neuroleptics, but can have a toxic effect on white blood cells

FIGURE 16.7 **Drug Therapy for Psychological Disorders** This figure summarizes the types of drugs used to treat various psychological disorders.

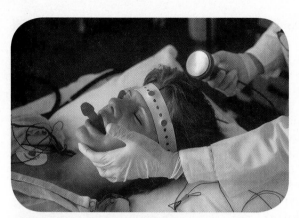

Electroconvulsive therapy (ECT), commonly called shock therapy, causes a seizure in the brain. ECT is still given to as many as 100,000 people a year, mainly to treat major depressive disorder.

● **electroconvulsive therapy (ECT)** A treatment, sometimes used for depression, that sets off a seizure in the brain; also called shock therapy.

Electroconvulsive Therapy

The goal of **electroconvulsive therapy (ECT),** commonly called *shock therapy,* is to set off a seizure in the brain. The notion that causing someone to have a seizure might help cure a psychological disorder may seem strange, but this idea has been around for quite some time. Hippocrates, the ancient Greek father of medicine, first noticed that malaria-induced convulsions would sometimes cure individuals who were thought to be insane (Endler, 1988). Following Hippocrates, many other medical doctors noted that head traumas, seizures, and convulsions brought on by fever would sometimes lead to the apparent cure of psychological problems.

In the early twentieth century, doctors induced seizures by insulin overdose and other means and used this procedure primarily to treat schizophrenia. In 1937, Ugo Cerletti, an Italian neurologist specializing in epilepsy, developed an efficient procedure to induce seizures using electrical shock, and ECT gained wide use in mental institutions (Faedda & others, 2010). Unfortunately, in earlier years, ECT was used indiscriminately, sometimes even to punish patients, as illustrated in the classic film *One Flew Over the Cuckoo's Nest,* starring Jack Nicholson.

Today, doctors use ECT primarily to treat severe depression (Bennett & others, 2013; Birkenhager & others, 2010; van Waarde & others, 2013), and it has shown some usefulness in treating severe, chronic post-traumatic stress disorder (Margoob, Zaffar Ali, & Andrade, 2010). ECT is given mainly to individuals who have not responded to drug therapy or psychotherapy, and its administration involves little discomfort. The patient receives anesthesia and muscle relaxants before the current is applied; this medication allows the individual to sleep through the procedure, minimizes convulsions, and reduces the risk of physical injury. Although in the past, electrical current was passed through the person's entire brain, increasingly ECT is applied only to the right side.

How effective is ECT? One analysis of the use of ECT compared its effectiveness in treating depression with that of cognitive therapy and antidepressant drugs (Seligman, 1994). ECT was as effective as cognitive therapy or drug therapy, with about four of five individuals showing marked improvement in all three therapies.

What sets electroconvulsive therapy apart from other treatments is the rapid relief it can produce in a person's mood (Merkl, Heuser, & Bajbouj, 2009). ECT may be especially effective as a treatment for acute depression in individuals who are at great risk of suicide (Kellner & others, 2006; Weiner & others, 2013). One study compared fMRI brain scans before and after ECT and found that the procedure reduced or weakened connections in the prefrontal cortex (Perrin & others, 2012).

ECT is controversial. Its potential side effects remain a source of debate and contradictory findings (Verwijk & others, 2012). These possible effects include memory loss and other cognitive impairments (Hirshbein, 2012). Some individuals treated with ECT have reported prolonged and profound memory loss (Koitabashi, Oyaizu, & Ouchi, 2009). Despite these potential problems, some psychiatrists argue that for certain individuals, this invasive treatment can have life-enhancing—and even life-saving—benefits (Huuhka & others, 2012; Martínez-Amorós & others, 2012).

More recently, practitioners are treating psychological disorders by applying electrical stimulation in very precise locations in the brain (Luigjes & others, 2012). In **deep brain stimulation,** doctors surgically implant electrodes in the brain that emit signals to alter the brain's electrical circuitry. For instance, deep brain stimulation of the nucleus accumbens (part of the brain's reward pathways) has been effective in treating severe depression (Bewernick & others, 2012).

● **deep brain stimulation** A procedure for treatment-resistant depression that involves the implantation of electrodes in the brain that emit signals to alter the brain's electrical circuitry.

Psychosurgery

● **psychosurgery** A biological therapy, with irreversible effects, that involves removal or destruction of brain tissue to improve the individual's adjustment.

Psychosurgery is a biological intervention that involves the removal or destruction of brain tissue to improve the individual's adjustment. The effects of psychosurgery cannot be reversed.

In the 1930s, Portuguese physician Antonio Egas Moniz developed a surgical procedure in which an instrument was inserted into the brain and rotated, severing fibers connecting the frontal lobe and the thalamus. Moniz theorized that by severing the connections between these structures, the surgeon could alleviate the symptoms of severe mental disorders (Soares & others, 2013). In 1949, Moniz received the Nobel Prize for developing the procedure, which he felt should be used with extreme caution and only as a last resort.

After hearing about Moniz's procedure, American neurologist Walter Freeman became the champion of *prefrontal lobotomies* (a term Freeman coined). Freeman developed his own technique, performed using a device similar to an ice pick, in surgeries that lasted mere minutes. A dynamic and charismatic advocate, in the 1950s and 60s Freeman traveled the country in a van he called the "lobotomobile," demonstrating the surgery in state-run mental institutions. In his career, Freeman performed over 3,000 lobotomies (El-Hai, 2005). Prefrontal lobotomies were conducted on tens of thousands of patients from the 1930s through the 1960s. These numbers speak not only to Freeman's persuasive charm but also to the desperation many physicians felt in treating institutionalized patients with severe psychological disorders (Lerner, 2005).

Subsequent research called the lobotomy procedure into question (Landis & Erlick, 1950; Mettler, 1952). Many individuals who received lobotomies suffered permanent and profound brain damage (Soares & others, 2013). Ethical concerns arose because, in many instances, giving consent for the lobotomy was a requirement for release from a mental hospital. Like ECT, lobotomies were being used as a form of punishment and control.

In the late 1970s new regulations classified the procedure as experimental and established safeguards for patients. Fortunately, crude lobotomies are no longer performed, and Freeman's technique is certainly not typical of contemporary psychosurgery. Modern psychosurgery is quite precise (Heller & others, 2006; Kopell, Machado, & Rezai, 2006) and involves making just a small lesion in the amygdala or another part of the limbic system (Fountas & Smith, 2007).

Today, only several hundred patients who have severely debilitating conditions undergo psychosurgery each year. Psychosurgery may be performed for OCD, major depression, or bipolar disorder rather than for schizophrenia (van Vliet & others, 2013; Shelton & others, 2010). Just as Moniz originally suggested, the procedure is now used only as a last resort—and with the utmost caution.

4· SOCIOCULTURAL APPROACHES AND ISSUES IN TREATMENT

In the treatment of psychological disorders, behavior therapies modify the person's behavior, cognitive therapies alter the person's thinking, and biological therapies change the person's body. This section focuses on sociocultural approaches to the treatment of psychological disorders. These methods view the individual as part of a system of relationships that are influenced by various social and cultural factors (Boyd-Franklin & others, 2013; Sue & others, 2014).

We first review some common sociocultural approaches, including group therapy, family and couples therapy, self-help support groups, and community mental health. We then examine various cultural perspectives on therapy.

Group Therapy

There is good reason to believe that individuals who share a psychological problem may benefit from observing others cope with a similar problem and that helping others cope can in turn improve individuals' feelings of competence and efficacy. The sociocultural approach known as **group therapy** brings together individuals who share a psychological disorder in sessions that are typically led by a mental health professional.

test yourself

1. How do antianxiety drugs work, and why do so many people take them?
2. What are SSRIs, and through what process do they have their effect?
3. Describe the procedure used in electroconvulsive therapy (ECT).

● **group therapy** A sociocultural approach to the treatment of psychological disorders that brings together individuals who share a particular psychological disorder in sessions that are typically led by a mental health professional.

Advocates of group therapy stress that individual therapy is limited because it puts the client outside the normal context of relationships. It is these very relationships, they argue, that may hold the key to successful therapy. Many psychological problems develop in the context of interpersonal relationships—within one's family, marriage, or peer group, for example. By taking into account the context of these important groups, therapy may be more successful.

Group therapy takes many diverse forms—including psychodynamic, humanistic, behavior, and cognitive therapy—plus approaches that do not reflect the major psychotherapeutic perspectives (Y. Chung & others, 2013; Piper & Sierra Hernandez, 2013). Six features characterize group therapy (Yalom & Leszcz, 2006):

- *Information:* Individuals receive information about their problems from either the group leader or other group members.

- *Universality:* Individuals are able to see that they are not alone. Others share their experiences.

- *Altruism:* Group members support one another with advice and sympathy and learn that they have something to offer others.

- *Experience of a positive family group:* A therapy group often resembles a family, with the leaders representing parents and the other members of the group representing siblings. In this new family, old wounds may be healed and new, more positive family ties made.

- *Development of social skills:* Corrective feedback from peers may correct flaws in the individual's interpersonal skills. An individual may come to see that he or she is self-centered if five other group members comment on the person's self-centeredness; in individual therapy, the individual might not believe the therapist.

- *Interpersonal learning:* The group can serve as a training ground for practicing new behaviors and relationships. A hostile person may learn that he or she can get along better with others by behaving less aggressively, for example.

● **family therapy** Group therapy with family members.

● **couples therapy** Group therapy with married or unmarried couples whose major problem lies within their relationship.

Family and Couples Therapy

Our relationships with family members and significant others are certainly an important part of human life. Sometimes these vital relationships can benefit from a helpful outsider. **Family therapy** is group therapy among family members (Wagenaar & Baars, 2012). **Couples therapy** is group therapy with married or unmarried couples whose major problem lies within their relationship. These approaches stress that although one person may have some abnormal symptoms, those symptoms are a function of the family or couple relationships (Lebow & Stroud, 2013). Psychodynamic, humanistic, and behavior therapies may be used in family and couples therapy.

Four of the most widely used family therapy techniques are

- *Validation:* The therapist expresses an understanding and acceptance of each family member's feelings and beliefs and thus validates the person. When the therapist talks with each family member, he or she finds something positive to say.

- *Reframing:* The therapist helps families reframe problems as family problems, not an individual's problems. A delinquent adolescent girl's problems are reframed in terms of how each family member contributed to the situation. The parents' lack of attention to the girl or marital conflict may be involved, for example.

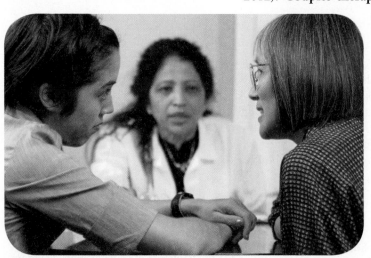

In family therapy, the assumption is that particular patterns of interaction among the family members cause the observed abnormal symptoms.

- *Structural change:* The family therapist tries to restructure the coalitions in a family. In a mother–son coalition, the therapist might suggest that the father take a stronger disciplinarian role to relieve the mother of some burden. Restructuring might be as simple as suggesting that the parents explore satisfying ways of being together, such as going out once a week for a quiet dinner.

- *Detriangulation:* In some families, one member is the scapegoat for two other members who are in conflict but pretend not to be. For example, parents of a girl with anorexia nervosa might insist that their marriage is fine but find themselves in subtle conflict over how to handle the child. The therapist tries to disentangle, or detriangulate, this situation by shifting attention away from the child to the conflict between the parents.

© David Sipress

Couples therapy proceeds in much the same way as family therapy. Couples therapy addresses diverse problems such as alcohol abuse, jealousy, sexual issues, infidelity, gender roles, two-career families, divorce, remarriage, and the special concerns of stepfamilies (Sandberg & Knestel, 2011). Conflict in close relationships frequently involves poor communication, and so the therapist tries to improve the communication between the partners (Meneses & Greenberg, 2011; Navidian & Bahari, 2013).

Self-Help Support Groups

Self-help support groups are voluntary organizations of individuals who get together on a regular basis to discuss topics of common interest. A professional does not conduct the group; rather, a paraprofessional or a member of the common-interest group takes the lead. *Paraprofessionals* are individuals who have been taught by a professional to provide some mental health services but who do not have formal mental health training. Some paraprofessionals may themselves have had a disorder; for example, a chemical dependency counselor may also be a recovering addict. The group leader and members provide support to help individuals with their problems.

Self-help support groups play a valuable role in Americans' mental health (Norcross & others, 2013). A survey in 2002 revealed that for mental health support, nearly 7,500 such groups existed in the United States, with more than 1 million members (Goldstrom & others, 2006). In addition to reaching so many people in need of help, these groups are important because they are relatively inexpensive. They also serve people who are otherwise unlikely to receive help, such as those with less education and few resources.

Self-help support groups provide members with a sympathetic audience for social sharing and emotional release. The social support, role modeling, and sharing of concrete strategies for solving problems that unfold in self-help groups add to their effectiveness. A woman who has been raped might not believe a therapist who tells her that, with time, she will put the pieces of her shattered life back together. The same message from another rape survivor—someone who has had to work through the same feelings of rage, fear, and violation—might be more believable.

Alcoholics Anonymous (AA), founded in 1935 by a reformed alcoholic and a physician, is one of the best-known self-help groups (Kelly, 2013). Some studies show a positive effect for AA (Pagano & others, 2013), but others do not (Kaskutas, 2009). Researchers continue to explore whether AA is beneficial (Blonigen, Timko, & Moos, 2013; Krentzman, Cranford & Robinson, 2013) and, if so, for whom (Krentzman & others, 2012).

For individuals who tend to cope by seeking information and affiliation with similar peers, self-help support groups can reduce stress and promote adjustment. However, as reviewed in Chapter 13, groups can be positive or negative influences on individuals, and group leaders may need to monitor these processes.

"We're organizing a tantrum support group."

© Randy Glasbergen

Community mental health counselors can serve as a lifeline to many local citizens.

Community Mental Health

The community mental health movement was born in the 1960s as society's attitude toward people with psychological disorders began to change. The deplorable conditions of some psychiatric facilities at the time were one catalyst for the movement. Advocates of community mental health maintained that individuals with psychological disorders ought to remain within society with their families rather than being locked away in institutions, and they should receive treatment in community mental health centers. This movement also reflected economic concerns, as it was thought that institutionalizing people was certainly more expensive than treating them in the community.

With the passage of the Community Mental Health Act of 1963, large numbers of individuals with psychological disorders were transferred from mental institutions to community-based facilities, a process called *deinstitutionalization*. Although at least partially motivated by a desire to treat individuals with psychological disorders more effectively and humanely, deinstitutionalization has been linked to rising rates of homelessness. The success of community mental health services depends on the resources and commitment of the communities in which they occur.

Community mental health involves training teachers, ministers, family physicians, nurses, and others who directly interact with community members to offer lay counseling and workshops. Clients receive help in areas ranging from coping with stress to reducing their drug use to developing assertiveness (A. Lim & others, 2012). Advocates and providers of community mental health believe that the best way to treat a psychological disorder is through prevention (Feinstein, Richter, & Foster, 2012; Thota & others, 2012).

An explicit goal of community mental health is to help people who are disenfranchised from society, such as those living in poverty, to lead happier, more productive lives (Cook & Kilmer, 2012; Simning & others, 2012). A key concept involved in this effort is *empowerment*—assisting individuals to develop the skills they need to control their own lives. Importantly, all of these programs may rely on financial support from local, state, and federal governments.

Cultural Perspectives

The psychotherapies discussed earlier in this chapter—psychodynamic, humanistic, behavior, and cognitive—center on the individual. This focus is compatible with the needs of people in Western cultures such as the United States, where the emphasis is on the individual rather than the group (family, community, or ethnic group). However, these psychotherapies may not be as effective with people who live in collectivistic cultures that place more importance on the group (Sue & others, 2013). Some psychologists argue that family therapy is likely to be more effective with people in cultures that place a high value on the family, such as Latino and Asian cultures (Y. Guo, 2005).

Considering psychotherapy within a cultural framework is enormously complex (Huey & others, 2014). Cultures may differ, for instance, in how they view the appropriateness of talking with an elder about personal problems or in talking about one's feelings at all (Asnaani & Hofmann, 2012; Naeem & others, 2009). Cultural issues in therapy include factors such as socioeconomic status, ethnicity, gender, country of origin, current culture, and religious beliefs and traditions (Farren, Snee, & McElroy, 2011; Joutsenniemi & others, 2012).

Cross-cultural competence refers both to how skilled a therapist feels about being able to manage cultural issues that might arise in therapy and to how the client

● **cross-cultural competence** A therapist's assessment of his or her ability to manage cultural issues in therapy and the client's perception of those abilities.

Clinical and Cultural Psychology: How Does Culture Influence Responses to Treatment?

All therapies seek to help people become psychologically healthier. What is a psychologically healthy person like? For many people, the answers are provided by culture. How well cultural values match up with the values inherent in therapeutic approaches is imperative.

For example, cognitive-behavior therapy (CBT) involves prompting individuals to question the validity of their beliefs and the reasonableness of their thoughts. From the CBT perspective, changing the way people think about their life experiences gives them a sense of control over their emotions and reactions. Consider, though, that some of our beliefs are embedded in our cultural worldview. Clients in therapy might view others' efforts to change such beliefs as judgmental or biased (Asnaami & Hofmann, 2012).

What makes a person psychologically healthy? How does your cultural experience influence your answer?

Cultures differ in terms of how well they match up with the values of CBT. For instance, in one study of college students in India, many felt that the goals of CBT conflicted with their personal, cultural, and religious beliefs (Scorzelli & Reinke-Scorzelli, 1994). Among these students, the notion that individuals might, through therapy, gain greater control over their life was viewed as clashing with cultural values emphasizing that supernatural forces define one's destiny and that a person should live in accord with familial and societal expectations. Similarly, a study in Pakistan found that students perceived being assertive, talking about one's feelings with an elder, and gaining control over one's feelings and life choices as inconsistent with their religious values (Naeem & others, 2009).

Culture plays a role, as well, in responsiveness to biological treatments, in a broad range of ways. For instance, culture influences diet, which can affect responses to drugs. Furthermore, cultural beliefs about the appropriateness of taking medication for psychological problems differ greatly (Wong & Pi, 2012). Ethnic differences exist in drug sensitivities as well, suggesting that optimal dosages across different ethnic groups may vary (Ninnemann, 2012). Finally, individuals from East Asian cultures may be more likely to use traditional herbal treatments that may influence the effects of psychoactive drugs (Wong & Pi, 2012).

Just as culture informs the meaning of normal and abnormal, it can influence the ways individuals respond to treatments for conditions deemed abnormal. To meet the needs of the diverse human population, practitioners of all forms of therapy must be ever mindful of these differences.

---

perceives the therapist's ability (Asnaani & Hofmann, 2012; Sue & others, 2014). Dominant features of cross-cultural competence are demonstrating respect for cultural beliefs and practices and balancing the goals of a particular therapeutic approach with the goals and values of a culture. To read more about the issues, see the Intersection.

ETHNICITY

Many ethnic minority individuals prefer discussing problems with parents, friends, and relatives rather than mental health professionals (Boyd-Franklin & others, 2013; Sue & others, 2014). Might therapy be most successful when the therapist and the client are from the same ethnic background? Researchers have found that when there is an ethnic match between the therapist and the client and when ethnic-specific services are provided, clients are less likely to drop out of therapy early and in many cases have better treatment outcomes (Jackson & Greene, 2000). Ethnic-specific services include culturally appropriate greetings and arrangements (for example, serving tea rather than coffee to Chinese American clients), providing flexible hours for treatment, and employing a bicultural/bilingual staff (Nystul, 1999).

Nonetheless, therapy can still be effective when the therapist and client are from different ethnic backgrounds if the therapist has excellent clinical skills and is culturally sensitive (Akhtar, 2006). Culturally skilled psychotherapists have good knowledge of their clients' cultural groups, understand sociopolitical influences, and have competence in working with culturally diverse groups (Austad, 2009; Sue & others, 2014).

GENDER

One byproduct of changing gender roles for women and men is reevaluation of the goal of psychotherapy (Bratini, Ampuero, & Miville, 2013; Corpus & Miville, 2013; Redway & Miville, 2013). Traditionally, the goal has been autonomy or self-determination for the client. However, those goals are often more central to men than to women, whose lives generally are more characterized by relatedness and connection with others. Thus, some psychologists argue that therapy goals should involve increased attention to relatedness and connection with others, especially for women, or should emphasize both autonomy/self-determination and relatedness/connection to others (Notman & Nadelson, 2002).

Feminist therapists believe that traditional psychotherapy continues to carry considerable gender bias and has not adequately addressed the specific concerns of women. Thus, several alternative nontraditional therapies have arisen that aim to help clients break free from traditional gender roles and stereotypes. In terms of improving clients' lives, the goals of feminist therapists are no different from those of other therapists. However, feminist therapists seek to challenge the power dynamic that is implied in the traditional therapist–client relationship and maintain a sense of equality across these roles. Feminist therapists believe that improvement depends in part on understanding how bias and discrimination in women's lives can contribute to the development of psychological disorders. These therapists work to facilitate client empowerment and to identify and harness client strengths, rather than fixing weaknesses (Enns, 2012).

test yourself

1. Why might group therapy be more successful than individual therapy?
2. What are four common family therapy techniques? Briefly describe each.
3. What social and economic forces drove the community mental health movement?

5· THERAPIES AND HEALTH AND WELLNESS

Therapy is generally aimed at relieving psychological symptoms. A therapy is considered effective if it frees a person from the negative effects of psychological disorders. Does therapy have larger implications related to a person's psychological wellness and even physical health? Researchers have examined this interesting question in a variety of ways.

For example, people who learn that they have cancer are undoubtedly under stress. Might psychotherapeutic help aimed at reducing this stress improve patients' ability to cope with the disease? Research indicates that therapy is having such a positive effect. One study revealed that group-based cognitive therapy that focused on improving prostate cancer patients' stress management skills was effective in improving their quality of life (Penedo & others, 2006). Another study found that individual cognitive-behavior therapy reduced symptom severity in cancer patients undergoing chemotherapy (Sikorskii & others, 2006).

As well, psychotherapy directed at relieving psychological disorders such as depression can have important benefits for physical health (Purdy, 2013). Depression is associated with coronary heart disease, for example (Linke & others, 2009). Psychotherapy that reduces depression is likely, then, to reduce the risk of heart disease (Mavrides & Nemeroff, 2013). A research review also showed evidence of positive effects of psychotherapy on health behavior and physical illness, including habits and ailments such as smoking, chronic pain, chronic fatigue syndrome, and asthma (Eells, 2000).

Psychotherapy might also be a way to *prevent* psychological and physical problems. One study demonstrated the benefits of incorporating therapy into physical healthcare (Smit & others, 2006). Individuals waiting to see their primary healthcare provider received either physical health treatment as usual or that same treatment plus brief psychotherapy (a simple version of minimal contact cognitive-behavior therapy). The brief psychotherapy included a self-help manual, instructions in mood management, and six short telephone conversations with a prevention worker. The overall rate of depression was lowered significantly in the psychotherapy group, and this difference was cost effective. That is, the use of brief psychotherapy as a part of regular physical checkups was both psychologically and economically advantageous.

Finally, although typically targeted at relieving distressing symptoms, might psychotherapy enhance psychological well-being? This question is important because the absence of psychological symptoms (the goal of most psychotherapy) is not the same thing as the presence of psychological wellness. Just as an individual who is without serious physical illness is not necessarily at the height of physical health, a person who is relatively free of psychological symptoms still might not show the qualities we associate with psychological thriving. Studies have found that a lack of psychological wellness may predispose individuals to relapse or make them vulnerable to problems (Ryff, Singer, & Love, 2004; Thunedborg, Black, & Bech, 1995). Research has demonstrated that individuals who show not only a decrease in symptoms but also an increase in well-being are less prone to relapse (Fava, 2006; Ruini & Fava, 2004).

Recently, therapists have developed a new type of treatment, aimed at enhancing well-being. **Well-being therapy (WBT)** is a short-term, problem-focused, directive therapy that encourages clients to accentuate the positive (Fava, 2006; Ruini & Fava, 2009). The first step in WBT is recognizing the good things in one's life when they happen. The initial WBT homework assignment asks clients to monitor their own happiness levels and keep track of moments of well-being. Clients are encouraged to note even small pleasures in their lives—a beautiful spring day, a relaxing chat with a friend, the great taste of morning coffee. Clients then identify thoughts and feelings that are related to the premature ending of these moments.

WBT is about learning to notice and savor positive experiences and coming up with ways to promote and celebrate life's good moments. WBT is effective in enhancing well-being, and it may also allow individuals to enjoy sustained recovery from mental disorders (Fava, Ruini, & Belaise, 2007; Ruini & Fava, 2009; Ruini & others, 2006).

Life is complicated and filled with potential pitfalls. We all need help from time to time, and therapy is one way to get that help. Through therapy we can improve ourselves—physically and psychologically—to become the best person we can be. Like all human relationships, a therapeutic relationship is complex and challenging but potentially rewarding, making positive change possible for an individual through a meaningful association with another (Joseph & Linley, 2004).

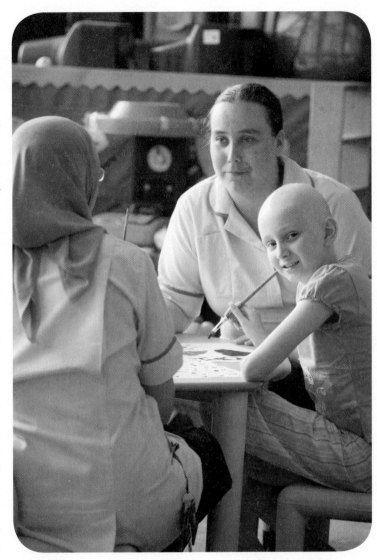

Psychotherapy can improve cancer patients' ability to cope with the disease.

● **well-being therapy (WBT)** A short-term, problem-focused, directive therapy that encourages clients to accentuate the positive.

test yourself

1. Discuss specific research findings about whether psychotherapy can improve a person's ability to cope with the effects of a disease such as cancer.
2. For what health-related behavior and chronic ailments is psychotherapy helpful, according to a research review?
3. What is well-being therapy, and what steps does it involve on the client's part?

1. APPROACHES TO TREATING PSYCHOLOGICAL DISORDERS

Two approaches to treating psychological disorders are psychotherapy and biological therapies. Psychotherapy, administered by a range of different professionals, is the process that mental health professionals use to help individuals recognize, define, and overcome their disorders and improve their adjustment. Biological treatments involve drugs and other procedures that change the functioning of the body. In most states, only medical doctors can prescribe drugs to treat psychological disorders. Psychologists have endeavored to obtain prescription privileges, arguing that doing so would make treatment more efficient for clients.

2. PSYCHOTHERAPY

Research strongly shows that psychotherapies are successful in treating psychological disorders, though no therapy is conclusively more effective than any other. Psychologists debate whether treatment decisions should be based on empirical research or clinical judgment. Evidence-based practice means taking research into account, combined with the clinician's judgment and client characteristics.

Three factors that influence the effectiveness of therapy are the therapeutic alliance, the therapist, and the client. Types of psychotherapy differ in terms of the how much they focus on gaining insight versus treating specific symptoms and gaining skills. They also differ in how directive or nondirective the therapist is.

Psychodynamic approaches to therapy focus on the unconscious and the need for the psychotherapist to interpret the client's thoughts, dreams, and childhood experiences. This form of therapy is based on the notion that gaining insight into unconscious conflicts is the key to treating psychological disorders.

Humanistic therapists encourage clients to understand themselves and to grow personally. Client-centered therapy, developed by Rogers, is a type of humanistic therapy that includes active listening, reflective speech, unconditional positive regard, empathy, and genuineness.

Behavior therapies use principles of learning to reduce or eliminate maladaptive behavior. They are based on the behavioral and social cognitive theories of personality. Behavior therapies seek to eliminate the symptoms or behaviors rather than to help individuals to gain insight into their problems.

Two behavior therapy techniques based on classical conditioning are systematic desensitization and aversive conditioning. In systematic desensitization, anxiety is treated by getting the individual to associate deep relaxation with increasingly intense anxiety-producing situations. In aversive conditioning, pairings of the undesirable behavior with aversive stimuli are repeated to decrease the behavior's pleasant associations.

In operant conditioning approaches to behavior therapy, a careful analysis of the person's environment is conducted to determine which factors need modification. Applied behavior analysis is the application of operant conditioning to change human behavior. Its main goal is to replace maladaptive behaviors with adaptive ones.

Cognitive therapies emphasize that the individual's cognitions (thoughts) are the main source of abnormal behavior. Cognitive therapies attempt to change the person's feelings and behaviors by changing cognitions. Cognitive-behavior therapy combines cognitive therapy and behavior therapy techniques. Self-efficacy and self-instructional methods are used in this approach.

As many as 50 percent of practicing therapists refer to themselves as "integrative" or "eclectic." Integrative therapy uses a combination of techniques from different therapies based on the therapist's judgment of which particular techniques will provide the greatest benefit for the client.

3. BIOLOGICAL THERAPIES

Biological approaches to therapy include drugs, electroconvulsive therapy (ECT), and psychosurgery. Psychotherapeutic drugs that treat psychological disorders fall into three main categories: antianxiety drugs, antidepressant drugs, medication for bipolar disorder, and antipsychotic drugs.

Benzodiazepines are the most commonly used antianxiety drugs. Antidepressant drugs regulate mood; the three main classes are tricyclics, MAO inhibitors, and SSRI drugs. Lithium is used to treat bipolar disorder. Antipsychotic drugs are administered to treat severe psychological disorders, especially schizophrenia.

Practitioners use electroconvulsive therapy to alleviate severe depression when other interventions have failed. Psychosurgery is an irreversible procedure in which brain tissue is destroyed. Though rarely used today, psychosurgery is more precise than in the days of prefrontal lobotomies.

4. SOCIOCULTURAL APPROACHES AND ISSUES IN TREATMENT

Group therapies emphasize that relationships can hold the key to successful therapy. Family therapy is group therapy with family members. Four widely used family therapy techniques are validation, reframing, structural change, and detriangulation. Couples therapy is group therapy with married or unmarried couples whose major problem is within their relationship.

Self-help support groups are voluntary organizations of individuals who get together on a regular basis to discuss topics of common interest. They are conducted without a professional therapist.

The community mental health movement was born out of the belief that individuals suffering from psychological disorders should not be locked away from their families and communities. The deinstitutionalization that resulted from the movement caused the homeless population to rise, however. Empowerment is often a goal of community mental health.

Psychotherapies' traditional focus on the individual may be successful in individualistic Western cultures. However, individual-centered psychotherapies may not work as well in collectivistic cultures. Therapy is often more effective when there is an ethnic match between the therapist and the client, although culturally sensitive therapy can be provided by a therapist with a different background than the client's.

Psychotherapies' emphasis on independence and self-reliance may be problematic for the many women who place a strong emphasis on connectedness in relationships. Feminist therapies have emerged to address that problem.

5. THERAPIES AND HEALTH AND WELLNESS

Psychotherapy has been shown to help individuals cope with serious physical diseases. Psychotherapy can also aid individuals by alleviating physical symptoms directly or by reducing psychological problems, such as depression, that are related to physical illness. Research has shown moreover that brief psychotherapy may be a cost-effective way to *prevent* serious psychological disorders.

Psychotherapy aims not only at reducing the presence of psychological illness but also at enhancing psychological wellness and personal growth. Individuals who gain in wellness are less likely to fall prey to recurrent psychological distress. Interventions such as well-being therapy have been designed to promote wellness itself.

key *terms*

apply your *knowledge*

1. To experience Rogerian therapy firsthand, watch a video of Carl Rogers describing his approach and participating in a session with a client at www.viddler.com/v/2b20cab0

2. To get a clear sense of how cognitive-behavior therapy works, see this clip at http://www.youtube.com/watch?v=ds3wHkwiuCo

3. Behavioral and cognitive approaches may be helpful in modifying a behavior that would not be considered abnormal but that an individual might still want to change (for example, procrastinating, eating unhealthy food, or watching too much TV). Think about a behavior that you would like to do more or less frequently; then imagine that you are a behavior therapist or a cognitive therapist, and describe the kinds of recommendations you might make during a therapy session.

4. For which kinds of problems would you be most likely to choose one of the sociocultural approaches to therapy? Which method would you choose? Do some research and see whether you can find a local group or therapist who would be helpful to someone with these kinds of problems. Where would you turn if an appropriate resource were not available in your area?

CHAPTER 17

Health Psychology

Is It a Disease or Just Gas?

Imagine that you are a parent of a 1-month-old infant.

Your baby's life generally involves eating, sleeping, pooping, and crying. You are tired all the time because your baby must be fed every 2 to 4 hours, even through the night. Days and nights blur together. You are exhausted. You notice that your baby, who is developing normally, has started to spit up a lot, sometimes quite suddenly, all over you. You start to worry that this frequent spitting up is a serious problem and take the baby to the doctor.

Laura Scherer and colleagues (2013) posed this scenario to parents while they waited for appointments with a pediatrician. For half, the scenario stated that the doctor diagnosed the baby with a disease called GERD (for gastrointestinal reflux disease). For the other half, the doctor never mentioned this label. The parents were asked whether they would seek medication for their child. Compared to those who were not given a disease label, parents who imagined their baby being diagnosed with GERD were strongly interested in medication, even when they had been told the medication was not effective.

This study shows what happens when physical symptoms are labeled as diseases and how psychological factors can influence health-related decisions.

Decision making is a psychological process even when it involves choices about medical treatments or between unhealthy and healthy behaviors. Indeed, physical health is influenced by contexts, behaviors, motivations, thoughts, and feelings—in other words, by factors at the very heart of the science of psychology. ●

PREVIEW

In this chapter, we focus on health psychology: the field devoted to promoting healthy practices and understanding the psychological processes that underlie health and illness. We begin by defining the field. Then we examine the various ways that psychologists explain the process of making healthy life changes and the resources on which individuals can draw to effect positive change. Next we survey what psychologists know about stress and coping, and we consider psychological perspectives on making wise choices in three vital areas: physical activity, diet, and the decision to smoke or not to smoke. We end with a look at psychology's role in shaping a good life.

1· HEALTH PSYCHOLOGY AND BEHAVIORAL MEDICINE

● **health psychology** A subfield of psychology that emphasizes psychology's role in establishing and maintaining health and preventing and treating illness.

● **behavioral medicine** An interdisciplinary field that focuses on developing and integrating behavioral and biomedical knowledge to promote health and reduce illness; overlaps with health psychology.

Health psychology emphasizes psychology's role in establishing and maintaining health and preventing and treating illness. Health psychologists emphasize that lifestyle choices, behaviors, and psychological characteristics can play important roles in health (Marks, 2013; Stowell, Robles, & Kane, 2013). A related discipline, **behavioral medicine,** is an interdisciplinary field that focuses on developing and integrating behavioral and biomedical knowledge to promote health and reduce illness. The concerns of health psychology and behavioral medicine overlap, but they are distinct. Health psychology primarily focuses on behavioral, social, and cognitive influences (Corsica & Perri, 2013; Xanthopoulos & Daniel, 2013), whereas behavioral medicine centers on behavioral, social, and biomedical factors (Aggarwal, Liao, & Mosca, 2013; Glei & others, 2013).

Health psychology and behavioral medicine both inform two related fields: health promotion and public health. *Health promotion* involves helping people change their lifestyle to optimize health and assisting them in achieving balance in physical, emotional, social, spiritual, and intellectual health and wellness. *Public health* is concerned with studying health and disease in large populations to guide policymakers. Public health experts identify public health concerns, set priorities, and design interventions for health promotion. An important goal of public health is to ensure that all populations have access to cost-effective healthcare, health promotion services, and health-promoting behaviors and resources.

The Biopsychosocial Model

The interests of health psychologists and behavioral medicine researchers are broad (Trudel-Fitzgerald, Savard, & Ivers, 2013; Turk & Wilson, 2013). The biopsychosocial model we examined in Chapter 15 in the context of psychological disorders applies to health psychology as well, because health psychology integrates biological, psychological, and social factors in health (Geller, Nelson, & Bonacquisti, 2013).

For example, stress is a focal point of study across the broad field of psychology. Study of the brain and behavior (Chapter 3), for instance, acknowledges the impact of stress on the autonomic nervous system. Furthermore, an individual's state of consciousness (Chapter 5), as well as the particular ways in which that person thinks about events (Chapter 8), can influence the experience of stress. Stressful events also affect our emotions (Chapter 10), which are themselves psychological and physical events. Aspects of our personalities, too, may be associated with stress (Chapter 12) and can influence our health. Finally, social contexts, relationships (Chapter 13), and work experiences (Chapter 14) can shape both an individual's experience of stress and his or her ability to cope with it.

The "Click It or Ticket" program, publicizing seatbelt use, reflects the efforts of individuals working in the related fields of health promotion and health psychology.

The Relationship Between Mind and Body

From the biopsychosocial perspective, the many diverse aspects of the person are strongly intertwined. Our bodies and minds are deeply connected, a link introduced in Chapter 1. After suffering a heart attack, one health psychologist ruefully noted that none of his colleagues in the field had thought to ask him whether heart disease was part of his family history, ignoring the obvious question that a medical doctor would ask first.

Although the mind is responsible for much of what happens in the body, it is not the only factor. Even as we consider the many ways that psychological processes contribute to health and disease, we must understand that sometimes illness happens for other reasons—affecting even those who have led healthy lives.

Although it might be more exciting to think about ways the mind may influence health, it is important to appreciate that the body may influence the mind as well. That is, how we feel physically may have implications for how we think. Health psychology and behavioral medicine are concerned not only with how psychological states influence health, but also with how health and illness may influence the person's psychological experience, including cognitive abilities, stress, and coping (O'Driscoll, 2013; Palgi, 2013). A person who is feeling psychologically run-down may not realize that the level of fatigue is in fact the beginning stage of an illness. In turn, being physically healthy can be a source of psychological wellness.

test yourself

1. What factors does the field of health psychology emphasize as keys to good health?
2. With what is the field of health promotion concerned?
3. Name three societal issues with which you might be concerned if you worked in the field of public health.

2· MAKING POSITIVE LIFE CHANGES

One of health psychology's missions is to help individuals identify and implement ways they can effectively change their behaviors for the better (Stowell, Robles, & Kane, 2013). **Health behaviors**—practices that have an impact on physical well-being—include adopting a healthy approach to stress, exercising, eating right, brushing one's teeth, performing breast and testicular exams, not smoking, drinking in moderation (or not at all), and practicing safe sex. Before exploring what health psychologists have learned about the best ways to make healthy behavioral changes, we focus on the process of change itself.

● **health behaviors** Practices that have an impact on physical well-being, such as adopting a healthy approach to stress, exercising, eating right, brushing one's teeth, performing breast and testicular exams, not smoking, drinking in moderation (or not at all), and practicing safe sex.

Theoretical Models of Change

In many instances, changing behaviors begins by changing attitudes. Psychologists have sought to understand specifically how changing attitudes can lead to behavioral changes.

What factors play a role in healthy behavior changes? One way this question has been answered is in the **theory of reasoned action** (Ajzen & Albarracin, 2007; Ajzen & Fishbein, 2005). The theory suggests that effective change requires that individuals

- Have specific intentions about their behaviors
- Hold positive attitudes about a new behavior
- Perceive that their social group looks favorably on the new behavior as well

● **theory of reasoned action** Theoretical model stating that effective change requires individuals to have specific intentions about their behaviors, as well as positive attitudes about a new behavior, and to perceive that their social group looks favorably on the new behavior as well.

The **theory of planned behavior** includes all of these three components but adds a fourth: the person's perceptions of *control* over the outcome (Ajzen, 2012a, 2012b). If you smoke and want to quit smoking, these theories tell us you will be more successful if you devise an explicit intention of quitting, feel good about it, believe that your friends support you, and believe that you have control over your smoking.

The theory of reasoned action and its extension, the theory of planned behavior, have accurately predicted whether individuals successfully engage in healthy behaviors (Ajzen & Manstead, 2007), including cancer screening (L. Ross & others, 2007), HIV prevention (Kalichman, 2007), prevention of smoking and marijuana use in adolescents and binge drinking in college students (Elliott & Ainsworth, 2012; Guo & others, 2007; Lac & others, 2009), exercise (B. H. Park & others, 2009; Plotnikoff & others, 2011), children's snack food consumption (Branscum & Sharma, 2013), self-medication with

● **theory of planned behavior** Theoretical model that includes the basic ideas of the theory of reasoned action but adds the person's perceptions of control over the outcome.

over-the-counter analgesics (Pineles & Parente, 2013), and cyberbullying in adolescence (Heirman & Walrave, 2012). Other theories have stressed the importance of awareness of the health threats posed by potentially harmful behaviors such as smoking and unprotected sex (Floyd, Prentice-Dunn, & Rogers, 2000; Fry & Prentice-Dunn, 2006).

Social cognitive theories emphasize the crucial role of beliefs about one's ability to make healthy changes, as well as of the individual's knowledge and skills (Bandura, 2009, 2012a). All theoretical models of health-related behavioral changes make predictions about the type of intervention that should be most successful in producing durable change.

The Stages of Change Model

● **stages of change model** Theoretical model describing a five-step process by which individuals give up bad habits and adopt healthier lifestyles.

The **stages of change model** describes the process by which individuals give up bad habits and adopt healthier lifestyles. The model breaks down behavioral changes into five steps, recognizing that real change does not occur overnight with one monumental decision (Norcross, Loberg, & Norcross, 2012; Prochaska, Norcross, & DiClemente, 1994) (Figure 17.1). Rather, change occurs in progressive stages, each characterized by particular issues and challenges. Those stages are

- Precontemplation
- Contemplation
- Preparation/Determination
- Action/Willpower
- Maintenance

PRECONTEMPLATION

The *precontemplation stage* occurs when individuals are not yet genuinely thinking about changing. They may not even be aware that they have a problem behavior. Individuals who drink to excess but are not aware that their drinking is affecting their work may be in this precontemplation phase. At this stage, raising one's consciousness about the problem is crucial.

FIGURE 17.1 Stages of Change Model Applied to Losing Weight
The stages of change model has been applied to many different health behaviors, including losing weight.

Stage	Description	Example
Precontemplation	Individuals are not yet ready to think about changing and may not be aware that they have a problem that needs to be changed.	Overweight individuals are not aware that they have a weight problem.
Contemplation	Individuals acknowledge that they have a problem but may not yet be ready to change.	Overweight individuals know they have a weight problem but aren't yet sure they want to commit to losing weight.
Preparation/ Determination	Individuals are preparing to take action.	Overweight individuals explore options they can pursue in losing weight.
Action/Willpower	Individuals commit to making a behavioral change and enact a plan.	Overweight individuals begin a diet and start an exercise program.
Maintenance	Individuals are successful in continuing their behavior change over time.	Overweight individuals are able to stick with their diet and exercise regimens for 6 months.

A woman who smokes may find her consciousness raised by the experience of becoming pregnant. A man who is stopped for drunk driving may be forced to take a good look at his drinking. Similarly, overweight individuals may not recognize their problem until they see photos of themselves taken at a family reunion—or until they learn that an order of a McDonald's Big Mac, large fries, and large chocolate shake amounts to over 2,000 calories, the recommended caloric intake for an adult woman for an entire day.

It is common for people in the precontemplation phase to deny that their current pattern of behavior is a problem. The individual might defend such behaviors, claiming that "I don't drink/smoke/eat that much." Those who are overweight may discover that they do eat "that much" when they start keeping track of calories.

CONTEMPLATION

In the *contemplation stage,* people acknowledge the problem but may not be ready to commit to change. As the name of the stage suggests, at this point individuals are actively thinking about change. They might reevaluate the place of this behavior in their life, and they may have mixed feelings about giving up a bad habit. For example, how will they deal with missing their friends on a smoke break? Or going out drinking? Or packing a healthy lunch instead of heading to the drive-thru? They may weigh the short-term gains of the harmful behavior against the long-term benefits of changing.

As we considered in Chapter 6, future rewards can be difficult to pursue when immediate pleasures beckon. Sure, it would be nice to be thinner, but losing weight is going to take time, and that hot fudge sundae is right there, looking very delicious. Nevertheless, in the contemplation phase, individuals may begin to separate themselves, mentally, from the typical overeater or smoker and start to define themselves as someone who is ready to change.

PREPARATION/DETERMINATION

At the *preparation/determination stage,* people are getting ready to take action. At this point, self-belief and especially beliefs about one's ability to "see it through" are very important. A key consideration in this stage is whether individuals truly feel they are ready to change. In a study of New Year's resolutions, readiness to change predicted success at achieving those resolutions (Norcross, Mrykalo, & Blagys, 2002).

During this stage, individuals start thinking concretely about how they might take on their new challenge. For example, they explore options for the best ways to quit smoking or drinking or to start an exercise program. Individuals who are seeking to lose weight might think about joining a gym to get regular exercise or setting the alarm clock for a 6 A.M. run.

ACTION/WILLPOWER

At the *action/willpower stage,* individuals commit to making a real behavioral change and enact an effective plan. An important challenge at this stage is to find ways to support the new, healthy behavior pattern. One approach is to find reinforcements or rewards for the new behavior. Individuals who have quit smoking might focus on how much better food tastes after they have given up cigarettes. Successful dieters might treat themselves to a shopping run to buy new, smaller-size clothes. Acknowledging, enjoying, and celebrating accomplishments can motivate consistent behavior.

Another source of support for new behaviors is the individual's social network (Skogstad & others, 2013; Vassilev & others, 2013). Friends, family, and members of a support group can help through their encouraging words and supportive behaviors. Members of a family might all quit smoking at the same time or join the individual in physical activities or healthier eating.

Finally, people may focus on alternative behaviors that replace the unhealthy ones. Perhaps, instead of bar hopping, they join a group dedicated to activities not associated with drinking alcohol, such as a dance club or community theater group. In other words, effective change also means avoiding tempting situations.

EVERY YEAR IT'S THE SAME THING. I RESOLVE TO LOSE A TON, AND YOU SAY YOU'RE GOING TO CONTROL YOUR ANGER.

© Ralph Hagen. www.CartoonStock.com.

MAINTENANCE

In the *maintenance stage,* individuals successfully avoid temptation and consistently pursue healthy behaviors. They may anticipate tempting situations and avoid them or actively prepare for them. If smokers seeking to kick the habit know that they always enjoy a cigarette after a big meal out with friends, they might mentally prepare themselves for that temptation before going out. Successful dieters might post a consciousness-raising photograph on the refrigerator.

At some point, people in maintenance may find that actively fighting the urge to indulge in unhealthy behaviors is no longer necessary. *Transcendence* means that they are no longer consciously engaged in maintaining their healthy lifestyle; rather, the lifestyle has become a part of who they are. They are now nonsmokers, healthy eaters, or committed runners.

RELAPSE

● **relapse** A return to former unhealthy patterns.

One challenge during the maintenance stage is to avoid **relapse,** a return to the former unhealthy patterns. Contrary to popular belief, relapse is a common aspect of change. That is, for most people, real change takes many attempts. Relapse can be discouraging and can lead a person to feel like a failure. However, the *majority* of people who eventually do change do not succeed on the first try. Rather, they try and fail and try again, cycling through the five stages several times before achieving a stable healthy lifestyle. Consequently, individuals who are experts in changing health behavior consider relapse to be normal (Norcross, Loberg, & Norcross, 2012; Prochaska & Norcross, 2010).

If you have ever tried to adopt a healthier lifestyle by dieting, starting an exercise program, or quitting smoking, you might know how bad you feel when you experience relapse. One slip, however, does not mean you will never reach your goal. Rather, when a slipup occurs, you have an opportunity to learn, to think about what led to the relapse, and to devise a strategy for preventing it in the future. Successful dieters, for example, do not let one lapse ruin the week. Individuals who successfully keep weight off are those who do not get too down on themselves when they relapse (Phelan & others, 2003).

EVALUATION OF THE STAGES OF CHANGE MODEL

The stages of change model has been applied successfully to a broad range of behaviors. These include cigarette smoking (C. L. Kohler & others, 2008; Schumann & others, 2006), exercise (Lippke & Plotnikoff, 2006), safe-sex practices (Arden & Armitage, 2008; Naar-King & others, 2006), marijuana use in teenagers (Walker & others, 2006), substance abuse more broadly (DiClemente, 2006; Migneault, Adams, & Read, 2005), and weight loss (MacQueen, Brynes, & Frost, 2002).

Although the stages of change model has proved to be relevant to a variety of behaviors, the model has its critics (Brug & others, 2004; Joseph, Breslin, & Skinner, 1999). Some have questioned whether the stages are mutually exclusive and whether individuals move from one stage to another sequentially as has been proposed (Littrell & Girvin, 2002). For example, some individuals might feel themselves to be in both action/willpower and maintenance at the same time or may move from contemplation back to precontemplation.

Critics of the model also point out that it refers more to attitudes that change than to behaviors (West, 2005). Recall from Chapter 13 that the relationship between attitudes and behavior can be complex. Furthermore, all of the stages might be understood as promoting readiness to change rather than change itself (West, 2005).

Nevertheless, research shows that the stages of change model does a good job of capturing the ways that individuals make positive life changes (Lippke &

BILL PROUD

"No, honestly, it's just diet and exercise."

© Bill Proud. www.CartoonStock.com.

others, 2009; Schuz & others, 2009). Experts have argued that the stages of change model can be a tool for therapists who are trying to help clients institute healthy behavior patterns. Sometimes, sharing the model with individuals who are trying to change provides them with a useful language to use in understanding the change process, to reduce uncertainty, and to develop realistic expectations for the difficult journey ahead (Hodgins, 2005; Schuz & others, 2009).

3· RESOURCES FOR EFFECTIVE LIFE CHANGE

Making positive changes to promote health can be challenging. Fortunately, there are various psychological, social, and cultural resources and tools at our disposal to help us in the journey to a healthier lifestyle. In this section we consider some of the tools that can help us achieve effective change and, ultimately, a healthier life.

Motivation

Recall from Chapter 10 that motivation refers to the "why" of behavior. Motivational tools for self-change involve changing for the right reasons. Change is most effective when you are doing it for you—because you want to. An analysis of intervention programs aimed at reducing childhood and adolescent obesity found that a strong predictor of weight loss was whether the participants had been required to join the program or had done so voluntarily (Stice, Shaw, & Marti, 2006). Those who had joined voluntarily were more likely to lose weight than their counterparts who had been required to join.

Self-determination theory, presented in Chapter 10, distinguishes between intrinsic motivation (doing something because you want to) and extrinsic motivation (doing something for external rewards) (Deci & Ryan, 2012b). Creating a context in which people feel more autonomous is associated with enhanced outcomes for a broad array of health behaviors, including controlling diabetes through diet (Julien, Senecal, & Guay, 2009), quitting smoking (Deci & Ryan, 2012b; Gwaltney & others, 2009), and getting regular physical exercise and playing sports (Curran, Hill, & Niemiec, 2013; Springer, Lamborn, & Pollard, 2013).

Planning and goal setting are also crucial to making effective change. Researchers have found that individuals who are able to come up with specific strategies, or **implementation intentions,** for dealing with the challenges of making a life change are more successful than others at negotiating the road to change (Armitage, 2006; Stern & others, 2013a). Setting short-term, achievable goals also allows individuals to experience the emotional payoff of small successes along the way to self-change (Kushner, 2007). The dieter who can take her skinny jeans out of the closet and zip them up is likely to feel a sense of accomplishment. The novice exerciser who catches a glimpse of his new biceps in the mirror gets a mood boost. These feelings of satisfaction can help to motivate continued effort toward achieving important health goals (Finch & others, 2005).

Enjoying the payoffs of our efforts to change also means that we must monitor our goal progress (Stadler, Oettingen, & Gollwitzer, 2010). As those who have watched *The Biggest Loser* will attest, stepping on a scale can be a scary prospect for someone who is trying to lose weight. However, it is important to get feedback on progress in the

test yourself

1. How does the theory of planned behavior expand upon, or extend, the theory of reasoned action?
2. Name and briefly describe the five stages of the stages of change model.
3. What positive advice would you give to someone who experiences relapse when dieting or trying to quit smoking?

● **implementation intentions** Specific strategies for dealing with the challenges of making a life change.

Children and adolescents who voluntarily join a weight-loss program are more likely to shed pounds than those who are required to join.

Experiencing the emotional payoff of small successes is important in achieving long-term goals. Being able to zip up skinny jeans, for example, gives a dieter a sense of accomplishment.

● **social support** Information and feedback from others indicating that one is loved and cared for, esteemed and valued, and included in a network of communication and mutual obligation.

pursuit of any goal. If an individual finds out that she is falling short, she can try to identify areas that need work. If, on the other hand, she discovers that she is doing well, it is a potent motivator for future progress.

Social Relationships

One way that social connections make a difference in our lives is through social support. **Social support** is information and feedback from others indicating that one is loved and cared for, esteemed and valued, and included in a network of communication and mutual obligation. Social support has three types of benefits: tangible assistance, information, and emotional support (Xanthopoulus & Daniel, 2013):

■ *Tangible assistance:* Family and friends can provide goods and services in stressful circumstances. For example, gifts of food are often given after the death of a loved one.

■ *Information:* Individuals who provide support can also recommend specific actions and plans to help the person under stress cope more successfully. Friends may notice that a coworker is overloaded with work and suggest ways for him or her to manage time or to delegate tasks more effectively.

■ *Emotional support:* In stressful situations, individuals often suffer emotionally and may develop depression, anxiety, and loss of self-esteem. Friends and family can reassure the person under stress that he or she is valuable and loved. Knowing that others care allows a person to manage stress with greater assurance.

One way that people gain support during difficult times is through *social sharing*—turning to others who act as a sounding board or a willing ear. Individuals who are striving to make healthy life changes might join a group of others who are also struggling with the same issue. Such social sharing can also occur in online support groups.

Getting support from others is important, but *giving* support can have benefits, too. A study of 423 older adult couples who were followed for 5 years revealed how helping others benefits physical health (S. L. Brown & others, 2003). At the beginning of the study, the couples were asked about the extent to which they had given or received emotional or practical help in the past year. Five years later, those who said they had helped others were half as likely to have died. One possible reason for this finding is that helping others may reduce the output of stress hormones, an effect that improves cardiovascular health and strengthens the immune system (Decety & Cacioppo, 2011; Emery, Anderson, & Goodwin, 2013; Norman & others, 2010).

Although research suggests a powerful role for social connections in health, research findings on the link between social support and health are not always so clear-cut. To read more about this issue, see the Intersection.

Religious Faith

Religious faith is strongly related to the maintenance of a healthy lifestyle and to good health (Balbuena, Baetz, & Bowen, 2013; George & others, 2013; Sapp, 2010). Many religions frown on excess and promote moderation. Indeed, weekly religious attendance relates to a host of healthy behaviors, including not smoking, taking vitamins, walking regularly, wearing seatbelts, exercising strenuously, sleeping soundly, and drinking moderately or not at all (Haber, Koenig, & Jacob, 2011; Hill & others, 2006).

A number of studies have linked religious participation to a longer and healthier life (Campbell, Yoon, & Johnstone, 2010; Koenig, 2012; Krause, 2006; McCullough & Willoughby, 2009). For example, one study revealed that religious affiliation, frequent attendance at religious services, and religious strength and comfort were linked to

Health Psychology and Cross-Cultural Psychology: How Does Culture Influence the Meaning of Social Support?

It is hard to imagine any factor as crucial to human survival as being part of a social group—having connections to a social network and friends to provide support in times of need. Yet many studies have found no relationship between individuals' perceptions of the emotional support they have received during stressful times and physical and psychological functioning (Bolger & Amarel, 2007). How might we understand such research?

Consider that being on the receiving end of social support can mean different things to different people. On the one hand, having someone express support and encouragement during times of stress might give a person a feeling of being genuinely cared for. In this sense, getting help might be truly helpful. However, receiving help from another might also make a person feel incompetent: Why am I unable to handle this problem on my own? Culture is one factor that illuminates when and for whom emotional support might come at a cost.

Jiyoung Park and her colleagues (2012) proposed that within Western cultures, which place a high value on personal independence, perceptions of support from others might entail concerns about being needy or incompetent. In this cultural context, receiving support may be viewed as threatening a person's sense of independence (Uchida & others, 2008). In contrast, in East Asian cultures that emphasize the interdependent nature of the self, providing and receiving help from others is an important way to enact cultural values. Rather than indicating that one is incompetent or a failure, in this context, getting help from others is a sign of succeeding at the culturally valued goal of being a member of one's group. Based on these proposed distinctions between Western and Eastern cultures, Park and her colleagues hypothesized that the link between health and perceptions of emotional support from others would be especially positive for individuals in East Asian cultures.

How and to whom do you typically offer support? When others have supported you in difficult times, how have you felt?

To test this prediction, the researchers surveyed over 1,000 adults in Japan and the United States. Participants completed questionnaires measuring stress, emotional support from others, and psychological and physical health. In support of the researchers' predictions, the relationship between perceptions of emotional support and health reports was strong and positive for Japanese but not for American respondents (J. Park & others, 2012). Interestingly, among Japanese participants, support was most likely to be associated with better health reports when individuals were experiencing high levels of stress. These results might indicate that within more interdependent cultures, it is important that support come during times when it is clearly warranted and does not indicate that the person is making unjustifiable demands on the social group (Uchida & others, 2008).

Does this research have a lesson for Westerners? Park and her colleagues suggest that Americans might benefit most from subtle forms of support that do not draw attention to their own coping capacities. Specifically, for Westerners, receiving help might be less emotionally costly when it occurs in ways that preserve the supported person's sense of self-efficacy and independence.

The researchers liken social support to an insurance policy: Just as insurance provides peace of mind when things are going well, knowing that we have a network of social support may promote health and well-being even when we do not feel the need to use it.

reduced risk of premature death from any cause (Schnall & others, 2010). The Psychological Inquiry breaks down the various factors that might play a role in the association between religious faith and health.

Religious participation may also benefit health through its relation to social support (George & others, 2013). Belonging to a faith community may give people access to a warm group of others who are available during times of need. This community is "there" to provide transportation to the doctor, to check in with the individual during hard times, and simply to stand next to the person during a worship service, as a fellow member of the community. The social connections promoted by religious activity can

Telomeres

psychological *inquiry*

Healthy Lifestyle
Not smoking, drinking moderately or not at all, walking regularly, wearing seatbelts, etc.

Social Support
Membership in a faith community, availability of help in times of need, buffer against loneliness

Sense of Life Meaning
Maintaining one's perspective, keeping a big-picture view on life's problems

Buffer Against the Effects of Stress
Hope and motivation for positive life change, slower disease progression, protection against job burnout

Religious Faith

Better health

Longer life

Praying for Good Health

This figure presents a model of the relationship between religious faith and health and longevity. Notice that the placement of the boxes and arrows suggests that religious faith has its influence on health through four intervening variables. Try to answer the questions below:

1. The model reflects results of correlational studies. How does this influence the causal conclusions one might wish to make?

2. Give another variable that ought to be added to this model. Where would it be placed?

3. According to this model, religious faith "comes first," and the other four variables are consequences of religious involvement. Do you think this schema is accurate, or would you change the placement of any of the variables? Explain.

4. How might this model be applied to individuals who are not religious at all?

test yourself

1. Name three tools or resources on which we can draw in trying to make positive life changes.
2. Discuss the importance of motivation in efforts at self-change.
3. Identify and describe three types of benefits provided by social support.

forestall anxiety and depression, help to prevent isolation and loneliness, and promote civic engagement (Lewis, MacGregor, & Putnam, 2013; Rosmarin, Krumrei, & Andersson, 2009).

Religious faith, and spirituality more generally, may also be important factors in good health because they provide a sense of life meaning and a buffer against the effects of stressful events (Emmons, 2005; C. L. Park, 2012, 2013). Religious thoughts can play a role in maintaining hope and stimulating motivation for positive life changes. Faith may also help individuals to avoid burnout at work (Murray-Swank & others, 2006) and to negotiate life's difficulties without feeling overwhelmed (Mascaro & Rosen, 2006). Belief in the enduring meaningfulness of one's life can help one keep perspective and see life's hassles in the context of the big picture (C. L. Park, 2012, 2013).

In summary, making positive life changes can be complex and challenging. Fortunately, though, we have powerful resources and tools to help us attain a healthier life.

4· TOWARD A HEALTHIER MIND (AND BODY): CONTROLLING STRESS

Complete the following sentence: "I wish I could stop_____." If you could change one thing about your behavior, what would you choose? Would the change perhaps have to do with feeling stressed out much of the time? Maybe you wish you could quit worrying so much or stop facing every daily challenge with tension. Let's look at the problems that can arise when you feel chronically stressed and the ways you can better manage your stress.

Stress and Its Stages

As described in Chapter 3, *stress* is an individual's response to environmental *stressors,* the circumstances and events that threaten the person and tax his or her coping abilities. We often think of negative life events as stressful, but positive occasions—such as graduating from college, getting married, and starting a new job—can also produce stress if these events present signifi-cant changes. Hans Selye (1974, 1983), the founder of stress research, focused on the physical response to stressors, especially the wear and tear on the body due to the demands placed on it. After observing patients with different problems—the death of someone close, loss of income, arrest for embezzlement—Selye concluded that any number of environmental events or stimuli would produce the same stress symptoms: loss of appetite, muscular weakness, and decreased interest in the world.

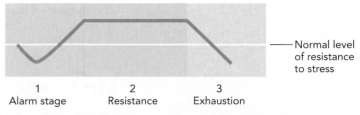

FIGURE 17.2   Selye's General Adaptation Syndrome
The general adaptation syndrome (GAS) describes an individual's response to stress in terms of three stages: (1) alarm, in which the body mobilizes its resources; (2) resistance, in which the body strives mightily to endure the stressor; and (3) exhaustion, in which resistance becomes depleted.

   General adaptation syndrome (GAS) is Selye's term for the common effects on the body when stressful demands are placed on it (Figure 17.2). The GAS consists of three stages: alarm, resistance, and exhaustion. Selye's model is especially useful in helping us understand the link between stress and health.

   The body's first reaction to a stressor, in the *alarm stage,* is a temporary state of shock during which resistance to illness and stress falls below normal limits. In trying to cope with the initial effects of stress, the body quickly releases hormones that, in a short time, adversely affect the functioning of the immune system, our body's net-work of natural defenses. During this time the individual is prone to infections from illness and injury.

   In the *resistance stage* of Selye's general adaptation syndrome, a number of glands throughout the body manufacture different hormones that protect the individual in many ways. Endocrine and sympathetic nervous system activity are not as high as in the alarm stage, although they still are elevated. During the resistance stage, the body's immune system can fight off infection with remarkable efficiency. Similarly, hormones that reduce the inflammation normally associated with injury circulate at high levels.

   If the body's all-out effort to combat stress fails and the stress persists, the individual moves into the *exhaustion stage.* At this point, the wear and tear on the body takes its toll; the person might collapse in a state of exhaustion, and vulnerability to disease increases. Serious, possibly irreversible damage to the body, such as a heart attack or even death, may occur.

   The body system that plays the greatest role in Selye's GAS is called the **hypotha-lamic-pituitary-adrenal axis (HPA axis).** The HPA axis is a complex set of interactions among the hypothalamus (part of the brain's limbic system), the pituitary gland (the master gland of the endocrine system), and the adrenal glands (endocrine system glands that are located on top of each kidney). The HPA axis regulates various body processes, including digestion, immune system responses, emotion, and energy expenditure. The axis also controls reactions to stressful events, and these responses will be our focus here.

   When the brain detects a threat in the environment, it signals the hypothalamus to produce corticotropin-releasing hormone (CRH). In turn, CRH stimulates the pituitary gland to produce another hormone that causes the adrenal glands to release cortisol. Cortisol is itself the "stress hormone" that directs cells to make sugar, fat, and protein available so the body can take quick action. Cortisol also suppresses the immune system.

   In Chapter 3 we distinguished between acute stress and chronic stress. Acute stress can sometimes be adaptive, and in acute stress cortisol plays an important role in help-ing us to take the necessary action to avoid dire consequences. Typically, once the body has dealt with a given stressor, our cortisol level returns to normal. However, under chronic stress, the HPA axis can remain activated over the long haul.

   The activity of the HPA axis varies from one person to the next. These differences may be explained by genes as well as by particular stressful experiences (Boersma & others, 2012). Research with rats has shown that prenatal stress can influence the

● **general adaptation syndrome (GAS)** Selye's term for the common effects of stressful demands on the body, consisting of three stages: alarm, resistance, and exhaustion.

● **hypothalamic-pituitary-adrenal axis (HPA axis)** The complex set of interactions among the hypothalamus, the pituitary gland, and the adrenal glands that regulates various body processes and controls reactions to stressful events.

development of the HPA axis (M. K. Green & others, 2011; O'Connor & others, 2013; Peters & others, 2012). When the HPA is chronically active, various systems in the body suffer, as we now consider.

Stress and the Immune System

● **psychoneuroimmunology** A new field of scientific inquiry that explores connections among psychological factors (such as attitudes and emotions), the nervous system, and the immune system.

Chronic stress can have serious implications for the body, in particular for the immune system. Interest in links between the immune system and stress spawned the field of **psychoneuroimmunology,** which explores connections among psychological factors (such as attitudes and emotions), the nervous system, and the immune system (Jaremka, Lindgren, & Kiecolt-Glaser, 2013; Kiecolt-Glaser, 2009, 2010; Stowell, Robles, & Kane, 2013).

The immune system and the central nervous system are similar in their modes of receiving, recognizing, and integrating signals from the external environment (Sternberg & Gold, 1996). The central nervous system and the immune system both possess "sensory" elements, which receive information from the environment and other parts of the body, and "motor" elements, which carry out an appropriate response. Both systems also rely on chemical mediators for communication. CRH, the hormone discussed above, is shared by the central nervous system and the immune system, uniting the stress and immune responses.

A variety of research supports the idea that stress can profoundly influence the immune system (Atanackovic & others, 2013; Ho & others, 2010; Iwata, Ota, & Duman, 2013). Acute stressors (sudden, stressful, one-time life events or stimuli) can produce immunological changes. For example, in relatively healthy HIV-infected individuals, as well as in individuals with cancer, acute stressors are associated with poorer immune system functioning (McIntosh & Rosselli, 2012; Pant & Ramaswamy, 2009). In addition to acute stressors, chronic stressors (long-lasting agents of stress) are associated with an increasing downturn in immune system responsiveness (Pervanidou & Chrousos, 2012). This effect has been documented in a number of circumstances, including worries about living next to a nuclear reactor, failures in close relationships (divorce, separation, and marital distress), negative relationships with family and friends, and burdensome caregiving for a family member with progressive illness (Friedman & others, 2012; Gouin & others, 2012).

A goal of psychoneuroimmunology is to determine the precise links among psychological factors, the brain, and the immune system (Priyadarshini & Aich, 2012; Stowell, Robles, & Kane, 2013). Preliminary hypotheses about the interaction that causes vulnerability to disease include the following:

- Stressful experiences lower the efficiency of immune systems, making individuals more susceptible to disease.
- Stress directly promotes disease-producing processes.
- Stressful experiences may cause the activation of dormant viruses that diminish the individual's ability to cope with disease.

These hypotheses may lead to better treatments for some of the most challenging diseases to conquer—cancer and AIDS among them (Carey, Scott-Sheldon, & Vanable, 2013; Nezu & others, 2013).

Sheldon Cohen and his colleagues have conducted a number of studies on the effects of stress, emotion, and social support on immunity and susceptibility to infectious disease (Cohen & Janicki-Deverts, 2009, 2012; Cohen & Shachar, 2012; Cohen & others, 2012, 2013; Sneed & others, 2012). Cohen and his colleagues (1998) found that adults who faced interpersonal or work-related stress for at least a month were more likely than their less-stressed counterparts to catch a cold after exposure to viruses. In the study, 276 adults were exposed to viruses and then quarantined for 5 days. The longer people had experienced major stress, the more likely they were to catch a cold. Individuals who reported high stress for the preceding 2 years tripled their risk of catching a cold (Figure 17.3). Those who experienced work-related stress for a month or longer were nearly five times more likely to develop colds than individuals without chronic stress. Those who experienced interpersonal stress for a month or more were twice as likely to catch a cold.

Cohen concluded that stress-triggered changes in the immune system and hormones might create greater vulnerability to infection. The findings suggest that when we know we are under stress, we need to take better care of ourselves than usual, although often we do just the opposite (Cohen & others, 2009, 2012, 2013).

Stress and Cardiovascular Disease

There is also reason to believe that stress can increase an individual's risk for cardiovascular disease (Emery, Anderson, & Goodwin, 2013). Chronic emotional stress is associated with high blood pressure, heart disease, and early death (Schulz, 2007). Apparently, the surge in adrenaline caused by severe emotional stress causes the blood to clot more rapidly, and blood clotting is a major factor in heart attacks (Strike & others, 2006).

Emotional stress also can contribute to cardiovascular disease in other ways. Individuals who have had major life changes (such as the loss of a loved one) have a higher incidence of cardiovascular disease and early death (Mostofsky & others, 2012). Job loss can also play a role. A longitudinal study of involuntary unemployment among workers 50 years and older over a 10-year period revealed that displaced workers have a twofold increase in the risk of stroke (Gallo & others, 2006). Recall the Type A behavior pattern described in Chapter 12. Individuals who are Type A tend to be highly reactive to stressful circumstances and to become hostile when frustrated.

The body's internal reactions to stress are not the only risk. People in a chronically stressed condition are more likely to take up smoking, start overeating, and avoid exercising. All of these stress-related behaviors are linked with the development of cardiovascular disease (Emery, Anderson, & Goodwin, 2013).

Stress and Cancer

Given the association of stress with poor health behaviors such as smoking, it is not surprising that stress has also been related to cancer risk (Hamer, Chida, & Molloy, 2009; Nezu & others, 2013). Stress sets in motion biological changes involving the autonomic, endocrine, and immune systems. If the immune system is not compromised, it appears to help provide resistance to cancer and slow its progress. Researchers have found, however, that the physiological effects of stress inhibit a number of cellular immune responses (Anderson, Golden-Kreutz, & DiLillo, 2001; Hayakawa, 2012). Cancer patients show diminished natural killer (NK)-cell activity in the blood (Bagnara & others, 2009; Rosental & others, 2012) (Figure 17.4). Low NK-cell activity is linked with the development of further malignancies, and the length of survival for the cancer patient is related to NK-cell activity (Buchser & others, 2012; Cho & Campana, 2009).

Thus, stress is clearly a factor not only in immune system functioning and cardiovascular health but also in the risk for cancer. In light of these links, understanding the psychological processes by which individuals can effectively handle stressful circumstances is a crucial topic in health psychology (Faul & others, 2009; Xanthopoulos & Daniel, 2013).

Coping with Stress

What stresses you out? Stressors can be anything from losing irreplaceable notes from a class, to being yelled at by a friend, to failing a test, to being in a car wreck.

Although everyone's body may have a similar response to stressors, not everyone perceives the same events as stressful (Schwarzer & Luszczynska, 2013). Indeed, whether or not an experience stresses us out depends on how we think about that experience.

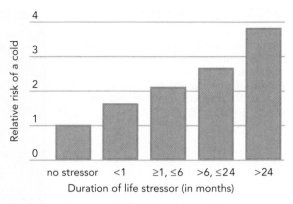

FIGURE 17.3 Stress and the Risk of Developing a Cold In a study by Cohen and others (1998), the longer individuals had a life stressor, the more likely they were to develop a cold. The four-point scale is based on the odds (0 = lower; 4 = higher) of getting a cold.

FIGURE 17.4 **NK Cells and Cancer** Two natural killer (NK) cells (*yellow*) are shown attacking a leukemia cell (*red*). Notice the blisters that the leukemia cell has developed to defend itself. Nonetheless, the NK cells are surrounding the leukemia cell and are about to destroy it.

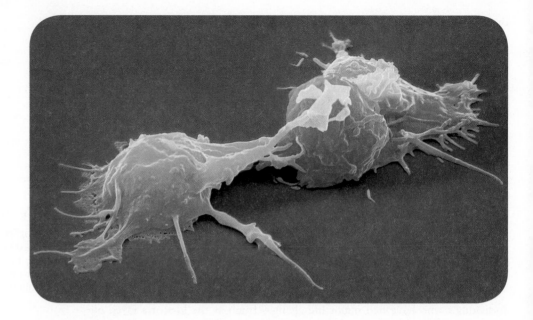

As reviewed in Chapter 8, *cognitive appraisal* refers to an individual's interpretation of an experience as either threatening or challenging, and the person's determination of whether he or she has the resources to cope effectively with the event. Coping means managing taxing circumstances, expending effort to solve life's problems, and seeking to master or reduce stress.

TYPES OF COPING

● **problem-focused coping** The coping strategy of squarely facing one's troubles and trying to solve them.

Research has identified two types of coping. **Problem-focused coping** is the cognitive strategy of squarely facing one's troubles and trying to solve them. For example, if you are having trouble with a class, you might go to the campus study skills center and sign up for a program to learn how to study more effectively. In taking this step, you have faced your problem and attempted to do something about it. Problem-focused coping might involve coming up with goals and implementation intentions, the problem-solving steps we examined earlier in this chapter. A meta-analysis revealed that problem-focused coping was linked to a lower level of psychopathology in areas such as anxiety, depression, eating disorders, and substance use disorders (Aldao, Nolen-Hoeksema, & Schweizer, 2010).

● **emotion-focused coping** The coping strategy that involves responding to the stress that one is feeling—trying to manage one's emotional reaction—rather than focusing on the problem itself.

Emotion-focused coping involves responding to the stress that you are feeling—trying to manage your emotional reaction—rather than confronting the problem itself. In emotion-focused coping, you might avoid the source of your stress, rationalize what has happened to you, deny the problem is occurring, laugh it off, or call on your religious faith for support. If you use emotion-focused coping, you might avoid going to a class that is a problem for you. You might say the class does not matter, deny that you are having difficulty with it, joke about it with your friends, or pray that you will do better.

Although problem-focused coping is generally associated with better outcomes, in some circumstances emotion-focused coping can be helpful. Denial is one of the main protective psychological mechanisms for navigating the flood of feelings that occurs when the reality of death or dying becomes too great.

For example, one study found that following the death of a loved one, bereaved individuals who directed their attention away from their negative feelings had fewer health problems and were rated as better adjusted by their friends, compared to bereaved individuals who did not use this coping strategy (Coifman & others, 2007). Denial can be used to avoid the destructive impact of shock by postponing the time when a person has to deal with stress. In other circumstances, however, emotion-focused coping can be problematic. Denying that your ex does not love you anymore keeps you from getting on with life. Yet emotion-focused coping may be useful in situations in which there is no solution to a problem, such as long-term grieving over the loss of a loved one. In such cases, the emotion itself might be the stressor.

Many individuals successfully use both problem-focused and emotion-focused coping when adjusting to a stressful circumstance. For example, in one study individuals said they used both problem-focused and emotion-focused coping strategies in 98 percent of the stressful encounters they face (Folkman & Lazarus, 1980). Over the long term, though, problem-focused coping usually works best (Nagase & others, 2009).

Strategies for Successful Coping

Successful coping can improve even the most stressful situations (Xanthopoulos & Daniel, 2013). Several specific factors are associated with effective coping, including a sense of personal control, a healthy immune system, personal resources, and positive emotions.

When one is experiencing stressful life events, multiple coping strategies often work better than a single strategy, as is true with any problem-solving challenge (Folkman & Moskowitz, 2004). People who have experienced a stressful life event or a cluster of difficulties (such as a parent's death, a divorce, and a significant loss of income) might actively embrace problem solving and consistently take advantage of opportunities for positive experiences, even in the context of the bad times they are going through. Positive emotion can give them a sense of the big picture, help them devise a variety of possible solutions, and allow them to make creative connections.

Optimism can play a strong role in effective coping (Goodin & Bulls, 2013). Recall from Chapter 12 that optimism is the expectancy that good things are likely to occur in the future (Carver & Scheier, 2009). Having an optimistic view of what lies ahead tends to help people engage constructively with potentially threatening information (Aspinwall, 1998, 2011; Aspinwall, Leaf, & Leachman, 2009; Aspinwall & Pengchit, 2013; Aspinwall & Tedeschi, 2010a, 2010b). Optimists are more likely than others to seek out genetic testing in order to learn about their risk for disease (Aspinwall, Leaf, & Leachman, 2009; Aspinwall & others, 2013).

Optimists face life's challenges from a position of strength. For instance, when an optimist finds out that tanning, a favorite pastime, is related to an elevated risk of skin cancer, the information is important but not overwhelming. In contrast, pessimists are already living in a bleak world and prefer not to hear more bad news.

Another personal quality that appears to promote thriving during difficult times is hardiness. **Hardiness** is characterized by a sense of commitment rather than alienation, and of control rather than powerlessness; a hardy individual sees problems as challenges rather than as threats (Maddi & others, 2006). Hardiness is exemplified by the basketball player whose team is down by two points with seconds remaining on the clock when he shouts, "Coach! Give me the ball!"

The links among hardiness, stress, and illness were the focus of the Chicago Stress Project, which studied male business managers 32 to 65 years of age over a 5-year period (Kobasa, Maddi, & Kahn, 1982; Maddi, 1998). During the 5 years, most of the managers experienced stressful events such as divorce, job transfers, the death of a close friend, inferior performance evaluations at work, and reporting to an unpleasant boss. In one aspect of the study, managers who developed an illness, ranging from the flu to a heart attack, were compared with those who did not (Kobasa, Maddi, & Kahn, 1982). Those who did not were more likely to have hardy personalities. Another aspect of the study investigated whether hardiness, along with exercise and social support, provided a buffer against stress and reduced illness in executives' lives (Kobasa & others, 1986). When all three factors were present in an executive's life, the level of illness dropped dramatically (Figure 17.5).

● **hardiness** A personality trait characterized by a sense of commitment rather than alienation and of control rather than powerlessness; a perception of problems as challenges rather than threats.

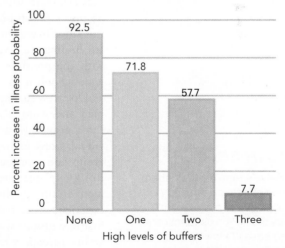

FIGURE 17.5 Illness in High-Stress Business Executives In one study of high-stress business executives (all of whom were selected for this analysis because they were above the stress mean for the entire year of the study), a low level of all three buffers (hardiness, exercise, and social support) involved a high probability of at least one serious illness in that year. High levels of one, two, and all three buffers decreased the likelihood of at least one serious illness occurring in the year of the study.

Other researchers also have found support for the role of hardiness in illness and health (Bartone & others, 2012; Sandvik & others, 2013). The results of this research on hardiness suggest the power of multiple factors, rather than any single factor, in cushioning individuals against stress and maintaining their health (Maddi, 1998, 2008; Maddi & others, 2006).

We have seen in this discussion that certain psychological capacities, such as optimism and hardiness, can help us avoid the effects of stress; we can thrive even during potentially threatening circumstances by changing the way we think. One significant stressor in life is illness itself. Can the way we think influence the likelihood of being diagnosed with a serious illness? Can it affect the eventual outcome of that illness? Research pointing to the links between psychological characteristics and better health outcomes can sometimes create a burden on individuals who are struggling with illness. To read about this issue, see the Critical Controversy.

Stress Management Programs

Nearly every day we are reminded that stress is bad for our health. "Avoid stress" may be a good prescription, but life is full of potentially stressful experiences. Sometimes just checking e-mail or answering a cell phone can be an invitation for stress. Sometimes, too, trying to manage stress on our own can be overwhelming. Thus, it makes sense to explore options for breaking the stress habit.

Because many people have difficulty in regulating stress, psychologists have developed various techniques that people can learn to apply themselves (Lopez & others, 2013; Matula, 2013). **Stress management programs** teach individuals how to appraise stressful events, develop coping skills, and put these skills into use in everyday life. Effective stress management programs are generally based on the principles of cognitive-behavior therapy (Mercer, 2009), as described in Chapter 16. Some stress management programs are broad in scope, teaching a range of techniques to handle stress; others teach a specific technique, such as relaxation or assertiveness training (Conley, Travers, & Bryant, 2013; Shiralkar & others, 2013).

Stress management programs are often taught through workshops, which are becoming more common in the workplace. Aware of the costs in lost productivity due to stress-related disorders, many organizations have become increasingly motivated to help their workers identify and cope with the stressful circumstances in their lives (Jex, Swanson, & Grubb, 2013; Sonnentag & Frese, 2013). Colleges and universities similarly run stress management programs for students (Conley, Travers, & Bryant, 2013). If you are finding the experience of college extremely stressful and having difficulty coping with the pressures, you might consider enrolling in a stress management program at your school or in your community.

Do stress management programs work? In one study, researchers randomly assigned men and women with hypertension (blood pressure greater than 140/90) to one of three groups (Linden, Lenz, & Con, 2001). One group received 10 hours of individual stress management training; a second group was placed in a waitlist control group and eventually received stress management training; and a third group (a control group) received no such training. The two groups that received the stress management training showed significantly reduced blood pressure. The control group experienced no reduction in blood pressure. Also, the reduced blood pressure in the first two groups was linked to a reported decrease in psychological stress and improved ability to cope with anger.

Coping effectively with stress is essential for physical and mental health (Xanthopoulos & Daniel, 2013). Still, there is a lot more we can do to promote our health. Healthful living—establishing healthy habits and evaluating and changing behaviors that interfere with good health—helps us avoid the damaging effects of stress (Jex, Swanson, & Grubb, 2013; Marks, 2013).

Just as the biopsychosocial perspective predicts, healthy changes in one area of life can have benefits that overflow to others. In the next section, we take a close look at habits and behaviors that directly influence our physical (and psychological) health and wellness.

● **stress management program** A regimen that teaches individuals how to appraise stressful events, how to develop skills for coping with stress, and how to put these skills into use in everyday life.

test yourself

1. What is Selye's term for the pattern of common effects on the body when demands are placed on it?

2. How does the HPA axis function in regulating stress? How is the body affected when the HPA axis is chronically active?

3. What personality characteristic applies to an individual who faces difficulties with a sense of commitment and control, and who perceives problems as challenges rather than threats?

CRITICAL CONTROVERSY

How Powerful Is the Power of Positive Thinking?

Research demonstrating the role of psychological variables in health, disease, and mortality is extremely appealing because it gives us a sense we have some control over our physical health. Yet as assuring as such findings might be, these factors are not a psychological recipe for immortality. When scientists find a link between some psychological factor and an important health outcome, the popular media often latch on to the results as if they mean that such factors play a causal role in disease. Such research can sometimes lead to victim blaming: thinking that a person is ill or has died because of a deficit of hardiness or optimism.

A compelling case in point is provided by research on "fighting spirit" in battling breast cancer. In a study published 35 years ago, 69 women were interviewed 3 months after undergoing surgery for breast cancer (Greer, Morris, & Pettingale, 1979). Based on the interviews, the researchers categorized the women's responses to breast cancer as denial, fighting spirit, quiet resignation, or helplessness. The researchers then contacted the women 5 years later to see whether they had experienced a recurrence. The results showed that women whose responses were characterized by either denial or fighting spirit were less likely to have had a recurrence of cancer. This study led to the conclusion that women with breast cancer should be encouraged to adopt a fighting attitude toward their cancer. The idea that a fighting spirit is important to breast cancer survival continues to hold sway in interventions for women coping with the disease (Coyne & Tennen, 2010).

Crucially, this finding—based on a single study with a relatively small sample—has not withstood the test of time. Subsequent research, especially studies employing much larger samples, has failed to show any link between adopting a fighting spirit and breast cancer outcomes (Petticrew, Bell, & Hunter, 2002; Phillips & others, 2008; M. Watson & others, 2005). Although the reality that a fighting spirit does not improve a woman's chances of beating cancer might seem disappointing, many have welcomed this news. As one expert commented, such findings "may help to remove any continuing feelings of guilt or sense of blame for breast cancer relapse from those women who

worry because they cannot always maintain a fighting spirit or a positive attitude" (Dobson, 2005, p. 865). The widespread belief that adopting a fighting spirit is key to cancer survival imposes a burden on individuals already dealing with a difficult life experience.

Does this conclusion mean that psychosocial variables have no role to play in disease? Certainly not. One study that found no effect of fighting spirit did show that initial helplessness in response to diagnoses was a predictor of poorer outcomes among women with breast cancer (M. Watson & others, 2005). Knowing that a person feels helpless early on may prompt professionals to provide much needed information about treatment and the potential for long-term recovery. Indeed, among the factors that (happily) complicate this type of research are that many cancers have effective treatments and that, especially with early detection, relatively few individuals die or experience a recurrence (Coyne & Tennen, 2010). Professionals can also use information about psychological characteristics to build in behavioral supports that might be needed to help a person stick with treatment and optimize her outcomes.

People deal with potentially life-threatening diagnoses in different ways. Dutch swimmer Maarten van der Weijden was diagnosed with leukemia in 2001 at the age of 20 but went on to win Olympic gold in 2008. With respect to his diagnosis, he remarked, "I . . . simply surrendered to the doctors. You always hear those stories that you have to think positively, that you have to fight to survive. This can be a great burden for patients. It has never been proven that you can cure cancer by thinking positively or by fighting" (quoted in Coyne, Tennen, & Ranchor, 2010, p. 40).

WHAT DO YOU THINK
- In the 1979 study, fighting and denial both were associated with better outcomes. Why do you think people latched on to fighting spirit rather than denial as a key intervention?

- If someone you love were diagnosed with cancer, how would the research reported here influence the support you would provide to that person?

5· TOWARD A HEALTHIER BODY (AND MIND): BEHAVING AS IF YOUR LIFE DEPENDS UPON IT

There's no escaping it: Getting stress under control is crucial for a healthy mind and body. Where health and wellness are concerned, it is also important to make wise behavioral choices when it comes to physical activity, diet and nutrition, and smoking.

Becoming Physically Active

Imagine that there was a time when, to change a TV channel, people had to get up and walk a few feet to turn a knob. Consider the time when people physically had to go to the library and hunt through card catalogs and shelves to find information rather than going online and Googling. As our daily tasks have become increasingly easy, we have become less active, and inactivity is a serious health problem (Donatelle, 2013).

Any activity that expends physical energy can be part of a healthy lifestyle. It can be as simple as taking the stairs instead of an elevator, walking or biking to class instead of driving, going ice skating instead of to a movie, or getting up and dancing instead of sitting at the bar. One study of older adults revealed that the more they expended energy in daily activities, the longer they were likely to live (Manini & others, 2006).

In addition to being related to life expectancy, physical activity correlates with a host of other positive outcomes, including a lower probability of developing cardiovascular disease (Fernhall, 2013; Swift & others, 2013), diabetes (Lee & Colagiuri, 2013), weight loss in overweight individuals (Hall, 2013), improved cognitive functioning (Mortimer & others, 2012), positive coping with stress (Head, Singh, & Bugg, 2012), and increased self-esteem and body image (Ginis, Bassett, & Conlin, 2012). Physical exercise has also been shown to reduce levels of anxiety (Petruzzello, 2012) and depression (Villaverde & others, 2012).

Even a real pig can benefit from exercise; Figure 17.6 shows a hog getting a workout. In this study, a group of hogs was trained to run approximately 100 miles a week (Bloor & White, 1983). After training, the researchers narrowed the arteries that supplied blood to the hogs' hearts. Compared to a control group of untrained hogs, the jogging hogs developed extensive alternative pathways that provided a blood supply to their hearts. These results suggest that being physically active is like investing energy in a wellness bank account: Activity enhances physical well-being and gives us the ability to face life's potential stressors energetically.

Exercise is one special type of physical activity. **Exercise** formally refers to structured activities whose goal is to improve health. Although exercise designed to strengthen muscles and bones or to improve flexibility is important to fitness, many health experts emphasize the benefits of **aerobic exercise,** which is sustained activity—jogging, swimming, or cycling, for example—that stimulates heart and lung functioning.

In one study, exercise literally meant the difference between life and death for middle-aged and older adults (Blair & others, 1989). More than 10,000 men and women were divided into categories of low fitness, medium fitness, and high fitness. Then they were studied over 8 years. Sedentary participants (low fitness) were more than twice as likely to die during the study's 8-year time span than those who were moderately fit, and more than three times as likely to die as those who were highly fit. The positive effects of physical fitness occurred for both men and women. The Psychological Inquiry examines the study's results.

One reason that exercise plays a role in how long people live may involve telomeres. Recall from Chapter 9 that telomeres protect the tips of chromosomes and become significantly shorter as individuals get older; that shortening is theorized to be a main reason for aging (Broer & others, 2013; C. Harrison, 2012). Researchers have recently found that habitual exercise and endurance exercise training may provide a protective effect on telomere length (J. H. Kim & others, 2012; Osthus & others, 2012).

● **exercise** Structured activities whose goal is to improve health.

● **aerobic exercise** Sustained activity—jogging, swimming, or cycling, for example—that stimulates heart and lung functioning.

FIGURE 17.6 The Jogging Hog Experiment Jogging hogs reveal the dramatic effects of exercise on health. In one investigation, a group of hogs was trained to run approximately 100 miles per week (Bloor & White, 1983). Then the researchers narrowed the arteries that supplied blood to the heart. The hearts of the jogging hogs developed extensive alternate pathways for blood supply, and 42 percent of the threatened heart tissue was salvaged, compared with only 17 percent in a control group of non-jogging hogs.

psychological *inquiry*

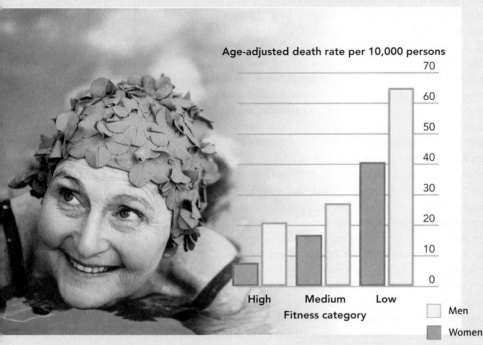

Age-adjusted death rate per 10,000 persons

(bar graph: Y axis labeled 0, 10, 20, 30, 40, 50, 60, 70; X axis "Fitness category" with categories High, Medium, Low; legend: Men (light), Women (dark))

Physical Activity: A Matter of Life and Death

This graph shows the results of an 8-year longitudinal study of over 10,000 men and women (Blair & others, 1989). The X (horizontal) axis shows the fitness level of participants, and the Y (vertical) axis shows the death rates within those groups. Note that results are separated for men and women. Using the figure, answer the questions below:

1. Which groups had the highest and lowest death rates?

2. Comparing the results for men and women separately, what role does gender play in mortality? What might explain this difference?

3. Because this is a correlational study, the results cannot be assumed to show that a low fitness level causes mortality. What third variables might explain the relationship between activity level and mortality?

Health experts recommend that adults engage in at least 30 minutes of moderate physical activity on most, preferably all, days of the week and that children exercise for 60 minutes. Most advise that you should try to raise your heart rate to at least 60 percent of your maximum rate. However, only about one-fifth of adults are active at these recommended levels of physical activity. Figure 17.7 lists examples of the physical activities that qualify as moderate (and, for comparison, vigorous) activities. Both moderate

Moderate	Vigorous
Walking briskly (3–4 mph)	Walking briskly uphill or with a load
Swimming, moderate effort	Swimming, fast treading crawl
Cycling for pleasure or transportation (≤10 mph)	Cycling, fast or racing (>10 mph)
Racket sports, table tennis	Racket sports, singles tennis, racketball
Conditioning exercise, general calisthenics	Conditioning exercise, stair ergometer, ski machine
Golf, pulling cart or carrying clubs	Golf, practice at driving range
Canoeing, leisurely (2.0–3.9 mph)	Canoeing, rapidly (≥4 mph)
Home care, general cleaning	Moving furniture
Mowing lawn, power mower	Mowing lawn, hand mower
Home repair, painting	Fix-up projects

FIGURE 17.7 Moderate and Vigorous Physical Activities At minimum, adults should strive for 30 minutes of moderate activity each day. That activity can become even more beneficial if we "pump it up" to vigorous.

and intense activities may produce important physical and psychological gains (Moran & Walsh, 2013; Morikawa & others, 2013).

A major obstacle to promoting exercise in the United States is that many U.S. cities are not designed in ways that promote walking or cycling. Advocates for change say that by making life too easy and far too accommodating to cars and drivers, urban designers have created an *obesogenic* (obesity-promoting) environment—a context where it is challenging for people to engage in healthy activities (Henderson, 2008; Lydon & others, 2011). Countries such as the Netherlands and Denmark have adopted urban planning strategies that promote walking and biking and discourage car use. In the Netherlands, 60 percent of all journeys taken by people over age 60 are by bicycle (Henderson, 2008).

Environmental contexts that invite physical activity increase activity levels. For example, one quasi-experimental study examined the effects of changes to the physical environment on activity. The study focused on an urban neighborhood in which a greenway (a biking and walking trail) was retrofitted to connect with pedestrian sidewalks. Researchers counted the number of people outside engaging in physical activity in that neighborhood for a 2-hour period at various times over 2 years. Compared to two other similar neighborhoods, the neighborhood with the trail featured more people being active, walking, and biking (Fitzhugh, Bassett, & Evans, 2010). Environmental features that welcome physical activity are also associated with health and wellness. In one study, elderly people who lived near parks, tree-lined streets, and areas for taking walks showed higher longevity over a 5-year study period (Takano, Nakamura, & Watanabe, 2002).

One hint for becoming more physically active is not to limit yourself to only a few options. There are many activities that require physical exertion. Choose one that you genuinely like. Important factors in sticking to an exercise plan include self-efficacy, making active choices, and experiencing positive reinforcement and social support (Cress & others, 2005). Finding a buddy who is interested in working out with you might be a powerful motivator.

One often-welcome payoff for increasing physical activity is weight loss. Researchers have found that one of the most effective components of weight-loss programs is regular exercise (Duncan, 2010; Strasser, 2013; Unick & others, 2013). Another way to combat weight problems is through changes in diet, our next topic.

Eating Right

The biggest health risk facing modern North Americans is being overweight or obese (Malhotra & others, 2013; Schiff, 2013). "Overweight" and "obese" are labels for ranges of weight that are greater than what experts consider healthy for an individual's height (CDC, 2012b). In recent years, the percentage of individuals who are overweight or obese has been increasing at an alarming rate. As Figure 17.8 indicates, the prevalence of being overweight or obese in the United States changed little from 1960 to 1980 (Flegal & others, 2012; Ogden & Carroll, 2010; C. L. Ogden & others, 2012). However,

FIGURE 17.8 Changes in the Percentage of U.S. Adults 20 to 74 Years of Age Classified as Overweight or Obese, 1960–2010 Being overweight or obese poses the greatest overall health risk for Americans today. In this graph, the vertical, or Y, axis shows the percentage of people considered overweight or obese, and the horizontal, or X, axis shows the years for these values.

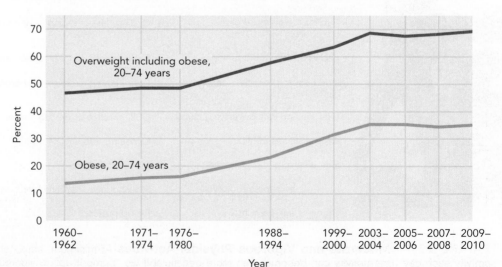

from 2009 to 2010, 69 percent of U.S. adults were overweight or obese, with 35 percent in the obese category (Flegal & others, 2012).

Exercising regularly is one great way to lose weight (Fahey, Insel, & Roth, 2013; Thompson, Manore, & Vaughan, 2013). Making healthy dietary choices is another (Hall, 2013). Eating right means eating sensible, nutritious foods. Despite the growing variety of choices Americans can make in the grocery store, many of us are unhealthy eaters. We take in too much sugar and not enough foods high in vitamins, minerals, and fiber, such as fruits, vegetables, and grains. We eat too much fast food and too few well-balanced meals—choices that increase our fat and cholesterol intake, both of which are implicated in long-term health problems (Schiff, 2013).

Healthy eating does not mean trying out every fad diet that comes along but rather incorporating tasty, healthy foods into meals and snacks. Healthy eating is not something that people should do just to lose weight—it is about committing to lifelong healthy food habits. Several health goals can be accomplished through a sound nutritional plan. Not only does a well-balanced diet provide more energy, but it also can lower blood pressure and lessen the risk for cancer and tooth decay (Fahey, Insel, & Roth, 2013).

Losing weight and opting for healthier foods can be difficult, especially when one is just starting out. Many weight-loss fads promise weight loss with no effort, no hunger, and no real change in one's food consumption. These promises are unrealistic. Making genuine, enduring changes in eating behavior is hard work. This reality does not mean adopting a pessimistic attitude. Rather, positive expectations and self-efficacy are important because the task at hand is a challenging one.

The National Weight Control Registry is an ongoing study of people who have lost at least 40 pounds and kept it off for at least 2 years. Research on these successful dieters gives us important tips on how people who keep the weight off achieve this goal (L. G. Ogden & others, 2012). Another study of approximately 2,000 U.S. adults found that exercising 30 minutes a day, planning meals, and weighing themselves daily were the main strategies of successful dieters (Kruger, Blanck, & Gillespie, 2006) (Figure 17.9).

The truth is that keeping weight off is an ongoing process. Moreover, the longer a dieter keeps the weight off, the less likely he or she is to gain it back (McGuire & others, 1999). The goal is difficult, but accomplishing it is a testament to the power of belief in oneself.

Quitting Smoking

Another health-related goal is giving up smoking. Evidence from a number of studies underscores the dangers of smoking and being around smokers (American Cancer Society, 2013). For example, smoking is linked to 30 percent of cancer deaths, 21 percent of heart disease deaths, and 82 percent of chronic pulmonary disease deaths. Secondhand smoke is implicated in as many as 9,000 lung cancer deaths a year. Children of smokers are at special risk for respiratory and middle-ear diseases (Accordini & others, 2012; Bisgaard, Jensen, & Bonnelykke, 2012).

Fewer people smoke today than in the past, and almost half of the living adults who ever smoked have quit. In 2011, 19 percent of all adults in the United States smoked, with men being more likely to smoke (21.6 percent) than women (16.5 percent) (CDC, 2013a). Although these numbers represent a substantial decline from 40 years ago, when 50 percent of men smoked, many individuals still smoke.

Quitting smoking has enormous health benefits. Figure 17.10 shows that when individuals quit smoking, their risk of fatal lung cancer declines over time. It is difficult to imagine that there is

FIGURE 17.9 **Comparison of Strategies in Successful and Unsuccessful Dieters** Losing weight—and keeping it off—can be challenging, but reaching these goals is not impossible. Success in dieting depends on engaging in physical activity, planning meals, and monitoring progress.

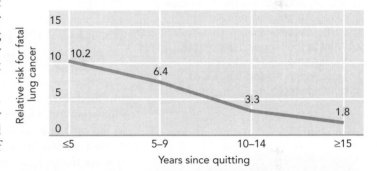

FIGURE 17.10 **Fatal Lung Cancer and Years Since Quitting Smoking** One study compared more than 43,000 former male smokers with almost 60,000 males who had never smoked (Enstrom, 1999). For comparison purposes, a zero level was assigned as the risk for fatal lung cancer for men who had never smoked. Over time, the relative risk for smokers who had quit declined, but even after 15 years it was still above that of nonsmokers.

"I told you smoking was bad for you."

© Adey Bryant. www.CartoonStock.com.

An experience as deceptively simple as taking in and perceiving a sunset becomes stunningly complex in the context of a human life.

a person living today who is not aware that smoking causes cancer, and there is little doubt that most smokers would like to quit. However, their addiction to nicotine makes quitting a challenge. Nicotine, the active drug in cigarettes, is a stimulant that increases the smoker's energy and alertness, a pleasurable and reinforcing experience. In addition, nicotine stimulates neurotransmitters that have a calming or pain-reducing effect (Johnstone & others, 2006; Plaza-Zabala & others, 2010).

Research confirms that giving up smoking can be difficult, especially in the early days of quitting (Pilnick & Coleman, 2010). There are various ways to quit smoking (Cahill, Stead, & Lancaster, 2012; Sachs & others, 2012; Tahiri & others, 2012). Common methods include:

- *Going cold turkey:* Some individuals succeed by simply stopping smoking without making any major changes in their lifestyle. They decide they are going to quit, and they do. Lighter smokers usually have more success with this approach than heavier smokers.

- *Using a substitute source of nicotine:* Nicotine gum, the nicotine patch, the nicotine inhaler, and nicotine spray work on the principle of supplying small amounts of nicotine to diminish the intensity of withdrawal (Larzelere & Williams, 2012).

- *Seeking therapeutic help:* Some smokers get professional help to kick the habit. Interventions may include psychotherapy and medications (Wynn & others, 2012), often in combination with each other (Gifford & others, 2011).

No one method is foolproof for quitting smoking (Fant & others, 2009). Often a combination of these approaches is the best strategy. Furthermore, quitting for good typically requires more than one try, as the stages of change model would suggest.

6· PSYCHOLOGY AND YOUR GOOD LIFE

In this chapter, we have examined how the mental and physical aspects of your existence intertwine and influence each other in dynamic ways. The field of health psychology serves to illustrate how all of the various areas of psychology converge to reveal that interplay.

As a human being, you are both a physical entity and a system of mental processes that are themselves reflected in that most complex of physical organs, the human brain. At every moment, both body and mind are present and affecting each other. Caring for your brain and mind—the resources that make it possible for you to read this book, study for tests, listen to lectures, fall in love, share with friends, help others, and make a difference in the world—is worthy of being a life mission.

Many pages ago, we defined psychology as the scientific study of behavior and mental processes, broadly meaning the things we do, think, and feel. Reflect for a moment on the psychological dimensions of vision. In Chapter 4 we examined the processes by which those amazing sense organs, our eyes, detect color, light, dark, shape, and depth. We probed the ways that the brain takes that information and turns it into perception—how a pattern of colors, shapes, and light comes to be perceived as a flower, a fall day, a sunset. Visual systems, we discovered, are generally the same from one person to the next. Thus, you can memorize the different parts of the human eye and know that your understanding is true for just about all the human eyes you will encounter in life.

However, even something as deceptively simple as perceiving a sunset through the sense of vision becomes amazingly complex when we put it in the context of a human life. Is that sunset the first you see while on your honeymoon, or right after a painful romantic breakup, or on the eve of the first day of your life as a new parent? Placing even the most ordinary moment in the framework of a human life renders it remarkably complex and undeniably fascinating.

This fascination is one of the primary motivations for the science of psychology itself. Individuals have always pondered the mysteries of human behavior, thought, and emotion. Why do we do the things we do? How do we think and feel? In this book, we have explored the broad range of topics that have interested psychologists throughout the history of this young science.

Coming to the close of this introduction to psychology allows you to look back but also ahead. It allows you to take stock of what psychology has come to mean to you now, as well as to consider what it might mean to you in the future. Whether or not you continue coursework in psychology, this book has highlighted opportunities for your future exploration about yourself and your world. In each of the real-life examples of human experience we have considered in the text—moments of heroism, weakness, joy, pain, and more—psychology has had a lesson to share with respect to the person that is *you*. Making the most of what you have learned about psychology means making the most of yourself and your life.

1. HEALTH PSYCHOLOGY AND BEHAVIORAL MEDICINE

Health psychology is a multidimensional field that emphasizes biological, psychological, and social factors in human health. Closely aligned with health psychology is behavioral medicine, which combines medical and behavioral knowledge to reduce illness and promote health. Related fields are health promotion, which is concerned with identifying ways to foster healthy behaviors, and public health, which focuses on understanding disease at the population level and directing public policy.

Health psychology and behavioral medicine demonstrate the biopsychosocial model by examining the interaction of biological, psychological, and social variables as they relate to health and illness. Stress is an example of a biological, psychological, and social construct.

Health psychology and behavioral medicine bring the relationship of the mind and body to the forefront. These approaches examine the reciprocal relationships between the mind and body: how the body is influenced by psychological states and how mental life is influenced by physical health.

2. MAKING POSITIVE LIFE CHANGES

The theory of reasoned action suggests that we can make changes by devising specific intentions for behavioral change. We are more likely to follow through on our intentions if we feel good about the change and if we feel that others around us also support the change. The theory of planned behavior incorporates these factors as well as our perceptions of control over the behavior.

The stages of change model posits that personal change occurs in a series of five steps: precontemplation, contemplation, preparation/determination, action/willpower, and maintenance. Each stage has its own challenges. Relapse is a natural part of the journey toward change.

3. RESOURCES FOR EFFECTIVE LIFE CHANGE

Motivation is an important part of sustaining behavioral change. Change is more effective when the person does it for intrinsic reasons (because he or she really wants to) rather than extrinsic reasons (to gain rewards). Implementation intentions are the specific ways individuals plan to institute changes successfully.

Social relationships are strongly related to health and survival. Social support refers to the aid provided by others to a person in need.

Support can take the form of tangible assistance, information, or emotional support. Social support has been found to have strong relations to functioning and coping with stress.

Religious faith is associated with enhanced health. One reason for this association is that religions often frown on excess and promote healthy behavior. Religious participation also allows individuals to benefit from a social group. Finally, religion provides a meaning system on which to rely in times of difficulty.

4. TOWARD A HEALTHIER MIND (AND BODY): CONTROLLING STRESS

Stress is the response of individuals when life circumstances threaten them and tax their ability to cope. Selye characterized the stress response with his concept of a general adaptation syndrome (GAS), which has three stages: alarm, resistance, and exhaustion.

The hypothalamic-pituitary-adrenal axis (HPA axis) comprises the interactions among the hypothalamus, pituitary gland, and adrenal glands. This axis plays an important role in human responses to stress. Chronic stress takes a toll on the body's natural disease-fighting abilities. Stress is also related to cardiovascular disease and cancer.

Kicking the stress habit means remembering that stress is a product of how we think about life events. Coping may be divided into the categories of problem-focused coping and emotion-focused coping. Overall, problem-focused coping is more adaptive than emotion-focused coping. Hardiness and optimism are associated with thriving during stressful times.

5. TOWARD A HEALTHIER BODY (AND MIND): BEHAVING AS IF YOUR LIFE DEPENDS UPON IT

Exercise has many positive psychological and physical benefits. Tips for increasing one's activity level include starting small by making changes in one's routine to incorporate physical activity (such as walking instead of driving to school); trying a variety of activities to find something one likes; finding an exercise partner; and swapping exercise for sedentary activities such as TV viewing. Keeping track of progress helps the individual to monitor his or her goal progress.

Overweight and obesity pose the greatest health risks to Americans today. They can be largely avoided by eating right, which means selecting nutritious foods and maintaining healthy eating habits for a lifetime, not just while on a diet. A combination of healthy eating and exercise is the best way to achieve weight loss.

Despite widespread knowledge that smoking causes cancer, some people still smoke. Methods of quitting include going cold turkey, using a substitute source of nicotine, and seeking therapy. Although difficult at first, quitting smoking can be achieved, though quitting for good usually takes more than one try. Usually a combination of methods is the best strategy for quitting.

6. PSYCHOLOGY AND YOUR GOOD LIFE

More than any other science, psychology is about you—understanding how you work. This book has aimed to show the relevance of psychology to your health and wellness and to help you appreciate the many, and deep, connections between this comparatively new science and your everyday life.

key *terms*

health psychology, p. 562

behavioral medicine, p. 562

health behaviors, p. 563

theory of reasoned action, p. 563

theory of planned behavior, p. 563

stages of change model, p. 564

relapse, p. 566

implementation intentions, p. 567

social support, p. 568

general adaptation syndrome (GAS), p. 571

hypothalamic-pituitary-adrenal axis (HPA axis), p. 571

psychoneuroimmunology, p. 572

problem-focused coping, p. 574

emotion-focused coping, p. 574

hardiness, p. 575

stress management program, p. 576

exercise, p. 578

aerobic exercise, p. 578

apply your *knowledge*

1. Take one day and become a stress detective. Every time a friend mentions how stressed out he or she is feeling, ask your friend to describe the source of the stress. What is the stressful event? How is the person appraising the event? How might he or she appraise the situation in ways that would help decrease stress?

2. Interview someone you know who has successfully lost weight, quit smoking, or started an exercise program. Ask the person about his or her experience of each of the stages of change. Does the theory fit your friend's experience? Why or why not?

3. Select one bad habit you would like to break for 1 week—for example, smoking, eating sugary foods, or putting off getting aerobic exercise. Keep a journal of your progress each day in avoiding the bad habit. How easy or difficult did you find this little test in healthy life change?

4. Search the web on the topic of stress management or coping with stress. Visit three or four sites and critically evaluate the suggestions made on the sites. How are they similar to the suggestions

given in the text? How much information is available to evaluate the claims on the sites? Based on your critical evaluation, is the advice something you would follow or not? Explain.

5. One method that has helped to decrease unhealthy behaviors, such as smoking, is to make them more expensive. Some local governments have suggested imposing taxes on unhealthy foods, such as sugary soft drinks. Would such a tax be useful? Would you be in favor of such a tax, or opposed? Why?

6. Turn to the Table of Contents of this book. Consider which chapters or topics you found most interesting as you explored psychology. Go to your school's library and locate the journals that are devoted to that area (you can ask a librarian for help). Browse a recent issue of one of the journals. What kinds of topics are scientists studying? If a particular study described in this book sounded interesting, you can probably obtain it online. Do a "Google scholar" search on the authors and take a look at the original article. What did the authors conclude? What did you learn?

GLOSSARY

abnormal behavior Behavior that is deviant, maladaptive, or personally distressful over a relatively long period of time.

absolute threshold The minimum amount of stimulus energy that a person can detect.

accommodation An individual's adjustment of his or her schemas to new information.

acquired immune deficiency syndrome (AIDS) A sexually transmitted infection, caused by the human immunodeficiency virus (HIV), that destroys the body's immune system.

acquisition The initial learning of the connection between the unconditioned stimulus and the conditioned stimulus when these two stimuli are paired.

action potential The brief wave of positive electrical charge that sweeps down the axon.

activation-synthesis theory of dreaming Theory that dreaming occurs when the cerebral cortex synthesizes neural signals generated from activity in the lower part of the brain and that dreams result from the brain's attempts to find logic in random brain activity that occurs during sleep.

addiction Either a physical or a psychological dependence, or both, on a drug.

adrenal glands Glands at the top of each kidney that are responsible for regulating moods, energy level, and the ability to cope with stress.

aerobic exercise Sustained activity—jogging, swimming, or cycling, for example—that stimulates heart and lung functioning.

affectionate or companionate love Love that occurs when individuals desire to have another person near and have a deep, caring affection for the person.

affective commitment A kind of job commitment deriving from the employee's emotional attachment to the workplace.

afferent nerves or sensory nerves Nerves that carry information about the external environment *to* the brain and spinal cord via sensory receptors.

aggression Behavior that is intended to harm another person.

aggression Social behavior with the objective of harming someone, either physically or verbally.

alcoholism A disorder that involves long-term, repeated, uncontrolled, compulsive, and excessive use of alcoholic beverages and that impairs the drinker's health and social relationships.

algorithms Strategies—including formulas, instructions, and the testing of all possible solutions—that guarantee a solution to a problem.

all-or-nothing principle The principle that once the electrical impulse reaches a certain level of intensity (its threshold), it fires and

moves all the way down the axon without losing any intensity.

altruism Unselfish interest in helping another person.

amnesia The loss of memory.

amygdala An almond-shaped structure within the base of the temporal lobe that is involved in the discrimination of objects that are necessary for the organism's survival, such as appropriate food, mates, and social rivals. There are two amygdalae in the brain, one on either hemisphere.

androgens The class of sex hormones that predominate in males, produced by the testes in males and by the adrenal glands in both males and females.

androgynous Having attributes that are typically associated with both genders.

anorexia nervosa An eating disorder that involves the relentless pursuit of thinness through starvation.

anterograde amnesia A memory disorder that affects the retention of new information and events.

antianxiety drugs Drugs that reduce anxiety by making the individual calmer and less excitable; commonly known as tranquilizers.

antidepressant drugs Drugs that regulate mood.

antipsychotic drugs Powerful drugs that diminish agitated behavior, reduce tension, decrease hallucinations, improve social behavior, and produce better sleep patterns in individuals with a severe psychological disorder, especially schizophrenia.

antisocial personality disorder (ASPD) Psychological disorder characterized by guiltlessness, law-breaking, exploitation of others, irresponsibility, and deceit.

anxiety disorders Disabling (uncontrollable and disruptive) psychological disorders that feature motor tension, hyperactivity, and apprehensive expectations and thoughts.

apparent movement The perception that a stationary object is moving.

applied behavior analysis or behavior modification The use of operant conditioning principles to change human behavior.

archetypes Jung's term for emotionally laden ideas and images in the collective unconscious that have rich and symbolic meaning for all people.

artificial intelligence (AI) A scientific field that focuses on creating machines capable of performing activities that require intelligence when they are done by people.

assimilation An individual's incorporation of new information into existing knowledge.

association cortex or association area The region of the cerebral cortex that is the site of the highest intellectual functions, such as thinking and problem solving.

associative learning Learning that occurs when an organism makes a connection, or an association, between two events.

Atkinson-Shiffrin theory Theory stating that memory storage involves three separate systems: sensory memory, short-term memory, and long-term memory.

attention The process of focusing awareness on a narrowed aspect of the environment.

attention-deficit/hyperactivity disorder (ADHD) A common psychological disorder in which the individual exhibits one or more of the following: inattention, hyperactivity, and impulsivity.

attitudes An individual's opinions and beliefs about people, objects, and ideas—how the person feels about the world.

attribution theory The view that people are motivated to discover the underlying causes of behavior as part of their effort to make sense of the behavior.

auditory nerve The nerve structure that receives information about sound from the hair cells of the inner ear and carries these neural impulses to the brain's auditory areas.

authoritarian parenting A restrictive, punitive style in which the parent exhorts the child to follow the parent's directions.

authoritative parenting A parenting style that encourages the child to be independent but that still places limits and controls on behavior.

autobiographical memory A special form of episodic memory, consisting of a person's recollections of his or her life experiences.

automatic processes States of consciousness that require little attention and do not interfere with other ongoing activities.

autonomic nervous system The body system that takes messages to and from the body's internal organs, monitoring such processes as breathing, heart rate, and digestion.

availability heuristic A prediction about the probability of an event based on the ease of recalling or imagining similar events.

aversive conditioning A form of treatment that consists of repeated pairings of a stimulus with a very unpleasant stimulus.

avoidance learning An organism's learning that it can altogether avoid a negative stimulus by making a particular response.

axon The part of the neuron that carries information away from the cell body toward other cells.

barbiturates Depressant drugs, such as Nembutal and Seconal, that decrease central nervous system activity.

basal ganglia Large neuron clusters located above the thalamus and under the cerebral cortex that work with the cerebellum and the cerebral cortex to control and coordinate voluntary movements.

base rate neglect The tendency to ignore information about general principles in favor of very specific but vivid information.

behavior Everything we do that can be directly observed.

behavioral approach An approach to psychology emphasizing the scientific study of observable behavioral responses and their environmental determinants.

behavioral genetics The study of the inherited underpinnings of behavioral characteristics.

behavioral medicine An interdisciplinary field that focuses on developing and integrating behavioral and biomedical knowledge to promote health and reduce illness; overlaps with health psychology.

behaviorism A theory of learning that focuses solely on observable behaviors, discounting the importance of mental activity such as thinking, wishing, and hoping.

behavior therapies Treatments, based on the behavioral and social cognitive theories of learning, that use principles of learning to reduce or eliminate maladaptive behavior.

big five factors of personality The five broad traits that are thought to describe the main dimensions of personality: neuroticism (emotional instability), extraversion, openness to experience, agreeableness, and conscientiousness.

binding In the sense of vision, the bringing together and integration of what is processed by different neural pathways or cells.

binge eating disorder (BED) An eating disorder characterized by recurrent episodes of eating more food in a short period of time than most people would eat, during which the person feels a lack of control over eating.

binocular cues Depth cues that depend on the combination of the images in the left and right eyes and on the way the two eyes work together.

biological approach An approach to psychology focusing on the body, especially the brain and nervous system.

biological rhythms Periodic physiological fluctuations in the body, such as the rise and fall of hormones and accelerated and decelerated cycles of brain activity, that can influence behavior.

biological therapies or biomedical therapies Treatments that reduce or eliminate the symptoms of psychological disorders by altering aspects of body functioning.

bipolar disorder Psychological disorder characterized by extreme mood swings that include one or more episodes of mania, an overexcited, unrealistically optimistic state.

bisexual Referring to a sexual orientation in which the individual is sexually attracted to people of both sexes.

borderline personality disorder (BPD) Psychological disorder characterized by a pervasive pattern of instability in interpersonal relationships, self-image, and emotions, and of marked impulsivity beginning by early adulthood and present in a variety of contexts.

bottom-up processing The operation in sensation and perception in which sensory receptors register information about the external environment and send it up to the brain for interpretation.

brain stem The stemlike brain area that includes much of the hindbrain (excluding the cerebellum) and the midbrain; it connects with the spinal cord at its lower end and then extends upward to encase the reticular formation in the midbrain.

broaden-and-build model Fredrickson's model of positive emotion, stating that the function of positive emotions lies in their effects on an individual's attention and ability to build resources.

bulimia nervosa An eating disorder in which the individual (typically female) consistently follows a binge-and-purge eating pattern.

burnout A distressed psychological state in which a person experiences emotional exhaustion and little motivation for work.

bystander effect The tendency of an individual who observes an emergency to help less when other people are present than when the observer is alone.

Cannon-Bard theory The proposition that emotion and physiological reactions occur simultaneously.

case study or **case history** An in-depth look at a single individual.

catatonia State of immobility and unresponsiveness lasting for long periods of time.

cell body The part of the neuron that contains the nucleus, which directs the manufacture of substances that the neuron needs for growth and maintenance.

central nervous system (CNS) The brain and spinal cord.

cerebral cortex Part of the forebrain, the outer layer of the brain, responsible for the most complex mental functions, such as thinking and planning.

chromosomes In the human cell, threadlike structures that come in 23 pairs, one member of each pair originating from each parent, and that contain the remarkable substance DNA.

circadian rhythms Daily behavioral or physiological cycles that involve the sleep/wake cycle, body temperature, blood pressure, and blood sugar level.

classical conditioning Learning process in which a neutral stimulus becomes associated with an innately meaningful stimulus and acquires the capacity to elicit a similar response.

client-centered therapy A form of humanistic therapy, developed by Rogers, in which the therapist provides a warm, supportive atmosphere to improve the client's self-concept and to encourage the client to gain insight into problems; also called Rogerian therapy or nondirective therapy.

clinical psychology The area of psychology that integrates science and theory to prevent and treat psychological disorders.

cognition The way in which information is processed and manipulated in remembering, thinking, and knowing.

cognitive affective processing systems (CAPS) Mischel's theoretical model for describing that individuals' thoughts and emotions about themselves and the world affect their behavior and become linked in ways that matter to that behavior.

cognitive appraisal Interpreting the events and experiences in one's life as harmful and threatening, or as challenging, and determining whether one has the resources to cope effectively.

cognitive approach An approach to psychology emphasizing the mental processes involved in knowing: how we direct our attention, perceive, remember, think, and solve problems.

cognitive-behavior therapy A therapy that combines cognitive therapy and behavior therapy with the goal of developing self-efficacy.

cognitive dissonance An individual's psychological discomfort (dissonance) caused by two inconsistent thoughts.

cognitive reappraisal Regulating one's feelings about an experience by reinterpreting that experience or thinking about it in a different way or from a different angle.

cognitive theory of dreaming Theory proposing that dreaming can be understood by applying the same cognitive concepts used to study the waking mind.

cognitive therapies Treatments emphasizing that cognitions (thoughts) are the main source of psychological problems and that attempt to change the individual's feelings and behaviors by changing cognitions.

collective unconscious Jung's term for the impersonal, deepest layer of the unconscious mind, shared by all human beings because of their common ancestral past.

concepts Mental categories that are used to group objects, events, and characteristics.

concrete operational stage Piaget's third stage of cognitive development, lasting from about 7 to 11 years of age, during which the individual uses operations and replaces intuitive reasoning with logical reasoning in concrete situations.

conditioned response (CR) The learned response to the conditioned stimulus that occurs after conditioned stimulus–unconditioned stimulus pairing.

conditioned stimulus (CS) A previously neutral stimulus that eventually elicits a conditioned response after being paired with the unconditioned stimulus.

conditions of worth The standards that the individual must live up to in order to receive positive regard from others.

cones The receptor cells in the retina that allow for color perception.

confederate A person who is given a role to play in a study so that the social context can be manipulated.

confirmation bias The tendency to search for and use information that supports one's ideas rather than refutes them.

conformity A change in a person's behavior to coincide more closely with a group standard.

connectionism or parallel distributed processing (PDP) The theory that memory is stored throughout the brain in connections among neurons, several of which may work together to process a single memory.

consciousness An individual's awareness of external events and internal sensations under a condition of arousal, including awareness of the self and thoughts about one's experiences.

continuance commitment A kind of job commitment deriving from the employee's perception that leaving the organization would be too costly, both economically and socially.

control group The participants in an experiment who are as much like the experimental group as possible and who are treated in every way like the experimental group except for a manipulated factor, the independent variable.

controlled processes The most alert states of human consciousness, during which individuals actively focus their efforts toward a goal.

convergence A binocular cue to depth and distance in which the muscle movements in an individual's two eyes provide information about how deep and/or far away something is.

convergent thinking Thinking that produces the single best solution to a problem.

coping Managing taxing circumstances, expending effort to solve life's problems, and seeking to master or reduce stress.

corpus callosum The large bundle of axons that connects the brain's two hemispheres, responsible for relaying information between the two sides.

correlational research Research that examines the relations between variables with the purpose of determining whether and how two variables change together.

counterconditioning A classical conditioning procedure for changing the relationship between

a conditioned stimulus and its conditioned response.

couples therapy Group therapy with married or unmarried couples whose major problem lies within their relationship.

creativity The ability to think about something in novel and unusual ways and to devise unconventional solutions to problems.

critical thinking The process of reflecting deeply and actively, asking questions, and evaluating the evidence.

cross-cultural competence A therapist's assessment of his or her ability to manage cultural issues in therapy and the client's perception of those abilities.

cross-sectional design A type of correlational study in which variables are measured at a single point in time.

culture-fair tests Intelligence tests that are intended to be culturally unbiased.

decay theory Theory stating that when an individual learns something new, a neurochemical memory trace forms, but over time this trace disintegrates; suggests that the passage of time always increases forgetting.

decision making The mental activity of evaluating alternatives and choosing among them.

deductive reasoning Reasoning from a general case that is known to be true to a specific instance.

deep brain stimulation A procedure for treatment-resistant depression that involves the implantation of electrodes in the brain that emit signals to alter the brain's electrical circuitry.

defense mechanisms The Freudian term for tactics the ego uses to reduce anxiety by unconsciously distorting reality.

deindividuation The reduction in personal identity and erosion of the sense of personal responsibility when one is part of a group.

delusions False, unusual, and sometimes magical beliefs that are not part of an individual's culture.

demand characteristics Any aspects of a study that communicate to the participants how the experimenter wants them to behave.

dendrites Treelike fibers projecting from a neuron, which receive information and orient it toward the neuron's cell body.

deoxyribonucleic acid (DNA) A complex molecule in the cell's chromosomes that carries genetic information.

dependent variable The outcome; the factor that can change in an experiment in response to changes in the independent variable.

depressants Psychoactive drugs that slow down mental and physical activity.

depressive disorders Psychological disorders in which the individual suffers from depression—an unrelenting lack of pleasure in life.

depth perception The ability to perceive objects three-dimensionally.

descriptive research Research that determines the basic dimensions of a phenomenon, defining what it is, how often it occurs, and so on.

descriptive statistics Mathematical procedures that are used to describe and summarize sets of data in a meaningful way.

development The pattern of continuity and change in human capabilities that occurs throughout life, involving both growth and decline.

difference threshold The degree of difference that must exist between two stimuli before the difference is detected.

discrimination An unjustified negative or harmful action toward a member of a group simply because the person belongs to that group.

discrimination (in classical conditioning) The process of learning to respond to certain stimuli and not others.

discrimination (in operant conditioning) Responding appropriately to stimuli that signal that a behavior will or will not be reinforced.

disorders of sexual development (DSD) Congenital conditions in which the development of chromosomal, gonadal, or anatomical sex is atypical; formerly called intersex conditions or hermaphroditism.

display rules Sociocultural standards that determine when, where, and how emotions should be expressed.

dissociative amnesia Dissociative disorder characterized by extreme memory loss that is caused by extensive psychological stress.

dissociative disorders Psychological disorders that involve a sudden loss of memory or change in identity due to the dissociation (separation) of the individual's conscious awareness from previous memories and thoughts.

dissociative identity disorder (DID) Dissociative disorder in which the individual has two or more distinct personalities or selves, each with its own memories, behaviors, and relationships; formerly called multiple personality disorder.

divergent thinking Thinking that produces many solutions to the same problem.

divided attention Concentrating on more than one activity at the same time.

divided consciousness view of hypnosis Hilgard's view that hypnosis involves a splitting of consciousness into two separate components, one that follows the hypnotist's commands and the other that acts as a "hidden observer."

dominant-recessive genes principle The principle that, if one gene of a pair is dominant and one is recessive, the dominant gene overrides the recessive gene. A recessive gene exerts its influence only if both genes of a pair are recessive.

double-blind experiment An experimental design in which neither the experimenter nor the participants are aware of which participants are in the experimental group and which are in the control group until the results are calculated.

downsizing A dramatic cutting of the workforce that has become a popular business strategy to enhance profitability.

dream analysis A psychoanalytic technique for interpreting a person's dreams.

drive An aroused state that occurs because of a physiological need.

DSM-5 The fifth edition of the *Diagnostic and Statistical Manual of Mental Disorders;* the major classification of psychological disorders in the United States.

efferent nerves or motor nerves Nerves that carry information *out of* the brain and spinal cord to other areas of the body.

ego The Freudian structure of personality that deals with the demands of reality.

egoism Giving to another person to ensure reciprocity; to gain self-esteem; to present oneself as powerful, competent, or caring; or to avoid censure from oneself and others for failing to live up to society's expectations.

elaboration The formation of a number of different connections around a stimulus at any given level of memory encoding.

elaboration likelihood model Theory identifying two ways to persuade: a central route and a peripheral route.

electroconvulsive therapy (ECT) A treatment, sometimes used for depression, that sets off a seizure in the brain; also called shock therapy.

emerging adulthood The transitional period from adolescence to adulthood, spanning approximately 18 to 25 years of age.

emotion Feeling, or affect, that can involve physiological arousal (such as a fast heartbeat), conscious experience (thinking about being in love with someone), and behavioral expression (a smile or grimace).

emotion-focused coping The coping strategy that involves responding to the stress that one is feeling—trying to manage one's emotional reaction—rather than focusing on the problem itself.

empathy A feeling of oneness with the emotional state of another person.

empirically keyed test A type of self-report test that presents many questionnaire items to two groups that are known to be different in some central way.

empirically supported treatment An approach to treating psychological disorders that advocates making treatment decisions based on the body of research that has shown which type of therapy works best.

empirical method Gaining knowledge through the observation of events, the collection of data, and logical reasoning.

encoding The first step in memory; the process by which information gets into memory storage.

endocrine system The body system consisting of a set of glands that regulate the activities of certain organs by releasing their chemical products into the bloodstream.

episodic memory The retention of information about the where, when, and what of life's happenings—that is, how individuals remember life's episodes.

ergonomics or human factors A field that combines engineering and psychology and that focuses on understanding and enhancing the safety and efficiency of the human–machine interaction.

estrogens The class of sex hormones that predominate in females, produced mainly by the ovaries.

ethnocentrism The tendency to favor one's own ethnic group over other groups.

evidence-based practice Integration of the best available research with clinical expertise in the context of client characteristics, culture, and preferences.

evolutionary approach An approach to psychology centered on evolutionary ideas such as adaptation, reproduction, and natural selection as the basis for explaining specific human behaviors.

executive function Higher-order, complex cognitive processes, including thinking, planning, and problem solving.

exercise Structured activities whose goal is to improve health.

experiment A carefully regulated procedure in which the researcher manipulates one or more variables that are believed to influence some other variable.

experimental group The participants in an experiment who receive the drug or other treatment under study—that is, those who are exposed to the change that the independent variable represents.

experimenter bias The influence of the experimenter's expectations on the outcome of research.

explicit memory or declarative memory The conscious recollection of information, such as specific facts or events and, at least in humans, information that can be verbally communicated.

external validity The degree to which an experimental design actually reflects the real-world issues it is supposed to address.

extinction (in classical conditioning) The weakening of the conditioned response when the unconditioned stimulus is absent.

extinction (in operant conditioning) Decreases in the frequency of a behavior when the behavior is no longer reinforced.

extrinsic motivation Motivation that involves external incentives such as rewards and punishments.

face validity The extent to which a test item appears to fit the particular trait it is measuring.

facial feedback hypothesis The idea that facial expressions can influence emotions as well as reflect them.

false consensus effect People's overestimation of the degree to which everybody else thinks or acts the way they themselves does.

family therapy Group therapy with family members.

feature detectors Neurons in the brain's visual system that respond to particular features of a stimulus.

fetish An object or activity that arouses sexual interest and desire.

figure-ground relationship The principle by which we organize the perceptual field into stimuli that stand out (figure) and those that are left over (ground).

fixation Using a prior strategy and failing to look at a problem from a fresh new perspective.

flashbulb memory The memory of emotionally significant events that people often recall with more accuracy and vivid imagery than everyday events.

flat affect The display of little or no emotion—a common negative symptom of schizophrenia.

flow The optimal experience of a match between one's skills and the challenge of a task.

forebrain The brain's largest division and its most forward part.

formal operational stage Piaget's fourth stage of cognitive development, which begins at 11 to 15 years of age and continues through the adult years; it features thinking about things that are not concrete, making predictions, and using logic to come up with hypotheses about the future.

frequency theory Theory on how the inner ear registers the frequency of sound, stating that the perception of a sound's frequency depends on how often the auditory nerve fires.

frontal lobes The portion of the cerebral cortex behind the forehead, involved in personality, intelligence, and the control of voluntary muscles.

functional fixedness Failing to solve a problem as a result of fixation on a thing's usual functions.

functionalism James's approach to mental processes, emphasizing the functions and purposes of the mind and behavior in the individual's adaptation to the environment.

fundamental attribution error Observers' overestimation of the importance of internal traits and underestimation of the importance of external situations when they seek explanations of an actor's behavior.

gender The social and psychological aspects of being female or male; gender goes beyond biological sex to include an individual's personal understanding of the meaning of being male or female.

gender identity An individual's multifaceted sense of belonging to the male or female sex.

gender roles Roles that reflect the individual's expectation for how females and males should think, act, and feel.

gender similarities hypothesis Hyde's proposition that men and women (and boys and girls) are much more similar than they are different.

gender stereotypes Overly general beliefs and expectations about what women and men are like.

general adaptation syndrome (GAS) Selye's term for the common effects of stressful demands on the body, consisting of three stages: alarm, resistance, and exhaustion.

generalization (in classical conditioning) The tendency of a new stimulus that is similar to the original conditioned stimulus to elicit a response that is similar to the conditioned response.

generalization (in operant conditioning) Performing a reinforced behavior in a different situation.

generalized anxiety disorder Anxiety disorder marked by persistent anxiety for at least 6 months, and in which the individual is unable to specify the reasons for the anxiety.

genes The units of hereditary information, consisting of short segments of chromosomes composed of DNA.

genotype An individual's genetic heritage; his or her actual genetic material.

gestalt psychology A school of thought interested in how people naturally organize their perceptions according to certain patterns.

gifted Possessing high intelligence (an IQ of 130 or higher) and/or superior talent in a particular area.

glands Organs or tissues in the body that create chemicals that control many of our bodily functions.

glial cells or glia The second of two types of cells in the nervous system; glial cells provide support, nutritional benefits, and other functions and keep neurons running smoothly.

gonads Glands that produce sex hormones and generate ova (eggs) in females and sperm in males; collectively called gametes, the ova and sperm are the cells that eventually will be used in reproduction.

group polarization effect The solidification and further strengthening of an individual's position as a consequence of a group discussion or interaction.

group therapy A sociocultural approach to the treatment of psychological disorders that brings together individuals who share a particular psychological disorder in sessions that are typically led by a mental health professional.

groupthink The impaired group decision making that occurs when making the right decision is less important than maintaining group harmony.

habituation Decreased responsiveness to a stimulus after repeated presentations.

hallucinations Sensory experiences that occur in the absence of real stimuli.

hallucinogens Psychoactive drugs that modify a person's perceptual experiences and produce visual images that are not real.

halo effect A bias, common in performance appraisals, that occurs when a rater gives an employee the same rating on all of the items being evaluated, even though the individual varies across the dimensions being assessed.

hardiness A personality trait characterized by a sense of commitment rather than alienation and of control rather than powerlessness; a perception of problems as challenges rather than threats.

Hawthorne effect The tendency of individuals to perform better simply because of being singled out and made to feel important.

health behaviors Practices that have an impact on physical well-being, such as adopting a healthy approach to stress, exercising, eating right, brushing one's teeth, performing breast and testicular exams, not smoking, drinking in moderation (or not at all), and practicing safe sex.

health psychology A subfield of psychology that emphasizes psychology's role in establishing and maintaining health and preventing and treating illness.

heritability The proportion of observable differences in a group that can be explained by differences in the genes of the group's members.

heterosexual Referring to a sexual orientation in which the individual is generally sexually attracted to members of the opposite sex.

heuristics Shortcut strategies or guidelines that suggest a solution to a problem but do not guarantee an answer.

hierarchy of needs Maslow's theory that human needs must be satisfied in the following sequence: physiological needs, safety, love and belongingness, esteem, and self-actualization.

hindbrain Located at the skull's rear, the lowest portion of the brain, consisting of the medulla, cerebellum, and pons.

hindsight bias The tendency to report falsely, after the fact, that one has accurately predicted an outcome.

hippocampus The structure in the limbic system that has a special role in the storage of memories.

homeostasis The body's tendency to maintain an equilibrium, or steady state or balance.

homosexual Referring to a sexual orientation in which the individual is generally sexually attracted to members of the same sex.

hormones Chemical messengers that are produced by the endocrine glands and carried by the bloodstream to all parts of the body.

human relations approach A management approach emphasizing the psychological characteristics of workers and managers, stressing the importance of factors such as morale, attitudes, values, and humane treatment of workers.

human sexual response pattern Masters and Johnson's model of human sexual response, consisting of four phases—excitement, plateau, orgasm, and resolution.

humanistic approach An approach to psychology emphasizing a person's positive qualities, the capacity for positive growth, and the freedom to choose any destiny.

humanistic perspectives Theoretical views stressing a person's capacity for personal growth and positive human qualities.

humanistic therapies Treatments, unique in their emphasis on people's self-healing capacities, that encourage clients to understand themselves and to grow personally.

hypnosis An altered state of consciousness or a psychological state of altered attention and expectation in which the individual is unusually receptive to suggestions.

hypothalamic-pituitary-adrenal axis (HPA axis) The complex set of interactions among the hypothalamus, the pituitary gland, and the adrenal glands that regulates various body processes and controls reactions to stressful events.

hypothalamus A small forebrain structure, located just below the thalamus, that monitors three pleasurable activities—eating, drinking, and sex—as well as emotion, stress, and reward.

hypothesis An educated guess that derives logically from a theory; a prediction that can be tested.

id The Freudian structure of personality consisting of unconscious drives; the individual's reservoir of sexual energy.

implementation intentions Specific strategies for dealing with the challenges of making a life change.

implicit memory or nondeclarative memory Memory in which behavior is affected by prior experience without a conscious recollection of that experience.

independent variable A manipulated experimental factor; the variable that the experimenter changes to see what its effects are.

individual psychology Adler's view that people are motivated by purposes and goals and that perfection, not pleasure, is thus the key motivator in human life.

inductive reasoning Reasoning from specific observations to make generalizations.

industrial and organizational (I-O) psychology The field of psychology that applies the science of human behavior to work and the workplace.

infant attachment The close emotional bond between an infant and its caregiver.

inferential statistics Mathematical methods that are used to indicate whether results for a sample are likely to generalize to a population.

informational social influence The influence other people have on us because we want to be right.

inner ear The part of the ear that includes the oval window, cochlea, and basilar membrane and whose function is to convert sound waves into neural impulses and send them to the brain.

insight learning A form of problem solving in which the organism develops a sudden insight into or understanding of a problem's solution.

instinct An innate (unlearned) biological pattern of behavior that is assumed to be universal throughout a species.

instinctive drift The tendency of animals to revert to instinctive behavior that interferes with learning.

integrative therapy Use of a combination of techniques from different therapies based on the therapist's judgment of which particular methods will provide the greatest benefit for the client.

integrity test A type of job-screening examination that is designed to assess whether a candidate will be honest on the job.

intellectual disability or intellectual developmental disorder A condition of limited mental ability that affects an individual's functioning in everyday life.

intelligence All-purpose ability to do well on cognitive tasks, to solve problems, and to learn from experience.

intelligence quotient (IQ) An individual's mental age divided by chronological age multiplied by 100.

interference theory The theory that people forget not because memories are lost from storage but because other information gets in the way of what they want to remember.

internal validity The degree to which changes in the dependent variable are due to the manipulation of the independent variable.

intrinsic motivation Motivation based on internal factors such as organismic needs (competence, relatedness, and autonomy), as well as curiosity, challenge, and fun.

investment model A model of long-term relationships that examines the ways that commitment, investment, and the availability of attractive alternative partners predict satisfaction and stability in relationships.

James-Lange theory The theory that emotion results from physiological states triggered by stimuli in the environment.

job analysis The process of generating a description of what a job involves, including the knowledge and skills that are necessary to carry out the job's functions.

job crafting The physical and cognitive changes individuals can make within the constraints of a task to make the work "their own."

job satisfaction The extent to which a person is content in his or her job.

job stress The experience of stress on the job and in the workplace setting.

kinesthetic senses Senses that provide information about movement, posture, and orientation.

KSAOs or KSAs Common elements in a person-oriented job analysis; an acronym for *k*nowledge, *s*kills, *a*bilities, and *o*ther characteristics.

language A form of communication—whether spoken, written, or signed—that is based on a system of symbols.

latent content According to Freud, a dream's hidden content; its unconscious and true meaning.

latent learning or implicit learning Unreinforced learning that is not immediately reflected in behavior.

law of effect Thorndike's law stating that behaviors followed by positive outcomes are strengthened and that behaviors followed by negative outcomes are weakened.

learned helplessness An organism's learning through experience with negative stimuli that it has no control over negative outcomes.

learning A systematic, relatively permanent change in behavior that occurs through experience.

leisure The pleasant times before or after work when individuals are free to pursue activities and interests of their own choosing, such as hobbies, sports, and reading.

levels of processing A continuum of memory processing from shallow to intermediate to deep, with deeper processing producing better memory.

limbic system A loosely connected network of structures under the cerebral cortex, important in both memory and emotion. Its two principal structures are the amygdala and the hippocampus.

lithium The lightest of the solid elements in the periodic table of elements, widely used to treat bipolar disorder.

longitudinal design A special kind of systematic observation, used by correlational researchers, that involves obtaining measures of the variables of interest in multiple waves over time.

long-term memory A relatively permanent type of memory that stores huge amounts of information for a long time.

major depressive disorder (MDD) Psychological disorder involving a significant depressive episode and depressed characteristics, such as lethargy and hopelessness, for at least 2 weeks.

manifest content According to Freud, the surface content of a dream, containing dream symbols that disguise the dream's true meaning.

mean A measure of central tendency that is the average for a sample.

median A measure of central tendency that is the middle score in a sample.

medical model The view that psychological disorders are medical diseases with a biological origin.

meditation The attainment of a peaceful state of mind in which thoughts are not occupied by worry; the meditator is mindfully present to his or her thoughts and feelings but is not consumed by them.

memory The retention of information or experience over time as the result of three key processes: encoding, storage, and retrieval.

mental age (MA) An individual's level of mental development relative to that of others.

mental processes The thoughts, feelings, and motives that each of us experiences privately but that cannot be observed directly.

mentoring A relationship between an experienced employee—a mentor—and a novice, in which the more experienced employee serves as an advisor, a sounding board, and a source of support for the newer employee.

mere exposure effect The phenomenon that the more individuals encounter someone or something, the more probable it is that they will start liking the person or thing even if they do not realize they have seen it before.

meta-analysis A method that allows researchers to combine the results of several different studies on a similar topic in order to establish the strength of an effect.

midbrain Located between the hindbrain and forebrain, an area in which many nerve-fiber systems ascend and descend to connect the higher and lower portions of the brain; in particular, the midbrain relays information between the brain and the eyes and ears.

middle ear The part of the ear that channels sound through the eardrum, hammer, anvil, and stirrup to the inner ear.

mindfulness The state of being alert and mentally present for one's everyday activities.

Minnesota Multiphasic Personality Inventory (MMPI) The most widely used and researched empirically keyed self-report personality test.

mode A measure of central tendency that is the most common score in a sample.

monocular cues Powerful depth cues available from the image in one eye, either the right or the left.

morphology A language's rules for word formation.

motivated forgetting Forgetting that occurs when something is so painful or anxiety-laden that remembering it is intolerable.

motivation The force that moves people to behave, think, and feel the way they do.

motor cortex A region in the cerebral cortex that processes information about voluntary movement, located just behind the frontal lobes.

movement disorders The unusual mannerisms, body movements, and facial expressions that are characteristic positive symptoms of schizophrenia.

myelin sheath A layer of fat cells that encases and insulates most axons.

natural selection Darwin's principle of an evolutionary process in which organisms that are best adapted to their environment will survive and produce offspring.

naturalistic observation The observation of behavior in a real-world setting.

nature An individual's biological inheritance, especially his or her genes.

need A deprivation that energizes the drive to eliminate or reduce the deprivation.

negative affect Negative emotions such as anger, guilt, and sadness.

negative punishment The removal of a stimulus following a given behavior in order to decrease the frequency of that behavior.

negative reinforcement The removal of a stimulus following a given behavior in order to increase the frequency of that behavior.

neglectful parenting A parenting style characterized by a lack of parental involvement in the child's life.

neocortex The outermost part of the cerebral cortex, making up 80 percent of the cortex in the human brain.

nervous system The body's electrochemical communication circuitry.

neural networks Networks of nerve cells that integrate sensory input and motor output.

neurons One of two types of cells in the nervous system; neurons are the nerve cells that handle the information-processing function.

neuroscience The scientific study of the structure, function, development, genetics, and biochemistry of the nervous system, emphasizing that the brain and nervous system are central to understanding behavior, thought, and emotion.

neurotransmitters Chemical substances that are stored in very tiny sacs within the terminal buttons and involved in transmitting information across a synaptic gap to the next neuron.

noise Irrelevant and competing stimuli—not only sounds but also any distracting stimuli for the senses.

normal distribution A symmetrical, bell-shaped curve, with a majority of the scores falling in the middle of the possible range and few scores appearing toward the extremes of the range.

normative commitment A kind of job commitment deriving from the employee's sense of obligation to the organization for the investment it has made in the individual's personal and professional development.

normative social influence The influence others have on us because we want them to like us.

nurture An individual's environmental and social experiences.

obedience Behavior that complies with the explicit demands of the individual in authority.

object permanence Piaget's term for the crucial accomplishment of understanding that objects and events continue to exist even when they cannot directly be seen, heard, or touched.

observational learning Learning that occurs through observing and imitating another's behavior.

obsessive-compulsive disorder (OCD) Psychological disorder in which the individual has anxiety-provoking thoughts that will not go away and/or urges to perform repetitive, ritualistic behaviors to prevent or produce some future situation.

occipital lobes Structures located at the back of the head that respond to visual stimuli.

Oedipus complex According to Freud, a boy's intense desire to replace his father and enjoy the affections of his mother.

olfactory epithelium The lining of the roof of the nasal cavity, containing a sheet of receptor cells for smell.

open-mindedness The state of being receptive to other ways of looking at things.

operant conditioning or instrumental conditioning A form of associative learning in which the consequences of a behavior change the probability of the behavior's occurrence.

operational definition A definition that provides an objective description of how a variable is going to be measured and observed in a particular study.

opiates Opium and its derivatives; narcotic drugs that depress the central nervous system's activity and eliminate pain.

opponent-process theory Theory stating that cells in the visual system respond to complementary pairs of red-green and blue-yellow colors; a given cell might be excited by red and inhibited by green, whereas another cell might be excited by yellow and inhibited by blue.

optic nerve The structure at the back of the eye, made up of axons of the ganglion cells, that carries visual information to the brain for further processing.

organizational citizenship behavior (OCB) Discretionary actions on the part of an employee that promote organizational effectiveness but are not included in the person's formal responsibilities.

organizational culture An organization's shared values, beliefs, norms, and customs.

organizational identity Employees' feelings of oneness with the organization and its goals.

orientation A program by which an organization introduces newly hired employees to the organization's goals, familiarizes them with its rules and regulations, and lets them know how to get things done.

outer ear The outermost part of the ear, consisting of the pinna and the external auditory canal.

ovaries Sex-related endocrine glands that produce hormones involved in women's sexual development and reproduction.

overlearning Learning to perform a task so well that it becomes automatic.

overt aggression Physically or verbally harming another person directly.

pain The sensation that warns an individual of damage to the body.

pancreas A dual-purpose gland under the stomach that performs both digestive and endocrine functions.

panic disorder Anxiety disorder in which the individual experiences recurrent, sudden onsets of intense terror, often without warning and with no specific cause.

papillae Rounded bumps above the tongue's surface that contain the taste buds, the receptors for taste.

parallel processing The simultaneous distribution of information across different neural pathways.

paraphilic disorders Sexual disorders that feature recurrent sexually arousing fantasies, urges, or behaviors involving nonhuman objects; the suffering or humiliation of oneself or one's partner; or children or other nonconsenting individuals.

parasympathetic nervous system The part of the autonomic nervous system that calms the body.

parietal lobes Structures at the top and toward the rear of the head that are involved in registering spatial location, attention, and motor control.

pedophilic disorder A paraphilic disorder in which an adult or an older adolescent sexually fantasizes about or engages in sexual behavior with individuals who have not reached puberty.

perception The process of organizing and interpreting sensory information so that it makes sense.

perceptual constancy The recognition that objects are constant and unchanging even though sensory input about them is changing.

perceptual set A predisposition or readiness to perceive something in a particular way.

performance appraisal The evaluation of a person's success at meeting his or her organization's goals.

peripheral nervous system (PNS) The network of nerves that connects the brain and spinal cord to other parts of the body.

permissive parenting A parenting style characterized by the placement of few limits on the child's behavior.

personality A pattern of enduring, distinctive thoughts, emotions, and behaviors that characterize the way an individual adapts to the world.

personality disorders Chronic, maladaptive cognitive-behavioral patterns that are thoroughly integrated into an individual's personality.

personological and life story perspectives Theoretical views stressing that the way to understand the person is to focus on his or her life history and life story.

phenotype An individual's observable characteristics.

phonology A language's sound system.

physical dependence The physiological need for a drug that causes unpleasant withdrawal symptoms such as physical pain and a craving for the drug when it is discontinued.

pituitary gland A pea-sized gland just beneath the hypothalamus that controls growth and regulates other glands.

placebo In a drug study, a harmless substance that has no physiological effect, given to participants in a control group so that they are treated identically to the experimental group except for the active agent.

placebo effect A phenomenon in which the participants' expectations, rather than an actual treatment, produce an outcome.

place theory Theory on how the inner ear registers the frequency of sound, stating that each frequency produces vibrations at a particular spot on the basilar membrane.

plasticity The brain's special capacity for change.

polygraph A machine, commonly called a lie detector, that monitors changes in the body, used to try to determine whether someone is lying.

population The entire group about which the investigator wants to draw conclusions.

positive affect Positive emotions such as joy, happiness, and interest.

positive illusions Favorable views of the self that are not necessarily rooted in reality.

positive psychology A branch of psychology that emphasizes human strengths.

positive punishment The presentation of a stimulus following a given behavior in order to decrease the frequency of that behavior.

positive reinforcement The presentation of a stimulus following a given behavior in order to increase the frequency of that behavior.

post-traumatic stress disorder (PTSD) Psychological disorder that develops through exposure to a traumatic event, a severely oppressive situation, cruel abuse, or a natural or an unnatural disaster.

pragmatics The useful character of language and the ability of language to communicate even more meaning than is verbalized.

preferential looking A research technique that involves giving an infant a choice of what object to look at.

prejudice An unjustified negative attitude toward an individual based on the individual's membership in a group.

preoperational stage Piaget's second stage of cognitive development, lasting from about 2 to 7 years of age, during which thought is more symbolic than sensorimotor thought.

preparedness The species-specific biological predisposition to learn in certain ways but not others.

primary reinforcer A reinforcer that is innately satisfying; one that does not take any learning on the organism's part to make it pleasurable.

priming The activation of information that people already have in storage to help them remember new information better and faster.

proactive interference Situation in which material that was learned earlier disrupts the recall of material that was learned later.

problem-focused coping The coping strategy of squarely facing one's troubles and trying to solve them.

problem solving The mental process of finding an appropriate way to attain a goal when the goal is not readily available.

procedural memory Memory for skills.

projective test A personality assessment test that presents individuals with an ambiguous stimulus and asks them to describe it or tell a story about it—to project their own meaning onto the stimulus.

prosocial behavior Behavior that is intended to benefit other people.

prospective memory Remembering information about doing something in the future; includes memory for intentions.

prototype model A model emphasizing that when people evaluate whether a given item reflects a certain concept, they compare the item with the most typical item(s) in that category and look for a "family resemblance" with that item's properties.

psychoactive drugs Drugs that act on the nervous system to alter consciousness, modify perception, and change mood.

psychoanalysis Freud's therapeutic technique for analyzing an individual's unconscious thoughts.

psychodynamic approach An approach to psychology emphasizing unconscious thought, the conflict between biological drives (such as the drive for sex) and society's demands, and early childhood family experiences.

psychodynamic perspectives Theoretical views emphasizing that personality is primarily unconscious (beyond awareness).

psychodynamic therapies Treatments that stress the importance of the unconscious

mind, extensive interpretation by the therapist, and the role of early childhood experiences in the development of an individual's problems.

psychological dependence The strong desire to repeat the use of a drug for emotional reasons, such as a feeling of well-being and reduction of stress.

psychology The scientific study of behavior and mental processes.

psychoneuroimmunology A new field of scientific inquiry that explores connections among psychological factors (such as attitudes and emotions), the nervous system, and the immune system.

psychopathology The scientific study of psychological disorders and the development of diagnostic categories and treatments for those disorders.

psychosis Psychological state in which a person's perceptions and thoughts are fundamentally removed from reality.

psychosurgery A biological therapy, with irreversible effects, that involves removal or destruction of brain tissue to improve the individual's adjustment.

psychotherapy A nonmedical process that helps individuals with psychological disorders recognize and overcome their problems.

puberty A period of rapid skeletal and sexual maturation that occurs mainly in early adolescence.

punishment A consequence that decreases the likelihood that a behavior will occur.

random assignment Researchers' assignment of participants to groups by chance, to reduce the likelihood that an experiment's results will be due to preexisting differences between groups.

random sample A sample that gives every member of the population an equal chance of being selected.

range A measure of dispersion that is the difference between the highest and lowest scores.

reasoning The mental activity of transforming information to reach conclusions.

referential thinking Ascribing personal meaning to completely random events.

reflective speech A technique in which the therapist mirrors the client's own feelings back to the client.

reinforcement The process by which a stimulus or event (a reinforcer) following a particular behavior increases the probability that the behavior will happen again.

relapse A return to former unhealthy patterns.

relational aggression Behavior that is meant to harm the social standing of another person.

reliability The extent to which a test yields a consistent, reproducible measure of performance.

REM sleep An active stage of sleep during which dreaming occurs.

renewal The recovery of the conditioned response when the organism is placed in a novel context.

representativeness heuristic The tendency to make judgments about group membership based on physical appearances or the match between a person and one's stereotype of a group rather than on available base rate information.

research participant bias In an experiment, the influence of participants' expectations, and of their thoughts on how they should behave, on their behavior.

resilience A person's ability to recover from or adapt to difficult times.

resting potential The stable, negative charge of an inactive neuron.

reticular formation A system in the midbrain comprising a diffuse collection of neurons involved in stereotyped patterns of behavior such as walking, sleeping, and turning to attend to a sudden noise.

retina The multilayered light-sensitive surface in the eye that records electromagnetic energy and converts it to neural impulses for processing in the brain.

retrieval The memory process that occurs when information that was retained in memory comes out of storage.

retroactive interference Situation in which material that was learned later disrupts the retrieval of information that was learned earlier.

retrograde amnesia Memory loss for a segment of the past but not for new events.

retrospective memory Remembering information from the past.

risky shift The tendency for a group decision to be riskier than the average decision made by the individual group members.

rods The receptor cells in the retina that are sensitive to light but not very useful for color vision.

role conflict The kind of stress that arises when a person tries to meet the demands of more than one important life role, such as worker and mother.

romantic or passionate love Love with strong components of sexuality and infatuation, often dominant in the early part of a love relationship.

Rorschach inkblot test A famous projective test that uses an individual's perception of inkblots to determine his or her personality.

sample The subset of the population chosen by the investigator for study.

schedules of reinforcement Specific patterns that determine when a behavior will be reinforced.

schema A preexisting mental concept or framework that helps people to organize and interpret information. Schemas from prior encounters with the environment influence the way individuals encode, make inferences about, and retrieve information.

schizophrenia Severe psychological disorder characterized by highly disordered thought processes; individuals suffering from schizophrenia may be referred to as psychotic because they are so far removed from reality.

science The use of systematic methods to observe the natural world, including human behavior, and to draw conclusions.

scientific management The managerial philosophy that emphasizes the worker as a well-oiled machine and the determination of the most efficient methods for performing any work-related task.

script A schema for an event, often containing information about physical features, people, and typical occurrences.

secondary reinforcer A reinforcer that acquires its positive value through an organism's experience; a secondary reinforcer is a learned or conditioned reinforcer.

secondary sex characteristics Traits that differ between the two sexes but are not part of the reproductive system; they include breasts in females and facial hair in males.

secure attachment The ways that infants use their caregiver, usually their mother, as a secure base from which to explore the environment.

selective attention The act of focusing on a specific aspect of experience while ignoring others.

self-actualization The motivation to develop one's full potential as a human being—the highest and most elusive of Maslow's proposed needs.

self-determination theory Deci and Ryan's theory asserting that all humans have three basic, innate organismic needs: competence, relatedness, and autonomy.

self-efficacy The belief that one can accomplish a given goal or task and produce positive change.

self-objectification The tendency to see oneself primarily as an object in the eyes of others.

self-perception theory Bem's theory on how behaviors influence attitudes, stating that individuals make inferences about their attitudes by perceiving their behavior.

self-regulation The process by which an organism effortfully controls behavior in order to pursue important objectives.

self-report test A method of measuring personality characteristics that directly asks people whether specific items describe their personality traits; also called an objective test or an inventory.

self-serving bias The tendency to take credit for one's successes and to deny responsibility for one's failures.

semantic memory A person's knowledge about the world, including his or her areas of expertise; general knowledge, such as of things learned in school, and everyday knowledge.

semantics The meaning of words and sentences in a particular language.

semicircular canals Three fluid-filled circular tubes in the inner ear containing the sensory receptors that detect head motion caused when an individual tilts or moves the head and/or the body.

sensation The process of receiving stimulus energies from the external environment and transforming those energies into neural energy.

sensorimotor stage Piaget's first stage of cognitive development, lasting from birth to about 2 years of age, during which infants construct an understanding of the world by coordinating sensory experiences with motor (physical) actions.

sensory adaptation A change in the responsiveness of the sensory system based on the average level of surrounding stimulation.

sensory memory Memory system that involves holding information from the world in its original sensory form for only an instant, not much longer than the brief time it is exposed to the visual, auditory, and other senses.

sensory receptors Specialized cells that detect stimulus information and transmit it to sensory (afferent) nerves and the brain.

serial position effect The tendency to recall the items at the beginning and end of a list more readily than those in the middle.

set point The weight maintained when the individual makes no effort to gain or lose weight.

sex The properties of a person that determine his or her classification as male or female.

sex chromosomes In humans, the pair of genes that differs between the sexes and determines a person's sex as male or female.

sexual harassment Unwelcome behavior or conduct of a sexual nature that offends, humiliates, or intimidates another person.

sexual orientation The direction of an individual's erotic interests.

sexual selection According to Darwin's theory of evolution, the differentiation between the male and female members of a species because of the differences between the two in competition and choice.

sexuality The ways people experience and express themselves as sexual beings.

sexually transmitted infection (STI) An infection that is contracted primarily through sexual activity—vaginal intercourse as well as oral and anal sex.

shaping Rewarding successive approximations of a desired behavior.

short-term memory Limited-capacity memory system in which information is usually retained for only as long as 30 seconds unless the individual uses strategies to retain it longer.

signal detection theory An approach to perception that focuses on decision making about stimuli under conditions of uncertainty.

situational judgment test A type of job-screening examination that presents job candidates with realistic, hypothetical scenarios and asks them to identify the most appropriate response.

sleep A natural state of rest for the body and mind that involves the reversible loss of consciousness.

social anxiety disorder or social phobia Anxiety disorder in which the individual has an intense fear of being humiliated or embarrassed in social situations.

social cognitive behavior view of hypnosis The perspective that hypnosis is a normal state in which the hypnotized person behaves the way he or she believes that a hypnotized person should behave.

social cognitive perspectives Theoretical views emphasizing conscious awareness, beliefs, expectations, and goals.

social comparison The process by which individuals evaluate their thoughts, feelings, behaviors, and abilities in relation to others.

social contagion Imitative behavior involving the spread of actions, emotions, and ideas.

social exchange theory The view of social relationships as involving an exchange of goods, the objective of which is to minimize costs and maximize benefits.

social facilitation Improvement in an individual's performance because of the presence of others.

social identity The way individuals define themselves in terms of their group membership.

social identity theory Tajfel's theory that social identity, based on group membership, is a crucial part of self-image and a valuable source of positive feelings about oneself.

social loafing Each person's tendency to exert less effort in a group because of reduced accountability for individual effort.

social psychology The study of how people think about, influence, and relate to other people.

social role theory Eagly's theory of gender development that acknowledges the physical differences between the sexes that have historically influenced different tasks performed by men and women; points out the ways that these differences color social expectations and create social structures that limit opportunities for both sexes.

social support Information and feedback from others indicating that one is loved and cared for, esteemed and valued, and included in a network of communication and mutual obligation.

sociocultural approach An approach to psychology that examines the ways in which social and cultural environments influence behavior.

somatic nervous system The body system consisting of the sensory nerves, whose function is to convey information from the skin and muscles to the CNS about conditions such as pain and temperature, and the motor nerves, whose function is to tell muscles what to do.

somatosensory cortex A region in the cerebral cortex that processes information about body sensations, located at the front of the parietal lobes.

specific phobia Anxiety disorder in which the individual experiences an irrational, overwhelming, persistent fear of a particular object or situation.

spontaneous recovery The process in classical conditioning by which a conditioned response can recur after a time delay, without further conditioning.

stages of change model Theoretical model describing a five-step process by which individuals give up bad habits and adopt healthier lifestyles.

standard deviation A measure of dispersion that tells us how much scores in a sample differ from the mean of the sample.

standardization The development of uniform procedures for administering and scoring a test, and the creation of norms (performance standards) for the test.

stem cells Unique primitive cells that have the capacity to develop into most types of human cells.

stereotype A generalization about a group's characteristics that does not consider any variations from one individual to another.

stereotype threat An individual's fast-acting, self-fulfilling fear of being judged based on a negative stereotype about his or her group.

stimulants Psychoactive drugs—including caffeine, nicotine, amphetamines, and cocaine—that increase the central nervous system's activity.

storage The retention of information over time and how this information is represented in memory.

stream of consciousness Term used by William James to describe the mind as a continuous flow of changing sensations, images, thoughts, and feelings.

strengths-based management A management style emphasizing that maximizing an employee's existing strengths is much easier than trying to build such attributes from the ground up.

stress management program A regimen that teaches individuals how to appraise stressful events, how to develop skills for coping with stress, and how to put these skills into use in everyday life.

stressors Circumstances and events that threaten individuals and tax their coping abilities and that cause physiological changes to ready the body to handle the assault of stress.

stress The responses of individuals to environmental stressors.

structuralism Wundt's approach to discovering the basic elements, or structures, of mental processes; so called because of its focus on identifying the structures of the human mind.

structured interview A kind of interview in which candidates are asked specific questions that methodically seek to obtain truly useful information for the interviewer.

subgoals Intermediate goals or intermediate problems devised to put the individual in a better position for reaching the final goal or solution.

subjective well-being A person's assessment of his or her own level of positive affect relative to negative affect, and an evaluation of his or her life in general.

subliminal perception The detection of information below the level of conscious awareness.

superego The Freudian structure of personality that serves as the harsh internal judge of our behavior; what we often call conscience.

suprachiasmatic nucleus (SCN) A small brain structure that uses input from the retina to synchronize its own rhythm with the daily cycle of light and dark; the body's way of monitoring the change from day to night.

sustained attention or vigilance The ability to maintain attention to a selected stimulus for a prolonged period of time.

sympathetic nervous system The part of the autonomic nervous system that arouses the body to mobilize it for action and thus is involved in the experience of stress.

synapses Tiny spaces between neurons; the gaps between neurons are referred to as synaptic gaps.

syntax A language's rules for combining words to form acceptable phrases and sentences.

systematic desensitization A method of behavior therapy that treats anxiety by teaching the client to associate deep relaxation with increasingly intense anxiety-producing situations.

temperament An individual's behavioral style and characteristic ways of responding.

temporal lobes Structures in the cerebral cortex that are located just above the ears and are involved in hearing, language processing, and memory.

testes Sex-related endocrine glands in the scrotum that produce hormones involved in men's sexual development and reproduction.

thalamus The forebrain structure that sits at the top of the brain stem in the brain's central core and serves as an important relay station.

Thematic Apperception Test (TAT) A projective test that is designed to elicit stories that reveal something about an individual's personality.

theory A broad idea or set of closely related ideas that attempts to explain observations and to make predictions about future observations.

theory of mind Individuals' understanding that they and others think, feel, perceive, and have private experiences.

theory of planned behavior Theoretical model that includes the basic ideas of the theory of reasoned action but adds the person's perceptions of control over the outcome.

theory of reasoned action Theoretical model stating that effective change requires individuals to have specific intentions about their behaviors, as well as positive attitudes about a new behavior, and to perceive that their social group looks favorably on the new behavior as well.

Theory X managers Managers who assume that work is innately unpleasant and that people have a strong desire to avoid it; such managers believe that employees need direction, dislike responsibility, and must be kept in line.

Theory Y managers Managers who assume that engaging in effortful behavior is natural to human beings; they recognize that people seek out responsibility and that motivation can come from allowing employees to suggest creative and meaningful solutions.

therapeutic alliance The relationship between the therapist and client—an important element of successful psychotherapy.

thermoreceptors Sensory nerve endings under the skin that respond to changes in temperature at or near the skin and provide input to keep the body's temperature at 98.6 degrees Fahrenheit.

thinking The process of manipulating information mentally by forming concepts, solving problems, making decisions, and reflecting critically or creatively.

third variable problem The circumstance where a variable that has not been measured accounts for the relationship between two other variables. Third variables are also known as confounds.

thought disorder The unusual, sometimes bizarre thought processes that are characteristic positive symptoms of schizophrenia.

360-degree feedback A method of performance appraisal whereby an employee's performance is rated by a variety of individuals, including himself or herself, a peer, a supervisor, a subordinate, and perhaps a customer or client.

tip-of-the-tongue (TOT) phenomenon A type of effortful retrieval associated with a person's feeling that he or she knows something (say, a word or a name) but cannot quite pull it out of memory.

tolerance The need to take increasing amounts of a drug to get the same effect.

top-down processing The operation in sensation and perception, launched by cognitive processing at the brain's higher levels, that allows the organism to sense what is happening and to apply that framework to information from the world.

training Teaching a new employee the essential requirements to do the job well.

trait theories Theoretical views stressing that personality consists of broad, enduring dispositions (traits) that tend to lead to characteristic responses.

tranquilizers Depressant drugs, such as Valium and Xanax, that reduce anxiety and induce relaxation.

transactional leader An individual in a leadership capacity who emphasizes the exchange relationship between the worker and the leader and who applies the principle that a good job should be rewarded.

transference A client's relating to the psychoanalyst in ways that reproduce or relive important relationships in the individual's life.

transformational leader An individual in a leadership capacity who is dynamic and who brings charisma, passion, and vision to the position.

transgender Experiencing one's psychological gender as different from one's physical sex, as in the cases of biological males who identify as female, and biological females who identify as male.

triarchic theory of intelligence Sternberg's theory that intelligence comes in three forms: analytical, creative, and practical.

trichromatic theory Theory stating that color perception is produced by three types of cone receptors in the retina that are particularly sensitive to different, but overlapping, ranges of wavelengths.

two-factor theory of emotion Schachter and Singer's theory that emotion is determined by two factors: physiological arousal and cognitive labeling.

Type A behavior pattern A cluster of characteristics—including being excessively competitive, hard-driven, impatient, and hostile—related to a higher incidence of heart disease.

Type B behavior pattern A cluster of characteristics—including being relaxed and easygoing—related to a lower incidence of heart disease.

Type D behavior pattern A cluster of characteristics—including being generally distressed, having negative emotions, and being socially inhibited—related to adverse cardiovascular outcomes.

unconditional positive regard Rogers's construct referring to the individual's need to be accepted, valued, and treated positively regardless of his or her behavior.

unconditioned response (UR) An unlearned reaction that is automatically elicited by the unconditioned stimulus.

unconditioned stimulus (US) A stimulus that produces a response without prior learning.

unconscious thought According to Freud, a reservoir of unacceptable wishes, feelings, and thoughts that are beyond conscious awareness.

validity The extent to which a test measures what it is intended to measure.

variable Anything that can change.

vestibular sense Sense that provides information about balance and movement.

volley principle Modification of frequency theory stating that a cluster of nerve cells can fire neural impulses in rapid succession, producing a volley of impulses.

vulnerability-stress hypothesis or diathesis-stress model Theory suggesting that preexisting conditions (such as genetic characteristics, personality dispositions, or experiences) may put a person at risk of developing a psychological disorder.

Weber's law The principle that two stimuli must differ by a constant minimum percentage (rather than a constant amount) to be perceived as different.

well-being therapy (WBT) A short-term, problem-focused, directive therapy that encourages clients to accentuate the positive.

wisdom Expert knowledge about the practical aspects of life.

working memory A combination of components, including short-term memory and attention, that allow individuals to hold information temporarily as they perform cognitive tasks; a kind of mental workbench on which the brain manipulates and assembles information to guide understanding, decision making, and problem solving.

Yerkes-Dodson law The psychological principle stating that performance is best under conditions of moderate arousal rather than either low or high arousal.

REFERENCES

A

Abbate, C., Trimarchi, P. D., Salvi, G. P., Quarenghi, A. M., Vergani, C., & Luzzatti, C. (2012). Delusion of inanimate doubles: Description of a case of focal retrograde amnesia. *Neurocase, 18* (6), 457–477.

Abbott, B. B., Schoen, L. S, & Badia, P. (1984). Predictable and unpredictable shock: Behavioral measures of aversion and physiological measures of stress. *Psychological Bulletin, 96,* 45–71.

ABC News. (2004, October 21). Poll: American sex survey. *ABC News.* http://abcnews.go.com/Primetime/PollVault/story?id=156921&page=1 (accessed May 9, 2013).

Abdeshahi, S. K., Hashemipoor, M., Mesgarzadeh, V., Shahidi P. A., & Halaj M. (2013). Effect of hypnosis on induction of local anaesthesia, pain perception, control of hemorrhage, and anxiety during extraction of third molars: A case-control study. *Journal of Craniomaxillofacial Surgery.* (in press)

Aberg, K. A., Liu, Y., Bukszár, J., McClay, J. L., Khachane, A. M., Andreassen, O. A., Blackwood, D., Corvin, A., Djurovic, S., Gurling, H., Ophoff, R., Pato, C. N., Pato, M. T., Riley, B., Webb, T., Kendler, K., O'Donovan, M., Craddock, N., Kirov, G., Owen, M., Rujescu, D., St. Clair, D., Werge, T., Hultman, C. M., Delisi, L. E., Sullivan, P., & van den Oord, E. J. (2013). A comprehensive family-based replications study of schizophrenia genes. *JAMA Psychiatry.* (in press)

Abramowitz, J. S., & Jacoby, R. J. (2014). Obsessive-compulsive behavior and related disorders. *Annual Review of Clinical Psychology* (vol. 10). Palo Alto, CA: Annual Reviews. (in press)

Abrams, L., & Rodriguez, E. L. (2005). Syntactic class influences phonological priming of tip-of-the-tongue resolution. *Psychonomic Bulletin and Review, 12* (6), 1018–1023.

Abramson, L. Y., Seligman, M. E. P., & Teasdale, J. (1978). Learned helplessness in humans: Critique and reformulation. *Journal of Abnormal Psychology, 87,* 49–74.

Accordini, S. Janson, C., Svanes, C., & Jarvis, D. (2012). The role of smoking in allergy and asthma: Lessons from the ECRHS. *Current Allergy and Asthma Reports, 12* (3), 185–191.

Acer, N., Uğurlu, N., Uysal, D.D., Unur E., Turgut M., & Camurdanoğlu, M. (2010). Comparison of two volumetric techniques for estimating volume of intracerebral ventricles using magnetic resonance imaging: A stereological study. *Anatomical Science International, 85* (3), 131–139.

Acheson, D. T., Forsyth, J. P., & Moses, E. (2012). Interoceptive fear conditioning and panic disorder: The role of conditioned stimulus–unconditioned stimulus predictability. *Behavior Therapy, 43,* 174–189.

Ackermann, K., Revell, V. L., Lao, O., Rombouts, E. J., Skene, D. J., & Kayser, M. (2012). Diurnal rhythms in blood cell populations and the effect of acute sleep deprivation in healthy young men. *Sleep, 35* (7), 933–940.

Adams, H. E., Wright, L. W., & Lohr, B. A. (1996). Is homophobia associated with homosexual arousal? *Journal of Abnormal Psychology, 105,* 440–445.

Addington, J., Cornblatt, B. A., Cadenhead, K. S., Cannon, T. D., McGlashan, T. H., Perkins, D. O., Seidman L. J., Tsuang, M. T., Walker, E. F., Woods S. W., & Heinssen, R. (2011). At clinical high risk for psychosis: Outcome for nonconverters. *American Journal of Psychiatry, 168* (8), 800–805.

Adelstein, J. S., Shehzad, Z., Mennes, M., DeYoung, C. G., Zuo, X., Kelly, C., Margulies, D. S., Bloomfield, A., Gray, J. R., Castellanos, F. X., & Milham, M. P. (2011). Personality is reflected in the brain's intrinsic functional architecture. *PLoS One, 6* (11), e27633.

Ader, R. (1974). Letter to the editor: Behaviorally conditioned immunosuppression. *Psychosomatic Medicine, 36,* 183–184.

Ader, R. (2000). On the development of psychoneuroimmunology. *European Journal of Pharmacology, 405,* 167–176.

Ader, R., & Cohen, N. (1975). Behaviorally conditioned immunosuppression. *Psychosomatic Medicine, 37,* 333–340.

Ader, R., & Cohen, N. (2000). Conditioning and immunity. In R. Ader, D. L. Felton, & N. Cohen (Eds.), *Psychoneuroimmunology* (3rd ed.). San Diego: Academic.

Adler, A. (1927). *The theory and practice of individual psychology.* Fort Worth: Harcourt Brace.

Adolph, K. E., & Berger, S. E. (2013). Development of the motor system. In H. Pashler, T. Crane, M. Kinsbourne, F. Ferreira, & R. Zemel (Eds.), *The encyclopedia of the mind.* Thousand Oaks, CA: Sage.

Adolph, K. E., & Robinson, S. R. R. (2013). The road to walking: What learning to walk tells us about development. In P. D. Zelazo (Ed.), *The Oxford handbook of developmental psychology.* New York: Oxford University Press.

Adolphs, R. (2009). The social brain: Neural basis of social knowledge. *Annual Review of Psychology* (vol. 60). Palo Alto, CA: Annual Reviews.

Ager, A. (2013). Annual research review: Resilience and child well-being—public policy implications. *Journal of Child Psychology and Psychiatry, 54* (4), 488–500.

Aggarwal, B., Liao, M., & Mosca, L. (2013). Medication adherence is associated with having a caregiver among cardiac patients. *Annals of Behavioral Medicine.* (in press)

Agnati, L. F., & others. (2012). Neuronal correlates to consciousness: The "Hall of Mirrors" metaphor describing consciousness as an epiphenomenon of multiple dynamic mosaics of cortical functional modules. *Brain Research, 1476,* 3–21.

Ago, Y., Tanaka T., Kita, Y., Tokumoto, H., Takuma, K., & Matsuda, T. (2012). Lithium attenuates methamphetamine-induced hyperlocomotion and behavioral sensitization via modulation of prefrontal monoamine release. *Neuropharmacology, 62* (4), 1634–1639.

Agorastos, A., Haasen, C., & Huber, C. G. (2012). Anxiety disorders through a transcultural perspective: Implications for migrants. *Psychopathology, 45,* 67–77.

Aguinis, H. (2009). *Performance management* (2nd ed.). Upper Saddle River, NJ: Prentice-Hall.

Aguinis, H. (2010). Organizational responsibility: Doing good and doing well. In S. Zedeck (Ed.), *APA handbook of industrial and organizational psychology.* Washington, DC: American Psychological Association.

Aguinis, H., & Kraiger, K. (2009). Benefits of training and development for individuals and teams, organizations, and society. *Annual Review of Psychology* (vol. 60). Palo Alto, CA: Annual Reviews.

Ahmadi, J., Kampman, K. M., Oslin, D. M., Pettinati, H. M., Dackis, C., & Sparkman, T. (2009). Predictors of treatment outcome in outpatient cocaine and alcohol dependency treatment. *American Journal of Addiction, 18,* 81–86.

Ahmed, N. U., Smith, G. L., Flores, A. M., Pamies, R. J., Mason, H. R., Woods, K. F., & Stain, S. C. (2005). Racial/ethnic disparity and predictors of leisure-time activity among U.S. men. *Ethnicity and Disease, 15,* 40–52.

Ahola, K., Honkonen, T., Kivimaki, M., Virtanen, M., Isometsa, E., Aromaa, A., & Lonnqvist, J. (2006). Contribution of burnout to the association between job strain and depression: The Health 2000 Study. *Journal of Occupational and Environmental Medicine, 48,* 1023–1030.

Ainsworth, M. D. S. (1979). Infant–mother attachment. *American Psychologist, 34,* 932–937.

Ainsworth, M. S., Blehar, M. C., Waters, E., & Wall, S. (1978). *Patterns of attachment: A psychological study of the strange situation.* Oxford, U.K.: Erlbaum.

Ajzen, I. (2001). Nature and operation of attitudes. *Annual Review of Psychology* (vol. 52). (pp. 27–58). Palo Alto, CA: Annual Reviews.

Ajzen, I. (2012a). Attitudes and persuasion. In K. Deaux & M. Snyder (Eds.), *The Oxford handbook of personality and social psychology.* (pp. 367–394). New York: Oxford University Press.

Ajzen, I. (2012b). The theory of planned behavior. In P. A. M. Lange, A. W. Kruglanski, & E. T. Higgins (Eds.), *Handbook of theories of social psychology.* Thousand Oaks, CA: Sage.

Ajzen, I., & Albarracin, D. (2007). Predicting and changing behavior: A reasoned action approach. In I. Ajzen, D. Albarracin, & R. Hornik (Eds.), *Prediction and change in health behavior.* Mahwah, NJ: Erlbaum.

Ajzen, I., & Fishbein, M. (2005). The influence of attitudes on behavior. In. D. Albarracin, B. T. Johnson, & M. P. Zanna (Eds.), *The handbook of attitudes* (pp. 173–221). Mahwah, NJ: Erlbaum.

Ajzen, I., & Manstead, A. S. R. (2007). Changing health-related behaviours: An approach based on the theory of planned behaviour. In M. Hewstone, H. Schut, J. de Wit, K. van den Bos, & M. S. Stroebe (Eds.), *The scope of social psychology: Theory and applications* (pp. 43–63). New York: Psychology Press.

Akaike, N., Shin, M., Wakita, M., Torii, Y., Harakawa, T., Ginnaga, A., Kato, K., Kaji, R., & Kozaki, S. (2013). Transynaptic inhibition of spinal transmission by A2 botulinum toxin. *Journal of Physiology.* (in press)

Akhtar, S. (2006). Technical challenges faced by the immigrant psychoanalyst. *Psychoanalytic Quarterly, 75,* 21–43.

Akkermann, K., Kaasik, K., Kiive, E., Nordquist, N., Oreland, L., & Harro, J. (2012). The impact of adverse life events and the serotonin transporter gene promoter polymorphism on the development of eating disorder symptoms. *Journal of Psychiatric Research, 46,* 38–43.

Aknin, L. B., Barrington-Leigh, C. P., Dunn, E. W., Helliwell, J. F., Burns, J., Biswas-Diener, R., Kemeza, I., Nyende, P., Ashton-James, C. E., & Norton, M. I. (2013). Prosocial spending and well-being: Cross-cultural evidence for a psychological universal. *Journal of Personality and Social Psychology, 104,* 635–652.

Albarracin, D., Durantini, M. R., & Earl, A. (2006). Empirical and theoretical conclusions of an analysis of outcomes of HIV-prevention interventions. *Current Directions in Psychological Science, 15,* 73–78.

Albarracin, D., Gillette, J. C., Earl, A. N., Glasman, L. R., Durantini, M. R., & Ho, M. (2005). A test of major assumptions about behavior change: A comprehensive look at the effects of passive and active HIV-prevention interventions since the beginning of the epidemic. *Psychological Bulletin, 131,* 856–897.

Albert, D., & Steinberg, L. (2011). Judgment and decision making in adolescence. *Journal of Research on Adolescence, 21,* 211–224.

Alberto, P. A., & Troutman, A. C. (2012). *Applied behavior analysis* (9th ed.). Upper Saddle River, NJ: Pearson.

Aldao, A., Nolen-Hoeksema, S., & Schweizer, S. (2010). Emotion-regulation strategies across psychopathology: A meta-analytic review. *Clinical Psychology Review, 30,* 217–237.

Aldwin, C. M. (2007). *Stress, coping, and development* (2nd ed.). New York: Guilford.

Aldwin, C. M., Levenson, M. R., & Kelly, L. L. (2009). Lifespan developmental perspectives on stress-related growth. In C. L. Park, S. Lechner, A. Stanton, & M. Antoni (Eds.), *Positive life changes in the context of medical illness.* Washington, DC: American Psychological Association.

Aldwin, C. M., Spiro, A., & Park, C. L. (2006). Health, behavior, and optimal aging. In J. E. Birren & K. W. Schaie (Eds.), *Handbook of the psychology of aging* (6th ed.). San Diego: Academic.

Aldwin, C. M., Yancura, L. A., & Boeninger, D. K. (2007). In C. M. Aldwin, C. L. Park, & A. Spiro (Eds.), *Handbook of health and aging.* New York: Guilford.

Alegría, M. (2011). Epidemiology of mental disorders in Latino and Asian populations. *Annual Review of Clinical Psychology* (vol. 7). Palo Alto, CA: Annual Reviews.

Alexander, B. (2013, February 13). Ongoing, severe epidemic of STDs in US, report finds. *NBC News.* http://vitals.nbcnews.com/_news/2013/02/13/16951432-ongoing-severe-epidemic-of-stds-in-us-report-finds?lite (accessed May 9, 2013)

Alexander, G. M., & Hines, M. (2002). Sex differences in response to children's toys in nonhuman primates (*Cercopithecus aethiops sabaeus*). *Evolution and Human Behavior, 23,* 467–479.

Alexander, G. M., Wilcox, T., & Woods, R. (2009). Sex differences in infants' visual interest in toys. *Archives of Sexual Behavior, 38,* 427–433.

Alexander, J., & Bickerstaff, S. (2013). Aripiprazole induced tardive dyskinesia-accruing evidence. *Australian and New Zealand Journal of Psychiatry, 47,* 289–290.

Alexander, M. G., & Fisher, T. D. (2003). Truth and consequences: Using the bogus pipeline to examine sex differences in self-reported sexuality. *Journal of Sex Research, 40,* 27–35.

Allen, T. D. (2013). The work-family role interface: A synthesis of the research from industrial and organizational psychology. In N. W. Schmitt, S. Highhouse, & I. B. Weiner (Eds.), *Handbook of psychology, 2nd Ed., Vol 12.* (pp. 698–718). Hoboken, NJ: Wiley.

Allport, G. W. (1954). *The nature of prejudice.* Cambridge, MA: Perseus.

Allport, G. W. (1961). *Pattern and growth in personality.* New York: Holt, Rinehart & Winston.

Allport, G. W., & Odbert, H. (1936). *Trait-names: A psycho-lexical study* (no. 211). Princeton, NJ: Psychological Review Monographs.

Almeida, J., & others. (2013). Affect of the unconscious: Visually suppressed angry faces modulate our decisions. *Cognitive, Affective, and Behavioral Neuroscience.* (in press)

Alonso, P., & others. (2012). Association between the NMDA glutamate receptor *GRIN2B* gene and obsessive-compulsive disorder. *Journal of Psychiatry and Neuroscience, 37* (4), 273–281.

Alonso, P., & others. (2013). The interaction between Comt and Bdnf variants influences obsessive-compulsive-related dysfunctional beliefs. *Journal of Anxiety Disorders, 27,* 321–327.

Alquist, J. L., Ainsworth, S. E., & Baumeister, R. F. (2013). Determined to conform: Disbelief in free will increases conformity. *Journal of Experimental Social Psychology, 49,* 80–86.

Alstermark, B., & Isa, T. (2012). Circuits for skilled reaching and grasping. *Annual Review of Neuroscience* (vol. 35). Palo Alto, CA: Annual Reviews.

Altemus, M. (2006). Sex differences in depression and anxiety disorders: Potential biological determinants. *Hormones and Behavior, 50,* 534–538.

Altenor, A., Volpicelli, J. R., & Seligman, M. E. P. (1979). Debilitated shock escape is produced by both short- and long-duration inescapable shock: Learned helplessness vs. learned inactivity. *Bulletin of the Psychonomic Society, 14,* 337–339.

Alter, A. L., Aronson, J., Darley, J. M., Rodriguez, C., & Ruble, D. N. (2010). Rising to the threat: Reducing stereotype threat by reframing the threat as a challenge. *Journal of Experimental Social Psychology, 46,* 166–171.

Althof, S. E., & others. (2010). Impact of tadalafil once daily in men with erectile dysfunction—including a report of the partner's evaluation. *Urology, 75* (6), 1358–1363.

Althoff, R. R., & others. (2012). Genetic and environmental contributions to self-reported thoughts of self-harm and suicide. *American Journal of Medical Genetics B: Neuropsychiatric Disorders, 159B,* 120–127.

Alvino, C., Kohlber, C., Barrett, F., Gur, R. E., Gur, R. C., & Verma, R. (2007). Computerized measurement of facial expression of emotions in schizophrenia. *Journal of Neuroscience Methods, 163,* 350–361.

Al-Wer, E. (2014). *Understanding sociolinguistics.* New York: Routledge. (in press)

Aly, M., & Yonelinas, A. P. (2012). Bridging consciousness and cognition in memory and preception: Evidence for both state and strength processes. *PLoS One, 7,* e30231.

Amano, T., Duvarci, S., Popa, D., & Pare, D. (2011). The fear circuit revisited: Contributions of the basal amygdala nuclei to conditioned fear. *Journal of Neuroscience, 31,* 15481–15489.

Ambady, N., Hallahan, M., & Conner, B. (1999). Accuracy of judgments of sexual orientation from thin slices of behavior. *Journal of Personality and Social Psychology, 77,* 538–547.

American Association of University Women (AAUW). (2006). *Drawing the line: Sexual harassment on campus (2006).* Washington, DC: Author.

American Cancer Society. (2013). Cigarette smoking. *American Cancer Society.* www.cancer.org/cancer/cancercauses/tobaccocancer/cigarettesmoking/cigarette-smoking-toc (accessed June 20, 2013)

American Psychiatric Association (APA). (2001). *Mental illness.* Washington, DC: Author.

American Psychiatric Association (APA). (2006). *American Psychiatric Association practice guidelines for the treatment of psychiatric disorders.* Washington, DC: Author.

American Psychiatric Association (APA). (2013a). *DSM-5: Diagnostic and statistical manual of mental disorders* (5th ed.). Washington, DC: Author.

American Psychiatric Association (APA). (2013b). *Gender dysphoria.* Arlington, VA: Author.

American Psychological Association. (2012). Research shows psychotherapy effective but underutilized. *APA.org.* www.apa.org/news/press/releases/2012/08/psychotherapy-effective.aspx (accessed June 6, 2013)

Amodio, D. M., & Mendoza, S. A. (2010). Implicit outgroup bias: Cognitive, affective, and motivational underpinnings. In B. Gawronski & B. K. Payne (Eds.), *Handbook of implicit social cognition.* New York: Guilford.

Amsterdam, J. D., Luo, L., & Shults, J. (2013). Effectiveness and mood conversion rate of short-term fluoxetine monotherapy in patients with rapid cycling bipolar II depression versus patients with nonrapid cycling bipolar II depression. *Journal of Clinical Psychopharmacology, 33* (3), 420–424.

Amunts, K., Schlaug, G., Jancke, L., Steinmetz, H., Schleicher, A., Dabringhaus, A., & Zilles, K. (1997). Motor cortex and hand motor skills: Structural compliance in the human brain. *Human Brain Mapping, 5* (3), 206–215.

Andel, R., Crowe, M., Pedersen, N. L., Mortimer, J., Crimmins, E., Johansson, B., & Gatz, M. (2005). Complexity of work and risk of Alzheimer's disease: A population-based study of Swedish twins. *Journals of Gerontology: Series B: Psychological Sciences and Social Sciences, 60B,* 251–258.

Anderman, E. M., Gray, D. L., & Chang, Y. (2013). Motivation and classroom learning. In W. M. Reynolds, G. F. Miller, & I. B. Weiner (Eds.), *Handbook of psychology* (2nd ed., vol. 7). Hoboken, NJ: Wiley.

Andersen, S. K., Müller, M. M., & Martinovic. J. (2012). Bottom-up biases in feature-selective attention. *Journal of Neuroscience, 32,* 16953–16958.

Anderson, B. A., Golden-Kreutz, D. M., & DiLillo, V. (2001). Cancer. In A. Baum, T. A. Revenson, & J. E. Singer (Eds.), *Handbook of health psychology.* Mahwah, NJ: Erlbaum.

Anderson, C. A., & Arciniegas, D. B. (2010). Cognitive sequelae of hypoxic-ischemic brain injury: A review. *NeuroRehabilitation, 26,* 47–63.

Anderson, C. A., Benjamin, A. J., Jr., & Bartholow, B. D. (1998). Does the gun pull the trigger? Automatic priming effects of weapon pictures and weapon names. *Psychological Science, 9,* 308–314.

Anderson, C. A., & Bushman, B. J. (2002). Human aggression. *Annual Review of Psychology* (vol. 53). (pp. 27–51). Palo Alto, CA: Annual Reviews.

Anderson, C. A., Shibuya, A., Ihori, N., Swing, E. L., Bushman, B. J., Sakamoto, A., Rothstein, H. R., & Saleem, M. (2010). Violent video game effects on aggression, empathy, and prosocial behavior in Eastern and Western countries: A meta-analytic review. *Psychological Bulletin, 136,* 151–173.

Anderson, N. H. (1965). Primacy effects in personality impression formation using a generalized order effect paradigm. *Journal of Personality and Social Psychology, 2,* 1–9.

Andersson, M., & Simmons, L. W. (2006). Sexual selection and mate choice. *Trends in Ecology and Evolution, 21,* 296–302.

Andre, J. B., & Morin, O. (2011). Questioning the cultural evolution of altruism. *Journal of Evolutionary Biology, 24,* 2531–2542.

Andreasen, N. J. C. (1987). Creativity and mental illness: Prevalence rates in writers and their first-degree relatives. *American Journal of Psychiatry, 144,* 1288–1292.

Andrews, G. (2014). Diagnostic issues in anxiety and related disorders. *Annual Review of Clinical Psychology* (vol. 10). Palo Alto, CA: Annual Reviews.

Andrillon, T., & others. (2011). Sleep spindles in humans: Insights from intracranial EEG and unit recordings. *Journal of Neuroscience, 31,* 17821–17824.

Ang, S., & van Dyne, L. (Eds.). (2009). *Handbook on cultural intelligence.* New York: M. E. Sharpe.

Angel, L., Fay, S., Bouazzaoui, B., & Isingrini, M. (2011). Two hemispheres for better memory in old age: Role of executive functioning. *Journal of Cognitive Neuroscience, 23,* 3767–3777.

Angel, L., & others. (2013). Differential effects of aging on the neural correlates of recollection and familiarity. *Cortex.* (in press)

Antón-Méndez, I., Schütze, C. T., Champion, M. K., Gollan, & Tamar. H. (2012). What the tip-of-the-tongue (TOT) says about homophone frequency inheritance. *Memory & Cognition, 40,* 802–811.

Antonucci, T. C., Birditt, K. S., & Ajrouch, K. J. (2013). Social relationships and aging. In R. M. Lerner, M. A. Easterbrooks, J. Mistry, & I. B. Weiner (Eds.), *Handbook of psychology* (2nd ed., vol. 6). Hoboken, NJ: Wiley.

APA Presidential Task Force on Evidence-Based Practice. (2006). Evidence-based practice in psychology. *American Psychologist, 61,* 271–285.

Appleby, L., Mortensen, P. B., Dunn, G., & Hiroeh, U. (2001). Death by homicide, suicide, and other unnatural causes in people with mental illness: A population-based study. *Lancet, 358,* 2110–2112.

Arber, C., & Li, M. (2013). Cortical interneurons from human pluripotent stem cells: Prospects for neurological and psychiatric disease. *Frontiers in Cellular Neuroscience.* (in press)

Arbib, M. A. (2012). *How the brain got language: The mirror system hypothesis.* New York: Oxford University Press.

Archer, J. (2004). Sex differences in aggression in real-world settings: A meta-analytic review. *Review of General Psychology, 8,* 291–322.

Arden, M., & Armitage, C. J. (2008). Predicting and explaining transtheoretical model stage transitions in relation to condom-carrying behaviour. *British Journal of Health Psychology, 13,* 719–735.

Ariely, D., & Norton, M. I. (2007). Psychology and experimental economics: A gap in abstraction. *Current Directions in Psychological Science, 16,* 336–339.

Armitage, C. J. (2006). Evidence that implementation intentions promote transitions between the stages of change. *Journal of Consulting and Clinical Psychology, 74,* 141–151.

Armor, D. A., Massey, C., & Sackett, A. M. (2008). Prescribed optimism. *Psychological Science, 19,* 329–331.

Arnett, J. J. (2004). *Emerging adulthood.* New York: Oxford University Press.

Arnett, J. J. (2006). Emerging adulthood: Understanding the new way of coming of age. In J. J. Arnett & J. L. Tanner (Eds.), *Emerging adults in America.* Washington, DC: American Psychological Association.

Arnett, J. J. (2007). Socialization in emerging adulthood. In J. E. Grusec & P. D. Hastings (Eds.), *Handbook of socialization.* New York: Oxford University Press.

Arnett, J. J. (2010). Oh, grow up! Generational grumbling and the new life stage of emerging adulthood. *Perspectives on Psychological Science.* 5 (1), 89–92.

Arnett, J. J. (Ed.). (2012). *Adolescent psychology around the world.* New York: Psychology Press.

Arnold, K., & others. (2013). Fetal alcohol spectrum disorders: Knowledge and screening practices of university hospital medical students and residents. *Journal of Population Therapeutics and Clinical Pharmacology, 20,* e18–25.

Arntz, A. (2005). Cognition and emotion in borderline personality disorder. *Journal of Behavior Therapy and Experimental Psychiatry, 36,* 167–172.

Aronson, E. (1986, August). *Teaching students things they think they already know all about: The case of prejudice and desegregation.* Paper presented at the meeting of the American Psychological Association, Washington, DC.

Aronson, J., Burgess, D., Phelan, S. M., & Juarez, L. (2013). Unhealthy interactions: The role of stereotype threat in health disparities. *American Journal of Public Health, 103,* 50–56.

Arpan, L., Rhodes, N., & Roskos-Ewoldsen, D. R. (2012). Attitudes: Theory, methods, and future directions. In D. R. Roskos-Ewoldsen & J. L. Monahan (Eds.), *Communication and social cognition.* New York: Psychology Press.

Arrow, H. (2007). The sharp end of altruism. *Science, 318,* 581–582.

Arthur, W. J., Bennett, W. J., Edens, P., & Bell, S. T. (2003). Effectiveness of training in organizations: A meta-analysis of design and evaluation features. *Journal of Applied Psychology, 88,* 234–245.

Asada, K., & Itakura, S. (2012). Social phenotypes of autism spectrum disorders and Williams syndrome: Similarities and differences. *Frontiers in Psychology, 3,* 247.

Asch, S. E. (1951). Effects of group pressure on the modification and distortion of judgments. In H. S. Guetzkow (Ed.), *Groups, leadership, and men.* Pittsburgh: Carnegie University Press.

Asherson, P., Adamou, M., Bolea, B., Muller, U., Dunn, S., Pitts, M., Thome, J., & Young, S. (2010). Is ADHD a valid diagnosis in adults? Yes. *British Medical Journal, 340,* 736–737.

Ashton, M. C., & Lee, K. (2008). The HEXACO model of personality structure and the importance of the H factor. *Social and Personality Psychology Compass, 2,* 1952–1962.

Asnaani, A., & Hofmann, S. G. (2012). Collaboration in multicultural therapy: Establishing a strong therapeutic alliance across cultural lines. *Journal of Clinical Psychology, 68,* 187–197.

Aspinwall, L. G. (1998). Rethinking the role of positive affect in self-regulation. *Motivation and Emotion, 22,* 1–32.

Aspinwall, L. G. (2011). Future-oriented thinking, proactive coping, and the management of potential threats to health and well-being. In S. Folkman (Ed.), *The Oxford handbook of stress, health, and coping.* New York: Oxford University Press.

Aspinwall, L. G., Leaf, S. L., & Leachman, S. A. (2009). Meaning and agency in the context of genetic testing for familial cancer. In P. T. P. Wong (Ed.), *The human quest for meaning* (2nd ed.). Hillsdale, NJ: Erlbaum.

Aspinwall, L. G., & Pengchit, W. (2013). Positive psychology. In M. D. Gellman & J. R. Turner (Eds.), *Encyclopedia of behavioral medicine.* New York: Springer.

Aspinwall, L. G., Taber, J. M., Kohlmann, W., & Leachman, S. A. (2013). Psychological aspects of hereditary cancer risk counseling and genetic testing. In B. I. Carr & J. Steel (Eds.), *Psychological approaches to cancer.* New York: Springer.

Aspinwall, L. G., & Tedeschi, R. G. (2010a). The value of positive psychology for health psychology: Progress and pitfalls in examining the relation of positive phenomena to health. *Annals of Behavioral Medicine, 39,* 4–15.

Aspinwall, L. G., & Tedeschi, R. G. (2010b). Of babies and bathwater: A reply to Coyne and Tennen's views on positive psychology and health. *Annals of Behavioral Medicine, 39,* 27–34.

Associated Press. (2007, February 7). College students think they're so special. *NBC News.* www.nbcnews.com/id/17349066/ns/health-mental_health/t/college-students-think-theyre-so-special/ (accessed March 9, 2013)

Astington, J. W., & Hughes, C. (2013). Theory of mind: Self-reflection and self-understanding. In P. D. Zelazo (Ed.), *The Oxford handbook of developmental psychology, Vol. 2.* (pp. 398–424). New York: Oxford University Press.

Atanackovic, D., & others. (2013). Acute psychological stress increases peripheral blood CD3$^+$CD56$^+$ natural killer T cells in healthy men: Possible implications for the development and treatment of allergic and autoimmune disorders. *Chronobiology International, 16* (4), 421–428.

Atkinson, J., & Braddick, O. (2013). Visual development. In P. D. Zelazo (Ed.), *The Oxford handbook of developmental psychology, Vol. 1.* (pp. 271–309). New York: Oxford University Press.

Atkinson, R. C., & Shiffrin, R. M. (1968). Human memory: A proposed system and its control processes. In K. W. Spence & J. T. Spence (Eds.), *The psychology of learning and motivation* (vol. 2). San Diego: Academic.

Aton, S. J., Seibt, J., Dumoulin, M., Steinmetz, N., Coleman, T., Naidoo, N., & Frank, M. G. (2009). Mechanisms of sleep-dependent consolidation of cortical plasticity. *Neuron, 61,* 454–466.

Austad, C. S. (2009). *Counseling and psychotherapy today.* New York: McGraw-Hill.

Austin, J. T., & Crespin, T. R. (2006). Problems of criteria in industrial and organizational psychology. In W. Bennett, C. E. Lance, & D. J. Woehr (Eds.), *Performance measurement.* Mahwah, NJ: Erlbaum.

Avey, J. B., Patera, J. L., & West, B. J. (2006). The implications of positive psychological capital on employee absenteeism. *Journal of Leadership and Organization Studies, 13,* 42–60.

Avolio, B. J., Sosik, J. J., & Berson, Y. (2013). Leadership models, methods, and applications: Progress and remaning blind spots. In N. W. Schmitt, S. Highhouse, & I. B. Weiner (Eds.), *Handbook of psychology, 2nd Ed., Vol 12.* (pp. 367–389). Hoboken, NJ: Wiley.

Axelsson, M., & others. (2012). Self-efficacy and adherence as mediating factors between personality traits and health-related quality of life. *Quality of Life Research, 22* (3), 567–575.

Azarbad, L., Corsica, J., Hall, B., & Hood, M. (2010). Psychosocial correlates of binge eating in Hispanic, African American, and Caucasian women presenting for bariatric surgery. *Eating Behaviors, 11,* 79–84.

B

Baars, B. J. (2010). Spontaneous repetitive thoughts can be adaptive: Postscript on "mind wandering." *Psychological Bulletin, 136,* 208–210.

Babiloni, C., Vecchio, F., Cappa, S., Pasqualetti, P., Rossi, S., Miniussi, C., & Rossini, P. M. (2006). Functional frontoparietal connectivity during encoding and retrieval processes follows HERA model: A high resolution study. *Brain Research Bulletin, 68,* 203–212.

Bachmann, T. (2011). Attention as a process of selection, perception as a process of representation, and phenomenal experience as the resulting process of perception being modulated by a dedicated consciousness mechanism. *Frontiers in Psychology.* doi: 10.3389/fpsyg.2011.00387

Bachschmid, M. M., & others. (2013). Vascular aging: Chronic oxidative stress and impairment of redox signaling—consequences for vascular homeostatis and disease. *Annals of Medicine, 45,* 17–36.

Baddeley, A. D. (1993). Working memory and conscious awareness. In A. F. Collins, S. E. Gatherhole, M. A. Conway, & P. E. Morris (Eds.), *Theories of memory.* Mahwah, NJ: Erlbaum.

Baddeley, A. D. (1998). *Human memory* (rev. ed.). Boston: Allyn & Bacon.

Baddeley, A. D. (2003). Working memory and language: An overview. *Journal of Communication Disorders, 36,* 189–208.

Baddeley, A. D. (2008). What's new in working memory? *Psychological Review, 13,* 2–5.

Baddeley, A. D. (2010a). Long-term and working memory: How do they interact? In L. Backman & L. Nyberg (Eds.), *Memory, aging, and the brain.* New York: Psychology Press.

Baddeley, A. D. (2010b). Working memory. *Current Biology, 20,* R136–R140.

Baddeley, A. D. (2012). Working memory: Theories, models, and controversies. *Annual Review of Psychology* (vol. 64). Palo Alto, CA: Annual Reviews.

Baddeley, J. L., & Pennebaker, J. W. (2009). Expressive writing. In W. T. O'Donohue & J. E. Fisher (Eds.), *General principles and empirically supported techniques of cognitive behavior therapy* (pp. 295–299). Hoboken, NJ: Wiley.

Baddeley, J. L., & Singer, J. A. (2008). Telling losses: Personality correlates and functions of bereavement narratives. *Journal of Research in Personality, 42,* 421–438.

Baddeley, J. L., & Singer, J. A. (2010). A loss in the family: Silence, memory, and narrative identity after bereavement. *Memory, 189,* 198–207.

Bagnara, D., & others. (2009). Adoptive immunotherapy mediated by ex vivo expanded natural killer T cells against CD1d-expressing lymphoid neoplasms. *Haematologica, 94* (7), 967–974.

Bahrick, H. P. (1984). Semantic memory content in permastore: Fifty years of memory for Spanish learned in school. *Journal of Experimental Psychology: General, 113,* 1–29.

Bahrick, H. P. (2000). Long-term maintenance of knowledge. In E. Tulving & F. I. M. Craik (Eds.), *The Oxford handbook of memory* (pp. 347–362). New York: Oxford University Press.

Bahrick, H. P. (2005). The long-term neglect of long-term memory: Reasons and remedies. In A. F. Healey (Ed.), *Experimental cognitive psychology and its applications* (pp. 89–100). Washington, DC: American Psychological Association.

Bahrick, H. P., Bahrick, P. O., & Wittlinger, R. P. (1974). Long-term memory: Those unforgettable high-school days. *Psychology Today, 8,* 50–56.

Bahrick, H. P., Hall, L. K., & Da Costa, L. A. (2008). Fifty years of memory of college grades: Accuracy and distortions. *Emotion, 8,* 13–22.

Bailey, J. M. (2003). Biological perspectives on sexual orientation. In L. D. Garnets & D.C. Kimmel (Eds.), *Psychological perspectives on lesbian, gay, and bisexual experiences* (2nd ed., pp. 50–85). New York: Columbia University Press.

Bailey, J. M., & Zucker, K. J. (1995). Childhood sex-typed behavior and sexual orientation: A conceptual and quantitative review. *Developmental Psychology, 31,* 43–55.

Baillargeon, R. (2014). Cognitive development in infancy. *Annual Review of Psychology* (vol. 65). Palo Alto, CA: Annual Reviews. (in press)

Baillargeon, R., Scott, R. M., & He, Z. (2010). False-belief understanding in infants. *Trends in Cognitive Sciences, 14,* 110–118.

Baillargeon, R., Stavans, M., Wu., D., Gerner, Y., Setoh, P., Kittredge, A. K., & Bernard, A. (2012). Object individuation and physical reasoning in infancy: An integrative account. *Language Learning and Development, 8,* 4–46.

Baillie, J. K., Barnett, M. W. , Upton, K. R., Gerhardt, D. J., Richmond, T. A., De Sapio, F., Brennan, P. M., Rizzu, P., Smith, S., Fell, M., Talbot, R. T., Gustincich, S., Freeman, T. C., Mattick, J. S., Hume, D. A., Heutink, P., Carninci, P., Jeddeloh, J. A., & Faulkner, G. J. (2011). Somatic retrotransposition alters the genetic landscape of the human brain. *Nature, 479,* 534–537.

Baio, J. (Ed.). (2012, March 30). Surveillance summaries: Prevalence of autism spectrum disorders—Autism and Developmental Disabilities Monitoring Network, 14 Sites, United States, 2008. Atlanta: Centers for Disease Control. www.cdc.gov/mmwr/preview/mmwrhtml/ss6103a1.htm?s_cid=ss6103a1_w (accessed June 25, 2013)

Baird, B., Smallwood, J., & Schooler, J. W. (2011). Back to the future: Autobiographical planning and the functionality of mind-wandering. *Consciousness and Cognition, 20,* 1604–1611.

Baker, C. I. (2013). Visual processing in the primate brain. In R. J. Nelson, S. J. Y. Mizumori, & I. B. Weiner (Eds.), *Handbook of psychology, 2nd ed., Vol. 3.* (pp. 81–114). Hoboken, NJ: Wiley.

Baker, D. B., & Joyce, N. R. (2013). Counseling psychology. In D. K. Freedheim & I. B. Weiner (Eds.), *Handbook of psychology, 2nd ed., Vol. 1.* (pp. 397–406). Hoboken, NJ: Wiley.

Baker, L. A., Raine, A., Liu, J., & Jacobson, K. C. (2008). Differential genetic and environmental influences on reactive and proactive aggression in children. *Journal of Abnormal Child Psychology, 36,* 1265–1278.

Balbuena, L., Baetz, M., & Bowen, R. (2013). Religious attendance, spirituality, and major depression in Canada: A 14-year follow-up study. *Canadian Journal of Psychology, 58,* 225–232.

Baldwin, T. T., & Padgett, M. Y. (1993). Management development: A review and commentary. In C. L. Cooper & I. T. Robertson (Eds.), *International review of industrial and organizational psychology* (pp. 35–38). Chichester, U.K.: Wiley.

Balliet, D., Li, N. P., & Joireman, J. (2011). Relating trait self-control and forgiveness within prosocials and proselfs: Compensatory versus synergistic models. *Journal of Personality and Social Psychology, 101,* 1090–1105.

Balodis, I. M., Molina, N. D., Kober, H., Worhunsky, P. D., White, M. A., Rajita, S., Grilo, C. M., & Potenza, M. N. (2013). Divergent neural substrates of inhibitory control in binge eating disorder relative to other manifestations of obesity. *Obesity, 21* (2), 367–377.

Balsam, K. F., Beauchaine, T. P., Rothblum, E. D., & Solomon, S. E. (2008). Three-year follow-up of same sex couple who had civil unions in Vermont, same-sex couples not in civil unions, and heterosexual married couples. *Developmental Psychology, 44,* 102–116.

Balter, M. (2010). Did working memory spark creative culture? *Science, 328,* 160–163.

Bandura, A. (1986). *Social foundations of thought and action.* Englewood Cliffs, NJ: Prentice-Hall.

Bandura, A. (1997). *Self-efficacy.* New York: Freeman.

Bandura, A. (2001). Social cognitive theory. *Annual Review of Psychology* (vol. 52). Palo Alto, CA: Annual Reviews.

Bandura, A. (2009). Social and policy impact of social cognitive theory. In M. Mark, S. Donaldson, & B. Campbell (Eds.), *Social psychology and program/policy evaluation.* New York: Guilford.

Bandura, A. (2010a). Vicarious learning. In D. Matsumoto (Ed.), *Cambridge dictionary of psychology.* New York: Cambridge University Press.

Bandura, A. (2010b). Self-efficacy. In D. Matsumoto (Ed.), *Cambridge dictionary of psychology.* New York: Cambridge University Press.

Bandura, A. (2011). Social cognitive theory. In P. A. M. van Lange, A. W. Kruglanski, & E. T. Higgins (Eds.), *Handbook of social psychological theories.* Thousand Oaks, CA: Sage.

Bandura, A. (2012a). Social cognitive theory. *Annual Review of Clinical Psychology* (vol. 8). Palo Alto, CA: Annual Reviews.

Bandura, A. (2012b). On the functional properties of perceived self-efficacy revisited. *Journal of Management, 38,* 9–44.

Bandura, A., & Bussey, K. (2004). On broadening the cognitive, motivational, and sociostructural scope of theorizing about gender development and functioning: Comment on Martin, Ruble, and Szkrybalo (2002). *Psychological Bulletin, 130,* 690–701.

Bandura, A., & Locke, E. A. (2003). Negative self-efficacy and goal effects revisited. *Journal of Applied Psychology, 88* (1), 87–99.

Bandura, A., Ross, D., & Ross, S. A. (1961). Transmission of aggression through imitation of aggressive models. *Journal of Abnormal and Social Psychology, 63,* 575–582.

Banthia, R., Malcarne, V. L., Ko, C. M., Varni, J. W., & Sadler, G. R. (2009). Fatigued breast cancer survivors: The role of sleep quality, depressed mood, stage, and age. *Psychology & Health, 24,* 965–980.

Banyard, V. L., & Williams, L. M. (2007). Women's voices on recovery: A multi-method study of the complexity of recovery from child sexual abuse. *Child Abuse and Neglect, 31,* 275–290.

Barber, N. (2009). Evolutionary social science: A new approach to violent crime. *Aggression and Violent Behavior, 13,* 237–250.

Barclay, L. J., & Aquino, K. (2010). Workplace aggression and violence. In S. Zedeck (Ed.), *APA handbook of industrial and organizational psychology.* Washington, DC: American Psychological Association.

Bard, P. (1934). Emotion. In C. Murchison (Ed.), *Handbook of general psychology.* Worcester, MA: Clark University Press.

Bardone-Cone, A. M., Abramson, L. Y., Vohs, K. D., Heatherton, T. F., & Joiner, T. E., Jr. (2006). Predicting bulimic symptoms: An interactive model of self-efficacy, perfectionism, and perceived weight status. *Behaviour Research and Therapy, 44,* 27–42.

Bargh, J. A., Gollwitzer, P. M., Lee-Chai, A., Barndollar, K., & Trotschel, R. (2001). The automated will: Nonconscious activation and pursuit of behavioral goals. *Journal of Personality and Social Psychology, 81,* 1014–1027.

Barker, A. T., Jalinous, R., & Freeston, I. L. (1985). Non-invasive magnetic stimulation of human motor cortex, *Lancet, 1,* 1106–1107.

Barkham, M., Stiles, W. B., Connell, J., & Mellor-Clark, J. (2012). Psychological treatment outcomes in routine NHS services: What do we mean by treatment effectiveness? *Psychology and Psychotherapy, 85* (1), 1–16.

Barkley, R., & 74 others. (2002). International consensus statement on ADHD. *Clinical Child and Family Psychology, 5,* 89–111.

Barling, J., Christie, A., & Hoption, C. (2010). Leadership. In S. Zedeck (Ed.), *APA handbook of industrial and organizational psychology.* Washington, DC: American Psychological Association.

Barling, J., Dupré, K., & Kelloway, E. K. (2009). Predicting workplace violence and aggression, *Annual Review of Psychology* (vol. 60). Palo Alto, CA: Annual Reviews.

Barling, J., Weber, T., & Kelloway E. K. (1996). Effects of transformational leadership training on attitudinal and financial outcomes: A field experiment. *Journal of Applied Psychology, 81,* 827–832.

Barloon, T., & Noyes, R., Jr. (1997). Charles Darwin and panic disorder. *Journal of the American Medical Association, 277,* 138–141.

Barlow, D. H., Bullis, J. R., Comer, J. S., & Ametaj, A. A. (2013). Evidence-based psychological treatments: An update and a way forward. *Annual Review of Clinical Psychology* (vol. 9). Palo Alto, CA: Annual Reviews.

Baron-Cohen, S. (1995). *Mindblindness: An essay on autism and theory of mind.* Cambridge, MA: MIT Press.

Baron-Cohen, S. (2002). The extreme male brain theory of autism. *Trends in Cognitive Science, 6,* 248–254.

Baron-Cohen, S. (2008). Autism, hypersystemizing, and the truth. *Quarterly Journal of Experimental Psychology, 61,* 64–75.

Baron-Cohen, S. (2011). The empathizing-systematizing (E-S) theory of autism: A cognitive developmental account. In U. Goswami (Ed.), *Wiley-Blackwell handbook of childhood cognitive development* (2nd ed.). New York: Wiley-Blackwell.

Baron-Cohen, S., Wheelwright, S., Hill, J., Raste, Y., & Plumb, I. (2001). The "reading of mind in the eyes" test revised version: A study with normal adults, and adults with Asperger syndrome or high-functioning autism. *Journal of Child Psychology and Psychiatry, 42* (2), 241–251.

Barrett, G. V., & Kernan, M. G. (1987). Performance appraisal and terminations: A review of court decisions since *Brito v. Zia* with implications for personnel practices. *Personnel Psychology, 40,* 489–503.

Barrett, L. F. (2011). Was Darwin wrong about emotional expressions? *Current Directions in Psychological Science, 20,* 400–406.

Barrick, M. R., Swider, B., & Stewart, G. L. (2010). Initial evaluations in the interview: Relationships with subsequent interviewer evaluations and employment offers. *Journal of Applied Psychology, 95,* 1037–1046.

Barrouillet, P., De Paepe, A., & Langerock, N. (2012). Time causes forgetting from working memory. *Psychonomic Bulletin and Review, 19,* 87–92.

Bartel, C. A., Wrzesniewski, A., & Wiesenfeld, B. (2007). The struggle to establish organizational membership: Newcomer socialization in remote work contexts. In C. A. Bartel., S. Blader, & A. Wrzesniewski (Eds.), *Identity and the modern organization.* Mahwah, NJ: Erlbaum.

Bartels, D. M., & Pizarro, D. A. (2011). The mismeasure of morals: Antisocial personality traits predict utilitarian responses to moral dilemmas. *Cognition, 121,* 154–161.

Bartels, S., & Desilets, R. (2012). *Health promotion programs for people with serious mental illness.* Washington, DC: SAMHSA-HRSA Center for Integrated Health Solutions.

Bartolo, A., Benuzzi, F., Nocetti, L., Baraldi, P., & Nichelli, P. (2006). Humor comprehension and appreciation: An fMRI study. *Journal of Cognitive Neuroscience, 18,* 1789–1798.

Bartolomei, F., & Naccache, L. (2011). The global workspace (GW) theory of consciousness and epilepsy. *Behavioral Neuroscience, 24,* 67–74.

Bartone, P. T., Hystad, S. W., Eid, J., & Brevik, J. L. (2012). Psychological hardiness and coping style as risk/resilience factors for alcohol abuse. *Military Medicine, 177,* 517–524.

Bartoshuk, L. (2008). Chemical senses: Taste and smell. *Annual Review of Psychology* (vol. 59). Palo Alto, CA: Annual Reviews.

Bass, B. M. (1985). *Leadership and performance beyond expectations.* New York: Free Press.

Bass, B. M., & Avolio, B. (1995). *MLQ Multifactor leadership questionnaire.* Redwood City, CA: Mind Garden.

Bassok, M., & Novick, L. R. (2012). Problem solving. In K. J. Holyoak & R. G. Morrison (Eds.), *The Oxford handbook of thinking and reasoning.* New York: Oxford University Press.

Bateman, A. J. (1948). Intra-sexual selection in *Drosophila. Heredity, 2,* 349–358.

Bateman, T. S., & Snell, S. A. (2011). *Management* (9th ed.). New York: McGraw-Hill.

Batson, C. D. (2002). Addressing the altruism question experimentally. In S. G. Post, L. G. Underwood, J. P. Schloss, & W. B. Hurlbut (Eds.), *Altruism and altruistic love.* New York: Oxford University Press.

Batson, C. D. (2006). "Not all self-interest after all": Economics of empathy-induced altruism. In D. DeCremer, M. Zeelenberg, & J. K. Murnigham (Eds.), *Social psychology and economics* (pp. 281–299). Mahwah, NJ: Erlbaum.

Batson, C. D. (2012). History of prosocial behavior research. In A. W. Kruglanski & W. Stroebe (Eds.), *Handbook of the history of social psychology.* New York: Psychology Press.

Batson, C. D., Duncan, B. D., Ackerman, P., Buckley, T., Birch, K., Cialdini, R. B., Schaller, M., Houlihan, D., Arps, K., Fultz, J., & Beaman, A. L. (2007). Issue 17: Does true altruism exist? In J. A. Nier (Ed.), *Taking sides: Clashing views in social psychology* (2nd ed., pp. 348–371). New York: McGraw-Hill.

Battaglia, M. (2012). Is behavioral genetics "too-big-to-know" science? *Behavioral and Brain Science, 35* (5), 360.

Bauer, J. J., McAdams, D. P., & Sakaeda, A. R. (2005). The crystallization of desire and the crystallization of discontent in narratives of life-changing decisions. *Journal of Personality, 73,* 1181–1213.

Bauer, J. J., Schwab, J. R., & McAdams, D. P. (2011). Self-actualizing: Where ego development finally feels good? *The Humanistic Psychologist, 39,* 1181–1213.

Bauer, M., Blumentritt, H., Finke, R., Schlattmann, P., Adli, M., Baethge, C., Bschor, T., Müller-Oerlinghausen, B., & Berghöfer, A. (2007). Using ultrasonography to determine thyroid size and prevalence of goiter in lithium-treated patients with affective disorders. *Journal of Affective Disorders, 104* (1-3), 45–51.

Bauer, P. J. (2009). Learning and memory: Like a horse and carriage. In A. Needham & A. Woodward (Eds.), *Learning and the infant mind.* New York: Oxford University Press.

Bauer, P. J., (2013). Memory. In P. D. Zelazo (Ed.), *The Oxford handbook of developmental psychology, Vol. 1.* (pp. 505–564). New York: Oxford University Press.

Bauer, P. J., Larkina, M., & Deocampo, J. (2011). Early memory development. In U. Goswami (Ed.), *Wiley-Blackwell handbook of childhood cognitive development* (2nd ed.). New York: Wiley-Blackwell.

Bauer, S. M., Schanda, H., Karakula, H., Olajossy-Hilkesberger, L., Rudaleviciene, P., Okribelashvili, N., Chaudhry, H. R., Idemudia, S. E., Gscheider, S., Ritter, K., Stompe, T. (2011). Culture and the prevalence of hallucinations in schizophrenia. *Comprehensive Psychiatry, 52,* 319–325.

Baumann, A. E. (2007). Stigmatization, social distance and exclusion because of mental illness: The individual with mental illness as a "stranger." *International Review of Psychiatry, 19,* 131–135.

Baumeister, R. F. (1999). *Evil: Inside human violence and cruelty.* New York: Freeman.

Baumeister, R. F. (2000). Gender differences in erotic plasticity: The female sex drive as socially flexible and responsive. *Psychological Bulletin, 126* (3), 347–374.

Baumeister, R. F., & Alquist, J. L. (2009). Self-regulation as limited resource: Strength model of control and depletion. In J. P. Forgas, R. F. Baumeister, & D. M. Tice (Eds.), *Psychology of self-regulation.* New York: Psychology Press.

Baumeister, R. F., & Leary, M. R. (2000). The need to belong: Desire for interpersonal attachments as a fundamental human motivation. In E. T. Higgins & A. W. Kruglanski (Eds.), *Motivational science: Social and personality perspectives* (pp. 24–49). New York: Psychology Press.

Baumgartner, T., Heinrichs, M., Vonlanthen, A., Fischbacher, U., & Fehr, E. (2008). Oxytocin shapes the neural circuitry of trust and trust adaptation in humans. *Neuron, 58* (4), 639–650.

Baumrind, D. (1991). Parenting styles and adolescent development. In J. Brooks-Gunn, R. Lerner, & A. C. Petersen (Eds.), *The encyclopedia of adolescence* (vol. 2). New York: Garland.

Baumrind, D. (1993). The average expectable environment is not good enough: A response to Scarr. *Child Development, 64,* 1299–1307.

Baumrind, D. (2012). Authoritative parenting revisited: History and current status. In R. Larzelere, A. S. Morris, & A. W. Harist (Eds.), *Authoritative parenting.* Washington, DC: American Psychological Association.

Bavelier, D., Green, C. S., Shrater, P., & Pouget, A. (2012). Brain plasticity in childhood. *Annual Review of Neuroscience* (vol. 35). Palo Alto, CA: Annual Reviews.

Baxter, L. R., Jr., Phelps, M. E., Mazziotta, J. C., Schwartz, J. M., Gerner, R. H., Selin, C. E., & Sumida, R. M. (1995). Cerebral metabolic rates for glucose in mood disorders: Studies with positron emission tomography and fluorodeoxyglucose F 18. *Archives of General Psychiatry, 42,* 441–447.

Baylor, D. (2001). *Seeing, hearing, and smelling the world.* www.hhmi.org/senses (accessed February 21, 2013)

Bayoglu, B., Cengiz, M., Karacetin, G., Uysal, O., Kocabasoğlu, N., Bayar, R., & Balcioglu, I. (2012). Genetic polymorphism of angiotensin 1-converting enzyme (ACE), but not angiotensin II type 1 receptor (ATr1), has a gender-specific role in panic disorder. *Psychiatry and Clinical Neurosciences, 66,* 130–137.

Beach, E., Williams, W., & Gilliver, M. (2013). Estimating young Australian adults' risk of hearing damage from selected leisure activities. *Ear and Hearing, 34,* 75–82.

Beard, C., Weisberg, R. B., & Keller, M. B. (2010). Health-related quality of life across the anxiety disorders: Findings from a sample of primary care patients. *Journal of Anxiety Disorders, 24,* 559–564.

Beck, A. (1967). *Depression.* New York: Harper & Row.

Beck, A. T. (2005). The current state of cognitive therapy: A 40-year retrospective. *Archives of General Psychiatry, 62,* 953–959.

Beck, A. T. (2006). How an anomalous finding led to a new system of psychotherapy. *Nature Medicine, 12,* 1139–1141.

Beck, A. T., & Haigh, E. (2014). The generic cognitive model. *Annual Review of Clinical Psychology* (vol. 10). Palo Alto, CA: Annual Reviews.

Becker, H., Kang, S. J., & Stuifbergen, A. (2012). Predictors of quality of life for long-term cancer survivors with preexisting disabling conditions. *Oncology Nursing Society, 39,* E122–E131.

Becker, M., & others. (2012). Culture and the distinctiveness motive: Constructing identity in individualistic and collectivist societies. *Journal of Personality and Social Psychology, 102* (4), 833–855.

Becker, M. W., Alzahabi, R., & Hopwood, C. J. (2013). Media multitasking is associated with symptoms of depression and social anxiety. *Cyberpsychology, Behavior, and Social Networking, 16* (2),132–135.

Becker-Weidman, E. G., Reinecke, M. A., Jacobs, R. H., Martinovich, Z., Silva, S. G., & March, J. S. (2009). Predictors of hopelessness among clinically depressed youth. *Behavioral and Cognitive Psychotherapy, 37* (3), 267–291.

Bedics, J. D., Atkins, D. C., Comtois, K. A., & Linehan, M. M. (2012). Treatment differences in the therapeutic relationship and introject during a 2-year randomized controlled trial of dialectical behavior therapy versus nonbehavioral psychotherapy experts for borderline personality disorder. *Journal of Consulting and Clinical Psychology, 80* (1), 66–77.

Bednark, J. G., Reynolds, J. N., Stafford, T., Redgrave, P., & Franz, E. A. (2013). Creating a movement heuristic for voluntary action: Electrophysiological correlates of movement-outcome learning. *Cortex, 49* (3), 771–780.

Beeler, C. K. (2010). Leader traits, skills, and behaviors. In M. D. Mumford (Ed.), *Leadership 101* (pp. 87–116). New York: Springer.

Beeli, G., Esslen, M., & Jancke, L. (2005). Synaesthesia: When coloured sounds taste sweet. *Nature, 434,* 38.

Behrens, K. Y., Parker, A. C., & Haltigan, J. D. (2011). Maternal sensitivity assessed during the strange situation procedure predicts child's attachment quality and reunion behaviors. *Infant Behavior and Development, 34* (2), 378–381.

Bélanger, J. J., Lafrenière, M. A., Vallerand, R. J., & Kruglanski, A. W. (2013). When passion makes the heart grow colder: The role of passion in alternative goal suppression. *Journal of Personality and Social Psychology, 104* (1), 126–147.

Belk, C., & Maier, V. B. (2013). *Biology* (4th ed.). Upper Saddle River, NJ: Pearson.

Bell, A. P., Weinberg, M. S., & Hammersmith, S. K. (1981). *Sexual preference: Its development in men and women.* Bloomington: Indiana University Press.

Bell, J. T., & Saffery, R. (2012). The value of twins in epigenetic epidemiology. *International Journal of Epidemiology, 4,* 140–150.

Bell, M. A., & Cuevas, K. (2013). Psychobiology of executive function in early development. In J. A. Griffin, L. S. Freund, & P. McCardle (Eds.), *Executive function in preschool children.* Washington, DC: American Psychological Association.

Bell, R. L., Franklin, K. M., Hauser, S. R., & Zhou, F. C. (2012). Introduction to the special issue, "Pharmacotherapies for the treatment of alcohol abuse and dependence" and a summary of patents targeting other neurotransmitter systems. *Recent Patents on CNS Drug Discovery, 7,* 93–112.

Belli, H., Ural, C., Vardar, M. K., Yesilyurt, S., & Oncu, F. (2012). Dissociative symptoms and dissociative disorder comorbidity in patients with obsessive-compulsive disorder. *Comprehensive Psychiatry, 53* (7), 975–980.

Beltz, A. M., Swanson, J. L., & Berenbaum, S. A. (2011). Gendered occupational interests: Prenatal androgen effects on psychological orientation to things versus people. *Hormones and Behavior, 60* (4), 313–617.

Bem, D. (1967). Self-perception: An alternative explanation of cognitive dissonance phenomena. *Psychological Review, 74,* 183–200.

Bem, D. J. (1996). The exotic becomes erotic: A developmental theory of sexual orientation. *Psychological Review, 103,* 320–335.

Bem, D. J. (2011). Feeling the future: Experimental evidence for anomalous retroactive influences on cognition and affect. *Journal of Personality and Social Psychology, 100,* 407–425.

Bem, S. L. (1983). Gender schema theory and its implications for child development: Raising gender-aschematic children in a gender-schematic society. *Signs, 8,* 598–616.

Bem, S. L. (1993). *The lenses of gender: Transforming the debate on sexual inequality.* New Haven, CT: Yale University Press.

Benedetti, F., & others. (2003). Conscious expectation and unconscious conditioning in analgesic; motor and hormonal placebo/nocebo responses. *Journal of Neuroscience, 23,* 4315–4323.

Benedict, C., Brooks, S. J., O'Daly, O. G., Almèn, M. S., Morell, A., Åberg, K., Gingnell, M., Schultes, B., Hallschmid, M., Broman, J. E., Larsson, E. M., & Schiöth, H. B. (2012). Acute sleep deprivation enhances the brain's response to hedonic food stimuli: An fMRI study. *Journal of Clinical Endocrinology & Metabolism, 97,* E443–E447.

Benham, B. (2008). The ubiquity of deception and the ethics of deceptive research. *Bioethics, 22,* 147–156.

Bennett, D. M., Fernie, G., Currie, J., & Reid, I. C. (2013). Usefulness of treatment reports for electroconvulsive therapy. *Journal of Electroconvulsive Therapy.* (in press)

Beraha, E., & others. (2012). Hemispheric asymmetry for affective processing in healthy subjects—an fMRI study. *PLoS One, 7* (10), e46931.

Berdahl, J. L., & Raver, J. L. (2010). Sexual harassment. In S. Zedeck (Ed.), *APA handbook of industrial and organizational psychology.* Washington, DC: American Psychological Association.

Berenbaum, S. A. (2006). Psychological outcome in children with disorders of sex development: Implications for treatment and understanding typical development. *Annual Review of Sex Research, 17,* 1–38.

Berenbaum, S. A., Blakemore, J. E. O., & Beltz, A. M. (2011). A role for biology in gender related behavior. *Sex Roles, 64,* 804–825.

Berenbaum, S. A., Bryk, K. L. K., & Beltz, A. M. (2012). Early androgen effects on spatial and mechanical abilities: Evidence from congenital adrenal hyperplasia. *Behavioral Neuroscience, 126,* 86–96.

Berg, J., Grant, A., & Johnson, V. (2010). When callings are calling: Crafting work and leisure in pursuit of unanswered occupational callings, *Organization Science, 21* (5), 973–994.

Berg, J. M., Wrzesniewski, A., & Dutton, J. E. (2010). Perceiving and responding to challenges in job crafting at different ranks: When proactivity requires adaptivity. *Journal of Organizational Behavior, 31,* 158–186.

Bergman, M. E., Langhout, R. D., Palmieri, P. A., Cortina, L. M., & Fitzgerald, L. F. (2002). The (un)reasonableness of reporting: Antecedents and consequences of reporting sexual harassment. *Journal of Applied Psychology, 87,* 230–242.

Bergman, M. E., Palmieri, P. A., Drasgow, F., & Ormerod, A. J. (2012). Racial/ethnic harassment and discrimination, its antecedents, and its effect on job-related outcomes. *Journal of Occupational Health Psychology, 17,* 65–78.

Berkman, E. T., Lieberman, M. D., & Gable, S. L. (2009). BIS, BAS, and response conflict: Testing predictions of the revised reinforcement sensitivity theory. *Personality and Individual Differences, 46,* 586–591.

Berkowitz, L. (1990). On the formation and regulation of anger and aggression: A cognitive neoassociationistic analysis. *American Psychologist, 45,* 494–503.

Berkowitz, L., & LePage, A. (1996). Weapons as aggression-eliciting stimuli. In S. Fein & S. Spencer (Eds.), *Readings in social psychology: The art and science of research* (pp. 67–73). Boston: Houghton Mifflin.

Berlim, M. T., Van den Eynde, F., & Daskalakis, Z. J. (2013). A systematic review and meta-analysis on the efficacy and acceptability of bilateral repetitive transcranial magnetic stimulation (rTMS) for treating major depression. *Psychological Medicine.* (in press)

Bermúdez, K., Bruner, C. A., & Lattal, K. A. (2013). Response acquisition with intermittent immediate and delayed conditioned reinforcement. *Journal of Experimental Analysis of Behavior, 99* (2), 189–199.

Bernadin, H. J. (2010). *Human resource management* (5th ed.). New York: McGraw-Hill.

Bernardy, N. C., Lund, B. C., Alexander, B., & Friedman, M. J. (2012). Prescribing trends in veterans with posttraumatic stress disorder. *Journal of Clinical Psychiatry, 73,* 297–319.

Berndt, N. C., Hayes, A. F., Verboon, P. Lechner, L., Bolman, C., & De Vries, H. (2012). Self-efficacy mediates the impact of craving on smoking abstinence in low to moderately anxious patients: Results of a moderated mediation approach. *Psychology of Addictive Behaviors, 27* (1), 113–124.

Berntsen, D. & Rubin, D. C. (2002). Emotionally charged autobiographical memories across the life span: The recall of happy, sad, traumatic, and involuntary memories. *Psychology and Aging, 17,* 636–652.

Berridge, K. C. (1996). Food reward: Brain substrates of wanting and liking. *Neuroscience Biobehavioral Reviews, 20,* 1–25.

Berridge, K. C., & Kringelbach, M. L. (2008). Affective neuroscience of pleasure: Reward in humans and animals. *Psychopharmacology, 199,* 457–480.

Berscheid, E. (1988). Some comments on love's anatomy. Or, whatever happened to an old-fashioned lust? In R. J. Sternberg & M. L. Barnes (Eds.), *Anatomy of love.* New Haven, CT: Yale University Press.

Berscheid, E. (2000). Attraction. In A. Kazdin (Ed.), *Encyclopedia of psychology.* Washington, DC, & New York: American Psychological Association and Oxford University Press.

Berscheid, E. (2006). Searching for the meaning of "love." In R. J. Sternberg & K. Weis (Eds.), *The new psychology of love* (pp. 171–183). New Haven, CT: Yale University Press.

Berscheid, E. (2010). Love in the fourth dimension. *Annual Review of Psychology,* (Vol. 61). (pp. 1–25). Palo Alto, CA: Annual Reviews.

Berscheid, E., & Regan, P. C. (2005). *The psychology of interpersonal relationships.* New York: Prentice-Hall.

Berthet, A., & others. (2012). L-dopa impairs proteasome activity in Parkinsonism through D1 dopamine receptor. *Journal of Neuroscience, 32* (2), 681– 691.

Bertram, L., & Tanzi, R. E. (2012). The genetics of Alzheimer's disease. *Progress in Molecular Biology and Translational Science, 107,* 79–100.

Bertrand, M., & Mullainathan, S. (2004). Are Emily and Greg more employable than Lakisha and Jamal? A field experiment on labor market discrimination. *American Economic Review, 94,* 991–1013.

Bertrand, R. M., Graham, E. K., & Lachman, M. E. (2013). Personality development in adulthood and old age. In R. M. Lerner, M. A. Easterbrooks, J. Mistry, & I. B. Weiner (Eds.), *Handbook of psychology, 2nd ed., Vol. 6.* (pp. 475–494). Hoboken, NJ: Wiley.

Besedovsky, L., Lange, T., & Born, J. (2012). Sleep and immune function. *European Journal of Physiology, 463,* 121–137.

Best, D. L. (2010). Gender. In M. H. Bornstein (Ed.), *Handbook of cultural developmental science.* New York: Psychology Press.

Bettencourt, B. A., Talley, A., Benjamin, A. J., & Valentine, J. (2006). Personality and aggressive behavior under provoking and neutral conditions: A meta-analytic review. *Psychological Bulletin, 132* (5), 751–777.

Beutel, M. E., & others. (2012). Type D personality as a cardiovascular risk marker in the general population: Results from the Gutenberg study. *Psychotherapy and Psychosomatics, 81,* 108–117.

Beutler, L. E., Forrester, B., Gallagher-Thompson, D., Thompson, L., & Tomlins, J. B. (2012). Common, specific, and treatment fit variables in psychotherapy outcome. *Journal of Psychotherapy Integration, 22* (3), 255–281.

Bewernick, B. H., Kayser, S., Sturm, V., & Schlaepfer, T. E. (2012). Long-term effects of nucleus accumbens deep brain stimulation in treatment-resistant depression: Evidence for sustained efficacy. *Neuropsychopharmacology, 37,* 1975–1985.

Beydoun, M. A., & Wang, Y. (2009). Gender-ethnic disparity in BMI and waist circumference distribution shifts in U.S. adults. *Obesity, 17,* 169–176.

Bhatia, T., Garg, K., Pogue-Geile, M., Nimaonkar, V. L., & Deshpande, S. N. (2009). Executive functions and cognitive deficits in schizophrenia: Comparisons between probands, parents, and controls in India. *Journal of Postgraduate Medicine, 55,* 3–7.

Biernat, M., & Deaux, K. (2012). History of social psychology research on gender. In A. W. Kruglanski & W. Stroebe (Eds.), *Handbook of the history of social psychology.* New York: Psychology Press.

Billig, M. (2012). The notion of "prejudice": Some rhetorical and ideological aspects. In J. Dixon & M. Levine (Eds.), *Beyond prejudice.* New York: Cambridge University Press.

Binder, D. (2012). Prep runner carries foe to finish line. *ESPN High School Sports.* http://espn.go.com/high-school/track-and-xc/story/_/id/8010251/high-school-runner-carries-fallen-opponent-finish-line (accessed May 13, 2013)

Birgegård, A., Norring, C., & Clinton, D. (2012). DSM-IV versus DSM-5: Implementation of proposed DSM-5 criteria in a large natural database. *International Journal of Eating Disorders, 45,* 353–361.

Birkenhager, T. K., & others. (2010). Influence of age on the efficacy of electroconvulsive therapy in major depression: A retrospective study. *Journal of Affective Disorders, 126,* 257–261.

Bisgaard, H., Jensen, S. M., & Bonnelykke, K. (2012). Interaction between asthma and lung function growth in early life. *American Journal of Respiratory and Critical Care Medicine, 185* (11), 1183–1189.

Bisson, J. L. (2013). What happened to harmonization of the PTSD diagnosis? The divergence of ICD11 and DSM5. *Epidemiology and Psychiatric Sciences.* (in press)

Biswas-Diener, R., Kashdan, T., & King, L. A. (2009). Two traditions of happiness research, not two distinct types of happiness. *Journal of Positive Psychology, 4,* 208–211.

Biswas-Diener, R., Vitterso, J., & Diener, E. (2005). Most people are pretty happy, but there is cultural variation: The Inughuit, the Amish, and the Maasai. *Journal of Happiness Studies, 6,* 205–226.

Bjork, R. A., Dunlosky, J., & Kornell, N. (2013). Self-regulated learning: Beliefs, techniques, and illusions. *Annual Review of Psychology* (vol. 64). Palo Alto, CA: Annual Reviews.

Bjorklund, D. F. (2012). *Children's thinking* (5th ed.). Boston: Cengage.

Blackman, M. (2008). The effective interview. In S. Cartwright & C. L. Cooper (Eds.), *The Oxford handbook of personnel psychology* (pp. 194–214). New York: Oxford University Press.

Blackwell, L. S., & Dweck, C. S. (2008). *The motivational impact of a computer-based program that teaches how the brain changes with learning.* Unpublished manuscript, Department of Psychology, Stanford University, Stanford, CA.

Blackwell, L. S., Trzesniewski, K. H., & Dweck, C. S. (2007). Implicit theories of intelligence predict achievement across an adolescent transition: A longitudinal study and an intervention. *Child Development, 78,* 246–263.

Blades, H. B. (2006). Killer coworker: The case of Michael McDermott, the Christmas killer. *Forensic Examiner, 156,* 49–52.

Blagrove, M., & Akehurst, L. (2000). Personality and dream recall frequency: Further negative findings. *Dreaming, 10,* 139–148.

Blair, C., & Razza, R. P. (2007). Relating effortful control, executive functioning, and false belief understanding to emerging math and literacy ability in kindergarten. *Child Development, 78,* 647–663.

Blair, S. N., Kohl, H. W., Paffenbarger, R. S., Clark, D. G., Cooper, K. H., & Gibbons, L. W. (1989). Physical fitness and all-cause mortality: A prospective study of healthy men and women. *Journal of the American Medical Association, 262,* 2395–2401.

Blakemore, J. E. O., Berenbaum, S. E., & Liben, L. S. (2009). *Gender development.* New York: Psychology Press.

Blakemore, S.-J., & Mills, K. (2014). The social brain in adolescence. *Annual Review of Psychology* (vol. 65). Palo Alto, CA: Annual Reviews. (in press)

Blanco, C., Alegría, A. A., Liu, S. M., Secades-Villa, R., Sugaya, L., Davies, C., & Nunes, E. V. (2012). Differences among major depressive disorder with and without co-occurring substance use disorders and substance-induced depressive disorder: Results from the National Epidemiologic Survey on Alcohol and Related Conditions. *Journal of Clinical Psychiatry, 73* (6), 865–873.

Blanco, M., & others. (2009). *Investigating critical incidents, driver restart period, sleep quantity, and crash countermeasures in commercial operations using naturalistic data collection: A final report* (Contract No. DTFH61-01-00049, Task Order #23). Washington, DC: Federal Motor Carrier Safety Administration.

Blanton, H., Jaccard, J., Klick, J., Mellers, B., Mitchell, G., & Tetlock, P. E. (2009). Strong claims and weak evidence: Reassessing the predictive validity of the IAT. *Journal of Applied Psychology, 94,* 567–582.

Blashfield, R. K. (2014). Diagnosis from DSM-1 through DSM-5. *Annual Review of Clinical Psychology* (vol. 10). Palo Alto, CA: Annual Reviews.

Blickle, G., Wendel, S., & Ferris, G. R. (2010). Political skill as moderator of personality—Job performance relationships in socioanalytic theory: Test of the getting ahead motive in automobile sales. *Journal of Vocational Behavior, 76,* 326–335.

Block, J. (1982). Assimilation, accommodation, and the dynamics of personality development. *Child Development, 53,* 281–295.

Block, J., & Kremen, A. M. (1996). IQ and ego-resiliency: Conceptual and empirical connections and separateness. *Journal of Personality and Social Psychology, 70,* 349–361.

Block, S. D., Shestowsky, D., Segovia, D. A., Goodman, G. S., Schaaf, J. M., & Alexander, K. W. (2012). "That never happened": Adults' discernment of children's true and false memory reports. *Law and Human Behavior, 36,* 365–374.

Blonigen, D. M., Carlson, M. D., Hicks, B. M., Krueger, R. F., & Iacono, W. G. (2008). Stability and change in personality traits from late adolescence to early adulthood: A longitudinal twin study. *Journal of Personality, 76,* 229–266.

Blonigen, D. M., Timko, C., & Moos, R. H. (2013). Alcoholics Anonymous and reduced impulsivity: A novel mechanism of change. *Substance Abuse, 34,* 4–12.

Bloom, B. (1985). *Developing talent in young people.* New York: Ballantine.

Bloom, F., Nelson, C. A., & Lazerson, A. (2001). *Brain, mind, and behavior* (3rd ed.). New York: Worth.

Bloom, P. (2004). Myths of word learning. In D. G. Hall & S. R. Waxman (Eds), *Weaving a lexicon.* (pp. 205–224). Cambridge, MA: MIT Press.

Bloor, C., & White, F. (1983). Unpublished manuscript. LaJolla, CA: University of California, San Diego.

Blumenfeld, P. C., Kempler, T. M., & Krajcik, J. S. (2006). Motivation and cognitive engagement in learning environments. In R. K. Sawyer (Ed.), *The Cambridge handbook of learning sciences.* New York: Cambridge University Press.

Blumenthal, H., Leen-Feldner, E. W., Babson, K. A., Gahr, J. L., Trainor, C. D., & Frala, J. L. (2011). Elevated social anxiety among early maturing girls. *Developmental Psychology, 47,* 1133–1140.

Blustein, D. L. (2013). The psychology of working: A new perspective for a new era. In D. L. Blustein (Ed.), *The Oxford handbook of the psychology of working.* New York: Oxford University Press.

Boals, A., & Rubin, D. C. (2011). The integration of emotions in traumatic memories: Cognitive-emotional distinctiveness and posttraumatic stress disorder. *Applied Cognitive Psychology, 25,* 811–816.

Boatright-Horowitz, S. L., Langley, M., & Gunnip, M. (2009). Depth-of-processing effects as college students use academic advising web sites. *CyberPsychology & Behavior, 12,* 331–335.

Bocanegra, B. R., & Zeelenberg, R. (2009). Dissociating emotion-induced blindness and hypervision. *Emotion, 9,* 865–873.

Bodenhausen, G. V., & Morales, J. R. (2013). Social cognition and perception. In H. A. Tennen, J. M. Suls, & I. B. Weiner (Eds.), *Handbook of psychology, 2nd ed., Vol. 5.* (pp. 225–246). Hoboken, NJ: Wiley.

Boeddeker, N., & Hemmi, J. M. (2010). Visual gaze control during peering flight manoeuvres in honeybees. *Proceedings: Biological Sciences, 277,* 1209–1217.

Boehm, J. K., & Kubzansky, L. D. (2012). The heart's content: The association between positive psychological well-being and cardiovascular health. *Psychological Bulletin, 138* (4), 655–691.

Boelen, P. A., & Carleton, R. N. (2012). Intolerance of uncertainty, hypochondriacal concerns, obsessive-compulsive symptoms, and worry. *Journal of Nervous and Mental Disease, 200,* 208–213.

Boeninger, D. K., Shiraishi, R. W., Aldwin, C. M., & Spiro, A. (2009). Why do older men report lower stress ratings? Findings from the Normative Aging Study. *International Journal of Aging and Human Development, 2,* 149–170.

Boersma, G. J., Salton, S. R., Sprizer, P. M., Steele, C. T., & Carbone, D. L. (2012). Models and mechanisms of metabolic regulation: Genes, stress, and the HPA and HPG axes. *Hormone and Metabolic Research, 44* (8), 598–606.

Boeve, B. F. (2010). REM sleep disorder: Updated review of the core features, the REM sleep disorder-neurodegenerative disease association, evolving concepts, controversies, and future directions. *Annals of the New York Academy of Sciences, 1184,* 15–54.

Bogaert, A. F. (2000). Birth order and sexual orientation in a national probability sample. *Journal of Sex Research, 37,* 361–368.

Bohart, A. C., & Tallman, K. (2010). Clients: The neglected common factor in psychotherapy. In B. L. Duncan, S. D. Miller, B. E. Wampold, & M. A. Hubble (Eds.), *The heart and soul of change: Delivering what works in therapy* (2nd ed., pp. 83–111). Washington, DC: American Psychological Association.

Bohn, A., & Berntsen, D. (2011). The reminiscence bump reconsidered: Children's prospective life stories show a bump in young adulthood. *Psychological Science, 22,* 197–202.

Bolger, N., & Amarel, D. (2007). Effects of social support visibility on adjustment to stress: Experimental evidence. *Journal of Personality and Social Psychology, 92* (3), 458–475.

Bolhuis, J. J., Brown, G. R., Richardson, R. C., & Laland, K. N. (2011). Darwin in mind: New opportunities for evolutionary psychology. *PLoS Biology, 9* (7), e1001109.

Bolino, M. C., Klotz, A. C., Turnley, W. H., & Harvey, J. (2013). Exploring the dark side of organizational citizenship behavior. *Journal of Organizational Behavior, 34* (4), 542–559.

Bonath, B., Tyll, S., Budinger, E., Krauel, K., Hopf, J. M., & Noesselt, T. (2013). Task-demands and audio-visual stimulus configurations modulate neural activity in the human thalamus. *NeuroImage, 66,* 110–118.

Bond, R., & Smith, P. B. (1996). Culture and conformity: A metaanalysis of studies using Asch's (1952, 1956) line judgment task. *Psychological Bulletin, 119,* 111–137.

Bonfatti, J. F. (2005). Hope holds the key: Finding inspiration. *Schizophrenia Digest* (Summer), 31–34.

Bonhomme, B. K., & others. (2013). Subclinical delusional thinking predicts lateral temporal cortex responses during social reflection. *Social Cognitive and Affective Neuroscience.* (in press)

Bonney, C. R., & Sternberg, R. J. (2011). Teaching and learning to think critically. In R. E. Mayer & P. A. Alexander (Eds.), *Handbook of research on learning and instruction.* New York: Routledge.

Bono, G., McCullough, M. E., & Root, L. M. (2008). Forgiveness, feeling connected to others, and well-being: Two longitudinal studies. *Personality and Social Psychology Bulletin, 34,* 182–195.

Bono, J. E., Hooper, A. H., & Yoon, D. J. (2012). Impact of rater personality on transformational and transactional leadership ratings. *Leadership Quarterly, 23,* 132–145.

Booker, C. L., & Sacker, A. (2012). Psychological well-being and reactions to multiple unemployment events: Adaptation or sensitisation? *Journal of Epidemiology and Community Health, 66* (9), 832–838.

Boonen, K., & others. (2010). Identification and relative quantification of neuropeptides from the endocrine tissues. *Methods in Molecular Biology, 615,* 191–206.

Bornstein, M. H., Jager, J., & Steinberg, L. D. (2013). Adolescents, parents, friends/peers: A relationship model. In R. M. Lerner, M. A. Easterbrooks, J. Mistry, & I. B. Weiner (Eds.), *Handbook of psychology* (2nd ed., vol. 6). Hoboken, NJ: Wiley.

Bornstein, R. F. (2012). Rorschach score validation as a model for 21st century personality assessment. *Journal of Personality Assessment, 94,* 26–38.

Bornstein, R. F., Denckla, C. A., & Chung, W.-J. (2013). Psychodynamic models of personality. In H. A. Tennen, J. M. Suls, & I. B. Weiner (Eds.), *Handbook of psychology* (2nd ed., vol. 5). Hoboken, NJ: Wiley.

Boschen, M. J. (2012). Pregabalin: Dose-response relationship in generalized anxiety disorder. *Pharmacopsychiatry, 45,* 51–56.

Bouchard, S. M., Brown, T. G., & Nadeau, L. (2012). Decision-making capacities and affective reward anticipation in DWI recidivists compared to non-offenders: A preliminary study. *Accident: Analysis and Prevention, 45,* 580–587.

Bouchard, T. J., Jr., & Loehlin, J. C. (2001). Genes, evolution, and personality. *Behavior Genetics, 31,* 243–273.

Bouchard, T. J., Lykken, D. T., Tellegen, A., & McGue, M. (1996). Genes, drives, environment, and experience. In D. Lubinski & C. Benbow (Eds.), *Psychometrics and social issues concerning intellectual talent.* Baltimore: Johns Hopkins University Press.

Bourque, F., van der Ven, E., Fusar-Polil, P., & Malia, A. (2012). Immigration, social environment, and onset of psychotic disorders. *Current Pharmaceutical Design, 18,* 518–526.

Bow, J. N., Flens, J. R., & Gould, J. W. (2010). MMPI-2 and MCMI-III in forensic evaluations: A survey of psychologists. *Journal of Forensic Psychology Practice, 10,* 37–52.

Bowen, B., Privitera, M. R., & Bowie, V. (2011). Reducing workplace violence by creating healthy workplace environments. *Journal of Aggression, Conflict and Peace Research, 3,* 4.

Bower, J. E., Moskowitz, J. T., & Epel, E. (2009). Is benefit finding good for your health? Pathways linking positive life changes after stress and physical health outcomes. *Current Directions in Psychological Science, 18,* 337–341.

Bowlby, J. (1969). *Attachment and loss* (vol. 1). London: Hogarth.

Bowlby, J. (1989). *Secure and insecure attachment.* New York: Basic.

Bowling, N. A. (2010). Effects of job satisfaction and conscientiousness on extra-role behaviors. *Journal of Business and Psychology, 25,* 119–130.

Bowman, N. A. (2010). College diversity experiences and cognitive development: A meta-analysis. *Review of Educational Research, 80,* 4–33.

Boyd-Franklin, N., Cleek, E. N., Wofsky, M., & Mundy, B. (Eds.). (2013). *Therapy in the real world.* New York: Guilford.

Boysen, G. A., & VanBergen, A. (2013). A review of published research on adult dissociative identiy disorder: 2000–2010. *Journal of Nervous and Mental Disorders, 201* (1), 5–11.

Boywitt, C. D., & Meiser, T. (2012). The role of attention for context-context binding of intrinsic and extrinsic features. *Journal of Experimental Psychology: Learning, Memory, and Cognition, 38* (4),1099–1107.

Brabec, J., & others. (2011). Volume of the amygdala is reduced in patients with narcolepsy—A structural MRI study. *Neuroendocrinology Letters, 32,* 652–656.

Brackett, M. A., Rivers, S. E., & Salovey, P. (2011). Emotional intelligence: Implications for personal, social, academic, and workplace success. *Social and Personality Psychology Compass, 5,* 88–103.

Bradbury, C., Cassin, S. E., & Rector, N. A. (2011). Motor inhibition and cognitive flexibility in obsessive-compulsive disorder. *Psychiatry Research, 187* (1-2), 160–165.

Brakel, T. M., Dijkstra, A., & Buunk, A. P. (2012). Effects of the source of social comparison information on former cancer patients' quality of life. *British Journal of Health Psychology, 17,* 667–681.

Brandes, N., Tienson, H., Lindemann, A., Vitvitsky, V., Reichmann, D., Banerjee, R., & Jakob, U. (2013). Time line of redox events in aging postmitotic cells. *eLife.* doi: http://dx.doi.org/10.7554/eLife.00306.001

Brannick, M. T., & Levine, E. L. (2002). *Job analysis: Methods, research, and applications.* Thousand Oaks, CA: Sage.

Brannon, L. (1999). *Gender: Psychological perspectives* (2nd ed.). Boston: Allyn & Bacon.

Branscum, P., & Sharma, M. (2013). Comparing the utility of the theory of planned behavior between boys and girls for predicting snack food consumption: Implications for practice. *Health Promotion Practice.* (in press)

Bransford, J., & others. (2006). Learning theories and education: Toward a decade of synergy. In P. A. Alexander & P. H. Winne (Eds.), *Handbook of educational psychology* (2nd ed.). Mahwah, NJ: Erlbaum.

Branstetter, S. A., & Furman, W. (2013). Buffering effect of parental monitoring knowledge and parent–adolescent relationships on consequences of adolescent substance use. *Journal of Child and Family Studies, 22,* 192–198.

Bratini, L., Ampuero, M. C., & Miville, M. L. (2013). Latina gender roles. In M. L. Miville (Ed.), *Multicultural gender roles: Applications for mental health and education.* New York: Wiley.

Braucher, J., Cohen, D., & Lawless, R. M. (2012). Race, attorney influence, and bankruptcy chapter choice. *Journal of Empirical Legal Studies.* http://papers. ssrn.com/sol3/papers.cfm?abstract_id=1989039 (accessed May 17, 2013)

Braun, M. H., Lukowiak, K., Karnik, V., & Lukowiak, K. (2012). Differences in neuronal activity explain differences in memory forming abilities of different populations of *Lymnaea stagnalis. Neurobiology of Learning and Memory, 97,* 173–182.

Breaugh, J. A. (2013). Employee recruitment. *Annual Review of Psychology* (vol. 64). Palo Alto, CA: Annual Reviews.

Brehm, J. W. (2000). Reactance. In A. E. Kazdin (Ed.), *Encyclopedia of psychology* (vol. 7, pp. 10–12). Washington, DC: American Psychological Association.

Breland, K., & Breland, M. (1961). The misbehavior of organisms. *American Psychologist, 16,* 681–684.

Brendgen, M., Boivin, M., Vitaro, F., Bukowski, W. M., Dionne, G., Tremblay, R. E., & Perusse, D. (2008). Linkages between children's and their friends' social and physical aggression: Evidence for a gene-environment interaction? *Child Development, 79,* 13–29.

Brennan, T. J. (2013, January 29). Women in combat? Some marines react. *AtWarBlogs.* http://atwar.blogs.nytimes.com/2013/01/29/women-in-combat-some-marines-react/ (accessed May 2, 2013)

Brent, B. K., & others. (2013). Subclinical delusional thinking predicts lateral temporal cortex responses during social reflection. *Social Cognitive and Affective Neuroscience.* (in press)

Bretherton, I. (2012). Afterward. In K. H. Brisch, *Treating attachment disorders* (2nd ed.). New York: Guilford.

Brewer, J. B., Zuo, Z., Desmond, J. E., Glover, G. H., & Gabrieli, J. D. E. (1998). Making memories: Brain activity that predicts how well visual experience will be remembered. *Science, 281,* 1185–1187.

Brewer, N., Barnes, J., & Sauer, J. (2011). The effects of peripheral message cues on clinicians' judgments about clients' psychological status. *British Journal of Clinical Psychology, 50* (1), 67–83.

Brewer, N., & Wells, G. L. (2011). Eyewitness identification. *Current Directions in Psychological Science, 20,* 24–27.

Brewin, C. R., Andrews, B., Hejdenberg, J., & Stewart, L. (2012). Objective predictors of delayed-onset post-traumatic stress disorder occurring after military discharge. *Psychological Medicine, 42,* 2119–2126.

Brickman, P., & Campbell, D. T. (1971). Hedonic relativism and planning the good society. In M. H. Appley (Ed.), *Adaptation-level theory* (pp. 287–302). New York: Academic.

Bridge, D. J., Chiao, J. Y., & Paller, K. A. (2010). Emotional context at learning systematically biases memory for facial information. *Memory and Cognition, 38,* 125–133.

Bridge, J. A., & others. (2008). Suicide trends among youth aged 10 to 19 years in the United States, 1996–2005. *Journal of the American Medical Association, 300,* 1025–1026.

Bridgman, T. (2007). Review of the three faces of leadership: Manager, artist, priest. *Personnel Review, 36,* 494–496.

Brigham, J. C., Bennett, L. B., Meissner, C. A., & Mitchell, T. L. (2007). The influence of race on eyewitness memory. In R. C. L. Lindsay, D. F. Ross, J. D. Read, & M. P. Toglia (Eds.), *The handbook of eyewitness memory: Vol II.* Mahwah, NJ: Erlbaum.

Brink, S. (2001, May 7). Your brain on alcohol. *U.S. News & World Report, 130* (18), 50–57.

Briñol, P., & Petty, R. E. (2012). History of attitudes and persuasion research. In A. W. Kruglanski & W. Stroebe (Eds.), *Handbook of the history of social psychology.* New York: Psychology Press.

Brisch, K. H. (2012). *Treating attachment disorders* (2nd ed.). New York: Guilford.

British Psychological Society. (2011). *Response to the American Psychiatric Association: DSM-5 development.* http://apps.bps.org.uk/_publicationfiles/consultation-responses/DSM-5%202011%20-%20BPS%20response.pdf (accessed May 20, 2013)

Brito-Melo, G. E., & others. (2012). Increase in dopaminergic, but not serotoninergic, receptors in T-cells as a marker for schizophrenia severity. *Journal of Psychiatric Research, 46* (6), 738–742.

Broadbelt, K. G., & others. (2012). Brainstem deficiency of the 14-3-3 regulator of serotonin synthesis: A proteomics analysis in the sudden infant death syndrome. *Molecular and Cellular Proteomics.* doi: 10.1074/mcp.M111.009530

Broberg, D. J., & Bernstein, I. L. (1987). Candy as a scapegoat in the prevention of food aversions in children receiving chemotherapy. *Cancer, 60,* 2344–2347.

Brockmole, J. R., & Logie, R. H. (2013). Age-related change in visual working memory: A study of 55,753 participants aged 8–75. *Frontiers in Psychology, 4,* 1–5.

Brody, L. R. (1999). *Gender emotion and the family.* Cambridge, MA: Harvard University Press.

Brody, N. (2007). Does education influence intelligence? In P. C. Kyllonen, R. D. Roberts, & L. Stankov (Eds.), *Extending intelligence.* Mahwah, NJ: Erlbaum.

Brody, S., & Costa, R. M. (2009). Satisfaction (sexual, life, relationship, and mental health) is associated directly with penile-vaginal intercourse, but inversely with other sexual behavior frequencies. *Journal of Sexual Medicine, 6,* 1947–1954.

Broer, L., & others. (2013). Meta-analysis of telomere length in 19, 713 subjects reveals high heritability, stronger maternal inheritance, and a paternal age effect. *European Journal of Human Genetics.* doi: 10.1038/ejhg.2012.303.

Brohan, E., Eglie, R., Sartorius, N., & Thornicroft, G. (2010). Self-stigma, empowerment, and perceived discrimination among people with schizophrenia in 14 European countries: The GAMIAN-Europe study. *Schizophrenia Research, 122,* 232–238.

Brooker, R. J., Widmaier, E. P., Graham, L. E., & Stiling, P. D. (2010). *Biology* (2nd ed.). New York: McGraw-Hill.

Brooks, J. G., & Brooks, M. G. (2001). *In search of understanding: The case for the constructivist classroom.* Upper Saddle River, NJ: Prentice-Hall.

Brown, A. R., & others. (2011). Aversive, appetitive, and flavor avoidance responses in the presence of contextual cues. *Learning and Behavior, 39,* 95–103.

Brown, A. S. (2012). *The tip of the tongue state.* New York: Taylor & Francis.

Brown, C. L., & others. (2013). Social activity and cognitive functioning over time: A coordinated analysis of four longitudinal studies. *Journal of Aging Research.* (in press)

Brown, D. (2007). Evidence-based hypnotherapy for asthma: A critical review. *International Journal of Clinical and Experimental Hypnosis, 55,* 220–249.

Brown, D. (2013). Morphological typology. In J. J. Song (Ed.), *The Oxford handbook of linguistic typology.* New York: Oxford University Press.

Brown, G. D. A., & Lewandowsky, S. (2010). Forgetting in memory models: Arguments against trace theory and consolidation failure. In S. D. Sala (Ed.), *Forgetting.* New York: Psychology Press.

Brown, K. G., & Sitzmann, T. (2010). Training and employee development for improved performance. In S. Zedeck (Ed.), *APA handbook of industrial and organizational psychology.* Washington, DC: American Psychological Association.

Brown, P., & Tierney, C. (2011). Media role in violence and the dynamics of bullying. *Pediatric Reviews, 32,* 453–454.

Brown, P. L., & Jenkins, H. M. (2009). On the law of effect. In D. Shanks (Ed.), *Psychology of learning.* Thousand Oaks, CA: Sage.

Brown, R. (1973). *A first language: The early stages.* Cambridge, MA: Harvard University Press.

Brown, R. E., & others. (2012). Control of sleep and wakefulness. *Physiological Reviews, 92,* 1087–1187.

Brown, S. D., Lent, R. W., Telander, K., & Tramayne, S. (2011). Social cognitive career theory, conscientiousness, and work performance: A meta-analytic path analysis. *Journal of Vocational Behavior, 79,* 81–90.

Brown, S. L., Nesse, R. N., Vinokur, A. D., & Smith, D. M. (2003). Providing social support may be more beneficial than receiving it: Results from a prospective study of mortality. *Psychological Science, 14,* 320–327.

Brüchmiller, K., Margraf, J., & Schneider, S. (2012). Is ADHD diagnosed in accord with diagnostic criteria? Overdiagnosis and influence of client gender on diagnosis. *Journal of Consulting and Clinical Psychology, 80,* 128–138.

Bruck, M., & Ceci, S. J. (2012). Forensic developmental psychology in the courtroom. In D. Faust & M. Ziskin (Eds.), *Coping with psychiatric and psychological testimony.* New York: Cambridge University Press.

Brug, J., Conner, M., Harré, N., Kremers, S., McKellar, S., & Whitelaw, S. (2004). The transtheoretical model and stages of change: A critique. Observations by five commentators on the paper by Adams, J. and White, M. (2004) Why don't stage-based activity promotion interventions work? *Health Education Research, 20,* 244–258.

Brumberg, J. S., & Guenther, F. H. (2010). Development of speech prostheses: Current status and recent advances. *Expert Review of Medical Devices, 7,* 667–679.

Brummett, B. H., Boyle, S. H., Kuhn, C. M., Siegler, I. C., & Williams, R. B. (2008). Associations among central nervous system serotonergic function and neuroticism are moderated by gender. *Biological Psychology, 78,* 200–203.

Brunelin, J., Fecteau, S., & Suad-Chagny, M. F. (2013). Abnormal striatal dopamine transmission in schizophrenia. *Current Medicinal Chemistry.* (in press)

Bruning, R. H., Schraw, G. J., Norby, M. M., & Ronning, R. R. (2004). *Cognitive psychology and instruction* (4th ed.). Upper Saddle River, NJ: Prentice-Hall.

Brunstein, J. (1993). Personal goals and subjective well-being: A longitudinal study. *Journal of Personality and Social Psychology, 65,* 1061–1070.

Brunstein, J., & Maier, G. W. (2005). Implicit and self-attributed motives to achieve: Two separate but interacting needs. *Journal of Personality and Social Psychology, 89,* 205–222.

Bryan, L. K., & Vinchur, A. J. (2013). Industrial-organizational psychology. In D. K. Freedheim & I. B. Weiner (Eds.), *Handbook of psychology, 2nd ed., Vol. 1.* (pp. 407–428). Hoboken, NJ: Wiley.

Bryan, S. M. (2012, January 28). Wolves' senses tapped to keep them clear of cattle. *Associated Press.* http://bangordailynews.com/2012/01/28/outdoors/wolves-senses-tapped-to-keep-them-clear-of-cattle/ (accessed April 3, 2013)

Bryant, J. B. (2012). Pragmatic development. In E. L. Bavin (Ed.), *The Cambridge handbook of child language.* New York: Cambridge University Press.

Bryant-Davis, T., Ullman, S. E., Tsong, Y., Tillman, S., & Smith, K. (2010). Struggling to survive: Sexual assault, poverty, and mental health outcomes of African American women. *American Journal of Orthopsychiatry, 80,* 61–70.

Bucherelli, C., Baldi, E., Mariottini, C., Passani, M. B., & Blandina, P. (2006). Aversive memory reactivation engages in the amygdala only some neurotransmitters involved in consolidation. *Learning and Memory, 13,* 426–430.

Buchser, W. J., Laskow, T. C., Pavlik, P. J., Lin, H. M., & Lotze, M. T. (2012). Cell-mediated autophagy promotes cancer cell survival. *Cancer Research, 72* (12), 1–10.

Bueno-Junior, L. S., & others. (2012). Muscarinic and icotinic modulation of thalamo-prefrontal cortex synaptic plasticity in vivo. *PLoS One, 7* (10), e47484.

Buhi, E. R., Goodson, P., Neilands, T. B., & Blunt, H. (2011). Adolescent sexual abstinence: A test of an integrative theoretical framework. *Health Education and Behavior, 38,* 63–79.

Bui, D. C., Maddox, G. B., & Balota, D. A. (2013). The roles of working memeory and intervening task difficulty in determining the benefits of repetition. *Psychonomic Bulletin and Review, 20* (2), 341–347.

Buján, A., Galdo-Álvarez, S., Lindín, M., & Díaz, F. (2012). An event-related potentials study of face naming: Evidence of phonological retrieval deficit in the tip-of-the-tongue state. *Psychophysiology, 49,* 980–990.

Bukowski, W. M., Brendgen, M., & Vitaro, F. (2007). Peers and socialization: Effects on externalizing and internalizing problems. In J. E. Grusec & P. D. Hastings (Eds.), *Handbook of socialization: Theory and research* (pp. 355–381). New York: Guilford.

Bulf, H., & Valenza, E. (2013). Object-based visual attention in 8-month-old infants: Evidence from an eye-tracking study. *Developmental Psychology.* doi: 10.1037/a0031310

Bullock, M. (2013). International psychology. In D. K. Freedheim & I. B. Weiner (Eds.), *Handbook of psychology, 2nd ed., Vol. 1.* (pp. 562–596). Hoboken, NJ: Wiley.

Burger, J. (2009). Replicating Milgram: Would people still obey today? *American Psychologist, 64,* 1–11.

Burks, D. J., & Kobus, A. M. (2012). The legacy of altruism in health care: The promotion of empathy, prosociality, and humanism. *Medical Education, 46,* 317–325.

Burnette, J. L., McCullough, M. E., Van Tongeren, D. R., & Davis, D. E. (2012). Forgiveness results from integrating information about relationship value and exploitation risk. *Personality and Social Psychology Bulletin, 38,* 345–465.

Burstein, M., & others. (2012). Specific phobia among U.S. adolescents: Phenomenology and typology. *Depression and Anxiety, 29* (12), 1072–1082.

Burton, C. M., & King, L. A. (2004). The health benefits of writing about peak experiences. *Journal of Research in Personality, 38,* 150–163.

Burton, C. M., & King, L. A. (2008). The effects of (very) brief writing on health: The 2-minute miracle. *British Journal of Health Psychology, 13,* 9–14.

Burton, C. M., & King, L. A. (2009). The benefits of writing about positive experiences: Applying the broaden and build model. *Psychology and Health, 24,* 867–879.

Buscemi, L., & Turchi, C. (2011). An overview of genetic susceptibility to alcoholism. *Medicine, Science, and the Law, 51,* Suppl. 1, S2–S6.

Busch, H., & Hofer, J. (2012). Self-regulation and milestones of adult development: Intimacy generativity. *Developmental Psychology, 48,* 282–293.

Busch, S. H., Frank, R. G., Leslie, D. L., Martin, A., Rosenheck, R. A., Martin, E. G., & Barry, C. L. (2010). Antidepressants and suicide risk: How did specific information in FDA safety warnings affect treatment patterns. *Psychiatric Services, 61,* 11–16.

Busch, S. H., Golberstein, E., & Meara, E. (2011). *The FDA and ABCs: The unintended consequences of antidepressant warnings on human capital.* Working Paper 17426. Cambridge, MA: National Bureau of Economic Research. www.nber.org/papers/w17426 (accessed June 17, 2013)

Buschkuehl, M., Jaeggi, S. M., & Jonides, J. (2012). Neuronal effects following working memory training. *Developmental Cognitive Neuroscience, 2,* Suppl. 1, S167–S179.

Bushman, L., & Huesmann, L. R. (2012). Effects of media violence on aggression. In D. G. Singer & J. L. Singer (Eds.), *Handbook of children and the media* (2nd ed.). Thousand Oaks, CA: Sage.

Buss, D. M. (2012). *Evolutionary psychology* (4th ed.). Upper Saddle River, NJ: Pearson.

Bussey, K., & Bandura, A. (2004). Social cognitive theory of gender development and functioning. In A. H. Eagly, A. Beall, & R. Sternberg (Eds.), *The psychology of gender* (2nd ed., pp. 92–119). New York: Guilford.

Bussy, G., Charrin, E., Brun, A., Curi, A., & des Portes, V. (2011). Implicit procedural learning in fragile X and Down syndrome. *Journal of Intellectual Disabilities Research, 55,* 521–528.

Butcher, J. N., Beutler, L. E., Harwood, T. M., & Blau, K. (2011). The MMPI-2. In T. M. Harwood, L. E. Beutler, & G. Groth-Marnat (Eds.), *Integrative assessment of adult personality* (3rd ed.). New York: Guilford.

Butcher, K. R., & Kintsch, W. (2013). Text comprehension and discourse processing. In A. F. Healy, R. W. Proctor, & I. B. Weiner (Eds.), *Handbook of psychology, 2nd ed., Vol. 4.* (pp. 578–604). Hoboken, NJ: Wiley.

Butler, A. C., Chapman, J. E., Forman, E. M., & Beck, A. T. (2006). The empirical status of cognitive-behavioral therapy: A review of meta-analyses. *Clinical Psychology Review, 26,* 17–31.

Butovskaya, M. L., & others. (2012). Aggression, digit ratio, and variation in the androgen receptor, serotonin transporter, and dopamine D4 receptor genes in Africa foragers: The Hadza. *Behavior Genetics, 42* (4), 647–462.

Buttenschøn, H. N., & others. (2011). The norepinephrine transporter gene is a candidate gene for panic disorder. *Journal of Neural Transmission, 118,* 969–976.

Buttermore, E. D., Thaxton, C. L., & Bhat, M. A. (2013). Organization and maintenance of molecular domains in myelinated axons. *Journal of Neuroscience Research, 91* (5), 603–622.

Buunk, B. P., & Van Yperen, N. W. (1991). Referential comparisons, relational comparisons, and exchange orientation: Their relation to marital satisfaction. *Personality and Social Psychology Bulletin, 17,* 709–717.

Byard, R. W., & Krous, H. F. (2004). Research and sudden infant death syndrome: Definitions, diagnostic difficulties, and discrepancies. *Journal of Paediatrics and Child Health, 40,* 419–421.

Byne, W., Bradley, S. J., Coleman, E., Eyler, A. E., Green, R., Mevielle, E. J., Meyer-Bahlburg, H. F. L., Pleak, R. R., & Tompkins, D. A. (2012). Report of the American Psychiatric Association Task Force on the Treatment of Gender Identity Disorder. *Archives of Sexual Behavior, 41,* 759–796.

Byrne, R. W., Hobaiter, C., & Klailova, M. (2011). Local traditions in gorilla manual skill: Evidence for observational learning of behavioral organization. *Animal Cognition, 14,* 683–693.

Byrne, S., Barry, D., & Petry, N. M. (2012). Predictors of weight loss success: Exercise vs. dietary self-efficacy and treatment attendance. *Appetite, 58,* 695–698.

Byrnes, J. P. (2012). How neuroscience contributes to our understanding of learning and development in typically developing and special needs students. In K. R. Harris, S. Graham, & T. Urdan (Eds.), *APA educational psychology handbook.* Washington, DC: American Psychological Association.

C

Cabaniss, D. L., Cherry, S., Douglas, C. J., Graver, R., & Schwartz, A. R. (2013). *Psychodynamic formulation.* New York: Wiley.

Cabeza, R. (2002). Hemispheric asymmetry reduction in older adults: The HAROLD model. *Psychology and Aging, 17,* 85–100.

Cabeza, R., Nyberg, L., & Park, D. (Eds.). (2005). *Cognitive neuroscience of aging.* New York: Oxford University Press.

Cahill, K., Stead, L. F., & Lancaster, T. (2012). Nicotine receptor partial agonists for smoking cessation. *Cochrane Database of Systematic Reviews, 4,* CD006103.

Caillouet, B. A., Boccaccini, M. T., Varela, J. G., Davis, R. D., & Rostow, C. D. (2010). Predictive validity of the MMPI-2 PSY-5 scales and facets for law enforcement officer employment outcomes. *Criminal Justice and Behavior, 37,* 217–238.

Caldwell, S. (2013). *Statistics unplugged* (4th ed.). Boston: Cengage.

Cale, E. M., & Lilienfeld, S. O. (2002). Sex differences in psychopathy and antisocial personality disorder: A review and integration. *Clinical Psychology Review, 22,* 1179–1207.

Calogero, R. M. (2013). Objects don't object: Evidence that self-objectification disrupts women's social activism. *Psychological Science, 24* (3), 312–318.

Calvo-Merino, B., Grezes, J., Glaser, D. E., Passingham, R. E., & Haggard, P. (2006). Seeing or doing? Influence of visual and motor familiarity inaction observation. *Current Biology, 16,* 1905–1910.

Camenisch, D. R., & Hilt, R. J. (2013). SSRIs for anxiety and depression in children. *Pediatric Annals, 42,* 62–66.

Cameron, J., Banko, K. M., & Pierce, W. D. (2001). Pervasive negative effects of rewards on intrinsic motivation: The myth continues. *Behavior Analyst, 24,* 1–44.

Cameron, J., & Pierce, W. D. (2002). *Rewards and intrinsic motivation: Resolving the controversy.* Westport, CT: Bergin & Garvey.

Cameron, J., Pierce, W. D., Banko, K. M., & Gear, A. (2005). Achievement-based rewards and intrinsic motivation: A test of cognitive mediators. *Journal of Educational Psychology, 97,* 641–655.

Cameron, K. S. (2003). Organizational virtuousness and performance. In K. S. Cameron, J. E. Dutton, & R. E. Quinn (Eds.), *Positive organizational scholarship: Foundations of a new discipline* (pp. 48–65). San Francisco: Berrett-Koehler.

Cameron, K. S. (2005). Organizational downsizing. In N. Nicholson, P. G. Audia, & M. M. Pilluta (Eds.), *The Blackwell encyclopedia of management.* Malden, MA: Blackwell.

Campbell, B. C., & Wang, S.-H. (2012). Familial linkage between neuropsychiatric disorders and intellectual interests. *PLoS One, 7* (1), e30405.

Campbell, J. D., Yoon, D. P., & Johnstone, B. (2010). Determining relationships between physical health and spiritual experience, religious practice, and congregational support in a heterogeneous sample. *Journal of Religion and Health, 49,* 3–17.

Campbell, L., Campbell, B., & Dickinson, D. (2004). *Teaching and learning through multiple intelligences.* Boston: Allyn & Bacon.

Canli, T. (2008a). Toward a neurogenetic theory of neuroticism. In D. W. Pfaff & B. L. Kieffer (Eds.), *Molecular and biophysical mechanisms of arousal, alertness, and attention.* (pp. 153–174). Malden, MA: Blackwell.

Canli, T. (2008b). Toward a "molecular psychology" of personality. In O. P. John, R. W. Robins, & L. A. Pervin (Eds.), *Handbook of personality theory and research* (3rd ed., pp. 311–327). New York: Guilford.

Cannon, M. J., Dominique, Y., O'Leary, L. A., Suiezek, J. F., & Floyd, R. L. (2012). Characteristics and behaviors of mothers who have a child with fetal alcohol syndrome. *Neurotoxicology and Teratology, 34,* 90–95.

Cannon, W. B. (1927). The James-Lange theory of emotions: A critical examination and an alternative theory. *American Journal of Psychology, 39,* 106–124.

Cannon, W. B., & Washburn, A. L. (1912). An explanation of hunger, *American Journal of Physiology, 29,* 441–454.

Canton-Cortes, D., Canton, J., & Cortes, M. R. (2012). The interactive effect of blame attribution with characteristics of child sexual abuse on posttraumatic stress disorder. *Journal of Nervous and Mental Disease, 200,* 329–335.

Cantor, J. M., & Blanchard, T. (2012). White matter volumes in pedophiles, hebephiles, and teleiophiles. *Archives of Sexual Behavior, 41,* 749–752.

Cantor, J. M., Kabani, N., Christensen, B. K., Zipursky, R. B., Barbaree, H. E., Dickey, R., Klassen, P. E., Mikulis, D. J., Kuban, M. E., Blak, T., Richards, B. A., Hanratty, M. K., & Blanchard, R. (2008). Cerebral white matter deficiencies in pedophilic men. *Journal of Psychiatric Research, 42,* 167–183.

Cantor, N., & Sanderson, C. A. (1999). Life task participation and well-being: The importance of taking part in daily life. In D. Kahneman, E. Diener, & N. Schwarz (Eds.), *Well-being: The foundations of hedonic psychology* (pp. 230–243). New York: Russell Sage Foundation.

Capaldi, E. J., & Martins, A. P. G. (2013). Animal cognition. In A. F. Healy, R. W. Proctor, & I. B. Weiner (Eds.), *Handbook of psychology* (2nd ed., vol. 4). Hoboken, NJ: Wiley.

Capasso, A., Putrella, C., & Milano, W. (2009). Recent clinical aspects of eating disorders. *Reviews on Recent Clinical Trials, 4,* 63–69.

Caplan, J. B., & Caplan, P. J. (2005). The perseverative search for sex differences in mathematics ability. In A. M. Gallagher & J. C. Kaufman (Eds.), *Gender differences in mathematics* (pp. 25–47). Cambridge, U.K.: Cambridge University Press.

Caprara, G. V., Alessandri, G., Di Giunta, L., Panerai, L., & Eisenberg, N. (2010). The contribution of agreeableness and self-efficacy beliefs to prosociality. *European Journal of Personality, 24,* 36–55.

Caprara, G. V., Fagnani, C., Alessandri, G., Steca, P., Gigantesco, A., Sforza, L., Cavalli, L., & Stazi, M. A. (2009). Human optimal functioning: The genetics of positive orientation towards self, life, and the future. *Behavior Genetics, 39,* 277–284.

Cardinali, D. P., Srinivasan, V., Brzezinski, A., & Brown, G. M. (2012). Melatonin and its analogs in insomnia and depression. *Journal of Pineal Research, 52* (4), 365–375.

Cardno, A. G., & Gottesman, I. I. (2000). Twin studies of schizophrenia: From bow-and-arrow concordances to Star Wars Mx and functional genomics. *American Journal of Medical Genetics, 97,* 12–17.

Carey, B. (2011a, November 25). Finding purpose after living with delusion. *New York Times,* A1.

Carey, B. (2011b, January 6). Journal's paper on ESP expected to prompt outrage. *New York Times,* A1.

Carey, M. P., Scott-Sheldon, L. A. J., & Vanable, P. A. (2013). HIV/AIDS. In A. M. Nezu, C. Maguth Nezu, P. A. Geller, & I. B. Weiner (Eds.), *Handbook of psychology* (2nd ed., vol. 9). Hoboken, NJ: Wiley.

Caricati, L. (2012). Upward and downward social comparison in the intermediate-status group: The role of social stratification stability. *British Journal of Social Psychology, 152* (6), 713–726.

Carlo, G., Knight, G. P., McGinley, M., & Hayes, R. (2011). The roles of parental inductions, moral emotions, and moral cognitions in prosocial tendencies among Mexican American and European American early adolescents. *Journal of Early Adolescence, 31,* 757–781.

Carlson, S. M., & White, R. (2011). Unpublished research, Institute of Child Development, University of Minnesota, Minneapolis.

Carlson, S. M., Zelazo, P. D., & Faja, S. (2013). Executive function. In P. D. Zelazo (Ed.), *The Oxford handbook of developmental psychology, Vol. 1.* (pp. 706–743). New York: Oxford University Press.

Carlston, D. E. (2013). On the nature of social cognition: My defining moment. In D. E. Carlson (Ed.), *The Oxford handbook of social cognition.* New York: Oxford University Press.

Carmona, J. E., Holland, A. K., & Harrison, D. W. (2009). Extending the functional cerebral theory of emotion to the vestibular modality: A systematic and integrative approach. *Psychological Bulletin, 135,* 286–302.

Carnahan, T., & McFarland, S. (2007). Revisiting the Stanford prison experiment: Could participant self-selection have led to the cruelty? *Personality and Social Psychology Bulletin, 33,* 603–614.

Carnell, S., Gibson, C., Benson, L., Ochner, C. N., & Geliebter, A. (2012). Neuroimaging and obesity: Current knowledge and future directions. *Obesity Reviews, 13,* 43–56.

Carney, D. R., Colvin, C. R., & Hall, J. A. (2007). A thin slice perspective on the accuracy of first impressions. *Journal of Research in Personality, 41,* 1054–1072.

Carothers, B. J., & Reis, H. T. (2013). Men and women are from Earth: Examining the latent structure of gender. *Journal of Personality and Social Psychology, 104* (2), 385–407.

Carr, R., & Peebles, R. (2012). Developmental considerations of media exposure risk for eating disorders. In J. Lock (Ed.), *The Oxford handbook of child and adolescent eating disorders: Developmental perspectives.* New York: Oxford University Press.

Carrard, I., der Linden, M. V., & Golay, A. (2012). Comparison of obese and nonobese individuals with binge eating disorder: Delicate boundary between binge eating disorder and non-purging bulimia nervosa. *European Eating Disorders Review.* doi: 10.1002/erv.2174.

Carskadon, M. A. (2006, March). *Too little, too late: Sleep bioregulatory processes across adolescence.* Paper presented at the meeting of the Society for Research on Adolescence, San Francisco.

Carskadon, M. A. (2011a). Sleep in adolescents: The perfect storm. *Pediatric Clinics of North America, 58,* 637–647.

Carskadon, M. A. (2011b). Sleep's effects on cognition and learning in adolescence. *Progress in Brain Research, 190,* 137–143.

Carson, C. M. (2005). A historical view of Douglas McGregor's Theory Y. *Management Decision, 43,* 450–460.

Carson, R. C., Butcher, J. N., & Mineka, S. (1996). *Abnormal psychology and life* (10th ed.). New York: HarperCollins.

Carstensen, L. L. (2006). The influence of a sense of time on human development. *Science, 312,* 1913–1915.

Carstensen, L. L. (2008, May). *Long life in the twenty-first century.* Paper presented at the meeting of the Association of Psychological Science, Chicago.

Carstensen, L. L. (2009). *A long bright future: An action plan for a lifetime of happiness, health, and financial security.* New York: Broadway Books.

Carstensen, L. L. (2011). *A long bright future: Happiness, health, and financial security in an age of increased longevity.* New York: Broadway Books.

Carstensen, L. L., & others. (2011). Emotional experience improves with age: Evidence based on over 10 years of sampling. *Psychology and Aging, 26,* 21–33.

Carver, C. S., & Connor-Smith, J. (2010). Personality and coping. *Annual Review of Psychology* (vol. 61). (pp. 679–704). Palo Alto, CA: Annual Reviews.

Carver, C. S., & Harmon-Jones, E. (2009). Anger is an approach-related affect: Evidence and implications. *Psychological Bulletin, 135,* 183–204.

Carver, C. S., & Scheier, M. F. (2009). Optimism. In M. R. Levy & R. H. Hoyle (Eds), *Handbook of individual differences in social behavior* (pp. 330–342). New York: Guilford.

Carver, C. S., & Scheier, M. F. (2013). Self-regulatory perspectives on personality. In H. A. Tennen, J. M. Suls, & I. B. Weiner (Eds.), *Handbook of psychology, 2nd ed., Vol. 5.* (pp. 119–140). Hoboken, NJ: Wiley.

Carver, C. S., Scheier, M. F., & Segerstrom, S. C. (2010). Optimism. *Clinical Psychology Review, 30,* 879–889.

Casalin, S., Luyten, P., Vliegen, N., & Meurs, P. (2012). The structure and stability of temperament from infancy to toddlerhood: a one-year prospective study. *Infant Behavior and Development, 35* (1), 94–108.

Cascio, W. F., & Aguinis, H. (2011). *Applied psychology in human resource management* (7th ed.). Upper Saddle River, NJ: Prentice-Hall.

Case, R. B., Moss, A. J., Case, N., McDermott, M., & Eberly, S. (1992). Living alone after myocardial infarction. Impact on prognosis. *Journal of the American Medical Association, 267,* 515–519.

Caserta, M., Lund, D., Utz, R., & de Vries, B. (2009). Stress-related growth among the recently bereaved. *Aging & Mental Health, 13,* 463–476.

Casey, B. J., & others. (2011). Behavioral and neural correlates of delay of gratification 40 years later. *Proceedings of the National Academy of Sciences USA, 108,* 14998–15003.

Caspi, A., McClay, J., Moffitt, T. E., Mill, J., Martin, J., Craig, I. W., Taylor, A., & Poulton, R. (2002). Role of genotype in the cycle of violence in maltreated children. *Science, 297,* 851–854.

Cassidy, J., Woodhouse, S. S., Sherman, L. J., Stupica, B., & Lejuez, C. W. (2011). Enhancing infant attachment security: An examination of treatment efficacy and differential susceptibility. *Development and Psychopathology, 23,* 131–148.

Castel, A. D., Vendetti, M., & Holyoak, K. J. (2012). Fire drill: Inattentional blindness and amnesia for the location of fire extinguishers. *Attention, Perception, and Psychophysics, 74,* 1391–1396.

Cathers-Schiffman, T. A., & Thompson, M. S. (2007). Assessment of English- and Spanish-speaking students with the WISC-III and Leiter-R. *Journal of Psychoeducational Assessment, 25,* 41–52.

Cauller, L. (2001, May). *Review of Santrock, Psychology* (7th ed.). New York: McGraw-Hill.

Cavallaro, F. I., & others. (2010). Hypnotizability-related EEG alpha and theta activities during visual and somesthetic imageries. *Neuroscience Letters, 470,* 13–18.

Cavina-Pratesi, C., Kentridge, R. W., Heywood, C. A., & Milner, A. D. (2010). Separate channels for processing form, texture, and color: Evidence from fMRI adaptation and visual object agnosia. *Cerebral Cortex, 20* (10), 2319–2332.

Caylak, E. (2012). Biochemical and genetic analyses of childhood attention deficit/hyperactivity disorder. *American Journal of Medical Genetics B: Neuropsychiatric Genetics, 159B*, 613–627.

CBS News. (2009, February 11). Ambien may prompt sleep-eating. *CBS News*. www.cbsnews.com/8301-500166_162-1404632.html (accessed February 25, 2013)

Center for Family and Demographic Research. (2002). *Ohio population news: Marriage in U.S. and Ohio*. Bowling Green, Ohio: Author.

Centers for Disease Control and Prevention (CDC). (2009). *Obesity: Halting the epidemic by making health easier*. Atlanta: Author.

Centers for Disease Control and Prevention (CDC). (2012a). Suicide: Facts at a glance. *Centers for Disease Control and Prevention*. www.cdc.gov/violenceprevention/pdf/suicide-datasheet-a.PDF (accessed May 30, 2013)

Centers for Disease Control and Prevention (CDC). (2012b). *Overweight and obesity*. Atlanta: Author.

Centers for Disease Control and Prevention (CDC). (2012c). Smoking and tobacco use. *Centers for Disease Control and Prevention*. www.cdc.gov/tobacco/data_statistics/fact_sheets/health_effects/effects_cig_smoking/ (accessed February 26, 2013)

Centers for Disease Control and Prevention (CDC). (2013a). Adult cigarette smoking in the United States: Current estimate. *Centers for Disease Control and Prevention*. www.cdc.gov/tobacco/data_statistics/fact_sheets/adult_data/cig_smoking/ (accessed June 20, 2013)

Centers for Disease Control and Prevention (CDC). (2013b). CDC's HIV prevention progress in the United States. *Centers for Disease Control and Prevention*. www.cdc.gov/hiv/dhap/prevention/index.html (accessed June 12, 2013)

Cervinka, R., Röderer, K., & Hefler, E. (2012). Are nature lovers happy? On various indicators of well-being and connectedness with nature. *Journal of Health Psychology, 17*, 379–388.

Cervone, D., & Pervin, L. A. (2013). Personality (12th ed.). New York: Wiley.

Chabardès, S., Polosan, M., Krack, P., Bastin, J., Krainik, A., David, O., Bougerol, T., & Benabid, A. L. (2012). Deep brain stimulation for obsessive-compulsive disorder: Subthalamic nucleus target. *World Neurosurgery*. doi: 10.1016/j.wneu.2012.03.010

Chabris, C., & Simons, D. (2010). *The invisible gorilla, and other ways our intuitions deceive us*. New York: Crown.

Chabris, C. F., Hebert, B. M., Benjamin, D. J., Beauchamp, J., Cesarini, D., van der Loos, M., Johannesson, M., Magnusson, P. K. E., Lichtenstein, P., Atwood, C. S., Freese, J., Hauser, T. S., Hauser, R. M., Christakis, N., & Laibson, D. (2012). Most reported genetic associations with general intelligence are probably false positives. *Psychological Science, 23*, 1314–1323.

Chae, Y., Goodman, G. S., Bederian-Gardner, D., & Lindsay, A. (2011). Methodological issues and practical strategies in research on child maltreatment victims' abilities and experiences as witnesses. *Journal of Child Abuse and Neglect, 35* (4), 240–248.

Chakraborty, S., Kaushik, D. K., Gupta, M., & Basu, A. (2010). Inflammasome signaling at the heart of central nervous system pathology. *Journal of Neuroscience Research, 88*, 1615–1631.

Chalabaev, A., Sarrazin, P., Fontayne, P., Boiché, J., & Clément-Guillotin, C. (2013). The influence of sex stereotypes and gender roles on participation and performance in sport and exercise: Review and future directions. *Psychology of Sport and Exercise*. (in press)

Chambless, D. L. (2002). Beware the dodo bird: The dangers of overgeneralization. *Clinical Psychology: Science and Practice, 9*, 13–16.

Chambon, V., Baudouin, J., & Franck, N. (2006). The role of configural information in facial emotion recognition in schizophrenia. *Neuropsychologia, 44*, 2437–2444.

Chan, R. W., Raboy, B., & Patterson, C. J. (1998). Psychosocial adjustment among children conceived via donor insemination by lesbian and heterosexual mothers. *Child Development, 69*, 326–332.

Chance, P. (2014). *Learning and behavior* (7th ed.). Boston: Cengage.

Chance, Z., Norton, M. I., Gino, F., & Ariely, D. (2011). Temporal view of the costs and benefits of self-deception. *Proceedings of the National Academy of Sciences USA, 108*, 15655–15659.

Chang, A. C. (2012). Primary prevention of sudden cardiac death of the young athlete: The controversy about the screening electrocardiogram and its innovative artificial intelligence solution. *Pediatric Cardiology, 33* (3), 428–433.

Chang, Y. K., Liu, S., Yu, H. H., & Lee, Y. H. (2012). Effect of acute exercise on executive function in children with attention deficit hyperactivity disorder. *Archives of Clinical Neuropsychology, 27*, 225–237.

Chang, Z., Lichtenstein, P., & Larsson, H. (2012). The effects of childhood ADHD symptoms on early-onset substance use: A Swedish twin study. *Journal of Abnormal Child Psychology, 40*, 425–435.

Chapeton, J., Fares, T., Lasota, D., & Steppanyants, A. (2013). Efficient associative memory storage in cortical circuits of inhibitory and excitatory neurons, *Proceedings of the National Academy of Sciences USA*. (in press)

Charbonneau, D., Barling, J., & Kelloway, E. K. (2001). Transformational leadership behaviors, upward trust, and satisfaction in self-managed work teams. *Organizational Development Journal, 17*, 13–28.

Charles, S. T., & Carstensen, L. L. (2010). Social and emotional aging. *Annual Review of Psychology* (vol. 61). (pp. 383–409). Palo Alto, CA: Annual Reviews.

Charney, E. (2012). Behavior genetics and postgenomics. *Behavioral and Brain Sciences, 35*, 331–358.

Chaudhuri, S. E., & Merfeld, D. M. (2013). Signal detection theory and vestibular perception: III. Estimating unbiased fit parameters for psychometric functions. *Experimental Brain Research, 225*, 133–146.

Chauvette, S., Seigneur, J., & Timofeev, I. (2012). Sleep oscillations in the thalamocortical system induce long-term neuronal plasticity. *Neuron, 75*, 1105–1113.

Chaves, J. F. (2000). Hypnosis. In A. Kazdin (Ed.), *Encyclopedia of psychology*. Washington, DC, & New York: American Psychological Association & Oxford University Press.

Chen, E., & Miller, G. E. (2013). Socioeconomic status and health: Mediating and moderating factors. *Annual Review of Clinical Psychology* (vol. 9). Palo Alto, CA: Annual Reviews.

Chen, P., & Jacobson, K. C. (2012). Developmental trajectories of substance use from early adolescence to young adulthood: Gender and racial/ethnic differences. *Journal of Adolescent Health, 50*, 154–163.

Cheng, C. (2005). Processes underlying gender-role flexibility: Do androgynous individuals know more or know how to cope? *Journal of Personality, 73*, 645–673.

Cheng, C. M., & Huang, C. L. (2011). Processes of conscious and unconscious memory: Evidence from current research on dissociation of memories within a test. *American Journal of Psychology, 124*, 421–440.

Chess, S., & Thomas, A. (1977). Temperamental individuality from childhood to adolescence. *Journal of Child Psychiatry, 16*, 218–226.

Chess, S., & Thomas, A. (1996). *Temperament: Theory and practice*. Philadelphia: Brunner/Mazel.

Chica, A. B., & Bartolomeo, P. (2012). Attentional routes to conscious perception. *Frontiers in Psychology, 3*, 1.

Chida, Y., & Steptoe, A. (2008). Positive psychological well-being and mortality: A quantitative review of prospective observational studies. *Psychosomatic Medicine, 70*, 741–756.

Chiesa, F., Primi, C., & Morsanyi, K. (2011). Developmental changes in probabilistic reasoning: The role of cognitive capacity, instructions, thinking styles, and relevant knowledge. *Thinking and Reasoning, 17*, 315–350.

Chiesa, M., & Hobbs, S. (2008). Making sense of social research: How useful is the Hawthorne effect? *European Journal of Social Psychology, 38*, 67–74.

Chiou, R., Stelter, M., & Rich, A. N. (2013). Beyond color perception: Auditory-visual synaesthesia induces experiences of geometric objects in specific locations. *Cortex*. (in press)

Chivers, M. L., Seto, M. C., & Blanchard, R. (2007). Gender and sexual orientation differences in sexual response to sexual activities versus gender of actors in sexual films. *Journal of Personality and Social Psychology, 93*, 1108–1121.

Cho, D., & Campana, D. (2009). Expansion and activation of natural killer cells for cancer immunotherapy. *Korean Journal of Laboratory Medicine, 29*, 89–96.

Choe, A. Y., Kim, B., Lee, K. S., Lee, J. E., Lee, J. Y., Choi, T. K., & Lee, S. H. (2013). Serotonergic genes (5-HTT and HTR1A) and separation life events: Gene-by-environment interaction for panic disorder. *Neuropsychobiology, 67*, 192–200.

Choi, J. K., & Bowles, S. (2007). The co-evolution of parochial altruism and war. *Science, 318*, 636–640.

Chomsky, N. (1975). *Reflections on language*. New York: Pantheon.

Chorost, M. (2011). *The worldwide mind: The coming integration of humans and machines*. New York: Free Press.

Chou, H. T., & Edge, N. (2012). "They are happier and having better lives than I am": The impact of using Facebook on perceptions of others' lives. *Cyberpsychology, Behavior, and Social Networking, 15*, 117–122.

Chou, S. P., Huang, B., Goldstein, R., & Grant, B. F. (2013). Temporal associations between physical illnesses and mental disorders—Results from the Wave 2 National Epidemiologic Survey on Alcohol and Related Conditions (NESARC). *Comprehensive Psychiatry*. (in press)

Chouinard, G. (2006). Interrelations between psychiatric symptoms and drug-induced movement disorder. *Journal of Psychiatry and Neuroscience, 31*, 177–180.

Christenfeld, N. J. S., & Mandler, G. (2013). Emotion. In D. K. Freedheim & I. B. Weiner (Eds.), *Handbook of psychology, 2nd ed., Vol. 1*. (pp. 117–197). Hoboken, NJ: Wiley.

Christensen, H., & others. (2010). Protocol for a randomized trial investigating the effectiveness of an online e-health application compared to attention placebo or sertraline in the treatment of generalized anxiety disorder. *Trials, 11,* 48.

Christopher Frueh, B., Grubaugh, A. L., Cusack, K. J., Kimble, M. O., Elhai, J. D., & Knapp, R. G. (2009). Exposure-based cognitive-behavioral treatment of PTSD in adults with schizophrenia or schizoaffective disorder: A pilot study. *Journal of Anxiety Disorders, 23,* 665–675.

Christopherson, E. R., & VanScoyoc, S. M. (2013). *Treatments that work with children: Empirically supported strategies for managing childhood problems* (2nd ed.). Washington, DC: American Psychological Association.

Chu, Y., & MacGregor, J. N. (2011). Human performance in insight problem solving: A review. *Journal of Problem Solving, 3,* 119–150.

Chudek, M., & Henrich, J. (2011). Culture-gene coevolution, norm-psychology, and the emergence of human prosociality. *Trends in Cognitive Sciences, 15* (5), 218–226.

Chung, T., & others. (2012). Drinking frequency as a brief screen for adolescent alcohol problems. *Pediatrics, 129* (2), 205–212.

Chung, Y., Yoon, K., Park, T., Yang, J., & Oh, K. (2013). Group cognitive-behavioral therapy for early psychosis. *Cognitive Therapy and Research, 37,* 403–411.

Cialdini, R. B. (1991). Altruism or egoism? That is (still) the question. *Psychological Inquiry, 2,* 124–126.

Cialdini, R. B. (1993). *Influence: Science and practice.* New York: HarperCollins.

Cialdini, R. B., Vincent, J. E., Lewis, S. K., Catalan, J., Wheeler, D., & Darby, B. L. (1975). Reciprocal concessions procedure for inducing compliance: The door-in-the-face technique. *Journal of Personality and Social Psychology, 31,* 206–215.

Ciani, K D., & Sheldon, K. M. (2010). Evaluating the mastery-avoidance goal construct: A study of elite college baseball players. *Psychology of Sport and Exercise, 11,* 127–132.

Claes, H. I. (2010). Understanding the effects of sildenafil on erection maintenance and erection hardness. *Journal of Sexual Medicine, 7,* 2184–2191.

Clark, B. (2008). *Growing up gifted* (7th ed.). Upper Saddle River, NJ: Prentice-Hall.

Clark, M. S., & Chrisman, K. (1994). Resource allocation in intimate relationships: Trying to make sense of a confusing literature. In M. J. Lerner & G. Mikula (Eds.), *Entitlement and the affectional bond: Justice in close relationships* (pp. 65–88). New York: Plenum.

Clark, R. D., & Hatfield, E. (1989). Gender differences in receptivity to sexual offers. *Journal of Psychology and Human Sexuality, 2,* 39–55.

Clark, R. E., Hales, J. B., Zola, S. M., & Thompson, R. F. (2013). Biological psychology. In D. K. Freedheim & I. B. Weiner (Eds.), *Handbook of psychology, 2nd ed., Vol. 1.* (pp. 55–78). Hoboken, NJ: Wiley.

Clarkin, J. F. (2012). An integrated approach to psychotherapy techniques for patients with personality disorders. *Journal of Personality Disorders, 26,* 43–62.

Clemens, N. A. (2010). Evidence base for psychotherapy: Two perspectives. *Journal of Psychiatric Practice, 16,* 183–186.

Cleveland, J. N., Barnes-Farrell, J. L., & Ratz, J. M. (1997). Accommodation in the workplace. *Human Resource Management Review, 7,* 77–107.

Clifton, C., Meyer, A. S., Wurm, L. H., & Treiman, R. (2013). Language comprehension and production. In A. F. Healy, R. W. Proctor, & I. B. Weiner (Eds.), *Handbook of psychology, 2nd ed., Vol. 4.* (pp. 523–547). Hoboken, NJ: Wiley.

Clifton, D. O., & Harter, J. K. (2003). Strengths investment. In K. S. Cameron, J. E. Dutton, & R. E. Quinn (Eds.), *Positive organizational scholarship* (pp. 111–121). San Francisco: Berrett & Koehler.

Clifton, D. O., & Nelson, P. (1992). Soar with your strengths. New York: Delacourt.

Cloud, J. (2008, August 27). Failing our geniuses. *Time,* 40–47.

Clutton-Brock, T. H. (2007). Sexual selection in males and females. *Science, 318,* 1882–1885.

Clutton-Brock, T. H. (2010). We do not need a sexual selection 2.0—nor a theory of genial selection. *Animal Behaviour, 79* (3), e7–e10.

Cobb, J. A., & others. (2013). Hippocampal volume and total cell numbers in major depressive disorder. *Journal of Psychiatric Research.* (in press)

Coelho, C. M., & Purkis, H. (2009). The origins of specific phobias: Influential theories and current perspectives. *Review of General Psychology, 13* (4), 335–348.

CogMed. (2013). *Cogmed: Working memory is the engine of learning.* Upper Saddle River, NJ: Pearson.

Cohen, D. (2001). Cultural variation: Considerations and implications. *Psychological Bulletin, 127,* 451–471.

Cohen, D., Nisbett, R. E., Bowdle, B. F., & Schwarz, N. (1996). Insult, aggression, and the southern culture of honor: An "experimental ethnography." *Journal of Personality and Social Psychology, 70,* 945–960.

Cohen, P. J. (2009). Medical marijuana: The conflict between scientific evidence and political ideology. Part one of two. *Journal of Pain & Palliative Care Pharmacotherapy, 23,* 4–25.

Cohen, S. (2011, August 20). Joplin tornado volunteers seek out owners of 27,000 photos found in rubble. www.huffingtonpost.com/2011/08/20/reuniting-tornado-victims_n_932115.html (accessed March 27, 2013)

Cohen, S., Alper, C. M., Doyle, W. J., Treanor, J. J., & Turner, R. B. (2006). Positive emotional style predicts resistance to illness after experimental exposure to rhinovirus or influenza a virus. *Psychosomatic Medicine, 68,* 809–815.

Cohen, S., Doyle, W. J., Alper, C. M., Janicki-Deverts, D., & Turner, R. B. (2009). Sleep habits and susceptibility to the common cold. *Archives of Internal Medicine, 169,* 62–67.

Cohen, S., Frank, E., Doyle, W., Skoner, D. P., Rabin, B. S., & Gwaltney, J. M. (1998). Types of stressors that increase susceptibility to the common cold in healthy adults. *Health Psychology, 17,* 214–223.

Cohen, S., & Janicki-Deverts, D. (2009). Can we improve our physical health by altering our social networks? *Perspectives on Psychological Science, 4* (4), 375–378.

Cohen, S., & Janicki-Deverts, D. (2012). Who's stressed? Distributions of psychological stress in the United States: Probability samples from 1983, 2006, and 2009. *Journal of Applied Social Psychology, 42,* 1320–1332.

Cohen, S., Janicki-Deverts, D., Crittenden, C. N., & Sneed, R. S. (2012). Personality and human immunity. In S. C. Segerstrom (Ed.), *The Oxford handbook of psychoneuroimmunology.* New York: Oxford University Press.

Cohen, S., Janicki-Deverts, D., & Miller, G. E. (2007). Psychological stress and disease. *Journal of the American Medical Association, 298,* 1685–1687.

Cohen, S., & Shachar, I. (2012). Cytokines as regulators of proliferation and survival of healthy and malignant peripheral B cells. *Cytokine, 60,* 13–22.

Cohen, S., & others. (2013). Association between telomere length and experimentally induced upper viral infection in healthy adults. *Journal of the American Medical Association, 309,* 699–705.

Cohen-Bendahan, C. C. C., van de Beek, C., & Berenbaum, S. (2005). Prenatal sex hormone effects on child and adult sex-typed behavior: Methods and findings. *Neuroscience & Biobehavioral Reviews, 29,* 353–384.

Cohen-Charash, Y., & Spector, P. E. (2001). The role of justice in organizations: A meta-analysis. *Organizational Behavior and Human Decision Processes, 86,* 278–321.

Cohen-Kettenis, P. T., & Pfafflin, F. (2010). The DSM diagnostic criteria for gender identity disorder in adolescents and adults. *Archives of Sexual Behavior, 39* (2), 499–513.

Cohen-Woods, S., Craig, I. W., & McGuffin, P. (2012). The current state of play on molecular genetics of depression. *Psychological Medicine.* doi:10.1017/S0033291712001286

Cohn, D. (2011, December 14). Marriage rate declines and marriage age rises. *Pew Research Social & Demographic Trends.* www.pewsocialtrends.org/2011/12/14/marriage-rate-declines-and-marriage-age-rises/ (accessed June 7, 2013)

Coifman, K. G., Bonanno, G. A., Ray, R. D., & Gross, J. J. (2007). Does repressing coping promote resilience? Affective-autonomic response discrepancy during bereavement. *Journal of Personality and Social Psychology, 92,* 745–758.

Cojan, Y., Archimi, A., Cheseaux, N., Waber, L., & Vuilleumier, P. (2013). Time-course of motor inhibition during hypnotic paralysis: EEG topographical and source analysis. *Cortex.* (in press)

Colapinto, J. (2000). *As nature made him.* New York: HarperAcademic.

Colella, A. J., & Bruyère, S. M. (2010). Disability and employment: New directions for industrial and organizational psychology. In S. Zedeck (Ed.), *APA handbook of industrial and organizational psychology.* Washington, DC: American Psychological Association.

Coleman, E., & others. (2011). Standards of care for the health of transsexual, transgender, and gender-nonconforming people, version 7. *International Journal of Transgenderism, 13,* 165–232.

Coleman-Jensen, A., Nord, M., Andrews, M., & Carlson, S. (2012, September). *Household food security in the United States in 2011.* Economic Research Report No. (ERR-141). USDA Economic Research Service, U.S. Department of Agriculture. www.ers.usda.gov/publications/err-economic-research-report/err141/report-summary.aspx#.UbYgYZztnps (accessed June 13, 2013)

Collin, G. B., & others. (2012). Meckelin is necessary for photoreceptor intraciliary transport and outer segment morphogenesis. *Investigative Ophthalmology and Visual Science, 53* (2), 967–974.

Colón, E. A., Callies, A. L., Popkin, M. K., & McGlave, P. B. (1991). Depressed mood and other variables related to bone marrow transplantation survival in acute leukemia. *Psychosomatics, 32,* 420–425.

Colquitt, J. A., LePine, J. A., & Wesson, M. J. (2011). *Organizational behavior* (2nd ed.). New York: McGraw-Hill.

Colrain, I. M., & Baker, F. C. (2011). Sleep EEG, the clearest window through which to view adolescent brain development. *Sleep, 34,* 1287–1288.

Colrain, I. M., & Baker, F. C. (2012). Editorial focus: The maturational trajectories of NREM and REM sleep durations differ across adolescence on both school-night and weekend sleep. *American Journal of Physiology: Regulatory, Integrative, and Comparative Physiology, 302* (5), R531–R532.

Committee to Review Adverse Effects of Vaccines. (2011, August). *Adverse effects of vaccines: Evidence and causality.* Institute of Medicine, National Academy of Sciences. Washington DC: National Academies Press.

Compton, J. A., & Pfau, M. (2004). Use of inoculation to foster resistance to credit card marketing targeting college students. *Journal of Applied Communication Research, 32,* 343–364.

Compton, J. A., & Pfau, M. (2008). Inoculating against pro-plagiarism justifications: Rational and affective strategies. *Journal of Applied Communication Research, 36,* 98–119.

Compton, W. M., & others. (2013). Transitions in illicit drug use status over three years: A prospective analysis of a general population sample. *American Journal of Psychiatry.* (in press)

Comstock, G. (2012). The use of television and other film-related media. In D. G. Singer & J. L. Singer (Eds.), *Handbook of children and the media* (2nd ed.). Thousand Oaks, CA: Sage.

Conley, C. S., Travers, L. V., & Bryant, F. B. (2013). Promoting psychosocial adjustment and stress management in first-year college students: The benefits of engagement in a psychosocial wellness seminar. *Journal of American College Health, 61,* 75–86.

Conley, T. D. (2011). Perceived proposer personality characteristics and gender differences in acceptance of casual sex offers. *Journal of Personality and Social Psychology, 100,* 309–329.

Connellan, J., Baron-Cohen, S., Wheelwright, S., Batki, A., & Ahluwalia, J. (2000). Sex differences in human neonatal social perception. *Infant Behavior & Development, 23,* 113–118.

Conner, K. R., Wood, J., Pisani, A. R., & Kemp, J. (2012). Evaluation of a suicide prevention training curriculum for substance abuse treatment providers based on treatment improvement protocol number 50. *Journal of Substance Abuse and Treatment, 44* (1), 13–6.

Connolly, T., Ordonez, L., & Barker, S. (2013). Judgment and decision making. In N. W. Schmitt, S. Highhouse, & I. B. Weiner (Eds.), *Handbook of psychology, 2nd ed., Vol. 12.* (pp. 493–522). Hoboken, NJ: Wiley.

Consortium on the Management of Disorders of Sexual Development. (2006). *Clinical guidelines for the management of disorders of sexual development.* Rohnert, CA: Intersex Society of North America.

Constantine, N. A. (2008). Converging evidence leaves policy behind: Sex education in the United States. *Journal of Adolescent Health, 42,* 324–326.

Constantinidou, F., & Baker, S. (2002). Stimulus modality and verbal learning performance in normal aging. *Brain and Language, 82,* 296–311.

Conway, M., & Rubin, D. (1993). The structure of autobiographical memory. In A. F. Collins, S. E. Gathercole, M. A. Conway, & P. E. Morris (Eds.), *Theories of memory.* Hillsdale, NJ: Erlbaum.

Cook, J. R., & Kilmer, R. P. (2012). Systems of care: New partnerships for community psychology. *American Journal of Community Psychology, 49,* 393–403.

Cooper, M. L. (2010). Toward a person × situation model of sexual risk-taking behaviors: Illuminating the conditional effects of traits across sexual situations and relationship contexts. *Journal of Personality and Social Psychology, 98,* 319–341.

Cooper, M. L., Barber, L. L., Zhaoyang, R., & Talley, A. E. (2011). Motivational pursuits in the context of human sexual relationships. *Journal of Personality, 79,* 1031–1066.

Cooper, M. L., Shapiro, C. M., & Powers, A. M. (1998). Motivations for sex and risky sexual behavior among adolescents and young adults: A functional perspective. *Journal of Personality and Social Psychology, 75,* 1528–1558.

Cooper, R. M., & Zubek, J. P. (1958). Effects of enriched and restricted early environments on the learning ability of bright and dull rats. *Canadian Journal of Psychology, 12,* 159–164.

Cooper-Hakim, A., & Viswesvaran, C. (2005). The construct of work commitment: Testing an integrative framework. *Psychological Bulletin, 131,* 241–259.

Copeland, D. E., Radvansky, G. A., & Goodwin, K. A. (2009). A novel study: Forgetting curves and the reminiscence bump. *Memory, 17,* 323–336.

Cordon, I. M., Melinder, A. M., Goodman, G. S., & Edelstein, R. S. (2013). Children's and adults' memory for emotional pictures: Examining age-related patterns using the developmental affective photo system. *Journal of Experimental Child Psychology, 114* (2), 339–356.

Coren, S. (2013). Sensation and perception. In D. K. Freedheim & I. B. Weiner (Eds.), *Handbook of psychology, 2nd ed., Vol. 1.* (pp. 100–289). Hoboken, NJ: Wiley.

Cornblatt, B. A., & others. (2012). Risk factors for psychosis: Impaired social and role functioning. *Schizophrenia Bulletin, 38,* 1247–1257.

Cornwell, E. Y., & Waite, L. J. (2009). Social disconnectedness, perceived isolation, and health among older adults. *Journal of Health and Social Behavior, 50,* 31–48.

Corpus, M. J., & Miville, M. L. (2013). Asian American female gender roles. In M. L. Miville (Ed.), *Multicultural gender roles: Applications for mental health and education.* New York: Wiley.

Corr, P. J. (2008). Reinforcement sensitivity theory (RST): Introduction. In P. J. Corr (Ed.), *The reinforcement sensitivity theory of personality* (pp. 1–43). New York: Cambridge University Press.

Correa, T., Hinsley, A. W., & de Zuniga, H. G. (2010). Who interacts on the web?: The intersection of users' personality and social media use. *Computers in Human Behavior, 26,* 247–253.

Corrigan, P. W. (2007). How clinical diagnosis might exacerbate the stigma of mental illness. *Social Work, 52,* 31–39.

Corrigan, P. W., & others. (2002). Challenging two mental illness stigmas: Personal responsibility and dangerousness. *Schizophrenia Bulletin, 28,* 293–309.

Corsica, J. A., & Perri, M. G. (2013). Understanding and managing obesity. In A. M. Nezu, C. Maguth Nezu, P. A. Geller, & I. B. Weiner (Eds.), *Handbook of psychology, 2nd ed., Vol. 9.* (pp. 128–148). Hoboken, NJ: Wiley.

Cortina, J. M., & Luchman, J. N. (2013). Personnel selection and employee performance. In N. W. Schmitt, S. Highhouse, & I. B. Weiner (Eds.), *Handbook of psychology, 2nd ed., Vol. 12.* (pp. 143–183). Hoboken, NJ: Wiley.

Cosci, F. (2012). Assessment of personality in psychosomatic medicine: Current concepts. *Advances in Psychosomatic Medicine, 32,* 133–159.

Cosgrove, V. E., Roybal, D., & Chang, K. D. (2013). Bipolar depression in pediatric populations: Epidemiology and management. *Pediatric Drugs, 15,* 83–91.

Cosmides, L. (2011). Evolutionary psychology. *Annual Review of Psychology* (vol. 62). Palo Alto, CA: Annual Reviews.

Cosmides, L., & Tooby, J. (2013). Evolutionary psychology: New perspectives on cognition and motivation. *Annual Review of Psychology* (vol. 64). Palo Alto, CA: Annual Reviews.

Costa, P. T., & McCrae, R. R. (1992). *Revised NEO personality inventory.* Odessa, FL: Psychological Assessment Resources.

Costa, P. T., & McCrae, R. R. (2006). Age changes in personality and their origins: Comment on Roberts, Walter, and Viechtbauer (2006). *Psychological Bulletin, 132,* 26–28.

Costa, P. T., & McCrae, R. R. (2013). A theoretical context for adult temperament. In T. D. Wachs & others (Eds.), *Temperament in context.* New York: Psychology Press.

Costa, P. T., Terraciano, A., McCrae, R. R., Scally, M., & Abecasis, G. (2010). An alternative to the search for single polymorphisms: Toward molecular personality scales for the five-factor model. *Journal of Personality and Social Psychology, 99* (6), 1014–1024.

Costandi, M. (2012, October 19). Scientists read dreams: Brain scans during sleep can decode visual content of dreams. *Nature.* www.nature.com/news/scientists-read-dreams-1.11625 (accessed March 28, 2013)

Cotugno, G., & others. (2011). Adherence to diet and quality of life in patients with phenylketonuria. *Acta Pediatrica, 100* (8), 1144–1149.

Coulson, S., & Wu, Y. C. (2005). Right hemisphere activation of joke-related information: An event-related brain potential study. *Journal of Cognitive Neuroscience, 17,* 494–506.

Couturier, J., Kimber, M., & Szatmari, P. (2013). Efficacy of family-based treatment for adolescents with eating disorders: A systematic review and meta-analysis. *International Journal of Eating Disorders, 46,* 3–11.

Cowan, N. (2008). What are the differences between long-term, short-term, and working memory? In W. S. Sossin, L. C. Lacaille, V. F. Castellucci, & S. Belleville (Eds.), *Essence of memory: Progress in brain research* (vol. 169, pp. 323–338). New York: Elsevier.

Cowan, N. (2010). The magical mystery four: How is working memory capacity limited, and why? *Current Directions in Psychological Science, 19,* 51–57.

Cowan, N., Morey, C. C., AuBuchon, A. M., Zwilling, C. E., Gilchrist, A. L., & Saults, J. S. (2011). New insights into an old problem: Distinguishing storage from processing in the development of working memory. In P. Barrouillet & V. Gaillard (Eds.), *Cognitive development and working memory: A dialogue between neo-Piagetian theories and cognitive approaches* (pp. 137–150). Hove, U.K.: Psychology Press.

Cowan, N., Rouder, J. N., Blume, C. L., & Saults, J. S. (2012). Models of verbal working memory capacity: What does it take to make them work? *Psychological Review, 119,* 480–499.

Cowan, R. L., Roberts, D. M., & Joers, J. M. (2008). Neuroimaging in human MDMA (Ecstasy) users. *Annals of the New York Academy of Sciences, 1139,* 291–298.

Cox, K., & McAdams, D. P. (2012). The transforming self: Service narratives and identity change in emerging adulthood. *Journal of Adolescent Research, 27,* 18–43.

Cox, K. S., Wilt, J., Olson, B., & McAdams, D. P. (2010). Generativity, the big five, and psychosocial adaptation in midlife adults. *Journal of Personality, 78,* 1185–1208.

Cox, R. E., & Bryant, R. A. (2008). Advances in hypnosis research: Methods, designs, and contributions of intrinsic and instrumental hypnosis. In M. R. Nash & A. J. Barnier (Eds.), *The Oxford handbook of hypnosis: Research theory and practice* (pp. 311–336). New York: Oxford University Press.

Coyne, J. C., & Tennen, H. (2010). Positive psychology in cancer care: Bad science, exaggerated claims, and unproven medicine. *Annals of Behavioral Medicine, 39,* 16–26.

Coyne, J. C., Tennen, H., & Ranchor, A. V. (2010). Positive psychology and cancer care: A story line resistant to evidence. *Annals of Behavioral Medicine, 39,* 35–42.

Craddock, N., & Forty, L. (2006). Genetics of affective (mood) disorders. *European Journal of Human Genetics, 14,* 660–668.

Craighead, E., Craighead, L. W., Ritschel, L. A., & Zagoloff, A. (2013). Behavior therapy and cognitive behavior therapy. In G. Stricker, T. A. Widiger, & I. B. Weiner (Eds.), *Handbook of psychology, 2nd ed., Vol. 8.* (pp. 291–319). Hoboken, NJ: Wiley.

Craik, F. I. M., & Lockhart, R. S. (1972). Levels of processing: A framework for memory research. *Journal of Verbal Learning and Verbal Behavior, 11,* 671–684.

Craik, F. I. M., & Tulving, E. (1975). Depth of processing and retention of words in episodic memory. *Journal of Experimental Psychology: General, 104,* 268–294.

Cramer, P. (2008a). Longitudinal study of defense mechanisms: Late childhood to late adolescence. *Journal of Personality, 75,* 1–23.

Cramer, P. (2008b). Seven pillars of defense mechanism theory. *Social and Personality Psychology Compass, 2,* 1963–1981.

Cramer, P. (2009a). The development of defense mechanisms from pre-adolescence to early adulthood: Do IQ and social class matter? A longitudinal study. *Journal of Research in Personality, 43,* 464–471.

Cramer, P. (2009b). An increase in early adolescent undercontrol is associated with the use of denial. *Journal of Personality Assessment, 91,* 331–339.

Cramer, P., & Jones, C. J. (2007). Defense mechanisms predict differential lifespan change in self-control and self-acceptance. *Journal of Research in Personality, 41,* 841–855.

Crampton, S. M., & Wagner, J. A., III. (1994). Percept-percept inflation in microorganizational research: An investigation of prevalence and effect. *Journal of Applied Psychology, 79,* 67–76.

Crandall, C. S. (2004). Social contagion of binge eating. In R. M. Kowalski & M. R. Leary (Eds.), *The interface of social and clinical psychology: Key readings* (pp. 99–115). New York: Psychology Press.

Crawford, T. J., & others. (2013). The role of working memory and attentional disengagement on inhibitory control: Effects of aging and Alzheimer's disease. *Journal of American Aging Association.* (in press)

Crede, M., Harms, P., Niehorster, S., & Gaye-Valentine, A. (2012). An evaluation of the consequences of using short measures of the big five personality traits. *Journal of Personality and Social Psychology, 102* (4), 874–888.

Creer, D. J., Romberg, C., Saksida, L. M., van Praag, H., & Bussey, T. J. (2010). Running enhances spatial pattern separation in mice. *Proceedings of the National Academy of Sciences USA, 107,* 2367–2372.

Cress, M. E., Buchner, D. M., Prohaska, T., Rimmer, J., Brown, M., Macera, C., DiPietro, L., & Chodzko-Zajko, W. (2005). Best practices for physical activity programs and behavior counseling in older adult populations. *Journal of Aging and Physical Activity, 13,* 61–74.

Crick, N. R., & Grotpeter, J. K. (1995). Relational aggression, gender, and social-psychological adjustment. *Child Development, 66,* 710–722.

Crisafulli, C., & others. (2013). Case-control association study of 36 single-nucleotide polymorphisms within 10 candidate genes for major depression and bipolar disorder. *Psychiatry Research.* (in press)

Crispin, G., & Mehler, M. (2012). 2012 sources of hire: Channels that influence. *Career Xroads.* www.ere.net/wp-content/uploads/2012/07/sources_of_hire_2012.pdf (accessed June 2, 2013)

Crocker, J., Major, B., & Steele, C. (1998). Social stigma. In D. T. Gilbert, S. T. Fiske, & G. Lindzey (Eds.), *Handbook of social psychology* (4th ed., vol. 2). New York: McGraw-Hill.

Crocker, J., & Park, L. E. (2012). Contingencies of self-worth. In M. R. Leary & J. P. Tangney (Eds.), *Handbook of self and identity* (2nd ed., pp. 309–326). New York: Guilford.

Crockett, M. J. (2009). The neurochemistry of fairness: Clarifying the link between serotonin and prosocial behavior. *Annals of New York Academy of Science, 1167,* 76–86.

Croft, W. (2012). *Verbs: Aspect and causal structure.* New York: Oxford University Press.

Cronbach, L. J. (1957). The two disciplines of scientific psychology. *American Psychologist, 12,* 671–684.

Crooks, R. L., & Baur, K. (2014). *Our sexuality* (12th ed.). Boston: Cengage.

Crossley, M. J., Madsen, N. R., & Ashby, F. B. (2012). Procedural learning of unstructured categories. *Psychonomic Bulletin and Review, 19,* 1202–1209.

Crowley, S. J., & Carskadon, M. A. (2010). Modifications to weekend recovery sleep delay circadian phase in older adolescents. *Chronobiology International, 27,* 1469–1492.

Crusio, W. E. (2012). Heritability estimates in behavior genetics: Wasn't that station passed long ago? *Behavioral and Brain Sciences, 35,* 361–362.

Csikszentmihalyi, M. (1990). *Flow: The psychology of optimal experience.* New York: HarperPerennial.

Cuijpers, P. (2001). Mortality and depressive symptoms in inhabitants of residential homes. *International Journal of Geriatric Psychiatry, 16,* 131–138.

Cukrowicz, K. C., Timmons, K. A., Sawyer, K., Caron, K. M., Gummelt, H. D., & Joiner, T. E. (2011). Improved treatment outcome associated with the shift to empirically supported treatments in an outpatient clinic is maintained over a ten-year period. *Professional Psychology, 42* (2), 145–152.

Cullen, K. (2010, January 14). The untouchable mean girls. *Boston Globe.* www.boston.com/news/local/massachusetts/articles/2010/01/24/the_untouchable_mean_girls/ (accessed May 8, 2013)

Cunningham, R. L., & McGinnis, M. Y. (2007). Factors influencing aggression toward females by male rats exposed to anabolic androgenic steroids during puberty. *Hormones and Behavior, 51,* 135–141.

Curran, K., DuCette, J., Eisenstein, J., & Hyman, I. A. (2001, August). *Statistical analysis of the cross-cultural data: The third year.* Paper presented at the meeting of the American Psychological Association, San Francisco.

Curran, T., Hill, A. P., & Niemiec, C. P. (2013). A conditional process model of children's behavioral engagement and behavioral disaffection in sport based on self-determination theory. *Journal of Sport and Exercise Psychology, 35,* 30–43.

Curtis, C. (2013, February 20). Vice President Biden honors public safety officers with Medal of Valor. *The White House Blog.* www.whitehouse.gov/blog/2013/02/20/vice-president-biden-honors-public-safety-officers-medal-valor (accessed June 8, 2013)

Curtis, M. A., Kam, M., & Faull, R. L. (2011). Neurogenesis in humans. *European Journal of Neuroscience, 33,* 1170–1174.

Curtiss, S. (1977). *Genie.* New York: Academic.

Cutrona, C. E. (1982). Transition to college: Loneliness and the process of social adjustment. In L. A. Peplau & D. Perlman (Eds.), *Loneliness.* New York: Wiley.

Cwir, D., Carr, P. B., Walton, G. M., & Spencer, S. J. (2011). Your heart makes my heart move: Cues of social connectedness cause shared emotions and physiological states among strangers. *Journal of Experimental Social Psychology, 47,* 661–664.

D

Dalal, R. S. (2013). Job attitudes: Cognition and affect. In N. W. Schmitt, S. Highhouse, & I. B. Weiner (Eds.), *Handbook of psychology, 2nd ed., Vol. 12.* (pp. 341–366). Hoboken, NJ: Wiley.

Dalton, J. H., Hill, J., Thomas, E., & Kloos, B. (2013). Community psychology. In D. K. Freedheim & I. B. Weiner (Eds.), *Handbook of psychology, 2nd ed., Vol. 1.* (pp. 468–488). Hoboken, NJ: Wiley.

Dalton, M., Hoyle, D. G., & Watts, M. W. (2011). *Human relations* (4th ed.). Boston: Cengage.

Damon, W. (2008). *The path to purpose: Helping our children find their calling in life.* New York: Free Press.

Damsa, C., Kosel, M., & Moussally, J. (2009). Current status of brain imaging in anxiety disorders. *Current Opinion in Psychiatry, 22,* 96–110.

Daniels, H. (2011). Vygotsky and psychology. In U. Goswami (Ed.), *Wiley-Blackwell handbook of childhood cognitive development* (2nd ed.). New York: Wiley-Blackwell.

Danner, D. D., Snowdon, D. A., & Friesen, W. V. (2001). Positive emotions in early life and longevity: Findings from the Nun Study. *Journal of Personality and Social Psychology, 80,* 804–813.

Dao, J. (2013, January 24). When the bullet flew, "they didn't care that I was a woman." *New York Times,* A1.

Darcy, E. (2012). Gender issues in child and adolescent eating disorders. In J. Lock (Ed.), *The Oxford handbook of child and adolescent eating disorders: Developmental perspectives.* New York: Oxford University Press.

Darley, J. M., & Latané, B. (1968). Bystander intervention in emergencies: Diffusion of responsibility. *Journal of Personality and Social Psychology, 8,* 377–383.

Darling, S., Allen, R. J., Havelka, J., Campbell, A., & Rattray, E. (2012). Visuospatial bootstrapping: Long-term memory representations are necessary for implicit binding of verbal and visuospatial working memory. *Psychonomic Bulletin and Review, 19* (2), 258–263.

Darnold, T. C., & Rynes, S. L. (2013). Recruitment and job choice research: Same as it ever was? In N. W. Schmitt, S. Highhouse, & I. B. Weiner (Eds.), *Handbook of psychology* (2nd ed., vol. 12). Hoboken, NJ: Wiley.

Darwin, C. (1862). *On the various contrivances by which British and foreign orchids are fertilised by insects, and on the good effects of intercrossing.* London: John Murray.

Darwin, C. (1871). *The descent of man and selection in relation to sex.* London: John Murray.

Darwin, C. (1965). *The expression of the emotions in man and animals*. Chicago: University of Chicago Press. (original work published 1872)

Darwin, C. (1979). *On the origin of species*. New York: Avenal Books. (original work published 1859)

Dating Sites Reviews. (2013). Online dating statistics & facts. *Dating Sites Reviews*. www.datingsitesreviews.com/staticpages/index.php?page=online-dating-industry-facts-statistics (accessed May 17, 2013)

D'Ausilio, A., Altenmuller, E., Olivetti, B. M., & Lotze, M. (2006). Cross-modal plasticity of motor cortex while listening to a rehearsed musical piece. *European Journal of Neuroscience, 24*, 955–958.

Davidson, P. S., Cook, S. P., & Glisky, E. L. (2006). Flashbulb memories for September 11th can be preserved in older adults. *Neuropsychology, Development, and Cognition B, 13*, 196–206.

Davidson, R. J. (2005). Neural substrates of affective style and value. In Y. Christen (Series Ed.) & J.-P. Changeux, A. R. Damasio, W. Singer, & Y. Christen (Vol. Eds.), *Research and perspectives in neurosciences: Neurobiology of human values* (pp. 67–90). Germany: Springer-Verlag.

Davidson, R. J., & Begley, S. (2012). *The emotional life of your brain*. New York: Hudson Street.

Davidson, R. J., Kabat-Zinn, J., Schumacher, J., Rosenkranz, M. M., Daniel, S., Saki, F., Urbanowski, F., Harrington, A., Bonus, K., & Sheridan, J. F. (2003). Alterations in brain and immune function produced by mindfulness meditation. *Psychosomatic Medicine, 65* (4), 564–570.

Davidson, R. J., Scherer, K. R., & Goldsmith, H. H. (Eds.). (2002). *Handbook of affective sciences*. New York: Oxford University Press.

Davis, C., Patte, K., Curtis, C., & Reid, C. (2010). Immediate pleasures and future consequences: A neuropsychological study of binge eating and obesity. *Appetite, 54*, 208–213.

Davis, J. I., Senghas, A., & Ochsner, K. N. (2009). How does facial feedback modulate emotional experience? *Journal of Research in Personality, 43*, 822–829.

Davis, M. C., Zautra, A. J., Johnson, L. M., Murray, K. E., & Okvat, H. A. (2007). Psychosocial stress, emotion regulation, and resilience among older adults. In C. M. Aldwin, C. L. Park, & A. Spiro (Eds.), *Handbook of health and aging*. New York: Guilford.

Deal, T. E., & Kennedy, A. A. (1982). *Corporate cultures: The rites and rituals of corporate life*. New York: Penguin.

De Angelis, T. (2002). Binge-eating disorder: What's the best treatment? *Monitor on Psychology, 33*, 30.

Deater-Deckard, K. (2013). The social environment and the development of psychopathology. In P. D. Zelazo (Ed.), *The Oxford handbook of developmental psychology, Vol. 2.* (pp. 527–548). New York: Oxford University Press.

Deaux, K. (2001). Social identity. In J. Worell (Ed.), *Encyclopedia of gender and women*. San Diego: Academic.

Deaux, K., & LaFrance, M. (1998). Gender. In D. T. Gilbert, S. T. Fiske, & G. Lindzey (Eds.), *The handbook of social psychology* (vols. 1 & 2, 4th ed., pp. 788–827). New York: McGraw-Hill.

Debiec, J., & LeDoux, J. E. (2006). Noradrenergic signaling in the amygdala contributes to the reconsolidation of fear memory: Treatment implications for PTSD. *Annals of the New York Academy of Science, 1071*, 521–524.

de Bloom, J., Geurts, S. A., & Kompier, M. A. (2012). Effects of short vacations, vacation activities and experiences on employee health and well-being. *Stress and Health, 28* (4), 305–318.

de Bloom, J., Geurts, S. A., Sonnentag, S., Taris, T., de Weerth, C., & Kompier, M. A. (2011). How does a vacation from work affect employee health and well-being? *Psychological Health, 26* (12), 1606–1622.

de Boer, B. J., Peper, C. E., & Beek, P. J. (2012). Development of temporal and spatial bimanual coordination during childhood. *Motor Control, 16*, 537–559.

Decety, J., & Cacioppo, J. T. (2011). *Handbook of social neuroscience*. New York: Oxford University Press.

Decety, J., Skelly, L. R., & Kiehl, K. A. (2013). Brain response to empathy-eliciting scenarios involving pain in incarcerated individuals with psychopathy. *JAMA Psychiatry, 24*, 1–8.

Deci, E., Koestner, R., & Ryan, R. (1999). The undermining effect is a reality after all—Extrinsic rewards, task interest, and self-determination: Repy to Eisenberger, Pierce, and Cameron (1999) and Lepper, Henderlong, and Gingras (1999). *Psychological Bulletin, 125*, 692–700.

Deci, E. L., & Ryan, R. M. (2000). The "what" and "why" of goal pursuits: Human needs and the self-determination of behavior. *Psychological Inquiry, 4*, 227–268.

Deci, E. L., & Ryan, R. M. (Eds.). (2002). *Handbook of self-determination research*. Rochester, NY: University of Rochester Press.

Deci, E. L., & Ryan, R. M. (2012a). Self-determination in health care and its relation to motivational interviewing: A few comments. *International Journal of Behavioral Nutrition and Physical Activity, 9*, 24.

Deci, E. L., & Ryan, R. M. (2012b). Self-determination theory. In P. A. M. Van Lange, A. W. Kruglanski, & E. T. Higgins (Eds.), *Handbook of theories of social psychology*. Thousand Oaks, CA: Sage.

Decimo, I., Bifari, F., Krampera, M., & Fumagalli, G. (2012). Neural stem cell niches in health and diseases. *Current Pharmaceutical Design, 18*, 1755–1783.

Declerck, C. H., Boone, C., & Kiyonari, T. (2010). Oxytocin and cooperation under conditions of uncertainty: The modulating role of incentives and social information. *Hormonal Behavior, 57* (3), 368–374.

De Cort, K., Griez, E., Büchler, M., & Schruers, K. (2012). The role of "interoceptive" fear conditioning in the development of panic disorder. *Behavior Therapy, 43*, 203–215.

Defilippis, M. S., & Wagner, K. D. (2013). Bipolar depression in children and adolescents. *CNS Spectrums.* (in press)

De Fruyt, F., & de Clercq, B. (2012). Childhood antecedents of personality disorders. In T. Widiger (Ed.), *The Oxford handbook of personality disorders*. New York: Oxford University Press.

Degenhardt, L., Bruno, R., & Topp, L. (2010). Is ecstasy a drug of dependence? *Drug and Alcohol Dependence, 107*, 1–10.

De Gennaro, L., Marzano, C., Cipolli, C., & Ferrara, M. (2012). How we remember the stuff that dreams are made of: Neurobiological approaches to the brain mechanisms of dream recall. *Behavioral Brain Research, 226*, 592–596.

Degnin, F. D. (2009). Difficult patients, overmedication, and groupthink. *Journal of Clinical Ethics, 20*, 64–74.

de Graaf, L. E., Huibers, J. J., Cuijpers, P., & Arntz, A. (2010). Minor and major depression in the general population: Does dysfunctional thinking play a role? *Comprehensive Psychiatry, 51*, 266–274.

de Graaf, T. A., Hsieh, P.-J., & Sack, A. T. (2012). The "correlates" in neural correlates of consciousness. *Neuroscience and Biobehavioral Reviews, 36*, 191–197.

de Groot, J. H. B., Smeets, M. A. M., Kaldewaij, A., Duijndam, M. J. A., & Semin, G. R. (2012). Chemosignals communicate human emotions. *Psychological Science, 23*, 1417–1424.

De Haan, E., Duckworth, A., Birch, D., & Jones, C. (2013). Executive coaching outcome research: The contribution of common factors such as relationship, personality match, and self-efficacy. *Consulting Psychology, 65*, 40–57.

Dehaene, S., & Changeux, J. P. (2011). Experimental and theoretical approaches to conscious processing. *Neuron, 70*, 200–207.

Dehaene, S., Changeux, J. P., Naccache, L., Sackur, J., & Sergent, C. (2006). Conscious, preconscious, and subliminal processing: A testable taxonomy. *Trends in Cognitive Sciences, 10*, 204–211.

de Hevia, M. D., & Spelke, E. S. (2010). Number-space mapping in human infants. *Psychological Science, 21* (5), 653–660.

DeJong W. (1994). Relapse prevention: An emerging technology for promoting long-term drug abstinence. *International Journal of Addiction, 29*, 681–705.

De Koninck, J. (2012). Sleep, dreams, and dreaming. In C. M. Morin & C. A. Espie (Eds.), *The Oxford handbook of sleep and sleep disorders*. New York: Oxford University Press.

DeLamater, J., & Moorman, S. M. (2007). Sexual behavior in later life. *Journal of Aging and Health, 19*, 921–945.

de Lange, F. P., van Gaal, S., Lamme, V. A., & Dehaene, S. (2011). How awareness changes the relative weights of evidence during human decision-making. *PLoS One, 9* (11), e1001203.

Del Casale, A., & others. (2012). Neurocognition under hypnosis: Findings from recent functional neuroimaging studies. *International Journal of Clinical and Experimental Hypnosis, 60*, 286–317.

Del Corso, J. J., & Rehfuss, M. C., & Galvin, K. (2011). Striving to adapt: Addressing Adler's work task in the 21st century. *Journal of Individual Psychology, 67*, 88–106.

Del Cul, A., Dehaene, S., Reyes, P., Bravo, E., & Slachevsky, A. (2009). Causal role of prefrontal cortex in the threshold for access to consciousness. *Brain, 132*, 2531–2540.

Del Giudice, M. J. (2010). What might this be? Rediscovering the Rorschach as a tool for personnel selection in organizations. *Journal of Personality Assessment, 92*, 78–89.

Dell, P. F. (2013). Three dimensions of dissociative amnesia. *Journal of Trauma and Dissociation, 14*, 25–39.

Dell'Osso, B., & Lader, M. (2012). Do benzodiazepines still deserve a major role in the treatment of psychiatric disorders? A critical reappraisal. *European Psychiatry, 28*, 7–20.

DeMarree, K. G., & Petty, R. E. (2007). The elaboration likelihood model of persuasion. In R. F. Baumeister & K. D. Vohs (Eds.), *Encyclopedia of social psychology*. Thousand Oaks, CA: Sage.

Demertzi, A., Soddu, A., & Laureys, S. (2013). Consciousness supporting networks. *Current Opinion in Neurobiology.* (in press)

Deming, W. E. (1986). *Out of the crisis*. Cambridge, MA: MIT Press.

Den Hartog, D. N., & Belschak, F. D. (2012). When does transformational leadership enhance employee proactive behavior? The role of autonomy and role breadth self-efficacy. *Journal of Applied Psychology, 97* (1), 194–202.

Dennis, A. A., Astell, A., & Dritschel, B. (2012). The effects of imagery on problem-solving ability and autobiographical memory. *Journal of Behavior Therapy and Experimental Psychiatry, 43,* Suppl. 1, S4–S11.

Denollet, J., & Conraads, V. M. (2011). Type D personality and vulnerability to adverse outcomes of heart disease. *Cleveland Clinic Journal of Medicine, 78,* Suppl. 1, S13–S19.

De Pauw, S. S., & Mervielde, I. (2010). Temperament, personality, and developmental psychopathology: A review on the conceptual dimensions underlying childhood traits. *Child Psychiatry and Human Development, 41,* 313–329.

Depue, R. A., & Collins, P. F. (1999). Neurobiology of the structure of personality: Dopamine, facilitation of incentive motivation, and extraversion. *Behavioural and Brain Sciences, 22,* 491–569.

De Raad, B., Barelds, D. P. H., Levert, E., Ostendorf, F., Mlacic, B., Di Blas, L., Hrebickova, M., Perugini, M., Church, A. T., & Katigbak, M. S. (2010). Only three factors of personality description are fully replicable across languages: A comparison of 14 trait taxonomies. *Journal of Personality and Social Psychology, 98,* 160–173.

De Raedt, R., & Koster, E. H. W. (2010). Understanding vulnerability for depression from a cognitive neuroscience perspective: A reappraisal of attentional factors and a new conceptual framework. *Cognitive, Affective, and Behavioral Neuroscience, 10,* 50–70.

Derks, D., Bos, A. E. R., & von Grumbkow, J. (2008). Emoticons in computer-mediated communication: Social motives and social context. *CyberPsychology & Behavior, 11,* 99–101.

Derntl, B., Habel, U., Robinson, S., Windischberger, C., Kryspin-Exner, I., Gur, R. C., & Moser, E. (2012). Culture but not gender modulates amygdala activation during explicit emotion recognition. *BMC Neuroscience, 13,* ArtID 54.

Derryberry, D., & Reed, M. (2002). Information processing approaches to individual differences in emotional reactivity. In R. J. Davidson, K. R. Scherer, & H. H. Goldsmith (Eds.), *Handbook of affective sciences.* New York: Oxford University Press.

Detour, J., Danion, J.-M., Gounot, D., Marrer, C., & Foucher, J. R. (2011). Prefrontal cortex recruitment during naturalistic remote memory: A factorial block-event fMRI study. *Brain Research, 1400,* 66–77.

de Villiers, J., & de Villiers, P. (2013). Syntax acquisition. In P. D. Zelazo (Ed.), *The Oxford handbook of developmental psychology, Vol 1.* (pp. 926–952). New York: Oxford University Press.

Devlin, S., & Arneill, A. B. (2003). Health care environments and patient outcomes: A review of the literature. *Environment and Behavior, 35,* 665–694.

De Vos, J. (2010). From Milgram to Zimbardo: The double birth of postwar psychology/psychologization. *History of the Human Sciences, 23,* 156–175.

de Waal, F. B. M., Leimgruber, K., & Greenberg, A. R. (2008). Giving is self-rewarding for monkeys. *Proceedings of the National Academy of Sciences USA, 105,* 13685–13689.

Dewsbury, D. A. (2013). Comparative psychology in historical perspective. In D. K. Freedheim & I. B. Weiner (Eds.), *Handbook of psychology* (2nd ed., vol. 1). Hoboken, NJ: Wiley.

DeYoung, C. G., Grazioplene, R. G., & Peterson, J. B. (2012). From madness to genius: The openness/intellect trait domain as a paradoxical circumplex. *Journal of Research in Personality, 46,* 63–78.

DeYoung, C. G., Hirsh, J. B., Shane, M. S., Papademetris, X., Rajeevan, N., & Gray, J. R. (2010). Testing predictions from personality neuroscience: Brain structure and the big five. *Psychological Science, 21,* 820–828.

de Zwaan, M., Mitchell, J. E., Crosby, R. D., Mussell, M. P., Raymond, N. C., Specker, S. M., & Seim, H. C. (2005). Short-term cognitive behavioral treatment does not improve outcome of a comprehensive very-low-calorie diet program in obese women with binge eating disorder. *Behavior Therapy, 36,* 89–99.

Dhillon, S. (2012). Aripiprazole: A review of its use in the management of mania in adults with bipolar 1 disorder. *Drugs, 72,* 133–162.

"Diabetes service dog saves man's life." (2013, January 9). *WLFI.* www.wlfi.com/dpp/news/local/diabetes-service-dog-saves-mans-life-mre1357748939474 (accessed March 27, 2013)

Diamond, A. (2013). Executive functions. *Annual Review of Psychology* (vol. 64). Palo Alto, CA: Annual Reviews.

Diamond, A., Casey, B. J., & Munakata, Y. (2011). *Developmental cognitive neuroscience.* New York: Oxford University Press.

Diamond, A., & Lee, K. (2011). Interventions shown to aid executive function development in children 4 to 12 years old. *Science, 333,* 959–964.

Diamond, L. M. (2008a). *Sexual fluidity: Understanding women's love and desire.* Cambridge, MA: Harvard University Press.

Diamond, L. M. (2008b). Female bisexuality from adolescence to adulthood: Results from a 10-year longitudinal study. *Developmental Psychology, 44,* 5–14.

Diamond, L. M. (2009). Emotion in relationships. In H. R. Reis & S. Sprecher (Eds.), *Encyclopedia of human relationships.* Thousand Oaks, CA: Sage.

Diamond, L. M. (2013a). Gender and same-sex sexuality. In D. T. Tolman & L. M. Diamond (Eds.), *APA handbook on sexuality and psychology.* Washington, DC: American Psychological Association.

Diamond, L. M. (2013b). Sexuality and same-sex sexuality in relationships. In J. Simpson & J. Davidio (Eds.), *Handbook of personality and social psychology.* Washington, DC: American Psychological Association.

Diamond, L. M., & Savin-Williams, R. C. (2013). Same-sex activity in adolescence: Multiple meanings and implications. In R. F. Fassinger & S. L. Morrow (Eds.), *Sex in the margins.* Washington, DC: American Psychological Association.

Diamond, M., & Sigmundson, H. K. (1997). Sex reassignment at birth. *Archives of Pediatric and Adolescent Medicine, 151,* 298–304.

Diaper, A., & others. (2012). Evaluation of the effects of venlafaxine and pregabalin on the carbon dioxide inhalation models of generalised anxiety disorder and panic. *Journal of Psychopharmacology, 27* (2), 135–145.

DiClemente, C. C. (2006). Natural change and the troublesome use of substances: A life-course perspective. W. R. Miller & K. M. Carroll (Eds.), *Rethinking substance abuse: What the science shows, and what we should do about it* (pp. 81–96). New York: Guilford.

DiDonato, T. E., & Krueger, J. I. (2010). Interpersonal affirmation and self-authenticity: A test of Rogers's self-growth hypothesis. *Self and Identity, 9,* 322–336.

Diederich, A., & Busemeyer, J. R. (2013). Judgment and decision making. In A. F. Healy, R. W. Proctor, & I. B. Weiner (Eds.), *Handbook of psychology, 2nd ed., Vol. 4.* (pp. 660–684). Hoboken, NJ: Wiley.

Diekelmann, S., Wilhelm, I., & Born, J. (2009). The whats and whens of sleep-dependent memory consolidation. *Sleep Medicine Reviews, 13,* 309–321.

Diekman, A. B., & Eagly, A. H. (2008). Of women, men, and motivation: A role congruity account. In J. Y. Shah & W. L. Gardner (Eds.), *Handbook of motivational science* (pp. 434–447). New York: Guilford.

Dien, J. (2009). A tale of two recognition systems: Implications of the fusiform face area and the visual word form area for lateralized object recognition models. *Neuropsychologia, 47,* 1–16.

Diener, E. (1999). Introduction to the special section on the structure of emotion. *Journal of Personality and Social Psychology, 76,* 803–804.

Diener, E. (2000). Subjective well-being: The science of happiness and a proposal for a national index. *American Psychologist, 55,* 34–43.

Diener, E. (2012a). New findings and future directions for subjective well-being research. *American Psychologist, 67,* 590–597.

Diener, E. (2012b). Positive psychology: Past, present, and future. In S. J. Lopez & C. R. Snyder (Eds.), *The Oxford handbook of positive psychology* (2nd ed.). New York: Oxford University Press.

Diener, E., & Chan, M. Y. (2011). Happy people live longer: Subjective well-being contributes to health and well-being. *Applied Psychology: Health and Well-Being, 3,* 1–43.

Diener, E., & Diener, C. (1996). Most people are happy. *Psychological Science, 7,* 181–185.

Diener, E., Emmons, R. A., Larsen, R. J., & Griffin, S. (1985). The Satisfaction with Life Scale. *Journal of Personality Assessment, 49,* 71–75.

Diener, E., & Seligman, M. E. P. (2002). Very happy people. *Psychological Science, 13,* 81–84.

Diener, E., Suh, E. M., Lucas, R. E., & Smith, H. L. (1999). Subjective well-being: Three decades of progress. *Psychological Bulletin, 125,* 276–302.

Digman, J. M. (1990). Personality structure: Emergence of the five-factor model. *Annual Review of Psychology* (vol. 41). (pp. 417–440). Palo Alto, CA: Annual Reviews.

Di Iorgi, N., Morana, G., Gallizia, A. L., & Maghnie, M. (2012). Pituitary gland imaging and outcome. *Endocrine Development, 23,* 16–29.

Dijksterhuis, A., Bos, M. W., Nordgren, L. F., & van Baaren, R. B. (2006). On making the right choice: The deliberation-without-attention effect. *Science, 311,* 1005–1007.

Dijksterhuis, A., Bos, M. W., Van der Leij, A., & Van Baaren, R. B. (2009). Predicting soccer matches after unconscious and conscious thought as a function of expertise. *Psychological Science, 20,* 1381–1387.

Dijksterhuis, A., & Nordgren, L. F. (2006). A theory of unconscious thought. *Perspectives on Psychological Science, 1,* 95–109.

Dijksterhuis, A., & Van Knippenberg, A. (1998). The relation between perception and behavior or how to win a game of Trivial Pursuit. *Journal of Personality and Social Psychology, 74,* 865–877.

Dillon, B. L. (2012). Workplace violence: Impact, causes, prevention. *Work, 42* (1), 15–20.

Di Lorenzo, P. M., & Youngentob, S. L. (2013). Taste and olfaction. In R. J. Nelson, S. J. Y. Mizumori, & I. B. Weiner (Eds.), *Handbook of psychology, 2nd ed., Vol. 3.* (pp. 272–305). Hoboken, NJ: Wiley.

Dimauro, J., Tolin, D. F., Frost, R. O., & Steketee, G. (2013). Do people with hoarding disorder under-report their symptoms? *Journal of Obsessive Compulsive and Related Disorders, 2*, 130–136.

Dinkelbach, H. J., Vitay, J., Beuth, F., & Hamker, F. H. (2012). Comparison of GPU- and CPU-implementations of mean-firing rate neural networks on parallel hardware. *Network, 23*, 212–236.

Dionisi, A. M., Barling, J., & Dupré, K. (2012). Revisiting the comparative outcomes of workplace aggression and sexual harassment. Journal of Occupational Health Psychology, *14*, 398–408.

Distel. M. A., Roeling, M. P., Tielbeek, J. J., van Toor, D., Derom, C. A., Trull, T. J., & Boomsma, D. I. (2012). The covariation of trait anger and borderline personality: A bivariate twin-siblings study. *Journal of Abnormal Psychology, 121* (2), 458–486.

Distel, M. A., Trull, T. J., Derom, C. A., Thiery, E. W., Grimmer, M. A., Martin, N. G., Willemsen, G., & Boomsma, D. I. (2008). Heritability of borderline personality disorder features is similar across three countries. *Psychological Medicine, 38*, 1219–1229.

Dixon, R. A., McFall, G. P., Whitehead, B. P., & Dolcos, S. (2013). Cognitive development in adulthood and aging. In R. M. Lerner, M. A. Easterbrooks, J. Mistry, & I. B. Weiner (Eds.), *Handbook of psychology, 2nd ed., Vol. 6.* (pp. 451–474). Hoboken, NJ: Wiley.

Dixon, R. M. W. (2012). *Basic linguistic theory* (vol. 3). New York: Oxford University Press.

Dobson, K. S. (2013). The science of CBT: Toward a metacognitive model of change? *Behavior Therapy, 44*, 224–227.

Dobson, R. (2005). "Fighting spirit" after cancer diagnosis does not improve outcome. *British Medical Journal, 330*, 865.

Dodge, E. (2012). Family evolution and process during the child and adolescent years in eating disorders. In J. Lock (Ed.), *The Oxford handbook of child and adolescent eating disorders: Developmental perspectives.* New York: Oxford University Press.

Dodge, K. A., Coie, J. D., & Lynam, D. (2006). Aggression and antisocial behavior in youth. In W. Damon & R. Lerner (Eds.), *Handbook of child psychology* (6th ed.). New York: Wiley.

Dollard, J., Doob, L. W., Miller, N. E., Mowrer, O. H., & Sears, R. R. (1939). *Frustration and aggression.* New Haven, CT: Yale University Press.

Dolnicar, S., Yanamandram, V., & Cliff, K. (2012). The contribution of vacations to quality of life. *Annals of Tourism Research, 39* (1), 59–83.

Domhoff, G. W. (2007). Realistic simulation and bizarreness in dream content: Past findings and suggestions for future research. In D. Barrett & P. McNamara (Eds.), *The new science of dreaming: Content, recall, and personality correlates* (vol. 2, pp. 1–27). Westport, CT: Praeger.

Domhoff, G. W. (2011). The neural substrate for dreaming: Is it a subsystem of the default network? *Consciousness and Cognition, 20*, 1163–1174.

Domino, M. E., & Swartz, M. S. (2008). Who are the new users of antipsychotic medications? *Psychiatric Services, 59*, 209–216.

Domjan, M. (2010). *The principles of learning and behavior* (6th ed.). Boston: Cengage.

Domschke, K., & others. (2011). Neuropeptide S receptor gene—Converging evidence for a role in panic disorder. *Molecular Psychiatry, 16*, 938–948.

Donahue, C. B., Odlaug, B. L., & Grant, J. E. (2011). Compulsive buying treated with motivational interviewing and imaginal desensitization. *Annals of Clinical Psychology, 23*, 226–227.

Donatelle, R. J. (2013). *Health: The basics* (10th ed.). Upper Saddle River, NJ: Pearson.

Donegan, E., & Dugas, M. J. (2012). Generalized anxiety disorder: A comparison of symptom change in adults receiving cognitive-behavioral therapy or applied relaxation. *Journal of Consulting and Clinical Psychology, 80*, 490–496.

Donnellan, M. B., Larsen-Rife, D., & Conger, R. D. (2005). Personality, family history, and competence in early adult romantic relationships. *Journal of Personality and Social Psychology, 88*, 562–576.

Donnellan, M. B., Lucas, R. E., & Fleeson, W. (2009). Introduction to personality and assessment at age 40: Reflections on the legacy of the person-situation debate and the future of person-situation integration. *Journal of Research in Personality, 43*, 117–119.

Donnellan, M. B., Trzesniewski, K. H., & Robins, R. W. (2009). An emerging epidemic of narcissism or much ado about nothing? *Journal of Research in Personality, 43*, 498–501.

Dougall, A. L., Biglan, M. C. W., Swanson, J. N., & Baum, A. (2013). Stress, coping, and immune function. In R. J. Nelson, S. J. Y. Mizumori, & I. B. Weiner (Eds.), *Handbook of psychology, 2nd ed., Vol. 3.* (pp. 440–460). Hoboken, NJ: Wiley.

Dougherty, S. (2010). Computing the unconscious. *Psychoanalytic Quarterly, 79*, 171–201.

Dougkas, A., Yaqoob, P., Givens, D. I., Reynolds, C. K., & Miihane, A. M. (2013). The impact of obesity-related SNP on appetite and energy intake. *British Journal of Nutrition.* (in press)

Dourley, J. (2011). Jung's equation of the ground of being with the ground of psyche. *Journal of Analytical Psychology, 56*, 514–531.

Dovidio, J. F., Kawakami, K., & Gaertner, S. L. (2002). Implicit and explicit prejudice and interracial interaction. *Journal of Personality and Social Psychology, 82*, 62–68.

Dovidio, J. F., Newheiser, A.-K., & Leyens, J.-P. (2012). History of intergroup relations research. In A. W. Kruglanski & W. Stroebe (Eds.), *Handbook of the history of social psychology.* New York: Psychology Press.

Dovidio, J. F., Saguy, T., Gaertner, S. L., & Thomas, E. L. (2012). From attitudes to (in) action: The darker side of "we." In J. Dixon & M. Levine (Eds.), *Beyond prejudice.* New York: Cambridge University Press.

Drasgow, F. (2013). Intelligence and the workplace. In N. W. Schmitt, S. Highhouse, & I. B. Weiner (Eds.), *Handbook of psychology, 2nd ed., Vol. 12.* (pp. 184–210). Hoboken, NJ: Wiley.

Drigotas, S. M., Safstrom, C. A., & Gentilia, T. (1999). An investment model prediction of dating infidelity. *Journal of Personality and Social Psychology, 77*, 509–524.

Dritschel, B., Kao, C., Astell, A., Neufeind, J., & Lai, T. (2011). How are depression and autobiographical memory retrieval related to culture? *Journal of Abnormal Psychology, 120*, 969–974.

Duke, A. A., Bègue, L., Bell, R., & Eisenlohr-Moul, T. (2013). Revisiting the serotonin-aggression relationship in humans: A meta-analysis. *Psychological Bulletin.* (in press)

Dulloo, A. G., Jacquet, J., & Montani, J. P. (2012). How dieting makes some fatter: From a perspective of human body composition auto-regulation. *Proceedings of the Nutrition Society, 71* (3), 379–389.

Dulmus, C. N., & Nisbet, B. C. (2013). *Person-centered recovery planner for adults with serious mental illness.* Hoboken, NJ: Wiley.

Duman, R. S., Li, N., Liu, R. J., Duric, V., & Aghajanian, G. (2012). Signaling pathways underlying the rapid antidepressant actions of ketamine. *Neuropharmacology, 62*, 35–41.

Dumontheil, I., & Klingberg, T. (2012). Brain activity during a visuospatial memory task predicts arithmetical performance 2 years later. *Cerebral Cortex, 22*, 1078–1085.

Duncan, A. E., Scherrer, J., Fu, Q., Bucholz, K. K., Heath, A. C., True, W. R., Haber, J. R., Howell, D., & Jacob, T. (2006). Exposure to paternal alcoholism does not predict development of alcohol-use disorders in offspring: Evidence from an offspring-of-twins study. *Journal of Studies on Alcohol, 67*, 649–656.

Duncan, B. L., Miller, S. D., Wampold, B. E., & Hubble, M. A. (Eds.). (2010). *The heart and soul of change: Delivering what works in therapy* (2nd ed.) Washington, DC: American Psychological Association.

Duncan, B. L., & Reese, R. J. (2013). Empirically supported treatments, evidence-based treatments, and evidence-based practice. In G. Stricker, T. A. Widiger, & I. B. Weiner (Eds.), *Handbook of psychology, 2nd ed., Vol. 8.* (pp. 489–514). Hoboken, NJ: Wiley.

Dunkel Schetter, C. (2011). Psychological science in the study of pregnancy and birth. *Annual Review of Psychology* (vol. 62). Palo Alto, CA: Annual Reviews.

Dunlop, W., & Tracy, J. L. (2013). Sobering stories: Narratives of self-redemption predict behavioral change and improved health among recovering alcoholics. *Journal of Personality and Social Psychology, 104* (3), 576–590.

Dunn, E. W., Aknin, L. B., & Norton, M. I. (2008). Spending money on others promotes happiness. *Science, 319*, 1687–1688.

Dunner, D. L. (2001). Management of anxiety disorders: The added challenge of comorbidity. *Depression and Anxiety, 13* (2), 57–71.

Dunnett, S. B. (2013). Neural tissue transplantation, repair, and rehabilitation. *Handbook of Clinical Psychology, 110*, 143–159.

Dupoux, E., de Gardelle, V., & Kouider, S. (2008). Subliminal speech perception and auditory streaming. *Cognition, 109*, 267–273.

Durantini, M. R., Albarracin, D., Mitchell, A. L., Earl, A. N., & Gillette, J. C. (2006). Conceptualizing the influence of social agents of behavior change: A meta-analysis of the effectiveness of HIV-prevention interventionists for different groups. *Psychological Bulletin, 132*, 212–248.

Duric, V., & Duman, R. S. (2013). Depression and treatment response: Dynamic interplay of signaling pathways and altered neural responses. *Cellular and Molecular Life Sciences, 70*, 39–53.

Durrant, R., & Ellis, B. J. (2013). Evolutionary psychology. In R. J. Nelson, S. J. Y. Mizumori, & I. B. Weiner (Eds.), *Handbook of psychology, 2nd ed., Vol. 3.* (pp. 26–51). Hoboken, NJ: Wiley.

Duvarci, S., Nader, K., & LeDoux, J. E. (2008). De novo mRNA synthesis is required for both consolidation and reconsolidation of fear memories in the amygdala. *Learning and Memory, 15,* 747–755.

Dweck, C. S. (2006). *Mindset.* New York: Random House.

Dweck, C. S. (2013). Social development. In P. D. Zelazo (Ed.), *The Oxford handbook of developmental psychology, Vol. 2.* (pp. 167–190). New York: Oxford University Press.

Dweck, C. S., & Master, A. (2009). Self-theories and motivation: Students' beliefs about intelligence. In K. R. Wentzel & A. Wigfield (Eds.), *Handbook of motivation at school.* New York: Routledge.

E

Eagly, A. H. (1987). *Sex differences in social behavior: A social-role interpretation.* Hillsdale, NJ: Erlbaum.

Eagly, A. H. (2009). The his and hers of prosocial behavior: An examination of the social psychology of gender. *American Psychologist, 64,* 644–658.

Eagly, A. H. (2010). Gender roles. In J. Levine & M. Hogg (Eds.), *Encyclopedia of group processes and intergroup relations.* Thousand Oaks, CA: Sage.

Eagly, A. H. (2012). Women as leaders: Paths through the labyrinth. In M. C. Bligh & R. Riggio (Eds.), *When near is far and far is near: Exploring distance in leader-follower relationships.* New York: Wiley-Blackwell.

Eagly, A. H., & Crowley, M. (1986). Gender and helping behavior: A meta-analytic review of the social psychological literature. *Psychological Bulletin, 100,* 283–308.

Eagly, A. H., & Diekman, A. B. (2003). The malleability of sex differences in response to changing social roles. In L. G. Aspinwall & U. M. Staudinger (Eds.), *A psychology of human strengths: Fundamental questions and future directions for a positive psychology* (pp. 103–115). Washington, DC: American Psychological Association.

Eagly, A. H., & Wood, W. (2010). Gender roles in a biosocial world. In P. van Lange, A. Kruglanski, & E. T. Higgins (Eds.), *Handbook of theories in social psychology.* Thousand Oaks, CA: Sage.

Eagly, A. H., Wood, W., & Johannesen-Schmidt, M. C. (2004). Social role theory of sex differences and similarities: Implications for the partner preferences of women and men. In A. H. Eagly, A. Beall, & R. S. Sternberg (Eds.), *The psychology of gender* (2nd ed., pp. 269–295). New York: Guilford.

Eastman, K. K. (1994). In the eyes of the beholder: An attributional approach to ingratiation and organizational citizenship behavior. *Academy of Management Journal, 37,* 1379–1391.

Eastwick, P. W., & Finkel, E. (2008). Sex differences in mate preferences revisited: Do people know what they initially desire in a romantic partner? *Journal of Personality and Social Psychology, 94,* 245–264.

Eaton, D. K., & others. (2012). Youth risk behavior surveillance—United States, 2011. *MMWR Surveillance Summary, 61* (4), 1–162.

Eberth, J., & Sedlmeier, P. (2012). The effects of mindfulness meditation: A meta-analysis. *Mindfulness, 3,* 174–189.

Ebner-Priemer, U. W., & Trull, T. J. (2012). Investigating temporal instability in psychological variables: Understanding the real world as time dependent. In M. R. Mehl & T. S. Conner (Eds.), *Handbook of research methods for studying daily life* (pp. 423–439). New York: Guilford.

Eby, L. T. (2010). Mentoring. In S. Zedeck (Ed.), *APA handbook of industrial and organizational psychology.* Washington, DC: American Psychological Association.

Eckerberg, B., Lowden, A., Nagai, R., & Akerstedt, T. (2012). Melatonin treatment effects on adolescent students' sleep timing and sleepiness in a placebo-controlled crossover study. *Chronobiology International, 29,* 1239–1248.

Eckert, A., Schmitt, K., & Gotz, J. (2011). Mitochondrial dysfunction—The beginning of the end in Alzheimer's disease? Separate and synergistic modesl of tau and amloyid-B toxicity. *Alzheimer's Research and Therapy, 3* (2),15.

Edgar, N., & Sibille, E. (2013). A putative role for oligodendrocytes in mood regulation. *Translational Psychiatry.* (in press)

Edinger, J. D., & Morin, C. M. (2012). Sleep disorders classification and diagnosis. In C. M. Morin & C. A. Espie (Eds.), *The Oxford handbook of sleep and sleep disorders.* New York: Oxford University Press.

Edwards, J., Peres, J., Monti, D. A., & Newberg, A. B. (2012). The neurobiological correlates of meditation and mindfulness. In A. Moreira-Almeida & F. S. Santos (Eds.), *Exploring frontiers of the mind–brain relationship* (pp. 97–112). New York: Springer.

Eells, T. D. (2000). Can therapy affect physical health? *Journal of Psychotherapy Practice and Research, 9,* 100–104.

Ehrensaft, D. (2013). "Look, Mom, I'm a boy—Don't tell anyone I was a girl." *Journal of LGBT Youth, 10,* 9–28.

Ehrhart, M. G., Ehrhart, K. H., Roesch, S. C., Chung-Herrera, B. G., Nadler, K., & Bradshaw, K. (2009). Testing the latent factor structure and construct validity of the Ten-Item Personality Inventory. *Personality and Individual Differences, 47,* 900–905.

Eichenbaum, H. (2013). Memory systems. In R. J. Nelson, S. J. Y. Mizumori, & I. B Weiner (Eds.), *Handbook of psychology, 2nd ed., Vol. 3.* (pp. 551–5734). Hoboken, NJ: Wiley.

Eidelman, P., Gershon, A., McGlinchey, E., & Harvey, A. G. (2012). Sleep and psychopathology. In C. M. Morin & C. A. Espie (Eds.), *The Oxford handbook of sleep and sleep disorders.* New York: Oxford University Press.

Ein-Dor, T., Mikulincer, M., Doron, G., & Shaver, P. R. (2010). The attachment paradox: How can so many of us (the insecure ones) have no adaptive advantages? *Perspectives on Psychological Science, 5,* 123–141.

Eisenberg, M. E., Madsen, N., Oliphant, J. A., & Sieving, R. E. (2013). Barriers to providing sexuality education that teachers believe students need. *Journal of School Health, 83,* 335–342.

Eisenberg, M. E., & others. (2008). Support for comprehensive sexuality education: Perspectives from parents of school-age youth. *Journal of Adolescent Health, 42,* 352–359.

Eisenberg, N., Fabes, R. A., & Spinrad, T. L. (2006). Prosocial development. In W. Damon & R. Lerner (Eds.), *Handbook of child psychology* (2nd ed.). New York: Wiley.

Eisenberg, N., Morris, A. S., McDaniel, B., & Spinrad, T. L. (2009). Moral cognitions and prosocial responding. In R. M. Lerner & L. Steinberg (Eds.), *Handbook of adolescent psychology* (3rd ed.). New York: Wiley.

Eisenberg, N., & Murphy, B. (1995). Parenting and children's moral development. In M. H. Bornstein (Ed.), *Children and parenting* (vol. 4). Hillsdale, NJ: Erlbaum.

Eisenberg, N., Spinrad, T. L., & Morris, A. S. (2013). Prosocial development. In P. D. Zelazo (Ed.), *The Oxford handbook of developmental psychology.* New York: Oxford University Press.

Eisenberg, N., Spinrad, T., & Sadovsky, A. (2013). Empathy-related responding in children. In M. Killen & J. G. Smetana (Eds.), *Handbook of moral development* (2nd ed.). New York: Routledge.

Eisenberg, N., & Valiente, C. (2002). Parenting and children's prosocial and moral development. In M. H. Bornstein (Ed.), *Handbook of parenting* (2nd ed.). Mahwah, NJ: Erlbaum.

Eisenberger, R., & Aselage, J. (2009). Incremental effects of reward on experienced performance pressure: Positive outcomes for intrinsic interest and creativity. *Journal of Organizational Behavior, 30,* 95–117.

Eiser, J. R. (2012). History of social judgment research. In A. W. Kruglanski & W. Stroebe (Eds.), *Handbook of the history of social psychology.* New York: Psychology Press.

Ekman, P. (1980). *The face of man.* New York: Garland.

Ekman, P. (1996). Lying and deception. In N. L. Stein, C. Brainerd, P. A. Ornstein, & B. Tversky (Eds.), *Memory for everyday emotional events.* Mahwah, NJ: Erlbaum.

Ekman, P. (2003). Emotions inside out: 130 years after Darwin's "The expression of emotions in man and animal." *Annals of the New York Academy of Science, 1000,* 1–6.

Ekman, P., Davidson, R. J., & Friesen, W. V. (1990). The Duchenne smile: Emotional expression and brain physiology: II. *Journal of Personality and Social Psychology, 58,* 342–353.

Ekman, P., & Friesen, W. V. (1969). The repertoire of nonverbal behavior: Categories, origins, usage, and coding. *Semiotica, 1,* 49–98.

Ekman, P., & Friesen, W. V. (1971). Constants across cultures in the face and emotion. *Journal of Personality and Social Psychology, 17,* 124–129.

Ekman, P., & O'Sullivan, M. (1991). Facial expressions: Methods, means, and moues. In R. S. Feldman & B. Rime (Eds.), *Fundamentals of nonverbal behavior.* Cambridge, U.K.: Cambridge University Press.

Elbert, T. (2012). Pain from brain: Can we remodel neural circuitry that generates phantom limb pain and other forms of neuropathic pain? *Neuroscience Letters, 507,* 95–96.

Eley, T. C., & others. (2004). Gene-environment interaction analysis of serotonin system markers with adolescent depression. *Molecular Psychiatry, 9* (10), 908–915.

El-Hai, J. (2005). *The lobotomist: A maverick medical genius and his tragic quest to rid the world of mental illness.* Hoboken, NJ: Wiley.

Elias, S. M., Gibson, L. A., & Barney, C. E. (2013). The role of social power in sexual harassment and job discrimination. *Deviant and Criminal Behavior in the Workplace,* 178–194.

Elkind, D. (1978). Understanding the young adolescent. *Adolescence, 13,* 127–134.

Elkins, G., Johnson, A., & Fisher, W. (2012). Cognitive hypnotherapy for pain management. *American Journal of Clinical Hypnosis, 54,* 294–310.

Elliott, M. A., & Ainsworth, K. (2012). Predicting university undergraduates' binge-drinking behavior: A comparative test of the one- and two-component theories of planned behavior. *Addictive Behaviors, 37,* 92–101.

Elliott, T., Kuang, X., Shadbolt, N. R., & Zauner, K. P. (2009). Adaptation in multisensory neurons:

Impact of cross-modal enhancement. *Network, 20,* 1–31.

Ellis, A. (2005). Why I (really) became a therapist. *Journal of Clinical Psychology, 61,* 945–948.

Ellis, M., Chambers, J. D., Gwynne, R. M., & Bornstein, J. C. (2013). Serotonin (5-HT) and cholecystokinin (CCK) mediate nutrient induced segmentation in guinea pig small intestine. *American Journal of Physiology and Gastrointestinal Liver Physiology, 304* (8), G749–G761.

Elmenhorst, D., Kroll, T., Matusch, A., & Bauer, A. (2012). Sleep deprivation increases cerebral serotonin 2A receptor binding in humans. *Sleep, 35,* 1615–1623.

Emery, C. F., Anderson, D. R., & Goodwin, C. L. (2013). Coronary heart disease and hypertension. In A. M. Nezu, C. Maguth Nezu, P. A. Geller, & I. B. Weiner (Eds.), *Handbook of psychology, 2nd ed., Vol. 9.* (pp. 340–364). Hoboken, NJ: Wiley.

Emes, R. D., & Grant, S. G. N. (2012). Evolution of synaptic complexity and diversity. *Annual Review of Neuroscience* (vol. 35). Palo Alto, CA: Annual Reviews.

Emmanouil, T. A., Burton, P., & Ro, T. (2013). Unconscious processing of unattended features in human visual cortex. *Journal of Cognitive Neuroscience, 25* (3), 329–337.

Emmons, R. A. (2005). Striving for the sacred: Personal goals, life meaning, and religion. *Journal of Social Issues, 61,* 731–745.

Emmons, R. A., & Diener, E. (1986). Situation selection as a moderator of response consistency and stability. *Journal of Personality and Social Psychology, 51,* 1013–1019.

Emmons, R. A., & King, L. A. (1988). Conflict among personal strivings: Immediate and long-term implications for psychological and physical well-being. *Journal of Personality and Social Psychology, 48,* 1040–1048.

Emmons, R. A., & McCullough, M. E. (2003). Counting blessings versus burdens: An experimental investigation of gratitude and subjective well-being in daily life. *Journal of Personality and Social Psychology, 84,* 377–389.

Emmons, R. A., & McCullough, M. E. (Eds.). (2004). *The psychology of gratitude.* New York: Oxford University Press.

Endler, N. S. (1988). The origins of electroconvulsive therapy (ECT). *Convulsive Therapy, 4,* 5–23.

Endrass, T., Kloft, L., Kaufmann, C., & Kathmann, N. (2011). Approach and avoidance learning in obsessive-compulsive disorder. *Depression and Anxiety, 28* (2), 166–172.

Endrass, T., Koehne, S., Riesel, A., & Kathmann, N. (2013). Neural correlates of feedback processing in obsessive-compulsive disorder. *Journal of Abnormal Psychology, 122,* 387–396.

Enea, V., & Dafinoiu, I. (2013). Flexibility in processing visual information: Effects of mood and hypnosis. *International Journal of Clinical and Experimental Hypnosis, 61,* 55–70.

Eng, P. M., Fitzmaurice, G., Kubzansky, L. D., Rimm, E. B., & Kawachi, I. (2003). Anger expression and risk of stroke and coronary heart disease among male health professionals. *Psychosomatic Medicine, 65,* 100–110.

Engel, A. K., & Singer, W. (2001). Temporal binding and the neural correlates of sensory awareness. *Trends in Cognitive Science, 5,* 16–25.

Engelmann, J. B., & Pogosyan, M. (2013). Emotion perception across cultures: The role of cognitive mechanisms. *Frontiers in Psychology.* doi: 10.3389/fpsyg.2013.00118

Englander, E. K. (2006). *Understanding violence* (3rd ed.). Mahwah, NJ: Erlbaum.

Engler, B. (2014). *Personality theories* (9th ed.). Boston: Cengage.

Enns, C. Z. (2012). Feminist approaches to counseling. In E. M. Altmaier & J. C. Hansen (Eds.), *The Oxford handbook of counseling psychology* (pp. 434–459). New York: Oxford University Press.

Enoch, M. A., & others. (2013). Independent effects of 5' and 3' functional variants in the serotonin transporter gene on suicidal behavior in the context of childhood trauma. *Journal of Psychiatric Research.* (in press)

Enstrom, J. E. (1999). Smoking cessation and mortality trends among two United States populations. *Journal of Clinical Epidemiology, 52,* 813–825.

Epstein-Ngo, Q. M., & others. (2013). A daily calendar analysis of substance use and dating violence among high risk urban youth. *Drug and Alcohol Dependence.* (in press)

Equal Employment Opportunity Commission (EEOC). (2012). *Sexual harassment charges EEOC & FEPAs combined FY 1997–2011.* Washington, DC: Author. www.eeoc.gov/eeoc/statistics/enforcement/sexual_harassment.cfm (accessed June 4, 2013)

Ericsson, K. A., & Moxley, J. H. (2012). A critique of Howard's argument for innate limits in chess performance or why we need an account based on acquired skill and deliberate practice. *Applied Cognitive Psychology, 26,* 649–653.

Erikson, E. H. (1968). *Identity: Youth and crisis.* New York: Norton.

Erikson, E. H. (1969). *Gandhi's truth.* New York: Norton.

Ernst, Z. R., Palmer, J., & Boynton, G. M. (2012). Dividing attention between two transparent motion surfaces in a failure of selective attention. *Journal of Vision.* doi: 10.1167/12.9.1334

Esler, M., Eikelis, N., Schlaich, M., Lambert, G., Alvarenga, M., Kaye, D., El-Osta, A., Guo, L., Barton, D., Pier, C., Brenchley, C., Dawood, T., Jennings, G., Lambert, E. (2009). Human sympathetic nerve biology: Parallel influences of stress and epigenetics in essential hypertension and panic disorder. In R. Kvetňanský, G. Aguilera, D. Goldstein, D. Jezova, O. Krizanova, E. L. Sabban, & K. Pacak (Eds.), *Stress, neurotransmitters, and hormones: Neuroendocrine and genetic mechanisms* (pp. 338–348). New York: New York Academy of Sciences.

Espana, R. A., & Jones, S. R. (2013). Presynaptic dopamine modulation by stimulant self-administration. *Frontiers in Bioscience, 5,* 261–276.

Espirito-Santo, H., & Pio-Abreu, J. L. (2009). Psychiatric symptoms and dissociation in conversion, somatization, and dissociative disorders. *Australian and New Zealand Journal of Psychiatry, 43,* 270–276.

Esposito, E. A., Grigorenko, E. L., & Sternberg, R. J. (2012). The nature-nurture issue: An illustration using behavior-genetic research on cognitive development. In A. Slater & J. Gavin-Bremmer (Eds.), *An introduction to developmental psychology* (2nd ed.). New York: Wiley-Blackwell.

Estes. A. C. (2013). Mental health and the dangers of oversimplifying gun control. *Motherboard Vice.* http://motherboard.vice.com/blog/mental-health-dangers-oversimplifying-gun-control (accessed May 30, 2013)

Evans, B. G., & Iverson, P. (2007). Plasticity in vowel perception and production: A study of accent change in young adults. *Journal of the Acoustical Society of America, 121* (6), 3814–3826.

Evans, C., & Diekman, A. B. (2009). On motivated role selection: Gender beliefs, distant goals, and career interest. *Psychology of Women Quarterly, 33,* 235–249.

Evans, St. J. B. T., & Stanovich, K. E. (2013). Dual-process theories of higher cognition: Advancing the debate. *Perspectives on Psychological Science.* (in press)

Evenson, R. J., & Simon, R. W. (2005). Clarifying the relationship between parenthood and depression. *Journal of Health and Social Behavior, 46,* 341–358.

Eysenck, H. J. (1967). *The biological basis of personality.* Springfield, IL: Thomas.

Eysenck, H. J. (1995). *Intelligence: A new look.* New York: Transaction.

Eysenck, M. W., & Keane, M. (2010). *Cognitive psychology.* New York: Psychology Press.

F

Faber, M. A., & Mayer, J. D. (2009). Resonance to archetypes in media: There's some accounting for taste. *Journal of Research in Personality, 43,* 307–322.

Faedda, G. L., Becker, I., Baroni, A., Tondo, L., Aspland, E., & Koukopoulos, A. (2010). The origins of electroconvulsive therapy: Prof. Bini's first report on ECT. *Journal of Affective Disorders, 120,* 12–15.

Fagan, T. K. (2013). School psychology. In D. K. Freedheim & I. B. Weiner (Eds.). *Handbook of psychology, 2nd ed., Vol. 1.* (pp. 448–467). Hoboken, NJ: Wiley.

Fagot, B. I. (1978). The influence of sex of child on parental reactions to toddler children. *Child Development,* 459–465.

Fahey, T. D., Insel, P. M., & Roth, W. T. (2013). *Fit and well* (10th ed.). New York: McGraw-Hill.

Faimberg, H. (2012). Listening to the psychic consequences of Nazism in psychoanalytic patients. *Psychoanalytic Quarterly, 81,* 157–169.

Fairweather, E., & Cramond, B. (2011). Infusing creative and critical thinking into the classroom. In R. A. Beghetto & J. C. Kaufman (Eds.), *Nurturing creativity in the classroom.* New York: Cambridge University Press.

Falk, C. F., Heine, S. J., Yuki, M., & Takemura, K. (2009). Why do Westerners self-enhance more than East Asians? *European Journal of Personality, 23,* 183–203.

Family and Youth Services Bureau. (2004). *Fact sheet: Section 510 state abstinence education program.* Bethesda, MD: U.S. Department of Health and Human Services.

Fant, R. V., Buchhalter, A. R., Buchman, A. C., & Heningfield, J. E. (2009). Pharmacotherapy for tobacco dependence. *Handbook of Experimental Pharmacology, 192,* 487–510.

Farr, R. H., & Patterson, C. J. (2013). Lesbian and gay adoptive parents and their children. In A. E. Goldberg & K. R. Allen (Eds.), *LGBT-parent families: Innovations in research and implications for practice* (pp. 39–55). New York: Springer.

Farren, C. K., Snee, L., & McElroy, S. (2011). Gender differences in outcome at 2-year follow-up of treated bipolar and depressed alcoholics. *Journal of Studies of Alcohol and Drugs, 72,* 872–880.

Fatemi, S. H., & Folsom, T. D. (2009). The neurodevelopmental hypothesis of schizophrenia, revisited. *Schizophrenia Bulletin, 35,* 528–548.

Faugeras, F., & others. (2012). Event related potentials elicited by violations of auditory regularities in patients with impaired consciousness. *Neuropsychologia, 50,* 403–418.

Faul, L. A., Jim, H. S., Williams, C., Loftus, L., & Jacobsen, P. B. (2009).Relationship of stress management skill to psychological distress and quality of life in adults with cancer. *Psychooncology, 19* (1), 102–109.

Fausto-Sterling, A., Garcia Coll, C., & Lamarre, M. (2012). Sexing the baby: Part 1–What do we really know about sex differentiation in the first three years of life? *Social Science and Medicine, 74,* 1684–1692.

Fava, G. A. (2006). The intellectual crisis in psychiatric research. *Psychotherapy and Psychosomatics, 75,* 202–208.

Fava, G. A., Ruini, C., & Belaise, C. (2007). The concept of recovery in depression. *Psychological Medicine, 37,* 307–317.

Fava, N. M., & Bay-Cheng, L. Y. (2012). Young women's adolescent experiences of oral sex: Relation of age of initiation to sexual motivation, sexual coercion, and psychological functioning. *Journal of Adolescence, 35,* 1191–1201.

Faymonville, M. E., Boly, M., & Laureys, S. (2006). Functional neuroanatomy of the hypnotic state. *Journal of Physiology, Paris, 99,* 463–469.

Fazio, R. H., Chen, J., McDonel, E. C., & Sherman, S. J. (1982). Attitude accessibility, attitude-behavior consistency, and the strength of the object-evaluation association. *Journal of Experimental Social Psychology, 18,* 339–357.

Fazio, R. H., & Olsen, A. (2007). Attitudes. In M. A. Hogg & J. Cooper (Eds.), *The Sage handbook of social psychology* (concise 2nd ed.). Thousand Oaks, CA: Sage.

Fei-Fei, L., Iyer, A., Koch, C., & Perona, P. (2007). What do we perceive in a glance at a real-world scene? *Journal of Vision, 7,* 10.

Feinberg, I., & Campell, I. G. (2013). Longitudinal sleep EEG trajectories indicate complex patterns of adolescent brain maturation. *American Journal of Physiology. Regulatory, Integrative, and Comparative Physiology.* (in press)

Feinstein, E. C., Richer, L., & Foster, S. E. (2012). Addressing the critical health problem of adolescent substance use through health care, research, and public policy. *Journal of Adolescent Health, 50* (5), 431–436.

Feinstein, J. S., Buzza, C., Hurlemann, R., Follmer, R. L., Dahdaleh, N. S., Coryell, W. H., Welsh, M. J., Tranel, D., & Wemmie, J. A. (2013). Fear and panic in humans with bilateral amygdala damage. *Nature Neuroscience, 16,* 270–272.

Feist, G. J. (1998). A meta-analysis of personality in scientific and artistic creativity. *Personality and Social Psychology Review, 2* (4), 290–309.

Felfe, J., & Schyns, B. (2006). Personality and the perception of transformational leadership: The impact of extraversion, neuroticism, personal need for structure, and occupational self-efficacy. *Journal of Applied Social Psychology, 36* (3), 708–739.

Feng, J., Spence, I., & Pratt, J. (2007). Playing an action video game reduces gender differences in spatial cognition. *Psychological Science, 18* (10), 850–855.

Fenn, K. M., & Hambrick, D. Z. (2013). What drives sleep-dependent memory consolidation: Greater gain or less loss? *Psychonomic Bulletin and Review.* (in press)

Ferguson, C. J., & Kilburn, J. (2010). Much ado about nothing: The misestimation and overinterpretation of violent video game effects in Eastern and Western nations: Comment on Anderson et al. (2010). *Psychological Bulletin, 136,* 174–178.

Ferguson, C. J., Rueda, S. M., Cruz, A. M., Ferguson, D. E., Fritz, S., & Smith, S. M. (2008). Violent video games and aggression: Causal relationship or byproduct of family violence and intrinsic violence motivation? *Criminal Justice and Behavior, 35,* 311–332.

Fergusson, D. M., McLeod, G. F., & Horwood, L. J. (2013). Childhood sexual abuse and adult developmental outcomes: Findings from a 30-year longitudinal study in New Zealand. *Child Abuse and Neglect.* (in press)

Ferguson, E., & Bibby, P. A. (2012). Openness to experience and all-cause mortality: A meta-analysis and r(equivalent) from risk ratios and odds ratios. *British Journal of Health Psychology, 17,* 85–102.

Feri, F., Meléndez-Jiménez, M. A., Ponti, G., & Vega-Redondo, F. (2011). Error cascades in observational learning: An experiment on the Chinos game. *Games and Economic Behavior, 73,* 136–146.

Fernhall, B. (2013). Long-term aerobic exercise maintains peak VO(2), improves quality of life, and reduces hospitalizations and mortality in patients with heart failure. *Journal of Physiotherapy, 59* (1), 56.

Ferrari, M., & Westrate, N. (Eds.). (2013). *Personal wisdom.* New York: Springer.

Ferretti, F., & Coluccia, A. (2009). Socio-economic factors and suicide rates in European Union countries. *Legal Medicine, 11,* Suppl. 1, S92–S94.

Ferrie, J. E., & others. (2011). Change in sleep duration and cognitive function: Findings from the Whitehall II Study. *Sleep, 34,* 565–573.

Festinger, L. (1954). A theory of social comparison processes. *Human Relations, 7,* 117–140.

Festinger, L. (1957). *A theory of cognitive dissonance.* Evanston, IL: Row Peterson.

Festinger, L., & Carlsmith, J. M. (1959). Cognitive consequences of forced compliance. *Journal of Abnormal and Social Psychology, 58,* 203–211.

Field, T. M., Diego, M., & Hernandez-Reif, M. (2011). Preterm infant massage therapy research: A review. *Infant Behavior and Development, 34,* 383–389.

Fields, R. (2013). *Drugs in perspective* (8th ed.). New York: McGraw-Hill.

Fifer, W. P., & Myers, M. M. (2002) Sudden fetal and infant deaths: Shared observations and distinctive features. *Seminar in Perinatology, 26,* 89–96.

Finch C. E. (2009). The neurobiology of middle-age has arrived. *Neurobiology and Aging, 30,* 515-520.

Finch, C. E. (2011). Inflammation and aging. In E. Masoro & S. Austad (Eds.), *Handbook of the biology of aging* (7th ed.). New York: Elsevier.

Finch, E. A., Linde, J. A., Jeffery, R. W., Rothman, A. J., King, C. M., & Levy, R. L. (2005). The effects of outcome expectations and satisfaction on weight loss and maintenance: Correlational and experimental analyses—A randomized trial. *Health Psychology, 24* (6), 608–616.

Fine, C. (2010). From scanner to sound bite: Issues in interpreting and reporting sex differences in the brain. *Current Directions in Psychological Science, 19,* 280–283.

Fingerhut, A. W., & Peplau, L. A. (2013). Same-sex romantic relationships. In C. J. Patterson & A. R. D'Augelli (Eds.), *Handbook of psychology and sexual orientation.* New York: Oxford University Press.

Fink, B., Brewer, G., Fehl, K., & Neave, N. (2007). Instrumentality and lifetime number of sexual partners. *Personality and Individual Differences, 43,* 747–756.

Firestone, D. (2012, November 9). The Republican bubble. *New York Times.* http://takingnote.blogs. nytimes.com/2012/11/09/the-republican-bubble/ (accessed April 9, 2013)

Fischer, R. (2006). Congruence and functions of personal and cultural values: Do my values reflect my culture's values? *Personality and Social Psychology Bulletin, 32,* 1419–1431.

Fischhoff, B., Bruine de Bruin, W., Parker, A. M., Millstein, S. G., & Halpern-Felsher, B. L. (2010). Adolescents' perceived risk of dying. *Journal of Adolescent Health, 46,* 265–269.

Fisher, A. J., Granger, D. A., & Newman, M. G. (2010). Sympathetic arousal moderates self-reported physiological arousal symptoms at baseline and physiological flexibility in response to a stressor in generalized anxiety disorder. *Biological Psychology, 83,* 191–200.

Fisher, M., Loewy, R., Hardy, K., Schlosser, D., & Vinogradov, S. (2013). Cognitive interventions targeting brain plasticity in the prodromal and early phases of schizophrenia. *Annual Review of Clinical Psychology* (vol. 9). Palo Alto, CA: Annual Reviews.

Fisher, T. D., Moore, Z. T., & Pittenger, M. J. (2012). Sex on the brain? An examination of frequency of sexual cognitions as a function of gender, erotophilia, and social desirability. *Journal of Sex Research, 49,* 69–77.

Fiske, A., Wetherell, J. L., & Gatz, M. (2009). Depression in older adults. *Annual Review of Clinical Psychology* (vol. 5). Palo Alto, CA: Annual Reviews.

Fitness, J., & Williams, V. (2013). The features and functions of positive emotions in close relationships. In M. Hojjat & D. Cramer (Eds.), *Positive psychology of love.* New York: Oxford University Press.

Fitzgerald, L. F. (2003). Sexual harassment and social justice: Reflections on the distance yet to go. *American Psychologist, 58,* 915–924.

Fitzhugh, E. C., Bassett, D. R., & Evans, M. F. (2010). Urban trails and physical activity: A natural experiment. *American Journal of Preventive Medicine, 39,* 259–262.

Fitzpatrick, K. K. (2012). Developmental considerations when treating anorexia nervosa in adolescents and young adults. In J. Lock (Ed.), *The Oxford handbook of child and adolescent eating disorders: Developmental perspectives.* New York: Oxford Univeristy Press.

Fivush, R. (2011). The development of autobiographical memory. *Annual Review of Psychology* (vol. 62). Palo Alto, CA: Annual Reviews.

Flagel, S. B., Akil, H., & Robinson, T. E. (2009). Individual differences in the attribution of incentive salience to reward-related cues: Implications for addition. *Neuropharmacology, 56,* 139–148.

Flanagan, K. S., Vanden Hoek, K. K., Ranter, J. M., & Reich, H. A. (2012). The potential of forgiveness as a response for coping with negative peer experiences. *Journal of Adolescence, 35,* 1215–1223.

Fleeson, W., Malanos, A. B., & Achille, N. M. (2002). An intraindividual process approach to the relationship between extraversion and positive affect: Is acting extraverted as "good" as being extraverted? *Journal of Personality and Social Psychology, 83,* 1409–1422.

Flegal, K. M., Carroll, M. D., Kit, B. K., & Ogden, C. L. (2012). Prevalence of obesity and trends in the distribution of body mass index among US adults, 1999–2010. *Journal of the American Medical Association, 307* (5), 491–497. http://jama.ama-assn.org/content/307/5/491 (accessed June 19, 2013)

Fleischmann, F., Phalet, K., & Klein, O. (2011). Religious affiliation and politicization in the face of discrimination: Support for political Islam and political action among the Turkish and Moroccan second generation in Europe. *British Journal of Social Psychology, 50,* 628–648.

Fleming, L., & Davidson, J. R. (2012). Sleep and medical disorders. In C. M. Morin & C. A. Espie (Eds.), *The Oxford handbook of sleep and sleep disorders.* New York: Oxford University Press.

Fleuret, F., & others. (2011). Comparing machines and humans on a visual categorization test. *Proceedings of the National Academy of Sciences USA, 108,* 17621–17625.

Flint, M. S., Baum, A., Chambers, W. H., & Jenkins, F. J. (2007). Induction of DNA damage, alteration of DNA repair, and transcriptional activation by stress hormones. *Psychoneuroendocrinology, 32,* 470–479.

Flor, H., & Diers, M. (2009). Sensorimotor training and cortical reorganization. *NeuroRehabilitation, 25,* 19–27.

Floyd, D. L., Prentice-Dunn, S., & Rogers, R. W. (2000). A meta-analysis of research on protection motivation theory. *Journal of Applied Social Psychology, 30,* 407–429.

Flynn, J. R. (1999). Searching for justice: The discovery of IQ gains over time. *American Psychologist, 54,* 5–20.

Flynn, J. R. (2006). The history of the American mind in the 20th century: A scenario to explain gains over time and a case for the irrelevance of *g.* In P. C. Kyllonen, R. D. Roberts, & L. Stankov (Eds.), *Extending intelligence.* Mahwah, NJ: Erlbaum.

Flynn, J. R. (2013). *Are we getting smarter?* New York: Cambridge University Press.

Fodor, I., & Epstein, J. (2002). Agoraphobia, panic disorder, and gender. In J. Worell (Ed.), *Encyclopedia of women and gender.* San Diego: Academic.

Foell, J., Bekrater-Bodmann, R., Flor, H., & Cole, J. (2011). Phantom limb after lower limb trauma: Origins and treatments. *International Journal of Lower Extremity Wounds, 10,* 224–235.

Foer, J. (2008). The unspeakable odyssey of the motionless boy. *Esquire.* www.esquire.com/features/unspeakable-odyssey-motionless-boy-1008 (accessed February 21, 2013)

Fok, H., Hui, C., Bond, M. H., Matsumoto, D., & Yoo, S. H. (2008). Integrating personality, context, relationship, and emotion type into a model of display rules. *Journal of Research in Personality, 42,* 133–150.

Foley, J. A., Kaschel, R., Logie, R. H., & Della Sala, S. (2011). Dual-task performance in Alzheimer's disease, mild cognitive impairment, and normal aging. *Archives of Clinical Neuropsychology, 26,* 340–348.

Foley, M., & Rauser, E. (2012). Evaluating progress in reducing workplace violence: Trends in Washington State workers' compensation claims rates, 1997–2007. *Work, 42* (1), 67–81.

Folkman, S., & Lazarus, R. S. (1980). An analysis of coping in a middle-aged community sample. *Journal of Health and Social Behavior, 21,* 219–239.

Folkman, S., & Moskowitz, J. T. (2004). Coping: Pitfalls and promises. *Annual Review of Psychology* (vol. 54). (pp. 745–744). Palo Alto, CA: Annual Reviews.

Fombonne, E. (2005). The changing epidemiology of autism. *Journal of Applied Research in Intellectual Disabilities, 18,* 281–295.

Fondell, E., & others. (2011). Short natural sleep is associated with higher T cell and lower NK cell activities. *Brain, Behavior, and Immunity, 25,* 1367–1375.

Fontana, A. P., Kilner, J. M., Rodrigues, E. C., Joffily, M., Nighoghossian, N., Vargas, C. D., & Sirigu, A. (2012). Role of the parietal cortex in predicting incoming actions. *NeuroImage, 59* (1), 556–564.

Fooladi, E., Bell, R. J., & Davis, S. R. (2012). Management strategies in SSRI-associated dysfunction in women at midlife. *Climacteric, 15,* 306–316.

Foote, B., Smolin, Y., Kaplan, M., Legatt, M. E., & Lipschitz, D. (2006). Prevalence of dissociative disorders in psychiatric outpatients. *American Journal of Psychiatry, 163,* 566–568.

Forbush, K., Heatherton, T. F., & Keel, P. K. (2007). Relationships between perfectionism and specific disordered eating behaviors. *International Journal of Eating Disorders, 40,* 37–41.

"Forecast for growth on campuses: More women, minorities." (2011, August 21). *Chronicle of higher education: Almanac of higher education 201.* http://chronicle.com/article/Forecast-for-Growth-on/128272/ (accessed March 30, 2013)

Forgas, J. P., Dunn, E., & Granland, S. (2008). Are you being served . . . ? An unobtrusive experiment of affective influences on helping in a department store. *European Journal of Social Psychology, 38,* 333–342.

Forgas, J. P., Fiedler, K., & Sedikides, C. (Eds.). (2012). *Social thinking and interpersonal behavior.* New York: Psychology Press.

Forman-Hoffman, V. L., & Cunningham, C. L. (2008). Geographical clustering of eating disordered behaviors in U.S. high school students. *International Journal of Eating Disorders, 41,* 209–214.

Forsythe, C., Bernard, M. L., & Goldsmith, T. E. (Eds.). (2006). *Cognitive systems.* Mahwah, NJ: Erlbaum.

Fouad, K., Bennett, D., Fischer, H., & Buchges, A. (2013). Comparative locomotor systems. In R. J. Nelson, S. J. Y. Mizumori, & I. B. Weiner (Eds.), *Handbook of psychology* (2nd ed., vol. 3). Hoboken, NJ: Wiley.

Fountas, K. N., & Smith, J. R. (2007). Historical evolution of stereotactic amygdalotomy for the management of severe aggression. *Journal of Neurosurgery, 106,* 710–713.

Fountoulakis, K. N. (2012). The possible involvement of NMDA glutamate receptor in the etiopathogenesis of bipolar disorder. *Current Pharmaceutical Design, 18,* 1605–1608.

Fowler, K. A., Lilienfeld, S. O., & Patrick, C. J. (2009). Detecting psychopathy from thin slices of behavior. *Psychological Assessment, 21,* 68–78.

Fox, R., & Millam, J. R. (2010). The use of ratings and direct behavioural observation to measure temperament traits in cockatiels (*Nymphicus hollandicus*). *Ethology, 116,* 59–75.

Fraley, R. C., Vicary, A. M., Brumbaugh, C. C., & Roisman, G. I. (2011). Patterns of stability in adult attachment: An empirical test of two models of continuity and change. *Journal of Personality and Social Psychology, 101,* 974–990.

Frank, M. G. (2006). The mystery of sleep function: Current perspectives and future directions. *Reviews in the Neurosciences, 17,* 375–392.

Franke, R. H., & Kaul, J. D. (1978). The Hawthorne experiments: First statistical interpretation. *American Sociological Review, 43,* 623–643.

Frankl, V. E. (2006). *Man's search for meaning* (3rd ed., reprint). I. Lasch (Trans.). Boston: Beacon. (original work published 1946)

Franklin, R. G., & Adams, R. B. (2011). The reward of a good joke: Neural correlates of viewing dynamic displays of stand-up comedy. *Cognitive, Affective, and Behavioral Neuroscience, 11,* 508–515.

Frattaroli, J. (2006). Experimental disclosure and its moderators: A meta-analysis. *Psychological Bulletin, 132,* 823–865.

Frazier, T. W. (2012). Friends not foes: Combined risperidone and behavior therapy for irritability in autism. *Journal of the American Academy of Child and Adolescent Psychiatry, 51,* 129–131.

Fredrick, S., & Loewenstein, G. (1999). Hedonic adaptation. In D. Kahneman, E. Diener, & N. Schwarz (Eds.), *Well-being: The foundations of hedonic psychology* (pp. 302–329). New York: Russell Sage Foundation.

Fredrickson, B. L. (1998). What good are positive emotions? *Review of General Psychology, 2,* 300–319.

Fredrickson, B. L. (2001). The role of positive emotions in positive psychology. *American Psychologist, 56,* 218–226.

Fredrickson, B. L. (2006). Unpacking positive emotions: Investigating the seeds of human flourishing. *Journal of Positive Psychology, 1,* 57–60.

Fredrickson, B. L. (2009). *Positivity.* New York: Crown.

Fredrickson, B. L. (2013a). *Love 2.0.* New York: Hudson Street.

Fredrickson, B. L. (2013b). Positive emotions broaden and build. In E. A. Plant & P. G. Devine (Eds.), *Advances on experimental social psychology.* (in press)

Fredrickson, B. L., & Roberts, T. (1997). Objectification theory: Toward understanding women's lived experiences and mental health risks. *Psychology of Women Quarterly, 21,* 173–206.

Fredrickson, B. L., Roberts, T., Noll, S. M., Quinn, D. M., & Twenge, J. M. (1998). That swimsuit becomes you: Sex differences in self-objectification, restrained eating, and math performance. *Journal of Personality and Social Psychology, 75,* 269–284.

Fredrickson, B. L., Tugade, M. M., Waugh, C. E., & Larkin, G. R. (2003). What good are positive emotions in crisis? A prospective study of resilience and emotions following the terrorist attacks on the United States on September 11th, 2001. *Journal of Personality and Social Psychology, 84,* 365–376.

Freedman, J. L., & Fraser, S. C. (1966). Compliance without pressure: The foot-in-the-door technique. *Journal of Personality and Social Psychology, 4,* 195–202.

Freedy, J. R., Carek, P. J., Diaz, V. A., & Thiedke, C. C. (2012). Integrating cognitive therapy into management of depression. *American Family Physician, 85,* 686–687.

Freeland, A., Manchanda, R., Chiu, S., Sharma, V., & Merskey, H. (1993). Four cases of supposed multiple personality disorder: Evidence of unjustified diagnoses. *Canadian Journal of Psychiatry, 38,* 245–247.

Freeman, D., & Freeman, J. (2012). *Anxiety.* New York: Oxford University Press.

Freestone, D. M., & Church, R. M. (2010). The importance of the reinforcer as a time marker. *Behavioral Processes, 84* (1), 500–505.

French, C. C., Santomauro, J., Hamilton, V., Fox, R., & Thalbourne, M. A. (2008). Psychological aspects of alien contact experience. *Cortex, 44,* 1387–1395.

Frenda, S. J., Nichols, R. M., & Loftus, E. F. (2011). Current issues and advances in misinformation research. *Current Directions in Psychological Science, 20,* 20–23.

Frensch, K. M., Pratt, M. W., & Norris, J. E. (2007). Foundations of generativity: Personal and family correlates of emerging adults' generative life-story themes. *Journal of Research in Personality, 41,* 45–62.

Freud, S. (1911). *The interpretation of dreams* (3rd ed.). A. A. Brill (Trans.). New York: Macmillan. (original work published 1899)

Freud, S. (1917). *A general introduction to psychoanalysis.* New York: Washington Square Press.

Freud, S. (1996). Number 23091. In R. Andrews, M. Seidel, & M. Biggs, (Eds.), *Columbia world of quotations.* New York: Columbia University Press. (original work published 1918)

Freund, A. M., Nikitin, J., & Riediger, M. (2013). Successful aging. In R. M. Lerner, M. A. Easterbrooks, J. Mistry, & I. B. Weiner (Eds.), *Handbook of psychology, 2nd ed., Vol. 6.* (pp. 615–638). Hoboken, NJ: Wiley.

Frey, B. N., & others. (2013). Biomarkers in bipolar disorder: A positional paper from the International Society for Bipolar Disorders Biomarkers Task Force, *47,* 321–332.

Fried, S. (2008, October 9). Commentary in "Think fat just hangs around, does nothing." *USA Today,* 6D.

Friedman, E. M., Karlamangla, A. S., Almeida, D. M., & Seeman, T. E. (2012). Social strain and cortisol regulation in midlife in the US. *Social Science & Medicine, 74* (4), 607–615.

Friedman, H. S. (2014). Personality and health. *Annual Review of Psychology* (vol. 65). Palo Alto, CA: Annual Reviews. (in press)

Friedman, M., & Rosenman, R. (1974). *Type A behavior and your heart.* New York: Knopf.

Friedman, R., Myers, P., & Benson, H. (1998). Meditation and the relaxation response. In H. S. Friedman (Ed.), *Encyclopedia of mental health* (vol. 2). San Diego: Academic.

Friese, M., Messner, C., & Schaffner, Y. (2012). Mindfulness meditation counteracts self-control depletion. *Consciousness and Cognition, 21,* 1016–1022.

Frijda, N. H. (2007). *The laws of emotion.* Mahwah, NJ: Erlbaum.

Fritz, C., & Sonnentag, S. (2006). Recovery, well-being, and performance-related outcomes: The role of work overload and vacation experiences. *Journal of Applied Psychology, 91,* 936–945.

Fromm, E. (1947). *Man for himself.* New York: Holt, Rinehart & Winston.

Fromm, E. (1973). *The anatomy of human destructiveness.* New York: Fawcett.

Frost, R. O., Steketee, G., & Tolin, D. F. (2012). Diagnosis and assessment of hoarding disorder. *Annual Review of Clinical Psychology* (vol. 8). Palo Alto: Annual Reviews.

Frost, R. O., Tolin, D. F., Steketee, G., & Oh, M. (2011). Indecisiveness and hoarding. *International Journal of Cognitive Therapy, 4,* 253–262.

Fry, P. S., & Debats, D. L. (2009). Perfectionism and the five-factor personality traits as predictors of mortality in older adults. *Journal of Health Psychology, 14,* 513–524.

Fry, R. B., & Prentice-Dunn, S. (2006). Effects of a psychosocial intervention on breast self-examination attitudes and behaviors. *Health Education Research, 21,* 287–295.

Fryberg, S. A., & Markus, H. R. (2003). On being American Indian: Current and possible selves. *Self and Identity, 2,* 325–344.

Fu, F. Q., Richards, K. A., Hughes, D. E., & Jones, E. (2010). Motivating salespeople to sell new products: The relative influence of attitudes, subjective norms, and self-efficacy. *Journal of Marketing, 74* (6), 61–76.

Fuchs, A. H., & Evans, R. B. (2013). Psychology as a science. In D. K. Freedheim & I. B. Weiner (Eds.), *Handbook of psychology, 2nd ed., Vol. 1.* (pp. 1–31). Hoboken, NJ: Wiley.

Funder, D. C. (2009). Persons, behaviors, and situations: An agenda for personality psychology in the postwar era. *Journal of Research in Personality, 43,* 120–126.

Fujiwara, E., Levine, B., & Anderson, A. K. (2008). Intact implicit and reduced explicit memory for negative self-related information in repressive coping. *Cognitive, Affective, and Behavioral Neuroscience, 8,* 254–263.

Fung, M. T., Raine, A., Loeber, R., Lynam, D. R., Steinhauer, S. R., Venables, P. H., & Stouthamer-Loeber, M. (2005). Reduced electrodermal activity in psychopathy-prone adolescents. *Journal of Abnormal Psychology, 114,* 187–196.

G

Gabert-Quillen, C. A., & others. (2012). The impact of social support on the relationship between trauma history and PTSD symptoms in motor vehicle accident victims. *International Journal of Stress Management, 19,* 69–79.

Gaig, C., & Iranzo, A. (2012). Sleep-disordered breathing in neurogenerative diseases. *Current Neurology and Neuroscience Reports,12* (2), 205–217.

Gaillard, R., Dehaene, S., Adam, C., Clémenceau, S., Hasboun, D., Baulac, M., Cohen, L., & Naccache, L. (2009). Converging intracranial markers of conscious access. *PLoS Biology, 7,* e1000061.

Gaines, S. O. (2012). Stereotyping, prejudice, and discrimination revisited: From Willliam James to W. E. B. Du Bois. In J. Dixon & M. Levine (Eds.), *Beyond prejudice.* New York: Cambridge University Press.

Gainotti, G. (2012). Unconscious processing of emotions and the right hemisphere. *Neuropsychologia, 50,* 205–218.

Galambos, N. L., Howard, A. L., & Maggs, J. L. (2011). Rise and fall of sleep quality with student experiences across the first year of the university. *Journal of Research on Adolescence, 21,* 342–349.

Gallagher, K. E., & Parrott, D. J. (2010). Influence of heavy episodic drinking on the relation between men's locus of control and aggression toward intimate partners. *Journal of Studies on Alcohol and Drugs, 71,* 299–306.

Gallagher, M. W., Lopez, S. J., & Pressman, S. D. (2013). Optimism is universal: Exploring the presence and benefits of optimism in a representative sample of the world. *Journal of Personality.* (in press)

Gallese, V., Gernsbacher, M. A., Heyes, C., Hickok, G., & Iacoboni, M. (2011). Mirror neuron forum. *Perspectives on Psychological Science, 6,* 369–407.

Gallo, K. P., Thompson-Hollands, J., Pincus, D. B., & Barlow, D. H. (2013). Anxiety disorders. In G. Stricker, T. A. Widiger, & I. B. Weiner (Eds.), *Handbook of psychology, 2nd ed., Vol. 8.* (pp. 147–170). Hoboken, NJ: Wiley.

Gallo, W. T., Bradley, E. H., Dubin, J. A., Jones, R. N., Falba, T. A., Teng, H. M., & Kasi, S. V. (2006). The persistence of depressive symptoms in older workers who experience involuntary job loss: Results from the health and retirement survey. *Journals of Gerontology B: Psychological Sciences and Social Sciences, 61,* S221–S228.

Gao, Y. J., & Ji, R. R. (2010). Chemokines, neuronal-glial interactions, and central processing of neuropathic pain. *Pharmacology & Therapeutics, 126,* 56–68.

Gao, Z., van Beugen, B. J., & de Zeeuw, C. I. (2012). Distributed synaptic plasticity and cerebellar learning. *Nature Review: Neuroscience, 13,* 619–635.

Garb, H. N., Wood, J. M., Nezworski, M. T., Grove, W. M., & Stejskal, W. J. (2001). Toward a resolution of the Rorschach controversy. *Psychological Assessment, 13,* 433–448.

Garcia, J. (1989). Food for Tolman: Cognition and cathexis in concert. In T. Archer & L. Nilsson (Eds.), *Aversion, avoidance, and anxiety.* Mahwah, NJ: Erlbaum.

Garcia, J., Ervin, F. E., & Koelling, R. A. (1966). Learning with prolonged delay of reinforcement. *Psychonomic Science, 5,* 121–122.

Garcia, J., & Koelling, R. A. (1966). Relation of cue to consequence in avoidance learning. *Psychonomic Science, 4,* 123–124.

Garcia, J., & Koelling, R. A. (2009). Specific hungers and poison avoidance as adaptive specializations of learning. In D. Shanks (Ed.), *Psychology of learning.* Thousand Oaks, CA: Sage.

Garcia, L. F., Aluja, A., Fibla, J., Cuevas, L., & Garcia, O. (2010). Incremental effect for antisocial personality disorder genetic risk combining 5-HTTLPR and 5-HTTVNTR polymorphisms. *Psychiatry Research, 177,* 161–166.

García-Bajos, E., & Migueles, M. (2013). Script-driven processing affords protection from retrieval-induced forgetting in the recall of everyday activities. *Quarterly Journal of Experimental Psychology.* doi:10.1080/17470218 .2012.739184

Gardner, H. (1983). *Frames of mind.* New York: Basic.

Gardner, H. (1993). *Multiple intelligences.* New York: Basic.

Gardner, H. (2002). The pursuit of excellence through education. In M. Ferrari (Ed.), *Learning from extraordinary minds.* Mahwah, NJ: Erlbaum.

Garfield, C. F., Dorsey, E. R., Zhu, S., Huskamp, H. A., Conti, R., Dusetzina, S. B., Higashi, A., Perrin, J. M., Kornfield, R., & Alexander, G. C. (2012). Trends in attention deficit hyperactivity disorder: Ambulatory diagnosis and medical treatment in the United States, 2000–2010. *Academic Pediatrics, 12,* 110–116.

Garrett, B. L. (2011). *Convicting the innocent: Where criminal prosecutions go wrong.* Cambridge, MA: Harvard University Press.

Gartland, N., O'Connor, D. B., & Lawton, R. (2012). The effects of conscientiousness on the appraisals of daily stressors. *Stress and Health, 28,* 80–86.

Gates, G. J. (2011). *How many people are lesbian, gay, bisexual, and transgender?* Los Angeles: Williams Institute, University of California, Los Angeles, School of Law. http://williamsinstitute. law.ucla.edu/wp-content/uploads/Gates-How-Many-People-LGBT-Apr-2011.pdf (accessed May 6, 2013)

Gathercole, S. E., & Alloway, T. P. (2008). *Working memory and learning: A practical guide.*Thousand Oaks, CA: Sage.

Gauvain, M. (2013). Sociocultural contexts of development. In P. D. Zelazo (Ed.), *The Oxford handbook of developmental psychology.* New York: Oxford University Press.

Gauvain, M., & Parke, R. D. (2010). Socialization. In M. H. Bornstein (Ed.), *Handbook of cultural developmental science*. New York: Psychology Press.

Gavlak, D. (2009, April 12). Jordan honor killing: Man confesses to brutally stabbing to death pregnant sister. www.huffingtonpost.com/2009/04/12/jordan-honor-killing-man-_n_185977.html (accessed May 15, 2013)

Gazzaley, A., & Nobre, A. C. (2012). Top-down modulation bridging selective attention and working memory. *Trends in Cognitive Science, 16* (2), 129–135.

Geary, D. C. (2010). *Male, female: The evolution of human sex differences* (2nd ed.). Washington, DC: American Psychological Association.

Gehring, W. J., Himle, J., & Nisenson, L. G. (2000). Action monitoring dysfunction in obsessive-compulsive disorder. *Psychological Science, 11*, 1–6.

Gehrman, P., Findley, J., & Perlis, M. (2012). Insomnia I: Etiology and conceptualization. In C. M. Morin & C. A. Espie (Eds.), *The Oxford handbook of sleep and sleep disorders*. New York: Oxford University Press.

Geier, A., Wansink, B., & Rozin, P. (2012). Red potato chips: Segmentation cues can substantially decrease food intake. *Health Psychology, 31*, 398–401.

Gelder, B. D., Meeren, H. K., Righart, R., Stock, J. V., van de Riet, W. A, & Tamietto, M. (2006). Beyond the face: Exploring rapid influences of context on face processing. *Progress in Brain Research, 155PB*, 37–48.

Gelfand, M., & others. (2012). The cultural contagion of conflict. *Philosophical Transactions of the Royal Society of London, 367*, 692–703.

Geisser, M. E., Roth, R. S., Theisen, M. E., Robinson, M. E., & Riley, J. L. (2000). Negative affect, self-report of depressive symptoms, and clinical depression: Relation to the experience of chronic pain. *Clinical Journal of Pain, 16*, 110–120.

Geller, E. S. (2002). The challenge of increasing proenvironmental behavior. In R. B. Bechtel & A. Churchman (Eds.), *Handbook of environmental psychology* (pp. 525–540). Hoboken, NJ: Wiley.

Geller, E. S. (2006). Occupational injury prevention and applied behavior analysis. In A. C. Gielen, D. A. Sleet, & R. J. DiClemente (Eds.), *Injury and violence prevention: Behavioral science theories, methods, and applications* (pp. 297–322). San Francisco: Jossey-Bass.

Geller, P. A., Nelson, A. R., & Bonacquisti, A. (2013). Women's health psychology. In A. M. Nezu, C. Maguth Nezu, P. A. Geller, & I. B. Weiner (Eds.), *Handbook of psychology, 2nd ed., Vol. 9.* (pp. 477–511). Hoboken, NJ: Wiley.

Gelo, O., Pritz, A., & Rieken, B. (Eds.). (2014). *Psychotherapy research*. New York: Springer.

Gems, D., & Partridge, L. (2013). Genetics of longevity in model organisms: Debates and paradigm shifts. *Annual Review of Physiology* (vol. 75). Palo Alto, CA: Annual Reviews.

Gentile, J. P., Dillon, K. S., & Gillig, P. M. (2013). Psychotherapy and pharmacotherapy for patients with dissociative identity disorder. *Innovations in Clinical Neuroscience, 10*, 22–29.

George, L. G., Helson, R., & John, O. P. (2011). The "CEO" of women's work lives: How big five conscientiousness, extraversion, and openness predict 50 years of work experiences in a changing sociocultural context. *Journal of Personality and Social Psychology, 101*, 812–830.

George, L. K. (2006). Perceived quality of life. In R. H. Binstock & L. K. George (Eds.), *Handbook of aging and the social sciences* (6th ed.). San Diego: Academic.

George, L. K., Kinghorn, W. A., Koenig, H. G., Gammon, P., & Blazer, D. G. (2013). Why gerontologists should care about empirical research on religion and health: Transdisciplinary perspectives. *Gerontologist, 111*, 563–568.

Geraerts, E., Lindsay, D. S., Merckelbach, H., Jelicic, M., Raymaekers, L., Arnold, M. M., & Schooler, J. W. (2009). Cognitive mechanisms underlying recovered-memory experiences of childhood sexual abuse. *Psychological Science, 20*, 92–98.

Germain, A. (2012). Parasomnias I: Nightmares. In C. M. Morin & C. A. Espie (Eds.), *The Oxford handbook of sleep and sleep disorders*. New York: Oxford University Press.

Germann, D., Kurylo, N., & Han, F. (2012). Risperidone. *Profiles of Drug Substances, Excipients, and Related Methodology, 37*, 313–361.

Germer, C. K., Siegel, R. D., & Fulton, P. R. (2013). *Mindfulness and psychotherapy*. New York: Guilford.

Gernsbacher, M. A., & Pripas-Kapit, S. R. (2012). Who's missing the point? A commentary on claims that autistic persons have a specific deficit in figurative language comprehension. *Metaphor and Symbol, 27*, 93–105.

Gervai, J. (2009). Environmental and genetic influences on early attachment. *Child and Adolescent Psychiatry and Mental Health, 3*, ArtID 25.

Geyer, T., Baumgartner, F., Müller, H. J., & Pollmann, S. (2013). Medial temporal lobe-dependent repetition suppression and enhancement due to implicit vs. explicit processing of individual repeated displays. *Frontiers in Human Neuroscience.* (in press)

Ghadirian, A.-M., Gregoire, P., & Kosmidis, H. (2001). Creativity and the evolution of psychopathologies. *Creativity Research Journal, 13*, 145–148.

Giang, D. W., & others. (1996). Conditioning of cyclophosphamide-induced leukopenia in humans. *Journal of Neuropsychiatry and Clinical Neuroscience, 8*, 194–201.

Gibbons, C. J., & others. (2010). The clinical effectiveness of cognitive behavior therapy in an outpatient clinic. *Journal of Affective Disorders, 110*, 161–166.

Gibbons, R. D., Brown, C. H., Hur, K., Marcus, S. M., Bhaumik, D. K., Erkens, J. A., Herings, R. M., & Mann, J. J. (2007) Early evidence on the effects of regulators' suicidality warnings on SSRI prescriptions and suicide in children and adolescents. *American Journal of Psychiatry, 164*, 1356–1363.

Gibbons, R. D., Hedeker, D., & DuToit, S. (2010). Advances in analysis of longitudinal data. *Annual Review of Clinical Psychology* (vol. 6). Palo Alto, CA: Annual Reviews.

Gibbons, R. D., Hur, K., Brown, C. H., Davis, J. M., & Mann, J. J. (2012). Benefits from antidepressants: Synthesis of 6-week patient-level outcomes from double-blind placebo-controlled randomized trials of fluoxetine and venlafaxine. *Archives of General Psychiatry, 69*, 572–579.

Gibbs, J. C. (2010). *Moral development and reality: Beyond the theories of Kohlberg and Hoffman* (2nd ed.). Boston: Allyn & Bacon.

Gibson, E. J. (2001). *Perceiving the affordances.* Mahwah, NJ: Erlbaum.

Gierisch, J. M., Nieuwsma, J. A., Bradford, D. W., Wilder, C. M., Mann-Wrobel, M. C., McBroom, A. J., Wing, L., Musty, M. D., Chobot, M. M., Hasselblad, V., & Williams, J. W., Jr. (2013, April 22). *Interventions to improve cardiovascular risk factors in people with serious mental illness.* Comparative Effectiveness Review No. 105. Rockville, MD: Agency for Healthcare Research and Quality. http://effectivehealthcare.ahrq.gov/index.cfm/search-for-guides-reviews-and-reports/?pageaction=displayproduct&productid=1464 (accessed July 2, 2013)

Gifford, E. V., Kohlenberg, B. S., Hayes, S. C., Pierson, H. M., Piasecki, M. P., Antonuccio, D. O., & Palm, K. M. (2011). Does acceptance and relationship focused behavior therapy contribute to bupropion outcomes? A randomized controlled trial of functional analytic psychotherapy and acceptance and commitment therapy for smoking cessation. *Behavior Therapy, 42*, 700–715.

Gigerenzer, G., & Gaissmaier, W. (2011). Heuristic decision making. *Annual Review of Psychology* (vol. 62). Palo Alto, CA: Annual Reviews.

Gijs, L. (2008). Paraphilia and paraphilia-related disorders: An introduction. In D. L. Rowland & L. Incrocci (Eds.), *Handbook of sexual and gender identity disorders* (pp. 491–528). Hoboken, NJ: Wiley.

Gilbert, A. L., Regier, T., Kay, P., & Ivry, R. B. (2006). Whorf hypothesis is supported in the right visual field but not the left. *Proceedings of the National Academy of Sciences USA, 103* (2), 489–494.

Gillen-O'Neel, C., Huynh, V. W., & Fuligni, A. J. (2013). To study or to sleep? The academic costs of extra studying at the expense of sleep. *Child Development, 84*, 133–142.

Gilligan, C. (1982). *In a different voice*. Cambridge, MA: Harvard University Press.

Gillihan, S. J., & Farah, M. J. (2005). Is self special? A critical review of evidence from experimental psychology and cognitive neuroscience. *Psychological Bulletin, 131*, 76–97.

Gil-Mohapel, J., Simpson, J. M., Ghilan, M., & Christie, B. R. (2011). Neurogenesis in Huntington's disease: Can studying adult neurogenesis lead to the development of new therapeutic strategies. *Brain Research, 1406*, 84–105.

Ginis, K. A., M., Bassett, R. L., & Conlin, C. (2012). Body image and exercise. In E. O. Acevedo (Ed.), *The Oxford handbook of exercise psychology*. New York: Oxford University Press.

Gino, F., Ayal, S., & Ariely, D. (2009). Contagion and differentiation in unethical behavior: The effect of one bad apple on the barrel. *Psychological Science, 20*, 393–398.

Giovannini, M., Verduci, E., Salvatici, E., Paci, S., & Riva, E. (2012). Phenylketonuria: Nutritional advances and challenges. *Nutrition and Metabolism.* doi: 10.1186/1743-7075-9-7

Gittelman, M. (2008). Editor's introduction: Why are the mentally ill dying? *International Journal of Mental Health, 37*, 3–12.

Glaw, X. M., Garrick, T. M., Terwee, P. J., Patching, J. R., Blake, H., & Harper, C. (2009). Brain donation: Who and why? *Cell and Tissue Banking, 10* (3), 241–246.

Glei, D. A., Goldman, N., Wu, C. H., & Weinstein, M. (2013). Does exposure to stressors predict changes in physiological dysregulation? *Annals of Behavioral Medicine.* (in press)

Gleitman, L., & Papafragou, A. (2012). Language and thought. In K. J. Holyoak & R. G. Morrison (Eds.), *The Oxford handbook of thinking and reasoning.* New York: Oxford University Press.

Glenberg, A. M. (2011). Positions in the mirror are closer than they appear. *Perspectives on Psychological Science, 6,* 408–410.

Glenn, D. (2010, February 5). Divided attention. *Chronicle of Higher Education, 56,* B5–B8.

Gobet, F., & Clarkson, G. (2004). Chunks in expert memory: Evidence for the magical number four . . . or is it two? *Memory, 12,* 732–747.

Godden, D. R., & Baddeley, A. D. (1975). Context-dependent memory in two natural environments: On land and under water. *British Journal of Psychology, 66,* 325–331.

Godsil, B. P., & Fanselow, M. S. (2013). Motivation. In A. F. Healy, R. W. Proctor, & I. B. Weiner (Eds.), *Handbook of psychology, 2nd ed., Vol. 4.* (pp. 32–60). Hoboken, NJ: Wiley.

Goel, A. K., & Davies, J. (2011). Artificial intelligence. In R. J. Sternberg & S. B. Kaufman (Eds.), *Handbook of intelligence.* New York: Cambridge University Press.

Goenjian, A. K., & others. (2012). Association of TPH1, TPH2, and 5HTTLPR with PTSD and depressive symptoms. *Journal of Affective Disorders,140* (3), 244–252.

Goethals, G. R., & Demorest, A. P. (1995). The risky shift is a sure bet. In M. E. Ware & D. E. Johnson (Eds.), *Demonstrations and activities in teaching of psychology* (vol. 3). Mahwah, NJ: Erlbaum.

Gogtay, N., & Thompson, P. M. (2010). Mapping gray matter development: implications for typical development and vulnerability to psychopathology. *Brain and Cognition, 72,* 6–15.

Gold, J., & Stricker, G. (2013). Psychotherapy integration and integrative psychotherapies. In G. Stricker, T. A. Widiger, & I. B. Weiner (Eds.), *Handbook of psychology, 2nd ed., Vol. 8.* (pp. 345–366). Hoboken, NJ: Wiley.

Goldberg, A., & Adriano, J. (2008, June 27). "I'm a girl"—Understanding transgender children: Parents of transgender 6-year-old support her choice. *ABC News.* http://abcnews.go.com/2020/story?id=5261464&page=1 (accessed May 3, 2013)

Goldberg, A. E. (2010). Introduction: Lesbian and gay parents and their children—Research and contemporary issues. In *Lesbian and gay parents and their children: Research on the family life cycle* (pp. 3–14). Washington, DC: American Psychological Association.

Goldberg, L. R., & Digman, J. M. (1994). Revealing structure in the data: Principles of exploratory factor analysis. In S. Strack & M. Lorr (Eds.), *Differentiating normal and abnormal personality* (pp. 216–242). New York: Springer.

Goldberg, L. S., & Grandey, A. A. (2007). Display rules versus display autonomy: Emotional regulation, emotional exhaustion, and task performance in a call center simulation. *Journal of Occupational Health Psychology, 12,* 301–318.

Goldberg, R. (2010). *Drugs across the spectrum* (6th ed.). Boston: Cengage.

Goldin-Meadow, S., & Alibali, M. W. (2013). Gesture's role in learning and development. In P. D. Zelazo (Ed.), *The Oxford handbook of developmental psychology.* New York: Oxford University Press.

Goldin-Meadow, S., & Cook, S. W. (2012). Gesture in thought. In K. J. Holyoak & R. G. Morrison (Eds.), *The Oxford handbook of thinking and reasoning, Vol. 1.* (pp. 953–973). New York: Oxford University Press.

Goldschmidt, L., Richardson, G. A., Willford, J., & Day, N. L. (2008). Prenatal marijuana exposure and intelligence test performance at age 6. *Journal of the American Academy of Child and Adolescent Psychiatry, 47,* 254–263.

Goldsmith, A. A., Thompson, R. D., Black, J. J., Tran, G. Q., & Smith, J. P. (2012). Drinking refusal self-efficacy and tension-reduction alcohol expectancies moderating the relationship between generalized anxiety and drinking behaviors in young adult drinkers. *Psychology of Addictive Behaviors, 26* (1), 59–67.

Goldstein, E. B. (2014). *Sensation and perception* (9th ed.). Boston: Cengage.

Goldstein, J. M., Seidman, L. J., Horton, N. J., Makris, N., Kennedy, D. N., Caviness, C., Faraone, S. V., & Tsuang, M. T. (2001). Normal sexual dimorphism of the adult human brain assessed by *in vivo* magnetic resonance imaging. *Cerebral Cortex, 11,* 490–497.

Goldstein, M. H., King, A. P., & West, M. J. (2003). Social interaction shapes babbling: Testing parallels between birdsong and speech. *Proceedings of the National Academy of Sciences USA, 100* (13), 8030–8035.

Goldston, D. B., Molock, S. D., Whibeck, L. B., Murakami, J. L., Zayas, L. H., & Hall, G. C. (2008). Cultural considerations in adolescent suicide prevention and psychosocial treatment. *American Psychologist, 63,* 14–31.

Goldstone, R. L., Kersten, A., & Carvalho, P. F. (2013). Concepts and categorization. In A. F. Healy, R. W. Proctor, & I. B. Weiner (Eds.), *Handbook of psychology* (2nd ed., vol. 4). Hoboken, NJ: Wiley.

Goldstrom, I. D., Campbell, J., Rogers, J. A., Lambert, D. B., Blacklow, B., Henderson, M. J., & Manderscheid, R. W. (2006). National estimates for mental health mutual support groups, self-help organizations, and consumer-operated services. *Administration and Policy in Mental Health, 33,* 92–103.

Goleman, D., Kaufman, P., & Ray, M. (1993). *The creative mind.* New York: Plume.

Goljevscek, S., & Carvalho, L. A. (2011). Current management of obsessive and phobic states. *Neuropsychiatric Diseases and Treatment, 7,* 599–610.

Gollnick, D. M., & Chinn, P. C. (2013). *Multicultural education in a pluralistic society* (9th ed.). Upper Saddle River, NJ: Pearson.

Golombok, S., Perry, B., Burston, A., Murray, C., Mooney-Somers, J., Stevens, M., & Golding, J. (2003). Children with lesbian parents: A community study. *Developmental Psychology, 39,* 20–33.

Golombok, S., & Tasker, F. (1996). Do parents influence the sexual orientation of their children? Findings from a longitudinal study of lesbian families. *Developmental Psychology, 32,* 3–11.

Gonda, X., & others. (2009). Association of the s allele of the 5-HTTLPR with neuroticism-related traits and temperaments in a psychiatrically healthy population. *European Archives of Psychiatry and Clinical Neuroscience, 259,* 106–113.

Gonzalez-Maeso, J., & Sealfon, S. C. (2009). Psychedelics and schizophrenia. *Trends in Neuroscience, 32,* 225–232.

Gonzalez-Vallejo, C., Lassiter, G. D., Bellezza, F. S., & Lindberg, M. J. (2008). "Save angels perhaps": A critical examination of unconscious thought theory and the deliberation-without-attention effect. *Review of General Psychology, 12,* 282–296.

Goodin, B. R., & Bulls, H. W. (2013). Optimism and the experience of pain: Benefits of seeing the glass half full. *Current Pain and Headache Reports, 17,* 329.

Gooding, P. A., Hurst, A., Johnson, J., & Tarrier, N. (2012). Psychological resilience in young and older adults. *International Journal of Geriatric Psychiatry, 27* (3), 262–270.

Goodman, G. S. (1991). Stress and children's testimony: Commentary on Peters. In J. Doris (Ed.) *The suggestibility of children's recollections* (pp. 77–82). Washington, DC: American Psychological Association.

Goodman, G. S. (2005). Wailing babies in her wake. *American Psychologist, 60,* 872–881.

Goodman, G. S. (2006). Children's eyewitness memory: A modern history and contemporary commentary. *Journal of Social Issues, 62,* 811–832.

Goodman, G. S., Quas, J. A., Batterman-Faunce, J. M., Riddlesberger, M., & Kuhn, J. (1997). Children's reactions to and memory for a stressful experience: Influences of age, knowledge, anatomical dolls, and parental attachment. *Applied Developmental Sciences, 1,* 54–75.

Goodwin, B. E., Sellborn, M., & Arbisi, P. A. (2013). Posttraumatic stress disorder in veterans: The utility of the MMPI-2-RF validity scales in detecting overreported symptoms. *Psychological Assessment.* (in press)

Goosens, K. A. (2011). Hippocampal regulation of aversive memories. *Current Opinion in Neurobiology, 21,* 460–466.

Goritz, C., & Frisén, J. (2012). Neural stem cells and neurogenesis in the adult. *Cell: Stem Cell, 10,* 657–659.

Gormley, B., & Lopez, F. G. (2010). Authoritarian and homophobic attitudes: Gender and adult attachment style differences. *Journal of Homosexuality, 57,* 525–538.

Gosling, S. D. (2008). Personality in nonhuman animals. *Social and Personality Psychology Compass, 2,* 985–1001.

Gosling, S. D., & John, O. P. (1999). Personality dimensions in nonhuman animals: A cross-species review. *Current Directions in Psychological Science, 8,* 69–75.

Gosling, S. D., Kwan, V. S. Y., & John, O. (2003). A dog's got personality: A cross-species comparison of personality judgments in dogs and humans. *Journal of Personality and Social Psychology, 85,* 1161–1169.

Gosling, S. D., Rentfrow, P. J., & Swann, W. B. (2003). A very brief measure of the big-five personality domains. *Journal of Research in Personality, 37,* 504–528.

Gottlieb, G. (2007). Probabilistic epigenesis. *Developmental Science, 10,* 1–11.

Gottman, J. M. (1994). *What predicts divorce?* Mahwah, NJ: Erlbaum.

Gottman, J. M. (2006, April, 29). Secrets of long-term love. *New Scientist, 2549,* 40.

Gottman, J. M., & Gottman, J. S. (2009). Gottman method of couple therapy. In A. S. Gurman (Ed.), *Clinical handbook of couple therapy* (4th ed.). New York: Guilford.

Gottman, J. M., Gottman, J. S., & Declaire, J. (2006). *10 lessons to transform your marriage: America's love lab experts share their strategies for strengthening your relationship.* New York: Random House.

Gottman, J. M., Levenson, R. W., Swanson, C., Swanson, K., Tyson, R., & Yoshimoto, D. (2003). Observing gay, lesbian and heterosexual couples' relationships: Mathematical modeling of conflict interaction. *Journal of Homosexuality, 45,* 65–91.

Gottman, J. M., & Silver, N. (1999). *The seven principles for making marriages work.* New York: Crown.

Gottman, J. M., Swanson, C., & Swanson, K. (2002). A general systems theory of marriage: Nonlinear difference equation modeling of marital interaction. *Personality and Social Psychology Review, 6,* 326–340.

Gouin, J. P., Glaser, R., Malarkey, W. B., Beversdorf, D., & Kiecolt-Glaser, J. K. (2012). Chronic stress, daily stressors, and circulating inflammatory markers. *Health Psychology, 31* (2), 264–268.

Gould, R. L., Coulson, M. C., & Howard, R. J. (2012). Efficacy of cognitive behavioral therapy for anxiety disorders in older people: A meta-analysis and meta-regression of randomized controlled trials. *Journal of the American Geriatrics Society, 60,* 218–229.

Gouzoulis-Mayfrank, E., & Daumann, J. (2009). Neurotoxity of drugs of abuse—the case of methylenedioxyampetamines (MDMA, ecstasy), and amphetamines. *Dialogues in Clinical Neuorscience, 11,* 305–317.

Graber, J. A. (2007). Pubertal and neuroendocrine development and risk for depressive disorders. In N. B. Allen & L. Sheeber (Eds.), *Adolescent emotional development and the emergence of depressive disorders.* New York: Cambridge University Press.

Graber, J. A., Brooks-Gunn, J., & Warren, M. P. (2006). Pubertal effects on adjustment in girls: Moving from demonstrating effects to identifying pathways. *Journal of Youth and Adolescence, 35,* 391–401.

Graeff, F. G. (2012). New perspective on the pathophysiology of panic: Merging serotonin and opioids in the periaqueductal gray. *Brazilian Journal of Medical and Biological Research, 45,* 366–375.

Graham, J. R. (2012). *MMPI-2: Assessing personality and psychopathology.* New York: Oxford University Press.

Grant, A. M., & Wrzesniewski, A. (2010). I won't let you down. . . or will I? Core self-evaluations, other orientation, anticipated guilt, and gratitude, and job performance. *Journal of Applied Psychology, 95,* 108–121.

Grant, B. F., Stinson, F. S., Dawson, D. A., Chou, P., Dufour, M. C., Compton, W., Pickering, R. P., & Kaplan, K. (2004). Prevalence and co-occurrence of substance use disorders and independent mood and anxiety disorders: Results from the national epidemiologic survey on alcohol and related conditions. *Archives of General Psychiatry, 61,* 807–816.

Gratz, K. L., Latzman, R. D., Young, J., Heiden, L. J., Damon, J. D., Hight, T. L., & Tull, M. T. (2012). Deliberate self-harm among community adolescents in an underserved area: Exploring the moderating roles of gender, race, and school-level and association with borderline personality features. *Personality Disorders, 3,* 39–54.

Gravetter, F. J., & Forzano, L. B. (2012). *Research methods for the behavioral sciences* (4th ed.). Boston: Cengage.

Gray, J. (2004). *Men are from Mars, women are from Venus.* New York: HarperCollins.

Gray, J. A. (1987). *The psychology of fear and stress.* Cambridge, U.K.: Cambridge University Press.

Gray, J. A., & McNaughton, N. (2000). *The neuropsychology of anxiety: An enquiry into the functions of the septo-hippocampal system.* Oxford, U.K.: Oxford University Press.

Graziano, A. M., & Raulin, M. L. (2013). *Research methods* (8th ed.). Boston: Allyn & Bacon.

Green, J. P., Page, R. A., Handley, G. W., & Rasekhy, R. (2005). The "hidden observer" and ideomotor responding: A real–simulator comparison. *Contemporary Hypnosis, 22,* 123–137.

Green, M. K., & others. (2011). Prenatal stress induces long term stress vulnerability, compromising stress response systems in the brain and impairing extinction of conditioned fear after adult stress. *Neuroscience, 192,* 438–451.

Green, R. (1987). *The "sissy boy syndrome" and the development of homosexuality.* New Haven, CT: Yale University Press.

Green, R. J., Bettinger, M., & Zacks, E. (1996). Are lesbian couples fused and gay male couples disengaged? Questioning gender straitjackets. In J. Laird & R. J. Green (Eds.), *Lesbian and gays in couples and families: A handbook for therapists* (pp. 185–230). New York: Jossey-Bass.

Greenberg, D. A., & Jin, K. (2013). Vascular endothelial factors (VEGFs) and stroke. *Cellular and Molecular Life Sciences.* (in press)

Greenberg, L., Elliott, R., Lietaer, G., & Watson, J. (2013). The humanistic-experiential approach. In G. Stricker, T. A. Widiger, & I. B. Weiner (Eds.), *Handbook of psychology* (2nd ed., vol. 8). Hoboken, NJ: Wiley.

Greene, J. & Haidt, J. (2002). How (and where) does moral judgment work? *Trends in Cognitive Sciences, 6,* 517–523.

Greene, R. L. (2011). *MMPI-2/MMPI-2-RF* (3rd ed.). Upper Saddle River, NJ: Pearson.

Greenhaus, J. H., & Callanan, G. A. (2013). Career dynamics. In N. W. Schmitt, S. Highhouse, & I. B. Weiner (Eds.), *Handbook of psychology* (2nd ed., vol. 12). Hoboken, NJ: Wiley.

Greenwald, A. G., Poehlman, T. A., Uhlmann, E., & Banaji, M. R. (2009). Understanding and using the Implicit Association Test: III. Meta-analysis of predictive validity. *Journal of Personality and Social Psychology, 97,* 17–41.

Greer, S., Morris, T., & Pettingale, K. W. (1979). Psychological response to breast cancer: Effect on outcome. *Lancet, 314,* 785–787.

Greeson, J. M., Lewis, J. G., Achanzar, K., Zimmerman, E., & Young K. H., & Suarez, E. C. (2009). Stress-induced changes in the expression of monocytic beta-2-integrins: The impact of arousal of negative affect and adrenergic responses to the Anger Recall interview. *Brain, Behavior, and Immunity, 23,* 251–256.

Gregan, M. J., Nelson, P. B., & Oxenham, A. (2011). Behavioral estimates of basilar-membrane compression: Additivity of forward masking in noise-masked normal-hearing listeners. *Journal of the Acoustical Society of America, 130,* 2835–2844.

Gregg, A. P., & Sedikides, C. (2010). Narcissistic fragility: Rethinking its link to explicit and implicit self-esteem. *Self and Identity, 9,* 142–146.

Gregory, S., Ffytche, D., Simmons, A., Kumari, V., Howard, M., Hodgins, S., & Blackwood, N. (2012). The antisocial brain: Psychopathy matters. *Archives of General Psychiatry, 69* (9), 962–972.

Greitemeyer, T. (2009). Effects of songs with prosocial lyrics on prosocial thoughts, affect, and behavior. *Journal of Experimental Social Psychology, 45,* 186–190.

Greitemeyer, T., & Osswald, S. (2010). Effects of prosocial video games on prosocial behavior. *Journal of Personality and Social Psychology, 98,* 211–221.

Greitemeyer, T., & Osswald, S. (2011). Playing prosocial video games increases the accessibility of prosocial thoughts. *Journal of Social Psychology, 151,* 121–128.

Griffin, D. (2012). Judgment heuristics. In K. J. Holyoak & R. G. Morrison (Eds.), *The Oxford handbook of thinking and reasoning.* New York: Oxford University Press.

Griffin, K. W., & others. (2012). Long-term effects of self-control on alcohol use and sexual behavior among urban minority young women. *International Journal of Environmental Research and Public Health, 9,* 1–23.

Griffin, M. A., & Clarke, S. (2010). Stress and well-being at work. In S. Zedeck (Ed.), *APA handbook of industrial and organizational psychology.* Washington, DC: American Psychological Association.

Griffin, R. W., & Moorhead, G. (2010). *Organizational behavior* (9th ed.). Boston: Cengage.

Griffiths, J. D., Marslen-Wilson, W. D., Stamatakis, E. A., & Tyler, L. K. (2013). Functional organization of the neural language system: Dorsal and ventral pathways are critical for syntax. *Cerebral Cortex.* (in press)

Grigoryan, G., Korkotian, E., & Segal, M. (2012). Selective facilitation of LPTP in the ventral hippocampus by calcium stores. *Hippocampus, 22* (7), 1635–1644.

Grilo, C. M., Masheb, R. M., & White, M. A. (2010). Significance of overvaluation of shape/weight in binge-eating disorder: Comparative study with overweight and bulimia nervosa. *Obesity, 18,* 499–504.

Grisso, T., & Brigham, J. C. (2013). Forensic psychology. In R. K. Otto & I. B. Weiner (Eds.), *Handbook of psychology* (2nd ed., vol. 11). Hoboken, NJ: Wiley.

Groenewold, N. A., Opmeer, E. M., de Jonge, P., Aleman, A., & Costafreda, S. G. (2013). Emotional valence modulates brain functional abnormalities in depression: Evidence for a meta-analysis of fMRI studies. *Neuroscience and Biobehavioral Reviews.* (in press)

Groffen, D. A., & others. (2013). Unhealthy lifestyles do not mediate the relationship between socioeconomic status and incident depressive symptoms: The Health ABC study. *American Journal of Geriatric Psychiatry.* (in press)

Grossi, E., Buscema, M. P., Snowdon, D., & Antuono, P. (2007). Neuropathological findings processed by artificial neural networks (ANNs) can perfectly distinguish Alzheimer's patients from controls in the Nun Study. *BMC Neurology, 7,* 15.

Grossman, I., Na, J., Varnum, M. E. W., Park, D. C., Kitayama, S., & Nisbett, R. E. (2010). Reasoning about social conflicts improves into old age. *Proceedings of the National Academy of Sciences USA, 107,* 7246–7250.

Grote, G. (2013). Adding a strategic edge to human factors/ergonomics: Principles for management of uncertainty as cornerstones for system design. *Applied Ergonomics.* (in press)

Grubin, D. (2010). The polygraph and forensic psychiatry. *Journal of the American Academy of Psychology and Law, 38,* 446–451.

Grunewaldt, K. H., Lohaugen, G. C., Austeng, D., Brubakk, A. M., & Skranes, J. (2013). Working memory training improves cognitive function in VLBW preschoolers. *Pediatrics, 131* (3), e747–e754.

Grusec, J. E. (2011). Socialization processes in the family: Social and emotional development. *Annual Review of Psychology* (vol. 62). Palo Alto, CA: Annual Reviews.

Guiney, H., & Machado, L. (2013). Benefits of regular aerobic exercise for executive functioning in healthy populations. *Psychonomic Bulletin and Review.* doi: 10.3758/s13423-012-0345-4

Gump, B., & Matthews, K. (2000, March). Are vacations good for your health? The 9-year mortality experience after the multiple risk factor intervention trial. *Psychosomatic Medicine, 62,* 608–612.

Gunderson, J. (2008). Borderline personality disorder: An overview. *Social Work in Mental Health, 6*, 5–12.

Gunderson, J. G., Bender, D., Sanislow, C., Yen, S., Rettew, J. B., Dolan-Sewell, R., Dyck, I., Morey, L. C., McGlashan, T. H., Shea, M. T., & Skodol, A. E. (2003). Plausibility and possible determinants of sudden "remissions" in borderline patients. *Psychiatry: Interpersonal and Biological Processes, 66,* 111–119.

Gunning, T. G. (2013). *Creating literature instruction for all children in grades pre-K to 4* (2nd ed.). Boston: Allyn & Bacon.

Gunty, A. L., Frazier, P. A., Tennen, H., Tomich, P., Yashiro, T., & Park, C. (2011). Moderators of the relation between perceived and actual posttraumatic growth. *Psychological Trauma: Theory, Research, Practice, and Policy, 3,* 61–66.

Guo, Q., Johnson, C. A., Unger, J. B., Lee, L., Xie, B., Chou, C. P., Palmer, P. H., Sun, P., Gallaher, P., & Pentz, M. (2007). Utility of theory of reasoned action and theory of planned behavior for predicting Chinese adolescent smoking. *Addictive Behaviors, 32,* 1066–1081.

Guo, X., & others. (2012). Effects of antipsychotic medications on quality of life and psychosocial functioning in patients with early-stage schizophrenia: 1-year follow-up naturalistic study. *Comprehensive Psychiatry, 53* (7), 1006–1012.

Guo, Y. (2005). Filial therapy for children's behavioral and emotional problems in mainland China. *Journal of Child and Adolescent Psychiatric Nursing, 18,* 171–180.

Gurin, P., Dey, E. L., Hurtado, S., & Gurin, G. (2002). Diversity and higher education: Theory and impact on educational outcomes. *Harvard Educational Review, 72,* 330–366.

Guttman, N., & Kalish, H. I. (1956). Discriminability and stimulus generalization. *Journal of Experimental Psychology, 51,* 79–88.

Gwaltney, C. J., Metrik, J., Kahler, C. W., & Shiffman, S. (2009). Self-efficacy and smoking cessation: A meta-analysis. *Psychology of Addictive Behaviors, 23,* 56–66.

Gwernan-Jones, R., & Burden, R. L. (2010). Are they just lazy? Student teachers' attitudes about dyslexia. *Dyslexia: An International Journal of Research and Practice, 16,* 66–86.

H

Haas, B. W., Omura, K., Constable, R. T., & Canli, T. (2007). Emotional conflict and neuroticism: Personality-dependent activation in the amygdala and subgenual anterior cingulate. *Behavioral Neuroscience, 121,* 249–256.

Haase, S. J., & Fisk, G. D. (2011). A comparison of signal detection theory to objective threshold/strategic model of unconscious perception. *Perceptual and Motor Skills, 113,* 242–256.

Habeck, C., Rakitin, B. C., Moeller, J., Scarmeas, N., Zarahn, E., Brown, T., & Stern, Y. (2004). An event-related fMRI study of the neurobehavioral impact of sleep deprivation on performance of a delayed-match-to-sample task. *Brain Research, 18,* 306–321.

Haber, J. R., Koenig, L. B., & Jacob, T. (2011). Alcoholism, personality, religion/spirituality: An integrative review. *Current Drug Abuse Reviews, 4,* 250–260.

Hackett, G. I. (2008). Disorders of male sexual desire. In D. L. Rowland & L. Incrocci (Eds.), *Handbook of sexual and gender identity disorders* (pp. 5–29). Hoboken, NJ: Wiley.

Hagadorn, J. A., & Seilacher. A. (2009). Hermit arthropods 500 million years ago? *Geology, 37,* 295–298.

Hagman, J. O., & Frank, G. K. W. (2012). Developmental concerns in psychopharmacological treatment of children and adolescents with eating disorders. In J. Lock (Ed.), *The Oxford handbook of child and adolescent eating disorders: Developmental perspectives.* New York: Oxford University Press.

Hagner, M. (2007). Mind reading, brain mirror, neuroimaging: Insight into the brain or the mind? In M. Ash & T. Sturm (Eds.), *Psychology's territories.* Mahwah, NJ: Erlbaum.

Hahn, D. B., Payne, W. A., & Lucas, E. B. (2013). *Focus on health* (11th ed.). New York: McGraw-Hill.

Hahn, U., & Oaksford, M. (2012). Rational argument. In K. J. Holyoak & R. G. Morrison (Eds.), *The Oxford handbook of thinking and reasoning.* New York: Oxford University Press.

Haidle, M. N. (2010). Working memory capacity and the evolution of modern cognitive capacities—Implications from animal and early human tool use. *Current Anthropology, 51/S1, Working memory: Beyond language and symbolism,* Wenner-Gren Symposium, Suppl. 1, S149–S166.

Haidt, J. (2001). The emotional dog and its rational tail: A social intuitionist approach to moral judgment. *Psychological Review, 108,* 814–834.

Haidt, J. (2003). The emotional dog does learn new tricks: A reply to Pizarro and Bloom (2003). *Psychological Review, 110,* 197–198.

Haidt, J., & Kesebir, S. (2010). Morality. In S. Fiske, D. Gilbert, & G. Lindzey (Eds.), *Handbook of social psychology* (5th ed., pp. 797–832). Hoboken, NJ: Wiley.

Halberstadt, J. (2010). Dumb but lucky: Fortuitous affect cues and their disruption by analytic thought. *Social and Personality Psychology Compass, 4,* 64–76.

Hald, G. M., Malamuth, N. M., & Yuen, C. (2010). Pornography and attitudes supporting violence against women: Revisiting the relationship in nonexperimental studies. *Aggressive Behavior, 36,* 14–20.

Hale, L., & others. (2013). Fibrinogen may mediate the association between long sleep duration and coronary heart disease. *Journal of Sleep Medicine.* (in press)

Hales, D. (2011). *An invitation to health* (14th ed.). Boston: Cengage.

Halgunseth, L. C., Ispa, J. M., & Rudy, D. (2006). Parental control in Latino families: An integrated review of the literature. *Child Development, 77,* 1282–1297.

Hall, J. A., & Matsumoto, D. (2004). Gender differences in judgments of multiple emotions from facial expressions. *Emotion, 14,* 201–206.

Hall, J. A., Park, N., Song, H., & Cody, M. J. (2010).Strategic misrepresentation in online dating: The effects of gender, self-monitoring, and personality traits. *Journal of Social and Personal Relationships, 27,* 117–135.

Hall, K. D. (2013). Diet versus exercise in "The Biggest Loser" weight loss competition. *Obesity.* doi: 10.1002/oby.20065

Hall, J. E., & Altmaier, E. M. (2013). Education, training, licensing, and credentialing in clinical psychology. In G. Stricker, T. A. Widiger, & I. B. Weiner (Eds.), *Handbook of psychology, 2nd ed., Vol. 8.* (pp. 517–532). Hoboken, NJ: Wiley.

Hall, R. C. W., & Hall, R. C. W. (2007). A profile of pedophilia: Definition, characteristics of offenders, recidivism, treatment outcomes, and forensic issues. *Mayo Clinic Proceedings, 82,* 457–471.

Hallahan, D. P., Kauffman, J. M., & Pullen, P. C. (2012). *Exceptional learners* (12th ed.): Boston: Allyn & Bacon.

Halpern, D. F. (2012). *Sex differences in cognitive abilities* (4th ed.). New York: Psychology Press.

Halpern, D. S., Benbow, C. P., Geary, D. C., Gur, R. C., Hyde, J. S. & Gernsbacher, M. A. (2007). The science of sex differences in science and mathematics. *Psychological Science in the Public Interest, 8,* 1–51.

Halter, M. J., Rolin-Kenny, D., & Grund, F. (2013). DSM-5: Historical perspectives. *Journal of Psychosocial Nursing and Mental Health Services, 51,* 22–29.

Hamer, M., Chida, Y., & Molloy, G. J. (2009). Psychological distress and cancer mortality. *Journal of Psychosomatic Research, 66,* 255–258.

Hames, J. L., Hagan, C. R., & Joiner, T. E. (2013). Interpersonal processes in depression. *Annual Review of Clinical Psychology* (vol. 9). Palo Alto, CA: Annual Reviews.

Hamilton, B. E., Martin, J. A., & Ventura, S. J. (2012). Births: Preliminary data for 2011. *National Vital Statistics Reports, 61* (5), Table 2.

Hamilton, D. L., & Carlston, D. E. (2013). The emergence of social cognition. In D. E. Carlston (Ed.), *The Oxford handbook of social cognition.* New York: Oxford University Press.

Hammad, T. A., Laughren, T., & Racoosin, J. (2006). Suicidality in pediatric patients treated with antidepressants. *Archives of General Psychiatry, 63* (3), 332–339.

Hammen, C., & Keenan-Miller, D. (2013). Mood disorders. In G. Stricker, T. A. Widiger, & I. B. Weiner (Eds.), *Handbook of psychology, 2nd ed., Vol. 8.* (pp. 121–146). Hoboken, NJ: Wiley.

Hamon, M., & Blier, P. (2013). Monoamine neurocircuitry in depression and strategies for new treatments. *Progress in Neuro-Psychopharmacology and Biological Psychiatry.* (in press)

Hampson, S. E., Edmonds, G. W., Goldberg, L. R., Dubanoski, J. P., & Hillier, T. A. (2013). Childhood conscientiousness relates to objectively measured adult physical health four decades later. *Health Psychology.* (in press)

Hampton, J. (2008). Abstinence-only programs under fire. *Journal of the American Medical Association, 17,* 2013–2015.

Han, K., Park, H. I., Weed, N. C., Lim, J., Johnson, A., & Joles, C. (2013). Gender differences in the MMPI across American and Korean adult and adolescent normative samples. *Journal of Personality Assessment, 95,* 197–206.

Han, S., O'Connor, A. R., Eslick, A. N., & Dobbins, I. G. (2012a). The role of the left ventrolateral prefrontal cortex during episodic decisions: Semantic elaboration or resolution of an episodic interference. *Journal of Cognitive Neuroscience, 24,* 223–234.

Han, S., & others. (2012b). NaV1.1 channels are critical for intercellular communication in the suprachiasmatic nucleus and for normal circadian rhythms. *Proceedings of the National Academy of Sciences USA.* doi: 10.1073/pnas.1115729109

Handley, E. (2012, August 21). Edinburgh Festival 2012: Ten funniest jokes at this year's Edinburgh Fringe revealed. *The Telegraph.* www.telegraph.co.uk/culture/theatre/edinburgh-festival/9488190/Edinburgh-Festival-2012-ten-funniest-jokes-at-this-years-Edinburgh-Fringe-revealed.html (accessed February 14, 2013)

Haney, C., Banks, C., & Zimbardo, P. (1973). Interpersonal dynamics in a simulated prison. *International Journal of Criminology and Penology, 1,* 69–97.

Hannum, R. D., Rosellini, R. A., & Seligman, M. E. P. (1976). Learned helplessness in the rat: Retention and immunization. *Developmental Psychology, 12,* 449–454.

Hanowski, R. J., Olson, R. L., Hickman, J. S., & Bocanegra, J. (2009, September). *Driver distraction in commercial vehicle operations.* Paper presented at the First International Conference on Driver Distraction and Inattention, Gothenburg, Sweden.

Hansen, K. B., Vilsboll, T., Bagger, J. L., Holst, J. J., & Knop, F. K. (2012). Impaired incretin-inducted amplification of insulin secretion after glucose homeostatic dysregulation in healthy subjects. *Journal of Clinical Endocrinology and Metabolism, 97* (4), 1363–1370.

Hansen, K. E., & Pronin, E. (2012). Illusions of self-knowledge. In S. Vazire & T.D. Wilson (Eds.), *Handbook of self knowledge.* New York: Guilford.

Hardwick, R. M., Rottschy, C., Miall, R. C., & Eickhoff, S. B. (2013). A quantitative meta-analysis and review of motor learning in the human brain. *NeuroImage.* (in press)

Hardy, L, Arthur, C. A., Jones, G., Shariff, A., Munnoch, K., Isaacs, I., & Allsopp, A. J. (2010). The relationship between transformational leadership behaviors, psychological, and training outcomes in elite military recruits. *Leadership Quarterly, 21,* 20–32.

Hardy, S. A., & Carlo, G. (2011). Moral identity: What is it, how does it develop, and is it linked to moral action? *Child Development Perspectives, 5,* 212–218.

Hare, R. D. (2003). *Manual for the revised psychopathy checklist* (2nd ed.). Toronto: Multi-Health Systems.

Harker, L. A., & Keltner, D. (2001). Expressions of positive emotion in women's college yearbook pictures and their relationship to personality and life outcomes across adulthood. *Journal of Personality and Social Psychology, 80,* 112–124.

Harlow, H. F. (1958). The nature of love. *American Psychologist, 13,* 673–685.

Harms, P. D., & Crede, M. (2010). Emotional intelligence and transformational and transactional leadership: A meta-analysis. *Journal of Leadership and Organizational Studies, 17,* 5–17.

Harned, M. S., Tkachuck, M. A., & Youngberg, K. A. (2013). Treatment preference among suicidal and self-injuring women with borderline personality disorder and PTSD. *Journal of Clinical Psychology, 69* (7), 749–761.

Harris, C. B., Sutton, J., & Barnier, A. J. (2010). Autobiographical forgetting. In S. D. Sala (Ed.), *Forgetting.* New York: Psychology Press.

Harris, D. M., & Kay, J. (1995). I recognize your face but I can't remember your name: Is it because names are unique? *British Journal of Psychology, 86,* 345–358.

Harris, J. A., Andrew, B. J., & Livesey, E. J. (2012). The content of compound conditioning. *Journal of Experimental Psychology: Animal Behavior and Processes, 38* (2), 157–166.

Harris, J. J., & Attwell, D. (2012). The energetics of CNS white matter. *Journal of Neuroscience, 32,* 356–371.

Harris Interactive. (2006, October 10). Seven out of ten heterosexuals today know someone gay. *Harris Interactive.* www.harrisinteractive.com/news/allnewsbydate.asp?NewsID=1099 (accessed May 9, 2013)

Harrison, B. F., & Michelson, M. R. (2012). Not that there's anything wrong with that: Messaging, source credibility, and marriage equality. *Political Behavior, 34* (2), 325–344.

Harrison, C. (2012). Ageing: Telomerase gene therapy increases longevity. *Nature Reviews: Drug Discovery, 11,* 518.

Harrison, Y. (2012). The functions of sleep. In C. M. Morin & C. A. Espie (Eds.), *The Oxford handbook of sleep and sleep disorders.* New York: Oxford University Press.

Harro, J., Merenakk, L., Nordquist, N., Konstabel, K., Comasco, E., & Oreland, L. (2009). Personality and the serotonin transporter gene: Associations in a longitudinal population-based study. *Biological Psychology, 81,* 9–13.

Hart, B., & Risley, T. R. (1995). *Meaningful differences in the everyday experience of young Americans.* Baltimore: Paul H. Brookes.

Hart, C. L., Ksir, C. J., & Ray, O. S. (2011). *Drugs, society, and human behavior* (14th ed.). New York: McGraw-Hill.

Hartenbaum, N., & others. (2006). Sleep apnea and commercial motor vehicle operators. *Chest, 130,* 902–905.

Harter, S. (2012). *The construction of the self* (2nd ed.). New York: Guilford.

Harter, S. (2013). Development of self-esteem. In M. H. Kernis (Ed.), *Self-esteem issues and answers.* New York: Psychology Press.

Hartley, B. L., & Sutton, R. M. (2013). A stereotype threat account of boys' academic underachievement. *Child Development.* (in press)

Hartmann, E. (1993). Nightmares. In M. A. Carskadon (Ed.), *Encyclopedia of sleep and dreams.* New York: Macmillan.

Hartmann, P., & Apaolaza-Ibanez, V. (2010). Beyond savanna: An evolutionary and environmental psychology approach to behavioral effects of nature scenery in green advertising. *Journal of Environmental Psychology, 30,* 119–128.

Harvey, P. D., & Bowie, C. R. (2013). Schizophrenia spectrum conditions. In G. Stricker, T. A. Widiger, & I. B. Weiner (Eds.), *Handbook of psychology, 2nd ed., Vol. 8.* (pp. 240–262). Hoboken, NJ: Wiley.

Hasan, Y., Bègue, L., & Bushman, B. J. (2013). Violent video games stress people out and make them more aggressive. *Aggressive Behavior, 39,* 64–70.

Hasegawa, H., & Unuma, H. (2010). Facial features in perceived intensity of schematic facial expressions. *Perceptual and Motor Skills, 110,* 129–149.

Haselton, M. G. (2006, April 29). How to pick a perfect mate. *New Scientist, 2549,* 36.

Haslam, S. A., & Reicher, S. D. (2003). Beyond Stanford: Questioning a role-based explanation of tyranny. *SPSP Dialogue, 18,* 22–25.

Haslam, S. A., Reicher, S. D., & Reynolds, K. J. (2012). Identity, influence, and change: Rediscovering John Turner's vision for social psychology. *British Journal of Social Psychology, 51* (2), 201–218.

Hassanpoor, H., Fallah, A., & Raza, M. (2012). New role for astroglia in learning: Formation of muscle memory. *Medical Hypotheses, 79,* 770–773.

Hassepass, F., & others. (2013). Unilateral deafness in children: Audiologic and subjective assessment of hearing ability after cochlear implantation. *Otology and Neurotology, 34,* 53–60.

Hassett, J. M., Siebert, E. R., & Wallen, K. (2008). Sex differences in rhesus monkey toy preferences parallel those of children. *Hormones and Behavior, 54,* 359–364.

Hattiangady, B., & Shetty, A. K. (2012). Neural stem cell grafting counteracts hippocampal injury-mediated impairments in mood, memory, and neurogenesis. *Stem Cells Translational Medicine, 1,* 696–708.

Haus, E. L., & Smolensky, M. H. (2012). Shift work and cancer risk: Potential mechanistic roles of circadian disruption, light at night, and sleep deprivation. *Sleep Medicine Reviews.* doi: 10.1016/j.smrv.2012.08.003

Haviland-Jones, J., Rosario, H. H., Wilson, P., & McGuire, T. R. (2005). An environmental approach to positive emotion: Flowers. *Evolutionary Psychology, 3,* 104–132.

Hawkley, L. C., & Cacioppo, J. T. (2009). Loneliness. In M. R. Leary & R. H. Hoyle (Eds.), *Handbook of individual differences in social behavior* (pp. 227–240). New York: Guilford.

Hawkley, L. C., Preacher, K. J., & Cacioppo, J. T. (2010). Loneliness impairs daytime functioning but not sleep duration. *Health Psychology, 29,* 124–129.

Hawkley, L. C., Thisted, R. A., & Cacioppo, J. T. (2009). Loneliness predicts reduced physical activity: Cross-sectional and longitudinal analyses. *Health Psychology, 28,* 354–363.

Haworth, C. M., Dale, P. S., & Plomin, R. (2009). The etiology of science performance: Decreasing heritability and increasing importance of shared environment from 9 to 12 years of age. *Child Development, 80,* 662–673.

Hay, P. P., Bacaltchuk, J., Stefano, S., & Kashyap, P. (2009). Psychological treatments for bulimia nervosa and binging. *Cochrane Database of Systematic Reviews, 4,* CD000562.

Hayakawa, Y. (2012). Targeting NKG2D in tumor surveillance. *Expert Opinion on Therapeutic Targets, 16* (6), 587–599.

Hayatbakhsh, M. R., & others. (2012). Birth outcomes associated with cannabis use before and during pregnancy. *Pediatric Research, 71,* 215–219.

Hayflick, L. (1977). The cellular basis for biological aging. In C. E. Finch & L. Hayflick (Eds.), *Handbook of the biology of aging.* New York: Van Nostrand.

Hayworth, K. J. (2012). Dynamically partitionable autoassociative networks as a solution to the neural binding problem. *Frontiers in Computational Neuroscience, 6,* 73.

Hazler, R. J. (2007). Person-centered therapy. In D. Capuzzi & D. Gross (Eds.), *Counseling and psychotherapy* (4th ed.). Upper Saddle River, NJ: Prentice-Hall.

Head, D., Singh, T., & Bugg, J. M. (2012). The moderating role of exercise on stress-related effects on the hippocampus and memory. *Neuropsychology, 26,* 133–143.

Head, L. S., & Gross, A. M. (2009). Systematic desensitization. In W. T. O'Donohue & J. E. Fisher (Eds.), *General principles and empirically supported techniques of cognitive behavior therapy.* Hoboken, NJ: Wiley.

Hearold, S. (1986). A synthesis of 1043 effects of television on social behavior. In G. Comstock (Ed.), *Public communication of behavior* (pp. 65–133). San Diego: Academic.

Hearst, E., & Jenkins, H. (1974). Sign tracking: The stimulus reinforce relation and directed action. *Monograph of the Psychonomic Society.* Austin, TX.

Hebb, D. O. (1949). *The organization of behavior: A neuropsychological theory.* New York: Wiley.

Hebb, D. O. (1980). *Essay on mind.* Mahwah, NJ: Erlbaum.

Hegarty, P. (2009). Toward an LGBT-informed paradigm for children who break gender norms: A comment on Drummond et al. (2008) and Rieger et al. (2008). *Developmental Psychology, 45,* 895–900.

Heidelbaugh, J. J. (2010). Management of erectile dysfunction. *American Family Physician, 81,* 305–312.

Heider, F. (1958). *The psychology of interpersonal relations.* Hoboken, NJ: Wiley.

Heine, S. J. (2005). Constructing good selves in Japan and North America. In R. M. Sorrentino, D. Cohen, J. M. Olson, & M. P. Zanna (Eds.), *Cultural and social behavior: The Ontario symposium* (vol. 10, pp. 95–116). Mahwah, NJ: Erlbaum.

Heine, S. J., & Hamamura, T. (2007). In search of East Asian self-enhancement. *Personality and Social Psychology Review, 11,* 1–24.

Heine, S. J., & Raineri, A. (2009). Self-improving motivations and collectivism: The case of Chileans. *Journal of Cross-Cultural Psychology, 40,* 158–163.

Heirman, W., & Walrave, M. (2012). Predicting adolescent perpetration in cyberbullying: An application of the theory of planned behavior. *Psicothema, 24,* 614–620.

Helgeson, V. S. (1994). Relation of agency and communion to well-being: Evidence and potential explanations. *Psychological Bulletin, 116,* 412–428.

Heller, A. C., Amar, A. P., Liu, C. Y., & Apuzzo, M. L. (2006). Surgery of the mind and mood: A mosaic of issues in time and evolution. *Neurosurgery, 59,* 720–733.

Hellriegel, D., & Slocum, J. W. (2011). *Organizational behavior* (13th ed.). Boston: Cengage.

Helsen, K., Goubert, L., Peters, M. L., & Vlaeyen, J. W. S. (2011). Observational learning and pain-related fear: An experimental study with colored cold pressor tasks. *Journal of Pain, 12,* 1230–1239.

Hemingway, H., & Marmot, M. (1999). Evidence based cardiology: Psychosocial factors in the aetiology and prognosis of coronary heart disease: Systematic review of prospective cohort studies. *British Medical Journal, 318,* 1460–1467.

Henderson, M. (2008, February 18). Welcome to the town that will make you lose weight. *Times Online.* www.thetimes.co.uk/tto/health/article1881007.ece (accessed June19, 2013)

Henderson, V. W. (2011). Gonadal hormones and cognitive aging: A midlife perspective. *Women's Health, 7* (1), 81–93.

Hendrick, C., & Hendrick, S. S. (2006). Styles of romantic love. In R. J. Sternberg & K. Weis (Eds.), *The new psychology of love* (pp. 149–170). New Haven, CT: Yale University Press.

Hendrick, C., & Hendrick, S. S. (2009). Love. In S. Lopez & C. R. Snyder, (Eds.), *The Oxford handbook of positive psychology* (2nd ed., pp. 447–454). New York: Oxford University Press.

Hendricks, J., & Hatch, L. R. (2006). Lifestyle and aging. In R. H. Binstock & L. K. George (Eds.), *Handbook of aging and the social sciences* (6th ed.). San Diego: Academic.

Hennessey, B. A. (2011). Intrinsic motivation and creativity: Have we come full circle? In R. A. Beghetto & J. C. Kaufman (Eds.), *Nurturing creativity in the classroom.* New York: Cambridge University Press.

Henry, J. D., MacLeod, M. S., Phillips, L. H., & Crawford, J. R. (2004). A meta-analytic review of prospective memory and aging. *Psychology and Aging, 19,* 27–39.

Hepper, E. G., & Sedikides, C. (2012). Self-enhancing feedback. In R. M. Sutton, M. J. Hornsey, & K. M. Douglas (Eds.), *Feedback: The communication of praise, criticism, and advice.* New York: Peter Lang.

Hepper, E. G., Sedikides, C., & Cai, H. (2013). Self-enhancement and self-protective strategies in China: Cultural expressions of a fundamental human motive. *Journal of Cross-Cultural Psychology, 44,* 5–23.

Hepting, U., & Solle, R. (1973). Sex-specific differences in color coding. *Archiv fur Psychologie, 125* (2-3), 184–202.

Herbers, J. E., & others. (2011). Direct and indirect effects of parenting on academic functioning of young homeless children. *Early Education and Development, 22,* 77–104.

Herberstein, M. E., & Kemp, D. J. (2012). A clearer view from fuzzy images. *Science, 335,* 409–410.

Herbert, J. (1988). The physiology of aggression. In J. Groebel & R. Hinde (Eds.), *Aggression and war: The biological and social bases.* New York: Cambridge University Press.

Hering, E. (1878). *Zur Lehre vom Lichtsinne* (illustration, 2nd ed.). Wien: C. Gerold's Sohn.

Herman, D., Macknight, J. M., Stromwall, A. E., & Mistry, D. J. (2011). The international athlete—Advances in management of jet lag disorder and anti-doping policy. *Clinical Sports Medicine, 30,* 641–659.

Hermes, M., Hagemann, D., Naumann, E., & Walter, C. (2011). Extraversion and its positive emotional core—further evidence from neuroscience. *Emotion, 11* (2), 367–378.

Hermundstad, A. M., Brown, K. S., Bassett, D. S., & Carlson, J. M. (2011). Learning, memory, and the role of neural network architecture. *PLoS Computational Biology, 7,* e1002063.

Hernandez Lallement, J., & others. (2013). Effort increases sensitivity to reward and loss magnitude in the human brain. *Social Cognitive and Affective Neuroscience.* (in press)

Herry, C., Bach, D. R., Esposito, F., Di Salle, F., Perrig, W. J., Scheffler, K., Luthi, A., & Seifritz, E. (2007). Processing of temporal unpredictability in human and animal amygdala. *Journal of Neuroscience, 27,* 5958–5966.

Hershfield, H., Scheibe, S., Sims, T., & Carstensen, L. L. (2013). When feeling bad can be good: Mixed emotions benefit physical health across adulthood. *Social Psychological and Personality Science, 4,* 54–61.

Hertwig, R., & Ortmann, A. (2008). Deception in experiments: Revisiting the arguments in its defense. *Ethics and Behavior, 18,* 59–92.

Herzog, H. (2006). Forty-two thousand and one Dalmatians: Fads, social contagion, and dog breed popularity. *Society & Animals, 14,* 383–397.

Hespos, S. J., & van Marle, K. (2012). Physics for infants: Characterizing the origins of knowledge about objects, substances, and number. *WIREs Cognitive Science, 3,* 19–27.

Hess, A. K., & Hess, C. E. (2013). Workplace violence: Prevention and aftermath. In S. M. Elias (Ed.), *Deviant and criminal behavior in the workplace* (pp. 221–246). New York: New York University Press.

Hess, E., & Cameron, K. S. (2006). *Developing management skills* (6th ed.). Upper Saddle River, NJ: Prentice-Hall.

Hess, Y. D., & Pickett, C. L. (2010). Social rejection and self- versus other-awareness. *Journal of Experimental Social Psychology, 46,* 453–456.

Hevey, D., McGee, H. M., & Horgan, J. H. (2013). Comparative optimism among patients with coronary heart disease is associated with fewer clinical events 12 months later. Journal of Behavioral Medicine. (in press)

Heward, W. L. (2013). *Exceptional children* (10th ed.). Upper Saddle River, NJ: Merrill.

Hewlin, P. F. (2009). Wearing the cloak: Antecedents and consequences of creating facades of conformity. *Journal of Applied Psychology, 94,* 727–741.

Heyes, C. (2010). Mesmerizing mirror neurons. *NeuroImage, 51,* 789–791.

Hickok, G. (2009). Eight problems for the mirror neuron theory of action understanding in monkeys and humans. *Journal of Cognitive Neuroscience, 17,* 282–293.

Hickok, G. (2010). The role of mirror neurons in speech and language processing. *Brain and Language, 112,* 1–2.

Hickok, G., & Hauser, M. (2010). (Mis)understanding mirror neurons. *Current Biology, 20,* 593–594.

Hicks, J. A., Cicero, D. C., Trent, J., Burton, C. M., & King, L. A. (2010). Positive affect, intuition, and the feeling of meaning. *Journal of Personality and Social Psychology. 98* (6), 967–979.

Hicks, J. A., Trent, J., Davis, W., & King, L. A. (2012). Positive affect, meaning in life, and future time perspective: An application of Socioemotional Selectivity Theory. *Psychology and Aging, 27,* 181–189.

Hidaka, B. H. (2012). Depression as a disease of modernity: Explanations for increasing prevalence. *Journal of Affective Disorders, 140* (3), 205–214.

Higa-McMillan, C. K., & Ebesutani, C. E. (2011). The etiology of social anxiety disorder in adolesents and young adults. In C. A. Alfano & D. C. Beidel (Eds.), *Social anxiety disorder in adolescents and young adults* (pp. 29–51). Washington, DC: American Psychological Association.

Higgins, E. T. (2005). Value from regulatory fit. *Current Directions in Psychological Science, 14,* 209–213.

Highhouse, S., & Schmitt, N. W. (2013). A snapshot in time: Industrial-organizational psychology today. In N. W. Schmitt, S. Highhouse, & I. B. Weiner (Eds.), *Handbook of psychology, 2nd ed., Vol. 12.* (pp. 3–13). Hoboken, NJ: Wiley.

Hildebrandt, T., Bacow, T., Markella, M., & Loeb, K. L. (2012). Anxiety in anorexia nervosa and its management using family-based treatment. *European Eating Disorders Review, 20,* e1–e16.

Hilgard, E. R. (1977). *Divided consciousness: Multiple controls in human thought and action.* New York: Wiley.

Hilgard, E. R. (1992). Dissociation and theories of hypnosis. In E. Fromm & M. R. Nash (Eds.), *Contemporary hypnosis research.* New York: Guilford.

Hill, C. E. (2000). Client-centered therapy. In A. Kazdin (Ed.), *Encyclopedia of psychology.* Washington, DC, & New York: American Psychological Association and Oxford University Press.

Hill, T. D., Burdette, A. M., Ellison, C. G., & Musick, M. A. (2006). Religious attendance and the health behaviors of Texas adults. *Preventive Medicine: An International Journal Devoted to Practice and Theory, 42,* 309–312.

Hines, M. (2013). Sex and sex differences. In P. D. Zelazo (Ed.), *The Oxford handbook of developmental psychology.* New York: Oxford University Press.

Hingson, R. W., Heeren, T., & Winter, M. R. (2006). Age at drinking onset and alcohol dependence: Age of onset, duration, and severity. *Archives of Pediatric and Adolescent Medicine, 160,* 739–746.

Hinkley, L. B., & others. (2012). The role of the corpus callosum development in functional connectivity and cognitive processing. *PLoS One, 7* (8), e39804.

Hinshaw, S. P. (2007). *The mark of shame: Stigma of mental illness and an agenda for change.* New York: Oxford University Press.

Hinton, D. E., Kredlow, M. A., Bui, E., Pollack, M. H., & Hofmann, S. G. (2012). Treatment change of somatic symptoms and cultural syndromes among Cambodian refugees with PTSD. *Depression and Anxiety, 29* (2), 147–154.

Hirata, A., & Castro-Alamancos, M. A. (2010). Neocortex network activation and deactivation states controlled by the thalamus. *Journal of Neurophysiology, 103* (3), 1147–1157.

Hirshbein, L. (2012). Historical essay: Electroconvulsive therapy, memory, and self in America. *Journal of the History of the Neurosciences, 21,* 147–169.

Hirsh-Pasek, K., & Golinkoff, R. M. (2013). Early language and literacy: Six principles. In S. Gilford (Ed.), *Head Start teacher's guide.* New York: Teacher's College Press.

Hnasko, T. S., & others. (2010). Vesicular glutamate transport promotes dopamine storage and glutamate corelease in vivo. *Neuron, 65,* 643–656.

Ho, M. L., & Brass, S. D. (2011). Obstructive sleep apnea. *Neurology International, 3,* e15.

Ho, R. C., Neo, L. F., Chua, A. N., Cheak, A. A., & Mak, A. (2010). Research on psychoneuroimmunology: Does stress influence immunity and cause coronary artery disease. *Annals of the Academy of Medicine, Singapore, 39,* 191–196.

Hobson, J. A. (1999). Dreams. In R. Conlan (Ed.), *States of mind.* New York: Wiley.

Hobson, J. A. (2000). Dreams: Physiology. In A. Kazdin (Ed.), *Encyclopedia of psychology.* Washington, DC, & New York: American Psychological Association and Oxford University Press.

Hobson, J. A. (2002). *Dreaming.* New York: Oxford University Press.

Hobson, J. A. (2004). Freud returns? Like a bad dream. *Scientific American, 290,* 89.

Hobson, J. A., & Friston, K. J. (2012). Waking and dreaming consciousness: Neurobiological and functional considerations. *Progress in Neurobiology, 98,* 82–98.

Hobson, J. A., Pace-Schott, E. F., & Stickgold, R. (2000). Dreaming and the brain. *Behavior and Brain Sciences, 23,* 793–842.

Hobson, J. A., & Voss, U. (2011). A mind to go out of: Reflections on primary and secondary consciousness. *Consciousness and Cognition, 20,* 993–997.

Hockett, C. F. (1960). The origin of speech. *Scientific American, 203,* 88–96.

Hodapp, R. M., Griffin, M. M., Burke, M. M., & Fisher, M. H. (2011). Intellectual disabilities. In R. J. Sternberg & S. B. Kaufman (Eds.), *Handbook of intelligence.* New York: Cambridge University Press.

Hodges, T. D., & Clifton, D. O. (2004). Strengths-based development in practice. In A. Linley & S. Joseph (Eds.), *Positive psychology in practice* (pp. 256–268). Hoboken, NJ: Wiley.

Hodgins, D. C. (2005). Weighing the pros and cons of changing change models: A comment on West (2005). *Addiction, 100,* 1042–1043.

Hodson, G., & Busseri, M. A. (2012). Bright minds and dark attitudes: Lower cognitive ability predicts greater prejudice through right-wing ideology and lower intergroup contact. *Psychological Science, 23* (2) 187–195.

Hoefnagels, M. (2012). *Biology* (2nd ed.). New York: McGraw-Hill.

Hoek, H. W. (2006). Incidence, prevalence and mortality of anorexia nervosa and other eating disorders. *Current Opinion in Psychiatry, 19,* 389–394.

Hoffman, J. (2012, February 23). Trying to find a cry of desperation amid Facebook drama. *New York Times,* A1.

Hofmann, S. G., Asmundson, G. J., & Beck, A. T. (2013). The science of cognitive therapy. *Behavior Therapy, 44,* 199–212.

Hogan, E. H., Hornick, B. A., & Bouchoux, A. (2002). Focus on communications: Communicating the message: Clarifying the controversies about caffeine. *Nutrition Today, 37,* 28–35.

Hogan, R. (2009). Much ado about nothing. *Journal of Research in Personality, 43,* 249.

Hogg, M. A. (2012). Social identity and the psychology of groups. In M. R. Leary & J. P. Tangney (Eds.), *Handbook of self and identity.* New York: Guilford.

Hogh, A., Henriksson, M. E., & Burr, H. (2005). A 5-year follow-up study of aggression at work and psychological health. *International Journal of Behavioral Medicine, 12,* 256–265.

Holbrook, C., & Fessler, D. M. (2013). Sizing up the threat: The envisioned physical formidability of terrorists tracks their leaders' failures and successes. *Cognition, 127,* 46–56.

Holland, A. C., Addis, D. R., & Kensinger, E. A. (2011). The neural correlates of specific versus general autobiographical memory construction and elaboration. *Neuropsychologia, 49,* 3164–3177.

Holland, A. S., & Roisman, G. I. (2010). Adult attachment security and young adults' dating relationships over time: Self-reported, observational, and physiological evidence. *Developmental Psychology, 46,* 552–557.

Holland, P. C. (1996). The effects of intertrial and feature-target intervals on operant serial feature-positive discrimination learning. *Animal Learning & Behavior, 24,* 411–428.

Hollins, M. (2010). The somesthetic senses. *Annual Review of Psychology* (vol. 61). (pp. 243–271). Palo Alto, CA: Annual Reviews.

Holmes, S. (1993). Food avoidance in patients undergoing cancer chemotherapy. *Support Care Cancer, 1* (6), 326–330.

Holtgraves, T. (2012). The role of the right hemisphere in speech act comprehension. *Brain and Language, 121,* 58–64.

Holzman, L. (2009). *Vygotsky at work and play.* Oxford, U.K.: Routledge.

Hooley, J. M., Maher, W. B., & Maher, B. A. (2013). Abnormal psychology. In D. K. Freedheim & I. B. Weiner (Eds.), *Handbook of psychology, 2nd ed., Vol. 1.* (pp. 340–376). Hoboken, NJ: Wiley

Hooper, J., & Teresi, D. (1993). *The 3-pound universe.* New York: Tarcher/Putnam.

Horney, K. (1945). *Our inner conflicts.* New York: Norton.

Horney, K. (1967). *Feminine psychology (collected essays, 1922–1937).* New York: Norton.

Horry, R., Wright, D. B., & Tredoux, C. G. (2010). Recognition and context memory for faces from own and other ethnic groups: A remember-know investigation. *Memory and Cognition, 38,* 134–141.

Horvath, A. O. (2013). You can't step into the same river twice, but you can stub your toes on the same rock: Psychotherapy outcome from a 50-year perspective. *Psychotherapy, 50* (1), 25–32.

Hoss, R. A., & Langlois, J. H. (2003). Infants prefer attractive faces. In O. Pascalis & A. Slater (Eds.), *The development of face processing in infancy and early childhood: Current perspectives* (pp. 27–38). Hauppauge, NY: Nova Science.

Hotard, S. R., McFatter, R. M., McWhirter, R. M., & Stegall, M. E. (1989). Interactive effects of extraversion, neuroticism, and social relationships on subjective well-being. *Journal of Personality and Social Psychology, 57,* 321–331.

Hough, L. M., & Johnson, J. W. (2013). Use and importance of personality variables in work settings. In N. W. Schmitt, S. Highhouse, & I. B. Weiner (Eds.), *Handbook of psychology, 2nd ed., Vol. 12.* (pp. 211–243). Hoboken, NJ: Wiley.

House, J. S., Landis, K. R., & Umberson, D. (1988). Social relationships and health. *Science, 241,* 540–545.

Houser-Marko, L., & Sheldon, K. M. (2008). Eyes on the prize or nose to the grindstone? The effects of level of goal evaluation on mood and motivation. *Personality and Social Psychology Bulletin, 34,* 1556–1569.

Houston, J. P., & others. (2012). Association of common variations in the norepinephrine transporter gene with response to olanzapine-fluoxetine combination versus continued fluoxetine treatment in patients with treatment-resistant depression: A candidate gene analysis. *Journal of Clinical Psychiatry, 73* (6), 878–885.

Houston, K. A., Clifford, B. R., Phillips, L. H., & Memon, A. (2013). The emotional eyewitness: The effects of emotion on specific aspects of eyewitness recall and recognition performance. *Emotion, 13* (1), 118–128.

Hovland, C. I., Janis, I. L., & Kelley, H. H. (1953). *Communication and persuasion.* New Haven, CT: Yale University Press.

Howe, M. J. A., Davidson, J. W., Moore, D. G., & Sloboda, J. A. (1995). Are there early childhood signs of musical ability? *Psychology of Music, 23,* 162–176.

Howes, M. B. (2006). *Human memory.* Thousand Oaks, CA: Sage.

Howes, O. D., & others. (2012). The nature of dopamine dysfunction in schizophrenia and what this means for treatment: Meta-analysis of imaging studies. *Archives of General Psychiatry, 69* (8), 776–786.

Howland, R. H. (2012). The use of dopaminergic and stimulant drugs for the treatment of depression. *Journal of Psychosocial Nursing and Mental Health Services, 50,* 11–14.

Howrey, B. T., & others. (2012). Self-reported sleep characteristics and mortality in older adults of Mexican origin: Results from the Hispanic established population for the epidemiologic study of the elderly. *Journal of the American Geriatrics Society, 60* (10), 1906–1911.

Hoyer, D., Hannon, J. P., & Martin, G. R. (2002). Molecular, pharmacological, and functional diversity of 5-HT receptors. *Pharmacology, Biochemistry, and Behavior, 71,* 533–554.

Hoyle, R. H. (2013). Self-knowledge and self-esteem. In M. H. Kernis (Ed.), *Self-esteem issues and answers.* New York: Psychology Press.

Hsiao, S. S., & Gomez-Ramirez, M. (2013). Neural mechanisms of tactile perception. In R. J. Nelson, S. J. Y. Mizumori, & I. B. Weiner (Eds.), *Handbook of psychology* (2nd ed., vol. 3). (pp. 206–239). Hoboken, NJ: Wiley.

Hu, S., & Kuh, G. D. (2003). Diversity learning experiences and college student learning and development. *Journal of College Student Development, 44,* 320–334.

Huang, C. C., & Chang, Y. C. (2009). The long-term effects of febrile seizures on the hippocampal neuronal plasticity—clinical and experimental evidence. *Brain and Development, 31,* 383–387.

Huart, C., Collet, S., & Rombaux, P. (2009). Chemosensory pathways: From periphery to cortex. *B-ENT, 5,* Suppl. 13, S3–S9.

Hubble, M. A., & Miller, S. D. (2004). The client: Psychotherapy's missing link for promoting a positive psychology. In A. Linley & S. Joseph (Eds.), *Positive psychology in practice* (pp. 335–353). Hoboken, NJ: Wiley.

Hubel, D. H., & Wiesel, T. N. (1963). Receptive fields of cells in striate cortex of very young, visually inexperienced kittens. *Journal of Neurophysiology, 26,* 994–1002.

Hudak, M. L., & others. (2012). Neonatal drug withdrawal. *Pediatrics, 129,* e540–e560.

Huey, S. J., Jones, E., Tilley, J., & Smith, C. (2014). The contribution of cultural competence to evidence-based care. *Annual Review of Clinical Psychology* (vol. 10). Palo Alto, CA: Annual Reviews.

Huffcutt, A. L., & Culbertson, S. S. (2010). Interviews. In S. Zedeck (Ed.), *APA handbook of industrial and organizational psychology.* Washington, DC: American Psychological Association.

Hugenberg, K., & Wilson, J. P. (2013). Faces are central to social cognition. In D. E. Carlston (Ed.), *The Oxford handbook of social cognition.* New York: Oxford University Press.

Hughes, A. E., Berg, C. A., & Wiebe D. J. (2012). Emotional processing and self-control in adolescents with type 1 diabetes. *Journal of Pediatric Psychology, 37* (8), 925–934.

Hughes, I. A., Houk, C., Ahmed, F., Lee, P. A., & LWPES-ESPE Consensus Group. (2006). Consensus statement on management of intersex disorders. *Archives of Disease in Childhood, 91,* 554–563.

Hunsley, J., & Bailey, J. M. (2001). Whither the Rorschach? An analysis of the evidence. *Psychological Assessment, 13,* 472–485.

Hunt, H. T. (2012). A collective unconscious reconsidered: Jung's archetypal imagination in the light of contemporary psychology and social science. *Journal of Analytical Psychology, 57,* 76–98.

Hunt, R. R., & Ellis, H. C. (2004). *Fundamentals of cognitive psychology* (7th ed.). New York: McGraw-Hill.

Huprich, S. K. (Ed.). (2013). *Rorschach assessment of the personality disorders.* New York: Routledge.

Huprich, S. K., & Hopwood, C. J. (Eds.). (2013). Personality assessment in *DSM-5.* New York: Routledge.

Hurleman, R., & others. (2010). Oxytocin enhances amygdala-dependent, socially reinforced learning and empathy in humans. *Journal of Neuroscience, 30,* 4999–5007.

Hurst, J. L. (2009). Female recognition and assessment of males through scent. *Behavioural Brain Research, 200,* 295–303.

Hutchinson, S. L., & Nimrod, G. (2012). Leisure as a resource for successful aging by older adults with chronic health conditions. *International Journal of Aging and Human Development, 74,* 41–65.

Hutson, J. R., & others. (2013). Adverse placental effect of formic acid on hCG secretion is mitigated by folic acid. *Alcohol and Alcoholism.* doi: 10.1093/alcalc/agt008

Huttenlocher, P. R. (1999). Dendritic synaptic development in human cerebral cortex: Time course and critical periods. *Developmental Neuropsychology, 16,* 347–349.

Huuhka, K., & others. (2012). One-year follow-up after discontinuing maintenance electroconvulsive therapy. *Journal of Electroconvulsive Therapy, 28* (4), 225–228.

Hyde, J. S. (2005). The gender similarities hypothesis. *American Psychologist, 60,* 581–592.

Hyde, J. S. (2006). Gender similarities in mathematics and science. *Science, 314,* 599–600.

Hyde, J. S. (2007). New directions in the study of gender similarities and differences. *Current Directions in Psychological Science, 16,* 259–263.

Hyde, J. S. (2014). Gender similarities and differences. *Annual Review of Psychology* (vol. 65). Palo Alto, CA: Annual Reviews.

Hyde, J. S., & DeLamater, J. D. (2011). *Understanding human sexuality* (11th ed.). New York: McGraw-Hill.

Hyde, J. S., & Else-Quest, N. (2013). *Half the human experience* (8th ed.). Boston: Cengage.

Hyland, M. E. (2011). Motivation and placebos: Do different mechanisms occur in different contexts. *Philosophical Transactions of the Royal Society of London. Series B, Biological Sciences, 366,* 1828–1837.

Hyman, R. (2010). Meta-analysis that conceals more than it reveals: Comment on Storm et al. (2010). *Psychological Bulletin, 136,* 486–490.

Hyman, S. (2001, October 23). *Basic and clinical neuroscience in the post-genomic era.* Paper presented at the centennial symposium on the Celebration of Excellence in Neuroscience, the Rockefeller University, New York City.

Hyman, S. E. (2010). The diagnosis of mental disorders: The problem of reification. *Annual Review of Clinical Psychology* (vol. 6). Palo Alto, CA: Annual Reviews.

Hyoun, S. C., Obican, S. G., & Scialli, A. R. (2012). Teratogen update: Methotrexate. *Birth Defects Research A: Clinical and Molecular Teratology, 94,* 187–204.

I

Iacono, W. G., & Lykken, D. T. (1997). The validity of the lie detector: Two surveys of scientific opinion. *Journal of Applied Psychology, 82,* 426–433.

Iannilli, E., & others. (2012). Taste laterality studied by means of umani and salt stimuli: An fMRI study. *NeuroImage, 60* (1), 426–435.

Ibanez, A., Huepe, D., Gempp, R., Gutiérrez, V., Rivera-Rei, A., & Toledo, M. I. (2013). Empathy, sex and fluid intelligence as predictors of theory of mind. *Personality and Individual Differences, 54,* 616–621.

Ibrahim, R., & Eviatar, Z. (2012). The contribution of the two hemispheres to lexical decision in different languages. *Behavior and Brain Functioning, 8,* 3.

Ideguchi, M., Palmer, T. D., Recht, L. D., & Weimann, J. M. (2010). Murine embryonic stem cell-derived pyramidal neurons integrate into the cerebral cortex and appropriate project axons to subcortical targets. *Journal of Neuroscience, 30,* 894–904.

Iglesias, P. A. (2012). A systems biology view of adaptation in sensory mechanisms. *Advances in Experimental Medicine and Biology, 736,* 499–516.

Ikeda, B. E., Collins, C. E., Alvaro, F., Marshall, G., & Garg, M. L. (2006). Well-being and nutrition-related side effects in children undergoing chemotherapy. *Nutrition and Dietetics, 63,* 227–239.

Ikeda, K., Sekiguchi, T., & Hayashi, A. (2010). Concentrated pitch discrimination modulates auditory brainstem responses during contralateral noise exposure. *Neuroreport, 21,* 359–366.

Imada, T. (2012). Cultural narratives of individualism and collectivism: A content analysis of textbook stories in the United States and Japan. *Journal of Cross-Cultural Psychology, 43,* 576–591.

Imada, T., & Ellsworth, P. C. (2011). Proud Americans and lucky Japanese: Cultural differences in appraisal and corresponding emotion. *Emotion, 11,* 329–345.

Imeri, L., & Opp, M. R. (2009). How (and why) the immune system makes us sleep. *Nature Reviews: Neuroscience, 10,* 199–210.

Impett, E. A., Peplau, L. A., & Gable, S. L. (2005). Approach and avoidance sexual motives: Implications for personal and interpersonal well-being. *Personal Relationships, 12,* 465–482.

Inaba, A., Thoits, P. A., Ueno, K., Gove, W. R., Evenson, R. J., & Sloan, M. (2005). Depression in the United States and Japan: Gender, marital status, and SES patterns. *Social Science & Medicine, 61,* 2280–2292.

Inelmen, E. M., & others. (2012). The importance of sexual health in the elderly: Breaking down barriers and taboos. *Aging: Clinical and Experimental Research, 24,* Suppl. 3, S31–S34.

Irwin, M. R., Wang, M., Campomayor, C. O., Coliado-Hidalgo, A., & Cole, S. (2006). Sleep deprivation and activation of morning levels of cellular and genomic markers of inflammation. *Archives of Internal Medicine, 166,* 1756–1762.

Iturbide, M. I., Raffaelli, M., & Carlo, G. (2009). Protective effects of ethnic identity on Mexican American college students' psychological well-being. *Hispanic Journal of Behavioral Sciences, 31,* 536–552.

Ivancevich, J. M., & Konopaske, R. (2011). *Organizational behavior and management* (9th ed.). New York: McGraw-Hill.

Iwassa, H., Masul, Y., Gondo, Y., Inagaki, H., Kawaal, C., & Suzuki, T. (2008). Personality and all-cause mortality among older adults dwelling in a Japanese community: A five-year population-based prospective study. *American Journal of Geriatric Psychiatry, 16,* 399–405.

Iwassa, H., & others. (2009). Personality and participation in mass health checkups among Japanese community-dwelling elderly. *Journal of Psychosomatic Research, 66,* 155–159.

Iwata, M., Ota, K. T., & Duman, R. S. (2013). The imflammasome: Pathways linking psychological stress, depression, and systemic illnesses. *Brain, Behavior, and Immunity, 31,* 105–114.

Izard, C. E. (2009). Emotion theory and research: Highlights, unanswered questions, and emerging issues. *Annual Review of Psychology* (vol. 60). (pp. 1–25). Palo Alto, CA: Annual Reviews.

J

Jablensky, E. (2000). Epidemiology of schizophrenia: The global burden of disease and disability. *European Archives of Psychiatry and Clinical Neuroscience, 250,* 274–285.

Jablensky, E., & others. (1992). Schizophrenia: Manifestations, incidence and course in different cultures: A World Health Organization 10-country study. *Psychological Medicine,* Monograph Suppl. 20, 1–97.

Jackendoff, R. (2012). *A user's guide to thought and meaning.* New York: Oxford University Press.

Jackson, L. C., & Greene, B. (2000). *Psychotherapy with African-American women.* New York: Guilford.

Jackson, M. L., & others. (2011). The effect of sleep deprivation on BOLD activity elicited by a divided attention task. *Brain Imaging and Behavior, 5,* 97–108.

Jackson, N. W. (2012). Equal discussion of significant findings? Possible confirmation bias in study of alcohol advertising. *Alcohol and Alcoholism, 47,* 79.

Jacobs, G. H. (2013). Comparative vision. In R. J. Nelson, S. J. Y. Mizumori, & I. B. Weiner (Eds.), *Handbook of psychology, 2nd ed., Vol. 3.* (pp. 52–80). Hoboken, NJ: Wiley.

Jacobs, T. L., Epel, E. S., Lin, J., Blackburn, E. H., Wolkowitz, O. M., Bridwell, D. A., Zanesco, A. P., Aichele, S. R., Sahdra, B. K., MacLean, K. A., King, B. G., Shaver, P. R., Rosenberg, E. L., Ferrer, E., Wallace, B. A., & Saron, C. D. (2011). Intensive meditation training, immune cell telomerase activity, and psychological mediators. *Psychoneuroendocrinology, 36,* 664–681.

Jacobsen, P. B., Bovbjerg, D. H., Schwartz, M. D., Andrykowski, M. A., Futterman, A. D., Gilewski, T., Norton, L., & Redd, W. H. (1993). Formation of food aversions in cancer patients receiving repeated infusions of chemotherapy. *Behavior Research Therapy, 31* (8), 739–748.

Jaeger, S. R., Bava, C. M., Worch, T., Dawson, J., & Marshall, D. W. (2011). The food choice kaleidoscope: A framework for structured description of product, place, and person as sources of variation in food choices. *Appetite, 56,* 412–423.

Jaeggi, S. M., Buschkuehl, M., Jonides, J., & Perrig, W. J. (2008). Improving fluid intelligence with training on working memory. *Proceedings of the National Academy of Sciences USA, 105* (19), 6829–6833.

Jahng, S., Solhan, M. B., Tomko, R. L., Wood, P. K., Piasecki, T. M., & Trull, T. J. (2011). Affect and alcohol use: An ecological momentary assessment study of outpatients with borderline personality disorder. *Journal of Abnormal Psychology, 120* (3), 572–584.

Jakupcak, M., Salters, K., Gratz, K. L., & Roemer, L. (2003). Masculinity and emotionality: An investigation of men's primary and secondary emotional responding. *Sex Roles, 49,* 111–120.

James, W. (1950). *Principles of psychology.* New York: Dover. (original work published 1890)

Jameson, D., & Hurvich, L. M. (1989). Essay concerning color constancy. *Annual Review of Psychology* (vol. 40). (pp. 1–22). Palo Alto, CA: Annual Reviews.

Jamison, K. R. (2009). *An unquiet mind: A memoir of moods and madness.* New York: Random House Digital.

Janak, P. H., Bowers, M.S., & Corbit, L. H. (2012). Compound stimulus presentation and the norepinephrine reuptake inhibitor Atomoxetine enhance long-term extinction of cocaine-seeking behavior. *Neuropsychopharmacology, 37,* 975–985.

Jang, K. L., Livesley, W. J., & Vernon, P. A. (1996). Heritability of the big five personality dimensions and their facets: A twin study. *Journal of Personality, 64,* 577–591.

Janis, I. (1972). *Victims of groupthink: A psychological study of foreign-policy decisions and fiascos.* Boston: Houghton Mifflin.

Janis, I. L., & Hovland, C. I. (1959). An overview of persuasability research. In C. I. Hovland & I. L. Janis (Eds.), **Personality** and *persuasability* (pp. 1–26). New Haven, CT: Yale University Press.

Janowsky, D. S., Addario, D., & Risch, S. C. (1987). *Psychopharmacology case studies* (2nd ed.). New York: Guilford.

"Japanese breaks pi memory record." (2005, July 2). *BBC News.* http://news.bbc.co.uk/2/hi/asia-pacific/4644103.stm (accessed March 30, 2013)

Jaremka, L. M., Lindgren, M. E., & Kiecolt-Glaser, J. K. (2013). Synergistic relationships among stress, depression, and troubled relationships: Insights from psychoneuroimmunology. *Depression and Anxiety, 30* (4), 288–296.

Jarrett, C. (2011). Ouch! The different ways people experience pain. *The Psychologist, 24,* Part 6.

Jaspal, R., & Cinnirella, M. (2012). Identity processes, threat, and interpersonal relations: Accounts from British Muslim gay men. *Journal of Homosexuality, 59,* 215–240.

Jensen-Campbell, L. A., & Malcolm, K. T. (2007). The importance of conscientiousness in adolescent interpersonal relationships. *Personality and Social Psychology Bulletin, 33,* 368–383.

Jeon, W. T., Eom, J. S., & Min, S. K. (2013). A 7-year follow-up study on the mental health of North Korean defectors in South Korea. *Journal of Traumatic Stress, 26,* 158–164.

Jeong, J., Kim, D. J., Kim, S. Y., Chae, J. H., Go, H. J., & Kim, K. S. (2001). Effect of total sleep deprivation on the dimensional complexity of the waking EEG. *Sleep, 15,* 197–202.

Jespersen, A. E., Lalumiere, M. L., & Seto, M. C. (2009). Sexual abuse history among adult sex offenders and non-sex offenders: Meta-analysis. *Child Abuse and Neglect, 33,* 179–192.

Jeste, D. V., & others. (2013). Association between older age and more successful aging: Critical role of resilience and depression. *American Journal of Psychiatry, 170,* 188–196.

Jex, S. M., Swanson, N., & Grubb, P. (2013). Healthy workplaces. In N. W. Schmitt, S. Highhouse, & I. B. Weiner (Eds.), *Handbook of psychology, 2nd ed., Vol. 12.* (pp. 615–642). Hoboken, NJ: Wiley.

Jiang, Y. H., & others. (2010). Clinical efficacy of acupuncture on the morphine-related side effects in patients undergoing spinal-epidural anesthesia and analgesia. *Chinese Journal of Integrative Medicine, 16,* 71–74.

Job, R. F. S. (1987). The effect of mood on helping behavior. *Journal of Social Psychology, 127,* 323–328.

Joel, S., MacDonald, G., & Shimotomai, A. (2011). Conflicting pressures on romantic relationship commitment for anxiously attached individuals. *Journal of Personality, 79,* 51–73.

Johansen, J. P., Wolff, S. B., Lüthi, A., & LeDoux, J. E. (2012). Controlling the elements: An optogenetic approach to understanding the neural circuits of fear. *Biological Psychiatry, 71* (12), 1053–1060.

Johnson, A. (2013). Procedural memory and skill acquisition. In A. F. Healy, R. W. Proctor, & I. B. Weiner (Eds.), *Handbook of psychology, 2nd ed., Vol. 4.* (pp. 495–520). Hoboken, NJ: Wiley.

Johnson, J. S., & Newport, E. L. (1991). Critical period effects on universal properties of language: The status of subjacency in the acquisition of a second language. *Cognition, 39,* 215–258.

Johnson, L. R., McGuire, J., Lazarus, R., & Palmer, A. A. (2012). Pavlovian fear memory circuits and phenotype models of PTSD. *Neuropharmacology, 62,* 638–646.

Johnson, R. E., & Chang, C. (2006). "I" is to continuance as "we" is to affective: The relevance of the self-concept for organizational commitment. *Journal of Organizational Behavior, 27* (5), 549–570.

Johnson, S. K., & Halpern, A. R. (2012). Semantic priming of familiar songs. *Memory and Cognition, 40* (4), 579–593.

Johnson, S. P. (2012). Development of the visual system. In P. Rakic & J. Rubenstein (Eds.), *Developmental neuroscience—Basic and clinical mechanisms.* New York: Oxford University Press.

Johnson, S. P. (2013). Object perception. In P. D. Zelazo (Ed.), *The Oxford handbook of developmental psychology.* New York: Oxford University Press.

Johnson-Laird, P. N., Mancini, F., & Gangemi, A. (2006). A hyper-emotion theory of psychological illnesses. *Psychological Review, 113,* 822–841.

Johnston, L. D., O'Malley, P. M., Bachman, J. G., & Schulenberg, J. E. (2012). *Monitoring the Future national results on adolescent drug use: Overview of key findings, 2011.* Ann Arbor, MI: Institute for Social Research, University of Michigan.

Johnstone, E., Benowitz, N., Cargill, A., Jacob, R., Hinks, L., Day, I., Murphy, M., & Walton, R. (2006). Determinants of the rate of nicotine metabolism and the effects on smoking behavior. *Clinical Pharmacology and Therapeutics, 80,* 319–330.

Joiner, T. E., Jr. (2005). *Why people die by suicide.* Cambridge, MA: Harvard University Press.

Joiner, T. E., & Ribeiro, J. D. (2011). Assessment and management of suicidal behavior in children and adolescents. *Pediatric Annals, 40,* 319–324.

Joiner, T. E., Ribeiro, J. D., & Silva, C. (2012). Nonsuicidal self-injury, suicidal behavior, and their co-occurrence as viewed through the lens of the interpersonal theory of suicide. *Current Directions in Psychological Science, 21* (5), 342–347.

Jones, E. E., & Harris, V. A. (1967). The attribution of attitudes. *Journal of Experimental Social Psychology, 3,* 1–24.

Jones, G. R., & George, J. M. (2007). *Essentials of contemporary management* (2nd ed.). New York: McGraw-Hill.

Jones, S. G., & Benca, R. M. (2013). Sleep and biological rhythms. In R. J. Nelson, S. J. Y. Mizumori, & I. B. Weiner (Eds.), *Handbook of psychology, 2nd ed., Vol. 3.* (pp. 365–395). Hoboken, NJ: Wiley.

Jordan, C. H., & Zeigler-Hill, V. (2013). Secure and fragile forms of self-esteem. In V. Zeigler-Hill (Ed.), *Self-esteem.* New York: Psychology Press.

Jordan-Young, R., & Rumiati, R. I. (2012). Hardwired for sexism? Approaches to sex/gender in neuroscience. *Neuroethics, 5,* 305–315.

Jose, A., O'Leary, K. D., & Moyer, A. (2010). Does premarital cohabitation predict subsequent marital stability and marital quality? A meta-analysis. *Journal of Marriage and the Family, 72,* 105–116.

Joseph, J. (2006). *The missing gene.* New York: Algora.

Joseph, J., Breslin, C., & Skinner, H. (1999). Critical perspectives on the transtheoretical model and stages of change. In J. A. Tucker, D. M. Donovan, & G. A. Marlatt (Eds.), *Changing addictive behavior: Bridging clinical and public health strategies* (pp. 160–190). New York: Guilford.

Joseph, S., & Linley, P. A. (2004). Positive therapy: A positive psychological approach to therapeutic practice. In P. A. Linley & S. Joseph (Eds.), *Positive psychology in practice* (pp. 354–368). Hoboken, NJ: Wiley.

Josephs, L., & Weinberger, J. (2013). Psychodynamic psychotherapy. In G. Stricker, T. A.

Widiger, & I. B. Weiner (Eds.), *Handbook of psychology, 2nd ed., Vol. 8.* (pp. 265–290). Hoboken, NJ: Wiley.

Joutsenniemi, K., & others. (2012). Prediction of the outcome of short- and long-term psychotherapy. *Journal of Affective Disorders, 141* (2-3), 331–342.

Jowsey, S. G., & others. (2012). Seligman's theory of attributional style: Optimism, pessimism, and quality of life after heart transplant. *Progress Transplant, 22,* 49–55.

Joy, J. E., Watson, S. J., & Benson, J. A. (Eds.). (1999). *Institute of medicine. Marijuana and medicine: Assessing the science base.* Washington, DC: National Academy Press.

Judd, F. K., Hickey, M., & Bryant, C. (2011). Depression and midlife: Are we overpathologising the menopause? *Journal of Affective Disorders, 136* (3), 199–211.

Judge, T. A., Bono, J. E., Ilies, R., & Gerhardt, M. W. (2002). Personality and leadership: A qualitative and quantitative review. *Journal of Applied Psychology, 87* (4), 765–780.

Judge, T. A., Piccolo, R. F., Podsakoff, J. C., & Rich, B. L. (2010). The relationship between pay satisfaction and job satisfaction. *Journal of Vocational Behavior, 77,* 157–167.

Judge, T. A., Thorson, C. J., Bono, J. E., & Patton, G. K. (2001). The job satisfaction–job performance relationship: A qualitative and quantitative review. *Psychological Bulletin, 127,* 376–407.

Julien, E., Senecal, C., & Guay, F. (2009). Longitudinal relations among perceived autonomy support from health care practitioners, motivation, coping strategies and dietary compliance in a sample of adults with type 2 diabetes. *Journal of Health Psychology, 14,* 457–470.

Jung, C. (1917). *Analytic psychology.* New York: Moffat, Yard.

Juntunen, C. L., & Bailey, T.-K. M (2013). Training and employment services for adult workers. In D. L. Blustein (Ed.), *The Oxford handbook of the psychology of working.* New York: Oxford University Press.

K

Kaas, J., O'Brien, B. M. J., & Hackett, T. A. (2013). Auditory processing in primate brains. In R. J. Nelson, S. J. Y. Mizumori, & I. B. Weiner (Eds.), *Handbook of psychology, 2nd ed., Vol. 3.* (pp. 157–195). Hoboken, NJ: Wiley.

Kabat-Zinn, J. (2006). Coming to our senses: Healing ourselves and the world through mindfulness. New York, NY: Hyperion.

Kabat-Zinn, J. (2009, March 18). *This analog life: Reconnecting with what is important in an always uncertain world.* Presentation at the 7th Annual Conference at the Center for Mindful Meditation, Worcester, MA.

Kabat-Zinn, J., & Davidson, R. (Eds.). (2012). *The mind's own physician.* Berkeley, CA: New Harbinger.

Kabat-Zinn, J., Lipworth, L., & Burney, R. (1985). The clinical use of mindfulness meditation for the self-regulation of chronic pain. *Journal of Behavioral Medicine, 8,* 163–190.

Kabat-Zinn, J., Wheeler, E., Light, T., Skillings, A., Scharf, M. J., Cropley, T. G., Hosmer, D., & Bernhard, J. D. (1998). Influence of a mindfulness meditation-based stress reduction intervention on rates of skin clearing in patients with moderate to severe psoriasis undergoing phototherapy (UVB) and photochemotherapy (PUVA). *Psychosomatic Medicine, 60,* 625–632.

Kagan, J. (2013). Temperamental contributions to inhibited and uninhibited profiles. In P. D. Zelazo (Ed.), *The Oxford handbook of developmental psychology.* New York: Oxford University Press.

Kahan, T. L., & Sullivan, K. T. (2012). Assessing metacognitive skills in waking and sleep: A psychometric analysis of the Metacognitive, Affective, Cognitive Experience (MACE) questionnaire. *Consciousness and Cognition, 21,* 340–352.

Kahana, M. J. (2012). *Foundations of human memory.* New York: Oxford University Press.

Kahn, A., & others. (1992) Sleep and cardiorespiratory characteristics of infant victim of sudden death: A prospective case-control study. *Sleep, 15,* 287–292.

Kahneman, D., & Klein, G. (2009). Conditions for intuitive experience: A failure to disagree. *American Psychologist, 64,* 515–526.

Kahneman, D., Krueger, A. B., Schkade, D. A., Schwarz, N., & Stone, A. A. (2004). A survey method for characterizing daily life experience: The day reconstruction method. *Science, 306,* 1776–1780.

Kahneman, D., Lovallo, D., & Sibony, O. (2011). Before you make that big decision. . . *Harvard Business Review, 89,* 50–60.

Kaiser, S., & others. (2010). Maintenance of real objects and their verbal designations in working memory. *Neuroscience Letters, 469,* 65–69.

Kalat, J. W., & Shiota, M. N. (2012). *Emotion* (2nd ed.). Boston: Cengage.

Kalichman, S. C. (2007). The theory of reasoned action and advances in HIV/AIDS prevention. In I. Ajzen, D. Albarracin, & R. Hornik (Eds.), *Prediction and change of health behavior.* Mahwah, NJ: Erlbaum.

Kalmbach, A., Hedrick, T., & Waters, J. (2012). Selective ooptogenetic stimulation of cholinergic axons in neocortex. *Journal of Neurophysiology, 107,* 2008–2019.

Kamin, L. J. (1968). Attention-like processes in classical conditioning. In M. R. Jones (Ed.), *Miami symposium on the prediction of behavior: Aversive stimuli.* Coral Gables, FL: University of Miami Press.

Kammrath, L. K., & Scholer, A. A. (2013). Cognitive-affective processing system. In H. A. Tennen, J. M. Suls, & I. B. Weiner (Eds.), *Handbook of psychology, 2nd ed., Vol. 5.* (pp. 161–182). Hoboken, NJ: Wiley.

Kandel, E. R., & Schwartz, J. H. (1982). Molecular biology of learning: Modulation of transmitter release. *Science, 218,* 433–443.

Kanov, J. M., Maitlis, S., Worline, M. C., Dutton, J. E., Frost, P. J., & Lilius, J. M. (2006). Compassion in organizational life. In J. V. Gallos (Ed.), *Organization development: A Jossey-Bass reader* (pp. 793–812). San Francisco: Jossey-Bass.

Kanter, J. W. (2013). The vision of a progressive clinical science to guide clinical practice. *Behavior Therapy, 44,* 228–233.

Kanwisher, N. (2006). Neuroscience: What's in a face? *Science, 311,* 617–618.

Kanwisher, N., & Yovel, G. (2010). Cortical specialization for face perception in humans. In J. T. Cacioppo & G. G. Berentson (Eds.), *Handbook of neuroscience for the behavioral sciences.* New York: Wiley.

Kaplan, H. S. (1974). *The new sex therapy: Active treatment of sexual dysfunctions.* New York: Routledge.

Kaplan, J. S. (2012). The effects of shared environment on adult intelligence: A critical review of adoption, twin, and MZA studies. *Developmental Psychology, 48* (5), 1292–1298.

Kaplan, R. A., Rossell, S. L., Enticott, P. G., & Castle, D. J. (2013). Own-body perception in body dysmorphic disorder. *Cognitive Neuropsychiatry.* (in press)

Kapur, S. (2003). Psychosis as a state of aberrant salience: A framework linking biology, phenomenology, and pharmacology. *American Journal of Psychiatry, 160,* 13–23.

Kar, B. R., Vijay, N., & Mishra, S. (2013). Development of cognitive and affective control networks and decision making. *Progress in Brain Research, 202,* 347–368.

Karau, S. J., & Williams, K. D. (1993). Social loafing: A meta-analytic review and theoretical integration. *Journal of Personality and Social Psychology, 65,* 681–706.

Karg, K., & Sen, S. (2012). Gene × environment interaction models in psychiatric genetics. *Current Topics in Behavioral Neuroscience, 12,* 441–462.

Karkazis, K., Tamar-Mattis, A., & Kon, A. A. (2010) Genital surgery for disorders of sex development: Implementing a shared decision-making approach. *Journal of Pediatric Endocrinology and Metabolism, 23* (8), 789–805.

Karlinsky, N., & Frost, M. (2012, April 27). Real "Beautiful Mind": College dropout became mathematical genius after mugging. *ABC News.* http://abcnews.go.com/blogs/health/2012/04/27/real-beautiful-mind-accidental-genius-draws-complex-math-formulas-photos/ (accessed March 13, 2013)

Karsten, J., & others. (2012). The state effect of depressive and anxiety disorders and the big five personality traits. *Journal of Psychiatric Research, 46* (5), 644–650.

Kaschel, R., Logie, R. H., Kazen, M., & Della Sala, S. (2009). Alzheimer's disease, but not aging or depression, affects dual-tasking. *Journal of Neurology, 256,* 1860–1868.

Kaskutas, L. A. (2009). Alcoholics Anonymous effectiveness: Faith meets science. *Journal of Addictive Diseases, 28,* 145–157.

Kaskutas, L. A., Subbaraman, M. S., Witbordt, J., & Zemore, S. E. (2009). Effectiveness of making Alcoholics Anonymous easier: A group format 12-step facilitation approach. *Journal of Substance Abuse Treatment, 37* (3), 228–239.

Kasser, T., & Ryan, R. M. (1993). A dark side of the American dream: Correlates of financial success as a central life aspiration. *Journal of Personality and Social Psychology, 65,* 410–422.

Kasser, T., & Ryan, R. M. (1996). Further examining the American dream: Differential correlates of intrinsic and extrinsic goals. *Personality and Social Psychology Bulletin, 22,* 280–287.

Kasser, T., Ryan, R. M., Couchman, C. E., & Sheldon, K. M. (2004). Materialistic values: Their causes and consequences. In T. Kasser & A. D. Kanner (Eds.), *Psychology and consumer culture: The struggle for a good life in a materialistic world* (pp. 11–28). Washington, DC: American Psychological Association.

Kasser, T., & Sharma, Y. S. (1999). Reproductive freedom, educational equality, and females' preference for resource-acquisition characteristics in mates. *Psychological Science, 10,* 374–377.

Kato, I., & others. (2003). Incomplete arousal processes in infants who were victims of sudden death. *American Journal of Respiratory Critical Care Medicine 168,* 1298–1303.

Kato, T., & others. (2013). Neurotransmitters, psychotropic drugs, and microglia: Clinical implications for psychiatry. *Current Medicinal Chemistry.* (in press)

Katz, J. N. (1995). *The invention of heterosexuality.* New York: Dutton.

Kaufman, J. C. (2005). Genius, lunatics, and poets: Mental illness in prize-winning authors. *Imagination, Cognition, and Personality, 20,* 305–314.

Kaufman, J. C., & Sternberg, R. J. (2013). The creative mind. In C. Jones, M. Lorenzen, & J. Sapsed (Eds.), *The Oxford handbook of creative industries.* New York: Oxford University Press.

Kavšek, M., & Granrud, C. E. (2012). Children's and adults' size estimates at near and far distances: A test of the perceptual learning theory of size constancy development. *Perception, 3,* 459–466.

Kawabata, Y., Tseng, W. L., Murray-Close, D., & Crick, N. R. (2013). Developmental trajectories of Chinese children's relational and physical aggression: Associations with social-psychological adjustment problems. *Journal of Abnormal Child Psychology.* (in press)

Kaye, W. H., Wierenga, C. E., Bailer, U. F., Simmons, A. N., & Bischoff-Grethe, A. (2013). Nothing tastes as good as skinny feels: The neurobiology of anorexia nervosa. *Trends in Neuroscience, 36,* 110–120.

Kazanis, I. (2013). Neurogenesis in the adult mammalian brain: How much do we need, how much do we have? *Current Topics in Behavioral Neuroscience.* (in press)

Keeley, J., Zayac, R., & Correia, C. (2008). Curvilinear relationships between statistics anxiety and performance among undergraduate students: Evidence for optimal anxiety. *Statistics Education Research Journal, 7,* 4–15.

Keen, R. (2011). The development of problem solving in young children: A critical cognitive skill. *Annual Review of Psychology* (vol. 63). (pp. 1–21). Palo Alto, CA: Annual Reviews.

Keeton, C. P., Kolos, A. C., & Walkup, J. T. (2009). Pediatric generalized anxiety disorder: Epidemiology, diagnosis, and management. *Pediatric Drugs, 11,* 171–183.

Keillor, J. M., Barrett, A. M., Crucian, G. P., Kortenkamp, S., & Heilman, K. M. (2002). Emotional experience and perception in the absence of facial feedback. *Journal of the International Neuropsychological Society, 8,* 130–135.

Keizer, R., Dykstra, P. A., & Poortman, A. R. (2010). Life outcomes of childless men and fathers. *European Sociological Review, 26,* 1–15.

Kellerman, A. L., & others. (1993). Gun ownership as a risk factor for homicide in the home. *New England Journal of Medicine, 329,* 1084–1091.

Kelley, H. H. (1973). The processes of causal attribution. *American Psychologist, 28,* 107–128.

Kellner, C. H., & others. (2006). Continuation electroconvulsive therapy vs pharmacotherapy for relapse prevention in major depression: A multisite study from the Consortium for Research in Electroconvulsive Therapy (CORE). *Archives of General Psychiatry, 63* (12), 1337–1344.

Kelly, G. F. (2006). *Sexuality today* (8th ed.). New York: McGraw-Hill.

Kelly, J. F. (2013). Alcoholics Anonymous science update: Introduction to the special issue. *Substance Abuse, 34,* 1–3.

Kelly, J. R., & Agnew, C. R. (2012). Behavior and behavioral assessment. In K. Deaux & M. Snyder (Eds.), *The Oxford handbook of personality and social psychology.* New York: Oxford University Press.

Kendler, K. S., Chen, X., Dick, D., Maes, H., Gillespie, N., Neale, M. C., & Riley, B. (2012). Recent advances in the genetic epidemiology and molecular genetics of substance use disorders. *Nature Neuroscience, 15,* 181–189.

Kendler, K. S., Gardner, C., & Dick, D. M. (2011). Predicting alcohol consumption in adolescence from alcohol-specific and general externalizing genetic risk factors, key environmental factors, and their interaction. *Psychological Medicine, 41,* 1507–1516.

Kennedy, B. L., & Most, S. B. (2012). Perceptual, not memorial, disruption underlies emotion-induced blindness. *Emotion, 12,* 199–202.

Kennedy, G. J., Haque, M., & Zarankow, B. (1997). Human sexuality in late life. *International Journal of Mental Health, 26,* 35–46.

Kenrick, D. T., Griskevicius, V., Neuberg, S. L., & Schaller, M. (2010). Renovating the pyramid of needs: Contemporary extensions built upon ancient foundations. *Perspectives on Psychological Science, 5,* 292–314.

Kensinger, E. A., & Choi, E. S. (2009). When side matters: Hemispheric processing and the visual specificty of emotional memories. *Journal of Experimental Psychology: Learning, Memory, and Cognition, 35,* 247–253.

Kerkhof, I., Vansteenwegen, D., Baeyens, F., & Hermans, D. (2011). Counterconditioning: An effective technique for changing conditioned preferences. *Experimental Psychology, 58,* 31–38.

Kern, M. L., & Friedman, H. S. (2008). Do conscientious individuals live longer? A quantitative review. *Health Psychology, 27,* 505–512.

Kernis, M. H. (2003). Toward a conceptualization of optimal self-esteem. *Psychological Inquiry, 14,* 1–26.

Kernis, M. H. (2013). *Self-esteem issues and answers.* New York: Psychology Press.

Kerns, J. G. (2007). Verbal communication impairments and cognitive control components in people with schizophrenia. *Journal of Abnormal Psychology, 116,* 279–289.

Kerns, J. G., Berenbaum, H., Barch, D. M., Banich, M. T., & Stolar, N. (1999). Word production in schizophrenia and its relationship to positive symptoms. *Psychiatry Research, 87,* 29–37.

Kessler, R. C., Chiu, W. T., Demler, O., & Walters, E. E. (2005). Prevalence, severity, and comorbidity of twelve-month DSM-IV disorders in the National Comorbidity Survey Replication (NCS-R). *Archives of General Psychiatry, 62,* 617–627.

Kessler, R. C., & others. (2012). Prevalence, persistence, and sociodemographic correlates of DSM-IV disorders in the National Comorbidity Survey Replication Adolescent Supplement. *Archives of General Psychiatry, 69,* 372–380.

Khare, K., & others. (2012). Accelerated MR imaging using compressive sensing with no free parameters. *Magnetic Resonance Imaging, 68* (5), 1450–1457.

Khodarahimi, S., & Ogletree, S. L. (2011). Birth order, family size, and positive pathological constructs: What roles do they play for Iranian adolescents and young adults. *Journal of Individual Psychology, 67,* 41–56.

Kickstarter.com. (2013). www.kickstarter.com/projects/search (accessed May 20, 2013)

Kiecolt-Glaser, J. K. (2009). Psychoneuroimmunology: Psychology's gateway to the biomedical future. *Perspectives on Psychological Science, 4,* 367–369.

Kiecolt-Glaser, J. K. (2010). Stress, food, and inflammation: Psychoneuroimmunology and nutrition at the cutting edge. *Psychosomatic Medicine, 72,* 365–372.

Kiess, H. O., & Green, B. A. (2010). *Statistical concepts for the behavioral sciences* (4th ed.). Boston: Allyn & Bacon.

Kihlstrom, J. (2005). Is hypnosis an altered state of consciousness or what?: Comment. *Contemporary Hypnosis, 22,* 34–38.

Kilicarslan, A., Isildak, M., Guven, G. S., Oz, S. G., Tannover, M. D., Duman, A. E., Saracbasi, O., & Sozen, T. (2006). Demographic, socio-economic, and educational aspects of obesity in an adult population. *Journal of the National Medical Association, 98,* 1313–1317.

Killeen, P. R. (2003). Complex dynamic processes in sign tracking with an omission contingency (negative automaintenance). *Journal of Experimental Psychology: Animal Behavior Processes, 29,* 49–61.

Killgore, W. D., Rosso, I. M., Gruber, S. A., & Yurgelun-Todd, D. A. (2009). Amygdala volume and verbal memory performance in schizophrenia and bipolar disorder. *Cognitive and Behavioral Neurology, 22,* 28–37.

Kim, H. (2011). Differential neural activity in the recognition of old and new events: An activation likelihood estimation meta-analysis. *Human Brain Mapping.* doi: 10.1002/hbm.21474.

Kim, J. H., Ko, J. H., Lee, D. C., Lim, I., & Bang, H. (2012). Habitual physical exercise has beneficial effects on telomere length in postmenopausal women. *Menopause, 19,* 1109–1115.

Kim, W., Woo, J. S., & Kim, W. (2012). Disrupted circadian rhythm in night shift workers: What can we do? *International Journal of Cardiology, 154* (1), 94–95.

Kimmel, A. J. (2012). Deception in research. In S. J. Knapp, M. C. Gottlieb, M. M. Handelsman, & L. D. VandeCreek (Eds.), *APA handbook of ethics in psychology, vol 2: Practice, teaching, and research* (pp. 401–421). Washington, DC: American Psychological Association.

King, B. M. (2005). *Human sexuality today* (5th ed.). Upper Saddle River, NJ: Prentice-Hall.

King, K. (2012). Aggravating conditions: Cynical hostility and neighborhood ambient stressors. *Social Science & Medicine, 75,* 2258–2266.

King, L. A. (2001). The health benefits of writing about life goals. *Personality and Social Psychology Bulletin, 27,* 798–807.

King, L. A. (2003). Measures and meanings: The use of qualitative data in social and personality psychology. In C. Sansone, C. Morf, & A. Panter (Eds.), *Handbook of methods in social psychology* (pp.173–194). New York: Sage.

King, L. A. (2008). Personal goals and life dreams: Positive psychology and motivation in daily life. In W. Gardner & J. Shah (Eds.), *Handbook of motivation science* (pp. 518–532). New York: Guilford.

King, L. A., Burton, C. M., & Geise, A. (2009). The good (gay) life: The search for signs of maturity in the narratives of gay adults. In P. Hammack & B. J. Kohler (Eds.), *The story of sexual identity: Narrative, social change, and the development of sexual orientation* (pp. 375–396). New York: Oxford University Press.

King, L. A., & Geise, A. C. (2011). Being forgotten: Implications for the experience of meaning in life. *Journal of Social Psychology, 151,* 696–709.

King, L. A., & Hicks, J. A. (2007). Whatever happened to "what might have been"? Regret, happiness, and maturity. *American Psychologist, 62,* 625–636.

King, L. A., Hicks, J. A., Krull, J., & Del Gaiso, A. K. (2006). Positive affect and the experience of meaning in life. *Journal of Personality and Social Psychology, 90,* 179–196.

King, L. A., & Miner, K. N. (2000). Writing about the perceived benefits of traumatic life events:

Implications for physical health. *Personality and Social Psychology Bulletin, 26,* 220–230.

King, L. A., Scollon, C. K., Ramsey, C. M., & Williams, T. (2000). Stories of life transition: Happy endings, subjective well-being, and ego development in parents of children with Down syndrome. *Journal of Research in Personality, 34,* 509–536.

King, L. A., & Smith, S. N. (2005). Happy, mature, and gay: Intimacy, power, and difficult times in coming out stories. *Journal of Research in Personality, 39,* 278–298.

King, L. A., & Trent, J. (2013). Personality strengths. In H. A. Tennen, J. M. Suls, & I. B. Weiner (Eds.), *Handbook of psychology, 2nd ed., Vol. 5.* (pp. 197–2224). Hoboken, NJ: Wiley.

King, P. E., Ramos, J. S., & Clardy, C. E. (2012). Searching for the sacred: Religious and spiritual development among adolescents. In K. I. Pargament, J. Exline, & J. Jones (Eds.), *APA handbook of psychology, religion, and spirituality.* Washington, DC: American Psychological Association.

Kinnish, K. K., Strassberg, D. S., & Turner, C. M. (2005). Sex differences in the flexibility of sexual orientation: A multidimensional retrospective assessment. *Archives of Sexual Behavior, 35,* 173–183.

Kinsey, A. C., Martin, C. E., & Pomeroy, W. B. (1953). *Sexual behavior in the human female.* Philadelphia: Saunders.

Kinsey, A. C., Pomeroy, W. B., & Martin, C. E. (1948). *Sexual behavior in the human male.* Philadelphia: Saunders.

Kinzler, K. D., Dupoux, E., & Spelke, E. S. (2013). "Native" objects and collaborators: Infants' object choices and acts of giving reflect favor for native over foreign speakers. *Journal of Cognition and Development, 13* (1), 67–81.

Kirby, D. B. (2008). The impact of abstinence and comprehensive sex and STD/HIV education programs on adolescent sexual behavior. *Sexuality Research & Social Policy, 5,* 18–27.

Kirby, D. B., Laris, B. A., & Rolleri, L. A. (2007). Sex and HIV education programs: Their impact on sexual behavior of young people throughout the world. *Journal of Adolescent Health, 40,* 206–217.

Kirby, E. D., Jensen, K., Goosens, K. A., & Kaufer, D. (2012). Stereotaxic surgery for excitotoxic lesion of specific brain areas in the adult rat. *Journal of Visual Experiments, 19,* e4079.

Kirk, R. E. (2013). Experimental design. In J. A. Schinka, W. F. Velicer, & I. B. Weiner (Eds.), *Handbook of psychology, 2nd ed., Vol. 2.* (pp. 3–33). Hoboken, NJ: Wiley.

Kirt, T., & Bachmann, T. (2013). Perceptual retouch theory derived modeling of interactions in the processing of successive visual objects for consciousness: Two-stage synchronization of neuronal oscillators. *Consciousness and Cognition.* (in press)

Kissileff, H. R., & others. (2012). Leptin reverses declines in satiation in weight-reduced obese humans. *American Journal of Clinical Nutrition, 95,* 309–317.

Kitayama, S. (2011). Psychology and culture: Cross-country or regional comparisons. *Annual Review of Psychology* (vol. 62). Palo Alto, CA: Annual Reviews.

Kitayama, S., & Bowman, N. A. (2010). Cultural consequences of voluntary settlement in the frontier: Evidence and implications. In M. Schaller, A. Norenzayan, S. J. Heine, T. Yamagishi, & T. Kameda (Eds.), *Evolution, culture, and the human mind* (pp. 205–227). New York: Psychology Press.

Kitayama, S., & Cohen, D. (Eds.). (2007). *Handbook of cultural psychology.* New York: Guilford.

Kitchener, K. S., King, P. M., & DeLuca, S. (2006). The development of reflective judgment in adulthood. In C. Hoare (Ed.), *Handbook of adult development and learning.* New York: Oxford University Press.

Kiuru, N., Burk, W. J., Laursen, B., Nurmi, J. E., & Salmela-Aro, K. (2012). Is depression contagious? A test of alternative peer socialization mechanisms of depressive symptoms in adolescent peer networks. *Journal of Adolescent Health, 50,* 250–255.

Klatzky, R. L., & Lederman, S. J. (2013). Touch. In A. F. Healy, R. W. Proctor, & I. B. Weiner (Eds.), *Handbook of psychology, 2nd ed., Vol. 4.* (pp. 152–178). Hoboken, NJ: Wiley.

Klemfuss, J. Z., & Ceci, S. J. (2012a). Legal and psychological perspectives on children's competence to testify in court. *Developmental Review, 32* (3), 268–286.

Klemfuss, J. Z., & Ceci, S. J. (2012b). The law and science of children's testimonial competence. In R. Holliday & T. Marche (Eds.), *Child forensic psychology.* New York: Macmillan.

Klimstra, T. A., Hale, W. W., Raaijmakers, Q. A., Branje, S. J., & Meeus, W. H. (2009). Maturation of personality in adolescence. *Journal of Personality and Social Psychology, 96,* 898–912.

Klimstra, T. A., Luyckx, K., Hale, W. A., Frijns, T., van Lier, P. A., & Meeus, W. H. (2010). Short-term fluctuations in identity: Introducing a micro-level approach to identity formation. *Journal of Personality and Social Psychology, 99,* 191–202.

Klintwall, L., & Eikeseth, S. (2012). Number and controllability of reinforcers as predictors of individual outcome for children with autism receiving early and intensive behavioral intervention: A preliminary study. *Research in Autism Spectrum Disorders, 6,* 493–499.

Klosterhalfen, S., Rüttgers, A., Krumrey, E., Otto, B., Stockhorst, U., Riepl, R. L., Probst, T., & Enck, P. (2000). Pavlovian conditioning of taste aversion using a motion sickness paradigm. *Psychosomatic Medicine, 62,* 671–677.

Klucharev, V., Hytonen, K., Rijpkema, M., Smidts, A., & Fernandez, G. (2009). Reinforcement learning signal predicts social conformity. *Neuron, 61,* 140–151.

Kluge, C., & others. (2011). Plasticity of human auditory-evoked fields induced by shock conditioning and contingency reversal. *Proceedings of the National Academy of Sciences USA, 108,* 12545–12550.

Kluver, J., Frazier, R., & Haidt, J. (2012). Psychology and business ethics. *Encyclopedia of management* (7th ed.). Boston: Gale Cengage.

Kluwe-Schiavon, B., Sanvicente-Vieira, B., Kristensen, C. H., & Grassi-Oliveira, R. (2013). Executive functions rehabilitation for schizophrenia: A critical systematic review. *Journal of Psychiatric Research, 47* (1), 91–104.

Knafo, A., Israel, S., & Ebstein, R. P. (2011). Heritability of children's prosocial behavior and differential susceptibility to parenting by variation in the dopamine receptor D4 gene. *Developmental Psychopathology, 23* (1), 53–67.

Knapp, S., & VandeCreek, L. (2000). Recovered memories of childhood abuse: Is there an underlying consensus. *Professional Psychology: Research and Practice, 31,* 365–371.

Knight, L. F., & Morales Hope, D. A. (2012). Correlates of same-sex attractions and behaviors

among self-identified heterosexual university students. *Archives of Sexual Behavior, 41,* 1199–1208.

Knoll, N., & others. (2013). Gene set of nuclear-encoded mitochondrial regulators is enriched for common inherited variation in obesity. *PLoS One, 8* (2), e55884.

Knox, M. T., & Kavanagh, E. C. (2012). CT perfusion imaging in the assessment of stroke. *American Journal of Roentgenology, 1999,* W417.

Kobasa, S., Maddi, S., & Kahn, S. (1982). Hardiness and health: A prospective study. *Journal of Personality and Social Psychology, 42,* 168–177.

Kobasa, S. C., Maddi, S. R., Puccetti, M. C., & Zola, M. (1986). Relative effectiveness of hardiness, exercise, and social support as resources against illness. *Journal of Psychosomatic Research, 29,* 525–533.

Koch, E. J. (2013). Examining the role of self-esteem in psychological functioning and well-being. In M. H. Kernis (Ed.), *Self-esteem issues and answers.* New York: Psychology Press.

Kochanek, K. D., Murphy, S. L., Anderson, R. N., & Scott, C. (2004, October 12). Deaths: Final data for 2002. *National Vital Statistics Reports, 53* (5). Washington, DC: U.S. Department of Health and Human Services.

Kochanska, G., Aksan, N., Prisco, T. R., & Adams, E. E. (2008). Mother-child and father-child mutually responsive orientation in the first two years and children's outcomes at preschool age: Mechanisms of influence. *Child Development, 79,* 30–44.

Kocsis, J. H. (2013). Review: SSRIs and TCAs equally effective at treating chronic depression and dysthemia; SSRIs are associated with fewer adverse events than TCAs. *Evidence Based Mental Health.* (in press)

Koelsch, S., Enge, J., & Jentschke, S. (2012). Cardiac signatures of personality. *PLoS One, 7* (2), e31441.

Koenig, H. G. (2012). Religious versus conventional psychotherapy for major depression in patients with chronic medical illness: Rationale, methods, and preliminary results. *Depression Research and Treatment.* doi: 10.1155/2012/460419

Koenigs, D., Young, L., Adolphs, R., Tranel, D., Cushman, F., Hauser, M., & Damasio, A. (2007). Damage to the prefrontal cortex increases utilitarian moral judgments. *Nature, 446,* 908–911.

Koenis, M. M., & others. (2013). Does sleep restore the topology of functional brain networks. *Human Brain Mapping, 34* (2), 487–500.

Koepp, M. J., Hammers, A., Lawrence, A. D., Asselin, M. C., Grasby, P. M., & Bench, C. J. (2009). Evidence for endogenous opioid release in the amygdala during positive emotion. *NeuroImage, 44,* 252–256.

Koerner, A. (2012). Social cognition and family communication. In D. R. Roskos-Ewoldsen & J. L. Monahan (Eds.), *Communication and social cognition.* New York: Psychology Press.

Koester, C., & others. (2012). Dissecting the role of diazepam-sensitive y-aminobutyric acid type A receptors in defensive behavioral reactivity to mild threat. *Pharmacology, Biochemistry, and Behavior, 103,* 541–549.

Kogan, A., Saslow, L. R., Impett, E. A., Oveis, C., & Keltner, D. (2011). Thin-slicing study of the oxytocin receptor (OXTR) gene and the evaluation and expression of the prosocial disposition. *Proceedings of the National Academy of Science, 108,* 19189–19192.

Kohlberg, L. (1958). *The development on modes of moral thinking and choice in the years 10 to 16.* Unpublished doctoral dissertation, University of Chicago.

Kohlberg, L. (1981). *Essays on moral development, vol. I: The philosophy of moral development.* San Francisco: Harper & Row.

Kohlberg, L. (1986). A current statement on some theoretical issues. In S. Modgil & C. Modgil (Eds.), *Lawrence Kohlberg.* Philadelphia: Falmer.

Kohler, C. L., Schoenberger, Y., Tseng, T., & Ross, L. (2008). Correlates of transitions in stage of change for quitting among adolescent smokers. *Addictive Behaviors, 33,* 1615–1618.

Kohler, P. K., Manhart, L. E., & Lafferty, W. E. (2008). Abstinence-only and comprehensive sex education and the initiation of sexual activity and teen pregnancy. *Journal of Adolescent Health, 42,* 344–351.

Köhler, W. (1925). *The mentality of apes.* New York: Harcourt Brace Jovanovich.

Kohut, H. (1977). *Restoration of the self.* New York: International Universities Press.

Koitabashi, T., Oyaizu, T., & Ouchi, T. (2009). Low bispectral index values following electroconvulsive therapy associated with memory impairment. *Journal of Anesthesiology, 23,* 182–187.

Kok, B. E., Catalino, L. I., & Fredrickson, B. L. (2008). The broadening, building, buffering effects of positive emotion. In S. J. Lopez (Ed.), *Positive psychology: Exploring the best of people* (vol. 3). Westport, CT: Greenwood.

Kok, G., & de Vries, N. K. (2006). Social psychology and health promotion. In P. A. M. Van Lange (Ed.), *Bridging social psychology.* Mahwah, NJ: Erlbaum.

Kolb, B., & Teskey, G. C. (2012). Age, experience, injury, and the changing brain. *Developmental Psychobiology, 54,* 311–325.

Koleva, S. P., Graham, J., Ditto, P., Iyer, R., & Haidt, J. (2012). Tracking the threads: How five moral concerns (especially purity) help explain culture war attitudes. *Journal of Research in Personality, 46,* 184–194.

Kolomeyer, A. M., & others. (2013). Software-assisted analysis during ocular health screening. *Telemedicine Journal and e-Health.* (in press)

Kopell, B. H., Machado, A. G., & Rezai, A. R. (2006). Not your father's lobotomy: Psychiatric surgery revisited. *Clinical Neurosurgery, 52,* 315–330.

Kort-Butler, L. A, & Hegewen, K. J. (2011). School-based extracurricular activity involvement and adolescent self-esteem: A growth-curve analysis. *Journal of Youth and Adolescence, 40,* 568–581.

Koski, J., Olson, I. R., & Newcombe, N. S. (2013). Tracking the eyes to see what children remember. *Memory.* (in press)

Kosslyn, S. M., Thompson, W. L., Kim, I. J., Rauch, S. L., & Alpert, N. M. (1996). Individual differences in cerebral blood flow in Area 17 predict the time to evaluate visualized letters. *Journal of Cognitive Neuroscience, 8,* 78–82.

Kotsis, V., Stabouli, S., Papakatsika, S., Rizos, Z., & Parati, G. (2010). Mechanisms of obesity-induced hypertension. *Hypertension Research, 33,* 386–393.

Kotter-Grühn, D., & Smith, J. (2011). When time is running out: Changes in positive future perception and their relationsips to changes in well-being in old age. *Psychology and Aging, 26,* 381–387.

Kovacs, A. M. (2009). Early bilingualism enhances mechanisms of false-belief reasoning. *Developmental Science, 12,* 48–54.

Kovacs, K., Lajtha, A., & Sershen, H. (2010). Effect of nicotine and cocaine on neurofilaments and receptors in whole brain tissue and synaptoneurosome preparations. *Brain Research Bulletin, 82,* 109–117.

Kovjanic, S., Schuh, S. C., Jonas, K., Van Quaquebeke, N., & van Dick, R. (2012). How do transformational leaders foster positive employee outcomes? A self-determination-based analysis of employees' needs as mediating links. *Journal of Organizational Behavior, 33* (8), 1031–1052.

Koziorynska, E. L., & Rodriquez, A. J. (2011). Narcolepsy: Clinical approach to etiology, diagnosis, and treatment. *Reviews in Neurological Diseases, 8,* e97–e106.

Kozlowski, S. W., & Bell, B. S. (2013). Work groups and teams in organizations. In N. W. Schmitt, S. Highhouse, & I. B. Weiner (Eds.), *Handbook of psychology, 2nd ed., Vol. 12.* (pp. 412–469). Hoboken, NJ: Wiley.

Kraemer, B., Noll, T., Delsignore, A., Milos, G., Schnyder, U., & Hepp, U. (2006). Finger length ratio (2D:4D) and dimensions of sexual orientation. *Neuropsychobiology, 53,* 210–214.

Kraft, T. L., & Pressman, S. D. (2012). Grin and bear it: The influence of manipulated facial expression on the stress response. *Psychological Science, 23* (11), 1372–1378.

Kraus, M. W., Piff, P. K., Mendoza-Denton, R., Rheinschmidt, M. L., & Keltner, D. (2012). Social class, solipsism, and contextualism: How the rich are different from the poor. *Psychological Review, 119* (3), 546–572.

Krause, N. (2006). Religion and health in late life. In J. E. Birren & K. W. Schaie (Eds.), *Handbook of the psychology of aging* (6th ed.). San Diego: Academic.

Krentzman, A. R., Brower, K. J., Cranford, J. A., Bradley, J. C., & Robinson, E. A. R. (2013). Gender and extroversion as moderators of the association between Alcoholics Anonymous and sobriety. *Journal of Studies on Alcohol and Drugs, 73,* 44–52.

Krentzman, A. R., Cranford, J. A., & Robinson, E. A. R. (2013). Multiple dimensions of spirituality in recovery: A lagged mediational analysis of Alcoholics Anonymous' principal theoretical mechanism of behavior change. *Substance Abuse, 34,* 20–32.

Kressel, L. M., & Uleman, J. S. (2010). Personality traits function as causal concepts. *Journal of Experimental Social Psychology, 46,* 213–216.

Kringelbach, M. L. (2005). The human orbitofrontal cortex: Linking reward to hedonic experience. *Nature Reviews: Neuroscience, 6,* 691–702.

Krishnamurthy, R., Archer, R. P., & Groth-Marnat, G. (2011). The Rorschach and performance-based assessment. In T. M. Harwood, L. E. Beutler, & G. Groth-Marnat (Eds.), *Integrative assessment of adult personality* (3rd ed.). New York: Guilford.

Kristof-Brown, A., & Guay, R. P. (2010). Person–environment fit. In S. Zedeck (Ed.), *APA handbook of industrial and organizational psychology.* Washington, DC: American Psychological Association.

Kroesbergen, E. H., van't Noordende, J. E., & Kolkman, M. E. (2013). Training working memory in kindergarten children: Effects on working memory and early numeracy. *Child Neuropsychology.* doi: 10.1080/09297049.2012.736483

Kroger, J. (2007). *Identity development* (2nd ed.). Thousand Oaks, CA: Sage.

Kroger, J. (2012). The status of identity developments in identity research. In P. K. Kerig, M. S. Schulz, & S. T. Hauser (Eds.), *Adolescence and beyond.* New York: Oxford University Press.

Kroger, J., Martinussen, M., & Marcia, J. E. (2010). Identity change in adolescence and young adulthood: A meta-analysis. *Journal of Adolescence, 33* (5), 683–698.

Kroneisen, M., Erdfelder, E., & Buchner, A. (2013). The proximate memory mechanism underlying the survival-processing effect: Richness of encoding or interactive imagery? *Memory, 21,* 143–149.

Kross, E., Mischel, W., & Shoda, Y. (2010). Enabling self-control: A cognitive affective processing system (CAPS) approach to problematic behavior. In J. Maddux & J. Tangney (Eds.), *Social psychological foundations of clinical psychology.* New York: Guilford.

Krueger, K. A., & Dayan, P. (2009). Flexible shaping: How learning in small steps helps. *Cognition, 110,* 380–394.

Krueger, R. F., Markon, K. E., & Bouchard, T. J. (2003). The extended genotype: The heritability of personality accounts for the heritability of recalled family environments in twins reared apart. *Journal of Personality, 71,* 809–833.

Kruger, J., Blanck, H. M., & Gillespie, C. (2006). Dietary and physical activity behaviors among adults successful at weight loss maintenance. *International Journal of Behavioral Nutrition and Physical Activity, 3,* 17.

Kruschke, J. K. (2011). Bayesian assessment of null values via parameter estimation and model comparison. *Perspectives on Psychological Science, 6,* 299–312.

Kuehnle, K., & Connell, M. (2013). Child sexual abuse evaluations. In R. K. Otto & I. B. Weiner (Eds.), *Handbook of psychology, 2nd ed., Vol. 11.* (pp. 579–614). Hoboken, NJ: Wiley.

Kuhl, P. K. (1993). Infant speech perception: A window on psycholinguistic development. *International Journal of Psycholinguistics, 9,* 33–56.

Kuhl, P. K. (2000). A new view of language acquisition. *Proceedings of the National Academy of Sciences USA, 97,* 11850–11857.

Kuhl, P. K. (2011). Early language learning and literacy: Neuroscience implications for education. *Mind, Brain, and Education, 5,* 128–142.

Kuhl, P. K. (2012). Language learning and the developing brain: Cross-cultural studies unravel the effects of biology and culture. *Journal of the Acoustical Society of America, 131* (4), 3207.

Kuhl, P. K., & Damasio, A. (2012). Language. In E. R. Kandel & others (Eds.), *Principles of neural science* (5th ed.). New York: McGraw-Hill.

Kuhn, D. (2009). Adolescent thinking. In R. M. Lerner & L. Steinberg (Eds.), *Handbook of adolescent psychology, volume 1: Individual bases of adolescent development* (3rd ed., pp. 152–186). Hoboken, NJ: Wiley.

Kuhn, D. (2011). What is scientific thinking and how does it develop? In U. Goswami (Ed.), *Wiley-Blackwell handbook of childhood cognitive development* (2nd ed.). New York: Wiley-Blackwell.

Kühnel, J., & Sonnentag, S. (2011). How long do you benefit from vacation? A closer look at the fade-out of vacation effect. *Journal of Organizational Behavior, 32* (1), 125–143.

Kujanik, S., & Mikulecky, M. (2010). Circadian and ultradian extrasystole rhythms in healthy individuals at elevated versus lowland altitudes. *International Journal of Biometeorology, 81* (2), 125–129.

Kumar, P. N., & George, B. (2013). Life events, social support, coping strategies, and quality of life in attempted suicide: A case-control study. *Indian Journal of Psychology, 55,* 46–41.

Kuper, K., Groh-Bordin, C., Zimmer, H. D., & Ecker, U. K. (2012). Electrophysiological correlates of exemplar-specific processes in implicit and explicit memory. *Cognitive, Affective, and Behavioral Neuroscience, 12,* 52–64.

Kurdek, L. (2004). Are gay and lesbian cohabiting couples *really* different from heterosexual married couples? *Journal of Marriage and Family, 66,* 880–900.

Kurose, K., & others. (2012). Genome-wide association study of SSRI/SNRI-induced sexual dysfunction in a Japanese cohort with major depression. *Psychiatry Research, 198,* 424–429.

Kurson, R. (2007). *Crashing through: A true story of risk, adventure, and the man who dared to see.* New York: Random House.

Kushner, R. F. (2007). Obesity management. *Gastroenterology Clinics of North America, 36,* 191–210.

Kusurkar, R. A., Ten Cate, T. J., Vos, C. M. P., Westers, P., & Croiset, G. (2013). How motivation affects academic performance: A structural equation modeling analysis. *Advances in Health Science Education: Theory and Practice, 18* (1), 57–69.

Kuyper, P. (1972). The cocktail party effect. *Audiology, 11,* 277–282.

Kwok, D. W., & Boakes, R. A. (2012). Blocking of acquisition of a taste aversion by a context experienced prior to the taste. *Behavioral Processes, 89,* 27–29.

L

Labouvie-Vief, G. (1986, August). *Modes of knowing and life-span cognition.* Paper presented at the meeting of the American Psychological Association, Washington, DC.

Labouvie-Vief, G. (2006). Emerging structures of adult thought. In J. J. Arnett & J. L. Tanner (Eds.), *Emerging adults in America* (pp. 60–84). Washington, DC: American Psychological Association.

Lac, A., Alvaro, E. M., Crano, W. D., & Siegel, J. T. (2009). Pathways from parental knowledge and warmth to adolescent marijuana use: An extension to the theory of planned behavior. *Prevention Science, 10,* 22–32.

Lachman, M. E., Rocke, C., Rosnick, C., & Ryff, C. D. (2008). Realism and illusion in Americans' temporal views of their life satisfaction: Age differences in reconstructing the past and anticipating the future. *Psychological Science, 19,* 89–897.

Lack, L. C., & Wright, H. R. (2012). Circadian rhythm disorders I: Phase-advanced and phase-delayed syndromes. In C. M. Morin & C. A. Espie (Eds.), *The Oxford handbook of sleep and sleep disorders.* New York: Oxford University Press.

Lader, M. (2012). Dependence and withdrawal: Comparison of the benzodiazepines and selective serotonin re-uptake inhibitors. *Addiction, 107,* 909–910.

LaFromboise, T. D., Albright, K., & Harris, A. (2010). Patterns of hopelessness among American Indian adolescents: Relationships by levels of acculturation and residence. *Cultural Diversity and Ethnic Minority Psychology, 16,* 68–76.

Laguna, M. (2013). Self-efficacy, self-esteem, and entrepreneurship among the unemployed. *Journal of Applied Social Psychology, 43,* 253–262.

Laible, D. J., & Thompson, R. A. (2000). Mother–child discourse, attachment security, shared positive affect, and early conscience development. *Child Development, 71,* 1424–1440.

Laible, D. J., & Thompson, R. A. (2002). Mother–child conflict in the toddler years: Lessons in emotion, morality, and relationships. *Child Development, 73,* 1187–1203.

Laible, D. J., & Thompson, R. A. (2007). Early socialization: A relationship perspective. In J. E. Grusec & P. D. Hastings (Eds.), *Handbook of socialization.* New York: Guilford.

Lam, C. B., & McBride-Chang, C. A. (2007).Resilience in young adulthood: The moderating influences of gender-related personality traits and coping flexibility. *Sex Roles, 56,* 159–172.

Lamb, M. E. (2013). Commentary: Early experience, neurobiology, plasticity, vulnerability, and resilience. In D. Narvaez, J. Panksepp, A. N. Schore, & T. R. Gleason (Eds.), *Evolution, early experience, and human development: From research to practice and policy.* New York: Oxford University Press.

Lambert, M. J. (2001). The effectiveness of psychotherapy: What a century of research tells us about the effects of treatment. *Psychotherapeutically speaking—Updates from the Division of Psychotherapy* (29). Washington, DC: American Psychological Association.

Lambert, M. J. (2013). Outcome in psychotherapy: The past and important advances. *Psychotherapy, 50* (1), 42–51.

Lamberton, L., & Minor-Evans, L. (2010). *Human relations* (4th ed.). New York: McGraw-Hill.

Laming, D. (2010). Serial position curves in free recall. *Psychological Review, 117,* 93–133.

Lampard, A. M., Byrne, S. M., McLean, N., & Fursland, A. (2012). The Eating Disorder Inventory-2 perfectionism scale: Factor structure and associations with dietary restraint and weight and shape concern in eating disorders. *Eating Behaviors, 13,* 49–53.

Lampe, L., & Sunderland, M. (2013). Social phobia and avoidant personality disorder: Similar but different? *Journal of Personality Disorders.* (in press)

Lamy, D., Leber, A. B., & Egeth, H. E. (2013). Selective attention. In A. F. Healy, R. W. Proctor, & I. B. Weiner (Eds.), *Handbook of psychology, 2nd ed., Vol. 4.* (pp. 267–294). Hoboken, NJ: Wiley.

Lanaj, K., Chang, C. D., & Johnson, R. E. (2012). Regulatory focus and work-related outcomes: A review and meta-analysis. *Psychological Bulletin, 138,* 998–1034.

Lanciano, T., Curci, A., Mastandrea, S., & Sartori, G. (2013). Do automatic mental associations detect a flashbulb memory? *Memory, 21,* 482–493.

Landgren, S., & others. (2011). Reward-related gender and personality traits in alcohol-dependent individuals: A pilot case control study. *Neuropsychobiology, 64,* 38–46.

Landis, C., & Erlick, D. (1950). An analysis of the Porteus Maze Test as affected by psychosurgery. *American Journal of Psychology, 63,* 557–566.

Landler, M. (2012, January 30). From Biden, a vivid account of Bin Laden raid. *New York Times.* http://thecaucus.blogs.nytimes.com/2012/01/30/from-biden-a-vivid-account-of-bin-laden-decision/ (accessed May 17, 2013)

Landsberg, L., & others. (2013). Obesity-related hypertension: Pathogenesis, cardiovascular risk, and treatment-A position paper of the Obesity Society and the American Society of Hypertension. *Journal of Clinical Hypertension, 15* (1), 14–33.

Lane, S. M., & Schooler, J. W. (2004). Skimming the surface: Verbal overshadowing of analogical retrieval. *Psychological Science, 15,* 715–719.

Lange, C. G. (1922). *The emotions.* Baltimore: Williams & Wilkins.

Laney, C., & Loftus, E. F. (2009). Eyewitness memory. In R. N. Kocsis (Ed.), *Applied criminal psychology.* Springfield, IL: Thomas.

Langer, E., Blank, A., & Chanowitz, B. (1978). The mindlessness of ostensibly thoughtful action: The role of "placebic" information in interpersonal interaction. *Journal of Personality and Social Psychology, 36* (6), 635–642.

Langer, E. J. (1997). *The power of mindful learning.* Reading, MA: Addison-Wesley.

Langer, E. J. (2000). Mindful learning. *Current Directions in Psychological Science, 9,* 220–223.

Langer, E. J. (2005). *On becoming an artist.* New York: Ballantine.

Langer, E. J., & Rodin, J. (1976). The effects of choice and enhanced personal responsibility for the aged: A field experiment in an institutional setting. *Journal of Personality and Social Psychology, 34,* 191–198.

Langer, J. J. (1991). *Holocaust testimonies: The ruins of memory.* New Haven, CT: Yale University Press.

Langlois, J. H., Kalakanis, L., Rubenstein, A. J., Larson, A., Hallam, M., & Smoot, M. (2000). Maxims or myths of beauty? A meta-analytic and theoretical review. *Psychological Bulletin, 126,* 390–423.

Langlois, J. H., Roggman, L. A., & Musselman, L. (1994). What is average and what is not average about attractive faces? *Psychological Science, 5,* 214–220.

Langstrom, N., Rahman, Q., Carlstrom, E., & Lichtenstein, P. (2010). Genetic and environmental effects on same-sex sexual behaviour: A population study of twins in Sweden. *Archives of Sexual Behavior, 39,* 75–80.

Lanius, R. A., Brand, B., Vermetten, E., Frewen, P. A., & Spiegel, D. (2012). The dissociative subtype of posttraumatic stress disorder: Rationale, clinical and neurobiological evidence, and implications. *Depression and Anxiety, 29* (8), 701–708.

Lapid, H., & others. (2011). Neural activity at the human olfactory epithelium reflects olfactory perception. *Nature Neuroscience, 14,* 1455–1461.

Lapierre, L. M., Spector, P. E., & Leck, J. D. (2005). Sexual versus non-sexual workplace aggression and victims' overall job satisfaction: A meta-analysis. *Journal of Occupational Health Psychology, 10,* 155–169.

Lapsley, D. K. (2013). Moral stage theory. In M. Killen & J. Smetana (Eds.), *Handbook of moral development* (2nd ed.). New York: Routledge.

Lapsley, D. K., & Yeager, D. (2013). Moral-character education. In W. M. Reynolds, G. F. Miller, & I. B. Weiner (Eds.), *Handbook of psychology, 2nd ed., Vol. 7.* (pp. 147–178). Hoboken, NJ: Wiley.

Larzelere, M. M., & Williams, D. E. (2012). Promoting smoking cessation. *American Family Physician, 85* (6), 591–598.

Lashley, K. (1950). In search of the engram. In *Symposium of the Society for Experimental Biology* (vol. 4). New York: Cambridge University Press.

Laszlo, S., & Plaut, D. C. (2012). A neurally plausible parallel distributed processing model of event-related potential reading data. *Brain and Language, 120,* 271–281.

Latané, B. (1981). The psychology of social impact. *American Psychologist, 36,* 343–356.

Latremoliere, A., & Woolf, C. J. (2009). Central sensitization: A generator of pain hypersensitivity by central neural plasticity. *Journal of Pain, 10,* 895–926.

Lau, C. Q. (2012). The stability of same-sex cohabitation, different-sex cohabitation, and marriage. *Journal of Marriage and Family, 74,* 973–988.

Laumann, E. O., Nicolosi, A., Glasser, D. B., Paik, A., & Gingell, C. (2005). Sexual problems among men and women aged 40–80 yrs: Prevalence and correlates identified in the global study of sexual attitudes and behaviours. *International Journal of Impotence Research, 17,* 39–57.

Laureys, S., & Schiff, N. D. (2012). Coma and consciousness: Paradigms (re)framed by neuroimaging. *NeuroImage.* doi: 10.1016/j.neuroimage.2011.12.041

Laursen, B, Hafen, C. A., Kerr, M., & Stattin, H. (2012). Friend influence over adolescent problem behaviors as a function of relative peer acceptance: To be liked is to be emulated. *Journal of Abnormal Psychology, 21,* 88–94.

Lauvin, M. A., & others. (2012). Functional morphological imaging of autism spectrum disorders: Current position and theories proposed. *Diagnostic and Interventional Imaging, 93,* 139–147.

Law, R., Groome, D., Thorn, L., Potts, R., & Buchanan, T. (2012). The relationship between retrieval-induced forgetting, anxiety, and personality. *Anxiety, Stress, and Coping, 25* (6), 711–718.

Lazar, A. S., & others. (2013). Circadian period and the timing of melatonin onset in men and women: Predictors of sleep during the weekend and in the laboratory. *Journal of Sleep Research.* (in press)

Lazarus, A. A., Beutler, L. E., & Norcross, J. C. (1992). The future of technical eclecticism. *Psychotherapy, 29,* 11–20.

Lazarus, R. S. (1991). On the primacy of cognition. *American Psychologist, 39,* 124–129.

Lazarus, R. S. (1993). Coping theory and research: Past, present, and future. *Psychosomatic Medicine, 55,* 234–247.

Lazarus, R. S. (2000). Toward better research on stress and coping. *American Psychologist, 55,* 665–673.

Lazarus, R. S. (2003). Does the positive psychology movement have legs? *Psychological Inquiry, 14,* 93–109.

Leahy, R. L., Holland, S. J. F., & McGinn, L. K. (2012). *Treatment plans and interventions for depression and anxiety disorders* (2nd ed.). New York: Guilford.

Leahy, R. L., & McGinn, L. K. (2012). Cognitive therapy for personality disorders. In T. Widiger (Ed.), *The Oxford handbook of personality disorders.* New York: Oxford University Press.

Leaper, C. (2013). Gender development. In P. D. Zelazo (Ed.), *The Oxford handbook of developmental psychology,Vol. 2.* (pp. 326–377). New York: Oxford University Press.

Leary, M. R., & Hoyle, R. H. (Eds.). (2009a). *Handbook of individual differences in social behavior.* New York: Guilford.

Leary, M. R., & Hoyle, R. H. (Eds.). (2009b). Situations, dispositions, and the study of social behavior. In M. R. Leary & R. H. Hoyle (Eds.), *Handbook of individual differences in social behavior* (pp. 3–11). New York: Guilford.

Leasure, J. L., & Decker, L. (2009). Social isolation prevents exercise-induced proliferation of hippocampal progenitor cells in female rats. *Hippocampus, 19,* 907–912.

Leatherwood, W. E., & Dragoo, J. L. (2012). Effect of airline travel on performance: A review of the literature. *British Journal of Sports Medicine.* doi: 10.1136/bjsports-2012-091449

LeBel, E. P., & Peters, K. R. (2011). Fearing the future of empirical psychology: Bem's (2011) evidence for psi as a case study of deficiencies in modal research practice. *Review of General Psychology, 15,* 371–379.

LeBlanc, L. A., & Gillis, J. M. (2012). Behavioral intervention for children with autism spectrum disorders. *Pediatric Clinics of North America, 59,* 147–164.

LeBoeuf, R. A., & Shafir, E. (2012). Decision making. In K. J. Holyoak & R. G. Morrison (Eds.), *The Oxford handbook of thinking and reasoning.* New York: Oxford University Press.

Lebow, J., & Stroud, C. B. (2013). Family therapy. In G. Stricker, T. A. Widiger, & I. B. Weiner (Eds.), *Handbook of psychology, 2nd ed., Vol. 8.* (pp. 384–407). Hoboken, NJ: Wiley.

Lebrun-Julien, F., & others. (2010). ProNGF induces TNF (alpha)-dependent death of retinal ganglion cells through a p75NTR non-cell-autonomous signaling pathway. *Proceedings of the National Academy of Sciences USA, 107,* 3817–3822.

Lederman, J. (2013, February 20). Biden honors police, firefighters with medals. *AP.* http://bigstory.ap.org/article/biden-honor-police-firefighters-medals (accessed April 21, 2013)

Ledikwe, J. H., Ello-Martin, J. A., & Rolls, B. J. (2005). Portion sizes and obesity epidemic. *Journal of Nutrition, 135,* 905–909.

LeDoux, J. E. (2009). Emotional coloration of consciousness: How feelings come about. In L. W. Weiskrantz & M. Davis (Eds.), *Frontiers of consciousness.* New York: Oxford University Press.

Ledoux, J. E. (2012). Evolution of human emotion: A view through fear. *Progress in Brain Research, 195,* 431–442.

Ledoux, J. E. (2013). The slippery slope of fear. *Trends in Cognitive Science, 17* (4), 155–156.

Lee, A. K., & Bishop, J. R. (2011). Pharmocogenetics of leptin in antipsychotic-associated weight gain and obesity-related complications. *Pharmacogenetics, 12,* 999–1016.

Lee, C. M., & Colagiuri, S. (2013). Risk scores for diabetes prediction: The International Diabetes Federation PREDICT-2 project. *Diabetes Research and Clinical Practice, 100* (2), 285–286.

Lee, E. A. E., & Troop-Gordon, W. (2011). Peer socialization of masculinity and femininity: Differential effects of overt and relational forms of peer victimization. *British Journal of Developmental Psychology, 29,* 197–213.

Lee, H., & Wallraven, C. (2013). Exploiting object constancy: Effects of active exploration and shape morphing on similarity judgments of novel objects. *Experimental Brain Research.* (in press)

Lee, J. H., & McDaniel, M. A. (2013). Discrepancy-plus-research processes in prospective memory retrieval. *Memory and Cognition, 41* (3), 443–451.

Lee, J. S., & Pyun, Y. D. (2012). Use of hypnosis in the treatment of pain. *Korean Journal of Pain, 25,* 75–80.

Lee, K., Ashton, M. C., Wiltshire, J., Bourdage, J. S., Visser, B. A., & Gallucci, A. (2013a). Sex, power, and money: Prediction from the Dark Triad and Honesty–Humility. *European Journal of Personality, 27,* 169–184.

Lee, K., Quinn, P. C., Pascalis, O., & Slater, A. (2013b). Development of face-processing ability in children. In P. D. Zelazo (Ed.), *The Oxford handbook of developmental psychology, Vol. 1.* (pp. 338–370). New York: Oxford University Press.

Lee, K. Y., & others. (2011). Effects of combined radiofrequency radiation exposure on the cell cycle and its regulatory proteins. *Bioelectromagnetics, 32,* 169–178.

Lee, P. A., Houk, C. P., Ahmed, S. F., & Hughes, I. A. (2006). Consensus statement on management of intersex disorders. *Pediatrics, 118,* e488–e500.

Lee, S., Choi, S., & Matejkowski, J. (2013). Comparison of major depressive disorder onset among foreign-born Asian Americans: Chinese, Filipino, and Vietnamese ethnic groups. *Psychiatry Research.* (in press)

Leedy, P. D., & Ormrod, J. E. (2013). *Practical research* (10th ed.). Upper Saddle River, NJ: Pearson.

Lefaucheur, J. P. (2012). Neurophysiology of cortical stimulation. *International Review of Neurobiology, 107,* 57–85.

Legate, N., Ryan, R. M., & Weinstein, N. (2012). Is coming out always a "good thing"? Exploring the relations of autonomy support, outness, and wellness for lesbian, gay, and bisexual individuals. *Social Psychological and Personality Science, 3,* 145–152.

Le Grange, D., Lock, J., Loeb, K., & Nicholls, D. (2010). Academy for Eating Disorders position paper: The role of the family in eating disorders. *International Journal of Eating Disorders, 43,* 1–5.

Leigh, E. G. (2010). The group selection controversy. *Journal of Evolutionary Biology, 23,* 6–19.

Leighton, J. P., & Sternberg, R. J. (2013). Reasoning and problem solving. In A. F. Healy, R. W. Proctor, & I. B. Weiner (Eds.), *Handbook of psychology, 2nd ed., Vol. 4.* (pp. 631–659). Hoboken, NJ: Wiley.

Leikas, S., Lönnqvist, J. E., & Verkasalo, M. (2012). Persons, situations, and behaviors: Consistency and variability of different behaviors in four interpersonal situations. *Journal of Personality and Social Psychology, 103* (6), 1007–1022.

Lenglet, C., & others. (2012). Comprehensive in vivo mapping of the human basal ganglia and thalamic connectome in individuals using 7T MRI. *PLoS One, 7* (1), e29153.

Lenhart, A., Purcell, K., Smith, A., & Zickuhr, K. (2010, February 3). Social media and young adults. *Pew Internet.* www.pewinternet.org/Reports/2010/Social-Media-and-Young-Adults.aspx (accessed June 6, 2013)

Lenneberg, E. H., Rebelsky, F. G., & Nichols, I. A. (1965). The vocalization of infants born to deaf and hearing parents. *Human Development, 8,* 23–37.

Leo, J. L. (2005). Editorial: Methylphenidate-induced neuropathology in the developing rat brain: Implications for humans. *Ethical Human Psychology and Psychiatry, 7,* 107–110.

Leonard, B. E., & Myint, A. (2009). The psychoneuroimmunology of stress. *Human Psychopharmacology, 24,* 165–175.

Leong, F. T. L., Holliday, B. G., Trimble, J. E., Padilla, A. M., & McCubbin, L. D. (2013). Ethnic minority psychology. In D. K. Freedheim & I. B. Weiner (Eds.), *Handbook of psychology, 2nd ed., Vol. 1.* (pp. 530–561). Hoboken, NJ: Wiley.

Lepage, M., Sergerie, K., Benoit, A., Czechowska, Y., Dickie, E., & Armony, J. L. (2011). Emotional face processing and flat affect in schizophrenia: Functional and structural neural correlates. *Psychological Medicine, 41,* 1833–1844.

Lepore, S. J., & Smyth, J. (Eds.). (2002). *The writing cure.* Washington, DC: American Psychological Association.

Lerner, B. H. (2005). Last-ditch medical therapy—Revisiting lobotomy. *New England Journal of Medicine, 353,* 119–121.

Lerner, J. V., & others. (2013). Positive youth development: Processes, philosophies, and programs. In R. M. Lerner, M. A. Easterbrooks, J. Mistry, & I. B. Weiner (Eds.), *Handbook of psychology, 2nd ed., Vol. 6.* (pp. 365–392). Hoboken, NJ: Wiley.

Lerner, R. D., Boyd, M., & Du, D. (2008). Adolescent development. In I. B. Weiner & C. B. Craighead (Eds.), *Encyclopedia of psychology* (4th ed.). New York: Wiley.

Leslie, L. M., Snyder, M., & Glomb, T. M. (2013). Who gives? Multilevel effects of gender and ethnicity on workplace charitable giving. *Journal of Applied Psychology, 98* (1), 49–62.

Leszczynski, J. P. (2009). A state conceptualization: Are individuals' masculine and feminine personality traits situationally influenced? *Personality and Individual Differences, 47,* 157–162.

Leung, A. K., Maddux, W. W., Galinsky, A. D., & Chiu, C. (2008). Multicultural experience enhances creativity. *American Psychologist, 63,* 169–181.

Lev, A. I. (2007). Transgender communities: Developing identity through connection. In K. J. Bieschke, R. M. Perez, & K. A. DeBord, (Eds.), *Handbook of counseling and psychotherapy with lesbian, gay, bisexual, and transgender clients* (2nd ed., pp. 147–175). Washington, DC: American Psychological Association.

Levenson, M. R., & Crumpler, C. (1996). Three models of adult development. *Human Development, 39,* 135–149.

Levin, C. (2010). The mind as a complex internal object: Inner estrangement. *Psychoanalytic Quarterly, 79,* 95–27.

Levin, J., & Fox, J. A. (2011). *Elementary statistics for social research* (3rd ed.). Upper Saddle River, NJ: Prentice-Hall.

Levine, F. M., & De Simone, L. L. (1991). The effects of experimenter gender on pain report in male and femals subjects. *Pain, 44,* 69–72.

Levine, M., Cassidy, C., & Jentzsch I. (2010). The implicit identity effect: Identity primes, group size, and helping. *British Journal of Social Psychology, 49* (4), 785–802.

Levine, S. C., Huttenlocher, J., Taylor, A., & Langrock, A. (1999). Early sex differences in spatial skill. *Developmental Psychology, 35,* 940–949.

Levine, S. C., Ratliff, K. R., Huttenlocher, J., & Cannon, J. (2012). Early puzzle play: A predictor of preschoolers' spatial transformation skill. *Developmental Psychology, 48* (2), 530–542.

Levinthal, C. F. (2010). *Drugs, behavior, and modern society* (6th ed.). Upper Saddle River, NJ: Prentice-Hall.

Levy, B. R., Slade, M. D., & Kasl, S. V. (2002). Increased longevity by positive self-perceptions of aging. *Journal of Personality and Social Psychology, 83,* 261–270.

Levy, J. C. (2013). *Adaptive learning and the human condition.* Upper Saddler River, NJ: Pearson.

Lewald, J., & Getzmann, S. (2011). When and where of auditory spatial processing in cortex: A novel approach using electromyography. *PLoS One, 6* (9), e25146.

Lewis, J. W., Talkington, W. J., Tallaksen, K. C., & Frum, C. A. (2012). Auditory object salience: Human cortical processing of non-biological action sounds and their acoustic signal attributes. *Frontiers in Systems Neuroscience, 6,* 27.

Lewis, M. D. (2013). The development of emotion regulation. In P. D. Zelazo (Ed.), *The Oxford handbook of developmental psychology.* New York: Oxford University Press.

Lewis, P. A., Cairney, S., Manning, L., & Critchley, H. D. (2011). The impact of overnight consolidation upon memory for emotional and neutral encoding contexts. *Neuropsychologia, 49,* 2619–2629.

Lewis, R. W., Yuan, J., & Wang, R. (2008). Male sexual arousal disorder. In D. L. Rowland & L. Incrocci (Eds.), *Handbook of sexual and gender identity disorders* (pp. 32–67). Hoboken, NJ: Wiley.

Lewis, V. A., MacGregor, C. A., & Putnam, R. D. (2013). Religion, networks, and neighborliness: The impact of religious social networks on civic engagement. *Social Science Research, 42,* 331–346.

Lewkowicz, D. J., & Hansen-Tift, A. M. (2012). Infants deploy selective attention to the mouth of a talking face when learning speech. *Proceedings of the National Academy of Sciences USA, 109* (5), 1431–1436.

Li, Y., & Epley, N. (2009). When the best appears to be saved for last: Serial position effects on choice. *Journal of Behavioral Decision Making, 22,* 378–389.

Liang, B., Williams, L. M., & Siegel, J. A. (2006). Relational outcomes of childhood sexual trauma in female survivors: A longitudinal study. *Journal of Interpersonal Violence, 21,* 42–57.

Liang, C.-Y., Xu, Z.-Y., Mei, W., Wang, L.-L., Xue, L., Lu, D. J., & Zhao, H. (2012). Neural correlates of feigned memory impairment are distinguishable from answering randomly and answering incorrectly: An fMRI and behavioral study. *Brain and Cognition, 79,* 70–77.

Libedinsky, C., & others. (2011). Sleep deprivation alters valuation signals in the ventromedial prefrontal cortex. *Frontiers in Behavioral Science.* doi: 10.3389/fnbeh.2011.00070

Lichstein, K. L., Vander Wal, G. S., & Dillon, H. R. (2012). Insomnia III: Therapeutic approaches. In C. M. Morin & C. A. Espie (Eds.), *The Oxford handbook of sleep and sleep disorders.* New York: Oxford University Press.

Lickliter, R. (2013). Biological development: Theoretical approaches, techniques, and key findings. In P. D. Zelazo (Ed.), *The Oxford handbook of developmental psychology.* New York: Oxford University Press.

Lieberman, J. A., & others. (2005). Effectiveness of antipsychotic drugs in patients with chronic schizophrenia. *New England Journal of Medicine, 353,* 1209–1223.

Lieberman, M. A. (2012). *Human learning and memory.* New York: Cambridge University Press.

Lieu, C. A., & Subramanian, T. (2012). The interhemispheric connections of the striatum: Implications for Parkinson's disease and drug-induced dyskinesias. *Brain Research Bulletin, 87,* 1–9.

Liew, J. (2012). Effortful control, executive functions, and education: Bringing self-regulatory and social competencies to the table. *Child Development Perspectives, 6* (2), 105–111.

Lilienfeld, S. O., Waldman, I. D., Landfield, K., Watts, A. L., Rubenzer, S., & Fasching, T. R. (2012). Fearless dominance and the U.S. presidency: Implications of psychopathic personality traits for successful and unsuccessful political leadership. *Journal of Personality and Social Psychology, 103* (3), 489–505.

Lilienfeld, S. O., Wood, J. M., & Garb, H. N. (2000, November). The scientific status of projective techniques. *Psychological Science in the Public Interest, 1* (2).

Lim, A., Nakamura, B. J., Higa-McMillan, C. K., Shimabukuro, S., & Slavin, L. (2012). Effects of workshop trainings on evidence-based practice knowledge and attitudes among youth community mental health providers. *Behavior Research and Therapy, 50* (6), 397–406.

Lim, I., & Merfeld, D. M. (2012). Signal detection theory and vestibular perception: II. Fitting perceptual thresholds as a function of frequency. *Experimental Brain Research, 222,* 303–320.

Lim, S. C., Kyung, K. U., & Kwon, D. S. (2012). Effect of frequency difference on sensitivity of beats perception. *Experimental Brain Research, 216,* 11–19.

Lin, H.-Y., & others. (2013). Psychiatric disorders of patients seeking obesity treatment. *BMC Psychiatry.* (in press)

Lin, X., Gang, D., Zhou, H., & Su, S. B. (2013). The expression of toll-like receptors in murine Muller cells, the glial cells of the retina. *Neurological Sciences.* (in press)

Lindau, S. T., & Gavrilova, N. (2010). Sex, health, and years of sexually active life gained due to good health: Evidence from two U.S. population based cross sectional surveys of aging. *British Medical Journal, 340,* c810.

Linden, W., Lenz, J. W., & Con, A. H. (2001). Individualized stress management for primary hypertension: A randomized trial. *Archives of Internal Medicine, 161,* 1071–1080.

Lindenberger, U., von Oertzen, T., Ghisletta, P., & Hertzogg, C. (2011). Cross-sectional age variance extraction: What's change got to do with it. *Psychology and Aging, 26,* 34–47.

Lindwall, M., & others. (2013). Dynamic associations of change in physical activity and change in cognitive function: Coordinated analyses across four studies with up to 21 years of longitudinal data. *Journal of Aging Research.* (in press)

Linebaugh, K. (2012, December 10). Service dogs pick up scent of diabetes danger. *Wall Street Journal.* http://online.wsj.com/article/SB10001424127887324001104578163423121970336.html?mod=WSJ_GoogleNews (accessed March 27, 2013)

Lingjaerde, O., Foreland, A. R., & Engvik, H. (2001). Personality structure in patients with winter depression, assessed in a depression-free state according to the five-factor model of personality. *Journal of Affective Disorders, 62,* 165–174.

Linke, S. E., & others. (2009). Depressive symptom dimensions and cardiovascular prognosis among women with suspected myocardial ischemia: A report from the National Heart, Lung, and Blood Institute-sponsored women's Ischemia Syndrome Foundation. *Archives of General Psychiatry, 66,* 499–507.

Linnman, C., Appel, L., Furark, T., Soderlund, A., Gordh, T., Langstrom, B., & Fredrikson, M. (2010). Ventromedial prefrontal neurokinin 1 receptor availability is reduced in chronic pain. *Pain, 149* (1), 64–70.

Linnman, C., & others. (2012). Resting amygdala and medial prefrontal metabolism predicts functional activation of the fear extinction circuit. *American Journal of Psychiatry, 169* (4), 415–423.

Lippa, R. (2000). Gender-related traits in gay men, lesbian women, and heterosexual men and women: The virtual identity of homosexual-heterosexual diagnosticity and gender diagnosticity. *Journal of Personality, 68,* 899–926.

Lippa, R. (2008). The relation between childhood gender nonconformity and adult masculinity-femininity and anxiety in heterosexual and homosexual men and women. *Sex Roles, 59,* 684–693.

Lippa, R. A. (2013). Men and women with bisexual identities show bisexual patterns of sexual attraction to male and female "swimsuit models." *Archives of Sexual Behavior, 42* (2), 187–196.

Lippke, S., & Plotnikoff, R. C. (2006). Stages of change in physical exercise: A test of stage discrimination and nonlinearity. *American Journal of Health Behavior, 30,* 290–301.

Lippke, S., Ziegelmann, J. P., Schwarzer, R., & Velicer, W. F. (2009). Validity of stage assessment in the adoption and maintenance of physical activity and fruit and vegetable consumption. *Health Psychology, 28,* 183–193.

Lipsey, M. W., & Wilson, D. B. (1993). The efficacy of psychological, educational, and behavioral treatment: Confirmation from meta-analysis. *American Psychologist, 48,* 1181–1209.

Lisman, J., & Sternberg, E. J. (2013). Habit and nonhabit systems for unconscious and conscious behavior: Implications for multitasking. *Journal of Cognitive Neuroscience, 25* (2), 273–283.

Lissek, S., Rabin, S., Heller, R. E., Lukenbaugh, D., Geraci, M., Pine, D. S., & Grillon, C. (2010). Overgeneralization of conditioned fear as a pathogenic marker of panic disorder. *American Journal of Psychiatry, 167,* 47–55.

Liszkowski, U., Schäffer, M., Carpenter, M., & Tomasello, M. (2009). Prelinguistic infants, but not chimpanzees, communicate about absent entities. *Psychological Science, 20,* 654–660.

Little, K. Y., Zhang, L., & Cook, E. (2006). Fluoxetine-induced alterations in human platelet serotonin transporter expression: Serotonin transporter polymorphism effects. *Psychiatry and Neuroscience, 31,* 333–339.

Little, T. D., Snyder, C. R., & Wehmeyer, M. (2006). The agentic self: On the nature and origins of personal agency across the life span. In D. K. Mroczek & T. D. Little (Eds.), *Handbook of personality development.* Mahwah, NJ: Erlbaum.

Littlefield, A. K., & Sher, K. J. (2010). Alcohol use disorders in young adulthood. In J. E. Grant (Ed.), *Young adult mental health* (pp. 292–310). New York: Oxford University Press.

Littlefield, A. K., & Sher, K. J. (2012). Smoking desistance and personality change in emerging and young adulthood. *Nicotine & Tobacco Research, 14,* 338–342.

Littrell, J. H., & Girvin, H. (2002). Stages of change: A critique. *Behavior Modification, 26,* 223–273.

Liu, C. M., & others. (2012). SOAP3: Ultra-fast GPU-based parallel alignment tool for short reads. *Bioinformatics.* doi:10.1093/bioinformatics/bts061

Liu, F., & Er, M. J. (2012). A novel efficient algorithm for self-generating fuzzy neural network with applications. *International Journal of Neural Systems, 22* (1), 21–35.

Liu, R., & Huang, X. (1999). A study on time-perceptual cues in visual information. *Acta Psychological Sinica, 31,* 15–20.

Lo, S. (2008). The nonverbal communication functions of emotions in computer-mediated communication. *CyberPsychology & Behavior, 11,* 595–597.

Lobbestael, J., & Arntz, A. (2010). Emotional, cognitive, and physiological correlates of abuse-related stress in borderline and antisocial personality disorder. *Behavior Research and Therapy, 48,* 116–124.

Lobbestael, J., Cima, M., & Arntz, A. (2013). The relationship between adult reactive and proactive aggression, hostile interpretation bias, and antisocial personality disorder. *Journal of Personality Disorders, 27* (special issue: The Social-Cognitive Basis of Personality Disorders), 53–66.

Lobo, F. A., & Schraag, S. (2011). Limitations of anesthesia depth monitoring. *Current Opinion in Anesthesia, 24,* 657–664.

Lock, J. (2012). Developmental translational research: Adolescence, brain circuity, cognitive processes and eating disorders. In J. Lock (Ed.), *The Oxford handbook of child and adolescent eating disorders: Developmental perspectives.* New York: Oxford University Press.

Loftus, E. F. (1975). Leading questions and the eyewitness report. *Cognitive Psychology, 7,* 560–572.

Loftus, E. F. (1993). Psychologists in the eyewitness world. *American Psychologist, 48,* 550–552.

Logue, A. W. (1995). *Self control: Waiting until tomorrow for what you want today.* Upper Saddle River, NJ: Pearson.

Lopez, C. R., & others. (2013). Stress management, depression, and immune status in lower income racia/ethnic minority women co-infected with HIV and HPV. *Journal of Applied Biobehavioral Research, 18,* 37–57.

Lopez, K. N., & Knudson, J. D. (2012). Obesity: From agricultural revolution to the contemporary pediatric epidemic. *Congenital Heart Disease, 7* (2), 189–199.

Lopez, S. J. (2013). *Making hope happen.* New York: Atria.

Lopez, S. J., & Gallagher, M. W. (2012). A case for positive psychology. In S. J. Lopez & C. R. Snyder (Eds.), *The Oxford handbook of positive psychology* (2nd ed.). New York: Oxford University Press.

Lorant, V., Croux, C., Weich, S., Deliege, D., Mackenbach, J., & Ansseau, M. (2007). Depression and socioeconomic risk factors: 7-year longitudinal population study. *British Journal of Psychiatry, 190,* 293–298.

Lorenz, K. Z. (1965). *Evolution and the modification of behavior.* Chicago: University of Chicago Press.

Loring-Meier, S., & Halpern, D. F. (1999). Sex differences in visual-spatial working memory: Components of cognitive processing. *Psychonomic Bulletin and Review, 6,* 464–471.

Lo Sauro, C., Ravaldi, C., Cabras, P. L., Faravelli, C., & Ricca, V. (2008). Stress, hypothalamic-pituitary-adrenal axis, and eating disorders. *Neuropsychobiology, 57,* 95–115.

LoSavio, S. T., Cohen, L. H., Laurenceau, J., Dasch, K. B., Parrish, B. P., & Park, C. L. (2011). Reports of stress-related growth from daily negative events. *Journal of Social and Clinical Psychology, 30,* 760–785.

Løvaas, O. I. (1987). Behavioral treatment and normal educational and intellectual functioning in young autistic children. *Journal of Consulting and Clinical Psychology, 55* (1), 3–9.

Lövdén, M., Wenger, E., Mårtensson, J., Lindenberger, U., & Bäckman, L. (2013). Structural brain plasticity in adult learning and development. *Neuroscience & Biobehavioral Reviews.* doi:10.1016/j.neubiorev.2013.02.014

Lovheim, H. (2012). A new three-dimensional model for emotions and monoamine neurotransmitters. *Medical Hypotheses, 78,* 341–348.

Low, C. A., Stanton, A., & Danoff-Burg, S. (2006). Expressive disclosure and benefit finding among breast cancer patients: Mechanisms for positive health effects. *Health Psychology, 25,* 181–189.

Lowmaster, S. E., & Morey, L. C. (2012). Predicting law enforcement officer job performance with the Personality Assessment Inventory. *Journal of Personality Assessment, 94* (3), 254–261.

Lu, J., Sherman, D., Devor, M., & Saper, C. B. (2006). A putative flip-flop switch for control of REM sleep. *Nature, 441,* 589–594.

Lubinski, D., Benbow, C. P., Webb, R. M., & Bleske-Rechek, A. (2006). Tracking exceptional human capital over two decades. *Psychological Science, 17,* 194–199.

Lubinski, D., Webb, R. M., Morelock, M. J., & Benbow, C. P. (2001). Top 1 in 10,000: A 10-year follow-up of the profoundly gifted. *Journal of Applied Psychology, 86,* 718–729.

Luborsky, L., Rosenthal, R., Diguer, L., Andrusyna, T. P., Berman, J. S., Levitt, J. T., Seligman, D. A., & Krause, E. D. (2002). The dodo bird verdict is alive and well—mostly. *Clinical Psychology: Science and Practice, 9,* 2–12.

Lucas, R. E. (2007). Extraversion. In R. Baumeister & K. Vohs (Eds.), *The encyclopedia of social psychology.* Thousand Oaks, CA: Sage.

Lucas, R. E. (2008). Personality and subjective well-being. In M. Eid & R. J. Larsen (Eds.), *The science of subjective well-being* (pp. 171–194). New York: Psychology Press.

Lucas, R. E., Clark, A. E., Yannis, G., & Diener, E. (2004). Unemployment alters the setpoint for life satisfaction. *Psychological Science, 15,* 8–13.

Ludlow, K. H., & others. (2009). Acute and chronic ethanol modulate dopamine d2-subtype receptor responses in ventral tegmental area GABA neurons. *Alcoholism: Clinical and Experimental Research, 33,* 804–811.

Ludwig, A. M. (1995). *The price of greatness: Resolving the creativity and madness controversy.* New York: Taylor & Francis.

Lueken, U., Krushwitz, J. D., Muehlhan, M., Siegert, J., Hoyer, J., & Wittchen, H.-U. (2011). How specific is specfic phobia? Different neural response patterns in two subtypes of specific phobia. *NeuroImage, 56* (1), 363–372.

Luhmann, M., Hofmann, W., Eid, M., & Lucas, R. E. (2012). Subjective well-being and adaptation to life events: A meta-analysis. *Journal of Personality and Social Psychology, 102,* 592–615.

Luigjes, J., & others. (2012). Surgery for psychiatric disorders. *World Neurosurgery,* doi: 10.1016/j.wneu.2012.03.009

Lund, H. G., Reider, B. D., Whiting, A. B., & Prichard, J. R. (2010). Sleep patterns and predictors of disturbed sleep in a large population of college students. *Journal of Adolescent Health, 46,* 124–132.

Luo, Y., & Baillargeon, R. (2005). Can a self-propelled box have a goal? Psychological reasoning in 5-month-old infants. *Psychological Science, 16,* 601–608.

Luo, Y., Kaufman, I., & Baillargeon, R. (2009). Young infants' reasoning about physical events involving inert and sef-propelled objects. *Cognitive Psychology, 58,* 441–486.

Lutchmaya, S., Baron-Cohen, S., Raggatt, P., Knickmeyer, R., & Manning, J. T. (2004). 2nd to 4th digit ratios, fetal testosterone and estradiol. *Early Human Development, 77,* 23–28.

Luthans, F., Avey, J. B., Avolio, B. J., Norman, S. M., & Combs, G. M. (2006). Psychological capital development: Toward a micro-intervention. *Journal of Organizational Behavior, 27,* 387–393.

Luthans, F., Youssef, C. M., & Avolio, B. J. (2007). *Psychological capital.* New York: Oxford University Press.

Lydon, C. A., Rohmeier, K. D., Yi, S. C., Mattaini, M. A., & Williams, W. L. (2011). How far do you have to go to get a cheeseburger around here? The realities of an environmental design approach to curbing the consumption of fast-food. *Behavior and Social Issues, 20,* 6–23.

Lyddon, R., & others. (2013). Serotonin 2c receptor RNA editing in major depression and suicide. *World Journal of Biological Psychiatry.* (in press)

Lykken, D. (1999). *Happiness: What studies on twins show us about nature, nurture, and the happiness set-point.* New York: Golden Books.

Lykken, D. T. (1987). The probity of the polygraph. In S. M. Kassin & L. S. Wrightsman (Eds.), *The psychology of evidence and trial procedures.* Newbury Park, CA: Sage.

Lykken, D. T. (2001). Lie detection. In W. E. Craighead & C. B. Nemeroff (Eds.), *The Corsini encyclopedia of psychology and behavioral science* (3rd ed.). New York: Wiley.

Lynam, D. R., Caspi, A., Moffitt, T. E., Loeber, R., & Stouthamer-Loeber, M. (2007). Longitudinal evidence that psychopathy scores in early adolescence predict adult psychopathy. *Journal of Abnormal Psychology, 116,* 155–165.

Lynam, D. R., & Miller, J. D. (2012). Fearless dominance and psychopathy: A response to Lilienfeld et al. *Personality Disoders, 3* (3), 341–353.

Lynn, S. J., & Green, J. P. (2011). The sociocognitive and dissociation theories of hypnosis: Toward a rapproachement. *International Journal of Clinical and Experimental Hypnosis, 59,* 277–293.

Lynn, S. J., Malakataris, A., Condon, L., Maxwell, R., & Cleere, C. (2012). Post-traumatic stress disorder: Cognitive hypnotherapy, mindfulness, and acceptance-based treatment approaches. *American Journal of Clinical Hypnosis, 54,* 311–330.

Lyon, G. J., & Wang, K. (2012). Identifying disease mutations in genomic medicine settings: Current challenges and how to accelerate the process. *Genome Medicine, 4,* 58.

Lyubomirsky, S. (2008). *The how of happiness: A scientific approach to getting the life you want.* New York: Penguin.

Lyubomirsky, S. (2011). *The way to happiness: Action plan for a happy life.* Yehuda, Israel: Kinneret.

Lyubomirsky, S. (2013). *The myth of happiness.* New York: Penguin.

Lyubomirsky, S., Boehm, J. K., Kasri, F., & Zehm, K. (2011a). The cognitive and hedonic costs of dwelling on achievement-related negative experiences: Implications for enduring happiness and unhappiness. *Emotion, 11,* 1152–1167.

Lyubomirsky, S., Dickerhoof, R., Boehm, J. K., & Sheldon, K. M. (2011b). Becoming happier takes both a will and a proper way: An experimental longitudinal intervention to boost well-being. *Emotion, 11,* 391–402.

M

Ma, J., & others. (2013). Magnetic stimulation modulates structural synaptic plasticity and regulates BDNF-TrkB signal pathway in cultured hippocampal neurons. *Neurochemistry International.* (in press)

Maccoby, E. E. (2002). Gender and group processes. *Current Directions in Psychological Science, 11,* 54–58.

Macdonald, J. S. P., & Lavie, N. (2008). Load induced blindness. *Journal of Experimental Psychology: Human Perception and Performance, 34,* 1078–1091.

MacDonald, K., & LaFreniere, P. J. (2012). The fate of heritability in the postgenomic era. *Behavioral and Brain Science, 35* (5), 370–371.

Machado, G. M., Oliveira, M. M., & Fernandes, L. A. (2009). A physiologically-based model for simulation of color vision deficiency. *IEEE Transactions on Visualization and Computer Graphics, 15,* 1291–1298.

MacIntosh, H., Reissing, E. D., & Andruff, H. (2010). Same-sex marriage in Canada: The impact of legal marriage on the first cohort of gay and lesbian Canadians to wed. *Canadian Journal of Human Sexuality, 19,* 79–90.

MacKenzie, S. B., Podsakoff, P. M., & Ahearne, M. (1998). Some possible antecedents and consequences of in-role and extra-role salesperson performance. *Journal of Marketing, 62,* 87–98.

MacQueen, C. E., Brynes, A. E., & Frost, G. S. (2002).Treating obesity: A follow-up study. Can the stages of change model be used as a postal screening tool? *Journal of Human Nutrition and Dietetics, 15* (1), 3–7.

Madan, A., Palaniappan, L., Urizar, G., Wang, Y., Formann, S. P., & Gould, J. B. (2006). Sociocultural factors that affect pregnancy outcomes in two dissimilar immigrant groups in the United States. *Journal of Pediatrics, 148,* 341–346.

Madden, D. J., Gottlob, L. R., Denny, L. L., Turkington, T. G., Provenzale, J. M., Hawk, T. C., & others. (1999). Aging and recognition memory: Changes in regional cerebral blood flow associated with components of reaction time distributions. *Journal of Cognitive Neuroscience, 11,* 511–520.

Madden, K., Middleton, P., Cyna, A. M., Matthewson, M., & Jones, L. (2012). Hypnosis for pain management during labor and childbirth. *Cochrane Database of Systematic Reviews, 11,* CD009356.

Maddi, S. (1998). Hardiness. In H. S. Friedman (Ed.), *Encyclopedia of mental health* (vol. 3). San Diego: Academic.

Maddi, S. R. (2008). The courage and strategies of hardiness as helpful in growing despite major, disruptive stresses. *American Psychologist, 63,* 563–564.

Maddi, S. R., Harvey, R. H., Khoshaba, D. M., Lu, J. L., Persico, M., & Brow, M. (2006). The personality construct of hardiness, III: Relationships with repression, innovativeness, authoritarianism, and performance. *Journal of Personality, 74,* 575–597.

Maddock, R. J., Buonocore, M. H. Copeland, L. E., & Richards, A. L. (2009). Elevated brain lactate responses to neural activation in panic disorder: A dynamic 1H-MRS study. *Molecular Psychiatry, 14,* 537–545.

Maddox, G. B., Naveh-Benjamin, M., Old, S., & Kilb, A. (2012). The role of attention in the associative building of emotionally arousing words. *Psychonomic Bulletin and Review, 19,* 1128–1134.

Maddux, W. W., & Galinsky, A. D. (2007, September). *Cultural borders and mental barriers: Living in and adapting to foreign countries facilitates creativity.* Working Paper No. 2007/51/B. Fountainbleau, France: INSEAD.

Madhyastha, T. M., Hamaker, E. L., & Gottman, J. M. (2011). Investigating spousal influence using moment-to-moment affect data from marital conflict. *Journal of Family Psychology, 25,* 292–300.

Madras, B. K. (2013). History of the discovery of the antipsychotic dopamine d2 receptor: A basis for the dopamine hypothesis of schizophrenia. *Journal of the History of the Neurosciences, 22* (1), 62–78.

Maeda, U., Shen, B. J., Schwarz, E. R., Farrell, K. A., & Mallon, S. (2012). Self-efficacy mediates the association of social support and depression with treatment adherence in heart failure patients. *International Journal of Behavioral Medicine, 20* (1), 88–96.

Maggio, N., & Segal, M. (2009). Differential corticosteroid modulation of inhibitory synaptic currents in the dorsal and ventral hippocampus. *Journal of Neuroscience, 29,* 2857–2866.

Magon, N., & Kaira, S. (2011). The orgasmic history of oxytocin: Love, lust, and labor. *Indian Journal of Endocrinology and Metabolism, 15,* Suppl. 3, S156–S161.

Maguire, E. A., Gadian, G. D., Johnsrude, I. S., Good, C. D., Ashburner, J., Frackowiak, R. S. J., & Frith, C. D. (2000). Navigation-related structural change in the hippocampi of taxi drivers. *Proceedings of the National Academy of Sciences USA, 97,* 4398–4403.

Mahler, D. A., Murray, J. A., Waterman, L. A., Ward, J., Kraemer, W. J., Zhang, X., & Baird, J. C. (2009). Endogenous opioids modify dyspnosa during treadmill exercise in patients with COPD. *European Respiratory Journal, 33,* 771–777.

Mahmoud, F. A., Aktas, A., Walsh, D., & Hullihen, B. (2011). A pilot study of taste changes among hospice inpatients with advanced cancer. *American Journal of Hospice and Palliative Care, 28,* 487–492.

Maier, N. R. F. (1931). Reasoning in humans. *Journal of Comparative Psychology, 12,* 181–194.

Maio, G. R., Olson, J. M., & Cheung, I. (2013). Attitudes in social behavior. In H. A. Tennen, J. M. Suls, & I. B. Weiner (Eds.), *Handbook of psychology, 2nd ed., Vol. 5.* (pp. 275–304). Hoboken, NJ: Wiley.

Majerus, S., Attout, L., D'Argembeau, A., Degueldre, C., Fias, W., Maquet, P., Perez, T. M., Stawarczyk, D., Salmon, E., Van der Linden, M., Phillips, C., & Balteau, E. (2012). Attention supports verbal short-term memory via competition between dorsal and ventral attention networks. *Cerebral Cortex, 22,* 1086–1097.

Major Depressive Disorder Working Group of the Psychiatric GWAS Consortium. (2013). A mega-analysis of genome-wide association studies for major depressive disorder. *Molecular Psychiatry.* (in press)

Makransky, G., Mortensen, E. L., & Glas, C. A. (2013). Improving personality facet scores with multidimensional computer adaptive testing: An illustration with the Neo Pi-R. *Assessment, 20* (1), 3–13.

Malamuth, N. M., Addison, T., & Koss, M. (2000). Pornography and sexual aggression: Are there reliable effects and can we understand them? *Annual Review of Sex Research, 11,* 26–91.

Malcolm-Smith, S., Solms, M., Turnbull, O., & Tredoux, C. (2008). Threat in dreams: An adaptation? *Consciousness and cognition, 17,* 1281–1291.

Malhotra, R. K., & Desai, A. K. (2010). Healthy brain aging: what has sleep got to do with it? *Clinics in Geriatric Medicine, 26,* 46–56.

Malhotra, R. K., Ostbye, T., Riley, C. M., & Finkelstein, E. A. (2013). Young adult weight trajectories through midlife by body mass category. *Obesity.* doi: 10.1002/oby.20318

Mallon, R., & Nichols, S. (2011). Dual processes and moral rules. *Emotion Review, 3,* 284–285.

Malloy, L. C., Lyon, T. D., & Quas, J. A. (2007). Fiilial dependency and recantation of child sexual abuse allegations. *Journal of the American Academy of Child & Adolescent Psychiatry, 46,* 162–170.

Malmberg, K. J., Criss, A. H., Gangwani, T. H., & Shiffrin, R. M. (2012). Overcoming the negative consequences of interference from recognition memory testing. *Psychological Science, 23* (2), 115–119.

Malón, A. (2012). Pedophilia: A diagnosis in search of a disorder. *Archives of Sexual Behavior, 41,* 1083–1097.

Mandal, I., & Sairam, N. (2012). Accurate prediction of coronary artery disease using reliable diagnosis system. *Journal of Medical Systems, 36* (5), 3353–3373.

Mandara, J. (2006). The impact of family functioning on African American males' academic achievement: A review and clarification of the empirical literature. *Teachers College Record, 108,* 206–233.

Mandler, G. (1980). Recognizing: The judgment of previous occurrence. *Psychological Review, 87,* 252–271.

Maner, J. K., Luce, C. L., Neuberg, S. L., Cialdini, R. B., Brown, S., & Sagarin, B. J. (2002). The effects of perspective taking on motivations for helping: Still no evidence for altruism. *Personality and Social Psychology Bulletin, 28,* 1601–1610.

Manini, T. M., & others. (2006). Daily activity energy expenditure and mortality among older adults. *Journal of the American Medical Association, 296,* 216–218.

Manning, J. T. (2002). *Digit ratio: A pointer to fertility, behavior, and health.* New Brunswick, NJ: Rutgers University Press.

Manning, R., Levine, M., & Collins, A. (2007). The Kitty Genovese murder and the social psychology of helping: The parable of the 38 witnesses. *American Psychologist, 62,* 555–562.

Manning, W. D., & Cohen, J. A. (2012). Premarital cohabitation and marital dissolution: An examination of recent marriages. *Journal of Marriage and the Family, 74,* 377–387.

Manrique, H. M., Völter, C. J. & Call, J. (2013). Repeated innovation in great apes. *Animal Behaviour, 85,* 195–202.

Mantonakis, A., Rodero, P., Lesschaeve, I., & Hastie, R. (2009). Order in choice: Effects of serial position on preferences. *Psychological Science, 20,* 1309–1312.

Manusov, V. (2012). Attributions and communication: Out of our heads and into behavior. In D. R. Roskos-Ewoldsen & J. L. Monahan (Eds.), *Communication and social cognition.* New York: Psychology Press.

Maoz, I. (2012). Contact and social change in an ongoing asymmetrical conflict: Four social-psychological models of reconciliation-aimed planned encounters between Israeli Jews and Palestinians. In J. Dixon & M. Levine (Eds.), *Beyond prejudice.* New York: Cambridge University Press.

Mar, R. A., Mason, M. F., & Litvack, A. (2012). How daydreaming relates to life satisfaction, loneliness, and social support: The importance of gender and daydream content. *Consciousness and Cognition, 21* (1), 401–407.

Marazziti, D., Carlini, M., & Dell'Osso, L. (2012). Treatment strategies of obsessive-compulsive disorder and panic disorder/agoraphobia. *Current Topics in Medicinal Chemistry, 12,* 238–253.

Marazziti, D., Corsi, M., Baroni, G., Consoli, M., & Catena-Dell'Osso, M. (2012). Latest advancements in the pharmacological treatment of binge eating disorder. *European Review for Medical and Pharmacological Science, 16,* 2102–2107.

Marchetti, I., Koster, E. H., & De Raedt, R. (2012). Mindwandering heightens the accessibility of negative to positive thought. *Consciousness and Cognition, 21,* 1517–1525.

Marcia, J. E. (1980). Ego identity development. In J. Adelson (Ed.), *Handbook of adolescent psychology.* New York: Wiley.

Marcia, J. E. (2002). Identity and psychosocial development in adulthood. *Identity, 2,* 7–28.

Marcus, G. F. (2001). *The algebraic mind.* Cambridge, MA: MIT Books.

Marewski, J. N., & Schooler, L. J. (2011). Cognitive niches: An ecological model of strategy selection. *Psychological Review, 118,* 393–437.

Margoob, M. A., Zaffar Ali, Z., & Andrade, C. (2010). Efficacy of ECT in chronic, severe, antidepressant- and CBT-refractory PTSD: An open, prospective study. *Brain Stimulation, 3,* 28–35.

Mariani, J. J., & Levin, F. R. (2012). Psychostimulant treatment of cocaine dependence. *Psychiatric Clinics of North America, 35,* 425–439.

Marine, A., Rutosalainen, J., Serra, C., & Verbeek, J. (2006). Preventing occupational stress in healthcare workers. *Cochrane Database System Review, 18* (4), CD002892.

Maris, R. W. (1998). Suicide. In H. S. Friedman (Ed.), *Encyclopedia of mental health* (vol. 3). San Diego: Academic.

Markant, J. C., & Thomas, K. M. (2013). Postnatal brain development. In P. D. Zelazo (Ed.), *The Oxford handbook of developmental psychology.* New York: Oxford University Press.

Markovits, H., Forgues, H. L., & Brunet, M. L. (2012). More evidence for a dual-process model of conditional reasoning. *Memory and Cognition, 40* (5), 736–747.

Markowitsch, H. J., & Staniloiu, A. (2012). Amnesic disorders. *Lancet, 380* (9851), 1429–1440.

Marks, A. K., Patton, F., & Coll, C. G. (2011). Being bicultural: A mixed-methods study of adolescents' implicitly and explicitly measured multi-ethnic identitities. *Developmental Psychology, 47,* 270–288.

Marks, D. F. (2013). Health psychology: Overview. In A. M. Nezu, C. Maguth Nezu, P. A. Geller, & I. B. Weiner (Eds.), *Handbook of psychology, 2nd ed., Vol. 9.* (pp. 3–26). Hoboken, NJ: Wiley.

Marlow, A. (1999). *How to stop time: Heroin from A to Z.* New York: Basic.

Marques, J. K., Wiederanders, M., Day, D. M., Nelson, C., & van Ommeren A. (2005). Effects of a relapse prevention program on sexual recidivism: Final results from California's Sex Offender Treatment Evaluation Project (SOTEP). *Sex Abuse, 17,* 79–107.

Marrazzo, J. M., Coffey, P., & Bingham, A. (2005). Sexual practices, risk perception, and knowledge of bacterial vaginosis among lesbian and bisexual women. *Perspectives on Sexual and Reproductive Health, 37,* 6–12.

Marsh, E. J., & Roediger, H. L. (2013). Episodic and autobiographical memory. In A. F. Healy, R. W. Proctor, & I. B. Weiner (Eds.), *Handbook of psychology, 2nd ed., Vol. 4.* (pp. 472–494). Hoboken, NJ: Wiley.

Marshall, D. S. (1971). Sexual behavior in Mangaia. In D. S. Marshall & R. C. Suggs (Eds.), *Human sexual behavior: Variations in the ethnographic spectrum* (pp. 103–162). New York: Basic.

Marston, O. J., & others. (2011). Neuropeptide Y cells represent a distinct glucose-sensing population in the lateral hypothalamus. *Endocrinology, 152,* 4046–4052.

Massa, L. J., & Mayer, R. E. (2006). Testing the ATI hypothesis: Should multimedia instruction accommodate verbalizer-visualizer cognitive style? *Learning and Individual Differences, 16,* 321–336.

Martin, C. L., & Ruble, D. N. (2010). Patterns of gender development. *Annual Review of Psychology* (vol. 61). (pp. 353–381). Palo Alto, CA: Annual Reviews.

Martin, G. L., & Pear, J. (2011). *Behavior modification* (9th ed.). Upper Saddle River, NJ: Pearson.

Martin, L. R., Friedman, H. S., & Schwartz, J. E. (2007). Personality and mortality risk across the lifespan: The importance of conscientiousness as biopsychosocial attribute. *Health Psychology, 26,* 428–436.

Martínez-Amorós, E., & others. (2012). Long-term treatment strategies in major depression: A 2-year provective naturalistic follow-up. *Journal of Electroconvulsive Therapy, 28* (2), 92–97.

Martin-Fardon, R., & Weiss, F. (2013). Modeling relapse in animals. *Current Topics in Behavioral Neuroscience, 13,* 403–432.

Martino, M., Rocchi, G., Escelsior, A., & Fornaro, M. (2012). Immunmodulation mechanism of antidepressants: Interactions between serotonin/norepinephrine balance and TH1/TH2 balance. *Current Neuropharmacology, 10,* 97–123.

Martins, A. T., Faisca, L. M., Esteves, R., Muresan, A., & Reis, A. (2012). Atypical moral judgment following traumatic brain injury. *Judgment and Decision Making, 7,* 478–487.

Maruyama, Y., Pereira, M., Margolskee, R. F., Chaudhari, N., & Roper, S. D. (2006). Umami responses in mouse taste cells indicate more than one receptor. *Journal of Neuroscience, 26,* 2227–2234.

Marx, R. F., & Didziulis, V. (2009, March 1). A life, interrupted. *New York Times.*

Marzano, C., & others. (2011). Recalling and forgetting dreams: Theta and alpha oscillations during sleep predict subsequent dream recall. *Journal of Neuroscience, 31,* 6674–6683.

Mas, S., & others. (2013). Common genetic background in anorexia nervosa and obsessive disorder: Preliminary results from an association study. *Journal of Psychiatric Research.* (in press)

Mascaro, N., & Rosen, D. H. (2006). The role of existential meaning as a buffer against stress. *Journal of Humanistic Psychology, 46,* 168–190.

Mash, E. J., & Wolfe, D. A. (2013). Disorders of childhood and adolescence. In G. Stricker, T. A. Widiger, & I. B. Weiner (Eds.), *Handbook of psychology, 2nd ed., Vol. 8.* (pp. 19–72). Hoboken, NJ: Wiley.

Maslow, A. H. (1954). *Motivation and personality.* New York: Harper & Row.

Maslow, A. H. (1971). *The farther reaches of human nature.* New York: Viking.

Massimini, F., & Delle Fave, A. (2000). Individual development in bio-cultural perspective. *American Psychologist, 55,* 24–33.

Masten, A. S. (2009). Ordinary magic: Lessons from research on human development. *Education Canada, 49,* 28–32.

Masten, A. S. (2011). Understanding and promoting resilience in children. *Current Opinion in Psychiatry, 24* (4), 267–273.

Masten, A. S. (2013). Risk and resilience in development. In P. D. Zelazo (Ed.), *The Oxford handbook of developmental psychology.* New York: Oxford University Press.

Masten, A. S., & others. (2008). School success in motion: Protective factors for academic achievement in homeless and highly mobile children in Minneapolis. *Center for Urban and Regional Affairs Reporter, 38,* 3–12.

Masters, W. H., & Johnson, V. E. (1966). *Human sexual response.* Boston: Little, Brown.

Mathew, K. L., Whitford, H. S., Kenny, M. A., & Denson, L. A. (2010). The long-term effects of mindfulness-based cognitive therapy as a relapse prevention treatment for major depressive disorder. *Behavioral and Cognitive Psychotherapy, 38,* 561–576.

Mathews, C. A., & others. (2012). Genome-wide linkage analysis of obsessive-compulsive disorder implicates chromosome 1p36. *Biological Psychiatry, 72* (8). 629–636.

Matlin, M. W. (2012). *Psychology of women* (7th ed.). Boston: Cengage.

Matlow, J. N., Jubetsky, A., Aleksa, K., Berger, H., & Koren, G. (2013). The transfer of ethyl glucuronide across the dually perfused human placenta. *Placenta, 34* (4), 369–373.

Matos, A. P., Ferreira, J. A., & Haase, R. F. (2012). Television and aggression: A test of a mediated model with a sample of Portuguese students. *Journal of Social Psychology, 152,* 75–91.

Matricciani, L. A., Olds, T. S., Blunden, S., Rigney, G., & Williams, M. T. (2012). Never enough sleep: A brief history of sleep recommendations for children. *Pediatrics, 129,* 548–556.

Matsumoto, D., & Juang, L. (2013). *Culture and psychology* (5th ed.). Boston: Cengage.

Matsumoto, D., & others. (2008) Mapping expressive differences around the world: The relationship between emotional display rules and individualism versus collectivism. *Journal of Cross-Cultural Psychology, 39,* 55–74.

Mattes, K., Spezio, M., Kim, H., Todorov, A., Adolphs, R., & Alvarez, R. M. (2010). Predicting election outcomes from positive and negative trait assessments of candidate images. *Political Psychology, 31,* 41–58.

Matthews, K. A., Gump, B. B., Harris, K. F., Haney, T. L., & Barefoot, J. C. (2004). Hostile behaviors predict cardiovascular motality among men enrolled in the multiple risk factor intervention trial. *Circulation, 109,* 66–70.

Matthews, R. A., Bulger, C. A., & Barnes-Farrell, J. L. (2010). Work social supports, role stressors, and work–family conflict: The moderating effect of age. *Journal of Vocational Behavior, 76,* 78–90.

Matula, B. (2013). Burnout/stress management: How to reduce burnout and stress in the workplace. *Journal of Healthcare Protection Management, 29,* 92–95.

Maurer, T. J., Mitchell, D. R. D., & Barbeite, F. G. (2002). Predictors of attitudes toward a 360-degree feedback system and involvement in post-feedback management development activity. *Journal of Occupational and Organizational Psychology, 75,* 87–107.

Maurer, T. J., Solamon, J. M., & Lippstreu, M. (2008). How does coaching interviewees affect the validity of a structured interview? *Journal of Organizational Behavior, 29* (3), 355–371.

Maxson, S. C. (2013). Behavioral genetics. In R. J. Nelson, S. J. Y. Mizumori, & I. B. Weiner (Eds.), *Handbook of psychology, 2nd ed., Vol. 3.* (pp. 1–254). Hoboken, NJ: Wiley.

May, M. (2003). Vision diary. *The Guardian.* www.guardian.co.uk/science/2003/aug/26/genetics.g2 (accessed February 21, 2013)

Mayer, J. D., Salovey, P., Caruso, D. R., & Cherkassky, L. (2011). Emotional intelligence. In R. J. Sternberg & S. B. Kaufman (Eds.), *Handbook of intelligence.* New York: Cambridge University Press.

Mayer, R. (2000). Problem solving. In M. A. Runco & S. Pritzker (Eds.), *Encyclopedia of psychology.* San Diego: Academic.

Mavrides, N., & Nemeroff, C. (2013). Treatment of depression in cardiovascular disease. *Depression and Anxiety, 30,* 328–341.

Mazur, J. E. (2013). *Learning and behavior* (7th ed.). Upper Saddle River, NJ: Pearson.

McAbee, S. T., & Oswald, F. L. (2013). The criterion-related validity of personality measures for predicting GPA: A meta-analytic validity comparison. *Psychological Assessment.* (in press)

McAdams, D. P. (1989). *Intimacy: The need to be close.* New York: Doubleday.

McAdams, D. P. (2001). The psychology of life stories. *Review of General Psychology, 5,* 100–122.

McAdams, D. P. (2006). *The redemptive self: Stories Americans live by.* New York: Oxford University Press.

McAdams, D. P. (2007, April 10). Understanding behavior (letter to the editor). *New York Times.* http://query.nytimes.com/gst/fullpage.html?res=9C0CE7DA153FF933A25757C0A9619C8B63&n=Top%2fReference%2fTimes%20Topics%2fSubjects%2fT%2fTerrorism (accessed May 16, 2013)

McAdams, D. P. (2009). *The person* (5th ed.). New York: Wiley.

McAdams, D. P. (2011). Life narratives. In K. L. Fingerman, C. A. Berg, J. Smith, & T. C. Antonucci (Eds.), *Handbook of lifespan development.* New York: Springer.

McAdams, D. P. (2012). Exploring psychological themes through life narrative accounts. In J. A. Holstein & J. F. Gubrium (Eds.), *Varieties of narrative analysis.* Thousand Oaks, CA: Sage.

McAdams, D. P. (2013). How actors, agents, and authors find meaning in life. In K. D. Markman, T. Proulx, & M. J. Lindberg (Eds.), *The psychology of meaning.* Washington, DC: American Psychological Association.

McAdams, D. P., & Bryant, F. B. (1987). Intimacy motivation and subjective mental health in a nationwide sample. *Journal of Personality, 55,* 395–413.

McAdams, D. P., & Olson, B. D. (2010). Personality development: Continuity and change over the lifespan. *Annual Review of Psychology* (vol. 61). Palo Alto, CA: Annual Reviews.

McAvinue, L. P. Vangkilde, S., Johnson, K. A., Habekost, T., Kyllingsbæk, S., Robertson, I. H., & Bundesen, C. (2012). The relationship between sustained attention, attentional selectivity, and capacity. *Journal of Cognitive Psychology, 24,* 313–328.

McCabe, J., Tanner, A., & Heiman, J. R. (2010). The impact of gender expectations on meanings of sex and sexuality: Results from a cognitive interview study. *Sex Roles, 62,* 252–263.

McCarrey, A. C., & others. (2012). Age differences in neural activity during slot machine gambling: An fMRI study. *PLoS One, 7* (11), e49787.

McCaslin, D. (2013). Infant hearing screening and the role of new technologies. *Journal of the American Academy of Audiology, 24* (1), 5–16.

McCauley, C., & Segal, M. E. (2009). Social psychology of terrorist groups. In J. Victoroff & A. W. Kruglanski (Eds), *Psychology of terrorism: Classic and contemporary insights* (pp. 331–346). New York: Psychology Press.

McClelland, J. L. (2011). Memory as a constructive process: The parallel-distributed processing approach. In S. Nalbantian, P. Matthews, & J. L. McClelland (Eds.), *The memory process.* Cambridge, MA: MIT Press.

McClelland, J. L., & others. (2010). Letting structure emerge: Connectionist and dynamical systems approaches to cognition. *Trends in Cognitive Science, 14,* 348–356.

McCombs, B. L. (2013). Educational psychology and educational transformation. In W. M. Reynolds, G. F. Miller, & I. B. Weiner (Eds.), *Handbook of psychology* (2nd ed., vol. 7). (pp. 493–534). Hoboken, NJ: Wiley.

McCormick, C. B., Dimmitt, C., & Sullivan, F. R. (2013). Metacognition, learning, and instruction. In W. M. Reynolds, G. F. Miller, & I. B. Weiner (Eds.), *Handbook of psychology, 2nd ed., Vol. 7.* (pp. 69–984). Hoboken, NJ: Wiley.

McCrae, R. R., & Costa, P. T. (2006). Cross-cultural perspectives on adult personality trait development. In D. K. Mroczek & T. D. Little (Eds.), *Handbook of personality development.* Mahwah, NJ: Erlbaum.

McCrae, R. R., Gaines, J. F., & Wellington, M. A. (2013). The five-factor model in fact and fiction. In H. A. Tennen, J. M. Suls, & I. B. Weiner (Eds.), *Handbook of psychology, 2nd ed., Vol. 5.* (pp. 65–92). Hoboken, NJ: Wiley.

McCrae, R. R., & Sutin, A. R. (2009). Openness to experience. In M. R. Leary & R. H. Hoyle (Eds.), *Handbook of individual differences in social behavior* (pp. 257–273). New York: Guilford.

McCullough, J. L., & Kelly, K. M. (2006). Prevention and treatment of skin aging. *Annals of the New York Academy of Science, 1067,* 323–331.

McCullough, M. E., Bono, G., & Root, L. M. (2007). Rumination, emotion, and forgiveness: Three longitudinal studies. *Journal of Personality and Social Psychology, 92,* 490–505.

McCullough, M. E., Emmons, R. A., & Tsang, J. (2002). The grateful disposition: A conceptual and empirical topography. *Journal of Personality and Social Psychology, 82,* 112–127.

McCullough, M. E., Kurzban, R., & Tabak, B. A. (2011). Evolved mechanisms for revenge and forgiveness. In M. Mikulincer & P. R. Shaver (Eds.), *Human aggression and violence: Causes, manifestations, and consequences* (pp. 221–239). Washington, DC: American Psychological Association.

McCullough, M. E., Luna, L. R., Berry, J. W., Tabak, B. A., & Bono, G. (2010). On the form and function of forgiving: Modeling the time–forgiveness relationship and testing the valuable relationships hypothesis. *Emotion, 10,* 358–376.

McCullough, M. E., Root, L. M., Tabak, B. A., & Witvliet, C. (2012). Forgiveness. In S. J. Lopez & C. R. Snyder (Eds.), *The Oxford handbook of positive psychology* (2nd ed.). New York: Oxford University Press.

McCullough, M. E., & Willoughby, B. L. (2009). Religion, self-regulation, and self-control: Associations, explanations, and implications. *Psychological Bulletin, 135,* 69–93.

McDaniel, M. A., & Einstein, G. O. (2007). *Prospective memory: An overview and synthesis of an emerging field.* Thousand Oaks, CA: Sage.

McDermott, R. (2009). Medical decision making: Lessons from psychology. *Urologic Oncology, 26,* 665–668.

McDonald, M., Asher, B. D., Kerr, N. L., & Navarrete, C. D. (2011). Fertility and intergroup bias in racial and minimal-group contexts: Evidence for shared architecture. *Psychological Science, 22,* 860–865.

McDonald, P. (2012). Workplace sexual harassment 30 years on: A review of the literature. *International Journal of Management Reviews, 14,* 1–17.

McEachin, J. J., Smith, T., & Løvaas, O. I. (1993). Long-term outcome for children with autism who received early intensive behavioral treatment. *American Journal on Mental Retardation, 97* (4), 359–372.

McFadden, D. (2008). What do sex, twins, spotted hyenas, ADHD, and sexual orientation have in common? *Perspectives on Psychological Science, 3,* 309–323.

McFadden, D., Loehlin, J. C., Breedlove, S. M., Lippa, R. A., Manning, J. T., & Rahman, Q. (2005). A reanalysis of five studies on sexual orientation and the relative length of the 2nd and 4th fingers (the 2D:4D ratio). *Archives of Sexual Behavior, 34,* 341–356.

McFadden, D., & Shubel, E. (2002). Relative lengths of fingers and toes in human males and females. *Hormones and Behavior, 42,* 492–500.

McGettigan, C., Evans, C., Rosen, S., Agnew, Z., Shah, P., & Scott, S. (2012). An application of univariate and multivariate approaches to fMRI to quantifying the hemispheric lateralization of acoustic and linguistic processes. *Journal of Cognitive Neuroscience, 24,* 636–652.

McGhee, K. E., & Travis, J. (2010). Repeatable behavioural type and stable dominance rank in the bluefin killifish. *Animal Behaviour, 79,* 497–507.

McGraw, A. P., Warren, C., Williams, L. E., & Leonard, B. (2012). Too close for comfort, or too far to care? Finding humor in distant tragedies and close mishaps. *Psychological Science, 23,* 1215–1223.

McGregor, D. M. (1960). *The human side of enterprise.* New York: McGraw-Hill.

McGuire, M. T., Wing, R. R., Klem, M. L., Lang, W., & Hill, J. O. (1999). What predicts weight regain in a group of successful weight losers? *Journal of Consulting and Clinical Psychology, 67,* 177–185.

McGuire, W. J. (2003). Doing psychology my way. In R. J. Sternberg (Ed.), *Psychologists defying the crowd: Stories of those who battled the establishment and won* (pp. 119–137). Washington, DC: American Psychological Association.

McGuire, W. J., & Papageorgis, D. (1961). The relative efficacy of various types of prior belief-defense in producing immunity against persuasion. *Public Opinion Quarterly, 26,* 24–34.

McIntosh, R. C., & Rosselli, M. (2012). Stress and coping in women living with HIV: A meta-analytic review. *AIDS and Behavior, 16* (8), 2144–2159.

McIntosh, W. D., Harlow, T. F., & Martin, L. L. (1995). Linkers and non-linkers: Goal beliefs as a moderator of the effects of everyday hassles on rumination, depression, and physical complaints. *Journal of Applied Social Psychology, 25,* 1231–1244.

McKay, K. M., Imel, Z. E., & Wampold, B. E. (2006). Psychiatrist effects in the psychopharmacological treatment of depression. *Journal of Affective Disorders, 92,* 287–290.

McKone, E., Crookes, K., & Kanwisher, N. (2010). The cognitive and neural development of face recognition in humans. In M. Gazzaniga (Ed.), *The cognitive neurosciences* (4th ed.). New York: Cambridge University Press.

McLanahan, S., & Adams, J. (1987). Parenthood and psychological well-being. *Annual Review of Sociology, 13,* 237–257.

McMahon, D. B., & Olson, C. R. (2009). Linearly additive shape and color signals in monkey inferotemporal cortex. *Journal of Neurophysiology, 101,* 1867–1875.

McMain, S., & Pos, A. E. (2007). Advances in psychotherapy of personality disorders: A research update. *Current Psychiatry Reports, 9,* 46–52.

McMains, S., & Kastner, S. (2011). Interaction of top-down and bottom-up mechanisms in the human visual cortex. *Journal of Neuroscience, 31,* 587–597.

McNamara, P., McLaren, D., & Durso, K. (2007). Representation of the self in REM and NREM dreams. *Dreaming, 17,* 113–126.

McNamara, T. P. (2013). Semantic memory and priming. In A. F. Healy, R. W. Proctor, & I. B. Weiner (Eds.), *Handbook of psychology* (2nd ed., vol. 4). Hoboken, NJ: Wiley.

McNaughton, N., & Corr, P. J. (2008). The neuropsychology of fear and anxiety: A foundation for reinforcement sensitivity theory. In P. J. Corr (Ed.), *The reinforcement sensitivity theory of personality* (pp. 44–94). New York: Cambridge University Press.

McNiel, J. M., Lowman, J. C., & Fleeson, W. (2010). The effect of state extraversion on four types of affect. *European Journal of Personality, 24,* 18–35.

McNulty, J. K. (2011). The dark side of forgiveness: The tendency to forgive predicts continued psychological and physical aggression in marriage. *Personality and Social Psychology Bulletin, 37,* 770–783.

McRae, K., Hughes, B., Chopra, S., Gabrieli, J. D. E., Gross, J. J., & Ochsner, K. N. (2010). The neural bases of distraction and reappraisal. *Journal of Cognitive Neuroscience, 22,* 248–262.

McRae, L. (2013). Rehabilitating antisocial personalities: Treatment through self-governance strategies. *Journal of Forensic Psychiatry & Psychology, 24* (1), 48–70.

McWilliams, L. A., & Bailey, S. J. (2010). Association between adult attachment rating and health conditions: Evidence from the National Comorbidity Survey replication. *Health Psychology, 29,* 446–453.

Mealor, A. D., & Dienes, Z. (2012). The speed of metacognition: Taking time to get to know one's structural knowledge. *Consciousness and Cognition, 22,* 123–136.

Medland, S. E., & Loehlin, J. C. (2008). Multivariate genetic analyses of the 2D:4D ratio: Examining the effects of hand and measurement technique in data from 757 twin families. *Twin Research and Human Genetics, 11,* 335–341.

MedlinePlus. (2012). *Alcoholism.* www.nlm.nih.gov/medlineplus/alcoholism.html (accessed February 26, 2013)

Meghnagi, D. (2011). From the dreams of a generation to the theory of dreams: Freud's Roman dreams. *International Journal of Psychoanalysis, 92* (3), 675–694.

Mehta, D. & Binder, E. B. (2012). Gene × environment vulnerability factors for PTSD: The HPA-axis. *Neuropharmacology, 62,* 654–662.

Mejia-Arauz, R., Rogoff, B., & Paradise, R. (2005). Cultural variation in children's observation during a demonstration. *International Journal of Behavioral Development, 29,* 282–291.

Melo, A., & others. (2011). Oxidative stress in neurodegenerative diseases: Mechanisms and therapeutic perspectives. *Oxidative Medicine and Cellular Longevity.* doi: 10.1155/2011/467180

Melton, L. (2005, December 17). How brain power can help you cheat old age. *New Scientist, 2530,* 32.

Meltzoff, A. N. (2011). Social cognition and the origins of imitation, empathy, and theory of mind. In U. Goswami (Ed.), *Wiley-Blackwell handbook of childhood cognitive development* (2nd ed.). New York: Wiley-Blackwell.

Meltzoff, A. N., & Williamson, R. A. (2013). Imitation: Social, cognitive, and theoretical perspectives. In P. D. Zelazo (Ed.), *The Oxford handbook of developmental psychology.* New York: Oxford University Press.

Mendel, R., & others. (2011). Confirmation bias: Why psychiatrists stick to wrong preliminary diagnoses. *Psychological Medicine, 20,* 1–9.

Mendes, N., Hanus, D., & Call, J. (2007). Raising the level: Orangutans use water as a tool. *Biology Letters, 3,* 453–455.

Mendes, W. B. (2007). Social facilitation. In R. Baumeister & K. Vohs (Eds.), *Encyclopedia of social psychology.* Thousand Oaks, CA: Sage.

Meneses, C. W., & Greenberg, L. S. (2011). The construction of a model of the process of couples' forgiveness in emotion-focused therapy for couples. *Journal of Marital and Family Therapy, 37* (4), 491–502.

Meng, M., Cherian, T., Singal, G., & Sinha, P. (2012). Lateralization of face processing in the human brain. *Proceedings: Biological Sciences, 279,* 2052–2061.

Menn, L., & Stoel-Gammon, C. (2009). Phonological development: Learning sounds and sound patterns. In J. Berko Gleason & N. Ratner (Eds.), *The development of language* (7th ed.). Boston: Allyn & Bacon.

Mercado, E., & Henderson, C. M. (2013). Neurally inspired models of psychological processes. In D. K. Freedheim & I. B. Weiner (Eds.), *Handbook of psychology, 2nd ed., Vol. 1.* (pp. 620–642). Hoboken, NJ: Wiley.

Mercer, C. H., Bailey, J. V., Johnson, A. M., Erens, B., Wellings, K., Fenton, K. A., & Copas, A. J. (2007). Women who report having sex with women: British national probability data on prevalence, sexual behaviors, and health outcomes. *American Journal of Public Health, 97,* 1126–1133.

Mercer, V. E. (2009). Stress management intervention. In W. T. O'Donohue & J. E. Fisher (Eds.), *General principles and empirically supported techniques of cognitive behavior therapy* (pp. 631–639). Hoboken, NJ: Wiley.

Meredith-Owen, W. (2011). Jung's shadow: Negation and naricissism of the self. *Journal of Analytical Psychology, 56,* 674–691.

Merkl, A., Heuser, I., & Bajbouj, M. (2009). Antidepressant electroconvulsive therapy: Mechanism of action, recent advances, and limitations. *Experimental Neurology, 219* (1), 20–26.

Mesquita, B. (2002). Emotions as dynamic cultural phenomena. In R. J. Davidson, K. R. Scherer, & H. H. Goldsmith (Eds.), *Handbook of affective sciences.* New York: Oxford University Press.

Messenger, J. C. (1971). Sex and repression in an Irish folk community. In D. S. Marshall & R. C. Suggs (Eds.), *Human sexual behavior.* New York: Basic.

Messer, S. B., & Abbass, A. A. (2010). Evidence-based psychodynamic therapy with personality disorders. In J. J. Magnavita (Ed.), *Evidence-based treatment of personality dysfunction: Principles, methods, and processes* (pp. 79–111). Washington, DC: American Psychological Association.

Meston, C. M., Seal, B. N., & Hamilton, L. D. (2008). Problems with arousal and orgasm in women. In D. L. Rowland & L. Incrocci (Eds.), *Handbook of sexual and gender identity disorders* (pp. 188–219). Hoboken, NJ: Wiley.

Metcalfe, J., & Mischel, W. (1999). A hot/cool system analysis of delay of gratification: Dynamics of will power. *Psychological Review, 106,* 3–19.

Mettler, F. A. (Ed.). (1952). *Psychosurgical problems.* Oxford: Blakiston.

Meyer, J. H. (2012). Neuroimaging markers of cellular function in major depressive disorder: Implications for therapeutics, personalized medicine, and prevention. *Clinical Pharmacology and Therapeutics, 91* (2), 201–214.

Meyer, J. P., Becker, T. E., & Vandenberghe, C. (2004). Employee commitment and motivation: A conceptual analysis and integrative model. *Journal of Applied Psychology, 89,* 991–1007.

Meyer, J. P., Stanley, D. J., Herscovitch, L., & Topolnytsky, L. (2002). Affective, continuance, and normative commitment to the organization: A meta-analysis of antecedents, correlates, and consequences. *Journal of Vocational Behavior, 61,* 20–52.

Meyer, K. (2011). Primary sensory cortices, top-down projections and conscious experience. *Progress in Neurobiology, 94,* 408–417.

Meyer, P. J., Meshul, C. K., & Phillips, T. J. (2009). Ethanol- and cocaine-induced locomotion are genetically related to increases in accumbal dopamine. *Genes, Brain, and Behavior, 8,* 346–355.

Meyer-Bahlburg, H. F. L. (1998). Gender assignment in intersexuality. *Journal of Psychology and Human Sexuality, 10,* 1–21.

Meyer-Bahlburg, H. F. L. (2005). Gender identity outcome in female-raised 46, XY persons with penile agenesis, cloacal exstrophy of the bladder, or penile ablation. *Archives of Sexual Behavior, 34,* 423–438.

Meyer-Bahlburg, H. F. L. (2010). From mental disorder to iatrogenic hypogonadism: Dilemmas in conceptualizing gender identity variants as psychiatric conditions. *Archives of Sexual Behavior, 39,* 461–476.

Meyer-Bahlburg, H. F. L, Dolezal, C., Baker, S. W., & New, M. I. (2008). Sexual orientation in women with classical or non-classical congenital adrenal hyperplasia as a function of degree of prenatal androgen excess. *Archives of Sexual Behavior, 37,* 85–99.

Miacic, B., & Goldberg, L. R. (2007). An analysis of a cross-cultural personality inventory: The IPIP big five factors markers in Croatia. *Journal of Personality Assessment, 88,* 168–177.

Michael, R. T., Gagnon, J. H., Laumann, E. O., & Kolata, G. (1994). *Sex in America.* Boston: Little, Brown.

Michalopoulou, P. G., Lewis, S. W., Wykes, T., Jaeger, J., & Kapur, S. (2013). Treating impaired cognition in schizophrenia: The case for combining cognitive-enhancing drugs with cognitive remediation. *European Neuropsychopharmacology.* doi: 10.1016/j.euroneuro.2013.03.012

Mickley, G. A., & others. (2013). Stimulation of the dorsal periaqueductal gray enhances spontaneous recovery of conditioned taste aversion. *Brain Research, 1493,* 27–39.

Middeldorp, C. M., de Geus, E. J. C., Beem, A. L., Lakenberg, N., Hottenga, J., Slagboom, P. E., & Boomsma, D. I. (2007). Family based association analyses between the serotonin transporter gene polymorphism (5-HTTLPR) and neuroticism, anxiety and depression. *Behavior Genetics, 37,* 294–301.

Middendorf, C. H., & Macan, T. H. (2002). Note-taking in the employment interview: Effects on recall and judgments *Journal of Applied Psychology, 87* (2), 293–303.

Migneault, J. P., Adams, T. B., & Read, J. P. (2005). Application of the transtheoretical model to substance abuse: Historical development and future directions. *Drug and Alcohol Review, 24,* 437–448.

Mikulincer, M., & Shaver, P. R. (2013a). Attachment theory expanded: A behavioral systems approach to personality. In K. Deaux & M. Snyder (Eds.), *The Oxford handbook of personality and social psychology.* New York: Oxford University Press.

Mikulincer, M., & Shaver, P. R. (2013b). Attachment-related contributions to the study of psychopathology. In P. Luyten & others (Eds.), *Handbook of contemporary psychodynamic approaches to psychopathology.* New York: Guilford.

Mikulincer, M., & Shaver, P. R. (2013c). The role of attachment security in adolescent and adult close relationships. In J. A. Simpson & L.

Campbell (Eds.), *The Oxford handbook of close relationships.* New York: Oxford University Press.

Mikulincer, M., Shaver, P. R., Bar-On, N., & Ein-Dor, T. (2010). The pushes and pulls of close relationships: Attachment insecurities and relational ambivalences. *Journal of Personality and Social Psychology, 98,* 450–468.

Milano, W., De Rosa, M., Milano, L., & Capasso, A. (2012). Night eating syndrome: An overview. *Journal of Pharmacy and Pharmacology, 64,* 2–10.

Milgram, S. (1965). Some conditions of obedience and disobedience to authority. *Human Relations, 18,* 56–76.

Milgram, S. (1974). *Obedience to authority.* New York: Harper & Row.

Millecamps, M., Seminowicz, D. A., Bushnell, M. C., & Coderre, T. J. (2013). The biopsychology of pain. In R. J. Nelson, S. J. Y. Mizumori, & I. B. Weiner (Eds.), *Handbook of psychology, 2nd ed., Vol. 3.* (pp. 240–271). Hoboken, NJ: Wiley.

Miller, A. B., Esposito-Smythers, C., Weismoore, J. T., & Renshaw, K.D. (2013). The relation between child maltreatment and adolescent suicidal behavior. *Clinical Child and Family Psychology Review.* (in press)

Miller, A. G. (2004). What can the Milgram obedience experiments tell us about the Holocaust? Generalizing from the social psychology laboratory. In A. G. Miller (Ed.), *The social psychology of good and evil* (pp. 193–239). New York: Guilford.

Miller, D. B., & O'Callaghan, J. P. (2006). The pharmacology of wakefulness. *Metabolism, 55,* Suppl. 2, S13–S19.

Miller, D. J., Vachon, D. D., & Lynam, D. R. (2009). Neuroticism, negative affect, and negative affect instability: Establishing convergent and discriminant validity using ecological momentary assessment. *Personality and Individual Differences, 47,* 873–877.

Miller, D. J., & others. (2012). Prolonged myelination in human neocortical evolution. *Proceedings of the National Academy of Sciences USA, 109,* 16480–16485.

Miller, G. (2011). ESP paper rekindles discussion about statistics. *Science, 331,* 272–273.

Miller, G., Chen, E., & Cole, S. W. (2009). Health psychology: Developing biologically plausible models linking the social world and physical health. *Annual Review of Psychology* (vol. 60). (pp. 501–524). Palo Alto, CA: Annual Reviews.

Miller, G. A. (1956). The magical number seven, plus or minus two: Some limits on our capacity for information processing. *Psychological Review, 48,* 337–442.

Miller, G. E., & Reynolds, W. M. (2013). Educational psychology: Contemporary perspectives. In W. M. Reynolds, G. F. Miller, & I. B. Weiner (Eds.), *Handbook of psychology* (2nd ed., vol. 7). Hoboken, NJ: Wiley.

Miller, J. (2013). Insights into moral development from cultural psychology. In M. Killen & J. G. Smetana (Eds.), *Handbook of moral development* (2nd ed.). New York: Routledge.

Miller, J. J., Fletcher, K., & Kabat-Zinn, J. (1995). Three-year follow-up and clinical implications of a mindfulness meditation-based stress reduction intervention in the treatment of anxiety disorders. *General Hospital Psychiatry, 17,* 192–200.

Miller, M. B., DeYoung, C. G., & McGue, M. (2012). Assumptions in studies of heritability and genotype-phenotype associations. *Behavioral and Brain Sciences, 35,* 372–373.

Miller, N. E. (1941). The frustration-aggression hypothesis. *Psychological Review, 48,* 337–442.

Miller, N. E. (1985). The value of behavioral research on animals. *American Psychologist, 40,* 432–440.

Miller, P. H. (2011). Piaget's theory: Past, present, and future. In U. Goswami (Ed.), *Wiley-Blackwell handbook of childhood cognitive development* (2nd ed.). New York: Wiley-Blackwell.

Miller, R., Perlman, D., & Brehm, S. S. (2009). *Intimate relationships* (5th ed.). New York: McGraw-Hill.

Miller, R. R., & Grace, R. C. (2013). Conditioning and learning. In A. F. Healy, R. W. Proctor, & I. B. Weiner (Eds.), *Handbook of psychology* (2nd ed., vol. 4). Hoboken, NJ: Wiley.

Miller, S. D., Hubble, M. A., Chow, D. L., & Seidel, J. A. (2013). The outcome of psychotherapy: Yesterday, today, and tomorrow. *Psychotherapy, 50,* 88–97.

Millet, B., & others. (2013). Obsessive compulsive disorder networks: Positron emission tomography and neuropsychology provide new insights. *PLoS One, 8* (1), e53241.

Miltenberger, R. G. (2012). *Behavior modification* (5th ed.). Boston: Cengage.

Mindell, J. A., Meltzer, L. J., Carskadon, M. A., & Chervin, R. D. (2009). Developmental aspects of sleep hygiene: Findings from the 2004 National Sleep in American Poll. *Sleep Medicine, 10,* 771–779.

Mineka, S. (2014). Behavioral models of anxiety disorders. *Annual Review of Clinical Psychology* (vol. 10). Palo Alto, CA: Annual Reviews.

Mineka, S., & Ohman, A. (2002). Phobias and preparedness: The selective, automatic, and encapsulated nature of fear. *Biological Psychiatry, 52,* 927–937.

Miner-Rubino, K., Twenge, J. M., & Fredrickson, B. L. (2002). Trait self-objectification in women: Affective and personality correlates. *Journal of Research in Personality, 36,* 147–172.

Miquez, G., Cham, H. X., & Miller, R. R. (2012). Spontaneous recovery and ABC renewal from retroactive cue interference. *Learning and Behavior, 40,* 42–53.

Mirilas, P., & others. (2010). Serum beta-endorphin response to stress before and after operation under fentanyl anesthesia in neonates, infants, and preschool children. *European Journal of Pediatric Surgery, 20* (2),106–110.

Mischel, W. (1968). *Personality and assessment.* New York: Wiley.

Mischel, W. (2004). Toward an integrative science of the person. *Annual Review of Psychology* (vol. 55). (pp. 1–22). Palo Alto, CA: Annual Reviews.

Mischel, W. (2009). From *Personality and Assessment* (1968) to personality science, 2009. *Journal of Research in Personality, 43,* 282–290.

Mischel, W., & Ayduk, O. (2011). Willpower in a cognitive-affective processing system: The dynamics of delay of gratification. In K. D. Vohs & R. F. Baumeister (Eds.), *Handbook of self-regulation* (2nd ed.). New York: Guilford.

Mischel, W., Cantor, N., & Feldman, S. (1996). Principles of self-regulation: The nature of will power and self-control. In E. T. Higgins & A. W. Kruglanski (Eds.), *Social psychology: Handbook of basic principles.* New York: Guilford.

Mischel, W., & Moore, B. S. (1980). The role of ideation in voluntary delay for symbolically presented rewards. *Cognitive Therapy and Research, 4,* 211–221.

Mischel, W., & Shoda, Y. (1999). Integrating dispositions and processing dynamics within a unified theory of personality: The cognitive-affective personality system. In L. A. Pervin & O. P. John (Eds.), *Handbook of personality: Theory and research* (2nd ed., pp. 197–218). New York: Guilford.

Mischel, W., & others. (2011). "Willpower" over the life span: Decomposing self-regulation. *Social Cognitive and Affective Neuroscience, 6,* 252–256.

Miserandino, M. (2012). *Personality psychology.* Upper Saddle River, NJ: Pearson.

Mistry, J., Contreras, M., & Dutta, R. (2013). Culture and child development. In R. M. Lerner, M. A. Easterbrooks, J. Mistry, & I. B. Weiner (Eds.), *Handbook of psychology, 2nd ed., Vol. 6.* (pp. 265–286). Hoboken, NJ: Wiley.

Mitchell, C. J., & others. (2010). Do reaction times in the Perruchet effect reflect variations in the strength of the associative link? *Journal of Experimental Psychology: Learning, Memory, and Cognition, 36,* 567–572.

Mitchell, K. E., Alliger, G. M., & Morfopoulos, R. (1997). Toward an ADA-appropriate job analysis. *Human Resource Management Review, 7,* 5–26.

Mitchell, M. B., & others. (2013). Cognitively stimulating activities: Effects on cognition across four studies with up to 21 years of longitudinal data. *Journal of Aging Research.* (in press)

Mitterauer, B. J. (2011). Possible role of glia in cognitive impairment in schizophrenia. *CNS Neuroscience and Therapeutics, 17,* 333–344.

Miyawaki, Y., Uchida, H., Yamashita, O., Sato, M., Morito, Y., Tanabe, C. T., Sadato, N., & Kamitani, Y. (2008). Visual image reconstruction from human brain activity using a combination of multiscale local image decoders. *Neuron, 60,* 915–929.

Mobbs, D., Greicius, M. D., Abdel-Azim, E., Menon, V., & Reiss, A. L. (2003). Humor modulates the mesolimbic reward centers. *Neuron, 40,* 1041–1048.

Mock, S., & Boerner, K. (2010). Sense making and benefit finding among patients with amyotrophic lateral sclerosis and their primary caregivers. *Journal of Health Psychology, 15,* 115–121.

Mock, S. E., & Eibach, R. P. (2011). Stability and change in sexual orientation identity over a 10-year period in adulthood. *Archives of Sexual Behavior.* doi: 10.1007/s10508-011-9761-1

Moffitt, T. E., & others. (2011). A gradient of childhood self-control predicts health, wealth, and public safety. *Proceedings of the National Academy of Sciences USA, 108,* 2693–2698.

Mohring, W., Libertus, M. E., & Bertin, E. (2012). Speed discrimination in 6- and 10-month-old infants follows Weber's law. *Journal of Experimental Child Psychology, 111,* 405–418.

Mojza, E. J., Lorenz, C., Sonnentag, S., & Binnewies, C. (2010). Daily recovery experiences: The role of volunteer work during leisure time. *Journal of Occupational Health Psychology, 15,* 60–74.

Mojzisch, A., & Schulz-Hardt, S. (2010). Knowing others' preferences degrades the quality of group decisions. *Journal of Personality and Social Psychology, 98,* 794–808.

Mokdad, A. H., Marks, J. S., Stroup, D. F., & Gerberding, J. L. (2004). Actual causes of death in the United States, 2000. *Journal of the American Medical Association, 291,* 1238–1245.

Molet, M., Miller, H. C., Laude, J. R., Kirk, C., Manning, B., & Zentall, T. R. (2012). Decision making by humans in a behavioral task: Do humans, like pigeons, show suboptimal choice? *Learning and Behavior, 40* (4), 439–447.

Molina, B., & Pelham, W. E. (2014). The attention deficit/hyperactivity disorder (ADHD) substance

use connection. *Annual Review of Clinical Psychology* (vol. 10). Palo Alto, CA: Annual Reviews.

Molloy, G. J., & others. (2012). Type D personality, self-efficacy, and medication adherence following an acute coronary syndrome. *Psychosomatic Medicine, 74,* 100–106.

Moncrieff, J., & Timimi, S. (2010). Is ADHD a valid diagnosis in adults? No. *British Medical Journal, 340,* 736–737.

Mondy, R. W. (2010). *Human resource management* (11th Ed.). Upper Saddle River, NJ: Prentice-Hall.

Monette, S., Bigras, M., & Guay, M. C. (2011). The role of executive functions in school achievement at the end of grade 1. *Journal of Experimental Child Psychology, 109,* 158–173.

Money, J., Hampson, J. G., & Hampson, J. L. (1955). Hermaphroditism: Recommendations concerning assignment of sex, change of sex, and psychological management. *Bulletin of Johns Hopkins Hospital, 97,* 284–300.

Money, J., Hampson, J. G., & Hampson, J. L. (1957). Imprinting and the establishment of gender role. *Archives of Neurology and Psychiatry, 77,* 333–336.

Money, J., & Tucker P. (1975). *Sexual signatures: On being a man or woman.* Boston: Little Brown.

Monk, T. H. (2012). Sleep and human performance. In C. M. Morin & C. A. Espie (Eds.), *The Oxford handbook of sleep and sleep disorders.* New York: Oxford University Press.

Montagna, P., Gambetti, P., Cortelli, P., & Lugaresi, E. (2003). Familial and sporadic fatal insomnia. *Lancet Neurology, 2,* 167–176.

Monteith, M. J., Woodcock, A., & Lybarger, J. E. (2013). Automaticity and control in stereotyping and prejudice: The revolutionary role of social cognition across three decades of research. In D. E. Carlston (Ed.), *The Oxford handbook of social cognition.* New York: Oxford University Press.

Moody, K. M., Schonberger, L. B., Maddox, R. A., Zuo, W., Cracco, L., & Cali, I. (2011). Sporadic fatal insomnia in a young woman: A diagnostic challenge: Case report. *BMC Neurology, 11,* 136–143.

Moore, A., Gruber, T., Derose, J., & Malinowski, P. (2012). Regular, brief mindfulness meditation practice improves electrophysiological markers of attentional control. *Frontiers in Human Neuroscience, 6,* ArtID 18.

Moore, D., & Barnard, T. (2012). With eloquence and humanity? Human factors/ergonomics in sustainable human development. *Human Factors, 54,* 940–951.

Moore, D. S. (2013). Behavioral genetics, genetics, and epigenetics. In P. D. Zelazo (Ed.), *The Oxford handbook of developmental psychology.* New York: Oxford University Press.

Moore, S. A., & Zoellner, L. A. (2012). The effects of expressive and experiential suppression on memory accuracy and memory distortion in women with and without PTSD. *Journal of Experimental Psychopathology, 3,* 368–392.

Moos, R. H. (1986). Work as a human context. In M. S. Pallack & R. Perloff (Eds.), *Psychology and work.* Washington, DC: American Psychological Association.

Moradi, B., & Huang, Y. (2008). Objectification theory and psychology of women: A decade of advances and future directions. *Psychology of Women Quarterly, 32,* 377–398.

Moran, B., & Walsh, T. (2013). Cardiovascular disease in women: How nurses can promote awareness and prevention. *Nursing for Women's Health, 17,* 63–68.

Moran, J. M., Wig, G. S., Adams, R. B., Jr., Janata, P., & Kelley, W. M. (2004). Neural correlates of humor detection and appreciation. *NeuroImage, 21,* 1055–1060.

Moreno, M. A., Jelenchick, L. A., Egan, K. G., Cox, E., Young, H., Gannon, K. E., & Becker, T. (2011). Feeling bad on Facebook: Depression disclosures by college students on a social networking site. *Depression and Anxiety, 28,* 447–455.

Morewedge, C. K., & Kahneman, D. (2010). Associative processes in intuitive judgment. *Trends in Cognitive Science, 14,* 435–440.

Morgan, C. D., & Murray, H. A. (1935). A method of investigating fantasies: The Thematic Apperception Test. *Archives of Neurology and Psychiatry, 34,* 289–306.

Morgan, H. (2012). "To paint the portrait of a bird": Analytic work from the perspective of a "developmental" Jungian. *Journal of Analytical Psychology, 57,* 40–56.

Morikawa, Y., & others. (2013). Aerobic interval exercise training in the afternoon reduces attacks of spastic angina in conjunction with improvement of endothelial function, oxidative stress, and inflammation. *Coronary Artery Disease, 24* (3), 177–182.

Moritsugu, J., Wong, F. Y., & Duffy, K. G. (2010). *Community psychology* (4th ed.). Boston: Allyn & Bacon.

Moritz, S., Alpers, G. W., Schilling, L., Jelinek, L., Brooks, A., Willenborg, B., & Nagel, M. (2011). Larger than life: Overestimation of object size is moderated by personal relevance in obsessive-compulsive disorder. *Journal of Behavior Therapy and Experimental Psychiatry, 42,* 481–487.

Morris, J. (2012). Interpersonal psychotherapy in child and adolescent mental health services. *Clinical Psychology and Psychotherapy, 19,* 141–149.

Morris, M. W., & Peng, K. (1994). Culture and cause: American and Chinese attributions for social and physical events. *Journal of Personality and Social Psychology, 67,* 949–971.

Morrison, A. S., & Heimberg, R. G. (2013). Social anxiety and social anxiety disorder. *Annual Review of Clinical Psychology* (vol. 9). Palo Alto, CA: Annual Reviews.

Morrison, F. J., Ponitz, C. C., & McClelland, M. M. (2010). Self-regulation and academic achievement in the transition to school. In S. D. Calkins & M. A. Bell (Eds.), *Child development at the intersection of emotion and cognition.* Washington, DC: American Psychological Association.

Morrison, G. S. (2012). *Early childhood education today* (12th ed.). Upper Saddle River, NJ: Merrill.

Morrow, R. L., Garland, E. J., Wright, J. M., Taylor, S., & Dormuth, C. R. (2012). Influence of relative age on diagnosis and treatment of attention-deficit/hyperactivity disorder in children. *Canadian Medical Association Journal, 184* (7) 755–762.

Mortimer, J. A., Ding, D., Borenstein, A. R., DeCarli, C., Guo, Q., Wu, Y., Zhao, Q., & Chu, S. (2012). Changes in brain volume and cognition in a randomized trial of exercise and social interaction in a community-based sample of non-demented Chinese elders. *Journal of Alzheimer's Disease, 30,* 757–766.

Mortimer, J. A., Snowdon, D. A., & Markesbery, W. R. (2009). The effect of APOE-epsilon4 on dementia is mediated by Alzheimer neuropathology. *Alzheimer Disease and Associated Disorders, 23,* 152–157.

Mortimer, J. A., & others. (2012). Changes in brain volume and cognition in a randomized trial of exercise and social interaction in a community-based sample of non-demented Chinese elders. *Journal of Alzheimer's Disease, 30,* 757–766.

Mortimer, J. T. (2012). The evolution, contributions, and prospects of the Youth Development Study: An investigation in life course social psychology. *Social Psychology Quarterly, 75,* 5–27.

Moscovici, S. (1985). Social influence and conformity. In G. Lindzey & E. Aronson (Eds.), *Handbook of social psychology* (3rd ed., vol. 2). New York: Random House.

Moses, T. (2010). Being treated differently: Stigma experiences with family, peers, and school staff among adolescents with mental health disorders. *Social Science Medicine, 70,* 985–993.

Mosher, C. E., & Danoff-Burg, S. (2008). Agentic and communal personality traits: Relations to disordered eating behavior, body shape concern, and depressive symptoms. *Eating Behaviors, 9,* 497–500.

Mosher, W. D., Chandra, A., & Jones, J. (2005). Sexual behavior and selected health measures: Men and women 15–44 years of age, United States, 2002. *Advance data from vital and health statistics, no. 362.* Hyattsville, MD: National Center for Health Statistics.

Moskowitz, D. S. (2010). Quarrelsomeness in daily life. *Journal of Personality, 78,* 39–66.

Moskowitz, J. T. (2003). Positive affect predicts lower risk of AIDS mortality. *Psychosomatic Medicine, 65,* 620–626.

Moss, C., Dhillo, W. S., Frost, G., & Hickson, M. (2012). Gastrointestinal hormones: The regulation of appetite and the anorexia of aging. *Journal of Human Nutrition and Dietetics, 25,* 3–15.

Moss, C. F., & Carr, C. E. (2013). Comparative audition. In R. J. Nelson, S. J. Y. Mizumori, & I. B. Weiner (Eds.), *Handbook of psychology, 2nd ed., Vol. 3.* (pp. 115–1564). Hoboken, NJ: Wiley.

Mostofsky, E., & others. (2012). Risk of acute myocardial infarction after the death of a significant person in one's life: The Determinants of Myocardial Infarction Onset Study. *Circulation, 125,* 3–15.

Motowidlo, S. J., & Kell, H. J. (2013). Job performance. In N. W. Schmitt, S. Highhouse, & I. B. Weiner (Eds.), *Handbook of psychology, 2nd ed., Vol. 12.* (pp. 82–103). Hoboken, NJ: Wiley.

Moustafa, A. A., Gilbertson, M. W., Orr, S. P., Herzallah, M. M., Servatius, R. J., & Myers, C. E. (2013). A model of amygdala–hippocampal–prefrontal interaction in fear conditioning and extinction in animals. *Brain and Cognition, 81,* 29–43.

Moyer, M. W. (2013). The myth of antioxidants. *Scientific American, 308,* 62–67.

Mroczek, B., Kurpas, D., Gronowska, M., Kotwas, A., & Karakiewicz, B. (2013). Psychosexual needs and sexual behaviors of nursing care home residents. *Archives of Gerontology and Geriatrics, 57* (1), 32–38.

Mroczek, D. K., & Spiro, A. (2005). Change in life satisfaction during adulthood: Findings from the Veterans Affairs Normative Aging Study. *Journal of Personality and Social Psychology, 88,* 189–202.

Mueller, D. L. (2010). Mechanisms maintaining peripheral tolerance. *Nature Immunology, 11,* 21–27.

Mulder, R. T. (2012). Cultural aspects of personality disorder. In T. Widiger (Ed.), *The Oxford handbook of personality disorders.* New York: Oxford University Press.

Mullis, I. V. S., Marting, M. O., Gonzales, E. J., & Kennedy, A. M. (2003). *PIRLS 2001 International Report: IEA's study of reading literacy achievement in primary schools.* Chestnut Hill, MA: Boston College.

Mumford, M. D., Scott, G., & Hunter, S. T. (2006). Theory—charismatic, ideological, and pragmatic leaders: How do they lead, why do they lead, and who do they lead? In M. D. Mumford (Ed.), *Pathways to outstanding leadership.* Mahwah, NJ: Erlbaum.

Munafo, M. R., Yalcin, B., Willis-Owen, S. A., & Flint, J. (2008). Association of the dopamine D4 receptor (DRD4) gene and approach-related personality traits: Meta-analysis and new data. *Biological Psychiatry, 63,* 197–206.

Muris, P., & Merckelbach, H. (2012). Specific phobia: Phenomenology, epidemiology, and etiology. In T. E. Davis, T. H. Ollendick, & L.-G. Öst (Eds.), *Intensive one-session treatment of specific phobias.* New York: Springer.

Muris, P., Meesters, C., & Timmermans, A. (2013). Some youths have a gloomy side: Correlates of the dark triad personality traits in non-clinical adolescents. *Child Psychiatry and Human Development.* (in press)

Murphy, B. S., Xu, J., & Kochanek, K. D. (2012). Deaths: Preliminary data for 2010. *National Vital Statistics Reports, 60* (4), 1–8.

Murphy, D. L., Moya, P. R., Fox, M. A., Rubenstein, L. M., Wendland, J. R., & Timpano, K. R. (2013). Anxiety and affective disorder comorbidity related to serotonin and other neurotransmitter systems: Obsessive-compulsive disorder as an example of overlapping clinical and genetic heterogeneity. *Philosophical Transactions of the Royal Society of London. Series B, Biological Sciences, 368* (1615), 20120435.

Murphy, M. L., Miller, G. E., & Wrosch, C. (2013). Conscientiousness and stress exposure and reactivity: A prospective study of adolescent females. *Journal of Behavioral Medicine, 36* (2), 153–164.

Murray, D. R., & Schaller, M. (2010). Historical prevalence of disease within 230 geopolitical regions: A tool for investigating origins of culture. *Journal of Cross-Cultural Psychology, 41,* 99–108.

Murray, D. R., Trudeau, R., & Schaller, M. (2011). On the origins of cultural differences in conformity: Four tests of the pathogen prevalence hypothesis. *Personality and Social Psychology Bulletin, 37,* 318–329.

Murray, M. (2013, April 11). NBC/WSJ poll: 53 percent support gay marriage. *NBC News.* http://firstread.nbcnews.com/_news/2013/04/11/17708688-nbcwsj-poll-53-percent-support-gay-marriage (accessed May 8, 2013)

Murray-Swank, A. B., Lucksted, A., Medoff, D. R., Yang, Y., Wohlheiter, K., & Dixon, L. B. (2006). Religiosity, psychosocial adjustment, and subjective burden of persons who care for those with mental illness. *Psychiatric Services, 57,* 361–365.

Mwendwa, D. T., Ali, M. K., Sims, R. C., Madhere, S., Levy, S. A., Callender, C. O., & Campbell, A. L. (2013). Psychometric properties of the Cook Medley Hostility Scale and its association with inflammatory markers in African Americans. *Psychology, Health, and Medicine.* (in press)

Myatchin, I., & Lagae, L. (2013). Developmental changes in visuo-spatial working memory in normally developing children: Event-related potentials study. *Brain Development.* (in press)

Myers, N. L. (2010). Culture, stress, and recovery form schizophrenia: Lessons from the field for global mlental health. *Culture, Medicine, and Psychiatry, 34,* 500–528.

N

Naar-King, S., Wright, K., Parsons, J. T., Frey, M., Templin, T., & Ondersma, S. (2006). Transtheoretical model and condom use in HIV-positive youths. *Health Psychology, 25,* 648–652.

Naeem, F., Gobbi, M., Ayub, M., & Kingdon, D. (2009). University students' views about compatibility of cognitive behaviour therapy (CBT) with their personal, social, and religious values (a study from Pakistan). *Mental Health, Religion, and Culture, 12* (8), 847–855.

Nagase, Y., & others. (2009). Coping strategies and their correlates with depression in the Japanese general population. *Psychiatry Research, 168,* 57–66.

Naismith, S. L., Lewis, S. J., & Rogers, N. L. (2011). Sleep-wake changes and cognition in neurogenerative diseases. *Progress in Brain Research, 190,* 21–52.

Nakamura, T. J., Nakamura, W., Yamazaki, S., Kudo, T., Cutler, T., Colwell, C. S., & Block, G. D. (2011). Age-related decline in circadian output. *Journal of Neuroscience, 30,* 10201–10205.

Nanda, S. (2008). Cross-cultural issues. In D. L. Rowland & L. Incrocci (Eds.), *Handbook of sexual and gender identity disorders* (pp. 457–485). Hoboken, NJ: Wiley.

Narayanan, J., & others. (2012). Accelerated long-term forgetting in temporal lobe epilepsy: Verbal, nonverbal, and autobiographical memory. *Epilepsy and Behavior, 22,* 622–630.

Narvaez, D. (2013). Integrative moral education. In M. Killen & J. G. Smetana (Eds.), *Handbook of moral development* (2nd ed.). New York: Routledge.

Narvaez, D., Panksepp, J., Schore, A. N., & Gleason, T. R. (Eds.). (2013). *Evolution, early experience, and human development: From research to practice and policy.* New York: Oxford University Press.

Nash, M. R. (2001). The truth and the hype about hypnosis. *Scientific American, 285,* 46–49, 52–55.

Nasser, J. (2013) Empirically supported treatments and efficacy trials: What steps do we still need to take? *Journal of Contemporary Psychotherapy.* doi: 10.1007/s10879-013-9236-x

Nassi, J. J., & Callaway, E. M. (2009). Parallel processing strategies of the primate visual system *Nature Review Neuroscience, 10,* 360–372.

Nath, A. (2010). Human immunodeficiency virus-associated neurocognitive disorder: Pathophysiology in relation to drug addiction. *Annals of the New York Academy of Sciences, 1187,* 122–128.

National Center for Health Statistics. (2005). *Early release of selected estimates from Jan–Mar 2005 National Health Interview Survey.* Washington, DC: Author.

National Center for PTSD. (2013). Gateway to post traumatic stress disorder information. *PTSD Info.* www.ptsdinfo.org/ (accessed May 24, 2013)

National Highway Traffic Safety Administration (NHTSA). (2007, December). *Traffic safety facts: Crash stats.* Washington, DC: NHTSA's Center for Statistics and Analysis.

National Human Genome Research Institute. (2012). Genome-wide association studies. *Genome.* www.genome.gov/12011238 (accessed February 15, 2013)

National Institute on Drug Abuse (NIDA). (2009a). *Research report series—MDMA (Ecstasy) abuse.* Bethesda, MD: Author.

National Institute on Drug Abuse (NIDA). (2009b). *NIDA infofacts: Marijuana.* Bethesda, MD: Author.

National Institute of Mental Health (NIMH). (2008). The numbers count: Mental disorders in America. *NIMH.* www.nimh.nih.gov/health/publications/the-numbers-count-mental-disorders-in-america/index.shtml (accessed May 24, 2013)

National Institute of Mental Health (NIMH). (2010). Suicide in the United States: Statistics and prevention. *NIMH.* www.nimh.nih.gov/health/publications/suicide-in-the-us-statistics-and-prevention/index.shtml (accessed May 30, 2013)

National Institute of Mental Health (NIMH). (2011). *Eating disorders. NIMH.* www.nimh.nih.gov/health/publications/eating-disorders/index.shtml (accessed May 30, 2013)

National Sleep Foundation. (2007, March 6). *Stressed-out American women have no time for sleep.* Washington DC: Author.

Naumann, L. P., Vazire, S., Rentfrow, P. J., & Gosling, S. D. (2009). Personality judgments based on physical appearance. *Personality and Social Psychology Bulletin, 35,* 1661–1671.

Naumova, E., & others. (2013). 16(th) IHIW: Immunogenetics of aging. *International Journal of Immunogenetics, 40,* 77–81.

Nauta, M. H., & others. (2012). Preventing mood and anxiety disorders in youth: A multi-centre RCT in the high risk offspring of depressed and anxious patients. *BMC Psychiatry, 12,* 31.

Navidian, A., & Bahari, F. (2013). The impact of mixed, hope, and forgiveness-focused marital counseling on interpersonal cognitive distortions of couples filing for divorce. *Journal of Psychiatric and Mental Health Nursing.* (in press)

Needham, A., Barrett, T., & Peterman, K. (2002). A pick-me-up for infants' exploratory skills: Early simulated experiences reaching for objects using "sticky mittens" enhances young infants' object exploration skills. *Infant Behavior and Development, 25,* 279–295.

Neely, M. N., Walter, E., Black, J. M., & Reiss, A. L. (2012). Neural correlates of humor detection and appreciation in children. *Journal of Neuroscience, 32,* 1784–1790.

Negriff, S., Susman, E. J., & Trickett, P. K. (2011). The development pathway from pubertal timing to delinquency and sexual activity from early to late adolescence. *Journal of Youth and Adolescence, 40* (10), 1343–1356.

Neikrug, A. B., & Ancoli-Israel, S. (2010). Sleep disorders in the older adult: A mini-review. *Gerontology, 56,* 181–189.

Neisser, U., Boodoo, G., Bouchard, T. J., Boykin, A. W., Brody, N., Ceci, S. J., Halpern, D. F., Loehlin, J. C., Perloff, R., Sternberg, R. J., & Urbina, S. (1996). Intelligence: Knowns & unknowns. *American Psychologist, 51,* 77–101.

Nelson, C. A. (2012). Brain development and behavior. In A. M. Rudolph, C. Rudolf, G. Lister, L. First, & A. A. Gershon (Eds.), *Rudolph's pediatrics* (22nd ed.). New York: McGraw-Hill.

Nelson, D. L., & Quick, J. C. (2011). *ORGB 2* (2nd ed.). Boston: Cengage.

Nelson, S. K., Kushlev, K., English, T., Dunn, E. W., & Lyubomirsky, S. (2013). In defense of parenthood: Children are associated with more joy than misery. *Psychological Science, 24,* 3–10.

Nestler, S., Blank, H., & Egloff, B. (2010). Hindsight ≠ hindsight: Experimentally induced dissociations between hindsight components. *Journal of Experimental Psychology: Learning, Memory, and Cognition, 36,* 1399–1413.

Nett, E. J., & others. (2012). Four-dimensional phase contrast MRI with accelerated dual velocity coding. *Journal of Magnetic Resonance Imaging, 35* (6), 1462–1471.

Neufeld, J., & others. (2012). The neural correlates of colored music: A functional MRI investigation of auditory-visual synesthesia. *Neuropsychologia, 50,* 85–89.

Neukrug, E. S., & Fawcett, R. C. (2010). *Essentials of testing and assessment* (2nd ed.). Boston: Cengage.

Neumann, I. D., & Landgraf, R. (2012). Balance of brain oxytocin and vasopressin: Implications for anxiety, depression, and social behaviors. *Trends in Neuroscience, 35,* 649–659.

Neumann, I. D., Veenema, A. H., & Beiderbeck, D. I. (2010). Aggression and anxiety: Social context and neurobiological links. *Frontiers in Behavioral Neuroscience.* doi: 10.3389/fnbeh.2010.00012

Neville, H. J. (2006). Different profiles of plasticity within human cognition. In Y. Munakata & M. H. Johnson (Eds.), *Attention and performance.* Oxford, U.K.: Oxford University Press.

Nevo, E., & Breznitz, Z. (2013). The development of working memory from kindergarten to first grade in children with different decoding skills. *Journal of Experimental Child Psychology, 114,* 217–228.

Nevsimalova, S. (2009). Narcolepsy in childhood. *Sleep Medicine Reviews, 13,* 169–180.

Newcombe, N. S. (2002). The nativist-empiricist controversy. *Psychological Science, 13,* 395–401.

Newport, F. (2011, May 20). For first time, majority of Americans favor legal gay marriage. *Gallup Politics.* www.gallup.com/poll/147662/first-time-majority-americans-favor-legal-gay-marriage.aspx (accessed May 8, 2013)

Newport, F. (2012, December 31). Hillary Clinton, Barack Obama most admired in 2012. *Gallup Politics.* www.gallup.com/poll/159587/hillary-clinton-barack-obama-admired-2012.aspx (accessed February 20, 2013)

Nezu, A. M., Nezu, C. M., Felgoise, S. H., & Greenberg, L. M. (2013). Psychological oncology. In A. M. Nezu, C. Maguth Nezu, P. A. Geller, & I. B. Weiner (Eds.), *Handbook of psychology, 2nd ed., Vol. 9.* (pp. 271–291). Hoboken, NJ: Wiley.

Niccolai, V., Wascher, E., & Stoerig, P. (2012). Distinct neural processes in grapheme-colour synaesthetes and semantic controls. *European Journal of Neuroscience, 36,* 3593–3601.

Nicholson, C. (2008). In the news: Scanning sexuality. *Nature Reviews: Neuroscience, 9,* 582.

Nickerson, R. S., & Adams, M. J. (1979). Long-term memory for a common object. *Cognitive Psychology, 11,* 287–307.

Nicolle, A., Symmonds, M., & Dolan, R. J. (2011). Optimistic biases in observational learning of value. *Cognition, 119,* 394–402.

Nielsen, J., & others. (2012). Geographical and temporal variations in clozapine prescription for schizophrenia. *European Neuropsychopharmacology, 22* (11), 818–824.

Nielsen, M. B., & Einarsen, S. (2012). Prospective relationships between workplace sexual harassment and psychological distress. *Occupational Medicine, 62* (3), 226–228.

Nijstad, B. (2009). *Group performance.* New York: Psychology Press.

Nilsson, H., Juslin, P., & Olsson, H. (2008). Exemplars in the mist: The cognitive substrate of the representativeness heuristic. *Scandinavian Journal of Psychology, 49,* 201–212.

Ni Mhaolain, A. M., & others. (2012). Subjective well-being amongst community-dwelling elders: What determines satisfaction with life? Findings from the Dublin Healthy Aging Study. *International Psychogeriatrics, 24,* 316–323.

Ninnemann, K. M. (2012). Variability in the efficacy of psychopharmaceuticals: Contributions from pharmacogenomics, ethnopsychopharmacology, and psychological and psychiatric anthropologies. *Culture, Medicine, and Psychiatry, 36,* 10–25.

Nisbet, E. K., Zelenski, J. M., & Murphy, S. (2011). Happiness is in our nature: Exploring nature relatedness as a contributor to subjective well-being. *Journal of Happiness Studies, 12,* 303–322.

Nisbet, R. E. (1987). Lay trait theory: Its nature, origins, and utility. In N. E. Grunberg, R. E. Nisbett, J. Rodin, & J. E. Singer (Eds.), *A distinctive approach to psychological research: The influence of Stanley Schachter.* Hillsdale, NJ: Erlbaum.

Nisbett, R. E. (2009). *Intelligence and how to get it: Why schools and cultures count.* New York: Norton.

Nisbett, R. E., Aronson, J., Blair, C., Dickens, W., Flynn, J., Halpern, D. F., & Turkheimer, E. (2012). Intelligence: New findings and theoretical developments. *American Psychologist, 67,* 130–159.

Nisbett, R. E., & Ross, L. (1980). *Human inference.* Upper Saddle River, NJ: Prentice-Hall.

Nishida, A., Miyaoka, T., Inagaki, T., & Horiguchi, J. (2009). New approaches to antidepressant drug design: Cytokine-regulated pathways. *Current Pharmaceutical Design, 15,* 1683–1687.

Nkomo, S. M., Fottler, M. D., & McAfee, R. B. (2011). *Human resource management applications* (7th ed.). Boston: Cengage.

Noe, R. A., Hollenbeck, J. R., Gerhart, B., & Wright, P. M. (2007). *Fundamentals of human resource management* (2nd ed.). New York: McGraw-Hill.

Noel, N. E., Maisto, S. A., Johnson, J. D., & Jackson, L. A. (2009). The effects of alcohol and cue salience on young men's acceptance of sexual aggression. *Addictive Behaviors, 34,* 386–394.

Nolen-Hoeksema, S. (2011). *Abnormal psychology* (5th ed.). New York: McGraw-Hill.

Norcross, J. C., Campbell, L. M., Grohol, J. M., Santrock, J. W., Selagea, F., & Sommer, R. (2013). *Self-help that works: Evidence-based resources for the public and professionals* (4th ed.). New York: Oxford University Press.

Norcross, J. C., Loberg, K., & Norcross, J. (2012). *Changeology: 5 steps to realizing your goals and resolutions.* New York: Simon & Schuster.

Norcross, J. C., Mrykalo, M. S., & Blagys, M. D. (2002). Auld lang syne: Success predictors, change processes, and self-reported outcomes of New Year's resolvers and nonresolvers. *Journal of Clinical Psychology, 58,* 397–405.

Nordgren, L. F., & Dijksterhuis, A. P. (2009). The devil is in the deliberation: Thinking too much reduces preference consistency. *Journal of Consumer Research, 36,* 39–46.

Nordstrom, B. R., & others. (2011). Neurocriminology. *Advances in Genetics, 75,* 255–283.

Norman, G. J., Devries, A. C., Cacioppo, J. T., & Bernsten, G. G. (2010). Multilevel analyses of stress. In J. Contrada & A. Baum (Eds.), *Handbook of stress science.* New York: Springer.

Norman, W. T. (1963). Toward an adequate taxonomy of personality attributes. *Journal of Abnormal and Social Psychology, 66,* 574–583.

North, M. S., & Fiske, S. T. (2012). History of social cognition. In A. W. Kruglanski & W. Stroebe (Eds.), *Handbook of the history of social psychology.* New York: Psychology Press.

Northoff, G. (2013). What the brain's intrinsic activity can tell us about consciousness: A tridimensional view. *Neuroscience and Biobehavioral Reviews.* (in press)

Nosek, B. A., & Banaji, M. R. (2007). Implicit attitude. In P. Wilken, T. Bayne, & A. Cleeremans

(Eds.), *The Oxford companion to consciousness.* Oxford: Oxford University Press.

Nosko, A., Tieu, T.-T., Lawford, H., & Pratt, M. W. (2011). How do I love thee? Let me count the ways: Parenting during adolescence, attachment styles, and romantic narratives in emerging adulthood. *Developmental Psychology, 47* (3), 645–657.

Notman, M. T., & Nadelson, C. C. (2002). Women's issues. In M. Hersen & W. H. Sledge (Eds.), *Encyclopedia of psychotherapy.* San Diego: Academic.

Nowak, M. A., Page, K. M., & Sigmund, K. (2000). Fairness versus reason in the ultimatum game. *Science, 289,* 1773–1775.

Nowotny, M., & Gummer, A. W. (2011). Vibration responses of the organ of Corti and the tectorial membrane to electrical stimulation. *Journal of the Acoustical Society of America, 130,* 3852.

Nozaki, T., & others. (2013). Effect of subthalamic nucleus stimulation during exercise on the mesolimbocortical dopaminergic region in Parkinson's disease: A positron emission topography study. *Journal of Cerebral Blood Flow and Metabolism.* (in press)

Nucci, L. (2013). Education for moral development. In M. Killen & J. G. Smetana (Eds.), *Handbook of moral development* (2nd ed.). New York: Routledge.

Nunez, P. L. (2012). Nested hierarchy, small worlds, brain complexity, and emergence. *Physics of Life Reviews, 9* (1), 45–46.

Nyberg, L. (2004, August). *Imaging cognition.* Paper presented at the 28th International Congress of Psychology, Beijing, China.

Nystul, M. S. (1999). *Introduction to counseling.* Boston: Allyn & Bacon.

O

Oakley, D. A., & Halligan, P. W. (2011). Using hypnosis to gain insights into healthy and pathological cognitive functioning. *Consciousness and Cognition, 20,* 328–331.

O'Barr, W. M. (2006). Multiculturalism in the marketplace: Targeting Latinas, African American women, and gay consumers. *Advertising and Society Review.* http://muse.jhu.edu/journals/advertising_and_society_review/v007/7.4unit11.html (accessed May 9, 2013)

Obler, L. K. (2009). Development in the adult years. In J. Berko Gleason & N. Ratner (Eds.), *The development of language* (7th ed.). Boston: Allyn & Bacon.

O'Brien, E. J., Bartoletti, M., & Leitzel, J. D. (2013). Self-esteem psychopathology, and psychotherapy. In M. H. Kernis (Ed.), *Self-esteem issues and answers.* New York: Psychology Press.

Occupational Safety and Health Administration (OSHA). (2002). www.osha.gov/pls/oshaweb/owadisp.show_document?p_id=3359&p_table=OSHACT (accessed June 4, 2013)

O'Connor, D. B., Conner, M., Jones, F., McMillan, B., & Ferguson, E. (2009). Exploring the benefits of conscientiousness: An investigation of the role of daily stressors and health behaviors. *Annals of Behavioral Medicine, 37,* 184–196.

O'Connor, T. G., Bergman, K., Sarkar, P., & Glover, V. (2013). Prenatal cortisol exposure predicts infant cortisol response to acute stress. *Developmental Psychobiology, 55* (2), 145–155.

O'Dell, K. R., Masters, K. S., Spielmans, G. I., & Maisto, S. A. (2011). Does Type-D personality predict outcomes among patients with

cardiovascular disease? A meta-analytic review. *Journal of Psychosomatic Research, 71,* 199–206.

O'Donovan, A., Lin, J., Tillie, J., Wolkowitz, O. M., Blackburn, E. H., & Epel, E. S. (2009). Pessimism correlates with leukocyte telomere shortness and elevated interleukin-6 in post-menopausal women. *Brain, Behavior, Immunology, 23* (4), 446–449.

O'Donovan, A., Tomiyama, A. J., Lin, J., Puterman, E., Adler, N. E., Kemeny, M., Wolkowitz, O. M., Blackburn, E. H., & Epel, E. S. (2012). Stress appraisals and cellular aging: A key role for anticipatory threat in the relationship between psychological stress and telomere length. *Brain, Behavior, and Immunity, 26,* 573–579.

O'Driscoll, M. P. (2013). Coping with stress: A challenge for theory, research, and practice. *Stress and Health, 29,* 89–90.

OECD. (2010). *Obesity and the economics of prevention—Fit or fat.* Paris: Author.

Ogden, C. L., & Carroll, M. D. (2010). Prevalence of overweight, obesity, and extreme obesity among adults: United States, trends 1960–1962 through 2007–2008. *NCHS Health E-Stat.* www.cdc.gov/nchs/data/hestat/obesity_adult_07_08/obesity_adult_07_08.pdf (accessed June 19, 2013)

Ogden, C. L., Carroll, M. D., Kit, B. K., & Flegal, K. M. (2012). Prevalence of obesity in the United States, 2009–2010. *NCHS Data Brief* (no. 82). www.cdc.gov/nchs/data/databriefs/db82.pdf (accessed June 19, 2013)

Ogden, L. G., Stroebele, N., Wyatt, H. R., Catenacci, V. A., Peters, J. C., Stuht, J., Wing, R. R., & Hill, J. O. (2012). Cluster analysis of the National Weight Control Registry to identify distinct subgroups maintaining successful weight loss. *Obesity, 20,* 2039–2047.

Ogilvie, R. D., & Wilkinson, R. T. (1988). Behavioral versus EEG-based monitoring of all-night sleep/wake patterns. *Sleep, 11* (2), 139–155.

Ogle, L., Sen, A., Pahlke, E., Jocelyn, L., Kostberg, D., Roey, S., & Williams, T. (2003). *International comparisons in fourth grade reading literacy: Finding from the Progress in International Literacy Study (PIRLS) of 2001.* (NCES 2003-073). Washington, DC: U.S. Government Printing Office.

Ohman, A., & Mineka, S. (2001). Fears, phobias, and preparedness: Toward an evolved module of fear and fear learning. *Psychological Review, 108,* 483–522.

Ohman, A., & Mineka, S. (2003). The malicious serpent: Snakes as a prototypical stimulus for an evolved module of fear. *Current Directions in Psychological Science, 12,* 5–9.

Ohman, A., & Soares, J. J. P. (1998). Emotional conditioning to masked stimuli: Expectancies for aversive outcomes following nonrecognized fear-relevant stimuli. *Journal of Experimental Psychology, 127,* 69–82.

Olatunji, B. O., Davis, M. L., Powers, M. B., & Smits, J. A. J. (2012). Cognitive-behavioral therapy for obsessive-compulsive disorder: A meta-analysis of treatment outcome and moderators. *Journal of Psychiatric Research, 47,* 33–41.

Olbrich, D., & Dittmer, M. (2011). Older poor-sleeping women display a smaller evening increase in melatonin secretion and lower values of melatonin and core body temperature than good sleepers. *Chronobiology Internatlional, 26,* 681–689.

Olds, J. M. (1958). Self-stimulation experiments and differential reward systems. In H. H. Jasper, L. D. Proctor, R. S. Knighton, W. C. Noshay, & R. T. Costello (Eds.), *Reticular formation of the brain.* Boston: Little, Brown.

Olds, J. M., & Milner, P. M. (1954). Positive reinforcement produced by electrical stimulation of the septal area and other areas of the rat brain. *Journal of Comparative and Physiological Psychology, 47,* 419–427.

O'Leary, E. (Ed.). (2013). *Gestalt therapy around the world.* New York: Wiley.

Olfson, M., & Marcus, S. C. (2009). National patterns in antidepressant medication treatment. *Archives of General Psychiatry, 66,* 848–856.

Oliver, P. L., & others. (2012). Disrupted circadian rhythms in a mouse model of schizophrenia. *Current Biology, 22* (4), 314–319.

Oliveras, A., & Schmieder, R. E. (2013). Clinical situations associated with difficult-to-control hypertension. *Journal of Hypertension, 31,* Suppl. 1, S3–S8.

Olness, K., & Ader, R. (1992). Conditioning as an adjunct in the pharmacotherapy of lupus erythematosus. *Journal of Developmental and Behavioral Pediatrics, 13,* 124–125.

Olson, M. H., & Hergenhahn, B. R. (2013). *Introduction to theories of learning* (9th ed.). Upper Saddle River, NJ: Pearson.

Olszewski-Kubilius, P., & Thomson, D. (2013). Gifted education programs and procedures. In W. M. Reynolds, G. F. Miller, & I. B. Weiner (Eds.), *Handbook of psychology, 2nd ed., Vol. 7.* (pp. 389–410). Hoboken, NJ: Wiley.

Omoto, A. M., & Snyder, M. (1995). Sustained helping without obligation: Motivation, longevity of service, and perceived attitude change among AIDS volunteers. *Journal of Personality and Social Psychology, 68,* 671–686.

"100 best companies to work for." (2013). *Fortune.* http://money.cnn.com/magazines/fortune/best-companies/2013/snapshots/1.html?iid=bc_lp_arrow1 (accessed May 31, 2013)

Ones, D. S., Viswesvaran, C., & Dilchert, S. (2005). Cognitive ability in personnel selection decisions. In A. Evers, N. Anderson, & O. Voskuijl (Eds.), *The Blackwell handbook of personnel selection* (pp. 255–275). Malden, MA: Blackwell.

Ophir, E., Nass, C., & Wagner, A. D. (2009). Cognitive control in media multitaskers. *Proceedings of the National Academy of Sciences USA, 106,* 15583–15587.

Oral, E., Aydin, N., Gulec, M., & Oral, M. (2012). Panic disorder and subthreshold panic in the light of comorbidity: A follow-up study. *Comprehensive Psychiatry, 53* (7), 988–594.

Orduña, V., García, A., & Hong, E. (2010). Choice behavior in spontaneously hypertensive rats: Variable vs. fixed schedules of reinforcement. *Behavioural Processes, 84* (1), 465–469.

Organ, D. W., Podsakoff, P. M., & Podsakoff, N. P. (2010). Expanding the criterion domain to include organizational citizenship behavior: Implications for employee selection. In S. Zedeck (Ed.), *APA handbook of industrial and organizational psychology.* Washington, DC: American Psychological Association.

Organ, D. W., & Ryan, K. (1995). A meta-analytic review of attitudinal and dispositional predictors of organizational citizenship behavior. *Personnel Psychology, 48,* 775–802.

O'Roak, B. J., & others. (2012). Sporadic autism exomes reveal a highly interconnected protein network of *de novo* mutations. *Nature, 485,* 246–250.

Ortega-Castro, N., & Vadillo, M. A. (2013). Retrieval-induced forgetting and interference between cues: Training a cue-outcome association attenuates retrieval by alternative cues. *Behavioural Processes, 94,* 19–25.

Osterman, L. L., & Brown, R. P. (2011). Culture of honor and violence against the self. *Personality and Social Psychology Bulletin, 37*, 1611–1623.

Osthus, I. B., & others. (2012). Telomere length and long-term endurance exercise: Does exercise affect biological age? A pilot study. *PLoS One, 7* (12), e52769.

Ostir, G. V., Markides, K. S., Black, S. A., & Goodwin, J. S. (2000). Emotional well-being predicts subsequent functional independence and survival. *Journal of the American Geriatrics Society, 48*, 473–478.

Ostroff, C., Kinicki, A. J., & Muhammad, R. S. (2013). Organizational culture and climate. In N. W. Schmitt, S. Highhouse, & I. B. Weiner (Eds.), *Handbook of psychology, 2nd ed., Vol. 12.* (pp. 643–676). Hoboken, NJ: Wiley.

Otonari, J., & others. (2012). Neuroticism and extraversion personality traits, health behaviors, and subjective well-being: The Fukuoka Study (Japan). *Quality of Life Research, 21* (10), 1847–1855.

Owens, J. A., Belon, K., & Moss, P. (2010). Impact of delaying school start time on adolescent sleep, mood, and behavior. *Archives of Pediatric and Adolescent Medicine, 164*, 608–614.

Oyserman, D., Elmore, K., & Smith, G. (2012). Self, self-concept, and identity. In M. R. Leary & J. P. Tangney (Eds.), *Handbook of self and identity* (2nd ed., pp. 69–104). New York: Guilford.

Oyserman, D., Kemmelmeier, M., Fryberg, S., Brosh, H., & Hart-Johnson, T. (2003). Racial-ethnic self-schemas. *Social Psychology Quarterly, 66*, 333–347.

Ozer, D. J., & Benet-Martinez, V. (2006). Personality and the prediction of consequential outcomes. *Annual Review of Psychology* (vol. 57). (pp. 401–421). Palo Alto, CA: Annual Reviews.

Oztop, E., Kawato, M., & Arbib, M. A. (2013). Mirror neurons: Functions, mechanisms, and models. *Neuroscience Letters.* (in press)

P

Packer, D. J. (2008). Identifying systematic disobedience in Milgram's obedience experiments: A meta-analytic review. *Perspectives on Psychological Science, 3*, 301–304.

Packer, D. J. (2009). Avoiding groupthink: Whereas weakly identified members stay silent, strongly identified members dissent about collective matters. *Psychological Science, 20*, 546–548.

Pagano, M. E., White, W. L., Kelly, J. F., Stout, R. L., & Tonigan, J. S. (2013). The 10-year course of Alcoholics Anonymous participation and long-term outcomes: A follow-up study of outpatient subjects in Project MATCH. *Substance Abuse, 34*, 51–59.

Page, S. (2012, December 5). Poll: Attitudes toward gays changing fast. *USA Today.* www.usatoday.com/story/news/politics/2012/12/05/poll-from-gay-marriage-to-adoption-attitudes-changing-fast/1748873/ (accessed May 7, 2013)

Paivio, A. (1971). *Imagery and verbal processes.* New York: Holt, Rinehart & Winston.

Paivio, A. (1986). *Mental representations: A dual coding approach.* New York: Oxford University Press.

Paivio, A. (2007). *Mind and its evolution: A dual coding theoretical approach..* Mahwah, NJ: Erlbaum.

Paivio, A., & Sadoski, M. (2011). Lexicons, contexts, events, and images: Commentary on Elman (2009) from the perspective of dual coding theory. *Cognitive Science, 35*, 198–209.

Palevsky, S. (2010, April 1). Best friends . . . again: Girls separated in Nazi Germany reunite after 76 years. *JWeekly.* www.jweekly.com/article/full/57605/best-friends-again-girls-separated-in-nazi-germany-reunite-after-76-years/ (accessed April 24, 2013)

Palgi, Y. (2013). Are ongoing cumulative chronic stressors associated with optimism and pessimism in the second half of life. *Anxiety, Stress, and Coping.* (in press)

Palmatier, M. I., Marks, K. R., Jones, S. A., Freeman, K. S., Wissman, K. M., & Sheppard, A. B. (2013). The effect of nicotine on sign-tracking and goal-tracking in a Pavlovian conditioned approach paradigm in rats. *Psychopharmacology, 226* (2), 247–259.

Pammer, K., & Blink, C. (2013). Attentional differences in driving judgments for country and city scenes: Semantic congruency in inattentional blindness. *Accident Analysis and Prevention, 50*, 955–963.

Pan, B. A., & Uccelli, P. (2009). Semantic development. In J. Berko Gleason & N. Ratner (Eds.), *The development of language* (7th ed.). Boston: Allyn & Bacon.

Pant, S., & Ramaswamy, B. (2009). Association of major stressors with elevated risk of breast cancer incidence or relapse. *Drugs Today, 45*, 115–126.

Papousek, I., Nauschnegg, K., Paechter, M., Lackner, H. K., Goswami, N., Schulter, G. (2010). Trait and state positive affect and cardiovascular recovery from experimental academic stress. *Biological Psychology, 83*, 108–115.

Papousek, I., Schulter, G., & Lang, B. (2009). Effects of emotionally contagious films on changes in hemisphere-specific cognitive performance. *Emotion, 9*, 510–519.

Parati, G., Lombardi, C., & Narkiewicz, K. (2007). Sleep apnea: Epidemiology, pathophysiology, and relation to cardiovascular risk. *American Journal of Physiology: Regulatory, Integrative, and Comparative Physiology, 293*, R1671–R1683.

Paris, J. (2012). The rise and fall of dissociative identity disorder. *Journal of Nervous and Mental Disease, 200*, 1076–1079.

Park, B. H., Lee, M. S., Hong, J. Y., Bas, S. H., Kim, E. Y., Kim, K. K., & Kim, D. K. (2009) The stages of physical activity and exercise behavior: An integrated approach to the theory of planned behavior. *Asia-Pacific Journal of Mental Health, 21*, 71–83.

Park, C. L. (2010). Making sense of the meaning literature: An integrative review of meaning making and its effects on adjustment to stressful life events. *Psychological Bulletin, 136*, 257–301.

Park, C. L. (2012). Meaning making in cancer survivorship. In P. T. P. Wong (Ed.), *The human quest for meaning* (2nd ed.). Thousand Oaks, CA: Sage.

Park, C. L. (2013). Religion and meaning. In R. F. Paloutzian & C. L. Park (Eds.), *Handbook of the psychology of religion and spirituality* (2nd ed.). New York: Guilford.

Park, C. L., Lechner, S. C., Antoni, M. H., & Stanton, A. L. (Eds.). (2009). *Medical illness and positive life change: Can crisis lead to personal transformation?* Washington, DC: American Psychological Association.

Park, D. C., & McDonough, I. M. (2013). The dynamic aging mind: Revelations from functional neuroimaging research. *Perspectives in Psychological Science, 8*, 62–67.

Park, D. H., Eve, D. J., Borlongan, C. V., Klasko, S. K., Cruz, L. E., & Sanberg, P. R. (2009). From the basics to application of cell therapy, a steppingstone to the conquest of neurodegeneration: A meeting report. *Medical Science Monitor, 15*, RA23–RA31.

Park, E. J., & others. (2013). Long-acting injectable formulations of antipsychotic drugs for the treatment of schizophrenia. *Archives of Pharmacal Research, 36*, 651–659.

Park, J., Kitayama, S., Karasawa, M., Curhan, K., Markus, H. R., Kawakami, N., Miyamoto, Y., Love, G. D., Coe, C. L., & Ryff, C. D. (2012). Clarifying the links between social support and health: Culture, stress, and neuroticism matter. *Journal of Health Psychology, 18* (2), 226–235.

Park, M. (2009, April 4). Teen tries to quiet the voices caused by schizophrenia. *CNN.* www.cnn.com/2009/HEALTH/04/24/schizophrenia.soloist.brain/index.html (accessed May 28, 2013)

Park, N., Peterson, C., & Seligman, M. (2004). Strengths of character and well-being. *Journal of Social and Clinical Psychology, 23*, 603–619.

Park, S. Y. (2012). *Sleep interrupted.* New York: Jodev Press.

Parker, P. S. (2006). *Race, gender, and leadership.* Mahwah, NJ: Erlbaum.

Parker, S. K. (2014). Work design for our times: Going beyond intrinsic motivation. *Annual Review of Psychology* (vol. 65). Palo Alto, CA: Annual Reviews. (in press)

Parks, M. R. (2007). *Personal relationships and personal networks.* Mahwah, NJ: Erlbaum.

Parpura, V., & others. (2013). Neuromodulation: Selected approaches and challenges. *Journal of Neurochemistry.* (in press)

Parr, E. B., Coffey, V. G., & Hawley, J. A. (2013). "Sarcobesity": A medical conundrum. *Maturitas, 74*, 109–113.

Parra Uribe, I., & others. (2013). Attempted and completed suicide: Not what we expected? *Journal of Affective Disorders.* (in press)

Parrish-Morris, J., Golinkoff, R. M., & Hirsh-Pasek, K. (2013). From coo to code: A brief story of language development. In P. D. Zelazo (Ed.), *The Oxford handbook of developmental psychology.* New York: Oxford University Press.

Parry, A., & Matthews, P. M. (2002). Functional magnetic resonance imaging: A window into the brain. *Interdisciplinary Science Reviews, 27*, 50–60.

Parsons, H. M. (1974). What happened at Hawthorne? *Science, 183*, 922–932.

Pascolo, P. B., & Cattarinussi, A. (2012). On the relationship between mouth opening and "broken mirror neurons" in autistic individuals. *Journal of Electromyography and Kinesiology, 22* (1), 98–102.

Pashler, H., McDaniel, M., Rohrer, D., & Bjork, R. (2008). Learning styles: Concepts and evidence. *Psychological Science in the Public Interest, 9*, 105–119.

Pasterski, V., Golombok, S., & Hines, M. (2011). Sex differences in social behavior. In P. K. Smith & C. H. Hart (Eds.), *Wiley-Blackwell handbook of childhood social development* (2nd ed.). New York: Wiley-Blackwell.

Patalano, A. L., Wengrovitz, S. M., & Sharpes, K. M. (2009). The influence of category coherence on inference about cross-classified entities. *Memory and Cognition, 37*, 21–38.

Patel, S. R., Zhu, X., Storfer-Isser, A., Mehra, A., Jenny, N. S., Tracy, R., & Redline, S. (2009). Sleep duration and biomarkers of inflammation. *Sleep, 32*, 200–204.

Patel, S. R., & others. (2012). A prospective study of sleep deprivation and pneumonia risk in women. *Sleep, 35*, 97–101.

Patell, E. A., Cooper, H., & Robinson, J. C. (2008). The effects of choice on intrinsic motivation and related outcomes: A meta-analysis of research findings. *Psychological Bulletin, 134,* 270–300.

Patten, S. B., Wang, J. L., Williams, J. V., Currie, S., Beck, C. A., Maxwell, C. A., & el-Guebaly, N. (2006). Descriptive epidemiology of major depression in Canada. *Canadian Journal of Psychology, 51,* 84–90.

Patterson, C. J., & Farr, R. H. (2010). Children of gay and lesbian parents: Reflections on the research-policy interface. In H. R. Schaffer & K. Durkin (Eds.), *Blackwell handbook of developmental psychology in action.* London: Blackwell.

Patterson, C. J., & Wainright, J. L. (2010). Adolescents with same-sex parents: Findings from the National Longitudinal Study of Adolescent Health. In D. Brodzinsky, A. Pertman, & D. Kunz (Eds.), *Lesbian and gay adoption: A new American reality.* New York: Oxford University Press.

Pattillo, R. (2010). Are students as good at multitasking as they think? *Nurse Educator, 35,* 24.

Paul, M. A., & others. (2011). Phase advance with separate and combined melatonin and light treatment. *Psychopharmcology, 214,* 515–523.

Paul-Samojedny, M., & others. (2010). Functional polymorphism in the interleukin-6 and interleukin-10 genes in patients with paranoid schizophrenia—A case control study. *Journal of Molecular Neuroscience, 42* (1), 112–119.

Paunonen, S., Jackson, D., Trzebinski, J., & Forserling, F. (1992). Personality structures across cultures: A multimethod evaluation. *Journal of Personality and Social Psychology, 62,* 447–456.

Paus, T., Toro, R., Leonard, G., Lerner, J. V., Lerner, R. M., Perron, M., Pike, G. B., Richer, L., Steinberg, L., Veillete, S., & Pausova, Z. (2008). Morphological properties of the action-observation cortical network in adolescents with low and high resistance to peer influence. *Social Neuroscience, 3,* 303–316.

Pavlov, I. P. (1927). *Conditioned reflexes.* G. V. Anrep (Trans.). New York: Dover.

Pavlov I. P. (1932). The reply of a physiologist to psychologists. *Psychological Review, 39,* 91–127.

Paxton, J. M., Ungar, L., & Greene, J. D. (2012). Reflection and reasoning in moral judgment. *Cognitive Science, 36,* 163–177.

Payne, E., & Fantz, A. (2013, February 28). Parents of trangendered first-grader file discrimination complaint. *CNN.* www.cnn.com/2013/02/27/us/colorado-transgender-girl-school (accessed May 3, 2013)

Pearson, N. J., Johnson, L. L., & Nahin, R. L. (2006). Insomnia, trouble sleeping, and complementary and alternative medicine: Analysis of the 2002 National Health Interview Survey data. *Archives of Internal Medicine, 166,* 1775–1782.

Peets, K., Hodges, E. V., & Salmivalli, C. (2013). Forgiveness and its determinants depending on the interpersonal context of hurt. *Journal of Experimental Child Psychology, 114* (1), 131–145.

Peigneux, P., Urbain, C., & Schmitz, R. (2012). Sleep and the brain. In C. M. Morin & C. A. Espie (Eds.), *The Oxford handbook of sleep and sleep disorders.* New York: Oxford University Press.

Pejic, T., Hermann, A., Vaitl, D., & Stark, R. (2013). Social anxiety modulates amygdala activation during social conditioning. *Social Cognitive Affective Neuroscience, 8* (3), 267–276.

Pel, J. J. M., van der Zee, Y. J., Boot, F. H., Evenhuis, H. M., & van der Steen, J. (2013). Remote eye tracking assesses age dependence processing of coherent motion in typically-developing

children. *Journal of Medical Engineering & Technology, 37,* 109–115.

Peleg, G., Katzier, G., Peleg, O., Kamara, M., Brodskey, L., Hel-Or, H., Keren, D., & Nevo, E. (2006). Hereditary family signature of facial expression. *Proceedings of the National Academy of Sciences USA, 103,* 15921–15926.

Pelleymounter, M. A., & others. (1995). Effects of the obese gene product on body weight regulation in ob/ob mice. *Science, 269,* 540–543.

Peñas-Liedó, E. M., Naranjo, M. E., & Lierena, A. (2013). Impact of cytochrome P450 genes on suicide attempt and risk. *European Archives of Psychiatry and Clinical Neuroscience.* (in press)

Penedo, F. J., Molton, I., Dahn, J. R., Shen, B. J., Kinsigner, D., Traeger, L., Siegel, S., Schneiderman, N., & Antoni, M. (2006). A randomized clinical trial of group-based cognitive-behavioral stress management in localized prostate cancer: Development of stress management skills improves quality of life and benefit finding. *Annals of Behavioral Medicine, 31,* 261–270.

Penfield, W. (1947). Some observations in the cerebral cortex of man. *Proceedings of the Royal Society, 134,* 349.

Pennebaker, J. W. (1997a). *Opening up: The healing power of expressing emotions* (rev. ed.). New York: Guilford.

Pennebaker, J. W. (1997b). Writing about emotional experiences as a therapeutic experience. *Psychological Science, 8,* 162–166.

Pennebaker, J. W. (2004). *Writing to heal: A guided journal for recovering from trauma emotional upheaval.* Oakland, CA: New Harbinger.

Pennebaker, J. W., & Chung, C. K. (2007). Expressive writing, emotional upheavals, and health. In H. S. Friedman & R. C. Silver (Eds.), *Foundations of health psychology* (pp. 263–284). New York: Oxford University Press.

Pennebaker, J. W., & Graybeal, A. (2001). Patterns of natural language use: Disclosure, personality, and social integration. *Current Directions in Psychological Science, 32,* 90–93.

Pennebaker, J. W., & O'Heeron, R. C. (1984). Confiding in others and illness rate among spouses of suicide and accidental-death victims. *Journal of Abnormal Psychology, 93,* 473–476.

Pepeu, G., Giovannini, M. G., & Bracco, L. (2013). Effect of cholinesterase inhibitors on attention. *Chemical-Biological Interactions.* (in press)

Peplau, L. A., Spalding, L. R., Conley, T. D., & Veniegas, R. C. (1999). The development of sexual orientation in women. *Annual Review of Sex Research, 10,* 70–99.

Perez-Costas, E., Melendez-Ferro, M., Rice, M. W., Conley, R. R., & Roberts, R. C. (2012). Dopamine pathology in schizophrenia: Analysis of total and phosphylated tyrosine hydroxlylase in the substantia nigra. *Frontiers in Psychology, 3,* 31.

Perkins, A. M., Inchley-Mort, S. L., Pickering, A. D., Corr, P. J., & Burgess, A. P. (2012). A facial expression for anxiety. *Journal of Personality and Social Psychology, 102* (5), 910–924.

Perkins, D. (1994, September). Creativity by design. *Educational Leadership,* 18–25.

Perrin, J. S., Merz, S., Bennett, D. M., Currie, J., Steele, D. J., Reid, I. C., & Schwarzbauer, C. (2012). Electroconvulsive therapy reduces frontal cortical connectivity in severe depressive disorder. *Proceedings of the National Academy of Sciences USA, 109,* 5464–5468.

Perrin, P. B., Heesacker, M., Pendley, C., & Smith, M. B. (2010). Social influence processes and persuation in psychotherapy and counseling. In

J. E. Maddux & J. P. Tagney (Eds.), *Social psychological foundations of clinical psychology.* New York: Guilford.

Pert, C. B. (1999). *Molecules of emotion.* New York: Simon & Schuster.

Pert, C. B., & Snyder, S. H. (1973). Opiate receptor: Demonstration in a nervous tissue. *Science, 179,* 1011.

Pervanidou, P., & Chrousos, G. P. (2012). Metabolic consequences of stress during childhood and adolescence. *Metabolism, 61* (5), 611–619.

Pescosolido, B. A., Medina, T. R., Martin, J. K., & Long, J. S. (2013). The "backbone" of stigma: Identifying the global core of public prejudice associated with mental illness. *American Journal of Public Health, 103,* 853–860.

Peters, J. L., Cohen, S., Staudenmayer, J., Hosen, J., Platts-Mills, T. A., & Wright, R. J. (2012). Prenatal negative life events increases cord blood IgE: Interaction with dust mite allergen and maternal atopy. *Allergy, 67* (4), 545–551.

Petersen, I. T., & others. (2012). Interaction between serotonin transporter polymorphism (5-HTTLPR) and stressful life events in adolescents' trajectories of anxious/depressed symptoms. *Developmental Psychology, 48,* 1463–1475.

Petersen, J. L., & Hyde, J. S. (2010). A meta-analytic review of research on gender differences in sexuality, 1973–2007. *Psychological Bulletin, 136,* 21–38.

Peterson, C., & Seligman, M. E. P. (2003). Character strengths before and after September 11. *Psychological Science, 14,* 381–384.

Petrosini, L., Cutuli, D., & De Bartolo, P. (2013). Environmental influences on development of the nervous system. In R. J. Nelson, S. J. Y. Mizumori, & I. B. Weiner (Eds.), *Handbook of psychology, 2nd ed., Vol. 3.* (pp. 461–480). Hoboken, NJ: Wiley.

Petrova, P., Schwarz, N., & Song, H. (2012). Fluency and social influence: Lessons from judgment and decision-making. In D. T. Kenrick, N. J. Goldstein, & S. L. Braver (Eds.), *Six degrees of social influence: Science, application, and the psychology of Robert Cialdini* (pp. 39–48). New York: Oxford University Press.

Petruzzello, S. J. (2012). The ultimate tranquilizer: Exercise and its influence on anxiety. In E. O. Acevedo (Ed.), *The Oxford handbook of exercise psychology.* New York: Oxford University Press.

Pettersson, E. T., & Turkheimer, E. (2013). Approach temperament, anger, and evaluation: Resolving a paradox. *Journal of Personality and Social Psychology, 105,* 285–300.

Petticrew, M., Bell, R., & Hunter, D. (2002). Influence of psychological coping on survival and recurrence in people with cancer: Systematic review. *British Medical Journal, 325,* 1066–1069.

Pettigrew, T. F., & Tropp, L. R. (2006). A meta-analytic test of intergroup contact theory. *Journal of Personality and Social Psychology, 90,* 751–783.

Petty, R. E., & Briñol, P. (2008). Persuasion: From single to multiple to metacognitive processes. *Perspectives on Psychological Science, 3,* 137–147.

Petty, R. E., & Cacioppo, J. T. (1986). The elaboration likelihood of persuasion. In L. Berkowitz (Ed.), *Advances in experimental social psychology* (vol. 19). New York: Academic.

Pezdek, K. (2003). Event memory and autobiographical memory for the events of September 11, 2001. *Applied Cognitive Psychology, 17,* 1033–1045.

Pezdek, K. (2012). Fallible eyewitness memory and identification. In B. L. Cutler (Ed.), *Conviction of the innocent: Lessons from psychological research* (pp. 105–124). Washington, DC: American Psychological Association.

Pezzo, M. V. (2011). Hindsight bias: A primer for motivational researchers. *Social and Personality Psychology Compass, 5,* 665–678.

Pfafflin, F. (2010). Understanding transgendered phenomena. In S. B. Levine, C. B. Risen, & S. E. Althof (Eds.), *Handbook of clinical sexuality for mental health professionals* (2nd ed., pp. 425–447). New York: Routledge/Taylor & Francis.

Pfaus, J. G., Kippin, T. E., Coria-Avila, G. A., Gelez, H., Afonso, V. M., & Ismail, N. (2012). Who, what, where, when (and maybe even why)? How the experience of sexual reward connects sexual desire, preference, and performance. *Archives of Sexual Behavior, 41,* 31–62.

Phaneuf, L., & McIntyre, L. L. (2007). Effects of individualized video feedback combined with group parent training on inappropriate maternal behavior. Journal of *Applied Behavior Analysis,* 40 (4), 737–741.

Phelan, J. E., & Basow, S. A. (2007). College students' attitudes toward mental illness: An examination of the stigma process. *Journal of Applied Social Psychology, 37,* 2877–2902.

Phelan, S., Hill, J. O., Lang, W., Dibello, J. R., Wing, R. R. (2003). Recovery from relapse among successful weight maintainers. *American Journal of Clinical Nutrition, 78,* 1079–1084.

Phillips, D. A., & Lowenstein, A. (2011). Early care, education, and child development. *Annual Review of Psychology* (vol. 62). (pp. 119–142). Palo Alto, CA: Annual Reviews.

Phillips, K. A., Osborne, R. H., Giles, G. G., Dite, G. S., Apicella, C., Hopper, J. L., & Milne, R. L. (2008). Psychosocial factors and survival of young women with breast cancer: A population-based prospective cohort study. *Journal of Clinical Oncology, 26* (28), 4666–4671.

Phillips, K. J., & Mudford, O. C. (2008). Functional analysis skills training for residential caregivers. *Behavioral Interventions,* 23 (1), 1–12.

Piaget, J. (1952). *The origins of intelligence in children.* New York: Oxford University Press.

Piber-Dabrowska, K., Sedek, G., & Kofta, M. (2010). The cognitive nature of prejudiced individuals. In T. Maruszewski, M. Fajkowska, & M. W. Eysenck (Eds.), *Personality from biological, cognitive, and social perspectives* (pp. 145–171). Clinton Corners, NY: Eliot Werner.

Pickering, A. D., & Smillie, L. D. (2008). The behavioral activation system: Challenges and opportunities. In P. J. Corr (Ed.), *The reinforcement sensitivity theory of personality* (pp. 120–154). New York: Cambridge University Press.

Pierce, B. H., & Gallo, D. A. (2011). Encoding modality can affect memory accuracy via retrieval orientation. *Journal of Experimental Psychology: Learning, Memory, and Cognition, 37,* 516–521.

Pierrehumbert, B., Torrisi, R., Laufer, D., Halfon, O., Ansermet, F., & Beck Popovic, M. (2010). Oxytocin response to an experimental psychosocial challenge in adults exposed to traumatic experiences during childhood or adolescence. *Neuroscience, 166,* 168–177.

Piff, P. K., Kraus, M. W., Côté, S., Cheng, B. H., & Keltner, D. (2010). Having less, giving more: The influence of social class on prosocial behavior. *Journal of Personality and Social Psychology, 99,* 771–784.

Pike, K. M., Yamamiya, Y., & Konishi, H. (2011). Eating disorders in Japan: Cultural context, clinical features, and future directions. In R. H. Striegel-Moore, S. A. Wonderlich, B. T. Walsh, & J. E. Mitchell (Eds.), *Developing an evidence-based classification of eating disorders: Scientific findings for DSM-5* (pp. 335–349). Washington, DC: American Psychiatric Association.

Pilecki, B., Arentoft, A., & McKay, D. (2011). An evidence-based causal model of panic disorder. *Journal of Anxiety Disorders, 25,* 381–388.

Pillemer, D. B. (1998). *Momentous events: Vivid memories.* Cambridge, MA: Harvard University Press.

Pilnick, A., & Coleman, T. (2010). "Do your best for me": The difficulties of finding a clinically effective endpoint in smoking cessation consultations in primary care. *Health, 14,* 57–74.

Pineles, L. L., & Parente, R. (2013). Using the theory of planned behavior to predict self-medication with over-the-counter analgesics. *Journal of Health Psychology.* (in press)

Piolino, P., Desgranges, B., Clarys, D., Guillery-Girard, B., Taconnat, L., Isingrini, M., & Eustache, F. (2006). Autobiographical memory, autonoetic consciousness, and self-perspective in aging. *Psychology and Aging, 21,* 510–525.

Piper, W. E., & Sierra Hernandez, C. A. (2013). Group psychotherapies. In G. Stricker, T. A. Widiger, & I. B. Weiner (Eds.), *Handbook of psychology* (2nd ed., vol. 8). (pp. 367–383). Hoboken, NJ: Wiley.

Pirooznia, M., & others. (2012). Data mining approaches for genome-wide association of mood disorders. *Psychiatric Genetics, 22,* 55–61.

Pitcher, D., Goldhaber, T., Duchaine, B., Walsh, V., & Kanswisher, N. (2012). Two critical and functionally distinct stages of face and body perception. *Journal of Neuroscience, 32,* 15877–15885.

Place, S. S., Todd, P. M., Zhuang, J., Penke, L., & Asendorpf, J. B. (2012). Judging romantic interest of others from thin slices is a cross-cultural ability. *Evolution and Human Behavior, 33,* 547–550.

Plaza-Zabala, A., Martin-Garcia, E., de Lecea, L., Maldonado, R., & Berrendero, F. (2010). Hypcretins regulate the anxiogenic-like effects of nicotine and induce reinstatement of nicotine-seeking behavior. *Journal of Neuroscience, 30,* 2300–2310.

Plotnikoff, R. C., & others. (2011). A test of the theory of planned behavior to explain physical activity in a large population sample of adolescents from Alberta, Canada. *Journal of Adolescent Health, 49* (5), 547–549.

Ployhart, R. E., & MacKenzie, W. I. (2010). Situational judgment tests: A critical review and agenda for the future. In S. Zedeck (Ed.), *APA handbook of industrial and organizational psychology.* Washington, DC: American Psychological Association.

Pluess, M., Belsky, J., Way, B. M., & Taylor, S. E. (2010). 5-HTTLPR moderates effects of current life events on neuroticism: Differential susceptibility to environmental influences. *Progress in Neuro-Psychopharmacology and Biological Psychiatry, 34* (6), 1070–1074.

Pogue, D. (2012, January 26). Embracing the mothers of invention. *New York Times.* www.nytimes.com/2012/01/26/technology/personaltech/financing-the-stuff-of-dreams-through-kickstarter-state-of-the-art.html?pagewanted=all (accessed April 8, 2013)

Poirier, J., & Cobb, N. K. (2012). Social influences as a driver of engagement in a web-based health intervention. *Journal of Medical Internet Research, 14* (1), e36.

Pomerantz, E. M., Saxon, J. L., & Oishi, S. (2000). The psychological trade-offs of goal investment. *Journal of Personality and Social Psychology, 79,* 617–630.

Pompili, M., & others. (2007). Suicide risk in schizophrenia: Learning from the past to change the future. *Annals of General Psychiatry, 6,* 10.

Poppenk, J., Moscovitch, M., McIntosh, A. R., Ozcelik, E., & Craik, F. L. (2010). Encoding the future: Successful processing of intentions engages predictive brain networks. *NeuroImage, 49,* 905–913.

Portnuff, C. D. F., & Fligor, B. J. (2006, October). *Output levels of portable music players.* Presented at the American Auditory Society Conference, Cincinnati.

Posner J., Russell J., & Peterson, B. S. (2005). The circumplex model of affect: An integrative approach to affective neuroscience, cognitive development, and psychopathology. *Developmental Psychopathology, 17,* 715–734.

Post, J. M., & Panis, L. K. (2011). Crimes of obedience: "Groupthink" at Abu Ghraib. *International Journal of Group Psychotherapy, 61,* 48–66.

Potter, N. N. (2012). Mad, bad, or virtuous? The moral, cultural, and pathologizing features of deviance. *Theory & Psychology, 22,* 23–45.

Poulin, M. J., Holman, E. A., & Buffone, A. (2012). The neurogenetics of nice: Receptor genes for oxytocin and vasopressin interact with threat to predict prosocial behavior. *Psychological Science, 23,* 446–452.

Powell, D. J., & Scholtz, W. (2012). Daily life stress and the cortisol awakening response: Testing the anticipation hypothesis. *PLoS One, 7* (12), e52067.

Powell, D. M., Spencer, M. B., & Petrie, K. J. (2011). Automated collection of fatigue ratings at the top of descent: A practical commercial airline tool. *Aviation, Space, and Environmental Science, 82,* 1037–1041.

Powell, R. A., & Honey, P. L. (2013). *Introduction to learning and behavior* (4th ed.). Boston: Cengage.

Prager, K. J., Shirvani, F., Garcia, J., & Coles, M. (2013). Intimacy and positive psychology. In M. Hojjat & D. Cramer (Eds.), *Positive psychology of love.* New York: Oxford University Press.

Prat, C. S. (2013). The neural basis of language faculties. In R. J. Nelson, S. J. Y. Mizumori, & I. B. Weiner (Eds.), *Handbook of psychology, 2nd ed., Vol. 3.* (pp. 595–619). Hoboken, NJ: Wiley.

Pratt, L. A., Brody, D. J., & Gu, Q. (2011, October). Antidepressant use in persons aged 12 and over: United States, 2005–2008. *NCHS Data Brief, 76,* 1–10.

Prescott, J., & others. (2011). Genome-wide association study of relative telomere length. *PLoS One, 10* (5), e19635.

Pressman, S. D., & Cohen, S. (2005) Does positive affect influence health? *Psychological Bulletin, 131,* 925–971.

Pressman, S. D., & Cohen, S. (2012). Positive emotion word use and longevity in famous deceased psychologists. *Health Psychology, 31,* 297–305.

Pressman, S. D., Gallagher, M. W., & Lopez, S. J. (2013). Is the emotion–health connection a "first-world problem"? *Psychological Science, 24,* 544–549.

Price, C. J. (2012). A review and synthesis of the first 20 years of PET and fMRI studies of heard speech, spoken language and reading. *NeuroImage, 62,* 816–847.

Price, D. D., Finniss, D. G., & Benedetti, F. (2008). A comprehensive review of the placebo effect. *Annual Review of Psychology* (vol. 59). (pp. 565–590). Palo Alto: Annual Reviews.

Prilleltensky, I., & Stead, G. B. (2013). Critical psychology, well-being, and work. In D. L. Blustein (Ed.), *The Oxford handbook of the psychology of working.* New York: Oxford University Press.

Prislin, R., & Crano, W. D. (2012). History of social influence research. In A. W. Kruglanski & W. Stroebe (Eds.), *Handbook of the history of social psychology.* New York: Psychology Press.

Priyadarshini, S., & Aich, P. (2012). Effects of psychological stress on innate immunity and metabolism in humans: A systematic analysis. *PLoS One, 7* (9), e43232.

Procaccini, C., Jirillo, E., & Matarese, G. (2012). Leptin as a neuromodulator. *Molecular Aspects of Medicine, 33,* 35–45.

Prochaska, J. O., & Norcross, J. C. (2010). *Systems of psychotherapy* (7th ed.). Pacific Grove, CA: Brooks/Cole.

Prochaska, J. O., Norcross, J. C., & DiClemente, C. C. (1994). *Changing for good: A revolutionary six-stage program for overcoming bad habits and moving your life positively forward.* New York: Avon.

Proffitt, D. R. & Caudek, C. (2013). Depth perception and the perception of events. In A. F. Healy, R. W. Proctor, & I. B. Weiner (Eds.), *Handbook of psychology, 2nd ed., Vol. 4.* (pp. 212–235). Hoboken, NJ: Wiley.

Pronin, E. (2007). Perception and misperception of bias in human judgment. *Trends in Cognitive Sciences, 11,* 37–43.

Pronin, E., & Kugler, M. B. (2007). Valuing thoughts, ignoring behavior: The introspection illusion as a source of the bias blind spot. *Journal of Experimental Social Psychology, 43,* 565–578.

Pronk, T. M., Karremans, J. C., Overbeek, G., Vermulst, A. A., & Wigboldus, D. H. J. (2010). What it takes to forgive: When and why executive functioning facilitates forgiveness. *Journal of Personality and Social Psychology, 98,* 119–131.

Provenzo, E. F. (2002). *Teaching, learning, and schooling in American culture: A critical perspective.* Boston: Allyn & Bacon.

Provine, R. R., Spencer, R. J., & Mandell, D. L. (2007). Emotional expression online: Emoticons punctuate website text messages. *Journal of Language and Social Psychology, 26,* 299–307.

Pryce, C. R., & others. (2011). Helplessness: A systematic translational review of theory and evidence for its relevance to understanding and treating of depression. *Pharmacology and Therapeutics, 132,* 242–267.

Pukrop, R., Sass, H., & Steinmeyer, E. M. (2000). Circumplex models for the similarity relationships between higher-order factors of personality and personality disorders: An empirical analysis. *Contemporary Psychiatry, 41,* 438–445.

Purdy, J. (2013). Chronic physical illness: A psychophysiological approach for chronic physical illness. *Yale Journal of Biology and Medicine, 86,* 15–28.

Puttonen, S., Viitasalo, K., & Härmä, M. (2011). Effect of shiftwork on systemic markers of inflammation. *Chronobiology International, 28,* 528–535.

Q

Qian, Z. (2009). Mate selection. In D. Carr (Ed.), *Encyclopedia of the life course and human development.* Boston: Gale Cengage.

Quang, P. N., & Schmidt, B. L. (2010). Endothelin-A receptor antagonism attenuates carcinoma-induced pain through opioids in mice. *Journal of Pain, 11* (7), 663–671.

Quinn, P. C. (2011). Born to categorize. In U. Goswami (Ed.), *Wiley-Blackwell handbook of childhood cognitive development* (2nd ed.). New York: Wiley-Blackwell.

R

Raabe, B., & Beehr, T. A. (2003). Formal mentoring versus supervisor and co-worker relationships: Differences in perceptions and impact. *Journal of Organizational Behavior, 24,* 271–293.

Racagni, G., & Popoli, M. (2010). The pharmacological properties of antidepressants. *International Clinical Psychopharmacology, 25,* 117–131.

Rachlin, H., & Green, L. (2009). The neural basis of drug craving: An incentive-sensitization theory of addiction. In D. Shanks (Ed.), *Psychology of learning.* Thousand Oaks, CA: Sage.

Racine, M., & others. (2012a). A systematic literature review of 10 years of research on sex/gender and experimental pain perception—Part 1: Are there really differences between women and men? *Pain, 153* (3), 602–618.

Racine, M., & others. (2012b). A systematic literature review of 10 years of research on sex/gender and pain perception—Part 2: Do biopsychosocial factors alter pain sensitivity differently in women and men? *Pain, 153* (3), 619–635.

Racz, S. J., & McMahon, R. J. (2011). The relationship between parental knowledge and monitoring and child and adolescent conduct problems: A 10-year update. *Clinical Child and Family Psychology Review, 14,* 377–398.

Radel, R., Sarrazin, P., & Pelletier, L. (2009). Evidence of subliminally primed motivational orientations: The effects of unconscious motivational processes on the performance of a new motor task. *Journal of Sport and Exercise Psychology, 31,* 657–674.

Radin, D. I. (2006). *Entangled minds: Extrasensory experiences in a quantum reality.* New York: Simon & Schuster.

Radulescu, L., & others. (2013). Multicenter evaluation of Neurelec Digisonic SP cochlear implant reliability. *European Archives of Otorhinolaryngology.* (in press)

Ragins, B. R., Cotton, J. L., & Miller, J. S. (2000). Marginal mentoring: The effects of type of mentor, quality of relationship, and program design on work and career attitudes. *Academy of Management Journal, 43,* 1177–1194.

Rahman, Q. (2005). The neurodevelopment of human sexual orientation. *Neuroscience & Biobehavioral Reviews, 29,* 1057–1066.

Rahman, Q., Clarke, K., & Morera, T. (2009). Hair whorl direction and sexual orientation in human males. *Behavioral Neuroscience, 123,* 252–256.

Rahman, Q., & Wilson, G. D. (2003). Sexual orientation and the 2nd to 4th finger length ratio: Evidence for organising effects of sex hormones or developmental instability? *Psychoneuroendocrinology, 28,* 288–303.

Raine, A. (2008). From genes to brain to antisocial behavior. *Current Directions in Psychological Science, 17,* 323–328.

Raine, A., Venables, P. H., & Williams, M. (1990). Relationships between N1, P300 and CNV recorded at age 15 and criminal behavior at age 24. *Psychophysiology, 27,* 567–575.

Rais, M., Cahn, W., Schnack, H. G., Hulshoff Pol, H. E., Kahn, R. S., & van Haren, N. E. M. (2012). Brain volume reductions in medication-naïve patients with schizophrenia in relation to intelligence quotient. *Psychological Medicine, 42* (9), 1847–1856.

Raj, T., & others. (2012). Alzheimer disease susceptibility loci: Evidence for a protein network under natural selection. *American Journal of Human Genetics, 90,* 720–726.

Rajaratnam, S. M., & others. (2011). Sleep disorders, health, and safety in police officers. *Journal of the American Medical Association, 306,* 2567–2578.

Ram, N., Morelli, S., Lindberg, C., & Carstensen, L. L. (2008). From static to dynamic: The ongoing dialetic about human development. In K. W. Schaie & R. P. Abeles (Eds.), *Social structures and aging individuals.* Mahwah, NJ: Erlbaum.

Ramachandran, V. S. (2000, May 31). Mirror neurons and imitation as the driving force behind "the great leap forward" in human evolution. *EDGE.* www.edge.org/ 3rd_culture/ramachandran/ ramachandran_index.html (accessed March 13, 2013)

Ramachandran V. S., & Oberman, L. S. (2006). Broken mirrors: A theory of autism. *Scientific American, 295,* 62–69.

Ramirez-Esparza, N., Gosling, S. D., Benet-Martinez, V., Potter, J. P., & Pennebaker, J. W. (2006). Do bilinguals have two personalities? A special case of cultural frame switching. *Journal of Research in Personality, 40,* 99–120.

Ramirez-Maestre, C., Esteve, R., & Lopez, A. E. (2012). The role of optimism and pessimism in chronic pain patients' adjustments. *Spanish Journal of Psychology, 15,* 286–294.

Ramsey, J. L., Langlois, J. H., Hoss, R. A., Rubenstein, A. J., & Griffin, A. M. (2004). Origins of a stereotype: Categorization of facial attractiveness by 6-month-old infants. *Developmental Science, 7* (2), 201–211.

Ramsey, R., & de C. Hamilton, A. F. (2010). Understanding actors and object-goals in the human brain. *NeuroImage, 50,* 1142–1147.

Ramsoy, T. Z., Liptrot, M. G., Skimminge, A., Lund, T. E., Sidaros, K., Christensen, M. S., Baare, W., Paulson, O. B., & Jernigan, T. L. (2009). Regional activation of the human medial temporal lobe during intentional encoding of objects and positions. *NeuroImage, 47,* 1863–1872.

Rand, M. K., & Shimansky, Y. P. (2013). Two-phase strategy of neural control for planar reaching movements: I. XY coordination variability and its relation to end-point variability. *Experimental Brain Research.* (in press)

Rapaport, D. (1967). On the psychoanalytic theory of thinking. In M. M. Gill (Ed.), *The collected papers of David Rapaport.* New York: Basic.

Rapaport, S. (1994, November 28). Interview. *U.S. News and World Report,* 94.

Rasmussen, K. A., & Wingate, L. R. (2011). The role of optimism in the interpersonal-psychological theory of suicidal behavior. *Suicide and Life-Threatening Behavior, 41,* 137–148.

Rathunde, K. (2010). Experimental wisdom and optimal experience: Interviews with three distinguished lifelong learners. *Journal of Adult Development, 17,* 81–93.

Rathunde, K., & Csikszentmihalyi, M. (2006). The developing person: An experiential perspective. In W. Damon & R. Lerner (Eds.), *Handbook of child psychology* (6th ed.). New York: Wiley.

Raudies, F., & Neumann, H. (2010). A neural model of the temporal dynamics of figure-ground segregation in motion perception. *Neural Networks, 23,* 160–176.

Raw, R. K., Wilkie, R. M., Culmer, P. R., & Mon-Williams, M. (2012). Reduced motor asymmetry in older adults when manually tracing paths. *Experimental Brain Research, 217,* 35–41.

Rawlins, W. K., & Russell, L. D. (2013). Friendship, positive being-with-others, and the edifying practices of storytelling and dialogue. In M. Hojjat & D. Cramer (Eds.), *Positive psychology and love.* New York: Oxford University Press.

Rayner, K., Pollatsek, A., & Schotter, E. R. (2013). Reading: Word identification and eye movements. In A. F. Healy, R. W. Proctor, & I. B. Weiner (Eds.), *Handbook of psychology, 2nd ed., Vol. 4.* (pp. 598–577). Hoboken, NJ: Wiley.

Recanzone, G. H., & Sutter, M. L. (2008). The biological basis of audition. *Annual Review of Psychology* (vol. 59). Palo Alto, CA: Annual Reviews.

Rector, N. A. (2013). Acceptance and commitment therapy: Empirical considerations. *Behavior Therapy, 44,* 213–217.

Rector, N. A., & Beck, A. T. (2001). Cognitive behavioral therapy for schizophrenia: An empirical review. *Journal of Nervous and Mental Disorders, 189,* 278–287.

Redway, J. A. K., & Miville, M. L. (2013). Gender roles among African American women. In M. L. Miville (Ed.), *Multicultural gender roles: Applications for mental health and education.* New York: Wiley.

Reece, B. L., Brandt, R., & Howie, K. T. (2011). *Effective human relations* (11th ed.). Boston: Cengage.

Reed, S. K. (2010). *Thinking visually.* New York: Psychology Press.

Reeder, G. D. (2013). Attribution. In D. Carlston (Ed.), *The Oxford handbook of social cognition.* New York: Oxford University Press.

Reel, L. A., & Hicks, P. B. (2012). Selective auditory attention in adults: Effects of rhythmic structure of the competing language. *Journal of Speech, Language, and Hearing Research, 55,* 89–104.

Reese, B. M., Haydon, A. A., Herring, A. H., & Halpern, C. T. (2013). The association between sequences of sexual initiation and the likelihood of teenage pregnancy. *Journal of Adolescent Health, 52,* 228–233.

Reeve, C. (2000, May 1). Use the body's repair kit. *Time, 155,* 18.

Reeve, C. L., & Charles, J. E. (2008). Survey of opinions on the primacy of *g* and social consequences of ability testing: A comparison of expert and non-expert views. *Intelligence, 36,* 681–688.

Regts, G., & Molleman, E. (2013). To leave or not to leave: When receiving interpersonal citizenship behavior influences an employee's turnover intention. *Human Relations, 66,* 193–218.

Rehfeldt, R. A. (2011). Toward a technology of derived stimulus relations: An analysis of articles published in the *Journal of Applied Behavior Analysis,* 1992–2009. *Journal of Applied Behavior Analysis, 44,* 109–119.

Reichardt, C. S. (2009). Quasi-experimental designs. In R. E. Millsap & A. Maydeu-Olivares (Eds.), *The Sage handbook of quantitative methods* (pp. 46–71). Thousand Oaks, CA: Sage.

Reif, A., & others. (2013). MAOA and mechanisms of panic disorder revisited: From bench to molecular psychotherapy. *Molecular Psychiatry.* (in press)

Reiner, W. G. (2011). Gender identity and sex-of-rearing in children with disorders of sexual differentiation. *Journal of Pediatric Endocrinology and Metabolism, 18,* 549–554,

Reis, H. T., Sheldon, K. M., Gable, S. L., Roscoe, J., & Ryan, R. M. (2000). Daily well-being: The role of autonomy, competence, and relatedness. *Personality and Social Psychology Bulletin, 26,* 419–435.

Reisner, S. L., Mimiaga, M. J., Skeer, M., & Mayer, K. H. (2009). Beyond anal sex: Sexual practices associated with HIV risk reduction among men who have sex with men in Boston, Massachusetts. *AIDS Patient Care and STDs, 23,* 545–550.

Reivich, K., & Gillham, J. (2003). Learned optimism: The measurement of explanatory style. In S. J. Lopez & C. R. Snyder (Eds.), *Positive psychological assessment: A handbook of models and measures* (pp. 57–74). Washington, DC: American Psychological Association.

Rendell, P. G., & Craik, F. I. M. (2000). Virtual week and actual week: Age-related differences in prospective memory. *Applied Cognitive Psychology, 14,* S43–S62.

Reniers, R. L., & others. (2012). Moral decision-making, ToM, empathy, and the mode default network. *Biological Psychology, 90,* 202–210.

Rescorla, R. A. (1966). Predictability and number of pairings in Pavlovian fear conditioning. *Psychonomic Science, 4,* 383–384.

Rescorla, R. A. (1988). Pavlovian conditioning: It's not what you think it is. *American Psychologist, 43,* 151–160.

Rescorla, R. A. (2003). Contemporary study of Pavlovian conditioning. *Spanish Journal of Psychology, 6,* 185–195.

Rescorla, R. A. (2004). Spontaneous recovery varies inversely with the training-extinction interval. *Learning and Behavior, 32,* 401–408.

Rescorla, R. A. (2005). Spontaneous recovery of excitation but not inhibition. *Journal of Experimental Psychology: Animal Behavior Processes, 31,* 277–288.

Rescorla, R. A. (2006a). Stimulus generalization of excitation and inhibition. *Quarterly Journal of Experimental Psychology, 59,* 53–67.

Rescorla, R. A. (2006b). Spontaneous recovery from overexpectation. *Learning and Behavior, 34,* 13–20.

Rescorla, R. A. (2006c). Deepened extinction from compound stimulus presentation. *Journal of Experimental Psychology: Animal Behavior Processes, 32* (2), 135–144.

Rescorla, R. A. (2009). A theory of Pavlovian conditioning: Variations in the effectiveness of reinforcement and nonreinforcement. In D. Shanks (Ed.), *Psychology of learning.* Thousand Oaks, CA: Sage.

Réthelyi, J. M., Benkovits, J., & Bitter, I. (2013). Genes and environments in schizophrenia: The different pieces of a manifold puzzle. *Neuroscience and Biobehavioral Reviews.* (in press)

Revelle, W. (2008). The contribution of reinforcement sensitivity theory to personality theory. In P. J. Corr (Ed.), *The reinforcement sensitivity theory of personality* (pp. 508–527). New York: Cambridge University Press.

Reynolds, C. R., Livingston, R., & Willson, V. (2006). *Measurement and assessment in education.* Boston: Allyn & Bacon.

Reynolds, C. R., & Suzuki, L. A. (2013). Bias in psychological assessment: An empirical review and recommendations. In J. R. Graham, N. A. Naglieri, & I. B. Weiner (Eds.), *Handbook of psychology, 2nd ed., Vol. 10.* (pp. 82–113). Hoboken, NJ: Wiley.

Reynolds, K. J., Haslam, S. A., & Turner, J. C. (2012). Prejudice, social identity, and social change: Resolving the Allportian problematic. In J. Dixon & M. Levine (Eds.), *Beyond prejudice.* New York: Cambridge University Press.

Reynolds, S., Wilson, C., Austin, J., & Hooper, L. (2012). Effects of psychotherapy for anxiety in children and adolescents: A meta-analytic review. *Clinical Psychology Review, 32* (4), 251–262.

Reznick, J. S. (2013). Working memory in infancy. In P. J. Bauer & R. Fivush (Eds.), *Handbook on the development of children's memory.* New York: Wiley.

Rezvani, A. H., Lawrence, A. J., Arolfo, M. P., Levin, E. D., & Overstreet, D. H. (2012). Novel medication targets for the treatment of alcoholism: Preclinical studies. *Recent Patents on CNS Drug Discovery, 7,* 151–162.

Rhoades, G. K., Stanley, S. M., & Markman, H. J. (2009). The pre-engagement cohabitation effect: A replication and extension of previous findings. *Journal of Family Psychology, 23,* 107–111.

Richardson, M. S., & Schaeffer, C. (2013). From work and family to a dual model of working. In D. L. Blustein (Ed.), *The Oxford handbook of the psychology of working.* New York: Oxford University Press.

Richter, M. A., & others. (2012). Evidence for cortical inhibitory and excitatory dysfunction in obsessive compulsive disorder. *Neuropsychopharmacology, 37,* 1144–1151.

Rieger, G., Linsenmeier, J. A. W., & Bailey, J. M. (2009). Childhood gender nonconformity remains a robust and neutral correlate of sexual orientation: Reply to Hegary (2009). *Developmental Psychology, 45,* 901–903.

Rieger, G., Linsenmeier, J. A. W., Gygax, L., & Bailey, J. M. (2008). Sexual orientation and childhood gender nonconformity: Evidence from home videos. Developmental Psychology, 44, 46–58.

Reiman, E. M., Fusselman, M. J., Fox, P. T., & Raichle, M. E. (1989). Neuroanatomical correlates of anticipatory anxiety. *Science, 243,* 1071–1074.

Ries, M. L., & others. (2012). Medial prefrontal functional connectivity—Relation to memory self-appraisal accuracy in older adults with and without memory disorders. *Neuropsychologia, 50* (5), 603–611.

Riezzo, I., Cerretani, D., Fiore, C., Bello, S., Centini, F., D'Errico, S., Fiaschi, A. I., Giorgi, G., Neri, M., Pomara, C., Turillazzi, E., & Fineschi, V. (2010). Enzymatic-nonenzymatic cellular antioxidant defense systems response and Immunohistochemical detection of MDMA, VMAT2, HSP70, and apoptosis as biomarkers for MDMA (ecstasy) neurotoxicity. *Journal of Neuroscience Research, 88,* 905–916.

Riketta, M. (2002). Attitudinal organizational commitment and job performance: A meta-analysis. *Journal of Organizational Behavior, 23,* 257–266.

Riley, B. D., Culver, J. O., Skrzynia, C., Senter, L. A., Peters, J. A., Costalas, J. W., Callif-Daley, F., Grumet, S. C., Hunt, K. S., Nagy, R. S., McKinnon, W. C., Petrucelli, N. M., Bennett, R. L., & Trepanier, A. M. (2012). Essential elements of genetic cancer risk assessment, counseling, and testing: Updated recommendations of the National Society of Genetic Counselors. *Journal of Genetic Counseling, 21,* 151–161.

Rimland, B. (1964). *Infantile autism.* East Norwalk, CT: Appleton-Century-Crofts.

Rimmele, U., Davachi, L., & Phelps, E. A. (2012). Memory for time and place contributes to enhanced confidence in memories for emotional events. *Emotion, 13,* 834–846.

Rips, L. J. (2011). Causation from perception. *Perspectives on Psychological Science, 6,* 77–97.

Rips, L. J., Smith, E. E., & Medin, D. L. (2012). Concepts and categories: Memory, meaning, and metaphysics. In K. J. Holyoak & R. G. Morrison (Eds.), *The Oxford handbook of thinking and reasoning.* New York: Oxford University Press.

Risbrough, V. B., & Stein, M. B. (2012). Neuropharmacology special issue on posttraumatic stress disorder (PTSD): Current state of the art in clinical and preclinical PTSD. *Neuropharmacology, 62,* 539–541.

Risen, J. L., & Gilovich, T. (2008). Why people are reluctant to tempt fate. *Journal of Personality and Social Psychology, 95,* 293–307.

Risley, T. R., & Hart, B. (2006). Promoting early language development. In N. F. Watt, C. Ayoub, R. H. Bradley, J. E. Puma, & W. A. LeBoeuf (Eds.), *The crisis in youth mental health: Critical issues and effective programs, vol. 4: Early intervention programs and policies* (pp. 83–88). Westport, CT: Praeger.

Rissman, J., & Wagner, A. D. (2012). Distributed representations in memory: Insights from functional brain imaging. *Annual Review of Psychology* (vol. 63). (pp. 101–128). Palo Alto, CA: Annual Reviews.

Ritchey, M., LaBar, K. S., & Cabeza, R. (2011). Level of processing modulates the neural correlates of emotional memory formation. *Journal of Cognitive Neuroscience, 23* (4), 757–771.

Ritchey, M., Wing, E. A., LaBar, K. S., & Cabeza, R. (2013). Neural similarity between encoding and retrieval is related to memory via hippocampal interactions. *Cerebral Cortex.* (in press)

Ritskes, R., Ritskes-Hoitinga, M., Stodkilde-Jorgensen, H., Baerentsen, K., & Hartman, T. (2003). MRI scanning during Zen meditation: The picture of enlightenment? *Constructivism in the Human Sciences, 8* (1), 85–90.

Ritter, D., & Elsea, M. (2005). Hot sauce, toy guns, and graffiti: A critical account of current laboratory aggression paradigms. *Aggressive Behavior, 31,* 407–419.

Rivas-Drake, D. (2012). Ethnic identity and adjustment: The mediating role of sense of community. *Cultural Diversity and Ethnic Minority Psychology, 18* (2), 210–215.

Rivet, T., & Matson, J. (2011). Review of gender differences in core symptomatology in autism spectrum disorders. *Research in Autism Spectrum Disorders, 5,* 957–976.

Rizzolatti, G., & Fabbri-Destro, M. (2010). Mirror neurons: From discovery to autism. *Experimental Brain Research, 200,* 233–237.

Rizzolatti, G., & Sinigaglia, C. (2010). The functional role of the parieto-frontal mirror circuit: Interpretations and misinterpretations. *Nature Reviews: Neuroscience, 11,* 264–274.

Roberts, B. W., Donnellan, M. B., & Hill, P. L. (2013). Personality trait development in adulthood. In H. A. Tennen, J. M. Suls, & I. B. Weiner (Eds.), *Handbook of psychology, 2nd ed., Vol. 5.* (pp. 183–196). Hoboken, NJ: Wiley.

Roberts, B. W., Jackson, J. J., Fayard, J. V., Edmonds, G., & Meints, J. O. (2009). Conscientiousness. In M. Leary & R. Hoyle (Eds.), *Handbook of individual differences in social behavior* (pp. 369–381). New York: Guilford.

Roberts, B. W., & Mroczek, D. (2008). Personality trait change in adulthood. *Current Directions in Psychological Science, 17,* 31–35.

Roberts, B. W., Walton, K. E., & Viechtbauer, W. (2006). Patterns of mean level change in personality traits across the life course: A meta-analysis of longitudinal studies. *Psychological Bulletin, 132,* 1–25.

Roberts, G., & others. (2011). Can improving working memory prevent academic difficulties? A school based randomized controlled trial. *BMC Pediatrics.* doi: 10.1186/1471-2431-11-57

Roberts, K. L., Lau, J. K., Chechlacz, M., & Humphreys, G. W. (2013). Spatial and temporal attention deficits following brain injury: A neuroanatomical decomposition of the temporal order judgment task. *Cognitive Neuropsychology.* (in press)

Robertson, E. M. (2012). New insights in human memory interference and consolidation. *Current Biology, 22,* R66–R71.

Robinson, A. J. (2008). McGregor's Theory X-Theory Y model. In J. Gordon (Ed.) *The Pfeiffer book of successful leadership development tools: The most enduring, effective, and valuable training activities for developing leaders* (pp. 63–66). San Francisco: Pfeiffer/Wiley.

Robinson-Riegler, B., & Robinson-Riegler, G. L. (2012). *Cognitive psychology* (3rd ed.). Upper Saddle River, NJ: Pearson.

Robson, D., Cole, F., Jalasi, S., Boojharut, B., Smith, S., Thompson, S., Jones, M., & Haddad, M. (2013). Smoking cessation and serious mental illness: A service evaluation of a drop-in stop smoking clinic on an acute in-patient unit *Journal of Clinical Nursing, 22,* 405–413.

Rodgers, J. L. (2007). The shape of things to come: Diagnosing social contagion from adolescent smoking and drinking curves. In T. D. Little, J. A. Bovaird, & N. A. Card (Eds.), *Modeling contextual effects in longitudinal studies* (pp. 343–362). Mahwah, NJ: Erlbaum.

Rodin, J. (1984, December). Interview: A sense of control. *Psychology Today,* 38–45.

Roelfs, D., Shor, E., Davidson, K. W., & Schwartz, J. E. (2011). Losing life and livelihood: A systematic review and meta-analysis of unemployment and all-cause mortality. *Social Science and Medicine, 72,* 840–854.

Roese, N. J., & Summerville, A. (2005). What we regret most . . . and why. *Personality and Social Psychology Bulletin, 31,* 1273–1285.

Roeser, R. W., & Zelazo, P. D. (2012). Contemplative science, education, and child development: Introduction to the special section. *Child Development Perspectives, 6,* 143–145.

Rogers, C. R. (1961). *On becoming a person.* Boston: Houghton Mifflin.

Rogers, C. R. (1980). *A way of being.* Boston: Houghton Mifflin.

Rogers, G., & others. (2009). The harmful health effects of recreational Ecstasy: A systematic review of observational evidence. *Health Technology Assessment, 13,* 1–315.

Rojas, Y., & Stenberg, S. A. (2010). Early life circumstances and male suicide—A 30-year follow-up of a Stockholm cohort born in 1953. *Social Science Medicine, 70,* 420–427.

Romero-Canyas, R., Downey, G., Berenson, K., Ayduk, O., & Kang, N. J. (2010). Rejection sensitivity and the rejection-hostility link in romantic relationships. *Journal of Personality, 78,* 119–148.

Roncero, M., Perpina, C., & Garcia-Soriano, G. (2011). Study of obsessive compulsive beliefs: Relationship with eating disorders. *Behavioral and Cognitive Psychotherapy, 39,* 457–470.

Rosack, J. (2007). Impact of FDA warning questioned in suicide rise. *Psychiatric News, 5,* 1.

Rose, N. S., & Craik, F. I. (2012). A processing approach to the working memory/long-term memory distinction: Evidence from the levels-of-processing span task. *Journal of Experimental Psychology: Learning, Memory, and Cognition, 38,* 1019–1029.

Rosell, D. R., & others. (2010). Increased serotonin 2A receptor availability in the orbitofrontal cortex of physically aggressive personality disordered patients. *Biological Psychiatry, 67* (12), 1154–1162.

Roseman, I. J., & Smith, C. A. (2009). Appraisal theory: Overview, assumptions, varieties, controversies. In K. R. Scherer, A. Schorr, & T. Johnstone (Eds.), *Appraisal processes in emotion: Theory, methods, research* (pp. 3–19). Oxford, U.K.: Oxford University Press.

Rosen, K., & Garety, P. (2005). Predicting recovery from schizophrenia: A retrospective comparison of characteristics at onset of people with single and multiple episodes. *Schizophrenia Bulletin, 31,* 735–750.

Rosenbaum, B., Harder, S., Knudsen, P., Køster, A., Lajer, M., Lindhardt, A., Valbak, K., & Winther, G. (2012). Supportive psychodynamic psychotherapy versus treatment as usual for first-episode psychosis: Two-year outcome. *Psychiatry: Interpersonal and Biological Processes, 75,* 331–341.

Rosenhan, D. L. (1973). On being sane in insane places. *Science, 179,* 250–258.

Rosental, B., & others. (2012). The effect of chemotherapy/radiotherapy on cancerous pattern recognition by NK cells. *Current Medicinal Chemistry, 19,* 1780–1791.

Rosenthal, E. S. (2012). The utility of EEG, SSEP, and other neurophysiologic tools to guide neurocritical care. *Neurotherapeutics, 9,* 24–36.

Rosenthal, L., Carroll-Scott, A., Earnshaw, V. A., Santilli, A., & Ickovics, J. R. (2012). The importance of full-time work for urban adults' mental and physical health. *Social Science and Medicine, 75* (9), 1692–1696.

Rosenthal, M. (2013). *Human sexuality.* Boston: Cengage.

Rosenthal, R. (1966). *Experimenter effects in behavioral research.* New York: Appleton-Century-Crofts.

Rosenthal, R., & Jacobsen, L. (1968). *Pygmalion in the classroom.* Fort Worth: Harcourt Brace.

Rosette, A. S., Brett, J. M., Barsness, Z., & Lytle, A. L. (2012). When cultures clash electronically: The impact of email and social norms on negotiation behavior and outcomes. *Journal of Cross-Cultural Psychology, 43,* 628–643.

Rosier, J. P., Stephan, K. E., den Ouden, H. E. M., Friston, K. J., & Joyce, E. M. (2010). Adaptive and aberrant reward prediction signals in the human brain. *NeuroImage, 50,* 657–664.

Rosmarin, D. H., Krumrei, E. J., & Andersson, G. (2009). Religion as a predictor of psychological distress in two religious communities. *Cognitive Behavior Therapy, 38,* 54–64.

Rosnow, R. L., & Rosenthal, R. (2013). *Beginning behavioral research* (7th ed.). Upper Saddle River, NJ: Pearson.

Ross, C. A., Keyes, B. B., Yan, H., Wang, Z., Zou, Z., Xu, Y., Chen, J., Zhang, H., & Xiao, Z. (2008). A cross-cultural test of the trauma model of dissociation. *Journal of Trauma and Dissociation, 9,* 35–49.

Ross, C. A., & Ness, L. (2010). Symptom patterns in dissociative identity disorder patients and the general population. *Journal of Trauma and Dissociation, 11,* 458–468.

Ross, C. E., & Van Willigen, M. (1996). Gender, parenthood, and anger. *Journal of Marriage and Family, 58,* 572–584.

Ross, L., Kohler, C. L., Grimley, D. M., & Anderson-Lewis, C. (2007). The theory of reasoned action and intention to seek cancer information. *American Journal of Health Behavior, 31,* 123–134.

Rosser, A., & Bachoud-Levi, A. C. (2012). Clinical trials of neural transplantation in Huntington's disease. *Progress in Brain Research, 200,* 347–371.

Rossi, E. L. (2009). The pyschosocial genomics of therapeutic hypnosis, psychotherapy, and rehabilitation. *American Journal of Clinical Hypnosis, 51,* 281–298.

Rossi, J. S. (2013). Statistical power analysis. In J. A. Schinka, W. F. Velicer, & I. B. Weiner (Eds.), *Handbook of psychology, 2nd ed., Vol. 2.* (pp. 71–108). Hoboken, NJ: Wiley.

Rotella, R. J. (2010). *Case studies in sport psychology.* Sudbury, MA: Jones & Bartlett.

Roten, R. G. (2007). *DSM-IV* and the taxonomy of roles: How can the taxonomy of roles complement the *DSM-IV* to create a more holistic diagnostic tool? *The Arts in Psychotherapy, 34,* 53–68.

Rotge, J. Y., & others. (2009). Inverse relationship between thalamic and orbitofrontal volumes in obsessive-compulsive disorder. *Progress in Neuro-Psychopharmacology & Biological Psychiatry, 33,* 682–686.

Rothbart, M. K., & Gartstein, M. A. (2008). Temperament. In M. M. Haith & J. B. Benson (Eds.), *Encyclopedia of infant and early childhood development.* London: Elsevier.

Rothbaum, F., Kakinuma, M., Nagaoka, R., & Azuma, H. (2007). Attachment and AMAE: Parent–child closeness in the United States and Japan. *Journal of Cross-Cultural Psychology, 38,* 465–486.

Rothbaum, F., Weisz, J., Pott, M., Miyake, K., & Morelli, G. (2000). Attachment and culture: Security in the United States and Japan. *American Psychologist, 55* (10), 1093–1104.

Rouder, J. N., & Morey, R. D. (2009). The nature of psychological thresholds. *Psychological Review, 116,* 655–660.

Rouder, J. N,., & Morey, R. D. (2011). A Bayes factor meta-analysis of Bem's ESP claim. *Psychonomic Bulletin and Review, 18,* 682–689.

Roughgarden, J., Oishi, M., & Akçay, E. (2006). Reproductive social behavior: Cooperative games to replace sexual selection. *Science, 311,* 965–968.

Routh, D. K. (2013). Clinical psychology. In D. K. Freedheim & I. B. Weiner (Eds.), *Handbook of psychology* (2nd ed., vol. 1). Hoboken, NJ: Wiley.

Rowland, D. L., & McMahon, C. G. (2008). Premature ejaculation. In D. L. Rowland & L. Incrocci (Eds.), *Handbook of sexual and gender identity disorders* (pp. 68–97). Hoboken, NJ: Wiley.

Rubin, D. C. (2011). The coherence of memories for trauma: Evidence from posttraumatic stress disorder. *Consciousness and Cognition, 20,* 857–865.

Rubin, Z., & Mitchell, C. (1976). Couples research as couples counseling: Some unintended effects of studying close relationships. *American Psychologist, 31,* 17–25.

Rubio-Fernández, P., & Geurts, B. (2013). How to pass the false-belief task before your fourth birthday. *Psychological Science, 24,* 27–33.

Rudy, D., & Grusec, J. E. (2006). Authoritarian parenting in individualist and collectivist groups: Associations with maternal emotion and cognition and children's self-esteem. *Journal of Family Psychology, 20,* 68–78.

Rueda, M. R., & Posner, M. I. (2013). Development of attentional networks. In P. D. Zelazo (Ed.), *The Oxford handbook of developmental psychology.* New York: Oxford University Press.

Rugg, M. D., & Vilberg, K. L. (2013). Brain networks underlying episodic memory retrieval. *Current Opinion in Neurobiology.* (in press)

Ruini, C., Belaise, C., Brombin, C., Caffo, E., & Fava, G. A. (2006). Well-being therapy in school settings: A pilot study. *Psychotherapy and Psychosomatics, 75,* 331–336.

Ruini, C., & Fava, G. A. (2004). Clinical applications of well-being therapy. In A. Linley & S. Joseph (Eds.), *Positive psychology in practice* (pp. 371–387). Hoboken, NJ: Wiley.

Ruini, C., & Fava, G. A. (2009). Well-being therapy for generalized anxiety disorder. *Journal of Clinical Psychology, 65,* 510–519.

Ruiz, A. (2012, November 7). School maintenance workers unsung heroes of Hurricane Sandy. *New York Daily News.* www.nydailynews.com/opinion/school-maintenance-workers-unsung-heroes-hurricane-sandy-article-1.1198412#ixzz2I9QyGgE6 (accessed February 20, 2013)

Rummel, J. (2010). Psychological distance to a prospective memory cue influences the probability of fulfilling a delayed intention. *Memory, 18* (3), 284–292.

Runyon, W. M. (2007). *Psychology and historical interpretation.* New York: Oxford University Press.

Rusbult, C. E., Agnew, C. R., & Arriaga, X. B. (2012). The investment model of commitment processes. In P. A. M. Van Lange, A. W. Kruglanski, & E. T. Higgins (Eds.), *Handbook of theories of social psychology.* Thousand Oaks, CA: Sage.

Rusbult, C. E., Finkel, E. J., & Kumashiro, M. (2009). The Michelangelo phenomenon. *Current Directions in Psychological Science, 18,* 305–309.

Rush, C. C., Becker, S. J., & Curry, J. F. (2009). Personality factors and styles among college students who binge eat and drink. *Psychology of Addictive Behaviors, 23,* 140–145.

Russell, P. J., Hertz, P. E., & McMillan, B. (2014). *Biology: The dynamic science* (3rd ed.). Boston: Cengage.

Russo, S. J., & others. (2010). The addicted synapse: Mechanisms of synaptic and structural plasticity in nucleus accumbens. *Trends in Neuroscience, 33* (6), 267–276.

Ryan, A. M., & Ployhart, R. E. (2014). Selection. *Annual Review of Psychology* (vol. 65). Palo Alto, CA: Annual Reviews. (in press)

Ryan, R. M., & Deci, E. L. (2000). Self-determination theory and the facilitation of intrinsic motivation, social development, and well-being. *American Psychologist, 55,* 68–78.

Ryan, R. M., & Deci, E. L. (2009). Promoting self-determined school engagement, motivation, learning, and well-being. In K. R. Wentzel & A. Wigfield (Eds.), *Handbook of research on schools, schooling, and human development.* New York: Routledge.

Rybakowski, J. K. (2013). Genetic influences on response to mood stabilizers in bipolar disorder: Current status and knowledge. *CNS Drugs, 27,* 165–173.

Rybakowski, J. K., & Klonowska, P. (2011). Bipolar mood disorder, creativity, and schizotypy: An experimental study. *Psychopathology, 44* (5), 296–302.

Ryckman, R. M. (2013). *Theories of personality* (10th ed.). Boston: Cengage.

Rydell, R. J., & Boucher, K. L. (2010). Capitalizing on multiple social identities to prevent stereotype threat: The moderating role of self-esteem. *Personality and Social Psychology Bulletin, 36,* 239–250.

Ryff, C. D., Singer, B. H., & Love, G. D. (2004). Positive health: Connecting well-being with biology. *Philosophical Transactions of the Royal Society of London, 359,* 1383–1394.

Rymer, R. (1993). *Genie.* New York: HarperCollins.

S

Sabanayagam, C., & Shankar, A. (2010). Sleep duration and cardiovascular disease: Results from the National Health Survey. *Sleep, 33,* 1037–1042.

Sacco, D. F., & Hugenberg, K. (2009). The look of anger and fear: Facial maturity modulates recognition of fearful and angry expressions. *Emotion, 9,* 39–49.

Sachs, J. (2009). Communication development in infancy. In J. Berko Gleason & N. Ratner (Eds.), *The development of language* (7th ed.). Boston: Allyn & Bacon.

Sachs, R., Wild, T. C., Thomas, L., Hammal, F., & Finegan, B. A. (2012). Smoking cessation interventions in the pre-admission clinic: Assessing two approaches. *Canadian Journal of Anaesthesiology, 59* (7), 662–669.

Sackett, P. R., Walmsley, P. T., & Laczo, R. M. (2013). Job and work analysis. In N. W. Schmitt, S. Highhouse, & I. B. Weiner (Eds.), *Handbook of psychology, 2nd ed., Vol. 12.* (pp. 61–81). Hoboken, NJ: Wiley.

Sacks, O. (2006, June 19). Stereo Sue. *New Yorker,* 64–73.

Sado, M., Knapp, M., Yamauchi, K., Fujisawa, D., So, M., Nakagawa, A., Kikuchi, T., & Ono, Y. (2009). Cost-effectiveness of combination therapy versus antidepressant therapy for management of depression in Japan. *Australian and New Zealand Journal of Psychiatry, 43,* 539–547.

Sahly, J., Shaffer, T. W., Erdberg, P., & O'Toole, S. (2011). Rorschach intercoder reliability for protocol-level comprehensive system variables in an international sample. *Journal of Personality Assessment, 93,* 592–596.

Sakolsky, D. J., McCracken, J. T., & Nurmi, E. L. (2012). Genetics of pediatric personality disorders. *Child and Adolescent Psychiatry Clinics of North America, 21,* 479–500.

Saleem, M., Anderson, C. A., & Gentile, D. A. (2012). Effects of prosocial, neutral, and violent video games on children's helpful and hurtful behaviors. *Aggressive Behavior, 38,* 281–287.

Salminen, N. H., Tiitnen, H., Yrttiaho, S., & May, P. J. (2010). The neural code for interaural time difference in human auditory cortex. *Journal of Acoustical Society of America, 127,* EL60.

Salthouse, T. A. (1994). The nature of the influence of speed on adult age differences in cognition. *Developmental Psychology, 30,* 240–259.

Salthouse, T. A. (2012). Consequences of age-related cognitive declines. *Annual Review of Psychology* (vol. 63). Palo Alto, CA: Annual Reviews.

Salvia, J., Ysseldyke, J. E., & Bolt, S. (2010). *Assessment* (11th ed.). Boston: Cengage.

Sandberg, J. G., & Knestel, A. (2011). The experience of learning Emotionally Focused Couples Therapy. *Journal of Marital and Family Therapy, 37* (4), 393–410.

Sandvik, A. M., Bartone, P. T., Hystad, S. W., Phillips, T. M., Thayer, J. F., & Hohensen, B. H. (2013). Psychological hardiness predicts neuroimmunological responses to stress. *Psychology, Health, and Medicine.* (in press)

Sanjuan, P., Arranz, H., & Castro, A. (2013). Effects of negative attributions on depressive symptoms of patients with coronary heart disease after controlling for physical functional impairment. *British Journal of Health Psychology.* (in press)

Santarcangelo, E. L., & others. (2012). Hypnotizability modulates the cardiovascular correlates of subjective relaxation. *International Journal of Clinical and Experimental Hypnosis, 60,* 383–396.

Santos, S., Torcato, I., & Castanho, M. A. (2012). Biomedical applications of bipeptides and tripeptides. *Biopolymers, 98* (4), 288–293.

Sapolsky, R. M. (2004). *Why zebras don't get ulcers* (3rd ed.). New York: Henry Holt.

Sapp, S. (2010). What have religion and spirituality to do with religion? Three approaches. *Gerontologist, 50* (2), 271–275.

Sar, V., Akyuz, G., & Dogan, O. (2007). Prevalence of dissociative disorders among women in the general population. *Psychiatry Research, 149,* 169–176.

Sarkar, U., Ali, S., & Whooley, M. A. (2009). Self-efficacy as a marker of cardiac function and predictor of heart failure hospitalization and mortality in patients with stable coronary heart disease: Findings from the Heart and Soul Study. *Health Psychology, 28,* 166–173.

Sarma, K., & Kola, S. (2010). Firearms, hanging, and drowning suicides in the Republic of Ireland. *Crisis, 31,* 69–75.

Saroglou, V. (2010). Religiousness as a cultural adaptation of basic traits: A five-factor model perspective. *Personality and Social Psychology Review, 14,* 108–125.

Sattler, C., Toro, P., Schönknecht, P., & Schröder, J. (2012). Cognitive activity, education and socioeconomic status as preventive factors for mild cognitive impairment and Alzheimer's disease. *Psychiatry Research, 196,* 90–95.

Saul, S. (2006, March 8). Some sleeping pill users range far beyond bed. *New York Times.* www.nytimes.com/2006/03/08/business/08ambien.html?pagewanted=all&_r=0 (accessed July 14, 2013)

Saurer, T. B., Ijames, S. G., Carrigan, K. A., & Lysle, D. T. (2008). Neuroimmune mechanisms of opioid-mediated conditioned immunomodulation. *Brain, Behavior, and Immunity, 22,* 89–97.

Sauter, D. A., Eisner, F., Ekman, P., & Scott, S. K. (2010). Cross-cultural recognition of basic emotions through nonverbal emotional vocalizations. *Proceedings of the National Academy of Sciences USA, 107,* 2408–2412.

Savage, J. (2008). The role of exposure to media violence in the etiology of violent behavior: A criminologist weighs in. *American Behavioral Scientist, 51,* 1123–1136.

Savage, J., & Yancey, C. (2008). The effects of media violence exposure on criminal aggression: A meta-analysis. *Criminal Justice and Behavior, 35,* 772–791.

Saver, C. (2013). Succession: Identifying and mentoring OR leaders. *OR Manager, 29,* 16–18.

Savic, I., & Lindström, P. (2008). PET and MRI show differences in cerebral asymmetry and functional connectivity between homo- and heterosexual subjects. *Proceedings of the National Academy of Science, 105,* 9403–9408.

Savin, H. B. (1973). Professors and psychological researchers: Conflicting values in conflicting roles. *Cognition, 2,* 147–149.

Savin-Williams, R. C. (2013). The new sexual-minority teenager. In J. S. Kaufman & D. A. Powell (Eds.), *Sexual identities.* Thousand Oaks, CA: Sage.

Sawatzky, R. G., & others. (2012). Stress and depression in students: The mediating role of stress management self-efficacy. *Nursing Research, 61,* 13–21.

Saxe, R., & Kanwisher, N. (2005). People thinking about thinking people: The role of the temporo-parietal junction in "theory of mind." In J. T. Cacioppo & G. G. Berntson (Eds.), *Social neuroscience: Key readings* (pp. 171–182). New York: Psychology Press.

Saxe, R., & Powell, L. (2006). It's the thought that counts: Specific brain regions for one component of theory of mind. *Psychological Science, 17* (8), 692–699.

Scarr, S. (1984, May). Interview. *Psychology Today,* 59–63.

Schachter, S., & Singer, J. E. (1962). Cognitive, social, and physiological determinants of emotional state. *Psychological Review, 69,* 379–399.

Schacter, D. L. (2001). *The seven sins of memory.* Boston: Houghton Mifflin.

Schacter, D. L. (2007). Memory: Defining the core. In H. L. Roediger, Y. Dudai, & S. M. Fitzpatrick (Eds.), *Science of memory: Concepts.* New York: Oxford University Press.

Schacter, D. L. & Wagner, A. D. (2011). Learning and memory. In E. R. Kandel, J. R. Schwartz, & T. M. Jessell (Eds.), *Principles of neural science* (5th ed.). New York: McGraw-Hill.

Schag, K., Schönleber, J., Teufel, M., Zipfel, S., & Giel, K. E. (2013). Food-related impulsivity in obesity and binge eating disorder—A systematic review. *Obesity Reviews.* (in press)

Schaie, K. W. (1994). The life course of adult intellectual abilities. *American Psychologist, 49,* 304–313.

Schaie, K. W. (2006). Intelligence. In R. Schultz (Ed.), *Encyclopedia of aging* (4th ed.). New York: Springer.

Schaie, K. W. (2007). Generational differences: The age-cohort period model. In J. E. Birren & K. W. Schaie (Eds.), *Encyclopedia of gerontology.* Oxford, U.K.: Elsevier.

Schaie, K. W. (2009). "When does age-related cognitive decline begin?" Salthouse again reifies the "cross-sectional fallacy." *Neurobiology of Aging, 30,* 528–529.

Schaie, K. W. (2010). Adult intellectual abilities. *Corsini encyclopedia of psychology.* New York: Wiley.

Schaie, K. W. (2012). *Developmental influences on adult intellectual development: The Seattle Longitudinal Study* (2nd ed.). New York: Oxford University Press.

Schaller, M., & Cialdini, R. B. (1988). The economics of empathic helping: Support for a mood management motive. *Journal of Experimental Social Psychology, 24,* 163–181.

Schank, R., & Abelson, R. (1977). *Scripts, plans, goals, and understanding.* Mahwah, NJ: Erlbaum.

Schaubroeck, J. M., Riolli, L. T., Peng, A. C., & Spain, E. S. (2011). Resilience to traumatic exposure among soldiers deployed in combat. *Journal of Occupational Health Psychology, 26,* 18–37.

Schedlowski, M., & Pacheco-Lopez, G. (2010). The learned immune response: Pavlov and beyond. *Brain, Behavior, and Immunity, 24,* 176–185.

Scheid, T. L., & Brown, T. N. (Eds.). (2010). *A handbook for the study of mental health: Social contexts, theories, and systems* (2nd ed.). New York: Cambridge University Press.

Scherer, L. D., Zikmund-Fisher, B. J., Fagerlin, A., & Tarini, B. A. (2013). Influence of "GERD" label on parents' decision to medicate infants. *Pediatrics, 131* (5), xi.

Schieffelin, B., & Ochs, E. (Eds.). (1986). *Language socialization across cultures.* Cambridge, U.K.: Cambridge University Press.

Schiff, W. J. (2013). *Nutrition for healthy living* (3rd ed.). New York: McGraw-Hill.

Schimmack, U. (2012). The ironic effect of significant results on the credibility of multiple-study articles. *Psychological Methods, 17,* 551–556.

Schirmer, A. (2013). Sex differences in emotion. In J. Armony & P. Vuilleumier (Eds.), *The Cambridge handbook of human affective neuroscience* (pp. 591–610). New York: Cambridge University Press.

Schkade, D. A., & Kahneman, D. (1998). Does living in California make people happy? A focusing illusion in judgments of life satisfaction. *Psychological Science, 9,* 340–346.

Schlegel, R. J., Hicks, J. A., Davis, W. E., Hirsch, K. A., & Smith, C. M. (2013). The dynamic interplay between perceived true self-knowledge and decision satisfaction. *Journal of Personality and Social Psychology, 104,* 542–558.

Schlegel, R. J., Hirsch, K. A., & Smith, C. M. (2013). The importance of who you really are: The role of the true self in eudaimonia. In A. S. Waterman (Ed.), *The best within us: Positive psychology perspectives on eudaimonia* (pp. 207–225). Washington, DC: American Psychological Association.

Schlesinger, J. (2012). *The insanity hoax: Exposing the myth of the mad genius.* Ardsley-on-Hudson, NY: Shrinktunes Media.

Schmeichel, B. J., Harmon-Jones, C., & Harmon-Jones, E. (2010). Exercising self-control increases approach motivation. *Journal of Personality and Social Psychology, 99,* 162–173.

Schmidt, A. M., Beck, J. W., & Gillespie, J. Z. (2013). Motivation. In N. W. Schmitt, S. Highhouse, & I. B. Weiner (Eds.), *Handbook of psychology, 2nd ed., Vol. 12.* (pp. 311–340). Hoboken, NJ: Wiley.

Schmidt, F. L. (2013). Meta-analysis. In J. A. Schinka, W. F. Velicer, & I. B. Weiner (Eds.), *Handbook of psychology, 2nd ed., Vol. 2.* (pp. 571–594). Hoboken, NJ: Wiley.

Schmidt, N. B., & Koselka, M. (2000). Gender differences in patients with panic disorder: Evaluating cognitive mediation of phobic avoidance. *Cognitive Therapy and Research, 24,* 533–550.

Schmidtke, J. I., & Heller, W. (2004). Personality, affect, and EEG: Predicting patterns of regional brain activity related to extraversion and neuroticism. *Personality and Individual Differences, 36,* 717–732.

Schmitz, M., & Wentura, D. (2012). Evaluative priming of naming and semantic categorization responses revisited: A mutual facilitation explanation. *Journal of Experimental Psychology: Learning, Memory, and Cognition, 38* (4), 984–1000.

Schmitz, W. M., & others. (2012). Preventing suicide through improved training in suicide risk assessment and care: An American Association of Suicidology Task Force report addressing serious gaps in U.S. mental health training. *Life Threatening Behavior, 42* (3), 292–304.

Schnall, E., & others. (2010). The relationship between religion and cardiovascular outcomes and all-cause mortality in the women's health initiative observational study. *Psychology and Health, 25,* 249–263.

Schneider, B., Ehrhart, M. G., & Macey, W. H. (2013). Organizational climate and culture. *Annual Review of Psychology* (vol. 64). Palo Alto, CA: Annual Reviews.

Schneider, K. J. (2002). Humanistic psychotherapy. In M. Hersen & W. H. Sledge (Eds.), *Encyclopedia of psychotherapy.* San Diego: Academic.

Schneider, K. J. (2009). Editor's commentary. *Journal of Humanistic Psychology, 49,* 6–8.

Schneiderman, I., Zagoory-Sharon, O., Leckman, J. F., & Feldman, R. (2012). Oxytocin during the initial stages of romantic attachment: Relations to couples' interactive reciprocity. *Psychoneuroendocrinology, 37,* 1277–1285.

Schönbucher, V., Schweizer, K., Rustige, L., Schützmann, K., Brunner, F., & Richter-Appelt, H. (2012). Sexual quality of life of individuals with 46, XY disorders of sex development. *Journal of Sexual Medicine, 9,* 3154–3170.

Schooler, J. W. (2002). Re-representing consciousness: Dissociations between experience and meta-consciousness. *Trends in Cognitive Sciences, 6,* 339–344.

Schooler, J. W., Ambadar, Z., & Bendiksen, M. (1997). A cognitive corroborative case study approach for investigating discovered memories of sexual abuse. In J. D. Read & D. S. Lindsay (Eds.), *Recollections of trauma: Scientific evidence and clinical practice* (pp. 379–387). New York: Plenum.

Schooler, J. W., Ariely, D., & Loewenstein, G. (2003). The explicit pursuit and assessment of happiness can be self-defeating. In I. Brocas & J. Carrillo (Eds.), *The psychology of economic decisions.* Oxford, U.K.: Oxford University Press.

Schooler, J. W., & Eich, E. (2000). Memory for emotional events. In E. Tulving & F. I. M. Craik (Eds.), *The Oxford handbook of memory* (pp. 379–392). New York: Oxford University Press.

Schooler, J. W., Smallwood, J., Christoff, K., Handy, T. C., Reichle, E. D., & Sayette, M. A. (2011). Meta-awareness, perceptual decoupling and the wandering mind. *Trends in Cognitive Sciences, 15,* 319–326.

Schredl, M. (2009). Dreams in patients with sleep disorders. *Sleep Medicine Reviews, 13,* 215–221.

Schredl, M. (2010). Nightmare frequency and nightmare topics in a representative German sample. *European Archives of Psychiatry and Clinical Neuroscience, 260,* 565–570.

Schultheiss, O. C., & Brunstein, J. C. (2005). An implicit motive perspective on competence. In A. J. Elliot & C. S. Dweck (Eds.), *Handbook of competence and motivation* (pp. 31–51). New York: Guilford.

Schultz, D. P., & Schultz, S. E. (2012). *A history of modern psychology* (10th ed.). Boston: Cengage.

Schultz, W. T. (Ed.) (2005). *The handbook of psychobiography.* New York: Oxford University Press.

Schulz, R. (2007). Cardiovascular health study. In K. S. Markides (Ed.), *Encyclopedia of health and aging.* Thousand Oaks, CA: Sage.

Schulz-Stubner, S., Krings, T., Meister, I. G., Rex, S., Thron, A., & Rossaint, R. (2004). Clinical hypnosis modulates functional magnetic resonance imaging signal intensities and pain perception in a thermal stimulation paradigm. *Regional Anesthesia and Pain Medicine, 29,* 549–556.

Schumann, A., John, U., Rumpf, H., Hapke, U., & Meyer, C. (2006). Changes in the "stages of change" as outcome measures of a smoking cessation intervention: A randomized controlled trial. *Preventive Medicine: An International Journal Devoted to Practice and Theory, 43,* 101–106.

Schunk, D. H. (2012). *Learning theories: An educational perspective* (6th ed.). Upper Saddle River, NJ: Pearson.

Schunk, D. H., & Zimmerman, B. J. (2013). Self-regulation and learning. In W. M. Reynolds, G. F. Miller, & I. B. Weiner (Eds.), *Handbook of psychology, 2nd ed., Vol. 7.* (pp. 45–68). Hoboken, NJ: Wiley.

Schur, E. A., Heckbert, S. R., & Goldberg, J. H. (2010). The association of restrained eating with weight change over time in a community-based sample of twins. *Obesity, 18* (6), 1146–1152.

Schuz, B., Sniehotta, F. F., Mallach, N., Wiedemann, A. U., & Schwarzer, R. (2009). Predicting transitions from preintentional, intentional, and actional stages of change. *Health Education Research, 24,* 64–75.

Schwartz, B. L., & Metcalfe, J. (2011). Tip-of-the-tongue (TOT) states: Retrieval, behavior, and experience. *Memory and Cognition, 39,* 737–749.

Schwartz, S. (2010). Life goes on in dreams. *Sleep, 33,* 15–16.

Schwartz, S. J., Donnellan, M. B., Ravert, R. D., Luyckx, K., & Zamboanga, B. L. (2013). Identity development, personality, and well-being in adolescence and emerging adulthood: Theory, research, and recent advances. In R. M. Lerner, M. A. Easterbrooks, J. Mistry, & I. B. Weiner (Eds.), *Handbook of psychology, 2nd ed., Vol. 6.* (pp. 339–364). Hoboken, NJ: Wiley.

Schwartz, S. J., Zamboanga, B. L., Meca, A., & Ritchie, R. A. (2012). Identity around the world: An overview. *New Directions in Child and Adolescent Development,* 1–18. doi: 10.1002/cad.20019

Schwartz, A. (2013, May 1). Attention-deficit drugs face new campus rules. *New York Times.* www.nytimes.com/2013/05/01/us/colleges-tackle-illicit-use-of-adhd-pills.html?pagewanted=all&_r=1& (accessed May 21, 2013)

Schwarz, N., Song, H., & Xu, J. (2009). When thinking is difficult: Metacognitive experiences as information. In M. Wanke (Ed.), *Social psychology of consumer behavior* (pp. 201–223). New York: Psychology Press.

Schwarzer, R., & Luszczynska, A. (2013). Stressful life events. In A. M. Nezu, C. Maguth Nezu, P. A. Geller, & I. B. Weiner (Eds.), *Handbook of psychology, 2nd ed., Vol. 9.* (pp. 29–56). Hoboken, NJ: Wiley.

Schyns, B., & Sanders, K. (2007). In the eyes of the beholder: Personality and the perception of leadership. *Journal of Applied Social Psychology, 37* (10), 2345–2363.

Schyns, B. & Schilling, J. (2013). How bad are the effects of bad leaders? A meta-analysis of destructive leadership and its outcomes. *Leadership Quarterly, 24* (1), 138–158.

Scorzelli, J. F., & Reinke-Scorzelli, M. (1994). Cultural sensitivity and cognitive therapy in India. *Counseling Psychologist, 22* (4), 603–610.

Scott, R. M., & Baillargeon, R. (2013). Do infants really expect others to act efficiently? A critical test of the rationality principle. *Psychological Science, 24,* 466–474.

Scott-Sheldon, L. A. J., & Johnson, B. T. (2006). Eroticizing creates safer sex: A research synthesis. *Journal of Primary Prevention, 27,* 619–640.

Sears, D. O. (2008). The American color line 50 years after *Brown v. Board:* Many "peoples of color" or Black exceptionalism? In G. Adams, M. Biernat, N. R. Branscombe, C. S. Crandall, & L. S. Wrightsman (Eds.), *Commemorating Brown: The social psychology of racism and discrimination.* Washington, DC: American Psychological Association.

Sebastian, C. L., & others. (2012). Neural responses to affective and cognitive theory of mind in children with conduct problems and varying levels of callous-unemotional traits. *Archives of General Psychiatry, 69,* 814–822.

Sedikides, C. (2009). On self-protection and self-enhancement regulation: The role of self-improvement and social norms. In J. P. Forgas, R. F. Baumeister, & D. Tice (Eds.), *The psychology of self-regulation.* New York: Psychology Press.

Sedikides, C., & Skowronski, J. J. (2009). Social cognition and self-cognition: Two sides of the same evolutionary coin? *European Journal of Social Psychology, 39,* 1245–1249.

Sedikides, C. & Skowronski, J. J. (2012). Construct accessibility and interpretation of self-behaviors: Tracing and reducing the signatures of self-protection and self-enhancement. In J. P. Forgas, K. Fielder, & C. Sedikides (Eds.), *Social thinking and interpersonal behavior.* New York: Psychology Press.

Seery, M. D. (2011). Challenge or threat? Cardiovascular indexes of resilience and vulnerability to potential stress in humans. *Neuroscience and Biobehavioral Reviews, 35,* 1603–1610.

Segerstrom, S. C. (2003). Individual differences, immunity, and cancer: Lessons from personality psychology. *Brain, Behavior and Immunity, 17,* Suppl. 1, S92–S97.

Segerstrom, S. C. (2006). *Breaking Murphy's law: How optimists get what they want from life and pessimists can too.* New York: Guilford.

Segerstrom, S. C., & Sephton, S. E. (2010). Optimistic expectations and cell-mediated immunity: The role of positive affect. *Psychological Science, 21,* 448–455.

Seidel, E. M., & others. (2012). Neural correlates of depressive realism—An fMRI study on causal attribution in depression. *Journal of Affective Disorders, 138,* 266–276.

Seligman, M. E. P. (1970). On the generality of the laws of learning. *Psychological Review, 77,* 406–418.

Seligman, M. E. P. (1990). *Learned optimism.* New York: Knopf.

Seligman, M. E. P. (1994). *What you can change and what you can't.* New York: Knopf.

Seligman, M. E. P., & Csikszentmihalyi, M. (2000). Positive psychology: An introduction. *American Psychologist, 55,* 5–14.

Seligman, M. E. P., & Maier, S. F. (1967). Failure to escape traumatic shock. *Journal of Experimental Psychology, 74,* 1–9.

Seligman, M. E. P., Rosellini, R. A., & Kozak, M. J. (1975). Learned helplessness in the rat: Time course, immunization, and reversibility. *Journal of Comparative and Physiological Psychology, 88,* 542–547.

Sellbom, M., Toomey, J. A., Wygant, D. B., Kucharski, L. T., & Duncan, S. (2010). Utility of the MMPI-2-RF (restructured form) validity scales in detecting malingering in a criminal forensic setting: A known-groups design. *Psychological Assessment, 22,* 22–31.

Sellers, R. M., Copeland-Linder, N., Martin, P. P., & Lewis, R. L. (2006). Racial identity matters: The relationship between racial discrimination and psychological functioning in African American adolescents. *Journal of Research on Adolescence, 16,* 187–216.

Selvaraj, V., Jiang, P., Chechneva, O., Lo, U. G., & Deng, W. (2012). Differentiating human stem cells into neurons and glial cells for neural repair. *Frontiers in Bioscience, 17,* 65–89.

Selye, H. (1974). *Stress without distress.* Philadelphia: Saunders.

Selye, H. (1983). The stress concept: Past, present, and future. In C. I. Cooper (Ed.), *Stress research.* New York: Wiley.

Semin, G. R., & Garrido, A. (2012). A systematic approach to impression formation: From verbal to multi-modal processes. In J. P. Forgas, K. Fiedler, & C. Sedikides (Eds.), *Social thinking and interpersonal behavior.* New York: Psychology Press.

Serafini, G., & others. (2013). Pharmacological properties of glutamatergic drugs targeting NMDA receptors and their application in major depression. *Current Pharmaceutical Design.* (in press)

Sergent, C., & Naccache, L. (2012). Imaging neural signatures of consciousness: "What," "when," "where," and "how" does it work? *Archives of Italian Biology, 150,* 91–106.

Sesardic, N. (2006). *Making sense of heritability.* New York: Cambridge University Press.

Seto, M. C. (2009). Pedophilia. *Annual Review of Clinical Psychology* (vol. 5). Palo Alto, CA: Annual Reviews.

Settles, R. E., Fischer, S., Cyders, M. A., Combs, J. L., Gunn, R. L., & Smith, G. T. (2012). Negative urgency: A personality predictor of externalizing behavior characterized by neuroticism, low conscientiousness, and disagreeableness. *Journal of Abnormal Psychology, 121* (1), 160–172.

Seymour, T. L., Seifert, C. M., Shafto, M. G., & Mosmann, A. L. (2000). Using response time measures to assess "guilty knowledge." *Journal of Applied Psychology, 85,* 30–37.

Shamay-Tsoory, S. G., Harari, H., Aharon-Peretz, J., & Levkovitz, Y. (2010). The role of the orbitofrontal cortex in affective theory of mind deficits in criminal offenders with psychopathic tendencies. *Cortex, 46,* 668–677.

Shariff, A. F., & Tracy, J. L. (2011). What are emotion expressions for? *Current Directions in Psychological Science, 20,* 395–399.

Sharma, N., Classen, J., & Cohen, L. G. (2013). Neural plasticity and its contribution to functional recovery. *Handbook of Clinical Psychology, 110,* 3–12.

Sharmila, D. (2012). Antidepressant–suicide link in children questioned. *Lancet, 379,* 791.

Sharp, E. S., Reynolds, C. A,. Pedersen, N. L., & Gatz, M. (2010). Cognitive engagement and cognitive aging: Is openness protective? *Psychology and Aging, 25,* 60–73.

Sheldon, K. M. (2002). The self-concordance model of healthy goal-striving: When personal goals correctly represent the person. In E. L. Deci & R. M. Ryan (Eds.), *Handbook of self-determination research* (pp. 65–86). Rochester, NY: University of Rochester Press.

Sheldon, K. M. (2013). Individual daimon, universal needs, and subjective well-being: Happiness as the natural consequence of a life well lived. In A. S. Waterman (Ed.), *The best within us: Positive psychology perspectives on eudaimonia* (pp. 119–137). Washington, DC: American Psychological Association.

Sheldon, K. M., Kasser, T., Houser-Marko, L., Jones, T., & Turban, D. (2005). Doing one's duty: Chronological age, felt autonomy, and subjective well-being. *European Journal of Personality, 19,* 97–115.

Sheldon, K. M., & Lyubomirsky, S. (2007). Is it possible to become happier? (And if so, how?). *Social and Personality Psychology Compass, 1,* 129–145.

Sheldon, K. M., & Lyubomirsky, S. (2012). The challenge of staying happier: Testing the happiness adaptation model. *Personality and Social Psychology Bulletin, 38,* 670–680.

Shelton, R. C., Osuntokun, O., Heinloth, A. N., & Corya, S. A. (2010). Therapeutic options for treatment-resistant depression. *CNS Drugs, 24,* 131–161.

Sherif, M., Harvey, O. J., White, B. J., Hood, W. R., & Sherif, C. W. (1961). *Intergroup cooperation and competition: The Robbers Cave experiment.* Norman: University of Oklahoma Press.

Sherman, R. A., Nave, C., & Funder, D. C. (2010). Situational similarity and personality predict behavioral consistency. *Journal of Personality and Social Psychology, 99,* 330–343.

Sherwood, L. (2013). *Human physiology* (8th ed.). Boston: Cengage.

Sherwood, L., Klandorf, H., & Yancey, P. (2013). *Animal physiology: From genes to organisms* (2nd ed.). Boston: Cengage.

Shetty, A. K., Rao, M. S., & Hattiangady, B. (2008). Behavior of hippocampal stem/progenitor cells following grafting into the injured hippocampus. *Journal of Neurosciece Research, 86,* 3062–3074.

Shields, S. A. (1991). Gender in the psychology of emotion. In K. T. Strongman (Ed.), *International Review of Studies of Emotion* (vol. 1). New York: Wiley.

Shin, M. S., & others. (2013). Treadmill exercise ameliorates symptoms of methimazole-induced hypothyroidism through enhancing neurogenesis and suppressing apotposis in the hippocampus of rat pups. *International Journal of Neuroscience.* (in press)

Shiner, R. L., & DeYoung, C. G. (2013). The structure of temperament and personality: A developmental approach. In P. D. Zelazo (Ed.), *The Oxford handbook of developmental psychology, Vol. 2.* (pp. 113–141). New York: Oxford University Press.

Shiralkar, M. T., Harris, T. B., Eddins-Folensbee, F. F., & Coverdale, J. H. (2013). A systematic review of stress-management programs for medical students. *Academic Psychiatry, 37* (3),158–164.

Shkurko, Y. S. (2013). The compatibility between sociological and cognitive neuroscientific ideas on consciousness: Is a neurosociology of consciousness possible? *Integrative Psychological and Behavioral Science.* (in press)

Shu, L. L., Gino, F., & Bazerman, M. H. (2011). Dishonest deed, clear conscience: When cheating leads to moral disengagement and motivated forgetting. *Personality and Social Psychology Bulletin, 37,* 330–349.

Shulman, J. L., Gotta, G., & Green, R. (2012). Will marriage matter? Effects of marriage anticipated by same-sex couples. *Journal of Family Issues, 33,* 158–181.

Shushruth, S., & others. (2012). Strong recurrent networks compute the orientation tuning of surround modulation in the primate visual cortex. *Journal of Neuroscience, 32,* 308–321.

Sibley, M. H., Pelham Jr., W. E., Molina, B. S. G., Gnagy, E. M., Waschbusch, D. A., Garefino, A. C., Kuriyan, A. B., Babinski, D. E., & Karch, K. M. (2012). Diagnosing ADHD in adolescence. *Journal of Consulting and Clinical Psychology, 80,* 139–150.

Sieber, W. J., Rodin, J., Larson, L., Ortega, S., & Cummings, N. (1992). Modulation of human natural killer cell activity by exposure to uncontrollable stress. *Brain, Behavior, and Immunity, 6,* 141–156.

Siegel J. M. (2005). Clues to the functions of mammalian sleep. *Nature, 437,* 1264–1271.

Siegel, J. M. (2011). REM sleep: A biological and psychological paradox. *Sleep Medicine Review, 15,* 139–142.

Siegel, S. (1988). State dependent learning and morphine tolerance. *Behavioral Neuroscience, 102,* 228–232.

Siegler, I. C., Bosworth, H. B., Davey, A., & Elias, M. F. (2013a). Disease, health, and aging in the first decade of the 21st century. In R. M. Lerner, M. A. Easterbrooks, J. Mistry, & I. B. Weiner (Eds.), *Handbook of psychology, 2nd ed., Vol. 6.* (pp. 437–450). Hoboken, NJ: Wiley.

Siegler, I. C., Elias, M. F., Brummett, B. H., & Bosworth, H. B. (2013b). Adult development and aging. In A. M. Nezu, C. Maguth Nezu, P. A. Geller, & I. B. Weiner (Eds.), *Handbook of psychology, 2nd ed., Vol. 9.* (pp. 459–476). Hoboken, NJ: Wiley.

Siegler, R. S. (2012). From theory to application and back: Following in the giant footsteps of David Klahr. In S. M. Carver & J. Shrager (Eds.), *The journey from child to scientist: Integrating cognitive development and the education sciences.* Thousand Oaks, CA: Sage.

Siegler, R. S., Fazio, L. K., Bailey, D. H. & Zhou, X. (2013). Fractions: The new frontier for theories of numerical development. *Trends in Cognitive Science, 17,* 13–19.

Sieswerda, S., Arntz, A., Mertens, I., & Vertommen, S. (2007). Hypervigilance in patients with borderline personality disorder: Specificity, automaticity, and predictors. *Behaviour Research and Therapy, 45,* 1011–1024.

Sikorskii, A., Given, C., Given, B., Jeon, S., & McCorkle, R. (2006). Testing the effects of treatment complications on a cognitive-behavioral intervention for reducing symptom severity. *Journal of Pain and Symptom Management, 32,* 129–139.

Silberstein, M., & Chemero, A. (2012). Complexity and extended phenomenological-cognitive systems. *Topics in Cognitive Science, 4,* 35–50.

Silva de Lima, M., Farrell, M., Lima Reisser, A. A., & Soares, B. (2010). WITHDRAWN: Antidepressants for cocaine dependence. *Cocharine Database of Systematic Reviews,* CD002950.

Silvia, P. J., Nusbaum, E. C., Berg, C., Martin, C., & O'Connor, A. (2009). Openness to experience, plasticity, and creativity: Exploring lower-order, high-order, and interactive effects. *Journal of Research in Personality, 43,* 1087–1090.

Simner, J. (2012a). Defining synesthesia. *British Journal of Psychology, 103,* 1–15.

Simner, J. (2012b). Defining synesthesia: A response to two excellent commentaries. *British Journal of Psychology, 103,* 24–27.

Simning, A., van Wijngaarden, E., Fisher, S. G., Richardson, T. M., & Conwell, Y. (2012). Mental healthcare need and service utilization in older adults living in public housing. *American Journal of Geriatric Psychiatry, 20,* 441–451.

Simola, S. K., Barling, J., & Turner, N. (2010). Transformational leadership and leader moral orientation: Contrasting an ethic of justice and an ethic of care. *Leadership Quarterly, 21,* 179–188.

Simon, H. A. (1969). *The sciences of the artificial.* Cambridge, MA: MIT Press.

Simons, D. J., & Chabris, C. F. (1999). Gorillas in our midst: Sustained inattentional blindness for dynamic events. *Perception, 28* (9), 1059–1074.

Simons, D. J., & Chabris, C. F. (2011). What people believe about how memory works: A representative survey of the U.S. population. *PLoS One, 6* (8), e22757.

Simon-Thomas, E. R., Godzik, J., Castle, E., Antonenko, O., Ponz, A., Kogan, A., & Keltner, D. J. (2012). An fMRI study of caring vs self-focus during induced compassion and pride. *Social Cognitive Affective Neuroscience, 7* (6), 635–648.

Simonton, D. K. (2010). So you want to become a creative genius? You must be crazy! In D. H. Cropley, A. J. Cropley, J. C. Kaufman, & M. A. Runco (Eds.), *The dark side of creativity* (pp. 218–234). New York: Cambridge University Press.

Simpkins, S. D., Bouffard, S. M., Dearing, E., Kreider, H., Wimer, C., Caronongan, P., & Weiss, H. B. (2009). Adolescent adjustment and patterns of parents' behaviors in early and middle adolescence. *Journal of Research on Adolescence, 19* (3), 530–557.

Simpson, H. B., & others. (2013). Treatment of obsessive-compulsive disorder complicated by comorbid eating disorders. *Cognitive Behavior Therapy, 42* (1), 64–76.

Sin, N. L., & Lyubomirsky, S. (2009). Enhancing well-being and alleviating depressive symptoms with positive psychology interventions: A practice-friendly meta-analysis. *Journal of Clinical Psychology, 65,* 467–487.

Singer, J. A., & Blagov, P. (2004). The integrative function of narrative processing: Autobiographical memory, self-defining memories, and the life story of identity. In D. R. Beike, J. M. Lampinen, & D. A. Behrend (Eds.), *The self and memory* (pp. 117–138). New York: Psychology Press.

Singer, J. A., & Conway, M. A. (2011). Reconsidering therapeutic action: Loewald, cognitive neuroscience, and the integration of memory's duality. *International Journal of Psychoanalysis, 92,* 1183–1207.

Singer, J. A., Singer, B. F., & Berry, M. (2013). A meaning-based intervention for addiction: Using narrative therapy to treat alcohol abuse. In J. Hicks & C. Routledge (Eds.), *The experience of meaning in life.* New York: Springer.

Singh, M., & others. (2010). Brain glutamatergic characteristics of pediatric offspring of parents with bipolar disorder. *Psychiatry Research, 182* (2), 165–171.

Singh-Manoux, A., Kivimaki, M., Glymour, M. M., Elbaz, A., Berr, C., Ebmeier, K. P., Ferrie, J. E., & Dugravot, A. (2012). Timing of onset of cognitive decline: Results from Whitehall II prospective cohort study. *British Journal of Medicine, 344,* 1–8.

Sinn, D. L., Gosling, S. D., & Moltschaniwskyj, N. A. (2008). Development of shy/bold behaviour in squid: Context-specific phenotypes associated with developmental plasticity. *Animal Behaviour, 75,* 433–442.

Sinn, D. L., Moltschaniwskyj, N. A., Wapstra, E., & Dall, S. R. X. (2010). Are behavioral syndromes invariant? Spatiotemporal variation in shy/bold behavior in squid. *Behavioral Ecology and Sociobiology, 64,* 693–702.

Sinnapah, S., Cadelis, G., Waltz, X., Lamarre, Y., & Connes, P. (2013). Overweight explains the increased red blood cell aggregation in patients with obstructive sleep apnea. *Clinical Hemorheology and Microcirculation.* (in press)

Sintov, N. D., & others. (2010). Empirically defined subtypes of alcohol dependence in an Irish family sample. *Drug and Alcohol Dependence, 107,* 230–236.

Sitnikova, T., Goff, D., & Kuperberg, G. R. (2009). Neurocognitive abnormalities during comprehension of real-world goal-directed behaviors in schizophrenia. *Journal of Abnormal Psychology, 118,* 256–277.

Sivacek, J., & Crano, W. D. (1982). Vested interest as a moderator of attitude-behavior consistency. *Journal of Personality and Social Psychology, 43* (2), 210–221.

Sivanathan, N., Arnold, K. A., Turner, N., & Barling, J. (2004). Leading well: Transformational leadership and well-being. In P. A. Linley & S. Joseph (Eds.), *Positive psychology in practice* (pp. 241–255). Hoboken, NJ: Wiley.

Skelton, K., Ressler, K. J., Norrholm, S. D., Jovanovic, T., & Bradley-Davino, B. (2012). PTSD and gene variants: New pathways and new thinking. *Neuropharmacology, 62,* 628–637.

Skinner, B. F. (1938). *The behavior of organisms: An experimental analysis.* New York: Appleton-Century-Crofts.

Skinner, B. F. (1957). *Verbal behavior.* New York: Appleton-Century-Crofts.

Skodol, A. (2012a). Diagnosis and DSM-5: Work in progress. In T. Widiger (Ed.), *The Oxford handbook of personality disorders.* New York: Oxford University Press.

Skodol, A. E. (2012b). Personality disorders in DSM-5. *Annual Review of Clinical Psychology* (vol. 8). Palo Alto, CA: Annual Reviews.

Skogstad, M., & others. (2013). Work-related post-traumatic stress disorder. *Occupational Medicine, 63,* 175–182.

Skolin I., Wahlin, Y. B., Broman, D. A., Koivisto Hursti, U., Vikström, L. M., & Hernell, O. (2006). Altered food intake and taste perception in children with cancer after start of chemotherapy: Perspectives of children, parents, and nurses. *Supportive Care in Cancer, 14,* 369–378.

Slater, A., Field, T., & Hernandez-Reif, M. (2007). The development of the senses. In A. Slater & M. Lewis (Eds.), *Introduction to infant development* (2nd ed.). New York: Oxford University Press.

Slater, C., & Dymond, S. (2011). Using differential reinforcement to improve equine welfare: Shaping appropriate truck loading and feet handling. *Behavioral Processes, 86,* 329–339.

Slattery, M. J., Grieve, A. J., Ames, M. E., Armstrong, J. M., & Essex, M. J. (2013). Neurocognitive function and state cognitive stress appraisal predict cortisol reactivity to an acute psychosocial stressor in adolescents. *Psychoneuroendocrinology.* (in press)

Slavin, R. E. (2006). Translating research into widespread practice: The case of success for all. In M. A. Constas & R. J. Sternberg (Eds.), *Translating theory and research into educational practice: Developments in content domains, large-scale reform, and intellectual capacity* (pp. 113–126). Mahwah, NJ: Erlbaum.

Slavin-Mulford, J., Sinclair, S. J., Malone, J., Stein, M., Bello, I., & Blais, M. A. (2013). External correlates of the Personality Assessment Inventory higher order structures. *Journal of Personality Assessment.* (in press)

Slof-Op't Landt, M. C. T., Bartels, M., Middeldorp, C. M., van Beijsterveldt, C. E. M., Slagboom, P. E., Boomsma, D. I., van Furth, E. F., & Meulenbelt, I. (2013). Genetic variation at the TPH2 gene influences impulsivity in addition to eating disorders. *Behavior Genetics, 43,* 24–33.

Slotnick, S. D., & Schacter, D. L. (2006). The nature of memory related activity in early visual areas. *Neuropsychologia, 44,* 2874–2886.

Smalarz, L., & Wells, G. L. (2013). Eyewitness certainty as a system variable. In B. L. Cutler (Ed.), *Reform of eyewitness identification procedures* (pp. 161–177). Washington, DC: American Psychological Association.

Smallwood, J., Schooler, J. W., Turk, D. J., Cunningham, S. J., Burns, P., & Macrae, C. N. (2011). Self-reflection and the temporal focus of the wandering mind. *Consciousness and Cognition, 20,* 1120–1126.

Smetana, J. G., Tasopoulos-Chan, M., Gettman, D. C., Villalobos, M., Campione-Barr, N., & Metzger, A. (2009). Adolescents' and parents' evaluations of helping versus fulfilling personal desires in family situations. *Child Development, 80,* 280–294.

Smieskova, R., & others. (2010). Neuroimaging predictors of transition to psychosis—A systematic review and meta-analysis. *Neuroscience and Biobehavioral Reviews, 34* (8), 1207–1222.

Smillie, L. D., Cooper, A., Wilt, J., & Revelle, W. (2012). Do extraverts get more bang for the buck? Refining the affective-reactivity hypothesis of extraversion. *Journal of Personality and Social Psychology, 103* (2), 306–326.

Smit, F., Willemse, G., Koopmanschap, M., Onrust, S., Cuijpers, P., & Beekman, A. (2006). Cost-effectiveness of preventing depression in primary care patients: Randomized trial. *British Journal of Psychiatry, 188,* 330–336.

Smit, Y., & others. (2012). The effectiveness of long-term psychoanalytic psychotherapy—A meta-analysis of randomized controlled trials. *Clinical Psychology Review, 32,* 81–92.

Smith, A. R., Silva, C., Covington, D. W., & Joiner, T. E. (2013). An assessment of suicide-related knowledge and skills among health professionals. *Health Psychology.* (in press)

Smith, C. A., & Kirby, L. D. (2009). Putting appraisal in context: Toward a relational model of appraisal and emotion. *Cognition and Emotion, 23,* 1352–1372.

Smith, C. P. (Ed.). (1992). *Thematic content analysis for motivation and personality research.* New York: Cambridge University Press.

Smith, D. (2004, February 7). Love that dare not squeak its name. *New York Times.* www.nytimes.com/2004/02/07/arts/07GAY.html (accessed May 9, 2013)

Smith, H. S. (2010). The role of genomic oxidative-reductive balance as predictor of complex regional pain syndrome development: A novel theory. *Pain Physician, 13,* 79–90.

Smith, M. C., Bibi, U., & Sheard, D. E. (2003). Evidence for the differential impact of time and emotion on personal and event memories for September 11, 2001. *Applied Cognitive Psychology, 17,* 1047–1055.

Smith, R. A., & Davis, S. F. (2013). *The psychologist as detective* (6th ed.). Upper Saddle River, NJ: Prentice-Hall.

Smith, R. E., Horn, S. S., & Bayen, U. J. (2012). Prospective memory in young and older adults: The effects of ongoing task load. *Neuropsychology, Development, and Cognition: Aging, Neuropsychology, and Cognition, 19* (4), 495–514.

Smith, R. L., Rose, R. J., & Schwartz-Mette, R. A. (2010). Relational and overt aggression in childhood and adolescence: Clarifying mean-level gender differences and associations with peer acceptance. *Social Development, 19,* 243–269.

Smith, S. J., Axelton, A. M., & Saucier, D. A. (2009). The effects of contact on sexual prejudice: A meta-analysis. *Sex Roles, 61,* 178–191.

Smyth, J. (1998). Written emotional expression: Effect sizes, outcome types, and moderating variables. *Journal of Consulting and Clinical Psychology, 66,* 174–184.

Sneed, R. S., Cohen, S., Turner, R. B., & Doyle, W. J. (2012). Parenthood and host resistance to the common cold. *Psychosomatic Medicine, 74,* 567–573.

Snell, R. S., & Wong, Y. L. (2007). Differentiating good soldiers from good actors. *Journal of Management Studies, 44* (6), 883–909.

Snowdon, D. A. (2003). Healthy aging and dementia: Findings from the Nun Study. *Annals of Internal Medicine, 139,* 450–454.

Snowdon, D. A. (2007, April). *Aging with grace: Findings from the Nun Study.* Paper presented at the 22nd annual Alzheimer's regional conference, Seattle.

Snyder, C. R., & Lopez, S. J. (Eds.). (2007). *Positive psychology: The scientific and practical explorations of human strengths.* Thousand Oaks, CA: Sage.

Snyder, J. A., Scherer, H. L., & Fisher, B. S. (2012). Social organization and social ties: Their effects on sexual harassment victimization in the workplace. *Work, 42* (1), 137–150.

Soares, M. S., Paiva, W. S., Guertzenstein, E. Z., Amorim, R. L., Bernardo, L. S., Pereira, J. F., Fonoff, E. T., & Teixeira, M. J. (2013). Psychosurgery for schizophrenia: History and perspectives. *Neuropsychiatric Disease and Treatment, 9,* 509–515.

Sofuoglu, M., Sugarman, D. E., & Carroll, K. M. (2010). Cognitive function as an emerging treatment target for marijuana addiction. *Experimental and Clinical Psychopharmacology, 18,* 109–119.

Sojcher, R., Fogerite, S. G., & Perlman, A. (2012). Evidence and potential mechanisms for mindfulness practices and energy psychology for obesity and binge-eating disorder. *Explore, 8,* 271–276.

Solesio-Jofre, E., & others. (2011). Age effects on retroactive interference during working memory maintenance. *Biological Psychology, 88,* 72–82.

Solomon, A. (2012, December 22). Anatomy of a murder-suicide. *New York Times Sunday Review.* www.nytimes.com/2012/12/23/opinion/sunday/anatomy-of-a-murder-suicide.html?pagewanted=all&_r=0 (accessed May 20, 2013)

Solomon, S. (2013). Self-esteem is central to human well-being. In M. H. Kernis (Ed.), *Self-esteem issues and answers.* New York: Psychology Press.

Solomon, Z., Horesh, D., Ein-Dor, T., & Ohry, A. (2012). Predictors of PTSD trajectories following captivity: A 35-year longitudinal study. *Psychiatry Research, 199,* 188–194.

Sommer, M., Hajak, G., Dohnel, K., Schwerdtner, J., Meinhardt, J., & Muller, J. L. (2006). Integration of emotion and cognition in patients with psychopathy. *Progress in Brain Research, 156C,* 457–466.

Sommer, M., Rothmayr, C., Dohnel, K., Meinhardt, J., Schwerdtner, J., Sodian, B., & Hajak, G. (2010). How should I decide? The neural correlates of everyday moral reasoning. *Neuropsychologia, 48,* 2018–2026.

Sommer, V., & Vasey, P. L. (Eds.). (2006). *Homosexual behaviour in animals: An evolutionary perspective.* New York: Cambridge University Press.

Song, A. V., & Halpern-Felsher, B. L. (2010). Predictive relationship between adolescent oral and vaginal sex: Results from a prospective, longitudinal study. *Archives of Pediatric and Adolescent Medicine, 165,* 243–249.

Song, S. (2006, March 27). Mind over medicine. *Time, 167,* 13.

Song, Y., Tian, M., & Liu, J. (2012). Top-down processing of symbolic meanings modulates the visual word form area. *Journal of Neuroscience, 32,* 12277–12283.

Sonnentag, S., & Frese, M. (2013). Stress in organizations. In N. W. Schmitt, S. Highhouse, & I. B. Weiner (Eds.), *Handbook of psychology, 2nd ed., Vol. 12.* (pp. 560–592). Hoboken, NJ: Wiley.

Sontag-Padilla, L. M., Dorn, L. D., Tissot, A., Susman, E. J., Beers, S. R., & Rose, S. R. (2012). Executive functioning, cortisol reactivity, and symptoms of psychopathology in girls with premature adrenarche. *Development and Psychopathology, 24,* 211–223.

Soomro, G. M. (2012). Obsessive-compulsive disorder. *Clinical Evidence, 12,* 1004.

Sourial-Bassillious, N., Rydelius, P. A., Aperia, A., & Aizman, O. (2009). Glutamate-mediated calcium signaling: A potential target for lithium action. *Neuroscience, 161* (4), 1126–1134.

South, S. C., & Krueger, R. F. (2008). And interactionist on genetic and environmental contributions to personality. *Social and Personality Psychology Compass, 2,* 929–948.

South, S. C., Reichborn-Kjennerud, T., Eaton, N. R., & Krueger, R. F. (2013). Genetics of personality. In H. A. Tennen, J. M. Suls, & I. B. Weiner (Eds.), *Handbook of psychology, 2nd ed., Vol. 5.* (pp. 3–26). Hoboken, NJ: Wiley.

Sozzi, M., Balconi, M., Arangio, R., Pisani, L., & Mariani, C. (2012). Top-down strategy in rehabilitation of spatial neglect: How about age effect? *Cognitive Processes, 13,* Suppl. 1, S339–S342.

Spanos, N. P. (1996). *Multiple identities and false memories: A sociocognitive perspective.* Washington, DC: American Psychological Association.

Sparks, J. R., & Areni, C. S. (2008). Style versus substance: Multiple roles of language power in persuasion. *Journal of Applied Social Psychology, 38,* 37–60.

Sparling, P., & Redican, K. (2012). *iHealth: An interactive framework.* New York: McGraw-Hill.

Sparrow, B., Liu, J., & Wegner, D. M. (2011). Google effects on memory: Cognitive consequences of having information at our fingertips. *Science, 333,* 776–778.

Spaulding, L. H. (1998). Florida's 1997 chemical castration law: A return to the dark ages. *Florida State University Law Review, 117,* 125–135.

Speakman, J. R., & others. (2011). Set points, settling points, and some alternative models: Theoretical options to understand how genes and environments combine to regulate body adiposity. *Disease Models and Mechanisms, 4,* 733–745.

Spearman, C. (1904). "General intelligence" objectively determined and measured. *American Journal of Psychology, 15,* 201–293.

Spelke, E. S., Bernier, E. P., & Snedeker, J. (2013). Core social cognition. In M. R. Banaji & S. A. Gelman (Eds.), *Navigating the social world: What infants, children, and other species can teach us.* New York: Oxford University Press.

Spelke, E. S., & Kinzler, K. D. (2007). Core knowledge. *Developmental Science, 10,* 89–96.

Spence, K. W. (1938). Gradual versus sudden solution of discrimination problems by chimpanzees. *Journal of Comparative Psychology, 25,* 213–224.

Spencer, J. P., Blumberg, M. S., McMurray, B., Robinson, S. R., Samuelson, L. K., & Tomblin, J. B. (2009). Short arms and talking eggs: Why we should no longer abide the nativist-empiricist debate, *Child Development Perspective, 3* (2), 79–87.

Spencer, S. J., Steele, C. M., & Quinn, D. M. (1999). Stereotype threat and women's math performance. *Journal of Experimental Social Psychology, 35,* 4–28.

Spencer-Smith, M. M., & Anderson, V. A. (2011). Plasticity in a pediatric population. In A. S. Davis (Ed.), *Handbook of pediatric neuropsychology* (pp. 177–189). New York: Springer.

Sperling, G. (1960). The information available in brief presentations. *Psychological Monographs, 74* (11).

Sperry, R. W. (1968). Hemisphere deconnection and unity in conscious awareness. *American Psychologist, 23,* 723–733.

Sperry, R. W. (1974). Lateral specialization in surgically separated hemispheres. In F. O. Schmitt & F. G. Worden (Eds.), *The neurosciences: Third study program.* Cambridge, MA: MIT Press.

Spiegel, D. (2006). Editorial: Recognizing traumatic dissociation. *American Journal of Psychiatry, 163,* 566–568.

Spiegel, D. (2010). Hypnosis testing. In A. F. Barabasz, K. Olness, R. Boland, & S. Kahn (Eds.), *Medical hypnosis primer: Clinical and research evidence* (pp. 11–18). New York: Routledge/Taylor & Francis.

Spiegel, D., Lewis-Fernandez, R., Lanius, R., Vermetten, E., Simeon, D., & Friedman, M. (2013). Dissociative disorders in DSM-5. *Annual Review of Clinical Psychology* (vol. 9). Palo Alto, CA: Annual Reviews.

Spielberger, C. D. (2004, August). *Type A behavior, anger-hostility, and heart disease.* Paper presented at the 28th International Congress of Psychology, Beijing, China.

Spring, J. (2013). *Deculturalization and the struggle for equality* (7th ed.). New York: McGraw-Hill.

Springer, J. B., Lamborn, S. D., & Pollard, D. M. (2013). Maintaining physical activity over time: The importance of basic psychological need satisfaction in developing the physically active self. *American Journal of Health Promotion, 27* (5), 284–293.

Sproesser, G. Strohbach, S., Schupp, H., & Renner, B. (2011). Candy or apple? How self-control resources and motives impact dietary healthiness in women. *Appetite, 56,* 784–787.

Squire, L. R. (1990, June). *Memory and brain systems.* Paper presented at the meeting of the American Psychological Society, Dallas.

Squire, L. R. (2004). Memory systems of the brain: A brief history and current perspective. *Neurobiology of Learning and Memory, 82,* 171–177.

Squire, L. R. (2007). Memory systems as a biological concept. In H. L. Roediger, Y. Dudai, & S. Fitzpatrick (Eds.), *Science of memory: Concepts.* New York: Oxford University Press.

Sriram, N., & Greenwald, A. G. (2009). The Brief Implicit Association Test. *Experimental Psychology, 56,* 283–204.

Sroufe, L. A., Coffino, B., & Carlson, E. A. (2010). Conceptualizing the role of early experience: Lessons from the Minnesota Longitudinal Study. *Developmental Review, 30,* 36–51.

Staddon, J. E., Chelaru, I. M., & Higa, J. J. (2002). A tune-trace theory of interval-timing dynamics. *Journal of the Experimental Analysis of Behavior, 77,* 105–124.

Stadler, G., Oettingen, G., & Gollwitzer, P. M. (2010). Intervention effects of information and self-regulation on eating fruits and vegetables over two years. *Health Psychology, 29,* 274–283.

Stallen, M., De Dreu, C. K., Shalvi, S., Smidts, A., & Sanfey, A. G. (2012). The herding hormone: Oxytocin stimulates in-group conformity. *Psychological Science, 23* (11), 1288–1292.

Standage, M., Gillison, F. B., Ntoumanis, N., & Treasure, D. C. (2012). Predicting students' physical activity and health-related well-being: A prospective cross-domain investigation of motivation across school physical education and exercise settings. *Journal of Sport and Exercise Psychology, 34,* 37–60.

Stangor, C. (2009). The study of stereotyping, prejudice, and discrimination within social psychology: A quick history of theory and research. In T. D. Nelson (Ed.), *Handbook of prejudice, stereotyping, and discrimination.* New York: Psychology Press.

Stankewitz, A., & May, A. (2011). Increased limbic and brainstem activity during migraine attacks following olfactory stimulation. *Neurology, 77,* 476–482.

Stanley, J. T., & Isaacowitz, D. M. (2012). Socioemotional perspectives on adult development. In S. K. Whitbourne & M. Sliwinski (Eds.), *Wiley-Blackwell handbook of adult development.* New York: Wiley-Blackwell.

Stanley, S. M., Rhoades, G. K., Amato, P. R., Markman, H. J., & Johnson, C. A. (2010). The timing of cohabitation and engagement: Impact on first and second marriages. *Journal of Marriage and the Family, 72,* 906–918.

Stanovich, K. E. (2013). *How to think straight about psychology* (10th ed.). Upper Saddle River, NJ: Pearson.

Stanovich, K. E., & West, R. F. (2007). Natural myside bias is independent of cognitive ability. *Thinking & Reasoning, 13,* 225–247

Starcevic, V. (2006). Anxiety states: A review of conceptual and treatment issues. *Current Opinions in Psychiatry, 19,* 79–83.

Staresina, B. P., Gray, J. C., & Davachi, L. (2009). Event congruency enhances episodic memory encoding through semantic elaboration and relational binding. *Cerebral Cortex, 19,* 1198–1207.

Starkstein, S.E. (2012). Apathy in Parkinson's disease: Diagnosic and etiological dilemmas. *Movement Disorders, 27,* 174–178.

Starr, C., Evers, C., & Starr, L. (2013). *Biology today and tomorrow with physiology* (4th ed.). Boston: Cengage.

Starr, C., Taggart, R., Evers, C., & Starr, L. (2013). *Evolution of life* (13th ed.). Boston: Cengage.

Stasiewicz, P. R., Brandon, T. H., & Bradizza, C. M. (2007). Effects of extinction context and retrieval cues on renewal of alcohol-cue reactivity among alcohol-dependent outpatients. *Psychology of Addictive Behaviors, 21* (2), 244–248.

Staub, E., & Vollhardt, J. (2008). Altruism born of suffering: The roots of caring and helping after victimization and other trauma. *American Journal of Orthopsychiatry, 78,* 267–280.

Staud, R., Price, D. D., Janicke, D., Andrade, E., Hadjipanayis, A. G., Eaton, W. T., Kaplan, L., & Wallace, M. R. (2011). Two novel mutations of SCN9A (Nav1.7) are associated with partial congenital insensitivity to pain. *European Journal of Pain, 15,* 223–230.

Staudinger, U. M., & Gluck, J. (2011). Psychological wisdom research. *Annual Review of Psychology* (vol. 62). Palo Alto, CA: Annual Reviews.

Staudt, M. (2010). Brain plasticity following early life brain injury: Insights from neuroimaging. *Seminars in Perinatology, 34,* 87–92.

Staw, B. M., Bell, N. E., & Clausen, J. A. (1986). The dispositional approach to job attitudes: A lifetime longitudinal test. *Administrative Science Quarterly, 31,* 56–77.

Stawarczyk, D., & others. (2012). Using the Daydreaming Frequency Scale to investigate the relationships between mind-wandering, psychological well-being, and present-moment awareness. *Frontiers in Psychology, 3,* 363.

StayClassy.org. (2011). *High school students start unique program to help feed families in need.* www.stayclassy.org/stories/high-school-students-start-unique-program-to-help-feed-families-in-need (accessed June 13, 2013)

Steblay, N., Dysart, J. & Wells, G. L. (2011). Seventy-two tests of the sequential lineup superiority effect: A meta-analysis and policy discussion. *Psychology, Public Policy, and Law, 17,* 99–139.

Steele, C. M., & Aronson, J. (1995). Stereotype threat and the intellectual test performance of African-Americans. *Journal of Personality and Social Psychology, 69,* 797–811.

Steele, C. M., & Aronson, J. A. (2004). Stereotype threat does not live by Steele and Aronson (1995) alone. *American Psychologist, 59,* 47–48.

Steger, M. F. (2012). Meaning in life. In S. J. Lopez & C. R. Snyder (Eds.), *The Oxford handbook of positive psychology* (2nd ed.). New York: Oxford University Press.

Steger, M. F., Frazier, P., Oishi, S., & Kaler, M. (2006). The meaning in life questionnaire:

Assessing the presence of and search for meaning in life. *Journal of Counseling Psychology, 53,* 80–93.

Stein, R. (2003). Blinded by the light. *The Age.* www.theage.com.au/articles/2003/09/01/1062403448264.html (accessed February 21, 2013)

Steinberg, L. (2012). Adolescent risk-taking: A social neuroscience perspective. In E. Amsel & J. Smetana (Eds.), *Adolescent vulnerabilities and opportunities: Constructivist developmental perspectives.* New York: Cambridge University Press.

Steinberg, L. (2013). How should the science of adolescent brain development inform legal policy? In J. Bhabha (Ed.), *Coming of age: A new framework for adolescent rights.* Philadelphia: University of Pennsylvania Press.

Stellar, J. E., Manzo, V. M., Kraus, M. W., & Keltner, D. (2012). Class and compassion: Socioeconomic factors predict responses to suffering. *Emotion, 12* (3), 449–459.

Stern, C., Cole, S., Gollwitzer, P. M., Oettingen, G., & Balcetis, E. (2013a). Effects of implementation intentions on anxiety, perceived proximity, and motor performance. *Personality and Social Psychology Bulletin, 39* (5), 623–635.

Stern, C., West, T. V., Jost, J. T., & Rule, N. O. (2013b). The politics of gaydar: Ideological differences in the use of gendered cues in categorizing sexual orientation. *Journal of Personality and Social Psychology, 104,* 520–541.

Stern, Y., Alexander, G. E., Prohovnik, I., & Mayeux, R. (1992). Inverse relationship between education and parietotemporal perfusion deficit in Alzheimer's disease. *Annals of Neurology, 32,* 371–375.

Stern, Y., Scarmeas, N., & Habeck, C. (2004). Imaging cognitive reserve. *International Journal of Psychology, 39,* 18–26.

Sternberg, E. M., & Gold, P. W. (1996). *The mind-body interaction in disease: Mysteries of the mind.* New York: Scientific American.

Sternberg, R. J. (1986). *Intelligence applied.* Fort Worth: Harcourt Brace.

Sternberg, R. J. (2008). The triarchic theory of human intelligence. In N. Salkind (Ed.), *Encyclopedia of educational psychology.* Thousand Oaks, CA: Sage.

Sternberg, R. J. (2011). The theory of successful intelligence. In R. J. Sternberg & S. B. Kaufman (Eds.), *Cambridge handbook of intelligence.* New York: Cambridge University Press.

Sternberg, R. J. (2012a). Intelligence in its cultural context. In M. Gelfand, C. Y. Chiu, & Y. Y. Hong (Eds.), *Advances in cultures and psychology* (vol. 2). New York: Oxford University Press.

Sternberg, R. J. (2012b). Giftedness and ethics. *Gifted Education International, 28* (3), 241–251.

Sternberg, R. J. (2012c). Human intelligence. In V. S. Ramachandran (Ed.), *Encyclopedia of human behavior* (2nd ed.). New York: Elsevier.

Sternberg, R. J. (2013a). Contemporary theories of intelligence. In W. M. Reynolds, G. F. Miller, & I. B. Weiner (Eds.), *Handbook of psychology, 2nd ed., Vol. 7.* (pp. 23–44). Hoboken, NJ: Wiley.

Sternberg, R. J. (2013b). The triarchic theory of successful intelligence. In D. P. Flanagan & P. L. Harrison (Eds.), *Contemporary intellectual assessment* (3rd ed.). New York: Guilford.

Sternberg, R. J. (2013c). Searching for love. *The Psychologist, 26,* 98–101.

Sterponi, L. (2010). Learning communicative competence. In D. F. Lancy, J. Bock, & S. Gaskins (Eds.), *The anthropology of learning in childhood* (pp. 235–259). Walnut Creek, CA: AltaMira.

Stevens, J. S., & Hamann, S. (2012). Sex differences in brain activation to emotional stimuli: A meta-analysis of neuroimaging studies. *Neuropsychologia, 50,* 1578–1593.

Stewart, A. D., & others. (2012). Body image, shape, and volumetric assessments using 3D whole body laser scanning and 2D digital photography in females with a diagnosed eating disorder: Preliminary novel findings. *British Journal of Psychology, 103,* 183–202.

Stewart, G. L., Dustin, S. L., Barrick, M. R., & Darnold, T. C. (2008). Handshake in employment interviews. *Journal of Applied Psychology, 93* (5), 1139–1146.

Stewart, J. L., Silton, R. L., Sass, S. M., Fisher, J. E., Edggar, J. C., Heller, W., & Miller, G. A. (2010). Attentional bias to negative emotion as a function of approach and withdrawal anger styles: An ERP investigation. *International Journal of Psychophysiology, 76,* 9–18.

Stewart, L. H., Ajina, S., Getov, S., Bahrami, B., Todorov, A., & Rees, G. (2012). Unconscious evaluations of faces on social dimensions. *Journal of Experimental Psychology and Genetics, 141* (4), 715–727.

Stewart, S. E., & others. (2013). Meta-analysis of association between obsessive-compulsive disorder and the 3' region of neuronal glutamate transporter gene SLC1A1. *American Journal of Medicine and Genetics B: Neuropsychiatry and Genetics.* (in press)

Stice, E., Marti, C. N., & Rohde, P. (2013). Prevalence, incidence, impairment, and course of the proposed DSM-5 eating disorder diagnoses in an 8-year prospective community study of young women. *Journal of Abnormal Psychology, 122,* 445–457.

Stice, E., Shaw, H., & Marti, C. N. (2006). A meta-analytic review of obesity prevention programs for children and adolescents: The skinny on interventions that work. *Psychological Bulletin, 132,* 667–691.

Stickgold, R. (2001). Watching the sleeping brain watch us: Sensory processing during sleep. *Trends in Neuroscience, 24,* 307–309.

Stiles-Shields, C., Hoste, R. R., Doyle, P. M., & Le Grange, D. (2012). A review of family-based treatment for adolescents with eating disorders. *Reviews on Recent Clinical Trials, 7,* 133–140.

Stillman, T. F., Maner, J. K., & Baumeister, R. F. (2010). A thin slice of violence: Distinguishing violent from nonviolent sex offenders at a glance. *Evolution and Human Behavior, 31,* 298–303.

Stirling, J. D. (2002). *Introducing neuropsychology.* East Sussex, U.K.: Psychology Press.

Stoklosa, J., & Öngür, D. (2011). Rational antipsychotic choice: Weighing the risk of tardive dyskinesia and metabolic syndrome. *Harvard Review of Psychiatry, 19,* 271–276.

Stone, A. A., Schwartz, J. E., Broderick, J. E., & Deaton, A. (2010). A snapshot of the age distribution of psychological well-being in the United States. *Proceedings of the National Academy of Sciences USA, 107,* 9985–9990.

Stone, J. (2002). Battling doubt by avoiding practice: The effects of stereotype threat on self-handicapping in white athletes. *Personality and Social Psychology Bulletin, 28,* 1667–1678.

Stoner, J. (1961). *A comparison of individual and group decisions, including risk.* Unpublished master's thesis, School of Industrial Management, MIT.

Stott, C., Drury, J., & Reicher, S. (2012). From prejudice to collective action. In J. Dixon & M. Levine (Eds.), *Beyond prejudice.* New York: Cambridge University Press.

Stowell, J. R., Robles, T. F., & Kane, H. S. (2013). Psychoneuroimmunology: Mechanisms, individual differences, and interventions. In A. M. Nezu, C. Maguth Nezu, P. A. Geller, & I. B. Weiner (Eds.), *Handbook of psychology* (2nd ed., vol. 9). Hoboken, NJ: Wiley.

Strahan, E., Spencer, S. J., & Zanna, M. P. (2002). Subliminal priming and persuasion: Striking while the iron is hot. *Journal of Experimental Social Psychology, 38*, 556–568.

Strasser, B. (2013). Physical activity in obesity and metabolic syndrome. *Annals of the New York Academy of Sciences, 1281*, 141–159.

Straube, T., Mothes-Lasch, M., & Miltner, W. H. (2011). Neural mechanisms of the automatic processing of emotional information from faces and voices. *British Journal of Psychology, 102*, 830–848.

Streff, F. M., & Geller, E. S. (1986). Strategies for motivating safety belt use: The application of applied behavior analysis. Health Education Research, 1 (1), 47–59.

Strickland, C. M., Drislane, L. E., Lucy, M., Krueger, R. F., & Patrick, C. J. (2013). Characterizing psychopathy using DSM-5 personality traits. *Assessment, 20*, 327–338.

Striegel-Moore, R. H., & Franko, D. L. (2008). Should binge eating disorder be included in the DSM-V? A critical review of the state of the evidence. *Annual Review of Clinical Psychology, 4*, 305–324.

Strike, P. C., Magid, K., Whitehead, D. L., Brydon, L., Bhattacharyya, M. R., & Steptoe, A. (2006). Pathophysiological processes underlying emotional triggering of acute cardiac events. *Proceedings of the National Academy of Sciences USA, 103*, 4322–4327.

Stroop, J. R. (1935). Studies of interference in serial verbal reactions. *Journal of Experimental Psychology, 28*, 643–662.

Strupp, H. H. (1995). The psychotherapist's skills revised. *Clinical Psychology: Science and Practice, 2*, 70–74.

Stulhofer, A., Busko, V., & Landripet, I. (2010). Pornography, sexual socialization, and satisfaction among young men. *Archives of Sexual Behavior, 39*, 168–178.

Sturmer, T., Hasselbach, P., & Amelang, M. (2006). Personality, lifestyle, and risk of cardiovascular disease and cancer: Follow-up of population-based cohort. *British Medical Journal, 332*, 1359.

Subedi, B., & Grossberg, G. T. (2011). Phantom limb pain: Mechanisms and treatment approaches. *Pain Research and Treatment.* doi: 10.1155/2011/864605

Sue, D., Sue, D. W., Sue, D. M., & Sue, S. (2014). *Essentials of understanding abnormal psychology* (2nd ed.). Boston: Cengage.

Sue, D., Sue, D. W., Sue, S., & Sue, D. M. (2013). *Understanding abnormal behavior* (10th ed.). Boston: Cengage.

Sueur, C., Deneubourg, J. L., & Petit, O. (2012). From social network (centralized vs. decentralized) to collective decision-making (unshared vs. shared consensus). *PLoS One, 7* (2), e32566.

Sugranyes, G., & others. (2012). Multimodal analyses identify linked functional and white matter abnormalities within the working memory network in schizophrenia. *Schizophrenia Research, 138* (2-3), 136–142.

Sullivan, H. S. (1953). *The interpersonal theory of psychiatry.* New York: Norton.

Sullivan, S. J., Mikels, J. A., & Carstensen, L. L. (2010). You never lose the ages you've been: Affective prospective taking in older adults. *Psychology and Aging, 251*, 229–234.

Suls, J., & Swain, A. (1998). Type A–Type B personalities. In H. S. Friedman (Ed.), *Encyclopedia of mental health* (vol. 3). San Diego: Academic.

Susman, E. J., & Dorn, L. D. (2013). Puberty: Its role in development. In R. M. Lerner, M. A. Easterbrooks, J. Mistry, & I. B. Weiner (Eds.), *Handbook of psychology, 2nd ed., Vol. 6.* (pp. 289–320). Hoboken, NJ: Wiley.

Sutin, A. R., Ferrucci, L., Zonderman, A. B., & Terracciano, A. (2011). Personality and obesity across the adult life span. *Journal of Personality and Social Psychology, 101*, 579–592.

Swaminathan, S. K., & Freedman, D. J. (2012). Preferential encoding of visual categories in the parietal cortex compared with the prefrontal cortex. *Nature Neuroscience, 15*, 315–320.

Swanson, J. (Ed.). (1999). *Sleep disorders sourcebook.* New York: Omnigraphics.

Swanson, S. A., Saito, N., Borges, G., Benjet, C., Aguilar-Gaxiola, S., Medina-Mora, M. E., & Breslan, J. (2012). Change in binge eating and binge eating disorder associated with migration from Mexico to the US. *Journal of Psychiatric Research, 46*, 31–37.

Swift, D. L., & others. (2013). Physical activity, cardiorespiratory fitness, and exercise training in primary and secondary coronary prevention. *Circulation Journal, 77*, 281–292.

Syed, M. (2013). Assessment of ethnic identity and acculturation. In K. Geisinger (Ed.), *APA handbook of testing and assessment in psychology.* Washington, DC: American Psychological Association.

T

Tabak, B. A., McCullough, M. E., Luna, L. R., Bono, G., & Berry, J. W. (2012). Conciliatory gestures facilitate forgiveness and feelings of friendship by making transgressors seem more agreeable. *Journal of Personality, 80* (2), 503–536.

Tacca, M. C. (2011). Commonalities between perception and cognition. *Frontiers in Perception Science.* doi: 10.3389/fpsyg.2011.00358

Taghipour, M., & Razmkon, A. (2012). Isolation and growth of neural stem cells derived from human hippocampus. *Journal of Injury and Violence Research.* http://jivresearch.org/jivr/index.php/jivr/article/view/365/249 (accessed April 16, 2013)

Tahiri, M., Mottillo, S., Joseph, L., Pilote, L., & Eisenberg, M. J. (2012). Alternative smoking cessation aids: A meta-analysis of randomized controlled trials. *American Journal of Medicine, 125*, 576–584.

Tajfel, H. (1978). The achievement of group differentiation. In H. Tajfel (Ed.), *Differentiation between social groups.* London: Academic.

Takahashi, Y., Roberts, B. W., & Hoshino, T. (2012). Conscientiousness mediates the relation between perceived parental socialisation and self-rated health. *Psychology & Health, 27* (9), 1048–1061.

Talbot, M. (2013, March 18). About a boy. *The New Yorker*, 56–65.

Tamis-LeMonda, C. S., & Song, L. (2013). Parent–infant communicative interactions in cultural context. In R. M. Lerner, M. A. Easterbrooks, J. Mistry, & I. B. Weiner (Eds.), *Handbook of psychology, 2nd ed., Vol. 6.* (pp. 143–173). Hoboken, NJ: Wiley.

Tannenbaum, S. I. (2006). Applied measurement: Practical issues and challenges. In W. Bennett, C. E. Lance, & D. J. Woehr (Eds.), *Performance measurement.* Mahwah, NJ: Erlbaum.

Tanofsky-Kraff, M., Bulik, C. M., Marcus, M. D., Striegel, R. H., Wilfley, D. E., Wonderlich, S. A., & Judson, J. I. (2013). Binge eating disorder—The next generation of research. *International Journal of Eating Disorders, 46*, 193–207.

Tao, R., Li, C., Newburn, E. N., Ye, T., Lipska, B. K., Herman, M. M., Weinberger, D. R., Kleinman, J. E., & Hyde, T. M. (2012). Transcript-specific associations of SLC12A5 (KCC2) in human prefrontal cortex with development, schizophrenic, and affective disorders. *Journal of Neuroscience, 32*, 5216–5522.

Tarokh, L., & Carskadon, M. A. (2010). Developmental changes in the human sleep EEG during early adolescence. *Sleep, 33*, 801–809.

Taga, K. A., Markey, C. N., & Friedman, H. S. (2006). A longitudinal investigation of associations between boys' pubertal timing and adult behavioral health and well-being. *Journal of Youth and Adolescence, 35*, 380–390.

Tagliamonte, S. A., & Denis, D. (2008). Linguistic ruin? LOL! Instant messaging and teen language. *American Speech, 83*, 3–34.

Takahashi, Y., Roberts, B. W., & Hoshino, T. (2012). Conscientiousness mediates the relation between perceived socialization and self-rated health. *Psychology and Health*, 1–14.

Takano, T., Nakamura, K., & Watanabe, M. (2002). Urban residential environments and senior citizens' longevity in mega-city areas: The importance of walkable green space. *Journal of Epidemiology and Community Health, 56*, 913–916.

Tanaka, J. W., Kaiser, M. D., Butler, S., & Le Grand, R. (2012). Mixed emotions: Holistic and analytic perception of facial expressions. *Cognition and Emotion, 26* (6), 961–977.

Tappan, M. B. (2013). Mediated moralities: Socio-cultural approaches to moral development. In M. Killen & J. G. Smetana (Eds.), *Handbook of moral development* (2nd ed.). New York: Routledge.

Tarter, R. E., Vanyukov, M., Kirisci, L., Reynolds, M., & Clark, D. B. (2006). Predictors of marijuana use in adolescents before and after illicit drug use: Examination of the gateway hypothesis. *American Journal of Psychiatry, 163*, 2134–2140.

Tateno, T., & Robinson, H. P. (2011). The mechanism of ethanol action on midbrain dopaminergic neuron firing: A dynamic clamp study of the role of I(h) and GABAergic synaptic integration. *Journal of Neurophysiology, 106*, 1901–1922.

Tavris, C., & Wade, C. (1984). *The longest war: Sex differences in perspective* (2nd ed.). Fort Worth: Harcourt Brace.

Tay, C., Ang, S., & Van Dyne, L. (2006). Personality, biographical characteristics, and job interview success: A longitudinal study of the mediating effects of self-efficacy and the moderating effects of internal locus of causality. *Journal of Applied Psychology, 91*, 446–454.

Taylor, F. W. (1911). *Scientific management.* New York: Harper & Row.

Taylor, H. G., & others (2010). Post-concussive symptoms in children with mild traumatic brain injury. *Neuropsychology, 24*, 148–159.

Taylor, J. G. (2012). The problem of "I": A new approach. *Journal of Consciousness Studies, 19*, 233–264.

Taylor, S. E. (2011a). Tend and befriend theory. In A. M. van Lange, A. W. Kruglanski, & E. T. Higgins (Eds.), *Handbook of theories of social psychology* (vol. 2). Thousand Oaks, CA: Sage.

Taylor, S. E. (2011b). Affiliation and stress. In S. S. Folkman (Ed.), *The Oxford handbook of stress, health, and coping*. New York: Oxford University Press.

Taylor, S. E. (2011c). Positive illusions: How ordinary people become extraordinary. In M. A. Gernsbacher, R. W. Pew, L. M. Hough, & J. R. Pomerantz (Eds.), *Psychology and the real world: Essays illustrating fundamental contributions to society* (pp. 224–228). New York: Worth.

Taylor, S. E. (2012). *Health psychology* (8th ed.). New York: McGraw-Hill.

Taylor, S. E. (2013). Social cognition and health. In D. E. Carlston (Ed.), *The Oxford handbook of social cognition*. New York: Oxford University Press.

Taylor, S. E., Brown, J. D., Colvin, C. R., Block, J., & Funder, D. C. (2007). Issue 6: Do positive illusions lead to healthy behavior? In J. A. Nier (Ed.). *Taking sides: Clashing views in social psychology* (2nd ed., pp. 116–137). New York: McGraw-Hill.

Taylor, S. E., Lerner, J. S., Sherman, D. K., Sage, R. M., & McDowell, N. K. (2003a). Are self-enhancing cognitions associated with healthy or unhealthy biological profiles? *Journal of Personality and Social Psychology, 85*, 605–615.

Taylor, S. E., Lerner, J. S., Sherman, D. K., Sage, R. M., & McDowell, N. K. (2003b). Portrait of the self-enhancer: Well adjusted and well liked or maladjusted and friendless? *Journal of Personality and Social Psychology, 84*, 165–176.

Taylor, S. E., & Sherman, D. K. (2008). Self-enhancement and self-affirmation: The consequences of positive self-thoughts for motivation and health. In W. Gardner & J. Shah (Eds.), *Handbook of motivation science*. New York: Guilford.

Tchanturia, K., & others. (2004). Cognitive flexibility in anorexia and bulimia nervosa. *Journal of the International Neuropsychological Society, 10*, 513–520.

Teesson, M., & Vogl, L. (2006). Major depressive disorder is common among Native Americans, women, the middle aged, the poor, the widowed, separated, or divorced people. *Evidence-Based Mental Health, 9*, 59.

Teffer, K., & Semendeferi, K. (2012). Human prefrontal cortex evolution, development, and pathology. *Progress in Brain Research, 195*, 191–218.

Teismann, N. A., Lenaghan, P., Stein, J., & Green, A. (2012). Will the real optic nerve please stand up? *Journal of Ultrasound Medicine, 31*, 130–131.

Temel, Y., & others. (2012). Neuromodulation in psychiatric disorders. *International Review of Neurobiology, 107*, 283–314.

Temple, J. R., Shorey, R. C., Fite, P., Stuart, G. L., & Le, V. D. (2013). Substance use as a longitudinal predictor of the perpetration of teen dating violence. *Journal of Youth and Adolescence*. (in press)

Tennie, C., Call, J., & Tomasello, M. (2010). Evidence for emulation in chimpanzees in social settings using the floating peanut task. *PLoS One, 5* (5), e10544.

ten Velden Hegelstad, W., & others. (2012). Long-term follow-up of the TIPS early detection in psychosis study: Effects on 10-year outcome. *American Journal of Psychiatry, 169* (4), 374–380.

Teodorescu, M., & others. (2006). Correlates of daytime sleepiness in patients with asthma. *Sleep Medicine, 7*, 607–613.

Tepper, B. J., Duffy, M. K., Hoobler, J., & Ensley, M. D. (2004). Moderators of the relationships between coworkers' organizational citizenship behavior and fellow employees' attitudes. *Journal of Applied Psychology, 89*, 455–465.

Terman, L. (1925). *Genetic studies of genius: Vol. 1: Mental and physical traits of a thousand gifted children*. Stanford, CA: Stanford University Press.

Terry, S. (2009). *Learning and memory* (4th ed.). Upper Saddle River, NJ: Prentice-Hall.

Thankachan, S., Kaur, S., & Shiromani, P. J. (2009). Activity of pontine neurons during sleep and cataplexy in hypocretin knock-out mice. *Journal of Neuroscience, 29*, 1580–1585.

Theeuwes, J., Belopolsky, A., & Olivers, C. N. (2009). Interactions between working memory, attention, and eye movements. *Acta Psychologica, 132*, 106–114.

Thigpen, C. H., & Cleckley, H. M. (1957). *Three faces of Eve*. New York. McGraw-Hill.

Thoeringer, C. K., Ripke, S., Unschuld, P. G., Lucae, S., Ising, M., Bettecken, T., Uhr, M., Keck, M. E., Mueller-Myhsok, B., Holsboer, F., Binder, E. B., & Erhardt, A. (2009). The GABA transporter 1 (SLC6A1): A novel candidate gene for anxiety disorders. *Journal of Neural Transmission, 116*, 649–657.

Thomas, M., Tyers, P., Lazic, S. E., Barker, R. A., Beazley, L., & Ziman, M. (2009). Graft outcomes influences by co-expression of Pax7 in graft and host tissue. *Journal of Anatomy, 214*, 396–405.

Thomas, M. S. C., & Johnson, M. H. (2008). New advances in understanding sensitive periods in brain development. *Current Directions in Psychological Science, 17*, 1–5.

Thompson, J., Manore, M., & Vaughan, L. (2013). *Nutrition for life* (3rd ed.). Upper Saddle River, NJ: Pearson.

Thompson, L., & others. (2005). Dispositional forgiveness of self, others, and situations. *Journal of Personality, 73*, 313–359.

Thompson, P. M., Giedd, J. N., MacDonald, D., Evans, A. C., & Toga, A. W. (2000). Growth patterns in the developing brain by using continuum sensor maps. *Nature, 404*, 190–193.

Thompson, R. A. (2013a). Attachment theory and research: Precis and prospect. In P. D. Zelazo (Ed.), *The Oxford handbook of developmental psychology, Vol. 2*. (pp. 191–216) New York: Oxford University Press.

Thompson, R. A. (2013b). Socialization of emotion regulation in the family. In J. Gross (Ed.), *Handbook of emotion regulation* (2nd ed.). New York: Guilford.

Thompson, R. A. (2013c). Relationships, regulation, and development. In R. M. Lerner (Ed.), *Handbook of child psychology* (7th ed.). New York: Wiley.

Thompson, S. C. (2001). The role of personal control in adaptive functioning. In C. R. Snyder & S. J. Lopez (Eds.), *Handbook of positive psychology*. New York: Oxford University Press.

Thompson, T. (2013). Autism research and services for young children: History, progress, and challenges. *Journal of Applied Research on Intellectual Disabilities, 26* (2), 1–27.

Thomson, D. R., & Milliken, B. (2012). Perceptual distinctiveness produces long-lasting priming of pop-out. *Psychonomic Bulletin and Review, 19* (2), 170–176.

Thorndike, E. L. (1898). *Animal intelligence: An experimental study of the associative processes in animals* (Psychological Review, monograph supplements, no. 8). New York: Macmillan.

Thornicroft, G., Brohan, E., Rose, D., Sartorius, N., Lees, M., & the INDIGO Study Group. (2009). Global pattern of experienced and anticipated discrimination against people with schizophrenia: A cross-sectional survey. *Lancet, 373*, 408–415.

Thota, A. B., & others. (2012). Collaborative care to improve the management of depressive disorders: A community guide systematic review and meta-analysis. *American Journal of Preventive Medicine, 42*, 525–538.

Thunedborg, K., Black, C. H., & Bech, P. (1995). Beyond the Hamilton depression scores in long-term treatment of manic-melancholic patients: Prediction of recurrence of depression by quality of life measurements. *Psychotherapy and Psychosomatics, 64*, 131–140.

Thyer, B. A. (2012). *Quasi-experimental research designs*. New York: Oxford University Press.

Tigani, X., & others. (2012). Self-rated health in centenarians: A nationwide cross-sectional Greek study. *Archives of Gerontology and Geriatrics, 54*, e342–e348.

Tikhomirov, A. A., & Spangler, W. D. (2010). Neocharismatic leadership and the fate of mergers and acquisitions: An institutional model of CEO leadership. *Journal of Leadership and Organizational Studies, 17*, 44–60.

Timofeev, I. (2011). Neuronal plasticity and thalamocortical sleep and waking oscillations. *Progress in Brain Research, 193*, 121–144.

Tinbergen, N. (1969). *The study of instinct*. New York: Oxford University Press.

Tindle, H., & others. (2012). Optimism, response to treatment of depression, and rehospitalization after coronary artery bypass graft surgery. *Psychosomatic Medicine, 74*, 200–207.

Ting-A-Kee, R., & others. (2013). Infusion of brain-derived neurotrophic factor into the ventral tegmental area switches the substrates mediating methanol motivation. *European Journal of Neuroscience*. (in press)

Todorov, A. (2013). Social psychology: Inference and person perception. *Annual Review of Psychology* (vol. 64). Palo Alto, CA: Annual Reviews.

Todorov, A., Mandisodza, A. N., Goren, A., & Hall, C. C. (2005). Inferences of competence from faces predict election outcomes. *Science, 308* (5728), 1623–1626.

Todd, R. M., Evans, J. W., Morris, D., Lewis, M. D., & Taylor, M. J. (2011). The changing face of emotion: Age-related patterns of amygdala activation to salient faces. *Social Cognitive and Affective Neuroscience, 6* (1), 12–23.

Todd, R. M., Talmi, D., Schmitz, T. W., Susskind, J., & Anderson, A. K. (2012). Psychophysical and neural evidence for emotion-enhanced perceptual vividness. *Journal of Neuroscience, 32*, 11201–11212.

Tol, W. A., Song, S., & Jordans, M. J. (2013). Annual research review: Resilience and mental health in children and adolescents living in areas of armed conflict—A systematic review of findings in low- and middle-income countries. *Journal of Child Psychology and Psychiatry, 54* (4), 445–460.

Tolman, E. C. (1932). *Purposive behavior in animals and man*. New York: Appleton-Century-Crofts.

Tolman, E. C., & Honzik, C. H. (1930). Degrees of hunger, reward and non-reward, and maze performance in rats. *University of California Publications in Psychology, 4*, 21–256.

Tomasi, D., & Volkow, N. D. (2012). Laterality patterns of brain functional connectivity: Gender effects. *Cerebral Cortex, 22* (6),1455–1462.

Tomé-Pires, C., & Miró, J. (2012). Hypnosis for the management of chronic and cancer procedure-related pain in children. *International Journal of Clinical and Experimental Hypnosis, 60*, 432–457.

Tomie, A., Brooks, W., & Zito, B. (1989). Sign tracking: The search for reward. In S. B. Klein & R. R. Mowrer (Eds.), *Contemporary learning theories* (pp. 191–223). Hillside, NJ: Erlbaum.

Tomie, A., Grimes, K. L., & Pohorecky, L. A. (2008). Behavioral characteristics and neurobiological substrates shared by Pavlovian sign-tracking and drug abuse. *Brain Research Reviews, 58,* 121–135.

Tomko, R. L., Trull, T. J., Wood, P. K., & Sher, K. J. (2013). Characteristics of borderline personality disorder in a community sample: Comorbidity, treatment utilization, and general functioning. *Journal of Personality Disorders.* (in press)

Tong, F., Nakayama, K., Moscovitch, M., Weinrib, O., & Kanwisher, N. (2000). Response properties of the human fusiform face area. *Cognitive Neuropsychology, 17,* 257–279.

Tononi, G., & Cirelli, C. (2011). Sleep and synaptic plasticity. *Annual Review of Psychology* (vol. 62). Palo Alto, CA: Annual Reviews.

Toplak, M. E., West, R. F., & Stanovich, K. E. (2011). The Cognitive Reflection Test as a predictor of performance on heuristics and biases tasks. *Memory & Cognition, 39,* 1275–1289.

Topolinski, S., & Strack, F. (2008). Where there's a will—there's no intuition: The unintentional basis of semantic coherence judgments. *Journal of Memory and Language, 58,* 1032–1048.

Topolinski, S., & Strack, F. (2009). Scanning the "fringe of consciousness": What is felt and what is not felt in intuition about semantic coherence. *Consciousness and Cognition, 18* (3), 608–618.

Torres, L., Yzaga, S. D., & Moore, K. M. (2011). Discrimination and Latino psychological distress: The moderating role of ethnic identity exploration and commitment. *American Journal of Orthopsychiatry, 81,* 526–534.

Travis, F., & Shear, J. (2010). Focused attention, open monitoring, and automatic self-transcending: Categories to organize meditations from Vedic, Buddhist, and Chinese traditions. *Consciousness and Cognition, 19* (4), 1110–1118.

Trawaiter, S., & Shapiro, J. R. (2010). Racial bias and stereotyping: Interpersonal processes. In B. Gawronski & B. K. Payne (Eds.), *Handbook of implicit cognition.* New York: Guilford.

Treasure, J., Claudino, A. M., & Zucker, N. (2010). Eating disorders. *Lancet, 375,* 583–593.

Tremblay, S., Beaule, V., Lepage, J. F., & Theoret, H. (2013). Anodal transcranial direct stimulation modulates GABAB-related intracortical inhibition in the M1 of healthy individuals. *Neuroreport, 24,* 46–50.

Trent, J., Lavelock, C., & King, L. A. (2013). Processing fluency, positive affect, and meaning in life. *Journal of Positive Psychology. 8,* 135–139.

Trevino, L. K. (2014). Ethical behavior in organizations. *Annual Review of Psychology* (vol. 65). Palo Alto, CA: Annual Reviews.

Triandis, H. C. (2007). Culture and psychology: A history of the study of their relationship. In S. Kitayama & D. Cohen (Eds.), *Handbook of cultural psychology* (pp. 59–76). New York: Guilford.

Trinkler, I., King, J. A., Doeller, C. F., Rugg, M. D., & Burgess, N. (2009). Neural bases of autobiographical support for episodic recollection of faces. *Hippocampus, 19,* 718–730.

Tropp, L. R., & Wright, S. C. (2003). Evaluations and perceptions of self, ingroup, and outgroup: Comparisons between Mexican-American and European-American children. *Self and Identity, 2,* 203–221.

Trudel-Fitzgerald, C., Savard, J., & Ivers, H. (2013). Which symptoms come first? Exploration of temporal relationships between cancer-related symptoms over an 18-month period. *Annals of Behavioral Medicine, 45* (3), 329–337.

Trull, T. J., & Brown, W. C. (2013). Borderline personality disorder: A five-factor model perspective. In T. A. Widiger & P. T. Costa (Eds.), *Personality disorders and the five-factor model of personality* (3rd ed., pp. 119–132). Washington, DC: American Psychological Association.

Trull, T. J., Carpenter, R. W., & Widiger, T. A. (2013). Personality disorders. In G. Stricker, T. A. Widiger, & I. B. Weiner (Eds.), *Handbook of psychology, 2nd ed., Vol. 8.* (pp. 94–120). Hoboken, NJ: Wiley.

Truxillo, D. M., & Bauer, T. N. (2010). Applicant reactions to organizations and selection systems. In S. Zedeck (Ed.), *APA handbook of industrial and organizational psychology.* Washington, DC: American Psychological Association.

Tryon, R. C. (1940). Genetic differences in maze-learning ability in rats. In *39th Yearbook, National Society for the Study of Education.* Chicago: University of Chicago Press.

Trzesniewski, K. H., & Donnellan, M. B. (2009). Reevaluating the evidence for increasingly positive self-views among high school students: More evidence for consistency across generations (1976–2006). *Psychological Science, 20,* 920–922.

Trzesniewski, K. H., & Donnellan, M. B. (2010). Rethinking "Generation Me": A study of cohort effects from 1976–2006. *Perspectives on Psychological Science, 5,* 58–75.

Trzesniewski, K. H., Donnellan, M. B., & Robins, R. W. (2008). Do today's young people really think they are so extraordinary? An examination of secular trends in narcissism and self-enhancement. *Psychological Science, 19,* 181–188.

Tsai, W., Chen, C., & Chiu, S. (2005). Exploring boundaries of the effects of applicant impression management tactics in job interviews. *Journal of Management, 31,* 108–125.

Tsang, S. Y., & others. (2013). Social cognitive role of schizophrenia candidate gene *GABRB2. PLoS One, 8* (4), e622322.

Tsiotra, P. C., Boutati, E., Dimitriadis, G., & Raptis, S. A. (2013). High insulin and leptin increase resistin and inflammatory cytokine production from human mononuclear cells. *BioMed Research International.* (in press)

Tsushima, Y., Sasaki, Y., & Watanabe, T. (2006). Greater disruption due to failure of inhibitory control on an ambiguous distractor. *Science, 314,* 1786–1788.

Tucker, J. S., & others. (2012). Resisting smoking when a best friend smokes: Do intrapersonal and contextual factors matter? *Journal of Research on Adolescence, 22,* 113–122.

Tuckman, A. M., Stern, Y., Basner, R. C., & Rakitin, B. C. (2011). The prefrontal model revisited: Double dissociations between young sleep deprived and elderly subjects on cognitive components of performance. *Sleep, 34,* 1039–1050.

Tugade, M. M., Fredrickson, B. L., & Feldman Barrett, L. (2004). Psychological resilience and positive emotional granularity: Examining the benefits of positive emotions on coping and health. *Journal of Personality, 72,* 1161–1190.

Tulving, E. (1972). Episodic and semantic memory. In E. Tulving & W. Donaldson (Eds.), *Origins of memory.* San Diego: Academic.

Tulving, E. (1983). *Elements of episodic memory.* New York: Oxford University Press.

Tulving, E. (1989). Remembering and knowing the past. *American Scientist, 77,* 361–367.

Tulving, E. (2000). Concepts of memory. In E. Tulving & F. I. M. Craik (Eds.), *The Oxford handbook of memory.* New York: Oxford University Press.

Turiano, N. A., & others. (2012). Personality trait level and change as predictors of health outcomes: Findings from a national study of Americans (MIDUS). *Journals of Gerontology B: Psychological Sciences and Social Sciences, 67B,* 4–12.

Turk, D. C., & Wilson, H. D. (2013). Chronic pain. In A. M. Nezu, C. Maguth Nezu, P. A. Geller, & I. B. Weiner (Eds.), *Handbook of psychology, 2nd ed., Vol. 9.* (pp. 292–317). Hoboken, NJ: Wiley.

Turkheimer, E. (2011). Genetics and human agency: Comment on Dar-Nimrod and Heine. *Psychological Bulletin, 137,* 825–828.

Turkheimer, E., Haley, A., Waldron, M., D'Onofrio, B., & Gottesman, I. I. (2003). Socioeconomic status modifies heritability of IQ in young children. *Psychological Science, 14,* 623–628.

Turnbull, A., Rutherford-Turnbull, H., Wehmeyer, M., & Shogren, K. A. (2013). *Exceptional lives* (7th ed.). Upper Saddle River, NJ: Merrill.

Turnbull, D. L., Cox, B. J., Oleski, J., & Katz, L. Y. (2013). The effects of borderline personality disorder and panic disorder on suicide attempts and the associated influence of affective dysregulation in the general population. *Journal of Nervous and Mental Disease, 201* (2), 130–135.

Tversky, A., & Kahneman, J. (1974). Judgment under uncertainty: Heuristics and biases. *Science, 185,* 1124–1131.

Twenge, J. M. (2006). *Generation Me: Why today's young Americans are more confident, assertive, entitled—and more miserable than ever before.* New York: Free Press.

Twenge, J. M. (2008). Social exclusion, motivation, and self-defeating behavior: Why breakups lead to drunkenness and ice cream. In J. Y. Shah & W. L. Gardner, (Eds.), *Handbook of motivation science* (pp. 508–517). New York: Guilford.

Twenge, J. M., & Campbell, W. K. (2008). Increases in positive self-views among high school students: Birth cohort changes in anticipated performance, self-satisfaction, self-liking, and self-competence. *Psychological Science, 19,* 1082–1086.

Twenge, J. M., & Campbell, W. K. (2009). *The narcissism epidemic: Living in the age of enlightenment.* New York: Free Press

Twenge, J. M., & Foster, J. D. (2008). Mapping the scale of the narcissism epidemic: Increases in narcissism 2002–2007 within ethnic groups. *Journal of Research in Personality, 42,* 1619–1622.

Tynes, B. M., Umaña-Taylor, A. J., Rose, C. A., Lin, J., & Anderson, C. J. (2012). Online racial discrimination and the protective function of ethnic identity and self-esteem for African America adolescents. *Developmental Psychology, 48,* 343–355.

U

Uchida, Y., Kitayama, S., Mesquita, B., Reyes, J. A. S., & Morling, B. (2008). Is perceived emotional support beneficial? Well-being and health in independent and interdependent cultures. *Personality and Social Psychology Bulletin, 34,* 741–754.

Uher, R., & Rutter, M. (2012). Classification of feeding and eating disorders: Review of evidence and proposals for ICD-11. *World Psychiatry, 11,* 80–92.

Uleman, J. S., & Kressel, L. M. (2013). Brief history of theory and research on impression formation. In D. E. Carlston (Ed.), *The Oxford handbook of social cognition.* New York: Oxford University Press.

Ullman, A. D. (1952). Review of "Antabuse" in the treatment of alcoholism. *Psychological Bulletin, 49*, 557–558.

Ulrich, R. S. (1991). Stress recovery during exposure to natural and urban environments. *Journal of Environmental Psychology, 11*, 201–230.

Umaña-Taylor, A. J., & Guimond, A. B. (2010). A longitudinal examination of parenting behaviors and perceived discrimination predicting Latino adolescents' ethnic identity. *Developmental Psychology, 46*, 636–650.

Umaña-Taylor, A. J., Updegraff, K. A., & Gonzales-Bracken, M. A. (2011). Mexican-origin adolescent mothers' stressors and psychological functioning: Examining ethnic identity affirmation and familism as moderators. *Journal of Youth and Adolescence, 40*, 140–157.

Umaña-Taylor, A. J., Wong, J. J., Gonzales, N. A., & Dumka, L. E. (2012). Ethnic identity and gender as moderators of the association between discrimination and academic adjustment among Mexican-origin adolescents. *Journal of Adolescence, 35* (4), 773–786.

Umanath, S., Sarezky, D., & Finger, S. (2011). Sleepwalking through history: Medicine, arts, and courts of law. *Journal of the History of the Neurosciences, 20*, 253–276.

Underhill, K., Montgomery, P., & Operario, D. (2007). Sexual abstinence programs to prevent HIV infection in high-income countries. *British Medical Journal, 335*, 248.

Underwood, M. K. (2011). Aggression. In M. K. Underwood & L. Rosen (Eds.), *Social development*. New York: Guilford.

Undurraga, J., & Baldessarini, R. J. (2012). Randomized, placebo-controlled trials of antidepressants for acute major depression: Thirty-year meta-analytic review. *Neuropsychopharmacology, 37*, 851–864.

Unick, J. L., & others. (2013). The long-term effectiveness of a lifestyle intervention in severely obese individuals. *American Journal of Medicine, 126*, 236–242.

United Nations Office on Drugs and Crime (UNODC). (2012). *World drug report*. www.unodc.org/documents/data-and-analysis/WDR2012/WDR_2012_web_small.pdf (accessed February 25, 2013)

United Nations World Youth Report. (2005). *World youth report 2005: Young people today and in 2015*. Geneva, Switzerland: United Nations.

Unkelbach, C. (2007). Reversing the truth effect: Learning the interpretation of processing fluency in judgments of truth. *Journal of Experimental Psychology: Learning, Memory, and Cognition, 33*, 219–230.

Unsworth, N., Brewer, G. A., & Spillers, G. J. (2011). Variation in working memory capacity and episodic memory: Examining the importance of encoding specificity. *Psychonomic Bulletin and Review, 18*, 1113–1118.

Urbina, S. (2011). Tests of intelligence. In R. J. Sternberg & S. B. Kaufman (Eds.), *Handbook of intelligence*. New York: Cambridge University Press.

Urry, H. L. (2010). Seeing, thinking, and feeling: Emotion-regulating effects of gaze-directed cognitive reappraisal. *Emotion, 10*, 125–135.

Urry, H. L., Nitschke, J. B., Dolski, I., Jackson, D. C., Dalton, K. M., Mueller, C. J., Rosenkranz, M. A., Ryff, C. D., Singer, B. H., & Davidson, R. J. (2004). Making a life worth living: Neural correlates of well-being. *Psychological Science, 15*, 367–372.

Ursache, A., Blair, C., & Raver, C. C. (2012). The promotion of self-regulation as a means of enhancing school readiness and early achievement in children at risk for school failure. *Child Development Perspectives, 6*, 122–128.

U.S. Department of Labor, Bureau of Labor Statistics. (2006). Survey of workplace violence prevention, 2005. *Bureau of Labor Statistics*. www.bls.gov/iif/oshwc/osnr0026.pdf (accessed June 4, 2013)

U.S. Department of Labor, Bureau of Labor Statistics. (2013). *Occupational outlook handbook, 2012–2013*. St. Paul: JIST Works.

U.S. Department of Labor. (2013). O*NET resource center. *O*NET Resource Center*. www.onetcenter.org/database.html (accessed June 1, 2013)

U.S. Food and Drug Administration. (2004, October 15). FDA launches a multi-pronged strategy to strengthen safeguards for children treated with antidepressant medications. *Food and Drug Administration news release*. Washington, DC: Author.

U.S. Food and Drug Administration. (2009). Office of Device Evaluation annual report, fiscal year 2008. *Food and Drug Administration*. Washington, DC: Center for Devices and Radiological Health.

U.S. General Accounting Office. (1996, September). *Cycle of sexual abuse: Research inconclusive about whether child victims become adult abusers*. Report to the Chairman, Subcommittee on the Judiciary, House of Representatives.

Uslaner, J. M., Acerbo, M. J., Jones, S. A., & Robinson, T. E. (2006). The attribution of incentive salience to a stimulus that signals an intravenous injection of cocaine. *Behavioral Brain Research, 169*, 320–324.

V

Vaes, J., Heflick, N. A., & Goldenberg, J. L. (2010). "We are people": Ingroup humanization as an existential defense. *Journal of Personality and Social Psychology, 98*, 750–760.

Vaillant, G. (2003). A 60-year follow-up of alcoholic men. *Addiction, 98*, 1043–1051.

Valenti, M., & others. (2013). Increased glutaminyl cyclase expression in peripheral blood of Alzheimer's disease patients. *Journal of Alzheimer's Disease*. (in press)

Vallières, A., & Bastille-Denis, E. (2012). Circadian rhythm disorders II: Shift-work and jet-lag. In C. M. Morin & C. A. Espie (Eds.), *The Oxford handbook of sleep and sleep disorders*. New York: Oxford University Press.

van Atteveldt, N. M, Blau, V. C., Blomert, L., & Goebel, R. (2010). fMR-adaptation indicates selectivity to audiovisual content congruency in distributed clusters in human superior temporal cortex. *BMC Neuroscience, 11*, 11.

van Bokhoven, I., van Goozen, S. H. M., van Engeland, H., Schaal, B., Arseneault, L., Seguin, J. R., Assaad, J., Nagin, D. S., Vitaro, F., & Tremblay, R. E. (2006). Salivary testosterone and aggression, delinquency, and social dominance in a population-based longitudinal study of adolescent males. *Hormones and Behavior, 50*, 118–125.

Vancouver, J. B. (2005). The depth of history and explanation as benefit and bane for psychological control theories. *Journal of Applied Psychology, 90*, 38–52.

Vancouver, J. B. (2012). Rhetorical reckoning: A response to Bandura. *Journal of Management, 38*, 465–474.

Vancouver, J. B., & Kendall, L. N. (2006). When self-efficacy negatively relates to motivation and performance in a learning context. *Journal of Applied Psychology, 91*, 1146–1153.

Vancouver, J. B., More, K. M., & Yoder, R. J. (2008). Self-efficacy and resource allocation: Support for a discontinuous model. *Journal of Applied Psychology, 93*, 35–47.

Vancouver, J. B., Thompson, C. M., Tischner, E. C., & Putka, D. J. (2002). Two studies examining the negative effect of self-efficacy on performance. *Journal of Applied Psychology, 87*, 506–516.

Vancouver, J. B., Thompson, C. M., & Williams, A. A. (2001). The changing signs in the relationships between self-efficacy, personal goals and performance. *Journal of Applied Psychology, 86*, 605–620.

Vandello, J. A., & Cohen, D. (2004). When believing is seeing: Sustaining norms of violence in cultures of honor. In M. Schaller & C. S. Crandall (Eds.), *The psychological foundations of culture* (pp. 281–304). Mahwah, NJ: Erlbaum.

Vandello, J. A., & Cohen, D. (2008). Culture, gender, and men's intimate partner violence. *Social and Personality Psychology Compass, 2*, 652–667.

Vandello, J. A., Cohen, D., Grandon, R., & Franiuk, R. (2009). Stand by your man: Indirect prescriptions for honorable violence and feminine loyalty in Canada, Chile, and the United States. *Journal of Cross-Cultural Psychology, 40*, 81–104.

van der Geest, V., Blokland, A., & Bijleveld, C. (2009). Delinquent development in a sample of high-risk youth: Shape, content, and predictors of delinquent trajectories from age 12 to 32. *Journal of Research in Crime and Delinquency, 46*, 111–143.

Vanderwert, R. E., Fox, N. A., & Ferrari, P. F. (2013). The mirror mechanism and mu rhythm in social development. *Neuroscience Letters*. (in press)

Van Dick, R., Becker, T. E., & Meyer, J. P. (2006). Commitment and identification: Forms, foci, and future. *Journal of Organizational Behavior, 27*, 545–548.

Van Doorn, G. S., & Taborsky, M. (2012). The evolution of generalized reciprocity on social interaction networks. *Evolution, 66*, 651–664.

van Gaal, S., & Lamme, V. A. F. (2011). Unconscious high-level information processing: Implications for neurobiological theories of consciousness. *Neuroscientist*. doi: 10.1177/107385841140407

van IJzendoorn, M. H., & Bakermans-Kranenburg, M. J. (2010). Invariance of adult attachment across gender, age, culture, and socioeconomic status? *Journal of Social and Personal Relationship, 27*, 200–208.

Vanini, G., Lydic, R., & Baghdoyan, H. A. (2012). GABA-to-ACh ratio in basal forebrain and cerebral cortex varies significantly during sleep. *Sleep, 35*, 1325–1334.

Van Ittersum, K., & Wansink, B. (2012). Plate size and color suggestibility: The Delboeuf illusion's bias on serving and eating behavior. *Journal of Consumer Research, 39* (2), 215–228.

van Kleef, E., Shimizu, M., & Wansink, B. (2013). Just a bite: Considerably smaller snack portions satisfy delayed hunger and craving. *Food Quality and Preference, 27*, 96–100.

Van Lange, P. A. M., Rusbult, C. E., Drigotas, S. M., & Arriaga, X. B. (1997). Willingness to sacrifice in close relationships. *Journal of Personality and Social Psychology, 72*, 1373–1395.

van Lankveld, J. (2008). Problems with sexual interest and desire in women. In D. L. Rowland & L. Incrocci (Eds.), *Handbook of sexual and gender identity disorders* (pp. 154–185). Hoboken, NJ: Wiley.

van Noordt, S. J., & Segalowitz, S. J. (2013). Performance monitoring and the medial prefrontal cortex: A review of individual differences and context effects as a window on self-regulation. *Frontiers in Human Neuroscience*. (in press)

Van Orden, K. A., Whitte, T. K., Gordon, K. H., Bender, T. W., & Joiner, T. E. (2008). Suicidal desire and the capability of suicide: Tests of the interpersonal-psychological theory of suicidal behavior among adults. *Journal of Consulting and Clinical Psychology, 76,* 72–83.

van Reedt Dortland, A. K. B., & others. (2012). Personality traits and childhood trauma as correlates of metabolic risk factors: The Netherlands Study of Depression and Anxiety (NESDA). *Progress in Neuropsychopharmacology and Biological Psychiatry, 36,* 85–91.

Van Riper, M. (2007). Families of children with Down syndrome: Responding to "a change in plans" with resilience. *Journal of Pediatric Nursing, 22,* 116–128.

van Vliet, I. M., van Well, E. P. L., Bruggeman, R., á Campo, J., Hijman, R., van Megen, H. J. G. M., van Balkom, A. J. L. M., & van Rijen, P. C. (2013). An evaluation of irreversible psychosurgical treatment of patients with obsessive-compulsive disorder in the Netherlands, 2001–2008. *Journal of Nervous and Mental Disease, 201,* 226–228.

van Waarde, J. A., van Oudheusden, L. J., Heslinga, O. B., Verwey, B., van der Mast, R. C., & Giltay, E. (2013). Patient, treatment, and anatomical predictors of outcome in electroconvulsive therapy: A prospective study. *Journal of Electroconvulsive Therapy, 29,* 113–121.

Vasco, V. R., Cardinale, G., & Polonia, P. (2012). Deletion of PLCB1 gene in schizophrenia-affected patients. *Journal of Cellular and Molecular Medicine, 16,* 844–851.

Vasselli, J. R., Scarpace, P. J., Harris, R. B., & Banks, W. A. (2013). Dietary components in the development of leptin resistance. *Advances in Nutrition, 4,* 164–175.

Vassilev, I., & others. (2013). Social networks, the "work" and work force of chronic illness self-management: A survey analysis of personal communities. *PLoS One, 8* (4), e59723.

Vaughn, S., Bos, C. S., & Schumm, J. S. (2003). *Teaching exceptional, diverse, and at-risk students in the general education classroom* (3rd ed.). Boston: Allyn & Bacon.

Vazquez, J., Hall, S. C., Witkowska, H. E., & Greco, M. A. (2008). Rapid alterations in cortical protein profiles underlie spontaneous sleep and wake bouts. *Journal of Cellular Biochemistry, 105,* 1472–1484.

Vazsonyi, A. T., & Huang, L. (2010). Where self-control comes from: On the development of self-control and its relationship to deviance over time. *Developmental Psychology, 46,* 245–257.

Veale, D., Murphy, P. Ellison, N., Kanakam, N., & Costa, A. (2013). Autobiographical memories of vomiting in people with a specific phobia of vomiting (emetophobia). *Journal of Behavioral Therapy and Experimental Psychiatry, 44* (1), 14–20.

Vega, V., & Malamuth, N. M. (2007). Predicting sexual aggression: The role of pornography in the context of general and specific risk factors. *Aggressive Behavior, 33,* 104–117.

Vega-Rivera, N. M., Ramírez-Rodríguez, G., & Estrada-Camarena, E. (2013). Acute stress further decreases the effect of ovariectomy on immobility behavior and hippocampal cell survival in rats. *Psychoneuroimmunology, 38,* 1407–1417.

Vella, E. J., Kamarck, T. W., Flory, J. D., & Manuck, S. (2012). Hostile mood and social strain during daily life: A test of the transactional model. *Annals of Behavioral Medicine, 44,* 341–352.

Vermetten, E., Schmahl, C., Lindner, S., Loewenstein, R. J., & Bremner, J. D. (2006). Hippocampal and amygdalar volumes in dissociative identity disorder. *American Journal of Psychiatry, 163,* 630–636.

Verquer, M. L., Beehr, T. A., & Wagner, S. H. (2003). A meta-analysis of relations between person–organization fit and work attitudes. *Journal of Vocational Behavior, 63,* 473–489.

Verschuere, B., Crombez, G., De Clercq, A., & Koster, E. H. W. (2005). Psychopathic traits and autonomic responding to concealed information in a prison sample. *Psychophysiology, 42,* 239–245.

Vervaet, M., van Heeringen, C., & Audenaert, K. (2004). Personality-related characteristics in restricting versus binging and purging eating disordered patients. *Comprehensive Psychiatry, 45,* 37–43.

Verwijk, E., Comijs, H. C., Kok, R. M., Spaans, H., Stek, M. L., & Scherder, E. J. A. (2012). Neurocognitive effects after brief pulse and ultrabrief pulse unilateral electroconvulsive therapy for major depression: A review. *Journal of Affective Disorders, 140,* 233–243.

Veselka, L., Schermer, J. A., Petrides, K. V., & Verson, P. A. (2009). Evidence for a heritable general factor of personality in two studies. *Twin Research and Human Genetics, 12,* 254–260.

Vezzali, L., Capozza, D., Stathi, S., & Giovannini, D. (2011). Increasing outgroup trust, reducing infrahumanization, and enhancing future contact intentions via imagined intergroup contact. *Journal of Experimental Social Psychology, 48* (1), 437–440.

Videtic, A., Zupanic, T., Pregelj, P., Balazic, J., Tomori, M., & Komel, R. (2009). Suicide, stress, and serotonin receptor 1A promotor polymorphism -1019,G in Slovenian suicide victims. *European Archives of Psychiatry and Clinical Neuroscience, 259,* 234–238.

Vilarroya, O. (2012). A straw man's neogenome. *Behavioral and Brain Science, 35* (5), 380–381.

Vilhauer, J. S., Cortes, J., Moali, N., Chung, S., Mirocha, J, & Ishak, W. W. (2013). Improving quality of life for patients with major depressive disorder by increasing hope and positive expectations with future directed therapy (FDT). *Innovations in Clinical Neuroscience, 10,* 12–22.

Villaverde, G. C., & others. (2012). Influence of exercise on mood in postmenopausal women. *Journal of Clinical Nursing, 21* (7-8), 923–928.

Vinberg, M., Mellerup, E., Andersen, P. K., Bennike, B., & Kessing, L. V. (2010). Variations in 5-HTTLPR: Relation to familiar risk of affective disorder, life events, neuroticism, and cortisol. *Progress in Neuro-Psychopharmacology & Biological Psychiatry, 34,* 86–91.

Vissers, D., & others. (2013). The effect of exercise on visceral adipose tissue in overweight adults: A systematic review and meta-analysis. *PLoS One, 8* (2), e56415.

Vitulano, N., & others. (2013). Obstructive sleep apnea and heart disease: The biomarkers point of view. *Frontiers in Bioscience, 5,* 588–599.

Vo, M. L., & Wolfe, J. M. (2013). The interplay of episodic and semantic memory in guiding repeated search in scenes. *Cognition, 126,* 198–212.

Vogel, M., Braungardt, T., Meyer, W., & Schneider, W. (2012). The effects of shift work on physical and mental health. *Journal of Neural Transmission, 119,* 1121–1132.

Vogt, T. M., Mullooly, J. P., Ernst, D., Pople, C. R., & Hollis, J. F. (1992). Social networks as predictors of ischemic heart disease, cancer, stroke, and hypertension. *Journal of Clinical Epidemiology, 45,* 659–666.

von Békésy, G. (1960). Vibratory patterns of the basilar membrane. In E. G. Wever (Ed.), *Experiments in hearing.* New York: McGraw-Hill.

von Helmholtz, H. (1852). On the theory of compound colors. *Philosophical Magazine, 4,* 519–534.

von Neumann, J. (1958). *The computer and the brain.* New Haven, CT: Yale University Press.

von Polier, G. G., Vloet, T. D., & Herpertz-Dahlmann, B. (2012). ADHD and delinquency—A developmental perspective. *Behavioral Sciences and the Law, 30,* 121–139.

Voracek, M., & Dressler, S. G. (2006). Lack of correlation between digit ratio (2D:4D) and Baron-Cohen's "reading the mind in the eyes" test, empathy, systemising, and autism-spectrum quotients in a general population sample. *Personality and Individual Differences, 41,* 1481–1491.

Voracek, M., Pietschnig, J., Nader, I. W., & Stieger, S. (2011). Digit ratio (2D:4D) and sex-role orientation: Further evidence and meta-analysis. *Personality and Individual Differences, 51,* 417–422.

Vrachnis, N., & others. (2011). The oxytocin-oxytocin receptor system and its antagonists as tocolytic agents. *International Journal of Endocrinology.* doi: 10.1155/2011/350546

Vuillermot, S., Weber, L., Feldon, J., & Meyer, U. (2010). A longitudinal examination of the neurodevelopmental impact of prenatal immune activation in mice reveals primary defects in dopaminergic development relevant to schizophrenia. *Journal of Neuroscience, 30,* 1270–1287.

Vukovic, J., & others. (2009). Lack of fibulin-3 alters regenerative tissue responses in the primary olfactory pathway. *Matrix Biology, 28,* 406–415.

Vuontela, V., Carlson, S., Troberg, A., Fontell, T., Simola, P., Saarinen, S., & Aronen, E. T. (2013). Working memory, attention, inhibition, and their relation to adaptive functioning and behavioral/emotional symptoms in school-aged children. *Child Psychiatry and Human Development, 44,* 105–122.

Vygotsky, L. S. (1962). *Thought and language.* Cambridge, MA: MIT Press.

W

Waage, S., & others. (2012). Subjective and objective sleepiness among oil rig workers during three different shift schedules. *Sleep Medicine, 13,* 64–72.

Wacker, J., Mueller, E. M., Hennig, J., & Stemmler, G. (2012). How to consistently link extraversion and intelligence to the catechol-O-methyltransferase (COMT) gene: On defining and measuring psychological phenotypes in neurogenetic research. *Journal of Personality and Social Psychology, 102,* 427–444.

Waenke, M., Samochowiecz, J., & Landwehr, J. (2012). Facial politics: Political judgment based on looks. In J. P. Forgas, K. Fiedler, & C. Sedikides (Eds.), *Social thinking and interpersonal behavior.* New York: Psychology Press.

Wagenaar, K., & Baars, J. (2012). Family and family therapy in the Netherlands. *International Review of Psychiatry, 24* (2), 144–148.

Wagenmakers, E. J., Wetzels, R., Borsboom, D., & van der Maas, H. L. J. (2011). Why psychologists must change the way they analyze their data: The case of psi: Comment on Bem (2011). *Journal of Personality and Social Psychology, 100,* 426–432.

Wagner, A. D., Schacter, D. L., Rotte, M., Koutstaal, B., Maril, A., Dale, A. M., Rosen, B. R., & Buckner, R. L. (1998). Building memories: Remembering and forgetting of verbal experiences as predicted by brain activity. *Science, 281,* 1185–1187.

Wagner, L., & Hoff, E. (2013). Language development. In R. M. Lerner, M. A. Easterbrooks, J. Mistry, & I. B. Weiner (Eds.), *Handbook of psychology, 2nd ed., Vol. 6.* (pp. 173–2144). Hoboken, NJ: Wiley.

Wai, J., Cacchio, M., Putallaz, M., & Makel, M. C. (2010). Sex differences in the right tail of cognitive abilities: A 30-year examination. *Intelligence, 38,* 412–413.

Wai, J., Lubinski, D., & Benbow, C. P. (2005) Creativity and occupational accomplishments among intellectually precocious youths: An age 13 to age 33 longitudinal study. *Journal of Educational Psychology, 97,* 484–492.

Wai, J., Putallaz, M., & Makel, M. C. (2012). Studying intellectual outliers: Are there sex differences and are the smart getting smarter? *Current Directions in Psychological Science, 21,* 382–390.

Wainright, J. L., & Patterson, C. J. (2008). Peer relations among adolescents with female same-sex parents. *Developmental Psychology, 44,* 117–126.

Wainryb, C. (2013). Moral development in culture: Diversity, tolerance, and justice. In M. Killen & J. G. Smetana (Eds.), *Handbook of moral development* (2nd ed.). New York: Routledge.

Wald, A., Langenberg, A. G., & Krantz, E. (2005). The relationship between condom use and herpes simplex virus acquisition. *Annals of Internal Medicine, 143,* 707–713.

Walder, D. J., Ospina, L., Daly, M., Statucka, M., & Raparia, E. (2012). Early neurodevelopment and psychosis risk: Role of neurohormones and biological sex in modulating genetic, prenatal, and sensory processing factors in brain development. In X. Anastassion-Hadjicharalambous (Ed.), *Psychosis: Causes, diagnosis and treatment.* Hauppauge, NY: Nova Science.

Walker, D. D., Roffman, R. A., Stephens, R. S., Wakana, K., & Berghuis, J. (2006). Motivational enhancement therapy for adolescent marijuana users: A preliminary randomized controlled trial. *Journal of Consulting and Clinical Psychology, 74,* 628–632.

Walker, L. E. A. (2009). *The battered woman syndrome* (3rd ed.). New York: Springer.

Walker, L. J. (2013). Moral personality, motivation, and identity. In M. Killen & J. G. Smetana (Eds.), *Handbook of moral development* (2nd ed.). New York: Routledge.

Walker, M. P. (2012). The role of sleep and neurocognitive function. In C. M. Morin & C. A. Espie (Eds.), *The Oxford handbook of sleep and sleep disorders.* New York: Oxford University Press.

Waller, E. A., Bendel, R. E., & Kaplan, J. (2008). Sleep disorders and the eye. *Mayo Clinic Proceedings, 83,* 1251–1261.

Waller, E. M., & Rose, A. J. (2013). Brief report: Adolescents' co-rumination with mothers, co-rumination with friends, and internalizing symptoms. *Journal of Adolescence, 36,* 429–433.

Wallerstein, R. S. (2012). Will psychoanalysis fulfill its promise? *International Journal of Psychoanalysis, 93,* 377–399.

Walter, S. (2010). One year later, horrific details of crime begin to come into focus. *Bay Citizen.* www.baycitizen.org/news/crime/hearing-reveals-horrific-details-crime/ (accessed May 14, 2013)

Walther, M. R., Snorrason, I., Flessnor, C. A., Franklin, M. E., Burkel, R., & Woods, D. W. (2013). The Trichotillomania Impact Project in Young Children (TIP-YC): Clinical characteristics, comorbidity, functional impairment, and treatment utilization. *Child Psychiatry and Human Development.* (in press)

Walton, K. E., & Roberts, B. W. (2004). On the relationship between substance use and personality traits: Abstainers are not maladjusted. *Journal of Research in Personality, 38,* 515–535.

Walton, N. M., & others. (2012). Adult neurogenesis transiently generates oxidative stress. *PLoS One, 7* (4), e35264.

Wampold, B. E. (2001). *The great psychotherapy debate: Models, methods, and findings.* Mahwah, NJ: Erlbaum.

Wampold, B. E. (2013). The good, the bad, and the ugly: A 50-year perspective on the outcome problem. *Psychotherapy, 50,* 16–24.

Wampold, B. E., & Brown, G. S. (2005). Estimating variability in outcomes attributable to therapists: A naturalistic study of outcomes of managed care. *Journal of Consulting and Clinical Psychology, 73,* 914–923.

Wan, C., Dach-Gruschow, K., No, S., & Hong, Y. (2011). Self-definitional functions of culture. In A. K. Leung & C. Y. Chiu (Eds.), *Cultural processes: A social psychological perspective* (pp. 111–135). New York: Cambridge University Press.

Wang, L., He, J. L., & Zhang, X. H. (2013). The efficacy of massage on preterm infants: A meta-analysis. *American Journal of Perinatology.* (in press)

Wang, L., Kennedy, B. L., & Most, S. B. (2012). When emotion blinds: A spatiotemporal competition account of emotion-induced blindness. *Frontiers in Psychology, 3,* 438.

Wang, Q. (2006). Earliest recollections of self and others in European American and Taiwanese young adults. *Psychological Science, 17,* 708–714.

Wang, Q. (2009a). Once upon a time: Explaining cultural differences in episodic specificity. *Social and Personality Psychology Compass, 3/4,* 413–432.

Wang, Q. (2009b). Are Asians forgetful? Perception, retention, and recall in episodic remembering. *Cognition, 111,* 123–131

Wang, Q., Hou, Y., Tang, H., & Wiprovnick, A. (2011). Travelling backwards and forwards in time: Culture and gender in the episodic specificity of past and future events. *Memory, 19,* 103–109.

Wanner, B., Vitaro, F., Tremblay, R. E., & Turecki, G. (2012). Childhood trajectories of anxiousness and disruptiveness explain the association between early-life adversity and attempted suicide. *Psychological Medicine, 42* (11), 2373–2382.

Wansink, B. (2013). Turning mindless eating into healthy eating. In E. Shafir (Ed.), *The behavioral foundations of public policy* (pp. 310–328). Princeton, NJ: Princeton University Press.

Wansink, B., & Cheney, M. M. (2005). Super bowls: Serving bowl size and food consumptions. *Journal of the American Medical Association, 293,* 1727–1728.

Wansink, B., Painter, J. E., & North, J. (2005). Bottomless bowls: Why visual cues of portion size may influence intake. *Obesity Research, 13,* 93–100.

Wansink, B., Van Ittersum, K., & Painter, J. E. (2006). Ice cream illusions: Bowl size, spoon size, and serving size. *American Journal of Preventive Medicine, 145,* 240–243.

Ward, J. (2010). *The student's guide to cognitive neuroscience* (2nd ed.). New York: Psychology Press.

Warden, M. R., & others. (2013). A prefrontal cortex-brainstem neuronal projection that controls response to behavioral challenge. *Nature.* (in press)

Warnecke, R. B., Morera, O., Turner, L., Mermelstein, R., Johnson, T. P., Parsons, J., Crittenden, K., Freels, S., & Flay, B. (2001). Changes in self-efficacy and readiness for smoking cessation among women with high school or less education. *Journal of Health and Social Behavior, 42,* 97–109.

Washington, D. L., Davis, T. D., Der-Martirosian, C., & Yano, E. M. (2013). PTSD risk and mental health care engagement in a multi-war era community sample of women veterans. *Journal of General Internal Medicine.* (in press)

Wasserman, E. A., & Castro, L. (2013). Comparative cognition. In R. J. Nelson, S. J. Y. Mizumori, & I. B. Weiner (Eds.), *Handbook of psychology, 2nd ed., Vol. 3.* (pp. 480–508). Hoboken, NJ: Wiley.

Waszak, F., Pfister, R., & Kiesel, A. (2013). Top-down versus bottom-up: When Instructions overcome automatic retrieval. *Psychological Research.* (in press)

Watabe-Uchida, M., Zhu, L., Ogawa, S. K., Vamanrao, A., & Uchida, N. (2012). Whole-brain mapping of direct inputs to midbrain dopamine neurons. *Neuron, 74,* 858–873.

Watanabe, H., & Mizunami, M. (2007). Pavlov's cockroach: Classical conditioning of salivation in an insect. *PLoS One, 6,* e529.

Waters, E., Merrick, S., Treboux, D., Crowell, J., & Albersheim, L. (2000). Attachment security in infancy and early adulthood: A 20-year longitudinal study. *Child Development, 71,* 684–689.

Watson, A., El-Deredy, W., Bentley, D. E., Vogt, B. A., & Jones, A. K. (2006). Categories of placebo response in the absence of site-specific stimulation of analgesia. *Pain, 126,* 115–122.

Watson, D. (2001). Positive affectivity: The disposition to experience pleasurable emotional states. In C. R. Snyder & S. J. Lopez (Eds.), *Handbook of positive psychology.* New York: Oxford University Press.

Watson, D., & Clark, L. A. (1997). Extraversion and its positive emotional core. In R. Hogan, J. A. Johnson, & S. R., Briggs (Eds.), *Handbook of personality psychology* (pp. 767–793). San Diego: Academic.

Watson, D., & Naragon, K. (2009). Positive affectivity: The disposition to experience positive emotional states. In S. J. Lopez & C. R. Snyder, (Eds.), *The Oxford handbook of positive psychology* (2nd ed., pp. 207–215). New York: Oxford University Press.

Watson, D., Stasik, S. M., Ro, E., & Clark, L. A. (2013). Integrating normal and pathological personality: Relating the DSM-5 trait-dimensional model to general traits of personality. *Assessment, 20,* 312–326.

Watson, D. L., & Tharp, R. G. (2014). *Self-directed behavior* (10th ed.). Boston: Cengage.

Watson, J. B., & Rayner, R. (1920). Conditioned emotional reactions. *Journal of Experimental Psychology, 3,* 1–14.

Watson, M., Homewood, J., Haviland, J., & Bliss, J. M. (2005). Influence of psychological response on breast cancer survival: A 10-year follow-up of a population-based cohort. *European Journal of Cancer, 41,* 1710–1714.

Watson, R. E., Desesso, J. M., Hurtt, M. E., & Cappon, G. D. (2006). Postnatal growth and morphological development of the brain: A species comparison. *Birth Defects Research Part B: Developmental and Reproductive Toxicology, 77,* 471–484.

Way, B. M., & Gurbaxani, B. M. (2008). A genetics primer for social health research. *Social and Personality Psychology Compass, 2* (2), 785–816.

Webb, R. T., & others. (2012). Suicide risk in primary care patients with major physical diseases: A case-control study. *Archives of General Psychiatry, 69,* 256–264.

Webb, W. B. (2000). Sleep. In A. Kazdin (Ed.), *Encyclopedia of psychology.* Washington, DC, & New York: American Psychological Association and Oxford University Press.

Wechsler, D. (1939). *The measurement of adult intelligence.* Baltimore: Williams & Wilkins.

Wechsler, H., Lee, J. E., Kuo, M., & Lee, H. (2000). College binge drinking in the 1990s—A continuing health problem: Results of the Harvard University School of Public Health 1999 College Alcohol Study. *Journal of American College Health, 48,* 199–210.

Wechsler, H., Lee, J. E., Kuo, M., Seibring, M., Nelson, T. F., & Lee, H. (2002). Trends in college binge drinking during a period of increased prevention efforts: Findings from 4 Harvard School of Public Health college alcohol study surveys: 1993–2001. *Journal of American College Health, 50,* 203–217.

Weekley, J. A., & Ployhart, R. E. (2005). *Situational judgment tests: Theory, measurement, and application.* New York: Psychology Press.

Wegener, D. T., & Petty, R. E. (2013). Attitudes and social cognition as social psychological siblings. In D. E. Carlston (Ed.), *The Oxford handbook of social cognition.* New York: Oxford University Press.

Weger, U. W., Hooper, N., Meier, B. P., & Hopthrow, T. (2012). Mindful maths: Reducing the impact of stereotype threat through a mindfulness exercise. *Consciousness and Cognition, 21,* 471–475.

Wei, F.-Y. F., Wang, Y. K., & Klausner, M. (2012). Rethinking college students' self-regulation and sustained attention: Does text messaging during class influence cognitive learning? *Communication Education, 61,* 185–204.

Weiner, B. (2006). *Social motivation, justice, and the moral emotions: An attributional approach.* Mahwah, NJ: Erlbaum.

Weiner, I. B. (2004). Rorschach assessment: Current status. In M. Hersen (Ed.), *Comprehensive handbook of psychological assessment* (vol. 2). New York: Wiley.

Weiner, R., & others. (2013). Electroconvulsive therapy device classification: Response to FDA advisory panel hearing and recommendations. *Journal of Clinical Psychiatry, 74,* 38–42.

Weinstein, N., Deci, E. L., & Ryan, R. M. (2011). Motivational determinants of integrating positive and negative past identities. *Journal of Personality and Social Psychology, 100,* 527–544.

Weinstein, N., Ryan, W. S., DeHaan, C. R., Przybylski, A. K., Legate, N., & Ryan, R. M. (2012). Parental autonomy support and discrepancies between implicit and explicit sexual identities: Dynamics of self-acceptance and defense. *Journal of Personality and Social Psychology, 102,* 815–832.

Weinstein, T. A. R., Capitanio, J. P., & Gosling, S. D. (2008). Personality in animals. In O. P. John, R. W. Robins, & L. A. Pervin (Eds.), *Handbook of personality theory and research* (3rd ed., pp. 328–350). New York: Guilford.

Weir, W. (1984, October 15). Another look at subliminal "facts." *Advertising Age,* 46.

Weisgram, E. S., Dinella, L. M., & Fulcher, M. (2011). The role of masculinity/femininity, values, and occupational value affordances in shaping young men's and women's occupational choices. *Sex Roles, 65,* 243–258.

Weiss, A., King, J. E., & Perkins, L. (2006). Personality and subjective well-being in orangutans (*Pongo pygmaeus* and *Pongo abelii*). *Journal of Personality and Social Psychology, 90,* 501–511.

Weiss, B., & Feldman, R. S. (2006). Looking good and lying to do it: Deception as an impression management strategy in job interviews. *Journal of Applied Social Psychology, 36,* 1070–1086.

Weissman, M., & Olfson, M. (1995). Depression in women: Implications for health care research. *Science, 269,* 99–801.

Welgampola, M. S., Bradshaw, A., & Halmagyi, G. M. (2011). Practical neurology—4: Dizziness on head movement. *Medical Journal of Australia, 195,* 518–522.

Wellman, H. M. (2011). Developing a theory of mind. In U. Goswami (Ed.), *Wiley-Blackwell handbook of childhood cognitive development* (2nd ed.). New York: Wiley-Blackwell.

Wells, G. L., & Loftus, E. F. (2013). Eyewitness memory for people and events. In E. K. Otto & I. B. Weiner (Eds.), *Handbook of psychology* (2nd ed., vol. 11). Hoboken, NJ: Wiley.

Wells, G. L., Steblay, N. K., & Dysart, J. E. (2011) *A test if the simultaneous vs. sequential lineup methods: An initial report of the AJS National Eyewitness Identification Field Studies.* Des Moines, IA: American Judicature Society.

Wentzel, K. R. (2013). School adjustment. In W. M. Reynolds, G. F. Miller, & I. B. Weiner (Eds.), *Handbook of psychology, 2nd ed., Vol. 7.* (pp. 213–232). Hoboken, NJ: Wiley.

Werbart, A., Levin, L., Andersson, H., & Sandell, R. (2013). Everyday evidence: Outcomes of psychotherapies in Swedish public health services. *Psychotherapy, 50* (1), 119–130.

Werner, J. M., & Bolino, M. C. (1997). Explaining U.S. courts of appeals decisions involving performance appraisal: Accuracy, fairness, and validation. *Personnel Psychology, 50,* 1–24.

Wesson, M. J., & Gogus, C. I. (2005). Shaking hands with a computer: An examination of two methods of organizational newcomer orientation. *Journal of Applied Psychology, 90,* 1018–1026.

West, R. (2005). Time for a change: Putting the transtheoretical (stages of change) model to rest. *Addiction, 100,* 1036–1039.

West, R. F., Meserve, R. J., & Stanovich, K. E. (2012). Cognitive sophistication does not attenuate the blindspot bias. *Journal of Personality and Social Psychology, 103,* 506–519.

West, R. F., Toplak, M. E., & Stanovich, K. E. (2008). Heuristics and biases as measures of critical thinking: Associations with cognitive ability and thinking dispositions. *Journal of Educational Psychology, 100,* 930–941.

Westen, D., Gabbard, G. O., & Soto, C. J. (2008). Psychoanalytic approaches to personality. In O. P. John, R. W. Robins, & L. A. Pervin (Eds.), *Handbook of personality theory and research* (3rd ed., pp. 61–113). New York: Guilford.

Wetherell, M. (2012). The prejudice problematic. In J. Dixon & M. Levine (Eds.), *Beyond prejudice.* New York: Cambridge University Press.

Wetzels, R., Matzke, D., Lee, M. D., Rouder, J. N., Iverson, G. J., & Wagenmakers, E. J. (2011). Statistical evidence in experimental psychology: An empirical comparison using 855 t-tests. *Perspectives on Psychological Science, 6,* 291–298.

Whalen, P. J., Raila, H., Bennett, R., Mattek, A., Brown, A., Taylor, J., van Tieghem, M., Tanner, A., Miner, M., & Palmer, A. (2013). Neuroscience and facial expressions of emotion: The role of amygdala–prefrontal interactions. *Emotion Review, 5,* 78–83.

Wheaton, S. (2012, January 10). When injuries to the brain tear at hearts. *New York Times,* D1.

Wheeler, D. S., & Miller, R. R. (2008). Determinants of cue interactions. *Behavioral Processes, 78,* 191–203.

Whelan, D. C., & Zelenski, J. M. (2012). Experimental evidence that positive moods cause sociability. *Social Psychological and Personality Science, 3,* 430–437.

Whitaker, J. L., & Bushman, B. J. (2012). "Remain calm. Be kind." Effects of relaxing video games on aggressive and prosocial behavior. *Social Psychological and Personality Science, 3,* 88–92.

White, J. W., & Frabutt, J. M. (2006). Violence against girls and women: An integrative developmental perspective. In J. Worell & C. D. Goodheart (Eds.), *Handbook of girls' and women's psychological health: Gender and well-being across the lifespan* (pp. 85–93). New York: Oxford University Press.

White, R. C., & Aimola Davies, A. M. (2012). Specular vision-touch synaesthesia: Two reference frames. *Perception, 41,* 871–874.

White, R. W. (1992). Exploring personality the long way: The study of lives. R. A. Zucker, A. I. Rabin, J. Aronoff, & S. J. Frank (Eds.), *Personality structure in the life course: Essays on personology in the Murray tradition* (pp. 3–21). New York: Springer.

Whitman, J. B., North, C. S., Downs, D. L., & Spitznagel, E. L. (2013). A prospective study of the onset of PTSD symptoms in the first month after trauma exposure. *Annals of Clinical Psychiatry, 25,* E8–E17.

Whorf, B. L. (1956). *Language, thought, and creativity.* New York: Wiley.

Widiger, T. A. (2009). Neuroticism. In M. R. Leary & R. H. Hoyle (Eds.), *Handbook of individual differences in social behavior* (pp. 129–146). New York: Guilford.

Widiger, T. A., & Crego, C. (2013). Diagnosis and classification. In G. Stricker, T. A. Widiger, & I. B. Weiner (Eds.), *Handbook of psychology, 2nd ed., Vol. 8.* (pp. 3–18). Hoboken, NJ: Wiley.

Wiebe, R. P. (2004). Delinquent behavior and the five factor model: Hiding in the adaptive landscape? *Individual Differences Research, 2,* 38–62.

Wiegand, D. M., & Geller, E. S. (2004). Connecting positive psychology and organizational behavior management: Achievement motivation and the power of positive reinforcement. *Journal of Organizational Behavior Management, 24,* 3–24.

Wiemer, J., Gerdes, A. B., & Pauli, P. (2012). The effects of an unexpected spider stimulus on skin conductance responses and eye movements: An inattentional blindness study. *Psychological Research.* doi: 10.1007/s00426-011-0407-7

Wiersma, D., Nienhuis, F. J., Slooff, C. J., & Giel, R. (1998). Natural course of schizophrenic disorders: A 15-year follow up of a Dutch incidence cohort. *Schizophrenia Bulletin, 24,* 75–85.

Wijesiri, L. (2005, October 21). Meditation's effect on the brain. *Maithri.* www.maithri.com/links/articles/meditation_effect_brain.htm (accessed March 29, 2013)

Wilcox, T., Alexander, G. M., Wheeler, L., & Norvell, J. (2012). Sex differences during visual scanning of occlusion events in infants. *Developmental Psychology, 48*, 1091–1105.

Wildman, J. L., Bedwell, W. L., Salas, E., & Smith-Jentsch, K. A. (2010). Performance measurement at work: A multilevel perspective. In S. Zedeck (Ed.), *APA handbook of industrial and organizational psychology*. Washington, DC: American Psychological Association.

Wilkowski, B. M., & Meier, B. P. (2010). Bring it on: Angry facial expressions potentiate approach-motivated motor behavior. *Journal of Personality and Social Psychology, 98*, 201–210.

Wilkowski, B. M., & Robinson, M. D. (2010). Associative and spontaneous appraisal processes independently contribute to anger elicitation in daily life. *Emotion, 10*, 181–189.

Willcox, D. C., Willcox, B. J., He, Q., Wang, N. C., & Suzuki, M. (2008). They really are that old: A validation study of centenarian prevalence in Okinawa. *Journals of Gerontology A: Biological Sciences and Medical Sciences, 63*, 338–349.

Williams, C. (2012). *Overcoming anxiety, stress, and panic: A five areas approach* (3rd ed.). New York: Oxford University Press.

Williams, D. R., Haile, R., Mohammed, S. A., Herman, A., Stein, D. J., Sonnega, J., & Jackson, J. S. (2012). Perceived discrimination and psychological well-being in the U.S.A. and South Africa. *Ethnicity and Health, 17*, 111–133.

Williams, J. D., & Gruzelier, J. H. (2001). Differentiation of hypnosis and relaxation by analysis of narrow band theta and alpha frequencies. *International Journal of Clinical and Experimental Hypnosis, 49*, 185–206.

Williams, K. D. (2007). Ostracism. *Annual Review of Psychology* (vol. 58). (pp. 425–452). Palo Alto, CA: Annual Reviews.

Williams, K. D. (2012). Ostracism: The impact of being rendered meaningless. In M. Mikulincer & P. Shaver (Eds.), *Meaning, mortality, and choice: The social psychology of existential concerns* (pp. 309–324). Washington, DC: American Psychological Association.

Williams, L. M. (1995). Recovered memories of abuse in women with documented child sexual victimization histories. *Journal of Traumatic Stress, 19*, 257–267.

Williams, L. M. (2003). Understanding child abuse and violence against women: A life-course perspective. *Journal of Interpersonal Violence, 18*, 441–451.

Williams, L. M. (2004). Researcher-advocate collaborations to end violence against women. *Journal of Interpersonal Violence, 19*, 1350–1357.

Williams, R. B. (2001). Hostility (and other psychosocial risk factors): Effects on health and the potential for successful behavioral approaches to prevention and treatment. In A. Baum, T. A. Revenson, & J. E. Singer (Eds.), *Handbook of health psychology*. Mahwah, NJ: Erlbaum.

Williams, R. B. (2002). Hostility, neuroendocrine changes, and health outcomes. In H. G. Koenig & H. J. Cohen (Eds.), *The link between religion and health*. New York: Oxford University Press.

Williamson, G. M., & Clark, M. S. (1989). Providing help and desired relationship type as determinants of changes in mood and self-evaluations. *Journal of Personality and Social Psychology, 56*, 722–734.

Willingham, D. T. (2011). Student "learning styles" theory is bunk. *Washington Post* guest blog post. http://voices.washingtonpost.com/answer-sheet/daniel-willingham/the-big-idea-behind-learning.html (accessed March 30, 2013)

Willis, J., & Todorov, A. (2006). First impressions: Making up your mind after a 100-ms exposure to a face. *Psychological Science, 17*, 592–598.

Wilsey, B., Marcotte, T., Tsodikov, A., Millman, J., Bentley, H., Gouaux, B., & Fishman, S. (2008). A randomized, placebo-controlled, crossover trial of cannabis cigarettes in neuropathic pain. *Journal of Pain, 9*, 506–521.

Wilson, A., & Godin, J. J. (2010). Boldness and intermittent locomotion in the bluegill sunfish, *Lepomis macrochirus. Behavioral Ecology, 21*, 57–62.

Wilson, G. T., Grilo, C. M., & Vitousek, K. M. (2007). Psychological treatment of eating disorders. *American Psychologist, 62*, 199–216.

Wilson, G. T., & Zandberg, L. J. (2012). Cognitive-behavioral guided self-help for eating disorders: Effectiveness and scalability. *Clinical Psychology Review, 32*, 343–357.

Wilson, J., Markie, D., & Fitches, A. (2012). Cholecystokinin system genes: Associations with panic and other psychiatric disorders. *Journal of Affective Disorders, 136*, 902–908.

Wilson, R. S., Barnes, L. L., Aggarwal, N. T., Boyle, P. A., Hebert, L. E., Mendes de Leon, C. F., & Evans, D. A. (2010). Cognitive activity and the cognitive morbidity of Alzheimer disease. *Neurology, 75* (11), 990–996.

Wilson, R. S., Mendes de Leon, D. F., Bienias, J. L., Evans, D. A., & Bennett, D. A. (2004). Personality and mortality in old age. *Journals of Gerontology: Psychological Sciences and Social Sciences, 59B*, 110–116.

Wilt, J., & Revelle, W. (2009) Extraversion. In M. Leary & R. Hoyle (Eds.), *Handbook of individual differences in social behavior* (pp. 27–45). New York: Guilford.

Wiltermuth, S. S. (2011). Cheating more when the spoils are split. *Organizational Behavior and Human Decision Processes, 115*, 157–168.

Wiltermuth, S. S., & Heath, C. (2009). Synchrony and cooperation. *Psychological Science, 20*, 1–5.

Windle, M. (2012). Longitudinal data analysis. In H. Cooper (Ed.), *APA handbook of research methods in psychology*. Washington, DC: American Psychological Association.

Windt, J. M., & Noreika, V. (2011). How to integrate dreaming into a general theory of consciousness—A critical review of existing positions and suggestions for future research. *Consciousness and Cognition, 20*, 1091–1107.

Winer, R. L., Hughes, J. P., Feng, O., O'Reilly, S., Kiviat, N. B., Holmes, K. K., & Koutsky, L. A. (2006). Condom use and the risk of genital human papilloma virus infection in young women. *New England Journal of Medicine, 354*, 2645–2654.

Winner, E. (1996). *Gifted children: Myths and realities*. New York: Basic.

Winner, E. (2000). The origins and ends of giftedness. *American Psychologist, 55*, 159–169.

Winner, E. (2006). Development in the arts. In W. Damon & R. Lerner (Eds.), *Handbook of child psychology* (6th ed.). New York: Wiley.

Winter, D. G. (2005). Measuring the motives of political actors at a distance. In J. M. Post (Ed.), *The psychological assessment of political leaders: With profiles of Saddam Hussein and Bill Clinton* (pp. 153–177). Ann Arbor: University of Michigan Press.

Wirth, T., Ober, K., Prager, G., Vogelsang, M., Benson, S., ven Witzke, O., Kribben, A., Engler, H., & Schedlowski, M. (2011). Repeated recall of learned immunosuppression: Evidence from rats and men. *Brain, Behavior, and Immunity, 25*, 1444–1451.

Wirtz, P. H., Siegrist, J., Schuhmacher, A., Hoefels, S., Maier, W., & Zobel, A. W. (2010). Higher overcommitment to work is associated with higher plasma cortisol but not ACTH responses in the combined dexamethasone/CRH test in apparently healthy men and women. *Psychoneuroendocrinology, 35*, 536–543.

Wiseman, R., & Watt, C. (2006). Belief in psychic ability and the misattribution hypothesis: A qualitative review. *British Journal of Psychology, 97*, 323–338.

Witelson, S. F., Kigar, D. L., & Harvey, T. (1999). The exceptional brain of Albert Einstein. *Lancet, 353*, 2149–2153.

Witelson, S. F., Kigar, D. L., Scamvougeras, A., Kideckel, D. M., Buck, B., Stanchev, P. L., Bronskill, M., & Black, S. (2008). Corpus callosum anatomy in right-handed homosexual and heterosexual men. *Archives of Sexual Behavior, 37*, 857–863.

Woike, B. A. (2001). Working with free response data: Let's not give up hope. *Psychological Inquiry, 12*, 157–159.

Woike, B. A. (2008). The state of the story in personality psychology. *Social and Personality Psychology Compass, 2*, 434–443.

Woike, B. A., & Matic, D. (2004). Cognitive complexity in response to traumatic experiences. *Journal of Personality, 72*, 633–657.

Wojtczak, M., & Oxenham, A. J. (2009). Pitfalls in behavioral estimates of basilar-membrane compression in humans. *Journal of the Acoustical Society of America, 125*, 270–281.

Wolf, S., Grein, S., & Queisser, G. (2013). Employing NeuGen 2.0 to automatically generate morphologies of hippocampal neurons and neural networks in 3D. *Neuroinformatics*. (in press)

Wolfe, D. (2013). Risk and resilience in the context of child maltreatment: The way forward. *Child Abuse and Neglect, 37*, 90–92.

Wolpe, J. (1990). *The practice of behavior therapy* (4th ed.). New York: Pergamon.

Wong, F. K., & Pi, E. H. (2012). Ethnopsychopharmacology considerations for Asians and Asian Americans. *Asian Journal of Psychiatry, 5*, 18–23.

Wong, Y. J., Kim, S. H., & Tran, K. K. (2010). Asian Americans' adherence to Asian values, attributions about depression, and coping strategies. *Cultural Diversity and Ethnic Minority Psychology, 16* (1), 1–8.

Woo, C. C., & Leon, M. (2013). Environmental enrichment as an effective treatment for autism: A randomized controlled trial. *Behavioral Neuroscience, 127*, 487–497.

Wood, D., Harms, P., & Vazire, S. (2010). Perceiver effects as projective tests: What your perceptions of others say about you. *Journal of Personality and Social Psychology, 99* (1), 174–190.

Wood, R. L., & Liossi, C. (2006). Neuropsychological and neurobehavioral correlates of aggression following traumatic brain injury. *Journal of Neuropsychiatry & Clinical Neurosciences, 18*, 333–341.

Wood, A. H., & Eagly, A. H. (2010). Gender. In S. Fiske, D. Gilbert, & G. Lindzey (Eds.), *Handbook of social psychology*. New York: Oxford University Press.

Wood, R. E., & Bandura, A. (1989). Impact of conceptions of ability on self-regulatory mechanisms and complex decision making. *Journal of Personality and Social Psychology, 56*, 407–415.

Woolfolk, A. (2013). *Educational psychology* (12th ed.). Upper Saddle River, NJ: Pearson.

World Health Organization (WHO). (2009). Suicide rates per 100,000 by country. *World Health Organization.* www.who.int/mental_health/prevention/suicide_rates/en/index.html (accessed May 30, 2013)

Worthington, R. L., Navarro, R. L., Savoy, H. B., & Hampton, D. (2008). Development, reliability, and validity of the Measure of Sexual Identity Exploration and Commitment (MoSIEC). *Developmental Psychology, 44.* 22–33.

Wrangham, R. W., & Glowacki, L. (2012). Intergroup aggression in chimpanzees and war in nomadic hunter gatherers: Evaluating the chimpanzee model. *Human Nature, 23* (1). 5–29.

Wright, J. W., & Harding, J. W. (2013). Importance of the brain angiotensin system in Parkinson's disease. *Parkinson's Disease.* (in press)

Wright, R. G. (2008). Sex offender post-incarceration sanctions: Are there any limits? *Criminal and Civil Confinement, 34,* 17–50.

Wright, R. H., Mindel, C. H., Tran, T. V., & Habenstein, R. W. (2012). *Ethnic families in America* (5th ed.). Upper Saddle River, NJ: Pearson.

Wrosch, C., Amir, E., & Miller, G. E. (2011). Goal adjustment capacities, coping, and subjective well-being: The sample case of caregiving for a family member with mental illness. *Journal of Personality and Social Psychology, 100,* 934–946.

Wrzesniewski, A. (2003). Finding positive meaning in work. In K. S. Cameron, J. E. Dutton, & R. E. Quinn (Eds.), *Positive organizational scholarship: Foundations of a new discipline* (pp. 296–308). San Francisco: Berrett-Koehler.

Wrzesniewski, A., Dutton, J. E., & Debebe, G. (2003). Interpersonal sense-making and the meaning of work. In R. M. Kramer, M. Roderick, & B. M. Staw (Eds.). *Research in organizational behavior: An annual series of analytical essays and critical reviews* (vol. 25, pp. 93–135). Oxford: Elsevier.

Wrzesniewski, A., McCauley, C. I., Rozin, P., & Schwartz, B. (1997). Jobs, careers, and callings: People's relations to their work. *Journal of Research in Personality, 31,* 21–33.

Wrzus, C., Hanel, M., Wagner, J., & Neyer, F. J. (2012). Social network changes and life events across the life span: A meta-analysis. *Psychological Bulletin, 139,* 53–80.

Wyatt, T. D. (2003). *Pheromones and animal behaviour: Communication by smell and taste.* Cambridge, U.K.: Cambridge University Press.

Wynn, T., & Coolidge, F. L. (2010). Beyond symbolism and language: An introduction to Supplement 1, working memory. *Current Anthropology, 51,* 5–16.

Wynn, T., Coolidge, F. L., & Bright, M. (2009). Hohlenstein-Stadel and the evolution of human conceptual thought. *Cambridge Archaeological Journal, 19,* 73–83.

Wynn, W. P., Stroman, R. T., Almgren, M. M., & Clark, K. J. (2012). The pharmacist "toolbox" for smoking cessation: A review of methods, medicines, and novel means to help patients along the path of smoking reduction to smoking cessation. *Journal of Pharmacy Practice, 25,* 591–599.

X

Xanthopoulos, M. S., & Daniel, L. C. (2013). Coping and social support. In A. M. Nezu, C. Maguth Nezu, P. A. Geller, & I. B. Weiner (Eds.), *Handbook of psychology, 2nd ed., Vol. 9.* (pp. 57–78). Hoboken, NJ: Wiley.

Xia, Q., & Grant, S. F. (2013). The genetics of human aging. *Annals of the New York Academy of Sciences.* (in press)

Xing, J., Zhang, Y., Han, K., Salem, A. H., Sen, S. K., Huff, C. D., & Jorde, L. B. (2009). Mobile elements create structural variation: Analysis of a complete human genome. *Genome Research, 19,* 1516–1526.

Xu, H., & others. (2013). The function of BMP4 during neurogenesis in the adult hippocampus in Alzheimer's disease. *Ageing Research and Reviews, 12* (1), 157–164.

Xu, J., & Potenza, M. N. (2012). White matter integrity and five-factor personality measures in healthy adults. *NeuroImage, 59,* 800–807.

Xue, S., Wang, Y., & Tang, Y. (2013). Personal and impersonal stimuli differentially engage brain networks during moral reasoning. *Brain and Cognition, 81,* 24–28.

Xue, Y. X., & others. (2012). A memory retrieval-extinction procedure to prevent drug craving and relapse. *Science, 336,* 241–245.

Y

Yalom, I. D., & Leszcz, M. (2006). *Theory and practice of group psychotherapy* (5th ed.). New York: Basic.

Yamamoto, S., & others. (2013). Activation of different signals identified with glia cells contribute to the progression of hyperalgesia. *Cellular and Molecular Neurobiology, 33,* 167–174.

Yamanishi, T., & others. (2009). Changes after behavior therapy among responsive and nonresponsive patients with obsessive-compulsive disorder. *Psychiatry Research, 172,* 242–250.

Yamasue, H., Abe, O., Suga, M., Yamada, H., Rogers, M. A., Aoki, S., Kato, N., & Kasai, K. (2008). Sex-linked neuroanatomical basis of human altruistic cooperativeness. *Cerebral Cortex, 18* (10), 2331–2340.

Yang, Y. (2008). Social inequalities in happiness in the United States, 1972–2004: An age-period-cohort analysis. *American Sociological Review, 73,* 204–226.

Yang, Y., Glenn, A. L., & Raine, A. (2008). Brain abnormalities in antisocial individuals: Implications for the law. *Behavioral Sciences and the Law, 26,* 65–83.

Yang, Y., & Raine, A. (2009). Prefrontal structural and functional brain imaging findings in antisocial, violent, and psychopathic individuals: A meta-analysis. *Psychiatry Research, 174,* 81–88.

Yang, Y., Roussotte, F., Kan, E., Sulik, K. K., Mattson, S. N., Riley, E. P., Jones, K. L., Adnams, C. M., May, P. A. O'Connor, M. J., Narr, K. L., & Sowell, E. R. (2012). Abnormal cortical thickness alterations in fetal alcohol spectrum disorders and their relationships with facial dysmorphology. *Cerebral Cortex, 22* (5), 1170–1179.

Yap, K., Mogan, C., & Kyrios, M. (2012). Obsessive-compulsive disorder and comorbid depression: The role of OCD-related and non-specific factors. *Journal of Anxiety Disorders, 26,* 565–573.

Yen, C. F., Chen, C. C., Lee, Y., Tang, T. C., Ko, C. H., & Yen, J. Y. (2009). Association between quality of life and self-stigma, insight, and adverse effects of medication in patients with depressive disorders. *Depression and Anxiety, 26* (11), 1033–1039.

Yi, Y., & Friedman, D. (2011). Event-related potential (ERP) measures reveal the timing of memory selection processes and proactive interference resolution in working memory. *Brain Research, 1411,* 41–56.

Yiend, J., Freestone, M., Vasquez-Montes, M., Holland, J., & Burns, T. (2013, May). The clinical profile of high-risk mentally disordered offenders. *Social Psychiatry and Psychiatric Epidemiology.* (in press)

Yip, T., Kiang, L., & Fuligni, A. J. (2008). Multiple social identities and reactivity to daily stress among ethnically diverse young adults. *Journal of Research in Personality, 42,* 1160–1172.

Yoo, J., Kim, H., & Hwang, D. Y. (2013). Stem cells as promising therapeutic options for neurological disorders. *Journal of Cellular Biochemistry.* (in press)

Yopchick, J. E., & Kim, N. S. (2012). Hindsight bias and causal reasoning: A minimalist approach. *Cognitive Processes, 13,* 63–72.

Yost, W. A. (2013). Audition. In A. F. Healy, R. W. Proctor, & I. B. Weiner (Eds.), *Handbook of psychology, 2nd ed., Vol. 4.* (pp. 120–151). Hoboken, NJ: Wiley.

Young, L. J. (2009). Being human: Love: Neuroscience reveals all. *Nature, 457,* 148.

Young, S. G., & Claypool, H. M. (2010). Mere exposure has differential effects on attention allocation to threatening and neutral stimuli. *Journal of Experimental Social Psychology, 46,* 424–427.

Young, T. (1802). On the theory of light and colors. *Philosophical Transactions of the Royal Society of London, 92,* 12–48.

Youssef, F. F., Dookeeram, K., Basdeo, V., Francis, E., Doman, M., Mamed, D., Maloo, S., Degannes, J., Dobo, L., Ditshotlo, P., & Legall, G. (2012). Stress alters personal moral decision making. *Psychoneuroimmunology, 37,* 491–498.

Yuan, J., Luo, Y., Yan, J. H., Meng, X., Yu, F., & Li, H. (2009). Neural correlates of the female's susceptibility to negative emotions: An insight into gender-related prevalence of affective disturbances. *Human Brain Mapping, 30,* 3676–3686.

Z

Zadra, A., & Domhoff, G. W. (2011). The content of dreams: Methods and findings. In M. Kryger, T. Roth, W. Dement (Eds.), *Principles and practices of sleep medicine* (5th ed., pp. 585–594). Philadelphia: Elsevier Saunders.

Zadra, A., & Pilon, M. (2012). Parasomnias II: Night terrors and somnambulism. In C. M. Morin & C. A. Espie (Eds.), *The Oxford handbook of sleep and sleep disorders.* New York: Oxford University Press.

Zajonc, R. B. (1965). Social facilitation. *Science, 149,* 269–274.

Zajonc, R. B. (1968). Attitudinal effects of mere exposure. *Journal of Personality and Social Psychology, 9,* 1–27.

Zajonc, R. B. (1984). On the primacy of affect. *American Psychologist, 39,* 117–123.

Zajonc, R. B. (2001). Mere exposure: A gateway to the subliminal. *Current Directions in Psychological Science, 10,* 224–228.

Zannas, A. S., & others. (2012). Stressful life events, perceived stress, and 12-month course of geriatric depression: Direct effects and moderation by the 5-HTTLPR and COMT Val158Met polymorphisms. *Stress, 15,* 425-434.

Zeifman, D., & Hazan, C. (2008). Pair bonds as attachments: Reevaluating the evidence in J. Cassidy & P. R. Shaver (Eds.), *Handbook of attachment* (2nd ed.). New York: Guilford.

Zeitzer, J. M., Friedman, L., & Yesavage, J. A. (2011). Effectiveness of evening phototherapy for insomnia is reduced by bright daytime light exposure. *Sleep Medicine, 12,* 805–807.

Zelazo, P. D. (2013). Developmental psychology: A new synthesis. In P. D. Zelazo (Ed.), *The Oxford handbook of developmental psychology.* New York: Oxford University Press.

Zelazo, P. D., & Lyons, K. E. (2012). The potential benefits of mindfulness training in early childhood: A developmental social cognitive neuroscience perspective. *Child Development Perspectives, 6,* 154–160.

Zelazo, P. D., & Muller, U. (2011). Executive function in typical and atypical development. In U. Goswami (Ed.), *Wiley-Blackwell handbook of childhood cognitive development.* New York: Wiley-Blackwell.

Zeman, M., & Herichova, I. (2013). Melotonin and clock genes in the cardiovascular system. *Frontiers in Bioscience, 5,* 743–753.

Zener, K. (1937). The significance of behavior accompanying conditioned salivary secretion for theories of the conditioned response. *American Journal of Psychology, 50,* 384–403.

Zhai, H., Miller, J., & Sammis, G. (2012). First enantioselective syntheses of the dopamine D1 and D2 receptor modulators, (+)- and (–)-govadine. *Bioorganic and Medicinal Chemistry Letters, 22* (4), 1557–1559.

Zhang, H., Chen, L., & Zhou, X. (2012). Adaptation to visual or auditory time intervals modulates the perception of visual apparent motion. *Frontiers of Integrative Neuroscience, 6,* 100.

Zhang, L.-F., & Sternberg, R. J. (2013). Learning in cross-cultural perspective. In T. Husén & T. N. Postlethwaite (Eds.), *International encyclopedia of education* (3rd ed.). New York: Elsevier.

Zhao, H., Seibert, S. E., & Lumpkin, G. T. (2010). The relationship of personality to entrepreneurial intentions and performance: A meta-analytic review. *Journal of Management, 36,* 381–404.

Zhao, J., Goldberg, J., & Vaccarino, V. (2012). Promoter methylation of serotonin transporter gene is associated with obesity measures: A monozygotic twin study. *International Journal of Obesity.* doi: 10.1038/ijo.2012.8

Zhou, N., Xu, L., & Pfingst, B. E. (2012). Characteristics of detection thresholds and maximum comfortable loudness levels as a function of pulse rate in cochlea implant users. *Hearing Research, 284* (1-2), 25–32.

Zhou, W., & Chen, D. (2009). Fear-related chemosignals modulate recognition of fear in ambiguous facial expressions. *Psychological Science, 20,* 177–183.

Zhou, X., Tang, W., Greenwood, T. A., Guo, S., He, L., Geyer, M. A., & Kelsoe, J. R. (2009). Transcription factor SP4 Is a susceptibility gene for bipolar disorder. *PLoS One, 4,* e5196.

Zhu, D. C., Zacks, R. T., & Slade, J. M. (2010). Brain activation during interference resolution in young and older adults: An fMRI study. *NeuroImage, 50,* 810–817.

Zietsch, B. P., Morley, K. I., Shekar, S. N., Verweij, K. J. H., Keller, M. C., Macgregor, S., Wright, M. J., Bailey, J. M., & Martin, N. G. (2008). Genetic factors predisposing to homosexuality may increase mating success in heterosexuals. *Evolution and Human Behavior, 29,* 424–433.

Zilney, L. A. (2011). *Drugs.* Upper Saddle River, NJ: Prentice-Hall.

Zimbardo, P. G. (1971). *The power and pathology of imprisonment.* Congressional Record (Serial No. 15, 1971-10-25). Hearings before Subcommittee No. 3, of the Committee on the Judiciary, House of Representatives, Ninety-Second Congress, First Session on Corrections, Part II, Prisons, Prison Reform and Prisoner's Rights: California. Washington, DC: U.S. Government Printing Office.

Zimbardo, P. G. (1972). Pathology of imprisonment. *Society, 6,* 4, 6, 8.

Zimbardo, P. G. (1973). On the ethics of intervention in human psychological research: With special reference to the Stanford prison experiment. *Cognition, 2,* 243–256.

Zimbardo, P. G. (1989). *Quiet rage: The Stanford prison study video.* Stanford, CA: Stanford University.

Zimbardo, P. G. (2007). *The Lucifer effect: Understanding how good people turn evil.* New York: Random House.

Zimbardo, P. G., Maslach, C., & Haney, C. (2000). Reflections on the Stanford prison experiment: Genesis, transformations, consequences. In T. Blass (Ed.), *Obedience to authority: Current perspectives on the Milgram paradigm* (pp. 193–237). Mahwah, NJ: Erlbaum.

Zimmer-Gembeck, M. J., Pronk, R. E., Goodwin, B., Mastro, S., & Crick, N. R. (2013). Connected and isolated victims of relational aggression: Associations with peer group status and differences between boys and girls. *Sex Roles, 68,* 363–377.

Zitner, A. (2002, November 10). Best defense may be a good, offensive stench. *Los Angeles Times.* http://articles.latimes.com/2002/nov/10/nation/na-odors10 (accessed March 13, 2013)

Zollig, J., & others. (2012). Plasticity of prospective memory through a familiarization intervention in old adults. *Neuropsychology, Development, and Cognition: Aging, Neuropsychology, and Cognition, 19* (1-2), 168–194.

Zopiatis, A., & Constanti, P. (2012). Extraversion, openness and conscientiousness: The route to transformational leadership in the hotel industry. *Leadership and Organization Development, 33,* 86–104.

Zorumski, C. F., & Izumi, Y. (2012). NMDA receptors and metaplasticity: Mechanisms and possible roles in neuropsychiatric disorders. *Neuroscience and Biobehaviorial Reviews, 36* (3), 989–1000.

Zorumski, C. F., Paul, S. M., Izumi, Y., Covey, D. F., & Mennerick, S. (2013). Neurosteroids, stress, and depression: Potential therapeutic opportunities. *Neuroscience and Biobehavioral Reviews, 37,* 109–122.

Zucker, K. J. (1999). Intersexuality and gender identity differentiation. *Annual Review of Sex Research, 10,* 1–69.

Zuckerman, M. (2013). Biological bases of personality. In H. A. Tennen, J. M. Suls, & I. B. Weiner (Eds.), *Handbook of psychology, 2nd ed., Vol. 5.* (pp. 27–42). Hoboken, NJ: Wiley.

CREDITS

Text and Line Art Credits

Chapter 2
Figure 2.1: (text) From Laura A. King, *Experience Psychology*, 1st ed. (Figure 1.3, p. 14). Copyright © 2010 by The McGraw-Hill Companies, Inc. Reprinted with permission.
p. 32, Psychology Inquiry: Diener, E., Emmons, R. A., Larsen, R. J., and Griffin, S. (1985). The Satisfaction With Life Scale. *Journal of Personality Assessment*, 49, 71–75 (Table 1, p. 72). Reprinted by permission of the publisher (Taylor & Francis Ltd, http://www.tandf.co.uk/journals).
Figure 2.3: From Laura A. King, *Experience Psychology*, 2nd ed. (Figure 1.5). Copyright © 2013 by The McGraw-Hill Companies, Inc. Reprinted with permission.

Chapter 3
Figure 3.1: From Laura A. King, *Experience Psychology*, 1st ed. Copyright © 2010 by The McGraw-Hill Companies, Inc. Reprinted with permission.
Figure 3.3: From R. Lewis, *Life*, 3rd ed. Copyright © 1998 by The McGraw-Hill Companies, Inc. Reprinted with permission.
Figure 3.4: From R. Lewis, *Life*, 3rd ed. Copyright © 1998 by The McGraw-Hill Companies, Inc. Reprinted with permission.
Figure 3.6: From *Mapping the Mind* by Rita Carter, 1998. Reprinted by permission of Moonrunner Design, Ltd.
Figure 3.11: From *Brain, Mind, and Behavior*, 3rd ed. by F. Bloom, C. A. Nelson, A. Lazerson. © 2001 by Educational Broadcasting Corporation. Used with the permission of W. H. Freeman and Company.
Figure 3.15: From *Brain, Mind, and Behavior*, 3rd ed. by F. Bloom, C. A. Nelson, A. Lazerson. © 2001 by Educational Broadcasting Corporation. Used with the permission of W. H. Freeman and Company.
Figure 3.16: From Laura A. King, *Experience Psychology*, 1st ed. Copyright © 2010 by The McGraw-Hill Companies, Inc. Reprinted with permission.
Figure 3.17: From Laura A. King, *Experience Psychology*, 1st ed. Copyright © 2010 by The McGraw-Hill Companies, Inc. Reprinted with permission.
Figure 3.18: From Laura A. King, *Experience Psychology*, 1st ed. Copyright © 2010 by The McGraw-Hill Companies, Inc. Reprinted with permission.

Chapter 4
Figure 4.2: From Laura A. King, *Experience Psychology*, 1st ed. (Figure 3.1, p. 80). Copyright © 2010 by The McGraw-Hill Companies, Inc. Reprinted with permission.
Figure 4.3: (line art) From Laura A. King, *Experience Psychology*, 1st ed. (Figure 3.1, p. 80). Copyright © 2010 by The McGraw-Hill Companies, Inc. Reprinted with permission.
Figure 4.17: The plates have been reproduced from *Ishihara's Tests for Colour Deficiency* published by KANEHARA TRADING INC., located at Tokyo in Japan. But tests for color deficiency cannot be conducted with this material. For accurate testing, the original plates should be used. Used with permission.
Figure 4.18: From Atkinson/Hilgard/Smith/Hoeksema/Fredrickson, *Atkinson and Hilgard's Introduction to Psychology*, 14th ed. © 2003 Wadsworth, a part of Cengage Learning. Reproduced by permission. www.cengage.com/permissions
Figure 4.25: From James J. Gibson, *The Perception of the Visual World*. © 1974 Wadsworth, a part of Cengage Learning, Inc. Reproduced by permission. www.cengage.com/permissions
Figure 4.27: From *Brain, Mind, and Behavior*, 3rd ed. by F. Bloom, C. A. Nelson, A. Lazerson. © 2001 by Educational Broadcasting Corporation. Used with the permission of W. H. Freeman and Company.

Chapter 5
Figure 5.6: Roffwarg, H. P., Muzio, J. N., & Dement, W. C. (1966, 29 April). Ontogenetic development of human dream-sleep cycle. *Science* 152, 604–619 (Figure 1, p. 608). Reprinted with permission from AAAS. http://www.sciencemag.org/content/152/3722/604.extract
p. 164, Psychology Inquiry: (line art) From Laura A. King, *Experience Psychology*, 2nd ed. (Figure 4.9, p. 146). Copyright © 2011 by The McGraw-Hill Companies, Inc. Reprinted with permission.
Figure 5.7: National Institute of Drug Abuse (2001). *Teaching Packet for Psychoactive Drugs*. Washington, DC: National Institute of Drug Abuse, Slide 9.
Figure 5.9: (line art) From Laura A. King, *Experience Psychology*, 1st ed. (Figure 4.11, p. 137). Copyright © 2010 by The McGraw-Hill Companies, Inc. Reprinted with permission.
Figure 5.10: (line art) From Laura A. King, *Experience Psychology*, 1st ed. (Figure 4.13, p. 140). Copyright © 2010 by The McGraw-Hill Companies, Inc. Reprinted with permission.
Figure 5.11: (line art) From Laura A. King, *Experience Psychology*, 2nd ed. (Figure 4.15, p. 153). Copyright © 2011 by The McGraw-Hill Companies, Inc. Reprinted with permission.

Chapter 6
Figure 6.3: From Laura A. King, *Experience Psychology*, 1st ed. (Figure 5.4, p. 166). Copyright © 2010 by The McGraw-Hill Companies, Inc. Reprinted with permission.

Chapter 7
Figure 7.9: From John W. Santrock, *Life-Span Development*, 11th ed. Copyright © 2008 by The McGraw-Hill Companies, Inc. Reprinted with permission.
Figure 7.15: David Barker, © Exploratorium, www.exploratorium.edu. Used with permission.

Chapter 8
Figure 8.1: (line art) From Laura A. King, *Experience Psychology*, 1st ed. (p. 230). Copyright © 2010 by The McGraw-Hill Companies, Inc. Reprinted with permission.
Figure 8.5: (text) From Laura A. King, *Experience Psychology*, 2nd ed. (Figure 7.6, p. 251). Copyright © 2010 by The McGraw-Hill Companies, Inc. Reprinted with permission.
p. 270, Psychology Inquiry: From John W. Santrock, *Children*, 7th ed. Copyright © 2003 by The McGraw-Hill Companies, Inc. Reprinted with permission.
Figure 8.9: From "The Increase in IQ Scores from 1932–1997," by Ulric Neisser. Used with permission.
Figure 8.11: From John W. Santrock, *Educational Psychology*. Copyright © 2001 by The McGraw-Hill Companies, Inc. Reprinted with permission.

Chapter 9
Figure 9.2: From Laura A. King, *Experience Psychology*, 1st ed. Copyright © 2010 by The McGraw-Hill Companies, Inc. Reprinted with permission.
Figure 9.6: From John W. Santrock, *A Topical Approach to Life-Span Development*. Copyright © 2002 by The McGraw-Hill Companies, Inc. Reprinted with permission.
Figure 9.8: (line art) From John W. Santrock, *Life-Span Development*, 9th ed. (Figure 8.8). Copyright © 2004 by The McGraw-Hill Companies, Inc. Reprinted with permission.
Figure 9.11: From John W. Santrock, *Life-Span Development*, 11th ed. (Figure 12.5). Copyright © 2008 by The McGraw-Hill Companies, Inc. Reprinted with permission.

Chapter 10
Figure 10.4: (text) From Laura A. King, *Experience Psychology*, 1st ed. (Figure 9.6, p. 323). Copyright © 2010 by The McGraw-Hill Companies, Inc. Reprinted with permission.
Figure 10.6: From Laura A. King, *Experience Psychology*, 1st ed. (Figure 9.7, p. 325). Copyright © 2010 by The McGraw-Hill Companies, Inc. Reprinted with permission.
p. 350, Psychology Inquiry: From Laura A. King, *Experience Psychology*, 1st ed. (Figure 9.11, p. 331). Copyright © 2010 by The McGraw-Hill Companies, Inc. Reprinted with permission.

Chapter 11
Figure 11.3: Adapted by permission from BMJ Publishing Group Limited. Tanner, J. M., Whitehouse, R. H., & Takaishi, M. (1966). Standards from birth to maturity for height, weight, height velocity, and weight velocity: British children, 1965. Part I. *Archives of Diseases in Childhood* 41, 454–471 (Figure 8, p. 466).
Figure 11.4: From John W. Santrock, *Child Development*, 10th ed. (Figure 13.3). Copyright © 2008 by The McGraw-

Chapter 12
p. 408, Psychology Inquiry: Ten-Item Personality Inventory—(TIPI) reprinted from *Journal of Research in Personality*, vol. 37, no. 6, Gosling, S. D., Rentfrow, P. J., & Swann, W. B., Jr., "A very brief measure of the Big-Five personality domains," pp. 504–528 (Appendix A, p. 525), 2003, with permission from Elsevier.

Chapter 13
p. 460, Psychology Inquiry: Image from *The Robbers Cave Experiment: Intergroup Conflict and Cooperation*, p. 197. © 1988 by Muzafer Sherif. Published by Wesleyan University Press. Reprinted by permission of Wesleyan University Press.

Chapter 15
p. 514, Psychology Inquiry: (graph) From Weissman, M. M., & Olfson, M. (1995, 11 August). Depression in women: Implications for health care research, *Science*, 269, 799–801 (Figure 1, p. 799). Reprinted with permission from AAAS. http://www.sciencemag.org/content/269/5225/799.abstract
Figure 15.4: From *Annual Review of Neuroscience*, vol. 20 (1997). Reproduced with permission of Annual Reviews in the format Textbook via Copyright Clearance Center.
p. 519, Psychology Inquiry: (graph) © Irving I. Gottesman, 2004. Used by permission.
Figure 15.11: From Laura A. King, *Experience Psychology*, 1st ed. (Figure 12.13, p. 444). Copyright © 2010 by The McGraw-Hill Companies, Inc. Reprinted with permission.

Chapter 16
p. 537, Psychology Inquiry: (graph) Reprinted with permission of Michael J. Lambert, professor of Psychology, Brigham Young University.
Figure 16.3: From Laura A. King, *Experience Psychology*, 1st ed. (Figure 13.4, p. 461). Copyright © 2010 by The McGraw-Hill Companies, Inc. Reprinted with permission.
p. 542, Psychology Inquiry: From Laura A. King, *Experience Psychology*, 1st ed. (Figure 13.5, p. 462). Copyright © 2010 by The McGraw-Hill Companies, Inc. Reprinted with permission.
Figure 16.5: From Laura A. King, *Experience Psychology*, 1st ed. (Figure 13.7, p. 466). Copyright © 2010 by The McGraw-Hill Companies, Inc. Reprinted with permission.

Chapter 17
Figure 17.1: From Laura A. King, *Experience Psychology*, 1st ed. (Figure 14.1, p. 483). Copyright © 2010 by The McGraw-Hill Companies, Inc. Reprinted with permission.

p. 570, Psychology Inquiry: (text) From Laura A. King, *Experience Psychology,* 1st ed. (Figure 14.3, p. 489). Copyright © 2010 by The McGraw-Hill Companies, Inc. Reprinted with permission.
Figure 17.2: From Hans Selye, *The Stress of Life,* 2nd ed., p. 476. Copyright © 1976 McGraw-Hill. Reprinted with permission.
Figure 17.3: Cohen, S., et al. (1988). Types of stressors that increase susceptibility to the common cold in healthy adults. *Health Psychology* 17, 214-233 (Figure 1, p. 219). Copyright © 1988 by the American Psychological Association. Reprinted with permission.
Figure 17.5: Reprinted with permission from *Journal of Psychosomatic Research,* vol. 29, no. 5, S. C. Kobasa, S. R. Maddi, M. C. Puccette, and M. A. Zola, "Relative effectiveness of hardiness, exercise and social support as resources against illness," pp. 525–533. Copyright 1985, with permission from Elsevier.
Figure 17.7: (text) From John W. Santrock, *Life-Span Development,* 11th ed. Copyright © 2008 by The McGraw-Hill Companies, Inc. Reprinted with permission.
Figure 17.10: From Laura A. King, *Experience Psychology,* 1st ed. (Figure 14.13, p. 504). Copyright © 2010 by The McGraw-Hill Companies, Inc. Reprinted with permission.

Photo Credits

Image Researcher: David Tietz
Design Elements: (orange cut in half) © Stockdisc/PunchStock RF; **(orange slice)** © Foodcollection RF; **(close-up of half an orange)** © Stockdisc/PunchStock RF; (© Fotosearch Premium/Getty Images RF) © Fotosearch Premium/Getty Images RF; **(two halves of an orange)** © Stewart Waller/fStop/Getty Images RF; **(oranges and apple, orange peel, half peeled orange)** © The McGraw-Hill Companies, Inc/Mark Dierker, photographer.

Front Matter

Page iv: Courtesy of Laura King; **p. xxi:** © Foodcollection; **p. xxiv:** © David Lees/Getty Images; **p. xxviii (manuscript):** © Burke/Triolo/Brand X Pictures/Jupiter Images RF; **p. xxviii (markers):** © The McGraw-Hill Companies, Inc./Ken Karp photographer; **p. xxix:** © RubberBall Productions RF.

Chapter 1

Opener: © Michael Blann/Digital Vision/Getty Images RF; **p. 5 (top):** © GlowImages/Alamy RF; **p. 5 (bottom):** © Brand X Pictures/PunchStock RF; **p. 8:** AP Photo/Carolyn Kaster; **p. 9 (both):** © Bettmann/Corbis; **p. 10:** © Michele Burgess/Corbis RF; **p. 11:** AP Photo; **p. 12:** © Time & Life Pictures/Getty Images; **p. 13:** © Kevin Dodge/Corbis; **p. 15:** Courtesy of Richard Davidson, University of Wisconsin, Madison. Photo by Jeff Miller; **p. 16:** Courtesy of Carol S. Dweck, Stanford University; **p. 17 (Tai Chi):** © Atlantide Phototravel/Corbis; **p. 17 (motorcycles):** © Chip Somodevilla/Getty Images; **p. 17 (gay pride):** © Peter Foley/Reuters/Corbis; **p. 17 (military departure):** © David McNew/Getty Images; **p. 17 (basketball):** © Dennis MacDonald/PhotoEdit; **p. 18:** U.S. Department of Health and Human Services; **p. 19:** © MistikaS/iStockphoto RF; **p. 20 (maze):** © artpartner-images.com/Alamy; **p. 21:** © Juergen Hasenkopf/ima/SuperStock.

Chapter 2

Opener: © PhotoAlto sas/Alamy RF; **p. 26 (flower):** © Dorling Kindersley/Getty Images; **p. 26 (couple):** © George Doyle & Ciaran Griffin/Stockbyte/Getty Images RF; **Fig 2.1 (gift):** © Stockdisc/PunchStock RF; **Fig 2.1 (money):** © Masterfile RF; **p. 28:** © Mirko Iannace/AGE Fotostock/Getty Images; **p. 30:** © The McGraw-Hill Companies, Inc./John Flournoy, photographer; **p. 31:** © Bettmann/Corbis; **Fig 2.2 (yawn):** © Doug Menuez/Getty Images RF; **Fig 2.2 (tired student):** © BananaStock/Jupiter Images RF; **Fig 2.2 (studying):** © Veer RF; **Fig 2.2 (socializing):** © Stockbyte/PunchStock RF; **p. 34 (ice-cream):** © Photodisc/PunchStock RF; **p. 35:** © Angel Chevrestt/ZumaPress.com/Alamy; **p. 36:** © Linda Steward/iStockphoto RF; **p. 38:** © Fuse/Getty Images RF; **p. 41:** © Nico Ferrando/Media Bakery RF; **p. 43:** Image courtesy of The Advertising Archives; **p. 45 (left):** © Justin Sullivan/Getty Images; **p. 45 (right):** © Elsa/Staff/Getty Images; **p. 46 (left):** © Michael Nichols/National Geographic/Getty Images; **p. 46 (right):** Courtesy of Barbara Fredrickson, University of North Carolina; **p. 48:** AP Photo/Ted S. Warren; **p. 49:** © Cyberstock/Alamy; **p. 51:** © Josef Lindau/Corbis; **p. 53 (letters):** © incamerastock/Alamy; **p. 54:** © AGE Fotostock/SuperStock; **p. 55:** © JGI/Jamie Grill/Blend Images/Getty Images RF; **p. 56:** Courtesy of James W. Pennebaker, University of Texas. Photo by Marsha Miller; **p. 57:** © Brand X Pictures RF.

Chapter 3

Opener: © Media Bakery RF; **p. 62 (left):** © DreamPictures/Blend Images/Getty Images; **p. 62 (right):** © Digital Vision/Getty Images RF; **p. 63:** Press Association via AP Images; **Fig 3.1:** © RubberBall Productions RF; **p. 66:** © Pascale Beroujon/Lonely Planet Images/Getty Images; **p. 68:** © Ida Mae Astute/ABC via Getty Images; **p. 72:** Centers for Disease Control; **Fig 3.8:** © annedde/E+/Getty Images RF; **p. 76:** © Blend Images/Alamy RF; **Fig 3.9:** © Peter Arnold, Inc./Stegerphoto/Getty Images; **Fig 3.10:** © Ralph Hutchings/Visuals Unlimited, Inc.; **p. 82:** © John Whiley, California Institute of Technology, estate of James Olds; **Fig 3.13:** © A. GlaubermanScience Source; **p. 83:** © Michael Kovac/Getty Images; **Fig 3.14:** © ER Productions/Getty Images RF; **p. 84:** From: Damasio H., Grabowski, T., Frank R., Galaburda A. M., Damasio A. R.: "The return of Phineas Gage: Clues about the brain from the skull of a famous patient." *Science,* 264:1102–1105, 1994; **Fig 3.19:** © PhotoAlto/PunchStock RF; **Fig 3.20:** © Lennart Nilsson/Scanpix; **p. 92:** © Riccardo Cassiani-Ingoni/Science Source; **p. 94:** © Rick Rickman; **Fig 3.22 (rat):** © PunchStock/BananaStock RF; **p. 96:** © Joe Murphy/NBAE via Getty Images; **p. 97:** © Enrico Ferorelli.

Chapter 4

Opener: © PhotoAlto/Alamy RF; **p. 105 (top):** © Ron Austing; Frank Lane Picture Agency/Corbis; **p. 105 (bottom):** © Image Source/PunchStock RF; **p. 106:** Library of Congress [LC-DIG-ds-00175]; **Fig 4.2 (eye):** © Barbara Penoyar/Getty Images RF; **Fig 4.2 (ear):** © The McGraw-Hill Companies, Inc./Eric Wise, photographer; **Fig 4.2 (foot):** © The McGraw-Hill Companies, Inc./Jill Braaten, photographer; **Fig 4.2 (smelling):** © ZenShui/Sigrid Olsson/Getty Images RF; **Fig 4.2 (eating):** © istockphoto.com/Zorani RF; **Fig 4.3:** © Stockbyte/PunchStock RF; **Fig 4.4:** © Photodisc RF; Fig 4.5: © Stockdisc RF; **p. 111:** © Markos Dolopikos/Alamy RF; **Fig 4.10:** Courtesy of X-Rite, Inc.; **Fig 4.12:** © Frank S. Werblin; **Fig 4.15:** © Editorial Image, LLC/Alamy; **Fig 4.16:** © RubberBall Productions/Getty Images RF; **p. 121:** © Silver Screen Collection/Hulton Archives/Getty Images; **Fig 4.22:** © Erich Lessing/Art Resource, NY ; **Fig 4.24:** © Steve Allen/Getty Images RF; **p. 135:** © John E Davidson/Getty Images RF; **p. 137:** © Tom Merton/OJO Images/Getty Images RF; **Fig 4.33:** © Thomas Coex/AFP/GettyImages; **Fig 4.33 (inset):** © Lennart Nilsson/Scanpix.

Chapter 5

Opener: © Corbis/Media Bakery RF; **p. 145:** © Comstock/Alamy RF; **p. 148:** © Mike Agliolo/Science Source; **p. 151 (bottom):** © Tim Pannell/Corbis RF; **Fig 5.3 (bat):** © Frank Greenaway/Getty Images; **Fig 5.3 (horse):** © Royalty Free/Corbis RF; **p. 153:** © Will and Deni McIntyre/Science Source; **Fig 5.5:** © Allan Hobson/Science Source; **p. 156:** © Rubberball/Alamy RF; **p. 157:** © Steve Cole/Getty Images RF; **p. 161:** © Thinkstock/PunchStock RF; **p. 163:** © Comstock/PunchStock RF; **p. 164:** © PhotoAlto/Picture Quest RF; **Fig 5.9:** © George Doyle/Stockbyte/Getty Images RF; **p. 166 (bottom):** © Ingram Publishing/Alamy RF; **p. 167:** © Royalty Free/Corbis RF; **p. 168:** © Ingram Publishing/SuperStock RF; **Fig 5.10:** © Image Source/Getty Images RF; **Fig 5.11:** © Digital Vision/PunchStock RF; **Fig 5.14:** © Stanford News Service; **p. 176:** © The McGraw-Hill Companies, Inc./Erin Koran; **p. 177:** © Jules Frazier/Getty Images RF.

Chapter 6

Opener: © Mike Kemp/Blend Images/Getty Images RF; **p. 182:** © John Fedele/Media Bakery; **Fig 6.1 (doctor's office):** © PunchStock RF; **Fig 6.1 (injection):** © Photodisc Collection/Getty Images RF; **Fig 6.1 (swimmer):** © Ryan McVay/Getty Images RF; **Fig 6.1 (award):** © Photodisc Inc./Getty Images RF; **p. 184:** The Granger Collection, New York; **p. 187 (pills):** © Brand X Pictures/PunchStock RF; **p. 187 (pipe):** © Karen Mower/E+/Getty Images RF; **p. 189:** Courtesy of Professor Benjamin Harris; **p. 191:** © Royalty Free/Corbis RF; **Fig 6.3 (pills):** © Thinkstock/Jupiter Images RF; **Fig 6.3 (water):** © Brand X Pictures/PunchStock RF; **Fig 6.3 (drinking):** © Rick Gomez/Corbis RF; **Fig 6.6:** © Nina Leen/Time & Life Pictures/Getty Images; **p. 195:** © Pilar Olivares/Reuters/Corbis; **Fig 6.8:** © Photodisc/Getty Images RF; **p. 198:** © David Sacks/The Image Bank/Getty Images; **p. 199:** © Royalty Free/Corbis RF; **p. 202:** © Samantha Mitchell/Media Bakery; **Fig 6.11 (all):** © SuperStock; **Fig 6.12:** © JP Laffont/Sygma/Corbis; **p. 208 (top):** © Paul Chesley/Stone/Getty Images; **p. 208 (bottom):** © Paul A. Souders/Corbis; **p. 210 (top):** © Purestock RF; **p. 210 (middle):** © John Lund/Marc Romanelli/Getty Images RF; **p. 210 (bottom):** © Steve Hix/Fuse/Getty Images RF; **p. 211:** © Image100 Ltd RF.

Chapter 7

Opener: © Ray Guy/Alamy; **Fig 7.1 (camera):** © iStockphoto.com/gbautista87 RF; **Fig 7.1 (box):** © iStockphoto.com/gvictoria RF; **Fig 7.1 (photo album):** © The McGraw-Hill Companies, Inc./Gary He, photographer; **p. 219:** © Image Source/Corbis RF; **Fig 7.6 (bird):** © Jeremy Woodhouse/Getty Images RF; **Fig 7.6 (ear):** © Geoff du Feu/Alamy RF; **Fig 7.6 (eye):** © ColorBlind Images/Blend Images LLC RF; **p. 225:** © Interfoto/Alamy; **p. 226:** © Ingram Publishing/Alamy RF; **p. 227:** © Lanny Ziering/Brand X Pictures/Getty Images RF; **p. 229:** © Jessica Peterson/Media Bakery RF; **p. 231:** AP Photo/Morry Gash; **p. 232:** © Tim Laman/Getty Images RF; **p. 235:** © PunchStock/Digital Vision RF; **Fig 7.12 (left):** © AP/Wide World Photos; **Fig 7.12 (right):** AP Photo/ho; **p. 237:** © Borut Furlan/WaterFrame/Getty Images; **p. 238:** AP Photo/Jason DeCrow; **p. 241:** © Lisa F. Young/Alamy RF; **p. 242 (left):** © Reuters/Corbis; **p. 242 (right):** AP Photo/Marie P. Marzi; **p. 243:** © Bettmann/Corbis; **Fig 7.15:** Photo illustration by David Tietz/Editorial Image, LLC; **p. 247:** © Design Pics/Monkey Business RF; **p. 249:** © Denkou Images/Alamy RF.

Chapter 8

Opener: © Felix Sanchez/Blend Images/Getty Images; **p. 254:** © Dilip Vishwanat/Getty Images for Honda; **Fig 8.1:** © Creatas/Picture Quest RF; **p. 256 (top):** © Shin Yoshino/Minden; **p. 256 (bottom):** © John Giustina/Getty Images RF; **Fig 8.5 (left):** © Digital Vision/SuperStock RF; **Fig 8.5 (right):** © Brand X Pictures RF; **p. 264:** © tiero/AGE Fotostock RF; **p. 266:** © Harry Hammond/V&A Images/Getty Images; **Fig 8.6 (left):** © David Austin/Stock Boston; **Fig 8.6 (right):** © Ben Simmons; **p. 269:** © Everett Collection Inc/Alamy; **p. 273:** © Elizabeth Crews/The Image Works; **p. 275:** © Heide Benser/zefa/Corbis; **p. 276:** © Dance By Beytan/Alamy; **p. 278 (top):** © SuperStock; **p. 278 (bottom):** © Holton Collection/SuperStock; **p. 280:** © epa european pressphoto agency b.v./Alamy; **Fig 8.10:** © Camille Tokerud/Photographer's Choice/Getty Images RF; **Fig 8.11 (top):** © Blend Images/SuperStock; **Fig 8.11 (bottom):** © Veer RF; **Fig 8.12 (both):** © 2003 University of Washington, Institute for Learning and Brain Sciences (I-LABS); **p. 284:** © Anthony Bannister/Animals Animals; **p. 285:** © Ariel Skelley/The Image Bank/Getty Images.

Chapter 9

Opener: © ICHIRO/Photodisc/Getty Images RF; **p. 290 (left):** © Katrina Wittkamp/Lifesize/Getty Images RF; **p. 290 (middle):** © Geri Engberg/The Image Works; **p. 290 (right):** © Syracuse Newspapers/J. Berry/The Image Works;

NAME INDEX

Note: Page numbers followed by "*f*" refer to figures.

A

Abbass, A. A., 539
Abbate, C., 246
Abbott, B. B., 211
ABC News, 384
Abdel-Azim, E., 83
Abdeshahi, S. K., 175
Abe, O., 368
Abecasis, G., 420
Abelson, R., 231
Aberg, K., 153
Aberg, K. A., 519
Abramowitz, J. S., 510
Abrams, L., 245
Abramson, L. Y., 334, 513
á Campo, J., 551
Accordini, S., 581
Acer, N., 519
Acerbo, M. J., 187
Achanzar, K., 343
Acheson, D. T., 507
Achille, N. M., 41
Ackerman, P., 441
Ackermann, K., 152
Adam, C., 145
Adamou, M., 505
Adams, E. E., 311
Adams, H. E., 399
Adams, J., 322
Adams, M. J., 243
Adams, R. B., 83
Adams, R. B., Jr., 83
Adams, T. B., 566
Addario, D., 520
Addington, J., 520
Addis, D. R., 220
Addison, T., 445
Adelstein, J. S., 418
Ader, R., 190
Adler, A., 401, 402
Adler, N. E., 285, 426
Adnams, C. M., 294
Adolph, K. E., 296
Adolphs, R., 81, 82, 148, 432
Adriano, J., 362
Afonso, V. M., 388
Ager, A., 293
Aggarwal, B., 562
Aggarwal, N. T., 249
Aghajanian, G., 512
Agnati, L. F., 255
Agnew, C. R., 423, 463
Agnew, Z., 280
Ago, Y., 547
Agorastos, A., 501
Aguilar-Gaxiola, S., 336
Aguinis, H., 473, 475, 478, 480, 490
Aharon-Peretz, J., 522
Ahearne, M., 482
Ahluwalia, J., 363
Ahmadi, J., 171
Ahmed, F., 361
Ahmed, N. U., 494
Ahmed, S. F., 361
Ahola, K., 494
Aich, P., 572
Aichele, S. R., 317

Aimola Davies, A., 107
Ainsworth, K., 563
Ainsworth, M. D. S., 305
Ainsworth, M. S., 305
Ainsworth, S. E., 451
Aizman, O., 515
Ajina, S., 432
Ajrouch, K. J., 293
Ajzen, I., 436, 563
Akaike, N., 72
Akçay, E., 367
Akehurst, L., 161
Akerstedt, T., 157
Akhtar, S., 556
Akil, H., 187
Akkermann, K., 335
Aknin, L. B., 27, 440
Aksan, N., 311
Aktas, A., 191
Akyuz, G., 515, 516
Albarracin, D., 361, 563
Albersheim, L., 306
Albert, D., 313
Alberto, P. A., 201, 202
Albright, K., 513
Aldao, A., 513, 574
Aldwin, C. M., 323
Alegría, A. A., 525
Alegría, M., 502
Aleksa, K., 294
Aleman, A., 77
Alessandri, G., 96, 409
Alexander, B., 390, 546
Alexander, G. C., 505
Alexander, G. E., 249
Alexander, G. M., 364, 372
Alexander, J., 549
Alexander, K. W., 240, 241
Alexander, M. G., 373
Ali, M. K., 427
Ali, S., 425
Alibali, M. W., 283
Allen, R. J., 147
Allen, T. D., 493
Alliger, G. M., 473
Allizia, A. L., 82
Alloway, T. P., 225
Allport, G. W., 406, 412, 460
Allsopp, A. J., 488
Almeida, D. M., 572
Almeida, J., 149
Almèn, M. S., 153
Almgren, M. M., 582
Alonso, P., 509
Alper, C. M., 573
Alpers, G. W., 510
Alpert, N. M., 76
Alquist, J. L., 425, 451
Alstermark, B., 63
Altemus, M., 507
Altenor, A., 196
Alter, A. L., 436
Althof, S. E., 389
Althoff, R. R., 525
Altmaier, E. M., 534
Aluja, A., 522
Alvarenga, M., 507

Alvarez, R. M., 432
Alvaro, E. M., 563
Alvaro, F., 191
Alvino, C., 518
Al-Wer, E., 278
Aly, M., 144
Alzahabi, R., 219
Amano, T., 343
Amar, A. P., 551
Amarel, D., 569
Amato, P. R., 5
Ambadar, Z., 239
Ambady, N., 433
Amelang, M., 425
American Association of University Women, 492
American Cancer Society, 581
American Psychiatric Association (APA), 333, 362, 382, 387, 501, 503, 511, 515
American Psychological Association, 536, 537
Ames, M. E., 285
Ametaj, A. A., 537
Amir, E., 323
Amodio, D. M., 458
Amorim, R. L., 551
Ampuero, M. C., 556
Amsterdam, J. D., 547
Amunts, K., 77
Ancoli-Israel, S., 158
Andel, R., 249
Anderman, E. M., 16, 204, 338
Andersen, P. K., 419, 512
Andersen, S. K., 104
Anderson, A. K., 238, 239
Anderson, B. A., 573
Anderson, C. A., 34, 91, 443, 444, 445
Anderson, C. J., 456
Anderson, D. R., 568, 573
Anderson, N. H., 433
Anderson, R. N., 526
Anderson, V. A., 91
Anderson-Lewis, C., 563
Andersson, G., 570
Andersson, H., 536
Andersson, M., 364
Andrade, C., 550
Andrade, E., 134
Andre, J. B., 440
Andreason, N. J. C., 267
Andrew, B. J., 186
Andrews, B., 511
Andrews, G., 503, 506, 509
Andrews, M., 431
Andrillon, T., 155
Andruff, H., 381
Andrusyna, T. P., 536
Andrykowski, M. A., 191
Ang, S., 271, 480
Angel, L., 75, 318
Ansseau, M., 513
Antonenko, O., 441
Antoni, M., 556
Antoni, M. H., 286
Antón-Méndez, I., 245
Antonucci, T. C., 293
Antonuccio, D. O., 582

Antuono, P., 37
Aoki, S., 368
Apaolaza-Ibanez, V., 18
Aperia, A., 515
Apicella, C., 577
Appel, L., 133
Appleby, L., 528
Apuzzo, M. L., 551
Aquino, K., 492
Arangio, R., 91
Arber, C., 318
Arbib, M. A., 65, 66, 280
Arbisi, P. A., 422
Archer, J., 373
Archer, R. P., 423
Archimi, A., 75
Arciniegas, D. B., 91
Arden, M., 566
Areni, C. S., 439
Arentoft, A., 502
Ariely, D., 53, 264, 353, 452
Armitage, C. J., 566, 567
Armony, J. L., 518
Armor, D. A., 292
Armstrong, J. M., 285
Arneill, A. B., 139
Arnett, J. J., 315, 316
Arnold, K., 294
Arnold, K. A., 488
Arnold, M. M., 239
Arntz, A., 513, 522, 524
Arolfo, M. P., 189
Aromaa, A., 494
Aronen, E. T., 303
Aronson, E., 461
Aronson, J., 272, 276, 436
Arpan, L., 436
Arps, K., 441
Arranz, H., 513
Arriaga, X. B., 463
Arrow, H., 442
Arseneault, L., 373, 443
Arthur, C. A., 488
Arthur, W. J., 478
Asada, K., 279
Asch, S. E., 446, 447
Aselage, J., 339
Asendorpf, J. B., 433
Ashburner, J., 63
Ashby, F. B., 229
Asher, B. D., 434
Asherson, P., 505
Ashton, M. C., 296, 411
Ashton-James, C. E., 440
Asmundson, G. J., 543
Asnaani, A., 554, 555
Aspinwall, L. G., 575
Aspland, E., 550
Assaad, J., 373, 443
Asselin, M. C., 343
Associated Press, 7
Astell, A., 221, 229
Astington, J. W., 145
Atanackovic, D., 572
Atkins, D. C., 545
Atkinson, J., 296
Atkinson, R. C., 222, 234
Aton, S. J., 152

Choi, S., 501
Choi, T. K., 507
Chomsky, N., 280, 280f
Chopra, S., 285
Chorost, M., 143
Chou, C. P., 563
Chou, H. T., 262
Chou, P., 521
Chou, S. P., 512, 528
Chow, D. L., 537, 538
Chrisman, K., 462
Christakis, N., 271
Christenfeld, N. J. S., 16, 341
Christensen, B. K., 388
Christensen, H., 509
Christensen, M. S., 224
Christie, A., 487
Christie, B. R., 92
Christoff, K., 147
Christopher Frueh, B., 544
Christopherson, E. R., 536
Chrousos, G. P., 572
Chu, S., 319, 578
Chu, Y., 205
Chua, A. N., 572
Chudek, M., 440
Chung, C. K., 56
Chung, S., 513
Chung, T., 166
Chung, W.-J., 396, 401
Chung, Y., 552
Chung-Herrera, B. G., 408
Church, A. T., 411
Church, R. M., 200
Cialdini, R. B., 439, 440, 441
Ciani, K. D., 338
Cicero, D. C., 261
Cima, M., 522
Cinnirella, M., 455
Cipolli, C., 161
Cirelli, C., 152
Claes, H. I., 389
Clardy, C. E., 455
Clark, A. E., 482, 493
Clark, B., 274
Clark, D. B., 172
Clark, D. G., 578, 579
Clark, K. J., 582
Clark, L. A., 427, 503
Clark, M. S., 440, 462
Clark, R. D., 374, 375
Clark, R. E., 9
Clarke, K., 378
Clarke, S., 493
Clarkin, J. F., 545
Clarkson, G., 223
Clarys, D., 237
Classen, J., 297
Claudino, A. M., 335
Clausen, J. A., 485
Claypool, H. M., 346
Cleckley, H. M., 516
Cleek, E. N., 545, 551, 555
Cleere, C., 174, 175
Clémenceau, S., 145
Clemens, N. A., 536
Clément-Guillotin, C., 367
Cleveland, J. N., 528
Cliff, K., 494
Clifford, B. R., 237, 240
Clifton, C., 277
Clifton, D. O., 484
Clinton, D., 334, 335
Clooney, G., 323
Cloud, J., 274
Clutton-Brock, T. H., 364
Cobb, J. A., 67
Cobb, N. K., 452
Cody, M. J., 409
Coe, C. L., 569

Coelho, C. M., 508
Coffey, P., 384
Coffey, V. G., 316
Coffino, B., 305
CogMed, 303
Cohen, D., 444, 445, 457
Cohen, J. A., 5
Cohen, L., 145
Cohen, L. G., 297
Cohen, L. H., 323
Cohen, N., 190
Cohen, P. J., 172
Cohen, S., 37, 217, 352, 463, 572, 573
Cohen-Bendahan, C. C. C., 379
Cohen-Charash, Y., 485
Cohen-Kettenis, P. T., 363
Cohen-Woods, S., 95
Cohn, D., 320
Coie, J. D., 311, 372
Coifman, K. G., 574
Cojan, Y., 75
Colagiuri, S., 578
Colapinto, J., 361, 361f
Cole, F., 529
Cole, J., 108
Cole, S., 158, 433, 567
Cole, S. W., 98
Colella, A. J., 472, 473
Coleman, E., 362, 363
Coleman, T., 152, 582
Coleman-Jensen, A., 431
Coles, M., 462
Coliado-Hidalgo, A., 158
Coll, C. G., 313
Collet, S., 135
Collin, G. B., 117
Collins, A., 442
Collins, C. E., 191
Collins, P. F., 419
Colón, E. A., 463
Colquitt, J. A., 471
Colrain, I. M., 155, 156
Coluccia, A., 526
Colvin, C. R., 433, 435
Colwell, C. S., 157
Comasco, E., 419
Combs, G. M., 480
Combs, J. L., 443
Comer, J. S., 537
Comijs, H. C., 550
Committee to Review Adverse Effects of Vaccines, 504
Compton, J. A., 439
Compton, W., 521
Compton, W. M., 524
Comstock, G., 445
Comtois, K. A., 545
Con, A. H., 576
Condon, L., 174, 175
Conger, R. D., 409
Conley, C. S., 576
Conley, R. R., 518
Conley, T. D., 375, 380
Conlin, C., 578
Connell, J., 15
Connell, M., 239
Connellan, J., 363
Conner, B., 433
Conner, K. R., 525
Conner, M., 425, 566
Connes, P., 160
Connolly, T., 483
Connor-Smith, J., 407, 425, 426
Conraads, V. M., 427
Consoli, M., 336
Consortium on the Management of Disorders of Sexual Development, 362
Constable, R. T., 418
Constanti, P., 488
Constantine, N. A., 386
Constantinidou, F., 210

Conti, R., 505
Contreras, M., 14, 208, 229
Conway, M., 237
Conway, M. A., 248
Conwell, Y., 554
Cook, E., 73
Cook, J. R., 554
Cook, S. P., 238
Cook, S. W., 278
Coolidge, F. L., 225
Cooper, A., 41, 419
Cooper, H., 338
Cooper, K. H., 578, 579
Cooper, M. L., 36, 391
Cooper, R. M., 95
Cooper-Hakim, A., 485
Copas, A. J., 384
Copeland, D. E., 237
Copeland, L. E., 507
Copeland-Linder, N., 314
Corbit, L. H., 73
Cordon, I. M., 240
Coren, S., 108
Coria-Avila, G. A., 388
Cornblatt, B. A., 520
Cornwell, E. Y., 463
Corpus, M. J., 556
Corr, P. J., 346, 419
Correa, T., 409
Correia, C., 329
Corrigan, P. W., 527, 528
Corsi, M., 336
Corsica, J., 335
Corsica, J. A., 18, 562
Cortelli, P., 153
Cortes, J., 513
Cortes, M. R., 511
Cortina, J. M., 472, 475, 476, 477
Cortina, L. M., 492
Corya, S. A., 551
Coryell, W. H., 507
Cosci, F., 427
Cosgrove, V. E., 515
Cosmides, L., 364, 442
Costa, A., 508
Costa, P. T., 407, 409, 420, 422
Costa, R. M., 384, 391
Costafreda, S. G., 77
Costalas, J. W., 94
Costandi, M., 163
Côté, S., 441
Cotton, J. L., 479
Cotugno, G., 292
Coulson, M. C., 536, 544
Coulson, S., 89
Couturier, J., 335
Coverdale, J. H., 576
Covey, D. F., 72
Covington, D. W., 525
Cowan, N., 224
Cowan, R. L., 171
Cox, B. J., 523
Cox, E., 533
Cox, K., 249
Cox, K. S., 320
Cox, R. E., 175
Coyne, J. C., 577
Cracco, L., 153
Craddock, N., 514
Craig, I. W., 95, 522
Craighead, E., 12, 16, 99, 189, 201, 540, 544
Craighead, L. W., 12, 16, 99, 189, 201, 540, 544
Craik, F. I., 219
Craik, F. I. M., 219, 234, 246
Craik, F. I., 233
Cramer, P., 403, 423
Cramond, B., 264
Crampton, S. M., 485

Crandall, C. S., 452
Cranford, J. A., 553
Crano, W. D., 437, 438, 563
Crawford, J. R., 246
Crawford, T. J., 225
Crede, M., 407, 488
Creer, D. J., 92
Crego, C., 503
Crespin, T. R., 480
Cress, M. E., 580
Crick, N. R., 372
Crimmins, E., 249
Crisafulli, C., 515
Crispin, G., 474, 475
Criss, A. H., 244
Critchley, H. D., 152
Crittenden, C. N., 572, 573
Crittenden, K., 425, 426
Crocker, J., 405, 456
Crockett, M. J., 441
Croft, W., 277
Croiset, G., 405
Crombez, G., 522
Cronbach, L. J., 409
Crookes, K., 89
Crooks, R. L., 380, 385
Cropley, T. G., 177
Crosby, R. D., 336
Crossley, M. J., 229
Croux, C., 513
Crowe, M., 249
Crowell, J., 306
Crowley, M., 370
Crowley, S. J., 157
Crucian, G. P., 347
Crumpler, C., 322
Crusio, W. E., 271, 420
Cruz, A. M., 444, 445
Cruz, L. E., 73
Csikszentmihalyi, M., 8, 323, 351, 495
Cuevas, K., 303
Cuevas, L., 522
Cuijpers, P., 463, 513, 557
Cukrowicz, K. C., 536
Culbertson, S. S., 472, 475, 476, 477
Cullen, K., 373
Culmer, P. R., 318
Culver, J. O., 94
Cummings, N., 212
Cunningham, C. L., 452
Cunningham, R. L., 443
Cunningham, S. J., 147
Curci, A., 238
Curhan, K., 569
Curi, A., 233
Curran, T., 567
Currie, J., 550
Currie, S., 493
Curry, J. F., 425
Curtis, C., 327, 335
Curtis, M. A., 318
Curtiss, S., 281
Cusack, K. J., 544
Cushman, F., 148
Cutler, T., 157
Cutrona, C. E., 463
Cutuli, D., 63
Cwir, D., 39
Cyders, M. A., 443
Cyna, A. M., 175
Czechowska, Y., 518

D

Dabringhaus, A., 77
Dach-Gruschow, K., 14
Dackis, C., 171
Da Costa, L. A., 227
Dafinoiu, I., 174
Dahdaleh, N. S., 507

Giovannini, M., 292
Giovannini, M. G., 72
Girvin, H., 566
Gittelman, M., 528
Given, B., 556
Given, C., 556
Givens, D. I., 331
Glas, C. A., 421
Glaser, D. E., 66
Glaser, R., 572
Glasman, L. R., 361
Glasser, D. B., 389
Glaw, X. M., 92
Gleason, T. R., 298
Glei, D. A., 562
Gleitman, L., 278
Glenberg, A. M., 66
Glenn, A. L., 443
Glenn, D., 219
Glisky, E. L., 238
Glomb, T. M., 370
Glover, G. H., 233
Glover, V., 572
Glowacki, L., 442
Gluck, J., 319
Glymour, M. M., 319
Gnagy, E. M., 505
Go, H. J., 153
Gobbi, M., 554, 555
Gobet, F., 223
Godden, D. R., 237
Godin, J. J., 411
Godsil, B. P., 468
Godzik, J., 441
Goebel, R., 108
Goel, A. K., 255
Goenjian, A. K., 512
Goethals, G. R., 453
Goff, D., 518
Gogtay, N., 298
Gogus, C. I., 478
Golay, A., 335
Golberstein, E., 548
Gold, J., 545
Gold, P. W., 572
Goldberg, A., 362
Goldberg, A. E., 382
Goldberg, J., 332
Goldberg, J. H., 335
Goldberg, L. R., 407, 411, 424
Goldberg, L. S., 347
Goldberg, R., 164
Goldenberg, J. L., 455
Golden-Kreutz, D. M., 573
Goldhaber, T., 89
Golding, J., 382
Goldin-Meadow, S., 278, 283
Goldman, N., 562
Goldschmidt, L., 172
Goldsmith, A. A., 425
Goldsmith, H. H., 341
Goldsmith, T. E., 254
Goldstein, E. B., 105
Goldstein, J. M., 368
Goldstein, M. H., 281
Goldstein, R., 512, 528
Goldston, D. B., 526
Goldstone, R. L., 256
Goldstrom, I. D., 553
Goleman, D., 267
Golinkoff, R. M., 281, 283
Goljevscek, S., 509
Gollan, 245
Gollnick, D. M., 14
Gollwitzer, P. M., 230, 433, 567
Golombok, S., 366, 377, 382
Gomez-Ramirez, M., 132
Gonda, X., 419
Gondo, Y., 425
Gonzales, E. J., 372
Gonzales, N. A., 314

Gonzales-Bracken, M. A., 314
Gonzalez-Maeso, J., 172
Gonzalez-Vallejo, C., 149
Good, C. D., 63
Goodall, J., 46f
Goodin, B. R., 575
Gooding, P. A., 293
Goodman, G. S., 240, 241
Goodson, P., 425
Goodwin, B., 372
Goodwin, B. E., 422
Goodwin, C. L., 568, 573
Goodwin, J. S., 35
Goodwin, K. A., 237
Goosens, K. A., 75, 239
Gordh, T., 133
Gordon, K. H., 526
Goren, A., 432
Goritz, C., 92
Gosling, S. D., 279, 408, 409, 411, 411f
Goswami, N., 351
Gotta, G., 381
Gottesman, I. I., 272
Gottlieb, G., 98
Gottlob, L. R., 318
Gottman, J. M., 320, 381
Gottman, J. S., 320
Gotz, J., 317
Gouaux, B., 172
Goubert, L., 203
Gouin, J. P., 572
Gould, J. B., 295
Gould, J. W., 422
Gould, R. L., 536, 544
Gounot, D., 233
Gouzoulis-Mayfrank, E., 171
Gove, W. R., 514
Graber, J. A., 312
Grace, R. C., 12, 16
Graeff, F. G., 507
Graham, E. K., 316, 415, 425
Graham, J., 148
Graham, L. E., 90
Grandey, A. A., 347
Grandon, R., 444
Granger, D. A., 506
Granland, S., 48
Granrud, C. E., 125
Grant, A., 487
Grant, A. M., 479
Grant, B. F., 512, 521, 528
Grant, J. E., 541
Grant, S. G. N., 63
Grasby, P. M., 343
Grassi-Oliveira, R., 518
Gratz, K. L., 370, 523
Graver, R., 539
Gravetter, R. J., 5, 43
Gray, D. L., 16, 204, 338
Gray, J., 376, 419
Gray, J. A., 419
Gray, J. C., 221
Gray, J. R., 441
Graybeal, A., 57
Graziano, A. M., 6, 20, 38, 52
Grazioplene, R. G., 266, 418
Greco, M. A., 152
Green, A., 118
Green, B. A., 33
Green, C. S., 12
Green, J. P., 174, 175
Green, L., 192
Green, M. K., 572
Green, R., 362, 363, 379, 381
Green, R. J., 381
Greenberg, A. R., 440
Greenberg, D. A., 318
Greenberg, L., 13, 540
Greenberg, L. M., 572, 573
Greenberg, L. S., 553
Greene, B., 555

Greene, J., 148, 311
Greene, J. D., 148
Greene, R. L., 422
Greenhaus, J. H., 486
Greenwald, A. G., 458
Greenwood, T. A., 411
Greer, S., 577
Greeson, J. M., 343
Gregan, M. J., 129
Gregg, A. P., 435
Gregoire, P., 266
Gregory, S., 522
Greicius, M. D., 83
Grein, S., 74
Greitemeyer, T., 442
Grezes, J., 66
Grieve, A. J., 285
Griez, E., 507
Griffin, A. M., 432
Griffin, D., 261
Griffin, K. W., 425
Griffin, M. A., 493
Griffin, M. M., 275
Griffin, R. W., 483, 490
Griffin, S., 28, 32
Griffiths, J. D., 280
Grigorenko, E. L., 272
Grigoryan, G., 233
Grillon, C., 507
Grilo, C. M., 335, 336, 545
Grimes, K. L., 187
Grimley, D. M., 563
Grimmer, M. A., 524
Griskevicius, V., 336
Grisso, T., 18
Groenewold, N. A., 77
Groffen, D. A., 513
Groh-Bordin, C., 226
Grohol, J. M., 54, 533, 553
Gronowska, M., 391
Groome, D., 244
Gross, A. M., 541
Gross, J. J., 285, 574
Grossberg, G. T., 108
Grossi, E., 37
Grossman, I., 319
Grote, G., 469
Groth-Marnat, G., 423
Grotpeter, J. K., 372
Grove, W. M., 423
Grubaugh, A. L., 544
Grubb, P., 493, 576
Gruber, S. A., 519
Gruber, T., 176
Grubin, D., 342
Grumet, S. C., 94
Grund, F., 503
Grunewaldt, K. H., 303
Grusec, J. E., 272, 309
Gruzelier, J. H., 174
Gu, Q., 547
Guay, F., 567
Guay, M. C., 303
Guay, R. P., 485
Guenther, F. H., 143
Guertzenstein, E. Z., 551
Guillery-Girard, B., 237
Guimond, A. B., 455
Guiney, H., 249
Gulec, M., 507
Gummelt, H. D., 536
Gummer, A. W., 129
Gump, B., 494
Gump, B. B., 427
Gunderson, J., 524
Gunderson, J. G., 524
Gunn, R. L., 443
Gunning, T. G., 282
Gunnip, M., 220
Gunty, A. L., 323
Guo, L., 507

Guo, Q., 319, 563, 578
Guo, S., 411
Guo, X., 547
Guo, Y., 554
Gupta, M., 67
Gur, R. C., 364, 370, 518
Gur, R. E., 518
Gurbaxani, B. M., 512
Gurin, G., 206
Gurin, P., 206
Gustincich, S., 271
Gutiérrez, V., 370
Guttman, N., 197, 197f
Guven, G. S., 493
Gwaltney, C. J., 567
Gwaltney, J. M., 463, 572
Gwernan-Jones, R., 212
Gwynne, R. M., 332
Gygax, L., 379

H

Haas, B. W., 418
Haase, R. F., 445
Haase, S. J., 112
Haasen, C., 501
Habeck, C., 153, 249
Habekost, T., 219
Habel, U., 370
Habenstein, R. W., 272
Haber, J. R., 167, 409, 568
Hackett, G. I., 389
Hackett, T. A., 108
Haddad, M., 529
Hadjipanayis, A. G., 134
Hafen, C. A., 315
Hagadorn, J. A., 78
Hagan, C. R., 525, 526
Hagemann, D., 419
Haggard, P., 66
Haggard, T., 399
Hagman, J. O., 335
Hagner, M., 21
Hahn, D. B., 410
Hahn, U., 260
Haidle, M. N., 225
Haidt, J., 148, 311
Haigh, E., 513
Haile, R., 459
Hajak, G., 148, 541
Halberstadt, J., 260, 261
Hald, G. M., 445
Hale, L., 158
Hale, W. A., 313
Hale, W. W., 313, 411
Hales, D., 165
Hales, J. B., 9
Haley, A., 272
Halgunseth, L. C., 309
Hall, B., 335
Hall, C. C., 432
Hall, G. C., 526
Hall, J. A., 370, 409, 433
Hall, J. E., 534
Hall, K. D., 578, 581
Hall, L. K., 227
Hall, R. C. W., 388
Hall, S. C., 152
Hallahan, D. P., 274
Hallahan, M., 433
Hallam, M., 432, 433
Halligan, P. W., 175
Hallschmid, M., 153
Halmagyi, G. M., 138
Halpern, A. R., 230
Halpern, C. T., 383
Halpern, D. F., 271, 272, 276, 372
Halpern, D. S., 364
Halpern-Felsher, B. L., 313, 382
Halter, M. J., 503

Malloy, L. C., 241
Malmberg, K. J., 244
Malón, A., 388
Malone, J., 421
Maloo, S., 148
Mamed, D., 148
Manchanda, R., 516
Mancini, F., 344
Mandal, I., 257
Mandara, J., 315
Mandell, D. L., 349
Manderscheid, R. W., 553
Mandisodza, A. N., 432
Mandler, G., 16, 231, 341
Maner, J. K., 433, 440
Manhart, L. E., 386
Manini, T. M., 578
Mann, J. J., 548
Manning, B., 260
Manning, J. T., 379
Manning, L., 152
Manning, R., 442
Manning, W. D., 5
Mann-Wrobel, M. C., 529
Manore, M., 410, 581
Manrique, H. M., 205
Manstead, A. S. R., 563
Mantonakis, A., 234
Manuck, S., 427
Manusov, V., 434
Manzo, V. M., 441
Maoz, I., 454
Maquet, P., 219
Mar, R. A., 147
Marazziti, D., 336, 546
March, J. S., 513
Marchetti, I., 147
Marcia, J. E., 313, 314
Marcotte, T., 172
Marcus, G. F., 232, 254
Marcus, M. D., 335
Marcus, S. C., 547
Marcus, S. M., 548
Marewski, J. N., 257
Margolskee, R. F., 134
Margoob, M. A., 550
Margraf, J., 505
Mariani, C., 91
Mariani, J. J., 73
Maril, A., 220
Marine, A., 427
Mariottini, C., 239
Maris, R. W., 526
Markant, J. C., 297
Markella, M., 334
Markesbery, W. R., 37
Markey, C. N., 312
Markham, H. J., 5
Markides, K. S., 35
Markie, D., 507
Markman, H. J., 5
Markon, K. E., 420
Markovits, H., 260
Markowitsch, H. J., 516
Marks, A. K., 313
Marks, D. F., 562, 576
Marks, J. S., 410
Marks, K. R., 187
Markus, H. R., 20, 569
Marlow, A., 192
Marmot, M., 352
Marques, J. K., 388
Marrazzo, J. M., 384
Marrer, C., 233
Marsh, E. J., 228, 237, 248
Marshall, D. S., 385, 385f
Marshall, D. W., 332
Marshall, G., 191
Marslen-Wilson, W. D., 280
Marston, O. J., 332
Mårtensson, J., 317

Marti, C. N., 333, 567
Martin, A., 548
Martin, C., 409
Martin, C. E., 383
Martin, C. L., 366
Martin, E. G., 548
Martin, G. L., 200, 201
Martin, G. R., 73
Martin, J., 522
Martin, J. A., 386
Martin, J. K., 503, 527
Martin, L. L., 353
Martin, L. R., 425
Martin, N. G., 377, 524
Martin, P. P., 314
Martínez-Amorós, E., 550
Martin-Fardon, R., 188
Marting, M. O., 372
Martin-Garcia, E., 582
Martino, M., 72
Martinovic, J., 104
Martinovich, Z., 513
Martins, A. P. G., 16
Martins, A. T., 148
Martinussen, M., 313
Maruyama, Y., 134
Marx, R. F., 516
Marzano, C., 155, 161
Mas, S., 335
Mascaro, N., 570
Mash, E. J., 505
Masheb, R. M., 335
Maslach, C., 450, 451
Maslow, A. H., 13, 44, 336, 337, 404
Mason, H. R., 494
Mason, M. F., 147
Massa, L. J., 210
Massey, C., 292
Massimini, F., 323
Mastandrea, S., 238
Masten, A. S., 293, 303
Master, A., 209, 211
Masters, K. S., 427
Masters, W. H., 384
Mastro, S., 372
Masul, Y., 425
Matarese, G., 331
Matejkowski, J., 501
Mathew, K. L., 513
Mathews, C. A., 509, 510
Matic, D., 423
Matlin, M. W., 14, 45
Matlow, J. N., 294
Matos, A. P., 445
Matricciani, L. A., 153
Matson, J., 370, 371
Matsumoto, D., 14, 20, 208, 229, 348, 370
Mattaini, M. A., 580
Mattek, A., 81
Mattes, K., 432
Matthews, K., 494
Matthews, K. A., 427
Matthews, P. M., 7
Matthews, R. A., 494
Matthewson, M., 175
Mattick, J. S., 271
Mattson, S. N., 294
Matula, B., 576
Matusch, A., 155
Matzke, D., 109
Maurer, T. J., 472, 475, 476, 477, 480
Mavrides, N., 557
Maxson, S. C., 96
Maxwell, C. A., 493
Maxwell, R., 174, 175
May, A., 135
May, M., 115, 116, 139
May, P. A., 294
May, P. J., 131
Mayer, J. D., 275, 402

Mayer, K. H., 384
Mayer, R., 257
Mayer, R. E., 210
Mayeux, R., 249
Mayo, E., 471f
Mazur, J. E., 189, 197, 202
Mazziotta, J. C., 515
McAbee, S. T., 409
McAdams, D. P., 44, 238, 248, 249, 320, 323, 411, 412, 413, 451
McAfee, R. B., 472
McAvinue, L. P., 219
McBride-Chang, C. A., 360
McBroom, A. J., 529
McCabe, J., 385
McCarrey, A. C., 74
McCaslin, D., 138
McCauley, C., 449
McCauley, C. I., 486
McClay, J., 522
McClelland, J. L., 231
McClelland, M. M., 415
McCombs, B. L., 265
McCorkle, R., 556
McCormick, C. B., 144
McCracken, J. T., 509
McCrae, R. R., 16, 406, 407, 409, 420, 422
McCubbin, L. D., 14, 45, 501
McCullough, J. L., 316
McCullough, M. E., 7, 8, 353, 407, 568
McDaniel, B., 311
McDaniel, M., 210
McDaniel, M. A., 245, 246
McDermott, M., 463, 492
McDermott, R., 262
McDonald, M., 434
McDonald, P., 491
McDonel, E. C., 436
McDonough, I. M., 293, 317
McDowell, N. K., 435
McEachin, J. J., 542
McElroy, S., 554
McFadden, D., 378, 379
McFall, G. P., 293, 319
McFarland, S., 451
McFatter, R. M., 427
McGee, H. M., 426
McGettigan, C., 280
McGhee, K. E., 411
McGinley, M., 311
McGinn, L. K., 510, 524
McGinnis, M. Y., 443
McGlashan, T. H., 524
McGlave, P. B., 463
McGlinchey, E., 158
McGraw, A. P., 83
McGregor, D. M., 484
McGue, M., 97, 272
McGuffin, P., 95
McGuire, J., 230
McGuire, M. T., 581
McGuire, T. R., 139
McGuire, W. J., 439
McIntosh, A. R., 233
McIntosh, R. C., 572
McIntosh, W. D., 353
McIntyre, L. L., 202
McKay, D., 502
McKay, K. M., 538
McKellar, S., 566
McKinnon, W. C., 94
McKone, E., 89
McLanahan, S., 322
McLaren, D., 155
McLean, N., 334
McLeod, G. F., 506
McMahon, C. G., 389
McMahon, D. B., 120
McMahon, R. J., 314
McMain, S., 544

McMains, S., 104
McMillan, B., 125, 425
McMurray, B., 302
McNamara, P., 155
McNamara, T. P., 228, 230
McNaughton, N., 419
McNiel, J. M., 427
McNulty, J. K., 8
McRae, K., 285
McRae, L., 522
McWhirter, R. M., 427
McWilliams, L. A., 306
Mealor, A. D., 149
Meara, E., 548
Meca, A., 14, 313
Medin, D. L., 256
Medina, T. R., 503, 527
Medina-Mora, M. E., 336
Medland, S. E., 379
MedlinePlus, 167
Medoff, D. R., 570
Meeren, H. K., 348
Meesters, C., 443
Meeus, W. H., 313, 411
Meghnagi, D., 539
Mehler, M., 474, 475
Mehta, D., 511
Mei, W., 233
Meier, B. P., 350, 436
Meinhardt, J., 148, 541
Meints, J. O., 424
Meiser, T., 236
Meissner, C. A., 241
Meister, I. G., 176
Mejia-Arauz, R., 208
Melendez-Ferro, M., 518
Meléndez-Jiménez, M. A., 203
Melinder, A. M., 240
Mellers, B., 458
Mellerup, E., 419, 512
Mellor-Clark, J., 15
Melo, A., 67
Melton, L., 249
Meltzer, L. J., 156
Meltzoff, A. N., 183, 202, 301
Memon, A., 237, 240
Mendel, G., 94
Mendel, R., 261
Mendes, N., 206
Mendes, W. B., 453
Mendes de Leon, C. F., 249
Mendes de Leon, D. F., 425
Mendoza, S. A., 458
Mendoza-Denton, R., 441
Meneses, C. W., 553
Meng, M., 87
Meng, X., 513
Menn, L., 283
Mennerick, S., 72
Menon, V., 83
Mercado, E., 12, 63
Mercer, C. H., 384
Mercer, V. E., 576
Merckelbach, H., 239, 508
Merenakk, L., 419
Merfeld, D. M., 112, 113
Merkl, A., 550
Mermelstein, R., 425, 426
Merrick, S., 306
Merskey, H., 516
Mertens, L., 524
Mervielde, I., 406
Merz, S., 550
Meserve, R. J., 264
Meshul, C. K., 167
Mesquita, B., 348, 569
Messenger, J. C., 385
Messer, S. B., 539
Messner, C., 176
Meston, C. M., 389
Metcalfe, J., 245, 340

Thome, J., 505
Thompson, C. M., 481
Thompson, J., 410, 581
Thompson, L., 409, 538
Thompson, M. S., 270
Thompson, P. M., 298
Thompson, R. A., 16, 307, 311
Thompson, R. D., 425
Thompson, R. F., 9
Thompson, S., 529
Thompson, S. C., 425
Thompson, T., 504, 541, 542
Thompson, W. L., 76
Thompson-Hollands, J., 99, 506, 509, 544
Thomson, D., 274
Thomson, D. R., 230
Thorn, L., 244
Thorndike, E. L., 193, 194f
Thornicroft, G., 528
Thorson, C. J., 485
Thota, A. B., 554
Thron, A., 176
Thunedborg, K., 557
Thyer, B. A., 40, 41
Tian, M., 104
Tielbeek, J. J., 524
Tienson, H., 317
Tierney, C., 445
Tieu, T.-T., 306
Tigani, X., 415, 426
Tiitnen, H., 131
Tikhomirov, A. A., 487, 488
Tilley, J., 554
Tillie, J., 426
Tillman, S., 513
Timimi, S., 505
Timko, C., 553
Timmermans, A., 443
Timmons, K. A., 536
Timofeev, I., 152
Timpano, K. R., 509
Tinbergen, N., 442
Tindle, H., 426, 513
Ting-A-Kee, R., 165
Tischner, E. C., 481
Tissot, A., 312
Tkachuck, M. A., 545
Todd, P. M., 433
Todd, R. M., 238, 346
Todorov, A., 432, 433, 434
Toga, A. W., 298
Tol, W. A., 293
Toledo, M. I., 370
Tolin, D. F., 510
Tolman, E. C., 204, 205
Tomasello, M., 206, 279
Tomasi, D., 368
Tomblin, J. B., 302
Tomé-Pires, C., 175
Tomich, P., 323
Tomie, A., 186, 187
Tomiyama, A. J., 285, 426
Tomko, R. L., 524
Tomlins, J. B., 538
Tomori, M., 525
Tompkins, D. A., 362, 363
Tondo, L., 550
Tong, F., 89
Tonigan, J. S., 553
Tononi, G., 152
Tooby, J., 364
Toomey, J. A., 422
Toplak, M. E., 263, 265
Topolinski, S., 261
Topolnytsky, L., 486
Topp, L., 171
Torcato, I., 70
Toro, P., 249
Toro, R., 312
Torres, L., 456

Tracy, J. L., 249, 348
Traeger, L., 556
Trainor, C. D., 312
Tramayne, S., 409
Tran, G. Q., 425
Tran, K. K., 513
Tran, T. V., 272
Tranel, D., 148, 507
Travers, L. V., 576
Travis, F., 178
Travis, J., 411
Trawaiter, S., 458
Treasure, D. C., 405
Treasure, J., 335
Treboux, D., 306
Tredoux, C., 162
Tredoux, C. G., 241
Treiman, R., 277
Tremblay, R. E., 373, 443, 525
Tremblay, S., 78
Trent, J., 38, 144, 261, 321, 407, 409
Trepanier, A. M., 94
Trevino, L. K., 491
Triandis, H. C., 20
Trickett, P. K., 312
Trimarchi, P. D., 246
Trimble, J. E., 14, 45, 501
Trinkler, I., 81
Troberg, A., 303
Troop-Gordon, W., 380
Tropp, L. R., 20, 460
Trotschel, R., 230
Troutman, A. C., 201, 202
Trudeau, R., 448
Trudel-Fitzgerald, C., 562
True, W. R., 167
Trull, T. J., 36, 521, 523, 524, 544
Truxillo, D. M., 473, 482
Tryon, R. C., 95
Trzebinski, J., 411
Trzesniewski, K. H., 7, 209
Tsai, W., 476
Tsang, J., 407
Tsang, S. Y., 519
Tseng, T., 566
Tseng, W. L., 372
Tsiotra, P. C., 331
Tsodikov, A., 172
Tsong, Y., 513
Tsuang, M. T., 368
Tsushima, Y., 111
Tucker, J. S., 315
Tucker, P., 361
Tuckman, A. M., 158
Tugade, M. M., 351
Tull, M. T., 523
Tulving, E., 227, 228, 234
Turban, D., 337
Turchi, C., 167
Turecki, G., 525
Turiano, N. A., 411, 425
Turillazzi, E., 171
Turk, D. C., 562
Turk, D. J., 147
Turkheimer, E., 272, 276, 292, 351
Turkington, T. G., 318
Turnbull, A., 275
Turnbull, D. L., 523
Turnbull, O., 162
Turner, C. M., 376
Turner, J. C., 454
Turner, J. M. W., 124f
Turner, L., 425, 426
Turner, N., 488
Turner, R. B., 572, 573
Turnley, W. H., 482
Tversky, A., 261
Twenge, J. M., 7, 337, 435
Tyers, P., 92
Tyler, L. K., 280
Tyll, S., 81

Tynes, B. M., 456
Tyson, R., 381

Uccelli, P., 277
Uchida, H., 163
Uchida, N., 79
Uchida, Y., 569
Ueno, K., 514
Uher, R., 334
Uhlmann, E., 458
Uhr, M., 507
Uleman, J. S., 433, 434
Ullman, A. D., 189
Ullman, S. E., 513
Ulrich, R. S., 139
Umaña-Taylor, A. J., 314, 455, 456
Umanath, S., 159
Umberson, D., 463
Underhill, K., 386
Underwood, M. K., 373
Undurraga, J., 546
Ungar, L., 148
Unger, J. B., 563
Unick, J. L., 580
United Nations Office on Drugs and Crime, 162
United Nations World Youth Report, 169–170
Unkelbach, C., 261
Unschuld, P. G., 507
Unsworth, N., 236
Unuma, H., 346
Updegraff, K. A., 314
Upp, H., 516
Upton, K. R., 271
Ural, C., 516
Urbain, C., 155
Urbanowski, F., 177
Urbina, S., 268, 271
Urizar, G. G., 295
Urry, H. L., 76, 285, 345
Ursache, A., 303
U.S. Department of Labor, 473, 474, 492
U.S. Food and Drug Administration, 129, 548
U.S. General Accounting Office, 388
Uslaner, J. M., 187
Utz, R., 323

Vaccarino, V., 332
Vachon, D. D., 427
Vadillo, M. A., 244
Vaes, J., 455
Vaillant, G., 168
Vaitl, D., 509
Valbak, K., 539
Valenti, M., 72
Valentine, J., 443
Valenza, E., 296
Valiente, C., 311
Vallerand, R. J., 266
Vallières, A., 151
Vamanrao, A., 79
Vanable, P. A., 572
van Atteveldt, N. M., 108
Van Baaren, R. B., 261
van Baaren, R. B., 261
van Balkom, A. J. L. M., 551
van Beijsterveldt, C. E. M., 335
VanBergen, A., 516
van Beugen, B. J., 72
van Bokhoven, I., 373, 443
Vancouver, J. B., 481
van de Beek, C., 379
VandeCreek, L., 240

Vandello, J. A., 444
Vandenberghe, C., 486
Van den Eynde, F., 78
Vanden Hoek, K. K., 8
van der Geest, V., 312
van de Riet, W. A., 348
Van der Leij, A., 261
Van der Linden, M., 219
van der Loos, M., 271
van der Maas, H. L. J., 109
van der Mast, R. C., 550
van der Steen, J., 296
van der Ven, E., 501
Vander Wal, G. S., 159
van der Weijden, M., 577
Vanderwert, R. E., 67
van der Zee, Y. J., 296
Van Dick, R., 486, 488
Van Doorn, G. S., 440
Van Dyne, L., 271, 480
van Engeland, H., 373, 443
van Furth, E. F., 335
van Gaal, S., 104, 146
Vangkilde, S., 219
van Goozen, S. H. M., 373, 443
van Haren, N. E. M., 519
van Heeringen, C., 334
van IJzendoorn, M. H., 305
Vanini, G., 79
Van Ittersum, K., 333
van Kleef, E., 333
Van Knippenberg, A., 230
Van Lange, P. A. M., 463
van Lankveld, J., 385, 389
van Lier, P. A., 313
van Marle, K., 302
van Megen, H. J. G. M., 551
van Noordt, S. J., 84
van Ommeren, A., 388
Van Orden, K. A., 526
van Oudheusden, L. J., 550
van Praag, H., 92
Van Quaquebeke, N., 488
van Reedt Dortland, A. K. B., 409
van Rijen, P. C., 551
Van Riper, M., 275
VanScoyoc, S. M., 536
Vansteenwegen, D., 189
van Tieghem, M., 81
van't Noordende, J. E., 303
Van Tongeren, D. R., 8
van Toor, D., 524
van Vliet, I. M., 551
van Waarde, J. A., 550
van Well, E. P. L., 551
van Wijngaarden, E., 554
Van Willigen, M., 322
Van Yperen, N. W., 462
Vanyukov, M., 172
Vardar, M. K., 516
Varela, J. G., 422
Vargas, C. D., 67
Varni, J. W., 158
Varnum, M. E. W., 319
Vasco, V. R., 519
Vasey, P. L., 377
Vasquez-Montes, M., 522
Vasselli, J. R., 331
Vassilev, I., 565
Vaughan, L., 410, 581
Vaughn, S., 275
Vazire, S., 409
Vazquez, J., 152
Vazsonyi, A. T., 309
Veale, D., 508
Vecchio, F., 233
Veenema, A. H., 443
Vega, V., 445
Vega-Redondo, F., 203
Vega-Rivera, N. M., 318
Veillete, S., 312

SUBJECT INDEX

Note: Page references in bold refer to definitions. Page references followed by "*f*" refer to figures.

electroconvulsive therapy (ECT), **550**, 550*f*
electroencephalographs (EEG), 75–76, 75*f*, 153–154, 154*f*, 163
electromagnetic spectrum, 116*f*
embedded marketing, 191
embryonic period, 78, 78*f*, 293, 294*f*
embryonic stem cells, 92
emerging adulthood, **315**–316
emoticons, 349
emotion, 340–353, **341**
 biological factors in, 341–344, 341*f*, 343*f*, 344*f*
 brain and, 81, 82, 89
 broaden-and-build model, 351
 Cannon-Bard theory, 342–343, 343*f*
 classifying, 349–351, 350*f*
 cognition and, 344–346, 345*f*
 in computer communications, 349
 culture and expression of, 348, 348*f*
 facial expressions and, 346–347, 346*f*
 gender influences in, 370
 helping behavior and, 48, 48*f*
 James-Lange theory, 342, 343*f*
 motivation and, 350–351
 nervous system in arousal, 341–342, 341*f*
 primacy debate, 345–346
 resilience and, 351
 sensation and, 137
 stress from, 573
 study of, 16
 two-factor theory of, 344–345, 345*f*
emotional memories, 233, 233*f*, 238–239
emotion-focused coping, **574**–575
emotion-induced blindness, 114
empathy, **370**, 371, 405, 441, 540
empirically keyed tests, **421**
empirically supported treatment, **536**
empirical method, **6**
empirical research, 27–28, 27*f*
empiricist approach, 302
employment
 employee commitment, 485–486
 employee development, 479
 employee selection, 474–478, 475*f*, 477*f*
 fastest-growing jobs, 475, 475*f*
 happiness and productivity, 29–30
 job analysis, 471–474, 473*f*, 474*f*
 job crafting, 487
 job satisfaction, 485
 leadership, 487–489
 meaning of work, 486–487
 night-shift, 151
 performance appraisals, 479–483, 482*f*
 sexual harassment in, 491–492, 492*f*
 stress at work, 493–495, 572–573, 573*f*
 training, 478–479
 unemployment, 493
 workplace aggression, 492–493
 work settings of psychologists, 15, 15*f*
encoding, 218–221, **219**
 attention in, 219
 context during, 235–236
 elaboration, 220–221, 220*f*
 failure in, 243, 244*f*
 imagery, 221, 221*f*
 levels of processing, 219–220, 220*f*
 specificity of, 236
 studying and, 247
encoding specificity principle, 236
endocrine system, **90**–91, 90*f*, 190. *See also* hormones
endorphins, 73–74, 133, 168, 343
environmental influences
 functionalism and, 9
 genes and, 10–11, 96–98
 on intelligence, 271–273, 273*f*

on language, 280–282, 282*f*
on obesity, 580
on wellness, 139
environmental psychology, 18
epilepsy, corpus callosum and, 87, 87*f*
epinephrine (adrenaline), 90, 98, 344
episodic memory, **228**, 228*f*, 229
erectile dysfunction, 389
ergonomics, **469**, 469*f*
erogenous zones, 400
ESM (experience sampling method), 35–36
ESP (extrasensory perception), 108, 109
estrogens, **312**, 358
ethical research, 51–54, 189, 189*f*, 449–450, 449*f*
ethnicity/ethnic groups. *See also* culture
 ethnic identity, 313–314, 455, 455*f*, 456*f*
 ethnocentrism, 456
 eyewitness testimony and, 241–242
 inclusion of, in research, 45–46
 in jigsaw classrooms, 461
 psychotherapies and, 555–556
 racial prejudice, 457–458, 459
 stereotype threat in, 436
 suicide in, 526
eugenics, 95
European American students, episodic memory and, 229
event-contingent responding, 36
event-specific knowledge, 238
evidence-based practice, 15, **537**
evolution
 of aggression, 442
 of altruism, 440
 of the brain, 80
 Darwin on, 10–11
 gender development and, 364, 367, 369*f*
 of language, 280
 of mirror neurons, 66
 of motivation, 328, 332
 of sexual behavior, 374
evolutionary approach, **13**–14
excoriation, 510
executive functions, 84, 86, **146**–147, 303
exercise, 92, **578**–581, 578*f*, 579*f*, 581*f*
exhibitionism, 387*f*
expectancy learning, 204–205
expectations, 204–205
experience sampling method (ESM), 35–36
experimental groups, **40**
experimental psychologists, 16
experimental research
 causation and, 37–38
 data analysis in, 28
 experimental and control groups in, 40
 experimenter bias in, 42–43
 independent and dependent variables in, 38–40
 methods summary, 44, 44*f*
 in a natural setting, 48, 48*f*
 participant bias and placebo effects, 43
 quasi-experimental designs, 35, 40–41
 validity in, 42
experimenter bias, **42**–43
experiments, **37**, 44
explicit memory, **226**–228, 227*f*, 228*f*, 233
explicit racism, 458
The Expression of the Emotions in Man and Animals (Darwin), 348
expressive aphasia, 86
expressiveness, 360
external locus of control, 414–415
external validity, **42**

extinction
 in classical conditioning, **188**, 188*f*
 in operant conditioning, **197**
extrasensory perception (ESP), 108, 109
extraversion, 73, 407–410, 407*f*, 418–419, 418*f*
extreme male brain theory, 371
extrinsic motivation, **338**, 339
extrinsic rewards, 29
eye, structure of, 117–118, 118*f*
eyewitness testimony, 240–243, 242*f*

F

Facebook, 395, 533
faces, in person perception, 432–433
face validity, **422**
facial attractiveness, 432–433
facial expressions, 346–347, 346*f*
facial feedback hypothesis, **347**
facial recognition, 89, 236, 236*f*
factor analysis, 407
fairness, in performance appraisals, 482
false consensus effect, **434**–435
families. *See* parenting
family therapy, **552**–553
FASD (fetal alcohol spectrum disorders), 294
fast pathway, 133
fatal familial insomnia (FFI), 153
faulty memories, 240–242, 242*f*
fearless dominance, 522, 523
fears
 brain and, 343–344, 344*f*
 classical conditioning and, 189, 189*f*, 208
 phobias, 508–509, 508*f*, 541, 549*f*
 of snakes, 344, 344*f*
feature detectors, **119**–120
feminist therapies, 402–403, 556
fetal alcohol spectrum disorders (FASD), 294
fetal period, 294, 294*f*
fetishes, **387**
FFA (fusiform face area), 89
FFI (fatal familial insomnia), 153
"fight or flight" response, 65, 74, 98, 341, 341*f*
figure-ground relationship, **122**–123, 123*f*
finger-length ratio, 378–379
first impressions, 433, 477
five-factor model of personality, **407**–411, 407*f*, 416
fixation, **258**, 400–401, 401*f*
fixed-interval schedules, 198, 199*f*
fixed mindset, 209–210
fixed-ratio schedules, 198, 199*f*
flashbacks, 511
flashbulb memories, **238**–239
flat affect, **518**
flow, **495**
Flynn effect, 272, 273*f*, 274
fMRI (functional magnetic resonance imaging), 77, 77*f*, 233
foot-in-the-door technique, 439
forebrain, **80**–82, 82*f*
forensic psychology, 18, 20
forgetting, 243–246
 amnesia, 228, 246, 516
 Ebbenhaus's forgetting curve, 243, 243*f*
 encoding failure, 243, 244*f*
 fake, 233
 motivated, 239–240
 prospective memory, 245–246
 retrieval failure, 244–246, 245*f*
forgiveness, 7–8
formal operational stage, 299*f*, **300**–301
fovea, 118, 118*f*
frame of mind, 5–6, 276

framing, 257, 552
free association, 539
free-radical theory of aging, 317
frequency, 127, 127*f*
frequency theory, **130**
Freud's psychoanalytic theory. *See* psychoanalysis
frontal lobes, **84**, 84*f*, 233, 233*f*
frotteuristic disorder, 387*f*
frustration, 212–213
frustration-aggression hypothesis, 443
functional fixedness, **258**–259
functionalism, **9**–10
functional magnetic resonance imaging (fMRI), 77, 77*f*, 233
fundamental attribution error, **434**–435, 434*f*
fusiform face area (FFA), 89

G

g (general ability), 267
GABA (gamma aminobutyric acid), 72, 166, 506, 507
ganglion cells, 118, 119*f*, 122*f*
GAS (general adaptation syndrome), **571**, 571*f*
gay and lesbian individuals. *See* sexual orientation
gender, **359**. *See also* gender differences; sex
 biological factors in, 363–364, 367–368
 cognitive differences in, 371–372
 differentiation of the sexes, 360–361
 evolutionary psychology on, 364, 367, 369*f*
 gender identity, 359–360, 361–362
 intersex conditions, 361–362, 361*f*
 sex *versus*, 359–360
 social cognitive approaches to, 365–366, 366*f*, 369*f*, 372, 373
 socialization and, 361–362, 361*f*
 social role theory, 366–367, 369*f*, 372, 373
 study of, 16
 transgender individuals, 362–363, 362*f*
gender bias, 45
gender differences
 in aggression, 372–373
 in alcohol effects, 165
 in autism spectrum disorders, 370, 371
 in brains, 368
 in cognition, 371–372
 in depression, 513–514, 514*f*
 in disordered eating, 333
 in emotions, 370
 in finger-length ratios, 378–379
 in language, 370, 371–372
 in moral development, 311
 in pain perception, 133–134
 in panic attacks, 507
 in psychotherapies, 556
 in pubertal changes, 312, 359, 359*f*
 in sexuality, 373–375, 374*f*
 in sexual selection, 364–365, 364*f*
gender dysphoria, 362
gender identity, **359**–360, 361–362
gender identity disorder (GID), 362
gender-nonconforming behavior, 366
gender roles, **367**
gender schema, 366
gender similarities hypothesis, **372**
gender stereotypes, **367**
general adaptation syndrome (GAS), **571**, 571*f*
generalization, in conditioning, **186**–187, **197**, 197*f*, 507
generalized anxiety disorder, **506**, 549*f*

visual cortex, 119–120
visual sensory memory, 222–223, 222*f*
visuo-spatial sketchpad, 225, 226*f*
volley principle, **130**
VTA (ventral tegmental area), 165, 165*f*, 447
vulnerability-stress hypothesis, **502,** 520

W

wavelength, 116, 116*f*, 117*f*
weapons effect, 444
Weber's law, **111**
weight. *See* obesity
weight loss
    exercise and, 580, 581, 581*f*
    motivation in, 332–333

stages of change model in, 564–566, 564*f*
    success of strategies for, 581, 581*f*
well-being therapy (WBT), 556–**557**
wellness
    cognitive appraisal and, 284–286
    good life and, 582–583
    human development and, 322–323
    job stress and, 493–495, 495*f*
    meditation and, 176–178, 317
    memory and, 248–250
    mind and body in, 21–22
    motivation, emotion, and, 352–353
    personality and, 411, 413, 425, 427–428
    scientific method and, 56–57
    sensation and perception and, 138–139
    sexual behavior and, 391
    sexual orientation and, 380–381

social psychology and, 463–464
stigma of psychological disorders, 503, 527–529, 528*f*
stress and, 284–285
therapies and, 556–557
writing about traumas and, 56–57
Wernicke's area, 86–87, 86*f*, 280
White, non-Latino students, 208
Williams syndrome, 279
wisdom, **319**
women and girls. *See also* gender differences; pregnancy
    brain in, 369
    in combat, 357
    Freud on, 396–397
    psychology of, 16
    self-objectification in, 435
    sex organs of, 359, 359*f*

sexual desire disorders in, 389
sexual harassment of, 491–492, 492*f*
in violent pornography, 445
working memory, **224**–226, 226*f*, 234, 303
workplace. *See* employment; industrial and organizational psychology
workplace aggression, 492–493
workplace incivility, 491
work settings of psychologists, 15, 15*f*
writing, healing power of, 56–57

X rays, 76

Yerkes-Dodson law, **329,** 330, 330*f*